Sixth Edition

Social and Personality Development

David R. Shaffer
University of Georgia

WADSWORTH

...pore • Spain • United Kingdom • United States

WADSWORTH
CENGAGE Learning

**Social and Personality Development,
Sixth Edition**
David R. Shaffer

Psychology Editor: Michele Sordi

Assistant Editor: Paige Leeds

Editorial Assistant: Trina Tom

Technology Project Manager: Amy Cohen

Marketing Manager: Kimberly Russell

Project Manager, Editorial Production:
Charlene M. Carpentier

Creative Director: Rob Hugel

Art Director: Vernon Boes

Print Buyer: Paula Vang

Permissions Editor: Roberta Broyer

Production Service: ICC Macmillan Inc.

Text Designer: Patrick Devine

Photo Researcher: Susan Lawson

Copy Editor: Jill Pellarin

Cover Designer: Cheryl Carrington

Cover Image: Banana Stock/Jupiterimages

Compositor: ICC Macmillan Inc.

For product information and technology assistance, contact us at
Cengage Learning Customer & Sales Support, 1-800-354-9706

For permission to use material from this text or product,
submit all requests online at **www.cengage.com/permissions**
Further permissions questions can be emailed to
permissionrequest@cengage.com

Library of Congress Control Number: 2008927143

ISBN-13: 978-0-495-60038-1

ISBN-10: 0-495-60038-5

Wadsworth
10 Davis Drive
Belmont, CA 94002-3098
USA

Cengage Learning is a leading provider of customized learning solutions with office locations around the globe, including Singapore, the United Kingdom, Australia, Mexico, Brazil, and Japan. Locate your local office at **international.cengage.com/region**

Cengage Learning products are represented in Canada by Nelson Education, Ltd.

For your course and learning solutions, visit **academic.cengage.com**

Purchase any of our products at your local college store or at our preferred online store **www.ichapters.com**

Printed in the United States of America
1 2 3 4 5 6 7 12 11 10 09 08

About the Author

Davidᴿ. ꜱʜᴀꜰꜰᴇʀ is a professor emeritus of psychology, past chair of the undergraduate program, and past chair of the Life-Span Developmental Psychology program and the Social Psychology program at the University of Georgia, where he taught courses in human development to graduate and undergraduate students for the past 35 years. His many research articles have concerned such topics as altruism, attitudes and persuasion, moral development, sex roles and social behavior, self-disclosure, and social psychology and the law. He has also served as associate editor for the *Journal of Personality and Social Psychology*, *Personality and Social Bulletin*, and *Journal of Personality*. In 1990, Dr. Shaffer received the Josiah Meigs Award for Excellence in Instruction, the University of Georgia's highest instructional honor.

Brief Contents

Contents

Chapter 12 Extrafamilial Influences I: Television, Computers, and Schooling   413

Chapter 13 Extrafamilial Influences II: Peers as Socialization Agents   451

Chapter 14 Epilogue: Fitting the Pieces Together 490

Preface

IN THE PREFACE of the first edition, I expressed an opinion that the study of social and personality development had come of age and the hope that my book reflected that fact. Clearly, the former premise turned out to be correct—so correct, in fact, that the information explosion that has occurred over the past 30 years has rendered earlier editions of this volume hopelessly obsolete.

My purpose in revising *Social and Personality Development* has been to produce a current and comprehensive overview of the discipline that reflects the best theories, research, and practical wisdom that developmentalists have to offer. Throughout my many years of teaching, I have tried to select rigorous, research-based textbooks that are also interesting, accurate, up to date, and written in concise, precise language that my students can easily understand. I believe that a good text should talk with, rather than at, its readers, anticipating their interests, questions, and concerns and treating readers as active participants in the learning process. A good "developmental" text should also stress the processes that underlie developmental change, so that students come away from the course with a firm understanding of the causes and complexities of whatever aspect(s) of development the text strives to present. Last, a good text is a relevant text—one that shows how the theory and research that students are asked to digest can be applied to a number of real-life settings. The present volume represents my attempt to accomplish all these objectives.

Philosophy

Certain philosophical views are inherent in any systematic treatment of a discipline as broad as social and personality development. My philosophy can be summarized as follows:

◆ I emphasize theory and believe in theoretical eclecticism. My reasons for doing so are straightforward: The study of social and personality development is now a well-established scientific discipline—one that has advanced because of the efforts of a large number of researchers who have taught us so much about developing children by formulating theory and systematically evaluating theoretical hypotheses. This area of study has a very rich theoretical tradition, and all the theories we will review have contributed in important ways to our understanding of social and personality development. Consequently, this book will not attempt to convince its readers that any one theoretical viewpoint is "best." The psychoanalytic, behavioristic, cognitive-developmental, social information-processing, ethological, ecological, sociocultural, and behavioral genetic viewpoints (as well as several less encompassing theories that address selected aspects of development) are all treated with respect.

◆ The best information about human development comes from systematic research. To teach this course effectively, I believe that one must convince students of the value of theory and systematic research. Although there are many ways to achieve these objectives, I have chosen to contrast modern developmental psychology with its "prescientific" origins and then to discuss and illustrate the many methodological approaches that researchers use to test their theories and answer important questions about developing children and adolescents. I've taken care to explain why there is no one best method for studying social and personality development, and I have repeatedly stressed that our most reliable knowledge is based on outcomes that can be replicated using a variety of methods.

◆ I favor a strong "process" orientation. A major complaint with many developmental texts is that they describe human development without adequately explaining why it occurs. In recent years, investigators have increasingly become concerned about identifying and understanding developmental processes—the biological and environmental factors that cause us to change—and this book clearly reflects this emphasis. My own "process orientation" is based on the belief that students are more likely to remember what develops when and if they know and understand the reasons these developments take place.

◆ I also favor a strong "contextual" orientation. One of the more important lessons that developmentalists have learned is that children and adolescents live in historical eras and sociocultural contexts that affect every aspect of their development. I have chosen to highlight these contextual influences in three major ways. First, cross-cultural comparisons are discussed throughout the text. Not only do students enjoy learning about the development of people in other cultures and ethnically diverse subcultures, but cross-cultural research also helps them to see how human beings can be so much alike and at the same time so different from one another. In addition, the impacts of such immediate contextual influences as our families, neighborhoods, schools, and peer groups are considered (1) throughout the first 10 chapters as we discuss important aspects of social and personality development, and (2) again in Chapters 11–13, as important topics in their own right.

◆ Human development is a holistic process. Although individual researchers may concentrate on particular topics such as physical development, cognitive development, emotional development, or the development of moral reasoning, development is not piecemeal but holistic: Human beings are at once physical, cognitive, social, and emotional creatures, and each of these components of "self" depends in part on the changes that are taking place in other areas of development. Clearly, this is a "specialty" book that focuses primarily on the social and emotional aspects of development. However, I have striven to paint a holistic portrait of the developing person by stressing the fundamental interplay between biological, cognitive, social, and ecological influences in my coverage of each facet of social and personality development.

◆ A developmental text should be a resource book for students—one that reflects current knowledge. I have chosen to cite more than 600 very recent studies and reviews (published since the 5th edition) to ensure that my coverage, as well as any outside readings that students may undertake, will represent our current understanding of a topic or topics. However, I have avoided the tendency, common in textbooks, to ignore older research simply because it is older. In fact, many of the "classics" of social and personality development are prominently displayed throughout the text to illustrate important breakthroughs and to show how our knowledge about developing persons gradually builds on these earlier findings and insights.

Content

Though not formally divided into parts, the book can be viewed in that way. The first three chapters (which could be construed as Part One) present an orientation to the discipline and the tools of the trade, including a through discussion and illustration of research methodologies (Chapter 1) and substantive reviews of both classical (Chapter 2) and contemporary (Chapter 3) theories of social and personality development. An important feature of this coverage is its analyses of the contributions and limitations of each research method and each of the major theoretical traditions.

Chapters 4–10 (which could be labeled as Part Two) focus on the "products," or outcomes, of social and personality development, including emotional development (Chapter 4), establishment of intimate relationships and their implications for later development (Chapter 5), development of the self (Chapter 6), achievement (Chapter 7), gender typing and gender-role development (Chapter 8), aggression and antisocial conduct (Chapter 9), and altruism and moral development (Chapter 10).

The third section (or Part Three) of the text explores the settings and contexts in which people develop and could be labeled the "ecology" of development. Here the focus is on the family as an agent of socialization (Chapter 11) and on four important extrafamilial influences: television, computers, schools (Chapter 12), and children's peer groups (Chapter 13).

Finally, a brief epilogue (Chapter 14) has been added to remind readers of the bigger picture—that is, the central themes and processes that underlie human social and personality development. My hope is that students will retain this knowledge and put it to good use in guiding their own transactions with developing persons, even if they should forget the many, many studies that they have read about and by which these important guiding principles have come to light.

New to This Edition

This sixth edition contains many important changes in the treatment of theoretical, empirical, and practical issues, reinforcing themes that are at the forefront of research today. At the most general level, these changes include (1) increased attention throughout to cultural/subcultural/historical influences, with emphasis on the impacts of economic disadvantage on child development; (2) an even stronger focus on the intricate interplays among biological and environmental forces in shaping development; (3) stronger and more frequent illustrations that developmental outcomes depend very crucially on the "goodness of fit" between persons and their socializing environments; (4) greater emphasis on the importance of good peer relations and high-quality friendships (and on the interplay between families and peers as socializing agents); and (5) expanded coverage of adolescent development. The empirical literature has been updated extensively, with the result that a sizable percentage of the references were published in the past 10 years, and most of the recent citations have appeared since late 2003, when the previous edition of this text went into production.

In a word, each chapter has been thoroughly revised and updated to add the new topics that reflect current trends in our discipline. To make way for the additions, I have condensed or otherwise reorganized other topics or, in some cases, have eliminated coverage that the newer evidence has rendered obsolete. Here is a small sampling of these changes:

- Introduction of the increasingly popular "diary study" methodology (Chapter 1)
- Addition of a social-developmental example of ethnographic research (Chapter 1)
- New coverage of psychophysiological methodologies (Chapter 1)
- New social-developmental examples of microgenetic research (Chapter 1)
- New research on emulation and imitative learning in infancy and toddlerhood (Chapter 2)
- Added discussion of mirror neurons as a possible mechanism underlying neonatal imitative capabilities (Chapter 2)
- Updated examples of Bronfenbrenner's environmental systems (Chapter 3)
- New findings regarding the ability of preschoolers to make trait-like inferences about others' behavior (Chapter 3)

- Discussion of mirror neurons as a possible mechanism underlying early empathic responding (Chapter 3)
- Expanded coverage of emotional understanding and social referencing among infants and toddlers (Chapter 4)
- Increased coverage of mixed emotions and their relevance to moral development (Chapter 4)
- New section that greatly expands coverage of parental influences on emotional understanding (Chapter 4)
- Updates on the stability of behavioral inhibition and on parental contributions to inhibition (Chapter 4)
- New box introducing effortful control (EC) as a component of temperament and its links to children's academic and social competencies (Chapter 4)
- New findings on the origins of disorganized/disoriented (D/D) attachments (Chapter 5)
- Expanded coverage of the long-term implications of secure and insecure attachments (Chapter 5)
- Extensive revision of the impacts of severe social deprivation on developing children, including a new look at the deprived child's prospects for recovery (Chapter 5)
- Significant updates on the links between alternative care, early social/emotional developments, and later problem behaviors (Chapter 5)
- New research on the contribution of joint attention to babies' evolving self-concepts (Chapter 6)
- Expanded coverage of social-cognitive precursors to children's belief-desire theory of mind (Chapter 6)
- New findings regarding parental contributions to children's mind-reading skills (Chapter 6)
- Research illustrating that a solid sense of self-esteem is a valuable resource that fosters positive developments (for most youngsters) rather than a mere reflection of positive life experiences (Chapter 6)
- Expanded coverage of ethnic identity formation and its correlates (Chapter 6)
- Additional evidence that very young preschoolers can make appropriate trait-like inferences (Chapter 6)
- New section illustrating that both parents and siblings contribute to children's role-taking skills (Chapter 6)
- Increased attention to the origins and bases of children's prejudicial attitudes and behaviors and to programs designed to overcome or lessen prejudice (Chapter 6)
- New research on goal framing and academic achievement (Chapter 7)
- An effective new intervention to prevent learned helplessness (Chapter 7)
- More coverage of cultural influences on achievement (Chapter 7)
- Expanded discussion of peer influences on academic achievement (Chapter 7)
- New research showing that family influences on children's achievement are more environmental than genetic in origin (Chapter 7)
- Major new section on parental expectancies and children's achievement behavior (Chapter 7)
- Expanded coverage of sex differences (or lack thereof) in risk-taking and mathematical performances and on the bases for sex differences in occupations requiring a math background (Chapter 8)

- More on the "social roles" critique of evolutionary theories of gender typing (Chapter 8)
- Research pointing to new components of gender identity and their influence on psychological well-being in childhood and adolescence (Chapter 8)
- New section on the influence of the Internet on adolescents' sexual identity seeking (Chapter 8)
- A closer look at the reasons for declines in sexual intercourse and out-of-wedlock births among adolescents (Chapter 8)
- Expanded coverage of social learning and social information-processing theories of aggression (Chapter 9)
- New research on Internet bullying/victimization (Chapter 9)
- Expanded coverage of peer influences on antisocial conduct (Chapter 9)
- New findings on the developmental course of sex differences in aggression (Chapter 9)
- Major new section on biological influences on aggression and antisocial conduct (Chapter 9)
- New research on contributions of marital conflict to children's aggression and internalizing disorders (Chapter 9)
- Findings that family contributions to antisocial conduct may differ for boys and girls (Chapter 9)
- New evidence that politically popular means of remediating adolescent offenders may do more harm than good (Chapter 9)
- Expanded coverage of programs designed to prevent aggression and violence at school (Chapter 9)
- New coverage of genetic influences on prosocial behavior (Chapter 10)
- New research on adolescent volunteerism and its impact on prosocial dispositions (Chapter 10)
- Significant updates on the development of conscience in toddlerhood, including work illustrating the components that comprise the early conscience (Chapter 10)
- Introduction of the concept of moral disengagement to account for many inconsistencies between moral reasoning and moral behavior (Chapter 10)
- Increased coverage of the development implications of experiencing behavioral versus psychological control (Chapter 11)
- New research pointing to genetic influences on parenting styles (Chapter 11)
- New findings on promoting healthy autonomy outcomes in adolescence (Chapter 11)
- New box examining parenting in affluent families and the adjustment difficulties that affluent children commonly display (Chapter 11)
- Increased attention to the disadvantages children could face from living with siblings (Chapter 11)
- New research seeking to determine whether the adjustment difficulties faced by children of divorce could be genetic in origin (Chapter 11)
- Evidence that genotype influences children's long-term reactions to child abuse (Chapter 11)
- New coverage of Bugental's social-cognitive model of child abuse and its implications for preventive interventions (Chapter 11)
- Evidence for the harmful influence of commercial television on young girls' body images (Chapter 12)

- Dramatically increased coverage of the potentially positive and negative impacts of Internet exposure on children and adolescents (Chapter 12)
- Suggestions to parents for limiting the potentially harmful effects of Internet exposure (Chapter 12)
- Expanded coverage of the determinants of effective schooling (Chapter 12)
- New research on the impacts of extracurricular activity participation on adolescent development (Chapter 12)
- Research showing that kindergarten transition programs boost parental involvement in learning activities and children's academic achievement (Chapter 12)
- The newest data on how America's children fare on the Nation's Report Card (Chapter 12)
- A preliminary evaluation of No Child Left Behind (NCLB) (Chapter 12)
- Evidence that even 6- to 10-month-old infants have clear peer preferences (Chapter 13)
- Increased attention to the evolution and growth of cross-sex friendships and the forms and functions of adolescent dating relationships (Chapter 13)
- New research pointing to the causal impact of one's sociometric status on psychological adjustment (Chapter 13)
- New section on age-related changes in the correlates of sociometric status (Chapter 13)
- Recent research illustrating advantages and some potential disadvantages of close friendships (Chapter 13)

Writing Style

My goal has been to write a book that treats its readers as active participants in an ongoing discussion. I have tried to be relatively informal and down to earth in my writing style and to rely heavily on questions, thought problems, and a number of other exercises to stimulate student interest and involvement. Many of the chapters were pretested on my own students, who provided many useful ideas for clarification and suggested several of the analogies and occasional anecdotes that I've used when introducing and explaining complex ideas. So, with the valuable assistance of my student critics, I have attempted to prepare a volume that is substantive and challenging but that reads more like a story than an encyclopedia.

Special Features

The pedagogical features of the text have been expanded considerably in this sixth edition. Among the important features that are included to encourage student interest and involvement and to make the material easier to learn are the following:

- *Outlines and chapter summaries.* An outline and brief introductory section at the beginning of each chapter provide the reader with a preview of what will be covered. Each chapter concludes with a summary, organized according to the chapter's major subdivisions and highlighting key terms, that allows one to quickly review the chapter's major themes.
- *Subheadings.* Subheadings are employed frequently to keep the material well organized and to divide the coverage into manageable bites.
- *Glossaries.* A running glossary provides on-the-spot definitions of more than 400 bold-faced key terms as they appear in the text. A complete glossary of key terms for the entire text appears at the end of the book.

◆ *Boxes.* Each chapter contains three to four boxes that call attention to important issues, ideas, or applications. The aim of the boxes is to permit a closer and more personal examination of selected topics while stimulating the reader to think about the questions, controversies, and practices under scrutiny. Some of these boxes are new to this edition, and most of the holdover have been substantially updated, as dictated by new findings that have emerged. The boxes fall into five categories: *Cultural Influences,* which examine the impacts of cultures, subcultures, or other social contexts on selected aspects of child/adolescent development (for example, "Cultural Differences in the Expression of Anger and Shame"); *Focus on Research,* which discuss a study or series of related studies that have been highly influential in illuminating the cause(s) of development or individual differences in development (for example, "How Girls are More Aggressive Than Boys"); *Current Controversies,* which address hotly debated issues today (for example, "Are Peers More Important than Parents?"); *Developmental Issues,* which examine a variety of developmentally significant topics or processes (for example, "Gangs and Antisocial Conduct"); and *Applying Developmental Research,* which focus on applying what we know to optimize developmental outcomes (for example, "Fostering Caregiver Sensitivity and Secure Mother/Infant Attachments"). All these boxes are carefully woven into the chapter narrative and were selected to reinforce central themes in the text.

◆ *Illustrations.* Photographs, figures, and tables appear frequently throughout the text. Although these features are designed in part to provide visual relief and to maintain student interest, they are not merely decorations. All visual aids, including occasional cartoons, were selected to illustrate important principles and outcomes and thereby further the educational goals of the text.

◆ *Instructor's Manual with Test Bank.* Available to all instructors who adopt *Social and Personality Development,* 6th Edition, the *Instructor's Manual with Test Bank* includes chapter outlines, InfoTrac® College Edition search terms, and annotated web links, as well as a robust assessment package with 70–115 multiple choice test items and 5–10 discussion questions, and each answer is labeled with its corresponding main text page reference. The test bank is also available electronically with ExamView®, an easy-to-use assessment and tutorial system that allows instructors to create, deliver, and customize tests and study guides (both print and online) in minutes.

◆ *Electronic Transparencies on eBank.* Available on eBank, this lecture and class preparation tool contains ready-to-use PowerPoint® slides featuring selected images from the text, allowing you to assemble, edit, publish, and present custom lectures for your course. Contact your local sales representative for more information.

◆ *Book Companion Website.* When you adopt *Social and Personality Development,* 6th Edition, you and your students will have access to a rich array of learning resources that you will not find anywhere else. This outstanding site features chapter outlines, chapter-by-chapter tutorial quizzes, essay questions, glossary, web links, flashcards, and more! Visit http://academic.cengage.com/psychology/shaffer for details.

Acknowledgments

As is always the case with projects as large as this one, there are many individuals whose assistance was invaluable in the planning and production of this volume. I extend my gratitude to the following expert reviewers for their many constructive and insightful comments on and suggestions for the sixth edition: Christia Spears Brown, University of California, Los Angeles; Keith Happaney, Lehman College, CUNY; Jon Hixon, Buena Vista University; Ravisha Mathur, San Jose State University; and Ashley Maynard, University of Hawaii.

Special thanks go once again to Pam Riddle, who managed the preparation of the manuscript and the *Instructor's Manual* at the University of Georgia. I am extremely grateful for the tireless efforts of this wonderful colleague on my behalf.

Once again, the staff at Cengage has displayed its skill and professionalism in the production of *Social and Personality Development,* 6th Edition. I am most grateful to Jill Pellarin, the copyeditor, for a skillful and meticulous job of editing; to Roberta Broyer, for securing the necessary permissions; to Patrick Devine, for lending his talent and creativity to the design of the book; to Susan Lawson, for securing photos that help the text content to "come alive"; to the indexer, Cheryl Duksta; and to Charlene Carpentier and to Lynn Lustberg of ICC Macmillan, who coordinated the efforts of these important contributors and carried out the production of the book with skill and efficiency.

Finally, my thanks go to Michele Sordi, my editor. Her strong beliefs in the merits of this project and her efforts to procure resources to significantly improve the design of the book are deeply appreciated at this end.

CHAPTER 1

Introduction

To THIS DAY I CAN RECALL how I made the decision to major in psychology. I was a first-quarter junior who had dabbled in premed, chemistry, zoology, and oceanography without firmly committing myself to any of these fields. Perhaps the single most important event that prompted me to walk over to the psychology table on that fateful fall registration day had actually occurred 18 months earlier. It was the birth of my niece.

This little girl fascinated me. I found it quite remarkable that by the tender age of 18 months she was already quite proficient at communicating with others. I was also puzzled by the fact that, although she and I were pals when she was 5 months old, she seemed somewhat wary around me 9 months later when I returned home for the summer. This toddler knew the names of a number of objects, animals, and people (mostly TV personalities), and she had already become very fond of certain individuals, particularly her mother and her grandmother. To my way of thinking she was well on her way to "becoming human," and the process intrigued me.

After studying human **development** for more than 30 years, I am more convinced than ever that the process of "becoming human," as I had called it, is remarkable in several respects. Consider the starting point. The newborn, or *neonate,* is often perceived as cute, cuddly, and lovable by its parents but is essentially an unknowing, dependent, and occasionally demanding little creature. Newborns have no prejudices or preconceptions; they speak no language; they obey no man-made laws; and they sometimes behave as if they were living for their next feeding. It is not hard to understand how John Locke (1690/1913) could describe the neonate as a *tabula rasa* (blank slate) who is receptive to any and all kinds of experience.

Irvin Child (1954, p. 655) has noted that, despite the enormous number of behavioral options available to the child, he or she is "led to develop actual behavior which is confined within a much narrower range—the range of what is customary and acceptable according to the standards of his group." Indeed, English children will learn to speak English while French children learn French. Jewish children will often develop an aversion to pork, Hindus will not eat the flesh of the sacred cow, and Christians learn that it is perfectly acceptable to consume either of these foods. American children are taught they will someday play an active role in electing their leaders, whereas Jordanian and Saudi Arabian children learn that their rulers assume that role as a birthright. Children who grow up in certain areas of the United States are likely to prefer square dancing and country music, whereas those who live in other areas will prefer hip-hop and rap music. Some children are permitted to "question" their parents' pronouncements, whereas others are taught to obey the commands of their elders without comment. In short, children develop in a manner and direction prescribed by their cultures, subcultures, and families.

What I had originally described as "becoming human" is more commonly labeled **socialization**—the process through which the child acquires the beliefs, behaviors, and values deemed significant and appropriate by other members of society. The socialization of each succeeding generation serves society in at least three ways. First, it is a means of regulating behavior. I suspect that the penalties for rape, robbery, and murder are not the most important inhibitors of these heinous acts. Any one of us could probably walk outside, snatch someone's purse, and stand a reasonably good chance of making a few dollars without getting caught. Then why don't we mug little old ladies or commit several other low-risk but socially inappropriate behaviors? Probably because the control of antisocial acts is largely a personal matter that stems from the standards of morality—right and wrong— that we have acquired from our interactions with parents, teachers, peers, and many other agents of socialization. Second, the socialization process helps to promote the personal growth of the individual. As children interact with and become like other members of their culture, they acquire the knowledge, skills, motives, and aspirations that will enable them to

development
the systematic continuities and changes in the individual that occur between conception (when a sperm penetrates an ovum creating a new organism) and death.

socialization
the process by which individuals acquire the beliefs, values, and behaviors considered desirable or appropriate by their culture or subculture.

function effectively within their communities. Finally, socialization perpetuates the social order. Socialized children become socialized adults who will impart what they have learned to their own children.

On the first day of class one year, I asked my students to write, in 50 words or less, the main reason they elected to take a course in social and personality development. One perceptive sophomore wrote, "I want to know why all of us turn out so much alike and, at the same time, so *different* from one another." Clearly, humans are alike in certain respects because as members of the same species, we share a common evolutionary heritage that tends to channel development along a similar path. What's more, those of us living within any given culture or subculture are also encouraged to adopt similar norms and values. Yet it is also true that no two individuals are exactly alike and that each of us has a unique personality. Why is this? One important reason is that no two of us, with the exception of identical twins, inherit precisely the same set of genes. A second and equally important contributor to our uniqueness is that every individual—even identical twins raised in the same home—has somewhat different (and often dramatically different) experiences while growing up. So social and personality development represents far more than the unfolding of a genetic program or the impact of cultures on individuals. As we will see, it is more accurately characterized as a long and involved interplay among a variety of social, cultural, and biological influences that conspire to make we humans similar in certain ways but very different from one another in many other respects.

❧ THE UNIVERSAL PARENTING MACHINE— A THOUGHT EXPERIMENT

Jones, Hendrick, and Epstein (1979) have described an interesting thought experiment that touches on the major issues that we will discuss throughout this book. They title their hypothetical experiment the "Universal Parenting Machine" and describe the project as follows:

> Suppose that six infants are placed immediately after birth into a "universal parenting machine" (the UPM). To enliven the scenario, we may suppose that three infants are male and three female. The UPM is . . . an enclosed building with advanced machinery and technology capable of taking care of all the infants' physical needs from immediately after birth to maturity. The most critical feature of the UPM is that it is constructed so that the infants will have no human contact other than with each other during their first 18 years of life. In fact, they will not even know that other human beings exist [p. 52].

Now imagine that the creation of a UPM is within the range of our technical capabilities. Let's also assume that the UPM can be set up in such a way as to create a modern-day Garden of Eden, complete with trees, flowers, the sounds of birds chirping, and a transparent domed room so that our experimental children are exposed to the sights and sounds of the weather and the movements of the sun, the moon, and the stars. In other words, try to imagine that we have simulated a very pleasant acre of the real world that lacks at least one potentially important feature: We have omitted all other people and, indeed, the concept of a culture. Were we to expose six infants to this environment, there are many questions we might wish to ask about their development. Here are but a few:

+ Perhaps the most basic question: Would these children interact with one another and become sociable creatures? If they did, several other questions might be asked.

+ Would the children love one another, depend on one another, or develop stable friendships?

+ Would the children ever develop a spoken language or some other efficient method of communicating complex ideas?

- ✦ Would this environment provide the kinds of stimulation that children need to develop intellectually so that they might have complex ideas to express?
- ✦ Would these children develop gender roles and/or become sexual beings at maturity?
- ✦ Would the children develop a sense of pride in their accomplishments (assuming, of course, that they were able to accomplish anything meaningful on their own)?
- ✦ Would the children's interactions be benevolent (guided by a spirit of togetherness, co-operation, and altruism) or belligerent (antagonistic and aggressive)?
- ✦ Would these children ever develop standards of good and evil or right and wrong to govern their day-to-day interactions?

How would the experiment turn out? That's hard to say, for this kind of project has not been conducted and, if current ethical guidelines prevail, never will be. But this is a thought experiment, and there is nothing to prevent us from speculating about possible outcomes, with the help of what we know about social and personality development.

Recall that a socialized person is one who has acquired the beliefs, values, and behaviors that are thought to be appropriate for members of his or her culture. How does the child become socialized? One point of view is that children are shaped by their culture. Were we to adopt this viewpoint quite literally, we might predict that our six experimental children would become semihuman, at best, in the absence of a prevailing social structure. The opposite side of the coin is that culture is shaped by people. So, it is conceivable that our six children would show enough initiative to interact, develop strong affectional ties, and create their own little culture, complete with a set of rules or customs to govern their interactions. Although this suggestion may seem improbable, there is at least one case in which a small group of Jewish war orphans did indeed form their own "society" in the absence of adult supervision while in a German prison camp during the Second World War (Freud & Dann, 1951). We will take a closer look at this intriguing "peer-only" culture in Chapter 13.

Of course, we can't be absolutely certain that infants raised by the UPM would create the same kind of social order the young war orphans did. Furthermore, the war orphans were integrated into adult society at a very early age, so they provide few clues about the kinds of people that our experimental children might eventually become. So where do we turn to develop some predictions about the outcome of our experiment? One possibility is to examine the existing theories of social and personality development to see what hints they provide.

There are now several such theories to examine, each of which makes assumptions about children and the ways they develop. In the following sections of this chapter, we will compare and contrast the different assumptions that theorists make about human nature and the character of human development. Our theoretical overview will then carry over into Chapters 2 and 3, where we will take an in-depth look at both classical and contemporary theories of social and personality development.

After examining the major theories, we will focus on emotional development and its relevance to virtually all other aspects of social life, including the child's earliest interpersonal relationships. You may have noticed that young infants are often drawn to their mothers and may lustily voice their distress if separated from this intimate companion. Why (and under what precise circumstances) are they likely to feel such distress? How might it affect the infant's reactions to strangers? And how might children learn to regulate and control negative emotions? These are but a few of the issues we will address in examining the emotional lives of infants, toddlers, children, and adolescents in Chapter 4.

Chapter 5 centers on other critically important issues. How do infants form close ties to their mothers or other close companions? And what happens to children who do not become securely attached to an older caregiver during the first two or three years of life? Answers to these questions—particularly the last—would almost certainly provide some basis for speculation about the development of children raised without adults by a universal parenting machine.

People clearly differ in their willingness to engage others in social interaction and to seek their attention or approval. Some individuals can be described as loners, whereas others are outgoing and gregarious. These two types differ in what is called *sociability,* or the value they place on the presence, attention, and approval of other people. Competence is another way in which people clearly differ. Some people take great pride in their accomplishments and seem highly motivated to achieve. Others do not appear to be terribly concerned about what they have accomplished or what they are likely to accomplish in the future. Would our six experimental children come to value the presence, attention, or approval of one another? Would they develop a motive to achieve? Perhaps a review of the factors that influence children's sociability, achievement motivation, and achievement behavior will help us to decide. These topics are discussed in Chapters 6 and 7, which explore the development of the self and the growth of one's propensities for achievement.

Recall that the children selected for our experiment were balanced with respect to biological sex (three males and three females). Would they eventually differentiate themselves on the basis of gender? Would they develop a sense of masculinity and femininity and pursue different activities? Would they become sexual beings at maturity? There are reasons for predicting that the answers to all these questions would be yes, for gender is, after all, a biological attribute. But we should keep in mind that gender roles and standards of sexual conduct are almost certainly affected by social values and customs. Thus, the gender typing and the sexual behavior of our six experimental children might well depend on the kind of social order they created, as well as on their biological heritage. The determinants of gender typing and gender-role behaviors are explored in detail in Chapter 8.

Earlier, we asked whether interactions among our six experimental children would turn out to be benevolent or belligerent. Children raised in a typical home setting display both kinds of behavior, but we should keep in mind that the socializing experiences provided by a UPM could hardly be described as typical. Nevertheless, it might be possible to make some educated guesses about the positive or negative character of these children's interactions if we had some information about the development of aggression and altruism in children reared under more normal circumstances. The factors that affect children's aggression and antisocial conduct are discussed in Chapter 9. The development of altruism and prosocial behavior (generosity, compassion, helpfulness, and cooperation) are covered in Chapter 10.

Of course, a major reason that human beings are able to live together in ordered societies is that they have devised laws and moral norms that distinguish right from wrong and govern their day-to-day interactions. How do children acquire a knowledge of these moral principles? What roles do parents, teachers, peers, and other agents of socialization play in a child's moral development? The answers to these questions may well provide some hints about the likelihood that children raised by a universal parenting machine would develop their own moral norms. Moral development is the primary focus of Chapter 10.

Because our experimental children are to be raised by a machine, they will not be exposed to a nuclear family as we know it, consisting of a mother, a father, and any number of brothers and sisters. How would the lack of family ties and familial influence affect their development? Perhaps we can gain some insight on this issue after focusing on the family as an agent of socialization in Chapter 11.

Although families have an enormous impact on their young throughout childhood and adolescence, it is only a matter of time before other societal agents begin to exert their influence. For example, infants and toddlers are frequently exposed to alternative caregivers and a host of new playmates when their working parents place them in some kind of day care. Even those toddlers who remain at home will soon begin to learn more about the outside world once they develop an interest in television and computer technology. And by age 6 to 7, virtually all youngsters in Western societies are venturing outside the home to school, a setting that requires them to adjust to the demands of a new authority figure—the classroom teacher—and to interact effectively with other little people who are similar to themselves. Does exposure to television, computers, and formal schooling contribute in any meaningful ways to the shaping of one's character? Do playmates and the peer group have a significant impact on a child's or an adolescent's social and personality development? The answers to these questions are of obvious importance to the development of our six experimental children, who are to be raised with no exposure to the electronic media and no companions other than peers. Thus, our overview of social and personality development will conclude with in-depth discussions of the major "extra-familial" agents of socialization—television, computers, and schools (Chapter 12) and children's peer groups (Chapter 13).

In sum, no one can specify *exactly* how children raised by a universal parenting machine would turn out. After all, there are no empirical precedents from which to work. Although we will not dwell further on our hypothetical children in the text, you may want to keep them in mind and to make some educated guesses about their future as we examine the major theories of social and personality development and review a portion of the data on developing children and adolescents that has been collected over the past 90 years. We will begin our discussion by briefly considering how scientists became interested in the socialization process and why they have settled upon theoretically inspired empirical research as the preferred method of acquiring knowledge about human development.

⌒ SOCIAL-PERSONALITY DEVELOPMENT IN HISTORICAL PERSPECTIVE

Childhood in Premodern Times

Childhood and adolescence were not always regarded as the special and sensitive periods we know them to be today. In the early days of recorded history, children had few if any rights, and their lives were not always valued by the elders. For example, archaeological research has shown that as far back as 7000 B.C., children were killed as religious sacrifices and sometimes embedded in the walls of buildings to "strengthen" these structures (Bjorklund & Bjorklund, 1992). Until the fourth century A.D., Roman parents were legally entitled to kill their deformed, illegitimate, or otherwise unwanted infants; and even after this active infanticide was outlawed, unwanted babies were often left to die in the wilderness or sold as servants upon reaching middle childhood (deMause, 1974).

Historian Philippe Aries (1962) has analyzed documents and paintings from medieval Europe and concluded that before 1600 European societies had little or no concept of childhood as we know it. Medieval children were closely cared for until they could feed, dress, and bathe themselves, but they were not often coddled by their elders (Aries, 1962;

Photo 1.1 Medieval children were often dressed and sometimes treated like miniature adults.

deMause, 1974). At about age 6, children were dressed in downsized versions of adult clothing and were depicted in artwork as working alongside adults (usually close relations) in shops or fields or as drinking and carousing with adults at parties and orgies. And except for exempting infants and toddlers from criminal culpability, medieval law generally made no distinctions between childhood and adult offenses (Borstelman, 1983; Kean, 1937).

During the 17th and 18th centuries, attitudes about children and child rearing began to change. Religious leaders of that era stressed that children were fragile creatures of God who should be shielded from the wild and wanton behavior of adults and at the same time diverted from their own stubborn and devilish ways. One method of accomplishing these objectives was to send young people to school. Although the primary purpose of schooling was to civilize children—to provide them with a proper moral and religious education— it was recognized that important subsidiary skills such as reading and writing should be taught in order to transform the innocents into "servants and workers" who would provide society "with a good labor force" (Aries, 1962, p. 10). Children were still considered family possessions, but parents were now discouraged from abusing their sons and daughters and were urged to treat them with more warmth and affection (Aries, 1962; Despert, 1965).

Children as Subjects: The Baby Biographies

The first glimmering of a systematic study of children can be traced to the late 19th century. This was a period in which investigators from a variety of academic backgrounds began to observe the development of their own children and to publish these data in works known as **baby biographies**.

Perhaps the most influential of the baby biographers was Charles Darwin, who made daily records of the early development of his son (Darwin, 1877; and see Charlesworth, 1992). Darwins's curiosity about child development stemmed from his earlier theory of evolution. Quite simply, he believed that young, untrained infants shared many characteristics with their nonhuman ancestors, and he advanced the (now discredited) *law of recapitulation*—the notion that an individual who develops from a single cell at conception into a marvelously complex, thinking human being as a young adult will retrace the entire evolutionary history of the species, thereby illustrating the "descent of man." So Darwin and many of his contemporaries viewed the baby biography as a means of answering questions about our evolutionary past.

baby biography
a detailed record of an infant's growth and development over a period of time.

Photo 1.2
American psychologist G. Stanley Hall (1844–1924) is recognized as one of the founders of developmental psychology.

Bettmann/Corbis

Unfortunately, baby biographies left much to be desired as works of science. Observations for many of the biographies were made at irregular intervals, and different biographers emphasized very different aspects of their children's behavior. Consequently, the data provided by various biographers were often not comparable. In addition, the persons making observations in these biographical studies were generally proud parents who were likely to selectively record pleasant or positive incidents while downplaying unpleasant or negative ones. Finally, almost every baby biography was based on observations of a single child, and it is difficult to know whether conclusions based on a single case would hold for other children.

Despite these shortcomings, baby biographies were a step in the right direction. The fact that eminent scientists such as Charles Darwin were now writing about developing children implied that human development was a topic worthy of scientific scrutiny.

Emergence of a Psychology of Childhood

Introductory textbooks in virtually all academic areas typically credit someone as the "founder" of the discipline. In the developmental sciences there are several influential pioneers who might merit consideration for this honor. Still, the person most often cited as the founder of developmental psychology is G. Stanley Hall.

Well aware of the shortcomings of baby biographies based on single children, Hall set out in the late 19th century to collect more objective data on larger samples. Specifically, he was interested in the character of children's thinking, and he developed a familiar research tool—the *questionnaire*—to "discover the contents of children's minds" (Hall, 1891). What he found was that children's understanding of worldly events increases rapidly over the course of childhood and that the "logic" of young children is not very logical at all. Hall later wrote an influential book titled *Adolescence* (1904) that was the first work to call attention to adolescence as a unique phase of the life span (see Box 1.1). Here, then, were the first large-scale scientific investigations of developing youth, and it is on this basis that G. Stanley Hall merits consideration as the founder of developmental psychology (White, 1992).

At about the time Hall was using questionnaires to study children's thinking, a young European neurologist was trying a different method of probing the mind and revealing its contents. The neurologist's approach was very fruitful, providing information that led him to propose a theory that revolutionized thinking about children and childhood. The neurologist was Sigmund Freud. His ideas came to be known as *psychoanalytic theory*.

In many areas of science, new theories are often revisions or modifications of old theories. But in Freud's day, there were few "old" theories of human behavior to modify. Freud was truly a pioneer, formulating his psychoanalytic theory from the thousands of notes and observations he made while treating patients for various kinds of emotional disturbances.

Freud's highly creative and unorthodox theorizing attracted a lot of attention. Shortly after the publication of his earliest theoretical monographs, the *International Journal of Psychoanalysis* was founded, and other researchers began to report their tests of Freud's thinking. By the mid-1930s much of Freud's work had been translated into other languages, and the impact of psychoanalytic theory was felt around the world. Over the years, Freud's theory proved to be quite *heuristic*—meaning that it continued to generate new research and to prompt other researchers to extend Freud's thinking. Clearly, the field of child development was alive and well by the time Freud died, in 1939.

The Role of Theory in the Scientific Enterprise

Freud's work, and other scientists' reactions to it, aptly illustrates the role theories play in the modern, scientific study of human development. Although the word *theory* is an

Box 1.1 Cultural Influences

On the "Invention" of Adolescence

Although modern-day concepts of childhood date to the 1700s, formal recognition of *adolescence* as a distinct phase of life came even later—during the early years of the 20th century (Hall, 1904). Ironically, the spread of industry in Western societies is probably the event most responsible for the "invention" of adolescence. As immigrants poured into industrialized nations and took jobs that had formerly been filled by children and teenagers, young people became economic liabilities rather than assets or, as one person put it, "economically worthless but emotionally priceless" (Zelizer, cited in Remley, 1988). Moreover, the increasingly complex technology of industrial operations placed a premium on obtaining an educated labor force. So the late 19th century was a period when laws were passed to restrict child labor and make schooling compulsory (Kett, 1977). Suddenly, teens were spending much of their time surrounded by age-mates and separated from adults. And as they hung out with friends and developed their own colorful "peer cultures," teenagers came to be viewed as a distinct class of individuals—those who had clearly emerged from the innocence of childhood but who were not yet ready to assume adult responsibilities (Hall, 1904).

After World War II, the adolescent experience broadened as increasing numbers of high school graduates postponed marriage and careers to pursue college (and postgraduate) education. Today, it is not at all unusual for young people to delay their entry into the workaday adult world until their mid to late 20s (Hartung & Sweeney, 1991; Vobejda, 1991). And we might add that society condones this "extended adolescence" by requiring workers to obtain increasingly specialized training to pursue their chosen careers (Elder, Liker, & Cross, 1984).

Interestingly, many of the world's cultures have no concept of adolescence as a distinct phase of life. The St. Lawrence Eskimos, for example, simply distinguish boys from men (or girls from women), following the tradition of many preliterate societies that passage to adulthood occurs at puberty (Keith, 1985). And yet, other cultures' depictions of the life span are much more intricate than our own. The Arasha of East Africa, for example, have at least *six* meaningful age strata for males: youths, junior warriors, senior warriors, junior elders, senior elders, and retired elders.

The fact that age does not have the same meaning in all eras or cultures reflects a basic truth that we have already touched on and will emphasize repeatedly throughout this book: The course of human development in one historical or cultural context is apt to differ, and to differ substantially, from that observed in other eras and

The Image Works

In some cultures, passage to adulthood occurs at puberty, and adolescents are expected to assume adult responsibilities.

cultural settings. Aside from our biological link to the human race, we are largely products of the times and places in which we live!

---

imposing term, it so happens that theories are something everyone has. If I were to ask you why males and females appear so different as adults when they seem so very similar as infants, you would undoubtedly have something to say on the issue. In answering, you would be stating or at least reflecting your own underlying theory of sex differences. So a **theory** is really nothing more than a set of concepts and propositions that allow the theorist to describe and explain some aspect of experience. In the field of psychology, theories help us to describe various patterns of behavior and to explain why those behaviors occur.

A *scientific* theory is a public pronouncement that indicates what a scientist believes to be true about his or her specific area of investigation (Miller, 2002). And the beauty of scientific theories is that they allow us to organize our thinking about a broad range of observations

theory
a set of concepts and propositions designed to organize, describe, and explain an existing set of observations.

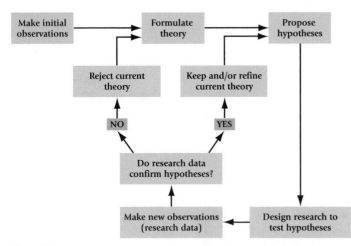

Figure 1.1
The role of theory in scientific investigation.

parsimony
a criterion for evaluating the scientific merit of theories; a parsimonious theory is one that uses relatively few explanatory principles to explain a broad set of observations.

falsifiability
a criterion for evaluating the scientific merit of theories; a theory is falsifiable when it is capable of generating predictions that could be disconfirmed.

heuristic value
a criterion for evaluating the scientific merit of theories. An heuristic theory is one that continues to stimulate new research and new discoveries.

hypothesis
a theoretical prediction about some aspect of experience.

original sin
the idea that children are inherently selfish egoists who must by controlled by society.

innate purity
the idea that infants are born with an intuitive sense of right and wrong that is often misdirected by the demands and restrictions of society.

and events. Imagine what life might be like for a researcher who plugs away at collecting data and recording fact after fact without organizing this information around a set of concepts and propositions. Chances are that this person would eventually be swamped by a large number of seemingly unconnected facts, thus qualifying as a trivia expert who lacks a "big picture." So theories are of critical importance to the developmental sciences (or any other scientific discipline), for each of them provides us with a "lens" though which we might interpret any number of specific observations about developing individuals.

What are the characteristics of a good theory? Ideally, it should be concise, or **parsimonious,** and yet be able to explain a broad range of phenomena. A theory with few principles that accounts for a large number of empirical observations is much more useful than a second theory that requires many more concepts and propositions to explain the same number (or a lesser number) of observations. In addition, good theories are **falsifiable**—that is, capable of making explicit predictions about future events so that the theory can be supported or disconfirmed. And as implied by the falsifiability criterion, good theories are **heuristic**—meaning that they build on existing knowledge by continuing to generate testable **hypotheses** that, if confirmed by future research, will lead to a much richer understanding of the phenomena under investigation (see Figure 1.1).

Today there are several "good" theories that have contributed to our understanding of social and personality development, and in Chapters 2 and 3 we will critically examine some of the more influential of these viewpoints. As we will see, each theory makes somewhat different assumptions about human nature as well as about the course and causes of development. So before we discuss the major theories of social and personality development, it may be helpful to consider some of the more basic issues on which they differ.

QUESTIONS AND CONTROVERSIES ABOUT HUMAN DEVELOPMENT

Developmental theorists have different points of view on at least five basic issues:

1. Are children inherently good or inherently bad?
2. Is nature (biological forces) or nurture (environmental forces) the primary influence on human development?
3. Are children actively involved in the developmental process; or, rather, are they passive recipients of social and biological influences?
4. Is development continuous or discontinuous?
5. Are the most noteworthy aspects of development "universals" that all humans display, or are they the "particularistic" or ideographic developments that characterize each individual?

Early Philosophical Perspectives on Human Nature

What kind of animal are we? After debating this issue for centuries, social philosophers have produced viewpoints ranging from Thomas Hobbes's (1651/1904) doctrine of **original sin,** which held that children are inherently selfish egoists who must be controlled by society, to Jean Jacques Rousseau's (1762/1955) doctrine of **innate purity**—the notion that children are born with an intuitive sense of right and wrong that is often misdirected by society. These two viewpoints clearly differ in their implications for child rearing. Proponents of original sin argued that parents must actively restrain their egoistic offspring, whereas the innate purists viewed children as "noble savages" who should be given the freedom to follow their inherently positive inclinations.

Another view on children and child rearing was offered by John Locke (1690/1913), who believed that the mind of an infant is a *tabula rasa,* or "blank slate," that is written upon by experience. In other words, children were portrayed as neither inherently good nor inherently bad, and how they will turn out should depend entirely on how they are raised. Like Hobbes, Locke argued in favor of disciplined child rearing to ensure that children develop good habits and acquire few if any unacceptable mannerisms and behaviors.

As it turns out, each of these three philosophical perspectives on human nature remains with us today in one or more contemporary theories of social and personality development. Although one may search in vain for explicit statements about human nature, the theorist will typically emphasize the positive or the negative aspects of children's character or perhaps will note that positivity or negativity of character depends on the child's experiences. These assumptions about human nature are important, for they influence the content of each developmental theory—particularly what the theory has to say about child rearing.

Nature versus Nurture

One of the oldest controversies among developmental theorists is the **nature versus nurture issue:** Are human beings a product of their heredity and other biological predispositions, or are they shaped by the environment in which they are raised? Here are two opposing viewpoints:

> Heredity and not environment is the chief maker of man. . . . Nearly all of the misery and nearly all of the happiness in the world are due not to environment. . . . The differences among men are due to differences in the germ cells with which they were born. [Wiggam, 1923, p. 42]

> Give me a dozen healthy infants, well formed, and my own specified world to bring them up in and I'll guarantee to take any one at random and train him to become any type of specialist I might select—doctor, lawyer, artist, merchant, chief, and yes, even beggar man and thief, regardless of his talents, penchants, tendencies, abilities, vocations, and race of his ancestors. There is no such thing as an inheritance of capacity, talent, temperament, mental constitution, and behavioral characteristics. [Watson, 1925, p. 82]

Of course, there is a middle ground, one that is endorsed by most contemporary developmentalists who believe that the relative contributions of nature and nurture depend on the particular aspect of development in question. However, today's developmentalists generally agree that all complex human attributes such as intelligence, temperament, and personality are the end products of a long and involved interplay between biological predispositions and environmental forces (see, for example, Bornstein & Lamb, 2005; Gottlieb, 2003). Their advice to us, then, is to think less about nature *versus* nurture and more about how these two sets of influences combine or *interact* to produce developmental change.

Activity versus Passivity

Another topic of theoretical debate is the **activity/passivity issue.** Are children curious, active creatures who largely determine how agents of society treat them? Or are they passive souls on whom society fixes its stamp? Consider the implications of these opposing viewpoints. If it could be shown that children are extremely malleable—literally at the mercy of

tabula rasa
the idea that the mind of an infant is a "blank slate" and that all knowledge, abilities, behaviors, and motives are acquired through experience.

nature versus nurture issue
debate within developmental psychology over the relative importance of biological predispositions (nature) and environmental influences (nurture) as determinants of human development.

activity/passivity issue
debate among developmental theorists about whether children are active contributors to their own development or, rather, passive recipients of environmental influence.

those who raise them—then perhaps individuals who turned out to be less than productive would be justified in suing their overseers for malfeasance. Indeed, a young man in the United States once used this logic to bring a malfeasance suit against his parents. Perhaps you can anticipate the defense that the parents' lawyer would offer. Counsel would surely argue that the parents tried many strategies in an attempt to raise their child right but that he responded favorably to none of them. The implication is that this young man played an active role in determining how his parents treated him and therefore bears a large share of the responsibility for creating the climate in which he was raised.

The activity/passivity issue goes beyond considering the child's conscious choices and behaviors. That is, developmentalists consider a child *active* in development whenever any child characteristic influences the environment he or she experiences. So a temperamentally difficult infant who challenges the patience of her loving but frustrated parents has an effect on the childbearing "environment" she experiences, even though she is not consciously choosing to be temperamentally difficult. Similarly, a preteen girl who has reached puberty long before her friends or classmates does not choose to be "early." Nevertheless, the fact that she appears so much more mature than her peers may have dramatic effects on the way others treat her and the social environment she experiences.

Which of these perspectives do you consider the more reasonable? Think about it, for very soon you will have an opportunity to state your views on this and other topics of theoretical debate.

Continuity versus Discontinuity

Now think for a moment about the concept of developmental change. Do you think that the changes we experience occur very gradually? Or would you say that these changes are rather abrupt?

continuity/discontinuity issue
debate among theorists about whether developmental changes are best characterized as gradual and quantitative or, rather, abrupt and qualitative.

On one side of the **continuity/discontinuity issue** are continuity theorists, who view human development as an additive process that occurs in small steps, without sudden changes. They might represent the course of developmental change with a smooth growth curve like the one in Figure 1.2A. By contrast, discontinuity theorists describe the road to maturity as a series of abrupt changes, each of which elevates the child to a new and presumably more advanced level of functioning. These levels, or "stages," are represented by the plateaus of the discontinuous growth curve in Figure 1.2B.

A second aspect of the continuity/discontinuity issue centers on whether developmental changes are quantitative or qualitative in nature. Quantitative changes are changes in *degree*.

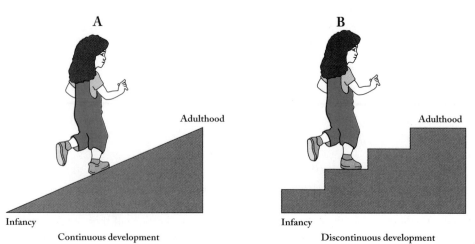

A

Adulthood

Infancy

Continuous development

B

Adulthood

Infancy

Discontinuous development

Figure 1.2 The course of development as described by continuity and discontinuity (stage) theorists.

For example, children gradually grow taller; they run a little faster with each passing year; and they acquire more and more knowledge about the world around them. By contrast, qualitative changes are changes in *kind*—changes that make the individual fundamentally different in some way than he or she was before. The transformation of a tadpole into a frog is a qualitative change. Similarly, we might regard the infant who lacks language as qualitatively different from a preschooler who speaks well, or the adolescent who is sexually mature as fundamentally different from a classmate who is yet to reach puberty. Continuity theorists generally think that developmental changes are both gradual and quantitative in nature, whereas discontinuity theorists tend to view such changes as more abrupt and qualitative. Indeed, discontinuity theorists are the ones who argue that we progress through **developmental stages**. Presumably, each of these stages represents a distinct phase within a larger sequence of development—a period of life characterized by a particular set of abilities, motives, behaviors, or emotions that occur together and form a coherent pattern. Furthermore, each of these stages is qualitatively different from the stage that proceeds or follows it. By contrast, continuity theorists view development as an additive process that occurs continuously and is not at all stagelike.

Finally, there is a third aspect of the continuity/discontinuity debate: Are there close connections between early developments and later ones, or, rather, do changes that occur early in life have little bearing on future outcomes? Continuity in this sense implies a sense of *connectiveness* between earlier and later developments. Those who argue against the concept of developmental stages might see such connectiveness in the *stability* of attributes over time, as might be indicated, for example, if aggressive toddlers routinely become aggressive grade-school children and adolescents or if particularly curious preschoolers are the ones most often recognized, as adults, for creative accomplishments. Even a theorist who proposes that we pass through qualitatively distinct stages might still see some connectiveness (or continuity) to development if the abilities that characterize each successive stage are thought to evolve from those of the previous stage.

Interestingly, societies often take different positions on the continuity/discontinuity issue. Some Pacific and Far Eastern cultures, for example, have words for infant qualities that are never used to describe older children, and adult terms such as *intelligent* or *angry* that are never used to characterize infants (Kagan, 1991). People in these cultures view personality development as discontinuous, and infants are regarded as so fundamentally different from adults that they cannot be judged on the same personality dimensions. By contrast, North Americans and Northern Europeans are more inclined to assume that personality development is a continuous process and to search for the seeds of adult personality in babies' temperaments.

In sum, the debate about developmental continuities and discontinuities is very complex. There is the issue of whether developmental change is gradual or abrupt, the issue of whether it is quantitative or qualitative, and the issue of whether it is or is not reliably connected to earlier developments.

developmental stage
a distinct phase within a larger sequence of development; a period characterized by a particular set of abilities, motives, behaviors, or emotions that occur together and form a coherent pattern.

Is Development Universal or Particularistic?

Finally, theorists often disagree about whether the most noteworthy aspects of development are **universal** (that is, normative outcomes that everyone is said to display) or **particularistic** (trends or outcomes that vary from person to person). Stage theorists typically believe that their developmental sequences apply to all normal people in all cultures and are therefore universal. For example, all normal humans begin to use language at 11–14 months of age, experience cognitive changes that prepare them for school at age 5–7 years, reach sexual maturity during the preteen or teenage period, and show some signs of aging (for example, wrinkles, a decline in certain sensory abilities) by midlife. From this perspective, then, the most important aspects of development are the universal patterns that all humans display.

universal development
normative developments that all individuals display.

particularistic development
developmental outcomes that vary from person to person.

How Do You Stand on Major Developmental Issues?

1. Children are
   a. creatures whose basically negative or selfish impulses must be controlled.
   b. neither inherently good nor inherently bad.
   c. creatures who are born with many positive and few negative tendencies.
2. Biological influences (heredity, maturational forces) and environmental influences (culture, parenting, styles, learning experiences) are thought to contribute to development. Overall,
   a. biological factors contribute more than environmental factors.
   b. biological and environmental factors are equally important.
   c. environmental factors contribute more than biological factors.
3. People are basically
   a. active beings who play a major role in determining their own abilities and traits.
   b. passive beings whose characteristics are molded either by social influences (parents and other significant people, outside events) or by biological factors beyond their control.
4. Development proceeds
   a. through stages, so that the individual changes rather abruptly into a quite different kind of person from the one he or she was in an earlier stage.
   b. continuously in small increments without abrupt changes or distinct stages.
5. Traits such as aggressiveness or dependency
   a. emerge in childhood and remain largely stable over the years.
   b. first appear in childhood but often disappear or give way to quite different traits at some later time.
6. A good analogy for a developing person might be
   a. a machine that becomes ever more complex as its parts (behaviors, emotions, abilities) grow more numerous and sophisticated.
   b. an entity that cannot be likened to a collection of parts and that blossoms over time much as a simple seed becomes a blooming rose.

Your pattern of answers:

___	___	___	___	___	___
1	2	3	4	5	6

However, other theorists believe that a singular focus on developmental universals is woefully incomplete. Why? Because it ignores all the factors that conspire to make each of us unique. Paths of development followed in one culture may be very different from those followed in another culture. And within any culture, developmental outcomes may vary across different subcultural or ethnic groups, from family to family, and from individual to individual. So the message of these "particularistic" theorists is that human development can (and does) proceed in many directions and is much less universal than stage theorists would have us believe.

These, then, are the major developmental controversies that different theories resolve in different ways. Perhaps you may wish to clarify your own stand on the issues by completing the brief questionnaire in Box 1.2. At the end of Chapter 3, Table 3.3 (on page 98) indicates how the major developmental theorists might answer these same questions so that you can compare their assumptions about human development with your own.

In the next section of the chapter, we will focus on the "tools of the trade"—that is, the research methods and designs that developmentalists use to test their theories and gain a better understanding of the social development of children and adolescents.

☞ RESEARCH METHODS

When detectives are assigned cases to solve, they will first gather the facts, formulate hunches, and then sift through the clues or collect additional information until one of their hunches proves correct. Unraveling the mysteries of social and personality development is in many ways a similar endeavor. Investigators must carefully observe their subjects, study the information they have collected, and then use it to draw conclusions about the ways people develop.

Our focus in this section is on the methods that researchers use to gather information about developing children and adolescents. Our first task is to understand why developmentalists consider it absolutely essential to gather all these facts. We will then discuss the advantages and disadvantages of several basic fact-finding strategies and see how these techniques might be used to detect developmental change.

The Scientific Method

The study of social and personality development is appropriately labeled a scientific enterprise because modern developmentalists have adopted a value system called the **scientific method** that guides their attempts at understanding. The scientific method is really more of an attitude or a value than a method; the attitude dictates that, above all, investigators must be *objective* and must allow their observations (or data) to decide the merits of their thinking.

In earlier eras, when social philosophers such as Hobbes, Locke, and Rousseau were presenting their views on children and childrearing, people were likely to interpret these pronouncements as fact. It was as if the public assumed that great minds always had great insights. Very few individuals questioned the word of well-known scholars, because the scientific method was not yet a widely accepted criterion for evaluating wisdom or knowledge.

The intent here is not to criticize the early social philosophers. In fact, today's developmentalists (and children) are indebted to these thinkers for helping to modify the ways in which society thought about, treated, and often exploited its young. However, great minds may on occasion produce miserable ideas that can do a great deal of harm if their errors in thinking are uncritically accepted and influence the way people are treated. The scientific method, then, is a valuable safeguard that helps to protect the scientific community and society at large against flawed reasoning. The protection comes from the practice of evaluating the merits of various theoretical pronouncements against objective observations, rather than simply relying on the academic, political, or social credibility of the theorist. Of course, this means that the theorist whose ideas are being evaluated must be equally objective and thus willing to discard pet notions when there is evidence against them.

Gathering Data: Basic Fact-Finding Strategies

No matter what aspect of social development we hope to study—be it the emotional responses of newborn infants, the growth of friendships among grade-school children, or the reasons some adolescents begin to use drugs—we must find ways to measure what interests us. Today researchers are fortunate to have many tried-and-true procedures that they can use to gather information and to test their hypotheses about human development. But regardless of the technique one employs, scientifically useful measures must always display two important qualities: **reliability** and **validity**.

A measure is *reliable* if it yields consistent information over time and across observers. Suppose you go into a classroom and record the number of times each child behaves in an aggressive manner towards others, but your research assistant, using the same scheme to observe the same children, does not agree with your measurements. Or you measure each child's aggressiveness one week but come up with very different aggressiveness scores while applying the same measure to the same children a week later. Clearly, your observational measure of aggression is unreliable because it yields highly inconsistent information. To be reliable and thus useful for scientific purposes, your measure would have to produce comparable estimates of children's aggression from independent observers (*interrater reliability*) and would yield similar scores for individual children from one testing to another shortly thereafter (*temporal stability*).

A measure is *valid* if it measures what it is supposed to measure. Perhaps you can see how an instrument must be reliable and measure consistently before it can possibly be valid.

scientific method
an attitude or value about the pursuit of knowledge that dictates that investigators must be objective and must allow their data to decide the merits of their theorizing.

reliability
the extent to which a measuring instrument yields consistent results, both over time and across observers.

validity
the extent to which a measuring instrument accurately reflects what the researchers intended to measure.

Yet reliability, by itself, does not guarantee validity. For example, a reliable observational scheme that is intended as a measure of children's aggression may provide badly overinflated estimates of aggressive behavior if the investigator simply classifies all acts of physical force as examples of aggression. What the researcher has failed to recognize is that many such high-intensity antics may simply represent enjoyable forms of rough-and-tumble play that children display without any harmful or aggressive intent. Clearly, researchers must demonstrate that they are measuring the attribute they say they are measuring before we can have much faith in the data they collect or the conclusions they reach.

With the importance of establishing the reliability and validity of measures in mind, let us consider some of the different ways in which aspects of social and personality development might be assessed.

Self-Report Methodologies   Three common procedures that developmentalists use to gather information and test hypotheses are interviews, questionnaires (including psychological tests), and the clinical method. Although these approaches are similar in that each asks subjects to answer questions posed by the investigator, they differ in the extent in which the investigator treats individual participants alike.

Interviews and Questionnaires   Researchers who opt for the interview or the questionnaire technique will ask the child (or the child's parents or teachers) a series of questions pertaining to such aspects of development as the child's feelings, beliefs, and characteristic patterns of behavior. Collecting data via a questionnaire (and most psychological tests) simply involves putting questions on paper and asking participants to respond to them in writing, whereas interviews require participants to respond orally to the investigator's queries. If the procedure is a **structured interview** or **structured questionnaire,** all who participate in the study are asked the same questions in the same order. The purpose of this standardized or structured format is to treat each person alike so that the responses of different participants can be compared.

One interesting use of the interview technique is a project in which kindergarten, second-grade, and fourth-grade children responded to 24 questions designed to assess their knowledge of social stereotypes about males and females (Williams, Bennett, & Best, 1975). Each question came in response to a different short story in which the central character was described by either stereotypically masculine adjectives (for example, *aggressive, forceful, tough*) or stereotypically feminine adjectives (for example, *emotional, excitable*). The child's task was to indicate whether the character in each story was male or female. Williams and his associates found that even kindergartners could usually tell whether the stories referred to boys or girls. In other words, these 5-year-olds were quite knowledgeable about gender stereotypes, although children's thinking became much more stereotyped between kindergarten and the second grade. One implication of these results is that stereotyping of the sexes must begin very early if kindergartners are already thinking along stereotyped lines.

A very creative use of interview or questionnaire methodologies is the so-called **diary study,** in which participants (usually adolescents or young adults) respond, in a diary or a notebook, to one or more standardized questions, either at a specified time (for example, at the end of the day) or whenever they are instructed to respond by a prompt from an electronic pager. Diary studies have proved invaluable for investigating a host of issues that may be difficult to study in other ways—issues such as the growth of moodiness and negativity as children transition into adolescence (Larson et al., 2002, and see Chapter 4) or the relationship between daily stressors and depression in adolescent boys and girls (Hankin, Mermelstein, & Roesch, 2007, and see Chapter 6).

Despite their versatility, interviews and questionnaires have some very real shortcomings. First, neither approach can be used with very young children who cannot read or comprehend speech very well. Second, investigators must hope that the answers they receive are

structured interview or structured questionnaire
a technique in which all participants are asked the same questions in precisely the same order so that the responses of different participants can be compared.

diary study
a self-report methodology in which participants respond to standardized questions, in a diary or notebook, at a specified time or whenever they are instructed to respond by prompt from an electronic pager.

honest and accurate and are not merely attempts by respondents to present themselves in a favorable manner. Many children, for example, may be reluctant to admit that they have snitched money from mother's purse or played "doctor" with the child next door. Clearly, inaccurate or untruthful responses will lead to erroneous conclusions. Investigators must also be careful to ensure participants of different ages interpret questions in the same way; otherwise, the age trends observed in one's study may reflect differences in participants' ability to comprehend and communicate rather than real underlying changes in children's feelings, thoughts, or behaviors. Finally, researchers who interview both developing children and their parents (or teachers) may have trouble determining which set of reports is the more accurate should the children's descriptions of their own feelings or behaviors differ from those of the other informants (Hussong et al., 2005).

Despite these potential shortcomings, structured interviews and questionnaires can be excellent methods of obtaining large amounts of useful information in a short period of time. Both approaches are particularly useful when the interviewer emphasizes to participants that their responses will be confidential and/or *challenges* them to report exactly what they know about an issue, thereby maximizing the likelihood or a truthful or accurate answer. In the gender stereotyping study, for example, the young participants probably considered each question a personal challenge or a puzzle to be solved and were thus motivated to answer accurately and to display exactly what they knew about males and females. Under the circumstances, then, the structured interview was an excellent method of assessing children's perceptions of the sexes.

The Clinical Method   The **clinical method** is a very close relative of the interview technique. The investigator is usually interested in testing an hypothesis by presenting the research participant with a task or problem of some sort and then inviting a response. When the participant has responded, the investigator will typically ask a second question or introduce a new problem in the hope of clarifying the participant's original answer. This questioning then continues until the investigator has the information needed to evaluate her hypothesis. Although participants are often asked the same questions in the initial stages of the research, their answers to each question determine what the investigator asks next. And because participants' answers often differ, it is possible that no two participants will ever receive exactly the same line of questioning. Thus, the clinical method considers each subject to be unique.

Jean Piaget, a famous Swiss psychologist, relied extensively on the clinical method to study children's moral reasoning and general intellectual development. The data from Piaget's research are largely protocol records of his interactions with individual children. Here is a small sample from Piaget's (1932/1965, p. 140) work on the development of moral reasoning—a sample which shows that this young child thinks about lying in a very different way than adults do.

Piaget: Do you know what a lie is?
Clai: It's when you say what isn't true.
Piaget: Is 2 + 2 = 5 a lie?
Clai: Yes, it's a lie.
Piaget: Why?
Clai: Because it isn't right.
Piaget: Did the boy who said 2 + 2 = 5 know it wasn't right or did he make a mistake?
Clai: He made a mistake.
Piaget: Then if he made a mistake, did he tell a lie or not?
Clai: Yes, he told a lie.

Like structured interviews, clinical methods are often useful for gathering large amounts of information in relatively brief periods. Proponents of this approach also cite its flexibility

clinical method
a type of interview in which a participant's response to each successive question (or problem) determines what the investigator will ask next.

as an advantage: By asking follow-up questions that are tailored to the participant's original answers (as Piaget did in the cited example), it is often possible to obtain a rich understanding of the meaning of those answers. However, the flexibility of the clinical method is also a potential shortcoming. Consider that it may be difficult, if not impossible, to directly compare the answers of participants who are asked different questions. Furthermore, this nonstandardized treatment of participants raises the possibility that the examiner's preexisting theoretical biases may affect the particular follow-up questions asked and the interpretations provided. Because conclusions drawn from the clinical method depend in part on the investigator's *subjective* interpretations, it is always desirable to verify these insights using other research techniques.

Observational Methodologies   Often researchers prefer to observe people's behavior directly rather than asking them questions about it. One method that many developmentalists favor is **naturalistic observation**—observing people in their common, everyday (that is, natural) surroundings. To observe children, this would usually mean going into homes, schools, or public parks and playgrounds and carefully recording what happens. Rarely will the investigator try to record every event that occurs; he or she will usually be testing a specific hypothesis about one type of behavior, such as cooperation or aggression, and will focus exclusively on acts of this kind. One strength of naturalistic observation is the ease with which it can be applied to infants and toddlers, who often cannot be studied though methods that demand verbal skills. But perhaps the greatest advantage of the observational technique is that it is the only method that can tell us how people actually behave in everyday life (Willems & Alexander, 1982).

However, naturalistic observation also has its limitations. First, some behaviors occur so infrequently (for example, heroic rescues) or are so socially undesirable (for example, overt sex play, thievery) that they are unlikely to be witnessed by a strange observer in the natural environment. Second, many events are usually happening at the same time in the natural setting, and any (or some combination) of them may be affecting people's behavior. This makes it difficult to pinpoint the causes of participants' actions or of any developmental trends in behavior. Finally, the mere presence of an observer can sometimes make people behave differently than they otherwise would. Children may "ham it up" when they have an audience, whereas parents may be on their best behavior, showing a strong reluctance, for example, to spank a misbehaving child. For these reasons, researchers will often attempt to minimize **observer influence** by (1) videotaping their participants from a concealed location or (2) by spending time in the setting before collecting their "real" data so that the individuals they are observing will grow accustomed to their presence and behave more naturally.

Several years ago, Mary Haskett and Janet Kistner (1991) conducted an excellent piece of naturalistic observation to compare the social behaviors of nonabused preschoolers with those of day-care classmates identified by child protection agencies as having been physically abused by their parents. The investigators first defined examples of the behaviors they wished to record—both *desirable* behaviors such as friendly social greetings and cooperative play, and *undesirable* behaviors such as physical aggression and name calling. They then monitored 14 abused and 14 nonabused preschool children as they mingled with peers in a play area of a day-care facility. Observations were made according to a **time-sampling** procedure: Each child was observed during three 10-minute play sessions on three different days. To minimize their influence on the play activities, observers stood outside the play area while making their observations.

The results were disturbing. As shown in Figure 1.3, abused children initiated fewer social interactions than their nonabused classmates and were somewhat

naturalistic observation
a method in which the scientist tests hypotheses by observing people as they engage in everyday activities in their natural habitats (for example, at home, at school, or on the playground).

observer influence
tendency of participants to react to an observer's presence by behaving in unusual ways.

time sampling
a procedure in which an investigator records the frequencies with which individuals display particular behaviors during the brief time intervals that each participant is observed.

Photo 1.3
Children's tendency to perform for an observer is one of the problems researchers must overcome when using the method of naturalistic observation.

PYMCA/Jupiter Images

socially withdrawn. And when they did interact with playmates, the abused youngsters displayed many more aggressive acts and other negative behaviors than did their nonabused companions. Indeed, nonabused children would often blatantly ignore any positive social initiations of an abused child, as if they did not want to get involved with him or her.

In sum, Haskett and Kistner's observational study shows that abused children are unattractive playmates who are likely to be disliked and even rejected by peers. But as is almost always the case in naturalistic observational research, it is difficult to pinpoint the exact cause of these findings. Did the negative behaviors of abused children cause their peers to back off and reject them? Or was it that peer rejection caused the abused children to display negative behaviors? Either possibility can account for Haskett and Kistner's results.

How might observational researchers study unusual or undesirable behaviors that they are unlikely to observe in the natural environment? One way is to conduct **structured observations** in the laboratory. In a structured observational study, each participant is exposed to a setting that might cue the behavior in question and is then surreptitiously observed (via hidden camera or through one-way mirror) to see whether he or she performs the behavior. For example, Leon Kuczynski (1983) got children to promise to help him with a boring task and then left them alone to work at it in a room where attractive toys were present. This procedure enabled Kuczynski to determine whether youngsters would break a promise to work (an undesirable act that some children displayed) when they thought there was no one present to observe their transgression.

Aside from being a most feasible way of studying behaviors that occur infrequently or are not openly displayed in the natural environment, structured observations also ensure that every participant in the sample is exposed to the *same* eliciting stimuli and has an *equal opportunity* to perform the target behavior—circumstances that are not always true in the natural setting. Of course, the major disadvantage of structured observations is that participants may not always respond to a contrived laboratory setting as they would in everyday life.

Case Studies Any or all of the data collection methods we have discussed—structured interviews, questionnaires, clinical methods, and behavioral observations—can be used to compile a detailed portrait of a single individual's development through the **case study** method. In preparing an individualized record, or "case," the investigator will typically seek many kinds of information about the participant, such as his or her family background, socioeconomic status, health records, academic or work history, and performance on psychological tests. Much of the information included in any case history comes from interviews with and observations of the individual, although the questions asked and observations made are typically not standardized and may vary considerably from case to case.

The baby biographies of the 19th and early 20th centuries are examples of case studies, and Sigmund Freud prepared many fascinating case studies of his clinical patients. In analyzing his cases, Freud noticed that different patients often described very similar events and experiences that had been noteworthy to them as they were growing up. He inferred from the observations that there must be important milestones in human development that all people share. As he continued to observe his patients and to listen to accounts of their lives, Freud concluded that each milestone in the life history of a patient was meaningfully related to earlier events. He then inferred that he had the data—the pieces of the puzzle—to construct a comprehensive explanation of human development—the account we know today as *psychoanalytic theory*.

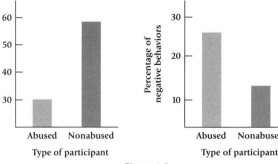

Figure 1.3
Social initiations and negative behaviors of abused and nonabused preschool children. Compared to their nonabused companions, abused youngsters initiate far fewer social interactions with peers and behave much more negatively toward them.

structured observation
an observational method in which the investigator cues the behavior of interest and observes participants' responses in a laboratory.

case study
a research method in which the investigator gathers extensive information about the life of an individual and then tests developmental hypotheses by analyzing the events of the person's life history.

Although Freud and many other developmentalists have used case studies to great advantage, there are major drawbacks to this approach. For example, it is often different to directly compare cases who have been asked different questions, have taken different tests, and have been observed under different circumstances. Case studies may also lack *generalizability*; that is, conclusions drawn from the experiences of the small number of individuals studied may simply not apply to most people. In fact, one recurring criticism of Freud's psychoanalytic theory is that it was formulated from the life histories of *emotionally disturbed patients*, who are hardly typical of the general population. For these reasons, any conclusions drawn from case studies should always be verified through the use of other research techniques.

Ethnography Ethnography—a form of participant observation often used in the field of anthropology—is becoming increasingly popular among researchers who hope to understand the impact of culture on developing children and adolescents. To collect their data, ethnographers sometimes live within the cultural or subcultural community they are studying for periods of months, or even years. The data they collect is typically diverse and extensive, consisting largely of naturalistic observations, notes made from conversations with members of the culture, and the researcher's initial interpretations of these events. These data are eventually used to compile a detailed portrait of the cultural community and to draw conclusions about how the community's unique values and traditions influence one or more aspects of the development of its children and adolescents.

A recent example of ethnographic research was conducted by Posada and associates (2004), who hoped to determine whether patterns of sensitive care that forecast secure attachments among white middle-class infants and their mothers in western industrialized societies were similar to or different from caregiving patterns associated with emotional security among infants in Bogata, Colombia. An observer made many extended visits to 27 Colombian homes. During the visits, mothers were told to carry on with daily routines, and the observer interacted naturally with family members. After each visit, observations and other notes were transcribed for further analysis by the research team.

From the many, many transcriptions, 10 dimensions of material caregiving were identified by two of the researchers and an ethnographic expert. These 10 caregiving dimensions, derived from in-depth analyses of mother-infant interactions, included domains such as quality of physical contact between mothers and infants, promptness of mothers' responses to infants' needs or bids for attention, smoothness of interactions between mothers and infants, and extent to which mothers and infants enjoyed their interactions.

Interestingly, these ethnographically derived caregiving dimensions were highly congruent with aspects of caregiving previously identified as components of sensitive care among white middle-class families from industrialized societies (see Chapter 5), thus implying that sensitive caregiving behaviors may be similar across cultures, at least during the infancy period.

Clearly, detailed ethnographic portraits of a culture or subculture that arise from close and enduring contact with members of the community can lead to a richer understanding of that community's traditions and values than is possible through a small number of visits in which outsiders make limited observations and conduct a couple interviews (LeVine et al., 1994). In fact, these extensive cultural or subcultural descriptions are particularly useful to investigators hoping to understand cultural conflicts and other developmental challenges faced by minority children and adolescents in diverse multicultural societies (Segal,

ethnography
method in which the researcher seeks to understand the unique values, traditions, and social processes of a culture or subculture by living with its members and making extensive observations and notes.

Photo 1.4
Ethnographic researchers attempt to understand cultural influences by living within the community and participating in all aspects of community life.

David Austen/Stock Boston

1991; see also Patel, Power, & Bhavnagri, 1996). But despite these clear strengths, ethnography is a highly subjective method—one in which researchers' own cultural values and theoretical biases can cause them to misinterpret what they have experienced. In addition, ethnographic conclusions pertain only to the culture or subculture studied and cannot be assumed to generalize to other contexts or social groups.

Psychophysiological Methods   In recent years, developmentalists have turned to **psychophysiological methods**—techniques that measure the relationship between physiological responses and behavior—to explore the biological underpinnings of children's perceptual, cognitive, and emotional responses. Psychophysiological methods are particularly useful for interpreting the mental and emotional experiences of infants and toddlers who are unable to report such events (Bornstein & Lamb, 2005).

Heart rate is an involuntary physiological response that is highly sensitive to one's psychological experiences. Compared to their normal resting, or baseline, levels, infants who are carefully attending to an interesting stimulus may show a decrease in heart rate, whereas those who are uninterested in it may show no heart rate change, and others, who are wary of or angered by the stimulus, may show a heart rate increase (Campos, Bertenthal, & Kermoian, 1992; Fox & Fitzgerald, 1990). Measures of brain function are also useful for assessing psychological state. For example, electroencephalogram (EEG) recording of brain wave activity can be obtained by attaching electrodes to the scalp. Because different patterns of EEG activity characterize different arousal states, investigators who hope to assess what infants perceive can present novel sights or sounds and look for changes in an infant's brain waves (called event-related potentials, or ERPs) to determine whether these stimuli have been detected, or even discriminated, for two stimuli perceived as different will produce different patterns of brain wave activity. Indeed, researchers have used ERPs to explore infants' reactions to others' displays of emotions, finding that 7-month-olds attend more to facial displays of negative rather than positive (or neutral) emotions (Leppanen et al., 2007) and that 12-month-olds are more inclined to use negative rather than positive (or neutral) facial expressions as a guide for how they should be feeling or behaving in new and uncertain situations (Carver & Vaccaro, 2007).

Though very useful, psychophysiological responses are far from perfect indicators of psychological states. Even though an infant's heart rate or brain wave activity may indicate that he or she is attending to a stimulus, it is often difficult to determine exactly which aspect of that stimulus (shape, color, and so on) has captured attention. Furthermore, changes in physiological responses often reflect mood swings, hunger, or even negative reactions to the physiological recording equipment rather than a change in the infant's attention to a stimulus or emotional reactions to it. For these reasons, physiological responses are more likely to be valid indicators of psychological experience when participants (particularly very young ones) are initially calm, alert, and contented.

Table 1.1 provides a brief review of the data-gathering schemes that we have examined thus far. In the sections that follow, we will consider how investigators relying on any one or some combination of these data gathering strategies might design their research to test hypotheses and detect developmental continuities and changes.

☞ DETECTING RELATIONSHIPS: CORRELATIONAL AND EXPERIMENTAL DESIGNS

Once researchers have decided what they want to study and how they will collect their data, they must then formulate a research plan, or design, that permits them to identify associations among events and behaviors and to specify the causes of these relationships. Here we consider two general research designs that investigators might employ: correlational and experimental.

psychophysiological methods methods that measure the relationships between physiological processes and aspects of children's physical, cognitive, social, or emotional behavior and development.

Table 1.1 Strengths and limitations of seven common research methods

Method	Strengths	Limitations
Self-reports		
Interviews and questionnaires	Relatively quick way to gather much information; standardized format allows the investigator to make direct comparisons between data provided by different participants.	Data collected may be inaccurate, or less than completely honest, or may reflect variations in respondents' verbal skills and ability to understand questions.
Clinical methods	Flexible methodology that treats subjects as unique individuals; freedom to probe can be an aid in ensuring that the participant understands the meaning of the questions asked.	Conclusions drawn may be unreliable in that participants are not all treated alike; flexible probes depend, in part, on the investigator's subjective interpretations of the participant's responses; can be used only with highly verbal participants.
Systematic observations		
Naturalistic observation	Allows study of behavior as it actually occurs in the natural environment.	Observed behaviors may be influenced by observer's presence; unusual or undesirable behaviors are unlikely to be observed during the periods when observations are made.
Structured observation	Offers a standardized environment that provides every child an opportunity to perform target behavior. Excellent way to observe infrequent or socially undesirable acts.	Contrived observations may not always capture the ways children behave in the natural environment.
Case studies	Very broad method that considers many sources of data when drawing inferences and conclusions about individual participants.	Kind of data collected often differs from case to case and may be inaccurate or less than honest; conclusions drawn from individual cases are subjective and may not apply to other people.
Ethnography	Provides a richer description of cultural beliefs, values, and traditions than is possible in brief observational or interview studies.	Conclusions may be biased by the investigator's values and theoretical viewpoints; results cannot be generalized beyond the groups and settings that were studied.
Psychophysiological methods	Useful for assessing biological underpinnings of development and identifying the perceptions, thoughts, and emotions of infants and toddlers who cannot report them verbally.	Cannot indicate with certainty what participants sense or feel; many factors other than the one being studied can produce a similar physiological response.

The Correlational Design

correlational design
a type of research design that indicates the strength of associations among variables; though correlated variables are systematically related, these relationships are not necessarily causal.

In a **correlational design,** the investigator gathers information to determine whether two or more variables of interest are meaningfully related. If the researcher is testing a specific hypothesis (rather than conducting preliminary exploratory research), he or she will be checking to see whether these variables are related as the hypothesis specifies they should be. No attempts are made to structure or to manipulate the participants' environment in any way. Instead, correlational researchers take people as they find them—already "manipulated" by natural life experiences—and try to determine whether variations in people's life experiences are associated with differences in their behaviors or patterns of development.

To illustrate the correlational approach to hypothesis testing, let's work with a simple theory specifying that youngsters learn a lot from watching television and are apt to imitate the actions of the characters they observe. One hypothesis we might derive from this theory is that the more often children observe TV characters who display violent and aggressive acts, the more inclined they will be to behave aggressively toward their own playmates. After selecting a sample of children to study, our next step in testing our hypothesis is to measure the two variables that we think are related. To assess children's exposure to aggressive themes on television, we might use the interview or naturalistic observational methods to determine what each child watches and then count the number of violent and aggressive acts that occur in this programming. To measure the frequency of the children's own aggressive behavior toward peers, we could observe our sample on a playground and record how often each child behaves in a hostile, aggressive manner toward playmates. Having now gathered the data, it is time to evaluate our hypothesis.

The presence (or absence) of a relationship between variables can be determined by subjecting the data to a statistical procedure that yields a **correlation coefficient.** A correlation coefficient (symbolized by an r) provides a numerical estimate of the strength and the direction of the association between two variables. It can range in value from $+1.00$ to -1.00. The absolute value of r (disregarding its sign) tells us the *strength* of the relationship. Thus, correlation coefficients of $-.70$ and $+.70$ are of equal strength, and both are stronger than a moderate correlation of $.50$. An r of $.00$ indicates that the two variables are unrelated.

The sign of the correlation coefficient indicates the *direction* of the relationship. If the sign is positive, this means that as one variable increases, the other variable also increases. For example, height and weight are positively correlated: As children grow taller, they (usually) get heavier (Tanner, 1990). Negative correlations, however, indicate inverse relationships; as one variable increases, the other *decreases*. Among grade-school students, for example, aggression and popularity are negatively correlated: Children who behave more aggressively are often less popular with their peers (Crick, 1996; LaFontana & Cillessen, 2002).

Now let's return to our hypothesized positive relationship between viewing televised violence and children's aggressive behavior. A number of investigators have conducted correlational studies similar to the one we have designed, and the results (reviewed in Liebert & Sprafkin, 1988) suggest a moderate positive correlation (between $+.30$ and $+.50$) between the two variables of interest: Children who watch a lot of violent television programming are more likely to behave aggressively toward playmates than do other youngsters who watch little violent programming (see Figure 1.4 for a visual display).

Do these correlational studies establish that exposure to violent TV programming *causes* children to behave more aggressively? *No, they do not!* Though we have detected a relationship between exposure to televised violence and children's aggressive behavior, the causal direction of the relationship is not at all clear. An equally plausible alternative explanation is that relatively aggressive children are more inclined to prefer violent programming. Another possibility is that the association between TV viewing and aggressive behavior is actually caused by a third variable we have not measured. Perhaps parents who fight a lot at home (an unmeasured variable) cause their children to become more aggressive *and* to favor violent TV programming. If this were true, the latter two variables may be correlated, even though their relationship to each other is not one of cause and effect.

In sum, the correlational design is a versatile approach that can detect systematic relationships between any two or more variables that we might be interested in and are capable of measuring. However, its major limitation is that *it cannot unambiguously indicate that one thing causes another.* How, then, might a researcher establish the underlying causes of various behaviors or other aspects of human development? One solution is to conduct experiments.

The Experimental Design

In contrast to correlational studies, **experimental designs** permit a precise assessment of the cause-and-effect relationship that may exist between two variables. Let's return to the issue of whether viewing violent television programming *causes* children to become more

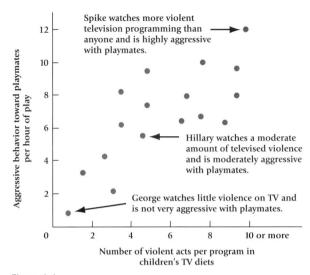

Figure 1.4

Plot of a hypothetical positive correlation between the amount of violence children see on television and the number of aggressive responses they display. Each dot represents a specific child who views a particular level of televised violence (shown on the horizontal axis) and commits a certain number of aggressive acts (shown on the vertical axis). Although the correlation is less than perfect, we see that children who watch more acts of violence on TV are generally more inclined to behave aggressively toward peers.

correlation coefficient
a numerical index, ranging from -1.00 to $+1.00$, of the strength and direction of the relationship between two variables.

experimental design
a research design in which the investigator introduces some change in the participant's environment and then measures the effect of that change on the participant's behavior.

aggressive. In conducting a laboratory experiment to test this (or any) hypothesis, we would bring participants to the lab, expose them to different treatments, and record as data their responses to these treatments.

The different treatments to which we expose our participants represent the **independent variable** of our experiment. To test the hypothesis that we have proposed, our independent variable (or treatments) would be the type of television program that our participants observe. Half the children might view a program in which one or more characters behave in a violent or otherwise aggressive manner toward others, whereas the other half would watch a program that contains little if any violence.

Children's reactions to the television shows would become the data, or **dependent variable,** in our experiment. Because our hypothesis centers on children's aggression, we would want to measure (as our dependent variable) how aggressively children behave after watching each type of television show. A dependent variable is called "dependent" because its value presumably depends on the independent variable. In the present case, we are hypothesizing that future aggression (our dependent variable) will be greater for children who watch violent programs (one level of the independent variable) than for children who watch nonviolent programs (the second level of the independent variable). If we are careful experimenters and exercise precise control over *all* other factors that may affect children's aggression, then the pattern of results that we have anticipated would allow us to draw a strong conclusion: Watching violent television programs *causes* children to behave more aggressively.

Many years ago, an experiment similar to the one we have proposed was actually conducted (Liebert & Baron, 1972). Half of the 5- to 9-year-olds in this study watched a violent 3½ minute clip from *The Untouchables*—one that contained two fistfights, two shootings, and a stabbing. The remaining children watched 3½ minutes of a nonviolent but exciting track meet. So the independent variable was the type of program children had watched. Then each child was taken into another room and seated before a box that had wires leading into the adjoining room. On the box was a green button labeled HELP, a red button labeled HURT, and a white light between the buttons. The experimenter noted that a child in the adjoining room would soon be playing a handle-turning game that would illuminate the white light. The child was told that, by pushing the buttons when the light was lit, he or she could either *help* the other child by making the handle easy to turn, or *hurt* the child by making the handle become very hot. When it was clear that the participant understood the instructions, the experimenter left the room, and the light came on 20 times over the next several minutes. So each participant had 20 opportunities to help or hurt another child. The total amount of time each participant spent pushing the HURT button served as a measure of his or her aggression—the dependent variable in this study.

The results were clear: Despite the availability of an alternative helping response, *both boys and girls were much more likely to press the HURT button (that is, behave aggressively) if they had watched the violent television program.* So it appears that a mere 3½-minute exposure to televised violence can cause children to behave more aggressively toward a peer, even though the aggressive acts they witnessed on television bore no resemblance to those they committed themselves.

When students discuss this experiment in class, someone invariably challenges this interpretation of the results. For example, one student proposed an alternative interpretation that "maybe kids who saw the violent film were naturally more sadistic than those who saw the track meet." In other words, he was suggesting that a **confounding variable**—children's *preexisting* levels of sadism—had determined their willingness to hurt a peer and that the independent variable (type of television programming) had had no effect at all! Could he have been correct? How do we know that children in the two experimental conditions didn't differ in some important way that may have affected their willingness to hurt a peer?

---

independent variable
the aspect of the environment that an experimenter modifies or manipulates in order to measure its impact on behavior.

dependent variable
the aspect of behavior that is measured in an experiment and assumed to be under the control of the independent variable.

confounding variable
some factor other than the independent variable that, if not controlled by the experimenter, could explain any differences across treatment conditions in participants' performance on the dependent variable.

This question brings us to the crucial issue of **experimental control.** In order to conclude that the independent variable is causally related to the dependent variable, the experimenter must ensure that all other factors that could affect the dependent variable are *controlled*—that is, equivalent in each experimental condition. One way to equalize these potentially confounding factors is to do what Liebert and Baron (1972) did: Randomly assign children to their experimental treatments. The concept of *randomization,* or **random assignment,** means that each research participant has an equal probability of being exposed to each experimental treatment or condition. Assignment of individual participants to a particular treatment is accomplished by an unbiased procedure such as the flip of a coin. If the assignment is truly random, there is only a very slim chance that participants in the two (or more) experimental conditions will differ on *any* characteristic that might affect their performance on the dependent variable: All these "confounding" characteristics will have been randomly distributed within each condition and equalized across the different conditions. Because Liebert and Baron randomly assigned children to experimental conditions, they could be reasonably certain that the group of children who watched the violent TV program were not naturally more sadistic than children who watched the nonviolent program. So it was reasonable for them to conclude that the former groups of children were the more aggressive group *because* they had watched a TV program in which violence and aggression was a central theme.

A Possible Limitation of Laboratory Experiments   Clearly, the greatest strength of the experimental method is its ability to establish conclusively that one thing causes another. Yet critics of laboratory experimentation have argued that the tightly controlled laboratory environment is often contrived and artificial and that children are likely to behave very differently in these surroundings than they would in a natural setting. Urie Bronfenbrenner (1977) has charged that a heavy reliance on laboratory experiments has made developmental psychology "the science of the strange behavior of children in strange situations with strange adults" (p. 19). Similarly, Robert McCall (1977) notes that experiments tell us what *can* cause a developmental change but do not necessarily pinpoint the factors that *actually do* cause such changes in natural settings. Consequently, it is quite possible that conclusions drawn from laboratory experiments will not always apply in the real world. In Box 1.3, we will consider a step that experimentalists can take to counter this criticism and assess the **ecological validity** of their laboratory findings.

The Natural (or Quasi) Experiment

There are many issues to which the experimental method cannot be applied or should not be used for ethical reasons. Suppose, for example, that we wish to study the effects of early social deprivation on infants' social and emotional development. Obviously, we cannot ask one group of parents to lock their infants in an attic for two years so that we can collect the data we need. It is simply unethical to submit children to any experimental treatment that may adversely affect their physical or psychological well-being.

However, we might be able to accomplish our research objectives through a **natural (or quasi) experiment**—a study in which we observe the consequences of a natural event to which participants have been exposed. So if we were able to locate a group of children who were raised in impoverished institutions with very little contact with caregivers over the first two years, we could compare their social and emotional development with that of children raised at home with their families. This comparison would provide some valuable information about the likely impact of early social deprivation on children's social and emotional development. (Indeed, precisely this kind of natural experiment is described in detail in Chapter 5.) The "independent variable" in a natural experiment is the "event" that participants experience (in our example, the social deprivation

experimental control
steps taken by an experimenter to ensure that all extraneous factors that could influence the dependent variable are roughly equivalent in each experimental condition; these precautions must be taken before an experimenter can be reasonably certain that observed changes in the dependent variable were caused by the manipulation of the independent variable.

random assignment
a control technique in which participants are assigned to experimental conditions through an unbiased procedure so that the members of the groups are not systematically different from one another.

ecological validity
state of affairs in which the findings of one's research are an accurate representation of processes that occur in the natural environment.

natural (or quasi) experiment
a study in which the investigator measures the impact of some naturally occurring event that is assumed to affect people's lives.

Assessing Causal Relationships in the Real World: The Field Experiment

How can we be more certain that a conclusion drawn from a laboratory experiment also applies in the real world? One way is to seek converging evidence for that conclusion by conducting a similar experiment *in a natural setting*—that is, a **field experiment.** This approach combines all the advantages of naturalistic observation with the more rigorous control that experimentation allows. In addition, subjects typically are not apprehensive about participating in a "strange" experiment because all the activities they undertake are everyday activities. Indeed, they may not even be aware that they are being observed or participating in an experiment.

Let's consider a field experiment (Leyens et al., 1975) that sought to test the hypothesis that heavy exposure to media violence can cause viewers to become more aggressive. The subjects were Belgian delinquents who lived together in cottages at a minimum-security institution for adolescent boys. Before the experiment began, the experimenters observed each boy in their research sample to measure his characteristic level of aggression. These initial assessments served as a *baseline* against which future increases in aggression could be measured. The baseline observations suggested that the institution's four cottages could be divided into two subgroups consisting of two cottages populated by relatively aggressive inmates and two cottages populated by less aggressive peers. Then the experiment began. For a period of one week, *violent* movies (such as *Bonnie and Clyde* and *The Dirty Dozen*) were shown each evening to one of the two cottages in each subgroup, and *neutral* films (such as *Daddy's Fiancée* and *La Belle Américaine*) were shown to the other cottages. Instances of physical and verbal aggression among residents of each cottage were recorded twice daily (at lunchtime and in the evenings after the movie) during the movie week and once daily (at lunchtime) during a posttreatment week.

The most striking result of this field experiment was the significant increase in *physical* aggression that occurred in the evenings among residents of both cottages assigned to the violent-film condition. Because the violent movies contained a large number of physically aggressive incidents, it appears that they evoked

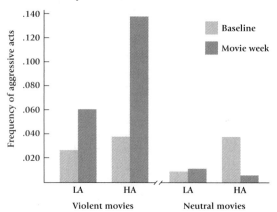

Mean physical aggression scores in the evening for highly aggressive (HA) and less aggressive (LA) boys under baseline conditions and after watching violent or neutral movies. (Adapted from Leyens et al., 1975.)

similar responses from the boys who watched them. But as shown in the figure, violent movies prompted larger increases in aggression among boys who were already relatively high in aggression. Furthermore, exposure to the violent movies caused the highly aggressive boys to become more *verbally aggressive* as well—an effect that these boys continued to display through the movie week *and* the posttreatment week.

Clearly, the results of the Belgian field experiment are consistent with Liebert and Baron's (1972) laboratory study in suggesting that exposure to media violence does indeed instigate aggressive behavior. Yet it also qualifies the laboratory findings by implying that the instigating effects of media violence *in the natural environment* are likely to be stronger and more enduring for the more aggressive members of the audience (and see Friedrich & Stein, 1973, for similar results with nursery-school children).

---

field experiment
an experiment that takes place in a naturalistic setting such as the home, the school, or a playground.

experienced by institutionalized infants). The "dependent variable" is whatever outcome measure one chooses to study (in our example, social and emotional development).

Note, however, that researchers conducting natural experiments do not control the independent variable, nor do they randomly assign participants to experimental conditions; they merely observe and record the apparent outcomes of a natural happening or event. So in the absence of tight experimental control, it is often hard to determine precisely what factor is responsible for any group differences that are found. Suppose, for example, that our socially deprived institutionalized children showed a poorer pattern of emotional outcomes than did children raised at home. Is the *social deprivation* that institutionalized children experienced the factor that accounts for this difference? Or is it that institutionalized children differed in other ways from family-reared children (for example, were more sickly as infants, were more poorly nourished) that might explain their poorer outcomes? Without randomly assigning participants to treatments and controlling other factors that may vary across treatments (for example, nutrition received), we simply *cannot* be certain that *social deprivation* is the factor responsible for the poor emotional outcomes that institutionalized children display.

Table 1.2 Strengths and limitations of general research designs

Design	Procedure	Strengths	Limitations
Correlational	Gathers information about two or more variables without researcher intervention.	Estimates the strength and direction of relationships among variables in the natural environment.	Does not permit determination of cause-and-effect relationships among variables.
Laboratory experiment	Manipulates some aspect of participants' environment (independent variable) and measures its impact on participants' behavior (dependent variable).	Permits determination of cause-and-effect relationships among variables.	Data obtained in artificial environment may lack generalizability to the real world.
Field experiment	Manipulates independent variable and measures its impact on the dependent variable in a natural setting.	Permits determination of cause-and-effect relationships and generalization of findings to the real world.	Experimental treatments may be less potent and harder to control when presented in the natural environment.
Natural (quasi) experiment	Gathers information about the behavior of people who experience a real-world (natural) manipulation of their environment.	Permits a study of the impact of natural events that would be difficult or impossible to simulate in an experiment; provides strong clues about cause-and-effect relationships.	Lack of precise control over the natural events or the participants exposed to them prevents the investigator from establishing definitive causal relationships.

Despite its inability to make precise statements about cause and effect, the natural experiment is useful nonetheless. Why? Because it can tell us whether a natural event could *possibly* have influenced those who experienced it and thus can provide some meaningful clues about cause and effect.

Table 1.2 summarizes the strengths and limitations of each of the general research designs we have discussed. Now let's consider designs that focus more specifically on detecting developmental continuities and changes.

DESIGNS FOR STUDYING DEVELOPMENT

Social developmentalists are not merely interested in examining children's behavior at one particular point in time; instead, they hope to determine how children's feelings, thoughts, abilities, and behaviors *develop* or *change* over time. How might we design research to chart these developmental trends? Let's briefly consider four approaches: the cross-sectional design, the longitudinal design, the sequential design, and the microgenetic design.

The Cross-Sectional Design

In a **cross-sectional design,** groups of children who *differ in age* are studied at *the same point in time.* For example, a researcher interested in determining whether children become more generous as they mature might place 6-, 8-, and 10-year-olds in a situation where they are afforded an opportunity to share a valuable commodity (say, candy or money) with needy youngsters who are less fortunate than themselves. By comparing the responses of children in the different age groups, investigators can often identify age-related changes in generosity (see Chapter 10 for a review of this topic) or in whatever aspect of development they have chosen to study.

An important advantage of the cross-sectional design is that the investigator can collect data from participants of different ages over a short time. For example, an investigator would not have to wait four years for her 6-year-olds to become 10-year-olds in order

cross-sectional design
a research design in which subjects from different age groups are studied at the same point in time.

to determine whether children's generosity increases over this age range. She can merely sample children of different ages and test all samples at approximately the same time.

Cohort Effects   Notice, however, that in cross-sectional research, participants at each age level are *different* people who come from different cohorts. A *cohort* is a group of people of the same age who are exposed to similar cultural environments or historical events as they are growing up. The fact that different cohorts are always involved in cross-sectional comparisons means that any age-related effects that are found in the study may not always be due to age or development but rather to some other feature that distinguishes individuals in different cohorts. For example, early cross-sectional research had consistently indicated that young adults score higher on intelligence tests than middle-aged adults, who, in turn, score higher than the elderly. But does intelligence decline with age, as these findings would seem to indicate? Not necessarily! More recent research (Schaie, 1986, 1990) reveals that individuals' intelligence test scores remain reasonably stable over the years and that the earlier studies were really measuring something quite different: cohort differences in education. The older adults in earlier cross-sectional studies had had less schooling, which could explain why they scored lower on intelligence tests than the middle-aged or young adult samples. Their test scores had not declined but rather had always been lower than those of the younger adults with whom they were compared. So the earlier cross-sectional research had discovered a **cohort effect,** not true developmental change.

Despite this important limitation, the cross-sectional comparison is still the design that developmentalists use most often. Why? Because it has the advantage of being quick and easy; we can go out this year, sample individuals of different ages, and be done with it. What's more, this design is likely to yield valid conclusions when there is little reason to believe that the cohorts being studied have had widely differing experiences while growing up. So if we compared the generosity of 6-, 8-, and 10-year-olds in the study proposed earlier, we might feel reasonably confident that history or the prevailing culture had not changed in major ways in the four years that separate these three cohorts. It is mainly in studies that attempt to make inferences about development over a span of many years that cohort effects present a major problem.

Data on Individual Development   There is a second noteworthy limitation of the cross-sectional method: It tells us nothing about the development of *individuals* because each person is observed *at only one point in time.* So cross-sectional comparisons cannot provide answers to questions such as "When will *my* child become more generous?" or "Will aggressive 2-year-olds become aggressive 5-year-olds?" To address issues like these, an investigator will often rely on a second kind of developmental comparison, the longitudinal design.

The Longitudinal Design

In a **longitudinal design**, the same participants are observed repeatedly over time. For example, a researcher interested in determining whether generosity increases over middle childhood might provide 6-year-olds an opportunity to behave in a charitable fashion toward needy youngsters and then follow up with similar assessments of the generosity of *these same children* at ages 8 and 10.

The period spanned by a longitudinal study may be very long or reasonably short. The investigators may be looking at one particular aspect of development, such as generosity, or at many. By repeatedly testing the same participants, investigators can assess the *stability* of various attributes and the patterns of developmental *change* for each person in the sample. In addition, they can identify *general* developmental trends by looking for commonalities in development that most or all individuals share. Finally, the tracking of several children over time will help investigators to understand the bases for *individual differences* in development,

cohort effect
age-related difference among cohorts that is attributable to cultural/historical differences in cohorts' growing-up experiences rather than to true developmental change.

longitudinal design
a research design in which one group of subjects is studied repeatedly over a period of months or years.

particularly if they are able to establish that different kinds of earlier experiences lead to very different outcomes.

Several very noteworthy longitudinal projects have followed children for decades and have assessed many aspects of development (see, for example, Kagan & Moss, 1962; Newman et al., 1997). However, most longitudinal studies are much more modest in direction and scope. For example, Carolee Howes and Catherine Matheson (1992) conducted a study in which the pretend play activities of a group of 1–2-year-olds were repeatedly observed at six-month intervals over the next three years. Using a classification scheme that assessed the cognitive complexity of play, Howes and Matheson sought to determine (1) whether play did reliably become more complex with age, (2) whether children reliably differed in the complexity of their play, and (3) whether the complexity of a child's play reliably forecasted his or her social competencies with peers. Not surprisingly, all children displayed increases in the complexity of their play over the three-year period, although there were reliable individual differences in play complexity at each observation point. In addition, there was a clear relationship between the complexity of a child's play and social competence with peers: Children who engaged in more complex forms of play at any given age were the ones who were rated as most outgoing and least aggressive at the next observation period six months later. So this longitudinal study shows that complexity of pretend play not only increases with age but is also a reliable predictor of children's future social competencies with peers.

Although we have focused on the important advantages of the longitudinal comparison, this procedure does have several drawbacks. For example, longitudinal research can be very costly and time-consuming, particularly if the project spans a period of several years. Moreover, the focus of theory and research in social and personality development is constantly changing, so that longitudinal questions that seem very exciting at the beginning of a long-term project may seem rather trivial by the time the study ends. **Selective attrition** may also become a problem: Children may move away, get sick, become bored with repeated testing, or have parents who, for one reason or another, will not allow them to continue in the study. The result is a smaller and potentially **nonrepresentative sample** that not only provides less information about the developmental issues in question but also may limit the conclusions of the study to those healthy children who do not move away and who remain cooperative over the long run.

There is another shortcoming of these very long-term longitudinal studies that students often see right away—the **cross-generational problem**. Children in longitudinal research are typically drawn from one cohort, and as a result, they will experience somewhat different cultural, family, and school environments than children in other cohorts. Consider, for example, how the times have changed since the 1930s and 1940s, when children in some of the early long-term longitudinal studies were growing up. In this age of dual-career families, more youngsters are attending day-care centers and nursery schools than ever before. Modern families are smaller than those of years past, meaning that children now have fewer brothers and sisters. Families also move more frequently than they did in the 1930s and 1940s, so that many children from the modern era are exposed to a wider variety of people and places than was typical in years gone by. And no matter where they may be living, today's youngsters grow up in front of television sets and computers, influences that were not available during the 1930s and 1940s. So children of earlier eras lived in a very different world, and we cannot be certain that these youngsters developed in precisely the same way as today's children. Stated another way, cross-generational changes in the environment may limit the conclusions of a longitudinal project to those participants who were growing up while the study was in progress.

We have seen that the cross-sectional and the longitudinal designs each have distinct advantages and disadvantages. Might it be possible to combine the best features of both approaches? A third kind of developmental comparison—the **sequential design**—tries to do just that.

selective attrition
nonrandom loss of participants during a study, resulting in a nonrepresentative sample.

nonrepresentative sample
a subgroup that differs in important ways from the larger group (or population) to which it belongs.

cross-generational problem
the fact that long-term changes in the environment may limit conclusions of a longitudinal project to that generation of children who were growing up while the study was in progress.

Photo 1.5 Leisure activities of the 1930s (left) and the 2000s (right).
As these photos illustrate, the kinds of experiences that children growing up in the 1930s had were very different from those of today's youth. Many believe that cross-generational changes in the environment may limit the results of a longitudinal study to the youngsters who were growing up while the research was in progress.

The Sequential Design

sequential design
a research design in which subjects from different age groups are studied repeatedly over a period of months or years.

Sequential designs combine the best features of cross-sectional and longitudinal studies by selecting participants of different ages and following each of these cohorts over time. To illustrate, imagine that we wished to study the development of children's moral reasoning between the ages of 6 and 12. We might begin in the year 2008 by testing the logical reasoning of a sample of 6-year olds (the 2002 birth cohort) and a sample of 8-year-olds (the 2000 birth cohort). We could then retest the reasoning abilities of both those groups in 2010 and 2012. Notice that the design calls for us to follow the 2002 cohort from ages 6 through 10 and the 2000 cohort from ages 8 through 12. A graphic representation of this research plan appears in Figure 1.5.

There are three major strengths of this sequential design. First, it allows us to determine whether cohort effects are influencing our results by comparing the moral reasoning of same-aged children who were born in different years. As shown in the figure, cohort effects are assessed by comparing the moral judgments of the two samples at ages 8 and 10. If the samples do not differ, we can assume that cohort effects are not operating. The figure also illustrates a second major advantage of our sequential design: It allows us to make both longitudinal and cross-sectional comparisons in the same study. If the age trends in reasoning are similar in both the longitudinal and the cross-sectional comparisons, we can be quite confident that they represent true developmental changes in moral reasoning abilities. Finally, sequential designs are often more efficient than standard longitudinal designs. In our example, we could trace the development of moral reasoning over a six-year age range, even though our study would take but four years to conduct. A standard longitudinal comparison that initially sampled 6-year-old participants would take six years to provide similar information. Clearly, this combination of the cross-sectional and longitudinal designs is a rather versatile alternative to either of these approaches.

The Microgenetic Design

Cross-sectional, longitudinal, and sequential designs provide only a broad outline of developmental changes without necessarily specifying why or how these changes take place. **Microgenetic designs** are used in an attempt to illuminate the processes that are thought to promote developmental changes. The logic is straightforward: Children who are thought to be ready for an important developmental change are exposed repeatedly to experiences that are thought to produce the change, and their behavior is monitored *as it is changing*.

Cognitive theorists have used this approach to specify how children come to rely on new and more efficient strategies for solving problems. By studying participants intensively over a period of hours, days, or weeks and carefully analyzing their problem-solving behavior, it is often possible to specify how their thinking and strategizing is changing to advance their cognitive competencies (Siegler & Svetina, 2002), arithmetic skills (Siegler & Jenkins, 1989), memory (Coyle & Bjorklund, 1997), and language skills (Gershkoff-Stowe & Smith, 1997). Although the microgenetic approach is a new method, it holds great promise for illuminating the kinds of experiences that can promote changes in such areas of social and personality development as self-concept and self-esteem, social cognition (that is, understanding others' behaviors and forming impressions of others), reasoning about moral issues, and thinking about gender-role stereotypes, to name a few.

Courage, Edison, and Howe (2005) have used the microgenetic design to investigate a major milestone in the development of self-concept: the ability to recognize oneself in a mirror or a recent photograph. One common method of assessing self-recognition is to place a dab of rouge (or some other colored substance) on an infant's face and shortly thereafter place him or her before a mirror. If the infant recognizes the mirror image as "me," he or she will investigate the strange colored mark by touching his or her *own* face (self-recognition) as opposed to doing nothing or perhaps reaching out to touch the mirror image (nonrecognition). Past cross-sectional research had revealed a sharp increase between 18 and 24 months of age in the percentage of toddlers displaying clear self-recognition. Does this imply that recognizing one's mirror image as one's self is a sudden "a--ha" kind of experience?

To find out, Courage et al. assessed self-recognition in each of 10 toddlers on a biweekly basis, starting when these youngsters were 15 months of age. These microgenetic assessments revealed that toddlers gradually evolved from nonrecognizers, through a brief (one- to two-week) ambiguous phase in which they successfully identified themselves on some testings but not on others, before showing reliable and unambiguous self-recognition at age 16–17 months on average. Clearly, one implication of these microgenetic data is that progression from not recognizing oneself to stable self-recognition is a gradual process rather than a sudden insight.

Although microgenetic techniques provide a unique opportunity to witness and record the actual process of developmental change as it occurs, there are disadvantages to this kind of research. First, it is difficult, time-consuming, and costly to track large numbers

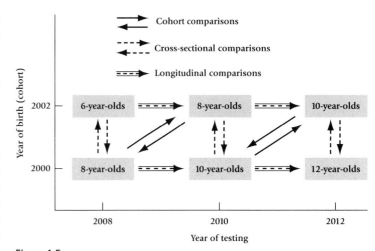

Figure 1.5

Example of a sequential design. Two samples of children, one born in 2000 and one born in 2002, are observed longitudinally over a 4-year period. The design permits the investigator to assess cohort effects by comparing children of the same age who were born in different years. In the absence of cohort effects, the longitudinal and cross-sectional comparisons in this design permit the researcher to make strong statements about the strength and direction of any developmental changes.

microgenetic design
a research design in which participants are studied intensively over a short period of time as developmental changes occur; attempts to specify how or why those changes occur.

Table 1-3 Strengths and limitations of four developmental designs

Design	Procedure	Strengths	Limitations
Cross-sectional	Observes people of different ages (or cohorts) at one point in time.	Demonstrates age differences; hints at developmental trends; is relatively inexpensive; takes little time to conduct.	Age trends may reflect extraneous differences between cohorts rather than true developmental change; provides no data on the development of individuals because each participant is observed at only one point in time.
Longitudinal	Observes people of one cohort repeatedly over time.	Provides data on the development of individuals; can reveal links between early experiences and later outcomes; indicates how individuals are alike and how they are different in the ways they change over time.	Relatively time-consuming and expensive; selective attrition may yield a nonrepresentative sample that limits the generalizability of one's conclusions; cross-generational changes may limit one's conclusions to the cohort that was studied.
Sequential	Combines the cross-sectional and the longitudinal approaches by observing different cohorts repeatedly over time.	Discriminates true developmental trends from cohort effects; indicates whether developmental changes experienced by one cohort are similar to those experienced by other cohorts; often less costly and time-consuming than the longitudinal approach.	More costly and time-consuming than cross-sectional research; despite being the strongest design, may still leave questions about whether a developmental change is generalizable beyond the cohorts studied.
Microgenetic	Children are observed extensively over a limited time period when a developmental change is thought to occur.	Extensive observation of changes as they occur can reveal how and why changes occur.	Too costly and time-consuming to use with large samples; Extensive experience given to stimulate change may be somewhat atypical.

of children in such a detailed way. What's more, the frequency of observations required in a microgenetic study may affect the development of the children involved. For example, the toddlers in Courage, Edison, and Howe's (2005) study had many, many opportunities to examine their images, and perhaps this extensive practice helps to explain why they achieved stable self-recognition somewhat earlier than toddlers participating in earlier cross-sectional studies, who were usually tested but once. In other words, the extensive experiences that children receive to stimulate development in a microgenetic study may not reflect what they would normally encounter and/or may misrepresent the processes that underlie developments in the natural environment. Nevertheless, when investigators use the microgenetic design as Courage and her associates (2005) did, investigating age-related changes at about the time they are already known to occur, the investigators are often able to specify more precisely how (or why) these developments take place.

To help you review and compare the four major developmental designs, Table 1.3 provides a brief description of each, along with its major strengths and weaknesses.

⌐ CROSS-CULTURAL COMPARISONS

Developmentalists are often hesitant to publish a new finding or conclusion until they have studied enough people to determine that their "discovery" is reliable. However, their conclusions are frequently based on participants living at one point in time within one particular culture or subculture, and it is difficult to know whether these conclusions will apply to future generations or even to children currently growing up in other societies or subcultures (Lerner, 1991). Today, the generalizability of findings across samples and settings has become an important issue, for many theorists have implied that there are "universals" in human development— events and outcomes that all children share as they progress from infancy to adulthood.

Cross-cultural studies are those in which participants from different cultural, subcultural, racial, or ethnic backgrounds are observed, tested, and compared on one or more aspects of development. Studies of this kind serve many purposes. For example, they allow the investigator to determine whether conclusions drawn about the development of children from one social context (such as middle-class, white youngsters in the United States) also characterize children growing up in other societies or even those from different ethnic or socioeconomic backgrounds within the same society (for example, American children of Latino ancestry or those from economically disadvantaged homes). So the **cross-cultural comparison** guards against the overgeneralization of research findings and indeed is the only way to determine whether there are truly "universals" in human development.

However, many investigators who favor the cross-cultural approach are looking for *differences* rather than similarities. They recognize that human beings develop in societies and subcultures that have very different ideas about issues such as the proper times and procedures for disciplining children, the activities that are most appropriate for boys and for girls, the time at which childhood ends and adulthood begins, the treatment of the aged, and countless other aspects of life (Fry, 1996). They have also learned that people from various cultures differ in the ways they perceive the world, express their emotions, think, and solve problems. So apart from its focus on universals in development, the cross-cultural approach also illustrates that human development is heavily influenced by the cultural context in which it occurs (see Box 1.4 for a dramatic illustration of cultural diversity in gender roles).

cross-cultural comparison
a study that compares the behavior and/or development of people from different cultural or subcultural backgrounds.

Box 1.4 Cultural Influences

A Cross-Cultural Comparison of Gender Roles

One of the greatest values of cross-cultural comparisons is that they can tell us whether a developmental phenomenon is or is not universal. Consider the roles that males and females play in our society. In our culture, the masculine role has traditionally required traits such as independence, assertiveness, and dominance. By contrast, females are expected to be more nurturing and sensitive to other people. Are these masculine and feminine roles universal? Could biological differences between the sexes lead to inevitable sex differences in behavior?

Many years ago, anthropologist Margaret Mead (1935) used ethnographic methods to compare the gender roles adopted by people in three tribal societies on the island of New Guinea, and her observations are certainly thought provoking. In the Arapesh tribe, both men and women were taught to play what we would regard as a feminine role: they were cooperative, nonaggressive, and sensitive to the needs of others. By contrast, both men and women of the Mundugumor tribe were brought up to be hostile, aggressive, and emotionally unresponsive to other people—a masculine pattern of behavior by Western standards. Finally, the Tchambuli displayed a pattern of gender-role development opposite to the Western pattern: males were passive, emotionally dependent, and socially sensitive, whereas females were dominant, independent, and assertive!

Mead's cross-cultural comparison suggests that cultural dictates may have as much as or more to do with the characteristic behavior patterns of men and women as biological differences do. So we very much need cross-cultural comparisons such as Mead's. Without them, we might easily make the mistake of assuming that whatever holds true in our society holds true everywhere; with their help, we can begin to understand the contributions of biology and environment to human development.

Owen Franken/Stock Boston

The roles assumed by men and women may vary dramatically from culture to culture.

Isn't it remarkable how many methods and designs developmentalists have at their disposal? This diversity of available procedures is a definite strength because findings gained through one procedure can then be confirmed (or perhaps disconfirmed) through other procedures. Indeed, providing *converging evidence* serves a most important function by demonstrating that the discovery one has made is truly a discovery and not merely an artifact of the method or the design used to collect the original data. So there is no "best method" for studying children and adolescents; each of the approaches we have considered has contributed substantially to our understanding of social and personality development.

POSTSCRIPT: ON BECOMING A WISE CONSUMER OF DEVELOPMENTAL RESEARCH

At this point, you may be wondering, "Why do I need to know so much about the methods developmentalists use to conduct research?" This is a reasonable question given that the vast majority who take this course will pursue other careers and will never conduct a scientific study of developing children or adolescents.

My answer is straightforward: Although survey courses such as this one are designed to provide a solid overview of theory and research in the discipline to which they pertain, they should also strive to help you evaluate the relevant information you may encounter in the years ahead. And you will encounter such information. Even if you don't read academic journals in your role as a teacher, school administrator, nurse, probation officer, social worker, or other professional who works with developing persons, then certainly you will be exposed to such information through the popular media—television, newspapers, magazines, and the like. How can you know whether that seemingly dramatic and important new finding you've just read or heard about can be taken seriously?

This is an important issue, for new information about social and personality development is often chronicled in the popular media several months or even years before the data on which the media reports are based finally make their appearance in professional journals (if they ever do). What's more, less than 30 percent of the papers developmentalists submit are judged sufficiently worthy of publication by reputable journals in our discipline. So, many media reports of "dramatic" new findings are based on research that other scientists don't view as very dramatic, or even worth publishing.

Even if a media report is based on a published article, coverage of the research and its conclusions is often misleading. For example, one bold network story reported on a published article saying that there was clear evidence that "alcoholism is inherited." As we will see in Chapter 3, this is a far more dramatic conclusion than the authors actually drew. Another metropolitan newspaper report summarized an article from the prestigious journal *Developmental Psychology* with the headline "Day care harmful for children." What was never made clear in the newspaper article was the researcher's (Howes, 1990) conclusion that *very low-quality* day care may be harmful to the social and intellectual development of *some* preschool children, but that most youngsters receiving good day care suffer no adverse effects. (The issue of day care and its impact on developing children is explored in depth in Chapter 5.)

I do not mean to imply that you can never trust what you read; rather, I'd caution you to be skeptical and to evaluate media (and journal) reports using the methodological information presented in this chapter. You might start by asking, "How were the data gathered and how was the study designed? Were appropriate conclusions drawn given the limitations of the method of data collection and the design (correlational versus experimental; cross-sectional versus longitudinal) that the investigators used? Were there proper control groups? Have the results of the study been reviewed by other experts in the field and published in a reputable academic journal?" And please don't assume that published articles are beyond criticism. Many theses and dissertations in the developmental sciences are based on problems and shortcomings that students have identified in previously published research. So take the time to read and evaluate published reports that seem especially relevant to your profession or to your role as a parent. Not only will you have a better understanding of the research and its conclusions, but any lingering questions and doubts you may have can often be addressed through a letter, a phone call, or an e-mail message to the author of the article.

In sum, one must become a knowledgeable consumer in order to get the most out of what the field of social and personality development has to offer. Our discussion of research methodology was undertaken with these objectives in mind, and a solid understanding of these methodological lessons should help you to properly evaluate the research you will encounter, not only throughout this text, but from many, many other sources in the years to come.

SUMMARY

+ **Development** refers to the systematic continuities and changes that occur between conception and death.
+ **Socialization** is the process through which children acquire the beliefs, behaviors, and values deemed significant and appropriate by members of society. Social and personality development is the product of a long and involved interplay among social, cultural, and biological influences that make humans similar in certain ways and very different from one another in many other respects.

THE UNIVERSAL PARENTING MACHINE—A THOUGHT EXPERIMENT

+ The universal parenting machine, a hypothetical thought experiment in which children are raised with peers and without parents or a prevailing culture, provides an interesting context for thinking about the processes and products of normal social and personality development.

SOCIAL-PERSONALITY DEVELOPMENT IN HISTORICAL PERSPECTIVE

+ In medieval times, children were afforded few of the rights and protections of today's youth. During the 17th and 18th centuries came a more humane outlook on children, and shortly thereafter some parents began to record the development of their infant sons and daughters in **baby biographies**. The scientific study of development did not emerge until nearly 1900, as G. Stanley Hall, in the United States, and Sigmund Freud, in Europe, began to collect data and formulate **theories** about human development. Soon, other researchers were deriving **hypotheses** and conducting research to evaluate and extend early theories.
+ A theory is a set of concepts and propositions that describe and explain observations one has made. Theories are particularly useful when they are **parsiminious, falsifiable,** and **heuristic.**

QUESTIONS AND CONTROVERSIES ABOUT HUMAN DEVELOPMENT

+ Theories of human development differ with respect to their stands on five basic issues: (1) Are human beings inherently good or bad? (As illustrated by the doctrines of **original sin, innate purity,** and **tabula rasa**); (2) the **nature/nurture issue;** the **activity/passivity issue;** (4) the **continuity/discontinuity issue;** and (5) the issue of whether the most important aspects of development are **universal** or **particularistic.**

RESEARCH METHODS

+ Today's developmentalists, guided by the **scientific method,** allow objective data to determine the adequacy of their thinking. Acceptable research methods are those that possess both **reliability** and **validity.** A method is reliable if it produces consistent, replicable results; it is valid if it accurately reflects what it was intended to measure.
+ The most common methods of data collection in the field of social and personality development are self-reports, observational methodologies, case studies, and ethnography. Self-reports include standardized procedures, such as **structured interviews** or **structured questionnaires** (including **diary studies**), that allow direct comparisons among research participants, and flexible approaches like the **clinical method,** which yields an individualized portrait of each participant's feelings, thoughts, and behaviors.
+ **Naturalistic observations** are obtained in the natural environments of children or adolescents, whereas **structured observations** take place in laboratories where the investigator cues the behavior of interest.
+ **Case studies** allow investigators to obtain an in-depth understanding of individual children or adolescents by collecting data based on interviews, observations, and test scores of the individual in question, as well as information about that person from such knowledgeable sources as teachers and parents.
+ **Ethnography,** used originally by anthropologists, is a descriptive procedure in which the researcher becomes a participant observer within a cultural or subcultural context. He or she will carefully observe the community members, make notes from conversations, and compile such information into a detailed portrait of the group's values and traditions and their impacts on developing children and adolescents.

- **Psychophysiological methods** measure the relationship between physiological responses and behavior. They are often used to reveal the biological underpinnings of children's perceptual, cognitive, or emotional responses.

DETECTING RELATIONSHIPS: CORRELATIONAL AND EXPERIMENTAL DESIGNS

- Two general research designs permit researchers to identify relationships among variables that interest them. **Correlational designs** examine relationships as they naturally occur, without any intervention. The **correlation coefficient** is used to estimate the strength and magnitude of the association between variables. However, correlational studies cannot specify whether correlated variables are causally related.
- The **experimental design** does point to cause-and-effect relationships. The experimenter manipulates one (or more) **independent variables,** exercises **experimental control** over all other **confounding variables** (often by **random assignment** of participants to treatments), and observes the effect(s) of the manipulation(s) on the **dependent variable.** Experiments may be performed in the laboratory or, alternatively, in the natural environment (that is, a **field experiment**), thereby increasing the **ecological validity** of the results. The impact of events that researchers cannot manipulate or control can be studied in **natural (quasi) experiments.** However, lack of control over natural events prevents the quasi-experimenter from drawing definitive conclusions about cause and effect.

DESIGNS FOR STUDYING DEVELOPMENT

- Cross-sectional, longitudinal, and sequential designs are employed to detect developmental change. The **cross-sectional** design, which compares different age groups at a single point in time, is easy to conduct; but it cannot tell us how individuals develop, and its results may be misleading if the age trends one observes are actually due to **cohort effects** rather than true developmental change.
- The **longitudinal design** detects developmental change by repeatedly examining the same participants as they grow older. Though it identifies developmental continuities and changes and individual differences in development, the longitudinal design is subject to such problems as **selective attrition**, which results in **nonrepresentative samples.** Moreover, the **cross-generational** problem of long-term longitudinal studies implies that results may be limited to the particular cohort studied.
- The **sequential design**, a combination of the cross-sectional and longitudinal designs, offers researchers the advantages of both approaches and allows them to discriminate true developmental trends from troublesome cohort effects.
- The **microgenetic design** studies children intensively over a brief period when developmental changes normally occur in an attempt to specify how or why these changes occur.

CROSS-CULTURAL COMPARISONS

- **Cross-cultural studies**, in which participants from different cultures or subcultures are compared on one or more aspects of development, are becoming increasingly important. Only by comparing people from many cultures can we identify "universal" patterns of development and at the same time demonstrate that other aspects of development are heavily influenced by the social context in which they occur.

CHAPTER 2

Classical Theories of Social and Personality Development

"That's only true in theory, not in practice."—Anonymous

"There is nothing as practical as a good theory."—Kurt Lewin

IN OUR INTRODUCTORY CHAPTER, we talked only briefly about theories, portraying them as sets of concepts and propositions that describe and explain certain aspects of our experience. We also noted that everyone is a "theorist," for each of us has definite points of view reflecting what we believe to be true about many issues, observations, and events. How important are theories to today's developmentalists? They are so important that many contemporary researchers cannot conceive of how knowledge might be advanced without them. In fact, when developmentalists describe themselves to other developmentalists, they are most likely to mention (1) their primary area of interest (for example, emotional development in infancy) and (2) the theoretical perspectives that guide their research. So a developmentalist's professional identity may depend in part on the theories he or she favors.

Our focus in this chapter is on some of the earliest and most highly influential ideas about human social and personality development—theories that guided the majority of research conducted before 1975 and remain influential today. We will begin by briefly considering Freud's *psychoanalytic* theory, an approach that depicts human beings as servants to inborn *biological* instincts that mature gradually over the course of childhood and play a major role in determining who we are and what we are likely to become. After reviewing Freud's theory and comparing it to a more recent psychoanalytic viewpoint, we will consider a very different perspective—*behaviorism* and *social-learning theory*—that downplays biological contributions to human development and portrays the child as a *tabula rasa* who is heavily influenced by his or her socializing *environment*. Finally, we conclude this chapter by examining the *cognitive-developmental* viewpoint of Jean Piaget—an *interactionist* theory which contends that biological forces (maturation) in concert with environmental experiences promote intellectual growth, which in turn has major implications for all aspects of social and personality development.

Of course, each of the three theoretical perspectives that we will examine in this chapter has its strengths and its weaknesses, and new theories of social-personality development—models that question and build on earlier insights—are constantly emerging. In Chapter 3, we will consider some of these newer ideas, focusing on models that emphasize biological contributions (for example, behavioral genetics and evolutionary perspectives), environmental forces (ecological systems theory), and cognitive underpinnings (sociocultural theory; social information-processing theory) of social and personality development.

Let's now begin our survey of the "classic" theories with Freud's psychoanalytic approach.

THE PSYCHOANALYTIC VIEWPOINT

With the possible exception of evolutionist Charles Darwin, it is difficult to think of a theorist who has had a greater impact on Western thought than Sigmund Freud, the Viennese physician who lived from 1856 to 1939. This revolutionary thinker challenged prevailing notions about human nature by proposing that we are driven by motives and conflicts *of which we are largely unaware* and that our personalities are shaped by early life experiences. In this section of the chapter, we will first consider Freud's fascinating **psychosexual theory** of human development and then compare Freud's theory with that of his best known follower, Erik Erikson.

psychosexual theory
Freud's theory that states that maturation of the sex instinct underlies stages of personality development and that how parents manage children's instinctual impulses will determine the traits children come to display.

Freud's Psychosexual Theory

Freud's view of human nature is essentially a restatement of Thomas Hobbes's *doctrine of original sin*. Central to his psychoanalytic theory is the notion that human beings are driven by powerful biological urges that must be satisfied. What kinds of urges? Undesirable ones! Freud (1940/1964) viewed the newborn as a "seething cauldron"—an inherently selfish creature who is relentlessly driven by two kinds of **instincts** that he called **Eros** and **Thanatos.** *Eros,* or the life instinct, was said to promote survival by directing life-sustaining activities such as breathing, eating, sex, and the fulfillment of all other bodily needs. By contrast, *Thanatos*—the death instinct—was viewed as a destructive force present in human beings that is expressed through such behaviors as arson, fistfights, sadistic aggression, murder, and even masochism (harm directed against the self).

Recall that Freud was a practicing neurologist who formulated his theory of human development from his analyses of the life histories of his emotionally disturbed patients. As he worked with his patients, seeking to relieve their nervous symptoms and anxieties, he came to rely heavily on such methods as hypnosis, *free association* (a quick spelling out of one's thoughts) and dream analysis because they gave some indication of **unconscious motives** that patients had **repressed** (that is, forced out of conscious awareness). By analyzing these motives and the events that had caused them to be suppressed, Freud concluded that human development is a conflictual process: As biological creatures, we have basic sexual and aggressive *instincts* that *must* be served; yet society dictates that many of these needs are undesirable and *must* be restrained. According to Freud, the ways in which parents have managed these sexual and aggressive urges in the first few years of life play a major role in shaping their child's conduct and character.

Three Components of Personality

Freud's psychosexual theory specifies that three components of personality—the id, ego, and superego—develop and gradually become integrated in a series of five psychosexual stages. The **id** is all that is present at birth. Its sole function is to satisfy inborn biological instincts, and it will try to do so immediately. If you think about it, young infants do seem to be "all id." When hungry or wet, they simply fuss and cry until their needs are met, and they are not known for their patience.

The **ego** is the conscious, rational component of the personality that reflects the child's emerging abilities to perceive, learn, remember, and reason. Its function is to find realistic means of gratifying the instincts, as when a hungry toddler, remembering how she gets food, seeks out her mom and says "cookie." As their egos mature, children become better at controlling their irrational ids and finding realistic ways to gratify needs on their own.

However, realistic solutions to needs are not always acceptable, as a hungry 3-year-old who is caught snitching cookies between meals may soon discover. The final component of personality, the **superego,** is the seat of the conscience. It develops between the ages of 3 and 6 as children *internalize* (take on as their own) the moral values and standards of their parents (Freud, 1933). Once the superego emerges, children do not need an adult to tell them they have been good or bad; they are now aware of their own transgressions and will feel guilty or ashamed of their unethical conduct. So the superego is truly an internal censor. It insists that the ego find socially acceptable outlets for the id's undesirable impulses.

Stages of Psychological Development

Freud thought that sex was the most important of the instincts because he discovered that the mental disturbances of his patients often revolved around childhood sexual conflicts that they had repressed. But are *young children* really sexual beings? Yes, said Freud (1940/1964), whose view of sex was very broad, encompassing such activities as thumb-sucking and urinating that we might not

Photo 2.1
The psychoanalytic theory of Sigmund Freud (1856–1939) changed our thinking about developing children.

Bettmann/Corbis

instinct
an inborn biological force that motivates a particular response or class of responses.

Eros
Freud's name for instincts such as respiration, hunger, and sex that help the individual (and the species) to survive.

Thanatos
Freud's name for inborn, self-destructive instincts that were said to characterize all human beings.

unconscious motives
Freud's term for feelings, experiences, and conflicts that influence a person's thinking and behavior but lie outside the person's awareness.

repression
a type of motivated forgetting in which anxiety-provoking thoughts and conflicts are forced out of conscious awareness.

id
psychoanalytic term for the inborn component of the personality that is driven by the instincts.

ego
psychoanalytic term for the rational component of the personality.

superego
psychoanalytic term for the component of the personality that consists of one's internalized moral standards.

Table 2.1 Freud's stages of psychosexual development

Psychosexual Stage	Age	Description
Oral	Birth–1 year	The sex instinct centers on the mouth, as infants derive pleasure from such oral activities as sucking, chewing, and biting. Feeding activities are particularly important. For example, an infant weaned too early or too abruptly may later crave close contact and become overdependent on a spouse.
Anal	1–3 years	Voluntary urination and defecation become the primary methods of gratifying the sex instinct. Toilet training produces major conflicts between children and parents. The emotional climate parents create can have lasting effects. For example, children punished for toileting "accidents" may become inhibited, messy, or wasteful.
Phallic	3–6 years	Pleasure is now derived from stimulating the genitals. Children develop an incestuous desire for the opposite-sex parent (called the *Oedipus complex* for boys and *Electra complex* for girls). Anxiety stemming from this conflict causes children to internalize the sex-role characteristics and moral standards of their same-sex parental rival.
Latency	6–11 years	Traumas of the phallic stage cause sexual conflicts to be repressed and sexual urges to be rechanneled into school work and vigorous play. The ego and superego continue to develop as the child gains more problem-solving abilities at school and internalizes societal values.
Genital	age 12 onward	Puberty triggers a reawakening of sexual urges. Adolescents must now learn how to express these urges in socially acceptable ways. If development has been healthy, the mature sex instinct is satisfied by marriage and child rearing.

phallic stage
Freud's third stage of psychosexual development (from 3 to 6 years of age), in which children gratify the sex instinct by fondling their genitals and developing an incestuous desire for the parent of the other sex.

Oedipus complex
Freud's term for the conflict that 3- to 6-year-old boys experience when they develop an incestuous desire for their mothers and, at the same time, a jealous and hostile rivalry with their fathers.

Electra complex
female version of Oedipus complex, in which a 3- to 6-year-old girl was believed to envy her father for possessing a penis and to seek him as a sex object in the hope of sharing the organ that she lacks.

identification
Freud's term for the child's tendency to emulate another person, usually the same-sex parent.

fixation
arrested development at a particular psychosexual stage, often occurring as a means of coping with existing conflicts and preventing movement to the next stage, where stress may be even greater.

consider at all erotic. Freud believed that as the sex instinct matured, its focus would shift from one part of the body to another, and that each shift brought on a new stage of psychosexual development. Table 2-1 briefly describes each of Freud's five stages of psychosexual development.

Clearly, the most controversial aspect of Freud's theory was his description of the **phallic stage**—a period when 3- to 6-year-olds were said to develop a hostile rivalry with their same-sex parent that stemmed from their own *incestuous* desire for the opposite-sex parent. This state of affairs (no pun intended) was called the **Oedipus complex** for boys and the **Electra complex** for girls. Freud believed that anxieties stemming from such rivalrous conflicts would build until children felt compelled to renounce their incestuous desires and to identify with their same-sex parental rival. As we will see in Chapters 8 and 10, this **identification** process was said to be the primary mechanism by which children acquire "masculine" or "feminine" identities and a strong internalized conscience, or superego.

Freud believed that parents must walk a fine line with their child at each psychosexual stage. Permitting either too much or too little gratification of sexual needs was thought to cause the child to become obsessed with whatever activity was strongly encouraged or discouraged. He might then **fixate** on that activity (that is, display arrested development) and retain some aspect of it throughout life. For example, an infant who was strongly punished for and thus conflicted about sucking her thumb might express this oral fixation through such substitute activities as chain smoking or oral sex as an adult. Note the implication here: Freud is saying that early childhood experiences and conflicts may haunt us for years and influence our adult interests, activities, and personalities.

Contributions and Criticisms of Freud's Theory

How plausible do you think Freud's ideas are? Do you think that we are all relentlessly driven by sexual and aggressive instincts? Or might the sexual conflicts that Freud thought so important merely have been reflections of the sexually repressive Victorian era in which he and his patients lived?

Few developmentalists today are strong proponents of Freud's theory. There is not much evidence that any of the oral, anal, and genital conflicts that Freud thought so important reliably predict one's later personality (see, for example, Bem, 1989; Crews, 1996). One reason for this may be that Freud's account of human development was based on the recollections of a relatively small number of emotionally disturbed adults whose experiences may not apply to most people.

Yet we should not reject all Freud's ideas simply because some of them may seem a bit outlandish. Perhaps Freud's greatest contribution was his concept of *unconscious motivation.* When psychology came into being in the mid-19th century, investigators were concerned with understanding isolated aspects of *conscious* experience, such as sensory processes and perceptual illusions. It was Freud who first noted that these scientists were studying the tip of an iceberg when he proclaimed that the vast majority of psychic experience lay below the level of conscious awareness. Freud also deserves considerable credit for focusing attention on the importance of early experience for later development. Debates continue about exactly how critical early experiences are, but few developmentalists today doubt that some early experiences *can* have lasting effects. Finally, we might thank Freud for studying the emotional side of human development—the loves, fears, anxieties, and other powerful emotions that play important roles in our lives. Unfortunately, these aspects of life have often been overlooked by developmentalists who have tended to concentrate on observable behaviors or on rational thought processes.

In sum, Freud was truly a great pioneer who dared to navigate murky, uncharted waters that his predecessors had not even thought to explore. In the process, he changed our views of humankind.

Erikson's Theory of Psychosocial Development

As Freud became widely read, he attracted many followers. However, Freud's pupils did not always agree with the master, and eventually they began to modify some of his ideas and became important theorists in their own right. Among the best known of these *neo-Freudian* scholars was Erik Erikson.

Comparing Erikson with Freud   Although Erikson (1963, 1982) accepted many of Freud's ideas, he differed from Freud in two important respects. First, Erikson (1963) stressed that children are *active,* curious explorers who seek to adapt to their environments, rather than passive slaves to biological urges who are molded by their parents. Erikson has been labeled an "ego" psychologist because he believed that at each stage of life, people must cope with social *realities* (in ego function) in order to adapt successfully and show a normal pattern of development. So in Erikson' theory, the ego is far more than a simple arbiter of the opposing demands of the id and superego.

A second critical difference between Erikson and Freud is that Erikson places much less emphasis on sexual urges and far more emphasis on cultural influences than Freud did. Clearly, Erikson's thinking was shaped by his own varied experiences. He was born in Denmark, raised in Germany, and spent much of his adolescence wandering throughout Europe. After receiving his professional training, Erikson came to the United States, where he studied college students, combat soldiers, civil rights workers in the South, and Native Americans. Having observed many similarities and differences in development across these diverse social groups, it is hardly surprising that Erikson would emphasize *social* and *cultural* aspects of development in his own **psychosocial theory.**

Photo 2.2
Erik Erikson (1902–1994) emphasized the sociocultural determinants of personality in his theory of psychosocial development.

psychosocial theory
Erikson's revision of Freud's theory, which emphasizes sociocultural (rather than sexual) determinants of development and posits a series of eight psychosocial conflicts that people must resolve successfully to display healthy psychological adjustment.

Table 2.2 Erikson's and Freud's stages of development

Approximate Age	Erikson's Stage or Psychosocial Crisis	Erikson's Viewpoint: Significant Events and Social Influences	Corresponding Freudian Stage
Birth to 1 year	Basic trust versus mistrust	Infants must learn to trust others to care for their basic needs. If caregivers are rejecting or inconsistent in their care, the infant may view the world as a dangerous place filled with untrustworthy or unreliable people. The mother or primary caregiver is the key social agent.	Oral
1 to 3 years	Autonomy versus shame and doubt	Children must learn to be "autonomous"—to feed and dress themselves, to look after their own hygiene, and so on. Failure to achieve this independence may force the child to doubt his or her own abilities and feel shameful. Parents are the key social agents.	Anal
3 to 6 years	Initiative versus guilt	Children attempt to act grown up and will try to accept responsibilities that are beyond their capacity to handle. They sometimes undertake goals or activities that conflict with those of parents and other family members, and these conflicts may make them feel guilty. Successful resolution of this crisis requires a balance: The child must retain a sense of initiative and yet learn not to impinge on the rights, privileges, or goals of others. The family is the key social agent.	Phallic
6 to 12 years	Industry versus inferiority	Children must master important social and academic skills. This is a period when the child compares himself or herself with peers. If sufficiently industrious, children will acquire the social and academic skills to feel self-assured. Failure to acquire these important attributes leads to feelings of inferiority. Significant social agents are teachers and peers.	Latency
12 to 20 years	Identity versus role confusion	This is the crossroad between childhood and maturity. The adolescent grapples with the question "Who am I?" Adolescents must establish basic social and occupational identities, or they will remain confused about the roles they should play as adults. The key social agent is the society of peers.	Early genital (adolescence)
20 to 40 years (young adulthood)	Intimacy versus isolation	The primary task at this stage is to form strong friendships and to achieve a sense of love and companionship (or a shared identity) with another person. Feelings of loneliness or isolation are likely to result from an inability to form friendships or an intimate relationship. Key social agents are lovers, spouses, and close friends (of both sexes).	Genital
40 to 65 years (middle adulthood)	Generativity versus stagnation	At this stage, adults face the tasks of becoming productive in their work and raising their families or otherwise looking after the needs of young people. These standards of "generativity" are defined by one's culture. Those who are unable or unwilling to assume these responsibilities will become stagnant and/or self-centered. Significant social agents are the spouse, children, and cultural norms.	Genital
Old age	Ego integrity versus despair	The older adult will look back at life, viewing it as either a meaningful, productive, and happy experience or a major disappointment full of unfulfilled promises and unrealized goals. One's life experiences, particularly social experiences, will determine the outcome of this final life crisis.	Genital

Eight Life Crises Erikson believed that human beings face eight major crises, or conflicts, during the course of their lives. Each conflict has its own time for emerging, as dictated by both biological maturation and the social demands that developing people experience at particular points in life. And each must be resolved successfully in order to prepare the individual for a satisfactory resolution of the next life crisis. Table 2.2 briefly describes each of Erikson's eight crises (or psychosocial stages) and lists the Freudian psychosexual stage to which it corresponds. Notice that Erikson's developmental stages do not end at adolescence or young adulthood as Freud's do. Erikson believed that the problems of adolescents and young adults are very different from those faced by parents who are raising children or by middle-age (or older) adults who might be striving to become better mentors for younger coworkers, make lasting contributions to their families or communities, and understand the meaning of life and their place in the natural order. Most contemporary developmentalists would definitely agree (see, for example, Sheldon & Kasser, 2001).

An analysis of the first psychosocial stage—**trust versus mistrust**—should help to illustrate Erikson's thinking. Recall that Freud emphasized the infant's oral activities during the first year of life, and he believed that a mother's feeding practices could have a lasting impact on her child's personality. Erikson agreed. However, he went on to argue that what is most important to an infant's later development is not merely the caregiver's feeding practices but rather her *overall responsiveness* to all the infant's needs. To develop a basic sense of *trust,* infants must be able to count on their primary caregivers to provide food, relieve discomfort, come when beckoned, smile when smiled upon, and display warmth and affection. But should close companions often neglect, reject, or respond inconsistently to an infant, that child will learn a very simple lesson: Other people are not to be trusted. Indeed, we will see in Chapters 5 and 13 that infants who establish untrusting, insecure relationships with their caregivers often make few, if any, close supportive friendships and tend to have conflictual, nonharmonious interactions with their peers.

trust versus mistrust
the first of Erikson's eight psychosocial stages, in which infants must learn to trust their closest companions or else run the risk of mistrusting other people later in life.

Contributions and Criticism of Erikson's Theory

Many people prefer Erikson's theory to Freud's because they simply refuse to believe that human beings are dominated by sexual instincts. An analyst like Erikson, who stresses our *rational, adaptive* nature, is so much easier to accept. In addition, Erikson emphasizes many of the social conflicts and personal dilemmas that people may remember, are currently experiencing, can easily anticipate, or can see affecting people they know.

Erikson does seem to have captured many of the central issues in life in his eight psychosocial stages. In fact, we will see just how stimulating his ideas have been as we discuss such topics as the emotional development of infants (Chapters 4 and 5), the growth of self-concept in childhood and the identity crisis facing adolescents (Chapter 6), and the influence of friends and playmates on social and personality development (Chapter 13) (see also Sigelman & Rider, 2006, for a discussion of Erikson's contributions to the field of adult development). On the other hand, Erikson's theory can be criticized for being vague about the *causes* of development. What kinds of experiences must a child have to develop autonomy as a toddler, initiative as a preschool child, or a stable identity during adolescence? Why, exactly, is a sense of trust so important for the development of autonomy, initiative, or industry? Unfortunately, Erikson is not very explicit about these important issues. So, Erikson's theory is really a *descriptive* overview of human social and emotional development that does not adequately *explain* how or why this development takes place.

Psychoanalytic Theory Today

Freud and Erikson are only two of many psychoanalysts who have had (or are having) a strong influence on the field of social and personality development (Tyson & Tyson, 1990). Karen Horney (1967), for example, has challenged Freud's ideas about sex differences in development and is now widely credited as a founder of the discipline we know today as the psychology of women. Alfred Adler (1929/1964), a contemporary of Freud, was among the first to suggest that *siblings* (and sibling rivalries) are critically important influences on social and personality development—a proposition that we will explore in detail in Chapter 11. And American psychoanalyst Harry Stack Sullivan (1953) wrote extensively about how *chumships* (close friendships) during preadolescence set the stage for the development of intimate love relationships later in life (see Chapter 13 for a discussion of this and other contributions that friends make to social and personality development). Although their theories clearly differ in focus, all these neo-Freudians place much more emphasis than Freud did on *social* contributions to personality development—and much less emphasis on the role of sexual instincts.

Despite the many important contributions that psychoanalytic theorists have made, only a small minority of contemporary developmentalists adhere strongly to this perspective. One reason that many researchers have abandoned the psychoanalytic approach (particularly Freud's theory) is because its propositions are difficult to verify or disconfirm. Suppose, for example, that we wanted to test the basic Freudian proposition that the healthy personality is one in which psychic energy is evenly distributed among the id, ego, and superego. How could we do it? There are objective tests that we could use to select "mentally healthy" subjects, but we have no instrument that measures psychic energy or the relative strengths of the id, ego, and superego. The point is that many psychoanalytic assertions are untestable by any method other than the interview or a clinical approach, and unfortunately, these techniques are time-consuming, expensive, and among the least objective of all methods used to study developing persons.

Of course, the main reason why so many developmentalists have abandoned the psychoanalytic perspective is that other theories seem more compelling. One perspective favored by many was the *behaviorist,* or *social-learning* approach, to which we will now turn.

THE BEHAVIORIST (OR SOCIAL-LEARNING) VIEWPOINT

In Chapter 1, we encountered a developmentalist who claimed that he could take a dozen healthy infants and train them to be whatever he chose—doctor, lawyer, beggar, and so on—regardless of their backgrounds or ancestry. What a bold statement! It implies that nurture is everything and that nature, or hereditary endowment, counts for nothing. The statement was made by John B. Watson, a strong proponent of the importance of learning in human development and the father of a school of psychology that came to be known as **behaviorism** (Horowitz, 1992).

Watson's Behaviorism

A basic premise of Watson's (1913) behaviorism is that conclusions about human development should be based on observations of overt behavior rather than on speculations about unconscious motives or cognitive processes that are unobservable. Furthermore, Watson believed that *well-learned* associations between external stimuli and observable responses (called **habits**) are the building blocks of human development. Like John Locke, Watson viewed the infant as a *tabula rasa* to be written on by experience; children have no inborn tendencies. Watson was a *social-learning* theorist who believed that how children turn out depends entirely on their rearing environments and the ways in which their parents and other significant people in their lives treat them. According to the behaviorist perspective, then, it is a mistake to assume that children progress through a series of distinct stages, dictated by biological maturation, as Freud (and others) had argued. Instead, development was viewed as a continuous process of behavioral change that is shaped by the person's unique environment and may differ dramatically from person to person.

behaviorism
a school of thinking in psychology that holds that conclusions about human development should be based on controlled observations of overt behavior rather than speculation about unconscious motives or other unobservable phenomena; the philosophical underpinning for social-learning theories.

habits
well-learned associations between stimuli and responses that represent the stable aspects of one's personality.

Photo 2.3
John B. Watson (1878–1958) was the father of behaviorism and the first social-learning theorist.

Archives of the History of American Psychology

To prove just how malleable children are, Watson set out to demonstrate that infantile fears and other emotional reactions are acquired rather than inborn. In one demonstration, for example, Watson and Rosalie Raynor (1920) presented a gentle white rat to a 9-month-old named Albert. Albert's initial reactions were positive ones; he crawled toward the rat and played with it as he had previously with a dog and a rabbit. Then, two months later, came an attempt to instill a fear response. Every time Albert reached for the white rat, Watson, standing behind him, would bang a steel rod with a hammer. Did little Albert eventually associate the white rat with the loud noise and come to fear his furry playmate? Indeed he did, thus illustrating that fears are easily learned.

Watson's belief that children are shaped by their social environments carried a stern message for parents—that it was they who were largely responsible for what their child would become. Watson (1928) cautioned parents that they should begin to train their child at birth and to cut back on the coddling if they hoped to instill good habits. Treat them, he said,

> . . . as though they were young adults. . . . Let your behavior always be objective and kindly firm. Never hug and kiss them, never let them sit on your lap. . . . Shake hands with them in the morning. Give them a pat on the head if they have made an extraordinally good job of a difficult task. . . . In a week's time, you will find how easy it is to be perfectly objective . . . [yet] kindly. You will be utterly ashamed at the mawkish, sentimental way you have been handling [your child]. (pp. 81–82)

Since Watson's day, several theories have been proposed to explain how we learn from our social experiences and form the habits that Watson viewed as "bricks in the edifice of human development." Perhaps the one theorist who did more than anyone to advance the behaviorist approach was B. F. Skinner.

Skinner's Operant-Learning Theory (Radical Behaviorism)

Through his research with animals, Skinner (1953) came to understand a very important form of learning that he believed to be the basis for most of the habits that organisms form. Quite simply, Skinner proposed that both animals and humans will repeat acts that lead to favorable outcomes and will suppress those that produce unfavorable outcomes. So a rat that presses a bar and receives a tasty food pellet is apt to perform that response again. In the language of Skinner's theory, the freely emitted bar-pressing response is called an *operant,* and the food pellet that strengthens this response (by making it more probable in the future) is called a **reinforcer.** Similarly, a girl may form a long-term habit of showing compassion toward distressed playmates if her parents consistently reinforce her kindly behavior with praise, or a teenage boy may become more studious should such conduct "pay off" in higher grades. **Punishers,** on the other hand, are consequences that suppress a response and decrease the likelihood that it will occur in the future. If the rat who had been reinforced for bar pressing were suddenly given a painful shock each time it pressed the bar, the bar-pressing habit would begin to disappear. Similarly, a teenage girl who is grounded every time she stays out beyond her curfew should become more concerned about being home on time.

Like Watson, then, Skinner believed that the habits that each of us develop result from our unique **operant learning** experiences. One boy's aggressive behavior may be reinforced over time because his playmates "give in to" (reinforce) his forceful tactics. Another boy may become relatively nonaggressive because his peers actively suppress (punish) aggressive conduct by fighting back. The two may develop in entirely different directions based on their different histories of reinforcement and punishment. According to Skinner, there is no need to speak of an "aggressive stage" in child development or of an "aggressive instinct" within human beings. Instead, he claims that the majority of habits that children acquire—the very responses

reinforcer
any consequence of an act that increases the probability that the act will recur.

punisher
any consequence of an act that suppresses that act and/or decreases the probability that it will recur.

operant learning
a form of learning in which voluntary acts (or operants) become either more or less probable, depending on the consequences they produce.

Photo 2.4
B. F. Skinner (1904–1990) proposed a social-learning theory that emphasized the role of external stimuli in controlling human behavior.

observational learning
learning that results from observing the behavior of others.

symbolic representations
the images and verbal labels that observers generate in order to retain the important aspects of a model's behavior.

Photo 2.5
Albert Bandura (1925–   ) has emphasized the cognitive aspects of learning in his social-learning theory.

that comprise a "personality" and make us unique—are freely emitted operants that have been shaped by their consequences. So Skinner's *operant learning theory* claims that the directions in which we develop depend very critically on *external* stimuli (reinforcers and punishers) rather than on internal forces such as instincts, drives, or biological maturation.

Today's developmentalists have come to appreciate that human behavior can take many forms and that habits can emerge and disappear over a lifetime, depending on whether they have positive or negative consequences (Gewirtz & Pelaez-Nogueras, 1992; Stricker et al., 2001). Yet many believe that Skinner placed far too much emphasis on operant behaviors shaped by *external* stimuli (reinforcers and punishers) while ignoring important *cognitive* contributors to social learning. One such critic is Albert Bandura, who has proposed a *social-cognitive* theory of human development that is widely respected today.

Bandura's Cognitive Social Learning Theory

Are we on firm ground in trying to explain human social learning on the basis of research with animals? Bandura (1977, 1986, 1992, 2001) doesn't think so. He agrees with Skinner that operant conditioning is an important type of learning, particularly for animals. However, Bandura stresses that humans are *cognitive* beings—active information processors—who, unlike animals, are likely to think about the relationships between their behavior and its consequences, and are often more affected by what they *believe* will happen than by the events they actually experience. Consider your own plight as a student. Your education is costly and time-consuming and may impose many demands that you find less than satisfying. Yet, you tolerate the costs and unpleasantries because you can probably *anticipate* greater rewards once you obtain your degree. Your behavior is not shaped by its immediate consequences; if it were, few students would ever make it through the trials and turmoils of college. Instead, you persist as a student because you have *thought about* the long-term benefits of obtaining an education and have decided that they outweigh the short-term costs you must endure.

Nowhere is Bandura's cognitive emphasis clearer than in his decision to highlight **observational learning** as a central developmental process. Observational learning is simply learning that results from observing the behavior of other people (called models). A 2-year-old may learn how to approach and pet the family dog by simply noting how his older sister does it. An 8-year-old may acquire a very negative attitude toward a minority group (as well as derogatory labels for these people) after hearing her parents talk about this group in a disparaging way. Observational learning simply could not occur unless cognitive processes were at work. We must *attend* carefully to the model's behavior, actively digest, or *encode*, what we observe, and then *store* this information in memory (as an image or a verbal label) if we are to imitate what we have observed at a later time. Indeed, as we will see in Box 2.1, children need not even be reinforced in order to learn this way.

Why does Bandura stress observational learning in his social-learning theory? Simply because this active, cognitive form of learning permits young children to quickly acquire literally thousands of new responses in a variety of settings where their "models" are simply pursuing their own interests and are not trying to teach them anything. In fact, many of the behaviors that children attend to, remember, and may imitate are actions that models display but would like to discourage—practices such as swearing, smoking, or eating between meals. So Bandura claims children are continually learning both desirable and undesirable responses by "keeping their eyes (and ears) open," and he is not at all surprised that human development proceeds so very rapidly along so many different paths.

Developmental Trends in Imitation and Observational Learning   Bandura's theory of observational learning assumes that an observer can construct images or other **symbolic representations** of a model's behavior and then use these mediators to reproduce what he or

Box 2.1 Focus on Research

An Example of No-Trial (Observational) Learning Without Reinforcement

In 1965, Bandura made what was then considered a radical statement: Children can learn by merely observing the behavior of a social model, *even without first performing the responses themselves or receiving any reinforcement for performing them.* Clearly, this "no-trial" learning is inconsistent with Skinner's theory, which claims that one must perform a response and then be reinforced to have learned that response.

Bandura (1965) conducted a now-classic experiment to prove his point. Nursery school children each watched a short film in which an adult model directed an unusual sequence of aggressive responses toward an inflatable Bobo doll, hitting the doll with a mallet while shouting "sockeroo," throwing rubber balls while shouting "bang, bang," and so on. There were three experimental conditions:

1. Children in the *model-rewarded* condition saw a second adult give the aggressive model candy and soda for a "championship performance."
2. Children in the *model-punished* condition saw a second adult scold and spank the model for beating up Bobo.
3. Children in the *no-consequence* condition simply saw the model behave aggressively.

When the film ended, each child was left alone in a playroom that contained a Bobo doll and the props that the model had used to work Bobo over. Hidden observers then recorded all instances in which the child imitated one or more of the model's unusual aggressive acts. These observations revealed how willing children were to *perform* the responses they had witnessed. The results of this "performance" test appear on the left-hand side of the figure. Notice that children in the model-rewarded and no-consequences conditions imitated more of the model's aggressive acts than those who had seen the model punished for aggressive behavior. Clearly, this looks very much like the kind of no-trial observational learning that Bandura had proposed.

But an important question remained. Had children in the first two conditions actually learned more from observing the model than those who had seen the model punished? To find out, Bandura devised a test to see just how much they had learned. Each child was now offered trinkets and fruit juice for reproducing all the model's behaviors he or she could recall. As we see in the right-hand side of the figure, this "learning test" revealed that children in

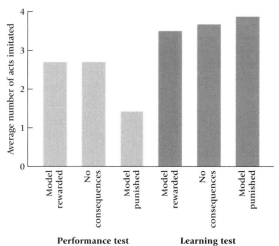

Average number of aggressive responses imitated during the performance test and the learning test for children who had seen a model rewarded, punished, or receiving no consequences for her actions. (Adapted from "Influence of Models' Reinforcement Contingencies on the Acquisition of Imitative Responses," by A. Bandura, 1965, *Journal of Personality and Social Psychology, 1,* 589–595. Copyright 1965 by the American Psychological Association. Adapted by permission.)

each of the three conditions had learned about the same amount by observing the model. Apparently, children in the model-punished condition had imitated fewer of the model's responses on the initial performance test because they felt that they too might be punished for striking Bobo. But when offered a reward, they showed that they had learned much more than their initial performances had implied.

In sum, it is important to distinguish what children *learn* by observation from their willingness to *perform* these responses. Clearly, reinforcement is not necessary for observational learning—that is, for the formation of images or verbal descriptions that would enable the observer to imitate the model's acts. However, the reinforcing or punishing consequences the model has received may well affect the observer's tendency to *perform* what he or she has already learned by observation.

---

she has witnessed. When do these capabilities first appear? When do children begin to take advantage of their emerging powers of observation to acquire important new skills? And how does the character of observational learning change over time? Although Bandura had little to say about these important issues, other researchers have addressed them and have provided some answers.

Origins of Imitation and Observational Learning   Although newborns are able to imitate a limited number of motor responses, such as sticking out their tongues (Kaitz et al., 1988), moving their heads as an adult model does (Meltzoff & Moore, 1989), and possibly even mimicking facial expressions of happiness and sadness (Field et al., 1982; and see Box 2.2 on page 56), these early imitative capabilities soon disappear and may be nothing more than involuntary reflexes (Abravanel & Sigafoos, 1984; Vinter, 1986). Voluntary imitation of novel responses first appears and becomes more reliable later in the first year (Piaget, 1951). Initially the model must be present and must continue to perform a new response before the child is able to imitate. But by 6 months of age, some infants are already able to imitate very simple acts (for example, pressing a button to activate a noise-making toy) 24 hours after seeing them modeled (Collie & Hayne, 1999). This **deferred imitation**—the ability to reproduce the actions of an adult model at sometime in the future—develops rapidly during the second year. Although many 14-month-olds will imitate the purposeful actions of a *televised* model after a 24-hour delay (Meltzoff, 1988a), these young toddlers are more likely to recall and imitate the actions of *live* rather than televised models (Barr & Hayne, 1999), even after a delay of one week (Meltzoff, 1988b).

Toddlers are more inclined to reproduce modeled acts (for example, opening a box) if the model's intentions are clear (to retrieve a toy) as opposed to ambiguous (nothing is retrieved) (Carpenter, Call, & Tomasello, 2002). And young toddlers are not mere mimics: They may devise even more efficient strategies than those the model used to produce interesting outcomes. In one study, 14-month-olds observed a chilly model wrapped in a blanket use her head to turn on a light. When given an opportunity, these toddlers also pressed the button to turn on the light but did so with their fingers rather than their heads (Gergely, Bekkering, & Kiraly, 2002). They thus replicated the model's goal (to turn on the light) while using a different means—a process known as **emulation.** Both imitation and emulation are common early in childhood; but starting at about age 2, children become more inclined to precisely imitate a model's specific actions (rather than to emulate), particularly if the model has been friendly to them rather than distant (Nielson, 2006) and/or the rationale for the model's specific actions is not clear to them (Williamson & Markman, 2006). They may choose to imitate the friendly model as a means of initiating or sustaining an interaction with this sociable individual. And they may choose to imitate a model's specific complex action that they don't fully understand because they are interested in reproducing the modeled outcome and think that precise imitation (rather than freelance emulation) is more likely to successfully achieve this aim. Yet, 3-year-olds are very selective imitators. They are not especially inclined to imitate a model's *unsuccessful* actions and are much more likely to precisely imitate a successful model when they have previously experienced difficulties at achieving the modeled objectives on their own (Williamson, Metzloff, & Markman, 2008).

In sum, the controlled *laboratory* evidence we have reviewed implies that 14- to 36-month-olds are highly receptive to social models, particularly warm and friendly models with whom they are motivated to interact. Their rapidly developing capacity for deferred imitation implies that they are already constructing symbolic representations of what they have witnessed and retrieving this information from memory to guide their reproduction of past events. Thus, older infants and toddlers should be prepared to learn a great deal from the behaviors of such real-world companions as parents, siblings, and playmates. Do they take advantage of their newly acquired imitative capabilities in the natural environment?

Yes, indeed! Leon Kuczynski and his associates (1987) asked mothers to record the immediate and the delayed reactions of their 12- to 20-month-old infants and their 25- to 33-month-old toddlers to the behavior of parental and peer models. The results were quite interesting. All the children imitated their models a fair percentage of the time, but there were clear age differences in the content of these imitations. The 12- to 20-month-olds tended to imitate affective displays, such as laughing and cheering, and other high-intensity antics like jumping, shaking the head to and fro, and pounding on the table. In other words, their imitations were largely playful in character. By contrast, the 25- to 33-month-olds more often imitated *instrumental* behaviors, such as household tasks and self-care routines. What's more, their imitations had more of a self-instructional quality to them, as if the older toddlers were now making an active attempt (1) to acquire

deferred imitation
reproduction of a modeled activity that has been witnessed at some point in the past.

emulation
reproduction of a modeled outcome by use of means other than those that the model displayed.

skills their models had displayed or (2) to understand the events they had witnessed. When imitating disciplinary encounters, for example, the 12- to 20-month-olds simply repeated verbal prohibitions and physical actions such as hand slapping, usually directing these responses to themselves. However, the older toddlers tended to reenact the entire scenario, including the social influence strategies the disciplinarian had used, and they usually directed these responses to another person, an animal, or a doll. So it seems that between the ages of 2 and 3, observational *learning* is becoming an important means by which children acquire basic personal and social competencies and gain a richer understanding of the rules and regulations they are expected to follow (see also Want & Harris, 2001).

A Later Development in Observational Learning: Use of Verbal Mediators   Although preschool children are rapidly acquiring language and becoming more accomplished as conversationalists, they are less likely than older children to rely on verbal labels to help them retain modeled sequences. In a study by Coates and Hartup (1969), 4- to 5-year-olds and 7- to 8-year-olds watched a short film in which an adult model displayed a number of unusual responses, such as shooting at a tower of blocks with a pop gun and throwing a beanbag between his legs. Some of the children from each age group were told to describe the model's actions as they observed them (*induced-verbalization condition*); others simply watched the model without having received any instructions (*passive-observation condition*). As shown in Figure 2.1, 4- to 5-year-olds who described what they were observing were later able to reproduce much more of the model's behavior than their age mates in the passive-observation condition. By contrast, 7- to 8-year-olds reproduced the same number of the model's responses whether or not they had been told to describe what the model was doing. This latter finding suggests that 7- to 8-year-olds will use verbal labels to describe what they have seen, *even if they are not told to*. One important implication of this study is that preschool children may generally learn *less* from social models because they, unlike older children, do not spontaneously produce the **verbal mediators** that would help them retain what they have observed.

Photo 2.6
By age 2, toddlers are already acquiring personal and social skills by imitating the adaptive acts of older social models.

verbal mediator
In Bandura's theory, a verbal encoding of modeled behavior that the observer stores in memory.

environmental determinism
the notion that children are passive creatures who are molded by their environments.

Social Learning as Reciprocal Determinism

Early versions of learning theory were largely tributes to Watson's doctrine of **environmental determinism**: Young, unknowing children were viewed as passive recipients of environmental influence—they would become whatever parents, teachers, and other agents of society groomed them to be. Bandura (1986, 1989, 2001) takes strong exception to this point of view, stressing that children and adolescents are active, thinking beings who contribute in many ways to their own development. Observational learning, for example, requires the observer to *actively* attend to, encode, and retain the behaviors displayed by social models. And children are often free to choose the models to whom they will attend; so they have some say about *what* they will learn from others.

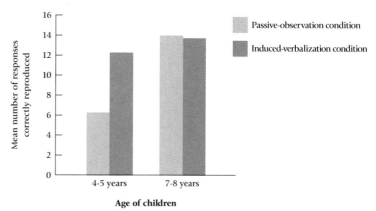

Figure 2.1
Children's ability to reproduce the behavior of a social model as a function of age and verbalization instructions. (Adapted from "Age and Verbalization in Observational Learning," by B. Coates and W. W. Hartup, 1969, *Developmental Psychology*, 1, 556–562. Copyright © 1969 by the American Psychological Association. Used by permission.)

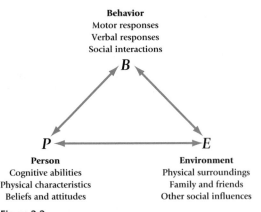

Figure 2.2
Bandura's model of reciprocal determinism. (Adapted from A. Bandura, 1978, "The Self System in Reciprocal Determinism." *American Psychologist*, 33, 344–358. Copyright © 1978 by the American Psychological Association. Used by permission.)

reciprocal determinism
the notion that the flow of influence between children and their environments is a two-way street; the environment may affect the child, but the child's behavior will also influence the environment.

Bandura (1986) has proposed the concept of **reciprocal determinism** to describe his view that human development reflects an interaction between the person (P), the person's behavior (B), and the environment (E) (see Figure 2.2). Unlike the early behaviorists, who maintained that the environment (E) shaped the child and his or her behavior. Bandura and others (most notably Richard Bell, 1979) propose that the links between the person, behaviors, and environments are bidirectional, so that children, for example, might influence their environments by virtue of their own conduct. Consider an example.

Suppose that a 4-year-old discovers that he can gain control over desirable toys by assaulting his playmates. In this case, control over a desired toy is a satisfying outcome that reinforces the child's aggressive behavior. But note that the reinforcer here is produced by the child himself—through his aggressive actions. Not only has bullying behavior been reinforced (by obtaining the toy), *but the character of the play environment has changed*. Our bully becomes more inclined to victimize his playmates in the future, whereas those playmates who are victimized may become even more inclined to "give in" to the bully (Putallaz et al., 2004; and see Figure 2.3).

In sum, cognitive-social-learning theorists describe development as a continuous *reciprocal interaction* between children and their environments. The situation or "environment" that a child experiences will surely affect her, but her behavior is thought to affect the environment as well. The implication is that children are actively involved in shaping the very environments that will influence their growth and development.

Contributions and Criticisms of the Social-Learning Perspective

Perhaps the major contribution of the social-learning viewpoint is the wealth of information it has provided about developing children and adolescents. Social-learning theories are very precise and testable (Horowitz, 1992). And by conducting tightly controlled experiments to determine how their participants react to various environmental influences,

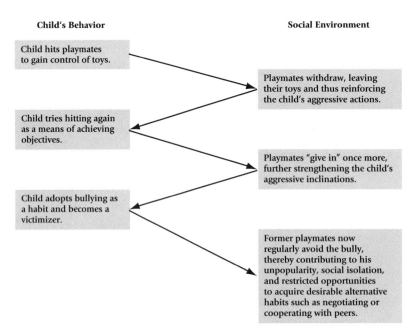

Figure 2.3 Reciprocal determinism: A hypothetical example showing how a child both influences and is influenced by the social environment.

social-learning theorists have begun to understand how and why developing persons might form emotional attachments, adopt gender roles, make friends, learn to abide by moral rules, and change in countless other ways over the course of childhood and adolescence. As we will see throughout the text, the social-learning perspective has contributed substantially to our knowledge of many aspects of social and personality development (Grusec, 1992).

The social-learning theorist's emphasis on overt behavior and its immediate causes has also produced a number of important clinical insights and practical applications. For example, many problem behaviors can now be quickly eliminated by behavioral modification techniques in which the therapist (1) identifies the reinforcers that sustain undesirable habits and eliminates them (2) modeling or reinforcing alternative behaviors that are more socially desirable. Thus, distressing antics such as bullying or name-calling can often be eliminated in a matter of days or weeks, rather than the months (or years) that a psychoanalyst might take, probing the child's unconscious, searching for a conflict that may underlie these hostilities.

Despite its strengths, many view the social-learning approach as an oversimplified account of social and personality development. Consider its explanation of individual differences. Presumably, individuals follow different developmental paths because no two persons grow up in exactly the same environment. Yet critics are quick to note that each person comes into the world with something else that is an equally plausible explanation for his or her "individuality"—a unique genetic inheritance. So social-learning theorists may have badly oversimplified the issue of individual differences in development by downplaying the contribution of important biological influences.

Yet another group of critics, whose viewpoint we will examine in Chapter 3, can agree with the behaviorists that development depends very heavily on the contexts in which it occurs. However, these *ecological systems theorists* argue that the "environment" that so powerfully influences development is really a series of social systems (for example, families, communities, and cultures) that interact with each other (and with the individual) in complex ways that are impossible to simulate in a laboratory. Their point is that only by studying the children and adolescents in their *natural settings* are we likely to understand how environments truly influence development.

One final criticism: Despite the popularity of recent cognitively oriented learning theories that stress the child's active role in the developmental process, some critics maintain that *no* learning theorist pays enough attention to *cognitive* influences on development. Proponents of this third, or "cognitive-developmental," viewpoint believe that the child's mental abilities undergo a series of qualitative changes (or stages) that behaviorists completely ignore. Further, they argue that a child's impressions of and reactions to the environment depend largely on his or her level of **cognitive development.** Let's now turn to this viewpoint and see what it has to offer.

cognitive development
age-related changes that occur in mental activities such as attending, perceiving, learning, thinking, and remembering.

🌀 PIAGET'S COGNITIVE-DEVELOPMENTAL VIEWPOINT

No theorist has contributed more to our understanding of children's thinking than Jean Piaget (1896–1980), a Swiss scholar who began to study intellectual development during the 1920s. Piaget was truly a remarkable individual. At age 10, he published his first scientific article about the behavior of a rare albino sparrow. His early interest in the ways that animals adapt to their environments eventually led him to pursue a Ph.D. in zoology, which he completed in 1918. Piaget's secondary interest was *epistemology* (the branch of philosophy concerned with the origins of knowledge), and he hoped to be able to integrate his two interests. Thinking that psychology was the answer, Piaget journeyed to Paris, where he accepted a position at the Alfred Binet laboratories, working on the first

Photo 2.7
In his cognitive-developmental theory. Swiss scholar Jean Piaget (1896–1980) focused on the growth of children's knowledge and reasoning skills.

scheme
an organized pattern of thought or action that a child constructs to make sense of some aspect of his or her experience; Piaget sometimes uses the term cognitive structure as a synonym for scheme.

behavioral schemes
organized patterns of behavior that are used to represent and respond to objects and experiences.

symbolic schemes
internal mental symbols (such as images or verbal codes) that one uses to represent aspects of experience.

operational schemes
Piaget's term for schemes that utilize cognitive operations, or mental "actions of the head," that enable one to transform objects of thought and to reason logically.

constructivist
one who gains knowledge by acting or otherwise operating on objects or events to discover their properties.

standardized intelligence test. His experiences in this position would have a profound influence on his career.

In the testing approach to the study of mental ability, an estimate is made of the person's intelligence based on the number and kinds of questions that he or she answers correctly. However, Piaget soon found that he was more interested in children's *incorrect* answers than their correct ones. He first noticed that children of about the same age were producing the same kinds of wrong answers. But why? As he proceeded to question children about their misconceptions, using the clinical method he had learned earlier while working in a psychiatric clinic, he began to realize that young children are not simply less intelligent than older children; their thought processes are completely different. Piaget then set up his own laboratory and spent 60 years charting the course of intellectual growth and attempting to determine how children progress from one mode (or stage) of thinking to another.

Piaget's View of Intelligence and Intellectual Growth

Influenced by his background in biology, Piaget (1950) defined intelligence as a basic life process that helps an organism to adapt to its environment. By adapting, Piaget means that the organism is able to cope with the demands of its immediate situation. For example, the hungry infant who grasps a bottle and brings it to her mouth is behaving adaptively, as is the adolescent who successfully interprets a road map while traveling or changes a tire should the need arise. As children mature, they acquire ever more complex "cognitive structures" that aid them in adapting to their environments.

Cognitive (Intellectual) Schemes   A cognitive structure—or what Piaget called a **scheme**— is an organized pattern of thought or action that is used to cope with or explain some aspect of experience. For example, many 3-year-olds may insist that the sun is alive because it comes up in the morning and goes down at night (Opfer & Gelman, 2001). These children are operating on the basis of a simple cognitive scheme—the idea that things that move are alive. The earliest *schemes*, formed in infancy, are simple motor habits such as reaching, grasping, and lifting that prove to be adaptive indeed. A curious infant who combines the responses of extending an arm (reaching) and grasping with the hand is suddenly capable of satisfying her curiosity by exploring almost any interesting object that is no more than an arm's length away. Simple as these **behavioral schemes** may be, they permit infants to operate toys, turn dials, open cabinets, and otherwise master their environments. Later in infancy, children are able to represent experiences mentally, forming such **symbolic schemes** as visual images. Shortly after entering grade school, children's schemes become **operational,** taking the form of internal mental activities or "actions of the head" (for example, cognitive addition or subtraction) that allow them to mentally manipulate information and think logically about the issues and problems they encounter in everyday life. At any age, children rely on their current cognitive schemes to understand the world around them. As a result, younger and older children, who construct very different kinds of schemes, will often interpret and respond to the same objects and events in very different ways.

Constructing Schemes: Piaget's Intellectual Functions   How do children develop more complex schemes and grow intellectually? Piaget claimed that infants have no inborn knowledge or ideas about reality as some philosophers have claimed. Nor are children simply handed information or passively taught how to think by adults. Instead, Piaget viewed children as **constructivists** who actively create new understandings of the world based on their own experiences. How? By being the curious and *active* explorers that they are.

Children watch what goes on around them; they experiment with objects they encounter; they make connections or associations between events; and they are puzzled when their current understanding (or schemes) fail to explain what they have experienced.

According to Piaget, children are able to construct new schemes because they have inherited two *intellectual functions,* which he calls *organization* and *adaptation.* **Organization** is the process by which children combine existing schemes into new and more complex intellectual structures. For example, a toddler may initially believe that anything that flies is a "birdie." As he gradually discovers that many things that are not birds can also fly, he may organize this knowledge into new and more complex hierarchical structures such as this one:

A flying object may be

a bird   a plane   Superman

According to Piaget, organization is inborn and automatic: Children are constantly organizing their available schemes into higher-order systems or structures.

The goal of organization is to further the process of adaptation. As its name implies, **adaptation** is the process of adjusting to the demands of the environment. According to Piaget, adaptation occurs through two complementary activities: assimilation and accommodation.

To illustrate the adaptive function, let's return to the 3-year-old who believes that the sun is alive. Surely this idea is not something the child learned from an adult; it was apparently constructed by the child on the basis of her own worldly experiences. After all, many things that move *are* alive. So long as the child clings to this understanding, she may regard any new moving object as alive; that is, new experiences will be interpreted in terms of her current cognitive structures, a process Piaget called **assimilation.** Eventually, however, this child will encounter moving objects that almost certainly couldn't be alive, such as a paper airplane that was nothing more than a sheet of newsprint before dad built it, or a wind-up toy that invariably stops moving unless she winds it again. Now here are contradictions (or what Piaget termed **disequilibriums**) between the child's understanding and the facts to be understood. It becomes clear to the child that her "objects-that-move-are-alive" scheme needs to be revised. So she will be prompted by these disconfirming experiences to **accommodate**—that is to alter her existing schemes so that they provide a better explanation of the events she has witnessed (perhaps by concluding that only things that move under their own power are alive).

So it goes through life; Piaget believes that we are continually relying on the complementary processes of assimilation and accommodation to adapt to our environments. Initially, we attempt to understand new experiences or to solve problems using our current cognitive structures (assimilation). But we will often find our existing schemes are inadequate for these tasks, which then prompts us to revise them (through accommodation) and to integrate them with other relevant schemes (organization) to provide a better "fit" with reality (Piaget, 1952). Biological maturation also plays an important role: As the brain and nervous system mature, children become capable of increasingly complex cognitive activities that help them to construct better understandings of what they have experienced (Piaget, 1970). Eventually, curious, active children, who are always forming new schemes and reorganizing this knowledge, will have progressed far enough to be thinking about old issues in entirely new ways; that is, they pass from one stage of cognitive development to the next higher stage.

Four Stages of Cognitive Development

Piaget proposed four major periods (or stages) of cognitive development: the *sensorimotor* stage (birth to age 2), the *preoperational* stage (ages 2 to 7), the *concrete-operational* stage (ages 7 to 11 or 12), and the *formal-operational* stage (ages 11–12 and beyond). These stages

organization
an inborn tendency to combine and integrate available schemes into coherent systems or bodies of knowledge.

adaptation
inborn tendency to adjust to the demands of the environment.

assimilation
Piaget's term for the process by which children interpret new experiences by incorporating them into their existing schemes.

disequilibriums
imbalances or contradictions between one's thought processes and environmental events. By contrast, *equilibrium* refers to a balanced, harmonious relationship between one's cognitive structures and the environment.

AN INFANT ACCOMMODATING HIS MOUTH TO THE SHAPE OF AN OBJECT

accommodation
Piaget's term for the process by which children modify their existing schemes in order to incorporate or adapt to new experiences.

invariant developmental sequence
a series of developments that occur in one particular order because each development in the sequence is a prerequisite for the next.

sensorimotor stage
Piaget's first stage of cognitive development, from birth to 2 years, when infants rely on behavioral schemes to adapt to the environment.

neonate
a newborn infant from birth to approximately one month of age.

primary circular reaction
a pleasurable response, centered on the infant's own body, that is discovered by chance and performed over and over.

secondary circular reaction
a pleasurable response, centered on an object external to the self, that is discovered by chance and performed over and over.

form what Piaget called an **invariant developmental sequence**—that is, all children progress through the stages in exactly the order in which they are listed. There is no skipping of stages because each successive stage builds on the previous stage and represents a more complex way of thinking.

The Sensorimotor Stage (Birth to Approximately 2 Years) The **sensorimotor stage** spans the first two years, or the period that developmentalists refer to as infancy. The dominant cognitive structures are behavioral schemes, which evolve as infants begin to coordinate their *sensory* input and *motor* responses in order to "act on" and get to "know" the environment.

During the first two years of life, infants evolve from reflexive creatures with very limited knowledge into planful problem solvers who have already learned a great deal about themselves, their close companions, and the objects and events in their everyday worlds. So dramatic are the infant's cognitive advances that Piaget divides the sensorimotor period into six substages (see Table 2.3 on p. 58), which describe the child's gradual transition from a reflexive to a reflective organism. Our review will concentrate on those aspects of sensorimotor development that have influenced thinking about children's social and personality development.

Growth of Intentional or Goal-Directed Behavior Over the first eight months, infants begin to act on objects and to discover that they can make interesting things happen. However, these discoveries emerge very gradually. Piaget believes that **neonates** are born with only a few basic reflexes (for example, sucking, grasping) that assist them in satisfying biological needs such as hunger. During the first month, their activities are pretty much confined to exercising their innate reflexes, assimilating new objects into these reflexive schemes (for example, sucking on objects other than nipples), and accommodating their reflexes to these novel objects.

The first coordinated habits emerge at 1–4 months of age as infants discover by chance that various responses that they can produce (for example, sucking their thumbs, making sounds by cooing) are satisfying and thus worthy of repetition. These responses, called **primary circular reactions,** are centered on the infant's own body. They are called "primary" because they are the first habits to appear and "circular" because the pleasure they bring stimulates their repetition.

Between 4 and 8 months of age, infants discover (again by chance) that they can make interesting things happen to *external* objects (such as making a rubber duck quack by squeezing it). These responses, called **secondary circular reactions,** also tend to be repeated for the pleasure they bring. Of what possible significance are these simple habits for social and personality development? According to Piaget, infants are discovering the limits and capabilities of their own bodies during the first four months and then recognizing that external objects are separate from their "physical selves" by the middle of the first year. Thus, making a distinction between "self" and "nonself" is viewed as the first step in the development of a personal identity, or self-concept.

Between 8 and 12 months of age, infants are suddenly able to coordinate two or more actions to achieve simple objectives. For example, were you to place a toy that the child wanted under a cushion, the child might lift the cushion with one hand while using the other to grab the toy. In this case, the act of lifting the cushion is not pleasurable in itself; nor is it emitted by chance. Rather, it represents part of a larger *intentional* scheme in which two initially unrelated responses—lifting and grasping—are coordinated as a means to an end. Piaget believed that these simple means-ends activities represent the earliest form of true problem solving.

At 12 to 18 months of age, infants begin to experiment with objects and will try to invent totally new methods of solving problems or reproducing interesting results. For example, a child who originally squeezed a rubber duck to make it quack may now decide to drop it, step on it, or crush it with a pillow to see whether these actions will have the same or different effects on the toy. These trial-and-error exploratory schemes, called **tertiary circular reactions,** signal the emergence of true curiosity.

A dramatic development takes place between 18 and 24 months of age: Children begin to internalize their behavioral schemes to construct mental symbols, or images. Suddenly, 18- to 24-month-olds are capable of solving problems mentally, without resorting to trial-and-error experimentation. This ability, called **inner experimentation,** is illustrated in Piaget's interaction with his son, Laurent:

> Laurent is seated before a table and I place a bread crust in front of him, out of reach. Also, to the right of the child I place a stick, about 25cm long. At first, Laurent tries to grasp the bread . . . and then he gives up. . . . Laurent again looks at the bread, and without moving, looks very briefly at the stick, then suddenly grasps it and directs it to the bread . . . [he then] draws the bread to him. (Piaget, 1952, p. 335)

Clearly, Laurent had an important insight: The stick can be used as an extension of his arm to obtain a distant object. Trial-and-error experimentation is not apparent in this case, for Laurent's "problem solving" occurred at an internal, symbolic level.

Development of Imitation   Imitation intrigued Piaget because, like Bandura, he viewed it as a highly adaptive activity—a means by which infants might actively participate in social exchanges and add many new skills to their behavioral repertoires. However, his own observations suggested that infants are incapable of imitating *novel* responses displayed by a model until 8 to 12 months of age (the same age at which they show clear evidence of intentionality in their own behavior). Furthermore, the imitative schemes of an 8-month-old are rather imprecise. Were you to bend and straighten your finger, the infant might mimic you by opening and closing her entire hand (Piaget, 1951). Voluntary imitation becomes much more precise between 12 and 18 months, and as we noted earlier, a major accomplishment of the second year is refinement of *deferred imitation*—the ability to reproduce actions modeled earlier in time. Clearly, this capacity for deferred imitation implies that infants are capable of generating the kinds of *symbolic* representations of their experiences that promote observational learning. [1]

What are we to make of recent claims that *neonates* are capable of imitating simple facial gestures and motor responses? In Box 2.2, we explore this phenomenon that Piaget overlooked and discuss its possible adaptive significance.

Development of Object Permanence   One of the more notable achievements of the sensorimotor period is the development of **object permanence**—the idea that objects continue to exist when they are no longer visible or detectable through the other senses. If you were to remove your watch and cover it with a coffee mug, you would be well aware that the watch continues to exist. Objects have a permanence for us; out of sight is not necessarily out of mind.

According to Piaget, babies are not initially aware of this basic fact of life. Throughout the first four months, infants will not search for attractive objects that vanish; were they interested in a watch that was then covered by a mug, they would soon lose interest, almost as if they believed that the watch had lost its identity by being transformed into a mug

tertiary circular reaction
an exploratory scheme in which infants devise new methods of acting on objects to reproduce interesting results.

inner experimentation
the ability to solve simple problems on a mental, or symbolic, level without having to rely on trial-and-error experimentation.

object permanence
the realization that objects continue to exist when they are no longer visible or detectable through the other senses.

---

[1]Piaget seems to be correct in stating that infants are slow to imitate truly novel motor responses that are not part of their existing behavioral repertoire. However, they can imitate responses they are already capable of performing by 6 months of age and will do so up to 24 hours after seeing a model perform them (Collie & Hayne, 1999). This very simple deferred initiation suggests that young infants have some symbolic capacity far earlier than Piaget gave them credit for.

Can Newborns Imitate?

Researchers once believed that infants were unable to imitate the actions of another person until the latter half of the first year (Piaget, 1951). But beginning in the late 1970s, a number of studies reported that babies less than 7 days old were apparently able to imitate a number of adult facial gestures, including sticking out their tongues, opening and closing their mouths, protruding their lower lips (as if they were sad), and even posing displays of happiness (Field et al., 1982; Meltzoff & Moore, 1977; Reissland, 1988; see the accompanying photos).

Some critics have argued that these early facial displays, particularly tongue protrusions and mouth openings (which are the most reliable responses)—are not imitative responses at all, but simply reflect the baby's attempts to explore with their mouths those sights they find particularly interesting (Jones, 1996). Others have wondered whether neonatal imitation might not reflect the activity of recently discovered *mirror neurons*—cells in the brain that fire both when the individual performs an action or observes the same action (Iacoboni, 2005; Winerman, 2005). The idea here is that observing an adult protrude her tongue may activate the mirror neurons of an observing infant, producing a somewhat similar motor response. Interestingly, those early matching displays become much harder to elicit over the first 3–4 months of life (Abravanel & Sigafoos, 1984). Some have interpreted this to mean that the neonate's limited capacity for mimicking is an *involuntary reflexive scheme* that disappears with age (as many

other reflexes do), only to be replaced later by voluntary imitation (Kaitz et al., 1988; Vinter, 1986).

However, Andrew Meltzoff (1990b; Meltzoff & Moore, 1992) contends that babies' early matching displays are *voluntary imitative responses*. He thinks this because babies only a few days old will often match an adult's facial expression *after a short delay*, even though the model is no longer posing that expression. According to Meltzoff, these imitative responses are possible because babies match facial movements they "see" in the model's face to movements they can "feel" in their own faces. Yet Meltzoff's critics contend that if neonatal imitation represented a *voluntary* imitative response, it should get stronger with age rather than disappearing (Bjorklund, 2005).

Clearly, the underlying meaning and causes of these early matching facial displays remain a topic of debate. But regardless of whether we choose to call it imitation, exploration, or reflexive behavior, a newborn's responsiveness to facial gestures almost certainly warms the hearts of caregivers and also helps to ensure that they and their baby get off to a good start. Indeed, we will see in Chapter 5 that very young infants have a number of other inborn characteristics that elicit the kinds of affectionate social contacts from caregivers that promote emotional attachments and healthy social and emotional development. So it is quite conceivable that the newborn's ability to match facial displays serves this same important function and is highly adaptive indeed!

     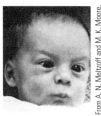

From A. N. Meltzoff and M. K. Moore, *Science*, 1977, 198, 75–78.

Sample photographs from videotaped recordings of 2- and 3-week-old infants imitating tongue protrusion, mouth opening, and lip protrusion.

(Bower, 1982). At age 4 to 8 months, infants will retrieve attractive objects that are partly concealed or hidden under a transparent cover; but their continuing failure to search for objects that are completely concealed suggests that, from their perspective, disappearing objects may no longer exist.[2]

According to Piaget, the first signs of an emerging object concept appear at 8 to 12 months of age. However, object permanence is far from complete, as we see in Piaget's demonstration with 10-month-old Jacqueline:

Jacqueline is seated on a mattress without anything to disturb or distract her. . . . I take her [toy] parrot from her hands and hide it twice in succession under the mattress, on her left [point A]. Both times Jacqueline looks for the object immediately and grabs it. Then I take it

---

[2]However, Piaget's conclusion has been hotly debated. Many investigators now believe that even very young infants *know* that objects continue to exist; they simply *forget* where the objects are if those objects remain hidden for more than a second or two (cf. Bjorklund, 2005, for a review).

from her hands and move it very slowly before her eyes to the corresponding place on her right, under the mattress [point B]. Jacqueline watches this movement . . . but at the moment when the parrot disappears [at point B], she turns to her left and looks where it was before [at point A]. [1954, p. 51]

Jacqueline's response is typical of children at this age. When searching for a disappearing object, the 8- to 12-month-old will often look in the place where it was previously *found* rather than the place where it was last seen. In other words, the child acts as if her *behavior* determined where the object was to appear, and consequently she does not treat the object as if it existed independent of her own activity.

Between 12 and 18 months of age, the object concept improves. Infants will now track the visible movements of objects and search for them where they were last seen. Yet the object concept is not complete because the child cannot make the mental inferences necessary to represent and understand *invisible* displacements. Thus, if you conceal an attractive toy in your hand, place your hand behind a barrier and deposit the toy there, remove your closed hand, and ask the child to find the toy, 12- to 18-month-olds will search where the toy was last seen—in your hand—rather than looking behind the barrier.

By 18 to 24 months of age, children are capable of mentally representing invisible displacements and using these mental inferences to guide their search for objects that disappear. The object concept is now complete.

Of what social significance is the object concept? In Chapter 5, we will see that it may play a very important role in the development of an infant's first true emotional attachments. Cognitive theorists (for example, Schaffer, 1977, 1991) have proposed that infants cannot form close emotional ties to regular companions unless these individuals have a "permanence" about them. After all, it would seem rather difficult to establish a meaningful and lasting relationship with a person who "ceases to exist" whenever he or she passes from view.

In sum, the child's intellectual achievements during the sensorimotor period are truly remarkable. In two short years, infants have evolved from reflexive and largely immobile creatures into planful thinkers who can move about on their own, solve some problems in their heads, form simple concepts, and even communicate many of their thoughts to their companions. Table 2.3 on page 58 presents a brief summary of the major intellectual accomplishments of the first two years.

The Preoperational Stage (Approximately 2 to 7 Years) During the **preoperational stage,** children become increasingly proficient at constructing and using mental symbols (words and images) to think about the objects, situations, and events they encounter. But despite these advances in symbolic reasoning, Piaget's descriptions of preoperational intelligence focus mainly on the limitations or deficiencies in children's thinking. Indeed, he called this period "preoperational" because he believed that preschool children have not yet acquired the **cognitive operations**—internal mental activities such as cognitive addition or subtraction—that would enable them to think logically. As we review this intellectual stage, we will once again focus on characteristics of preoperational thought that have implications for social and personality development.

Symbolism and Pretend Play   The early preoperational period (ages 2–3) is marked by a dramatic increase in children's use of the **symbolic function**—the ability to make one thing—a word or an object—stand for, or represent, something else. Consider, for example, that because 2- to 3-year-olds can use words and images to represent their experiences, they are now quite capable of reconstructing past events and thinking about or even comparing objects that are no longer present.

A second hallmark of the early preoperational period—one made possible by the growth of symbolism—is a dramatic increase in both the frequency and complexity of *pretend play:* Toddlers often pretend to be people they are not (mommies, superheroes),

preoperational stage
Piaget's second stage of cognitive development, lasting from about ages 2 to 7, when children are thinking at a symbolic level but are not yet using cognitive operations.

cognitive operation
an internal mental activity that one performs on objects of thought.

symbolic function
the ability to use symbols (for example, images and words) to represent objects and experiences.

Table 2.3 Summary of the substages and intellectual accomplishments of the sensorimotor period

Piagetian Substage	Methods of Solving Problems or Producing Interesting Outcomes	Imitation Skills	Object Concept
1. Reflex activity (0–1 month)	Exercising and accommodating inborn reflexes	Some imitation of facial expressions and gross motor responses[1]	Tracks moving object but ignores its disappearance
2. Primary circular reactions (1–4 months)	Repeating interesting acts that are centered on one's own body	Repetition of own behavior that is mimicked by a companion	Looks intently at the spot where an object disappeared[2]
3. Secondary circular reactions (4–8 months)	Repeating interesting acts that are directed toward external objects	Same as in substage 2	Searches for partly concealed object
4. Coordination of secondary schemes (8–12 months)	Combining actions to solve simple problems (first evidence of intentionality)	Ability to eventually imitate novel responses after gradually accommodating a crude first attempt at imitation	Searches for and finds concealed object that has not been visibly displaced—first glimmering of notion of object permanence
5. Tertiary circular reactions (12–18 months)	Experimenting to find new ways to solve problems or reproduce interesting outcomes	Systematic imitation of novel responses; deferred imitation of simple motor acts	Searches for and finds object that has been visibly displaced
6. Invention of new means through mental combinations (18–24 months)	Solving problems at an internal symbolic level—first evidence of child's using insight	Deferred imitation of complex behavioral sequences	Searches for and finds objects that have been hidden through invisible displacements—object concept is complete

[1]Imitation of facial expressions is apparently an inborn ability that may bear little relation to the voluntary imitation that appears later in the first year.

[2]Many researchers now believe that the object concept may be present very early and that Piaget's research badly underestimates what young infants may know about objects (see Bjorklund, 2005).

Sources: Adapted from T. M. Field, R. Woodson, R. Greenberg, & D. Cohen, 1982, "Discrimination and Imitation of Facial Expressions by Neonates." *Science,* 218, 179–181; also A. N. Meltzoff & M. K. Moore, 1977, "Imitation of Facial and Manual Gestures by Human Neonates." *Science,* 198, 75–78.

and they may assume these roles with props (such as a shoe box or a stick) that symbolize role-relevant objects (for example, a baby's crib or a ray gun). Although parents are occasionally concerned when their preschoolers immerse themselves in a world of make believe, Piaget viewed pretend play as serious business—an activity that promotes the child's social, emotional, and intellectual development. And there is ample support for Piaget's argument. For example, many children create "imaginary playmates" early in life, and their play dramas with imaginary companions may help them practice and perfect such social routines as interacting amicably with or providing support and comfort to friends (Gleason, 2002; Gleason, Sebanc, & Hartup, 2000). In the real world, social pretend play requires children to adopt different roles, coordinate their play activities, and resolve any disputes that arise. Children may also learn about and prepare for adult roles by playing "house" or "school" and stepping into the shoes of their mothers, fathers, or nursery-school teachers (Pellegrini & Bjorklund, 2004). Perhaps due to the social skills they acquire through play (for example, an ability to cooperate), preschool children who pretend a lot are judged to be more creative and more socially mature by their preschool teachers and more popular with their peers than age-mates who pretend less often (Connolly & Doyle, 1984; Howes & Matheson, 1992).

Finally, pretend play may foster healthy emotional development by allowing children to freely express feelings that bother them or to resolve emotional conflicts (Fein, 1986). If Jennie, for example, has been scolded at lunch for failing to eat her peas, she may gain control of the situation at play as she scolds her doll for picky eating or persuades the doll to "eat healthy" and consume the peas. Playful resolution of such emotional conflicts may even be an important contributor to children's understanding of authority and to the rationales that underlie the rules they must follow (Piaget & Inhelder, 1969).

Let it never be said, then, that play is useless. Although children play because it is fun, not because it sharpens their skills, players indirectly contribute to their own social, emotional, and intellectual development, enjoying themselves all the while. In this sense, play is truly the child's work—and is serious business indeed!

Deficiencies in Preoperational Reasoning   Despite the adaptive characteristics of children's symbolism and pretend play, much of what Piaget had to say about preoperational thought dwelled on its limitations. The most striking deficiency that he saw was the child's **egocentrism**—a tendency to view the world from one's own perspective and to have difficulty recognizing another person's divergent point of view. Piaget demonstrated this by first familiarizing children with an asymmetrical mountain scene (see Figure 2.4) and then asking them what an observer would see as he gazed at the scene from a vantage point other than their own. Often 3- to 4-year-olds said that the other person would see exactly what they see, which Piaget interpreted as the child's failure to consider the other's divergent perspective.

If young children often have trouble with *perceptual perspective-taking,* or inferring what others can see and hear, imagine the difficulties they must face with *conceptual perspective taking*—that is, correctly inferring what another person may be feeling, thinking, or intending. Indeed, we will see that preschoolers do often rely on their own perspectives and thus fail to make accurate judgments about other people's motives, intentions, and desires; also, they do often assume that if they know something, others will too (Hala & Chandler, 1996; Ruffman et al., 1993). Furthermore, the egocentrism that younger children display may help to explain why they may sometimes appear rather cruel, selfish, inconsiderate, or unwilling to help one another. If these "insensitive" youngsters do not realize how their own actions make others feel, they may not readily experience the remorse and sympathy that might inhibit antisocial behavior or promote acts of kindness. This hypothesized link between children's cognitive abilities (namely their empathic capabilities and role-taking skills) and their social conduct will be explored in detail when we consider the topics of aggression, altruism, and moral development in Chapters 9 and 10.

Between the ages of 4 and 7, egocentrism declines somewhat and children become much more proficient at classifying objects on the basis of shared perceptual features such as size, shape, and color. In fact, Piaget characterized the thinking of the 4-to 6-year-old as **"intuitive"** because her understanding of objects and events tends to "center" on their single, most salient *perceptual* feature—the way things appear to be—rather than or logical on rational thought processes.

The deficiencies of intuitive reasoning are quite clear if we examine the results of Piaget's famous *conservation* studies (Flavell, 1963). One of these experiments begins with the child adjusting the volumes of liquid in two identical containers until each is said to have "the same amount to drink." Next the child sees the experimenter pour the liquid from one of these tall, thin containers into a short, broad container. He is then asked whether the remaining tall, thin container and the shorter, broader container have the same amount of liquid (see Figure 2.5 for an illustration of the procedure). Children younger than 6 or 7 will usually say that the tall, thin receptacle contains more liquid than the short, broad one. The child's thinking about liquids is apparently **centered** on one perceptual feature—the relative heights of the columns (tall column = more liquid). In Piaget's terminology, preoperational children are incapable of **conservation:** They do not yet realize that certain properties of a substance (such as its volume or mass) remain unchanged when its appearance is altered in some superficial way.

egocentrism
the tendency to view the world from one's own perspective while failing to recognize that others may have different points of view.

intuitive thought
Piaget's term for reasoning that is dominated by appearances (or perceptual characteristics of objects and events) rather than by rational thought processes.

centered thinking (centration)
the tendency to focus on only one aspect of a problem when two or more aspects are relevant.

conservation
the recognition that the properties of an object or substance do not change when its appearance is altered in some superficial way.

Figure 2.4
Piaget's three-mountain problem. Young preoperational children are egocentric. They cannot easily assume another person's perspective and will often say that another child viewing the mountain from a different vantage point will see exactly what they see from their own location.

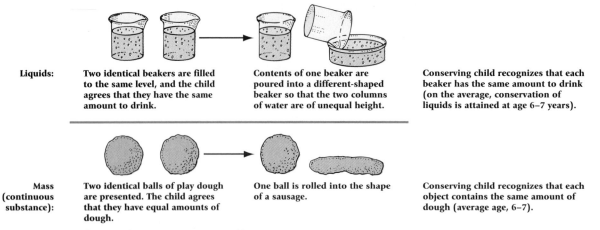

Liquids: **Two identical beakers are filled to the same level, and the child agrees that they have the same amount to drink.** **Contents of one beaker are poured into a different-shaped beaker so that the two columns of water are of unequal height.** **Conserving child recognizes that each beaker has the same amount to drink (on the average, conservation of liquids is attained at age 6–7 years).**

Mass (continuous substance): **Two identical balls of play dough are presented. The child agrees that they have equal amounts of dough.** **One ball is rolled into the shape of a sausage.** **Conserving child recognizes that each object contains the same amount of dough (average age, 6–7).**

Figure 2.5 Two of Piaget's famous conservation problems.

reversibility
the ability to reverse, or negate, an action by mentally performing the opposite action.

compensation
the ability to consider more than one aspect of a problem at a time (also called decentration).

concrete-operational stage
Piaget's third stage of cognitive development, lasting from about ages 7 to 11, when children are acquiring cognitive operations and thinking more logically about tangible objects and experiences.

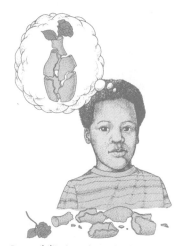

Reversibility is an important cognitive operation that develops during middle childhood.

Why do preoperational children fail to conserve? Simply because their thinking is not yet *operational*. According to Piaget, either of two cognitive operations is necessary for conservation. The first is **reversibility**—the ability to mentally undo, or reverse, an action. At the intuitive level, the child is incapable of mentally reversing the flow of action and therefore does not realize that the liquid in the short, broad container would attain its former height if it were poured back into the tall, thin container. Second, the child must be able to overcome his or her "centered" thinking in order to recognize that immediate appearances can be deceiving. Piaget suggests that children begin to "decenter" as they acquire a cognitive operation called **compensation**—the ability to focus on several aspects of a problem at the same time. Children at the intuitive stage are unable to attend simultaneously to both height and width when trying to solve the liquid conservation problem. Consequently, they fail to recognize that increases in the width of the column of liquid compensate for decreases in its height to preserve its absolute amount.

Let's consider one implication of the young child's intuitive reasoning for social and personality development. Three- to 5-year-olds clearly understand that they are boys or girls and that everyone can be classified according to gender. But the thinking of these young children about gender and its implications is quite egocentric and is dominated by appearances. Thus, a 4-year-old boy might well say he could become a mommy if he really wanted to or might conclude that a woman who cuts her hair short, wears men's clothing, and has a job as a construction worker is now a man (McConaghy, 1979; Slaby & Frey, 1975). Impressions such as these suggest that preschool children have not yet conserved the concept of gender. In Chapter 8, we will see that the conservation of gender is an important contributor to gender-role development that is often not attained until age 5 to 7—precisely the age at which children begin to conserve "nonsocial" attributes such as liquids and mass.

The Concrete-Operational Stage (Approximately 7 to 11 Years) According to Piaget, children at the **concrete-operational stage** are rapidly acquiring cognitive operations and applying these important new skills when thinking about objects and events that they've seen, heard, or otherwise experienced. Recall from our earlier discussion that a cognitive operation is an internal mental activity that enables the child to modify and reorganize her images and symbols to reach a logical conclusion. For example, the operation of *reversibility* allows a child to mentally reverse the flow of action and thereby recognize that a column of water that has assumed a new appearance would once again look the same if she were to pour it back into its original container. Armed with this cognitive operation, then, the concrete operator now *knows* that the two different containers have the same amount of liquid; he uses *logic*, not misleading appearances, to reach his conclusion. So the ability to operate on one's objects of thought takes the 7- to 11-year-old far beyond the static and centered thinking of the preoperational stage.

The Growth of Relational Logic   One of the hallmarks of preoperational thinking—an ability that permits us to (among other things) sharpen our self-concepts by comparing our skills and attributes with those of other people—is a better understanding of relations and relational logic. Can you remember an occasion when your gym teacher said, "Line up by height from tallest to shortest"? Carrying out such a request is really quite easy for concrete operators who are now capable of **seriation**—the ability to mentally arrange items along a quantifiable dimension such as height and weight. By contrast, preoperational youngsters perform miserably on mental seriation tasks and would struggle to comply with the gym teacher's request.

Closely related to seriation is the concept of **transitivity**—the ability to accurately infer the relations among elements in a serial order. If, for example, Jane is taller than Susan, who is taller than Jo, then Jane has to be taller than Jo. Elementary as this inference may seem to us, Piaget claimed that children show little awareness of the logical necessity of the transitivity principle before the stage of concrete operations (Markovits & Dumas, 1999).

Interestingly, however, the transitive inferences of concrete operators are generally limited to *real objects* that are *physically present;* 7- to 11- year-olds cannot yet apply this relational logic to abstract signifiers such as the *x*'s, *y*'s and *z*'s that we use in algebra. Indeed, Piaget names this period *concrete* operations because his research implied that 7- to-11-year-olds are not yet able to apply their operational schemes to think *logically* about abstract ideas or about any hypothetical proposition that violates their conceptions of reality. Let's see why he came to this conclusion.

The Formal-Operational Stage (Age 11–12 and Beyond)   By age 11 or 12, many children are entering the last of Piaget's intellectual stages: **formal operations.** Recall that concrete operations are mental actions performed on material aspects of experience and that concrete operators can think quite logically about tangible objects and events. By contrast, formal operations are mental actions performed on *ideas* and *propositions*. No longer is thinking tied to the factual or observable, for formal operators can reason quite logically about hypothetical processes and events that may have no basis in reality.

Reactions to Hypothetical Propositions   One way to determine whether a preadolescent has crossed over into the stage of formal operations is to present a thought problem that violates her views about the real world. The concrete operator, whose thinking is tied to objective reality, will often balk at hypothetical propositions. In fact, she may even reply that it is impossible to think logically about objects that don't exist or events that could never happen. By contrast, formal operators enjoy thinking about hypotheticals and are likely to generate some very unusual and creative responses. In Box 2.3, we see the differences between concrete-operational and formal-operational thinking as children consider a hypothetical proposition that was presented in the form of an art assignment.

Hypothetico-Deductive Reasoning: The Systematic Search for Answers and Solutions   The formal operator's approach to problem solving becomes increasingly systematic and abstract—much like the **hypothetico-deductive reasoning** of a scientist. We can easily compare the reasoning of formal operators with that of their youngest counterparts by examining their responses to Piaget's famous *pendulum problem* (Inhelder & Piaget, 1958). Given strings of different lengths, objects of different weights to attach to one end of the

seriation
a cognitive operation that allows one to order a set of stimuli along a quantifiable dimension such as height or weight.

transitivity
the ability to infer relations among elements in a serial order (for example, if $A > B$ and $B > C$, then $A >$ than C).

formal-operational stage
Piaget's fourth and final stage of cognitive development, from age 11 to 12 and beyond, when the individual begins to think more rationally and systematically about abstract concepts and hypothetical events.

hypothetico-deductive reasoning
a style of problem solving in which all possible solutions to a problem are generated and then systematically evaluated to determine the correct answer(s).

| Box 2.3 | Focus on Research |

Children's Responses to a Hypothetical Proposition

Piaget (1970) has argued that the thinking of concrete operators is reality bound. Presumably most 9-year-olds would have a difficult time thinking about objects that don't exist or events that could never happen. By contrast, children entering the stage of formal operations were said to be quite capable of considering hypothetical propositions and carrying them to a logical conclusion. Indeed, Piaget suspected that many formal operators would even enjoy this type of cognitive challenge.

Several years ago a group of concrete operators (9-year-old fourth-graders) and a group of children who were at or rapidly approaching formal operations (11- to 12-year-old sixth-graders) completed the following assignment:

> Suppose that you were given a third eye and that you could choose to place this eye anywhere on your body. Draw me a picture to show where you would place your "extra" eye, and then tell me why you would put it there.

All the 9-year-olds placed the third eye *on the forehead between their two natural eyes.* It seems as if these children called on their concrete experiences to complete their assignment: Eyes are found somewhere around the middle of the face in all people. One 9-year-old boy remarked that the third eye should go between the other two because "that's where a cyclops has his eye." The rationales for this eye placement were rather unimaginative. Consider the following examples:

> *Jim* (age 9½): I would like an eye beside my two other eyes so that if one eye went out, I could still see with two.
>
> *Vickie* (age 9): I want an extra eye so I can see you three times.
>
> *Tanya* (age 9½): I want a third eye so I could see better.

By contrast, the older, formal-operational children gave a wide variety of responses that were not at all dependent on what they had seen previously. Furthermore, these children thought out the advantages of this hypothetical situation and provided rather imaginative rationales for placing the "extra" eye in unique locations. Here are some sample responses:

> *Ken* (age 11½): (*Draws the extra eye on top of a tuft of hair.*) I could revolve the eye to look in all directions.
>
> *John* (age 11½): (*Draws his extra eye in the palm of his left hand.*) I could see around corners and see what kind of cookie I'll get out of the cookie jar.
>
> *Tony* (age 11): (*Draws a close-up of a third eye in his mouth.*) I want a third eye in my mouth because I want to see what I am eating.

When asked their opinions of the "three eye" assignment, many of the younger children considered it rather silly and uninteresting. One 9-year-old remarked, "This is stupid. Nobody has three eyes." However, the 11–12-year-olds enjoyed the task and continued to pester their teacher for "fun" art assignments "like the eye problem" for the remainder of the school year (Shaffer, 1973).

So the results of this demonstration are generally consistent with Piaget's theory. Older children who are at or rapidly approaching the stage of formal operations are more likely than younger, concrete operators to generate logical and creative responses to a hypothetical proposition and to enjoy this type of reasoning.

Tanya's, Ken's, and John's responses to the "third eye" problem.

strings, and a hook on which to hang the other end, the subject's task is to discover which factor influences how fast the pendulum oscillates (that is, swings back and forth during a given time period). Is it the length of the string? The heaviness of the weight? The force with which the weight is pushed? The height from which the weight is released? Or might two or more of these variables be important?

The key to solving this problem is to first identify the four factors that might control the pendulum's oscillation and then systematically test all of these "hypotheses," varying one factor at a time while holding all the other factors constant. Formal operators, who rely on this systematic approach to hypothesis generation and testing, eventually discover that the oscillation of the pendulum depends on only one factor: the length of the string. By contrast, 9- to 10-year-old concrete operators are not able to generate and systematically test the full range of possibilities that would permit them to draw a logical conclusion. They often test one variable (say, string length) without holding another (weight) constant; and should they find that a short string with a heavy weight oscillates faster than a longer one with a lighter weight, they are apt to erroneously conclude that both string length and weight control the pendulum's oscillation.

In sum, formational-operational reasoning is rational, systematic, and abstract; the formal operator can think logically about *ideas* and *possibilities* as well as tangible objects and events.

Personal and Social Consequences of Formal Thought   Formal-operational thinking is a powerful tool that may change the adolescent in many ways—some good and some not so good. First the good news: As we will see in Chapter 6, formal operations may pave the way for thinking about what is possible in one's life, forming a stable identity, and achieving a much richer understanding of other people's psychological perspectives and the underlying causes of their behavior. The formal operator is also better equipped to make difficult personal decisions that involve weighing alternative courses of action and their probable consequences for oneself and other people (see Chapter 10, for example, on the development of moral reasoning). So advances in cognitive growth do help to lay the groundwork for changes in other aspects of social and personality development.

Now the bad news: Formal operations may also be related to some of the more painful aspects of the adolescent experience. Unlike younger children, who tend to accept the world as it is and to heed the dictates of authority figures, formal operators, who can imagine hypothetical alternatives to present realities, may begin to question everything—from their parents' authority to restrict their choice of friends, to the need for spending billions on space exploration and missle defense shields when so many people are hungry and homeless. Indeed, the more logical inconsistencies and other flaws that adolescents detect in the real world, the more inclined they are to become frustrated with or even rebelliously angry toward the agents (for example, parents, the government) they hold responsible for these imperfect states of affairs. Piaget (1970) viewed this idealistic fascination with the way things "ought to be" as a perfectly normal outgrowth of the adolescent's newly acquired abstract reasoning abilities, and he proclaimed formal operations the primary cause of the "generation gap."

According to Piaget, adolescents can be so focused on themselves and their thinking that they actually appear more egocentric than they were during the grade-school years. David Elkind (1967, 1981) has identified two kinds of "egocentrism" that adolescents often display. The **imaginary audience** phenomenon refers to the adolescent's feeling that she is constantly "on stage" and that everyone around her is just as concerned with and as critical of her actions or appearance as she is. Thus, a teenage girl who has spent hours making up her face to hide a few pimples may be convinced that her date is repulsed by them whenever he looks away—when, in truth, the equally self-conscious boy may be turning away because he's convinced that her looks of concern imply that his mouthwash has failed him.

The second form of adolescent egocentrism is what Elkind calls the **personal fable**—a belief in the *uniqueness* of oneself and one's thinking. For example, a teenager who has just been dumped by his first love may feel that no one in human history has ever experienced anything quite like *his* crushing agony. The personal fable may also help to explain many of the risks that adolescents take. After all, *they* are unique and are unlikely to be harmed by snorting cocaine or

imaginary audience
allegedly a form of adolescent egocentrism that involves confusing one's own thoughts with those of a hypothesized audience and concluding that others share your preoccupations.

personal fable
allegedly a form of adolescent egocentrism in which the individual thinks that he and his thoughts and feelings are special or unique.

Photo 2.8
An adolescent may feel that others are as preoccupied with her appearance or her conduct as she is—allegedly a form of egocentrism known as the imaginary audience phenomenon.

having unsafe sex: The negative consequences are much more likely to happen to others, not to me.

Elkind believed that both forms of adolescent egocentrism would increase as youngsters are first acquiring formal operations and would gradually decline over time as idealism wanes. However, the data are not always consistent with his point of view. Apparently, teenagers perceive just as many personal dangers in risky acts such as drug use, driving while intoxicated, and having unsafe sex as middle-age adults do, thus questioning the idea that adolescents feel especially unique or invulnerable (Beyth-Marom et al., 1993). Indeed, much of adolescent risk taking apparently reflects a desire to take risks and have exciting experiences rather than any feelings of invulnerability (Arnett & Balle-Jensen, 1993; Gardner & Steinberg, 2005). And although the imaginary audience phenomenon is stronger among 13- to 15-year-olds than among older adolescents, it is often the 13- to 15-year-olds still functioning at the *concrete-operational* level who show more of this self-consciousness (Gray & Hudson, 1984; O'Connor & Nikolic, 1990)—just the reverse of what Elkind would expect. Consequently, some developmentalists now believe that the apparent self-preoccupation that adolescents display may be linked less closely to formal-operational thinking than to the development of advanced role-taking skills (discussed in Chapter 6) that allow teenagers to contemplate how *other people* might perceive them or react to their behavior (Lapsley et al., 1986; Vartanian & Powlishta, 1996). Viewed in this way, adolescent egocentrism is not very "egocentric" after all.

Contributions and Criticisms of Piaget's Viewpoint

Like Freud and Watson, Piaget was an innovative renegade. He was unpopular with psychometricians because he claimed that their intelligence tests only measure what children know, and tell us nothing about the most important aspect of intellect—how children think. In addition, Piaget dared to study an unobservable, mentalistic concept, "cognition," which had fallen from favor among psychologists from the behaviorist tradition (Beilin, 1992).

By the 1960s, the times had clearly changed. Not only had Piaget's early theorizing and research legitimized the study of children's thinking, but his early work linking moral development to cognitive development (see Chapter 10 for an extended discussion) has contributed immensely to a whole new area of developmental research—the study of **social cognition.** Recent social-cognitive theorists such as Lawrence Kohlberg and Robert Selman have found that the same mind that gradually constructs increasingly sophisticated understandings of the physical world also comes, with age, to form more complex ideas about sex differences, moral values, the significance of human emotions, the meaning and obligations of friendship, and countless other aspects of social life. The development of social cognition is a primary focus of Chapter 6, and the links between one's social-cognitive abilities and various aspects of social and personality development are discussed throughout the text.

Piaget's theory has also had a strong impact on education. For example, popular *discovery-based* educational programs are based on the premise that young children do not think like adults and will learn best by having "hands-on" educational experiences with familiar aspects of their environment. So a preschool teacher in a Piagetian classroom might introduce the difficult concept of number by presenting her pupils with different numbers of objects to stack, color, or arrange. Presumably, new concepts like number are best transmitted by methods in which curious, active children can apply their existing schemes and make the critical "discoveries" for themselves.

Although Piaget is clearly a giant among behavioral scientists, whose work has left deep and lasting imprints on our thinking about human development (Fischer & Bidell, 1998; Flavell, 1996), many of his ideas have now been challenged. For example, we noted earlier that Piaget's ideas that young infants totally lack object permanence for the first 8 months or any capacity for symbolism throughout the first year now seem to be incorrect. Indeed,

social cognition
the thinking that people display about the thoughts, feelings, motives, and behaviors of themselves and other people.

Piaget often underestimated children's reasoning abilities, as we will see once again when we examine his theory of moral reasoning in Chapter 10. What's more, Piaget's notion that cognitive growth proceeds through a universal and invariant sequence of stages has been questioned, both in theory and in research (Bjorklund, 2005). In his own *sociocultural theory*, Russian developmentalist Lev Vygotsky (1978) focused on how *culture*—the beliefs, values, traditions, and skills of a social group—is transmitted from generation to generation. Rather than depicting children as independent explorers who make critical discoveries on their own, Vygotsky viewed cognitive growth as a *socially mediated activity*—one in which children gradually acquire new ways of thinking and behaving through cooperative dialogues with more knowledgeable members of society. Vygotsky also rejected the notion that all children progress through the same stages of cognitive growth. Why? Because the new skills that children master through their interactions with more competent associates are often specific to their culture rather than universal cognitive structures. So from Vygotsky's perspective (which we will explore more carefully in Chapter 3), Piaget largely ignores important social and cultural influences on human development.

Despite these and other criticisms, almost no one today would challenge Piaget's notion that social and personality development depends, in part, on cognitive development. And the reason is simple: Social-developmentalists of the past half century have found—over and over again—that many important social and emotional developments occur at roughly the same time that children reach noteworthy Piagetian cognitive milestones. So Piaget's theory does have its shortcomings; but it nonetheless provides a valuable framework for understanding changes that occur in many aspects of development. It is truly a classic in the field of developmental psychology.

SUMMARY

+ This chapter examines three classic perspectives on social and personality development: the *psychoanalytic* viewpoint, *behaviorism* (or the *social-learning* viewpoint), and Piaget's *cognitive-developmental* viewpoint.

THE PSYCHOANALYTIC VIEWPOINT

+ The psychoanalytic perspective originated with Sigmund Freud, whose **psychosexual theory** claimed that humans are driven by inborn sexual and aggressive instincts (**Eros** and **Thonatos**) that must be controlled. Much of human behavior was said to reflect **unconscious motives** that people have **repressed**. Freud proposed five stages of psychosexual development—oral, anal, phallic, latency, and genital—in which three components of personality, the **id, ego,** and **superego**, emerge and become closely integrated.

+ Freud's description of the **phallic stage**, and the **Oedipus** and **Electra complexes** that 3- to 6-year-olds were said to experience, has been highly controversial. According the Freud, parents must handle these sexual conflicts carefully to prevent their children from **fixating** on immature activities and showing arrested development.

+ Eric Erikson's **psychosocial theory** revises and extends Freud's theory by concentrating less on the sex instinct and more on important sociocultural determinants of human development. According to Erikson, people progress through a series of eight psychosocial conflicts, beginning with **"trust versus mistrust"** in infancy and concluding with "integrity versus despair" in old age. Each conflict must be resolved in favor of the positive trait (trust, for example) if development is to be healthy.

THE BEHAVIORIST (OR SOCIAL-LEARNING) VIEWPOINT

+ The learning viewpoint, or **behaviorism,** originated with John B. Watson, who argued that infants are **tabulae rasae** who develop **habits** as a result of their social experiences. Development was viewed as a continuous process that could proceed in many different directions, depending on the kinds of environments to which a person is exposed. B. F. Skinner, who extended Watson's theory, claimed that development reflects the **operant** conditioning of children who are *passively* shaped by the **reinforcers** and **punishments** that accompany their behaviors. By contrast, Albert Bandura's cognitive social-learning theory viewed children as *active* information processors who quickly develop many new habits through **observational learning**. Bandura rejects Watson's **environmental determinism,** proposing instead that children have a hand in creating the environments that influence their development (**reciprocal determinism**).

PIAGET'S COGNITIVE-DEVELOPMENTAL VIEWPOINT

+ Jean Piaget's theory of intellectual development has many important implications for social and personality development. According to Piaget, intellectual activity is a basic life function that helps the child to adapt to the environment. He describes children as active, inventive explorers (that is, **constructivists**) who are constantly constructing **schemes** to represent what they know and modifying these cognitive structures throughout the processes of **organization** and **adaptation.** Organization is the process by which children rearrange their existing knowledge into higher-order schemes.

Adaptation is the process of adjusting successfully to the environment, and it occurs through two complementary activities: **assimilation** and **accommodation.**

+ Piaget believed that intellectual growth proceeds through an **invariant sequence** of stages that can be summarized as follows:

    + **Sensorimotor period (0–2 years)**. Over the first two years, infants come to "know" and understand objects and events by acting on them. The **behavioral (or sensorimotor) schemes** that a child creates to adapt to his surroundings are eventually internalized to form mental symbols (or **symbolic schemes**) that enable the child to understand **object permanence**, to display **deferred imitation**, and to solve simple problems on a mental level without resorting to trial and error.

    + **Preoperational period (roughly 2–7 years.** Symbolic reasoning becomes increasingly apparent during the **preoperational period** as children begin to use words and images in inventive ways in their play activities. Although 2- to 7-year olds are becoming more and more knowledgeable about the world in which they live, their thinking is quite deficient by adult standards. Piaget describes preschool children as highly **egocentric:** They view events from their own perspective and have difficulty assuming another person's point of view. And their thinking is characterized by **centration:** When they encounter something new, they tend to focus only on one aspect of it—its most obvious, or perceptually salient, feature. Consequently, these **intuitive thinkers** often fail to solve such problems as **conservation** tasks that require them to evaluate several pieces of information simultaneously.

    + **Concrete operations (roughly 7–11 years).** During the period of **concrete operations**, children can think logically and systematically about concrete objects, events, and experiences. They can now perform arithmetical operations in their heads and mentally **reverse** the outcomes of physical actions and behavioral sequences. The acquisition of these and other **cognitive operations** permit the child to conserve, seriate, and make transitive inferences. However, concrete operators still cannot think logically about hypothetical propositions that violate their conceptions of reality.

    + **Formal operations (age 11–12 and beyond).** Formal-operational thinking is rational, abstract, and much like the **hypothetico-deductive reasoning** of a scientist. At this stage, adolescents can "think about thinking" and operate on ideas as well as tangible objects and events. These newly emerging cognitive powers may help to explain why adolescents are so idealistic and display such thinking as the **imaginary audience** and the **personal fable.**

+ Although Piaget has accurately described the general *sequences* of intellectual development, some investigators have challenged Piaget's assumption that development occurs in stages, while others have criticized his theory for underestimating children's cognitive capabilities and for largely ignoring social and cultural influences. But despite its shortcomings, Piaget's theory has contributed enormously to our understanding of cognitive development, has been applied extensively in the field of education, has helped spawn the field of *social cognition,* and has provided important insights about many other aspects of social and personality development.

CHAPTER 3

Recent Perspectives on Social and Personality Development

IMAGINE THAT WE HAVE BEEN transported back to 1974 and are in the second week of a new semester, taking the first course in social and personality development that our college has ever offered. Having already reviewed the psychoanalytic and behavioristic perspectives on developing children, our professor introduced what she calls the "new look" at child development—Piaget's cognitive-developmental theory. Indeed, Piaget's theory does appear to be a fresh insight. After all, children are portrayed not as passive agents shaped by biological instincts or environmental influences but rather as *active* beings who play a prominent role in their own development. Furthermore, Piaget emphasizes neither nature nor nurture, choosing instead to characterize development as an intricate interplay between biological maturation and the experiences that curious, active children have and create for themselves.

Piaget's theory clearly qualified as the "new look" at social-personality development in the early 1970s. However, several new theories have emerged over the past 25 years—models that challenged, built on, and extended earlier viewpoints. Some of these recent theories emphasize biological forces, whereas others concentrate more on either environmental influences or on cognitive contributors to social and personality development. But as we will see in reviewing these theories, they all acknowledge the two points that Piaget sought to emphasize, namely that (1) developing persons are *active* rather than passive beings, and (2) development results from a variety of complex transactions between the forces of nature and nurture.

In the first two sections of the chapter, we will become acquainted with two kinds of "biological" theories. The first has strong evolutionary overtones, focusing heavily on inherited attributes that characterize all members of the species and conspire to make us *alike* (that is, contribute to normative developmental outcomes). By contrast, the second, or *behavioral genetics* viewpoint is concerned mainly with determining how the unique combination of genes that each person inherits might be implicated in making individuals *different* from one another.

⌒ MODERN EVOLUTIONARY PERSPECTIVES

Biological theories of human development have a long and illustrious history. Freud's psychoanalytic theory obviously had strong biological overtones. Not only were inborn instincts the motivational components of Freud's theory, but *maturation* of the sex instinct was said to determine the course (or at least the stages) of social and personality development.

Interestingly, behaviorist John B. Watson may have taken his extreme environmental stance partly in response to Freud and to other prominent biological theorists of his day, most notably Arnold Gesell (1880–1961), who argued that human development is largely a matter of biological maturation. Gesell's (1933) view was that children, much like plants, simply "bloomed," following a pattern and timetable laid out in their genes; how parents raised their young was thought to be of little importance.

Although today's developmentalists have largely rejected Gesell's radical claims, the notion that biological influences play a significant role in human development is alive and well in **ethology**—the scientific study of the evolutionary basis of behavior and the contributions of such evolved responses to a species's survival and development (Archer, 1992). The origins of this discipline can be traced to Charles Darwin; however, modern ethology arose from the work of Konrad Lorenz and Niko Tinbergen, two European zoologists whose animal research highlighted some important links between evolutionary processes and adaptive behaviors (Dewsbury, 1992). Here we will briefly examine the central assumptions of classical ethology and their implications for human development.

ethology
the study of the bioevolutionary bases of behavior and development.

Assumptions of Classical Ethology

According to Lorenz (1937, 1981) and Tinbergen (1973), members of all animal species are born with a number of "biologically programmed" behaviors that are (1) products of evolution and (2) adaptive in that they contribute to survival. Many species of birds, for example, come biologically prepared to engage in such instinctual behaviors as following their mothers (a response called *imprinting*, which helps to protect the young from predators and to ensure they find food), building nests, and singing songs. These biologically programmed characteristics are thought to have evolved as a result of the Darwinian process of **natural selection;** that is, over the course of evolution, birds with genes responsible for these "adaptive" behaviors were more likely to survive and to pass their genes on to future generations than were birds lacking these adaptive characteristics. Over many, many generations, then, the genes underlying the most adaptive behaviors would become more widespread in the species, characterizing nearly all individuals.

So ethologists focus on inborn or instinctual responses that (1) members of a species share and (2) seem to steer individuals along similar developmental paths. Where might one search for these adaptive behaviors and study their developmental implications? Ethologists have always preferred to study their subjects in the natural environment. Why? Simply because they believe that the inborn attributes that shape human (or animal) development are most easily identified and understood if observed in the natural settings where they evolved and have proven to be adaptive (Hinde, 1989).

natural selection
an evolutionary process, proposed by Charles Darwin, stating that individuals with characteristics that promote adaptation to the environment will survive, reproduce, and pass these adaptive characteristics to offspring; those lacking these adaptive characteristics will eventually die out.

Ethology and Human Development

Instinctual responses that promote survival are relatively easy to spot in animals. But do humans really display such behaviors? And if they do, how might these preprogrammed responses influence their development?

Human ethologists such as John Bowlby (1969, 1973) not only believe that children display a wide variety of preprogrammed behaviors, they also claim that each of these responses promotes a particular kind of experience that will help the individual to survive and develop normally. For example, the cry of a human infant is thought to be a biologically programmed "distress signal" that brings caregivers running. Not only are infants said to be biologically programmed to convey their distress with loud, lusty cries, but ethologists also believe that caregivers are biologically predisposed to respond to such signals. So the adaptive significance of an infant's crying is to ensure (1) the infant's basic needs (for example, hunger, thirst, safety) will be met, and (2) the infant will have sufficient contact with other human beings to bond with humans by forming social and emotional attachments (Bowlby, 1973).

Although ethologists are especially critical of learning theorists for largely ignoring the biological basis of human development, they are well aware that development could not progress very far without learning. For example, the cry of an infant may be an innate signal that promotes the human contact from which emotional attachments emerge. However, these emotional attachments do not simply "happen" automatically. The infant must first *learn* to discriminate familiar faces from those of strangers before he will show any evidence of being emotionally attached to a regular companion. Presumably, the adaptive significance of this discriminatory learning goes back to that period in evolutionary history when humans traveled in nomadic tribes and spent much of their time outdoors. In those days, it was crucial that an infant become attached to familiar companions and fearful of strangers, for failure to cry in response to a strange face might make the infant an easy target for a predatory animal.

Photo 3.1
The cry is the distress signal that attracts the attention of caregivers.

Bob Daemmrich/Stock Boston

Now consider the opposite side of the coin. Some caregivers who suffer from various life stresses of their own (for example, prolonged illnesses, depression, an unhappy marriage, or even a habitually cranky baby) may be routinely inattentive or neglectful, so that the infant's cries rarely promote any contact with them. Such an infant is not likely to form strong emotional attachments to her caregivers and could remain rather shy and emotionally unresponsive to other people for years to come (Ainsworth, 1979, 1989). What this infant has *learned* from her early experiences is that her closest companions are undependable and not to be trusted. Consequently, she may become ambivalent or wary around her caregivers and may later assume that other regular associates, such as teachers and peers, are equally untrustworthy individuals who should be avoided whenever possible.

How important are an individual's early learning experiences? Like Freud, the ethologists believe that they are *very* important. In fact, they have argued that there may be "critical periods" for the development of many attributes and behaviors. A *critical period* is a short part of the life cycle during which the developing organism is uniquely sensitive or responsive to specific environmental influences; outside this period, the same environmental events or influences are thought to have no lasting effects (Bruer, 2001). Although this concept of critical period does seem to explain certain aspects of animal development, such as imprinting in young fowl, many human ethologists think that the term *sensitive period* is a more accurate portrayal of human development. A **sensitive period** refers to a time that is optimal for the emergence of particular competencies or behaviors and in which the individual is particularly sensitive to environmental influences. The time frames of sensitive periods are less rigid, or well-defined, than those of critical periods. And it is possible for development to occur outside of a sensitive period but then it is much more difficult to foster (Bjorklund & Pellegrini, 2002).

To illustrate, some ethologists believe that the first three years of life are a sensitive period for the development of social and emotional responsiveness in human beings (Bowlby, 1973). Presumably, we are most susceptible to forming close emotional ties during the first three years, and should we have little or no opportunity to do so during this period, we would find it difficult to make close friends or to enter into intimate emotional relationships with other people later in life. Clearly, this is a most interesting and provocative claim about the emotional lives of human beings—one that we will examine carefully when we consider the long-term effects of early social and emotional development in Chapter 5.

In sum, ethologists clearly acknowledge that we are heavily influenced by our experiences. Yet they are quick to remind us that we are inherently biological creatures whose inborn characteristics affect the kinds of learning experiences we are likely to have.

Modern Evolutionary Theory

Like ethologists, proponents of a movement known as *modern evolutionary theory* are also interested in specifying how natural selection might predispose us to develop adaptive traits, motives, and behaviors. However, evolutionary theorists make different assumptions about the workings of evolution than ethologists do. Recall the ethological notion that preselected adaptive behaviors are those that ensure survival of the *individual*. Modern evolutionary theorists disagree, arguing instead that preselected, adaptive motives and behaviors are those that ensure the survival and spread of the *individual's genes*. This may seem like a subtle distinction, but it is an important one. Consider the personal sacrifice made by a father who perished after saving his four children from a house fire. This is hard for an ethologist to explain, for the father's selflessness does not promote his survival. Evolutionary theorists, however, view the father's motives and behavior as highly adaptive. Why? Because his children carry his genes and have many more reproductive years ahead of the four of them than he does. Thus, from the modern evolutionary perspective, the

sensitive period
period of time that is optimal for the development of particular capacities or behaviors, and in which the individual is particularly sensitive to environmental influences that would foster these attributes.

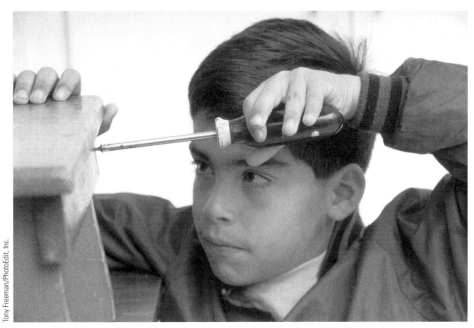

Photo 3.2 Compared with other animal species, humans mature very slowly, an evolutionary advantage that allows them to acquire the many physical, motor, cognitive, and social skills that permit them to shape their environments to their needs.

father has ensured the survival and spread of *his genes* (or, literally, of those who carry his genes), even if he should perish from his actions.

Let's briefly consider how the evolutionary history of our species might have led to sex differences in one socially significant attribute—human mating preferences (Buss, 1995, 2000). The average male produces billions of sperm in his lifetime, making sperm plentiful compared to ova. Thus, if males are interested in spreading and preserving their genes, it stands to reason from an evolutionary perspective that they might best serve this unconscious biological motive by seeking to fertilize many females. Moreover, males ought to seek youthful, attractive partners because these attributes imply fertility, sexual interest, and hence reproductive success. Females should be just as interested as males are in preserving their genes for posterity. But because a women can produce fewer offspring than a man and her investment in her offspring is great (having to bear, nurse, and raise them), she should be inclined to seek *one* mate who has the tangible resources (wealth, power) and psychological attributes (kindness, a capacity for love) that will aid her in protecting and nurturing her children.

Interestingly, men's and women's mating preferences do tend to confirm these predictions, with men the world over being more inclined than women to seek mates who are younger and attractive, and women being more inclined to seek an older and kindly mate with ample resources who is emotionally attracted to her (see Buss, 1995, 2000). So modern evolutionary theorists contend that the largely unconscious purpose of protecting and maximizing the number of genes we leave to posterity can explain sex differences in mating preferences. (Of course, other interpretations are possible. As an exercise, you might see whether you can explain the findings cited here using one or more of the other theories covered in this or the previous chapter.)

Consider another issue: Compared to other animal species, human beings develop very slowly, remaining immature and requiring others' nurturance and protection for many years. Modern evolutionary theorists view this long period of immaturity as a necessary evolutionary adaptation. Perhaps more than other species, human beings must survive by their wits. Armed with a large, powerful brain, itself an evolutionary adaption, humans use tools to shape their environments to their needs. They also create intricate cultures with complex rules and social conventions that the young of each generation must learn in order to survive and thrive within these social systems. Thus, a lengthy period of development, accompanied by the protections provided by older individuals (particularly from genetic relatives who are interested in preserving their genes), is adaptive in that it allows juveniles to acquire all the physical and cognitive competencies, knowledge, and social skills to occupy niches as productive members of modern human cultures (see Geary & Bjorklund, 2000; Bjorklund & Pellegrini, 2002, for more on the adaptive value of prolonged period of immaturity in humans).

Contributions and Criticisms of Evolutionary Viewpoints

If this text had been written in 1974, it would not have included any evolutionary perspectives. Although ethology came into its own during the 1960s, the early ethologists studied animal behavior; only within the past 25–35 years have proponents of ethology or modern evolutionary theory made a serious attempt to specify evolutionary contributions to human development, and many of their hypotheses could still be considered speculative. Nevertheless, proponents of evolutionary perspectives have already contributed importantly to our discipline by reminding us that every child is a biological creature who comes equipped with a number of adaptive, genetically programmed characteristics—attributes that will influence other people's reactions to the child and thus the course that development is likely to take. In addition, the ethologists have made a major methodological contribution by showing us the value of (1) studying human development in normal, everyday settings and (2) comparing human development with that of other species.

One very intriguing ethological notion that we will discuss in detail in Chapter 5 is that infants are inherently sociable creatures who are quite capable of promoting and sustaining social interactions from the day they are born. This viewpoint contrasts sharply with that of behaviorists, who portray the newborn as a *tabula rasa,* or with Piaget's "asocial" infant, who is said to enter the world equipped only with a few basic reflexes. Evolutionary theorists also believe that we humans have evolved in ways that predispose us to develop and display prosocial motives such as **altruism** that contribute to the common good and permit us to live and work together in harmony. Box 3.1 describes some observations suggesting that there may be a biological basis for certain aspects of altruism.

By way of criticism, evolutionary approaches are like psychoanalytic theory in being very hard to test. How does one demonstrate that various motives, mannerisms, and behaviors are inborn, adaptive, or products of evolutionary history? Such claims are difficult to confirm. Harvard paleontologist Steven Jay Gould (1978) has criticized all evolutionary theorists for constructing "just-so stories" to explain how various forms of social behavior have been naturally selected because of their adaptive value. A just-so story is an explanation that sounds plausible and in fact may be true but is not supported by any *conclusive* evidence. (Indeed, the explanation given in Box 3.1 for the evolution of altruism in group contexts could be considered a just-so story.) This is a strong critique, for theories that easily lend themselves to just-so stories lack one important characteristic of a *useful* scientific model—they are nearly impossible to falsify. Evolutionary theories have also been criticized as being *retrospective* or "post hoc" explanations of development. One can easily apply evolutionary concepts to explain what has already happened, but can the theories *predict* what is likely to happen in the future? Many developmentalists believe that they cannot.

Finally, proponents of other viewpoints (mostly notably, social-learning theory) have argued that, even if the bases for certain motives or behaviors are biologically programmed, these innate responses will soon become so modified by learning that it may not be helpful to spend much time wondering about their prior evolutionary significance. Even some

altruism
a selfless concern for the welfare of others that is expressed through prosocial acts such as sharing, cooperating, comforting others, or helping.

Box 3.1 Focus on Research

Is Altruism a Part of Human Nature?

Darwin's notion of "survival of the fittest" seems to argue against altruism as an inborn motive. Many have interpreted Darwin's idea to mean that powerful, self-serving individuals who place their own needs ahead of others' are the ones who are most likely to survive. If this were so, evolution would favor the development of selfish, egoistic motives—not altruism—as basic components of human nature.

Martin Hoffman (1981) has challenged this point of view, listing several reasons that the concept of "survival of the fittest" actually implies altruism. His arguments hinge on the assumption that human beings are more likely to receive protection from natural enemies, satisfy all their basic needs, and successfully reproduce if they have genes that predispose them to be socially outgoing and to live together in cooperative social groups. If this assumption is correct, cooperative, altruistic individuals would be the ones who are most likely to survive long enough to pass along their "altruistic genes" to their offspring; individualists who "go it alone" would probably succumb to famine, predators, or some other natural disaster that they could not cope with by themselves. So over thousands of generations, natural selection would favor the development of innate social motives such as altruism. Presumably, the tremendous survival value of being "social" makes altruism, cooperation, and other social motives much more plausible as components of human nature than competition, selfishness, and the like.

It is obviously absurd to argue that infants routinely help other people. However, Hoffman believes that even newborn babies are capable of recognizing and *experiencing* the emotions of others. This ability, known as **empathy**, is thought to be an important con-

tributor to altruism, for a person must recognize that others are distressed in some way and sympathize with them before he or she is likely to help. So Hoffman is suggesting that at least one precursor of altruism—empathy—is present at birth.

Hoffman's claim is based on an experiment (Sagi & Hoffman, 1976) in which infants less than 36 hours old listened to (1) another infant's cries, (2) an equally loud computer simulation of a crying infant, or (3) no sounds at all (silence). The infants who heard a real infant crying soon began to cry themselves, display physical signs of agitation such as kicking, and grimace. Infants exposed to the simulated cry or to silence cried much less and seemed not to be very discomforted. (Studies by Dondi, Simion, & Caltran, 1999, and Martin & Clark, 1982, have confirmed these observations.)

Hoffman argues that there is something quite distinctive about the human cry. His contention is that infants listen to and experience the distress of (that is, empathize with) another crying infant and become distressed themselves. How is this possible? Although the answer is by no means firmly established, recent findings from the field of cognitive neuroscience suggest that activation of *mirror neurons*—brain cells that fire both when a person performs or merely witnesses an action or event—is the neurological mechanism responsible for early empathic responding (Iacoboni, 2005; Winerman, 2005). Of course, none of these findings conclusively demonstrates that humans are altruistic by nature. But they do imply that a capacity for empathy may be present at birth and thus serve as a biological foundation for the eventual development of altruistic behavior (see Chapter 10 for an in-depth analysis of how empathy comes to promote altruism).

strong, genetically influenced attributes can easily be modified by experience. Consider, for example, that young mallard ducklings clearly prefer their mothers' vocal calls to those of other birds (for example, chickens), a behavior that ethologists say is innate, adaptive, and a product of mallard evolution. Yet Gilbert Gottlieb (1991) has shown that duckling embryos that were exposed to chicken calls before hatching come to prefer the call of a chicken to that of a mallard mother! In this case, the ducklings' prenatal *experiences* overrode a genetic predisposition. Of course, human beings have a much greater capacity for learning than ducklings do, thus leading many critics to argue that cultural learning experiences quickly overshadow innate evolutionary mechanisms in shaping human conduct and character. Albert Bandura (1973), for example, made the following observation when comparing the aggressive behavior of humans and animals:

> [Unlike animals], man does not rely heavily on auditory, postural, or olfactory signals for conveying aggressive intent or appeasement. He has [developed] a much more intricate system of communication—namely language—for controlling aggression. National leaders can. . . better safeguard against catastrophic violence by verbal communiques than by snapping their teeth or erecting their hair, especially in view of the prevalence of baldness among the higher echelons. [p. 16]

Despite these criticisms, evolutionary viewpoints are most valuable additions to the developmental sciences. Not only has their emphasis on biological processes provided a healthy balance to the heavily environmental emphasis of learning theories, but they have also convinced more developmentalists to look for the causes of development in the *natural environment*, where it actually occurs.

empathy
the ability to experience the same emotions that someone else is experiencing.

Now let's turn to a second modern biological perspective that is becoming increasingly influential—the *behavioral genetics* approach.

BEHAVIORAL GENETICS: BIOLOGICAL BASES FOR INDIVIDUAL DIFFERENCES

In recent years, investigators from a number of academic disciplines have asked the question, "Are there specific abilities, traits, and patterns of behavior that depend very heavily on the *particular combination* of genes that an individual inherits, and if so, are these attributes likely to be modified by one's experiences?" Those who focus on these issues in their research are known as *behavioral geneticists*.

behavioral genetics
the scientific study of how genotype interacts with environment to determine behavioral attributes such as intelligence, personality, and mental health.

genotype
the genetic endowment that an individual inherits.

phenotype
the ways in which a person's genotype is expressed in observable or measurable characteristics.

Before we take a closer look at the field of **behavioral genetics,** let's dispel a common myth. Although behavioral geneticists view development as the process through which one's **genotype** (the set of genes one inherits) comes to be expressed as a **phenotype** (one's observable characteristics and behaviors), they are *not* strict hereditarians. Instead, they claim that most behavioral attributes are the end product of a long and involved interplay between hereditary predispositions and environmental influences. Consider an example. A child who inherits genes for tall stature will almost certainly grow taller than one who inherits genes for short stature if these children are raised in the same environment. But if the first child receives very poor nutrition early in life and the second is well nourished, they may well be about the same height as adults. Thus, the behavioral geneticist is well aware that even attributes such as physical stature that seem to have a very strong hereditary component are often modified in important ways by environmental influences.

How, then, do behavioral geneticists differ from ethologists and modern evolutionary theorists, who are also interested in the biological bases of development? The answer is relatively simple. As we noted earlier, proponents of evolutionary viewpoints study inherited attributes that characterize *all* members of a species and conspire to make them *alike* (that is, attributes that contribute to *common* developmental outcomes). By contrast, behavioral geneticists focus on the biological bases for *variation* among members of a species. They are concerned with determining how the unique combination of genes that each of us inherits might be implicated in making us *different* from one another. Let's now consider the methods they use to approach this task.

Methods of Studying Hereditary Influences

There are two major strategies that behavioral geneticists use to assess hereditary contributions to behavior: *selective breeding* and *family studies*. Each of these approaches attempts to specify the **heritability** of various attributes—that is, the amount of variation in a trait or a class of behavior that is attributable to hereditary factors.

heritability
the amount of variability in a trait that is attributable to hereditary factors.

selective breeding experiment
a method of studying genetic influences by determining whether traits can be bred in animals through selective mating.

Selective Breeding   Some investigators have looked for hereditary contributions to various behavioral attributes by deliberately manipulating animal genotypes in an attempt to "breed" for these attributes. A classic example of such a **selective breeding experiment** is R. C. Tryon's (1940) attempt to show that maze-learning ability is a heritable attribute in rats. Tryon first tested a large number of rats for the ability to run a complex maze. Rats that made few errors were labeled "maze-bright"; those that made many errors were termed "maze-dull." Then, across several generations, Tryon mated bright rats with other bright rats, and dull rats with dull rats. He also controlled the environments to which the rats were exposed to rule out their contribution to differences in maze-learning performance. As we see in Figure 3.1, differences across generations in the maze-learning

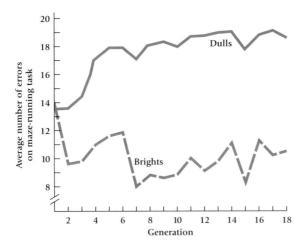

Figure 3.1   Maze-running performance by inbred maze-bright and maze-dull rats over 18 generations. (From Plomin et al., 2001.)

performances of the maze-bright and maze-dull groups became progressively greater. Clearly, Tryon showed that maze-learning ability in rats is influenced by their genetic makeup. Other investigators have used this same selective breeding technique to show that genes contribute to such attributes as activity level, emotionality, aggressiveness, and sex drive in rats, mice, and chickens (Plomin et al., 2001).

Family Studies   Because people don't take kindly to the idea of being selectively bred by experimenters, human behavioral genetics relies on an alternative methodology known as the family study. In a typical family study, persons who live in the same household are compared to see how similar they are on one or more attributes. If the attribute in question is heritable, then the similarity between any two pairs of individuals who live in the same environment should increase as a function of their **kinship**—that is, the extent to which they have the same genes.

Two kinds of family (or kinship) studies are common today. The first is the **twin design,** or **twin study,** which asks the question, "Are pairs of identical twins reared together more similar to each other on various attributes than pairs of fraternal twins reared together?" If genes affect the attribute(s) in question, then identical twins should be more similar, for they have 100 percent of their genes in common (kinship = 1.00), whereas fraternal twins, on average, share only 50 percent (kinship = .50).

The second common family study, **adoption design,** focuses on adoptees who are genetically unrelated to other members of their adoptive families. A researcher searching for hereditary influences would ask, "Are adopted children similar to their biological parents, whose *genes* they share (kinship = .50), or are they similar to their adoptive parents, whose *environment* they share?" If adoptees resemble their biological parents in temperament or personality, even though these parents did not raise them, then genes must be influential in determining such attributes.

Family studies can also help us to estimate the extent to which various abilities and behaviors are influenced by the environment. To illustrate, consider a case in which two genetically unrelated adopted children are raised in the same home. Their degree of kinship with each other and with their adoptive parents is .00. Consequently, there is no reason to suspect that these children

kinship
the extent to which two individuals have genes in common.

twin design
a study in which sets of twins that differ in zygosity (kinship) are compared to determine the heritability of an attribute.

adoption design
a study in which adoptees are compared with their biological relatives and their adoptive relatives to estimate the heritability of an attribute.

Photo 3.3
Because identical twins have identical genotypes, they are a rich source of information about possible hereditary contributions to personality and social behavior.

Mary Kay Denny/PhotoEdit, Inc.

Recent Perspectives on Social and Personality Development   **75**

will resemble each other or their adoptive parents unless their common environment plays some part in determining their standing on the attribute in question. Another way the effects of environment can be inferred is to compare identical twins raised in the same environment with identical twins raised in different environments. The kinship of all pairs of identical twins, reared together or apart, is 1.00. So, if identical twins reared together are more alike on an attribute than identical twins reared apart, we can infer that the environment plays a role in determining that attribute.

Estimating the Contributions of Genes and Environment

Behavioral geneticists rely on some reasonably simple mathematical calculations to determine (1) whether a trait is genetically influenced and (2) the degree to which heredity *and* environment account for individual differences in that trait. When studying traits that a person either does or does not display (for example, a drug habit or clinical depression), researchers calculate and compare **concordance rates**—the percentages of pairs of people (for example, identical twins, fraternal twins, parents and their adoptive children) in which *both* members of the pair display the trait if one member does. Suppose that you are interested in determining whether homosexuality in men is genetically influenced. You might locate gay men who have a twin, either identical or fraternal, and then track down their twin siblings to determine whether they too are gay. As shown in Figure 3.2, the concordance rate for identical twins in one such study was much higher (29 of the 56 co-twins of gay men were also gay) than the concordance rate for fraternal twins (12 of the 54 co-twins were also gay). This suggests that genotype does contribute to a man's sexual orientation. But because identical twins are not perfectly concordant for sexual orientation, we can also conclude that their *experiences* (that is, environmental influences) must also influence their sexual orientations, despite their identical genes.

For continuous traits that can assume many values (for example, aggressiveness, intelligence), behavioral geneticists estimate hereditary contributions by calculating *correlation coefficients* rather than concordance rates. In a study of IQ scores, for example, a correlation coefficient indicates whether the IQ scores of twins are systematically related to the IQ scores of their co-twins. Larger correlations indicate closer resemblances in IQ, thus implying that if one twin is bright, the other is bright too, and if one twin is dull, the other is probably dull as well.

As we noted earlier, behavioral genetics studies always tell us about *both* genetic and environmental influences on development. This point is easily illustrated by considering a review of family studies of intellectual performance (IQ) based on 112,942 pairs of children, adolescents, or adults, the results of which appear in Table 3.1. Here we will focus on the twin correlations (identical and fraternal) to show how behavioral geneticists can estimate the contributions of three factors to individual differences in intellectual performance (IQ).

Gene Influences   Genetic influences on IQ are clearly evident in Table 3.1. The correlations become higher when pairs of people are more closely related genetically and are highest when the pairs are identical twins. But just how strong is the hereditary influence?

Behavioral geneticists use statistical techniques to estimate the amount of variation in a trait that is attributable to hereditary factors. This index, called a **heritability coefficient,** is calculated as follows from twin data:

$$H = (r\text{ identical twins} - r\text{ fraternal twins}) \times 2$$

Translated, the equation reads: Heritability of an attribute equals the correlation between identical twins minus the correlation between fraternal twins, all multiplied by a factor of 2 (Plomin, 1990).

concordance rate
the percentage of cases in which a particular attribute is present for one member of a twin pair if it is present for the other.

heritability coefficient
a numerical estimate, ranging from .00 to +1.00, of the amount of variation in an attribute that is due to hereditary factors.

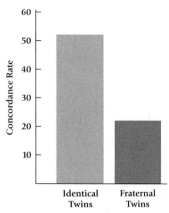

Figure 3.2
Concordance rates for homosexuality in 110 male twin pairs. From the higher concordance for identical twin pairs, we can infer that genes influence one's sexual orientation. Yet the fact that only half the identical twin pairs share the same sexual orientation despite their identical genes also implies that environment contributes to one's sexual orientation as well. (Adapted from Bailey & Pillard, 1991.)

Table 3.1 Average correlation coefficients for intelligence-test scores from family studies involving persons at four levels of kinship

Genetic Relationship (Kinship)	Reared Together (in Same Home)	Reared Apart (in Different Homes)
Unrelated siblings (kinship = .00)	+.34	−.01[a]
Adoptive parent/adoptive offspring (kinship = .00)	+.19	—
Half-siblings (kinship = .25)	+.31	—
Biological parent/child (kinship = .50)	+.42	+.22
Siblings (kinship = .50)	+.47	+.24
Twins		
Fraternal (kinship = .50)	+.60	+.52
Identical (kinship = 1.00)	+.86	+.72

[a]This is the correlation obtained from random pairings of unrelated people living apart.

Source: Bouchard & McGue, 1981.

Now we can estimate the contribution that genes make to individual differences in intellectual performance. If we focus on sets of twins raised together from Table 3.1, our estimate becomes:

$$H = (.86 - .60) \times 2 = .52$$

The resulting heritability estimate for IQ is .52, which on a scale ranging from 0 (not at all heritable) to 1.00 (totally heritable) is moderate at best. We might conclude that, within the population from which our twins reared together came, IQ is influenced to a moderate extent by hereditary factors. However, it appears that much of the variability among people on this trait is attributable to nonhereditary factors—that is, to environmental influences and to errors we may have made in measuring the trait (no measure is perfect).

Interestingly, the data in Table 3.1 also allows us to estimate the contributions of *two* sources of environmental influence.

Nonshared Environmental Influences (NSE)   These are experiences that are unique to the individual—experiences that are *not* shared by other members of the family and thus make family members *different* from each other (Rowe & Plomin, 1981; Rowe, 1994). Where is evidence of **nonshared environmental influence** in Table 3.1? Notice that identical twins raised together are not perfectly similar in IQ, even though they share 100 percent of their genes and the same family environment: a correlation of +.86, though substantial, is less than a perfect correlation of +1.00. Because identical twins share the same genes and family environment, any *differences* between twins raised together must necessarily be due to *differences* in their experiences. Perhaps they were treated differently by friends, or perhaps one twin favors puzzles and other intellectual games more than the other twin does. Because the only factor that can make identical twins raised together any *different* from one another are experiences they do *not* share, we can estimate the influence of nonshared environmental influences by the following formula (Rowe & Plomin, 1981):

NSE = 1 − *r* (identical twins reared together)

So the contribution of nonshared environmental influences to individual differences in IQ performance (that is, 1 − .86 = .14) is small, but detectable nevertheless. As we will see, nonshared environmental influences make a greater contribution to other attributes, most notably personality traits.

nonshared environmental influence (NSE)
an environmental influence that people living together do not share and that should make these individuals different from one another.

Shared Environmental Influences (SE)   These are experiences that individuals living in the same home environment share and that conspire to make them *similar* to each other. As you can see in Table 3.1, both identical and fraternal twins (and, indeed, biological siblings and pairs of unrelated individuals) show a greater intellectual resemblance if they live together than if they live apart. One reason that growing up in the same home may increase children's degree of intellectual similarity is that parents model similar interests for *all* their children and tend to rely on similar strategies to foster their intellectual growth (Hoffman, 1991; Lewin et al., 1993).

How do we estimate the contribution of **shared environmental influence** (SE) to a trait? One rough estimate can be made as follows:

$$SE = 1 - (H + NSE)$$

Translated, the equation reads: Shared environmental influences on a trait equal 1 (the total variation for that trait) minus the variation attributable to genes (*H*) *and* nonshared environmental influences (NSE). Previously, we found that the heritability of IQ in our twins-reared-together sample was .52, and the contribution of nonshared environment was a .14. So the contribution of shared environmental influences to individual differences in IQ (that is, SE = 1 − [.52 + .14] = **.34**) is moderate and meaningful.

One final note: Although heritability coefficients are useful for estimating whether genes make any meaningful contribution to various human attributes, these statistics are poorly understood and often misinterpreted. In Box 3.2, we will take a closer look at what heritability estimates *can* and *cannot* tell us.

Hereditary Contributions to Personality and Mental Health

Although psychologists have typically assumed that the relatively stable habits and traits that make up our personalities are shaped by our environments, family studies and other longitudinal projects reveal that many core dimensions of personality are genetically influenced (Loehlin, 1992; Plomin, 1994). For example, **introversion/extroversion**—the extent to which a person is shy, retiring, and uncomfortable around others versus outgoing and socially oriented—shows about the same moderate level of heritability as IQ does (Martin & Jardine, 1986).

Another important attribute that may be genetically influenced is **empathic concern.** A person high in empathy recognizes the needs of others and is concerned about their welfare. In Box 3.1, we saw that newborn infants will react to the distress of another infant by becoming distressed themselves—a finding that implies that the capacity for empathy may be innate. But are there any biological bases for *individual differences* in empathic concern?

Indeed there are. As early as 14 to 20 months of age, identical twin infants are already more similar in their levels of concern for distressed companions than fraternal twin infants are (Zahn-Waxler, Robinson, & Emde, 1992). And by middle age, identical twins who have lived apart for many years since leaving home still resemble each other on measures of empathic concern ($r = +.41$), whereas fraternal twins do not ($r = +.05$), thus suggesting that this attribute is a reasonably heritable trait (Matthews et al., 1981). In fact, the authors of this adult twin study noted that "If empathic concern . . . leads to altruistic motivation, [our] study provides evidence for a genetic basis for individual differences in altruism" (p. 246).

How Much Genetic Influence?   To what extent are our personalities influenced by the genes we have inherited? We get some idea by looking at personality resemblances among family members, as shown in Table 3.2. Note that identical twins are more similar to each other on this composite measure of personality than are fraternal twins. Were we to use the twin data to estimate the genetic contribution to personality, we might conclude that many personality traits are moderately heritable (that is, $H = +.40$ in this

shared environmental influences (SE)
an environmental influence that people living together share and that should make these individuals similar to one another.

introversion/extroversion
the opposite poles of a personality dimension: Introverts are shy and anxious around others, and tend to withdraw from social situations; extroverts are highly sociable and enjoy being with others.

empathic concern
a measure of the extent to which an individual recognizes the needs of others and is concerned about their welfare.

Box 3.2 Current Controversies

Some Common Misconceptions about Heritability Estimates

Heritability coefficients are controversial statistics that are poorly understood and frequently misapplied. One of the biggest misconceptions that people hold is the notion that heritability coefficients can tell us whether we have inherited a trait. *This idea is simply incorrect.* When we talk about the heritability of an attribute, we are referring to the extent to which *differences* among individuals on that attribute are related to differences in the genes that they have inherited—it does not tell us that there is a gene (or genes) that absolutely determine whether one will display that trait (Plomin, 1994). To illustrate that *heritable* means something other than *inherited*, consider that all humans inherit two eyes. Agreed? Yet the heritability of eyes is .00, simply because everyone has two and there are no individual differences in "eyeness" (except for those attributable to environmental events such as accidents).

In interpreting heritability coefficients, it is important to recognize that these estimates apply only to populations and *never to individuals.* So if you studied the heights of many pairs of 5-year-old twins and estimated the heritability of height to be .90, you could infer that a major reason that 5-year-olds *differ* in height is that they have different genes. But because heritability estimates say nothing about individuals, it is clearly inappropriate to conclude from an *H* of .90 that 90 percent of Freddie Jones's height is inherited, while the remaining 10 percent reflects the contribution of environment.

Let's also note that heritability estimates refer only to the particular trait in question as displayed by members of a *particular population* under *particular environmental circumstances.* Indeed, heritability coefficients may differ substantially for different populations raised in different environments. Suppose, for example, we located a large number of identical and fraternal twin infants, each of whom was raised in an impoverished orphanage in which his or her crib was lined with sheets that prevented much visual or social contact with other infants or with adult caregivers. Previous research (that we will examine in Chapter 5) suggests that if we measured how sociable these infants are, we would find that they vary somewhat in sociability but that virtually all of them would be much less sociable than babies raised at home—a finding we could reasonably attribute to their socially depriving early environment. But because these twins experienced *the same depriving environment*, the only reason they might show any *differences* in sociability is due to differences in their genetic predispositions. The heritability coefficient for sociability would actually approach 1.0 in this sample—a far cry from the *H*s of .25 to .40 found in studies of other infants raised at home with parents (Plomin, 1994).

Finally, people have often assumed that genetically influenced traits cannot be modified by environmental influences. *This too is a false assumption!* In Chapter 5, for example, we will see that the depressed sociability of institutionalized infants can be improved substantially by placing them with responsive, socially stimulating adoptive families. To assume that *heritable* means *unchangeable* (as some critics of social programs for the socially and intellectually disadvantaged have done) is to commit a potentially grievous error based on a common misconception about the meaning of heritability coefficients.

In sum, the term *heritable* is not a synonym for *inherited*, and heritability estimates, which may vary widely across populations and environments, can tell us nothing about the development of individuals. And though heritability estimates are useful for helping us to determine whether there is any hereditary basis for the *differences* people display on any attribute we might care to study, they say nothing about children's capacity for change and should not be used to make public policy decisions that could constrain children's development or adversely affect their welfare.

---

sample). Of course, one implication of a moderate heritability coefficient is that personality is strongly influenced by environmental factors.

Which Aspects of Environment Influence Personality? Developmentalists have traditionally assumed that the home environment that individuals *share* is especially important in shaping their personalities. Now examine Table 3.2 again and see whether you can find

Table 3.2 Personality resemblances among family members at three levels of kinship

	Kinship			
	1.00 (Identical Twins)	.50 (Fraternal Twins)	.50 (Nontwin Siblings)	.00 (Unrelated Children Raised in the Same Household)
Personality attributes (average correlations across several personality traits)	.50	.30	.20	.07

Sources: J. C. Loehlin, "Fitting Heredity-Environment Models Jointly to Twin and Adoption Data from the California Psychological Inventory." *Behavior Genetics*, 1985, *15*, 199–221. Also J. C. Loehlin & R. C. Nichols, *Heredity, Environment, and Personality: A Study of 850 Sets of Twins.* Austin, TX: University of Texas Press, 1976. Copyright © 1976 by the University of Texas Press.

some problems with this logic. Notice, for example, that genetically unrelated individuals who live in the same home barely resemble each other on the composite personality measure ($r = .07$). Therefore, aspects of the home environment that all family members *share* must not contribute much to the development of personality.

How, then, does environment affect personality? According to behavioral geneticists David Rowe and Robert Plomin (1981; Rowe, 1994), the aspects of environment that contribute most heavily to personality are *nonshared environmental influences*—influences that make individuals *different* from each other. And there are many sources of nonshared experience in a typical home. Parents, for example, often treat sons differently than daughters, or first-born children differently than later-borns. To the extent that siblings are not treated alike by parents, they will experience different environments, which will increase the likelihood that their personalities will differ in important ways. Interactions among siblings provide another source of nonshared environmental influence. For example, an older sibling who habitually dominates a younger one may become generally assertive and dominant as a result of these home experiences. But for the younger child, this home environment is a dominating environment that may foster the development of such personality traits as passivity, tolerance, and cooperation.

Measuring the Effects of Nonshared Environments   How could we ever measure the impact of something as broad as nonshared environments? One strategy used by Denise Daniels and her associates (Daniels, 1986; Daniels & Plomin, 1985) is simply to ask pairs of adolescent siblings whether they have been treated differently by parents and teachers or have experienced other important differences in their lives (for example, differences in their popularity with peers). Daniels finds that siblings do report such differences, and more important, the greater the *differences* in parental treatment and other experiences that siblings report, the more dissimilar siblings are in their personalities. Although correlational studies of this sort do not conclusively establish that differences in experiences *cause* differences in personality, they do suggest that some of the most important environmental influences on development may be nonshared experiences unique to each member of the family (Dunn & Plomin, 1990).

Now an important question: Do siblings have different experiences because they have different genes? Stated another way, isn't it possible that a child's genetically influenced attributes might affect how other people respond to her, so that a physically attractive youngster, for example, is apt to be treated very differently by parents and peers than a less attractive sibling would be? Although genes do contribute to some extent to the different experiences that siblings have (Baker & Daniels, 1990; McGue et al., 2005), there is ample reason to believe that our highly individualized, unique environments are not entirely due to our having inherited different genes. How do we know this?

The most important clue comes from studies of identical twins. Because identical twins are perfectly matched from a genetic standpoint, any *differences* between them must necessarily reflect the contribution of environmental influences that they do *not* share. Indeed, identical twins do report differences in their environments that have implications for their personalities and social adjustment. For example, one recent study found that a twin who receives warmer treatment from a parent (an NSE) or who establishes closer relationships with teachers (an NSE) is typically less emotionally distressed than his or her identical co-twin (Crosnoe & Elder, 2002). And the greater the discrepanices in the ways that identical twins are treated by their parents, the less similiar the twins are in their personalities and social behaviors (Asbury et al., 2003; Burt et al., 2006). Clearly, these nonshared environmental influences cannot be attributed to the twins' different genes, because identical twins have identical genotypes! This is why the formula for estimating the contribution of nonshared environmental influences (that is, $1 - r$ [identical twins raised together]) makes sense, because the estimate it provides is based on environmental influences that are *not* in any way influenced by genes.

With these facts in mind, let's return to Table 3.2. Here we see that the average correlation for identical twins across many personality traits is only +.50, which implies that identical twins are alike in some respects and different in others. Applying the formula for estimating NSE ($1 - .50 = .50$) tells us that nonshared environmental influences are very important contributors to personality—at least as important as genes are.

In sum, the family environment does contribute importantly to personality, but not simply because it has a standard effect on all family members that makes them alike. True, there are some important areas of socialization for which parents do treat all their children alike and foster similarities among them (Hoffman, 1991). For example, parents often model and encourage the same moral, religious, and political interests and values in all their children. For these and many other psychological characteristics, *shared environmental influences* are often as important or even more important than genes are in creating likenesses between brothers and sisters (Hoffman, 1991, 1994; Plomin, 1990). But when it comes to the shaping of many other basic personality traits, it is the *nonshared* experiences people have—in concert with genetic influences—that contribute most to their phenotypes (Plomin et al., 2001; Reiss et al., 2000).

Hereditary Contributions to Behavior Disorders and Mental Illnesses

Is there a hereditary basis for mental illness? Might some people be genetically predisposed to commit deviant or antisocial acts? Although these ideas seemed absurd 30 years ago, it now appears that the answer to both questions is a qualified yes.

Consider the evidence for **schizophrenia**—a serious mental illness characterized by severe disturbances in logical thinking, emotional expression, and social behavior, which typically emerges in late adolescence or early adulthood. A survey of several twin studies of schizophrenia suggests an average concordance rate of .46 for identical twins but only .14 for fraternal twins (Gottesman & Shields, 1982). In addition, children who have a biological parent who is schizophrenic are at increased risk of becoming schizophrenic themselves, even if they are adopted and raised by another family early in life (Loehlin, 1992). These are strong indications that schizophrenia is genetically influenced.

In recent years, it has also become quite clear that heredity contributes to abnormal behaviors and conditions such as alcoholism, susceptibility to problem behaviors, criminality and delinquency, depression, hyperactivity, *manic-depressive* psychosis, and a number of *neurotic disorders* (Baker, et al., 1989; Bartels et al., 2004; Plomin et al., 2001; Rowe, 1994). Now, you may have or have had close relatives who were diagnosed as alcoholic, neurotic, manic-depressive, or schizophrenic. Rest assured that does *not* mean that you or your children will develop these problems. Only 5–10 percent of children who have one schizophrenic parent ever develop any symptoms that might be labeled "schizophrenic." Even if you are an identical twin whose co-twin has a serious psychiatric disorder, the odds are only between 1 in 2 (for schizophrenia) and 1 in 20 (for most other disorders) that you would ever experience anything that even approaches the problem that affects your twin.

Because identical twins are often *discordant* (that is, not alike) with respect to mental illness and behavioral disorders, environment must be a very important contributor to these conditions. In other words, people do not inherit behavioral disorders; instead, they inherit *predispositions* to develop certain illnesses or deviant patterns of behavior. And even when a child's family history suggests that such a genetic predisposition may exist, it usually takes one or more very stressful experiences (for example, rejecting parents, a failure or series of failures at school, or dissolution of the family due to divorce) to trigger a disorder (Plomin & Rende, 1991; Rutter, 1979). Clearly, these latter findings provide some basis for optimism, for it may be possible someday to prevent the onset of most genetically influenced disorders should we (1) learn more about the environmental triggers that precipitate these disturbances while (2) striving to develop interventions or therapeutic techniques that will

schizophrenia
a serious form of mental illness characterized by disturbances in logical thinking, emotional expression, and interpersonal behavior.

help "high-risk" individuals to maintain their emotional stability in the face of environmental stress.

Heredity and Environment as Developmental Co-Conspirators

After reviewing a portion of the literature and seeing how behavioral geneticists estimate the contribution of heredity to various attributes, it should be clear that both heredity and environment contribute in important ways to our cognitive performances, personalities, and mental health. But how? From our discussion thus far, one might get the impression that heredity and environment are *independent* sources of influence, much as they were portrayed 35 years ago when developmentalists were embroiled in the great nature/nurture debate. Today, behavioral geneticists believe that our genes may actually influence the kinds of environments we are likely to experience (Plomin et al., 2001; Scarr & McCartney, 1983). How? In at least three ways.

Passive Genotype/Environmental Correlations   According to Sandra Scarr and Kathleen McCartney (1983), the home environment parents provide for their children is influenced in part by the parents' own genotypes. And because parents also provide their children with genes, it so happens that the rearing environments to which children are exposed are correlated with (and are likely to suit) their own genotypes.

The following example illustrates a developmental implication of these **passive genotype/environment correlations.** Parents who are genetically predisposed to be athletic may create a very athletic home environment by encouraging their children to play vigorously and to take an interest in sports. Besides being exposed to an athletic environment, the children may have inherited their parents' genetic predisposition for athletics, which might make them particularly responsive to that environment. So children of athletic parents may come to enjoy athletic pursuits for *both* hereditary and environmental reasons, and the influences of heredity and environment are tightly intertwined.

Evocative Genotype/Environment Correlations   Earlier, we noted that the environmental influences that contribute most heavily to many aspects of personality are "nonshared" experiences that make individuals *different* from one another. Might the differences in environments that children experience be partly due to the fact that they have inherited different genes and may elicit different reactions from their companions?

Scarr and McCartney (1983) think so. Their notion of **evocative genotype/environment correlations** assumes that a child's genetically influenced attributes will affect the behavior of others toward him or her. For example, smiley, active babies may receive more attention and social stimulation than moody, passive ones. Teachers may respond more favorably to physically attractive students than to their less attractive classmates. Clearly, these *reactions* of other people to the child (and the child's genetically influenced attributes) are environmental influences that play an important role in shaping that child's personality. So once again, we see an intermingling of hereditary and environmental influences: One's genetically influenced characteristics affect the character of the social environment in which the personality develops.

Active Genotype/Environment Correlations   Finally, Scarr and McCartney propose that the environments children prefer and seek out will be those that are most compatible with their genetic predispositions. For example, a child genetically predisposed to be extroverted is likely to invite friends to the house, be an avid party-goer, and generally prefer activities that are socially stimulating. By contrast, a child genetically predisposed to be shy and introverted may actively avoid large social gatherings and choose instead to pursue activities such as coin collecting that can be done alone. So one implication of

passive genotype/environment correlations
the notion that the rearing environments that biological parents provide are influenced by the parents' own genes and hence are correlated with the child's own genotype.

evocative genotype/environment correlations
the notion that our heritable attributes affect others' behavior toward us and thus influence the social environment in which development takes place.

these **active genotype/environment correlations** is that people with different genotypes will *select* different "environmental niches" for themselves—niches that may then have a powerful effect on their future social, emotional, and intellectual development.

active genotype/environment correlations
the notion that our genotypes affect the types of environments that we prefer and seek out.

How Do Genotype/Environment Correlations Influence Development?

According to Scarr and McCartney (1983), the relative importance of active, passive, and evocative gene influences changes over the course of development. During the first few years, infants, toddlers, and preschool children are not free to roam the neighborhood, choosing friends and building environmental niches. Most of their time is spent at home in an environment that parents structure for them, so that passive genotype/environment interactions are particularly important early in life. But once children reach school age and venture away from home on a daily basis, they suddenly become much freer to pick their own interests, activities, friends, and hangouts. Thus, active, niche-building interactions should exert more and more influence on development as the child matures (see Figure 3.3). Finally, evocative genotype/environment interactions are always important; that is, a person's genetically influenced attributes and patterns of behavior may influence the ways other people react to him or her throughout life.

If Scarr and McCartney's theory has any merit, then virtually all siblings other than identical twins should become much less similar over time as they emerge from the relatively similar rearing environments parents impose during the early years and begin to actively select different environmental niches for themselves. Indeed, there is ample support for this idea. Pairs of genetically unrelated adoptees who live in the same home do show some definite similarities in conduct and in intellectual performance during early and middle childhood (Scarr & Weinberg, 1978). Because these adoptees share no genes with each other or with their adoptive parents, their resemblances must be due to their common rearing environments. Yet by late adolescence, genetically unrelated siblings no longer resemble each other in intelligence or personality, presumably because they have selected very different environmental niches, which in turn have steered them along differing developmental paths (Scarr & McCartney, 1983; Scarr et al., 1981). Even fraternal twins, who have 50 percent of their genes in common, are much less alike as adolescents and adults than they were as children (McCartney, Harris, & Bernieri, 1990). Apparently the genes that fraternal twins do *not* share cause these individuals to select somewhat different environmental niches, which in turn will contribute to their declining resemblance over time. By contrast, pairs of identical twins continue to display some very noteworthy similarities throughout life. Not only do identical twins elicit similar reactions from other people, but (2) their identical genotypes predispose them to prefer and to select very *similar* environments (that is, friends, interests, and activities), which in turn exert comparable influences on these twin pairs and virtually guarantee that they will continue to resemble one another over time. Even identical twins raised *apart* should be similar in some respects if their identical genes cause them to seek out and to prefer similar activities and experiences. Let's take a closer look.

Separated Identical Twins Thomas Bouchard and his associates (Bouchard et al., 1990; Farber, 1981) have studied more than 30 pairs of *separated identical twins* who were raised in different home environments. One such pair was Oscar Stohr and Jack Yufe. Oscar was raised as a Catholic by his mother in Nazi-dominated Europe. He became involved in the Hitler Youth Movement during World War II and is now employed as a factory supervisor in Germany. Jack, a store owner, was raised as a Jew and came to

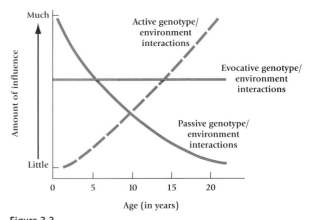

Figure 3.3
Relative influence of passive, evocative, and active (niche-picking) genotype/environment interactions as a function of age.

Photo 3.4
Jack Yufe (left) and
Oscar Stohr (right).

loathe Nazis while growing up in a Caribbean country halfway around the world. Today, Jack is a political liberal, whereas Oscar is very conservative.

Like every pair of separated identical twins that Bouchard has studied, Oscar and Jack are different in some very noteworthy respects. One twin is usually more self-assured, outgoing, or aggressive than the other, or perhaps has a different religious or political philosophy (as Jack and Oscar do). Yet perhaps the more remarkable finding is that all these twin pairs also show a number of striking similarities as well. As young men, for example, Oscar and Jack both excelled at sports and had difficulty with math. They have similar mannerisms, and both tend to be absent-minded. And then there are the little things, such as their common tastes for spicy foods and sweet liqueurs, their habit of storing rubber bands on their wrists, and their preference for flushing the toilet *before* and after using it.

How can separated identical twins be so different and, at the same time, so similar to each other? The concept of *active gene influences* helps to explain the uncanny resemblances. When we learn that twins grow in different environments, we tend to think of these settings as more dissimilar than they really are. In fact, identical twins raised apart are members of the same life cohort who are likely to be exposed to many of the same kinds of objects, activities, educational experiences, and historical events as they are growing up. So, if identical twins are genetically predisposed to select comparable aspects of the environment for special attention, and if their "different" environments provide them with reasonably similar sets of experiences from which to build their environmental niches, then these individuals should resemble each other in many of their habits, mannerisms, abilities, and interests.

Why, then, do separated identical twins often differ? According to Scarr and McCartney (1983), twins could be expected to differ on any attribute for which their rearing environments are so dissimilar as to prevent them from ever establishing comparable niches. Oscar Stohr and Jack Yufe are a prime example. They are alike in many ways because their separate rearing environments permitted them access to many of the same kinds of experiences (for example, sports, math classes, spicy foods, rubber bands), thereby enabling these genetically identical individuals to develop several similar habits, mannerisms, and interests. However, it was almost inevitable that they would differ in their political ideologies because their sociopolitical environments (Nazi-dominated Europe versus the laid-back Caribbean) were so *dissimilar* as to prevent them from ever building the kinds of "niches" that would make them staunch political allies.

Contributions and Criticisms of the Behavioral Genetics Approach

Behavioral genetics is a relatively new discipline that is having a strong influence on the way scientists look at human development. We now know, for example, that many attributes previously thought to be shaped by environment are influenced in part by genes. As Scarr and McCartney put it, we are products of "cooperative efforts of the nature/ nurture team, directed by the genetic quarterback" (1983, p. 433). In effect, genes may exert many of their influences on human development by affecting the experiences we have, which in turn influence our behavior. And one very important implication of their viewpoint is that many of the "environmental" influences on development that have previously been identified may reflect in part the workings of genes (Jaffee et al., 2004; Plomin et al., 2001).

Need Parenting Be "Good" or Simply "Good Enough"?

True or false?
Within typical families, parenting practices have a major influence on children's development.

In Chapter 2, we saw that John Watson (1928) advised parents to take their role very seriously, for he believed that parents had the power to shape their children's destiny. Sandra Scarr (1992) disagrees, arguing that parents do not have the power to mold children in any way they see fit. Yet, in some ways, Scarr's viewpoint is every bit as controversial as Watson's. She believes that human beings have evolved in ways that make them responsive to a wide range of environments and that:

1. Within the broad range of home environments that are typical of the human species, children display normal, adaptive patterns of development.
2. Particular child-rearing practices do not influence developmental outcomes to any great extent.
3. Only those home environments that fall far outside the normal range (for example, those in which parents are violent, abusive, or neglectful) are likely to seriously constrain development and produce maladaptive outcomes.

Of course, Scarr assumes that different children respond in somewhat different ways to the typical (or "average expectable") home environment due, in large part, to the fact that they have different genes. However, she also believes that a child's or an adolescent's development is so heavily influenced by the reactions he or she evokes from people other than parents and by the environmental niches he or she constructs that parental child-rearing practices have little effect on development—provided that these practices are "good enough" (that is, within the range of what might be considered normal for human beings). So, in contrast to Watson, who advocated superparenting, Scarr states that parents need only provide an "average expectable environment" in order to foster healthy development and fulfill their own role as effective guardians. She states that:

> Children's outcomes do not depend on whether parents take (them) to a ball game or a museum so much as they depend on genetic transmission, on plentiful opportunities, and on having a *good enough* environment that supports children's development to become themselves (Scarr, 1992, p. 15, emphasis added).

What do you think about Scarr's propositions? Many developmentalists were quick to criticize them. Diana Baumrind (1993), for example, points out that different child-rearing practices that

fall well within what Scarr considers the range of "good enough" parenting produce *very large differences* in children's and adolescents' developmental outcomes. In her own research, Baumrind consistently finds that "highly demanding–highly responsive" parents have children and adolescents who perform better academically and who show better social adjustment than do parents who are only moderately demanding or responsive but well within the "normal range" on these parenting dimensions. Baumrind also argues that just because children are active agents who, in part, shape their own environments in no way implies that parents are powerless to influence those environments in ways that might promote (or inhibit) adaptive outcomes. Finally, Baumrind worries that telling parents they need only be "good enough" may cause them to become less invested in promoting children's competencies and quicker to absolve themselves of responsibility should their children founder. This would be unfortunate, in her view, because research consistently indicates that parents who feel personally responsible for fostering adaptive development typically have competent, well-adjusted sons and daughters, whereas those who are less personally involved tend to have offspring whose outcomes are less adaptive. For all those reasons, Baumrind concludes that Scarr's "good enough" parenting is simply *not* good enough.

Other critics (for example, Jackson, 1993) are concerned about the possible implications of Scarr's views for public policy were they to be accepted by those in power. Specifically, if we endorse Scarr's ideas that the "average expectable environment" is all children need to approximate their genetically influenced developmental potentials, then there would be little reason to intervene in an attempt to optimize the development of economically disadvantaged children from homes that fall within the normal range of family environments. Yet Jackson (1993) notes that many such interventions designed to promote the cognitive and emotional development of African-American (and other) populations have had impressive results. If we assumed that these interventions are unnecessary, as Scarr's theory implies to Jackson, then we would hardly be serving the best interests of perhaps 25–30 percent of America's children (not to mention the majority of children in many other countries around the world; see Baumrind, 1993).

Clearly, this debate about the influence of parenting practices illustrates the very different perspectives on development taken by behavioral geneticists (Scarr) and environmentalists (Baumrind, Jackson). At this point, the debate is far from resolved, although we will see throughout the text that parenting does seem to have a meaningful effect on the developmental outcomes of children and adolescents and that many developmentalists would advise parents to strive to be much better than "good enough."

Of course, not all developmentalists would agree that genetic endowment is the "quarterback" of the "nature/nurture team" (Gottlieb, 1996; Greenberg, 2005; Partridge, 2005; and see the debate about parenting in Box 3.3). Students often object to Scarr and McCartney's theory because they sometimes read it to mean that genes *determine* environments. But this is not what the theory implies. What Scarr and McCartney are saying is this:

1. People with different genotypes are likely to evoke different responses from others and to select different environmental niches for themselves.

2. Yet the responses they evoke and the niches they select depend to no small extent on the particular individuals, settings, and circumstances they encounter. Although a child must be genetically predisposed to be outgoing and extroverted, for example, it would be difficult to act on this predisposition if she lived in the wilds of Alaska with a reclusive father. In fact, this youngster could well become rather shy and reserved when raised in such an asocial environment.

In sum, genotypes and environments *interact* to produce developmental change and variations in developmental outcomes. True, genes exert some influence on those aspects of the environment that we are likely to experience. But the particular environments available to us limit the possible phenotypes that are likely to emerge from a particular genotype (Gottlieb, 1991, 1996). Perhaps Donald Hebb (1980) was not too far off when he said that behavior is determined 100 percent by heredity and 100 percent by the environment, for it seems that these two sets of influences are complexly intertwined.

Interesting as these new ideas may be, critics argue that the behavioral genetics approach is merely a descriptive overview of how development might proceed rather than a well-articulated *explanation* of development. One reason for this sentiment is that we know so little about how genes exert their effects (Partridge, 2005). Genes are encoded to manufacture proteins and amino acids, not to produce such attributes as intelligence or sociability. Though we now suspect that genes affect behavior *indirectly* by influencing the experiences we evoke from others or create for ourselves, we still know very little about how or why genes might impel us to prefer particular kinds of stimulation or to find certain activities especially satisfying (Plomin & Rutter, 1998). In addition, behavioral geneticists apply the term *environment* in a very global way, making few if any attempts to measure environmental influences directly or to specify *how* environments act on individuals to influence their behavior. Perhaps you can see the problem: The critics contend that one has not *explained* development by merely postulating that *unspecified* environmental forces influenced in *unknown* ways by our genes *somehow* shape our abilities, conduct, and character (Gottlieb, 1996; Partridge, 2005).

How exactly do environments impinge on children and adolescents to influence their abilities, conduct, and character? What environmental influences, at what ages, are particularly important? These are questions that we will be seeking to answer throughout the remainder of this text. Recall that we briefly examined one *environmentalist* perspective—the social learning approach in Chapter 2—that relies on laboratory experimentation to describe how children and adolescents learn from their experiences. Now let's consider a very different environmentalist viewpoint—one that criticizes the heavy experimental emphasis of social-learning theory and that insists that only by studying people in their *natural settings* are we likely to understand how environments truly influence development.

ECOLOGICAL SYSTEMS THEORY: A MODERN ENVIRONMENTALIST PERSPECTIVE

Imagine a discussion in which leading "environmentalists" are brought together and asked a very straightforward question: "What is this entity you people call *environment?*" We have just criticized behavioral geneticists for being vague on this issue, and interestingly enough, social-learning theorists aren't much better. Behaviorists John B. Watson and B. F. Skinner depicted "environment" as any and all external forces that shape the individual's development. Although current social-learning theorists such as Bandura (1986, 1989) have backed away from this extremely mechanistic view by acknowledging that environments both influence and *are influenced by* developing individuals, they continue to provide only vague descriptions of the environmental contexts in which development takes place.

Photo 3.5
In his ecological systems theory, Urie Bronfenbrenner (1917–2005) describes how multiple levels of the surrounding environment influence child and adolescent development.

Chris Hildreth/Cornell University

By contrast, Urie Bronfenbrenner's (1979, 1989; Bronfenbrenner & Morris, 2006) **ecological systems theory** is an exciting new look at human development that provides the most detailed analyses of environmental influences that has appeared to date. And because it also concedes that a person's biologically influenced characteristics interact with environmental forces to shape development, it is probably more accurate to describe this perspective as a **bioecological theory.**

Bronfenbrenner (1979) begins by assuming that *natural* environments are the major source of influence on developing persons—and one that is often overlooked (or simply ignored) by researchers who choose to study development in the highly artificial context of the laboratory. He then proceeds to define "environment" (or the natural ecology) as "a set of nested structures, each inside the next, like a set of Russian dolls" (p. 22). In other words, the developing person is said to be at the center of and embedded in several environmental systems, ranging from immediate settings such as the family to more remote contexts such as the broader culture (see Figure 3.4). Each of these systems is thought to interact with the others and with the individual to influence development in important ways.

ecological systems theory
Bronfenbrenner's model emphasizing that the developing person is embedded in a series of environmental systems that interact with one another and with the person to influence development (sometimes called **bioecological theory).**

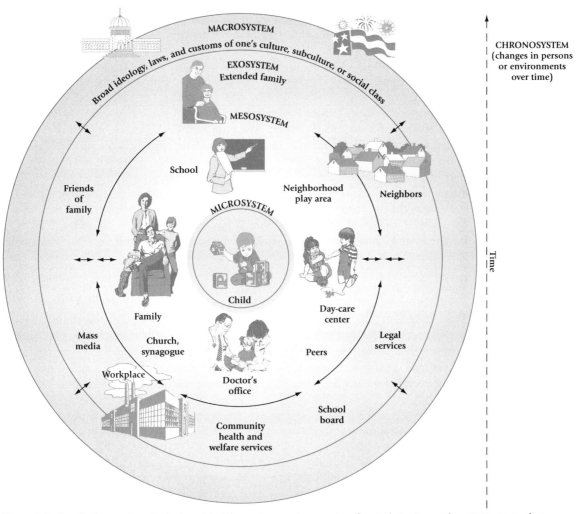

Figure 3.4 Bronfenbrenner's ecological model of the environment as a series of nested structures. The microsystem refers to relations between the child and the immediate environment, the mesosystem to connections among the child's immediate settings, the exosystem to social settings that affect but do not contain the child, and the macrosystem to the overarching ideology of the culture. (Based on Bronfenbrenner, 1979.)

Bronfenbrenner's Contexts for Development

microsystem
the immediate settings (including role relationships and activities) that the person actually encounters; the innermost of Bronfenbrenner's environmental layers, or contexts.

The Microsystem   Bronfenbrenner's innermost environmental layer, or **microsystem,** refers to the activities and interactions that occur in the person's immediate surroundings. For most young infants, the microsystem may be limited to the family. Yet the natural environment eventually becomes much more complex as children are exposed to such other microsystems as day care, preschool classes, youth groups, and peers in neighborhood play areas. Not only are children influenced by the people in their microsystems, but their own biologically and socially influenced characteristics—their habits, temperaments, physical characteristics, and capabilities—influence the behavior of companions as well. For example, an extremely irritable or temperamentally difficult infant can alienate her parents or even create friction between them that may be sufficient to impair their marital relationship (Belsky, Rosenberger, & Crnic, 1995). And interactions between any two individuals in a microsystem are likely to be influenced by third parties. Fathers, for example, clearly influence mother/infant interactions: Happily married mothers who have close supportive relationships with their spouses tend to interact much more patiently and sensitively with their infants than mothers who experience marital tension, receive little support from their spouses, and feel that they are raising their children on their own (Cox et al., 1989, 1992). So microsystems are truly dynamic contexts for development in which each person influences and is influenced by all other persons in the system.

mesosystem
the interconnections among an individual's immediate settings, or microsystems. The second of Bronfenbrenner's environmental layers, or contexts.

The Mesosystem   The second of Bronfenbrenner's environmental layers, or **mesosystem,** refers to the connections or interrelationships among such microsystems as homes, schools, and peer groups. Bronfenbrenner believes that development is likely to be optimized by strong, supportive links between microsystems. For example, youngsters who have established secure and harmonious relationships with parents are inclined to be socially competent, accepted by peers, and to enjoy close, supportive friendships during childhood and adolescence (Gavin & Furman, 1996; Kerns, Klepec, & Cole, 1996; NICHD Early Child Care Research Network, 2006; Shulman, Elicker, & Sroufe, 1994). A child's ability to master lessons at school depends not only on the quality of instruction his teachers provide, but also on the extent to which parents value these scholastic activities and consult or cooperate with teachers (Luster & McAdoo, 1996; Schulting, Malone, & Dodge, 2005). On the other hand, nonsupportive links between microsystems can spell trouble. For example, when peer groups devalue academics, they often undermine an adolescent's scholastic performance, despite the best efforts of parents and teachers to encourage academic achievement (Chen et al., 2005; Steinberg, Dornbusch, & Brown, 1992).

exosystem
social systems that children and adolescents do not directly experience but that may nonetheless influence their development; the third of Bronfenbrenner's environmental layers, or contexts.

The Exosystem   Bronfenbrenner's third environmental layer, the **exosystem,** consists of contexts that children and adolescents are not a part of but which may nevertheless influence their development. For example, parents' work environment is an exosystem influence, and children's emotional relationships at home and at school can be influenced considerably by whether their parents work regular hours (Hsueh & Yoshikawa, 2007) and enjoy their work (Greenberger, O'Neal, & Nagel, 1994). Similarly, children's experiences in school may also be affected by their exosystem—by a social integration plan adopted by the school board, or by a plant closing in their community that results in a decline in the school's revenue.

macrosystem
the larger cultural or subcultural context in which development occurs; Bronfenbrenner's outermost environmental layer, or context.

The Macrosystem   Bronfenbrenner also stresses that development occurs in a **macrosystem**—that is, a cultural, or subcultural, or social class context in which microsystems, mesosystems, and exosystems are embedded. The macrosystem is really a broad, overarching ideology that dictates (among other things) how children should be treated, what they should be taught, and the goals for which they should strive. Of course, these values differ from culture to culture (and across subcultures and social classes) and can greatly influence the kinds of experiences children have in their homes, neighborhoods, schools, and all other contexts that affect them, directly or indirectly. To cite one example, the incidence of child abuse in families (a microsystem experience) is much lower in those cultures (or macrosystems) that discourage physical punishment of children and advocate nonviolent ways of resolving interpersonal conflict (Belsky, 1993; U.S. Department of State, 2002).

Finally, Bronfenbrenner's model includes a temporal dimension, or **chronosystem,** which emphasizes that changes *in the child* or in any of the ecological contexts of development can affect the direction development is likely to take. Cognitive and biological changes that occur at puberty, for example, seem to contribute to increased conflict between young adolescents and their parents (Paikoff & Brooks-Gunn, 1991; Steinberg, 1996). And the impacts of environmental changes also depend upon another chronological variable—the age of the child. For example, even though a divorce hits hard at youngsters of all ages, adolescents are less likely than younger children to experience the strong blow of feeling that *they* were the cause of the break-up (Hetherington & Clingempeel, 1992).

chronosystem
in ecological systems theory, changes in the individual or the environment that occur over time and influence the direction development takes.

Contributions and Criticisms of Ecological Systems Theory

Though we have touched briefly on the ecological perspective here and will explore its propositions through the text, perhaps you can already see that it provides a much richer description of environment (and environmental influences) than anything offered by learning theorists. Each of us functions in particular microsystems that are linked by a mesosystem and embedded in the larger contexts of an exosystem and a macrosystem. It makes little sense to an ecological theorist to try to study environmental influences in contrived laboratory contexts. Instead, they argue that only by observing transactions between developing persons and their ever-changing *natural* settings will we ever understand how individuals influence and are influenced by their environments.

Bronfenbrenner's detailed analyses of environmental influences has suggested many ways in which the development of children and adolescents might be optimized. To illustrate, imagine a working mother who is having a tough time establishing a pleasant relationship with her temperamentally difficult infant. At the level of the microsystem, a successful intervention might assist the father to become a more sensitive companion—one who assumes some of the drudgery of child care and who encourages the mother to be more responsive to and patient with their baby (Cowan, Powell, & Cowan, 1998). At the level of the exosystem, mothers (and fathers) can often be helped to improve their relationships with their children if their community has parenting classes available in the adult education curriculum or, alternatively, if parenting groups exist in which parents with problems can express their concerns, enlist one another's emotional support, and learn from each other how to elicit more favorable reactions from their children (Lyons-Ruth et al., 1990). And at the level of the macrosystem, a social policy guaranteeing parents the right to take paid or unpaid leave from their jobs to attend to family matters might be an especially important intervention indeed—one that not only allows working parents more time to resolve any difficulties that may arise with their children (Clarke et al., 1997), but also conveys an attitude that society views the resolution of family problems as important to children's (and ultimately, to society's) well-being (Bronfenbrenner & Neville, 1995).

Yet, despite its strengths, ecological systems theory falls far short of being a complete account of human development. Though Bronfenbrenner characterizes the theory as a

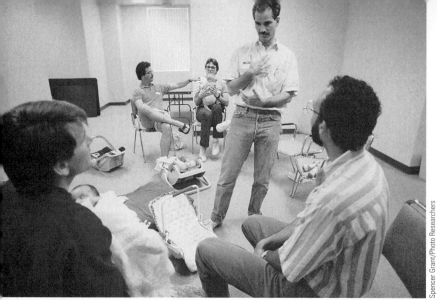

Spencer Grant/Photo Researchers

*bio*ecological model, it really has very little to say about specific biological contributors to development. And even though developmentalists are indebted to the ecological systems perspective for describing the complexities of the natural environments that influence and are influenced by developing persons, we must still understand how children and adolescents *process* environmental *information* and *learn* from their experiences before we can fully comprehend how environments influence human development. So the ecological systems approach is an important addition to the field—but one that is best described as a complement to, rather than a replacement for, other developmental theories.

Photo 3.6
Parenting classes are an "exosystem" influence that can help parents establish more harmonious relationships with their children.

sociocultural theory
Vygotsky's perspective on development, in which children acquire their culture's values, beliefs, and problem-solving strategies through collaborative dialogues with more knowledgeable members of society.

tools of intellectual adaptation
Vygotsky's term for methods of thinking and problem-solving strategies that children internalize from their interactions with more competent members of society.

Courtesy Archives of the History of American Psychology

Photo 3.7
The sociocultural theory of Lev Vygotsky (1896–1934) views human development as a socially mediated process that may vary from culture to culture.

MODERN COGNITIVE PERSPECTIVES

In this section of the chapter, we will complete our review of recent perspectives on human development by examining two influential cognitive approaches: Vygotsky's *sociocultural theory* and the *social information-processing* approach.

Vygotsky's Sociocultural Theory

Earlier in Chapter 2, we reviewed the cognitive-developmental theory of Jean Piaget—a viewpoint which specifies that children progress through a universal and invariant sequence of cognitive stages that have many implications for their social and personality development. In order to view Piaget's work from a new vantage point, let's consider a perspective on cognitive development and its implications that has been arousing a great deal of interest lately—the **sociocultural theory** of Russian developmentalist Lev Vygotsky (1934/1962, 1930–1935/1978; and see Rogoff, 1990, 1998; Wertsch & Tulviste, 1992). Vygotsky was an active scholar in the 1920s and 1930s when Piaget was formulating his theory, and his ideas qualify as "recent" only in the sense that they are now being translated from Russian and have begun to influence Western thinking in important ways. Vygotsky died of tuberculosis at age 38, before his own theory was fully developed. Nevertheless, he left us with important food for thought by insisting that (1) human development occurs in a particular sociocultural context that influences the form that it takes, and (2) many of a child's most noteworthy personal characteristics and cognitive skills evolve from *social interactions* with parents, teachers, and other more competent associates.

The Role of Culture in Intellectual Development   Vygotsky (1930–1935/1978) claimed that infants are born with a few *elementary mental functions*—attention, sensation, perception, and memory—that are eventually transformed by the culture into new and more sophisticated mental processes that he called *higher mental functions*. Take memory, for example. Young children's early memorial capabilities are limited by biological constraints to the images and impressions they can produce. However, each culture provides its children **tools of intellectual adaptation** that permit them to use their basic mental functions more adaptively. Thus, children in Western societies may learn to remember more efficiently by taking notes on what to remember, whereas their age-mates in preliterate societies may have learned other memory strategies, such as representing each object they must remember by tying a knot in a string or by tying a string around a finger to remind them to perform a chore. Such *socially transmitted* memory strategies and other cultural tools teach children how to use their minds—in short, *how* to think. And because each culture also transmits specific beliefs and values, it teaches children *what* to think as well.

In sum, Vygotsky claimed that human cognition, even when carried out in isolation, is inherently *sociocultural* because it is affected by the beliefs, values, and tools of intellectual adaptation passed to individuals by their culture. And because these values and intellectual tools may vary dramatically from culture to culture, Vygotsky believed that neither the course nor the content of intellectual growth was as "universal" as Piaget had assumed.

The Social Origins of Early Competencies   Vygotsky agreed with Piaget that young children are curious explorers who are actively involved in learning and discovering new principles. However, he placed much less emphasis than Piaget did on *self*-initiated discovery, choosing instead to stress the importance of *social* contributions to personal growth.

According to Vygotsky, many of the truly important "discoveries" that children make occur within the context of cooperative or collaborative *dialogues* between a skillful tutor, who may model the activity and transmit verbal instructions, and a novice pupil, who first seeks to understand the tutor's instruction and eventually internalizes this information, using it to regulate his or her own performance.

Vygotsky claims that **collaborative (or guided) learning** occurs most readily within the child's **zone of proximal development**—a term he uses to describe the difference between what a learner can accomplish independently and what he or she can accomplish with the guidance and encouragement of a more skilled partner. To illustrate collaborative learning as Vygotsky sees it, let's imagine that a 4-year-old boy is eager to learn to hit a whiffle ball with his plastic bat; but try as he might, he cannot make contact when Dad pitches to him. His father, noticing that the boy always takes his eye off the ball and holds his arms too close to his body, quickly concludes that his son is not about to become the next Barry Bonds without assistance. How might this father help his son to become a better hitter?

One feature of social collaboration that fosters cognitive growth and the acquisition of other skills is **scaffolding**—willingness of the more expert participants to carefully tailor the support they provide to the novice learner's current abilities so that he can profit from this assistance and increase his understanding of the problem. So our father, observing that his son can't hit what he doesn't track, might first build a tee, allowing the whiffle ball to remain *stationary*. He then places the boy before the tee and gives relevant verbal instructions ("bring your arms out," "keep your head up," and "WATCH THE BALL") before encouraging his son to knock the ball into the next county.

Vygotsky assumes that the child's role in collaborative learning is to take the language of the verbal instructions and to use it to guide his own activities. Thus, our 4-year-old's **private speech** might include such statements as "arms out" or "watch the ball" as he takes his first several dozen swings at it. As the boy learns these initial lessons, the father will provide new and more complex instructions (such as, "turn your hips as you swing") to further his son's skills, whereas the boy will verbalize these new directives (out loud or to himself) as he continues to refine his techniques. After several such dialogues (or exchanges of information), the boy should have internalized the instructions and gained a pretty fair verbal representation of the component skills involved in batting. He may now be ready to put this "private speech" to good use in guiding his attempts to hit a *moving* ball.

It is important to note that collaborative learning is a form of *social learning*—but one very different than the kinds of learning emphasized by social-learning theorists. It does not depend on the shaping of new responses through administration of tangible reinforcers, nor does it rest solely on lessons learned by observation (although the tutor's demonstrations of the new skill or activity may often help to clarify his verbal instructions). Instead, guided learning is really more of an "apprenticeship" in thinking and doing—one in which

collaborative (or guided) learning
The process of learning or acquiring new skills that occurs as novices participate in activities under the guidance of a more skillful tutor.

zone of proximal development
Vygotsky's term for the range of tasks that are too complex to be mastered alone but can be accomplished with guidance and encouragement from a more skillful partner.

scaffolding
process by which an expert, when instructing a novice, responds contingently to the novice's behavior in a learning situation so that the novice gradually increases his or her understanding of a problem.

private speech
Vygotsky's term for the subset of a child's verbal utterances that serve a self-communicative function and guide the child's activities.

Photo 3.8
According to Vygotsky, new skills are often easier to acquire if children receive guidance and encouragement from a more competent associate.

inner speech
internalized private speech; covert verbal thought.

novice children learn any number of culturally relevant skills and activities through their day-to-day, "hands-on" participation in such activities as preparing food, tracking prey, harvesting crops, solving puzzles, or hitting a baseball, with the guidance of their parents, teachers, older siblings, or their more skillful and accomplished peers (Rogoff, 1998). So collaborative (or guided) learning, which can only occur through *social* transactions between tutor and tutee, appears to be a very meaningful socialization process—and one that social learning theorists seem to have overlooked.

Contributions and Criticisms of the Sociocultural Perspective

Vygotsky's sociocultural theory offers a new lens through which to view human development by stressing the importance of specific social processes other theorists have not emphasized. According to Vygotsky, children's minds, skills, and personalities develop as they (1) take part in cooperative dialogues with skilled partners on tasks that are within their zone of proximal development and (2) incorporate what skillful tutors say to them into what they say to themselves. As social speech is translated into private speech and ultimately into covert **inner speech,** the culture's preferred methods of thinking and problem solving—or tools of intellectual adaptation—work their way from the language of competent tutors into the child's own thinking.

Unlike Piaget, who stressed *universal* sequences of cognitive growth, which were said to promote *universal* stages of social-personality development, Vygotsky's theory leads us to expect wide variations across cultures in the course of development—variations that reflect differences in children's cultural learning experiences. For example, children in Western cultures often learn to work *independently* on puzzles and other intellectual challenges that adults provide—experiences that prepare them for the *individual mastery* of academic assignments in highly structured Western classrooms. By contrast, children in some Australian and African bushman hunter societies are encouraged to *collaborate* early and to acquire elaborate spatial reasoning skills that prepare them to successfully track and corner the prey on which their livelihoods absolutely depend. Neither orientation to problems or set of cognitive capacities is necessarily any better or more advanced than the other; instead, they represent alternative forms of development that have evolved because they enable children to adapt successfully to values and traditions of their own cultures (Rogoff, 1998; Vygotsky, 1978).

Vygotsky's emphasis on collaborative learning has caused many (particularly developmentalists interested in education) to look anew at the roles that peers may play as agents of socialization. Indeed, research in educational settings reveals that children are often quicker to master important lessons and to report that they enjoy what they are learning when they collaborate with fellow students as opposed to working alone (Azmitia, 1992; Brown, 1997; Johnson & Johnson, 1989), and the youngsters who gain the most from these collaborations are usually the less competent collaborators who clearly profit from the guidance provided by their more skillful peers (Azmitia, 1988; Tudge, 1992). Not only are such collaborative learning projects of some academic benefit to participants, but as we will see in Chapter 12, they may also help to foster racial harmony and to improve the social standing and self-esteem of children with learning disabilities and other special needs.

Criticisms? Many of Vygotsky's writings are only now being translated from Russian to other languages (Wertsch & Tulviste, 1992), and his theory has not received the intense scrutiny that Piaget's theory has. Nevertheless, at least some of his ideas already have been challenged. Barbara Rogoff (1990, 1998), for example, argues that guided participations that rely heavily on the kinds of verbal instruction that Vygotsky emphasized may be less adaptive in some cultures or less useful for some forms of learning than for others. A young child learning to stalk prey in Australia's outback or to plant, care for, and harvest rice in Southeast Asia may profit more from observation and practice than from verbal instruction and encouragement (see also Rogoff et al., 1993). Other investigators are finding that collaborative problem solving among peers does not always benefit the collaborators and may actually *undermine* task performance if the more competent collaborator is not very confident about what he knows or fails to adapt his instruction to a partner's level of understanding (Levin & Druyan, 1993; Tudge, 1992). But despite whatever criticism his theory should generate in the years ahead, Vygotsky has provided a valuable service by reminding us that both cognitive growth and social development are (1) much less universal than some theorists contend and (2) are best understood when studied in the cultural and social contexts in which they occur.

The Social Information-Processing (or Attributional) Perspective

Our final "grand theory" pertaining to social and personality development stems from the efforts of cognitive theorists, social psychologists, and social-developmentalists who were concerned with explaining (1) how people process social information and interpret their experiences and/or (2) how these interpretations influence their social behavior and personality development. Today, many developmentalists call this viewpoint the **social information-processing (or attributional) perspective.**

Premises of Social Information-Processing Theory Social information-processing theorists depict human beings as active processors of social information who are constantly generating explanations, or **causal attributions,** for their own and other people's behavior. These "attribution" theorists propose that children's impressions of themselves, other people, and their social experiences will change, becoming much deeper and more abstract, as they become better at inferring the reasons that people behave as they do. Unlike Piaget, however, many social information-processing theorists view the course of both cognitive growth and social information processing as a *continuous, incremental* process that is not at all stagelike.

Theorizing about attributional processes can be traced to Fritz Heider (1958), a social psychologist who believed that all human beings are characterized by two strong motives: (1) the need to form a coherent understanding of the world and (2) the need to exert some control over the environment and thus become the "captain of one's own ship." To satisfy these motives, a person must be able to predict how people are likely to behave in a variety of situations and to understand why they behave in these ways.

According to Heider, a person who is seeking to explain some noteworthy behavior will tend to attribute it either to *internal* causes (for example, some characteristic or disposition of the actor) or to *external* causes (for example, something about the situation that elicited the actor's behavior or is otherwise responsible for it). This is an important distinction, for the kinds of causal attributions we make about our own or other people's behavior can influence our reactions to that behavior. Consider the following example.

Suppose a 10-year-old boy is walking across the playground when he is suddenly smacked in the back of the head by a Frisbee. He turns around and sees a single classmate, who is laughing at this turn of events. What kind of attribution does the child make about his classmate's behavior? It is likely that the boy will interpret the laughter as a sign that the classmate *intended* to hit him, and he will probably attribute the classmate's behavior to some internal (or dispositional) cause, such as the classmate's aggressiveness. Consequently, the boy is likely to be angry and may respond with some form of rejection

social information-processing (or attribution) theory
social-cognitive theory stating that the explanations we construct for social experiences largely determine how we react to those experiences.

causal attributions
conclusions drawn about the underlying causes of our own or another person's behavior.

or counteraggression. Had the classmate expressed concern about having hit the boy with the Frisbee, and had there been another classmate present to whom the Frisbee was apparently being thrown, it is more likely that the boy would view the harm done to him as *unintentional* and perhaps attribute it to some external (or situational) cause, such as the wind deflecting the Frisbee's path. Given this kind of attribution, the victim is not as likely to be angry, and his behavior might be very different than if he had held the classmate personally responsible for the harm that he had experienced.

In sum, social information-processing theorists contend that the implications of our experiences for our social conduct and personality development depend not so much on what these experiences are as on the attributions we make about them. Stated another way, we are largely products of our *interpretations* of our social experiences (that is, social information processing) rather than the objective character of those experiences. Of course, one implication of this viewpoint is that the same experience can have very different effects on individuals who make different attributions about it.

Heider and other early attribution theorists (for example, Kelley, 1973) were social psychologists who studied the causal attributions of adults and were not interested in developmental issues. Yet, once the principles underlying adult attributions had been established, an obvious next step was to study children's interpretations of social behavior, seeking to determine how their causal attributions differ from those of adults and why they change over time. To provide a flavor of this research, let's briefly consider how children come to view people as possessing stable dispositions, or *traits*—a milestone that critically influences the kinds of impressions they form of themselves and their companions.

Inferring Dispositional Attributes   If asked to characterize yourself or another person you know well, you are likely to mention several psychological qualities that you or your companion display—perhaps **traits** such as friendliness, integrity, and intelligence. Interestingly, children younger than 8 or 9 years old rarely make trait-like attributions about themselves or anyone else. Why not? Early thinking about this issue (Secord & Peevers, 1974) presumed that to describe oneself or another person in trait-like terms, a child must (1) know that individuals can be the *cause* of various behaviors, (2) recognize that such actions are often guided by *intentions*, and (3) realize that particular individuals are likely to behave in *consistent* and *predictable* ways over time and across situations.

Interestingly, even very young children understand that people are *causal* agents who often perform acts fully *intending* to produce a given effect. By age 2, toddlers frequently display their awareness of causality and intentionality in their own language (for example, "I left it [TV] on '*cause* I want to watch it"). What's more, 2-year-olds are much more likely to recall causal event sequences than noncausal ones two weeks after observing them (Bauer & Mandler, 1989; Miller & Aloise, 1989) and are more inclined to faithfully imitate a model's complex behavior if they understand the model's purpose (or intention) for performing it (Call, Carpenter, & Tomasello, 2005; Carpenter, Call, & Tomasello, 2002). And 3-year-olds recognize that actors clearly *intend* to succeed when striving to achieve a goal and that failures are unintentional (Shultz & Wells, 1985; Stipek, Recchia, & McClintic, 1992). In fact, the attributional error most often made by preschool children is to assume that *most effects that other people produce are intentional*; consequently, children younger than 6 or 7 may often fail to distinguish deliberate acts from either accidents or from other behaviors that produce consequences the actor could not have foreseen (Nelson-LeGall, 1985; Schultz & Wells, 1985).

Yet the knowledge that an actor has caused a foreseeable and intended outcome is not, in itself, an indication that the actor possesses a stable trait. Attribution theorists argue that to view someone as exhibiting a trait, the perceiver must first (1) judge the actor's behavior to be *internally* caused, rather than attribute it to situational constraints, and then (2) infer that this internal cause is reasonably *stable over time and across situations*.

trait
a dispositional characteristic that is stable over time and across situations.

Understanding Trait-like Attributions If preschool children often make *dispositional* attributions, deciding that an actor's behavior reflects her personal *motives* or *intentions* (internal causes), then why do they not use psychological constructs, or traits, to describe themselves or their companions? A study by Steven Rholes and Diane Ruble (1984) suggests one answer.

In Rholes and Ruble's study, 5- to 10-year-olds first heard stories in which an actor's behavior varied in its consistency. Some actors produced outcomes that were highly *consistent* over time, whereas other actors produced *inconsistent* outcomes. Earlier research (Kelley, 1973) had shown that adults often relay on a **consistency schema,** generally making trait-like attributions about actors who behave consistently over time and across situations. Here is a sample of a "high consistency" story that might lead perceivers to attribute the actor's behavior to a trait he displays, namely *high ability:*

> Yesterday Sam threw the basketball through the hoop almost every time he tried. In the past, Sam has almost always thrown the ball through the hoop when he tried.

After hearing such consistent (or inconsistent) stories, the 5- to 10-year-olds in Rholes and Ruble's study were asked to make either dispositional or situational attributions for the actor's behavior and to answer a series of questions to determine whether they viewed an actor's dispositions as *stable* causes of his or her outcomes. In the basketball story, for example, children might be asked, "How many times do you think Sam could throw the ball through the hoop in the future?" (stability over time) or "How many other kinds of throwing games would Sam do well at?" (stability over situations).

Rholes and Ruble found that even 5- and 6-year-olds made dispositional attributions about the actor's *current behavior* if the action was high in consistency. But when it came to the *prediction* questions, children younger than 9 did not seem to recognize that dispositions are stable across situations. Thus, 5- to 8-year-olds who viewed Sam as being good at basketball today did not realize that Sam probably has the perceptual-motor skills to do well at other, similar games, today or in the future.

In sum, children younger than 8 or 9 may fail to describe the self and others in "trait-like" terms not because they fail to make dispositional attributions (as attribution theorists had originally thought) but because they are often uncertain about the *stability* of these dispositions. Stated another way, younger children do not think about traits in the same ways that older ones do. They believe that many traits (particularly negative ones) will change, becoming more positive with age (Lockart, Chang, & Story, 2002). And should they hear a teacher describe a classmate as "smart" because he made the highest grade on a recent test, they are likely to treat this term more as a evaluation of how well the classmate did on that test than as an indication of his enduring intellectual abilities (Alvarez, Ruble, & Bolger, 2001; Rholes & Ruble, 1984). By contrast, trait-like terms are much more meaningful to a 9-year-old, who can use a label like "smart" as a brief and convenient way of expressing her knowledge that the person who is smart in one situation is likely to display the same inclination (and be smart) in other similar situations. Of course, understanding the implications of traits is an important advance in person perception because it enables us to more confidently predict how associates who display the traits we attribute to them are likely to behave in a variety of social settings.

Photo 3.9
Although this 5-year-old knows that his brother is good at fixing his bike (a dispositional attribution), he is unlikely to describe him in trait-like terms (in other words, mechanical) because he may not realize that his brother probably has the mechanical skill to perform many kinds of repairs.

consistency schema
attributional heuristic implying that actions that a person consistently performs are likely to be internally caused (reflecting a dispositional characteristic).

Contributions and Criticisms of the Social Information-Processing Perspective

Clearly, we have touched only briefly here on the social information-processing perspective. Yet we will see over and over again that its proponents have contributed importantly to our understanding of such central social-developmental issues as the development of our self-concepts and self-esteem (Chapter 6), the growth of achievement orientations (Chapter 7), gender-role socialization (Chapter 8), and the bases for individual differences in aggressive behavior (Chapter 9), moral conduct (Chapter 10), and peer acceptance/popularity (Chapter 13), to name a few. Indeed, the central proposition of social information-processing theory—that developing persons are active information seekers who are often influenced more by their *interpretations* of social experiences than by the objective character of these experiences—has proved to be a crucial theoretical insight.

By way of criticism, social information-processing theorists can be rather vague about the factors responsible for developmental changes in the attributions children make. For example, why do children younger than 8 or 9 not understand that dispositional characteristics can be stable over time and across situations, thereby implying the existence of psychological *traits*? Social information-processing theorists answer by arguing that younger children simply have not had enough *experience* at appraising the causes of their own and other people's behavior, and at comparing actors' behaviors over time and across situations, to have developed the concept of consistent and enduring psychological traits (Rholes & Ruble, 1984). Yet newer research demonstrates that preschool children, who are socially inexperienced from Rholes and Ruble's perspective, can make realistic and appropriate trait inferences if they have ample social information to process. For example, one recent experiment found that even some 3- and 4-year-olds (and more 5- and 6-year-olds) were quicker to appropriately label an actor "nice" when presented with five examples (rather than only one example) of the actor's kindly behavior (Boseovski & Lee, 2006). In addition, the "social experience" hypothesis leaves many other questions unanswered. For example, what kinds of social experience, and with whom, are most likely to foster the growth of trait-like attributions? The social information-processing perspective is largely silent on this and other potentially important contributors to children's social-cognitive development.

What's more, many alternative explanations for the emergence of trait-like attributions are possible and highly plausible. We will see in Chapter 6, for example, that theorists influenced by Piaget would argue that young children make few trait-like attributions because of their *cognitive immaturity;* that is, they are highly egocentric, lack role-taking skills, and display centered thinking, focusing on the way things appear to be at present—all of which may hinder them from detecting regularities or invariances in conduct over time (and across situations) that might lead to stable trait-like attributions. Other researchers (for example, Eder, 1989) have shown that even 3- to 5-year-old preschool children are aware of regularities in the conduct of well-known playmates but apparently do not yet know what words to use to describe the rudimentary "traits" they have detected. So although social information-processing theory is a valuable addition to the field of social and personality development, it rarely provides a complete account of the phenomena to which it applies and is best viewed as a compliment to, rather than a replacement for, the other theoretical viewpoints we have considered.

THEORIES AND WORLDVIEWS

Now that we have completed our survey of the major theories of human development, how might we compare them? One way is to group the theories into even grander categories, for each is grounded in a broader set of philosophical assumptions, or *worldview*. By examining the fundamental assumptions that underlie different theories, we can perhaps appreciate just how deeply some of their disagreements run.

Early developmental theories adopted either of two broad worldviews (Overton, 1984). The first, the **mechanistic model,** likens human beings to machines by viewing them (1) as a collection of parts (behaviors) that can be decomposed, much as machines can be taken apart piece by piece; (2) as *passive,* changing mostly in response to outside influences (much as machines depend on external energy sources to operate); and (3) as changing gradually or *continuously* as their parts (specific cognitive, emotional, and behavioral capabilities) are added. By contrast, the **organismic model** compares humans to plants and other living organisms by viewing them (1) as whole beings who cannot be understood as a simple collection of parts; (2) as *active* in the developmental process, changing under the guidance of internal forces (such as instincts or maturation); and (3) as evolving through distinct (discontinuous) *stages* as they mature.

mechanistic model
view of children as passive entities whose developmental paths are primarily determined by external (environmental) influences.

organismic model
view of children as active entities whose developmental paths are primarily determined by forces from within themselves.

Which theorists have adopted which model? Clearly, early learning theorists such as Watson and Skinner favored the mechanistic worldview, for they saw human beings as passively shaped by environmental events and they analyzed human behavior response by response. Bandura's social-learning theory is primarily mechanistic; yet it does reflect the important organismic assumption that human beings are active creatures who both influence and are influenced by their environments. By contrast, psychoanalytic theorists such as Freud and Erikson and cognitive-developmentalists from the Piagetian tradition all base their theories primarily on the organismic model: Given some nourishment from their surroundings, human beings will progress through discontinuous steps or stages as directed by forces lying within themselves—much as seeds evolve into blooming plants. Finally, ethologists and behavioral geneticists also could be classified as organismic models. They clearly portray humans as active, holistic beings with biological predispositions that channel or guide development. Although both theories view development as more continuous than stagelike, ethologists stress that some developments can be abrupt, or discontinuous, as when a new and adaptive behavior emerges during its sensitive period (an organismic premise).

Another broad worldview, the **contextual model,** has recently evolved and become the perspective that many developmentalists favor (Lerner, 1996). The contextual model views development as the product of a dynamic interplay between person and environment. People are assumed to be active in the developmental process (as in the organismic model) *and* the environment is active as well (as in the mechanistic model). Development may have both universal aspects *and* aspects peculiar to certain cultures, times, or individuals. The potential exists for both continuous and discontinuous change, and development may proceed along many different paths, depending on the intricate interplay between internal forces (nature) and external influences (environment).

contextual model
view of children as active entities whose developmental paths represent a continuous, dynamic interplay between internal forces (nature) and external influences (nurture).

Although none of the theories we've reviewed provides a pure example of the contextual worldview, some come reasonably close: Information-processing theorists describe children and adolescents as active processors of environmental input whose processing capabilities are influenced by biological maturation *and* by the kinds of social and cultural experiences they encounter. (Note that Vygotsky's sociocultural theory makes similar assumptions.) Although they view development as basically continuous rather than stagelike, many information-processing theorists concede that changes within particular developmental domains may be uneven and that qualitative leaps in one's intellectual performances or social information-processing capabilities are not unknown.

Bronfenbrenner's ecological systems theory also adopts a contextual worldview. Bronfenbrenner does make the "mechanistic" assumption that humans are heavily influenced by many environmental contexts, ranging from our home settings to the wider society in which we live. Yet he is keenly aware that children and adolescents are active biological beings who change as they mature and whose behaviors and biologically influenced attributes influence the very environments that are influencing their development. So development is viewed as the product of a truly dynamic interplay between an active person and an ever-changing "active" environment, and it is on this basis that the ecological systems approach qualifies as a contextual theory.

Table 3.3 Summary of the philosophies underlying eight major developmental perspectives

Theory	Active versus Passive Person	Continuous versus Discontinuous Development	Nature versus Nurture	Worldview
Psychoanalyic perspective	*Active:* Children are driven by inborn instincts that are channeled (with the assistance of others) into socially desirable outlets.	*Discontinuous:* Emphasizes stages of psychosexual development (Freud) or psychosocial development (Erikson).	*Both nature and nurture:* Biological forces (instincts, maturation) precipitate psychosexual stages and psychosocial crises; parental child-rearing practices influence the outcomes of these stages.	Organismic
Learning perspective	*Passive:* Children are molded by their environments (although Bandura claims that developing persons also influence these environments).	*Continuous:* Emphasizes the gradual addition of learned responses (habits) that make up one's personality.	*Nurture most important:* Environmental input rather than biological influences determines the course of development.	Mechanistic
Piaget's cognitive developmental theory	*Active:* Children actively construct more sophisticated understandings of the self, others, and the environment to which they adapt.	*Discontinuous:* Emphasizes an invariant sequence of qualitatively distinct cognitive stages.	*Both nature and nurture:* Children have an inborn need to adapt to the environment; they are nurtured by a stimulating environment that provides many adaptive challenges.	Organismic
Ethological perspective	*Active:* Humans are born with biologically determined behaviors that promote adaptive developmental outcomes.	*Both:* Emphasizes that adaptive behaviors are added continuously, but that some adaptive capabilities emerge abruptly (or fail to emerge) during sensitive periods of their development.	*Nature:* Biologically programmed adaptive behaviors are stressed, although an appropriate environment (which is influenced by the biological predispositions of companions) is necessary for successful adaptation.	Organismic

Table 3.3 summarizes the philosophical assumptions and worldviews underlying each of the broad theoretical perspectives we have reviewed. As you compare the viewpoints you expressed in Box 1.2 (on page 14) with those of the theorists, see whether you can clearly determine your own worldview on human nature and the character of human development.

Although we have loosely classified the major theories as "biological," "environmental," or "cognitive" viewpoints, it should be clear by now that each of these models (with the possible exceptions of the radical behaviorism of Watson and Skinner) acknowledges the contributions of forces other than those it emphasizes. In other words, all modern-day theorists are well aware that biological factors, cognitive growth, and environmental influences are complexly intertwined and that changes in one aspect of development may have important implications for other developmental domains. Consider the following example.

What determines a person's popularity with peers? If you were to say that social skills are important, you would be right. Social skills such as warmth, friendliness, and a willingness to cooperate—all of which are heavily influenced by rearing environments—are characteristics that popular children typically display. And yet we will see in Chapter 13 that such

Table 3.3 (continued)

Theory	Active versus Passive Person	Continuous versus Discontinuous Development	Nature versus Nurture	Worldview
Behavioral genetics	*Active:* By virtue of genetically influenced characteristics, we elicit responses from others and we select environmental niches for ourselves.	*Continuous:* Genotype/environment interactions occur continuously, influencing the form that development takes.	*Both nature and nurture:* Emphasis is on nature; however, genes are said to exert a heavy influence on the environments in which development takes place.	Organismic
Ecological systems perspective	*Both:* Humans actively influence the environmental contexts that influence their development.	*Both:* Emphasizes that transactions between ever-changing individuals and ever-changing environments lead to quantitative developmental changes. However, discontinuous personal or environmental events (for example, reaching puberty, parents' divorce) can produce abrupt qualitative changes.	*Nurture:* Impacts of environmental contexts on development are most clearly emphasized, although children's biologically influenced attributes can affect their environments.	Contextual
Modern cognitive viewpoints Vygotsky Social information-processing theory	*Active:* Children actively possess environmental information to answer questions, interpret the causes of their own and others' behavior, and acquire culturally valued attributes and modes of thinking.	*Continuous:* Emphasizes gradual acquisition of social information-processing skills and of other culturally valued attributes.	*Emphasis on nurture:* Capabilities that develop are heavily influenced by one's social and cultural experiences. However, some information-processing theorists clearly acknowledge that biological maturation permits older children and adolescents to process information faster.	Contextual
My viewpoint (Review Box 1.2)	_____	_____	_____	_____

genetically influenced attributes as facial attractiveness and the age at which a child reaches puberty can have a very real effect on social life. For example, boys who reach puberty early enjoy better relations with their peers than boys who reach puberty later. Let's also note that bright children who do well in school tend to be more popular with their peers than children of average intelligence or below who perform somewhat less admirably in the classroom.

In sum, one's popularity depends not only on social skills but also on cognitive prowess and physical characteristics. As this example illustrates, development is not piecemeal but **holistic**—human beings are biological, cognitive, and social creatures, and each of these components of "self" depends in part on changes that are taking place in other areas of development. This holistic perspective is perhaps the dominant theme of human development today—and the theme around which the remainder of this book is organized.

In case you are wondering, no one expects you to choose one of the major theories as a favorite and to reject the others. The fact that each theory emphasizes different aspects of development, combined with the realization that human development is truly a *holistic* enterprise, has led many developmentalists to become theoretical **eclectics:** individuals who

holistic perspective
a unified view of the developmental process that emphasizes the interrelationships among the physical/biological, mental, social, and emotional aspects of human development.

eclectics
those who borrow from many theories in their attempts to predict and explain human development.

recognize that none of the grand theories can explain all aspects of social and personality development and that each has contributed to what we know about developing children and adolescents. The plan for the remainder of this book is to take an *eclectic approach*, borrowing from many theories to integrate their contributions into a unified, holistic portrait of the developing person.

SUMMARY

♦ This chapter examines several recent perspectives on social and personality development—theories that have challenged, built on, and extended the three classical viewpoints we reviewed in Chapter 2.

MODERN EVOLUTIONARY PERSPECTIVES

♦ The evolutionary viewpoint, as expressed in **ethology,** is that humans are born with a number of adaptive attributes that have evolved through **natural selection** and channel development in ways that promote adaptive outcomes. Ethologists recognize that humans are influenced by their experiences and even claim that certain adaptive characteristics are most likely to develop during **sensitive periods,** provided that the environment fosters this development. Modern evolutionary theorists have searched for preselected motives, such as **altruism,** and other behaviors that ensure the survival not of individuals, but of individuals' genes.

BEHAVIORAL GENETICS: BIOLOGICAL BASES FOR INDIVIDUAL DIFFERENCES

♦ *Behavioral genetics* is the study of how **genotypes** and environment contribute to individual variations in **phenotypes.** Although animals can be studied in *selective breeding* experiments, human behavioral geneticists must conduct family studies (often **twin designs** or **adoption designs**), estimating the **heritability** of various attributes from similarities and differences among family members who differ in **kinship.** Hereditary contributions to various attributes are estimated by evaluating **concordance rates** and **heritability coefficients.** Behavioral geneticists can also determine the amount of variability in a trait that is attributable to **nonshared environmental influences** and **shared environmental influences.**

♦ Family studies reveal that the genes people inherit influence their intellectual performances, such core dimensions of personality as **introversion/extroversion** and **empathic concern,** and even their predispositions to display such abnormalities as **schizophrenia,** neurotic disorders, alcoholism, and criminality. However, none of these complex attributes is genetically "determined"; all are heavily influenced by environment.

♦ Behavioral geneticists have sought to explain how hereditary and environment combine to produce developmental change. One recent model proposes three avenues by which genes influence the environments we are likely to experience: through **passive genotype/environment correlations, evocative genotype/ environment correlations,** and **active** (or **niche-building**) **genotype/environment correlations.** However, the behavioral genetics approach has been criticized as an incomplete theory of development that describes, but fails to *explain,* how either genes or environment influence our abilities, conduct, and character.

ECOLOGICAL SYSTEMS THEORY: A MODERN ENVIRONMENTALIST PERSPECTIVE

♦ Urie Bronfenbrenner's **ecological systems theory** views development as the product of transactions between an ever-changing person and an ever-changing environment. Bronfenbrenner proposes that the natural environment in which development occurs actually consists of several interacting contexts or systems—**microsystem, mesosystem, exosystem,** and **macrosystem**—each of which is also influenced by the **chronosystem**—that is, by changes that occur over time in the individual or in other environmental contexts. This detailed analysis of person/environment interactions has suggested many new interventions to optimize development.

MODERN COGNITIVE PERSPECTIVES

♦ Vygotsky's **sociocultural theory** proposes that children's minds, skills, and personalities develop as they acquire the **tools of intellectual adaption** that pertain to their culture. Children acquire cultural beliefs, values, and problem-solving strategies in the context of *collaborative dialogues* with more skillful partners as they gradually internalize their tutors' instructions to master tasks within their **zone of proximal development. Collaborative learning** is most effective when more skillful associates properly **scaffold** their instruction, thereby allowing the child to profit from it and begin to function more independently.

♦ Social information processing theorists propose that children's reactions to their social experiences depend largely on the **causal attributions** they make about their own and other people's behavior. This crucial insight has been supported consistently by research and has contributed importantly to our understanding of many social-developmental issues. However, social information-processing theory rarely provides a complete account of the phenomena to which it applies and is best viewed as an important complement to, rather than a replacement for, other theoretical viewpoints.

THEORIES AND WORLDVIEWS

♦ Theories can be grouped into families based on the worldviews that underlie them. As developmentalists have come to appreciate the incredible complexity and **holistic character** of human development, more of them are favoring a **contextual model** over the **mechanistic model** that guides learning theories or the **organismic model** that underlies stage theories. Indeed, most contemporary developmentalists are theoretically **eclectic,** recognizing that no single theory offers a totally adequate account of human development and that each contributes importantly to our understanding of developing persons.

CHAPTER 4

Emotional Development and Temperament

Two 18-month-olds, Caryn and Cherry, are each holding their mothers' hand, patiently awaiting the entrance of a department store Santa. Upon appearing and seeing these toddlers, Santa quickly approaches them, bends over, belts out a deep, "HO! HO! HO!" and inquires rather intrusively, "Have you been good little girls this year?" Cherry, obviously startled and fearful, whimpers and nearly falls over backward as she turns away to clutch at her mother. Caryn too is cautious, but she's highly curious as well. She looks intently at Santa, then at her mother, who says, "Tell Santa, 'Yes, I've been good and I'd like a doll for Christmas this year.'" Caryn then turns and approaches Santa, allowing him to pick her up and place her on his lap.

Clearly, these toddlers had very different emotional reactions on meeting this loud, bearded stranger in a bright red suit. Cherry, noticeably upset, sought comfort from her mother, whereas Caryn, more intrigued than scared, first looked at her mother for clarification and guidance before exploring the situation for herself. Why might these two children have reacted so differently to the same novel experience?

In this chapter, we address such issues by turning to the literature on children's emotional development. We begin by charting age-related changes in children's experience and displays of emotion and their growing abilities to recognize and interpret the emotions of other people. We will then examine how children come to regulate and control their emotions, a tremendously important achievement that allows them to interact effectively with other people and to accomplish any number of other personal goals.

Of course, not everyone shows the same patterns of emotional development, and parents who have more than one child often believe that their children were very different in their emotional reactions to everyday events from birth onward. Social-developmentalists have learned over the past 40 years that parents are quite correct: Babies do differ in their patterns of emotional and behavioral reactivity, or *temperaments*. As we explore the temperamental differences that children display and the hereditary and environmental influences that influence temperament, we will see why the early temperamental attributes that help to explain why children react so differently to novel and to everyday events are now considered by many developmentalists to be important building blocks of our adult personalities.

🔊 AN OVERVIEW OF EMOTIONS AND EMOTIONAL DEVELOPMENT

Before we begin our explorations into the emotional lives of developing persons, we might first ask, "What are emotions?" My students typically answer this question by saying something like "the feelings we have about our experiences" or "patterns of positive or negative moods that all of us show." Developmentalists would not disagree with these definitions but would add that an emotion represents much more than a "feeling." In their view, **emotions** have several components including:

1. *feelings* (generally positive or negative in character)
2. *physiological correlates,* including changes in heart rate, galvanic skin response (that is sweat gland activity), brain wave activity, and so forth.
3. *cognitions* that elicit or accompany feelings and physiological changes, and
4. *goals,* or the desire to take such actions as escaping noxious stimuli, approaching pleasant ones, influencing the behavior of others, communicating needs, or desires, and so on.

emotion
a motivational construct that is characterized by changes in affect (or feelings), physiological responses, cognitions, and overt behavior.

A simple example may help to illustrate all four components of emotion in action. Imagine a boy whose face lights up upon seeing the new truck he receives for his third birthday. His very positive feeling is accompanied by an increase in heart rate and perhaps by the cognition "I got what I wanted," and he is immediately motivated by all these concomitants of his "happiness" to approach the toy (and, perhaps, to convey his thanks to the persons responsible for granting his wish).

Two Theories of Emotions and Emotional Development

Although many theorists have had something to say about the development of emotions and their adaptive significance, two theories are especially influential today. The first of these approaches, **discrete emotions theory** has strong evolutionary overtones, tracing back to 1872, when Charles Darwin proposed that most basic emotions that humans display are products of our evolutionary history that have some adaptive value (see Darwin, 1965). For example, the *disgust* that babies show should they suck on a bitter solution may be an inborn reaction that protects them from tainted food by causing them to reject or spit out the offending substance; the distress cries that newborns emit when hungry or otherwise discomforted promote a baby's well-being by communicating to caregivers that all is not well and the infant has some need to which they should attend (Saarni, Mumme, & Campos, 1998). Like Darwin, modern proponents of discrete emotions theory (for example, Eckman, 2003; Izard et al., 2000) continue to argue that many basic human emotions are inborn products of our evolutionary history. Each "discrete" emotion (sadness versus anger, for example) is accompanied by a particular set of facial (and bodily) reactions (see Figure 4.1) and is apparent very early in life.

discrete emotions theory
a theory of emotions specifying that specific emotions are biologically programmed, accompanied by distinct sets of bodily and facial cues, and discriminable from early in life.

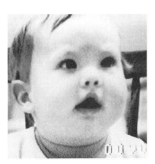

Interest: brows raised; mouth may be rounded; lips may be pursed.

Fear: mouth retracted; brows level and drawn up and in; eyelids lifted.

Disgust: tongue protruding; upper lip raised; nose wrinkled.

Joy: bright eyes; cheeks lifted; mouth forms a smile.

Sadness: corners of mouth turned down; inner portion of brows raised.

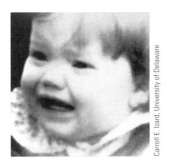

Anger: mouth squared at corners; brows drawn together and pointing down; eyes fixed straight ahead.

Carroll E. Izard, University of Delaware

Figure 4.1 Young infants display a variety of emotional expressions.

functionalist perspective (on emotions)
a theory specifying the major purpose of an emotion is to establish, maintain, or change one's relationship with the environment to accomplish a goal; emotions are not viewed as discrete early in life but as entities that emerge with age.

By contrast, theorists who take a **functionalist perspective** to emotional development believe that newborns and very young infants do not display discrete emotions; their emotional lives may consist mainly of global experiences of positivity (excitement) and negativity (distress) (Campos, Mumme, et al., 1994; Sroufe, 1995). Functional theorists also propose that the most basic purpose of emotions is to influence behavior and promote some action toward achieving a goal (Campos, Mumme, et al., 1994; Witherington, Campos, & Hertenstein, 2001), and they emphasize environmental influences on emotional development. So a newborn whose arms are restrained or who receives a shot is likely to become extremely distressed by the frustration or pain she experiences. Yet it may take her two to three months of interacting with other people (that is, social experience) before she is able to understand that someone is causing her distress. She may now look or turn toward this agent, become red in the face, and perhaps squirm, kick, or take other actions, thereby communicating her *anger* (rather than her distress) in an attempt to eliminate the cause of her pain or discomfort or to elicit a comforting response from her companions. And should she succeed, her angry display would have been "functional" indeed (Saarni, Mumme, & Campos, 1998).

Functional theorists also emphasize that successful adaption to their environments often requires children to control their emotions rather than expressing them freely. Although taking some sort of direct, forceful action may be an expedient way for a 2-year-old to deal with a playmate who angers him, neither nearby adults nor other children are likely to tolerate free expression of unbridled anger for long, and the child who persists in acting out this way is likely to find himself in the corner or without willing playmates. Indeed, a crucially important aspect of children's emotional development involves learning to *regulate* emotions to maintain social harmony or achieve other important goals. As we will see, expressions of emotions do become more socially appropriate with age, as children learn the circumstances under which it is acceptable (or unacceptable) to display particular emotions.

Let's now begin our examination of children's emotional development by examining the sequencing of discrete emotions in infancy and toddlerhood.

APPEARANCE AND DEVELOPMENT OF DISCRETE EMOTIONS

I often begin my own class discussion of emotional development with the same questions theorists have debated: Do babies have feelings? Do they display specific emotions such as happiness, sadness, fear, and anger the way that older children and adults do? Most new parents think so. In one study, more then half the mothers of 1-month-olds claimed that their babies displayed at least five distinct emotional expressions: Interest, surprise, joy, anger, and fear (Johnson et al., 1982). Although these data appear to be quite consistent with the premise of discrete emotions theory, namely that many basic human emotions are innate, critics might argue that this is simply a case of proud mothers reading too much into the behavior of their infants. How might we tell whether infants experience specific emotions?

Carroll Izard and his colleagues at the University of Delaware have studied infants' emotional expressions by videotaping babies' responses to such events as grasping an ice cube, having a toy taken away, or seeing their mothers return after a separation (Izard, 1982, 1993). Izard's procedure is to ask raters, who are *unaware* of the events that an infant has experienced, to tell him what emotion the infant is experiencing from the facial expression the infant displays. These studies reveal that different adult raters observing the same expressions reliably see the same emotion in a baby's face (review Figure 4.1.) What's more, infants respond in predictable ways to particular kinds of experiences. For example, soft sounds and novel visual displays are likely to elicit smiles and looks of interest, whereas inoculations and other painful stimuli will elicit distress from a younger infant and anger from an older one (Izard, Hembree, and Huebner, 1987). Babies also express emotions vocally. For example, 2-month-olds often coo when contented and may also display "blurts" of excitation when they are happy or interested in something—signals that parents interpret as positive emotions and will attempt to prolong by talking to or playing with their babies (Keller & Scholmerich, 1987).

Interestingly, adults can usually tell what *positive* emotion a baby is experiencing (for example, interest versus joy) from facial expressions, but specific negative emotions (fear versus anger, for example) are much more difficult to pinpoint on the basis of facial cues alone (Izard et al., 1995; Matias & Cohn, 1993). Nevertheless, most researchers agree that babies communicate a variety of feelings through their facial and vocal expressions and that each expression becomes a more recognizable sign of a particular emotion with age (Camras et al., 1992; Izard et al., 1995).

Sequencing of Discrete Emotions in the First Year

Various emotions appear at different times over the first year of life. At birth, babies show facial expressions of interest, distress, disgust, and contentment (as indicated by a rudimentary smile). Other **primary (or basic) emotions** that emerge between age 2 and 7 months are anger, sadness, joy, surprise, and fear (Izard et al., 1995). These so-called primary emotions may have deep biological roots in that they emerge at roughly the same age in all normal infants and are displayed and interpreted similarly in all cultures (Camras et al., 1992; Izard, 1993). Yet some learning (or cognitive development) may be necessary before babies will express any emotion not present at birth. Indeed, one of the strongest elicitors of surprise and joy among 2- to 8-month-olds is their discovery that they can exert some control over objects and events. And disconfirmation of these *learned* expectancies (as when someone or something prevents them from exerting control) is likely to *anger* many 2- to 4- month-olds and may *sadden* the 4- to 6- month-olds as well (Lewis, Alessandri, & Sullivan, 1990; Sullivan, Lewis, & Allesandri, 1992).

Of course, each of these primary emotions changes considerably over time from the form it took and the functions it served when it first appeared. Let's first consider changes that occur in a positive emotion—happiness—before turning to the development of such negative emotions as anger, sadness, and fear.

primary (or basic) emotions
the set of emotions present at birth or emerging early in the first year that some theorists believe to be biologically programmed.

Development of a Positive Emotion: Happiness

As noted above, babies' first signs of happiness (or contentment) are the rudimentary smiles they show primarily in response to a full stomach or to such soothing stimuli as gentle rocking, stroking of the skin, and high-pitched vocalizations that caregivers may provide. In fact, these smiles often occur while a baby is sleeping and are thought to be reflexive responses attributable more to changes in biological state (tension release) than to social stimuli or social interaction (Sroufe & Waters, 1976).

By the end of the second month, babies begin to display **social smiles** that are most often seen in interactions with caregivers who are likely to be delighted at a baby's positive reaction to them and to smile back and continue whatever they are doing that the baby enjoys (Lavelli & Fogel, 2005; Malatesta & Haviland, 1982). By age 3 months, babies

social smile
smile directed at people; first appears at 6–10 weeks of age.

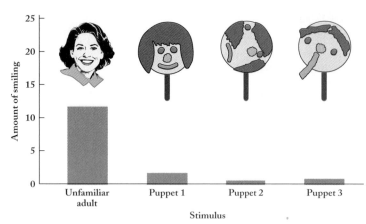

Figure 4.2
Three-month-old infants' smiling at an unfamiliar adult and three hand puppets varying in resemblance to a human face. Although infants spent just as much time looking at each of the four stimuli, they spent much more time smiling at the human face. (From Ellsworth, Muir, & Hains, 1993.)

are more likely to smile at real people than at other interesting and animated puppets that beckon to them (Ellsworth, Muir, & Hains, 1993; see Figure 4.2). And between 3 and 6 months of age, babies increasingly display raised-check and open-mouth (that is BIG) smiles while gazing or interacting pleasantly with a *smiling* caregiver, a sign that some interpret as indicating that young infants are beginning to share positive affect with a companion (Legerstee & Varghese, 2001; Messinger, Fogel, & Dickson, 2001).

Although smiling does become increasingly "social" with age, even very young infants are likely to smile and (later) laugh when they operate and control toys or other inanimate aspects in their environments. In one study, 2-month-old infants had strings attached to their arms. The infants in an experimental group caused music to play whenever they moved their arms, whereas "control" infants heard the same music at intervals unrelated to their arm movements. The results were striking: Infants who had caused the music to play smiled more as the music played than did infants whose arm movements had nothing to do with the music they heard (Lewis, Alessandri, & Sullivan, 1990). What made the first group of infants so happy was not that pleasant music came on, but that *they could make it come on*.

By age 6 or 7 months, infants begin to reserve their biggest smiles for familiar companions and may often seem wary rather than happy to encounter a person they don't know. At this point, infants regularly use smiles and other signs of positive affect as sociable gestures as they share their delight with or attempt to prolong positive social interactions with familiar companions (Fogel et al., 2006; Saarni, Mumme, & Campos, 1998).

Photo 4.1 Few signals attract as much attention as a baby's social smile.

Development of Negative Emotions

Although newborns show generalized distress to hunger, pain, and a wide range of other discomforting stimuli, particular negative emotions begin to appear over the first six months of life. Red-faced anger (as opposed to general distress) is sometimes seen in the faces of 2-month-olds who receive painful inoculations or who cannot exert control over toys and other events, and these angry reactions become increasingly intense by the middle of the first year (Izard et al., 1995; Lewis, Alessandri, & Sullivan, 1990; Sullivan & Lewis, 2003; Sullivan, Lewis, & Alessandri, 1992).

Sadness shows a similar developmental trend, with 2- to 6-month-olds becoming sullen in some of the same situations that elicit angry displays (for example, when experiencing painful medical procedures or loss of control; see Izard et al., 1995; Lewis, Alessandri, & Sullivan, 1990). One situation in particular that may sadden young infants is when they cannot seem to elicit a positive response from a caregiver. In one research program, mothers were asked to adopt a still and sullen expression while interacting with their babies. These infants became saddened (and occasionally angry) by their mothers' "still face" (Tronick et al., 1978; see also Lewis & Ramsey, 2005). Simarily, expressions of sadness are common in 2- to 3-month-old infants of caregivers who are chronically depressed; indeed, these babies may begin to match their caregivers' depressive symptoms, becoming more sullen and socially unresponsive over time (Campbell, Cohn, & Myers 1995; Field, 1995).

Why do expressions of anger and sadness increase with age? Learning and cognitive development probably play important roles. As young infants increasingly recognize that they can exert control over objects and people in their environment, they begin to react negatively to a loss of control or to people who are thwarting their objectives (Sullivan & Lewis, 2003). For example, the 2- to 6-month-olds who had previously been able to turn on the music by waving their arms often became angry (and sometimes saddened) when arm-waving would no longer play the tune (Lewis, Alessandri, & Sullivan, 1990; Sullivan, Lewis, & Alessandri, 1992). By age 3 to 4 months, infants expect caregivers to respond to their social overtures (Van Egeren, Barratt, & Roach, 2001), and violation of an infants' learned expectancies, as when a mother adopts a "still face" or is having a serious depressive episode, is often enough not only to distress an infant, but to sadden her as well. It is important to note that by 4 months of age (and possibly sooner), anger and sadness are clearly discrete emotions that convey different messages and have different psychophysiological consequences. For example, the anger that accompanies a baby's loss of control over a tune by arm movements is often accompanied by even more vigorous arm movements but few signs of adrenocortical activity (a physiological indicator of stress). These angered infants are behaving adaptively by trying to reestablish control. By contrast, infants who become saddened over a loss of control become *less* animated; they have essentially "given up," and their sadness is marked by an increase in adrenocortical indicators of stress (Lewis & Ramsey, 2005).

Fear and Fearful Reactions   Fear is one of the last primary emotions to emerge (Witherington, Campos, & Hertenstein, 2001). Young infants are occasionally startled by loud, unexpected noises or sudden changes in body position, but reactions that clearly indicate that an infant considers a person, object, or situation to be a distinct *threat* (and thus cause him to be fearful) begin to appear at 6 to 7 months of age.

There are two particular fears that most infants display between 7 and 8 months of age. To illustrate the first, imagine 8-month-old Billy sitting on the floor in the den as his mother leads a strange person into the room. The stranger suddenly walks closer, bends over, and says, "Hi, Billy! How are you?" If Billy is like many 8-month-olds, he may stare at the stranger for a moment and then turn away, whimper, and crawl toward his mother.

Box 4.1 Applying Developmental Research

Combating Stranger Anxiety: Some Helpful Hints for Doctors and Child-Care Professionals

It is not at all unusual for toddlers visiting the doctor's office to break into tears and to cling tenaciously to their parents. Some youngsters who remember previous visits may be suffering from "shot anxiety" rather than stranger anxiety, but many are simply reacting fearfully to the approach of an intrusive physician who may poke, prod, and handle them in ways that are atypical and upsetting. Fortunately, there are steps that caregivers and medical personnel (or any other stranger) can take to make such encounters less terrifying for an infant or toddler. What can we suggest?

1. *Keep familiar companions available.* Infants react much more negatively to strangers when they are separated from their mothers or other close companions. Indeed, most 6- to 12-month-olds are not particularly wary of an approaching stranger if they are sitting on their mothers' laps; however, they will frequently whimper and cry at the stranger's approach if seated only a few feet from their mothers (Morgan & Ricciuti, 1969; and see Bohlin & Hagekull, 1993). Clearly, doctors and nurses can expect a more constructive response from their youngest patients if they can avoid separating them from their caregivers.

2. *Arrange for companions to respond positively to the stranger.* Stranger anxiety is less likely to occur if the caregiver issues a warm greeting to the stranger or uses a positive tone of voice when talking to the infant about the stranger (Feinman, 1992). These actions permit the child to engage in *social referencing*

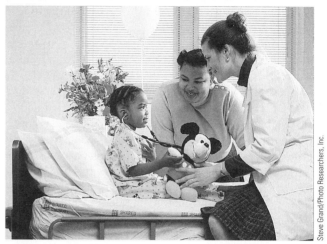

Most toddlers respond favorably to a friendly stranger—even a doctor—who offers a toy.

and to conclude that maybe the stranger really isn't all that scary if mom and dad seem to like him. It might not hurt, then, for medical personnel to strike up a pleasant conversation with the caregiver before directing their attention to the child.

---

stranger anxiety
a wary or fretful reaction that infants and toddlers often display when approached by an unfamiliar person.

This wary reaction to a stranger, or **stranger anxiety,** stands in marked contrast to the smiling, babbling, and other positive greetings that infants often display when approached by a familiar companion. Most infants react positively to strangers until they form their first emotional attachment, and then become apprehensive shortly thereafter (Schaffer & Emerson, 1964). Wary reactions to strangers—which are often mixed with signs of interest—peak at 8–10 months of age and gradually decline in intensity over the second year (Sroufe, 1977). However, even an 8- to 10-month-old is not afraid of every strange face she sees and may occasionally react rather positively to strangers. In Box 4.1, we will consider the circumstances under which stranger anxiety is most likely to occur and see how medical personnel and other child-care professionals might use this knowledge to head off outbreaks of fear and trembling in their offices.

Many infants who have formed emotional attachments also begin to display obvious signs of discomfort when separated from their mothers or other attachment objects. Ten-month-old Tony, for example, is likely to cry as he sees his mother put on a coat and pick up her purse as she prepares to go shopping, whereas 15-month-old Doris might even follow her mother to the door while whining and pleading not to be left at home. These reactions reflect the children's **separation anxiety.** Separation anxiety normally appears at 6–8 months of age, peaks at 14–18 months, and gradually becomes less frequent and less intense throughout infancy and the preschool period (Kagan, Kearsley, & Zelazo, 1978; Weinraub & Lewis, 1977). However, grade-school children and even adolescents may still show signs of anxiety or sadness when separated for long periods from their loved ones (Thurber, 1995).

separation anxiety
a wary or fretful reaction that infants and toddlers often display when separated from persons to whom they are attached.

Why do infants come to fear strangers and separations from primary caregivers and other close companions? And why do these concerns take six to eight months to emerge? Many theorists have speculated about these issues, and two viewpoints in particular have

3. *Make the setting more "familiar."* Stranger anxiety occurs less frequently in familiar settings than in unfamiliar ones. For example, few 10-month-olds are especially wary of strangers at home, but most react negatively to strange companions when tested in an unfamiliar laboratory (Sroufe, Waters, & Matas, 1974). Although it may be unrealistic to advise modern physicians to make home visits, they could make at least one of their examination rooms more homelike for young children, perhaps by placing an attractive mobile in one corner and posters of cartoon characters on the wall, or by having a stuffed toy or two available for the child to play with. The infant's familiarity with a strange setting also makes a difference: Whereas the vast majority (90 percent) of 10-month-olds become upset if a stranger approaches them within a minute after being placed in an unfamiliar room, only about half will react negatively to the stranger when they have had 10 minutes to grow accustomed to this setting (Sroufe, Waters, & Matas, 1974). Perhaps trips to the doctor would become more tolerable for an infant or toddler if medical personnel gave the child a few minutes to familiarize himself with the examination room before making their entrance.

4. *Be a sensitive, unobtrusive stranger.* Not surprisingly, an infant's response to a stranger depends on the stranger's behavior (Sroufe, 1977). The meeting is likely to go best if the stranger initially keeps his or her distance and then approaches slowly while smiling, talking, and offering a familiar toy or suggesting a familiar activity (Bretherton, Stolberg, & Kreye, 1981; Sroufe, 1977). It also helps if the stranger, like any sensitive caregiver, takes his or her cues from the infant (Mangelsdorf, 1992). Babies prefer strangers they can control! Intrusive strangers who approach quickly and force themselves on the child (for example, by trying to pick infants up before they have time to adjust) probably get the response they deserve.

5. *Try looking a little less strange to the child.* Stranger anxiety depends, in part, on the stranger's physical appearance. Jerome Kagan (1972) has argued that infants form mental representations, or *schemas,* for the faces that they encounter in daily life and are most likely to be afraid of people whose appearance is not easily assimilated into these existing schemas. So a doctor in a sterile white lab coat with a strange stethoscope around her neck (or a nurse with a pointed hat that may give her a "witchlike" look) can make infants and toddlers rather wary indeed! Pediatric professionals may not be able to alter various physical features (for example, a huge nose or a facial scar) that might make children wary; but they can and often do shed their strange instruments and white uniforms in favor of more "normal" attire that will help their youngest patients to recognize them as members of the human race. Babysitters with spiked hair or nose rings might also heed this advice if establishing rapport with their young companions is a priority.

received some empirical support. *Evolutionary theorists* (for example, Bowlby, 1973) claim that many situations that infants face qualify as *natural clues to danger*—situations that have been so frequently associated with danger throughout human evolutionary history that a fear or avoidance response has become biologically programmed. Among the situations that infants may be programmed to fear, once they can readily discriminate familiar objects and events from unfamiliar ones, are strange faces (which in earlier eras may have been predatory animals), strange settings, and the "strange" circumstance of being separated from familiar companions. Consistent with this evolutionary viewpoint, infants show more fearful reactions to separations and strangers in unfamiliar laboratory environments than they do at home; presumably the strangeness of a laboratory magnifies whatever apprehension infants ordinarily experience on encountering a stranger or having to endure a separation. The evolutionary viewpoint also explains an interesting cross-cultural variation in separation anxiety. Infants from many nonindustrialzed societies, who sleep with their mothers and are nearly always in close contact with them, begin to protest separations about two to three months earlier than Western infants do (Ainsworth, 1967). Why? Because these infants are so rarely apart from their caregivers that almost any separation is a very strange, fear-provoking event.

Cognitive-developmental theorists view stranger anxiety and separation anxiety as natural outgrowths of an infant's perceptual and cognitive development. Jerome Kagan (1972, 1976) suggests that 6- to 10-month-olds have finally developed stable schemes for (1) the faces of familiar companions and (2) these companions' probable whereabouts at home (if they are not present). Suddenly a strange face that is discrepant with the infants' schemes for caregivers *appears* and upsets children because they can't *explain* who this is or what has become of familiar caregivers. Kagan also proposes that 7- to 10-month-olds will not protest most separations at home because they have a pretty good idea where a caregiver has gone should he leave them in the living room and proceed to a familiar locale, such as the kitchen. But should a caregiver violate this "familiar faces in familiar places" scheme by lifting his briefcase and walking out the front door, an infant cannot easily account for his whereabouts and will probably fuss. Consistent with this notion, infants observed at home are more likely to protest when caregivers depart through an unfamiliar doorway (such as the entrance to the cellar) than through a familiar one (Littenberg, Tulkin, & Kagan, 1971); and a 9-month-old infant who has played quietly during a separation soon becomes extremely upset after looking for his mother and discovering she is not where he thought she was (Corter, Zucker, & Galligan, 1980).

In sum, stranger anxiety and separation anxiety are complex emotional reactions that may stem in part from an infant's general *apprehension of the unfamiliar* (the evolutionary viewpoint) and his inability to *explain* who a stranger may be or what has become of a familiar companion (the cognitive-developmental viewpoint). Yet it is important to note that infants vary dramatically in their responses to separations and strangers: Some are almost indifferent to these events, whereas others act as if they are terrified. Why the variations? As we will see later in this chapter and in Chapter 5, developmentalists believe that individual differences in fearfulness often reflect variations in (1) temperament or (2) the quality, or security, of infants' attachment relationships.

Development of Self-Conscious Emotions

From later in the second year until well into the third, infants begin to display such **secondary** or **complex emotions** as embarrassment, shame, guilt, envy, and pride. These emotional responses are often called **self-conscious emotions** because each involves some damage to or enhancement of the sense of self. Michael Lewis (1998) believes that embarrassment, the simplest self-conscious emotion, will not emerge until the child can recognize herself in a mirror or a photograph (a crucial self-referential milestone we touched on in Chapter 1 and will discuss in detail in Chapter 6), whereas *self-evaluative* emotions such as shame, guilt, and pride require both self-recognition *and* an understanding of rules and standards for evaluating one's conduct.

Most of the available evidence is consistent with Lewis's theory. For example, the only toddlers who became noticeably embarrassed by lavish praise or by requests to "show off" for strangers are those who display clear signs of self-recognition (Lewis, Stanger, & Sullivan, 1989). By about age 3, when children are better able to evaluate their performances as good or bad, they begin to show clear signs of *pride* (smiling, applauding, or shouting "I did it") when they succeed at a difficult task, as well as *shame* (a downward gaze with a slumped posture, often accompanied by statements such as "I'm no good at this") should they fail at a seemingly easy task (Lewis, Alessandri, & Sullivan, 1992; Stipek, Recchia, & McClintic, 1992). Preschool children may also show *evaluative embarrassment,* characterized by nervous smiles, self-touching, and gaze aversion, when they fail to complete a task in the allotted time or to otherwise match a standard (Alessandri & Lewis, 1996). Evaluative embarrassment stems from a negative *evaluation* of one's performance and is much more stressful than the "simple" embarrassment of being the object of others' attention (Lewis & Ramsay, 2002). Is evaluative embarrassment merely a milder form of shame? Possibly, although Lewis and Ramsay (2002) reported that preschoolers who experience evaluative embarrassment do *not* slump, turn their eyes downward, and turn down the corners of their mouth as children do when they feel ashamed; in fact, the 4-year-olds who failed to master a challenge in this study typically displayed either evaluative embarrassment or shame, but not both, thus suggesting that these are different emotions.

secondary (or complex) emotions
self-conscious or self-evaluative emotions that emerge in the second and third years and depend in part on cognitive development (sometimes called **self-conscious emotions**).

self-conscious emotions
see **secondary (or complex) emotions.**

Photo 4.2
By age 3, children are capable of evaluating their conduct and may experience such self-evaluative emotions as shame over a transgression or a personal failure.

Lori C. Diehl/PhotoEdit, Inc.

Other investigators make clear distinctions between shame and guilt. Guilt implies that we have in some way failed to live up to our obligations to other people; a child who feels guilty is likely to focus on the interpersonal consequences of his wrongdoing and may try to *approach* others to make reparations for his harmful acts (Higgins, 1987; M. L. Hoffman, 2000). By contrast, shame is more self-focused than based on a concern for others. Whether it stems from a moral transgression, personal failure, or a social blunder, shame causes children to focus (negatively) on themselves and may motivate them to hide out and *avoid* other people (Tangney & Dearing, 2002).

Parental Influence on Self-Conscious Emotions   Parents can clearly influence a child's susceptibility to particular self-conscious emotions. For example, Allessandri and Lewis (1996) observed mothers' reactions as their 4- and 5-year-olds succeeded or failed at a variety of puzzles. As expected, children generally showed some signs of pride over their successes and shame over their failures. Yet the amounts of pride and shame they displayed largely depended on their mothers' reactions to these outcomes. Mothers who accentuated the negative by being especially critical of failures tended to have children who displayed high levels of shame after a failure and little pride after successes. By contrast, mothers who were more inclined to react positively to successes had children who displayed more pride in their accomplishments and less shame on those occasions when they failed to achieve their objectives.

Consider another interesting parental influence. Clear rule-breaking and other moral transgressions have the potential to make children feel guilty, shameful, or both. But how parents react to transgressions may determine whether children feel guilty or shameful. Children are more inclined to feel ashamed if parents belittle *them* (Claire, you are so *bad, stupid, thoughtless,* and so on), whereas they are more likely to feel guilty rather than shameful if parents criticize their *inappropriate behavior* by emphasizing why it was wrong and how it may have harmed others, while encouraging them to do what they can to repair any harm they've done (M. L. Hoffman, 2000; Tangney & Dearing, 2002).

Initially, toddlers and young preschool children are most likely to display self-evaluative emotions when an adult is present to observe their conduct (Harter & Whitesell, 1989; Stipek, Recchia, & McClintic, 1992). As Michael Lewis (1998) points out, young children's initial self-evaluations may reflect how they think they will be evaluated by parents or other important persons in their lives. In fact, many children may be well into the elementary school years before they fully internalize very many rules or evaluative standards and come to feel especially prideful, shameful, or guilty about their conduct in the absence of external surveillance (Bussey, 1992; Harter & Whitesell, 1989).

Later Developments in Emotional Expressivity

The majority of distinct or discrete emotions have appeared, at least in rudimentary form, over the first few years of life. What changes most dramatically in childhood are the situations or events that trigger various emotions. For example, we will see in Chapters 7 and 8 that the causes of children's anxieties and fears shift from threats (real or imagined) that they cannot explain or cope with directly to important real-life issues such as meeting academic challenges or establishing good relations with and gaining acceptance from peers. In Chapter 9, we will see how changes in children's social-cognitive abilities influence the circumstances that are likely to anger them and provoke aggressive responses. And in Chapter 10, we will explore how children gradually acquire a greater capacity to experience such complex emotions as pride, guilt, shame, and genuine concern for others' welfare as they internalize more and more rules, ethical principles, and performance standards and increasingly come to monitor and evaluate their own (and others') conduct.

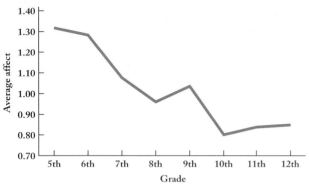

Figure 4.3
Average affect displayed by preadolescents and adolescents over an 8-year period. Notice that although the average valance of emotions declines between 5th and 10th grades, it remains a positive number. This means that the typical adolescent is more often in a positive mood than a negative one. (From Larson et al., 2002.)

One change in emotional life that deserves comment here is the common assumption that developing persons become increasingly moody and show a dramatic increase in negative emotions as they reach sexual maturity and make the transition from childhood to adolescence. There is some support for the notion that daily experience of emotion becomes somewhat more negative and somewhat less positive from early to mid-adolescence, particularly among young adolescents who describe themselves as lonely, low in self-esteem, or who display minor conduct disorders (Collins & Steinberg, 2006; Schneiders et al., 2006). However, this downward trend in "mood" has generally leveled off by mid-adolescence (Larson & Lampman-Petraitis, 1989; Larson et al., 2002; see Figure 4.3) and becomes more positive once again in early adulthood and beyond (Carstensen et al., 2000; Mroczek & Kolarz, 1998). Although the vast majority of adolescents manage these changes in emotionality quite well and remain well adjusted, bouts of serious and subclinical depression do increase early in adolescence (Wichstrom, 1999), affecting as many as 15-20 percent of teenagers in one study (Hankin et al., 1998), with more girls than boys showing elevated depressive symptomotology (Hankin, Mermelstein, & Roesch, 2007; Twenge & Nolen-Hoeksma, 2002).

Why might young adolescents suddenly experience more negative emotions? Physiological and hormonal changes that accompany sexual maturation may contribute something to increased moodiness and restlessness (Buchanan, Eccles, & Becker, 1992; Udry, 1990). However, many researchers believe that a dramatic increase in daily hassles with parents, teachers, and peers is primarily responsible for the less positive trend in emotional experience early in adolescence. Consistent with this life stress perspective, conflicts between parents and their children about personal responsibilities and self-governance issues peak in early to mid-adolescence and gradually decline in frequency over the teenage years (Laursen, Coy, & Collins, 1998; Smetana & Gaines, 1999). Thus, as hassles within the family decline, the downward trend in adolescent emotions levels off. And in their recent longitudinal study, Reed Larson and his associates (2002) found that life stress was a good predictor of adolescent affect: At any given age, the adolescents who were experiencing more life stress reported less favorable daily emotional experiences (see also Schneiders et al., 2006).

Not surprisingly, elevated levels of stress (of many kinds) are also major contributors to the negative affect of adolescents who become seriously depressed. Indeed, girls may be more susceptible than boys to depression for two reasons. In a recent diary study, 13- to 15-year-old girls (1) not only reported *more* stressful experiences with family members, peers, and romantic partners than boys did, but (2) they also reacted more negatively to these kinds of stressors as well, particularly to the hassles they experienced with peers (Hankin, Mermestein, & Roesch, 2007). From early in the preschool period, girls are quicker than boys to emphasize the importance of maintaining harmonious relationships with their playmates and other peer associates (see Chapter 8 for an extended discussion). And given this orientation, hassles with friends and other peer acquaintances may simply be more noticeable and/or more disturbing to girls, thus contributing in part to their greater susceptibility to depressed affect.

⌒ IDENTIFYING AND UNDERSTANDING OTHERS' EMOTIONS

As children mature, they not only experience and display a wider variety of emotions, but they also become much better at recognizing others' feelings and at properly interpreting the causes and the functions served by their own and others' displays of emotion. Acquiring knowledge about emotions is an important developmental hurdle that enables us to infer how people are feeling and tailor our behavior to achieve our objectives (for example, displaying compassion, rather than joy or anger, toward a companion who is distressed). As we will see, children's understanding of emotions is tenuous at best in infancy and toddlerhood but develops very rapidly during the preschool and grade-school years.

Early Identification and Interpretion of Emotions

When do infants first notice and respond to the emotional expressions of other people? Surprising as it may seem, they are prepared to react to certain vocal signals at birth or shortly thereafter. In Box 3.1, for example, we learned that newborns who hear another infant cry will soon begin to cry themselves, thus showing their responsiveness to the distress of another baby. Over the first year, parents the world over speak to infants in high-pitched tones that are acoustic concomitants of positive emotions such as happiness (Fernald & Mazzie, 1991; Grieser & Kuhl, 1988), and even 2-day-old infants pay more attention to this highly intonated speech than to the "flatter" speech that adults use when communicating with each other (Kaplan et al., 1996).

Currently there is some debate about when babies begin to recognize and interpret the facial expressions of emotion that others display. Although 3-month-olds prefer to look at photos of happy faces rather than photos of neutral, sad, or angry ones (La Barbera et al., 1976; Kuchuk, Vibbert, & Bornstein, 1986), their looking preferences may simply reflect their powers of visual discrimination and do not necessarily imply that infants this young interpret various expressions as "happy," "angry," or "sad." Yet there is some evidence to suggest that young infants do attend carefully and *react appropriately* to more natural displays of emotion. For example, 3-month-olds will not only discriminate their mothers' happy, sad, or angry expressions when these facial configurations are accompanied by a happy, sad, or angry tone of voice, but they also become rather gleeful in response to a happy expression and distressed by their mothers' anger or sadness (Haviland & Lelwica, 1987). By 4 months of age, infants can discriminate changes in a *stranger's* naturalistic displays of emotion (a happy person becoming sad, for example), and by age 7 months, they not only discriminate others' simple emotions on the basis of only one kind of sensory imput (vocal cues or facial expressions, for example) (Flom & Bahrick, 2007), but show different patterns of brain wave activity (ERPs) to photos posing different emotions (Leppanen et al., 2007). Interestingly, 7-month-olds, who have just begun to experience and express fear themselves, now look longer at and show stronger ERPs to fearful rather than happy or neutral faces (Leppanen et al., 2007), perhaps implying that there is something about a fearful face that is of special significance. So, are 7-month-olds on the verge of actually *interpreting* the meaning or personal relevance of others' emotional displays?

Social Referencing Infants' ability to interpret particular emotional expressions does become more obvious between ages 7 and 10 months (Soken & Pick, 1999)—the point at which they begin to monitor their parents' emotional reactions to uncertain situations and to use this information to regulate their own behavior (Feinman, 1992). This **social referencing** becomes more common with age (Walden & Baxter, 1989) and soon extends to people other than parents. By the end of the first year, for example, infants will typically approach and play with unfamiliar toys if a nearby stranger is smiling but are apt to avoid these objects if the stranger displays a fearful expression (Klinnert et al., 1986). In one recent study, 12-month-old infants even social referenced from a televised segment, avoiding and reacting negatively themselves to presentation of an object that had elicited a fearful reaction from an adult on TV (Mumme & Fernald, 2003). Interestingly, 12-month-olds display stronger ERPs to an adults' display of negative rather than positive emotions in social referencing situations (Carver & Vaccaro, 2007), and vocal expressions of emotion

social referencing
the use of others' emotional expressions to gain information or infer the meaning of otherwise ambiguous situations.

seem to convey as much or more information to a 12-month-old as facial expressions do (Mumme, Fernald, & Herrera, 1996). Some investigators have wondered whether adult emotional signals might not be best interpreted as simple commands that infants respond to (for example, "don't touch") rather than as active information seeking on the infant's part (Baldwin & Moses, 1996). One line of evidence consistent with this interpretation is a recent study in which 18-month-olds watched an experimenter either become angry or remain neutral after a third party had performed an interesting action (pulling a toy apart). Although witnessing this scene had little effect on the emotions of the infant-observers, they were much less inclined to imitate the actors' behavior in the presence of the experimenter who had become angry, as if they were using the experimenter's angry emotions as a cue that "pulling the toy apart is a forbidden act that I should not perform" (Repacholi & Meltzoff, 2007). Yet social referencing in older toddlers is often more easily interpreted as active information seeking on a child's part rather than a simple response to a command or a directive. For example, toddlers will often look to their companions *after* they have approached or avoided a new object or situation, thereby suggesting that they are now using others' emotional reactions as information to assess the merits or accuracy of their own appraisals (Hornik & Gunner, 1988).

Emotions, Emotional Understanding, and Early Social Development Although infants only display primary emotions throughout the first year and have only a primitive understanding of others' feelings, let's recognize that their emotional capabilities are very important contributors to early social development. Clearly, a baby's displays of emotion serve a *communicative* function that is likely to affect the behavior of caregivers. For example, cries of distress summon close companions. Early suggestions of a smile or expressions of interest may convince caregivers that their babies are willing and even eager to strike up a social relationship with them. Later expressions of fear or sadness may indicate that the infant is insecure or feeling blue and needs some attention or comforting. Anger may imply that the infant wishes her companions to cease whatever they are doing that is upsetting her, whereas joy serves as a prompt for caregivers to prolong an ongoing interaction or perhaps signals the baby's willingness to accept new challenges. So infant emotions are adaptive in that they promote social contact and help caregivers to adjust their behavior to the infant's needs and goals. Stated another way, the emotional expressions of infancy help nonlinguistic infants and their close companions to communicate and "get to know each other" (Tronick, 1989).

   At the same time, the infant's emerging ability to recognize and interpret others' emotions is an important achievement that enables him to infer how he should be feeling or behaving in a variety of situations. The beauty of this "social referencing" is that children can quickly acquire *knowledge* in this way. For example, a sibling's joyful reaction to the family dog should indicate that this "ball of fur" is a friend rather than an unspeakable monster. A mothers' pained expression and accompanying vocal concern might immediately suggest that the knife in one's hand is an implement to be avoided. And given the frequency with which expressive caregivers direct an infant's attention to important aspects of the environment or display their feelings about an infant's appraisal of objects and events, it is likely that the information contained in their emotional displays will contribute in a major way to the child's understanding of the world in which he lives (Rosen, Adamson, & Bakeman, 1992).

Later Developments in Identifying Others' Emotions

Before age 3, children are notoriously bad at identifying and labeling the emotional expressions posed by people in pictures or on puppets' faces (see Widen & Russell, 2003, for a review). In fact, they often fail to label others' facial expressions or use the label "happy" to characterize most emotions. This may simply reflect the fact that 2- to 3-year-olds have not acquired (or cannot retrieve) the words to label various emotions, because even 18-month-olds can draw some appropriate behavioral inferences from others' emotional expressions. In a study by Repacholi and Gopnik (1997), for example, 18-month-olds who earlier saw a woman express *disgust* at the thought of eating crackers knew enough to understand that she would prefer raw vegetables to the crackers that they personally favored when offered a choice between these snacks.

Between ages 3 and 5, children become better and better at correctly identifying and labeling the simple emotions on people's (or puppets') faces (Laible, 2004b; Widen & Russell, 2003). Three-year-olds are likely to correctly label happy expressions but will often use the label "happy" to describe other positive emotions such as surprise. Between ages 3 and 4 children begin to rely on the labels "sad" (or "mad") to characterize negative emotions, with "scared" (the label used for fear) becoming more common and applied more appropriately by 4- and 5-year-olds (Widen & Russell, 2003). Yet even 5-year-olds rarely used the labels "surprised" or "disgusted" to characterize emotions—these emotions, and the more complex ones such as pride, shame, and guilt are not correctly labeled until the early to middle grade-school years.

However, it is important to note that facial cues are not the only information that children use to recognize others' emotions. Thomas Boone and Joseph Cunningham (1998) exposed 4-, 5-, and 8-year-olds to adults dancing with expressive bodily movements that might suggest that they were happy, sad, angry, or fearful. Even 5-year-olds could tell from expressive movements which of the dancers was the sad, fearful, or happy one, and 8-year-olds were as skilled as adults, correctly identifying all four emotions implied by the dancers' expressive movements.

Understanding the Causes of Emotions

Over the preschool and early grade-school years, children show rapid advances in their ability to identify the emotions that other people are likely to feel in particular situations. A common method for assessing children's understanding of the causes of emotions is to expose them to short stories that are accompanied by pictures or drawings, such as those in Figure 4.4, and to ask them to describe or pick out a face showing how the story character feels. Even 3-year-olds are good at recognizing that positive events such as a birthday party are likely to evoke happiness, and by age 4, they recognize that events such as one's dog running away are likely to make a character feel sad (Denham, Zoller, & Couchoud, 1994; Michalson & Lewis, 1985). Yet children are often not very good at identifying situations likely to evoke anger, fear, surprise, or disgust until very late in the preschool or into the early elementary-school years.

However, some investigators believe that the story-telling methodology may underestimate preschool children's understanding of the negative emotions of people they know. Richard Fabes and his associates (1988, 1991), for example, found that 3- to 5-year-olds actually had a better understanding of day-care classmates' *negative* emotions (that is, distress, anger, and so on) than their positive emotions (that is, happy displays). This finding might be expected from other research showing that when parents of 2- to 5-year-olds discuss emotions with their children, they talk much more about the causes of negative emotions than about the causes of positive emotions (Lagattuta & Wellman, 2002). But even though there is some disagreement about whether children know more about positive than about negative emotions early on, virtually everyone agrees that (1) children learn a great deal about the causes of all primary emotions during the preschool period, but (2) it may be well into the late-elementary-school or middle-school years before they are proficient at telling us the situations and circumstances likely to evoke pride, guilt, shame, envy, jealousy, and other *complex* emotions (Saarni, Mumme, & Campos, 1998).

Figure 4.4 A measure of children's ability to recognize others' emotions. Children are told short stories, each of which is accompanied by a drawing to match the story. The child's task is to identify the emotion the story character might be experiencing. (Adapted from Michalson & Lewis, 1985.)

Birthday party

Mother with pink hair

Dog runs away

Awful-tasting food

Sister knocks over tower of blocks

Lost in a grocery store

Other Milestones in Emotional Understanding Interestingly, even 4- and 5-year-olds know that a persons' current feelings (particularly negative emotions such as sadness) may stem from reflections on past events (Lagattuta & Wellman, 2001). In one study, children heard a story about a girl named Mary whose pet rabbit was chased away by a dog, never to be seen again. Much later, Mary sees something to remind her of her rabbit (for example, a photo of the rabbit or of the offending dog), and children were asked, "Why is Mary now feeling sad?" Very few of the 3-year-olds, but more then 80 percent of the 4-year-olds and 100 percent of the 5-year-olds, realized that the present reminder of her rabbit caused Mary to think about the rabbit's previous disappearance and to become saddened again about that unhappy event (Laguttuta, Wellman, & Flavell, 1997).

As grade-school children become better at using personal, situational, and historical information to understand and interpret emotions, they achieve several important breakthroughs in emotional understanding. For example, between ages 5 and 7, children understand that they can feel two compatible emotions at the same time (for example, "I am happy to be at Disneyland and excited about meeting Mickey Mouse") (Harter, 1999), and by age 8, they recognize that the same situation (for example, the rapid approach of a big friendly dog) may elicit very different emotions (fear versus joy) from different individuals (Gnepp & Klayman, 1992). And between the ages of 6 and 10, children begin to acknowledge that they or people they know can have positive and negative (that is, mixed) feelings about the same situation (for example, John's happy to be at the party but sad that Henry wasn't invited) (Brown & Dunn, 1996; Harter, 1999).

Age differences in children's understanding of mixed emotions is relevant to many areas of social development, including moral development. Consider a situation in which a child kicks his ball into a busy street and then runs to retrieve it, despite having been told that he is *never* to run into the street. When asked how this child would feel under these circumstances, 4- and 5-year-olds typically say he feels good (his desire to retrieve the ball was fulfilled) rather than bad (about having violated a prohibition). By contrast, 7-year-olds are more inclined to acknowledge the character's experience of mixed emotions, saying that although he might feel good about retrieving the ball, this emotion would likely be overshadowed by negative feelings about having broken a rule and doing something that could have proved harmful (Lagattuta, 2005). This acknowledgment of mixed emotions implies a stronger respect for rules and obligations among older children, as well as knowledge that compliance with or violations of rules can have a strong impact on such moral emotions as pride, shame, and guilt (see Chapter 10 for an in-depth analysis of moral development).

Notice that many of these later advances in emotional understanding emerge at about the same age that children can integrate more than one piece of information (for example, height and width of a column of liquid) in Piagetian conservation tasks, and they may depend in part on the same underlying cognitive developments. However, social experiences are also important. Jane Brown and Judy Dunn (1996), for example, found that 6-year-olds who show an early understanding of conflicting emotions have often discussed the causes of emotions with their parents earlier in childhood. Apparently, these discussions prepared them to analyze mixed feelings that might have arisen from squabbles with siblings and peers.

Let's now consider how parents might contribute to young children's understanding of emotions.

Parental Contributions to Early Emotional Understanding

In recent years, it has become increasingly apparent that conversations between parents and children about emotions and their causes play a crucial role in fostering children's emotional understanding, beginning in infancy when children start to talk about their feelings. For example, mothers may often talk about *desires* their toddlers express ("I know you want a cookie, Todd") and about the emotions that accompany the thwarting or fulfillment of these desires ("I'm sorry you are sad, but no cookies before dinner"; "You'll be happy later when we have cookies for dessert"), thereby linking the child's goal achievements or blockages with particular emotional consequences. Indeed, 15-month-olds whose mothers often use this kind of "desire" language when conversing with them are, by age 2, already better

Photo 4.3
Conversations about the emotional consequences of toddlers' thwarted and fulfilled desires foster early emotional understanding.

Michael Newman/PhotoEdit, Inc.

at recognizing the emotions of story characters than are age-mates whose mothers have talked less frequently about the emotional consequences of fulfilled and thwarted desires earlier in infancy (Taumoepean & Ruffman, 2006).

Emotional dialogues with children become much richer throughout the preschool period, due in part to children's rapidly increasing linquistic capabilities and growing interest in emotional experiences. By discussing the emotions of storybook characters with young children or encouraging them to reminisce about their own memorable emotional experiences, parents are teaching children to recognize discrete emotions, understand the events that caused these emotions, and learn the circumstances under which it is acceptable or unacceptable to express particular emotions (Laible, 2004a). These kinds of conversations should remind us of Vygotsky's ideas about the social construction of new knowledge through a process in which an older, more knowledgeable person scaffolds an interaction—in this case, a dialogue about emotions—in such a way as to further a child's attention, recollection, and understanding of salient emotional events.

However, parents clearly differ in how they choose to talk about emotions. Some use a highly *elaborative* style in which they frequently ask their children open-ended questions about the emotions of storybook characters or provide ample background information and pose open-ended questions when conversing with their children about past events that have evoked noteworthy emotions. Other parents are far less elaborative in their emotional dialogues; they are more inclined to simply read stories without commenting on characters' emotions and are likely to ask simple yes-no questions about their children's emotional experiences (for example, "You were scared at the zoo, weren't you?") rather than open-ended questions that require a child to provide a more detailed analysis and interpretation of his or her feelings. Does discourse style matter? Yes, indeed! Three- to 5-year-olds whose mothers use a more elaborative style are much better able to recognize and discriminate others' facial expressions of emotion and are better at predicting how a puppet will react emotionally to particular events (for example, going to a movie, being approached by a big, but friendly dog) compared to age-mates whose mothers have been less elaborative when discussing emotions (Laible, 2004b).

So it seems that parents do contribute to advances in their children's emotional understanding early in life (see also Denham & Auerbach, 1995; Laible & Thompson, 2000) and that highly elaborative conversations that stimulate the child to think about and analyze her emotions (and allow the more knowledgeable adult to correct misconceptions) is a particularly effective method of emotional socialization.

LEARNING TO REGULATE EMOTIONS

emotional self-regulation
the process of adjusting one's emotions to appropriate levels of intensity in order to accomplish one's goals.

From infancy onward, an ability to successfully regulate one's emotions is a tremendously important skill that is not only crucial to achieving one's personal objectives but will also affect the character of social interactions a person is likely to have and the kinds of social relationships and alliances she is likely to form. **Emotional self-regulation** involves the capacity to control emotions and to adjust emotional arousal to an appropriate level of intensity to achieve one's aims. Appropriate regulation of emotion involves the abilities to manage our feelings, our physiological reactions associated with these feelings, our emotion-related cognitions (for example, thoughts about how the situation producing the emotion should be interpreted), and our emotion-related behavior (for example, the facial expressions we display). Consider an example of a situation calling for emotional regulation which illustrates all these regulatory components:

Billy skins his knee after he is knocked down by Sean, one of his bigger and tougher classmates. It is unclear exactly why this happened, but it could have been unintentional. Nevertheless,

Billy's first reaction is anger. He hopes to avoid a fight but still wants to let Sean know that he has done some harm through his carelessness and should pay more attention to what he is doing. To successfully accomplish these goals, Billy may have to dampen his anger (regulate feelings) and his arousal (regulate physiology) to stay focused on the idea that the harm done may have been an accident (regulate emotion-related cognitions) that does not call for harsh words and angry facial expressions (regulate emotion-relevant behavior) that could provoke the fight Billy is hoping to avoid.

This particular regulatory challenge is one that would be much too difficult for toddlers, most preschoolers, and many early-elementary-school children, let alone infants, who quickly become emotionally aroused by a multitude of events and experiences (for example, hunger, gas, pain, loud noises) and must rely on caregivers to soothe and settle them. Clearly, the emergence of emotional self-regulation is a long and involved process that is heavily influenced by lessons learned both within and outside the home.

Early Socialization of Emotional Self-Regulation

In the first few months of life, it is caregivers who regulate babies' emotional arousal by controlling their exposure to events likely to overstimulate them, and by rocking, stroking, holding, singing, or providing pacifiers to their overaroused infants (Campos, 1989; Jahromi, Putnam, & Stifter, 2004; Rock, Trainer, & Addison, 1999). But by the middle of the first year, babies are making some progress at regulating their negative emotions. Six-months-olds, for example, do manage to reduce at least some of their negative arousal by turning their bodies away from unpleasant stimuli or by seeking objects to suck, such as their thumbs or a pacifier (Mangelsdorf, Shapiro, & Marzolf, 1995). These self-initiated actions are particularly effective at reducing distress when mothers notice them and offer their own comforting to draw their babies' attention away from the source of discomfort (Crockenberg & Leerkes, 2004). Interestingly, 6-month-old boys find it harder than 6-month-old girls to regulate unpleasant arousal and are more inclined than girls are to emit negative emotions to elicit regulatory support (soothing) from caregivers (Weinberg et al., 1999).

Parents are much quicker to regulate an infant's negative emotions than her positive ones, which they typically enjoy and try to promote (Denham, 1998). Consider that when mothers play with 7-month-old infants, they restrict themselves mainly to displays of joy, interest, and surprise, thus serving as models of positive emotions for their babies (Malatesta & Haviland, 1982). Mothers also respond selectively to their infants' emotions; over the first several months, they become increasingly attentive to babies' expressions of interest or surprise and less responsive to the infant's negative emotions (Malatesta et al., 1986). Through basic learning processes, then, babies are being trained to display more pleasant faces and fewer unpleasant ones—and they do just that over time.

However, the emotions that are considered socially acceptable may be quite different in one culture than in another. American parents love to stimulate their babies until they reach peaks of delight. By contrast, caregivers among the Gusii and the Aka tribes of central Africa rarely take part in face-to-face play with their babies, seeking instead to keep young infants as calm and contented as possible (Hewlett et al., 1998; LeVine et al., 1994). So American babies learn that intense displays of emotion are okay *as long as they are positive,* whereas Gusii and Aka babies learn to restrain both positive and negative emotions.

By the end of the first year, infants develop other strategies for reducing negative arousal, such as rocking themselves, chewing on objects, and moving away from people or events that upset them (Mangelsdorf, Shapiro, & Marzolf, 1995). And by age 18–24 months, toddlers are now more likely to try to control the actions of people or objects (for example, mechanical toys) that upset them (Mangelsdorf, Shapiro, & Marzolf, 1995), and they are beginning to cope with frustrations of having to wait for snacks or gifts by talking to companions, playing with toys, or otherwise distracting themselves from the source of their disappointments (Grolnick, Bridges, & Connell, 1996). In fact, toddlers this young have even been observed to knit their brows or to compress their lips as they actively attempt to suppress their anger or sadness (Malatesta et al., 1989). Yet even 18-month old toddlers have a very difficult time regulating any *fear* they may experience (Buss & Goldsmith, 1998); instead, fearful toddlers often develop styles of emotional expression that are more likely to attract attention and soothing from caregivers (Horstmann, 2003). Consider, for example, that when 2-year-olds are made angry (by having a toy snatched away, for instance) or fearful (by the approach of a stranger), they often choose not to express the anger or fear they are actually experiencing, but turn to a caregiver and look *sad*, which is more successful at eliciting regulatory support (Buss & Kiel, 2004).

Emerging Cognitive Strategies for Regulating Emotions

By 18–24 months of age, toddlers begin to talk about emotions, and these conversations about the causes and consequences of their own and others' emotions contribute greatly to their emotional understanding and to their emotional self-regulation. Interestingly, parents talk just as much about positive emotions as about negative emotions to their 2- to 5-year-olds, although discussions about negative emotions center more heavily on their causes, their relationships to other mental states and goals, and on regulating issues (Lagattuta & Wellman, 2002). Preschoolers, then, are continuing to learn about the importance of controlling intense negative emotions, which are disruptive and unpleasant and may adversely affect their interactions with parents, siblings, and other playmates, thereby interfering with the accomplishment of personal or social goals.

Conversations about emotions with parents often help preschool children develop cognitive strategies for emotional self-regulation. One common approach that parents take is to instruct children to distract themselves from stressors they cannot control by focusing attention on something more pleasant (for example, telling a child about to receive an

Photo 4.4
Family conversations about emotional experiences help young children to better understand their own and other people's feelings.

Jeff Greenberg/Stock Boston

inoculation to look at a brightly colored poster on the wall) or by otherwise helping them to understand frightening, frustrating, or disappointing experiences (Thompson, 1994, 1998). These supportive interventions are a form of guided instruction of the kind that Vygotsky wrote about—experiences that should help preschoolers to devise their own effective strategies for regulating emotions. Indeed, 3- to 6-year-olds do become better and better at coping with unpleasant emotional arousal through such cognitive strategies as directing their attention away from frightening events ("I scared of shark [Jaws]. Close my eyes!"), by thinking pleasant thoughts to overcome unpleasant ones ("Mommy left me, but when she comes back, we're going to the movies"), and by reinterpreting the cause of their distress in a more satisfying way ("He [movie actor] didn't die . . . it's just pretend"). (Thompson, 1994; see also Carrick & Quas, 2006).

Although we have been talking as if competent regulation of emotions involves the suppression of feelings and emotionally-relevant behaviors, adaptive regulation may sometimes involve maintaining or *intensifying* one's emotions rather than suppressing them. For example, children may learn that *conveying* their anger helps them to stand up to a bully (Thompson, 1994). And as we will see in Chapter 10, parents often call attention to (and thereby seek to maintain) the uneasiness young children experience after causing another person distress or breaking a rule. Why? Because they hope to persuade youngsters to *reinterpret* these feelings in ways that cause them (1) to *sympathize* with victims of distress and to act on this concern or (2) to feel *guilty* about their transgressions and become less inclined to repeat them (Dunn, Brown, & Macguire, 1995; Kochanska, 1991).

Another form of emotional arousal that we may seek to maintain or enhance is pride in our accomplishments—an important contributor to a healthy sense of achievement motivation and to the development of a positive academic self-concept (see Chapter 7 for further discussion of this point). So effective regulation of emotions involves an ability to suppress, maintain, or even intensify our emotional arousal in order to remain productively engaged with the challenges we face or the people we encounter (Buss & Goldsmith, 1998; Thompson, 1994).

Learning and Abiding by Emotional Display Rules

Each society has a set of **emotional display rules** that specify the circumstances under which various emotions should or should not be expressed. Children in many cultures, for example, learn that they are supposed to express happiness or gratitude when they receive a gift from grandma and, by all means, to suppress any disappointment they may feel should the gift turn out to be underwear. These emotional "codes of conduct" are rules that children must acquire and use in order to get along with other people and to maintain their approval.

An ability to dampen specific emotions is obviously an important skill that children must acquire to comply with a culture's display rules. But such compliance also requires a little deception or faking, as well. That is, a display rule may require us not only to suppress whatever unacceptable emotions we are actually experiencing but also to *replace* them (outwardly, at least) with whatever emotion the display rule calls for in that situation (for example, acting happy rather than sad upon receiving underwear as a birthday gift).

By about age 3, children are beginning to show some limited ability to hide their true feelings. Michael Lewis and his associates (Lewis, Stanger, and Sullivan, 1989), for example, found that 3-year-olds who had lied about peeking at a forbidden toy showed subtle signs of anguish (detectable on film played in slow motion); however, they were able to mask their feelings well enough to make it impossible for uninformed adult judges to discriminate them from other children who truthfully reported that they hadn't peeked. With each passing year, preschool children become a little better at posing outward expressions that differ from their inner feelings (Peskin, 1992; Ruffman et al., 1993). Still, even 5-year-olds are not especially skilled at disguising their true emotions or at convincing others who may be skeptical that their lies are true (Polak & Harris, 1999).

Throughout the grade-school years, children become increasingly aware of socially sanctioned display rules, learning more and more about which emotions to express (and which to suppress) in particular social situations (Jones, Abbey, & Cumberland, 1998; Zeman & Shipman, 1997). Perhaps because parents place stronger pressures on girls to "act nice" in social situations, girls are both more motivated and more skilled at complying with display rules than boys are (Davis, 1995). Furthermore, mothers who emphasize positive emotions and who deemphasize negative feelings in their parent-child interactions tend to have children who are better able to mask disappointment and other negative emotions (Garner & Power, 1996; Jones, Abbey, & Cumberland, 1998). By contrast, children who are exposed to frequent displays of negative emotion at home, whether it is directed at them or not,

emotional display rules
culturally defined rules specifying which emotions should or should not be expressed under which circumstances.

Box 4.2 Cultural Influences

Cultural Differences in the Expressions of Anger and Shame

Recently, Pamela Cole, Carole Bruschi, and Babu Tamang (2002) reported a cross-cultural study comparing how children in three cultures—the United States, the Brahman of Nepal, and the Tamang of Nepal—react to unpleasant situations that have the potential to elicit anger or shame. The two Nepalese cultural groups are often described as *collectivistic:* They stress the importance of respecting authority, maintaining social harmony, and subordinating individual aims and goals in the interest of promoting group welfare. Within these cultures, experience and expression of shame acknowledges one's wrongdoing and willingness to submit to authority for the greater good of the group. Anger, on the other hand, is discouraged in Asian collectivist societies because it signals self-assertion and threatens authority and social harmony. By contrast, U.S. children live in an *individualistic* society that values individual autonomy, self-expression, and the pursuit of individual goals. American society is more tolerant of anger expressed in the interest of self-assertion and protection of individual rights, provided that it is expressed in socially acceptable (that is, nonhostile) ways. Shame on the other hand, is often viewed by Americans as harmful to one's self-esteem and thus is not as highly valued as it is in collectivist cultures.

Do these broad cultural values influence the reaction of children to difficult situations that have the potential to elicit anger or shame? To find out, Cole and her associates provided 8- to 12-year-old Brahman, Tamang, and American grade-school children with stories to think about. Here is one example:

You are doing your homework. Your father is sitting next to you. You want to use the eraser and you see it by his hand.

You take the eraser and your father slaps your hand and says, "Don't grab things—wait until I am finished!"

Having heard each story, children were asked how they would feel if the situation had happened to them and what feelings they would express outwardly. They answered by picking among schematic drawings of faces expressing anger, shame, happiness, and a neutral expression (called "okay").

In examining an interesting pattern of results, we'll focus on the shame and anger expressed by the oldest (11- to 12-year-old) participants in each culture—that is, children who had more time to assimilate their culture's emotional display rules. As revealed in the accompanying figure, U.S. children were much more likely to express anger in response to these difficult situations than were children from either of the Nepalese collectivist groups. Tamang youngsters were relatively high in expression of shame, and Brahman children expressed very little anger or shame (or any other emotion) in response to the same story situations. When explaining their responses, a typical reaction of an angry U.S. child was to exclaim, "You can have the eraser but you don't need to *hit* me!" More shameful Tamang children typically said something like, "Why be angry?" as they acknowledged self-blame for acting inappropriately ("I snatched the eraser"). By contrast, Brahman children, who said they would not act angry or shameful, typically felt angry themselves but said it is wrong to display anger in the eraser story because "Father gave me life. [I should] just sit quietly."

Why did the Tamang children from Nepal show more shame than Brahman Nepalese age-mates? Follow-up in-home

---

often display high levels of negative emotionality themselves that they are not very good at regulating (Davies & Cummings, 1994; Eisenberg, Gershoff et al., 2001; Jenkins et al., 2005; Maughan & Cicchetti, 2002; Paulussen-Hoogeboom et al., 2007).

Yet even under the best of circumstances, simple display rules often take some time to master fully. As we see in Figure 4.5, many 7- to 9-year-olds (especially boys) are still unable to hide all their disappointment and act thrilled about receiving a lousy gift. And many 12- and 13-year-olds will fail to suppress all their anger when taunted by a peer (Underwood et al., 1999) or when their plans are thwarted by a respected adult exercising authority (Underwood, Coie, & Herbsman, 1992).

Compliance with culturally specified rules for displaying emotions occurs earlier and is especially strong among collectivist peoples such as the Japanese or the Brahman people of Nepal—cultures that suppress individualism, stress the importance of maintaining social harmony, and place the needs of the social order above those of individuals (Cole & Tamang, 1998). And as we see in Box 4.2, there is considerable variation across cultures in the particular emotions that children are permitted to express and are expected to inhibit. But regardless of the specific display rules a culture prescribes, these guidelines for appropriate emotional expression help developing persons to "fit in" and thus work for the good of society. Even in *individualistic* societies such as the United States, in which children have considerable freedom to express a broad range of emotions, a growing compliance with emotional display rules is largely motivated by a desire to maintain others' approval and to avoid

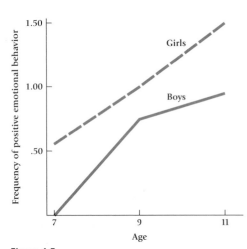

Figure 4.5
With age, children are more able to display positive emotional reactions after receiving a disappointing gift. (Based on C. Saarni, 1984.)

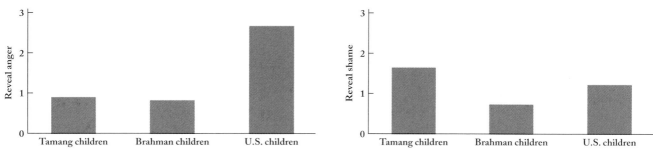

Cultural differences in the expression of anger and shame in response to unpleasant situations that could elicit either emotion. (Adapted from Cole, Bruschi, & Tamang, 2002).

observations of emotions expressed by 3- to 5-year-old Tamang and Brahman children and elders' reactions to those emotions revealed very different patterns of emotional socialization. The Tamang strongly disapprove of angry displays but will attend to and reason with a child who appears ashamed, thereby sending a message that competent children are those who are humble, socially graceful, and never angry. By contrast, Brahman parents largely ignore children who express shame and will attend to and reason with angry children, perhaps sending the message that anger is understandable but can be addressed and that competent children should not be overly shameful (Cole, Tamang, & Shrestha, 2006). Why do these two collectivist groups show these different patterns of emotional socialization? Cole and her associates speculate that status differences between the Tamang

and the Brahman people may be partially responsible. Tamangs in Nepal are of much lower social status than Brahmans are. Thus, Tamang children's expressions of self-blame (shame) may reflect an acknowledgment of powerlessness and a submissive role that is consistent with their lower caste status as members of a disadvantaged minority group.

As this study illustrates, people from different societies (and from different subgroups within a society) have very different ideas about appropriate and inappropriate displays of emotion. Although all human beings may be quite capable of experiencing and displaying a full range of human emotions, the feelings that they express outwardly, and the situations in which they express them, will vary from group to group in accordance with the underlying values and explicit display rules of each social group.

criticism (Saarni, 1990; Zeman & Garber, 1996), and children who have mastered these emotional codes of conduct are viewed as more likable and more competent by their teachers and peers (Jones, Abbey, & Cumberland, 1998).

EMOTIONAL COMPETENCE, SOCIAL COMPETENCE, AND PERSONAL ADJUSTMENT

Having now examined developmental trends in children's expression of emotions, their knowledge or understanding of their own and others' emotions, and their ability to regulate emotions (see Table 4.1 for a brief review), we come to an interesting question: Just how important are these developments to a child's social competencies, social standing, and personal adjustment?

Developmentalists who investigate these issues believe that achieving emotional competence is crucial to children's **social competence**—that is, their ability to achieve personal goals in social interactions while continuing to maintain positive relationships with others (Rubin, Bukowski, & Parker, 1998). **Emotional competence** has three components: *Competent emotional expressivity,* which involves frequent expression of more positive emotions and relatively infrequent displays of negative ones; *competent emotional knowledge,* which involves the abilities to correctly identify other people's feelings and the events responsible for those emotions; and *competent emotional regulation,* or the ability to adjust one's experience and expression of emotional arousal to an appropriate level of intensity to successfully achieve one's goals (Denham et al., 2003). Research has consistently revealed that each of

social competence
the ability to achieve personal goals in social interactions while maintaining positive relationships with others.

emotional competence
abilities to display predominantly positive (rather than negative) emotions, correctly identify others' emotions and respond appropriately to them, and adjust one's own emotions to appropriate levels of intensity in order to achieve one's goals.

Table 4.1 An overview of emotional development

Age	Emotional Expressions/Regulations	Emotional Understandings
Birth to 6 months	◆ All primary emotions appear. ◆ Displays of positive emotion are encouraged and become more commonplace. ◆ Attempts to regulate negative emotions by sucking or turning away are observed.	◆ Child can discriminate such facial expressions as happiness, anger, and sadness.
7 to 12 months	◆ Primary emotions such as anger, fear, and sadness become more apparent. ◆ Emotional self-regulation improves as infants rock themselves, chew on objects, or move away from distressing stimuli.	◆ Recognition of others' primary emotions improves. ◆ Social referencing appears.
1 to 3 years	◆ Secondary (self-conscious) emotions appear. ◆ Emotional self-regulation improves as toddlers distract themselves from or attempt to control stimuli that upset them.	◆ Toddlers begin to talk about and play-act emotions. ◆ Social referencing becomes more widespread.
3 to 6 years	◆ Cognitive strategies for regulating emotions appear and are refined. ◆ Some masking of emotions and compliance with simple display rules appear.	◆ Emerging abilities to identify and understand the causes of primary emotion. ◆ Recognition of others' emotions from expressive body movements. ◆ Understanding that a person can experience two compatible emotions at the same time. ◆ Awareness that thinking about past events can elicit emotions.
6 to 12 years	◆ Compliance with display rules improves. ◆ Self-conscious emotions become more closely tied to internalized standards of "right" or "competent" behavior. ◆ Self-regulation strategies (including those allowing one to intensify emotions when appropriate) become more varied and more complex.	◆ Emerging awareness that different people may experience different emotions about the same event. ◆ Awareness that people can simultaneously experience incompatible or mixed emotions. ◆ Understanding of the causes of self-conscious emotions improves.
13 to 18 years	◆ Increase in negative emotions associated with hormonal changes accompanying puberty and with daily hassles adolescents experience, both within and outside the family.	◆ All aspects of emotional understanding continue to improve.

these components of emotional competence is related to children's social competence. For example, children who express predominately positive affect and relatively little anger or sadness tend to be appraised more favorably by teachers and to establish more favorable relationships with peers than those who are angry, sad, or otherwise moody much of the time (Hubbard, 2001; Eisenberg, Liew, & Pidada, 2004; Ladd, Birch, & Buhs, 1999). Children who score high on tests of emotional understanding tend to be rated high in social competence by their teachers and to display social skills that enable them to make friends easily and establish positive relations with their classmates (Brown & Dunn, 1996; Dunn, Cutting, & Fisher, 2002; Mostow et al., 2002). Finally, children who have difficulties appropriately regulating their emotions (particularly anger) are often disliked and rejected by peers (Eisenberg, Liew, & Pidada, 2004; Rubin, Bukowski, & Parker, 1998) and face such adjustment problems as over-impulsivity and a general lack of self-control, inappropriate aggression, anxiety, depression, and social withdrawal (Eisenberg, Cumberland, et al., 2001; Gilliom et al., 2002; Hill et al., 2006; Maughan & Cicchetti, 2002).

Susanne Denham and her associates (2003) conducted an interesting longitudinal study in which all three components of emotional competence were assessed in 3- to 4-year-olds to determine which aspect or aspects of early emotional development are most clearly linked to children's emerging social competencies, both during the preschool period and later in kindergarten. Emotional expressivity was assessed by *time sampling:* Each 3- to 4-year-old was observed for 24 5-minute periods to assess the frequency with which he or she was displaying positive or negative emotions. Emotional knowledge was measured by assessing children's ability to identify the emotion a puppet would be experiencing in eight common situations (for example, after receiving an ice cream cone, after having a nightmare, and so forth). Finally, emotional self-regulation was measured by mothers' reports of the frequency of their children's regulatory lapses and by examples of dysregulated behaviors observed during the time-sampled observations of children's positive and negative emotions mentioned above. Social competence was assessed at age 3 to 4 and again when the children were in kindergarten. These measures consisted of teachers' and day-care providers' assessments of their cooperativeness and sensitivity to the feelings of peers, and by peer assessment of their likability.

The results were complex but very informative. At age 3 to 4, children's emotional expressivity predicted both their emotional knowledge and emotional regulation. That is, children who expressed predominately positive emotions were generally more knowledgeable about emotions and better at regulating emotions then those whose expressed emotions were less positive. Yet only emotional regulation predicted children's social competence, with children high in emotional self-regulation being rated more socially competent by day-care providers and more likable by day-care classmates than dysregulated children were. But the picture had changed by kindergarten, when both competent emotional expressivity (that is, displaying predominately positive emotions) and competent emotional knowledge became strong predictors of kindergartners' social competencies, with emotional self-regulation playing a more secondary role.

What is so interesting about those results is not so much the particulars as the bigger picture: All three aspects of emotional competence *assessed early in life* have implications for children's emerging social competence and, ultimately, for their likely patterns of social adjustment. Clearly, what children are learning early on about the desirability of expressing particular emotions, inhibiting or otherwise regulating less desirable feelings, and about the meaning of the emotions that other people express and how they, as perceivers, should respond to these signals are all crucial lessons that are apt to serve them well throughout childhood, adolescence, and the rest of their lives.

TEMPERAMENT AND DEVELOPMENT

We've seen some overall similarities among children in the development of emotional expression, emotional understanding, and emotional self-regulation. However, there are also some striking differences in emotional functioning as well. Think back to the scene that opened this chapter: Two toddlers, Cherry and Caryn, displayed strikingly different emotional reactions to an intrusive bearded stranger, Santa, who bid for their attention. Clearly, the strong stranger anxiety Cherry displayed stands in marked contrast to Caryn's slight wariness but obvious curiosity. Are differences in early socialization of emotions involved? We might suspect from what we have learned thus far that perhaps Caryn's parents have talked more than Cherry's parents have about the causes of emotions and have taken a more active role in helping her to develop strategies for regulating emotions. And recall that these two toddlers used their mothers in different ways, with Cherry clutching hers for protection and Caryn looking to her mother for information about Santa (social referencing). Thus, it is quite possible, as we will see in Chapter 5, that the toddlers' different responses to Santa reflect variations in the security of the emotional ties, or *attachments,* that these little girls have established with their mothers. And yet differences in the two girls' feelings and behaviors may reflect something else—perfectly normal variations in *temperament.*

What Is Temperament and How Is It Measured?

As parents and day-care providers well know, every baby has a distinct "personality." In trying to describe infant personalities, researchers have focused on aspects of **temperament,** which Mary Rothbart and John Bates (1998) define as "*constitutionally based*" individual differences in emotional, motor, and attentional reactivity and self-regulation" (p. 109, italics added) that many believe to be the emotional and behavioral building blocks of the adult personality. What kinds of emotional and behavioral variations? Although different researchers do not always define or measure temperament in precisely the same ways, many would agree that the following six dimensions provide a fairly good description of individual differences in infant temperament (Rothbart & Bates, 1998):

1. *Fearful distress (fearfulness)*—wariness, distress, and withdrawal in new situations or in response to novel stimuli.

2. *Irritable distress*—fussiness, crying, and showing distress when desires are frustrated (sometimes called frustration/anger).

3. *Positive affect*—frequency of smiling, laughing, willingness to approach others and to cooperate with them (called sociability by some researchers).

4. *Activity level*—amount of gross motor activity (for example, kicking, crawling).

5. *Attention span/persistence*—length of time child orients to and focuses on objects or events of interest.

6. *Rhythmicity*—regularity/predictability of bodily functions such as eating, sleeping, and bowel functioning.

Notice, then, that infant temperament reflects two kinds of negative emotionality (fearfulness and irritability) as well as global positive affect. What's more, the first five of these six temperamental components are also useful for describing temperamental variations that preschool and older children display (Rothbart & Bates, 1998).

Variations on some temperamental dimensions take some time to appear and are undoubtedly influenced by biological maturation and experience (Rothbart et al., 2001). For example, fearful distress does not appear until age 6 to 7 months, and variations in attention span, although certainly apparent early, become more noticeable later in the first year as the frontal lobes of the brain mature and babies become more capable of regulating attention.

Measurement of Temperament   There are many different methods and approaches to measuring temperamental variations in infants and older children, but perhaps the most common approach is to ask adults who know the child well to characterize his or her behavior on questions designed to assess particular temperamental attributes. On Mary Rothbart's *Infant Behavior Questionnaire (IBQ),* for example, parents might be asked to describe how often (on a 7-point scale on which 1 = never and 7 = often) their baby cries in response to the sound of a vacuum cleaner (fearful distress), fusses while waiting for a bottle (irritability), smiles and laughs (positive affect), squirms or kicks (activity level), and so on. Similar items, designed to be more age-appropriate, comprise Rothbart's *Child Behavior Questionnaire (CBQ),* which is usually completed by parents, teachers, or day-care providers to assess temperamental variations of children ranging from toddlers to the early grade-school years. Sample items from the CBQ ask the adult reporter to indicate how often the child in question is afraid of loud noises, large animals, and so forth (fearful distress), has temper tantrums (irritability), runs rather than walks from room to room (activity level), and so on. The major advantage of instruments such as the IBQ and CBQ is that the adults who complete them usually have extensive knowledge of the child's behavior and emotional reactivity in many different situations (Rothbart & Bates, 1998). However, a potential disadvantage, particularly when parents are involved, is that their reports may not be completely objective.

Other investigators prefer to assess temperament (or more precisely the component of temperament in which they are particularly interested) by exposing children to laboratory situations in which temperamental variations of interest are likely to be observed. If one hoped to study variations in fearful distress (or what some would label behavioral inhibition), the procedure might be to expose children to strangers or to unusual toys that may move, make noise, or involve some element of uncertainty, and note children's responses to these objects and situations (Kagan, 1992). Investigators who favor laboratory assessments view them as more objective and less biased assessments of temperament (Kagan, 1998), although potentially important disadvantages of the laboratory observation approach are (1) that such measures may be heavily influenced by transient factors such as the child's mood on a particular day, and (2) they typically provide information about one or two temperamental attributes rather than reflecting broader temperamental differences.

Hereditary and Environmental Influences on Temperament

Hereditary Influences   To many, the very term *temperament* implies a biological foundation for individual differences in behavior—a foundation that is genetically influenced and stable over time (Buss & Plomin, 1984; Rothbart & Bates, 2006). Behavioral geneticists have looked for hereditary influences by comparing the temperamental similarities of pairs of identical and fraternal twins. By the middle of the first year, identical twins are already more similar than fraternal twins on such temperamental attributes as activity level, irritability, and positive affect (Braungart et al.,1992; Emde et al., 1992; see Figure 4.6). Although the heritability coefficients for most temperamental attributes are moderate at best throughout infancy and the preschool period (Goldsmith, Buss, & Lemery, 1997), many important components of temperament are genetically influenced.

Environmental Influences   The fact that temperamental attributes are only moderately heritable means that environment also influences children's temperaments. Which aspects of environment are most important? Some research implies that the home environments that siblings share most clearly influence *positively toned* temperamental attributes such as smiling/positive affect; yet shared environment contributes very little to *negatively toned* attributes such as irritability and fearful distress because siblings living together often do not resemble each other on these aspects of temperament (Goldsmith, Buss, & Lemery, 1997; Goldsmith et al., 1999). Instead, negatively toned temperamental attributes are shaped more by *nonshared environmental influences*—those aspects of environment that siblings do not share and that conspire to make them temperamentally *dissimilar*. This can easily happen if parents notice early behavioral differences among their children and adjust their parenting to them. For example, if a mother observes that her infant Jimmy is much less outgoing with strangers than her 3-year-old Jennifer was at Jimmy's age, she may allow Jimmy more freedom to avoid social contacts and to pursue solitary activities, thereby encouraging him to become more reclusive and socially inhibited than his sister is (Park et al., 1997).

Stability of Temperament

How stable is early temperament over time? Is the "fearful" 8-month-old who is highly upset by a strange face likely to remain wary of strangers at 24 months and to shun new playmates as a 4-year-old? Longitudinal research indicates that several components of

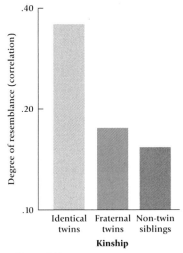

Figure 4.6
Average correlations in infant temperament among identical twins, fraternal twins, and nontwin siblings born at different times. (From Braungart et al., 1992; Emde et al., 1992.)

temperament—namely activity level, irritability, and positive affect/sociability—are moderately stable through infancy, childhood, and sometimes even into the early adult years (Caspi & Silva, 1995; Jaffari-Bimmel et al., 2006; Lemery et al., 1999). In fact, one longitudinal study in New Zealand found that several components of temperament measured at age 3 were not only moderately stable between ages 3 and 18, but also predicted individual differences in participants' antisocial tendencies and the quality of their personal and family relationships at ages 18 to 21 (Caspi & Silva, 1995; Henry et al., 1996; Newman et al., 1997). Findings such as these illustrate why many developmentalists consider temperament to be the cornerstone of the adult personality. However, not all individuals are so temperamentally stable.

Consider what Jerome Kagan and his associates found while conducting longitudinal studies of a temperamental attribute they call **behavioral inhibition:** the tendency to withdraw from unfamiliar people or situations (Kagan, 1992, 2003). At age 4 months, inhibited infants are already fussing and showing heightened motor activity to such novel objects as a brightly colored mobile, and they often display intense physiological arousal (for example, high heart rates) to situations that barely phase uninhibited infants. When tested at age 21 months, toddlers classified as inhibited were rather shy and sometimes even fearful when they encountered unfamiliar people, toys, or settings, whereas most uninhibited children responded quite adaptively to these events. And when retested at ages 4, 5½, and 7½, inhibited youngsters were still less sociable with strange adults and peers and more cautious than uninhibited children were about engaging in activities that involved an element of risk (for example, walking a balance beam). What's more, infants and toddlers who fit the inhibited profile are at risk for developing exaggerated fears (for example, fear of being kidnapped) as grade-school children (Kagan et al., 1999) and becoming shy and socially anxious as adolescents (Kagan et al., 2007; Schwartz, Snidman, & Kagan, 1999).

So behavioral inhibition is a moderately stable attribute that may have deep biological roots. Indeed, researchers have been finding that infants easily upset by novelty show greater electrical activity in the right cerebral hemisphere of the brain (the center for negative emotions) than in the left hemisphere, whereas infants who are less reactive show either the opposite pattern or no hemispheric differences in electrical activity (Calkins, Fox, & Marshall, 1996; Fox, Bell, & Jones, 1992). Moreover, children classified as inhibited or uninhibited in infancy are still showing different physiological responses to novelty as preadolescents and young adults (Schwartz et al., 2003; Woodward et al., 2001), and family studies clearly indicate that behavioral inhibition is a genetically influenced attribute (Bartels et al., 2004; DiLalla, Kagan, & Resnick, 1994; Robinson et al., 1992). Nevertheless, both Kagan (1998) and other researchers (Kerr et al., 1994; Pfeifer et al., 2002) found that it was mainly those children at the extremes of the continuum—the most highly inhibited and most highly uninhibited youngsters—who displayed such long-term stability, with most other children showing considerable fluctuation in their levels of inhibition over time. Of course, the finding that many children show meaningful variations in their levels of inhibition implies that this attribute is subject to environmental influence. Indeed, environmental factors can even contribute to the stability of inhibition, for it appears that children are likely to remain highly inhibited over time if their caregivers (1) are overprotective and allow them little autonomy (Fox, 2007), or alternatively, (2) are not very accurate at appraising their feelings or are insensitive to them, and are inclined to make such snide remarks about their wariness as "Don't be such a baby!" (Kiel & Buss, 2006; Rubin, Burgess, and Hastings, 2002).

Here, then, is another example of how genetically influenced temperamental attributes are often modified (or even maintained) by environmental factors. Interestingly, we will see similar processes at work as we examine Alexander Thomas and Stella Chess's classic longitudinal research on the stability of *temperamental profiles* from infancy to adulthood.

behavioral inhibition
a temperamental attribute reflecting the fearful distress children display and their tendency to withdraw from unfamiliar people and situations.

Early Temperamental Profiles and Later Development

In their earliest reports, Thomas and Chess (1977; Thomas, Chess, & Birch, 1970) noted that certain aspects of infant temperament tend to cluster in predictable ways, forming broader temperamental profiles. In fact, the majority of the 141 infants in their *New York Longitudinal Study* could be placed into one of three temperamental profiles:

1. **Easy temperament** (40 percent of the sample): Easygoing children are even-tempered, typically in a positive mood, and quite open and adaptable to new experiences. Their habits are regular and predictable.

2. **Difficult temperament** (10 percent of the sample): Difficult children are active, irritable, and irregular in their habits. They often react very vigorously to changes in routine and are very slow to adapt to new persons or situations.

3. **Slow-to-warm-up temperament** (15 percent of the sample): These children are quite inactive, somewhat moody, and can be slow to adapt to new persons and situations. But, unlike the difficult child, they typically respond to novelty in mildly, rather than intensely, negative ways. For example, they may resist cuddling by looking away rather than by kicking or screaming.

The remaining children fit none of these profiles, showing their own unique patterns of temperamental attributes.

easy temperament
temperamental profile in which the child quickly establishes regular routines, is generally good natured, and adapts easily to novelty.

difficult temperament
temperamental profile in which the child is irregular in daily routines and adapts slowly to new experiences, often responding negatively and intensely.

slow-to-warm-up temperament
temperamental profile in which the child is inactive and moody and displays mild passive resistance to new routines and experiences.

Temperamental Profiles and Children's Adjustment   Apparently, these broader temperamental patterns may persist over time and influence a child's adjustment to a variety of settings later in life. For example, temperamentally "difficult" children are more likely than other children to have problems adjusting to school activities, and they are often irritable and aggressive in their interactions with siblings and peers (Rubin et al., 2003; Stams, Juffer, & van IJzendoorn, 2002; Chess & Thomas, 1999). By contrast, about half of all children who are "slow to warm up" show a different kind of adjustment problem, as their hesitancy to embrace new activities and challenges may cause them to be ignored or neglected by peers (Chess & Thomas, 1999).

Child Rearing and Temperament   Do those observations imply that early temperamental profiles are difficult to alter and will largely determine our personalities and social adjustment? No, they do not! Chess and Thomas (1999) find that early temperamental characteristics *sometimes do* and *sometimes do not* carry over into later life. In other words, temperamental profiles can change, and one factor that often determines whether they do change is the **"goodness of fit"** between the child's temperamental style and patterns of child rearing used by parents. Let's first consider a "good fit" between temperament and child rearing. Difficult infants and toddlers who fuss a lot and have trouble adapting to new routines often become less cranky and more adaptable over the long run if parents can remain calm as they insist that their children comply with rules, while also exercising restraint and allowing them to respond to new routines at a more leisurely pace. Indeed, many difficult infants who experience such patient and sensitive caregiving are no longer classifiable as especially difficult or showing any adjustment problems later in childhood or adolescence (Bates et al., 1998; Jaffari-Bimmel et al., 2006). Yet it is not always easy for parents to be patient and sensitive with highly active, moody children who resist their bids for attention; in fact, many parents become irritable, impatient, demanding, and punitive with difficult children (Sanson, Hemphill, & Smart, 2004; van den Boom, 1995). Unfortunately, these attitudes and behaviors constitute a "poor fit" with a difficult child, who is apt to become all the more fussy and resistant in response to the parent's forceful and punitive tactics, which in turn may induce parents to become even more irritable and less involved with their children over time (Lengua, 2006). And true to form, difficult infants

"goodness-of-fit" model
Thomas and Chess's notion that development is likely to be optimized when parents' child-rearing practices are sensitively adapted to the child's temperamental characteristics.

are especially likely to remain difficult and to display behavior problems later in life if their parents are often impatient, angry, demanding, and forceful with them (Chess & Thomas, 1999; Rubin et al., 2003).

Part of the reason that difficult children may be prone to experience adjustment problems is that many of them are not particularly skillful at regulating emotions—especially negative emotions. In Box 4.3, we once again touch on regulatory issues as we examine a temperamental attribute that has been receiving a lot of attention lately—*effortful control*.

Cross-Cultural Variations in the Developmental Implications of Temperament

The research we have reviewed linking temperament and developmental outcomes is limited in one very important respect: Most of it was conducted in Western cultures such as the United States, Canada, and the countries of Western Europe. This is a potentially serious limitation because at least some preliminary evidence indicates that what qualifies as a "desirable" temperament, and outcomes associated with it, may vary from culture to culture. Let's consider one example: the implications of childhood and adolescent shyness.

In the United States, children who are shy and reserved are at a social disadvantage. They run the risk of being neglected or even rejected by peers—an outcome that can lead to low self-esteem, depression, and a number of other adjustment problems that we will discuss in detail in Chapter 13. Furthermore, even if shy adolescents or young adults are otherwise well-adjusted, they often fail to act boldly or assertively enough to take advantage of many opportunities, and they typically lag far behind non-shy peers at getting married, having children, and firmly establishing themselves in a career (Caspi, Elder, & Bem, 1988).

By contrast, many Asian cultures have historically valued what Americans would call a shy and somewhat inhibited demeanor. Past research from China, for example, consistently found that children who were shy and reserved were perceived as socially mature by their teachers (Chen, Rubin, & Li, 1995) and were much more likely than active, assertive children to be popular with their peers—precisely the opposite pattern of what we see in the United States and Canada (Chen, Rubin, & Sun, 1992). And the boisterous classroom behaviors that most Western children display on occasion (and that American teachers view as normal) are likely to be branded as conduct disorders by teachers in Thailand, who expect their pupils to be reserved, respectful, and obedient (Weisz et al., 1995). There is, however, an interesting update to report on recent data coming out of China. As China has moved to a market economy over the past 15 years, undertaken social reforms, and gradually introduced advanced technologies and such Western ideals as valuing individual freedom and initiative (all of which have been most enthusiastically accepted in the younger generation), a change seems to be emerging in the extent to which Chinese *children* see shyness as a social advantage. Xinyin Chen, Cen, and associates (2005), for example, recently reported that shy Chinese children are now less likely than their more assertive and outgoing peers to be popular and, like Western children from earlier studies, are currently at some risk of being rejected by peers. Thus, as the values of a culture change (an historical effect), so too can the perceived desirability of particular temperamental attributes.

There are even differences among Western cultures in outcomes associated with shyness. Swedes, for example, view shyness somewhat more positively than Americans do and prefer shy, reserved behaviors to bold, assertive, or attention-seeking antics. Consequently, shyness is not really a disadvantage for Swedish men. Like shy American men, shy Swedish men married and had children later than their non-shy counterparts; however, shyness did not constrain their careers in the same way it does for American men (Kerr, Lambert,

Photo 4.5
Difficult infants are likely to retain their difficult temperaments if parents are impatient and forceful with them.

Bob Daemmerich/Stock Boston

Box 4.3 Focus on Research

Effortful Control, Emotional Self-Regulation, and Social Development

Recall that the ability to properly regulate emotions is a very important attribute that has meaningful implications for the future: Competent regulators are less aggressive, anxious, withdrawn, or depressed, and generally get along better with teachers and peers. Recently, social-developmentalists have focused on temperamental contributions to self-regulation by studying variations in children's **effortful control**—an attribute that is so closely linked to regulatory ability that it is occasionally used to measure emotional self-regulation by some researchers (Eisenberg, Zhou, et al., 2005).

Effortful control (EC) is defined as "the efficiency of executive attention, including the ability to inhibit a dominant response and/or to activate a subdominant response" (Rothbart & Bates, 2006). It consists of a variety of related capacities such as the abilities to (1) focus attention on a task or a situation, (2) shift attention as needed to deal with changing situational demands, (3) suppress inappropriate responses, and (4) plan and select a response that is more appropriate for the situation at hand. There is ample reason to suspect that EC would be related to the successful regulation of emotions. To behave appropriately at his birthday party, for example, a 6-year-old must stay focused on the celebration (rather than wandering off to his room), shift attention from stuffing his face with cake when told to come open his grandmother's gift, suppress a dominant but inappropriate response (expressions of anger or sadness) should the unwrapped gift prove to be disappointing, and plan to select a response more appropriate to the situation ("Thanks, Grandma, for the underwear—I really needed it!").

EC is usually measured with a subset of items from Rothbart's Child Behavior Questionnaire (CBQ), for which parents or teachers report how true or untrue particular behaviors are of the target child (for example, "gets angry when called in from play," "remains calm about upcoming treats", "shows strong concentration while coloring," "can easily stop an activity when told 'No!'"). Although considered a genetically influenced temperamental attribute, EC is quite susceptible to environmental influence. In fact, one twin study found that environmental factors accounted for a clear majority of the variance in children's EC scores, with genes playing a secondary role (Goldsmith, Buss, & Lemery, 1997). Although limited to date, the evidence consistently reveals that warm, supportive parenting tends to foster children's effortful control, whereas harsh parenting and inconsistent discipline tends to inhibit it (Eisenberg, Zhou, et al., 2005; Rothbart & Bates, 2006; Spinrad et al., 2007).

Developmental trends in effortful control generally parallel the growth of emotional self-regulation, with children showing large improvements in EC between 2 and 3 years of age (Carlson, Mandell, & Williams; 2004; Kochanska, Murray, & Harlan, 2000). And though children generally become better with age at focusing attention and controlling their impulses (Jacques & Zelazo, 2001), there are clear individual differences in EC that are moderately stable throughout the preschool years, middle childhood, and adolescence (Lengua, 2006; Li-Grining, 2007; Zhou et al., 2007). So are children who display more effortful control in any way advantaged?

It certainly appears that they are, at least from the limited evidence currently available. For example, preschool children higher in EC (particularly in the ability to inhibit dominant but possibly inappropriate responses) are already performing better academically one year later in kindergarten than their classmates who were lower in EC (Blair & Razza, 2007). Moreover, grade-school children and adolescents who test *low* in EC are more prone to developing such externalizing problem behaviors as inappropriate aggression and delinquency, and to displaying internalizing problems such as anxiety, depression, and social withdrawal, compared to classmates who display a good sense of effortful control (Eisenberg, Sadovsky, et al., 2005; Eisenberg, Zhou, et al., 2005; Zhou et al., 2007).

In sum, effortful control appears to be a most important temperamental attribute—one that has already been linked to children's emerging emotional and academic competencies, as well as their risk of displaying a variety of problem behaviors, and that may prove in the years ahead to have implications for many other aspects of social behavior and personality development.

& Bem, 1996). What about Swedish women? Shyness posed no problems for them in establishing intimate relationships, for shy Swedish girls married and had children at roughly the same age as their non-shy peers. But unlike shy American women, who were generally well educated and who married successful men, shy Swedish women completed *fewer* years of education than their non-shy counterparts and married men who made less money, thus suggesting that shyness may place them at some risk of economic disadvantage. Why did shy Swedish girls receive less education than their non-shy peers? Margaret Kerr and her associates (1996) speculate that Swedish teachers are more likely to encourage shy students to continue their education if the students are males. So lacking the initiative to approach teachers and seek their guidance, shy Swedish girls end up having fewer educational opportunities than their non-shy female peers or shy boys do.

We see, then, that outcomes associated with shyness can vary dramatically across cultures (and even within a culture, depending on one's gender or even the historical era in which the research is conducted). Clearly, some temperamental qualities provide better fits with a culture's specific values and traditions that others do. And because cultural traditions vary so widely, we can safely conclude that there is no one temperamental profile that is most adaptive in all cultures.

effortful control
temperamental attribute that reflects one's ability to focus and/or shift attention as called for by the situation and to suppress dominant or inappropriate responses in favor of those more appropriate for the situation.

SUMMARY

AN OVERVIEW OF EMOTIONS AND EMOTIONAL DEVELOPMENT

✦ An emotion is a complex construct consisting of a feeling (positive or negative), physiological responses, cognitions that elicit or accompany feelings and physiological changes, and a goal or desire to take some action.

✦ **Discrete-emotions theory** claims that each human emotion is accompanied by a particular set of facial and bodily reactions; these emotional states are said to be products of our evolutionary history and apparent very early in life. By contrast, proponents of a **functional perspective** believe that emotions develop over time and that their purpose is to promote some action toward achieving a goal.

APPEARANCE AND DEVELOPMENT OF DISCRETE EMOTIONS

✦ Human infants are clearly emotional beings. At birth, babies show facial expressions of interest, distress, disgust, and contentment, with the remaining **primary emotions** appearing by the middle of the first year.

✦ Between age 6 and 10 weeks, babies begin to display **social smiles** that become more frequent over time. By age 2 months, infants smile to indicate their pleasure at exerting some control over toys or other events, and by age 6 to 7 months, are reserving their biggest social smiles for familiar companions.

✦ Anger and sadness (as distinguished from generalized distress) first appear at about age 2 months and become more recognizable as discrete emotions over the first year. Fear normally appears at 6 to 7 months of age. Two particularly interesting early fears are a fear of strangers, or **stranger anxiety,** and a discomfort at being separated from caregivers, or **separation anxiety.**

✦ **Secondary,** or **self-conscious, emotions** such as embarrassment, pride, shame, and guilt emerge in the second (or third) year, after children reach such cognitive milestones as self-recognition and have acquired standards for evaluating their conduct.

✦ The situations that evoke particular emotions change over the course of childhood. Young adolescents often show an increase in the display of negative emotions that may reflect hormonal changes associated with puberty, and an increase in daily hassles that they may experience with parents, teachers, and peers.

IDENTIFYING AND UNDERSTANDING OTHERS' EMOTIONS

✦ The infant's ability to discriminate facial displays of emotion and to derive information from them improves dramatically over the first year. By 7 to 10 months of age, infants are capable of **social referencing,** which enables them to assess how they ought to be feeling or behaving in a variety of uncertain situations.

✦ Between ages 3 and 5 years, children become better and better at using facial cues and even expressive bodily movements to identify the primary emotions that others are experiencing.

✦ Children gradually become better at identifying the causes of particular emotions and the situations or events that evoke them. Four- to 5-year olds are quite aware that a current emotion may be caused by thinking about past events. Between ages 6 and 10 years, they become increasingly aware that different people may experience different emotions to the same event and that a person can experience two or more emotions simultaneously.

✦ Parents and other caregivers may promote young children's understanding of emotions by talking about the child's mental states and their emotional consequences. Adults' use of a rich, *elaborative style* when conducting these emotional dialogues is a particularly effective means of emotional socialization.

LEARNING TO REGULATE EMOTIONS

✦ **Emotional self-regulation** refers to the process of adjusting one's emotions to an appropriate level of intensity to accomplish one's goals.

✦ Young infants are almost totally dependent on caregivers to calm them and regulate their distress. By the end of the first year, infants develop simple strategies for regulating negative emotions, and during the preschool years, children, often aided by parents and other adults, develop cognitive strategies to moderate (or in some cases to intensify) emotional arousal to achieve their objectives.

✦ Improvements in emotional regulation help children to comply with culturally defined **emotional display rules.** Although all human beings are capable of experiencing the full range of human emotions, the feelings that they express outwardly, and the situations in which they display them, vary considerably from culture to culture.

EMOTIONAL COMPETENCE, SOCIAL COMPETENCE, AND PERSONAL ADJUSTMENT

✦ **Emotional competence** consists of three components: (1) competent emotional expressivity, (2) competent emotional understanding, and (3) competent emotional self-regulation.

✦ As early as the preschool years, all three aspects of emotional competence are associated with children's **social competence** and personal adjustment.

TEMPERAMENT AND DEVELOPMENT

✦ Many components of **temperament** are genetically influenced. Environment also contributes heavily to temperament, with shared environmental influences having the larger impact on positively valenced temperamental attributes and nonshared environmental influences affecting negatively valenced aspects of temperament.

✦ Such components of temperament as activity level, irritability, fearful distress, and **behavioral inhibition** are moderately stable over time and forecast later variations in adult personality. Stability is greatest for individuals at the extremes of a temperamental dimension.

✦ Temperamental attributes often cluster in predictable patterns such as the **easy, difficult,** and **slow-to-warm-up profiles.** Although children with difficult and slow-to-warm-up temperaments are at greater risk of experiencing adjustment problems, whether they actually develop these problems depends on the **goodness of fit** between the parenting they receive and their own temperamental attributes.

✦ **Effortful control,** the ability to focus and/or shift attention and to inhibit dominant responses to behave more appropriately for the situation at hand is a strong temperamental contributor to emotional self-regulation and to competent patterns of social behavior.

✦ Temperamental attributes considered desirable or undesirable may vary from culture to culture in accordance with how well they match the values of those cultures.

CHAPTER 5

Establishment of Intimate Relationships and Their Implications for Future Development

In 1960, JOHN BOWLBY published an article describing the behavior of 15- to 30-month-old toddlers who had been separated for long periods from their mothers while hospitalized for chronic illnesses. The progress of these sickly but otherwise normal children was anything but normal. According to Bowlby, most of these children progressed through three behavioral phases during their prolonged hospitalization:

1. In an initial *protest phase,* children tried to regain their mothers by crying, demanding her return, and resisting the attention of substitute caregivers. This phase lasted from a few hours to more than a week.

2. In a second *phase of despair,* children seemed to lose hope of ever being reunited with their mothers. They often became apathetic and unresponsive to toys and other people and seemed to be in a deep state of mourning.

3. Finally, many children progressed to what Bowlby called the *detachment phase.* They appeared to have "recovered" in that they showed renewed interest in toys and substitute caregivers; but their relationships with their mothers had changed. When the mother visited, her child was often cool and indifferent, showing little if any protest when she left once again. It almost seemed as if the children were in the process of undoing their emotional ties to their mothers.

Bowlby noted that a fourth separation phase, *permanent withdrawal from human relationships,* may occur if a child's separation from the mother is extremely prolonged or if he loses a series of temporary attachment objects, such as nurses or babysitters, while separated from his mother. In either case, these children often become less interested in human contact. They are still able to communicate with other people on their initiative but become more egocentric as their attention shifts from human beings to fuzzy toys or other inanimate objects.

Bowlby's study was prompted in part by even earlier work that we will examine later in this chapter—research implying that children reared in orphanages and other institutional settings, apart from a primary caregiver, often failed to form close emotional ties to anyone and would sink into a state of depression and despair, becoming unresponsive to other human beings and seemingly almost unwilling to live (Spitz, 1945, 1949). These observations had suggested to Bowlby that the establishment of close affectional ties, or *attachments,* between infants and their primary caregivers may be a necessary prerequisite for normal social and emotional development. His own later observations of hospitalized toddlers reinforced this conclusion by suggesting that long after they have formed, attachments continue to play a crucial role in children's lives and that anything that might undermine these bonds (such as a prolonged separation from loved ones) can trigger grief and despair and set the stage for poor developmental outcomes.

In this chapter, we will evaluate these and other claims about the importance of early affectional ties to children's social, emotional, and even their intellectual development. We will begin by considering how infants and their caregivers establish these intimate relationships. We will then evaluate the significance of early attachments in two ways. First, we will review a rapidly expanding base of evidence suggesting that the relationships that infants form with caregivers differ in their quality, or *security,* and that the kinds of emotional attachments that emerge can have important implications for children's short-term and long-term development. Second, we will chart the progress of infants who have had little or no contact with a primary caregiver and do not appear to become attached to anyone. Finally, we conclude by considering an important and widely debated practical issue: Are young children likely to suffer emotionally and to display less than optimal patterns of development should their parents work and they spend much of their early years in some sort of alternative care?

WHAT ARE EMOTIONAL ATTACHMENTS?

Although babies can communicate many of their feelings right from the start, their social lives will change rather dramatically as they become emotionally attached to their caregivers. What is an emotional **attachment?** John Bowlby (1969) used the term to describe the strong affectional ties that we feel for the special people in our lives. According to Bowlby, people who are securely attached take pleasure in their interactions and feel comforted by their partner's presence in times of stress or uncertainty. So 10-month-old Michael may reflect the attachment relationship he shares with his mother by reserving his biggest grins for her and by crying out to her or crawling in her direction whenever he is upset, discomforted, or afraid.

attachment
a close emotional relationship between two persons, characterized by mutual affection and a desire to maintain proximity.

Attachments Are Reciprocal Relationships

Bowlby also stressed that parent-child attachments are reciprocal relationships; infants become attached to parents, and parents become attached to infants.

Parents clearly have an edge on infants when it comes to forming these intimate affectional ties, although people sometimes find it hard to understand how a parent might become emotionally involved with a **neonate.** Many years ago, a classmate of mine, listening to our professor describing just how drawn he was to his newborn son, remarked:

neonate
a newborn infant from birth to approximately 1 month of age.

emotional bonding
term used to describe the strong affectional ties that parents may feel toward a neonate; some theorists believe that the strongest bonding occurs shortly after birth, during a sensitive period.

> Why do you feel that way? Newborn infants drool, spit up, fuss, cry, dirty their diapers on a regular basis, and often require lots of attention at all hours of the day and night. Because babies are associated with so many unpleasant consequences, wouldn't learning theory predict that their parents should learn to dislike them?

Since that day nearly 40 years ago, social-developmentalists have come to understand how parents might be drawn to a newborn infant. Even before their baby is born, many parents display their readiness to become attached by talking blissfully about the baby, formulating grand plans for him or her, and expressing delight in such milestones as feeling their fetus kick, hearing his heart beat with the aid of a stethoscope, or seeing his image on ultrasound (Grossman et al., 1980). What's more, research conducted and widely reported in the 1970s and 1980s implied that parents who had had extensive close contact (and ideally, skin-to-skin contact) with their newborn in the first few hours after birth would quickly become **emotionally bonded** to her, and that the parental bond that forms during this early "sensitive period" would be stronger and remain stronger than those later established by other parents who had had no contact with their babies shortly after birth (Klaus & Kennell, 1976, 1982).

This "sensitive period" hypothesis was a radical claim that other researchers quickly sought to evaluate. What later research has told us is that having close contact with a newborn can intensify positive feelings that parents may already have for their baby and help them get off to a good start with him or her, especially when mothers are very young, economically disadvantaged, and know very little themselves about how to stimulate or to care for an infant (Eyer, 1992). But there is no compelling evidence that parents who haven't had early contact with a newborn will later have difficulties establishing intimate ties to that child. In fact, there is evidence to the contrary: Most adoptive parents are quite satisfied with and end up establishing very close emotional ties to their adoptees, even though they have often had no contact with their adopted infants for days, weeks, or even months after birth (Jaffari-Bimmel et al., 2006; Levy-Shiff, Goldschmidt, & Har-Even, 1991). Indeed, the likelihood that a mother and her infant will become securely attached is just as high (or higher) in adoptive families as in nonadoptive ones (Stams, Juffer, & Van IJzendoorn, 2002; Singer et al., 1985).

Photo 5.1
Children and caregivers who are securely attached interact often and try to maintain proximity.

© Ellen Senisi/The Image Works

In sum, secure attachments between infants and caregivers are not formed in the first few hours (or days) after birth; they build gradually from social interactions that take place over a period of months, and there is simply no reason for parents who have not had early skin-to-skin contact with their new-born to assume that they will have problems establishing a warm and loving relationship with him or her.

Interactional Synchrony and Attachment

One important contributor to the growth of attachments is the **synchronized routines** that infants and caregivers often establish over the first few months of a baby's life. Infants normally begin to gaze quite intently and to show more interest in their mothers' faces between 4 and 9 weeks of age (Lavelli & Fogel, 2002), and by age 2 to 3 months, they are beginning to understand some simple social contingencies as well. Thus, if a mother smiles at her 3-month-old when the baby is alert and attentive, he will often become delighted, crack a big smile in return, and expect a meaningful response from Mom (Lavelli & Fogel, 2002, 2005; Legerstee & Varghese, 2001). By contrast, when social expectancies are violated, as they are in the "still face" procedure when a parent is instructed to look sullen, 2- to 6-month-olds usually smile briefly at the parent to regain her attention before becoming distressed by her lack of responsiveness (Moore, Cohn, & Campbell, 2001). So even very young infants have come to expect some degree of "synchrony" between their own gestures and those of caregivers, and these expectancies are one reason that face-to-face play interactions with regular companions become increasingly coordinated and complex over the first several months (Stern, 1977).

Interactional synchrony is most likely to develop if the caregiver attends carefully to the baby's state, provides playful stimulation when the child is alert and attentive, and avoids pushing things when an overexcited or tired infant is fussy and sending the message "Cool it! I just need a break from all this excitement." Edward Tronick (1989, p. 112) described one very synchronous interaction that unfolded as a mother played peek-a-boo with her infant:

> . . . The infant abruptly turns away from his mother as the game reaches its "peek" of intensity and begins to suck on his thumb and stare into space with a dull facial expression. The mother stops playing and sits back watching . . . After a few seconds the infant turns back to her with an inviting expression. The mother moves closer, smiles, and says in a high-pitched, exaggerated voice, "Oh, now you're back!" He smiles in response and vocalizes. As they finish crowing together, the infant reinserts his thumb and looks away. The mother again waits. [Soon] the infant turns . . . to her and they greet each other with big smiles.

Notice that much information is exchanged in this simple but synchronous exchange. By turning away and sucking, the excited infant is saying, "Hey, I need to mellow out and regulate my emotional state." His mother tells him she understands by patiently awaiting his return. As he returns, Mom smiles to tell him she's glad he's back, and he acknowledges that signal with a smile and an excitable blurt. And when the baby becomes overstimulated a minute or two later, his mother waits for him to calm once again, and he communicates his thanks by smiling big for her when he turns back the second time. Clearly, this is a dyad that not only interacts smoothly but quickly repairs any interactive errors.

How important are synchronous exchanges to the establishment of affectional ties? We can get some idea by contrasting synchronous interactions with conflictual, nonsynchronous ones. Suppose the mother in the example had been less patient when her infant turned away, choosing instead to click her tongue to attract his attention and to follow up by sticking her face in the baby's line of vision. According to Tronick (1989), what might well happen is that the baby would grimace, turn further away, and perhaps even push at his mother's face. The mother's intrusive actions have communicated something like "Cut the coy stuff and come play with me," whereas the infant's negative response implies "No, you cool it and give me some space." Here, then, is an exchange in which messages go unheeded and interactive errors persist—one that is undoubtedly much less pleasant for both the mother and her baby than the highly affectionate, synchronous interplay described earlier.

Photo 5.2
Early synchrony of affect and behavior is one of the best predictors of strong, mutually satisfying attachments between infants and their caregivers.

In sum, infants play an important role in winning others' affection by virtue of their responsiveness to social overtures and their emerging ability to synchronize their behaviors with those of sensitive companions. Smooth synchronous interactions are most likely to develop if parents limit their social stimulation to those periods when the baby is alert and receptive, and avoid pushing things too far when the infant's message is "Hey, I need to chill out." Parents may have a difficult time establishing synchronized routines with temperamentally irritable or unresponsive infants (Feldman, 2006). But under normal circumstances, synchronized exchanges between 3-month-olds and their caregivers may occur several times a day and are particularly important contributors to emotional attachments (Stern, 1977). As an infant continues to interact with a responsive caregiver, he will learn what this person is like and how he can regulate her attention (Keller et al., 1999). Of course, the caregiver should become better at interpreting the baby's signals and will learn how to adjust her behavior to successfully capture and maintain his attention. As the caregiver and the infant practice their routines and become better play partners, their relationship should become more satisfying for both parties and eventually blossom into a strong reciprocal attachment (Isabella, 1993; Isabella & Belsky, 1991).

HOW DO INFANTS BECOME ATTACHED?

Although many parents begin to form emotional ties to their infant very soon after the baby is born, an infant requires some time before she is developmentally ready to form a genuine attachment to another human being. Many theories have been proposed to explain how and why infants become emotionally involved with the people around them. But before we consider these theories, we should briefly discuss the phases that babies go through in becoming attached to a close companion.

The Growth of Primary Attachments

Many years ago, Rudolph Schaffer and Peggy Emerson (1964) studied the development of emotional attachments by following a group of Scottish infants from early infancy to 18 months of age. Once a month, mothers were interviewed to determine (1) how the infant responded when separated from close companions in seven situations (for example, being left in a crib, being left in the presence of strangers) and (2) the persons to whom the infant's separation responses were directed. A child was judged to be attached to someone if separation from that person reliably elicited a protest.

Schaffer and Emerson found that infants pass through the following phases as they develop close ties with their caregivers:

1. The **asocial phase** (0–6 weeks). Very young infants are somewhat "asocial" in that many kinds of social or nonsocial stimuli will produce a favorable reaction, and few produce any kind of protest. By the end of this period, infants are beginning to show a preference for such social stimuli as a smiling face.

2. The **phase of indiscriminate attachments** (6 weeks to 6–7 months). Now infants clearly enjoy human company but tend to be somewhat indiscriminate: They smile more at people than at such other life like objects as talking puppets (Ellsworth, Muir, & Hains, 1993) and are likely to fuss whenever any adult puts them down. Although 3- to 6-month-olds reserve their biggest grins for familiar companions and are more quickly soothed by a regular caregiver, they seem to enjoy the attention they receive from just about anyone (including strangers).

3. The **specific attachment phase** (about age 7–9 months). Between 7 and 9 months of age, infants begin to protest only when separated from one particular individual, usually the mother. Now able to crawl, infants may try to follow along behind mother to stay close and will often greet her warmly when she returns. They also become somewhat wary of strangers. According to Schaffer and Emerson, these babies have established their first genuine attachments.

The formation of a secure attachment to a caregiver has another important consequence: It promotes the development of exploratory behavior. Mary Ainsworth (1979) emphasizes that an attachment object serves as a **secure base** for exploration—a point of safety from which an infant can feel free to venture away. Thus Juan, a securely attached infant visiting a neighbor's home with his mother, may be quite comfortable exploring the far corners of the living room as long as he can check back occasionally to see that Mom is still seated on the sofa. But should she disappear into the bathroom, Juan may become wary and reluctant

Photo 5.3 An infants who is securely attached uses her attachment object as a secure base from which to explore the environment.

to explore. Paradoxical as it may seem, then, infants apparently need to rely on another person in order to feel confident about acting independently.

4. The **phase of multiple attachments.** Within weeks after forming their initial attachments, about half the infants in Schaffer and Emerson's study were becoming attached to other people (fathers, siblings, grandparents, or perhaps even a regular babysitter). By 18 months of age, very few infants were attached to only one person, and some were attached to five or more.

Schaffer and Emerson originally believed that infants who are multiply attached have a "hierarchy" of attachment objects and that the individual at the top of the list is their most preferred companion. However, later research indicates that each of the infant's attachment objects may serve different functions, so that the person whom an infant prefers most may depend on the situation. For example, most infants prefer the mother's company if they are upset or frightened. However, fathers seem to be preferred as playmates, possibly because much of the time they spend with their infants is "play time" (Bretherton, 1985; Parke, 2002). Schaffer (1977) later concluded that "being attached to several people does not necessarily imply a shallower feeling toward each one, for an infant's capacity for attachment is not like a cake that has to be [divided]. Love, even in babies, has no limits" (p. 100).

Theories of Attachment

If you have ever had a kitten or a puppy, you may have noticed that pets often seem especially responsive and affectionate to the person who feeds them. Might the same be true of human infants? Developmentalists have long debated this very point, as we will see in examining four influential theories of attachment: psychoanalytic theory, learning theory, cognitive-developmental theory, and ethological theory.

Psychoanalytic Theory: I Love You Because You Feed Me

According to Freud, young infants are "oral" creatures who derive satisfaction from sucking and mouthing objects and should be attracted to any person who provides oral pleasure. Because it is usually mothers who "pleasure" oral infants by feeding them, it seemed logical to Freud that the mother would become the baby's primary object of security and affection, particularly if she were relaxed and generous in her feeding practices.

Erik Erikson also believed that a mother's feeding practices will influence the strength or security of her infant's attachment. However, he claimed that a mother's *overall responsiveness* to all her child's needs is more important than feeding itself. According to Erikson, a caregiver who consistently responds to an infant's needs will foster the infant's sense of *trust* in other people, whereas unresponsive or inconsistent caregiving breeds *mistrust*. He adds that children who have learned not to trust caregivers during infancy may come to avoid or to remain skeptical about close mutual-trust relationships throughout life.

Before we examine the research on feeding practices and attachments, we need to consider another viewpoint that assumes that feeding is important—learning theory.

Learning Theory: Rewardingness Leads to Love

For quite different reasons, some learning theorists have also assumed that infants will become attached to persons who feed them and gratify their needs. Feeding was thought to be particularly important for two reasons (Sears, 1963). First, it should elicit positive responses from a contented infant (smiles, coos) that are likely to increase a caregiver's affection for the baby. Second, feeding is often an occasion when mothers can provide an infant with *many comforts*—food, warmth, tender touches, soft reassuring vocalizations, changes in scenery, and even a dry diaper (if necessary)—*all in one sitting*. Over time, then, an infant should come to associate

Photo 5.4
The "wire" and "cloth" surrogate mothers used in Harlow's research. Infants became attached to the cloth mother even if it was the wire mother who fed them.

Martin Rogers/Stock Boston

secondary reinforcer
an initially neutral stimulus that acquires reinforcement value by virtue of its repeated association with other reinforcing stimuli.

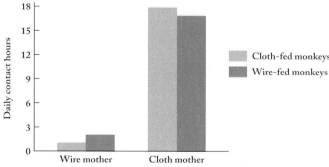

Figure 5.1
By 25 days of age, infants were spending much more time in contact with their cloth mother than their wire mother surrogate, regardless of which "mother" fed them. These contact differences persisted across the 165-day rearing period. (Adapted from Harlow & Zimmerman, 1959.)

his mother with pleasant or pleasurable sensations, so that the mother herself becomes a valuable commodity. Once the mother (or any other caregiver) has attained this status as a **secondary reinforcer**, the infant is attached—he or she will now do whatever is necessary (smile, cry, coo, babble, or follow) in order to attract the caregiver's attention or to remain near this valuable and rewarding individual.

Just how important *is* feeding? In 1959, Harry Harlow and Robert Zimmerman reported the results of a study designed to compare the importance of feeding and tactile stimulation for the development of attachments in infant monkeys. The monkeys were separated from their mothers in the first day of life and reared for the next 165 days by two surrogate mothers. As you can see in Photo 5.4, each surrogate mother had a face and well-proportioned body constructed of wire. However, the body of one surrogate (the "cloth mother") was wrapped in foam rubber and covered with terry cloth. Half the infants were always fed by this warm, comfortable cloth mother, the remaining half by the rather uncomfortable "wire mother."

The research question was simple: Would these infants become attached to the "mother" who fed them, or would they instead prefer the soft, cuddly terry cloth mother? It was no contest! Even if fed by the wire mother, infants clearly preferred the cloth mother, spending more than 15 hours a day clutching her, compared with only an hour or so (mostly at mealtimes) with the wire mother (see Figure 5.1). Furthermore, all infants ran directly to the cloth mother when they were frightened by such novel stimuli as marching toy bears. Clearly Harlow and Zimmerman's classic study implies that *contact comfort* is a more powerful contributor to attachment in monkeys than feeding or the reduction of hunger.

Apparently, feeding is not any more important to human infants than to baby monkeys. When Schaffer and Emerson (1964) asked mothers the feeding schedules (regular interval versus demand feeding) they had used and the age at which they had weaned their infants, they found that the generosity of a mother's feeding practices simply did not predict the quality of her infant's attachment to her. In fact, for 39 percent of these infants, the person who usually fed, bathed, and changed a baby was not even the child's primary attachment object!

Current Viewpoints   Although it is now quite clear that feeding is *not* the primary contributor to attachments in either monkeys or humans, learning theorists continued to argue that *reinforcement* is the mechanism responsible for emotional attachments (Gewirtz & Petrovich, 1982). Their revised viewpoint, which is similar to that of Erik Erikson, is that infants will be attracted to any individual who is quick to respond to *all their needs* and who provides them with a variety of pleasant or rewarding experiences. Indeed, Schaffer and Emerson (1964) found that the two aspects of a mother's behavior that predicted the character of her infant's attachment to her were her *responsiveness* to the infant's behavior and the *total amount of stimulation* that she provided. Mothers who responded reliably and appropriately to their infants' bids for attention and who often played with their babies had infants who were closely attached to them.

Cognitive-Developmental Theory: To Love You, I Must Know You Will Be There
Cognitive-developmental theory has little to say about which adults are most likely to

appeal to infants, but it does remind us of the holistic character of development by suggesting that the ability to form attachments depends in part on the infant's level of cognitive development. Before an attachment can occur, the infant must be able to discriminate familiar companions from strangers. She must also recognize that familiar companions have a "permanence" about them (object permanence), for it would be difficult indeed to form a stable relationship with a person who ceases to exist whenever she passes from view (Schaffer, 1971). So perhaps it is no accident that attachments first emerge at age 7–9 months—precisely the time when infants are entering Piaget's *fourth sensorimotor substage,* the point at which they first begin to search for and find objects that they've seen someone hide from them.

Barry Lester and his associates (1974) evaluated this hypothesis by giving 9-month-old infants a test of object permanence before exposing them to brief separations from their mothers, their fathers, and a stranger. They found that 9-month-olds who scored high (substage 4 or above) in object permanence only protested when separated from their mothers, whereas age-mates who scored lower (substage 3 or below) did not reliably protest separations from anyone. So it seemed that only the cognitively advanced 9-month-olds had formed a primary attachment (to their mothers)—a finding which implies that the timing of this important emotional milestone does depend in part on the infant's level of object permanence.

Bowlby's Ethological Theory: Perhaps I Was Born to Relate and Love Ethologists have proposed an interesting explanation for emotional attachments that has strong evolutionary overtones. A major assumption of the ethological approach is that all species, including human beings, are born with a number of innate behavioral tendencies that have in some way contributed to the survival of the species over the course of evolution. Indeed, John Bowlby (1969, 1980), who was originally a proponent of Freudian psychoanalytic theory, came to believe that many of these built-in behaviors are specifically designed to promote attachments between infants and their caregivers. Even the attachment relationship itself is said to have adaptive significance, serving to protect the young from predators and other natural calamities and to ensure that their needs are met. Of course, ethologists would argue that the long-range purpose of the primary attachment is to permit members of each successive generation to survive and live to reproduce, thereby enabling the species to survive (Geary, 2002).

Origins of the Ethological Viewpoint Interestingly, the ethological theory of attachment was prompted by research with animals. In 1937, Konrad Lorenz reported that very young goslings would follow almost any moving object—their mothers, a duck, or even a human being—a behavior he labeled **imprinting.** Lorenz also noted that (1) imprinting is automatic—young fowl do not have to be taught to follow; (2) imprinting occurs only within a narrowly delimited *critical period* after the bird has hatched; and (3) imprinting is irreversible—once the bird begins to follow a particular object, it will remain attached to it.

Lorenz then concluded that imprinting was an adaptive response. Young birds should generally survive if they follow their mothers so that they are led to food and afforded protection. Those that wander away may starve or be eaten by predators and thus fail to pass their genes to future generations. So over the course of many, many generations, then, the imprinting response eventually became an inborn, **preadapted characteristic** that attaches a young fowl to its mother, thereby increasing its chances of survival.

Attachment in Humans Although human infants do not imprint on their mothers in the same way that young fowl do, they have inherited a number of attributes that help them to maintain contact with others and to elicit caregiving. Lorenz (1943), for example, suggested that a baby's "kewpie doll" appearance (that is, large forehead, chubby cheeks, and soft, rounded features (see Figure 5.2) makes the infant appear cute or lovable to caregivers. Thomas Alley (1981) agreed. Alley found that adults judged line drawings of infant faces

imprinting
an innate or instinctual form of learning in which the young of certain species will follow and become attached to moving objects (usually their mothers).

preadapted characteristic
an innate attribute that is a product of evolution and serves some function that increases the chances of survival for the individual and the species.

Figure 5.2
Infants of many species display the "kewpie-doll" effect that makes them appear lovable and elicits caregivers' attention. (Adapted from Lorenz, 1943.)

(and profiles) to be "adorable"—much cuter than those of 2-, 3-, and 4-year-old children. So babyish facial features may well help to elicit the kinds of positive attention from others that will promote emotional attachments, and the more attractive the baby, the more favorably mothers and other companions respond to him or her (Barden et al., 1989; Langlois et al., 1995). Nevertheless, babies need not be adorable to foster close attachments, for a clear majority of relatively unattractive infants end up securely attached to their caregivers (Speltz et al., 1997).

Not only do most infants have "cute" faces, but many of their inborn, reflexive responses may have an endearing quality about them (Bowlby, 1969). For example, an infant's sucking and grasping reflexes may lead parents to believe that their baby enjoys being close to them. Smiling, which is initially a reflexive response to almost any pleasing stimulus, is a particularly potent signal to caregivers (Lavelli & Fogel, 2005), as are cooing, excitable blurting, and spontaneous babbling (Keller & Scholmerich, 1987). From 3 to 6 months of age, infants become more likely to emit raised-cheek, open-mouth (or big) smiles in response to a smiling caregiver, as if they are signaling their willingness to share positive affect with her (Messinger, Fogel, & Dickson, 2001), and parents often interpret their babies' big social smiles as an indication that "My baby is happy and I am an effective caregiver." So a smiling infant can reinforce caregiving activities and thereby increase the likelihood that parents or other nearby companions will want to attend to this happy little person in the future.

Finally, Bowlby insists that under normal circumstances, adults are just as biologically predisposed to respond favorably to a baby's signals as the baby is to emit them. It is difficult, he claims, for parents to ignore an urgent cry or fail to warm up to a baby's big grin. In sum, human infants and their caregivers are said to have evolved in ways that predispose them to respond favorably to each other and form close attachments, thus enabling infants (and ultimately, the species) to survive.

Does this mean that attachments are automatic? No, it does not! Bowlby claims that secure attachments develop gradually as parents become more proficient at reading and reacting appropriately to the baby's signals, and the baby is *learning* what his parents are like and how he might regulate their behavior. Yet the process can easily go awry, as illustrated by observations that an infant's preprogrammed signals will eventually wane if they fail to produce favorable reactions from an unresponsive caregiver, such as a depressed mother or an unhappily married father. So while Bowlby believes that human beings are biologically *prepared* to form close attachments, he also stresses that secure emotional bonds will not develop unless each participant has *learned* how to respond appropriately to the behavior of the other.

Comparing the Four Theoretical Approaches Although the four theories we have reviewed differ in many respects, each has something to offer. Clearly, feeding practices are not as important to human attachments as psychoanalysts had originally thought; but it was Freud who stressed that we will need to know more about mother/infant interactions if we hope to understand how babies form attachments. Erik Erikson and the learning theorists pursued Freud's early leads and concluded that caregivers do play an important role in an infant's emotional development. Presumably infants are likely to view a responsive companion who provides many comforts as a trustworthy and rewarding individual who is worthy of affection. Ethologists can agree with this point of view, but they add that infants are *active participants* in the attachment process who emit preprogrammed responses that enable them to promote the very interactions from which attachments are likely to develop. Finally, cognitive theorists have contributed by showing that the timing of emotional attachments is related to the infant's level of cognitive development. So it makes little sense to tag one of these theories as "correct" and to ignore the others, for each theory has helped us to understand how infants become attached to their closest companions.

INDIVIDUAL DIFFERENCES IN ATTACHMENT SECURITY

The attachment relationships that virtually all home-reared infants establish with caregivers clearly differ in quality. Some infants are quite comfortable and relaxed around their attachment objects, whereas others seem highly anxious or uncertain about what to expect next. Some infants become extremely sad or angry (or both) when their parents leave them with a babysitter, whereas others react more adaptively to these separations, quickly composing themselves by playing with toys or with their sitter (see Box 5.1 for some helpful

Box 5.1 Applying Developmental Research

On Easing the Pain of Separation

At some point, most parents find it necessary to leave their infants and toddlers in an unfamiliar setting (such as a nursery or a day-care center) or in the company of a stranger (for example, a baby- sitter) for hours at a time. How can they make these necessary separations easier for their child to bear? Here are three simple recommendations:

1. *Provide an explanation for the separation.* Cognitive-developmental theorists tell us that separations are most upsetting when infants and toddlers cannot explain where caregivers have gone or when they will return. Thus, an explanation for the separation may help immensely. Indeed, toddlers who are left in unfamiliar settings cry less and play much more constructively if their mothers have taken a moment to explain that they are leaving and will soon return (Weinraub & Lewis, 1977). Brief explanations work better than lengthy ones (Adams & Passman, 1981), and one need not prepare a toddler days in advance for an upcoming separation. In fact, 2-year-olds who are prepared in advance often worry in advance; moreover, they protest more and play less constructively once the separation actually occurs than do age-mates who have received little advance preparation (Adams & Passman, 1980).

2. *Provide some reminder of home.* Ethologists tell us that separations involving a *strange* caregiver in a *strange* setting are likely to be particularly upsetting. Not surprisingly, then, separations can be made less painful for older infants and toddlers if they have some reminder of home with them, such as a favorite stuffed animal or a security blanket (Passman & Weisberg, 1975). Indeed, giving the toddler a sharply focused photograph of his mother (or having one available for the substitute caregiver to show the child) may also help him to respond more constructively to a necessary separation (Passman & Longeway, 1982).

3. *Choose a sensitive substitute caregiver.* Finally, all developmentalists advise parents to select a substitute caregiver who enjoys children and is sensitive to their concerns. Although infants 8 months of age and older are likely to become visibly upset when first left with an unfamiliar sitter, their adjustment to this arrangement clearly depends on the sitter's behavior (Gunnar et al., 1992). If the sitter assumes a "caretaker" role by first settling the child in and then pursuing her own interests, most infants and toddlers will continue to display signs of distress. But if the sitter acts as a "playmate" by providing toys and attracting the child's interest, most infants and toddlers will

Necessary separations are easier to bear when toddlers have their favorite toys with them and their sitters act more like playmates than like caretakers.

quickly stop protesting and join in the fun (Gunnar et al., 1992). Clearly, a sitter who enjoys interacting with young children is a far better choice than one who sees her function as quickly attending to the child's most basic needs before heading to the telephone or refrigerator.

Table 5.1 The eight episodes of the strange situation

Episode	Events	Potential Attachment Behaviors Noted
1.	Experimenter introduces parent and baby to playroom and leaves.	
2.	Parent sits while baby plays.	Parent as a secure base
3.	Stranger enters, sits, and talks to parent.	Stranger anxiety
4.	Parent leaves, stranger offers comfort if the baby is upset.	Separation anxiety
5.	Parent returns, greets baby, and offers comfort if baby is upset. Stranger leaves.	Reunion behaviors
6.	Parent leaves room.	Separation anxiety
7.	Stranger enters and offers comfort.	Ability to be soothed by stranger
8.	Parent returns, greets baby, offers comfort if necessary, and tries to interest baby in toys.	Reunion behaviors

Note: All episodes except the first last 3 minutes, although separation episodes may be abbreviated and reunion episodes extended for babies who become extremely upset.

hints that parents and substitute caregivers might heed to make necessary separations easier for infants and toddlers to bear). Why are some infants seemingly secure and others insecure in their attachment relationships? And does the security of a child's early attachments have any impact on later development? To answer these questions, researchers first had to find ways of measuring attachment security.

Assessing Attachment Security

The most widely used technique for measuring the quality of attachments that 1- to 2-year-olds have established with their mothers or other caregivers is Mary Ainsworth's Strange Situation procedure (Ainsworth et al., 1978). The **Strange Situation** consists of a series of eight episodes (summarized in Table 5.1) that attempt to simulate (1) naturalistic caregiver/infant interactions in the presence of toys (to see whether the infant uses the caregiver as a *secure base* from which to explore); (2) brief separations from the caregiver and encounters with strangers (which often stresses the infant); and (3) reunion episodes (to determine whether a stressed infant derives any comfort and reassurance from the caregiver and can once again become involved with toys). By recording and analyzing an infant's responses to these episodes—that is, exploratory activities, reactions to strangers and separations, and, in particular, behaviors when reunited with the close companion—it is usually possible to characterize his or her attachment to the caregiver in one of four ways.

1. **Secure attachment.** About 60–65 percent of 1-year-old American infants fall into this category. The securely attached infant actively explores while alone with the mother and may be visibly upset by separations. The infant *often greets the mother warmly when she returns and, if highly distressed, will often seek physical contact with her,* which helps to alleviate that distress. The child may be outgoing with strangers while the mother is present.

2. **Resistant attachment.** About 10 percent of 1-year-olds show this type of "insecure" attachment. These infants try to stay close to their mothers but explore very little while she is present. They become very distressed as the mother departs. But when she returns, the infants are ambivalent: They *remain near her,* although they seem angry at her for having left them and are likely to *resist physical contact initiated by the mother.* Resistant infants are quite wary of strangers, even when their mothers are present.

Strange Situation
a series of eight separations and reunion episodes to which infants are exposed in order to determine the quality of their attachments.

secure attachment
an infant/caregiver bond in which the child welcomes contact with a close companion and uses this person as a secure base from which to explore the environment.

resistant attachment
an insecure infant/caregiver bond characterized by strong separation protest and a tendency of the child to remain near but resist contact initiated by the caregiver, particularly after a separation.

3. **Avoidant attachment.** These infants (about 20 percent of 1-year-olds) also display an "insecure" attachment. They often show little distress when separated from the mother and will generally *turn away from and may continue to ignore their mothers, even when she tries to gain their attention.* Avoidant infants are often rather sociable with strangers but may occasionally avoid or ignore them in much the same way that they avoid or ignore their mothers.

4. **Disorganized/disoriented attachment.** This recently discovered attachment pattern characterizes the 5–15 percent of American infants who are most stressed by the Strange Situation and who seem to be the most insecure (NICHD Early Child Care Research Network, 2001b). It appears to be a curious combination of the resistant and the avoidant patterns that reflects confusion about whether to approach or avoid the caregiver (Main & Solomon, 1990). When reunited with their mothers, these infants may cringe and look fearful, freeze, or curl up on the floor; or they may move closer but then abruptly move away as the mother draws near.

Measurement Issues   A clear majority of infants in any research sample can be classified into one of the four attachment categories that Ainsworth and her associates have described. Nevertheless, the Strange Situation procedure has been criticized. Urie Bronfenbrenner (1979), for example, believes that the very "strangeness" of the Strange Situation (rapid exposure to strange environments, strangers, and abrupt separations from the caregiver) may prompt exaggerated emotional reactions that are not true indicators of an infant's day-to-day behavior at home or the true character of her relationships with caregivers. Others have argued that the four discrete attachment "types" that Ainsworth and her followers have identified are somewhat artificial and that it might be better to characterize attachment differences among infants in terms of continuous dimensions, such as overall security with the caregiver (see, for example, Waters et al., 1995) or differences on such attachment-related behavioral dimensions as proximity seeking and displays of anger and resistance to comforting (Fraley & Spieker, 2003; but see Cassidy, 2003, and Sroufe, 2003, for criticisms of these notions). And unfortunately, the Strange Situation isn't very useful for characterizing the attachments of children much older than 2, who have become quite accustomed to (and less stressed by) brief separations from caregivers and encounters with strangers.

Although the Strange Situation remains the most widely used measure of attachment security for researchers studying infants and toddlers, alternative methods have been developed to assess the attachment representations of older children, adolescents, and adults. One such measure, the **Attachment Q-set (AQS),** is appropriate for use with 1- to 5-year-olds. Using this instrument, a parent or trained observer sorts 90 descriptions of attachment-related behaviors (for example, "Child seeks reassurance from caregiver when wary, . . . greets caregiver with big smiles") into categories ranging from "most like" to "least like" the child's behavior *at home.* The resulting profile represents how secure the child is with his or her caregivers at home (Waters et al., 1995). Q-set data can also be scored to indicate the particular "type" of attachment the child has with a caregiver, and these assessments generally match those derived from the Strange Situation procedure (van IJzendoorn et al., 2004). Other methods used with adolescents and adults include the **Adult Attachment Interview (AAI),** in which respondents are questioned extensively about their recollections and feelings about their early childhood relationships with parents, and based on their reports, are classified as having secure, avoidant/dismissing, resistant/preoccupied, or unresolved/disoriented mental representations of attachment relationships (Hesse, 1999; Main & Goldwyn, 1994).

These newer assessments of attachments and attachment representations in older children and adults are very useful because they permit us to seek answers to some intriguing questions. For example, is the quality of an infant's primary attachment stable over time?

avoidant attachment
an insecure infant/caregiver bond characterized by little separation protest and a tendency of the child to avoid or ignore the caregiver.

disorganized/disoriented attachment
an insecure infant/caregiver bond characterized by the infant's dazed appearance on reunion or a tendency to first seek and then abruptly avoid the caregiver.

Attachment Q-set
alterative method of assessing attachment security that is based on observations of the child's attachment-related behaviors at home; can be used with infants, toddlers, and preschool children.

Adult Attachment Interview
clinical interview used with adolescents and adults to tap respondents' memories of their childhood relationships with parents in order to assess the character of respondents' attachment representations.

Do early attachments forecast the kind of attachment relationships a child will later establish with other people, such as her spouse or her own children? Later in the chapter we will address these very issues and discuss some of the other ways that an early history of secure or insecure attachments might influence a person's outcomes later in life.

Cultural Variations in Attachment

The percentages of infants and toddlers who fall into the various attachment categories differ somewhat from culture to culture and seem to reflect cultural variations in child rearing. For example, parents in northern Germany deliberately encourage their infants to be independent and tend to discourage close, clingy contact, perhaps explaining why more German than American babies show reunion behaviors characteristic of the avoidant attachment pattern (Grossman et al., 1985). Furthermore, intense separation and stranger anxieties, which characterize resistant attachments, are much more common in cultures such as Japan, where parents rarely leave their infants with substitute caregivers (Takahashi, 1986), and Israel, where communally reared kibbutz children sleep in "infant houses" managed by substitute caregivers without having their parents available to them at night (Aviezer et al., 1999).

Western researchers generally interpret these findings as evidence that the meanings of attachment relationships and attachment security are culturally universal, and that cultural variations in attachment classifications simply illustrate how different patterns of caregiving across cultures lead to varying percentages of securely and insecurely attached infants (van IJzendoorn & Sagi, 1999; Waters & Cummings, 2000). However, other researchers disagree, arguing that what qualifies as a secure (or an insecure) behavioral profile varies from culture to culture.

In Japan, for example, mothers respond very differently to babies than Western mothers do (Rothbaum, Pott, et al., 2000; Rothbaum, Weisz, et al., 2000). Compared to American mothers, Japanese mothers have much more close contact with their infants and strive to *anticipate* all their babies' needs, rather than simply reacting to a needy baby's cries. Japanese mothers emphasize social routines more and exploration less than American mothers do, and they seek to promote the infant's *Amae*—a state of total dependence on the mother and a presumption of mother love and indulgence. Given these child-rearing practices, it is hardly surprising that Japanese infants are upset by separations and will cling to their mothers on reunion—behaviors that cause some of them to be classified as insecurely attached in the Strange Situation. Yet the establishment of a healthy sense of *Amae* is considered highly adaptive in Japan, a hallmark of a healthy attachment, because it sets the stage for the development of a culturally valued communal orientation—one in which Japanese children learn to become *interdependent* by accommodating to others' needs, cooperating, and working toward the accomplishment of *group* goals (Rothbaum, Weisz, et al., 2000). By contrast, a healthy, secure attachment in Western societies is one in which infants have been encouraged to *separate* themselves from their watchful and protective caregivers to explore the environment, become *independent* and autonomous, and pursue mostly *individual* goals.

Don't misunderstand; a majority of Japanese babies (and babies in all cultures) are classified as secure rather than insecure in the Strange Situation. Yet the dependence and strong stranger/separation anxieties that are quite common among Japanese babies may not reflect the

Amae
Japanese term that refers to an infant's feeling of total dependance on his or her mother and presumption of the mother's love and indulgence.

Photo 5.5
Although child-rearing traditions vary dramatically across cultures, secure attachments are more common than insecure attachments around the world.

Keren Su/Stone/Getty Images

heightened emotional *in*securities that underlie the same behaviors in Western infants. What seems to be universal about attachments is that parents around the world prefer that their youngsters feel secure in their relationships with them and that most parents try to promote culturally valued forms of security (Behrens, Hesse, & Main, 2007; Posada & Jacobs, 2001; Rothbaum, Pott, et al., 2000). However, much of what we know about the origins of secure and insecure attachments comes from research conducted in European and North American cultures. With this limitation in mind, let's use what researchers have learned about how infants become securely and insecurely attached.

⌒ FACTORS THAT INFLUENCE ATTACHMENT SECURITY

Among the many factors that seem to influence the kinds of attachments that infants establish are the quality of caregiving they receive, the character or emotional climate of their homes, and their own temperaments.

Quality of Caregiving

Mary Ainsworth (1979) believes that the quality of an infant's attachment to his mother (or any other close companion) depends largely on the kind of attention he has received. According to this **caregiving hypothesis,** mothers of *securely attached* infants are thought to be sensitive, responsive caregivers from the very beginning. And apparently they are. One review of 66 studies found that mothers who display the characteristics described in Table 5.2 tend to have infants who form secure attachments with them (De Wolff & van IJzendoorn, 1997). In addition, mothers of securely attached infants and toddlers are **insightful;** that is, they understand the causes of the child's emotions and the motives underlying his behavior—abilities that help them to respond in an appropriate way to his needs and concerns (Koren-Karie et al., 2002). So if a caregiver has a positive attitude toward her baby; understands, appreciates, and is sensitive to his needs and goals; has established interactional synchrony with him; and provides ample stimulation and emotional support, the infant will often derive comfort and pleasure from their interactions and is likely to become securely attached.

Babies who show a *resistant* rather than secure pattern of attachment often have parents who are *inconsistent* in their caregiving—reacting enthusiastically or indifferently depending on their moods and being unresponsive a good deal of the time (Ainsworth, 1979; Isabella, 1993; Isabella & Belsky, 1991). The infant copes with this unreliable caregiving by

caregiving hypothesis
Ainsworth's notion that the type of attachment an infant develops with a particular caregiver depends primarily on the kind of caregiving he has received from that person.

insightfulness
caregiver capacity to understand an infant's motives, emotions, and behaviors and to take them into account when responding to the infant; thought to be an important contributor to sensitive caregiving.

Table 5.2 Aspects of caregiving that promote secure mother-infant attachments

Characteristic	Description
Sensitivity	Responding promptly and appropriately to the infant's signals
Positive attitude	Expressing positive affect and affection for the infant
Synchrony	Structuring smooth, reciprocal interactions with the infant
Mutuality	Structuring interactions in which mother and infant attend to the same thing
Support	Attending closely to and providing emotional support for the infant's activities
Stimulation	Frequently directing actions toward the infant

Note: These six aspects of caregiving are moderately correlated with each other.

Source: De Wolff and van IJzendoorn, 1997.

trying desperately—through clinging, crying, and other attachment behaviors—to obtain emotional support and comfort, and then becomes *angry* or *resentful* when these efforts often fail.

There are at least two patterns of caregiving that place infants at risk of developing *avoidant* attachments. Ainsworth and others (for example, Isabella, 1993) find that some mothers of avoidant infants are often impatient with their babies and unresponsive to their signals, are likely to express negative feelings about their infants, and seem to derive little pleasure from close contact with them. Ainsworth (1979) believes that these mothers are rigid, self-centered people who are likely to *reject* their babies. In other cases, however, avoidant babies have overzealous parents who chatter endlessly and provide high levels of stimulation, even when their babies do not want it (Belsky, Rovine, & Taylor, 1984; Isabella & Belsky, 1991). Infants may be responding quite adaptively by learning to avoid or ignore adults who seem to dislike their company or who bombard them with stimulation they cannot handle. Whereas resistant infants make vigorous attempts to gain emotional support, avoidant infants seem to have learned to do without it (Isabella, 1993).

Finally, Mary Main believes that infants who develop *disorganized/disoriented* attachments are often drawn to their caregivers, but also *fearful* of them because of past episodes in which they were frightened by the caregiver's actions, neglected, or physically abused (Main & Solomon, 1990). Indeed, the infant's approach/avoidance (or totally dazed demeanor) at reunion is quite understandable if she has experienced cycles of acceptance and abuse, fright, or neglect and doesn't know whether to approach the caregiver for comfort or to retreat from her to safety. Available research supports Main's theorizing: Although disorganized/disoriented attachments are occasionally observed in any research sample, they seem to be especially common among physically abused infants (Carlson, 1998; Carlson et al., 1989).

Disorganized/disoriented attachments are also common among infants whose mothers are severely depressed or who abuse alcohol or drugs and may, as a result, mistreat or neglect their babies (Beckwith, Rozga, & Sigman, 2002). What's more, these very insecure attachments often emerge if the baby's primary caregiver has suffered a devastating interpersonal loss or trauma and is currently displaying an unresolved or disoriented mental representation of attachment relationships (Green & Goldwyn, 2002). An unresolved/disoriented caregiver appears to foster a disorganized/disoriented attachment by virtue of her extremely insensitive caregiving behaviors (for example, laughing at rather than comforting a distressed infant) and other actions that likely seem quite frightening to a baby (for example, startling or pretending to attack the child, or handling the child roughly as though he were an inanimate doll) (Madigan, Moran, & Pederson, 2006; Forbes et al., 2007; True, Pisani, & Oumar, 2001). Is it any wonder, then, that infants who are repeatedly abused, neglected, rebuffed, or ridiculed when they seek comfort, or frightened in any number of other ways, might become conflicted about whether to approach or avoid an extremely insensitive and unpredictable caregiver on whom his welfare absolutely depends?

Who Is at Risk of Becoming an Insensitive Caregiver?   Several personal characteristics place parents at risk of displaying the insensitive patterns of parenting that contribute to insecure attachments. For example, insecure attachments of one kind or the other are the *rule* rather than the exception when a child's primary caregiver has been diagnosed as clinically depressed (Radke-Yarrow et al., 1985; Teti et al., 1995). Depressed parents often ignore babies' social signals and generally fail to establish satisfying and synchronous relationships with them, particularly if their infants are irritable or inattentive (Poehlmann & Fiese, 2001). And infants often become distressed at these caregivers' lack of responsiveness and may soon begin to match their depressive symptoms, even when interacting with other *nondepressed* adults (Campbell, Cohn, & Meyers, 1995; Field, 1995).

Another group of parents who are often insensitive caregivers are those who themselves felt unloved, neglected, or abused as children. These formerly mistreated caregivers often start out with the best intentions, vowing never to do to their children what was done to them—but they often expect their infants to be "perfect" and to love them right away. So when their babies are irritable, fussy, or inattentive (as all infants will be at times), these emotionally insecure adults are likely to feel as if they are being rejected once again (Steele & Pollack, 1974). They may then back off or withdraw their own affection (Biringen, 1990; Crowell & Feldman, 1991; Madigan, Moran, & Pederson, 2006), sometimes to the point of neglecting or even abusing their babies.

Finally, adults whose pregnancies were unplanned and their babies unwanted can be particularly insensitive caregivers whose children fare rather poorly in all aspects of development. In one longitudinal study in Czechoslovakia (Matejcek, Dytrych, & Schuller, 1979), mothers who had been denied permission to abort an unwanted pregnancy were judged to be less closely attached to their children than a group of same-aged mothers of similar marital and socioeconomic status who had not requested an abortion. Although both the "wanted" and the "unwanted" children were physically healthy at birth, over the next nine years the unwanted children were more frequently hospitalized, made lower grades in school, had less stable family lives and poorer relations with peers, and were generally more irritable and antisocial than the children whose parents had wanted them. Follow-up observations in young adulthood tell much the same story: Compared to their "wanted" peers, the formerly "unwanted" children were now much less satisfied with their marriages, their jobs, their friendships, and their general mental health, having more often sought treatment for a variety of psychological disorders (David, 1992, 1994). What's more, older siblings of the unwanted children—siblings who were "wanted"—generally fared much better in their psychosocial development than the unwanted children did—a finding which indicates that the social and emotional deficiencies that unwanted children displayed was tied to their own "unwanted" status and not to their parents' general lack of competence at parenting (David, Dytrych, & Matejeck, 2003). Clearly, parents are unlikely to be very sensitive to and foster the development of children they do not care to raise.

Ecological Constraints on Caregiving Sensitivity Of course, parent/child interactions always take place in a broader ecological context that may influence how caregivers respond to their children (Bronfenbrenner & Morris, 2006). Insensitive parenting, for example, is much more likely among caregivers who are experiencing health-related, legal, or financial problems, and it is hardly surprising that the incidence of insecure attachments is highest among poverty-stricken families that receive inadequate health care (Murray et al., 1996; NICHD Early Child Care Research Network, 1997).

The quality of a caregiver's relationship with his or her spouse can also have a dramatic effect on parent/infant interactions. Consider that parents who were unhappily married before the birth of their child (1) are less sensitive caregivers after the baby is born, (2) express less favorable attitudes about their infants and the parenting role, and (3) establish less secure ties with their infants and toddlers, compared to other parents from similar socioeconomic backgrounds whose marriages are close and confiding (Cox et al., 1989; Howes & Markman, 1989). Happily married couples, on the other hand, usually support each other's parenting efforts, and this positive social support for parenting is especially important if the baby has already shown a tendency to be irritable and unresponsive. In fact, Jay Belsky (1981) found that newborns who are "at risk" for later emotional difficulties (as indicated by their sluggish reactions to social stimulation and the ease at which they become irritated) are likely to have nonsynchronous interactions with their parents *only when the parents are unhappily married*. So it seems that a stormy marriage is a major environmental hazard that can hinder or even prevent the establishment of secure emotional ties between parents and their infants.

Box 5.2 Applying Developmental Research

Fostering Caregiver Sensitivity and Secure Mother-Infant Attachments

As we have noted, parents who are clinically depressed and those who are economically disadvantaged and have little social support are clearly at risk of becoming insensitive caregivers whose infants may establish insecure attachments with them. In recent years, developmentalists have designed intervention experiments to see whether they could help at-risk caregivers to become more sensitive, hoping to promote secure emotional ties between these mothers and their babies. In one intervention, *depressed, poverty-stricken* mothers were visited regularly by a social services professional who first established a friendly, supportive relationship and then improved mothers' interactive skills by teaching them how to elicit more favorable responses from their babies. Mothers were also encouraged to attend weekly parenting classes. Children whose mothers had received this support later scored higher on intelligence tests and were more likely to be securely attached than infants of other depressed mothers who hadn't participated in the intervention (Lyons-Ruth et al., 1990).

A second intervention study conducted in the Netherlands (van den Boom, 1994) targeted *economically disadvantaged* mothers who had babies who were extremely *irritable*—a temperamental attribute that can hinder the establishment of interactional synchrony and place babies at greater risk of establishing insecure attachments. When the infants were 6 months old, half of their mothers were randomly assigned to participate in the intervention for a three-month period, whereas the remaining mothers in the control group received no intervention. The intervention consisted of helping mothers to adjust their caregiving behaviors to their infants' needs and unique temperamental characteristics in order to evoke more positive responses from the babies and promote smoother interactions. At the end of the intervention, mothers and infants were observed at play and in routine care situations to assess maternal sensitivity and the infants' social responsiveness. When the infants were 12 months old, the security of their attachments to their mothers was assessed in the Strange Situation.

The results were striking. By the time the intervention ended, mothers in the intervention group were more attentive, sensitive, and responsive to their babies than control mothers were, and their infants were more sociable, more willing to explore, and cried less than did infants of control mothers. At age 12 months, 63 percent of the babies of the intervention mothers had established secure attachments with them, compared to only 22 percent of the babies of control mothers who had established secure attachments. What's more, these effects persisted over time (van den Boom, 1995). Nine months after the intervention ended, intervention mothers were still much more sensitive while playing with their toddlers than control mothers were, and 74 percent of their now 18-month old children were securely attached to them (as opposed to 26 percent of the toddlers of control mothers who were securely attached). And at age 3½ years, children in the intervention group still had more secure emotional ties to their mothers (as assessed by the *Attachment Q-set*) then did children in the control group.

So these intervention *experiments* clearly indicate that caregiver sensitivity can be fostered and is *causally* related to attachment security. Obviously, the sensitivity training in these experiments was extensive, lasting for months. But the best news is that even brief interventions with mothers of *newborns* can help them to respond more sensitively to their babies, thereby fostering the development of secure attachments (Bakermans-Kranenburg, van IJzendoorn, & Juffer, 2003).

Fortunately, there are ways of assisting at-risk parents to become more sensitive, responsive caregivers. Two studies designed with this goal in mind are presented in Box 5.2.

Infant Temperament

Thus far, we have talked as if parents are responsible for the kind of attachments that infants establish. But because it takes two people to form an attachment *relationship*, we might suspect that babies can also influence the quality of parent/infant emotional ties. Do the large temperamental variations that infants display influence attachment classifications? Jerome Kagan (1984, 1989) certainly thinks so. He argues that the Strange Situation really measures individual differences in infants' temperaments rather than the quality of their attachments. This idea grew from his observation that the percentages of 1-year-olds who have established *secure, resistant,* and *avoidant* attachments corresponds closely to the percentages of babies who fall into Thomas and Chess's *easy, difficult,* and *slow-to-warm-up* temperamental profiles (see Table 5.3). And the linkages even make some sense. Kagan suggests that a temperamentally "difficult" infant who actively resists changes in routine and is upset by novelty may become so distressed by the rapidly changing circumstances of Strange Situation that he is unable to respond constructively to his mother's comforting and is thus classified as *resistant*. By contrast, a friendly, easygoing child is apt to be classified as *securely attached*, whereas one who is shy or "slow to warm up" may appear distant or detached in the Strange Situation and will probably be classified as *avoidant*. So Kagan's

Table 5.3 Comparison of the percentages of young infants who can be classified as temperamentally "easy," "difficult," and "slow to warm up" with the percentages of 1-year-olds who have established secure, resistant, and avoidant attachments with their mothers

Temperamental Profile	Percentage of "Classifiable" Infants	Attachment Classification	Percentage of 1-Year-Olds
Easy	60	Secure	65
Difficult	15	Resistant	10
Slow to warm up	23	Avoidant	20

Sources: Ainsworth et al., 1978; Thomas & Chess, 1977.

temperament hypothesis implies that infants, not caregivers, are the primary architects of their attachment classifications. Presumably, the attachment behaviors that a child displays reflect his or her own temperament.

Does Temperament Explain Attachment Security?   Although such components of temperament as irritability or negative emotionality do predict certain attachment behaviors (for example, intensity of separation protests) and can certainly contribute to the quality of an infant's attachments (Goldsmith & Alansky, 1987; Kochanska & Coy, 2002; Poehlmann & Fiese, 2001), most experts view Kagan's temperament hypothesis as far too extreme. Consider, for example, that many infants are securely attached to one close companion and insecurely attached to another—a pattern that we would not expect to see if attachment classifications were merely reflections of the child's relatively stable temperamental characteristics (Goossens & van IJzendoorn, 1990; Sroufe, 1985). In addition, we have already seen in Box 5.2 that when mothers of temperamentally difficult Dutch infants were trained to be more patient, sensitive, and responsive, the vast majority of their babies establish secure rather than insecure attachments—a finding which indicates that sensitive caregiving is *causally* related to attachment quality (van den Boom, 1995). What's more, one review of 34 studies revealed that maternal characteristics that often predict insensitive parenting—factors such as illness, depression, and other life stress—were associated with a sharp increase in insecure attachments (see Figure 5.3). However, child problems such as prematurity, illness, and other psychological disorders had virtually no impact on attachment quality (van IJzendoorn et al., 1992).

Finally, a study of identical and same-sex fraternal twins revealed that 70 percent of the identical twins pairs and 64 percent of the fraternal twins established the same kind of attachments (that is, both twins secure or both insecure) with their caregiver (O'Connor & Croft, 2001; see also Bokhorst et al., 2003, and Roisman & Fraley, 2006, for similar results). These findings have two important implications. First, because concordance in attachment classifications was not appreciably higher for the identical twins pairs, it appears that genetic contributions to children's attachments (including the contribution of genetically influenced components of temperament) were very modest at best. Second, because most twins were concordant in their attachment classifications, shared environmental influences (for example, interacting with the same sensitive or insensitive caregiver) must have contributed substantially to the resemblances in attachments that twin siblings displayed. Even among twin pairs who have *different* attachment relationships with their caregivers, the differences reflect contributions of nonshared environmental influences rather than differences in any genetically influenced attribute such as temperament (Fearon et al., 2006).

temperament hypothesis
Kagan's view that the Strange Situation measures individual differences in infants' temperaments rather than the quality of their attachments.

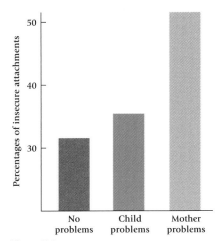

Figure 5.3
Comparing the impact of maternal and child problem behaviors on the incidence of insecure attachments. Maternal problems were associated with a sharp increase in insecure attachments, whereas child problems were not.

Box 5.3 Focus on Research

On the Intricate Interplay between Caregiving and Temperament in Shaping Infant Attachments

Several years ago, Grazyna Kochanska (1998) sought to test an integrative theory of infant/caregiver attachments—one specifying that (1) quality of caregiving is most important in determining whether an infant's emerging attachments are secure or insecure, but (2) infant temperament is the better predictor of the *type* of insecurity infants display, should their attachments be insecure. Kochanska began by measuring quality of caregiving mothers provided (that is, maternal responsiveness to her infant; the synchrony of positive emotions between mother and infant) when their babies were 8–10 and 13–15 months old. She also assessed the aspect of infant temperament known as fearful distress. *Fearful* children are prone to showing strong distress in new and uncertain situations and are similar to those children that Kagan calls behaviorally *inhibited*. *Fearless* children, by contrast, are largely unperturbed by strange settings, people, or separations and are similar to children whom Kagan refers to as behaviorally *uninhibited*. Finally, Kochanska used the Strange Situation to assess the quality of infants' attachments to their mothers at age 13–15 months. Thus, she had data allowing her to determine whether caregiving or temperament contributed more strongly to the security and specific type of attachments that infants display.

The study produced two particularly interesting sets of results. First, as anticipated by the integrative theory, quality of caregiving (but not infant temperament) clearly predicted whether infants

established secure or insecure attachments with their mothers, with positive, responsive parenting being associated with secure attachments. And yet, quality of caregiving did *not* predict the specific *type* of insecurity that infants with insecure attachments displayed.

What, then, predicted *type* of insecurity? Infant fearfulness did! As anticipated by the integrative theory and a knowledge of the fearful/fearless dimension, temperamentally fearful children who had insecure attachments were prone to display *resistant* attachments, whereas the insecure infants who were temperamentally fearless were more likely to display *avoidant* attachments.

Clearly, these findings imply that strong versions of both the caregiving hypothesis and the temperament hypothesis are overstatements. In fact, the data are actually quite consistent with Thomas & Chess's *goodness-of-fit model:* Secure attachments evolve from relationships in which there is a good fit between the caregiving an infant receives and his or her own temperament, whereas insecure attachments are likely to develop when highly stressed or otherwise inflexible caregivers fail to accommodate to their infants' temperamental characteristics. Indeed, one reason why caregiver sensitivity consistently predicts attachment security is that the very notion of sensitive care implies an ability to tailor one's caregiving practices to whatever temperamental qualities a baby might display (van den Boom, 1995).

Although the findings cited all seem to favor Ainsworth's caregiving hypothesis over Kagan's temperament model, look carefully at the research presented in Box 5.3. This research clearly illustrates the important link between sensitive caregiving and secure attachments while also demonstrating how child temperament can sometimes contribute to the kinds of attachments infants establish.

To this point we have focused only on the quality of the infant's attachment to her mother. Do you think that the kind of attachment an infant has with her mother will have any effect on the infant's relationship with her father? We will explore this issue in the next section as we look at some of the ways fathers contribute to their children's social and emotional development.

FATHERS AS ATTACHMENT OBJECTS

In 1975, Michael Lamb described fathers as the "forgotten contributors to child development." And he was right. Until the mid-1970s, fathers were treated as biological necessities who played only a minor role in the social and emotional development of their infants and toddlers. One reason for overlooking or discounting the father's early contributions may have been that fathers spend less time interacting with babies than mothers do (Parke, 2002; Yeung et al., 2001). Nevertheless, fathers appear to be just as fascinated with their *newborn* infants as mothers are (Hrdy & Batten, 2007; Nichols, 1993), and they become increasingly involved with their babies over the first year of life, spending an average of nearly an hour a day interacting with their 9-month-olds (Ninio & Rinott, 1988). Fathers are most highly involved with their infants, toddlers, and preschool children and hold more favorable attitudes about them when they are happily married or otherwise have a cordial relationship with the mother (Belsky, 1996; Coley & Hernandez, 2006; Cox et al., 1989, 1992) and when mothers encourage them to become an important part of their children's lives (DeLuccie, 1995; Palkovitz, 1984).

Fathers as Caregivers

Many infants form secure attachments to their fathers during the latter half of the first year, particularly if the father has a positive attitude about parenting, spends considerable time with the child, and is a sensitive caregiver (van IJzendoorn & De Wolff, 1997). How do fathers compare to mothers as companions? Research conducted in Australia, Israel, India, Italy, Japan, and the United States reveals that mothers and fathers in all these societies tend to play some-

Creatas/Jupiter Images

Photo 5.6
The "playmate" role is only one of many that fathers assume.

what different roles in a baby's life. Mothers are more likely than fathers to hold their infants, soothe and talk to them, play traditional games such as peekaboo, and care for their physical needs; fathers are more likely than mothers to provide playful physical stimulation and initiate unusual or unpredictable games that infants often enjoy (Parke & Buriel, 2006). Although most infants prefer their mothers' company when upset or afraid, fathers are often preferred as playmates (Lamb, 1997).

However, the playmate role is but one of many that modern fathers fulfill, particularly if their wives are working and they must necessarily assume at least some of the caregiving burden (Grych & Clark, 1999; Pleck & Masciadrelli, 2004). And what kinds of caregivers do dads make? Many of them are (or soon become) rather skillful at virtually all phases of routine care (including diapering, bathing, and soothing a distressed infant). Moreover, once fathers become objects of affection, they begin to serve as a *secure base* from which their babies will venture to explore the environment (Lamb, 1997). So fathers are rather versatile companions who can assume any and all functions normally served by the other parent (of course, the same is true of mothers).

Fathers as Contributors to Emotional Security and Other Social Competencies

Although many infants form the same kind of attachment with their fathers that they have established with their mothers (Fox, Kimmerly, & Schafer, 1991; Rosen & Rothbaum, 1993), it is not at all unusual for a child to be securely attached to one parent and insecure with the other (van IJzendoorn & De Wolff, 1997). For example, when Mary Main and Donna Weston (1981) used the Strange Situation to measure the quality of 44 toddlers' attachments to their mothers and their fathers, they found that 12 toddlers were securely attached to both parents, 11 were secure with the mother but insecure with the father, 10 were insecure with the mother but secure with the father, and 11 were insecurely attached to both parents.

What does the father add to a child's social and emotional development? One way to find out is to compare the social behavior of children who are securely attached to their fathers to those whose relationships with their fathers are insecure. Main and Weston did just that by exposing their four groups of toddlers to a friendly stranger in a clown outfit who spent several minutes trying to play with the child and then turned around and cried when a person at the door told the clown he would have to leave. As the clown went through his routine, the toddlers were each observed and rated for (1) the extent to which they were willing to establish a positive relationship with the clown (low ratings indicated

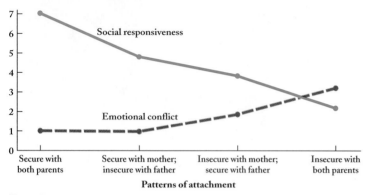

Figure 5.4
Average levels of social responsiveness and emotional conflict shown by toddlers who were either securely or insecurely attached to their mothers and fathers. (Adapted from Main & Weston, 1981.)

that the infant was wary or distressed) and (2) signs of emotional conflict (that is, indications of psychological disturbance such as curling up in the fetal position on the floor or vocalizing in a "social" manner to a wall). Figure 5.4 shows the results of this stranger test. Note that toddlers who were securely attached to *both* parents were the most socially responsive group. Equally important is the finding that toddlers who were securely attached to *at least one parent* were more friendly toward the clown and less emotionally conflicted than those who had insecure relationships with both parents. Other recent research has shown that, compared to children who are securely attached to only one or neither parent, those who are secure with *both* parents are less anxious and socially withdrawn and make better adjustments to the challenges of attending school (Verschueren & Marcoen, 1999). Children who are secure with fathers who are involved with them also display better emotional self-regulation, greater social competencies with peers, and lower levels of problem behaviors and delinquency throughout childhood and adolescence (Cabrera et al., 2000; Coley & Medeiros, 2007; Lieberman, Doyle, & Markiewicz, 1999; Pleck & Masciadrelli, 2004). Indeed, the positive benefits of having a secure, supportive relationship with one's father often occur even if he may no longer be residing in the home (Black, Dubowitz, & Starr, Jr., 1999; Coley & Medeiros, 2007). So not only are fathers potentially important contributors to many (perhaps *all*) aspects of child development, but it seems that a secure attachment to one's father may help to compensate for the potentially harmful effects of an insecure mother/child attachment relationship (Main & Weston, 1981; Verschueren & Marcoen, 1999).

⤳ ATTACHMENT AND LATER DEVELOPMENT

Both psychoanalytic theorists (Erikson, 1963; Freud, 1905/1930) and ethologists (Bowlby, 1969) believe that the feelings of warmth, trust, and security that infants gain from secure attachments will set the stage for healthy psychological development later in life. Of course one implication of this viewpoint is that insecure attachments may forecast less than optimal developmental outcomes in the years ahead.

Long-Term Correlates of Secure and Insecure Attachments

Although the existing data are somewhat limited in that they focus almost exclusively on infants' attachments to their mothers, it seems that infants who have established secure primary attachments are likely to display more favorable developmental outcomes. For example, babies who were securely attached at age 12–18 months are better problem solvers as 2-year-olds (Frankel & Bates, 1990), are more complex and creative in their symbolic play (Pipp, Easterbrooks, & Harmon, 1992), display more positive and fewer negative emotions (Kochanska, 2001), and are more attractive to toddlers as playmates (Fagot, 1997; Jacobson & Willie, 1986) than children who were insecurely attached. In fact, infants whose primary attachments are disorganized/disoriented are at risk of becoming hostile and aggressive preschool and grade-school children whom peers are likely to reject (Lyons-Ruth, Alpern, & Repacholi, 1993; Lyons-Ruth, Easterbrooks, & Cibelli, 1997).

Many longer-term studies of securely and insecurely attached children paint a similar picture. Everett Waters and his associates (1979), for example, first measured the quality of children's attachments at 15 months of age and then observed these children in a nursery-school setting at age 3½. Children who had been securely attached to their mothers at age 15 months were now social leaders in the nursery school: They often initiated play activities, were generally sensitive to the needs and feelings of other children, and were very popular with their peers. Observers described these children as curious, self-directed, and eager to learn. By contrast, children who had been insecurely attached at age 15 months were somewhat socially and emotionally withdrawn, hesitant to engage other children in play activities, and were described by observers as less curious, less interested in learning, and much less forceful in pursuing their goals. A follow-up in a camp setting when these children were 11–12 and 15–16 years old revealed that those who had been securely attached as infants and toddlers displayed better social skills and were more likely to have close friends than age-mates whose primary attachments had been insecure (Englund et al., 2000; Elicker, England, & Sroufe, 1992; Shulman, Elicker, & Sroufe, 1994). And recent studies with other samples reveal that youngsters whose early attachment relationships were or are currently insecure are more likely than those with secure attachments to have conflicted emotional dialogues with parents rather than the synchronous dialogues that promote emotional self-regulation (Oppenheim, Koren-Kaire, & Sagi-Schwartz, 2007); to be less enthused about mastering challenges (Moss & St-Laurent, 2001) and less prepared to deal constructively with the social and academic stresses surrounding their transition to college (Larose, Bernier, Tarabulsy, 2005); and to display poorer relations with peers, fewer close friendships, and more deviant behaviors (for example, disobedience at school) and other psychopathological symptoms throughout childhood and adolescence (Allen et al., 1998, 2007; Demulder et al., 2000; Jaffari-Bimmel et al., 2006; NICHD Early Child Care Research Network, 2006; Schneider, Atkinson, & Tardif, 2001). These longer-term relationships between early parent/child attachments and later social, emotional, and intellectual outcomes are sometimes indirect. In a prospective longitudinal study, for example, Geertjan Overbeek and associates (2007) found that the quality of parent/child bonds in middle childhood was indirectly associated with the quality of the relationship that these children had with their spouses at age 25. That is, children who had poor relations with parents at ages 4–10 subsequently experienced more conflict with parents during adolescence, but it was parent/adolescent conflict (which was strongly influenced by quality of adolescents' earlier relationships with parents) that best predicted how well these individuals got along with their spouses (see also Jaffari-Bimmel et al., 2006, for indirect effects of early attachment classifications on adolescent social competencies).

So it seems that children can be influenced, either directly or indirectly, by the quality of their earlier attachments for many years to come. And one reason is that attachments are often stable over time. In middle-class samples, most children (84 percent in one American sample and 85 percent in a German sample) experienced the same kind of attachment relationships with their parents during the grade-school years that they did in infancy (Main & Cassidy, 1988; Wartner et al., 1994). In fact, a sizeable number of adolescents and young adults from stable family backgrounds continue to display the same kinds of attachments that they had established in infancy with their parents (Hamilton, 2000; Waters et al., 2000), with many nondepressed, middle-class adolescents becoming even more secure with their parents over time (Allen et al., 2004).

Why Might Attachment Quality Forecast Later Outcomes?

Why is the quality of one's early attachments so often stable over time? And how might attachments shape one's behavior and influence the character of future interpersonal relationships?

MODEL OF SELF

	Positive	Negative
Positive	**SECURE** (Secure primary attachments)	**PREOCCUPIED** (Resistant primary attachments)
Negative	**DISMISSING** (Avoidant primary attachments)	**FEARFUL** (Disorganized/disoriented primary attachments)

MODEL OF OTHERS (vertical label on left, Positive / Negative)

Figure 5.5

Four perspectives on close emotional relationships that evolve from the positive or negative "working models" of self and others that people construct from their experiences with intimate companions. (Adapted from Bartholomew & Horowitz, 1991.)

internal working models
cognitive representations of self, others, and relationships that infants construct from their interactions with caregivers.

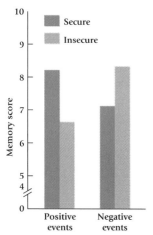

Figure 5.6

Due to differences in their internal working models, securely attached children are biased to remember positive experiences and insecurely attached children to remember negative experiences. (Based on means in Table 1, p. 113, in J. Belsky, B. Spritz, & K. Crnic, "Infant Attachment Security and Affective-Cognitive Information Processing at Age 3." *Psychological Science, 7,* 1996, 111–114.)

Attachments as Working Models of Self and Others John Bowlby (1980, 1988) and Inge Bretherton (1985, 1990) have proposed an interesting explanation for both the stability and any enduring effects of early attachment classifications. They believe that as infants continue to interact with primary caregivers, they will develop **internal working models**—that is, cognitive representations of *themselves* and *other people*—that are used to interpret events and form expectations about the character of human relationships. Sensitive, responsive caregiving should lead the child to conclude that people are dependable (positive working model of others), whereas insensitive, neglectful, or abusive caregiving may lead to insecurity and a lack of trust (negative working model of others). Although this sounds very similar to Erik Erikson's earlier ideas about the importance of trust, ethologists proceed one step further, arguing that an infant will also develop a working model of the self based largely on her ability to elicit attention and comfort *when she needs it*. So an infant whose caregivers respond quickly and appropriately to her bids for attention is likely to believe that "I'm lovable" (positive working model of self), whereas one whose signals are ignored or misinterpreted may conclude that "I'm unworthy or loathful" (negative working model of self). Presumably, these two models will combine to influence the quality of the child's primary attachments and the expectations she has about future relationships. What kinds of expectations might she form?

One version of this "working models" theory appears in Figure 5.5. As shown, infants who construct positive working models of themselves and their caregivers are the ones who should (1) form secure primary attachments, (2) have the *self*-confidence to approach and to master new challenges, and (3) be inclined to establish secure, mutual-trust relationships with friends and spouses later in life. By contrast, a positive model of self coupled with a negative model of others (as might result when infants can successfully attract the attention of an insensitive, overly intrusive caregiver) is thought to predispose the infant to form *avoidant* attachments and to "dismiss" the importance of close emotional bonds. A negative model of self and a positive model of others (as might result when infants sometimes can but often cannot attract the attention and care they need) should be associated with *resistant* attachments and a "preoccupation" with establishing secure emotional ties. Finally, a negative working model of both the self and others is thought to underlie *disorganized/disoriented* attachments and an emerging "fear" of being hurt (either physically or emotionally) in intimate relationships (Bartholomew & Horowitz, 1991).

Jay Belsky, Becky Spritz, and Keith Crnic (1996) were among the first to demonstrate that children who had secure and insecure attachments as infants have different styles of processing information that suggest they have formed very different internal working models of self and others. These researchers treated 3-year-olds to a series of puppet shows dramatizing positive events such as getting a birthday present and negative ones such as spilling juice. They expected children who had been securely attached as infants to expect positive experiences in life and to attend to them and remember them especially well; they expected children with histories of insecure attachment to expect and tend to recall the more negative events. The securely and insecurely attached children in the study did not differ in their attention to positive and negative events, but as Figure 5.6 shows, securely attached children excelled at remembering positive events, whereas insecurely attached children excelled at remembering negative events. This was true even when group differences in temperament were controlled. The implication? Bowlby was on the right track in theorizing that differences in the internal working models that securely and insecurely attached individuals form may be significant for later development.

Caregivers' Working Models of Attachments   Interestingly, caregivers also have positive or negative working models of themselves and others based on their own life experiences. Several methods now exist to measure adults' working models, based either on a detailed analysis of their memories of childhood attachment experiences as indicated in the *Adult Attachment Interview,* or by their current views of themselves, other people, and the character of interpersonal relationships as reported on paper-and-pencil measures (Bartholomew & Horowitz, 1991; Main & Goldwyn, 1994). Using these instruments, adults can be reliably cast into the classifications described earlier in Figure 5.5. Do parents' own working models influence the kinds of attachments their babies form?

Indeed they do. Peter Fonagy and his associates (1991), for example, found that English mothers' working models of attachment relationships measured *before their babies were born* accurately predicted about 75 percent of the time whether their infants would establish secure or insecure attachments with them. Similar results have now been reported in studies conducted in Canada, Germany, the Netherlands, Japan, and the United States (Behrens et al., 2007; Benoit & Parker, 1994; Das Eiden, Teti, & Corns, 1995; Steele, Steele, & Fonagy, 1996; van IJzendoorn, 1995), with an exact matching of working models occurring in 60–70 percent of the mother/infant dyads. One contributor to these working model matches is that mothers with more positive working models of self and others are more likely to provide the kind of sensitive, responsive, and nonintrusive caregiving that fosters secure infant attachments (Slade et al., 1999; van Bakel & Riksen-Walraven, 2002; Tarabulsy et al., 2005). Why is this? An important clue comes from a prospective longitudinal study in New Zealand that found that mothers who themselves as children had received warm, sensitive parenting—the kind of parenting that promotes secure attachments—tend to care for their own children in the warm, sensitive ways to which they themselves were accustomed (Belsky et al., 2005). However, sensitivity of care provided is not the only contributor to working-model "matches" between mothers and their infants. Another contributor is that mothers with secure attachment representations experience more joy and pleasure from interacting with their babies than do those whose attachment representations are insecure (Slade et al., 1999), and it appears that these two factors may contribute *independently* to the kinds of attachments infants form (Pederson et al., 1998).

So it seems that cognitive representations of intimate relationships are often transmitted from generation to generation. Indeed, Bowlby (1988) proposed that once formed early in life, working models may stabilize, becoming an aspect of personality that continues to influence the character of one's close emotional ties throughout life.

Is Attachment History Destiny?

Although it appears that early working models can be long lasting, and that there are some clear advantages to having formed secure emotional attachments early in life, the future is not always so bleak for infants who are insecurely attached. As we learned earlier in this chapter, a secure relationship with another person such as the father (or perhaps a grandparent or a day-care provider) can help to offset whatever undesirable consequences might otherwise result from an insecure attachment with the mother. What's more, if an insensitive mother becomes more sensitive and responsive over time, her child becomes much less susceptible to the behavioral problems and other shortcomings commonly associated with having an insecure early attachment with her (Forbes et al., 2007; NICHD Early Child Care Research Network, 2006).

Let's also note that secure attachments can become insecure should a mother return to work, deliver another baby that requires undue attention, or experience such life stresses as martial problems, depression, a major illness, or financial woes that dramatically alter the way that she and her child respond to one another (Lewis, Feiring, & Rosenthal, 2000; Moss et al., 2005; NICHD Early Child Care Research Network, 2006; Waters et al., 2000). One reason why Bowbly used the term *working* models was to underscore that a child's cognitive representations of self, others, and close emotional relationships are dynamic and can change (for better or for worse) if later experiences with caregivers, close friends, romantic partners, or spouses imply that a revision is necessary.

In sum, secure attachment histories are no guarantee of positive adjustment later in life; nor are insecure early attachments a certain indicator of poor life outcomes (Thompson, 1998). Yet we should not underestimate the adaptive significance of secure early attachments. Children who have functioned adequately as infants but very poorly (due to one or more major life stresses) during the preschool period are more likely to recover and to display good social skills and self-confidence during the grade-school years if their early attachment histories were secure rather than insecure (Sroufe, Egeland, & Kreutzer, 1990). The message? Although it provides no absolute guarantee of experiencing adaptive outcomes, an early *secure* attachment history appears to be an important source of emotional strength—a resource on which a child (or an adolescent) might draw to better cope with and function adaptively in the face of stress and adversity.

THE UNATTACHED INFANT

Some infants have very limited contacts with adults during the first year or two of life and do not appear to become attached to anyone. Occasionally, these socially deprived youngsters are reared at home by very abusive or neglectful caregivers, but most of them are found in understaffed institutions where they may see a caregiver only when it is time to be fed, changed, or bathed. Will these infants suffer as a result of their early experiences?

Correlates of Social Deprivation in Infancy and Childhood

In the 1940s, physicians and psychologists began to discover and study infants who were living under conditions of extreme social deprivation. It was not uncommon for the institutions in which these infants lived to have but one caregiver for every 10–20 infants. Caregivers rarely interacted with the infants except to bathe and change them or to prop a bottle against their pillows at feeding time. Infants were often housed in separate cribs with sheets hung over the railings so that, in effect, they were isolated from the world around them. By today's standards, these babies were victims of extreme neglect.

Infants raised under these conditions appear quite normal for the first three to six months of life: They cry for attention, smile and babble at caregivers, and make the proper postural adjustments when they are about to be picked up. But in the second half of the first year, their behavior changes. Now they seldom cry, coo, or babble; they become rigid and fail to accommodate to the handling of caregivers; and they often appear rather depressed and uninterested in social contact (Goldfarb, 1943; Provence & Lipton, 1962; Ribble, 1943; Spitz, 1945). Here is a description of one such infant:

> Outstanding were his soberness, his forlorn appearance, and lack of animation. . . . He did not turn to adults to relieve his distress. . . . He made no demands. . . . As one made active and persistent efforts at a social exchange he became somewhat more responsive, animated and . . . active, but lapsed into his depressed . . . appearance when the adult became less active. . . . If you crank his motor you can get him to go a little; but he can't start on his own. (Provence & Lipton, 1962, pp. 134–135)

More recently, grave concerns have arisen about the serious maladjustment of many children raised in deprived institutions in Romania after the social upheavals surrounding the fall of the Romanian government in 1990. These Romanian children spent their time in orphanages with 20 to 30 children in a room and only one caregiver for every 10 to 20 children.

Photo 5.7
Children raised in barren, understaffed institutions show many signs of development impairment.

Much of their time was spent rocking back and forth in their cribs, with few occasions to play or experience human affection and virtually no opportunities to establish synchronous routines with anyone (Fisher et al., 1997). A large number of these children were either extremely withdrawn and unresponsive to social overtures or indiscriminately friendly, approaching and seeking attention as readily from strangers as from familiar caregivers (Smyke, Dumitrescu, & Zeanah, 2002). These withdrawn/inhibited and indiscriminately friendly/disinhibited patterns describe a clinical syndrome known as **reactive attachment disorder**—an inability to bond, securely or otherwise, to adoptive or foster parents (American Psychiatric Association, 2000), even when these new caregivers have secure working models of attachment relationships (Marcovitch et al., 1997).

How serious is the problem? One estimate comes from a recent study in which the Strange Situation was used to compare the attachment classifications of 95 12- to 31-month-old institutionalized Romanian children to those of 50 Romanian age-mates who had never been institutionalized. The institutionalized children participated with their "favorite" caregiver, whereas the comparison group participated with their mothers. As shown in Figure 5.7, a large majority of the never institutionalized children had formed secure attachments, whereas an even larger majority of the institutionalized children were either unclassifiable (little evidence of any attachment) or displayed a disorganized/disoriented attachment to a favorite caregiver (Zeanah et al., 2005). What's more the "secure" attachments of those few institutionalized children who formed them were rated as significantly less close and comfortable than the secure attachments of the home-reared children. Even after having been adopted and

reactive attachment disorder
inability to form secure attachment bonds with other people; characterizes many victims of early social deprivation and/or abuse.

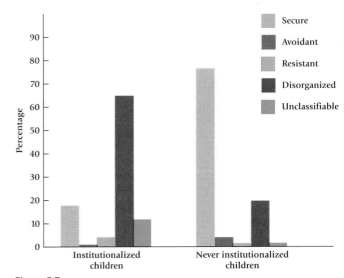

Figure 5.7
Percentages of secure, avoidant, resistant, disorganized and unclassifiable attachments in 12- to 31-month-old institutionalized and never institutionalized Romanian children. (Adapted from Zeanah et al., 2005.)

having spent considerable time in middle-class homes, adoptees who had spent their first six to eight months in understaffed Romanian orphanages were far less likely to become securely attached and more likely to show abnormal patterns of insecure behavior than age-mates raised at home (Chisholm, 1998, O'Connor et al., 2003).

What are these institutionalized infants like as schoolchildren and adolescents? The answer depends in part on how long they remain in the institution. William Goldfarb (1943, 1947) compared children who left an understaffed orphanage during the first year with similar children who spent their first three years at the orphanage before departing for foster homes. After interviewing, observing, and testing these children at ages 3½, 6½, 8½, and 12, Goldfarb found that youngsters who had spent three years in the institution lagged behind the early adoptees in virtually all aspects of development. They scored poorly on IQ tests, were socially immature, remarkably dependent on adults, had poor language skills, and were prone to behavior problems such as aggression and hyperactivity. By early adolescence, they were often loners who had a difficult time relating to peers or to members of their adoptive families (see also Croft et al., 2007; Kreppner et al., 2007). Intellectual performance may be impaired by as little as six months of institutionalization. One recent study found that despite having lived many years in good adoptive homes, Romanian adoptees who had spent their first six months or longer in an institution were continuing to show substantially lower IQs at age 11 than English or Romanian age-mates who had been adopted prior to age 6 months (Beckett et al., 2006). Yet about a third of the adoptees who had spent more than six months in depriving institutions were functioning normally with no serious impairments by age 11 (Kreppner et al., 2007).

Why Might Early Deprivation Be Harmful?

No one today questions that early social deprivation can have lasting effects, but there is some disagreement about why this is so. The fact that as little as six months of institution-alization can have measurable long-term effects on intellectual performance has prompted some to presume that the early years represent a "sensitive" period in which inadequate social stimulation inhibits normal growth and development of the brain, provided that the deprivation continues for longer than six months (Nelson, 2007; Rutter, 2006).

With regard to the social implications of early deprivation, proponents of the **maternal deprivation hypothesis** (Bowlby, 1969; Spitz, 1965) think that children in understaffed institutions develop abnormally because they lack the warm, loving attention of a single mother figure to whom they can become attached. But despite its popularity, there are many observations the maternal deprivation hypothesis cannot easily explain. Studies of adequately staffed institutions in Russia, China, and Israel, for example, reveal that infants who are cared for by many responsive caregivers appear quite normal and are as well adjusted later in childhood as those who are reared at home (Bronfenbrenner, 1970a, Kessen, 1975; Oppenheim, Sagi, & Lamb, 1988). Similarly, Efe (Pygmy) infants in Zaire seem to thrive from birth on being cared for and even nursed by a variety of caregivers (Tronick, Morelli, & Ivey, 1992). So it seems that the impairments characterizing children in understaffed institutions probably reflect something other than their lack of an exclusive primary attachment to a singular mother figure.

Might socially deprived infants develop abnormally simply because they have little contact with anyone who responds to their social signals? Proponents of the **social stimulation hypothesis** think so, arguing that the normal development of Chinese, Russian, Israeli, and Efe infants raised by multiple caregivers implies that infants need *sustained* interactions with *responsive* companions—either one or several—in order to develop normally. Such stimulation may be particularly important because it often depends in part on the infant's own behavior: People often attend to the infant when he or she cries, smiles, babbles, burps, or gazes at them. This kind of association between one's own behavior and

maternal deprivation hypothesis the notion that socially deprived infants develop abnormally because they have failed to establish attachments to a primary caregiver.

social stimulation hypothesis the notion that socially deprived infants develop abnormally because they have had little contact with companions who respond contingently to their social overtures.

the behavior of caregivers may lead an infant to believe that she has some *control* over the social environment—an important contributor to a positive working model of self. And as she exerts this "control" and receives others' attention and affection, she should develop a positive working model of others and become more outgoing.

Now consider the plight of socially deprived infants who may emit many signals and rarely receive a response from their overburdened or inattentive caregivers. What are these children likely to learn from their early experiences? Probably that their attempts to attract the attention of others are useless (negative working model of self), for nothing they do seems to matter to anyone (negative working model of others). Consequently they may develop a sense of **"learned helplessness"** and simply stop trying to elicit responses from other people (Finkelstein & Ramey, 1977). Here, then, is a very plausible reason why socially deprived infants are often rather passive, withdrawn, and apathetic.

learned helplessness
the failure to learn how to respond appropriately in a situation because of previous exposures to uncontrollable events in the same or similar situations.

Can Children Recover from Early Deprivation Experiences?

Fortunately, socially deprived (or otherwise maltreated) infants and toddlers can overcome many of their initial handicaps if placed in homes where they receive lots of attention from sensitive, responsive caregivers (Clarke & Clarke, 2000; Nelson, 2007). Recovery seems to go especially well when children have not been abused and are placed by age 6 months with *highly educated* and *relatively affluent* adoptive or foster parents who themselves have positive (that is, secure) working models of attachment relationships (Dozier et al., 2001; Kreppner et al., 2007; Stams, Juffer, & van IJzendoorn, 2002). Audrey Clark and Jeannette Hanisee (1982), for example, studied a group of Asian orphans who had lived in institutions, foster homes, or hospitals before coming to the United States. Many were war orphans who had early histories of malnutrition or serious illness. But despite the severe environmental insults they had endured, these children made remarkable progress. After only two to three years in their highly stimulating, middle-class adoptive homes, the Asian adoptees scored significantly *above* average on both a standardized intelligence test and an assessment of social maturity.

On the other hand, the lingering deficiencies and reactive attachment disorders that some early abuse victims and many late adoptees display suggest that the first six months of life may be a *sensitive period* for developments that would help infants to establish *secure* affectional ties and other capacities that these ties may foster. Can they make complete recoveries? We don't really know yet (see Beckett et al., 2006; Kreppner et al., 2007), although it is likely that especially severe or prolonged adversity may take longer to overcome and may require stronger interventions than merely placing these children in good homes. Current thinking is that severe and prolonged early deprivation probably affects the development of the brain in ways that may help to account for some of the long-term deficiencies that many institutionalized children display (Nelson, 2007; Rutter, 2006). This might be good news, for the brain remains plastic (changeable) until well into adolescence or young adulthood (Huttenlocher, 2002). Thus, if neural bases of their lingering deficiencies can be identified, it may be possible to design effective interventions to help institutionalized or otherwise abused children to place most of their problems behind them.

MATERNAL EMPLOYMENT, DAY CARE, AND EARLY EMOTIONAL DEVELOPMENT

In recent years an important question has arisen about the ways in which our infants, toddlers, and preschool children spend their time. Should they be cared for at home by a parent, or can they pursue their developmental agendas just as well in a day-care setting? Now that more than 60 percent of all mothers and more than 50 percent of mothers with infants less than 1 year old work outside the home at least part time (National Research Council and Institute for Medicine, 2000; Tran & Weinraub, 2006), more and more young children are receiving alternative forms of care. In the United States, about 40 percent of infants and toddlers are cared for regularly by their parents, whereas 21 percent receive care from other relatives, 4 percent are cared for at home by a sitter, 14 percent receive care in day-care homes (typically run by a woman who takes a few children into her own home for payment), and 31 percent are enrolled in large child-care centers (Scarr, 1998).[1]

Do infants who attend day-care homes or centers have trouble establishing or maintaining secure attachments to working mothers? Do they suffer in any way compared to those who stay at home with a parent? Research to date suggests that they usually do not (Ahnert, Rickert, & Lamb, 2000; NICHD Early Child Research Network, 1997, 2000, 2001a, 2001b, 2003a). In fact, high-quality day care promotes both the social responsiveness and the intellectual development of children from disadvantaged backgrounds, who are otherwise at risk of experiencing behavior problems and serious developmental delays (Love et al., 2003; Ramey & Ramey, 1998). Furthermore, a large, well-controlled longitudinal study of 1,153 children in alternative care that began in 1991 and continues today revealed that neither the age at which children enter day care nor the amount of care they receive was related in any simple way to the security of their attachments to their mothers or their emotional well-being (NICHD Early Child Care Research Network, 1997, 2001b). The one cause for concern in this large longitudinal study was that children who had spent more time in alternative care throughout the first four and a half years of life were somewhat more aggressive and disobedient in elementary school than those who had experienced less out-of-home care (NICHD, 2003a). What's more, higher levels of problem behaviors were still detectable at age 12 among youngsters who had spent greater amounts of time in one particular kind of alternative care—group day-care centers (Belsky et al., 2007). Yet these "amount of care" effects are not large and are *not* always found in other well-controlled studies (see Love et al., 2003).

Unfortunately, these broad generalizations do not tell the full story. Let's briefly consider two factors that are likely to influence how well an infant or toddler adjusts to maternal employment and day care.

Quality of Alternative Care

Table 5.4 lists what experts believe to be the most important characteristics of high-quality day care for infants and toddlers (Burchinal et al., 2000; de Schipper, Riksen-Walraven, & Guerts, 2006; Howes, 1997). Unfortunately, the quality of alternative care in the United States is very uneven compared to that widely available in many Western European countries. Large numbers of American infants and toddlers are cared for by sitters who have little knowledge of or training in child development, or in unlicensed day-care homes or centers that often fail to meet minimum health and safety standards (Scarr, 1998).

How important is high-quality care? Apparently there is far less risk that children will display insecure attachments (or any other adverse outcome) when they receive excellent day care—*even when that care begins very early.* Jerome Kagan and his associates (1978), for example, found that the vast majority of infants who entered a high-quality, university-sponsored day-care program at age 3½ to 5½ months not only developed secure

---

[1]These figures total more than 100 percent because a substantial number of American children have more than one regular care arrangement, such as morning enrollment in a day-care center and parental care at home during other hours. Moreover, as many as 30–40 percent of very young infants in day care experience at least one change in primary day care providers over the first 12–15 months of life (Tran & Weinraub, 2006).

Table 5.4 Characteristics of high-quality infant and toddler day care

Physical setting	The indoor environment is clean, well lighted, and ventilated; outdoor play areas are fenced, spacious, and free of hazards; they include age-appropriate implements (slides, swings, sandbox, and so on).
Child/caregiver ratio	No more than three infants or four to six toddlers per adult caregiver.
Caregiver characteristics/ qualifications	Caregivers should have some training in child development and first aid; they should be warm, emotionally expressive, and responsive to children's bids for attention. Ideally, staffing is consistent so that infants and toddlers can form relationships (even attachment relationships) with their caregivers.
Toys/activities	Toys and activities are age appropriate; infants and toddlers are always supervised, even during free play indoors.
Family links	Parents are always welcome and caregivers confer freely with them about their child's progress.
Licensing	Day-care setting is licensed by the state and (ideally) accredited by the National Family Day Care Program or the National Academy of Early Childhood Programs.

attachments to their mothers but were just as socially, emotionally, and intellectually mature over the first two years of life as children from similar backgrounds who had been cared for at home. Studies conducted in Sweden (where day care is government subsidized, closely monitored, and typically of high quality) report similar positive outcomes (Broberg et al., 1997), and it seems that the earlier Swedish infants enter high-quality day care, the better their cognitive, social, and emotional development years later in elementary and junior high school (Andersson, 1989, 1992). Finally, studies of U.S. children in day-care arrangements of varying quality reveal that early entry into high-quality care is a reasonably good predictor of favorable social, emotional, and (especially) intellectual outcomes (for example, language skills, readiness for school, and performance on standardized tests) at age 3, 4½, and during the primary grades at school, with low-quality care being associated with much poorer outcomes (Burchinal et al., 2000; Howes, 1997; Love et al., 2003; NICHD Early Child Care Research Network, 2000, 2001a, 2003b; 2005b).

Unfortunately, children who receive the poorest and most unstable day care are often those whose parents are living complex, stressful lives of their own that may constrain their sensitivity as parents and their involvement in children's lives and learning activities (Fuller, Holloway, & Liang, 1996; Howes, 1990). So a child's poor progress in day care may often stem as much from a disordered home life, in which stress-ridden parents are not all that enthused about parenting, as from the less than optimal alternative care that he or she receives (NICHD Early Child Care Research Network, 1997, 1998a). Let's explore this idea further.

Parenting and Parents' Attitudes about Work

According to Lois Hoffman (1989), a mother's attitudes about working and child care may be as important to her child's social and emotional well-being as her actual employment status. Mothers tend to be much happier and more sensitive as caregivers when their employment statuses are consistent with their desire to be either employed or a full-time homemaker (Harrison & Ungerer, 2002; NICHD Early Child Care Research Network, 1998b). Working mothers do spend less time per day with their infants, toddlers, and preschool children; but they

Photo 5.8
High-quality day care can have beneficial effects on children's social, emotional, and intellectual development.

Jim Whitmer/Stock Boston

often compensate for their absences during the work day by creating stimulating home environments and spending a greater percentage of their evening and weekend time holding and playing with their children (and less time on housework, instrumental child care, and their own social activities) compared to mothers who remain unemployed (Huston & Rosenkrantz Aronson, 2005). So if a mother wants to (or needs to) work, she can still be a sensitive caregiver, and it may make little sense to pressure her into staying home to care for her child when she might be hostile, depressed, or otherwise unresponsive in that role.

Does it matter when a mother returns to work? Unfortunately, there is no simple answer to this question. Some researchers have found that infants may face a slightly elevated risk of insecure attachments (and, in some studies, risk of lower scores on tests of school readiness and primary grade reading and math performance) if their mothers returned to work within the first 9 to 12 months after giving birth (see, for example, Barglow, Vaughn, & Molitor, 1987; Belsky & Rovine, 1988; Brooks-Gunn, Han, & Waldfogel, 2002; Han, 2005; Hill et al., 2005). Yet we must not read too much into these findings because most infants whose mothers return early to work still end up securely attached and display no serious cognitive shortcomings later in childhood, particularly when their mothers are working because they want to and are themselves sensitive caregivers (Belsky & Rovine, 1988; Belsky et al., 2007; Harrison & Ungerer, 2002).

Even when children receive far less than optimal alternative care, their outcomes will depend greatly on the parenting they receive (NICHD Early Child Care Research Network, 1997, 1998b, 2001a, 2001b, 2003a). Outcomes are likely to be better if a working mother has positive attitudes *both* about working and about being a mother (Belsky & Rovine, 1988; Huston & Rosenkrantz, 2005). And it also helps immensely if her spouse approves of her working and supports her in her parenting role (Cabrera et al., 2000). Ultimately, parents' attitudes about parenting and the quality of care they provide at home have far more to do with an infant's, a toddler's, or an older child's development than the kind of alternative care he receives (Belsky et al., 2007; NICHD Early Child Care Research Network, 1997, 1998a, 2001b).

What conclusions can we draw, then, about maternal employment, alternative care, and children's early social and emotional development? Considered together, the evidence suggests that (1) children of working mothers who receive sensitive, responsive care at home are at little risk of poor emotional outcomes and that (2) excellent alternative care helps to buffer children against emotional insecurity (and other adverse outcomes) should the parenting they receive be far less than optimal. One way that stimulating, high-quality day care serves this protective function is by helping to make children more socially and intellectually responsive, which may often have the effect of inducing parents to become more sensitive and responsive to them (see Burchinal et al., 2000; NICHD Early Child Care Research Network, 1999). In the final analysis, it seems that maternal employment and day care are most likely to be associated with poor emotional (and other negative) outcomes when infants and toddlers face the *dual risk* of insensitive parenting and poor alternative care (NICHD Child Care Research Network, 1997, 2001b).

How Might We Assist Working Parents?

What, then, might be done to help working parents to establish and maintain more secure ties with their infants and toddlers and to otherwise optimize their development? A national policy governing parental leave for child care is certainly one step in the right direction. In 1993, the United States Congress passed the *Family and Medical Leave Act*—a law guaranteeing workers in firms with 50 or more employees the right to take 12 weeks of *unpaid* leave to spend time with their infants, without jeopardizing their jobs. Yet this guarantee (1) does not apply to nearly half of American workers, who are employed by firms with fewer than 50 employees (Kamerman, 2000) and (2) seems almost miserly compared

Table 5.5 Sample parental-leave policies in modern industrialized nations

Canada	Mothers receive 15 weeks of leave at 55 percent of pay. An additional 10 weeks of parental leave is available to either parent.
Finland	Mothers receive 18 weeks of leave at 70 percent pay. Additional parental leave of 26 weeks at 70 percent pay is available to either parent.
Germany	Mothers receive 14 weeks at 100 percent pay and up to $2^1/_2$ years of additional leave at partial pay.
Sweden	Mothers receive 14 weeks of leave at 80 percent pay; the mother or father may take an additional 38 weeks of parental leave at 60 percent pay, and may extend leave benefits for at another 6 months, receiving a similar fraction of pay.
United Kingdom	Mothers receive 6 weeks of 90 percent pay and 12 additional weeks in which they receive a flat-rate monetary stipend. Thirteen weeks of additional unpaid leave can be taken by either parent.
United States	Either parent may take 12 weeks of *unpaid* leave in firms of 50 or more employees.

Source: Kamerman, 2000.

to the often generous parental-leave policies that many other industrialized societies have established (see Table 5.5).

An early report on the impact of maternal leave reveals that longer leaves are more beneficial than shorter ones. Specifically, American mothers who took four-month leaves after giving birth displayed less negative affect when interacting with their babies than did mothers whose leaves lasted only two months (Clark et al., 1997; see also Feldman, Sussman, & Zigler, 2004). The benefits of longer leaves were most noticeable among mothers who reported depressive symptoms or who had babies with difficult temperaments: These mothers were much more *positively* involved with their infants and had more sensitivity in their face-to-face interactions if their leave had lasted a full four months. Longer leaves may allow depressed mothers to become more involved with their babies and confident as caregivers, while allowing more time for those with difficult infants to establish a "good fit" between their parenting and the babies' temperamental attributes. Unfortunately, many mothers cannot afford to take four-month, *unpaid* leaves, thus prompting researchers and child care advocates to recommend that the *Family and Medical Leave Act* of 1993 be revised to provide four to six months of leave with partial pay to employees in all firms, regardless of their size (Clark et al., 1997; Kamerman, 2000).

A workable national policy governing day care may be equally (or more) important. At present, middle-class families are the ones caught most directly in a day-care squeeze. Upper-income families have the resources to purchase excellent day care; and the compensatory education (or other subsidized alternative care) that many lower-income children receive is typically of higher quality than that middle-class parents can afford to purchase (Scarr, 1998)[2]. Meanwhile parents from all social backgrounds must often struggle to find and keep competent sitters or other high-quality day-care placements, which are in short supply—due in part to the continuing reluctance of the U.S. government to subsidize day care for all citizens and carefully monitor its quality, as many European countries have done. Increasingly, employers are realizing that it is in their best interest to help workers

[2]Unfortunately, high-quality commercial day care in the United States is rather expensive and a real burden to many families who have more than one child enrolled. In the Athens, Georgia, area, for example, day-care fees in 2006 ran approximately $8000 per year per child (and slightly higher for infants) for commercial or nonprofit placements that meet the criteria for good or excellent care.

obtain quality day care. According to Sandra Scarr (1998), many corporations vie each year to be on the *Working Women* magazine list of the top 100 most family-friendly companies, and some larger employers have even established day-care centers at the work site. Edward Zigler (Zigler & Finn-Stevenson, 1996) has proposed that public schools, which are already established institutions in all communities, could be a relatively economical way to provide day care for preschool children, with costs funded by a mix of federal, state, and local tax dollars and parental fees. In fact, Zigler has prompted more than 400 school systems in the United States to incorporate child care into their educational programs. Yet these efforts by corporations and the public schools are not widespread and appear unlikely to become public policy any time soon. So until more options are available, most working parents in the United States will continue to face the very real challenge of finding good alternative care at a cost they can afford.

SUMMARY

WHAT ARE EMOTIONAL ATTACHMENTS?

✦ Infants normally form affectional ties to their close companions during the first year of life. These **attachments** are reciprocal relationships, for an infant's attachment objects (parents and other intimate companions) will normally become attached to him or her. Parents' initial **emotional bonding** with their infant builds in strength as they gear their behavior to the infant's social signals and establish **synchronized routines.** These exquisite interactions are pleasing for both parents and infants and are thought to contribute to strong reciprocal attachments.

HOW DO INFANTS BECOME ATTACHED?

✦ Infants pass through an **asocial phase** and a **phase of indiscriminate attachment** before forming their first true attachments at 7–9 months of age during the **phase of specific attachments.** Attached infants become more curious, using their attachment object as a **secure base** for exploration. They eventually enter the **phase of multiple attachments,** forming affectional ties to more than one person.

THEORIES OF ATTACHMENT

✦ Early *psychoanalytic* and *learning* theories were called into question by the finding that feeding plays much less of a role in human attachments than these models expected. The *cognitive-developmental* notion that attachments depend in part on cognitive development has received some support. *Ethological* theory, which specifies that humans have **preadapted characteristics** that predispose them to form attachments, has become especially influential in recent years. Yet all these theories have contributed to our understanding of infant attachments.

INDIVIDUAL DIFFERENCES IN ATTACHMENT QUALITY

✦ Ainsworth's **Strange Situation** is most commonly used to assess the quality of attachments that 1- to 2-year-olds have formed, although the **Attachment Q-set** and the **Adult Attachment Interview** are versatile alternatives that enable researchers to assess the security of attachment representations in older children, adolescents, and adults. Four attachment classifications have been identified: **secure, resistant, avoidant,** and **disorganized/disoriented.**

✦ Although the distribution of various attachment classifications varies across cultures and often reflects cultural differences in child rearing, parents around the world prefer that their infants form secure attachments, and more infants around the world establish secure attachments than any other pattern.

FACTORS THAT INFLUENCE ATTACHMENT SECURITY

✦ Sensitive, responsive, **insightful** caregiving is associated with the development of secure attachments, whereas inconsistent, neglectful, overly intrusive, and abusive caregiving predict insecure attachments. Thus, there is ample support for the **caregiving hypothesis.** Fortunately, parents who are at risk of promoting insecure attachments can be trained to become more sensitive, responsive caregivers.

✦ Infant characteristics and temperamental attributes may also influence attachment quality by affecting the character of caregiver/infant interactions. However, the **temperament hypothesis**—that attachments are merely reflections of infant temperament—is clearly an overstatement.

✦ Today, some developmentalists favor an integrative theory—one which holds that caregiving largely determines whether attachments are secure or not, whereas child temperament largely influences the type of insecurity that a child who receives insensitive caregiving might display.

FATHERS AS ATTACHMENT OBJECTS

✦ Infants often form attachments to their fathers soon after they become attached to their mothers. Sensitivity of paternal caregiving promotes secure attachments, whereas insensitivity is likely to foster insecure father/infant attachments. Fathers often assume the role of playmate in infants' and toddlers lives, although they are (or can be) quite proficient at all aspects of caregiving.

✦ A secure attachment to the father contributes in many ways to a child's social and emotional development and may help to compensate for the potentially harmful effects of an insecure mother/child attachment relationship.

ATTACHMENT AND LATER DEVELOPMENT

✦ Secure attachment during infancy predicts intellectual curiosity and social competence later in childhood. One reason for this is that infants form **internal working models** of themselves and others that are often stable over time and influence their reactions to people and challenges for years to come. Parents' working models correspond closely with those of their children; thus attachment representations are often transmitted from generation to generation. However, children's working models can change, so that a secure attachment history is no guarantee of positive adjustment later in life; nor are insecure attachments a certain indication of poor life outcomes.

THE UNATTACHED INFANT

✦ Some infants have had very limited contacts with caregivers early in life and don't seem attached to anyone. Children who were socially deprived as infants are withdrawn and apathetic and (in the case of humans) may later display intellectual deficits, behavior problems, and **reactive attachment disorders.** Current speculation is that early deprivation may adversely affect brain development. Deprived children's problems appear to stem more from their lack of responsive social stimulation **(social stimulation hypothesis)** than from failure to receive care from a singular mother figure **(maternal deprivation**

hypothesis), and they often display some capacity for recovery, overcoming many of their initial handicaps. However, special interventions yet to be discovered may be necessary to allow victims of severe and prolonged social deprivation to place any lingering deficiencies behind them.

MATERNAL EMPLOYMENT, DAY CARE, AND EARLY EMOTIONAL DEVELOPMENT

✦ It was once feared that regular separations from working parents and placement into day care might prevent infants from establishing secure attachments or undermine the quality of attachments that were already secure. However, there is little evidence that either a mother's employment outside the home or alternative caregiving will have harmful effects unless children face the dual risks of insensitive care at home and poor day care.

✦ Stronger family-leave policies and national policies to make affordable, high-quality day care available to all parents are among the most important supports working parents need to optimize their children's social, emotional, and intellectual development.

CHAPTER 6

Development of the Self and Social Cognition

Who Am I?

I am a free man, an American, a United States Senator, a Democrat,
a liberal, a conservative, a Texan, a taxpayer, a rancher, a businessman, a
consumer, a parent, a voter, and not as young as I used to be nor as old
as I expect to be, and I am all these things in no fixed order.—Lyndon B.
Johnson, U.S. Senator and 37th President of the United States
(as quoted by Gordon, 1968)

How would you answer the "Who am I" question? Although not all adults think
of themselves in the same ways mentioned by former president Lyndon Johnson, college
students often respond by mentioning some of the most noteworthy personality characteristics (for example, honesty, friendliness), some of the roles they may be playing in life
(for example, student, peer tutor, hospital volunteer), their religious or moral views, their
future aspirations, and perhaps their political leanings. In so doing, they are describing that
elusive concept that psychologists call the **self.**

self
the combination of physical and
psychological attributes that is
unique to each individual.

Although no one else knows you as well as you do, it is a safe bet that much of what you
know about yourself stems from your contacts and experiences with other people. When
a college sophomore tells us that he is a friendly and energetic person who is active in his
fraternity, the Young Republicans, and the Campus Crusade for Christ, he is saying that
his past experiences with others and the groups to which he belongs are important determinants of his personal identity. Many years ago, sociologists Charles Cooley (1902) and
George Herbert Mead (1934) proposed that the self-concept evolves from social interactions and will undergo many changes over the course of a lifetime. Cooley used the term
looking-glass self to emphasize that a person's understanding of self is a reflection of how
other people react to him: The self-concept is the image cast by a social mirror.

looking-glass self
the idea that a child's self-concept
is largely determined by the ways
other people respond to him or her.

Cooley and Mead believed that the self and social development are completely intertwined—that they emerge together and that neither can progress far without the other.
Presumably, newborns experience people and events as simple "streams of impressions" and
will have absolutely no concept of "self" until they realize that they exist independent of
the objects and individuals that they encounter regularly. Once infants make this important distinction between self and nonself, they will establish interactive routines with close
companions (that is, develop socially) and will learn that their behavior elicits predictable
reactions from others. In other words, they are acquiring information about the "social self"
based on the ways people respond to them. Mead (1934) concluded that:

> the self has a character that is different from that of the physiological organism proper. The
> self is something which . . . is not initially there at birth but arises in the process of social de-
> velopment. That is, it develops in a given individual as a result of his relations to that process
> as a whole and to other individuals within the process.

Do babies really have no sense of self at birth? We explore this issue in the first section of
the chapter, as we trace the growth of the self-concept from infancy through adolescence.
We will then consider how children and adolescents evaluate the self and construct a sense
of *self-esteem*. Our focus will then shift to a major developmental hurdle that adolescents
face: the need to establish a firm, future-oriented self-portrait, or *identity*, with which to
approach the responsibilities of young adulthood. Finally, we will consider what developing children know about other people and interpersonal relationships and will see that this

aspect of **social cognition,** which parallels the development of the self-concept, nicely illustrates Cooley's and Mead's point that personal (self) and social aspects of development are complexly intertwined.

Of course, there are several other aspects of self-development that warrant more extended coverage as important topics in their own right. In Chapter 7, for example, we will see how curious infants and toddlers become fascinated by and begin to take pride in their ability to make things happen—a pride that may (or may not) blossom into a strong motive to achieve and a favorable academic self-concept. And we all develop conceptions of ourselves (and others) as males or females, as prosocial or antisocial beings, and as moral (or immoral) individuals. Research on these topics is now so extensive that each merits a chapter of its own (see Chapters 8–10).

For now, let's return to the starting point and see how children come to know this entity we call the *self.*

DEVELOPMENT OF THE SELF-CONCEPT

When do infants first distinguish themselves from other people, objects, and environmental events? At what point do they become consciously aware of their uniqueness. What kinds of information do young children use to define the self? And how do their self-images and feelings of self-worth change over time? These are some of the issues we will explore as we trace the development of the **self-concept** from infancy through adolescence.

The Emerging Self: Differentiation, Discrimination, and Self-Recognition

Like Mead, many developmentalists believe that infants are born without a sense of self. Psychoanalyst Margaret Mahler (Mahler, Pine, & Bergman, 1975) likens the newborn to a "chick in an egg" who has no reason to differentiate the self from the surrounding environment. After all, every need that the child has is soon satisfied by his or her ever-present companions, who are simply "there" and have no identities of their own.

By contrast, other developmentalists (see Brown, 1998; Meltzoff, 1990a) believe that even newborn infants have the *capacity* to distinguish the self from the surrounding environment. For example, newborns cry at hearing a recording of another baby's cries but *not* upon hearing a recording of their *own* cries, thus implying that a differentiation of self and others is possible at birth (Dondi et al., 1999). Furthermore, newborns anticipate the arrival of their own hands at their mouths and, as we noted in Box 2.2, seem capable of using **proprioceptive feedback** from their own facial expressions to mimic at least some of the facial expressions their caregivers display. These kinds of observations suggested to Andrew Meltzoff (1990a) that:

> The young infant possess an embryonic "body scheme" . . . [Although] this body scheme develops [over time], some body scheme kernel is present as a "psychological primitive" right from the earliest phases of infancy. (p. 160)

Of course, these observations are subject to alternative interpretations (many believe them to be mere reflexes), and it is by no means an easy task to clearly establish when infants first become self-aware. Yet almost everyone agrees that the first glimmerings of this capacity can be seen in the first two or three months (Samuels, 1986; Stern, 1995). Recall Piaget's (and others') descriptions of cognitive development early in infancy. During the first two months, babies are exercising their reflexive schemes and repeating pleasurable acts centered in their own bodies (for example, sucking their thumbs and waving their arms). In other words, they are becoming acquainted with their own physical capabilities, and by 3 months of age, an infant who sees legs kicking on a TV monitor can already use proprioceptive and spatial cues about the directionality of those kicks to decide whether the legs he is observing are his own (Rochat & Morgan, 1995). We also learned in Chapter 4 that infants only 1 to 3 months old delight at producing interesting sights and sounds by kicking their legs or pulling their arms (which are attached by strings to mobiles or to audiovisual machinery; Lewis, Alessandri, & Sullivan, 1990; Rovee-Collier, 1995). Even an 8-week-old infant can recall how to produce these interesting events for two or three days; and if the strings are disconnected so she can no longer exert any control, she may pull or kick all the harder and become rather distressed (Lewis, Alessandri, & Sullivan, 1990; Sullivan, Lewis, & Alessandri, 1992). Thus it seems that 2-month-old infants may have some limited sense of **personal agency,** or understanding that *they* are responsible for at least some of the events that so fascinate them.

So it is still an open question whether newborn infants can truly differentiate themselves from the surrounding environment. But even if they can't, it is likely that they learn the limits of their own bodies during the first month or two and differentiate this "physical self" from the external objects they can control shortly thereafter (Samuels, 1986). So if a 2- to 4-month-old could talk, he might answer the "Who am I" question by saying, "I am a looker, a chewer, a reacher, and a grabber who acts on objects and makes things happen."

In the second half of the first year, infants recognize that they and their companions are separate beings with different perspectives that can be shared (Thompson, 1998). For example, infants 9 months of age and older recognize that they and a companion can share perceptual experiences by *joint attention*—that is, by both attending to the same object at the same time. And by the end of the first year, babies have already learned to direct a companion's attention to an interesting object or event by pointing at it a—skill that some believe to represent an early cooperative kind of communication by which an infant attempts to influence her companion's perspective or mental state (Tomasello, Carpenter, & Liszkowski, 2007).

Self-Recognition   Once infants know that they *are* (that they exist independent of other people and other objects), they are in a position to find out *who* or *what* they are (Harter, 1983). When do infants perceive themselves as having unique physical characteristics? When do they construct firm self-images and view themselves as an object that has a sense of permanence over time?

One way to answer these questions is to expose infants to some visual representation of the self (that is, a videotape or mirror reflection) and see how they respond to these images. Research of this type reveals that infants only 4 to 5 months old seem to treat their own faces as familiar social stimuli (Legerstee, Anderson, & Schaffer, 1998; Rochat & Striano, 2002). For example, Marie Legerstee and her associates (1998) found that 5-month-olds who viewed moving images of themselves and an age-mate (on videotape) could clearly discriminate their own image from that of the peer, as indicated by their preference to gaze at the peer's face (which was novel and interesting to them) rather than at their own (which was presumably familiar and hence less interesting). How might infants this young come to discriminate their own faces from those of other people? One explanation is that babies (in Western cultures, at least) often find themselves in front of mirrors, usually beside a caregiver who is playing a social game with them (Fogel, 1995; Stern, 1995). Such experiences may thus allow ample opportunity for an infant to become familiar with her mirror image and to match her own movement-produced proprioceptive information with the actions of one of the figures in the mirror, thereby discriminating this "self" from the other person present, whose movements do not correspond so closely with her own (Legerstee, Anderson, & Schaffer, 1998).

Over the next several months, infants become better able to discriminate visual representations of themselves and other people and to perceive others as potential social partners.

personal agency
the recognition that one can be the cause of an event or events.

In one study (Rochat & Straiano, 2002), 9-month-olds saw either a video representation of themselves or of an adult who mimicked the actions the infant was performing. Not only did these 9-month-olds pay more attention to the mimicking adult than to their own images, but they were much more inclined to treat the adult as a "playmate" by smiling and trying to reengage this person when the video paused and the mimicry stopped.

Yet the remarkable skills that young infants display at differentiating self from others may simply represent their powers of visual discrimination rather than any conscious, cognitive awareness that the reflection of self in a mirror or on videotape is *"me."* How might we determine whether infants have truly constructed a firm *self*-image (realizing "Hey, that's *me!*") that is stable over time?

Michael Lewis and Jeanne Brooks-Gunn (1979) have studied the development of **self-recognition** by asking mothers to surreptitiously apply a spot of rouge to their infants' noses (under the pretext of wiping the infants' faces) and then place the infants before a mirror. If infants have a scheme for their own faces and recognize their mirror images as themselves, they should soon notice the new red spot and reach for or wipe their *own* noses. When infants 9 to 24 months old were given this **rouge test,** the younger ones showed no self-recognition: They often did nothing or tried to wipe the rouge off the person in the mirror. Signs of self-recognition were observed among some of the 15- to 17-month olds, but only among the 18- to 24-month-olds did a majority of children touch their own noses, apparently realizing that they had a strange mark on their faces. They knew exactly who that kid in the mirror was (see also Lewis & Ramsay, 2004).

Interestingly, infants from nomadic tribes, who have no experience with mirrors, begin to display self-recognition on the rouge test at the same age as city-reared infants (Priel & deSchonen, 1986). And many 18- to 24-month-olds can even recognize themselves in

self-recognition
the ability to recognize oneself in a mirror or a photograph, coupled with the conscious awareness that the mirror or photographic image is a representation of "me."

rouge test
test of self-recognition that involves marking a toddler's face and observing his or her reaction to the mark when he or she is placed before a mirror.

Photo 6.1 Recognizing one's mirror image as "me" is a crucial milestone in the development of self.

Lon C. Diehl/PhotoEdit, Inc.

current photographs and will often use a personal pronoun ("me") or their own name to label their photographic image (Lewis & Brooks-Gunn, 1979; Lewis & Ramsey, 2004). But children this young are not yet fully aware that the self is an entity that is stable over time. Not until age 3½ will they retrieve a brightly colored sticker placed surreptitiously on their heads if their first glimpse of it comes after a 2–3 minute delay on videotape or in a photograph (Povinelli, Landau, & Perilloux, 1996). Apparently 2- to 3-year-olds who display some self-recognition do not retrieve the sticker because their concept of self is limited to that of a **present self,** and they don't yet appreciate that events that occurred in the past have implications for them now. By contrast, 4- and 5-year olds quickly retrieve the sticker after a *brief delay* but do not retrieve it if the videotape depicts events that happened a week earlier. These older preschoolers have developed the concept of **extended self:** They recognize that the self is stable over time and that (1) events that happened very recently have implications for the present, whereas (2) a sticker they see a week later on film is *not* still on their heads because this event happened to them a long time ago (Povinelli et al., 1999; Povinelli & Simon, 1998).

Cognitive and Social Contributors to Self-Recognition

Why do 18- to 24-month-olds suddenly recognize an already familiar mirror image as "me"? Recall that this is precisely the age when toddlers are said to internalize their sensorimotor schemes to form mental symbols—one of the first of which may be a now-clear image of their own bodies and facial features (Nielsen, Suddendorf, & Slaughter 2006). How might this happen? It seems that these older toddlers, who are on the verge of creating mental symbols, begin to notice the contingency between actions they can see in the mirror and proprioceptive information they can sense from their own bodily movements, thus recognizing that "the guy in the mirror who is doing what I am doing must be 'me'" (Miyazaki & Hiraki, 2006). Even children with severe mental retardation will display self-recognition on the rouge test if they have attained a mental age of 18–20 months (Hill & Tomlin, 1981).

Although a certain level of cognitive development may be necessary for self-recognition, social experiences are probably of equal importance. Gordon Gallup (1979) found that adolescent chimpanzees can easily recognize themselves in a mirror (as shown by the rouge test) unless they have been reared in complete social isolation. In contrast to normal chimps, social isolates react to their mirror images as if they were looking at another animal! So the term *looking-glass self* may apply to chimpanzees as well as to humans: Reflections in a "social mirror" enable normal chimps to develop some self-awareness, whereas a chimpanzee that is denied these experiences will fail to acquire a clear self-image.

One social experience that contributes to self-awareness in humans is a secure attachment to a primary caregiver. Sandra Pipp and her associates (1992) administered a complex test of self knowledge to 2- and 3-year-olds, a test assessing the child's awareness of his name and gender as well as tasks to assess self-recognition. As we see in Figure 6.1, securely attached 2-year-olds were outperforming their insecurely attached age-mates on the test, and differences in self-knowledge between secure and insecure 3-year-olds were even greater.

Parents also contribute to a child's expanding self-concept by providing descriptive information ("You're a big girl"; "You're such a smart boy") and by evaluating the child's behavior ("That's wrong, Billy; big boys don't snatch their baby sisters' toys"). Parents also talk with their children about noteworthy events they have shared with them, such as a trip to the zoo or to Disneyworld. In these conversations, children are typically asked such questions as "Where did we go last week? What was your favorite thing about the trip?" These interchanges help young children to organize their experiences into story-line narratives and to recall them as events that have personal significance—as things that happened to *"me"* (Farrant & Reese, 2000). And autobiographical memories of noteworthy events, which are initially co-constructed with the

present self
early self-representation in which 2- and 3-year-olds recognize current representations of self but are largely unaware that past self-representations or self-relevant events have implications for the future.

extended self
more mature self-representation, emerging between ages 3½ and 5 years, in which children are able to integrate past, present, and unknown future self-representations into a notion of a self that endures over time.

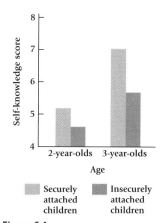

Figure 6.1
Average scores on a test of self-knowledge as a function of age and attachment quality. (Adapted from Pipp, Easterbrooks, & Harmon, 1992.)

aid of an adult, help to illustrate that the self is stable over time (for example, "I am an older version of the kid who went to Disneyworld last summer"), thus contributing to a growing sense of *extended self* (Povinelli & Simon, 1998).

Social and Emotional Consequences of Self-Recognition   The achievement of self-recognition paves the way for several new social and emotional competencies. For example, we saw in Chapter 4 that the ability to experience *self-conscious* emotions such as embarrassment depends on self-recognition. Furthermore, toddlers who have reached this self-referential milestone soon become more outgoing and socially skilled. They now take great pleasure in imitating a playmate's activities (Asendorph & Baudonniere, 1993; Asendorph, Warkentin, & Baudonniere, 1996), begin to display more complex forms of social pretend play (Lewis & Ramsay, 2004), and will occasionally even cooperate to achieve shared goals (as illustrated by one child's operating a handle so that another can retrieve toys from a container) (Brownell & Carriger, 1990; see also Brownell, Ramani, & Zerwas, 2006). This early emerging ability to share intentions and thus cooperate with social partners is so significant that some see it as the foundation for human culture (Tomasello, 1999). Indeed, 2-year-old self-aware children readily partake in cooperative problem-solving activities with social partners, whereas even mature chimpanzees show little interest in cooperative problem solving (Warneken, Chen, & Tomasello, 2006).

Emergence of Categorical Self   Once toddlers display clear evidence of self-recognition, they also become more sensitive to the ways in which people differ, and begin to categorize themselves on these dimensions—a classification called the **categorical self** (Stipek, Gralinski, & Kopp, 1990). Age, sex, and such evaluative dimensions as good–bad are the first social categories that toddlers incorporate into their self-concepts, as illustrated by such statements as "I *big* boy, not a *baby*" or "Jennie *good girl*."

Interestingly, young children are even becoming aware of racial and ethnic categories, although it may take a while before they can classify themselves correctly. Native American 3- to 5-year-olds, for example, can easily discriminate Indians from whites in photographs but are less often accurate in specifying which category they most resemble (Spencer & Markstrom-Adams, 1990). A similar "misidentifications" phenomenon has been observed among African-American preschoolers, who show a clear pro-white bias and associate fewer positive attributes with the color black or with African-American people (Cross, 1985; Spencer, 1988). However, these "misidentifications" and pro-white biases do not necessarily mean that minority youngsters are unaware of their own ethnicity or are especially critical of themselves, for minority children often display a pro-white sentiment *and* highly favorable self-concepts (see Spencer & Markstrom-Adams, 1990). Instead, the so-called "misidentifications" that minority preschoolers display may simply reflect the same early awareness of negative stereotypes about minorities that white children display (Bigler & Liben, 1993) and a desire to align themselves with what they believe to be the most advantaged group (Spencer & Markstrom-Adams, 1990).

categorical self
a person's classification of the self along socially significant dimensions such as age and sex.

Who Am I? Responses of Preschool Children

I'm three years old and I live in a big house with my mother and father and my brother, Jason, and my sister, Lisa. I have blue eyes and a kitty that is orange and a television in my room. I know all of my ABC's—listen: A, B, C, D, E, F, G, H, J ,K, L, O, M, P, Q, X, Z. I can run real fast. I like pizza and I have a nice teacher at preschool. I can count to 10, want to hear me? I love my dog, Skipper. I can climb to the top of the jungle gym . . . I'm really strong. I can lift this chair, watch me! (Harter, 1999, p. 37)

This composite statement, which actually reflects the "Who am I?" responses of several 3- to 4-year-olds, nicely illustrates why many developmentalists claim that the self-concepts of preschool children are concrete, physicalistic, and nearly devoid of any psychological self-awareness. Notice that these preschoolers seem to be defining the self in terms of their *physical attributes* ("I have blue eyes"), their *preferences* ("I like pizza"), their *possessions* ("... a television in my room"), and the *actions* that they can perform and feel proud of (for example, running fast, climbing to the top of the jungle gym). By contrast, psychological descriptors such as "I'm friendly" or "I'm helpful" are rarely used by children this young (Damon & Hart, 1988; Harter, 1999). Even descriptions that sound like traits (for example, "I'm really strong") are usually referring to physical capabilities in a particular context ("I can lift this chair") rather than the child's assessment of how strong she is compared to other children.

Photo 6.2
Preschool children are already aware of their behavioral patterns and preferences and are using this information to form an early "psychological" portrait of the self.

These findings would hardly surprise Erik Erikson. In his theory of psychosocial development, Erikson (1963) proposes that 2- to 3-year-olds are struggling to become independent or autonomous, while 4- to 5-year-olds who have achieved some sense of autonomy are now acquiring new skills, achieving important objectives, and taking great pride in their accomplishments. According to Erikson, it is a healthy sign when preschool children largely define themselves in terms of their activities and physical capabilities, because an activity-based self-concept reflects the sense of *initiative* they will need in order to cope with the many new lessons they must learn at school.

Evidence for an Early "Psychological" Self-Concept   However, not everyone agrees that preschoolers' self-concepts are limited to observable characteristics and devoid of any "psychological" self-awareness. Rebecca Eder (1989, 1990) finds that when 3½- to 5-year olds are asked to respond to contrasting *forced choice* statements that require fewer verbal skills than open-ended "Who am I" questions, they can quickly characterize themselves on *psychological* dimensions such as sociability (by choosing, for example, between such statements as "I like to play by myself" versus "I like to play with my friends"). Furthermore, they characterize themselves differently on different dimensions, and these self-characterizations are stable over time (Eder, 1990). Although preschool children may not be consciously aware of what it means to be "sociable" or "athletic" or to be an "achiever," Eder's research implies that they have rudimentary psychological conceptions of self long before they can express this knowledge in trait-like terminology.

Children's Theory of Mind and Emergence of the Private Self

When adults think about the self, they know that it consists of a **public self** (or **me**) that others can see and a **private self** (or **I**) that has an inner, reflective (thinking) character not directly available to others. Are young children aware of both the public and private aspects of self? Such a distinction implies that they have a **theory of mind**—an understanding that people have mental states, such as desires, beliefs, and intentions, that are not always shared with or accessible to others, and that often guide their behavior.

Early Understandings of Mental States   The first step toward acquiring a theory of mind is the realization that oneself and other humans are animate (rather then inanimate) objects whose behaviors reflect goals and intentions. Remarkably, 2-month-old infants are making some progress; they are already more likely to repeat simple gestures displayed by a human rather than an inanimate object, thereby suggesting that they may already identify with human models (Legerstee, 1991). By age 6 months, infants perceive human actions as purposeful and know that humans behave differently toward people than they do toward inanimate objects. For example, if 6-month-olds see an actor *talking* to an unseen stimulus behind a screen, they expect a person to appear when the screen is removed and are

public self (or me)
those aspects of self that others can see or infer.

private self (or I)
those inner, or subjective, aspects of self that are known only to the individual and are not available for public scrutiny.

theory of mind
an understanding that people are cognitive beings with mental states that are not always accessible to others and that often guide their behavior.

joint attention
the act of attending to the same object at the same time as someone else; a way in which infants share experiences and intentions with their caregivers.

desire theory
an early theory of mind in which a person's actions are thought to be a reflection of her desires rather than other mental states such as beliefs.

belief-desire theory
theory of mind that develops between ages 3 and 4; the child now realizes that both beliefs and desires may determine behavior and that people will often act on their beliefs, even if they are inaccurate.

false-belief task
method of assessing one's understanding that people can hold inaccurate beliefs that can influence their conduct, wrong as these beliefs may be.

surprised if an inanimate object appears instead. By contrast, if the actor had *manipulated* the unseen stimulus, 6-month-olds expect to see an object and are surprised if a person appears (Legerstee, Barna, & DiAdamo, 2000). By age 9 months, infants can discriminate an adult's negative intent (teasing them by withholding a toy) from a more positive one (attempting to give them the toy) (Behne et al., 2005). Age 9–12 months is also when infants engage in a good deal of **joint attention,** often pointing at or otherwise directing a companion's attention to objects or events, thus implying that they perceive a social partner as capable of understanding or sharing their own perspectives and intentions (Tomasello, Carpenter, & Liszkowski, 2007). And by 18 months, toddlers have discovered that *desires* influence behavior, and can often reason accurately about other people's desires. So having seen a woman express disgust at the thought of eating crackers, they know that she would prefer vegetables to the crackers that they personally favor when offered a choice between these snacks (Repacholi & Gopnik, 1997).

Young children's understanding of the workings of the mind expands rapidly between ages 2 and 5. Two- to 3-year-olds often talk about their feelings and desires and even display some understanding of the connections between different mental states. They know, for example, that a child who *desires* a cookie will *feel good* (happy) if he receives it and *feel bad* (sad, angry) if he doesn't (Moses, Coon, & Wusinich, 2000; Wellman, Phillips, & Rodriguez, 2000). What's more, 2- to 3-year-olds are well aware that (1) they may know something that others don't (O'Neill, 1996; see also Moll & Tomasello, 2007) and (2) people cannot actually observe their thoughts (Flavell et al., 1993). Yet, even though 3-year-olds have become more mindful of the human mind and an emerging private self, they still have a primitive understanding of such constructive and interpretive mental products as beliefs and inferences. In fact, they have been labeled **desire theorists** because they think that a person's actions generally reflect his *desires* and do not yet understand that what a person *believes* might also affect his behavior (Cassidy, 1998; Wellman & Liu, 2004).

Between ages 3 and 4, most children develop a **belief-desire theory of mind** in which they recognize, as we adults do, that beliefs and desires are different mental states and that either or both can influence one's conduct (Wellman, Cross, & Watson, 2001). So a 4-year-old who has broken a vase while roughhousing may now try to overcome his mother's apparent *desire* to punish him by changing her mental state—that is, by trying to make her *believe* that his breaking the vase was unintentional ("I didn't mean to, Mama—it was an accident!").

Origins of a Belief-Desire Theory of Mind Very young children may view desire as the most important determinant of behavior because their own actions are so often triggered by desires and they may assume that other people's conduct reflects similar motives. In addition, 3 year-olds have a very curious view of beliefs, thinking that they are accurate reflections of reality that everyone shares. They don't seem to appreciate, as older children and adults do, that beliefs are merely *interpretations* of reality that may differ from person to person and may be *inaccurate*. Consider children's reactions to the following story—a **false-belief task** that assesses the understanding that people can hold incorrect beliefs and be influenced by them, wrong though they may be:

> Sam puts some chocolate in a blue cupboard and goes out to play. In his absence, his mother moves the chocolate to the green cupboard. When Sam returns, he wants his chocolate. Where does he look for it?

Three-year-olds say "in the green cupboard." They know where the chocolate is, and because beliefs reflect reality for them, they assume that Sam will be driven by his *desire* for chocolate to look in the right place. By contrast, most

Photo 6.3
Even 1-year-olds show awareness that other people can have mental states (perceptions) different from their own when they point at objects so that their companions and they can jointly attend to the same object.

Asia Images/Jupiter Images

4- to 5-year-olds display a *belief-desire theory of mind:* They now understand that beliefs are merely mental representations of reality that may be inaccurate and that someone else may not share; thus, they know that Sam will look for his chocolate in the blue cupboard where he *believes* it is (beliefs often influence behavior, even if they are false) rather than in the green cupboard where they know it is (Wellman, Cross, & Watson, 2001).

Once children understand that people will act on the basis of false beliefs, they may use this knowledge to their own advantage by lying or attempting other deceptive ploys (Talwar, Gordon, & Lee, 2007). For example, 4-year olds (but not 3-year olds) who are playing hide-the-object games will *spontaneously* generate false clues, trying to *mislead* their opponent about the object's true location (Sodian et al., 1991). Notice that these 4-year-olds are now making a clear distinction between public and private self, for they recognize that their deceptive *public* behavior (the false clues) may lead their opponent to adapt a belief that differs from their own *private* knowledge about the object's location.

It's not that younger children haven't any capacity to recognize a false belief or its implications. For example, 3-year-olds can tell from thought-bubble depictions or from knowledge that a story character is participating in pretense that the incorrect beliefs that story characters have expressed really do contradict reality (Cassidy, 1998; Wellman, Hollander, & Schult, 1996). And if they have collaborated with an adult in formulating a deceptive strategy in a hide-the-object game, their performance improves dramatically on other false-belief tasks (Hala & Chandler, 1996). Nevertheless, between ages 3 and 4 is when children normally begin to achieve a much richer understanding of mental life, distinguishing desires from beliefs and clearly discriminating the private-self-as-knower from the public self they present to others.

However, it is more accurate to think of theory of mind as a set of understandings that children begin to develop in infancy and continue to refine and use throughout life than to view it as something that suddenly emerges at age 4 (Wellman & Liu, 2004). How important are these early developments? David Bjorklund (2005) answers by claiming that the development of a belief-desire theory of mind is the foundation for all later social-cognitive development. If children never learned to read minds and failed to recognize that public appearances do not necessarily reflect private realities, they would be largely incapable of drawing meaningful *psychological* inferences about their own or others' behavior, and the intricate social interactions and cooperative, conciliatory activities that we humans display would be virtually impossible. Indeed, young children who have mastered false-belief tasks do tend to display more advanced social skills and better social adjustment than age-mates who have not (Keenan, 2003; Repacholi & Slaughter, 2003).

How Does a Theory of Mind Originate?   How do children manage to construct a theory of mind so early in life? One perspective is that human infants may be just as biologically prepared and as motivated to acquire information about mental states as they are to share meaning through language (Meltzoff, 1995). As Box 6.1 illustrates, there are even those who believe that theory of mind is a product of evolution and that the human brain has specialized modules that allow children to construct a rich understanding of their own and others' mental activities.

But even if humans are biologically predisposed to develop a theory of mind, there are many social experiences that foster its development. Pretend play, for example, is an activity that prompts children to think about mental states. As toddlers and preschool children conspire to make one object represent another or to enact pretend roles such as Spiderman and Harry Potter, they become increasingly aware of the creative potential of the human mind—an awareness that beliefs are merely mental constructions that can influence ongoing activities, even if they misrepresent reality (as they do during pretend play) (Hughes & Dunn, 1998; Taylor & Carlson, 1997). Young children also have ample opportunity to learn how the mind works from family discussions centering on discussions of motives,

Box 6.1 Current Controversies

Is Theory of Mind Biologically Programmed?

Some theorists claim that the capacities underlying self-consciousness and complex theories of mind are products of human evolution and are the basis for our social intelligence and the development of cultures (Baron-Cohen, 1995, 2000, Mitchell, 1997). Presumably our human ancestors would have found it highly adaptive to understand beliefs, desires, and other mental states because this ability to "read minds" allows for the evolution of cooperative divisions of labor and more accurate assessments of the motives of rival groups that might threaten survival.

Simon Baron-Cohen (1995) has proposed that humans possess brain modules that are specialized for mind reading. One such module is the *shared attention mechanism (SAM)*, which is said to develop between 9 and 18 months of age and allows two or more individuals to understand that they are attending to the same thing. Another such mechanism is the *theory of mind module (TOMM)*, which allegedly develops between 18 and 48 months of age and permits children to eventually discriminate and interpret such mental states as intentions, desires, and beliefs.

Indeed, there is some evidence that the development of a belief-desire theory of mind may reflect processing skills that are *domain-specific*—that is, apart from normal intelligence. For example, about 85 percent of both 4-year-olds with normal intelligence and most older mentally retarded individuals pass false-belief problems. Yet joint attention and understanding of false beliefs are lacking (or delayed for years) in children with *autism* (Peterson, Wellman, & Liu, 2005), even though these autistic children might perform quite well on other intellectual tasks (Baron-Cohen, 2000). Autism is a severe psychiatric disorder; affected children cannot easily share attention with others, seem to be in a world of their own, and have difficulties with most forms of social interaction. Baron-Cohen (1995) claims that autistic individuals lack a TOMM and display profound deficits in reading minds, or *mindblindness*. Imagine how confusing and even frightening it would be to interact with other humans if you lacked the capacity to understand their motives and desires or to recognize that they may try to deceive you. Temple Grandin (1996), a woman with autism who is intelligent enough to be a college professor, described having to compensate for her lack of mind-reading skills by actively creating a memory bank of

how people behave and what emotions they are likely to express in particular situations. Although she can grasp simple emotions such as anger and happiness, she never could quite understand what *Romeo and Juliet* was all about.

Baron-Cohen's biological model of theory of mind is new and is already proving to be controversial. Using neuroimaging techniques, researchers have begun to identify areas of the brain that are activated during theory of mind tasks and seem to be uniquely involved in thinking about others' beliefs (Gallagher & Firth, 2003; Saxe, Carey, & Kanwisher, 2004). Yet these findings may represent normal maturational changes in the developing brain and do not establish that autistic children's mind-reading problems are attributable to their lack of a specialized TOMM. Instead, their mindblindness may stem from deficits in shared attention and thus limited experience conversing with parents and siblings about the meaning of mental states. This alternative hypothesis gains some support from studies of deaf children, who often show little understanding of false belief until late childhood or early adolescence (Peterson & Siegal, 2000), particularly when they have hearing parents who do not use sign language and have little opportunity to "converse" about desires, beliefs, and intentions (Woolfe, Want, & Siegal, 2000). By contrast, deaf children of signing deaf parents often converse with them in sign language and show little if any delay in acquiring a theory of mind (Schick et al., 2007).

It is also clear that not all aspects of self-consciousness or theory of mind are uniquely human. Chimpanzees, for example, show self-recognition on the rouge test, and apes can share attention by following the gaze of another ape to an object, communicate by calls and gestures, and even deceive others to get what they want (Tomasello, Call, & Hare, 2003). Yet Joseph Call and Michael Tomasello (1999) found that orangutans and chimpanzees could not pass a nonverbal false-belief task—a task that 4- and 5-year-olds passed at about the same time they passed other false-belief problems that mark them as acquiring a belief-desire theory of mind. So it is conceivable that humans have something like a TOMM that helps to explain the rich social-cognitive abilities that only humans display, although more research will be necessary to properly evaluate this claim.

intentions, beliefs, and other mental states (Jenkins et al., 2003). Conversations with parents and other adults may contribute to an emerging theory of mind in at least two ways. First, they foster general language development, which is consistently associated with preschoolers' performance on the false-belief tasks (Milligan, Astington, & Dack, 2007). In addition, the more often mothers talk about mental states with their infants, toddlers, and preschool children, the more inclined children become to refer to mental states in their own speech (Taumoepeau & Ruffman, 2006) and the better their performances on false-belief and other theory of mind tasks (Meins et al., 2002; Ruffman, Slade, & Crowe, 2002).

Might interactions among siblings contribute as well? Results are somewhat mixed, although some researchers have found that preschoolers with *older* siblings consistently do better on false-belief tasks and are quicker to acquire a belief–desire theory of mind than other children are (see Ruffman et al., 1998, for a review). Having older siblings may provide the younger child with more opportunities for complex pretend play and more interactions involving deception and trickery—experiences that illustrate that beliefs need not reflect reality to influence one's own or others' behavior. By contrast, having a twin sibling whose mind is at the same developmental level as one's own confers no advantage whatsoever, as twins with no other siblings typically perform like only children do on theory mind tasks (Wright Cassidy et al., 2005).

Cultural Influences   Do children in all cultures construct such a rich understanding of how the mind works during the preschool period? Apparently not. Even 8-year-olds among the Junin Quechua people of Peru have difficulties understanding that beliefs can be false (Vinden, 1996). Why? Probably because Junin Quechua speakers do not often talk about their own or others' mental states. Most of these people are subsistence farmers who work from dawn to dusk just to survive, and they do not need to reflect very often on what they or others may feel or believe in order to live productive lives. In fact, their language has few mental state words, and references to mental states are largely absent from their folktales. Similarly, even adolescents in some New Guinea tribes could not answer questions about other people's thoughts that 5-year-olds in our society handle easily (Vinden & Astington, 2000). So the appearance of a belief-desire theory of mind by age 4 is not universal and is likely to be delayed in cultures that lack the social supports for its emergence.

Conceptions of Self in Middle Childhood and Adolescence

Once children develop a theory of mind and clearly differentiate their public and private selves, their self-descriptions very gradually evolve from listings of their physical, behavioral, and other "external" attributes to sketches of their enduring inner qualities—that is, their traits, values, beliefs, and ideologies (Damon & Hart, 1988; Harter, 1999). This developmental shift toward a more abstract or "psychological" portrayal of self from middle childhood to preadolescence can be seen in the following two responses to the "Who am I?" question (Montemayor & Eisen, 1977, pp. 317–318):

> **9-year-old:** My name is Bruce C. I have brown eyes. I have brown hair. I love! sports. I have seven people in my family. I have great! eye sight. I have lots! of friends. I live at. . . . I have an uncle who is almost 7 feet tall. My teacher is Mrs. V. I play hockey! I'm almost the smartest boy in the class. I love! food. . . . I love! school.

> **11½-year-old:** My name is A. I'm a human being . . . a girl . . . a truthful person. I'm not pretty. I do so-so in my studies. I'm a very good cellist. I'm a little tall for my age. I like several boys. . . . I'm old fashioned. I am a very good swimmer. . . . I try to be helpful. . . . Mostly I'm good, but I lose my temper. I'm not well liked by some girls and boys. I don't know if boys like me. . . .

Notice that our 9-year-old continues to list physical attributes (for example, brown hair, blue eyes) as important aspects of self. However, his self-portrait is more "psychological" than those of younger children in that it focuses heavily on his preferences ("I love sports"; "I love school"), relationships ("I have lots of friends"; "My teacher is..."), and occasionally on his psychological traits ("I am almost the smartest boy in the class"). Peer relationships become especially important to grade-school children who are concerned about displaying behaviors and traits that will solidify their standing with peers:

> *What are you like?* I am friendly. *Why is that important?* Other kids won't like you if you aren't. (Damon & Hart, 1988, p. 60)

Now contrast the 9-year-old's self-portrait with that of our 11½-year-old preadolescent. The older girl is still concerned about peer relationships ("I like several boys"; "I'm not well liked by some boys and girls"). However, her self-description is dominated by enduring

dispositional qualities, or traits, that allegedly characterize her personality (for example, truthful, old-fashioned, helpful, somewhat temperamental). Moreover, the self-concepts of older children are not so uniformly positive (Harter, 1999). Children increasingly come to compare themselves to other people (mostly peers) and to acknowledge that there are dimensions on which they may fall short by comparison (for example, "I'm not pretty"; "I do so-so in my studies").

The Self in Adolescence Now consider a sample self-description of a 17-year-old adolescent:

> I am a human being . . . a girl . . . an individual. . . . I am a Pisces. I am a moody person . . . an indecisive person . . . an ambitious person. I am a big curious person. . . . I am lonely. I am an American (God help me). I am a Democrat. I am a liberal person. I am a radical. I am conservative. I am a pseudoliberal. I am an Atheist. I am not a classifiable person (i.e., I don't want to be). (Montemayor & Eisen, 1977, p. 318)

At first glance, this self-portrait may not seem appreciably different from that of the 11½-year-old above: Both persons describe their most notable personality traits and lament somewhat about their social lives ("I'm not well liked by . . ." versus. "I am lonely"). Yet we see evidence of broader value, or ideological, categorizations in the adolescent portrait (for example, Democrat, radical, atheist) and something else that stands out—inconsistencies (for example, "I am liberal . . . , I am conservative"; "I am an American [*God* help me]. . . . I am an Atheist" [italics added]).

Inconsistencies in self-portrayals are fairly typical of adolescents who are becoming much more aware that they may not be the same person in all situations—a fact that may puzzle or even annoy them. Susan Harter and Ann Monsour (1992) asked 13-, 15-, and 17-year-olds to describe themselves when they are with (1) parents, (2) friends, (3) romantic partners, and (4) teachers and classmates. Then each participant was asked to sort through the four self-descriptions, picking out any inconsistencies and indicating how confusing or upsetting they were. As we see in Figure 6.2, 13-year-olds reported few inconsistencies and were not bothered much by those they did detect. By contrast, 15-year-olds listed many oppositional attributes and were often confused about them. One 15-year-old talked about her tendency to be happy with friends but depressed at home. "I really think of myself as happy—and want to be that way because I think that's my true self, but I get depressed with my family and it bugs me" (Harter & Monsour, 1992, p. 253). These 15-year-olds seemed to feel that there were several different selves inside them and were concerned about finding the "real me." Interestingly, adolescents who are most upset over inconsistencies in their self-portrayals are those who put on false fronts, acting out of character in an attempt to improve their images or win the approval of parents or peers. Unfortunately, those who most often display these **false self-behaviors** are the ones who feel least confident that they know who they truly are (Harter et al., 1996).

Inconsistent self-portrayals are somewhat less bothersome to older adolescents, who have often integrated them into a higher-order, more coherent view of themselves. A 17-year-old boy, for example,

false self-behavior
acting in ways that do not reflect one's true self or the "true me."

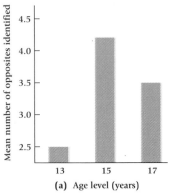
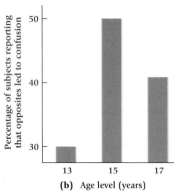

Figure 6.2
Average number of oppositional attributes reported by 13-, 15-, and 17-year-olds (panel a) and the percentages of 13-, 15-, and 17-year-olds who said they were confused or "mixed up" by these inconsistencies in their self-portraits (panel b). (Adapted from Harter & Monsour, 1992.)

might conclude that it is perfectly understandable to be relaxed and confident with parents and classmates but nervous on dates if one has not yet had much dating experience, or that "moodiness" can explain his being cheerful with friends on some occasions but irritable on others. Harter and Monsour believe that cognitive development—specifically the formal-operational ability to compare abstract traits like "cheerful" and "irritable" and to ultimately integrate them into more general concepts like "moodiness"—is behind this change in self-perceptions.

In sum, one's self-concept becomes more psychological, more abstract, and more of a coherent, integrated self-portrait from childhood throughout adolescence. Truly, the adolescent becomes a sophisticated self-theorist who can reflect on and understand the workings of his or her personality.

One final point, but an important one: The overview of self-concept development presented here stems largely from research conducted in Western industrialized societies that value independence and view *personal* attributes as the hallmark of one's character. Yet as we will see in Box 6.2, this Eurocentric perspective on the meaning of "self" may not completely capture the experiences of people from many *collectivist* societies around the world.

⤳ SELF-ESTEEM: THE EVALUATIVE COMPONENT OF SELF

As children develop, they not only come to understand more and more about themselves and to construct more intricate self-portraits, but they also begin to *evaluate* the qualities that they perceive themselves as having. This evaluative aspect of self is called **self-esteem.** Children with high self-esteem are fundamentally satisfied with the type of person they are; they recognize their strong points, can acknowledge their weaknesses (often hoping to overcome them), and generally feel quite positive about the characteristics and competencies they display. By contrast, children with low self-esteem view the self in a less favorable light, often choosing to dwell on perceived inadequacies rather than on any strengths they may happen to have.

self-esteem
One's evaluation of one's worth as a person based on an assessment of the qualities that make up the self-concept.

Origins of Self-Esteem

Children's evaluations of themselves and their competencies is a most important aspect of self that can influence many other aspects of their conduct and their psychological well-being. How does self-esteem originate and when do children first establish a realistic sense of self-worth?

These questions are not easy to answer, but Bowlby's (1988) "working models" theory that we discussed in Chapter 5 provides some meaningful clues. The theory predicts that securely attached children, who construct *positive* working models of self and others, should soon begin to evaluate themselves more favorably than insecurely attached children, whose working models of self and others are not so uniformly positive. And apparently they do. In studies conducted in Belgium, 4- to 5-year-olds were asked questions about their worthiness, which they answered through a hand puppet (for example, "Do you [puppet] like to play with [this child]?"; "Is [this child] a good [bad] boy/girl?"). Children with secure ties to their mothers not only described themselves more favorably (through the puppet) than did children who were insecurely attached, but they were also rated as more competent and more socially skilled by their preschool teachers (Verschueren, Marcoen, & Schoefs, 1996). What's more, the positivity of children's self-descriptions was highest for those children who were securely attached to both of their parents (Verschueren &

Box 6.2 Cultural Influences

Cultural Influences on the Self-Concept

On the following scale, indicate the extent to which you agree or disagree with each of the items below:

1	2	3	4	5	6	7
Strongly disagree						Strongly agree

_____ 1. I have respect for authority figures with whom I interact.

_____ 2. I am comfortable with being singled out for praise or rewards.

_____ 3. My happiness depends on the happiness of those around me.

_____ 4. Speaking up in class is not a problem for me.

_____ 5. I should take my parents' advice into consideration when making education/career plans.

_____ 6. My identity independent of others is very important to me.

(Adapted from Singelis, 1994.)

What is considered desirable in the way of a self-concept may vary dramatically across cultures. Western societies such as the United States, Canada, Australia, and the industrialized countries of Europe might be termed **individualistic societies:** They value competition and individual initiative and tend to emphasize ways in which people differ from each other. By contrast, many Asian cultures (for example, India, Japan, and China) could be considered **collectivist** or **communal** societies: People are more cooperative and interdependent rather than competitive and independent, and their identities are closely tied to the groups to which they belong (for example, families, religious organizations, and communities) rather than to their own accomplishments and personal characteristics (Triandis, 1995). In fact, people in East Asian cultures such as China, Korea, and Japan tend to value self-effacement and to view individuals who are preoccupied with personal concerns as somewhat abnormal and maladjusted (Markus & Kitayama, 1994; Triandis, 1995).

Indeed, cross-cultural variations in the nature or content of people's self-concepts are quite clear in the responses of older American and Japanese adolescents to a "Who Am I" questionnaire (Cousins, 1989). The questionnaire required them to first rate themselves on *personal/individualistic* attributes (for example, "I am honest"; "I am smart") and *social/relational* attributes (for example, "I'm a student"; "I'm a good son"). Then participants were asked to place a check mark by the five responses that they viewed as most self-descriptive and central to their self-concepts.

The results of this study were quite clear. As shown in the accompanying figure, the majority of American students' core self-descriptors (59 percent) were personal/individualistic attributes, whereas these same attributes made up only 19 percent of the core self-descriptors of the Japanese students. By contrast, Japanese students were much more inclined than American students were to list social/relational attributes as especially noteworthy components of their self-concepts. In terms of developmental trends, older Japanese and Chinese adolescents

individualistic society
society that values personalism and individual accomplishments, which often take precedence over group goals. These societies tend to emphasize ways in which individuals differ from each other.

collectivist (or communal) society
society that values cooperative interdependence, social harmony, and adherence to group norms. These societies generally hold that the group's well-being is more important than that of the individual.

Marcoen, 1999) and proved to be stable over time when reassessed at age 8 (Verschueren, Buyck, & Marcoen, 2001). So it seems that by age 4 or 5 (and possibly sooner), children have already established an early and meaningful sense of self-esteem—one that is influenced by their attachment history and is a reasonably accurate reflection of how teachers evaluate their competencies.

Components of Self-Esteem in Childhood

When we adults think about self-esteem, a global appraisal of self comes to mind, based on the strengths and weaknesses we display in several different life domains. The same is true for children, who first evaluate their competencies in many different areas and integrate these impressions into an overall self-evaluation (Harter, 1999; Marsh & Ayotte, 2003).

Susan Harter (1982, 1999, 2005) has proposed such a hierarchical model of childhood self-esteem, which is shown in Figure 6.3. To test her model, she asks children to complete a *Self-Perception Scale for Children* on which they evaluate themselves in five domains: *scholastic competence, social acceptance, physical appearance, athletic competence,* and *behavioral conduct.* They also indicate their overall feelings of self-worth, or *global self-esteem.* They make these assessments by indicating whether statements

Figure 6.3
A multidimensional and hierarchical model of self-esteem. (Adapted from Harter, 1996.)

are less inclined than preadolescents are to make distinctions among people on the basis of *individualistic* attributes, whereas American participants become more inclined to make such distinctions as they grow older (Crystal et al., 1998). Differences among children from individualistic and collectivist cultures may appear early in childhood. For example, Heidi Keller and associates (2004) found that more that 95 percent of 18- to 20-month-old toddlers of African Nso farmers (a collectivist group that discourages infant independence and advocates providing lots of bodily contact to infants and toddlers) had yet to recognize themselves as unique individuals on the rouge test, whereas 65 percent of Greek age-mates raised according to Western standards had already achieved self-recognition. Differences are not always found in all domains. For example, in learning contexts, Chinese adolescents are more concerned about displaying *individual* mastery of new materials rather than seeking social recognition or pursing other group objectives (Li, 2006). But in many other life domains, children and adolescents from collectivist cultures appear to be more socially and less individually oriented than their Western age-mates. Indeed, research reveals that Asian-American adolescents, whose families often retain many collectivist values even after immigrating to the United States, tend to place more emphasis on their social identities and connections to other people than European-American adolescents do (Chao, 2001; Fuligini, Yip, & Tseng, 2002).

Where do you stand on the individualist/collectivist continuum? If you are like most people from individualistic societies, you probably indicated greater agreement with items 2, 4, and 6 (which tap independence and individualistic concerns), whereas

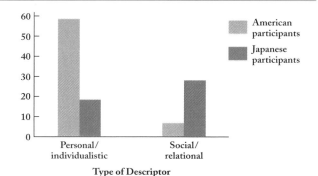

Type of Descriptor

Average percentages of personal/individualistic and social/relational attributes listed as core dimensions of the self-concept by American and Japanese students who responded to a "Who Am I?" questionnaire. (Adapted from Cousins, 1989.)

people from collectivist societies usually find it easier to agree with items 1, 3, and 5 (which tap interdependence or communal concerns).

Clearly, the traditional values and beliefs of one's culture can dramatically influence the kinds of self-concepts that emerge. And as we will see throughout the remainder of the text, the distinctions between individualistic and collectivist cultures and value systems are important ones that have implications for such aspects of self as the ways in which individuals look at and evaluate achievement behavior, aggression, altruism, and moral development, to name just a few.

pertinent to each competency domain (and global self-worth) are true or not true of themselves (see Figure 6.4 on page 184).

According to Harter, 4- to 7-year-olds could be accused of having inflated egos because they tend to rate themselves positively in all domains. Some researchers think that these very positive assessments reflect a *desire* to be liked or to be good at various activities rather than the foundation for a firm sense of self-worth (Eccles et al., 1993; Harter & Pike, 1984). However, the self-appraisals of 4- to 7-year-olds are not totally unrealistic because they are modestly correlated with children's achievement test scores and with ratings teachers give them on the same competency domains (Marsh, Ellis, & Craven, 2002; Measelle et al., 1998).

Starting at about age 8, children's own competency appraisals began to more closely reflect other people's evaluations of them (Harter, 1982; Marsh, Craven, & Debus, 1998). For example, personal assessments of social competencies are now confirmed by peers who had been asked to rate their classmates' social competencies; and children with high athletic self-esteem are more frequently chosen for team sports and are rated higher in physical competence by gym teachers than classmates who feel physically inadequate. Taken together, these findings suggest that both self-knowledge and self-esteem may depend to a large extent on the way others perceive and react to our behavior. This is precisely the point that Charles Cooley (1902) was making when he coined the term *looking-glass self* to explain how we construct a self-image.

Yet Harter also found that children differ in terms of the *importance* they assign to the various competency domains assessed by her scale. What's more, youngsters who rate

Type of item	Really true for me	Sort of true for me		But		Really true for me	Sort of true for me
Scholastic competence	1	2	Some kids have trouble figuring out the answers at school	But	Other kids almost always can figure out the answers	3	4
Social acceptance	1	2	Some kids find it hard to make friends	But	Other kids find it easy to make friends	3	4
Athletic competence	1	2	Some kids don't feel that they are very good when it comes to sports	But	Other kids do very well at all kinds of sports	3	4
Physical appearance	4	3	Some kids are happy with the way they look	But	Other kids are not happy with the way they look	2	1
Behavioral conduct	1	2	Some kids usually get in trouble because of the things they do	But	Other kids usually don't do things that get them in trouble	3	4
Global self-esteem	4	3	Some kids are pretty pleased with themselves	But	Other kids are often unhappy with themselves	2	1

Figure 6.4 Sample items from Harter's Self-Perception Scale for Children. Numbers in each box indicate the number of points a child would receive were he or she to give that response on that item. (Adapted from Harter, 1988.)

themselves as very competent in the areas that *they* see as most important tend to be highest in overall self-worth. So it seems that older children's feelings of self-esteem depend both on how they think others evaluate them (that is, the social looking-glass) and on how they choose to evaluate themselves (Harter, 2005).

Self-Esteem in Adolescence

By early adolescence, one's perceptions of self-worth become increasingly differentiated and increasingly centered on interpersonal relationships. Harter, Waters, and Whitesell (1998) coined the term **relational self-worth** to describe their finding that adolescents often begin to perceive their self-worth somewhat differently in different relational contexts (for example, with parents, with teachers, with male classmates, and with female classmates). Clearly, all these domains of relational self-worth contribute to one's global self-esteem, although any particular domain may be much more important for some teenagers than for others. Thus, one adolescent may enjoy high global self-esteem because he views himself as especially bright and as receiving ample support and admiration from his teachers, even though peers may consider him nerdy; another may enjoy equally high global self-esteem because she views her competencies with peers in a very favorable way, even though she feels much less efficacious in her relations with parents and teachers. Here, then, is another example of how self-appraisals depend not only on how others might evaluate us, but also on *how we choose to evaluate ourselves* (that is, on the kind of relationships and aspects of relational self-worth that we view as most central or important to our self-concepts).

Given the increasing importance of interpersonal relationships, it is hardly surprising that new relationship-oriented dimensions such as *romantic appeal* and *quality of close friendships* become very important contributors to an adolescent's global self-esteem

relational self-worth
feelings of self-worth within a particular relationship context (for example, with parents, with male classmates); may differ across relationship contexts.

(Masden et al., 1995; Richards et al., 1998), although they may influence the self-appraisals of boys and girls in somewhat different ways (Thorne & Michaelieu, 1996). Girls who enjoy very high self-esteem are often those who have had *supportive* relationships with friends, whereas boys are more likely to derive high self-esteem from their ability to successfully *influence* their friends. Low self-esteem in girls is most strongly associated with a failure to win friends' support and approval, whereas a major contributor to low self-esteem in adolescent boys is a lack of romantic competence, as reflected by their failure to win or maintain the affection of girls.

Jeff Greenberg/Photo Researchers, Inc.

Photo 6.4
In adolescence, the quality of one's friendships becomes one of the strongest determinants of self-esteem.

Is Self-Esteem Stable over Time?

How stable are one's feelings of self-worth? Is a child who enjoys high self-esteem as an 8-year-old likely to feel especially good about himself as an adolescent? Or is it more reasonable to assume that the stresses and strains of adolescence cause most teenagers to doubt themselves and their competencies, thereby undermining their self-esteem?

Erik Erikson (1963) favored the latter point of view, arguing that young adolescents who experience the many physical, cognitive, and social changes associated with puberty often become confused and show at least some erosion of self-esteem as they leave childhood behind and begin to search for stable adult identity. Indeed, longitudinal studies that assess children's and adolescents' perceptions of their competencies in particular domains such as academics, social acceptance, physical skills/sports, appearance, and so on often find that children's and adolescents' competencey beliefs gradually decline across the elementary, middle, and secondary school years (see Fredricks & Eccles, 2002, and Jacobs et al., 2002, for pertinent findings and reviews), with particularly noticeable dips for some domains (for example, academics, sporting competence) early in adolescence (Cole et al., 2001; Watt, 2004). These declining competency beliefs may partially reflect the more realistic self-appraisals that older children provide as they move from smaller elementary schools to larger junior high schools, encounter much larger peer groups, and discover that they may not be as skilled as they thought they were in one or more competency domains. As Herbert Marsh and Kit-Tai Hau (2003) put it, if our goal is to maintain high self-esteem, it may be better to be a big fish in a small pond rather than a smaller one in a big pond. So, do most younger adolescents show the sudden confusion and erosion in self-esteem that Erikson anticipated?

Small-sample studies designed to answer this question have been highly inconsistent, with several reporting significant dips in global self-worth across the transition from childhood to adolescence, whereas others report no such decline and even gradual gains in self-esteem throughout the adolescent period (see Robins et al., 2002, for a review). However, recent studies of larger, more representative samples suggest that Erikson may have been correct in thinking that early adolescence is a time when many youngsters experience some erosion in self-worth. Richard Robins and his associates (2002), for example, surveyed the global self-esteem of more than 300,000 individuals between the ages of 9 and 90, reporting that the trends for both males and females was for self-esteem to show a meaningful decline between ages 9 and 20, followed by a recovery and gradual increase in self-worth from young adulthood to about age 65, when self-esteem began to decline again among the elderly. Another recent longitudinal study revealed a similar pattern of rising self-esteem and psychological well-being between ages 18 and 25, with the largest increases shown by emerging adults who had gotten married and/or experienced increases in social support from family, friends, coworkers, and romantic partners (Galambos, Barker, & Krahn, 2006).

But before we conclude that adolescence is hazardous to our sense of self-worth, let's note the results of a recent **meta-analysis** of 50 studies of self-esteem across the life span, which found that the temporal stability of self-esteem is lowest in childhood and early adolescence and becomes much stronger later in adolescence and early adulthood (Trzesniewski, Donnellan, & Robins, 2003). What these data imply is that there are tremendous individual variations in the ways children experience the transition to adolescence: Many do show a loss of self-esteem, whereas many others may not fluctuate much or may even post gains in self-worth. Erosion of self esteem is likely to be observed in those youth who are experiencing *multiple stressors* as they enter adolescence—those who are transitioning from elementary schools to more rigorous junior high schools where they are the youngest and the least competent students, while also coping with pubertal changes, beginning to date, and perhaps dealing with family transitions such as a move to a new town or their parents' divorce (Gray-Little & Hafdahl, 2000; Simmons et al., 1987). Because girls mature faster than boys, they are more likely than boys to be experiencing school transitions *and* pubertal changes at the same time. What's more, girls are more likely than boys to be dissatisfied with their bodies and physical appearance during the adolescent years (Paxton, Eisenberg, & Neumark-Sztainer, 2006; Rosenblum & Lewis, 1999). And girls, who are more concerned with maintaining others approval (Rudolph, Caldwell, & Conley, 2005), are bothered more by hassles with family members and peers than boys are (Gutman & Eccles, 2007; Hankin, Mermelstein, & Roesch, 2007). All these findings help to explain why more girls than boys become depressed during adolescence (Wichstrom, 1999; Stice & Bearman, 2001) and why adolescent girls tend to show more sizable drops in perceived self-worth than adolescent boys do (Robins et al., 2002). (One suggestion for improving girl's body images and fostering a healthier sense of self-esteem appears in Box 6.3.)

Don't misunderstand: Most teenagers manage to cope rather well with whatever changes in self-esteem they may experience. And we should recall that despite some absolute fluctuation (either up or down), self-esteem does show some meaningful *temporal stability* during the adolescent years (Trzesniewski, Donnellan, & Robins, 2003). So those who enter their teens with a reasonably favorable sense of self-worth are likely exit adolescence with their self-esteem intact—and can look forward to a gradual increase in self-esteem as they successfully negotiate the developmental challenges of young adulthood (Robins et al., 2002; Galambos, Barker, & Krahn, 2006).

How Important is Self-Esteem?   Recently, a controversy has risen about the importance self-esteem plays at influencing life outcomes. Some theorists contend that self-esteem is somewhat epiphenomenal—if good things happen, self-esteem is high; if not, self-esteem is low (Baumeister et al., 2003; Seligman, 1993). According to this viewpoint, high self-esteem is a consequence rather than a cause of positive social adjustment. However, other theorists (for example, Donnellan et al., 2005) assert that a solid sense of self-esteem is a positive *resource* that facilitates productive achievement experiences and offers some protection against mental health problems, substance abuse, and antisocial behavior. So which is it? Is high self-esteem a resource that promotes positive development or merely a consequence of favorable life outcomes?

Although the controversy is far from resolved, at least two recent studies imply that a positive self-evaluation predicts favorable outcomes ahead, whereas low self-esteem forecasts a less rosy future. In their longitudinal study of adolescents from high-risk environments, Jean Gerard and Cheryl Buehler (2004) found that youth with higher levels of self-esteem were less inclined to become depressed or to display future conduct disorders. A second longitudinal study in New Zealand found that adolescents with low self-esteem displayed poorer mental and physical health, worse economic prospects, and higher levels of criminal behavior in their mid-20s than did adolescents with high self-esteem (Trzesniewski et al., 2006). What's more, one meta-analytic review reported that programs designed to boost

Box 6.3 Focus on Research

Sports Participation and Self-Esteem among Adolescent Females

Researchers who study children's physical development find that boys and girls are nearly equal in physical strength and abilities until puberty, when boys continue to post gains in large-muscle strength whereas girls level off or decline. These sex differences are attributable in part to biology: Adolescent boys have more muscle, less fat, and higher concentrations of male sex hormones (for example, testosterone) than adolescent girls do (Tanner, 1990). Yet these biological differences do not explain the *decline* in large-muscle strength that many teenage girls display, even as they are growing taller and heavier (Smoll & Schutz, 1990). Instead, it seems that upon reaching puberty, girls historically have been encouraged to become less tomboyish and more interested in traditionally feminine (and less active) pursuits, and that their lack of physical activity during adolescence is a major contributor to their declining physical strength—a decline not seen among female athletes who remain highly active (Whipp & Ward, 1992).

One purpose for enacting Title IX, a 1972 federal law banning discrimination on the basis of gender in federally funded institutions, was to encourage girls to remain more physically active throughout adolescence and young adulthood. This law has resulted in dramatic increases in funding for female athletic programs at the college level, and high school programs for female athletics have also expanded greatly over the past 30 years. Even private corporations such as Nike have entered the playing field with a 1990s ad campaign featuring young girls pleading, "If you let me play sports . . . ," and then citing various health and social benefits that can result from sport participation. One of the benefits to which the ads alluded was an enhanced sense of self-esteem.

Is there any basis for the latter claim? To find out, Erin Richman and David Shaffer (2000) constructed an elaborate questionnaire to measure both the depth and breadth of female freshman college students' participation in formal and informal sporting activities during their high school years. These researchers also asked their participants to complete instruments designed to assess their current (1) levels of self-esteem, (2) feelings of physical competence, (3) body image, and (4) possession of such desirable "masculine" attributes as assertiveness and a healthy sense of competition.

The results provided some support for claims made in the Nike ad campaign. First, there was a clear relation between girls' participation in sports during high school and their later self-esteem: Girls who had earlier participated to a greater extent in sports enjoyed higher levels of general self-worth as college students. Further analysis revealed that the apparently salutary effect of earlier sporting activities on girls' college self-esteem reflected the findings that (1) sports participation was associated with increases in perceived physical competencies, development of a more favorable body image, and acquisition of desirable masculine attributes (such as assertiveness), and (2) all these developments in turn were positively correlated with (and apparently fostered) participants' college self-esteem.

Clearly, these are correlational data that should be interpreted cautiously. However, they are consistent with the proposition that girls' participation in sporting activities during the adolescent years may well contribute to an enhanced sense of self-worth. Sports-related gains in self-esteem are greatest for girls who enjoy sports; but girls who enjoy sports the most are those who perceive that their participation in sporting activities does foster physical competencies, more favorable body images, and such desirable personal attributes as assertiveness (Shaffer & Wittes, 2006). These findings imply that gym classes and formal team sports might be more beneficial to a larger number of girls if educators and coaches were to emphasize and devise ways to measure and to illustrate the physical gains and psychological benefits of formal and informal sporting activities, while concentrating less on the outcomes of competitive sports or the physical deficiencies of the less athletically competent girls under their tutelage.

Steve Skjold/PhotoEdit, Inc.

Girls who enjoy sporting activities experience many benefits, including an increase in self-esteem.

the self-worth of low self-esteem children and adolescents produce notable improvements in participants' personal adjustment and academic performances (Haney & Durlak, 1998). Taken together, these findings do seem to imply that a solid sense of self-worth is a potentially valuable resource that helps children and adolescents to cope with adversity and achieve favorable development outcomes.

However, let's note that there can be a dark side to having high self-esteem for some children. Consider the aggressive bully who derives (and maintains) his high self-esteem by dominating other children. In a recent short-term longitudinal study, Medhavi Menon and associates (2007) found that aggressive preadolescents with high self-esteem came to increasingly value the rewards they gained by behaving aggressively and to increasingly belittle their victims—cognitions known to perpetuate or even intensify future aggression and antisocial conduct (see Chapter 9 for an extended discussion of the determinants of childhood and adolescent aggression). So it is probably more accurate to conclude that high self-esteem is likely to foster adaptive development in the years ahead to the extent that it derives from prosocial or otherwise adaptive life experiences rather than antisocial or maladaptive conduct.

Parental and Peer Contributions to Self-Esteem

Parenting Styles   Parents can play a crucial role in shaping a child's self-esteem. As we noted in Chapter 5, the sensitivity of parenting early in childhood clearly influences whether infants and toddlers construct positive or negative working models of self. Furthermore, grade-school children and adolescents with high self-esteem tend to have parents who are warm and supportive, set clear standards for them to live up to, and allow them a voice in making decisions that affect them personally (Coopersmith, 1967; Gutman & Eccles, 2007; Lamborn et al., 1991). What's more, the link between high self-esteem and this nurturing/democratic parental style is much the same in Taiwan and Australia as it is in the United States and Canada (Scott, Scott, & McCabe, 1991). Although these child-rearing studies are correlational and we cannot be sure that warm, supportive parenting *causes* high self-esteem, it is easy to imagine such a causal process at work. Certainly, sending a message that "You're a good kid whom I trust to follow rules and make good decisions" is apt to promote higher self-esteem than more aloof or more controlling styles in which parents may be saying, in effect, "Your inadequacies turn me off."

Peer Influences   As early as age 5 or 6, children are beginning to recognize differences among themselves and their classmates as they use **social comparison** information to tell them whether they perform better or worse in various domains than their peers (Pomerantz et al., 1995). For example, they glance at each others' papers and ask, "How many did you miss?" or make such statements as "I'm faster than you" after winning a footrace (Frey & Ruble, 1985). This kind of comparison increases and becomes more subtle with age (Pomerantz et al., 1995) and plays an important role in shaping children's perceived competencies and global self-esteem (Altermatt et al., 2002), particularly in Western cultures where competition and individual accomplishments are stressed. Interestingly, this preoccupation with evaluating oneself in comparison to peers is not nearly as strong among communally reared kibbutz children in Israel, perhaps because cooperation and teamwork are so strongly emphasized in the kibbutzim (Butler & Ruzany, 1993).

Peer influences on self-esteem become even more apparent in adolescence (Harter, 1999). Young adolescents who receive ample and balanced social support from both parents and peers tend to display high levels of self-esteem and few problem behaviors (DuBois et al., 2002b). And recall that some of the strongest contributions to adolescent self-appraisals are the quality of one's relationships with particularly close friends. In fact, when young adults reflect back on life experiences that were noteworthy to them and that may have influenced their self-esteem, they mention experiences with friends and romantic partners as frequently or even more frequently than experiences with parents and family members (McLean & Thorne, 2003; Thorne & Michaelieu, 1996).

social comparison
the process of defining and evaluating the self by comparing oneself to other people.

Culture, Ethnicity, and Self-Esteem

Children and adolescents from such collectivist societies as China, Japan, and Korea tend to report lower levels of global self-esteem than their age-mates from individualistic countries such as the United States, Canada, and Australia (Harter, 1999). Why is this? The differences seem to reflect the different emphases that collectivist and individualistic societies place on individual accomplishments and self-promotion. In Western societies, people often compete as they pursue individual objectives and take pride in (and even brag about) their individual accomplishments. By contrast, people from collectivist societies are more interdependent than independent. They tend to value humility and self-effacement and to derive self-worth from contributing to the welfare of the groups (for example, families, communities, classrooms, or even the larger society) to which they belong. In fact, acknowledging one's weaknesses and needs for self-improvement—admissions that may lower one's reported self-worth on traditional measures of self-esteem—can actually make children from collectivist societies feel *good* about themselves because these behaviors are likely to be viewed by others as evidence of appropriate humility and increased commitment to the group's welfare (Heine et al., 1999).

There are also ethnic differences in self-esteem among people in multicultural societies. Consider findings from the United States. Throughout elementary school, disadvantaged African-American and Hispanic children, who are becoming aware of negative ethnic stereotypes and possibly even experiencing prejudice from some adults and peers, often express lower levels of self-esteem as compared to their European-American age-mates; by contrast, Asian-American elementary school children tend to report as high or higher levels of self-esteem than European-American children do (Twenge & Crocker, 2002). However, the picture changes somewhat by adolescence. Now African-American and Hispanic youth are likely to express about the same or even higher levels of self-esteem than European Americans do (Gerard & Buehler, 2004; Gray-Little & Hafdahl, 2000; Twenge & Crocker, 2002), particularly if they have ample social support from parents and have been encouraged to identify with and take pride in their ethnic group and its cultural traditions (Caldwell et al., 2002; Hughes et al., 2006; Umana-Taylor, Diversi, & Fine, 2002).

Interestingly, Asian Americans begin to report lower levels of self-esteem as adolescents than their European-American classmates do (Twenge & Crocker, 2002). This finding may reflect the fact that many Asian-American families retain some of the collectivist values of their country of origin (see Chao, 2001), including the prescriptions that one should display appropriate personal humility, respect parental authority, and be willing to subordinate individual motives and concerns for the greater good of the family.

Now that we have considered how developing children and adolescents acquire information about the self and evaluate this information to gain a sense of self-esteem, we turn to another crucial aspect of self development: the need to form a firm, future-oriented personal identity.

⤳ WHO AM I TO BE? FORGING AN IDENTITY

According to Erik Erikson (1963), the major developmental hurdle that adolescents face is establishing an **identity**—a firm and coherent sense of who they are, where they are heading, and where they fit into society. Forging an identity involves grappling with many important choices: What kind of career do I want? What spiritual, moral, and political values should I adopt? Who am I as a man or a woman, and as a sexual being? Just where do I fit into society? All this is, of course, a lot for teenagers to have on their minds, and Erikson used the term **identity crisis** to capture the sense of confusion, and even anxiety,

identity
a mature self-definition; a sense of who one is, where one is going in life, and how one fits into society.

identity crisis
Erikson's term for the uncertainty and discomfort that adolescents experience when they become confused about their present and future roles in life.

that adolescents may feel as they think about who they are today and try to decide "What kind of self can (or should) I become?"

Can you recall a time during the teenage years when you were confused about who you were, what you should be, and what you were likely to become? Is it possible that you have not yet resolved these identity issues and are still seeking answers? If so, does that make you abnormal or maladjusted?

James Marcia (1980) has developed a structured interview that allows researchers to classify adolescents into one of four identity statuses—*identity diffusion, foreclosure, moratorium*, and *identity achievement*—based on whether they have explored various alternatives and made firm commitments to an occupation, a religious ideology, a sexual orientation, and a set of political values. These identity statuses are as follows:

1. **Identity diffusion:** Persons classified as "diffuse" have not yet thought about or resolved identity issues and have failed to chart future life directions, *Example:* "I haven't really thought much about religion, and I guess I don't know exactly what I believe."

2. **Foreclosure:** Persons classified as "foreclosed" are committed to an identity but have made this commitment without experiencing the "crisis" of deciding what really suits them best. *Example:* "My parents are Baptists and so I'm a Baptist; it's just the way I grew up."

3. **Moratorium:** Persons in the status are experiencing what Erikson called an identity crisis and are actively asking questions about life commitments and seeking answers. *Example:* "I'm evaluating my beliefs and hope that I will be able to describe what's right for me. I like many of the answers provided by my Catholic upbringing, but I'm skeptical about some teachings as well. I have been looking into Unitarianism to see whether it might help me answer my questions."

4. **Identity Achievement:** Identity-achieved individuals have resolved identity issues by making *personal* commitments to particular goals, beliefs, and values. *Example:* "After a lot of soul-searching about my religion and other religions too, I finally know what I believe and what I don't."

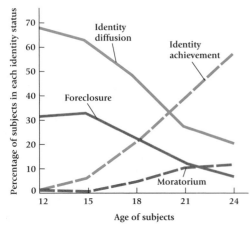

Figure 6.5 Percentages of subjects in each of Marcia's four identity statuses as a function of age. Note that resolution of the identity crisis occurs much later than Erikson assumed: only 4 percent of the 15-year-olds and 20 percent of the 18-year-olds had achieved a stable identity. (Adapted from Meilman, "Cross-sectional age changed in ego identity status during adolescence," *Developmental Psychology*, 15, p. 230–231. Copyright © 1979 by the American Psychological Association. Reprinted by permission.)

identity diffusion
identity status characterizing individuals who are not questioning who they are and have not yet committed themselves to an identity.

foreclosure
identity status characterizing individuals who have prematurely committed themselves to occupations or ideologies without really thinking about these commitments.

moratorium
identity status characterizing individuals who are currently experiencing an identity crisis and are actively exploring occupational and ideological positions in which to invest themselves.

identity achievement
identity status characterizing individuals who have carefully considered identity issues and have made firm commitments to an occupation and ideologies.

Developmental Trends in Identity Formation

Although Erikson assumed that the identity crisis occurs in early adolescence and is often resolved by age 15–18, his age norms were overly optimistic. When Philip Meilman (1979) measured the identity statuses of males between the ages of 12 and 24, he observed a clear developmental progression. But as shown in Figure 6.5, the vast majority of 12- to 18-year-olds were identity diffuse or foreclosed, and not until age 21 or older had the majority of participants reached the moratorium status or achieved stable identities.

Is the identity formation process different for girls and women than it is for boys and men? In most respects, no (Archer, 1992; Kroger, 2005). Girls make progress toward achieving a clear sense of identity at about the same ages that boys do. However, one intriguing sex difference has been observed: Although today's college women are just as concerned about establishing a career identity as men are, they attach greater importance to the aspects of identity that center on sexuality, gender roles, and the issue of balancing family and career goals (Archer, 1992; Kroger, 2005).

Judging from this research, identity formation takes quite a bit of time. Not until late adolescence—during the college years—do many young men and women move from the diffusion or foreclosure status into the moratorium status and then achieve a sense of identity (Waterman, 1982; Kroger,

2005). But this is by no means the end of the identity formation process. Many adults are *still* struggling with identity issues or have reopened the question of who they are after thinking they had all the answers earlier in life (Kroger, 2005; Yip, Seaton, & Sellers, 2006). A divorce, for example, may cause a homemaker to rethink what it means to be a woman and raise again questions about other aspects of her identity as well.

The process of achieving identity is also quite uneven (Archer, 1982; Kroger, 2005). For example, Sally Archer (1982) assessed the identity statuses of 6th- to 12th-graders in four domains: occupational choice, gender-role attitudes, religious beliefs, and political ideologies. Only 5 percent of her adolescents were in the same identity status in all four areas, with 95 percent being in two or even three statuses across the four domains. So adolescents can achieve a strong sense of identity in one area and still be searching in others.

How Painful is Identity Formation?

Perhaps it is unfortunate that Erikson used the term "crisis" to describe the adolescent's active search for an identity (or identities), because adolescents in the moratorium status often do not appear all that "stressed out." In fact, James Marcia and his associates (1993) find that these active identity seekers feel much better about themselves and their futures than do age-mates in the diffusion and foreclosure statuses (but see Meeus et al., 1999, for an opposing viewpoint). Yet Erikson was right in characterizing identity achievement as a very healthy and adaptive development, because identity achievers do enjoy higher self-esteem and are less self-conscious or preoccupied with personal concerns than their counterparts in the other three identity statuses (Adams, Abraham, & Markstrom, 1987; O'Connor, 1995; Seaton, Scottham, & Sellers, 2006). Moreover, Erikson viewed the achievement of a stable identity as a prerequisite for establishing a truly intimate relationship (or *shared identity*) with another person during the psychological crisis of **intimacy versus isolation** that young adults face. And true to form, college students displaying mature identity statuses as freshman and sophomores had often established intimate relationships one year later, whereas those with diffuse identities had rarely established intimacy with anyone over the next 12 months (Fitch & Adams, 1983; see also Peterson, Ewigman, & Kivlahan, 1993). So the establishment of a stable personal identity is a significant milestone indeed—one that helps pave the way for positive psychological adjustment and the growth of deep and trusting emotional commitments that could conceivably last a lifetime.

What may be most painful or "crisis-like" about identity seeking is a long-term failure to establish one. Erikson believed that individuals without a clear identity would eventually become depressed and lacking in self-confidence as they drift aimlessly, trapped in the "diffusion" status. Or alternatively, they might heartily embrace what Erikson called a **negative identity,** becoming a "black sheep," a "delinquent," or a "loser." Why? Because for these foundering souls, it is better to become everything that one is not supposed to be than to have no identity at all

intimacy versus isolation
the sixth of Erikson's psychosocial conflicts, in which young adults must commit themselves to a shared identity with another person (that is, intimacy) or else remain aloof and unconnected to others.

negative identity
Erikson's term for an identity that is in direct opposition to that which parents and most adults would advocate.

Photo 6.5
Adopting a "negative identity" sometimes boosts the self-esteem of adolescents who are identity diffused.

A. Ramey/PhotoEdit, Inc.

(Erikson, 1963). Indeed, many adolescents who are stuck in the diffusion status are highly apathetic and do express a sense of hopelessness about the future, sometimes even becoming suicidal (Chandler et al., 2003; Waterman & Archer, 1990). Others who enter high school with very low self-esteem often drift into delinquency and view their deviant self-image as having provided them with a boost in self-worth (Loeber & Stouthamer-Loeber, 1998; Wells, 1989). So it seems that a small minority of adolescents and young adults experience what might be termed an identity *crisis* after all.

Personal, Social, and Cultural Influences on Identity Formation

The adolescent's progress toward identity achievement is influenced by at least four factors: cognitive growth, parenting, schooling, and the broader social-cultural context.

Cognitive Influences   Cognitive development plays an important role in identity achievement. Adolescents who have achieved solid mastery of formal operational thought and who can reason logically about hypotheticals are now better able to imagine and contemplate future identities. Consequently, they are more likely to raise and resolve identity issues than are age-mates who are less intellectually mature (Berzonsky & Kuk, 2000; Boyes & Chandler, 1992).

Parenting Influences   The relationships that adolescents have with their parents can also affect their progress at forging an identity (Grotevant & Cooper, 1998; Markstrom-Adams, 1992). Adolescents in the diffusion status are more likely than those in other statuses to feel neglected or rejected by their parents and to be distant from them (Archer, 1994). Perhaps it is difficult to establish one's own identity without first having the opportunity to identify with respected parental figures and take on some of their desirable qualities. At the other extreme, adolescents in the identity foreclosure status are often extremely close to and may sometimes fear rejection from relatively controlling parents (Berzonsky & Adams, 1999). Foreclosed adolescents may never question parental authority or feel any need to construct a separate identity. These youth are more likely to forge independent identities when they move out of the house as opposed to living at home during the college years (Jordyn & Byrd, 2003).

By contrast, adolescents who move easily into the moratorium and identity achievement statuses appear to have a solid base of affection at home combined with considerable freedom to be individuals in their own right (Grotevant & Cooper, 1998). In family discussions, for example, these adolescents experience a sense of closeness and mutual respect while feeling free to disagree with their parents and to be individuals in their own right. So the same loving and democratic style of parenting that helps children gain a strong sense of self-esteem is also associated with healthy and adaptive identity outcomes in adolescence.

Scholastic Influences   Does attending college help one to forge an identity? The answer is yes—and no. Attending college does seem to push people toward setting career goals and making stable occupational commitments (Waterman, 1982); but college students are often far behind their working peers in terms of establishing firm political and religious identities (Munro & Adams, 1977). In fact, some collegians will regress from identity achievement to the moratorium or even the diffusion status in certain areas, most notably religion. But let's not be too critical of the college environment, for, like college students, many adults will later reopen the question of who they are if exposed to people or situations that challenge old viewpoints and offer new alternatives (Kroger, 2005).

Cultural-Historical Influences   Finally, identity formation is strongly influenced by the broader social and historical context in which it occurs (Bosma & Kunnen, 2001)—a point that Erikson himself emphasized. In fact, the very idea that adolescents should choose a personal identity after carefully exploring many options may well be peculiar to industrialized societies of the 20th century (Cote & Levine, 1988). As in past centuries, adolescents in many nonindustrialized societies today will simply adopt the adult roles they are expected to adopt, without any soul-searching or experimentation: Sons of farmers will become farmers, the children of fishermen will become (or perhaps marry) fishermen, and so on. For many of the world's adolescents, then, what Marcia calls identity foreclosure is probably the most adaptive route to adulthood. In addition, the specific life goals that adolescents pursue are necessarily constrained somewhat by whatever options are available and valued in their society at any given point in time (Bosma & Kunnen, 2001; Matsumoto, 2000).

Identity Formation among Minority Youth

In addition to identity issues that confront all adolescents, members of ethnic minority groups must also decide upon the merits of establishing an **ethnic identity**—a personal identification with an ethnic group and its values and traditions (Phinney, 1996). This is not always an easy task. As we saw earlier, some minority children may even identify at first with the culture's ethnic majority, apparently wanting to affiliate with the group that has the most status in society (Spencer & Markstrom-Adams, 1990). One Hispanic adolescent who had done this said, "I remember I would not say I was Hispanic. My friends . . . were white and Oriental and I tried so hard to fit in with them" (Phinney & Rosenthal, 1992, p. 158). It is not that young children have no knowledge of their subcultural traditions. Mexican-American preschoolers, for example, may learn such culturally relevant behaviors as giving a Chicano handshake; yet not until about age 8 are they likely to fully understand which ethnic labels apply to them, what they mean, or that one's ethnicity is a lifelong attribute (Bernal & Knight, 1997).

Forming a positive ethnic identity during adolescence seems to involve the same steps, or statuses, as forming a vocational or religious identity (Phinney, 1993; Seaton, Scottham, & Sellers, 2006). Young adolescents often say that they identify with their own ethnic group because their parents and other members of the group influenced them to do so (foreclosure status) or because that is what they are and they have not given the issue much thought (diffusion status). But between ages 15 and 19, many minority youths move into the moratorium or achievement phase of ethnic identity (French et al., 2006; Pahl & Way, 2006). One Mexican-American girl describes her moratorium period this way: "I want to know what we do and how our culture is different from others. Going to festivals and cultural events helps me to learn more about my own culture and about myself" (Phinney, 1993, p. 70). Once ethnic identity is achieved, minority youth tend to display higher self-esteem, better academic adjustment, better relations with parents, and more favorable assessments of peers of other ethnicities than their counterparts who merely label themselves as a minority and are still ethnically diffuse or foreclosed (Chavous et al., 2003; Fuligni, Witkow, & Garcia, 2005; Phinney, Ferguson, & Tate, 1997; Supple et al., 2006; Yip & Fuligni, 2002). So it seems as if establishing a strong identification with one's ethnic group is an important personal resource that promotes adaptive outcomes. Indeed, Lisa Kiang and her associates (2006) found that even after controlling for the effects of another important personal resource—self-esteem—minority adolescents who had achieved strong ethnic identities were better able their less identified age-mates to maintain their happiness and sense of well-being in the face of daily hassles.

Questions regarding ethnic identity are sometimes triggered by the stresses associated with others' prejudicial comments or by being discriminated against because of one's ethnicity (see Caldwell et al., 2002; DuBois et al., 2002a; Pahl & Way, 2006). Minority youth also face thorny identity questions when they encounter conflicts between the

ethnic identity
sense of belonging to an ethnic group and committing oneself to that group's traditions or culture.

values of their subculture and those of the majority culture, and members of their sub-cultural communities (especially peers) often discourage identity explorations that clash with the traditions of their own group (Ogbu, 1988). Virtually all North American minorities have a term for community members who are "too white" in orientation, be it the "apple" for Native Americans (red on the outside, white on the inside), the Hispanic "coconut," the Asian "twinkie," or the African-American "oreo." Yet, even though social pressures are likely to stimulate identity explorations and push one into the moratorium phase, ethnic identity achievement is a very personal matter—minority adolescents must grapple with social taunts and other value conflicts and decide *for themselves* what they are inside (Pahl & Way, 2006).

Interestingly, mixed-ethnicity adolescents and cross-ethnic adoptees in white adoptive homes sometimes face even greater conflicts. These youngsters may feel pressured to choose between minority and white peer groups, thereby encountering social barriers to achieving an identity as *both* African American (for example) and white (DeBerry, Scarr, & Weinberg, 1996; Kerwin et al., 1993). About half the cross-ethnic adoptees in Scarr's classic Minnesota Transracial Adoption Study (1983) were showing some signs of social maladjustment at age 17. Although African American in appearance, many of these adoptees looked to whites as their primary reference group. Thus, their maladjustment could reflect the fact that (1) they were not prepared to function effectively within the African-American community, and (2) they were likely to face some prejudice and discrimination as black persons trying to fit into a white ecological niche (DeBerry, Scarr, & Weinberg, 1996). Yet a stronger identification with *either* a white or an African-American reference group predicted better adjustment outcomes that did maintaining a more ethnically diffuse orientation. So here is another sign that establishing some kind of ethnic identity, or point of reference, is an adaptive developmental outcome for members of a minority group.

Finally, various ethnicities in a multicultural society such as the United States differ in the extent to which the ideal self is more personal (individualistic) or collective. Most European Americans who derive originally from individualistic cultures usually describe their ethnicity with a general label such as "white" and may (or may not) mention a collective identity as simply "American." By contrast, Native American cultures are typically collectivist in origin, and Native American youth often develop strong bicultural collective identities as both Native Americans and Americans (Whitesell et al., 2006; see also Fuligni, Witkow, & Garcia, 2005, for evidence that such groups as Chinese Americans seek to create bicultural ethnic identities that represent a combination of their ethnic origin with their status as American youth). Thus, ethnically achieved minority youths in the United States often construct multifaceted collective identities and take pride in being *both* an American and a member of their particular racial or ethnic group.

How can we help minority youths to forge positive ethnic identities and to achieve more favorable adjustment outcomes? Their parents can play a major role, starting in the preschool period, by (1) teaching them about their group's cultural traditions and fostering ethnic pride, (2) preparing them to deal constructively with the prejudices and value conflicts they may encounter, and (3) simply being warm and supportive confidants (Bernal & Knight, 1997; Caldwell et al., 2002; Caughy et al., 2002; Hughes et al., 2006; McHale et al., 2006). Schools and communities can also help by promoting a greater understanding and appreciation of ethnic diversity, starting early in the preschool years (Burnette, 1997), and by continuing their efforts to ensure that educational and economic opportunities are extended to all (Spencer & Markstrom-Adams, 1990).

Photo 6.6
Forging a positive ethnic identity is an adaptive development for minority youths.

Jonathan Nourok/PhotoEdit, Inc.

THE OTHER SIDE OF SOCIAL COGNITION: KNOWING ABOUT OTHERS

Being appropriately "social" requires us to interact with other people, and these interactions are more likely to be harmonious if we know what our social partners are thinking or feeling and can predict how they are likely to behave (Heyman & Gelman, 1998). Although research on theory of mind tells us that even preschool children are budding psychologists, they still have much to learn about other people's personalities and behavioral tendencies. The development of children's knowledge about other people—their descriptions of others' characteristics and the inferences they make about others' thoughts and behaviors—represents perhaps the largest area of social-cognitive research. And there are so many questions to be answered. For example, what kinds of information do children use to form impressions of others? How do these impressions change over time? And what skills are children acquiring that might explain such changes in person perception? These are the issues that we will now explore.

Age Trends in Person Perception

Children younger than 7 or 8 are likely to characterize people they know in the same concrete, observable terms that they use to describe the self (Livesley & Bromley, 1973; Ruble & Dweck, 1995; and see Box 6.4). Five-year-old Jenny, for example, said: "My daddy is big. He has hairy legs and eats mustard. Yuck! My daddy likes dogs—do you?" Not much of a personality profile there! When young children do use a psychological term to describe others, it is typically a very general attribute such as "He's *nice*" or "She's *mean*" that they may use more as a description or evaluation of the other person's recent behavior than as an explanation of the person's enduring qualities (Rholes & Ruble, 1984; Ruble & Dweck, 1995).

It's not that preschoolers have no appreciation for the inner qualities that people display. As we noted earlier in the chapter, even 18-month-olds are aware that other people's behavior reflects their goals or desires, and they can occasionally interpret these mental states correctly and respond appropriately to them (Repacholi & Gopnik, 1997). By age 3 to 5, children are aware of how their closest peer companions typically behave in a variety of different situations (Eder, 1989). And kindergartners already know that their classmates differ in academic competencies and social skills; furthermore, they reliably choose the "smart" ones as teammates for academic competitions and the "socially skilled" classmates as partners for play activities (Droege & Stipek, 1993).

Not only are 5- to 6-year-olds becoming more aware of *behavioral consistencies* that their companions display, but they are also beginning to make other kinds of "trait-like" inferences based largely on their emerging understanding of such subjective mental states as desires and motives that might *explain* other people's conduct. For example, 5-year-olds who hear stories about a child who has often shared and a second child who rarely has can correctly infer that the first child will be *motivated* to share in the future and is "generous" (as opposed to selfish), whereas the second child will be *unmotivated* to share and is "selfish" (Yuill & Pearson, 1998). Thus, 5-year-olds assume that individual differences in past behaviors imply different *motives* with different implications for future behavior. And the links between thinking about motives and making trait-like behavioral predictions is even clearer when the children in this study were asked to identify the emotions that children with contrasting traits might display to the same outcome. Five-year-olds were quite capable of making appropriate emotional inferences, saying, for example, that the generous child would feel "happy" were she to share her birthday cake with other children, whereas a selfish child would feel "sad" were his stingy motive thwarted by being made to share. Yet these findings may actually underestimate the capabilities of young children, for more

Ethnic Categorization and Prejudice In Children and Adolescents

Because toddlers and preschool children tend to define others in terms of their observable characteristics, it may come as no surprise to learn that even 3- and 4-year-olds notice differences in skin color and can apply labels such as *black* and *white* to different people or to photos of blacks and whites. Furthermore, studies conducted in Australia, Canada, and the United States reveal that by age 5 or 6, many white children have some knowledge of ethnic stereotypes (Bigler & Liben, 1993) and display at least some prejudicial attitudes toward blacks and Native Americans (Aboud, 2003; Black-Gutman & Hickson, 1996; Doyle & Aboud, 1995; Dunham, Baron, & Banaji, 2006).

Interestingly, parents often believe that their own children are largely oblivious to ethnic diversity and that prejudicial attitudes and behaviors in other children arise when their bigoted parents pass their own intolerant views to them (Burnette, 1997). However, research suggests otherwise, because the ethnic attitudes of young children often bear little relationship to those of their parents or their friends (Aboud, 1988; Burnette, 1997). Indeed, young children show strong inclinations to sort people into categories and to identify with and prefer the category to which they belong. To illustrate, 3- to 5-year-olds who are sorted into "red" and "blue" groups (based on the color of work shirts they wore) came over time to develop much more favorable attitudes to their own color groups, even though preschool teachers used the labels "red group" and "blue group" in simple descriptive and nonevaluative ways (Patterson & Bigler, 2006). What's more, first-graders already prefer loyal in-group members who choose to play exclusively with playmates of their own ethnicity (Castelli, De Amicis, & Sherman, 2007). Labels denoting ethnic groups (blacks, Jews, and Arabs, for example) lead children to expect that members of various ethnicities will differ in important ways; in fact, when making inferences about another person's preferences or behaviors, the label "Arab" or "Jew" had as much as or more to do with the conclusions that 5-year-old Israeli children drew as the person's physical appearance did (Diesendruck & haLevi, 2006). So the origins of ethnic bias may be more *cognitive* than social, reflecting the tendency of egocentric youngsters to rigidly categorize people by skin color (or ethnic labels) and

to strongly favor the group to which they belong, without necessarily being overly hostile toward people of other ethnicities (Aboud, 2003).

There is some debate about the growth of prejudical attitudes beyond the preschool period. As children enter the stage of concrete operations and become more flexible in their thinking, *overt* ethnic bias often declines in strength. This increased tolerance of 8- to 9-year-olds reflects a more realistic evaluation of ethnic groups in which out-groups are viewed more favorably and their own group somewhat less favorably than was true during the preschool years (Doyle & Aboud, 1995; Teichman, 2001). It also reflects a little self-presentation, for young grade-school children are learning and increasingly coming to comply with norms advocating the suppression of prejudicial actions (Rutland et al., 2005). Yet implicit (private) indicators of prejudicial attitudes are quite apparent during middle childhood (Dunham, Baron, & Banaji, 2006), and 7- to 9-year-olds may suddenly dislike members of other groups if their own reference group is close and exclusionary and they are in some way threatened by the presence of an out-group (Nesdale et al., 2005). Nevertheless, the in-group bias that elementary school children display is primarily in-group favoritism rather than out-group derogation or hatred (Pfeifer, Ruble, et al., 2007). Simply stated, it's not that out-groups are loathful; they simply "come up short" compared to one's own group.

Social forces can play a role in maintaining and even increasing ethnic prejudice among preadolescents and adolescents. Daisa Black-Gutman and Fay Hickson (1996) found that Euro-Australian children's prejudice toward black Aborigines declined between ages 5 and 9, and then intensified at age 10 to 12, returning to the levels displayed by 5- to 6-year-olds! Because the 10- to 12-year-olds were no longer constrained by the egocentrism and rigid categorization schemes of a 5- or 6-year-old, their increased prejudice apparently reflected the influence of adult attitudes, namely the deep-seated animosity that many Euro-Australians feel toward black Aborigines. However, increases in prejudice during early adolescence may also reflect the fact that personal identity issues are becoming increasingly important; thus, praising the virtues of one's own group and the shortcomings of other groups is a

recent research has found that even 3- and 4-year-olds can draw appropriate trait-like inferences (viewing someone as either "nice" or "mean") if they encounter clear examples of the target person's generous or harmful behavior (Boseovski & Lee, 2006; Liu, Gelman, & Wellman, 2007). What's more, 4- and 5-year-olds can use trait labels to *predict* trait-relevant behaviors in the near future. So, if told that Bobby is *"selfish,"* they predict that he will take his toys away from his sister rather than allowing her to continue playing with them (Liu, Gelman, & Wellman, 2007).

So certainly by age 4 to 5 (or slightly sooner) children appear to be capable of thinking about traits in psychologically meaningful ways. Why, then, do they not use many trait words to describe the people they know well? Very possibly because they do not truly understand that a personality trait implies notable consistencies in one's behavior *over time and across situations.* Consider the following example. Children hear a story in which a child either shares or refuses to share toys with kids who have none, and are then asked to predict how many toys that child will share in a similar context in the future. Even 5-year-olds

way of solidifying one's group identity and enhancing self-worth (Teichman, 2001).

Developmentalists now believe that the best way to combat ethnic prejudice is for parents and teachers to talk openly about the merits of ethnic diversity and the harmful effects of prejudice, beginning in the preschool period when strong favoritism of one's own in-group and early indications of prejudice often take root (Burnette, 1997). Three major approaches to prejudice reduction have been implemented in U.S. schools with varying degrees of success (Pfeifer, Brown, & Juvonen, 2007):

1. *Multicultural curricula*: programs designed to expose children to the customs and histories of diverse groups, present them with stories about minority group members, and depict various ethnic groups in nonsterotypical ways.

2. *Cooperative learning programs:* programs designed to promote equal-status contact in which children of different races and ethnicities must pull together to pursue common goals. These groups are evaluated or receive rewards and recognition based on the degree to which they increase the academic performance of each group member. This encourages inter-ethnic cooperation as the performance of each child, regardless of ethnicity, matters to the whole group.

3. *Anti-bias/social-cognitive programs:* programs that typically discuss causes of racial prejudice and ways to promote inter-ethnic cooperation. Children may role-play or read about discriminatory acts and are encouraged to imagine what the child being discriminated against is thinking (perspective taking) or how he or she feels (empathy training).

By themselves, multicultural curricular interventions are of limited effectiveness, sometimes improving but often failing to influence children's attitudes toward out-groups. Cooperative learning programs have fared better, often promoting more positive attitudes toward out-groups and cross-ethnic friendships (as well as increased academic achievement), whereas anti-bias/social cognitive interventions have also enjoyed some success at promoting more positive attitudes and behaviors toward out-group members (Pfeifer, Brown, & Juvonen, 2007; see also Hughes, Bigler, & Levy, 2007). Of course, it is likely that some

Mixed-ethnicity discussion groups can help to foster an appreciation of diverse subcultural traditions and combat the formation of prejudicial attitudes.

combination of all three approaches will prove more effective than any single program.

Should we be devoting limited educational resources to try to reduce prejudice in the schools? Jennifer Pfeifer and her associates (2007) think so and suggest that it " . . . might be appropriate to incorporate prejudice reduction programs into the 'character education' component of the No Child Left Behind policy" (p. 13). One major challenge, they claim, is to find effective and personal ways to be honest and forthright with young children about prejudice and discrimination rather than shunning the issue or covering it up. Indeed, strong straitforward talk about prejudice that begins even before children go to school may be necessary because, once established, prejudicial attitudes are difficult to modify. As developmentalist Vonnie McLoyd (cited in Burnette, 1997, p. 33) has noted, "Racism is so deeply rooted that [overcoming it] is going to take hard work by open, honest, fair-minded people who are not easily discouraged."

say that the child who shared will share more toys later than the child who didn't and, if descriptors are supplied to them, they may even choose the appropriate trait label (generous versus selfish) to describe the characters they heard about. Yet these "trait-like" inferences could conceivably be attributable to *evaluative reasoning* rather than trait-like reasoning. A 5-year-old may think: "He shared; that's *good;* therefore, he'll do something *good* in the future, and sharing is good." Given a choice between describing the child as generous or selfish, generous is the *good* descriptor; so our 5-year-old picks that label. He may be making the appropriate trait-like predictions by evaluating the story character as a good person who may do good again rather than by first inferring that the story character is *generous* and that current generosity—a stable trait—implies future generosity.

Jeannette Alarvez and her associates (2001) tested this hypothesis by exposing 5- to 6-year-olds and 9- to 10-year-olds to story scenarios and asking questions about them. For example, children heard stores about story characters who either shared or refused to share toys with other kids. They were then asked to predict how many toys that child might share in a similar future context (in other words, none, a few, many, a lot). They were also asked to indicate whether the character's behavior was good or bad and to rate how good (or bad) the behavior was (for example, a little good/bad, pretty good/bad, very good/bad). Finally, after picking a trait (generous versus selfish) to describe the character's behavior, they indicated how much of that trait the character displayed (for example, for generous: a little generous, pretty generous, very generous). The results were clear. Children from both age groups made appropriate behavioral inferences, saying that the child who had shared would share more toys in the future than the child who hadn't shared. But the rationale for these inferences differed by age. For 5- to 6-year-olds, *evaluations* of the story character's behavior as good or bad is what predicted their assessments of how many toys he or she would share in the future, and the extent to which they evaluated the character as generous or selfish did not. It was just the reverse for 9- to 10-year-olds, whose assessments of the story character's future sharing reflected their assessments of how generous (or selfish) the character was rather than how good (or bad) they viewed his behavior.

In sum, 5- to 6-year-olds often seem to use traits as *evaluative* labels for other's behaviors (for example, a sharing child is labeled generous because he was good [and may well do good in the future]) rather than as descriptions of dispositional characteristics that are very stable over time and across situations (see also Rholes & Ruble, 1984). Yet the finding that even 4-year-olds can predict a person's future behavior if that person is described as possessing a trait (selfishness, for example) implies that they have a primitive understanding of traits as dispositions, even though they are not yet able to spontaneously generate trait labels to both characterize others' past behavior and make predictions about future conduct (see Liu, Gelman, & Wellman, 2007).

Changes in Person Perception across Middle Childhood and Adolescence   Data from the studies we have reviewed imply that children should reliably come to view others as characterized by stable dispositional attributes (that is, traits) at some point during middle childhood. This is precisely what the literature indicates (Rholes & Ruble, 1984). Between ages 7 and 16, children begin to rely less and less on concrete attributes and more on psychological descriptors to characterize their friends and family members. These changes are nicely illustrated in a program of research by Carl Barenboim (1981), who asked 6- to 11-year-olds to describe three persons they knew well. Rather than simply listing the behaviors that close companions display, 6- to 8-year-olds often *compared* others on noteworthy behavioral dimensions, making such statements as "Billy *runs faster* than Jason" or "She *draws the best* pictures in our whole class." As shown in Figure 6.6, use of these **behavioral comparisons** increased between ages 6 and 8 and declined rapidly after age 9. One outgrowth of the behavioral comparison process is that children become increasingly aware of regularities in a companion's behavior and eventually begin to attribute them to stable **psychological constructs,** or traits, that the person is now presumed to have. So a 10-year-old who formerly described one of her acquaintances as drawing best of anyone in her class may now convey the same impression by saying that the acquaintance is very artistic. Notice in reexamining the figure that children's use of these psychological constructs increased rapidly between ages 8 and 11—the same period when behavioral comparisons became less common. Eventually, children begin to compare and contrast others on important psychological dimensions, making such statements as "Bill is more shy than Ted" or "Susie is the most artistic person in our class." Although few 11-year-olds generate these **psychological comparisons** when describing others (see Figure 6.6), the majority of 12- to 16-year-olds in Barenboim's second study were actively comparing their associates on noteworthy psychological dimensions.

Person perception changes in many other ways as children approach and enter adolescence. Unlike younger children, who tend to take people at their word, 10- to 11-year-olds are much more aware that others are motivated to present themselves in socially desirable

behavioral comparisons phase the tendency to form impressions of others by comparing and contrasting their overt behaviors.

psychological constructs phase tendency to base one's impressions of others on the stable traits these individuals are presumed to have.

psychological comparisons phase tendency to form impressions of others by comparing and contrasting these individuals on abstract psychological dimensions.

ways. Consequently, they are much more skeptical than 6- to 7-year-olds are about another person's self-reports of attributes such as honesty or intelligence, choosing instead to base their own conclusions on personal observations (or teacher reports) (Heyman & Legare, 2005).

By age 14 to 16, adolescents are not only more aware of the *dispositional* similarities and dissimilarities that characterize their acquaintances, they are also beginning to recognize that any number of *situational* factors (for example, illness, family strife) can cause a person to act "out of character" (Damon & Hart, 1988). They now view people as unique individuals with distinctive combinations of personality traits and are able to analyze how a person's diverse and often inconsistent traits "fit together" and make sense, much as they do when construct- ing their own self-concepts. Todd, for example, may notice that Juanita brags about her abilities at times but seems very unsure of herself at other times, and he may integrate these seemingly discrepant impressions by concluding that Juanita is basically insecure and boasts to hide that insecurity. So by mid- to late adolescence, young people are becoming sophisticated person- ality theorists and have grown quite proficient at looking both "inside" and "outside" their regular companions to understand

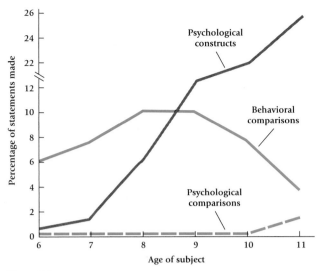

Figure 6.6
Percentages of descriptive statements classified as behavioral comparisons, psychological (trait-like) constructs, and psychological comparisons for children between the ages of 6 and 11. (From Barenboim, 1981.)

what really makes them tick. Why do children's self-concepts and their impressions of others become increasingly abstract and coherent with age? In addressing these issues, we will first examine two "cognitive" points of view before considering how social forces might contribute, both directly and indirectly, to the growth of social cognition.

Theories of Social-Cognitive Development

Cognitive Theories of Social Cognition   The two cognitive theories that are most often used to explain developmental trends in social cognition are Piaget's cognitive-developmental approach and Robert Selman's role-taking theory.

Cognitive-Developmental Theory   According to cognitive-developmental theorists, the ways that children think about the self and other people largely depend on their own levels of cognitive development. Recall that the thinking of 3- to 6-year-old "preoperational" children tends to center on the most salient *perceptual* aspects of stimuli and events. So it would hardly surprise a Piagetian to find that 3- to 6-year-olds describe their associates in very concrete, observable terms, mentioning their appearances and possessions, their likes and dislikes, and the actions that they can perform.

The thinking of 7- to 10-year-olds will change in many ways as these youngsters enter Piaget's concrete-operational stage. Not only is egocentrism becoming less pronounced, but children are now *decentering* from perceptual illusions and beginning to recognize that certain properties of an object remain unchanged despite changes in the object's ap- pearance (*conservation*). Clearly, these emerging abilities to look beyond immediate appear- ances and to infer underlying invariances might help to explain why 7- to 10-year-olds, who are actively comparing themselves with their peers, become more attuned to regulari- ties in their own and others' conduct and use psychological constructs, or traits, to describe these patterns.

By age 12 to 14, children are entering formal operations and are now able to think more logically and systematically about abstractions. Although the concept of a psycho- logical trait is itself an abstraction, it is one based on regularities in concrete, observable behaviors, perhaps explaining why older *concrete* operators can think in these terms. However, a trait *dimension* is even more of a mental inference or abstraction that has few if any concrete referents. Thus, the ability to think in dimensional terms and to reliably order people along these continua (as is necessary in making psychological comparisons) implies that a person is able to operate on abstract concepts—a formal-operational ability (O'Mahoney, 1989).

Although children do begin to make behavioral comparisons at age 6–8 and psychological comparisons at age 11–12—precisely the times that Piaget's theory implies that they should—cognitive-developmental theory clearly underestimates the social-cognitive abilities of young children. We've seen, for example, that 4-year-olds with a belief-desire theory of mind are achieving a much richer understanding of the *subjective* nature of such mental states as desires and beliefs, and that by age 4 to 5—still the *preoperational* period in Piaget's theory—children can use their knowledge of mental states, along with their observations of behavioral regularities, to make at least some very accurate inferences and predictions about a person's future behavior (Alvarez, Ruble, & Bolger, 2001; Boseovski & Lee, 2006; Yuill & Pearson, 1998). Clearly, general cognitive development contributes to the growth of social cognition as proponents of cognitive-developmental theory have claimed. Yet Robert Selman (1980) believes that there is one particular aspect of cognitive growth that underlies a mature understanding of the self and other people—the growth of **role-taking skills.**

Selman's Role-Taking Theory　According to Selman (1980; Yeates & Selman, 1989), children will gain much richer understandings of themselves and other people as they acquire the ability to discriminate their own perspectives from those of their companions and to see the relationships between these potentially discrepant points of view. Role-taking skills have been described as one's theory of mind in action (Blair, 2003). Simply stated, Selman believes that in order to "know" a person, one must be able to assume his perspective and understand his thoughts, feelings, beliefs, motives, and intentions—in short, the *internal* factors that account for his behavior. If a child has not yet acquired these important role-taking skills, she may have little choice but to describe her acquaintances in terms of their external attributes—that is, their appearance, their activities, and the things they possess.

Selman has studied the development of role-taking skills by asking children to comment on a number of interpersonal dilemmas. Here is one example (Selman, 1976, p. 302):

> Holly is an 8-year-old girl who likes to climb trees. She is the best tree climber in the neighborhood. One day while climbing down from a tall tree, she falls . . . but does not hurt herself. Her father sees her fall. He is upset and asks her to promise not to climb trees any more. Holly promises. Later that day, Holly and her friends meet Shawn. Shawn's kitten is caught in a tree and can't get down. Something has to be done right away or the kitten may fall. Holly is the only one who climbs trees well enough to reach the kitten and get it down, but she remembers her promise to her father.

To assess how well a child understands the perspectives of Holly, her father, and Shawn, Selman asks: Does Holly know how Shawn feels about the kitten? How will Holly's father feel if he finds out she climbed the tree? What does Holly think her father will do if he finds out she climbed the tree? What would you do? Children's responses to such probes led Selman to conclude that role-taking skills develop in a stagelike manner, as shown in Table 6.1.

Notice in examining the table that children progress from largely egocentric beings, who seem unaware of any perspective other than their own (stage 0), to sophisticated social-cognitive theorists, who can keep several perspectives in mind and compare each with the viewpoint that "most people" would adopt (Stage 4). Apparently, these role-taking skills represent a true developmental sequence, for 40 of 41 boys who were repeatedly

role taking
the ability to assume another person's perspective and understand his or her intentions, thoughts, feelings, and behaviors.

Photo 6.7
Robert Selman (1942–) has emphasized the relationship between the development of role-taking skills and the growth of interpersonal understanding.

Table 6.1 Selman's stages of social perspective taking

Stage of Role Taking	Typical Responses to the "Holly" Dilemma
0. Egocentric or undifferentiated perspective (roughly 3 to 6 years) Children are unaware of any perspective other than their own. They assume that whatever they feel is right for Holly to do will be agreed with by others.	Children often assume that Holly will save the kitten. When asked how Holly's father will react to her transgression, these children think he will be "happy because he likes kittens." In other words, these children like kittens themselves, and they assume that Holly and her father also like kittens.
1. Social-informational role taking (roughly 6 to 8 years) Children now recognize that people can have perspectives that differ from their own but believe that this happens *only* because these individuals have received different information.	When asked whether Holly's father will be angry because she climbed the tree, the child may say, "If he didn't know why she climbed the tree, he would be angry. But if he knew why she did it, he would realize that she had a good reason."
2. Self-reflective role taking (roughly 8 to 10 years) Children now know that their own and others' points of view may conflict even if they have received the same information. They are now able to consider the other person's viewpoint. They also recognize that the other person can put himself in their shoes, so they are now able to anticipate the person's reactions to their behavior. However, the child cannot consider his own perspective and that of another person at the same time.	If asked whether Holly will climb the tree, the child might say, "Yes. She knows that her father will understand why she did it." In so doing, the child is focusing on the father's consideration of Holly's perspective. But if asked whether the father would want Holly to climb the tree, the child usually says no, thereby indicating that he is now assuming the father's perspective and considering the father's concern for Holly's safety.
3. Mutual role taking (roughly 10 to 12 years) The child can now simultaneously consider her own and another person's points of view and recognize that the other person can do the same. The child can also assume the perspective of a disinterested third party and anticipate how each participant (self and other) will react to the viewpoint of his or her partner.	At this stage, a child might describe the outcome of the "Holly" dilemma by taking the perspective of a disinterested third party and indicating that she knows that both Holly and her father are thinking about what the other is thinking. For example, one child remarked: "Holly wanted to get the kitten because she likes kittens, but she knew that she wasn't supposed to climb trees. Holly's father knew that Holly had been told not to climb trees, but he couldn't have known about [the kitten]."
4. Societal role taking (roughly 12 to 15 and older) The adolescent now attempts to understand another person's perspective by comparing it with that of the social system in which he operates (that is, the view of the "generalized other"). In other words, the adolescent expects others to consider and typically assume perspectives on events that most people in their social group would take.	When asked whether Holly should be punished for climbing the tree, the stage 4 adolescent is likely to say "No" and claim that the value of humane treatment of animals justifies Holly's act and that most fathers would recognize this point.

Source: Adapted from Selman, 1976.

tested over a 5-year period showed a steady forward progression from stage to stage, with no skipping of stages (Gurucharri & Selman, 1982). Perhaps the reason that they develop in one particular order is that they are loosely related to Piaget's invariant sequence of cognitive stages (Keating & Clark, 1980): Preoperational children are at Selman's first or second level of role taking (stage 0 or 1), whereas most concrete operators are at the third or fourth level (stage 2 or 3), and formal operators are about equally distributed between the fourth and fifth levels of role taking (stages 3 and 4).

Role Taking and Thinking about Relationships   As children acquire role-taking skills, their understanding of the meaning and character of human relationships begins to change. Consider what children of different ages say about the meaning of *friendship*. Preschoolers at Selman's egocentric (level 0) stage think that virtually any pleasant interactions between themselves and available playmates qualify those playmates as "friends." So 5-year-old Chang might describe Terry as a close friend simply because "He lives next door and plays games with me" (Damon, 1977).

Common activity continues to be the principal basis for friendship among 6- to 8-year-olds (Hartup, 1992). But because these youngsters have reached Selman's stage 1 and recognize that others may not always share their perspectives, they begin to view a friend as someone who *chooses* to "do nice things for me." Friendships are often one-way at this stage, for the child feels no strong pressure to reciprocate these considerations. And should a friend fail to serve the child's interests (for example, by spurning an invitation to camp out in the back yard), she may quickly become a nonfriend.

Later, at Selman's stage 2, 8- to 10-year-olds show increasing concern for the needs of a friend and begin to see friendships as reciprocal relationships, based on *mutual trust,* in which two people exchange respect, kindness, and affection (Selman, 1980). No longer are common activities sufficient to brand someone a friend; as children appreciate how their own interests and perspectives and those of their peers can be similar or different, they insist that their friends be *psychologically* similar to themselves.

By early adolescence, many youngsters have reached Selman's stage 3 or 4. Although they still view friends as psychologically similar people who like, trust, and assist each other, they have expanded their notions of the obligations of friendship to emphasize the exchange of *intimate* thoughts and feelings (Berndt & Perry, 1990). They also expect their friends to stick up for them and be *loyal,* standing ready to provide close emotional support whenever they may need it (Berndt & Perry, 1990; Buhrmester, 1990).

So, with the growth of role-taking skills, children's conceptions of friendship gradually change from the one-sided, self-centered view of friends as "people who benefit me" to a harmonious, reciprocal perspective in which each party truly understands the other, enjoys providing him or her with emotional support and other niceties, and expects these same considerations in return. Perhaps because they rest on a firmer basis of intimacy and inter-personal understanding, the close friendships of older children and adolescents are viewed as more important and are more stable, or long-lasting, than those of younger children (Berndt, 1989; Berndt & Hoyle, 1985; Furman & Buhrmester, 1992).

Table 6.2 briefly summarizes the changes in thinking about the self and others that we have discussed—changes that are clearly influenced by cognitive development. Yet, as we will see in concluding the chapter, the growth of *social* cognition is also heavily influenced by *social* interactions and experiences that children and adolescents have had.

Social Influences on Social-Cognitive Development   Many developmentalists have wondered whether the growth of children's self-awareness and their understanding of other people are as closely tied to cognitive development as cognitive theorists have assumed. Consider, for example, that even though children's role-taking abilities are related to their performances on Piagetian measures and IQ tests (Pellegrini, 1985), it is quite possible for a child to grow less egocentric and to mature intellectually without becoming an especially skillful role-taker (Shantz, 1983). So there must be other, *noncognitive* factors that contribute to the growth of role-taking skills and that may even exert their own unique effects on children's social-cognitive development. Might social experiences play such a role? No less an authority than Jean Piaget thought so.

Social Experience as a Contributor to Role-Taking   Many years ago, Piaget (1965) argued that playful interactions among grade-school children promote the development of role-taking skills and mature social judgments. Piaget's view was that, by assuming

Table 6.2 Milestones in the development of self and social cognition

Age (years)	Self-Concept/Self-Esteem	Social Cognition
0–1	Can differentiate self from the external environment Sense of personal agency emerges Can discriminate own face from other faces Recognizes that oneself and a companion can share experiences	Discriminates familiar from unfamiliar people Prefers familiar companions (attachment objects)
1–2	Self-recognition emerges Categorical self develops	Recognizes that others' behavior reflects intentions Recognition that others act on desires Categorization of others on socially significant dimensions
3–5	Self-concept emphasizes physical attributes, possessions, and actions Sense of self-esteem emerges Appearance of belief-desire theory of mind and private self	Impressions are based largely on others' actions and concrete attributes Knowledge of ethnic stereotypes and prejudicial attitudes emerge Friendships are based on shared activities
6–11	Self-concepts gradually come to emphasize personality traits Self-esteem is based largely on one's academic, physical, and social competencies	Impressions come to be based largely on the traits others display (psychological constructs) Prejudicial attitudes often decline in strength Friendships are based largely on psychological similarities and mutual trust
12 and older	Friendships and romantic appeal become important to one's self-esteem Self-concepts now reflect one's values and ideologies, and become more integrated and abstract Identity is achieved (later in adolescence or young adulthood)	Impressions are now based largely on others' dispositional similarities and dissimilarities (psychological comparisons) Prejudicial attitudes may decline or intensify, depending on social influences Friendships are based on loyalty and sharing of intimacies

different roles while playing together, young children become more aware of discrepancies between their own perspectives and those of their playmates. When conflicts arise in play, children must learn to coordinate their points of view with those of their companions (that is, compromise) in order for play to continue. So Piaget assumed that *equal-status contacts among peers* are a very important contributor to social perspective taking and the growth of interpersonal understanding.

Not only has research consistently supported Piaget's viewpoint, but it appears that some forms of peer contact may be better than others at fostering the growth of interpersonal understanding. Specifically, Janice Nelson and Frances Aboud (1985) proposed that disagreements among *friends* are particularly important because children tend to be more open and honest with their friends than with mere acquaintances and are more motivated to resolve disputes with friends. As a result, disagreeing friends should be more likely than disagreeing acquaintances to provide each other with the information needed to understand and appreciate their conflicting points of view. Indeed, when 8- to 10-year-olds discuss an interpersonal issue on which they disagree, pairs of friends are much more critical

Photo 6.8
Disagreements among peers are important contributors to role-taking skills and the growth of interpersonal understanding.

Robert Brenner/PhotoEdit, Inc.

of their partners than pairs of acquaintances are; but friends are also more likely to fully explain the rationales for their own points of view. Furthermore, disagreeing friends display increases in social understanding after these discussions are over, whereas disagreeing acquaintances do not (Nelson & Aboud, 1985). So it seems that equal-status contacts among friends may be especially important for the growth of role-taking skills and interpersonal understanding.

Parental and Sibling Influences on Role-Taking Of course, children with siblings are often exposed to divergent perspectives during conflicts with brothers and sisters, and parental interventions in these disputes can foster the growth of role-taking. Julie Smith and Hildy Ross (2007) found that when mothers of squabbling 5- to 10-year-olds intervene as *mediators*—that is, by setting ground rules for settling arguments that limit contentious strategies and prevent the escalation of hostilities while (1) allowing each sibling to have his or her say to identify points of contention, (2) encouraging each to discuss his or her goals and feelings, and (3) prompting *them* to brainstorm their own solutions to their disputes—siblings become much more proficient at understanding each other's perspectives and resolving disputes *amicably*, even on future occasions when the mother is not present to intervene. Yet when mothers intervened to impose solutions to conflict, siblings were less likely to appreciate each other's point of view, and contentious issues were likely to remain unresolved or were resolved in ways that seemed like a win for one sibling and a loss for the other. So parental input into sibling disputes is more likely to foster the growth of role-taking when parents intervene as mediators rather than adjudicators.

Yet another clue that parents contribute meaningfully to the development of social understanding is the finding that abused or otherwise maltreated children and adolescents tend to remain more egocentric and are seriously delayed in the development of role-taking skills when compared to nonabused age-mates whose parents have taken their responsibility as caregivers more seriously (Burack et al., 2006). Indeed, it may be especially difficult for a neglected or abused child to learn to understand and regulate emotions, discover how the human mind works, and recognize and appreciate others' divergent perspectives if his or her maltreating caregivers offer little in the way of affection, support, playful social interactions, and opportunities to converse about feelings, goals, intentions, and other mental states.

Social Experience as a Direct Contributor to Person Perception Social contacts with parents, siblings and peers not only contribute *indirectly* to person perception by fostering the development of role-taking skills, but they are also a form of *direct experience* by which children can learn what others are like. In other words, the more experience a child has with social partners, the more *motivated* she should be to try to understand them and the more *practiced* she should become at appraising the causes of their behavior (Higgins & Parsons, 1983).

Popularity is a convenient measure of social experience; that is, popular children interact more often with a wider variety of peers than do their less popular age-mates (LeMare & Rubin, 1987). So, if the amount of direct experience a child has with peers exerts its own unique influence on his or her social cognitive judgments, then popular children should outperform less popular age-mates on tests of social understanding, *even when their role-taking skills are comparable*. This is precisely what Jackie Gnepp (1989) found when she tested the ability of popular and less popular 8-year-olds to make appropriate trait-like inferences about an unfamiliar child from a small sample of the child's previous behaviors. So it seems that both social experience (as indexed by popularity) and cognitive competence (role-taking skills) each contribute in their own way to the development of children's understanding of other people. Apparently, Cooley (1902) and Mead (1934) were quite correct in suggesting that social cognition and social experience are completely intertwined—that they develop together, are reciprocally related, and neither can progress very far without the other.

SUMMARY

◆ The **self** is thought to arise from social interactions and to largely reflect other people's reactions to us (that is, a **looking-glass self**). The development of **social cognition** deals with how children's understandings of the self and other people change with age.

DEVELOPMENT OF THE SELF-CONCEPT

◆ Although there is some disagreement, most developmentalists believe that babies are born without a **self-concept** and will gradually differentiate themselves from the external environment over the first 2–6 months as they gain a sense of **personal agency** and learn (from their experiences before mirrors) to discriminate their faces from those of other people.

◆ Later in the first year, infants recognize that they and their companions are separate beings who, nevertheless, can share experiences.

◆ By 18–24 months of age, toddlers begin to pass the **rouge test** and display true **self-recognition**—a milestone that depends on cognitive development and social experiences with companions. Initial self-recognition provides evidence for a toddler's conception of a **present self,** which gradually evolves into a conception of **extended self,** or a self that is stable over time. Toddlers also classify themselves along socially significant dimensions such as age and sex, forming a **categorical self**.

◆ Although preschool children know how they typically behave in many situations and can classify themselves along psychological dimensions if asked to do so in ways that do not tax their verbal skills, the self-descriptions of 3- to 5-year-olds are typically very concrete, focusing mostly on their physical features, possessions, and the activities they can perform.

◆ Between ages 3 and 4, children's **theory of mind** progresses from a **desire theory** to a **belief-desire theory** that more closely resembles adults' conception of how the mind works. Once a child achieves this milestone, which is fostered by pretend play, increasing linguistic ability, and conversations about mental states with parents, siblings and other adults, she more clearly distinguishes the **private self** from the **public self** and is better prepared to make meaningful psychological inferences about her own and others' behavior.

◆ Over the course of middle childhood, children begin to describe themselves in terms of their inner and enduring psychological attributes. Adolescents have an even more integrated and abstract self-concept that includes not only their dispositional qualities (that is, traits, beliefs, attitudes, and values) but a knowledge of how these characteristics might interact with each other and with situational influences to affect their behavior. However, frequent displays of **false self-behaviors** can leave adolescents confused about who they really are.

◆ Core aspects of self-concept tend to be personal characteristics among people in **individualistic societies** but social or relational attributes among people in **collectivist (or communal) societies.**

SELF-ESTEEM: THE EVALUATIVE COMPONENT OF SELF

◆ **Self-esteem**, the judgments we make about our self-worth, begin to take shape early in life as infants form positive or negative working models of self and others from their interactions with caregivers. By age 8, children's self-evaluations become more accurate reflections of how others evaluate their physical, behavioral, academic, and social competencies. In adolescence, feelings of **relational self-worth** and new dimensions such as romantic appeal and quality of close friendships also become important contributors to global self-esteem. Self-esteem often declines during adolescence, particularly for teens who experience a large number of new life stressors all at once, only to recover and gradually increase throughout young adulthood and middle age.

◆ A solid and realistic sense of self-esteem is a valuable resource that helps children and adolescents cope with adversity and achieve favorable developmental outcomes.

◆ Warm, responsive, democratic parenting appears to foster self-esteem, whereas aloof or controlling parenting styles appear to undermine it. Peers influence each other's self-esteem through **social comparison** during the grade-school years. For adolescents, some of the strongest determinants of self-worth are the quality of one's relationships with peers—particularly with close friends and romantic partners.

◆ Children and adolescents from collectivist societies, where self-criticism is viewed as adaptive, tend to express lower levels of global self-esteem than age-mates from individualistic societies. During the elementary-school years, African-American and Hispanic children report lower levels of self-esteem than European-American and Asian-American children do. Yet African-American and Hispanic *adolescents* often report as high or even higher levels of self-esteem than adolescents of other ethnicities, particularly if they have been encouraged to take pride in their ethnicity and its cultural traditions.

WHO AM I TO BE? FORGING AN IDENTITY

◆ One of the more challenging tasks of adolescence is to resolve the **identity crisis** by forming a stable **identity** (or identities) with which to embrace the responsibilities of young adulthood. From the **diffusion** and **foreclosure** statuses, many college-age youths progress to the **moratorium** status (where they are experimenting to find an identity) and ultimately to **identity achievement.** Identity formation is an uneven process that often continues well into adulthood.

◆ The process of seeking an identity is a lot less crisis-like than Erik Erikson assumed. Identity achievement and moratorium are psychologically healthy statuses. If there is a crisis surrounding the identity formation process, it is a long-term failure to form one, for adolescents stuck in the diffusion status often assume a **negative identity** and display poor psychological adjustment.

◆ Healthy identity outcomes are fostered by cognitive development, by warm, supportive parents who encourage individual self-expression, and by a culture that permits and expects adolescents to find their own niches. For minority youth, achieving a positive **ethnic identity** fosters healthy identity outcomes in other life domains.

THE OTHER SIDE OF SOCIAL COGNITION: KNOWING ABOUT OTHERS

◆ Although preschool children are not oblivious to other people's inner qualities and can make some accurate and appropriate trait-like inferences, children younger than age 7 to 8 are more likely to describe friends and acquaintances in the same concrete observable terms that they use to describe the self. As they compare themselves and others on noteworthy behavioral dimensions, they become more attuned to regularities in their own and others' conduct (**behavioral comparisons** phase) and later begin to rely on stable psychological constructs, or traits, to describe these patterns (**psychological constructs** phase). Young adolescents' impressions of others become even more abstract as they begin to make **psychological comparisons** among their friends and acquaintances. And by age 14 to 16, adolescents are becoming sophisticated "personality theorists" who know that any number of situational influences can cause a person to act "out of character."

♦ The growth of children's social-cognitive abilities is related to cognitive development in general and to the emergence of **role-taking** skills in particular: To truly "know" a person, one must be able to assume her perspective and understand her thoughts, feelings, motives, and intentions. However, *social interactions*—particularly contacts with parents, siblings, friends and peers—are important contributors to social-cognitive development. They contribute indirectly by fostering the growth of role-taking skills and in a more direct way by providing the experiences children need to learn what others are like.

CHAPTER 7

Achievement

Father: David, your mother told me that you are not doing very well in English composition and that your teacher says you put little effort into your story writing. What do you have to say?

9th-grader: Ah, Dad . . . I don't like English and I'm just not good at thinking up stories.

Father: That's not true! You certainly have a vivid imagination when describing your camping experiences and all the fish that you had hooked but that got away. I think you just need to work harder at putting your thoughts and experiences on paper.

9th-grader: But I don't want to write stuff. Writing's not important to me.

Father: Son, we all have to do things in life that we'd rather not do. Think how long you'd last at a job if your supervisor gave you a work assignment and you said, "Ah, boss, I really don't want to do that . . . I'm no good at it." To be successful, you have to work at the challenges you face and do your best to master them. Doing a good job—regardless of whether the task is something you'd choose to work at yourself—can really boost your self-confidence and make you feel that you might accomplish anything that you set your mind to. So the next time you have to write a story, I'd like you to take the assignment seriously and to work at it until you've done the best job that you can do—that's all anyone can ask. What do you say?

9th-grader: Oh . . . all right; but don't expect any miracles!

Father: Oh, I don't expect to get Hemingway . . . but I know that you have the ability to craft a better than average ninth-grade short story or essay if you work at it. And you may even come to like writing if you take it seriously.

Have you ever had a conversation remotely like this one with a parent or a teacher? Many of my students say that they have, and that is hardly surprising. One of the most basic aims of socialization is to urge children to pursue important objectives, to work hard to achieve them, and to take pride in their accomplishments. During my junior high and high school years, I had several such conversations with my parents (the passage above is one of them) about the value of working at assignments such as writing essays or memorizing the Gettysburg Address, which I saw as busy work and of no use whatsoever. Both of my parents took the position that you can never be certain what will prove to be useful in the years ahead and that I should strive to do my best, whatever the assignment, because successful completion of these scholastic activities would help to build the self-confidence I would need to be successful in life.

My parents' outlook was typical of many adults in Western societies where children are often encouraged to be self-reliant, and even competitive, and to do well in whatever activities they may undertake—in short, to become "achievers." As we will see, not all cultures believe that *competitive* successes and *individual* accomplishments are the best indicators of what it means to have "achieved." But even though the meaning of achievement varies somewhat from society to society, one survey of 30 cultures revealed that people all over the world value personal attributes such as self-reliance, responsibility, and a willingness to work hard to attain important objectives (Fyans et al., 1983).

Must these valued attributes be taught? Social-learning theorists thought so, although others have a somewhat different opinion. Many years ago, psychoanalyst Robert White (1959) proposed that from infancy onward, human beings are intrinsically motivated to "master" their environments—to have an effect on or to cope successfully with a world of people and objects. We see this **mastery motive** in action as we watch infants struggle to turn knobs, open cabinets, and operate toys—and then notice their pleasure when they succeed (Jennings & Dietz, 2003).[1] Even infants and toddlers who are mentally retarded

mastery motivation
an inborn motive to explore, understand, and control one's environment.

[1]White used the term *effectance motivation* to describe the infant's need for mastery, although most developmentalists today refer to it as mastery motivation.

will actively seek out challenges just for the joy of mastering them (Hausen-Corn, 1995). Notice that White's viewpoint is very similar to that of Jean Piaget, who believed that children are intrinsically motivated to *adapt* to the environment by assimilating new experiences and then accommodating to these experiences.

If all infants are truly mastery-oriented and experience satisfaction over the effects they produce, then why is it that school-age children vary so dramatically in their achievement strivings? Is there a "motive to achieve" that children must acquire? How do children's self-images and their expectations about succeeding or failing affect their aspirations and accomplishments? And what kinds of home settings and social influences are likely to promote (or hinder) achievement behavior? These are some of the major issues that we will consider in the pages that follow.

THE CONCEPT OF ACHIEVEMENT MOTIVATION

One reason that some children try harder than others to master their school assignments, music lessons, or the position they play on the neighborhood T-ball team is that they differ in **achievement motivation**—their willingness to strive to succeed at challenging tasks and to meet high standards of accomplishment. Achievement motivation is reflected differently in different cultures. In Western industrialized societies, which tend to be *individualistic* cultures, achievement motivation is inferred from individual (and often competitive) accomplishments that can be compared against some standard of excellence. As we will see, most of the research on the growth of achievement motivation has been conducted in Western societies and reflects this largely Eurocentric view of achievement. By contrast, people from *collectivist* societies would argue that achievement motivation reflects a willingness to strive to succeed at objectives that promote *social welfare* or that *maximize the goals* of the groups to which they belong (see Triandis, 1995).

Yet, regardless of the culture in which one lives, the concept of "achievement" presumes some learning on the child's part. Not only must he or she acquire some idea of what constitutes acceptable or unacceptable performance in any given domain, or context, but an achiever has also learned to use these standards to *evaluate* her accomplishments. Even though there is widespread agreement that one's propensity for achievement is largely an acquired attribute, different theorists look at this construct in very different ways.

achievement motivation
a willingness to strive to succeed at challenging tasks and to meet high standards of accomplishment.

The Motivational View of Achievement

David McClelland and his associates (1953) speak of the child's **need for achievement (*n* Ach),** which they define as a "learned motive to compete and to strive for success whenever one's behavior can be evaluated against a standard of excellence" (p. 78). In other words, high "need-achievers" have learned to take *pride* in their ability to meet or exceed high standards, and it is this sense of *self*-fulfillment that motivates them to work hard, to be successful, and to try to outperform others when faced with new challenges.

McClelland measured achievement motivation by asking participants to examine a set of four pictures and then write a story about each as part of a test of "creative imagination." These four pictures show people working or studying, although each is sufficiently ambiguous to suggest any number of themes (see Photo 7.1). A person's need for achievement (*n* Ach) is determined by counting the achievement-related statements that he or she includes in the four stories (the assumption being that participants are projecting themselves and their motives into their themes). For example, a high need-achiever might respond to Photo 7.1 by saying that these men have been working for months on a new

need for achievement (*n* Ach)
McClelland's depiction of achievement motivation as a learned motive to compete and to strive for success in situations in which one's performance can be evaluated against some standard of excellence.

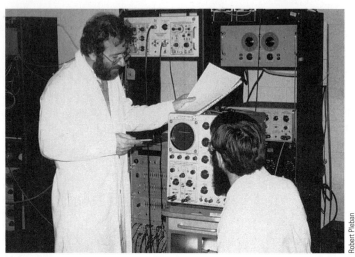

Photo 7.1
Scenes like this one were used by David McClelland and his associates to measure achievement motivation.

scientific breakthrough that will revolutionize the field of medicine, whereas a low need-achiever might say that the workers are glad the day is over so that they can go home and relax.

A Behavioral View of Achievement

In contrast to McClelland's viewpoint, Vaughn Crandell and his associates define achievement in behavioral rather than motivational terms. According to Crandall, Katkovsky, and Preston (1960), "Achievement is any *behavior* directed toward the *attainment of approval or the avoidance of disapproval* for competence in performance in situations where standards of excellence are operable" (p. 789; italics added). Crandall and associates argue that there is no single, overriding motive to achieve that applies to all achievement tasks. Instead, they propose that children will show different strivings in different skill areas (for example, art, schoolwork, sports), depending on the extent to which they *value* doing well in each area, and they *expect* to succeed and be recognized for their accomplishments.

Notice that McClelland and Crandall clearly differ on the issue of what reinforces achievement behavior. McClelland argues that the sense of *personal pride* stemming from one's high accomplishments is reinforcing (and will sustain achievement behavior in the future) because it satisfies an *intrinsic* need for competence or achievement. However, Crandall and his associates counterargue that one need not talk about internal needs that must be satisfied in order to explain why people strive to meet exacting standards. Instead, they propose that achievement behaviors are simply a class of instrumental responses designed to win the *approval* (or to avoid the disapproval) of significant others, such as parents, teachers, and peers.

Which of these viewpoints is correct? Perhaps both of them are. Susan Harter (1981) found that some children do view achievement tasks as a means of satisfying personal needs for competence or mastery (an **intrinsic orientation** very similar to McClelland's view of *n* Ach), whereas others strive to do well primarily to earn external incentives such as grades, prizes, or social approval (an **extrinsic orientation** that other theorists have called "social achievement"). Harter measured children's orientations to achievement with a 30-item questionnaire that asked whether the reasons they perform various activities are intrinsic justifications ("I like challenging tasks"; "I like to solve problems myself") or extrinsic ones ("I do things to get good grades, to win the teacher's approval," and so on). Her research revealed that children who are intrinsically oriented are more likely than those who are extrinsically oriented to prefer challenging problems over simpler ones and to view themselves as highly competent at schoolwork. Indeed, people who are intrinsically motivated truly enjoy the process of working toward accomplishing their objectives rather than viewing these efforts as onerous (Deci, Koestner, & Ryan, 2001; Harackiewicz, 1998), and young adolescents willingly devote more effort to homework assignments when homework is perceived as a valuable tool for helping them to achieve mastery goals (Trautwein et al., 2006).

Might clever teachers become more successful at achieving curricular objectives if they can find ways to persuade students to pursue intrinsic rather than extrinsic goals as they learn new material? Mararten Vansteenkiste and associates (2005) think so. They found that young adolescents became more involved in learning new nutritional information and achieved a much richer conceptual understanding of this material when told that following these nutritional guidelines was important to help them maintain physical health (intrinsic goal) as opposed to being told that compliance would help them to be

intrinsic orientation
a desire to achieve in order to satisfy one's personal needs for competence or mastery.

extrinsic orientation
a desire to achieve in order to earn external incentives such as grades, prizes, or the approval of others.

more physically attractive to others (extrinsic goal). Simply stated, students seem more personally invested in new learning when they are intrinsically oriented (or are pursing an intrinsic goal).

So by the early elementary school years, children in Western societies already differ in their orientations to achievement. And as we will soon see, many theories have been proposed to explain how and why grade-school children (and, indeed, adolescents and adults) respond so differently to the challenges they face. But before we discuss these theoretical claims, let's first consider some of the milestones that toddlers and preschool children reach as they begin to evaluate their accomplishments.

EARLY REACTIONS TO ONE'S ACCOMPLISHMENTS: FROM MASTERY TO SELF-EVALUATION

As we have noted, even infants can take pleasure in "mastering" a new toy or in producing other interesting outcomes. But when do they first acquire performance standards and begin to evaluate their outcomes as "successes" or "failures"? At what age do they understand the implications of winning or losing at a competitive activity with an age-mate? These are important questions in that Western definitions of achievement typically portray high achievers as those who reliably *evaluate* their accomplishments against standards of excellence and will often try to *outperform* others when faced with new challenges.

Deborah Stipek and her associates (Stipek, Recchia, & McClintic, 1992) have conducted a series of studies with 1- to 5-year-olds to find out when children develop the capacity to evaluate their accomplishments against performance standards—a capacity central to achievement motivation. In Stipek's research, children were observed as they undertook activities that had clear-cut achievement goals (for example, hammering pegs into pegboards, working puzzles, knocking down plastic pins with a bowling ball). Tasks were structured so that children either could or could not master them so that reactions to success or failure could be observed. One of these studies even had 2- to 5-year-olds compete with a peer at a block-stacking task, and their reactions to winning or losing were noted. Based on this research, Stipek and her colleagues found that children progress through three phases in learning to evaluate their performances in achievement situations, phases we will call *joy in mastery, approval seeking,* and *use of standards.*

◆ *Phase 1: Joy in mastery.* Before the age of two, infants and toddlers are visibly pleased to master challenges, displaying the mastery motivation White (1959) wrote about. However, they do not call other people's attention to their triumphs or otherwise seek recognition, and rather than being bothered by failures, they simply shift goals and attempt to master other toys. They are not yet evaluating their outcomes in relation to performance standards that define success and failure.

◆ *Phase 2: Approval seeking.* As they near age 2, toddlers begin to anticipate how others will evaluate their performances. They seek recognition when they master challenges and expect disapproval when they fail. For example, children as young as 2 who succeeded on a task often smiled, held their heads and chins up high, and made such statements as "I did it" as they called the experimenter's attention to their feats. Meanwhile, 2-year-olds who failed to master a challenge would often turn away from the experimenter as though they hoped to avoid criticism. It seems, then, that 2-year-olds are already appraising their outcomes as *mastery* successes or nonsuccesses and have already learned that they can expect approval after successes and disapproval after failures.

◆ *Phase 3: Use of standards.* An important breakthrough occurred around age 3 as children began to react more independently to their successes and failures. They seemed to have adopted objective standards for appraising their performance and were not as dependent on others to tell them when they had done well or poorly. These phase 3 children seemed capable of experiencing a self-focused *pride* (rather than mere pleasure) in their achievements and *shame* or *evaluative embarrassment* (rather than mere disappointment) after failing to achieve an objective (see also Lewis, Alessandri, & Sullivan, et al., 1992; Lewis & Ramsay, 2002).

How do young children respond to competitive activities? Prior to age 33 months, competitors were neither happy about winning nor sad about losing. Instead, successfully completing (mastering) their individual tasks was what was most important to 24- to 32-month-olds. By contrast, 33- to 41-month-olds expressed much more positive affect upon mastering a task if they finished first (and won a competition) than if they finished second. And by age 42–60 months, losers tended to slow down or stop working when a winner had been declared; apparently, they understood the competitive nature of the game and that there was little reason for them to rush to finish once an opponent had "won." Nevertheless, shameful responses were very infrequent among preschoolers who "lost" at a competitive activity. So for 3½- to 5-year-olds, it appears winning is divine but that losing is not typically interpreted as a clear failure.

In sum, infants are guided by a mastery motive and take pleasure in their everyday accomplishments; 2-year-olds begin to anticipate others' approval or disapproval of their performances; and children 3 and older evaluate their accomplishments against performance standards defining success and failure and are capable of experiencing pride or shame/evaluative embarrassment, depending on how successfully they match those standards. Of course, Stipek's work looks at *normative* trends in young children's reactions to achievement outcomes and, as such, has little to say about the development of *individual differences* in achievement motivation. To address this issue, we now turn to the major theories of achievement—models that do seek to explain why individuals might adopt different achievement orientations and how this choice of an orientation might influence their future accomplishments.

⤳ THEORIES OF ACHIEVEMENT MOTIVATION AND ACHIEVEMENT BEHAVIOR

The theories that have contributed most to our understanding of achievement motivation and achievement behavior are the McClelland/Atkinson need achievement models and more recent attributional (or social information-processing) approaches. In this section of the chapter, we will compare and contrast these influential points of view.

Need Achievement Theories

The first major theory of achievement was the "need achievement" approach, a motivational model that stemmed from the pioneering efforts of David McClelland and his associates at Wesleyan University and was later revised by John Atkinson of the University of Michigan.

McClelland's Theory of Achievement Motivation   In 1938, Henry Murray published *Explorations in Personality,* a text that had a profound influence on students of human behavior. Murray outlined a personality theory that included a taxonomy of human needs. He discussed 28 basic human needs—for example, the need for sex, the need for affiliation, the need for nurturance—including the need for achievement (*n* Ach), which he defined as "the desire of tendency to do things as rapidly and . . . as well as possible" (p. 164).

McClelland and his associates at Wesleyan University read Murray's work and became interested in the development of achievement motivation. McClelland and his colleagues

(1953) viewed *n* Ach as a learned motive that, like all other complex social motives, is acquired on the basis of rewards and punishments that accompany certain kinds of behavior. If children are frequently reinforced for independence, competitiveness, and success and if they meet with disapproval when they fail, their achievement motivation should be rather strong. But a child can hardly be expected to develop a strong need for achievement if he or she is not often encouraged to be self-reliant, competitive, and highly competent in day-to-day activities. In sum, the strength of an individual's achievement motive was thought to depend on the quality of his or her "achievement" training. McClelland and his associates believed that the quality of achievement training received by children varied as a function of their culture, their social class, and the attitudes of their parents about the value of independence and achievement.

The first task faced by the Wesleyan group was to develop a method of measuring achievement motivation. What was needed was an instrument that measured the strength of one's desire to compete and to excel in situations where standards of excellence are operable.

McClelland and his associates settled on the story-writing technique described earlier because they believed that a person's true underlying motives might well be reflected in his fantasy life—that is, dreams, wishes, idle thoughts, and daydreams. They soon discovered that people varied a great deal in the amount of achievement imagery they displayed when writing stories about ambiguous work or study scenes. The next step, then, was to validate this measure by showing that people who scored high in the need for achievement would actually turn out to be high achievers, whereas those who scored low would display more modest accomplishments.

AP Photo/HO

Photo 7.2
David McClelland (1917–1998) proposed a theory of achievement motivation that guided research on children's propensities for achievement throughout the 1950s and 1960s.

The Relationship between Achievement Motivation and Achievement Behavior Is achievement motivation related in some meaningful way to achievement behavior? Early returns suggested that it was. Several studies conducted during the 1950s revealed that college students who score high in *n* Ach tend to have higher grade-point averages than those who score low, and they aspire to higher-status occupations as well (Bendig, 1958; McClelland et al., 1953; Minor & Neel, 1958). So it seemed that people who express a strong desire to achieve on the McClelland fantasy measure of *n* Ach often do achieve at higher levels than those who test low in achievement motivation.

The Achieving Society What would happen if large numbers of high need-achievers were present in a culture at a given time? Would that culture take large strides forward, showing clear signs of technological or economic growth in the years ahead?

A direct test of this hypothesis appears in McClelland's (1961) book *The Achieving Society.* McClelland assessed the mean *n* Ach of each of 23 countries in a most interesting way. He simply obtained readers used in the primary grades in each country and scored the stories in these books for achievement imagery in the same way he typically scored stories that children might produce themselves. Children's readers were selected for study because they represent the popular culture of the country and, as such, are probably a reasonably good indication of the amount of achievement training that grade-school children are receiving at any given time. Readers from the 1920s and the year 1950 were sampled. McClelland's goal was to see whether he could predict the subsequent economic growth of a country from the amount of achievement imagery present in its readers during the 1920s.

As anticipated, McClelland (1961) found a significant positive correlation ($r = +.53$) between the number of achievement themes in a country's readers during the 1920s and the country's increase in economic productivity for the period 1929 to 1950. Although this correlational relationship is consistent with his hypothesis, it does not necessarily mean that the *n* Ach of a society affects its subsequent economic growth. One rival hypothesis is that economic growth already underway during the 1920s was responsible for both a country's preoccupation with achievement during the 1920s *and* its later economic growth.

But if prior economic growth had been the causal agent, then the country's economic growth between 1929 and 1950 should be highly correlated with the number of achievement themes in its readers in 1950. *No such relationship was observed.* Thus, McClelland's cross-cultural data suggest that achievement motivation precedes economic growth and that a nation's mean *n* Ach is a barometer of its future economic accomplishments.[2]

Problems with McClelland's Approach   Although McClelland's work seems to imply that achievement motivation is a reliable predictor of achievement behavior at both the individual and the group (or cultural) level, other investigators were having some difficulty replicating his findings. Virginia Crandall (1967), for example, found that children high in *n* Ach outperformed their low-need-achieving age-mates in fewer than half the studies she reviewed. Other studies (reviewed in Winter, 1996) reveal that McClelland's measure of *n* Ach is a better predictor of future success in entrepreneurial activities, such as establishing a business, than it is of success in the sciences or professions. Finally, John Atkinson (1964) noticed that people who actually do accomplish a lot (high achievers) often differed from people who accomplish much less (low achievers) in their *emotional reactions* to achievement contexts: High achievers welcomed new challenges, whereas low achievers seemed to dread them. Why is it that achievement motivation often fails to forecast achievement behavior? Could there be other, competing motives that make achievement contexts so threatening to some people that their performance is impeded? Atkinson thought so, as we will see in his revision of McClelland's theory.

Atkinson's Revision of Need Achievement Theory   In outlining his theory of achievement motivation, Atkinson (1964) proposed that:

> in addition to a general disposition to achieve success [called the **motive to achieve success (M$_s$)**, or the achievement motive], there is also a general disposition to avoid failure, called **motive to avoid failure [M$_{af}$]**. Where the motive to achieve might be characterized as a capacity for reacting with pride in accomplishment, the motive to avoid failure can be conceived as a capacity for reacting with shame and embarrassment when the outcome of performance is failure. When this disposition is aroused in a person, as it is aroused whenever it is clear . . . that his performance will be evaluated and failure is a distinct possibility, the result is anxiety and a tendency to withdraw from the situation. (p. 244)

So Aktinson claimed that a person's tendency to approach or avoid achievement activities depends on the relative strength of *two* competing motives. A person who willingly accepts new challenges and accomplishes a lot was presumed to have a motive to attain success that is considerably stronger than his or her motive to avoid failure (that is, $M_s > M_{af}$). By contrast, the low achiever who shies away from challenges and accomplishes little was thought to have a motive to avoid failure that is stronger than his or her motive is attain success (that is, $M_{af} > M_s$). In Atkinson's theory, then, the relationship between one's achievement motivation (M$_s$) and achievement behavior is clearly influenced by the strength of the motive to avoid failure (M$_{af}$).

Is It Worth Accomplishing? The Value of a Particular Goal   Atkinson also believed that the *value* one places on the success he might attain is an important determinant of achievement behavior. Virginia Crandall (1967) agreed. She noted that there are many, many areas in which children might achieve, including schoolwork, sports, hobbies, domestic

---

motive to achieve success (M$_s$)
Atkinson's term for the disposition describing one's tendency to approach challenging tasks and take pride in mastering them; analogous to McClelland's need for achievement.

motive to avoid failure (M$_{af}$)
Atkinson's term for the disposition describing one's tendency to shy away from challenging tasks so as to avoid the embarrassment of failing.

---

[2]This conclusion was strengthened by the results of a second study in which the *n* Ach scores for readers used in 39 countries in the year 1950 predicted the economic growth of those countries between 1952 and 1958 (McClelland, 1961).

activities, and making friends, to name a few. Presumably, a child's willingness to set high standards and to work to attain them may differ from area to area, depending in part on the **achievement value** of accomplishing these objectives or winning recognition for one's efforts.

Joel Raynor (1970) tested this hypothesis in an interesting study of introductory psychology students. Each student took McClelland's fantasy measure of *n* Ach (used to define M_s) and the *Test Anxiety Questionnaire*, an objective paper-and-pencil test that measures one's anxiety about being evaluated (used to define M_{af}). These students also made judgments about how relevant (hence, valuable) they thought their introductory psychology course would be to their future careers. Raynor's major prediction was that students high in achievement motivation (that is, those for whom $M_s > M_{af}$) would do much better in their intro psychology course if they considered the course relevant to their future (high value) as opposed to irrelevant (low value).

Table 7.1 shows the results. As predicted, students for whom $M_s > M_{af}$ (those in the top row) did make significantly *higher* grades if they considered introductory psychology relevant to their future careers. Apparently, achievement motivation is more likely to forecast noteworthy accomplishments when the goals one might attain are considered valuable or important. Notice also that participants for whom $M_{af} > M_s$ actually obtained *lower* grades if their psychology course was considered career-relevant. So as Atkinson had suspected, a high fear of failure can actually undermine progress toward *valuable* goals.

We see, then, that one's performance in achievement contexts depends on far more than his or her absolute level of *n* Ach. To predict how a person is likely to fare when faced with a challenge, it also helps to know something about (1) the person's fear of failure (M_{af}) and (2) the perceived *value* of success—a *cognitive* variable that differs across individuals and achievement domains and is a crucial determinant of achievement behavior.

Can I Achieve? The Role of Expectancies in Achievement Behavior Finally, Atkinson (1964) proposed that a second *cognitive* variable—our expectations of succeeding or failing should we try to achieve an objective—is a critical determinant of achievement behavior. He claimed that people are more likely to work hard when they feel that they have a reasonable prospect of succeeding than when they see little chance of attaining a goal. How important are these **achievement expectancies?** Very important, and we can illustrate this point with the following example. Were we to review a massive literature, we would find the IQ is a moderate to strong correlate of academic achievement, with brighter children typically outperforming their average-IQ or low-IQ classmates (Neisser et al., 1996). Yet it is not uncommon for children with high IQs and low academic expectancies to earn *poorer* grades than their classmates with lower IQs but higher expectancies (Battle, 1966; Crandall, 1967; Phillips, 1984). In other words, expectations of success and failure are a powerful determinant of achievement behavior; children who expect to achieve usually do, whereas those who expect to fail may spend little time and effort pursuing goals they believe to be "out of reach" (Dweck, 2001; Heckhausen & Dweck, 1999).

Summing Up Atkinson's need achievement theory is a significant revision and extension of McClelland's earlier theory—a model that held that individual differences in achievement behavior are primarily attributable to the overall levels of achievement motivation (*n* Ach) that people display. Atkinson's theory is properly classified as a motivational model in that one's willingness to work hard to obtain various objectives is said to depend

Table 7.1 Mean grade-point averages in introductory psychology as a function of achievement-related motives and the relevance of the course to future careers

Achievement Profiles	Relevance of Course to One's Future	
	Low	High
$M_s > M_{af}$	2.93	3.37
$M_{af} > M_s$	3.00	2.59

Note: Mean grade-point averages are computed on a 4.00 scale where A = 4, B = 3, C = 2, D = 1, F = 0.

Source: Raynor, J. O. (1970). Relationships between achievement-related motives, future orientation, and academic performance. *Journal of Personality and Social Psychology*, 15, 28–33. Reprinted by permission of the American Psychology Association.

achievement value perceived value of attaining a particular goal should one strive to achieve it.

achievement expectancies cognitive expectations of succeeding or failing at a particular achievement-related activity.

on the relative strength of two achievement-related motives: the motive to attain success (M_s) and the motive to avoid failure (M_{af}). But Atkinson also claims that two cognitive variables—*expectancies* of success (or failure) and the *value* of various objectives—are every bit as important as the motivational variables in determining our achievement strivings and our actual accomplishments.

Recently, social information-processing theorists have focused more extensively on cognitive determinants of achievement in general and on the origins of achievement expectancies in particular. Let's now turn to the attributional perspective to see what it can tell us about children's propensities for achievement.

Weiner's Attribution Theory

Earlier in this chapter and throughout the text, we have noted that infants and toddlers are apt to view themselves as efficacious and to master many challenges when they have had ample opportunities to *control* their environments—that is, to regulate the behavior of responsive companions and to satisfy other objectives, such as successfully operating age-appropriate toys. Just how important is this sense of personal control to children's achievement expectancies and to the value they are likely to attach to their successes and failures?

Bernard Weiner (1974, 1986) has proposed an attributional theory of achievement that claims that a person's achievement behavior depends very critically on how he interprets prior successes and failures and on whether he thinks he can *control* these outcomes. Weiner believes that human beings are active information processors who will sift through the data available to them and formulate explanations, or **causal attributions,** for their achievement outcomes. What kinds of attributions will they make? Though they might not always use these precise labels, Weiner argues that people are likely to attribute their successes or failures to any of four causes: (1) their *ability* (or lack thereof), (2) the amount of *effort* expended, (3) the *difficulty* (or easiness) of the task, or (4) the influence of *luck* (either good or bad).

Notice that two of these causes, ability and effort, are *internal* causes, or qualities of the individual, whereas the other two, task difficulty and luck, are *external,* or environmental, factors. This grouping of causes along an "internal/external" dimension follows from Virginia Crandall's earlier research on a dimension or personality called **locus of control** (Crandall, 1967). Individuals with an *internal locus of control* assume that they are personally responsible for what happens to them. If they received an A grade on an essay, they would probably attribute the mark to their superior writing ability or their own hard work (internal causes). Individuals with an *external locus of control* believe that their outcomes depend more on luck, fate, or the actions of others than on their own abilities or efforts. They might say that an A grade was due to luck ("The teacher happened to like this one"), easy grading, or some other *external* cause. Crandall proposed that an internal locus of control is conducive to achievement: Children must necessarily believe that *they* can produce positive outcomes if they are to strive for success and become high achievers. Children with an external locus of control were not expected to strive for success or to become high achievers, because they assume that their efforts do not necessarily determine their outcomes.

Children's locus of control is often measured by administering the *Intellectual Achievement Responsibility Questionnaire,* a 34-item scale that taps one's perceptions of responsibility for pleasant and unpleasant outcomes. Each item describes an achievement-related experience and asks the child to select either an internal or an external cause for that experience (see Figure 7.1 for sample items). The more "internal" responses the child selects, the higher his internality score. Children who choose few internal responses are classified as externalizers.

causal attributions
conclusions drawn about the underlying causes of one's own or another person's behavior.

locus of control
personality dimension distinguishing people who assume that they are personally responsible for their life outcomes (internal locus) from those who believe that their outcomes depend more on circumstances beyond their control (external locus).

1. *If a teacher passes you to the next grade, it would probably be*
   _____ a. because she liked you or
   *_____ b. because of the work that you did

2. *When you do well on a test at school, it is more likely to be*
   *_____ a. because you studied for it
   _____ b. because the test was especially easy

3. *When you read a story and can't remember much of it, it is usually*
   _____ a. because the story wasn't well written or
   *_____ b. because you weren't interested in the story

*Denotes the "internal" response for each sample item.

Figure 7.1
Sample items from the Intellectual Achievement Responsibility Questionnaire. (From V. C. Crandall, *Intellectual Achievement Responsibility Questionnaire.* Wright State University School of Medicine, Yellow Springs, Ohio.)

In their review of more than 100 studies, Maureen Findley and Harris Cooper (1983) found that internalizers do earn higher grades and will typically outperform externalizers on standardized tests of academic achievement. In fact, one rather extensive study of minority students in the United States revealed that children's beliefs in internal control were a better predictor of their academic achievements than were their *n* Ach scores, their parents' child-rearing practices, or the type of classroom and teaching styles to which these students had been exposed (Coleman et al., 1966). So Crandall was right in assuming that a willingness to take personal responsibility for one's successes is conducive to achievement behavior.

How, then, does Weiner's theory differ from Crandall's earlier ideas about locus of control? The answer is straightforward: Weiner claims that the four possible causes for achievement outcomes also differ along a *stability* dimension. Ability and task difficulty are relatively stable or unchangeable. If you have high verbal ability today, you'll have roughly the same high ability tomorrow; and if a particular kind of verbal problem is particularly difficult, similar problems are also likely to be difficult. By contrast, the amount of effort one expends on a task or the workings of luck are variable, or unstable, from situation to situation. So Weiner classifies the four possible causes for successes and failures along *both* a locus of causality and a stability dimension, as shown in Table 7.2.

Contributions of "Stability" and "Locus of Control" Attributions to Future Achievement Behavior Why is it important to consider both *locus* of causality and *stability* to classify causal attributions? Simply because each of these judgments has different consequences. According to Weiner, it is the stability dimension that determines achievement *expectancies:* Outcomes attributed to stable causes lead to stronger expectancies than those attributed to unstable causes. To illustrate, a *success* that you attribute to your high ability leads you to confidently predict similar successes in the future. Had you attributed that same success to an unstable cause that can vary from situation to situation (such as effort or luck), you should not be quite so confident of future successes. Conversely, *failures* attributed to stable causes we can do little about (such as low ability or task difficulty) also lead to strong expectancies—this time to negative expectancies that lead us to anticipate similar failures in the future. By contrast, attributing a failure to an unstable cause (such as not trying very hard) allows for the possibility of improvement and hence a less negative expectancy.

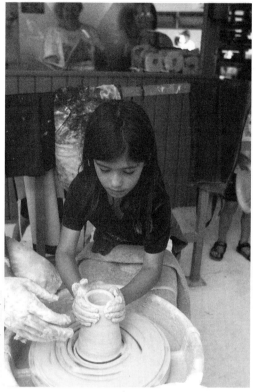

Michale Newman/PhotoEdit, Inc.

Photo 7.3
If youngsters believe they are personally responsible for their successes, they are more likely to become high achievers.

Table 7.2 Weiner's classification of the causes of achievement outcomes (and examples of how you might explain a terrible test grade)

	Locus of Causality	
	Internal Cause	**External Cause**
Stable Cause	*Ability* "I'm hopeless in math."	*Task difficulty* "That test was incredibly hard and much too long."
Unstable Cause	*Effort* "I should have studied more instead of going out to the concert."	*Luck* "What luck! Every question seemed to be about something taught on the days of class I missed."

If the perceived stability of an achievement-related outcome determines achievement expectancies, what role does locus of causality (or control) play? According to Weiner, judgments about the internality or externality of an outcome determine its *value* to the perceiver. Presumably, successes are most valuable when attributed to *internal* causes that one can take credit for, such as hard work or high ability, and few of us would feel especially proud if we succeeded because of external causes such as blind luck or a ridiculously easy task. Yet *failures* attributed to internal causes (especially to low ability) can be damaging to our self-esteem and may make us less inclined to strive for future success. Clearly, it seems fruitless to work hard to reverse a poor grade if we think we have little ability in the subject matter; in fact, the course may suddenly seem less valuable or important, and we might be inclined to drop it. But if we can attribute our poor mark to an *external* cause such as bad luck or to an especially difficult (or ambiguous) exam, the failure should not make us feel especially critical of ourselves or necessarily undermine our feelings about the value of the course.

According to Weiner, it is adaptive to attribute our successes to high ability, for this internal and stable attribution causes us to *value* what we have accomplished and leads us to *expect* that we can repeat our successes. By contrast, it is more adaptive to attribute *failures* to low effort (rather than low ability) because effort is unstable and we are more likely to believe that we can do better in the future if we just try harder.

In sum, Weiner's attribution model is like Atkinson's theory in stressing the importance of two cognitive variables: achievement expectancies and achievement value. But Weiner's approach assigns a primary role to the cognitive variables. Presumably, the perceived locus of causality for achievement outcomes affects our *valuation* of these successes and failures, whereas our attributions about the stability of these outcomes affect our *achievement expectancies*. Together, these two judgments (expectancy and value) determine our willingness (motivation) to undertake similar achievement-related activities in the future (see Figure 7.2 for a schematic overview of Weiner's theory).

Age Differences in Achievement-Related Attributions If it seems to you as if Weiner's theory sounds a little too cognitive and too abstract to explain the achievement attributions that young children display, you would be right. Before age 7 or so, children tend to be unrealistic optimists who think they have the ability to succeed on almost any task, even those they have repeatedly failed to master in the past (Stipek & Mac Iver, 1989). Preschool and primary-grade teachers may contribute to this rosy optimism by setting mastery goals and by praising children more for their efforts than for the quality of their work, thus leading them to believe that they can accomplish much and "be smart" by working hard (Rosenholtz & Simpson, 1984; Stipek & Mac Iver, 1989). By age 5, children are well aware of the relationship between task difficulty and ability, knowing, for example, that a child who finds a task to be easy is smarter than a child who finds the same task to be difficult (Heyman, Gee, & Giles, 2003). However, even 7-year-olds tend to equate

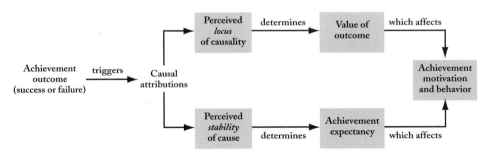

Figure 7.2 An overview of Weiner's attribution theory of achievement.

effort expended with ability. They may say, for example, that John, who spent four hours at a task, is smarter than Jose, who accomplished the same result in only two hours; or they may claim that two children who expend the same amount of effort should achieve equal outcomes (see Nicholls & Miller, 1984; Nicholls, 1989). When recalling a story about a child who did not try very hard at his schoolwork but got everything right (thus implying high ability), young children tended to *mis*remember the child as putting forth a high level of effort (Heyman, Gee, & Giles, 2003). Indeed, younger children seem to display an **incremental view of ability:** They believe that ability is changeable, not stable, and that they can get smarter or become more capable through increased effort and lots of practice (Droege & Stipek, 1993; Dweck & Leggett, 1988).

incremental view of ability
belief that one's ability can be improved through increased effort and practice.

Of course, we adults generally view effort and ability as *inversely related*, saying, for example, that John must have less ability than Jose if he had to expend twice as much effort to accomplish the same end. And judging from Weiner's (1982, 1986) findings, young adults see ability as more stable over time than young children do. So when do children begin to distinguish ability from effort? When do they move toward an **entity view of ability**—a perspective that ability is a fixed or stable trait that is not influenced much by effort or practice? It turns out that many 8- to 12-year-olds are beginning to distinguish effort from ability (Nicholls & Miller, 1984; Pomerantz & Ruble, 1997), due in part to cognitive development—particularly their concrete-operational ability to simultaneously classify objects, events, and outcomes on more than one dimension.

entity view of ability
belief that one's ability is a highly stable trait that is not influenced much by effort or practice.

However, social experiences—especially the changing character of experiences at school—also contribute greatly to changes in children's thinking about ability and effort. Elementary school teachers gradually place more and more emphasis on *ability* appraisals; they assign grades that reflect the quality of work students perform rather than the amount of effort expended, and these performance evaluations are supplemented by such competitive activities as science fairs, spelling bees, and flash card contests, which also place a premium on the speed or *quality* rather than the quantity of students' work. Furthermore, older grade-school children are often placed into "ability groups" based on the teacher's appraisal of their competencies (Rosenholtz & Simpson, 1984; Stipek & Mac Iver, 1989). So all these practices, coupled with children's increased use of social comparison to appraise their abilities (Altermatt et al., 2002; Pomerantz et al., 1995), help to explain why older grade-school students begin to distinguish effort from ability and begin to make the kind of causal attributions for their successes and failures that Weiner's theory anticipates.

Interestingly, the late elementary school period (fourth through sixth grades) is also the time when many students begin to value academic achievement less and to develop rather negative academic self-concepts, a trend that becomes even stronger during the junior high and high school years (Blackwell, Trzesniewski, & Dweck, 2007; Eccles, 2004; Jacobs et al., 2002). And as we are about to see, children's tendencies to distinguish ability and effort and to adopt an *entity view* of ability are major contributors to these trends.

Dweck's Learned Helplessness Theory

All children founder on occasion as they attempt to master challenges, but they don't all respond to failure in the same way. Building on Weiner's attribution theory, Carol Dweck and her colleagues have tried to understand why some children persist in the face of failure and ultimately achieve their objectives, whereas others who fail may simply stop trying and "give up." Their findings reveal that these two types of children explain their achievement outcomes in very different ways (Dweck, 2001; Dweck & Leggett, 1988).

Some children are **mastery-oriented:** They tend to attribute success to their high ability but tend to externalize the blame for their failures ("That test was ambiguous and unfair") or attribute them to *unstable* causes that they can easily overcome ("I'll do better if I try harder"). These students are called "mastery-oriented" because they persist in the face of

mastery orientation
a tendency to persist at challenging tasks because of a belief that one has the ability to succeed and/or that earlier failures can be overcome by trying harder.

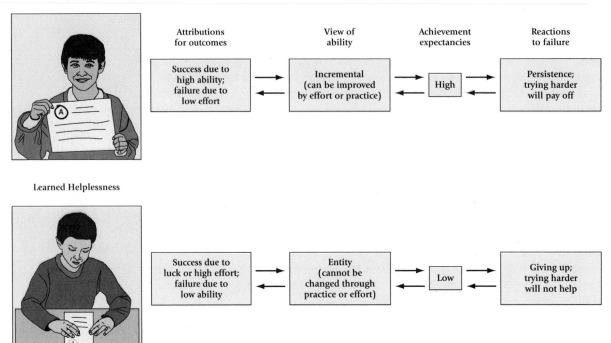

Figure 7.3 Characteristics of the mastery-oriented and learned-helplessness achievement orientations.

failure, believing that their increased effort will ultimately allow them to succeed. Although they see their ability as a reasonably stable attribute that doesn't fluctuate radically from day to day (which allows them to feel confident about repeating their successes), they still think that they can eventually improve their competencies (an *incremental* viewpoint) by trying harder after failures. So mastery-oriented youngsters are highly motivated to "master" new challenges, regardless of whether they have previously succeeded or failed at similar tasks (see Figure 7.3).

By contrast, other children often attribute their successes to the *unstable* factors of hard work or luck; they do not experience the pride and self-esteem that come from viewing themselves as highly competent. Yet they often attribute their failures to a stable and internal cause—namely, their *lack of ability*—which causes them to form low expectations of future successes and to give up. It appeared to Dweck as if these youngsters were displaying a **learned helplessness orientation:** If failures are attributed to a *stable* cause—lack of ability—that the child thinks he can do little about (an *entity view* of ability), he becomes frustrated and sees little reason to try to improve. So he stops trying and acts helpless (see Figure 7.3).

It is important to note that children who come to display helpless orientations are *not* merely the least competent members of a typical classroom. Instead, even highly talented students may adopt this unhealthy attributional style, which, once established, tends to persist over time and will eventually undermine their academic performances in subjects in which they feel helpless (Fincham, Hokoda, & Sanders, 1989; Phillips, 1984; Ziegert et al., 2001).

How Does Learned Helplessness Develop? According to Dweck (1978), parents and teachers may unwittingly foster the development of a helpless achievement orientation if they simply note that the child *worked hard* when she succeeds but criticize her *lack of ability*

learned helplessness orientation a tendency to give up or to stop trying after failing because these failures have been attributed to a lack of ability that one can do little about.

when she fails. Apparently even 4- to 6-year-olds can begin to develop a helpless orienta-tion if their failures are often punished or otherwise criticized in ways that cause them to doubt their abilities (Burhans & Dweck, 1995; Ziegert et al., 2001). By contrast, if parents and teachers praise the child's efforts at devising effective problem-solving strategies when she succeeds but emphasize her *lack of effort* when she fails, the child may conclude that she is certainly capable enough and would do even better if she tried harder—the viewpoint adopted by mastery-oriented youngsters (Dweck, 2001). In one clever experiment, Dweck and her associates (1978) demonstrated that fifth-graders who received the *helplessness-producing* pattern of evaluation while working at unfamiliar problems did indeed begin to attribute their failures to a lack of ability, whereas classmates who received the *mastery-oriented* evaluative pattern attributed their failures to a lack of effort, saying, in effect, "I need to try harder." These strikingly different attributional styles were created in less than one hour in this experiment, thus implying that similar patterns of evaluative feedback from parents or teachers, given consistently over a period of months or years, might well contribute to the development of the contrasting "helpless" and "mastery" orientations so often observed among grade-school (and older) students.

On Helping the Helpless to Achieve   Obviously, giving up as soon as one begins to founder is not the kind of achievement orientation that adults would hope to encourage. What can be done to help these "helpless" children to persist at tasks they have failed? According to Dweck, one effective therapy might be a form of **attribution retraining** in which children are persuaded to attribute their failures to unstable causes—namely insuf-ficient effort—that they can do something about, rather than continuing to view them as stemming from their lack of ability, which is not so easy to change.

Dweck (1975) tested her hypothesis by exposing children who had become "helpless" after failing a series of tough math problems to either of two "therapies." Over a period of 25 therapy sessions, half the children received a *success-only* therapy in which they worked problems they could solve and received tokens for their successes. The other half received *attribution retraining*—they experienced nearly as many successes over the 25 sessions as did the children in the other group but were also told after each of several prearranged failures that they had not concentrated enough or worked fast enough and *should have tried harder.* Thus, an explicit attempt was made to convince these youngsters that failures can reflect a lack of effort rather than a lack of ability. Did this therapy work? Yes, indeed! At the end of the experiment, "helpless" children in the attribution-retraining condition now performed much better on the tough math problems they had initially failed; and when they did fail one, they usually attributed their outcome to a lack of effort and tried all the harder. By contrast, children in the success—only condition showed no such improve-ments, giving up once again after failing the original problems. So merely showing children who act helpless that they are capable of succeeding is not enough! To alleviate learned helplessness, one must teach children to respond more constructively to their *failures* by viewing these experiences as something they can overcome if they try harder.

Can we do better than this? Certainly we can by taking steps to *prevent* learned helpless-ness from developing. Parents and teachers can play a major part in these preventive efforts by simply praising the child's noteworthy successes and taking care not to undermine her self-worth by suggesting that failures reflect a lack of ability (Burhans & Dweck, 1995). Yet, as the research in Box 7.1 indicates, there are right ways and wrong ways to praise success. Simply telling a child who succeeds that he is really "smart" or "intelligent" can actually do more harm than good.

Yet another preventive strategy that might easily be implemented at school is to per-suade students to modify their theory of intelligence—that is, to convince them that *ability* can be developed by increased effort (incremental viewpoint), thereby contradict-ing their emerging belief that ability is stable and unchangeable (entity viewpoint). Lisa

Box 7.1 Applying Developmental Research

Caution—Praise Can Be Dangerous

Recently, Dweck and her associates have argued that there are right ways and wrong ways to praise a child's accomplishments if one hopes to promote a mastery orientation and prevent learned helplessness. Because mastery-oriented children tend to attribute success to their high ability, it might seem that praise telling them how "smart," "intelligent," or "good" they are at the task would be the best way to acknowledge their triumphs. Yet Dweck (2001) argues that this kind of **person (or trait) praise** may prove harmful in the long run. If children are often told that they are "good at this" or "smart" when they succeed at tasks, they may become more interested in **performance goals** than in new learning when faced with challenges. That is, they may hope to do well primarily *to show how smart they are!* A subsequent failure quickly undermines this performance goal, perhaps causing the child to conclude "I'm not so smart after all" and to give up and act helpless. By contrast, Dweck argues that children who receive **process praise** when they succeed—feedback that praises the *effort* they have expended at *formulating effective problem-solving strategies*—should become more interested in **learning goals.** That is, they may come to view the prospect of improving their competencies (rather than displaying their smarts) as the most important objective when faced with novel challenges. A subsequent failure at a new problem does not immediately undermine a learning goal. It simply informs the child that she "needs to work harder and devise a more effective strategy"—in other words, to be persistent—if she hopes to master the task and *increase her abilities.*

Melissa Kamins and Carol Dweck (1999) tested these hypotheses in an experiment with kindergartners. Each child role-played the part of a youngster who had succeeded at several tasks, such as completing a puzzle, stacking blocks, and making a house with Legos. After each success, some children were told they did very well and received *person praise* for their successes ("I'm really proud of you; you are really good at this"). Other children were told they had done very well and received *process praise* for their successes ("You tried really hard; you found a good way to do it"). Then children were asked to evaluate themselves (for example, how good . . . smart are you?) and to tell how they were feeling (ranging on a 5-point scale from very sad to very happy) about their successes. To measure later persistence in the face of failure, children role-played scenarios involving two more tasks (in other words, a drawing task and an arithmetic task) in which they were told that mistakes had been made. They were then given choices between working further at the tasks that had ended in success or at those at which mistakes had been made.

The results were clear. As we see in the figure (panels a & b), children who received process praise for successes evaluated themselves more favorably (for example, smarter, better at the task) and felt better about their successes than those who received person praise. Apparently, these kindergartners viewed information about high-effort expenditure as more indicative of their capabilities than

(a) Self-evaluation

Type of praise received

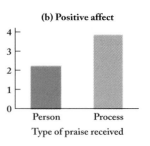

(b) Positive affect

Type of praise received

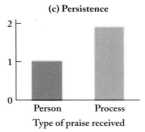

(c) Persistence

Type of praise received

Average assessments of one's competencies and feelings after succeeding and willingness to persist at a task that one has failed. Note: Higher number = greater perceived competencies (panel a), more positive feelings about one's successes (panel b), and stronger tendencies to choose to work at a task that one had failed (panel c). (Adapted from Kamins and Dweck, "Person versus process praise and criticism," *Developmental Psychology*, 35, p. 835–947. Copyright © 1999 by the American Psychological Association. Used with permission.)

such specific person praise as "You are really good at this." What's more, we see in the figure (panel c) that children who received process praise were more inclined than those receiving person praise to be persistent by choosing to work at tasks that had not been mastered, as if learning goals or improving their skills were their primary objectives. By comparison, children who had received person praise were more inclined to select tasks that had been completed successfully, as if they were more interested in displaying their competencies and not looking bad (performance goals) than in acquiring new skills (see also Mueller & Dweck, 1998, for a similar pattern of results with fifth-graders working at age-appropriate challenges.)

So there does seem to be a right way and a wrong way to praise children's successes in order to promote a mastery orientation and prevent learned helplessness. As Dweck anticipated, process praise, focusing heavily on children's efforts and the successful strategies they devised, proved superior to person praise at fostering children's perceived competencies (or self-efficacy) and at encouraging them to persist at challenges that they initially failed to master.

---

person (or trait) praise
praise focusing on desirable personality traits such as intelligence; this praise fosters performance goals in achievement contexts.

Blackwell and her associates (2007) adopted this strategy with low-achieving seventh-grade math students. Half of the students were randomly assigned to an experimental group that, over eight weeks during advisory periods, received lessons focusing on such topics as "You can grow your intelligence" and "Learning makes you smarter" that were designed to foster an incremental theory of intelligence. Control participants received an equal number of alternative lessons centering on improving memory strategies and other study skills. The major dependent variable in this longitudinal study was the grades that participants earned in math. As we see in Figure 7.4, participants in both groups were already beginning to show declines in math performance between the spring of sixth grade (time 1) and the beginning of spring term in the seventh grade (time 2) when the treatments began. But notice that this downward trajectory in math grades was reversed by the end of the Spring semester (time 3) for students in the intervention group, whereas it continued unabated for classmates in the control group. What's more, further analysis revealed that students who benefited most from the "incremental theory" intervention were those who had had stronger entity views of intelligence prior to participating in the intervention.

So work on properly praising successes (see Box 7.1) and at fostering adaptive theories of intelligence implies that preventing learning helplessness may depend most critically on convincing children that ability is something that anyone can develop if he or she works hard enough. Indeed, this crucial lesson, in conjunction with attempts by educators to make new learning objectives more interesting by framing them in ways to promote intrinsic (rather than extrinsic) goals (see Vansteenkiste et al., 2005), could go a long way toward reversing or eliminating the downward trajectories in academic interest and performance often seen early in adolescence (Eccles, 2004) and possibly even reduce the large number of unmotivated high school students who set themselves up for future economic disadvantage by dropping out of school.

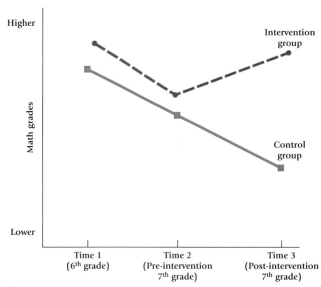

Figure 7.4
Changes in math grades for students in the intervention and control conditions. (Adapted from Blackwell, Trzesniewski, & Dweck, 2007.)

performance goal
state of affairs in which one's primary objective in an achievement context is to display one's competencies (or to avoid looking incompetent).

process praise
praise of effort expended to formulate good ideas and effective problem-solving strategies; this praise fosters learning goals in achievement contexts.

learning goal
state of affairs in which one's primary objective in a achievement context is to increase one's skills or objectives.

Reflections on Theories of Achievement

Having now reviewed four major achievement theories, it should be obvious that children's propensities for achievement involve far more than an innate mastery motive or a global need for achievement. Clearly McClelland and his associates made an important contribution by showing that people reliably differ in their *motivation* to achieve and by suggesting how this motive might be nurtured, although their notion that achievement motivation was a global attribute that predicted one's reactions to all achievement tasks now seems badly overstated. Atkinson's revision of need achievement theory pointed to the existence of a competing "motive to avoid failure" that can make people shy away from challenging tasks to avoid the embarrassment of failing. Of course, Atkinson's model also broke important new ground by emphasizing that achievement-related cognitions, namely one's *expectancies* of succeeding and the *value* of success, are important determinants of achievement behavior. Weiner's later attribution theory, which grew out of Crandall's earlier work on locus of control, has illustrated how our explanations, or *causal attributions,* for achievement outcomes contribute to our achievement expectancies and to the perceived value of our success and failure experiences. Finally, Dweck's learned-helplessness theory takes us back to the starting point by demonstrating how well-ingrained attributional styles affect children's *motivation* to persist at challenging tasks that they have initially failed to master. So, as we concluded when reviewing the various theories of attachment in Chapter 5, it makes no sense to brand any single achievement theory as "correct" and to ignore the others. Each of these theories has helped us to understand why children differ so dramatically when responding to the challenges they face.

∽ CULTURAL AND SUBCULTURAL INFLUENCES ON ACHIEVEMENT

Individualistic versus Collectivistic Perspectives on Achievement

There is now ample evidence that a child's cultural heritage affects his or her orientation toward achievement. In *individualistic* societies such as the United States, Canada, and the countries of Western Europe, child-rearing practices promote self-reliance and individual assertion, and children are given a great deal of freedom to pursue *personal* (and often highly creative) objectives. By contrast, *collectivist* societies in Africa, Asia, and Latin America emphasize the importance of maintaining social harmony and pursuing goals that are considered honorable by other members of one's social network and/or that maximize *social* welfare (Berry et al., 1992; Triandis, 1995). How might these diverse cultural values affect people's reactions to achievement tasks?

Consider first a cross-cultural study that challenged people to make correct judgments about visual stimuli when access to social norms were available (Berry, 1967). Participants were Arctic Eskimos, members of an individualistic society who are forced by their geography to hunt and fish for a living, and the Temne of Sierra Leone, a collectivist people whose livelihood depends on their pulling together to successfully plant, harvest, and ration a single crop (rice). Individuals from each culture were asked to make comparisons among lines that differed in length. For each comparison, the participant was shown a standard line and eight test lines. The participant's task was to select the test line that was the same length as the standard. Before each judgment, the experimenter presented fictitious group norms by telling the subject "Most Temne (or Eskimo) people say this line [an incorrect choice] is equal in length to the standard." The incorrect line that was five lines away from the correct one served as the contrived group norm for each trial (see Figure 7.5). The distance of the participant's choice away from the correct line and in the direction of the contrived norm served as a measure of conformity for that trial. A total conformity score was determined by simply adding across trials the number of lines a participant's choices were away from the correct lines.

As expected, Berry found that the Temne largely conformed to the contrived group norms, whereas the Eskimos disregarded normative information and displayed their independence by selecting the correct lines (or lines very close to the correct ones). One Temne illustrated the cultural roots of his conformity by stating, "When Temne people choose a thing, we must all agree with the decision—that is what we call cooperation" (Berry, 1967, p. 417). Eskimo participants spoke infrequently while making their judgments, although they sometimes flashed confident smiles as they rejected the group norm in favor of a line much nearer to the correct one.

Cultural differences in children's achievement orientations are especially clear in so-called *mixed-motive* contexts that pit self-interest against that of the group. A mixed-motive game is one in which participants can choose either to compete or to cooperate in order to earn enough points, credits, and so on to win a valuable prize; but unknown to them, the best way for any player to earn a prize is for all of them to begin to cooperate early on and to continue to cooperate until they reach their objective. Children from a collectivist society (Mexico), who are taught to cooperate, clearly outperform their more competitive Mexican-American and European-American age-mates at these mixed-motive challenges (Kagan & Masden, 1971, 1972). In fact, many 7- to 9-year-old American children are already so competitive in mixed-motive contexts that upon discovering that they can't win a prize, they then seek to lower their partner's score (with the apparent objective of "beating" him or her at a personal contest).

We see, then, that people from different cultures do think of achievement in very different ways. To a person from an individualistic culture,

The top line on the stimulus card is the standard. On each trial, the subject is informed that one of the other lines (designated here by the asterisk) was most often perceived to be the same length as the standard by members of a reference group. The correct choice for this card is the second line from the bottom.

Figure 7.5
A common method of measuring conformity to group norms. (Adapted from Berry, 1967.)

individual accomplishments and evidence of personal merit are the most common indications that one has achieved. By contrast, to a person from a collectivist culture, achievement implies that one must often suppress individualism and pull together with partners or coworkers to work for the greater good of the group. This does not mean that collectivist people never compete with one another. In China, for example, academic competitions are intense because parents demand that their children do well in school, and only the very best students, fewer than 10 percent, will have an opportunity to receive a higher education. Indeed, Jin Li (2006) recently reported that Chinese adolescents pursue mostly individual rather then collective goals in academic contexts. Yet, even though Chinese children compete academically and pursue individual goals, an important rationale for striving to excel at school is to honor the family (a collectivist objective), and their peer groups—the very persons with whom they are competing—are instrumental at reinforcing demands for academic achievement and will often work together as a group, trying to promote better academic performances (Chen, Li, et al., 2000; Chen, Chang, & He, 2003).

Of course, an emphasis on individualism or collectivism is only one of many general beliefs and values that vary across cultures and influence children's achievement orientations. To cite another example, there are clear cultural differences in the connections that people make between effort and achievement: Compared to American mothers, Chinese and Japanese mothers believe that scholastic achievement is far more dependent on the amount of effort a child expends than on his or her innate intelligence (Stevenson & Lee, 1990). In other words, Asian parents adopt more of an *incremental* perspective on ability than American parents do—a perspective that seems to carry over to their children and may prevent Asian youngsters from acting helpless when they experience difficulties with their lessons. We will explore this intriguing cultural difference in more detail when we consider the topic of schooling and scholastic influences in Chapter 12.

Ethnic Variations in Achievement

Several reviews of the literature suggest that there are clear ethnic variations in achievement—at least in the area of academic achievement, which has been most heavily studied. Although there are tremendous individual differences *within* any ethnic group, African-American, Native American, and Latino children tend to earn poorer grades at school and lower scores on standardized scholastic achievement tests than their European-American classmates, whereas Asian Americans (particularly recent immigrants) tend to outperform European Americans at school (Chen & Stevenson, 1995; Fuligni, 1997; Tseng, 2006). What might explain these ethnic variations?

One early hypothesis was that ethnic differences in scholastic achievement reflect group differences in intelligence. Indeed, students from underachieving ethnic minority groups do perform at lower levels on IQ tests than European-American or Asian-American students (Neisser et al., 1996). But research also indicates that much (perhaps a large majority) of ethnic variations in IQ-test performance is really a hidden social class effect, and that minority and majority students raised in comparable environments score at about the same levels on IQ tests (Brooks-Gunn, Klebanor, & Duncan, 1996; Scarr & Weinberg, 1983; Waldman, Weinberg, & Scarr, 1994).

Yet another explanation for ethnic variations in achievement is that a larger percentage of students from underachieving ethnic minority groups are from lower socioeconomic backgrounds—a factor that we will see is associated with poorer academic performance. In other words, the argument was that ethnic variations in scholastic achievement, like ethnic variations in IQ, largely represent social-class effects. Consistent with this viewpoint, Charlotte Patterson and her associates (1990) found that variation in family income (an indicator of socioeconomic status) is a better predictor of the academic competencies of African-American and white schoolchildren than is race per se (see also Greenberg et al., 1999).

Still, *even after controlling for social class,* African-American students did not perform as well academically as their white classmates. Why is this?

Certainly *not* because their parents devalue the importance of schooling or academic achievement. African-American and Latino-American parents seem to value education at least as much (if not more) than European-American parents do (Galper, Wigfield, & Seefeldt, 1997; Steinberg, Dornbusch, & Brown, 1992), and they are actually more likely to appreciate the value of homework, competency testing, and a longer school day (Stevenson, Chen, & Uttal, 1990). Today many developmentalists believe that ethnic variations in academic achievement may be attributable not so much to differences in parental attitudes about the value of education as to (1) subtle subcultural differences in parenting practices, (2) differences across ethnic groups in peer endorsement of academics, and (3) the negative influence of social stereotypes on academic performance.

Ethnic Variations in Parenting   Subtle differences in parenting across ethnic groups may well influence children's propensity for achievement, even when the families studied are of the same socioeconomic status. Elsie Moore (1986), for example, found that African-American and European-American mothers from middle-class families clearly differed as they monitored their children's reactions to a tough cognitive challenge. In general, children from European-American homes seemed to enjoy testing sessions, whereas children from the African-American homes did not, often answering questions quickly, as if they hoped to escape from an unpleasant experience. These contrasting reactions appeared to be linked to parenting practices that mothers used while supervising their children's problem-solving activities. Compared with the African-American mothers, European-American mothers provided a great deal of *positive* encouragement. They joked to relieve tension, often cheered when their children showed some progress, and seemed to be conveying an attitude that mastering challenges can be fun. By contrast, African-American mothers were more inclined to try to urge their children onward by showing mild signs of *displeasure* at a child's *lack of progress* (perhaps conveying to the child that tackling challenges involves a risk of disapproval), and their evaluations of their children's performance were somewhat more negative than those of European-American mothers. Perhaps this is why their children were less comfortable during the problem-solving session. In sum, Moore's findings suggest that even when children from different ethnic backgrounds all grow up in advantaged homes, there may still be subtle differences in parenting styles that contribute to ethnic variations in scholastic achievement (see also Alexander & Entwisle, 1988; Slaughter-Defoe et al., 1990; Bradley, Corwyn, Burchinal, et al., 2001; Bradley, Corwyn, McAdoo, et al., 2001; and Raver, Gershoff, & Aber, 2007, for further discussion of this point).

Interestingly, Asian-American students often experience a stringent style of parenting that is more similar to the pattern Moore observed of middle-class African-American than of white mothers. However, this strict, somewhat critical pattern of parenting, coupled with the *very strong* emphasis on education and *very high* achievement standards that many Asian-American parents set for their children, actually *promotes* academic success. Why? Probably because Asian-American families often retain at least some collectivist values from the family's culture of origin—especially those which specify to Asian-American children that they must remain *respectful* of and *obey* their elders, who have the duty to train them to be socially responsible and competent human beings (Chao, 1994, 2001). Indeed, the cultural roots of these Asian-American child-rearing practices can be seen in cross-cultural studies. For example, Chinese mothers are less likely than American mothers to emphasize a child's successes but are more likely than American mothers to attend to and constructively criticize failures. What Chinese mothers are doing is transmitting their culturally ingrained value of striving for self-improvement by communicating that a failure signals a needs for corrective action—in this case, a need to work harder to improve one's competencies (an incremental view of ability) (Ng, Pomerantz, & Lam, 2007).

Peer Group Influences   Peers are also an important influence on grade-school children and adolescents, who may sometimes support and at other times undermine parents' attempts to encourage academic achievement. Peer pressures that interfere with academic achievement may be especially acute for many lower-income African-American and Latino students. Lawrence Steinberg and his colleagues (1992) found that the African-American and Latino peer cultures in many low-income areas actively *discourage* academic achievement, whereas European-American and Asian-American peer groups are more inclined to value and encourage it. High-achieving African-American students in some inner-city schools actually run the risk of being rejected by their African-American peers if their academic accomplishments cause them to be perceived as "acting white" (Ford & Harris, 1996; Fordham & Ogbu, 1986).

Yet, regardless of your ethnicity, you can probably remember preadolescent or adolescent peer groups that tended to be somewhat rebellious, scoffed at adult advice, endorsed antisocial norms, and were rather unenthused about school and academic achievement. In his recent study of 11- to 13-year-old predominantly white youth, Thomas Kindermann (2007) found that sixth-graders who started the school year hanging out with peers who were not academically engaged showed significant declines in their own academic motivation by the end of the year. Even in China, a collectivist society that values both respect for elders and academic achievement, a child's affiliation with a rebellious, antisocial peer group can have a negative impact on academic achievement (Chen, Chang, et al., 2005). As we see in Figure 7.6, the more supportive the mothers of these antisocial youth were in trying to foster academic achievement at the beginning of the study, the worse their children's academic performance *two years later*—a finding that implies that antisocial peer groups may often undermine parents' best attempts to promote achievement behavior.

On the other hand, Figure 7.6 also shows that parents who work hard to promote responsible behaviors are largely successful at fostering academic achievement as long as their children have not affiliated with antisocial peers (Chen, Chang, et al., 2005). Clearly, supportive parenting contributes to positive achievement outcomes (as we will see in the pages that follow). But so too might peer influences, for children whose parents value education highly tend to associate with peers who share those values. In his study of Latino, East Asian, Filipino, and European immigrant families, Andrew Fuligni (1997) found that immigrant adolescents tend to make higher grades at school and to express higher educational and occupational aspirations than native-born U.S. adolescents do, despite the fact that their parents are not highly educated and often speak little English at home (see also Georgiades, Boyle, & Duku, 2007; Tseng, 2006). Why? Because the parents of these high achievers strongly endorsed the value of academics, a value that was clearly reinforced by their friends, who often studied together with them, shared class notes, and encouraged them to do well in school. This kind of peer support for parental values also fosters the academic achievement of talented African-American students (Ford & Harris, 1996; Gutman, Sameroff, & Eccles, 2002) and seems to be a strong contributor to the academic successes of students from any background (Ryan, 2001). Clearly, it is easier to remain focused on academic goals if one is not receiving mixed messages about their value from parents and peers.

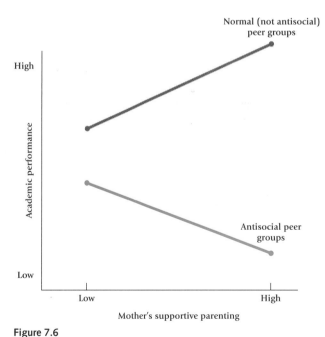

Figure 7.6

Effects of mothers' attempts to promote responsible behaviors as a function of children's peer group affiliations. Notice that mothers who try the hardest to promote academic achievement had children who were performing very poorly at school two years later if they hung out with antisocial peers but were performing very well if they affiliated with other, more typical Chinese peer groups. (Adapted from Chen, Chang, He, 2005.)

A Threat in the Air: How Social Stereotypes Can Influence Academic Performance

Two students, one black and the other white, sit next to each other in a college English class. Both are from middle-class families and attended top-flight high schools, where they earned good grades. Yet the black student is now flunking out of college, whereas the white student is not. Why are their performances so different?

Claude Steele (1997) believes that the answer may have little to do with race differences in genetics, parenting, social class, or family dysfunction. Instead, he argues that any member of an ethnic group characterized by such negative stereotypes as "blacks are less intelligent" or "Latinos are lazy" often experience **stereotype threat** in testing situations—an underlying suspicion that the stereotypes about his social group could be true and a fear that he will be judged to have traits associated with the negative stereotype. Once aroused, this stereotype threat creates a disruptive anxiety that impairs the student's ability to concentrate and do his best in testing situations (Wheeler & Petty, 2001). So according to Steele, a stigmatized minority student might still be influenced by a negative stereotype, even if he has publicly proclaimed it to be false.

To test his theory, Steele and Joshua Aronson (1995) administered a very difficult verbal-skills test to older adolescent females after telling them that these problems were either (1) designed to assess their abilities (which might trigger stereotype threat among stigmatized minorities) or (2) simply of interest to the researchers (no stereotype threat). As the figure indicates, African Americans performed *poorly* when they thought their abilities were being assessed but performed much better—in fact, *just as well as white students did*—when the test was portrayed as a nonevaluative exercise. In a second study, Steele and Aronson found that simply having black students indicate their race on the test booklet is sufficient to trigger stereotype threat and undermine test performance.

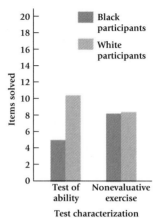

Average performance on a difficult verbal test as a function of race and test characterization. African-American students perform poorly on tests of mental abilities when they think they are taking a test that may result in their being branded as unintelligent. (Adapted from Steele & Aronson, 1995.)

Perhaps results of this kind should be labeled stereotype salience effects because making a stereotype salient does not always have harmful consequences. For example, there is a stereotype that Asian Americans are academically talented—especially in mathematics. Consistent with this stereotype, Asian-American women in one study actually performed *better* on a math test when reminded of their Asian-American identity than when not prompted

---

stereotype threat
a fear that one will be judged to have traits associated with negative social stereotypes about his or her ethnic group.

Finally, the research in Box 7.2 points to a subtle way in which negative social stereotypes may undermine the scholastic performance of students from some ethnic minorities—even talented students who are highly motivated to achieve.

Social Class Differences in Achievement

socioeconomic status (SES)
one's position within a society that is stratified according to status and power.

In addition to their membership in particular ethnic groups, children also differ in their social class standing or **socioeconomic status (SES)**—that is, their position within a society that is stratified according to status and power. In Western societies, the most common measures of a family's social class—family income, prestige of parents' occupations, and parents' educational levels—are based on the family's current or prior accomplishments. So in these cultures, social class is clearly an achievement-related construct, and it is perhaps not surprising to find that children from middle- and upper-class backgrounds score higher in *n* Ach and are more likely to do well in school than children from the lower socioeconomic strata (see Bradley, Corwyn, McAdoo, et al., 2001b; Patterson, Kupersmidt, & Vaden, 1990; Schoon et al., 2002). Children from families living in *poverty* are especially likely to underperform academically, and the impacts of poverty on achievement behavior appear to be cumulative. That is, longitudinal data reveal that the longer children and adolescents live under impoverished conditions, the poorer their educational attainments and the greater the likelihood that they will be employed at menial lower-status occupations

to consider their ethnic identity (Shih, Pittinsky, & Ambady, 1999). Yet, consistent with the stereotype that women are not as good at math as men, Asian-American women in this same study performed *worse* on the math test when prompted to think of their identity as women than when not prompted to consider their gender identity (see also Muzzatti & Agnoli, 2007, for a similar undermining effect of stereotypes on the math performance of Italian girls).

Interestingly, 6- to 10-year-olds, particularly those from ethnically stigmatized groups, are becoming increasingly aware of others' stereotyped beliefs; what's more, those stigmatized 6- to 10-year-olds who are aware of others' beliefs about their lack of academic ability are already showing the effects of stereotype threat, performing worse on cognitive challenges when they believe that the test is diagnostic of their ability (threat condition) as opposed to a simple learning exercise (nonthreat condition) (McKown & Weinstein, 2003).

So from middle childhood, it appears that stereotype threat can handicap stigmatized minority students and contribute most importantly to ethnic differences in intellectual and academic performances. And there is more. Joshua Aronson and colleagues (2002) find that students who experience stereotype threat over academics can become extremely frustrated and actually disidentify with school or with those domains of schooling to which the stereotypes apply, coming to view them as less important to their own life outcomes. This disidentifcation may thus close the door on many career options and even contribute to a decision to drop out of school. How might these vulnerabilities to harmful stereotypes be overcome?

One approach might be to help stigmatized minority students to achieve healthy ethnic identities. Recently Inna Altschul, Daphna Oyserman, and Deborah Bybee (2006) found that African-American

and Latino adolescents from low-income families attained significantly higher grade-point averages at school when they identified with and felt closely connected to their ethnic groups *and* they felt that it was important to their families and their ethnic community that they succeed at school. Adolescents who believe that achievement is part of what it means to be African American or Latino seem to be able to override stereotyped depictions of their ability and to stay focused on succeeding at school, particularly if they have an incremental view of ability and believe that anyone can become more capable if he or she works hard enough (see Good, Aronson, & Inzlicht, 2003).

Another approach that Steele favors is a program in which stigmatized minority students and whites regularly study together, discussing personal and social issues, as well as participating in mastery workshops in their academic subjects. By avoiding self-segregation, these cross-ethnic collaborative programs can help minority students see that students from all ethnic backgrounds must often struggle to master their lessons and that members of no race or ethnicity are inherently inferior intellectually to any other—perceptions that should surely go a long way toward defusing stereotype threat. Interestingly, both black and white college students who have participated in such programs show increases in their grade-point averages, with the improvement being especially striking for black students (Steele, cited in Woo, 1995). Steele also claims that schools might further reduce stereotype threat by (1) ending remedial programs that set only minimal goals and (2) relying less on those kinds of affirmative-action efforts that in subtle ways send minorities the message that they can't compete or succeed without assistance. If there is one single principle, Steele says, it is to "challenge [minorities], don't remediate them. Challenge conveys faith in their [own] potential" (cited in Woo, 1995).

during young adulthood (Duncan & Brooks-Gunn, 1997, 2000; NICHD Early Child Care Research Network, 2005a; Schoon et al., 2002).

As was true with ethnic variations in achievement, social class differences in achievement were first attributed to group differences in intelligence. Middle- and upper-class children do tend to score somewhat higher on IQ tests than lower- and working-class youngsters do (Neisser et al., 1996), thus implying that children from the higher socioeconomic strata may have an "intellectual advantage" that contributes to their greater achievements. Nevertheless, most contemporary theorists believe that class-linked variations in parenting and family life are probably more important than intelligence in explaining social class differences in academic achievement. Indeed, it has been argued (and repeatedly shown) that economic hardship creates psychological distress—a strong discomfort and dissatisfaction with life's conditions that makes lower-income adults edgy and irritable and reduces their capacity to be sensitive, supportive, and highly involved in their children's learning activities, either as a direct participant or as a monitor of the child's (or adolescent's) educational progress (Conger et al., 1992; Conger, Patterson, & Ge, 1995; McLoyd, 1998; Raver, Gershoff, & Aber, 2007). What's more, lower-income parents are often poorly educated themselves and may have neither the knowledge nor the monetary resources to provide their children with age-appropriate books and other educational toys, games, and experiences that foster an interest in learning and a readiness for scholastic challenges (Duncan & Brooks-Gunn, 2000; Gershoff et al., 2007; Klebanov et al., 1998).

Box 7.3 Applying Developmental Research

Recipes for Effective Compensatory Interventions

Evaluations of compensatory education programs conducted over the past 30 years point strongly to two conclusions: Outcomes can be improved dramatically if (1) disadvantaged children are exposed to compensatory education earlier in life and for longer periods, and (2) ways are found to help parents become more involved in their children's learning activities.

The Importance of Parental Involvement

Regardless of their format, compensatory education programs are almost always more effective when they involve the parents of disadvantaged children in one way or another. Today, many developmentalists favor involving parents through **two-generation interventions** that not only provide disadvantaged children with high-quality preschool education but also provide parents with social support, information about child rearing and other family matters, and the educational and vocational training parents need to lift themselves out of poverty (Ramey & Ramey, 1998).

Victoria Seitz and Nancy Apfel (1994; see also Seitz, Rosenbaum, & Apfel, 1985) conducted such an invention, targeting poverty-stricken mothers who had recently delivered their firstborn children. Other impoverished mothers and their firstborns received no intervention and served as a control group. Ten years later, Seitz and her associates (1985) followed up on the firstborn children of these families. They found that children who had received the compensatory intervention were much more likely than nonparticipants to be making normal scholastic progress and were much *less* likely to have been retained in a grade or to have required costly remedial services such as special education. And there was more. In what might be called a *diffusion* effect, the younger siblings of the "intervention" and the "control" participants displayed precisely the same differences in scholastic outcomes that the firstborns did, even though these younger brothers and sisters of program participants had not been born *until after the intervention was over* (Seitz & Apfel, 1994). Apparently, this family intervention made disadvantaged mothers who participated more involved in their children's lives and more confident and effective in their parenting—a change

that not only benefited their firstborn children who received stimulating preschool care, but all their subsequent children as well. It was an effective intervention indeed. (See also Brooks-Gunn, Berlin, & Fuligni, 2000, and Ryan et al., 2002, for other examples of two-generation interventions that produced clear social and intellectual benefits for children of poor parents who took advantage of the parenting skills training and child-care services offered by the programs).

The Importance of Intervening Early

Critics of Head Start and other similar programs argue that they begin too late (often after age 3) and are too brief to have any lasting impact. Indeed, interventions that begin in infancy and last for several years produce more enduring gains in IQ and academic performance.

Two-generation family interventions that target disadvantaged children and their parents can lead to changes in parenting that benefit all children in the family.

Finally, lower-income families are often living in poverty-stricken (or otherwise economically disadvantaged) neighborhoods where there is little sense of community, cohesion, and support among neighbors, and few such community resources as libraries and preschool or youth programs to provide children with stimulating, enriching activities that foster intellectual curiosity and an interest in achieving (Duncan & Brooks-Gunn, 1997; Kohen et al., 2002). Yet when lower-income parents find ways to stimulate children by reading to them, teaching new skills, and providing many age-appropriate challenges to master, their children (1) perform well academically and show as much intrinsic interest in scholastic achievement as middle-class youngsters do (Bradley, Corwyn, McAdoo, et al., 2001; DeGarmo, Forgatch, & Martinez, 1999; Gottfried, Fleming, & Gottfried, 1998; Schulting, Malone, & Dodge, 2005), and (2) later aspire to higher-status occupations as adolescents than do lower-income classmates whose parents are less involved (Hill et al., 2004).

What can be done to improve the educational and, ultimately, the occupational prospects of America's economically disadvantaged children? Perhaps the most enduring legacy of President Lyndon Johnson's War on Poverty of the 1960s is a variety of preschool

The Carolina Abecedarian project is one such program (Campbell & Ramey, 1994, 1995; Campbell et al., 2001). Program children came from families on welfare in which mothers scored far below average in IQ tests. The project provided stimulating day care and (later) compensatory education for eight hours a day, five days a week, starting when participants were 6 to 12 *weeks* old and continuing to age 5. Other children from the same disadvantaged backgrounds did not participate and served as a control group. At regular intervals over the next 21 years, the progress of these two groups of high-risk children was assessed by administering periodic IQ tests and tests of academic achievement. The results were striking. The program participants began to outperform their counterparts in the control group on IQ tests, starting at age 18 months and maintaining this IQ advantage through age 21. Here, then, is evidence that high-quality preschool interventions that begin very early have *lasting* intellectual benefits. They can have lasting educational benefits too, for program participants outperformed the control group in all areas of academic achievement from the third year of school onward. And as adults, program participants were generally less depressed than their counterparts from the control group, even though many of them had grown up in very unstimulating home environments, which often foster the development of depressive symptoms (McLaughlin et al., 2007).

In a similar early intervention in Chicago, program participants who received additional compensatory education services that continued for their first two or three years at school performed exceptionally well academically, scoring about half a grade level higher in math and reading achievement in the third and the seventh grades then program participants whose compensatory education ended at school entry (Reynolds & Temple, 1998). So extended compensatory education that helps disadvantaged children to make the transition to a structured classroom environment can be most beneficial. However, participants who completed even the preschool portion of the Chicago study displayed long-term effects of their participation, showing significantly lower rates of grade retention and special education placements throughout the school years, significantly fewer arrests for delinquent activities by age 18,

and significantly higher high school graduation rates by age 20 than program nonparticipants did (Reynolds, Ou, & Topitzes, 2004).

This research has had a major impact on the way today's interventions are conducted. A notable example is the Early Head Start program, which targets disadvantaged families with infants and toddlers and provides both center-based child care and family/parenting support services. An early evaluation of this program conducted at 17 sites around the United States was quite positive: Compared to control parents who did not participate in the program, Early Head Start parents were more emotionally supportive toward their children, read to them more, and provided them with more learning opportunities. And by age 3, children who participated in Early Head Start were already scoring higher than control children in cognitive and language development, and displayed less aggressive behavior as well (Love et al., 2005).

Of course, two-generation family interventions and long-term programs such as the Abecedarian and the Chicago projects are expensive to administer, and there are critics who claim that they would not be worth the high costs of providing them to all disadvantaged families. However, such an attitude may be "penny wise and pound foolish," for Victoria Seitz and her associates (1985) found that extensive two-generation interventions emphasizing quality day care often pay for themselves by (1) allowing more parents freedom from full-time child care to work, thereby reducing their need for public assistance; and (2) providing the foundation for cognitive growth that enables *most* disadvantaged children to avoid costly special education services at school—a savings that, by itself, would justify the expense of the interventions (Karoly et al., 1998). And when we consider the long-term economic benefits that could accrue later in life when gainfully employed adult graduates of highly successful interventions pay more taxes than disadvantaged nonparticipants, need less public assistance, and are less often maintained at public expense in penal institutions (costs that may run as much as $350 billion *a year* by one estimate; see Reynolds, Ou, & Topitzes, 2004), the net return on each dollar invested in compensatory education could be very impressive indeed (Duncan & Magnusson, 2007).

compensatory interventions (Head Start being the best known) that were aimed at (1) compensating for the cognitive disadvantages that poverty-stricken children typically display upon entering school (see, for example, Stipek & Ryan, 1997) and (2) placing them on a roughly equal footing with their middle-class peers. Long-term follow-ups of some of the better of the early compensatory interventions suggested that they rarely produced any permanent boosts in the IQs of disadvantaged children. However, this does not mean these programs failed, for program participants were much more likely than other low-SES nonparticipants to have positive attitudes about school, meet their school's basic requirements, and graduate from high school, while also being less likely to be retained in grade or to require costly special educational services (Barnett, 1993; Darlington, 1991). Indeed, there is now ample reason to believe that the outcomes of compensatory education will be even better in the future, as we will see in examining some of the more effective of these programs in Box 7.3.

In sum, a person's propensity for achievement may indeed by influenced by the teachings, attitudes, and values that prevail within his or her culture, subculture, and socioeconomic

compensatory interventions
special educational programs designed to further the cognitive growth and scholastic achievements of disadvantaged children.

two-generation interventions
interventions with goals of (1) stimulating children's intellectual development and readiness for school through preschool day care and education and (2) assisting parents to gain parenting skills and move out of poverty.

niche within society. Yet there are truly dramatic individual differences in achievement within any cultural, ethnic, or socioeconomic group—differences that are heavily influenced by variations in home and family lives.

⌇ HOME AND FAMILY INFLUENCES ON ACHIEVEMENT

Over the years, researchers have identified four particularly important home influences on children's mastery and achievement motivations and actual achievement behaviors: the quality of the child's attachments, the character of the home environment, the child-rearing practices that parents use—practices that can either foster or inhibit a child's will to achieve, and the expectancies that parents have for their children.

Quality of Attachments and Achievement

In Chapter 5, we reviewed a portion of the evidence suggesting that secure attachments to parents promote mastery behaviors. Recall that infants and toddlers who were securely attached to their primary caregivers at age 12 to 18 months are more likely than those who were insecurely attached to solve problems successfully as 2-year-olds and to display a strong sense of curiosity, self-reliance, and an eagerness to solve problems some 3 to 5 years later as they enter elementary school. And children whose attachments are secure upon entering school tend to remain more self-assured and to do better in school than their insecurely attached peers through middle childhood and into adolescence—even when other factors known to affect academic achievement, such as IQ and social class, are held constant (Jacobsen & Hofmann, 1997). However, securely attached youngsters are not any more intellectually competent, on average, than their insecurely attached age-mates; instead, they seem more *eager* to *apply* their competencies to the challenges they encounter (Belsky, Garduque, & Hrncir, 1984; Moss & St-Laurent, 2001). So children apparently need the "secure base" provided by a loving, responsive parent to feel comfortable about taking risks and *seeking* challenges.

The Home Environment

A young child's tendency to explore, acquire new skills, and solve problems will also depend on the character of the home environment and the challenges it provides. Bettye Caldwell and Robert Bradley have developed an instrument called the **HOME Inventory** (*H*ome *O*bservation for *M*easurement of the *E*nvironment) that allows a researcher to visit an infant, a toddler, or a preschool child at home and gain a good idea of just how stimulating that home environment is (Caldwell & Bradley, 1984). The infant-toddler version of the HOME inventory consists of 45 statements, each of which can be scored *yes* (the statement is true of this home) or *no* (the statement is not true of this home). In order to gather the information to complete the inventory, the researcher (1) asks the child's mother to describe her daily routine and child-rearing practices, (2) carefully observes the mother as she interacts with her child, and (3) notes the kinds of play materials that the parent makes available for the child. The 45 bits of information collected are then grouped into the six categories, or subscales, in Table 7.3. The home then receives a score on each subscale. The higher the scores across all six subscales, the more stimulating the home environment.

Does the quality of the home environment predict children's achievement behavior? To find out, William van Doorninck and his associates (1981) visited the homes of 50 12-month-old infants from economically disadvantaged backgrounds and used the

HOME inventory
a measure of the amount and type of intellectual stimulation provided by a child's home environment.

Table 7.3 Subscales and sample items from the HOME inventory (Infant version)

Subscale 1: Emotional and Verbal Responsivity of Parent (11 items)	
Sample Items:	Parent responds verbally to child's vocalizations or verbalizations.
	Parent's speech is distinct, clear, and audible.
	Parent caresses or kisses child at least once.

Subscale 2: Avoidance of Restriction and Punishment (8 items)	
Sample Items:	Parent neither slaps nor spanks child during visit.
	Parent does not scold or criticize child during visit.
	Parent does not interfere with or restrict child more than three times during visit.

Subscale 3: Organization of Physical and Temporal Environment (6 items)	
Sample Items:	Child gets out of house at least four times a week.
	Child's play environment is safe.

Subscale 4: Provision of Appropriate Play Materials (9 items)	
Sample Items:	Child has a push or pull toy.
	Parent provides learning facilitators appropriate to age—mobile, table and chairs, highchair, playpen, and so on.
	Parent provides toys for child to play with during visit.

Subscale 5: Parental Involvement with Child (6 items)	
Sample Items:	Parent talks to child while doing household work.
	Parent structures child's play periods.

Subscale 6: Opportunities for Variety in Daily Stimulation (5 items)	
Sample Items:	Father provides some care daily.
	Child has three or more books in his or her room.

Source: Adapted from Bradley & Caldwell, 1984.

HOME inventory to classify these settings as relatively stimulating (high HOME scores) or unstimulating (low HOME scores). Five to nine years later, the research team followed up on these children by looking at their standardized achievement test scores and the grades they had earned at school. As we see in Table 7.4, the quality of the home environment at age 12 months predicted children's academic achievement several years later. Two out of three children from stimulating homes were now performing quite well at school, whereas 70 percent of those from unstimulating homes were doing very poorly. And in a large multiethnic longitudinal study of families from around the United States, Bradley, Corwyn, Burchinal, and associates (2001) found that children *of all ethnicities and social classes* performed better academically throughout childhood and into the adolescent years if they lived in homes scoring relatively high (as opposed to moderate or low) on the HOME inventory. Not only do stimulating home environments promote good academic achievement, but they also promote an *intrinsic orientation* to achievement—a strong willingness to seek out and master challenges to satisfy *personal* needs for competence or mastery (Gottfried, Fleming, & Gottfried, 1998). So even though the seeds of mastery motivation may well be

Table 7.4 Relationship between quality of home environment at 12 months of age and children's grade-school academic achievement five to nine years later

	Academic Achievement	
Quality of Home Environment at Age 12 Months	**Average or High (Top 70%)**	**Low (Bottom 30%)**
Stimulating	20 children	10 children
Unstimulating	6 children	14 children

Source: Adapted from van Doorninck et al., 1981.

innate, as White and Piaget claimed, the joy of discovery and problem solving is most likely to blossom in an intellectually stimulating home environment that provides children with many age-appropriate challenges and the encouragement to master them (Bradley, Corwyn, Burchinal, et al., 2001).

Of course, the demands that parents make of their child and the ways they respond to her accomplishments can also influence the child's will to achieve. Let's now consider some of the child-rearing practices that seem to encourage (or discourage) the development of a healthy achievement orientation.

Child Rearing and Achievement

What kinds of child-rearing practices foster achievement motivation? In their book *The Achievement Motive,* McClelland and associates (1953) proposed that parents who stress **independence training**—doing things on one's own—and who warmly reinforce such self-reliant behavior will contribute in a positive way to the growth of achievement motivation; and research bears this out (Peterson & Steen, 2002; Winterbottom, 1958). However, it is important to note that successfully fostering autonomy and self-reliance requires far more than isolating a child to accomplish objectives alone. Consistent with Vygotsky's viewpoint on the importance of collaborative learning, one longitudinal study found that 2-year-olds whose parents had carefully scaffolded their efforts, allowing them to successfully master challenges that would have been impossible without such gentle parental guidance, were the ones who felt most comfortable and most motivated in achievement contexts one year later, as 3-year-olds (Kelly, Brownell, & Campbell, 2000).

In addition, other investigators (for example, Rosen & D'Andrade, 1959) have found that direct **achievement training**—setting *high but attainable standards* for children to meet and stressing the objective of *doing things well*—also fosters achievement motivation. Children may need a helpful hint now and then (that is, a little parental scaffolding) to work to the best of their abilities and reach lofty objectives. Yet it is important for parents not to become too directive, for they should want their child to believe that it was she who actually mastered the challenge, rather than the parent (Grolnick et al., 2002). These kinds of experiences at performing well at tough challenges can feed on themselves and help youngsters to view challenging tasks as intrinsically interesting.

Finally, the patterns of praise (or punishment) that accompany the child's accomplishments are also important. Children who seek challenges and display high levels of achievement motivation have parents who *praise their successes and are not overly critical of an occasional failure;* by contrast, children who shy away from challenges and are low in achievement motivation have parents who are slow to acknowledge their successes (or who do so in a "matter-of-fact" way) and are inclined to *criticize* or *punish* their failures (Burhans & Dweck, 1995; Kelly, Brownell, & Campbell, 2000; Teeven & McGhee, 1972).

We see, then, that parents of youngsters high in achievement motivation possess three characteristics: (1) They are warm, accepting, and quick to praise the child's accomplishments; (2) they provide noninvasive guidance and control by setting reasonable standards for the child to live up to and then monitoring her progress to ensure that she does; and (3) they permit the child some independence or autonomy, allowing her a say in deciding how best to master challenges and meet their expectations. Diana Baumrind (1973) calls this warm, firm, but democratic

independence training
encouraging children to become self-reliant by accomplishing goals without others' assistance.

achievement training
encouraging children to do things well—that is, to meet or exceed high standards as they strive to accomplish various objectives.

Photo 7.4
Parents who encourage achievement and who respond warmly to successes are likely to raise mastery-oriented children who enjoy challenges.

Robert Pleban

parenting an **authoritative parenting** style—a style that she and others have found to foster positive attitudes about achievement and considerable academic success among grade-school children and adolescents, both in Western societies (Glasgow et al., 1997; Lamborn et al., 1991) and in Asia (Chen, Dong, & Zhou, 1997; Lin & Fu, 1990).[3] If children are encouraged and supported in a positive manner as they tackle their schoolwork, they are likely to enjoy new challenges and feel confident of mastering them (McGrath & Repetti, 2000). By contrast, parents can undermine a child's school performance and motivation to succeed if they (1) are uninvolved and offer little in the way of guidance or (2) are highly controlling and do such things as nag continually about homework, induce guilt when the child performs poorly, offer tangible bribes for good grades, or harp incessantly about bad ones (Aunola & Nurmi, 2004; Ginsburg & Bronstein, 1993).

Family Environmental Influences or Genetic Influences?   At this point, we may wish to consider whether the family contributions that we have discussed truly represent *environmental* influences. Is it plausible that parents' genotypes might influence their patterns of caregiving, child rearing, and the amounts of stimulation they provide their children? Alternatively, might variations in children's IQs or temperaments—two genetically influenced attributes—prompt parents to rely more (or less) on the authoritative pattern of child-rearing that fosters academic achievement? Affirmative answers to these questions would imply that family influences of the kind we have been discussing could represent hidden genetic effects rather than influences attributable to family environments.

In addressing this issue, let's first recall findings from Chapter 5 indicating that the quality of attachments that twin siblings establish with primary caregivers—an attribute we've seen to affect achievement motivation and behavior—is influenced primarily by the sensitivity of caregiving children receive (a shared environmental influence) and barely at all by genes and children's genetically influenced attributes. Consider also recent findings surrounding *school readiness*—children's basic knowledge at school entry of letters, numbers, colors, shapes, pre-reading and writing skills—which is a very good predictor of future academic achievement (see, for example, Duncan et al., 2007). A recent twin study of 5-year-olds' school readiness (Lemelin et al., 2007) did find modest genetic contributions to most school readiness skills. Yet by far the largest contributor to school readiness was *shared environmental influence*, which would include (among other things) the quality of attachments twins have with parents, the character of the home environment that they shared, and the similarities in child rearing that they experienced, as well as such shared contextual influences as family socioeconomic status. So even though variations in genotype do contribute to individual differences in children's achievement propensities, the homes in which children reside are indeed potent *environmental* influences that play an important rule in shaping their achievement motivation and achievement behavior.

Parental Expectancies and Achievement

Although a child's expectancies of succeeding or failing at a particular challenge clearly influence her motivation to achieve, let's also note that the parents have expectancies for their children as well—expectancies that can affect their child's achievement cognitions and achievement behavior. How well parents expect a child to perform in a particular

---

[3]However, some investigators report that Chinese and first-generation Chinese-American students perform better academically if their parents are more stern and controlling rather than authoritative (see, for example, Chao, 2001). We will explore this issue in greater detail when we consider ethnic variations in parenting in Chapter 11.

achievement domain (for example, mathematics) does depend in part on the child's earlier performances. So parents whose children do well in subjects such as math or English come to view their children as more competent in those domains and expect more of them than will parents whose children have performed poorly in these subjects (Frome & Eccles, 1998). Yet once parents develop clear impressions of their children's competencies, something very interesting unfolds over time: Parents' perceptions of their children's competencies influence children's perceptions of their *own* competencies—so much so that children's own self-concepts of ability become more closely aligned with parents' views of their ability than they are with their own past achievement performances (Frome & Eccles, 1998; Jodl et al., 2001)!

What's more, how parents perceive their children's competencies can influence how they socialize their children, thereby affecting a child's achievement behavior. So if parents think that their son lacks academic ability, for example, they may not invest much effort helping him to develop academic skills and may even encourage him to look to achieve in other domains, such as sports. By contrast, parents who perceive their child to be an academic star are likely to provide the materials and opportunities to hone her intellectual skills, thereby fostering academic achievement. Indeed, there is clear evidence that parental expectations do influence children's academic performances. Even after controlling for children's past performances in math and reading, parents' earlier impressions of their children's competencies in these areas were found to predict children's performances on standardized tests of math and reading that were administered nine months later (Halle, Kurtz-Costes, & Mahoney, 1997). It is almost as if what parents think about their child's talents (or lack thereof) strongly affect the child's self-perceptions, achievement motivation, and achievement behavior, thus creating a self-fulfilling prophecy.

Obviously, parental assessments of competence are most likely to undermine achievement behavior when the parent thinks that his or her child lacks ability. Yet Eva Pomerantz and Wei Dong (2006) have argued that whether these negative parental assessments actually do undermine a child's achievement may depend very crucially on yet another factor—the *parent's* own theory of intelligence. Parents who themselves are *entity* theorists may subtly (or not so subtly) communicate that the child's incompetence in a given domain is fixed or unchangeable, thereby undermining his or her motivation to achieve. By contrast, parents who reject the entity theory (favoring an *incremental* viewpoint) may be more inclined to encourage a child who seems to lack ability to work harder to improve his competencies. If so, we might expect that a parent's negative assessment of a child's ability is likely to result in poor achievement performances— the self-fulfilling prophecy—only if the parent strongly endorses an entity theory of intelligence.

Pomerantz and Dong (2006) tested this hypothesis in a one-year longitudinal study of fourth- through sixth-graders. At the beginning of the study, mothers were interviewed to determine (1) their perceptions of their children's academic competencies in six subjects and (2) the strength of their belief in an entity theory of intelligence. Mothers who clearly favored the entity viewpoint strongly agreed with statements such as "You have a certain amount of intelligence and can't do much to change it," whereas mothers who rejected this viewpoint (low-entity mothers) clearly disagreed with such items. To control for earlier academic performances, children's grades at the beginning of the project were recorded. The major dependent variable was the grades children were making one year later at the end of the study.

The results, shown in Figure 7.7, provide clear support for Pomerantz and Dong's hypotheses. Notice in examining the figure that children's academic performances closely matched their mothers' perceptions of their high or low levels of academic competence (the self-filling prophecy) only if their mothers strongly endorsed an entity theory of intelligence and thought that academic competencies were stable or unchangeable. Particularly noteworthy is the finding that low maternal perceptions of children's competencies seriously *undermined* academic performances only when mothers strongly believed that competence is stable. By contrast, children apparently overcame their mothers' low expectations if mothers did not endorse an entity theory of intelligence. Why? Possibly because low-entity mothers are more likely to believe that academic competencies can be improved through hard work and are sending that message to their children.

So a parent's impression that her child lacks competence can undermine achievement behavior if that parent also favors an entity theory of intelligence. How might we deal with this issue? Given that children's theories of intelligence can be altered with relatively simple interventions (Blackwell, Trzesniewski, & Dweck, 2007), the same should be true for parents. Pomerantz & Dong (2006) suggest that it may be possible for schools to implement parental education programs to teach parents that academic competence is something that must be cultivated over time (an incremental view of ability), although it is likely that these kind of interventions will be most effective if they are implemented early in a child's academic career (before parents have well-developed impressions of their children's competencies) and if parents are provided with explicit strategies (such as those summarized below) for developing academic talents.

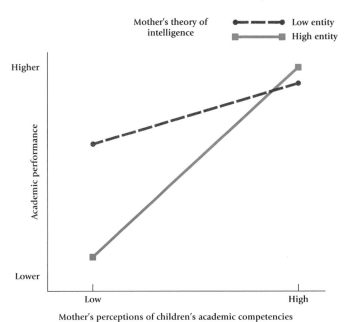

Figure 7.7 Children's grades at the end of the study as a function of mothers' perceptions of their academic competencies and mothers' endorsement of an entity theory of intelligence. (Adapted from Pomerantz & Dong, 2006.)

Summing Up After reviewing what we know about home and family contributions to achievement, we can point to many steps that parents can take to help their children cope effectively with the challenges they face. They might begin by striving to become sensitive, responsive caregivers, thereby prompting their infants to use them as secure bases from which to explore and seek challenges. Of course, providing a stimulating home environment with many age-appropriate challenges will further the joy of problem solving and promote other mastery behaviors, particularly if parents take interest in their child's learning, set reasonable goals for him or her to accomplish, and provide whatever support (or scaffolding) that that child needs to succeed and feel that she has personally mastered something truly meaningful (independence training), while taking care to praise the effortful persistence (process praise) that enabled her to do things well (achievement training). Finally, it may be particularly important for parents to communicate the positive impressions they have about a child's competencies while at the same time taking care to stress that the lack of competence that a foundering child may feel is something that can be overcome if he or she is willing to work hard enough to develop these talents (incremental view of ability).

So it may not be that difficult (in theory, at least) to foster achievement motivation and achievement behavior in young children. Perhaps the biggest hurdles we face rest not with trying to interest curious youngsters to seek challenges but rather to convince more adults to follow the simple guidelines outlined above. We must also find ways to assist more parents to cope with the many other stresses and challenges they may be facing (for example, depression, job stress, martial stress, or poverty) so that they have the time, energy, and resources to invest in their children's lives.

SUMMARY

+ A basic aim of socialization is to build on children's inborn **mastery motivation** to encourage them to pursue important objectives and to take pride in their accomplishments.

THE CONCEPT OF ACHIEVEMENT MOTIVATION

+ **Achievement motivation** has been conceptualized in very different ways. McClelland regarded it as a learned motive to compete and strive for success (that is the **need for achievement**, or *n* Ach). This viewpoint depicts the high achiever as having an **intrinsic orientation.** However, behavioral theorists view the motivation to achieve as a need to attain social approval and other external incentives; thus, the high achiever is presumed to have an **extrinsic orientation.**

EARLY REACTIONS TO ONE'S ACCOMPLISHMENTS: FROM MASTERY TO SELF-EVALUATION

+ Infants are guided by a mastery motive and take pleasure in their everyday accomplishments. By age 2, toddlers have begun to anticipate others' approval or disapproval of their performances, and children 3 and older evaluate their accomplishments against performance standards and can experience true pride or shame, depending on how successfully they match those standards. For 3½- to 5-year-olds, winning a competition is bliss, but losing is not yet considered a "failure."

THEORIES OF ACHIEVEMENT MOTIVATION AND ACHIEVEMENT BEHAVIOR

+ Research testing McClelland's need achievement theory demonstrated that people reliably differ in achievement motivation (*n* Ach). However, McClelland's notion that this one global motive would predict achievement behaviors in all contexts was badly overstated.

+ Atkinson's revision of need achievement theory pointed to two competing motives—**the motive to achieve success (M_s)** and the **motive to avoid failure (M_{af})**—that influence achievement behavior. Atkinson also broke new ground by stressing that two achievement-related cognitions—**achievement expectancies** and **achievement value**—are important determinants of achievement behaviors.

+ Weiner's attribution theory grew out of earlier work on **locus of control** and focused on how the **causal attributions** we make for our successes and failures influence our **achievement expectancies** and the perceived **value** of success (or failure).

+ Dweck's theory identified two contrasting achievement orientations. **Mastery-oriented** children and adolescents attribute their successes to stable, internal causes (such as high ability), their failures to unstable causes (lack of effort), and they retain an **incremental view of ability.** Consequently, they feel quite competent and will work hard to overcome failures. By contrast, children with a **learned helplessness orientation** often stop trying after a failure because they display an **entity view of ability** and attribute their failures to a lack of ability that they feel they can do little about. Children who are often criticized for their lack of ability and who feel pressured to adopt **performance goals** rather than **learning goals** are

at risk of becoming helpless. Helpless children can become more mastery-oriented if they are taught (through **attribution training**) that their failures can and often should be attributed to unstable causes, such as a lack of effort, that they can overcome by trying harder. Parents and teachers can help to *prevent* learned helplessness by praising children for their accomplishments, although **process praise** is likely to be much more effective than **person praise.** Fortunately, maladaptive entity theories of ability that can place children at risk academically can be modified by relatively simple interventions.

CULTURAL AND SUBCULTURAL INFLUENCES ON ACHIEVEMENT

+ One's cultural heritage can clearly affect one's orientation toward achievement. People from *collectivistic* societies are taught to suppress individualism and to work for the greater good of their social groups. By contrast, people from *individualistic* societies are taught to be more self-reliant and will come to stress personal accomplishments as indications of achievement.

+ Academic achievement varies as a function of ethnicity and **socioeconomic status (SES).** Subtle differences in parenting style, as well as disruptive peer influences and **stereotype threat,** seem to contribute to the poor academic performances of underachieving ethnic minorities.

+ Regardless of ethnicity, children from disadvantaged backgrounds face serious risks of becoming academic underachievers. **Compensatory interventions,** especially **two-generation interventions** and/or those that start very early and last at least throughout the preschool period, can significantly reduce the academic risks that disadvantaged children face.

HOME AND FAMILY INFLUENCES ON ACHIEVEMENT

+ Infants and toddlers who are securely attached to primary caregivers are likely to become curious preschoolers who seek challenges and will tend to do well later at school.

+ Research with the **HOME Inventory** reveals that stimulating home environments that provide young children with a variety of age-appropriate challenges and the encouragement and support to master them will foster academic achievement in the years ahead.

+ Early **independence training** and **achievement training** promote achievement motivation, particularly if parents warmly reinforce successes and are not overly critical of occasional failures. Parents who combine all these practices into one parenting style **(authoritative parenting)** tend to raise children who achieve considerable academic success.

+ Parents' perceptions of their children's abilities affect children's own competency appraisals and their achievement behavior, thus creating self-fulfilling prophecies. Negative competency appraisals by parents can seriously undermine a child's academic performance if parents themselves are entity theorists, thereby implying to the child that his or her shortcomings are stable and unchangeable.

CHAPTER 8

Sex Differences, Gender-Role Development, and Sexuality

How important is a child's gender to his or her development? Many people would say, "Very important!" Often the first bit of information that parents receive about their child is his or her sex, and the question "Is it a boy or a girl?" is the very first one that most friends and relatives ask when proud new parents telephone to announce the birth of their baby (Intons-Peterson & Reddel, 1984). Indeed, the ramifications of this gender labeling are normally swift in coming and rather direct. In the hospital nursery or delivery room, parents often call an infant son things like "big guy" or "tiger," and they are likely to comment on the vigor of his cries, kicks, or grasps. By contrast, infant daughters are more likely to be labeled "sugar" or "sweetie" and described as soft, cuddly, and adorable (Maccoby, 1980; MacFarlane, 1977). A newborn infant is usually blessed with a name that reflects his or her sex, and in many Western societies children are immediately adorned in either blue or pink. Mavis Hetherington and Ross Parke (1975, pp. 354–355) describe the predicament of a developmental psychologist who "did not want her observers to know whether they were watching boys or girls":

> Even in the first few days of life some infant girls were brought to the laboratory with pink bows tied to wisps of their hair or taped to their little bald heads . . . When another attempt at concealment of sex was made by asking mothers to dress their infants in overalls, girls appeared in pink and boys in blue overalls, and "Would you believe overalls with ruffles?"

This gender indoctrination continues during the first year as parents provide their children with "gender-appropriate" clothing, toys, and hairstyles (Pomerleau et al., 1990). They also play differently with and expect different reactions from their young sons and daughters (Bornstein et al., 1999; Caldera, Huston, and O'Brien, 1989). So it is clear that a child's companions view gender as an important attribute—one that often determines how they will respond to him or her.

Why do people react differently to males and females—especially *infant* males and females? One explanation centers on the biological differences between the sexes. Recall that fathers determine the sex of their offspring. A zygote that receives an X chromosome from each parent is a genetic (XX) female that will develop into a baby girl, whereas a zygote that receives a Y chromosome from the father is a genetic (XY) male that will normally assume the appearance of a baby boy. Could it be that this basic genetic difference between the sexes is ultimately responsible for *sex differences in behavior*—differences that might explain why parents often do not treat their sons and daughters alike? We will explore this interesting idea in some detail in a later section of the chapter.

However, there is more to sex differences than biological heritage. The vast majority of the world's societies expect males and females to behave differently and to assume different roles. In order to conform to these expectations, the child must understand that he is a boy or that she is a girl and must incorporate this information into his or her self-concept. In this chapter, we will concentrate on the interesting and controversial topic of **gender typing**—the process by which children acquire not only a gender identity but also the motives, values, and behaviors considered appropriate in their culture for members of their biological sex.

We begin the chapter by summarizing what people generally believe to be true about sex differences in cognition, personality, and social behavior. As it turns out, some of these beliefs have an element of truth to them, although many others are best described as fictions or fables that have no basis in fact. We will then look at developmental trends in gender typing and see that youngsters are often well aware of gender-role stereotypes and are displaying gender-typed patterns of behavior long before they are old enough to go to

gender typing
the process by which a child becomes aware of his or her gender and acquires motives, values, and behaviors considered appropriate for members of that sex.

Photo 8.1
Gender-role socialization begins very early as parents provide their infants with "gender-appropriate" clothing, toys, and hairstyles.

Tony Anderson/Getty Images

kindergarten. And how do children learn so much about the sexes and gender roles at such an early age? We will address this issue by reviewing several influential theories that specify how biological forces, social experiences, and cognitive development might combine or interact to influence the gender typing process. And after examining an interesting perspective, which asserts that traditional gender roles have outlived their usefulness in today's modern society, we will conclude by briefly considering another self-aspect that is central to our concept of self as male or female—the self as a sexual being.

CATEGORIZING MALES AND FEMALES: GENDER-ROLE STANDARDS

Most of us have learned a great deal about males and females by the time we enter college. In fact, if you and your classmates were asked to jot down 10 psychological dimensions on which men and women are thought to differ, it is likely that every member of the class could easily generate such a list. Here's a head start: Which gender is most likely to display emotions? To be tidy? To be competitive? To use harsh language?

A **gender-role standard** is a value, a motive, or a class of behavior that is considered more appropriate for members of one sex than the other. Taken together, a society's gender-role standards describe how males and females are expected to behave, and reflect the stereotypes by which we categorize and respond to members of each sex.

The female's role as child bearer is largely responsible for the gender-role standards and stereotypes that have prevailed in many societies, including our own. Girls have typically been encouraged to assume an **expressive role** that involves being kind, nurturant, cooperative, and sensitive to the needs of others (Conway & Vartanian, 2000; Parsons, 1955). These psychological traits, it was assumed, would prepare girls to play the wife and mother roles—to keep the family functioning and raise children successfully. By contrast, boys have been encouraged to adopt an **instrumental role,** for as a traditional husband and father, a male would face the tasks of providing for the family and protecting it from harm. Thus, young boys are expected to become dominant, assertive, independent, and competitive. Similar norms and role prescriptions are found in many, though certainly not all, societies (Wade & Tavris, 1999; Williams & Best, 1990). In one rather ambitious project, Herbert Barry, Margaret Bacon, and Irving Child (1957) analyzed the gender-typing practices of 110 nonindustrialized societies, looking for sex differences in the socialization of five attributes: nurturance, obedience, responsibility, achievement, and self-reliance. As shown in Table 8.1, achievement and self-reliance were more strongly encouraged in young boys, whereas young girls were encouraged to become nurturant, responsible, and obedient (see also Best & Williams, 1997).

Children in modern industrialized societies also face strong gender-typing pressures, though not always to the same extent and in the same ways that children in nonindustrialized societies do. (For example, parents in many Western societies place roughly equal emphasis on achievement for sons and for daughters; Lytton & Romney, 1991). Furthermore, the findings in Table 8.1 do not imply that self-reliance in girls is frowned on or that disobedience by young boys is acceptable. In fact, all five attributes that Barry and his colleagues studied were encouraged of *both* boys and girls, but with different emphases on different attributes depending on the sex of the child (Zern, 1984; see also Pomerantz & Ruble, 1998). So it appears that the first goal of socialization is to encourage

gender-role standard
a behavior, value, or motive that members of a society consider more typical or appropriate for members of one sex.

expressive role
a social prescription, usually directed toward females, that one should be cooperative, kind, nurturant, and sensitive to the needs of others.

instrumental role
a social prescription, usually directed toward males, that one should be dominant, independent, assertive, competitive, and goal-oriented.

Table 8.1 Sex differences in the socialization of five attributes in 110 societies

Attribute	Percentage of Societies in Which Socialization Pressures Were Greater for	
	Boys	Girls
Nurturance	0	82
Obedience	3	35
Responsibility	11	61
Achievement	87	3
Self-reliance	85	0

Note: The percentages for each attribute do not add to 100 because some of the societies did not place differential pressure on boys and girls with respect to that particular attribute. For example, 18 percent of the societies for which pertinent data were available did not differentiate between the sexes in the socialization of nurturance.

Source: Adapted from Barry, Bacon, & Child, 1957.

children to acquire those traits that will enable them to become well-behaved, contributing members of society. A second goal (but one that many adults view as important nevertheless) is to "gender-type" the child by stressing the importance of relationship-oriented (or expressive) attributes for girls and individualistic (or instrumental) attributes for boys.

Because cultural norms specify that girls should assume an expressive role and boys an instrumental role, we may be inclined to assume that girls and women actually display expressive traits and that boys and men possess instrumental traits (Broverman et al., 1972; Williams & Best, 1990). If you are thinking that these stereotypes have disappeared as attention to women's rights has increased and as more women have entered the labor force, think again. Although some change has occurred in the latter half of the 20th century in the direction of more egalitarian gender roles and norms (at least in Western societies) (Botkin, Weeks, & Morris, 2000; Eagly, Wood, & Deakman, 2000), adolescents and young adults still endorse many traditional stereotypes and prefer men and women who display stereotyped attributes (Lueptow, Garovich-Szabo, & Lueptow, 2001; Twenge, 1997; test yourself in Box 8.1). For example, college students in one recent study (Prentice & Carranza, 2002) insisted that women ought to be friendly, cheerful, compassionate, emotionally expressive, and patient, while not being stubborn, arrogant, intimidating, or domineering. Men, by contrast, ought to be rational ambitious, assertive, athletic, and leaders with strong

Box 8.1 Developmental Issues

Do You Display Characteristics Commonly Attributed to Men or Women?

Several surveys (for example, Ruble, 1983; Williams, Satterwhite, & Best, 1999) have asked college students to respond to lists of mannerisms and personal characteristics, indicating which of these traits characterize the "typical" man or the "typical" woman. As an exercise, rate yourself using the scale below to indicate the extent to which you think you display each attribute. (Be frank and honest; there are no right or wrong answers.)

Scale:	1	2	3	4	5
	Really unlike me	Sort of unlike me	Neither unlike nor like me	Sort of like me	Really like me

Trait
1. Active _____
2. Adventurous _____
3. Aggressive _____
4. Ambitious _____
5. Competitive _____
6. Dominant _____
7. Independent _____
8. Good leader _____
9. Mathematical _____
10. Decisive _____
11. Mechanical _____
12. Outspoken _____
13. Persistent _____
14. Self-confident _____
15. Strong _____
16. Tough _____

Σ traits 1–16 _____

Trait
17. Aware of others' feelings _____
18. Considerate _____
19. Creative _____
20. Curious _____
21. Other-oriented _____
22. Sexy _____
23. Artistic _____
24. Excitable _____
25. Empathic _____
26. Affectionate _____
27. Charming _____
28. Neat _____
29. Sensitive _____
30. Soft-hearted _____
31. Tactful _____
32. Understanding _____

Σ traits 17–32 _____

Traits 1–16 are attributes more commonly associated with men, whereas traits 17–32 are traits more commonly associated with women. Add and record your scores for each set of attributes.

We will return to this example when we discuss the topics of masculinity, femininity, and androgyny later in the chapter.

personalities, and by all means ought not be emotional, gullible, or weak and approval seeking. Might these presumed (and preferred) differences between the sexes have any factual basis? Let's see whether they do.

∽ SOME FACTS AND FICTIONS ABOUT SEX DIFFERENCES

The old French maxim *vive la différence* reflects a fact that we all know to be true: Males and females are anatomically different. Adult males are typically taller, heavier, and more muscular than adult females, whereas females may be hardier in the sense that they live longer (Giampaoli, 2000). But although these physical variations are fairly obvious, the evidence for sex differences in psychological functioning is not as clear as most of us might think.

Actual Psychological Differences between the Sexes

In a classic review of more than 1500 studies comparing males and females, Eleanor Maccoby and Carol Jacklin (1974) concluded that few traditional gender stereotypes have any basis in fact. In fact, their review pointed to only four *small* but reliable differences between the sexes that were consistently supported by research. Here are their conclusions, with some updates and amendments:

1. *Verbal ability.* When differences are found, girls display greater verbal abilities than boys on many measures. Girls acquire language and develop verbal skills at an earlier age than boys (Bornstein & Haynes, 1998) and display a small but consistent verbal advantage on tests of reading comprehension and speech fluency throughout childhood and adolescence (Halpern, 2004; Wicks-Nelson & Israel, 2006). Boys, however, perform slightly better than girls on tests of verbal analogies (Lips, 2006).

2. *Visual/spatial abilities.* Boys outperform girls on some tests of **visual/spatial abilities**—that is, the ability to draw inferences about or to otherwise mentally manipulate pictorial information (see Figure 8.1 for two kinds of visual/spatial tasks on which sex differences have been found). The male advantage in spatial abilities is moderately robust, detectable by age 4, and persists across the life span (Choi & Silverman, 2003; Halpern, 2004; Voyer, Voyer, & Bryden, 1995).

   visual/spatial ability
   the ability to mentally manipulate or otherwise draw inferences about pictorial information.

3. *Mathematical reasoning.* Beginning in adolescence, boys show a small but consistent advantage over girls on tests of *arithmetic reasoning* (Halpern, 1997, 2004; Hyde, Fennema, & Lamon, 1990; and see Figure 8.2). Girls actually exceed boys in computational skills and even earn higher grades in math, in part because girls are more inclined than boys to adopt learning rather than performance goals, thereby working harder to improve their mathematical competencies (Kenney-Benson et al., 2006). Nevertheless, boys feel more self-efficacious in math than girls do (Simpkins, Davis-Kean, & Eccles, 2006) and have acquired more mathematical problem-solving strategies that enable them to outperform girls on complex word problems, geometry, and the mathematics portion of the Scholastic Assessment Test (SAT) (Byrnes & Takahira, 1993; Casey, 1996; Lips, 2006). The male advantage in mathematical problem solving is most apparent among high math achievers; more males than females are exceptionally talented in math (Lips, 2006; Stumpf & Stanley, 1996). And it seems that sex differences in visual/spatial abilities and the problem-solving strategies they support contribute to sex differences in arithmetic reasoning (Casey, Nuttal, & Pezaris, 1997). However, we will soon see that social forces—namely the messages boys and girls receive about their respective abilities—can also influence their mathematical, verbal, and visual/spatial reasoning skills.

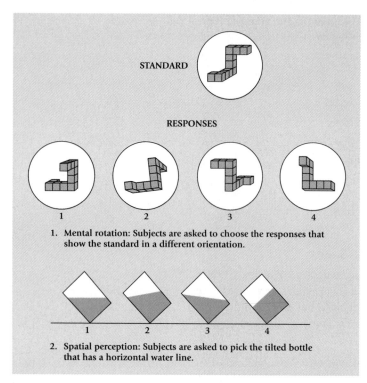

1. **Mental rotation:** Subjects are asked to choose the responses that show the standard in a different orientation.

2. **Spatial perception:** Subjects are asked to pick the tilted bottle that has a horizontal water line.

Figure 8.1
Two spatial tasks for which sex differences in performance have been found. (From Linn & Petersen, 1985.)

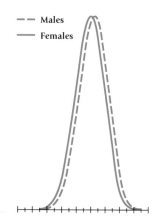

Figure 8.2
These two distributions of scores—one for males, one for females—give some idea of the size of the gap between the sexes in abilities for which sex differences are consistently found. Despite a small difference in average performance, the scores of males and females overlap considerably. (Adapted from Hyde, Fennema, & Lamon, 1990.)

4. *Aggression.* Finally, boys are more physically and verbally *aggressive* than girls, starting as early as age 2, and are about 10 times more likely than girls are to be involved in violent crime during adolescence (Barash, 2002; Snyder, 2003). However, girls are more likely than boys to display covert forms of hostility toward others by snubbing or ignoring them or by trying to undermine their relationships or social status (Crick, Casas, & Mosher, 1997; Crick & Grotpeter, 1995).

Other sex differences: Critics were quick to challenge Maccoby and Jacklin's review, claiming that the procedures they used to gather and tabulate their results led them to underestimate the number of sex differences that actually exist (Block, 1976; Huston, 1983). More recent research, which often combines the results of several studies and provides a better estimate of the reliability of sex-related differences, points to several additional sex differences in personality and social behavior. For example:

5. *Activity level.* Even before they are born, boys are more physically active than girls (Almli, Ball, & Wheeler, 2001), and they remain more active throughout childhood, especially when interacting with peers (Eaton & Enns, 1986; Eaton & Yu, 1989). In fact, the heightened activity that boys display may help to explain why they are more likely than girls to initiate and to be receptive to bouts of nonaggressive, *rough-and-tumble* play (Pellegrini & Smith, 1998).

6. *Fear, timidity, and risk-taking.* As early as the first year of life, girls appear to be more fearful or timid in uncertain situations than boys are. They are also more cautious and less assertive in these situations than boys are, taking far fewer risks than boys do (Christopherson, 1989; Feingold, 1994). Sex differences in risk taking may stem in part from boys heightened activity levels. But parental responses to risk taking are also important. Mothers of 6- to 10-year-olds report that they try harder with daughters than with sons to enforce rules against risk taking. Why? Partly because they have had less success at modifying sons' risky behaviors and have concluded that "boys will be boys" and that taking risks is "in their nature" (Morrongiello & Hogg, 2004). Boys continue to take more risks (and to suffer more negative consequences as a result) throughout childhood and adolescence, although girls do engage in some risky behaviors (for example, cigarette smoking, binge drinking) about as often as boys do (Blakemore, Berenbaum, & Liben, in press).

7. *Developmental vulnerability.* From conception, boys are more physically vulnerable than girls to prenatal and perinatal birth hazards and to the effects of disease (Raz et al., 1994, 1995). Boys are also more likely than girls to display a variety of developmental problems, including autism, reading and language-related disabilities, attention-deficit, hyperactivity syndrome, emotional disorders, and mental retardation (Halpern, 1997; Holden, 2005; Thompson, Caruso, & Ellerbeck, 2003).

8. *Emotional expressivity/sensitivity.* As infants, boys and girls do not differ much in their displays of emotion (Brody, 1998). But from toddlerhood onward, boys are more likely

than girls to display one emotion—anger—whereas girls more frequently display most other emotions (Fabes et al., 1991; Kochanska, 2001). Two-year-old girls are already using more emotion-related words than 2-year-old boys do (Cervantes & Callanan, 1998), and parents of preschoolers talk more with daughters than with sons about emotions and memorable emotional events (Kuebli, Butler, & Fivush, 1995). Indeed, this social support for reflecting on their feelings may help to explain why girls and women characterize their emotions as deeper, or more intense, and feel freer to express them than boys and men do (Fuchs & Thelen, 1988; Saarni, 1999).

The evidence for sex differences in empathic sensitivities is mixed. Girls and women consistently *rate themselves* (and are described by others) as more nurturant and empathic than boys and men (Baron-Cohen, 2003; Feingold, 1994). Yet laboratory studies designed to induce empathy (by exposing children to others' distress or misfortunes) reveal that boys express nearly as much facial distress and concern and as much physiological arousal to others' misfortunes as girls do (Blakemore, Berenbaum, & Liben, in press; Eisenberg & Fabes, 1998). And in naturalistic contexts, boys have been found to be at least as affectionate toward and concerned about the welfare of pets and older relatives as girls are (Melson, Peet, & Sparks, 1991).

9. *Compliance.* From early in the preschool period, girls are more compliant than boys to the requests and demands of parents, teachers, and other authority figures (Feingold, 1994; Smith et al., 2004). And when trying to persuade others to comply with them, girls are especially inclined to rely on tact and polite suggestions (Baron-Cohen, 2003), whereas boys, who are quite capable of being tactful and who *usually do* collaborate amicably, are nevertheless more likely than girls to resort to demanding or controlling strategies (Leaper, Tennenbaum, & Shaffer, 1999; Strough & Berg, 2000).

10. *Self-esteem.* Boys show a small edge over girls in global self-esteem (Kling et al., 1999). This sex difference becomes more noticeable in early adolescence and persists throughout adulthood (Robins et al., 2002).

Photo 8.2
Rough-and-tumble play is more common among boys than among girls.

In reviewing the evidence for "real" sex differences, we must keep in mind that the data reflect *group averages* that may or may not characterize the behavior of any particular individual. For example, gender accounts for about 5 percent of the variation children display in overt aggressive behaviors (Hyde, 1984), so the remaining 95 percent is due to differences between people other than their sex. Furthermore, the sex differences in verbal, spatial, and mathematical abilities that Maccoby and Jacklin identified are not large, are most apparent at the extreme (that is, very high or very low) ends of the ability distributions (Halpern, 1997, 2004), and may not be evident elsewhere (Lips, 2006; Stetsenko et al., 2000). For example, women do better on tests of mathematical ability, sometimes even outperforming men, in societies like Israel, where women have excellent opportunities in technical training and technical occupations (Baker & Jones, 1992). Even within the United States, expected sex differences do not emerge in all ethnic groups. For example, Chinese-American girls perform as well as Chinese-American boys in higher-level mathematics, including the Scholastic Aptitude test, even though European-American boys out perform European-American girls on the SAT by about 40 to 50 points (Lips, 2006). Findings such as these imply that most sex differences are not biologically inevitable and that cultural, subcultural, and other social influences play an important role in the development of males and females (Halpern, 1997).

What, then, should we conclude about psychological differences between the sexes? Although contemporary scholars may quibble at times about which sex differences are real or meaningful (Eagly, 1995; Hyde & Plant, 1995), most developmentalists can agree on this: *Males and females are far more psychologically similar than they are different,* and even the most well-documented differences seem to be modest and subject to qualification (Blakemore, Berenbaum, & Liben, in press). So it is impossible to accurately predict the aggressiveness, mathematical skills, activity level, or emotional expressivity of any individual simply by knowing his or her gender. Only when group averages are computed do the sex differences emerge.

Cultural Myths

Another conclusion that most developmentalists now endorse is Maccoby and Jacklin's (1974) proposition that many (perhaps most) gender-role stereotypes are "cultural myths" that have no basis in fact. Among the most widely accepted of these "myths" are those in Table 8.2.

Why do these inaccuracies persist? Maccoby and Jacklin (1974) propose that:

a . . . likely explanation for the perpetuation of "myths" is the fact that stereotypes are such powerful things. An ancient truth is worth restating here: if a generalization about a group of people is believed, whenever a member of the group behaves in the expected way the observer notes it and his belief is confirmed and strengthened; when a member of the group behaves in a way that is not consistent with the observer's expectations, the instance is likely to pass unnoticed, and the observer's generalized belief is protected from disconfirmation. . . . [This] well-documented [selective attention] . . . process . . . results in the perpetuation of myths that would otherwise die out under the impact of negative evidence. (p. 355)

In other words, gender-role stereotypes are well-ingrained cognitive schemes that we use to interpret and often to distort the behavior of males and females (Martin & Halverson, 1981; see also Box 8.2). People even use these schemes to classify the behavior

Table 8.2 Some unfounded beliefs about sex differences

Beliefs	Facts
1. Girls are more "social" than boys.	The two sexes are equally interested in social stimuli, equally responsive to social reinforcement, and equally proficient at learning from social models. At certain ages, boys actually spend more time than girls with playmates.
2. Girls are more "suggestible" than boys.	Most studies of children's conformity find no sex differences. However, sometimes boys are more likely than girls to accept peer-group values that conflict with their own.
3. Girls are better at simple repetitive tasks, whereas boys excel at tasks that require higher-level cognitive processing.	The evidence does not support these assertions. Neither sex is superior at rote learning, probability learning, or concept learning.
4. Boys are more "analytic" than girls.	With the exception of the modest sex differences in cognitive abilities that we have already discussed, boys and girls do not differ on tests of analytical or logical reasoning.
5. Girls lack achievement motivation.	No such differences exist! Perhaps the myth of lesser achievement motivation for females has persisted because males and females have generally directed their achievement strivings toward different goals.

Source: Adapted from Maccoby & Jacklin, 1974.

Do Gender Stereotypes Color Children's Interpretations of Counterstereotypic Information?

Maccoby and Jacklin (1974) proposed that, once people learn gender stereotypes, they are more likely to attend to and remember events that are consistent with these beliefs than events that would disconfirm them. Carol Martin and Charles Halverson (1981) agree, arguing that gender stereotypes are well-ingrained schemes or naïve theories that people use to organize and represent experience. Once established, these gender schemes should have at least two important effects on a child's (or an adult's) cognitive processes: (1) an *organizational* effect on memory, such that information consistent with the scheme will be easier to remember than counterstereotypic events, and (2) a *distortion* effect, such that counterstereotypic information will tend to be remembered as much more consistent with one's gender scheme that the information really is. For example, it should be easier for people to remember that they saw a girl at the stove cooking (gender-consistent information) than a boy partaking in the same activity (gender-inconsistent information). And if people were to witness the latter event, they might distort what they had seen to make it more consistent with their stereotypes—perhaps by remembering the actor as a girl rather than a boy or by reconstructing the boy's activities as *fixing* the stove rather than cooking.

Martin & Halverson (1983) tested their hypotheses in an interesting study with 5- and 6-year-olds. During a first session, each child was shown 16 pictures, half of which depicted a child performing *gender-consistent* activities (for example, a boy playing with a truck)

and half showing children displaying *gender-inconsistent* behaviors (for example, a girl chopping wood). One week later, children's memory for what they had seen was assessed.

The results of this experiment were indeed interesting. Children easily recalled the sex of the actor for scenes in which actors had performed gender-consistent activities. But when the actor's behavior was gender *inconsistent,* these youngsters often distorted the scene by saying that the actor's sex was consistent with the activity they recalled (for example, they were likely to say that it had been a boy rather than a girl who had chopped wood). As predicted, children's *confidence* about the sex of the actors was greater for gender-consistent scenes than for gender-inconsistent ones, suggesting that counterstereotypic information is harder to remember. But it was interesting to note that when children actually distorted a gender-inconsistent scene, they were just as confident about the sex of the actor (which they recalled *incorrectly*) as they were for the gender-consistent scenes in which they correctly recalled the actor's sex. So it seems that children are likely to distort counterstereotypic information to be more consistent with their stereotypes and that these memory distortions are "real" to them as stereotypical information that has not been distorted.

Why, then, do inaccurate gender stereotypes persist? Because we find disconfirming evidence harder to recall and in fact often distort that information in ways that will confirm our initial (and inaccurate) beliefs.

of infants. In one study (Condry & Condry, 1976), college students watched a videotape of a 9-month-old child who was introduced as either a girl ("Dana") or a boy ("David"). As the students observed the child at play, they were asked to interpret his/her reactions to toys such as a teddy bear or a jack-in-the-box. The resulting impressions of the infant's behavior clearly depended on his or her presumed sex. For example, a strong reaction to the jack-in-the-box was labeled "anger" when the child was presumed to be a boy and "fear" when the child had been introduced as a girl.

As it turns out, the persistence of unfounded or inaccurate gender-role stereotypes has important consequences for both boys and girls. Some of the more negative implications of these cultural myths are discussed in the following section.

Do Cultural Myths Contribute to Sex Differences in Ability (and Vocational Opportunity)?

In 1968, Phillip Goldberg asked college women to judge the merits of several scientific articles that were attributed to a male author ("John McKay") or to a female author ("Joan McKay"). Although these manuscripts were identical in every other respect, participants judged the articles written by a male to be of higher quality than those by a female.

These young women were reflecting a belief, common to people in many societies, that girls and women lack the potential to excel in either math and science courses or in occupations that require this training (Eccles et al., 2000; Tennenbaum & Leaper, 2003). Kindergarten and first-grade girls already believe that they are not as good as boys are in arithmetic; and throughout the grade-school years, children increasingly come to regard reading, art, and music as girls' domains and mathematics, science, athletics, and mechanical subjects as more appropriate for boys (Eccles, Jacobs, & Harold, 1990; Eccles et al., 1993, 2002). Furthermore, an examination of the percentages of U.S. male and female practioners in various occupations reveals that women are overrepresented in fields that call for verbal ability (for example, library science, elementary education) and are seriously underrepresented in most other professions, particularly the sciences and other technical fields (for example, engineering) that require a math/science background (Eccles et al., 2000; National Council for Research on Women, 2002), and these imbalances are also seen in Europe (DeWandre, 2002). How do we explain these dramatic sex differences? Are the relatively small sex-related differences in verbal, mathematical, or visual/spatial performances responsible? Or rather, do gender-role stereotypes create a **self-fulfilling prophecy**—one that *promotes* sex differences in cognitive performance and steers boys and girls along different career paths? Today, many developmentalists favor the latter viewpoint. Let's take a closer look.

Home Influences   Parents may often contribute to sex differences in ability and self-perceptions by treating their sons and daughters differently. Jacquelynne Eccles and her colleagues have conducted a number of studies aimed at understanding why girls tend to shy away from math and science courses and are underrepresented in occupations that involve math and science. They find that parental expectations about sex differences in mathematical ability do become self-fulfilling prophecies. The plot goes something like this:

1. Parents, influenced by gender stereotypes, expect their sons to outperform their daughters in math. Even before their children have received any formal math instruction, mothers in the United States, Japan, and Taiwan express a belief that boys have more mathematical ability than girls (Lummis & Stevenson, 1990), and this parental belief becomes stronger as children grow older (Frome & Eccles, 1998).

2. Parents attribute their sons' successes in math to ability but credit their daughters' successes to hard work (Parsons, Adler, & Kaczala, 1982). These attributions further reinforce the belief that girls lack mathematical talent and turn in respectable performances only through plodding effort (see also Pomerantz & Ruble, 1998). Parents often communicate this message in subtle ways. If a child seeking help with her homework hears her mother say, "Go see Dad; he's the math brain," or hears her dad remark, "It's okay, honey; even your mom has trouble with math," she is learning that math is perceived as a male domain for which girls are not well suited (Lips, 2006).

3. Children begin to internalize their parents' views, so that boys feel relatively self-confident, whereas girls are somewhat more inclined to underestimate both their general academic abilities (Cole et al., 1999; Stetsenko et al., 2000) and, in particular, their proficiencies in math (Fredricks & Eccles, 2002; Simpkins, Davis-Keane, & Eccles, 2006).

4. Suspecting that they lack ability, girls become less interested in math, value it less, are less likely to take elective math courses, and become less inclined than boys to pursue career possibilities that involve math after high school (Benbow & Arjimand, 1990; Jacobs et al., 2002). Even female college students who perceive themselves to be strong in math and science are less likely than male counterparts to anticipate future study or careers in these areas (Lips, 2004).

In short, parents who expect their daughters to struggle with numbers and to shy away from math may often get what they expect. Eccles and her colleagues (1990) have ruled out the possibility that parents (and girls themselves) expect less of girls because girls actually do worse in math than boys do. The negative effects of low parental expectancies on girls' self-perceptions are evident even when boys and girls perform *equally well* on tests of math aptitude and attain similar grades in math (Eccles, Jacobs, & Harold, 1990). Parental

self-fulling prophecy
phenomenon whereby people cause others to act in accordance with the expectations they have about those others.

beliefs that girls excel in English and that boys are more talented in sports and science contribute to sex differences in interests and competencies in these areas as well (Eccles et al., 2000; Fredricks & Eccles, 2002; Tennenbaum & Leaper, 2003).

Scholastic Influences   Teachers also have stereotyped beliefs about the relative abilities of boys and girls in particular subjects. Sixth-grade math instructors, for example, believe that boys have more ability in math but that girls try harder at it (Jussim & Eccles, 1992). And even though these teachers often reward girls' greater efforts by assigning them equal or higher grades than they give to boys (Jussim & Eccles, 1992; Kenney-Benson et al., 2006), their subtle message that girls must try harder to succeed in math may nonetheless convince many girls that their talents might be best directed toward other nonquantitative achievement domains for which they are better suited . . . like music or English.

In sum, unfounded beliefs about sex differences in cognitive abilities may indeed contribute to the small sex-related ability differences we have discussed and, ultimately, to the large underrepresentation of women in the sciences and other occupations requiring quantitative skills. Clearly, the chain of events that Eccles describes is not inevitable. For example, girls whose parents are nontraditional in their gender-role attitudes and behaviors do not show the age-related declines in math and science achievement that girls from traditional families are likely to display (Updegraff, McHale, & Crouter, 1996). But even so, girls, to a greater extent than boys, tend to be generalists at school, striving to do well in most or all of their classes. Thus, girls may be less likely to become exceptionally proficient in any subject (particularly in "masculine" subjects like math and science) when their time, energies, and talents are so broadly invested across many academic domains (Denissen, Zarrett, & Eccles, 2007).

Efforts have been made in recent years to educate parents, teachers, and counselors about the subtle ways that unfounded gender stereotypes can undermine the educational and occupational aspirations of talented female students, and there are signs that progress is being made. In one longitudinal study, Eccles and her colleagues (Fredricks & Eccles, 2002; Jacobs et al., 2002) found that by 12th grade, girls valued mathematics as much as boys did and viewed themselves just as competent at it as boys (although the fact remained that both sexes showed declines in their perceived competencies and valuation of math across the high school years). And although women make up only 23 percent of the total science and engineering workforce in the United States today, larger percentages of women than men are entering and graduating from college (Lips, 2006). In addition, women in 2005 earned 49 percent of all law degrees, 47 percent of all medical degrees, and 44 percent of all graduate degrees in engineering and science. Corresponding percentages in 1976 were about 10 percent for science and engineering, 18 percent for law, and 28 percent for medicine (Cynkar, 2007b). In 2006, Nancy Pelosi became the first female congressional leader (Speaker of the U.S. House of Representatives), and 2007 witnessed the emergence of the first serious female contender for president of the United States. So there is reason to suspect that many of the constraining stereotypes about women's competencies will eventually crumble as women achieve, in ever-increasing numbers, in politics, professional occupations, the sciences, skilled trades, and virtually all other walks of life. To oppose such a trend is to waste a most valuable resource: the abilities and efforts of more than half the world's population.

Now let's examine the gender typing process to see why it is that boys and girls may come to view themselves so differently and will often choose to assume different roles.

☞ DEVELOPMENTAL TRENDS IN GENDER TYPING

Gender-typing research has traditionally focused on three separate but interrelated topics: (1) the development of **gender identity,** or the knowledge that one is either a boy or a girl and that gender is an unchanging attribute; (2) the development of

gender identity
one's awareness of one's gender and its implications.

gender-role stereotypes, or ideas about what males and females are supposed to be like; and (3) the development of *gender-typed* patterns of *behavior*—that is, the child's tendencies to select same-sex playmates and to favor same-sex activities over those normally associated with the other sex.

Development of the Gender Concept

The first step in the development of a gender identity is to discriminate males from females and to place oneself into one of these categories. By 6 months of age, infants are using differences in vocal pitch to discriminate female speech from that of males (Miller, 1983); and by the end of the first year, they can reliably discriminate photographs of men and women (women are the long-haired ones) and are beginning to match male and female voices with faces in tests of intermodal perception (Leinbach & Fagot, 1993; Poulin-Dubois et al., 1994).[1]

Between ages 2 and 3, children begin to tell us what they know about gender as they acquire and correctly use such labels as "mommy" and "daddy" and (slightly later) "boy" and "girl" (Leinbach & Fagot, 1986). By age 2½ to 3, almost all children can accurately label themselves as either boys or girls (Thompson, 1975; Warin, 2000), although it will take longer for them to grasp the fact that gender is a permanent attribute. Many 3- to 5 year-olds, for example, think that boys could become mommies or girls daddies if they really wanted to, or that a person who changes clothing and hairstyles can become a member of the other sex (Fagot, 1985b; Warin, 2000). Children normally begin to understand that sex is an unchanging attribute between the ages of 5 and 7, so that most youngsters have a firm, future-oriented identity as a boy or a girl by the time they enter grade school or shortly thereafter (Szkrybalo & Ruble, 1999).

More recently, Susan Egan and David Perry (2001) have argued that one's sense of gender identity includes not only the knowledge that "I am a boy/girl and will always be a boy/girl," but also such judgments as "I am a typical/atypical member of my gender," "I am content/not content with my biological sex," "I feel free/not free to explore cross-sex options," and "I feel that my sex is/is not superior to the other sex." As we will see later in the chapter, these latter aspects of gender identity have emerged by the elementary school years and play a meaningful role in influencing a child's personal and social adjustment.

Development of Gender-Role Stereotypes

Remarkable as it may seem, toddlers begin to acquire gender-role stereotypes at about the same time that they become aware of their basic identities as boys or girls. Deanna Kuhn and her associates (1978) showed a male doll ("Michael") and a female doll ("Lisa") to 2½ to 3½-year-olds and then asked each child which of the two dolls would engage in gender-stereotyped activities such as cooking; sewing; playing with dolls, trucks, or trains; talking a lot; giving kisses; fighting; or climbing trees. Almost all the 2½-year-olds had some knowledge of gender-role stereotypes. For example, boys and girls agreed that girls talk a lot, never hit, often need help, like to play with dolls, and like to help their mothers with chores such as cooking and cleaning. By contrast, these young children felt that boys like to play with cars, like to help their fathers, like to build things, and are apt to make statements such as "I can hit you" (see also Blakemore, 2003). The 2- to 3-year-olds who know the most about gender stereotypes are those who can correctly label photographs of

---

[1]*Intermodal perception* refers to one's ability to use one sensory channel (say, vision) to identify a stimulus that is already familiar through modality (such as audition, or hearing).

Photo 8.3 By age 2½ to 3, children know that boys and girls prefer different kinds of activities, and they have already begun to play in gender-stereotyped ways.

other children as boys and girls (Fagot, Leinbach, & O'Boyle, 1992). So an understanding of gender labels seems to accelerate the process of gender stereotyping.

Over the preschool and early grade-school years, children learn more and more about the toys, activities, and achievement domains considered appropriate for boys and for girls (Blakemore, 2003; Serbin, Powlishta, & Gulko, 1993). Eventually, grade-school children draw sharp distinctions between the sexes on *psychological* dimensions, learning first the positive traits that characterize their own gender and the negative traits associated with the other sex (Serbin, Powlishta, & Gulko, 1993). By age 10 to 11, children's stereotyping of personality traits is beginning to rival that of adults. In one well-known cross-cultural study, Deborah Best and her colleagues (1977) found that fourth- and fifth-graders in England, Ireland, and the United States generally agree that women are weak, emotional, soft-hearted, sophisticated, and affectionate, whereas men are ambitious, assertive, aggressive, dominating, and cruel. Later research reveals that these same personality dimensions (and many others) are reliably attributed to men and women by male and female participants from many countries around the world (Williams, Satterwhite, & Best, 1999).

How seriously do children take the gender-role prescriptions they are rapidly learning? Do they believe that they must conform to these stereotypes? Many 3- to 7-year-olds do; they often reason like little chauvinists, treating gender-role standards as blanket rules that are not to be violated (Banerjee & Lintern, 2000; Ruble & Martin, 1998). Consider the reaction of one 6-year-old to a boy named George who likes to play with dolls:

(*Why do you think people tell George not to play with dolls?*) Well, he should only play with things that boys play with. The things that he is playing with now is girls' stuff . . . (*Can George play with Barbie dolls if he wants to?*) No sir! . . . (*What should George do?*) He should stop playing with girls' dolls and start playing with G.I. Joe. (*Why can a boy play with G.I. Joe and not a Barbie doll?*) Because if a boy is playing with a Barbie doll, then he's just going to get people teasing him . . . and if he tries to play more, to get girls to like him, then the girls won't like him either. (Damon, 1977, p. 255; italics added)

Why are young children so rigid and intolerant of gender-role transgressions? Possibly because gender-related issues are very important to them between ages 3 and 7: After all, this is the time when they are firmly classifying themselves as boys or girls and beginning to suspect that they will *always be* boys and girls. Thus, they may exaggerate gender-role stereotypes to "get them cognitively clear" so that they can live up to their male or female self-images (Maccoby, 1998).

By age 8 to 9, however, children are becoming more flexible and less chauvinistic in their thinking about gender (Blakemore, 2003; Levy, Taylor, & Gelman, 1995; McHale, Crouter, & Tucker, 2001). Notice how 9-year-old James makes a clear distinction between moral rules that people are obligated to obey and gender-role standards that are customary but *nonobligatory*.

> (*What do you think his parents should do?*) They should . . . get him trucks and stuff, and see if he will play with those. (*What if . . . he kept on playing with dolls? Do you think they would punish him?*) No. (*How come?*) It's not really doing anything bad. (*Why isn't it bad?*) Because . . . if he was breaking a window, and he kept on doing that, they could punish him, because you're not supposed to break windows. But if you want to you can play with dolls. (*What's the difference? . . .*) Well, breaking windows you're not supposed to do. And if you play with dolls, you can, but boys usually don't. (Damon, 1977, p. 263; italics added)

However, just because grade-school children say that boys and girls can legitimately pursue cross-sex interests and activities does not necessarily imply that they *approve* of those who do. When asked about whether they could be friends with a boy who wears lipstick or a girl who plays football, and to evaluate such gender-role transgressions, grade-school children (and adults) were reasonably tolerant of violations by girls. However, participants (especially boys) came down hard on boys who tried to look and behave like girls, viewing these transgressions as almost as bad as violating a moral rule. Here, then, is an indication of the greater pressure placed on boys to conform to gender roles (Blakemore, 2003; Levy, Taylor, & Gelman, 1995).

Cultural Influences   Although 8- to 10-year-olds from Western individualistic societies are becoming more flexible in their thinking about many violations of gender stereotypes, the same pattern may not be apparent elsewhere. In Taiwan, a collectivist society with an emphasis on maintaining social harmony and living up to social expectations, children are strongly encouraged to accept and conform to appropriate gender-role prescriptions. As a result, Taiwanese 8- to 10-year-olds are less accepting of gender-role violations (particularly by boys) than their age-mates from a Western individualistic society (urban Israelis) (Lobel et al., 2001).

Adolescent Thinking about Gender Stereotypes   Thinking about the traits that males and females might display and the hobbies and occupations they might pursue becomes increasingly flexible (among Western youths, at least) during early adolescence, as children make the transition from elementary school to junior high. But soon thereafter, gender-role prescriptions once again become less flexible, with both boys and girls showing a strong intolerance of cross-sex mannerisms that reflect atypical identities (for example, boys wearing lipstick or girls sporting crew cuts), whether displayed by males or females (Alfieri, Ruble, & Higgins, 1996; Sigelman, Carr, & Begley, 1986; Signorella, Bigler, & Liben, 1993). How might we explain this second round of gender chauvinism?

Apparently, an adolescent's increasing intolerance of cross-sex mannerisms and behaviors is tied to a larger process of **gender intensification**—a magnification of sex differences that is associated with increased pressure to conform to gender roles as one reaches puberty (Boldizar, 1991; Galambos, Almeida, & Petersen, 1990; Hill and Lynch, 1983). Boys begin to see themselves as more masculine; girls emphasize their feminine side (McHale, Updegraff, et al., 2001; McHale, Shanahan, et al., 2004). Why might gender intensification occur? Parental influence is one contributor: As children enter adolescence, mothers become more involved in joint activities with daughters and fathers more involved with sons (Crouter, Manke, & McHale, 1995)—especially in families with both sons and daughters in which

gender intensification
a magnification of sex differences early in adolescence; associated with increased pressure to conform to traditional gender roles.

each parent may take primary responsibility for properly socializing children of the same sex (McHale & Crouter, 2003; Shanahan, McHale, Crouter, & Osgood, 2007). However, peer influences may be even more important. For example, adolescents increasingly find that they must conform to traditional gender norms in order to succeed in the dating scene. A girl who was a tomboy and thought nothing of it may find during adolescence that she must dress and behave in more "feminine" ways to attract boys, and a boy may find that he is more popular if he projects a more sharply "masculine" image (Burn, O'Neil, & Nederend, 1996; Katz, 1979). Social pressures on adolescents to conform to traditional roles may even help explain why sex differences in various cognitive abilties sometimes become more noticeable as children enter adolescence (Hill & Lynch, 1983; Roberts et al., 1990). Later in high school, teenagers become more comfortable with their identities as young men or women and more flexibile once again in their thinking about gender (Urberg, 1979). Yet even adults may remain highly intolerant of males who blatantly disregard gender-role prescriptions (Levy, Taylor, & Gelman, 1995).

Development of Gender-Typed Behavior

The most common method of assessing the "gender appropriateness" of children's behavior is to observe whom and what they like to play with. Sex differences in playful gestures and toy preferences develop very early—even before the child has established a basic gender identity or can correctly label various toys as "boy things" or "girl things" (Blakemore, LaRue, & Olejnik, 1979; Fagot, Leinbach, & Hagan, 1986). For example, Leif Stennes and associates (2005) found that in the early pretend play of 13-month-olds, girls emitted more actions and communication gestures centering on themes of pretending to be a parent, whereas boys' play actions and gestures were often imitations of such masculine activities as pounding with a hammer or digging with a shovel. By age 14 to 22 months, boys have come to prefer trucks and cars to other objects, whereas girls of this age would rather play with dolls and soft toys (Smith & Daglish, 1977). In fact, 18- to 24-month-old toddlers will often refuse to play with cross-sex toys, even when there are no other objects available for them to play with (Caldera, Huston, & O'Brien, 1989).

Gender Segregation   Children's preferences for same-sex playmates also develop very early. In nursery school, 2-year-old girls already prefer to play with other girls (La Freniere, Strayer, & Gauthier, 1984), and by age 3, boys are reliably selecting boys rather than girls as companions. This **gender segregation,** which has been observed in a wide variety of cultures (Leaper, 1994; Whiting & Edwards, 1988), becomes progressively stronger with each passing year. By age 6½, children spend more than 10 times as much time with the same-sex as with opposite-sex companions (Maccoby, 1998), and when a young child does play with other-sex peers, there is usually at least one same-sex comrade present (Fabes, Martin, & Hanish, 2003). Grade-school and preadolescent children generally find cross-gender contacts less pleasing and are likely to behave more negatively toward opposite-sex than same-sex peers (Underwood, Schockner, & Hurley, 2001). Interestingly, even young children believe that it is wrong to exclude a child from such contexts as doll play or playing with trucks on the basis of gender (Killen et al., 2001), but they often do so anyway (see also Brown & Bigler, 2004). Alan Sroufe and his colleagues (1993) found that those 10- to 11-year-olds who insist most strongly on maintaining clear gender boundaries and who avoid consorting with the "enemy" tend to be viewed as socially competent and popular, whereas children who violate gender segregation rules tend to be much less popular and less well adjusted. In fact, children who display a *preference* for cross-sex friendships are likely to be *rejected* by their peers (Kovacs, Parker, & Hoffman, 1996). However, gender boundaries and biases against other-sex companions decline in adolescence when the social and physiological events of puberty trigger an interest in members of the opposite sex (Bukowski, Sippola, & Newcomb, 2000; Serbin, Powlishta, & Gulk, 1993).

gender segregation
children's tendency to associate with same-sex playmates and to think of the other sex as an out-group.

Why does gender segregation occur? Eleanor Maccoby (1998) believes that it largely reflects differences between boys' and girls' play styles—an incompatibility that may stem from boys' heightened levels of androgen, which fosters active, rambunctious behavior. In one study (Jacklin & Maccoby, 1978), an adult observer recorded how often pairs of same-sex and mixed-sex toddlers played together or played alone when placed in a playroom with several interesting toys. As we see in Figure 8.3, boys directed far more social responses to boys than to girls, whereas girls were more sociable with girls than with boys. Interactions between playmates in the same-sex pairings were lively and positive in character. By contrast, girls tended to withdraw from boys in the mixed-sex pairs. Boys were simply too boisterous and domineering to suit the taste of many girls, who prefer less roughhousing and would rather rely on polite negotiations than demands or shows of force when settling disputes with their playmates (see also Martin & Fabes, 2001). Throughout childhood, boys prefer playing or working together in same-sex *groups,* whereas girls are more likely than boys to withdraw in group settings, choosing instead to focus attention on individuals and functioning best in same-sex *dyads* (Benenson & Heath, 2006). Girls are expected to play quietly and gently and are subject to criticism (by both boys and girls) should they become loud and rough like the boys (Blakemore, 2003).

Cognitive and social-cognitive development also contribute to the increasing gender segregation children display. Once preschoolers label themselves as boys or girls and begin to acquire gender stereotypes, they come to favor the group to which they belong and will eventually view the other sex as a homogeneous out-group with many negative characteristics (Martin, 1994; Powlishta, 1995). In fact, children who hold the more stereotyped views of the sexes are the ones most likely to maintain gender segregation in their own play activities and to make few if any opposite-sex friends (Kovacs, Parker, & Hoffman, 1996; Martin, 1994).

Sex Differences in Gender-Typed Behavior

Many cultures, including our own, assign greater status to males and the male gender role (Blakemore, Berenbaum, & Liben, in press; Turner & Gervai, 1995), and boys face stronger pressures than girls to adhere to gender-appropriate codes of conduct (Bussey & Bandura, 1992). Consider that fathers of baby girls are generally willing to offer a truck to their 12-month-old daughters, whereas fathers of baby boys are likely to withhold dolls from their sons (Snow, Jacklin, & Maccoby, 1983). And boys are quicker than girls to adopt gender-typed toy preferences. Judith Blakemore and her associates (1979), for example, found that 2-year-old boys clearly favor gender-appropriate toys, whereas some 2-year-old girls may not. By 18 months to 2 years of age, many children (and more boys than girls) develop *extremely intense* interests in such gender-typed objects and activities as vehicles for boys and dolls or dressing up for girls (DeLoache, Simcock, & Macari, 2007). And by age 3 to 5, boys (1) are much more likely than girls to say that they *dislike* opposite-sex toys (Bussey & Bandura, 1992; Eisenberg, Murray, & Hite, 1982) and (2) *may* even prefer

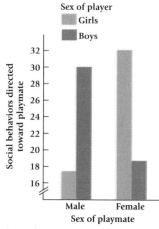

Figure 8.3
By age 33 months, toddlers already prefer playmates of their own sex. Boys are much more sociable with boys than with girls, whereas girls are more outgoing with girls than with boys. (Adapted from Jacklin & Maccoby, 1978.)

a girl playmate who likes "boy" toys to a boy playmate who prefers girls' activities (Alexander & Hines, 1994).

Between the ages of 4 and 10, both boys and girls are becoming more aware of what is expected of them and conforming to these cultural prescriptions (Huston, 1983). Yet girls are more likely than boys to retain an interest in cross-sex toys, games, and activities. Consider what John Richardson and Carl Simpson (1982) found when recording the toy preferences of 750 5- to 9-year-olds as expressed in their letters to Santa Claus. Although most requests were clearly gender-typed, we see in Table 8.3 that more girls than boys were asking for "opposite-sex" items. With respect to their actual gender-role preferences, young girls often wish they were boys, and nearly half of today's college women claim that they were tomboys when they were young (Bailey, Bechtold, & Berenbaum, 2002). Yet it is unusual for a boy to wish he were a girl (Martin, 1990).

Table 8.3 Percentages of boys and girls who requested popular "masculine" and "feminine" items from Santa Claus

	Percentage of Boys Requesting	Percentage of Girls Requesting
Masculine items		
Vehicles	43.5	8.2
Sports equipment	25.1	15.1
Spatial/temporal toys (construction sets, clocks, and so on)	24.5	15.6
Feminine items		
Dolls (adult female)	.6	27.4
Dolls (babies)	.6	23.4
Domestic accessories	1.7	21.7

Source: Adapted from Richardson & Simpson, 1982.

There are probably several reasons that girls are drawn to male activities and the masculine role during middle childhood. For one thing, they are becoming increasingly aware that masculine behavior is more highly valued, and perhaps it is only natural that girls would want to be what is "best" (or at least something other than a second-class citizen) (Frey and Ruble, 1992). Furthermore, girls are given much more leeway than boys are to partake in cross-sex activities; it is okay to be a "tomboy" but a sign of ridicule and rejection should a boy be labeled a "sissy" (Martin, 1990). Finally, fast-moving masculine games and "action" toys may simply be more interesting than the playthings and pastimes (dolls, dollhouses, dish sets, cleaning and caretaking utensils) often imposed on girls to encourage their adoption of a nurturant, expressive orientation. Consider the reaction of Gina, a 5-year-old who literally squealed with delight when she received an "action garage" (complete with lube racks, gas pumps, cars, tools, and spare parts) from Santa one Christmas. At the unveiling of this treasure, Gina and her three female cousins (aged 3, 5, and 7) immediately ignored their dolls, dollhouses, and unopened gifts to cluster around and play with this unusual and intriguing toy.

In spite of their earlier interest in masculine activities, most girls come to prefer (or at least to comply with) many of the prescriptions for the feminine role by mid-adolescence (McHale, Shanahan, et al., 2004). Why? Probably for biological, cognitive, and social reasons. Once they reach puberty and their bodies assume a more womanly appearance (*biological growth*), girls often feel the need to become more "feminine" if they hope to be attractive to members of the other sex (Burn, O'Neil, & Nederend, 1996; Katz, 1979). Furthermore, these young adolescents are also attaining formal operations and advanced role-taking skills (*cognitive growth*), which may help to explain why they become (1) self-conscious about their changing body images (Jones, 2004; McCabe & Ricciardelli, 2005), (2) so concerned about people's evaluations of them (Elkind, 1981; remember the *imaginary audience* phenomenon), and (3) more susceptible to gender intensification pressures and thus more inclined to conform to the *social* prescriptions of the female role.

Subcultural Variations in Gender Typing

Although not extensive, research on social-class and ethnic variations in gender typing reveals that (1) middle-class adolescents (but not children) hold more flexible gender-role attitudes than their low-SES peers (Bardwell, Cochran, & Walker, 1986; Canter & Ageton, 1984) and (2) African-American children hold less stereotyped views of women than European-American children do (Bardwell, Cochran, & Walker, 1986; see also Leaper, Tennenbaum, & Shaffer, 1999).

Researchers have attributed these social class and ethnic variations in gender typing to differences in education and family life. For example, people from middle-class backgrounds typically have a wider array of educational and occupational options available to them, perhaps explaining why they eventually adopt more flexible attitudes about the roles that men and women should play.

Why might African-American children hold less stereotyped views of the sexes? One reason may be that the African-American community has historically endorsed more favorable attitudes toward gender equality in the sharing of family responsibilities (King, Harris, & Heard, 2004), so that the behavior of mothers and fathers toward their children may not differ as much as is true in other ethnic communities. Indeed, Jaipaul Roopnarine and associates (2005) recently found that unlike the mother-nurturer/father-playmate roles that parents often assume with infants in European-American families, African-American fathers are less constrained and are as inclined (or even more so) than mothers to provide their infants with nurturing comfort, vocal stimulation, and lots of affection. As caregivers, their behavior was strikingly similar to that of mothers. What's more, a greater percentage of African-American than European-American children are living in *single-parent* homes and/or have mothers who are *employed* outside the house (U.S. Bureau of the Census, 2001). So the less stereotyped portrayal of women observed among African-American youngsters may also reflect the fact that their mothers are more likely than European-American mothers to be assuming both instrumental (male) and expressive (female) functions in their own roles as parents (Leaper, Tennenbaum, & Shaffer, 1999).

Finally, children raised in "countercultural" or "avant-garde" homes (in which parents strive to promote egalitarian gender-role attitudes) are indeed less gender-stereotyped than children from traditional families in their *beliefs* about which activities and occupations are appropriate for males and females (Weisner & Wilson-Mitchell, 1990). Nevertheless, these "countercultural" children are quite aware of traditional gender stereotypes and are just as "gender-typed" in their toy and activity preferences as children from more traditional families.

In sum, gender-role development proceeds at a remarkable pace (Ruble, Martin, & Berenbaum, 2006; and see Table 8.4 for a brief overview). By the time they enter school, children have long been aware of their basic gender identities, have acquired many,

Table 8.4 An overview of gender typing

Age in Years	Gender Identity	Gender Stereotyping	Gender-Typed Behavior
0–2½	✦ Ability to discriminate males from females emerges and improves. ✦ Child accurately labels the self as a boy or a girl.	✦ Some gender stereotypes emerge.	✦ Gender-typed toy/activity preferences emerge. ✦ Preferences for same-sex playmates emerge (gender segregation).
3–6	✦ Conservation of gender (recognition that one's gender is unchanging) emerges.	✦ Gender stereotyping of interests, activities, and occupations emerges and becomes quite rigid.	✦ Gender-typed play/toy preferences become stronger, particularly for boys. ✦ Gender segregation intensifies.
7–11	✦ Expansion of gender identity to include perceptions of one's gender typicality and gender contentedness.	✦ Gender stereotyping of personality traits and achievement domains emerges. ✦ Gender stereotyping becomes less rigid.	✦ Gender segregation continues to strengthen. ✦ Gender-typed toy/activity preferences continue to strengthen for boys; girls develop (or retain) interest in some masculine activities.
12 & beyond	✦ Gender identity becomes more salient, reflecting gender intensification pressures.	✦ Intolerance of cross-sex mannerisms increases early in adolescence. ✦ Gender stereotyping becomes more flexible in most respects later in adolescence.	✦ Conformity to gender-typed behaviors increases early in adolescence, reflecting gender intensification. ✦ Gender segregation becomes less pronounced.

many stereotypes about how the sexes differ, and have come to prefer gender-appropriate activities and same-sex playmates. During middle childhood, their knowledge continues to expand as they learn more about gender-stereotyped *psychological* traits, and they become more flexible in their thinking about gender roles. Yet their *behavior*, especially if they are boys, becomes even more gender-typed, and they segregate themselves even more from the other sex. Now a most intriguing question: How does all this happen so fast?

THEORIES OF GENDER TYPING AND GENDER-ROLE DEVELOPMENT

Several theories have been proposed to account for sex differences and the development of gender roles. Some theories emphasize the role of biological differences between the sexes, whereas others emphasize *social* influences on children. Some emphasize what society does to children, others what children do to themselves as they try to understand gender and all its implications. Let's briefly examine two biological theories and then consider the more "social" approaches offered by psychoanalytic theory, social-learning theory, cognitive-developmental theory, and gender schema theory.

Evolutionary Theory

"Once there was a baby named Chris . . . [who] went to live on a beautiful island . . . [where] there were only boys and men; Chris was the only girl. Chris lived a very happy life on this island, but she never saw another girl or woman" (Taylor, 1996, p. 1559). What would Chris be like?

When Marianne Taylor (1996) asked 4- to 10-year-olds to indicate Chris's toy preferences, occupational aspirations, and personality traits, 4- to 8-year-olds assigned stereotypically feminine attributes to her, despite the fact that she was raised in a masculinizing environment and never saw a girl or woman. In other words, preschool and young grade-school children display an *essentialist bias,* assuming that Chris's biological status as a girl will determine what she will become. Only the 9- to 10-year-olds in this study showed any awareness that Chris's masculinizing environment might influence her activities, aspirations, and personality characteristics.

The biological perspective that comes closest to displaying a similar essentialist bias is the evolutionary approach. Evolutionary psychologists (for example, Buss, 1995, 2000; Geary, 1999, 2005) contend that men and women faced different evolutionary pressures over the course of human history and that natural selection process conspired to create fundamental differences among males and females that determined gender divisions of labor. In Chapter 3, for example, we noted how evolutionary theorists explain different mating strategies favored by men and women to preserve their genes. Males, who need only contribute sperm to produce offspring, can best ensure that their genes survive by mating with multiple partners and producing many children. By contrast, females must invest much more to achieve the same objective, taking nine months from conception to the birth of each offspring and years to raise each to ensure that their genes survive. To successfully raise children, women presumably evolved in ways that would make them kind, gentle, and nurturant (expressive characteristics) and to prefer men who would display kindness toward them and would provide resources (food and protection) to help ensure children's survival. Men, by contrast, should become more competitive, assertive, and aggressive (instrumental traits) because these attributes should increase their chances of successfully attracting mates and procuring resources (Geary, 1999).

According to evolutionary theorists (Buss, 1995, 2000), males and females may be psychologically similar in many ways but should differ in any domain in which they have faced different adaptive problems throughout evolutionary history. Consider the male superiority in visual spatial performance. Spatial skills are essential for hunting; few kills would be made if hunters could not anticipate the trajectory of their spears (or rocks, or arrows) with the path of a moving prey animal. Thus, the pressure to provide food necessary for survival might ensure that males, who were most often the hunter-providers, would develop greater spatial skills than females.

Criticisms of the Evolutionary Approach The evolutionary account of sex-differences and gender typing has been roundly criticized. It applies mainly to sex differences that are consistent across cultures and largely ignores differences that are limited to particular cultures or historical periods (Blakemore, Berenbaum, & Liben, in press). What's more, proponents of the **social-roles hypothesis** have argued that psychological sex differences do not reflect biologically evolved dispositions. Instead, they emerge because of variations in (1) roles that cultures *assign* to men and women (provider versus homemaker, for example) and in (2) agreed-upon socialization practices to promote traits in boys and girls (assertion versus nurturance, for example) to properly enact these roles (Eagly, Wood, & Diekman, 2000). Clearly, proponents of the social-roles viewpoint are not critics of the concept of natural selection for such attributes as good spatial skills among our hunter-gatherer ancestors. Yet they might also argue that unless the selected genes that influence such attributes as spatial skills are located on the Y chromosome that all females lack, they should be transmitted equally to *both sons and daughters,* meaning that neither sex should have a genetic advantage for this attribute. The implication, then, is that males might develop spatial skills to a greater extent than females by virtue of their hunting for food (that is, spatial activities stemming from a socially assigned role) rather than any biological evolved difference between themselves and females.

Today, most biologically oriented theorists take a softer, less essentialist stance, arguing that biological and social influences interact to determine a person's behaviors and role preferences. What biological differences between the sexes might be important? For one, males have a Y chromosome and hence some genes that all females lack. But perhaps far more important is that the sexes clearly differ in hormonal balance, with males having higher concentrations of androgens (including testosterone) and lower levels of estrogen than females do. According to the best-known interactive theory of gender typing, these biological correlates of gender, in concert with important social influences, steer boys and girls toward different patterns of behavior and gender roles. Let's now consider this influential theory.

Money and Ehrhardt's Biosocial Theory

Overview of Sexual Differentiation and Gender-Role Development John Money and Anke Ehrhardt (1972) describe a number of critical episodes or events that will affect a person's eventual preference for the masculine or the feminine gender role. The first critical event occurs at conception as the child inherits either an X or a Y chromosome from the father. Over the next six weeks, the developing embryo has only an undifferentiated gonad, and the sex chromosomes determine whether this structure becomes the male testes or the female ovaries. If a Y chromosome is present, the embryo develops testes; otherwise ovaries will form.

These newly formed gonads then determine the outcome of episode 2. The testes of a male embryo secrete two hormones—*testosterone*, which stimulates the development of a male internal reproductive system, and *mullerian inhibiting substance* (MIS), which inhibits

---

social-roles hypothesis
the notion that psychological differences between the sexes and other gender-role stereotypes are created and maintained by differences in *socially assigned* roles that men and women play (rather than attributable to biologically evolved dispositions).

the development of female organs. In the absence of these hormones, the embryo develops the internal reproductive system of a female.

At a third critical point, three to four months after conception, continuing secretion of testosterone by the testes normally leads to the growth of a penis and scrotum. If testosterone is absent (as in normal females), or if the male fetus has inherited a rare recessive disorder, called **testicular feminization syndrome (TFS),** which makes his body insensitive to male sex hormones, female external genitalia (labia and clitoris) will form. Testosterone also alters the development of the brain and nervous system. For example, it signals the male brain to stop secreting hormones in a cyclical pattern so that males do not experience menstrual cycles at puberty.

Once a child is born, *social* factors immediately come into play. Parents and other people label and begin to react to the child based on the appearance of his or her genitals. If one's genitals are abnormal so that he or she is mislabeled as a member of the other sex, this incorrect label can affect his or her future development. For example, if a biological male were consistently labeled and treated as a girl (as a boy with TFS syndrome and female external genitalia might be), he would, by about age 2½ to 3, acquire the gender identity (though not the biological characteristics) of a girl. Finally, biological factors enter the scene again at puberty, when large quantities of hormones are released, stimulating the growth of the reproductive system, the appearance of secondary sex characteristics, and the development of sexual urges. These events, in combination with one's earlier self-concept as a male or a female, provide the basis for an adult gender identity and gender-role preference (see Figure 8.4).

Evidence for Biological Influences on Gender-Role Development

How much influence *do* biological factors have on the behavior of males and females? To answer this question, we must consider what investigators have learned about genetic and hormonal influences.

Genetic Influences   Genetic factors may contribute to some sex differences in personality, cognitive abilities, and social behavior. Corrine Hutt (1972), for example, suspects that several of the developmental disorders more commonly seen among boys may be **X-linked recessive traits** for which their mother is a carrier (genetic [XX] females

testicular feminization syndrome (TFS)
a genetic anomaly in which a male fetus is insensitive to the effects of male sex hormones and will develop female-like external genitalia.

X-linked recessive trait
an attribute determined by recessive gene that appears only on X chromosomes; because the gene determining these characteristics is recessive (that is, dominated by other genes that might appear at the same location on X chromosomes), such characteristics are more common among males, who have only one X chromosome; also called *sex-linked trait*.

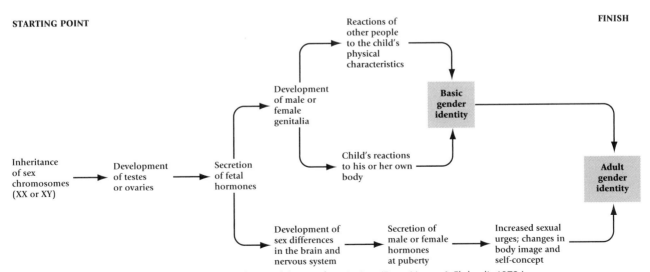

Figure 8.4   Critical events in Money and Ehrhardt's biosocial theory of sex typing. (From Money & Ehrhardt, 1972.)

Photo 8.4 Girls who often play with visual/spatial toys tend to perform better on tests of spatial ability.

timing of puberty effect
the finding that people who reach puberty late preform better on visual/spatial tasks than those who mature early.

would have to inherit a recessive gene from each parent to show the same disorders). Furthermore, **timing of puberty,** a biological variable regulated in part by our genotypes, has a slight effect on visual/spatial performances. Both boys and girls who mature *late* tend to outperform early maturers of their own sex on some visual/spatial tasks, allegedly because slow maturation promotes increasing specialization of the brain's right hemisphere, which serves spatial functions (see Newcombe & Dubas, 1987). However, later research indicates that the spatial performances of both boys and girls are more heavily influenced by their *previous involvement* in spatial activities and their *self-concepts* than by the timing of puberty (Levine et al., 1999; Newcombe & Dubas 1992; Signorella, Jamison, & Krupa, 1989). Specifically, it appears that having a strong masculine self-concept and ample experience with spatial toys and activities will foster the growth of spatial skills in both boys and girls, whereas having restricted spatial experiences and a feminine self-concept seems to inhibit spatial abilities.

How closely are our masculine and feminine self-concepts related to the genes that we have inherited? Results from several behavioral genetics studies of adolescent twins suggest that genotype accounts for about 50 percent of the variability in people's masculine self-concepts but only 0–20 percent of the variability in their feminine self-concepts (Loehlin, 1992; Mitchell, Baker, & Jacklin, 1989). What's more, a recent twin study found moderate genetic and moderate shared environmental influences on the gender-typed toy and activity preferences of 3- to 4-year-old boys and girls (Iervolino et al., 2002). So even though genes determine our biological sex and clearly have some influence on the outcome of gender typing, it appears that much of the variability in people's gender-typed behaviors and their masculine and feminine self-concepts is attributable to environmental influence.

Hormonal Influences   Biological influences on development are much more apparent in studies of children who have been exposed to the "wrong" hormones during the prenatal period. Before the consequences were known, some mothers who had problems carrying pregnancies to term were given drugs containing progestin, which are converted to the male hormone testosterone by the body. Other children with a condition known as **congenital adrenal hyperplasia (CAH)** have a genetic defect which causes their adrenal glands to produce unusually high levels of androgen from the prenatal period onward. These conditions usually have no effect on males; but female fetuses are often masculinized so that, despite their XX genetic endowment and female internal organs, they are often born with external

congenital adrenal hyperplasia (CAH)
a genetic anomaly that causes one's adrenal glands to produce unusually high levels of androgen from the prenatal period onward; often has masculinizing effects on female fetuses.

genitalia that resemble those of a boy (for example, a large clitoris that looks like a penis and fused labia that resemble a scrotum).

Money and Ehrhardt (1972; Ehrhardt & Baker, 1974) have followed several of these **androgenized females** whose external organs were surgically altered and who were then raised as girls. Compared with their sisters and other girls, many more androgenized girls were tomboys who often played with boys and who preferred boys' toys and activities to traditionally feminine pursuits (see also Berenbaum & Snyder, 1995; Servin et al., 2003). In fact, this strong preference for masculine toys and activities persists over time, even when the mothers of these girls have strongly encouraged more girl-typical play and have praised them lavishly for playing with feminine toys (Pasterski et al., 2005). As adolescents, androgenized girls began dating somewhat later than other girls and felt that marriage should be delayed until they had established their careers. A high proportion (37 percent) described themselves as homosexual or bisexual (Money, 1985; see also Berenbaum, 2002). Androgenized females also perform better than most girls and women on tests of spatial ability, further suggesting that early exposure to male hormones may have "masculinizing" effects on a female fetus's brain (Berenbaum, 1998; Hines, 2004). Indeed, one recent Swedish study showed a dose-related effect: Girls with more severe cases of CAH (and thus greater prenatal exposure to male sex hormones) showed the strongest interest in masculine toys and careers (Servin et al., 2003). Although a skeptic might wonder whether other family members had reacted to the girls' abnormal genitalia early in life, treating those girls more like boys, interviews with the girls' parents suggested that they had not (Ehrhardt & Baker, 1974). Even *normal* variations in girls' exposure to testosterone (produced by their mothers) prior to their birth are associated with girls' play behavior at age 3½: Girls exposed to high-normal levels of testosterone before birth show stronger preferences for masculine toys and activities than do female age-mates exposed to lower levels of testosterone (Hines et al., 2002; but see Knickmeyer et al., 2005, for a failure to replicate this finding). So we must seriously consider the possibilities that (1) some differences between males and females may be hormonally mediated and may reflect the impact of hormones on the organization of the brain (Cahill, 2005), thus implying that (2) heavy prenatal exposure to male sex hormones can influence the attitudes, interests, and activities of human females.

androgenized females females who develop male-like external genitalia because of exposure to male sex hormones during the prenatal period.

Evidence for Social-Labeling Influences   Although biological forces may steer boys and girls toward different activities and interests, Money and Ehrhardt (1972) insist that social-labeling influences are also important—so important, in fact, that they can modify or even *reverse* biological predispositions. Indeed, some of the evidence for this provocative claim comes from Money's own work with androgenized girls.

Recall that Money's androgenized girls were born with the internal reproductive organs of a normal female even though their external genitalia resembled a penis and scrotum. In the past, some androgenized girls were labeled boys at birth and raised as such until their abnormalities were detected. Money (1965) reports that the discovery and correction of this condition (by surgery and gender reassignment) presents few if any adjustment problems, provided that the sex change occurs *before age 18 months*. But after age 3, gender reassignment is exceedingly difficult because these genetic females have experienced prolonged masculine gender typing and have already labeled themselves as boys. These data led Money to conclude that there is a "critical period" between 18 months and 3 years of age for the establishment of gender identity. As illustrated in Box 8.3, it may be more accurate to call the first three years a *sensitive* period, for other investigators have claimed that it is possible under certain circumstances to assume a new identity later in adolescence. Nevertheless, Money's findings indicate that early social labeling and gender-role socialization can play a very prominent role in determining a child's gender identity and role preferences.

Box 8.3 Current Controversies

Is Biology Destiny?

When biological sex and social labeling conflict, which wins? Consider the case of a male identical twin whose penis was damaged beyond repair during circumcision (Money & Tucker, 1975). After seeking medical advice and considering the alternatives, the parents agreed to a surgical castration to remove all outward evidence of their son's maleness. After the operation, the family began to raise this child as a girl, changing her hairstyle, dressing her in frilly blouses, dresses, and the like, purchasing feminine toys for her to play with, and teaching such feminine behaviors as sitting to urinate. By age 5, the girl twin was described by Money as very different from her genetically identical brother. Allegedly, she knew she was a girl and was far neater and daintier than her brother. Here, then, was a case in which assigned sex and gender-role socialization seemed to overcome biological predispositions. Or did they?

Milton Diamond and Keith Sigmundson (1997) followed up on this "Bruce" turned "Brenda" and found that the story had a twist ending (see also Colapinto, 2000, for a fascinating documentary on this case, including excerpts from interviews with the individual, her parents, brother, and peers). Almost from the beginning "Brenda" (and her twin) reported that she was never really comfortable with feminine toys and clothing. Brenda preferred her brother's playthings and loved to take things apart to see how they worked. Not knowing of her birth as a male, Brenda at age 10 suspected she was not really a girl. Not only did she have "feelings" for girls and often had fistfights with boys, but "I thought I was a freak or something. . . . But I didn't want to admit it" (pp. 299–300). Being rejected by peers for her somewhat masculine looks also took its toll, as did continued pressures to act more feminine and to submit to surgery to construct a vagina and complete her feminization. Finally, at age 14 and after years of inner turmoil and suicidal thinking, Brenda had had it; she refused vaginal surgery and quit taking female hormones, choosing instead to have a mastectomy, take male hormones, and receive surgery to construct a penis. What emerged was a handsome young man (now "David") who became very popular, dated girls, married at age 25, and reports that he is thrilled with his hard-won identity as a man (Colapinto, 2000). Perhaps we should back off from the notion that early gender-role socialization is all that matters. Biology matters too.

A second source of evidence that biology matters is a study of 18 biological males in the Dominican Republic who had a genetic condition (TFS syndrome) that made them insensitive prenatally to the effects of male hormones (Imperato-McGinley et al., 1979). They began life with ambiguous genitals and were said to have been labeled and raised as girls. However, under the influence of male hormones produced at puberty, they sprouted beards and became masculine in appearance. How, in light of Money and Ehrhardt's critical-period hypothesis, could a person adjust to becoming a man after leading an entire childhood as a girl?

Amazingly, 16 of these 18 individuals seemed able to accept their late conversion from female to male and to adopt masculine lifestyles, including the establishment of heterosexual relationships. One retained a female identity and gender role, and the remaining individual switched to a male gender identity but still dressed as a female. Clearly, this study also casts doubt on the notion that socialization during the first three years is absolutely critical to later gender-role development. Instead, it suggests that hormonal influences may be more important than social influences.

However, Imperato-McGinley's conclusions have been challenged (Ehrhardt, 1985). Little information was reported about

Bruce-Brenda-David

Reuters/Corbis

how these individuals were raised, and it is quite possible that Dominican parents, knowing TFS syndrome was common in their society, treated these girls-turned-boys differently from other "girls" when they were young. Furthermore, the girls-turned-boys had genitals that were not completely normal in appearance, and the practice of river bathing in Dominican culture almost certainly means that these youngsters compared themselves to normal girls (and boys) and may have recognized early that they were "different." So these children may not have received an exclusively feminine upbringing and *may never have fully committed themselves to being girls*. Nor should we automatically assume that their later incorporation of the masculine role was due to hormones. One study of TFS males raised as females among the Sambia of New Guinea found that *social pressures*—namely, the argument that they could not bear children—is what appeared most responsible for the gender switches that occurred after puberty (Herdt & Davidson, 1988).

Finally, another Canadian boy, whose penis was damaged during circumcision and who was raised as a girl from 7 months of age, has now reached adulthood and continues to live quite comfortably within her *female* gender identity (Bradley et al., 1998). Clearly, biology is not destiny and social influences are important in shaping one's gender identity.

What studies like these of individuals with genital abnormalities appear to teach us is this: We are predisposed by our biology to develop as males or females; the first three years of life are a *sensitive period* perhaps, but not a critical period, for the establishment of gender identity; and *neither* biology nor social labeling can fully account for gender-role development.

Photo 8.5 Gender-role behaviors are often specific to one's culture. Like many Peruvian boys, this youngster routinely washes clothes and attends to household tasks.

Cultural Influences   The fact that most societies promote instrumental traits in males and expressive traits in females has led some theorists to conclude that traditional gender roles are part of the natural order of things—a product of our bioevolutionary history (Buss, 1995, 2000). Yet there are sizable differences across cultures in what people expect of boys and girls. In Tahiti, for example, few distinctions are made among males and females; even the native language lacks gender pronouns, and most names are used for both boys and girls (Wade & Tavris, 1999). And consider Margaret Mead's (1935) study of three tribal societies in New Guinea. *Both* males and females among the Arapesh were taught to be cooperative, nonaggressive, and sensitive to the needs of others. This behavioral profile would be considered "expressive" or "feminine" in Western cultures. By contrast, *both* men and women of the Mundugumor tribe were expected to be assertive, aggressive, and emotionally unresponsive in their interpersonal relationships—a masculine pattern of behavior by Western standards. Finally, the Tchambuli displayed a pattern of gender-role development *opposite* to that of Western societies: Males were passive, emotionally dependent, and socially sensitive, whereas females were dominant, independent, and assertive. So members of these three tribes developed in accordance with the gender roles that were *socially* prescribed by their culture—none of which matched the female/expressive–male/instrumental pattern seen in Western societies. Clearly, social forces contribute heavily to gender typing.

In sum, Money and Ehrhardt's biosocial theory stresses the importance of early biological developments that influence how parents and other social agents label a child at birth and that possibly also affect behavior more directly. However, the theory also holds that whether children are socialized as boys or girls strongly influences their gender-role development—in short, that biological and social forces *interact*. But how, exactly, do they interact?

A Psychobiosocial Viewpoint   Diane Halpern (1997) has offered a **psychobiosocial model** to explain how nature and nurture might jointly influence the development of many gender-typed attributes. Halpern agrees with Money and Ehrhardt that prenatal exposure to male or female hormones initially influences the organization of male and female brains

psychobiosocial model perspective on nature/nurture interactions specifying that specific early experiences affect the organization of the brain, which in turn influences one's responsiveness to similar experiences in the future.

in ways that might make boys, for example, somewhat more receptive to spatial activities and girls somewhat more susceptible to quiet verbal exchanges. These heightened sensitivities, in concert with parents' beliefs about the kinds of experiences most appropriate for boys and for girls, means that boys are likely to (and actually do) receive a richer array of spatial experiences than girls do, whereas girls will be exposed more often to verbal play activities (Bornstein et al., 1999).

Drawing on recent advances in the field of cognitive neuroscience, Halpern then proposes that the different early experiences that boys and girls have will influence the neural pathways laid down in their immature and highly *plastic* (that, is changeable) brains. Although the genetic code imposes some constraints on brain development, it does not provide specific "wiring" instructions, and the precise architecture of the brain is heavily influenced by the early experiences one has (Johnson, 1998). So according to Halpern (1997), boys, who receive more early spatial experiences than girls do, may develop a richer array of neural pathways in areas of the brain's right cerebral hemisphere that serve spatial functions, which in turn may make them ever more receptive to spatial activities and to acquiring spatial skills. By contrast, girls may develop a richer array of neural interconnections in areas of the brain's left cerebral hemisphere serving verbal functions, thereby becoming ever more receptive to verbal activities and to acquiring verbal skills. From a psychobiosocial perspective then, nature and nurture feed on each other and are a false dichotomy. In Halpern's words, " . . . biology and environment are as inseparable as conjoined twins who share a common heart" (p. 1097).

What both biosocial theory and the psychobiosocial model do *not* do is to specify the precise social processes that contribute most heavily to children's emerging gender identities and gender-typed patterns of behavior. Let's turn now to the social theories of gender typing, the first of which was Sigmund Freud's psychoanalytic approach.

Freud's Psychoanalytic Theory

Recall from Chapter 2 that Freud thought that sexuality (the sex instinct) was inborn. However, he believed that one's preference for a particular gender role emerges during the **phallic stage** of psychosexual development as children begin to emulate and to **identify** with their same-sex parent. Specifically, Freud claimed that a 3- to 6-year-old boy will internalize masculine attributes and behaviors when he is forced to identify with his father as a means of renouncing his incestuous desire for his mother, reducing his **castration anxiety** and thus resolving his **Oedipus complex.** However, Freud believed that gender typing is more difficult for a young girl, who lacks a penis, already feels castrated, and will experience no overriding fear that would compel her to strongly identify with her mother and resolve her **Electra complex.** Why, then, would a girl ever develop a preference for the feminine role? Freud offered several suggestions, one of which was that the object of a girl's affection, her father, was likely to encourage her feminine behavior—an act that increases the attractiveness of the mother, who serves as the girl's model of femininity. So by trying to please her father (or to prepare for relationships with other males after she recognizes the implausibility of possessing her father), a girl should be motivated to incorporate her mother's feminine attributes and will eventually become gender-typed (Freud, 1924/1961).

Evaluating Freud's Theory Although children are rapidly learning gender stereotypes and developing gender-typed playmate and activity preferences at roughly the ages Freud says they should, his psychoanalytic theory of gender typing has not fared well at all. Many 4- to 6-year-olds are so ignorant about differences between male and female genitalia that it is hard to see how most boys could fear castration or how most girls could feel castrated as Freud says they do (Bem, 1989; Katcher, 1955). Furthermore, Freud assumed that a boy's identification with his father is based on fear; but most researchers find that boys

phallic stage
Freud's third stage of psychosexual development (from 3 to 6 years of age) in which children gratify the sex instinct by fondling their genitals and developing an incestuous desire for the parent of the other sex.

identification
Freud's term for the child's tendency to emulate another person, usually the same-sex parent.

castration anxiety
in Freud's theory, a young boy's fear that his father will castrate him as punishment for his rivalrous conduct.

Oedipus complex
Freud's term for the conflict that 3- to 6-year-old boys were said to experience when they develop an incestuous desire for their mothers and a jealous and hostile rivalry with their fathers.

Electra complex
female version of the Oedipus complex, in which a 3- to 6-year-old girl was thought to envy her father for possessing a penis and would choose him as a sex object in the hope that he would share with her this valuable organ that she lacked.

identify more strongly with fathers who are warm and nurturant rather than overly punitive and threatening (Hetherington & Frankie, 1967). Finally, studies of parent/child resemblances reveal that school-age children and adolescents are not all that similar psychologically to either parent (Maccoby & Jacklin, 1974). Clearly, these findings are damaging to the Freudian notion that children acquire important personality traits by identifying with the same-sex parent.

Let's now consider the social-learning interpretation of gender typing to see whether this approach looks any more promising.

Social-Learning Theory

According to social-learning theorists such as Albert Bandura (1989; Bussey & Bandura, 1999), children acquire their gender identities and gender-role preferences in two ways. First, through **direct tuition** (or *differential reinforcement*), children are encouraged and rewarded for gender-appropriate behaviors and are punished or otherwise discouraged for behaviors considered more appropriate for members of the other sex. Second, through *observational learning,* children adopt the attitudes and behaviors of a variety of same-sex models.

direct tuition
teaching young children how to behave by reinforcing "appropriate" behaviors and by punishing or otherwise discouraging inappropriate conduct.

Direct Tuition of Gender Roles   Are parents actively involved in teaching boys how to be boys and girls how to be girls? Yes, indeed (Leaper, Anderson, & Sanders, 1998; Lytton & Rommney, 1991), and their shaping of gender-typed behaviors begins rather early. Beverly Fagot and Mary Leinbach (1989), for example, found that parents are already encouraging gender-appropriate activities and discouraging cross-gender play during the second year of life, *before* children have acquired their basic gender identities or display clear preferences for male or female activities. By age 20–24 months, daughters are consistently reinforced for dancing, dressing up (as women), following parents around, asking for help, and playing with dolls; and they are generally discouraged from manipulating objects, running, jumping, and climbing. By contrast, sons are often reprimanded for such "feminine" behaviors as doll play or seeking help and are actively encouraged to play with masculine items such as blocks, trucks, and push-and-pull toys that require large muscle activity (Fagot, 1978).

Are children influenced by the "gender curriculum" their parents provide? They certainly are! In fact, parents who show the clearest patterns of differential reinforcement have children who are relatively quick to (1) label themselves as boys or girls, (2) develop strong gender-typed toy and activity preferences, and (3) acquire an understanding of gender stereotypes (Fagot & Leinbach, 1989; Fagot, Leinbach, & O'Boyle, 1992). And fathers are even more likely than mothers to encourage "gender-typed" behaviors and to discourage behavior considered more appropriate for the other sex (Leve & Fagot, 1997; Lytton & Romney, 1991). So it seems that children's earliest preferences for gender-typed toys and activities may well result from their parents' (particularly fathers') successful attempts to reinforce these interests.

Throughout the preschool period, parents become less and less inclined to carefully monitor and differentially reinforce their children's gender-typed activities (Fagot & Hagan, 1991; Lytton & Romney, 1991). Why? Because many other factors conspire to maintain these interests, not the least of which is the behavior of siblings and same-sex peers (Beal, 1994; McHale, Crouter, & Tucker, 1999). Even before they have established their basic gender identities, 2-year-old boys will often belittle or disrupt each other for playing with girl toys or with girls, and 2-year-old girls are quite critical of other girls who choose to play with boys (Fagot, 1985a). And there is evidence that these early peer influences are important, for the greater the amount of time that preschool children spend with same-sex peers, the more gender-typed they become in their behaviors and toy preferences 6 months later (Martin & Fabes, 2001). So one's toddler playmates are already beginning to differentially reinforce gender-typed attitudes and behaviors and will continue to do so throughout childhood (McHale, Kim et al., 2004), even as parents are becoming somewhat less likely to do so.

Observational Learning   According to Bandura (1989), children acquire many of their gender-typed attributes and interests by observing and imitating a variety of same-sex models. The assumption is that boys, for example, will see which toys, activities, and behaviors are "for boys" and girls will learn which activities and behaviors are "for girls" by selectively attending to and imitating a variety of *same-sex* models, including peers, teachers, older siblings, and media personalities, as well as their mothers or their fathers (Fagot, Rodgers, & Leinbach, 2000).

Yet there is some question as to just how important *same-sex* modeling influences are during the *preschool* period, for researchers often find that 3- to 6-year-olds learn from models of both sexes (Leaper, 2000; Ruble & Martin, 1998). For example, children of employed mothers (who play the *masculine* instrumental role) or of fathers who routinely perform such *feminine* household tasks as cooking, cleaning, and child care are less aware of gender stereotypes than children of more traditional parents are (Sabattini & Leaper, 2004; Turner & Gervai, 1995). Similarly, boys with sisters and girls with brothers have less gender-typed activity preferences than children who have only same-sex siblings (Colley et al., 1996; Rust et al., 2000). What's more, John Masters and his associates (1979) found that preschool children are much more concerned about the sex-appropriateness of the *behavior* they are observing than the sex of the model who displays it. Four- to 5-year-old boys, for example, will play with objects labeled "boys' toys" even after they have seen a girl playing with them. However, these youngsters are reluctant to play with "girls' toys" that boy models have played with earlier, and they think that other boys would also shun objects labeled as girls' toys (Martin, Eisenbud, & Rose, 1995). So children's toy choices are affected more by the labels attached to the toys than by the sex of the child who served as a model. But once they recognize that gender is an unchanging aspect of their personalities (at age 5 to 7), children do begin to attend more selectively to same-sex models and are now likely to avoid toys and activities that other-sex models seem to enjoy (Frey & Ruble, 1992; Ruble, Ballaban, & Cooper, 1981).

Media Influences   Not only do children learn by observing other children and adult models with whom they interact, but they also learn about gender roles from reading stories and watching television. Although sexism in children's books has declined over the past 50 years, male characters are still more likely than female characters to engage in active, instrumental pursuits such as climbing, riding bikes, or making things, whereas female characters are often depicted as passive and dependent individuals who spend much of their time playing quietly indoors and creating problems that require masculine solutions (Diekman & Murnen, 2004; Turner-Bowker, 1996). It is similar in the world of television. Males are usually portrayed as influential individuals who work at a profession, whereas females, particularly if they are married women, are often depicted as passive, emotional creatures who support a prominent male character, manage a home, or work at "feminine" occupations such as nursing (Ogletree et al., 2004; Signorielli & Kahlenberg, 2001). Apparently, children are influenced by these highly traditional role portrayals because those who watch a lot of television are more likely to prefer gender-typed toys and activities and to hold highly stereotyped views of men and women than their classmates who watch little television (McGhee & Frueh, 1980; Signorielli & Lears, 1992).

In sum, there is a lot of evidence that differential reinforcement and observational learning contribute to gender-role development. However, social-learning theorists have often portrayed children as *passive pawns* in the process: Parents, peers, and TV characters show them what to do and reinforce them for doing it. Might this perspective miss something, namely the child's *own* contribution to gender-role socialization? Consider, for example, that children do not always receive gender-stereotyped Christmas presents because their sexist parents force these objects upon them. Many parents who would rather buy gender-neutral or educational toys end up "giving in" to sons who beg for trucks or daughters who want tea sets (Robinson & Morris, 1986).

Kohlberg's Cognitive-Developmental Theory

Lawrence Kohlberg (1966) has proposed a cognitive theory of gender typing that is quite different from the other theories we have considered and helps to explain why boys and girls adopt traditional gender roles even when their parents may not want them to. Kohlberg's major themes are:

1. Gender-role development depends on cognitive development; children must acquire certain understandings about gender before they will be influenced by their social experiences.

2. Children *actively socialize themselves;* they are not merely passive pawns of social influence.

According to both psychoanalytic theory and social-learning theory, children first learn to do "boy" or "girl" things because their parents encourage these activities; then they come to identify with or habitually imitate same-sex models, thereby acquiring a stable gender identity. By contrast, Kohlberg suggests that children *first* establish a stable gender identity and then *actively* seek out same-sex models and other information to learn how to act like a boy or a girl. To Kohlberg, it's not "I'm treated like a boy; therefore, I must be one" (social-learning position). It's more like "Hey, I'm a boy; therefore, I'd better do everything I can do find out how to behave like one" (cognitive—self-socialization position).

Kohlberg believes that children pass through the following three stages as they acquire a mature understanding of what it means to be a male or a female:

1. **Basic gender identity.** By age 3, children have labeled themselves as boys or girls.

2. **Gender stability**. Somewhat later, gender is perceived as *stable over time*. Boys invariably become men and girls grow up to be women.

3. **Gender consistency.** The gender concept is complete when the child realizes that one's sex is also *stable across situations*. Five- to 7-year-olds who have reached this stage are no longer fooled by appearances. They know, for example, that one's gender cannot be altered by cross-dressing or taking up cross-sex activities.

When do children become motivated to socialize themselves—that is, to seek out same-sex models and learn how to act like males and females? According to Kohlberg, self-socialization begins only after children reach *gender consistency*. So for Kohlberg, a mature understanding of gender (1) instigates true gender typing and (2) is the *cause* rather than the consequence of attending to same-sex models.

Studies conducted in more than 20 different cultures reveal that preschool children do proceed through Kohlberg's three stages of gender identity in the sequence he describes and that attainment of gender consistency (or conservation of gender) is clearly associated with other relevant aspects of cognitive development, such as the conservation of liquids and mass (Munroe, Shimmin, & Munroe, 1984; Szkrybalo & Ruble, 1999). Furthermore, children who have achieved gender consistency display more gender-stereotypic play preferences (Warin, 2000) and begin to pay more attention to same-sex models on television (Luecke-Aleska et al., 1995); and boys now clearly favor novel toys that male models prefer to those that female models like—even when the toys they are passing on are the

basic gender identity
the stage of gender identity in which the child first labels the self as a boy or a girl.

gender stability
the stage of gender identity in which the child recognizes that gender is stable over time.

gender consistency
the stage of gender identity in which the child recognizes that a person's gender is invariant despite changes in the person's activities or appearance (also known as gender constancy).

more attractive objects (Frey & Ruble, 1992). So children with a mature gender identity (especially boys) often play it safe and select the toy or activity that other members of their gender view as more appropriate for them.

Criticisms of Kohlberg's Theory   The major problem with Kohlberg's theory is that gender typing is well underway before the child acquires a mature gender identity. We have seen, for example, that 2-year-old boys prefer masculine toys before they have achieved a basic gender identity and that 3-year-olds of each sex have learned many gender-role stereotypes and already prefer same-sex activities and playmates long before they begin to attend more selectively to same sex models. Furthermore, we've noted that gender reassignment can be exceedingly difficult after children reach age 3 (Kohlberg's basic identity stage) and have initially categorized themselves as boys or girls. In fact, one's level of gender identity may rest as much on social experience as on cognitive development, for even 3- and 4-year-olds who have often seen members of the other sex naked may display gender consistency on gender identity tests (Bem, 1989). What's more, the rigidity of children's thinking about gender and gender-role stereotypes appears to be more closely related to their level of gender stability (rather than gender consistency), and once they reach gender consistency, they actually become more *flexible* in their thinking about gender stereotypes (see Ruble, Martin, & Berenbaum, 2006; Ruble et al., 2007). So Kohlberg badly overstates the case in arguing that a mature understanding of gender is necessary for gender typing to begin. As we will see in the next section, only a rudimentary understanding of gender permits children to acquire gender stereotypes and develop strong gender-typed toy and activity preferences.

Gender Schema Theory

Carol Martin and Charles Halverson (1981, 1987) have proposed a somewhat different cognitive theory of gender typing (actually, an information-processing theory) that appears quite promising. Like Kohlberg, Martin and Halverson believe that children are intrinsically motivated to acquire interests, values, and behaviors that are consistent with their "boy" or "girl" self-images. But unlike Kohlberg, they argue that this "self-socialization" begins as soon as the child acquires a *basic gender identity* at age 2½ or 3 and is well underway by age 6 to 7, when the child achieves gender consistency.

According to Martin and Halverson's "gender schema" theory, establishment of a basic gender identity motivates a child to learn about the sexes and to incorporate this information into **gender schemas**—that is, organized sets of beliefs and expectations about males and females that will influence the kinds of information the child attends to, elaborates, and remembers. First, children construct a simple **"in-group/out-group schema"** that allows them to classify some objects, behaviors, and roles as "for boys" and others as "for girls" (for example, trucks are for boys; dolls are for girls; girls can cry but boys should not, and so on). This is the kind of information that researchers normally tap when studying children's knowledge of gender stereotypes. And this initial categorization of objects and activities clearly affects children's thinking. In one research program, 4- and 5-year-olds were shown unfamiliar gender-neutral toys (for example, spinning bells, a magnet stand), were told that these objects were either "for boys" or "for girls," and were asked whether they and other boys or girls would like them. Children clearly relied on the labels to guide their thinking. Boys, for example, liked "boy" objects better than girls did, and children assumed that other boys would also like these objects better than other girls would. Just the opposite pattern of reasoning was observed when *these same objects* were labeled as "for girls." As Martin & Ruble (2004) put it, "children are gender detectives who search for cues about gender—who should or should not engage in a particular activity, who can play with whom, and why boys and girls are different" (p. 67). Thus, highly attractive toys will soon lose their

gender schemas
organized sets of beliefs and expectations about males and females that guide information processing.

"in-group/out-group" schema
one's general knowledge of the mannerisms, roles, activities, and behaviors that characterize males and females.

luster if they are labeled as for the other sex (Martin, Eisenbud, & Rose, 1995).

In addition, children are said to construct an **own-sex schema**, which consists of detailed plans of action that they will need to perform various gender-consistent behaviors and enact a gender role. So a girl who has a basic gender identity might first learn that sewing is "for girls" and building model airplanes is "for boys." Then, because she is a girl and wants to act consistently with her own self-concept, she may gather a great deal of information about sewing to add to her own-sex schema, while largely ignoring information about building model airplanes (see also Figure 8.5). To test this notion, 4- to 9-year-olds were given boxes of gender-neutral objects (for example, burglar alarms, pizza cutters) and told that these objects were either "boy" items or "girl" items (Bradbard et al., 1986). As predicted, boys subsequently explored "boy" items more than girls did, whereas girls explored more than boys when the objects were described as things girls enjoy. One week later, boys recalled much more in-depth information about "boy items" than girls did, whereas girls recalled more than boys about these very same objects if they had been labeled "girl"

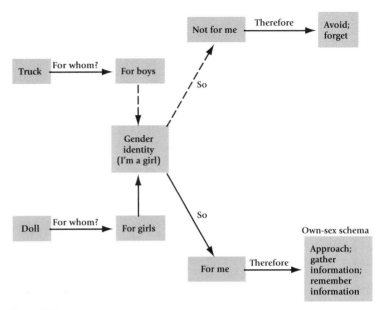

Figure 8.5

Gender schema theory in action. A young girl classifies new information according to an "in-group/out-group schema" as either "for boys" or "for girls." Information about boys' toys and activities is ignored, but information about toys and activities for girls is relevant to the self and so is added to an ever-larger "own-sex schema." (Adapted from Martin & Halverson, 1987.)

items. If children's information-gathering efforts are consistently guided by their own-sex schemas in this way, we can easily see how boys and girls might acquire very different stores of knowledge and develop different interests and competencies as they mature.

Once formed, gender schemas "structure" experience by providing a framework for processing social information. The idea here is that children are likely to encode and remember information consistent with their gender schemas and to forget schema-inconsistent information or to otherwise distort it so that it becomes more consistent with their stereotypes (Liben & Signorella, 1993; Martin & Halverson, 1983), especially if they have reached age 6 to 7, when their own stereotyped knowledge and preferences have crystallized and are especially strong (Welch-Ross & Schmidt, 1996). Support for this idea was presented in Box 8.2; recall that children who heard stories in which actors performed gender-atypical behaviors (for example, a girl chopping wood) tended to recall the action but to alter the scene to conform to their gender stereotypes (saying that a boy had been chopping). Surely these strong tendencies to forget or to distort counterstereotypic information help to explain why unfounded beliefs about males and females are so slow to die.

In sum, Martin and Halverson's gender schema theory is an interesting "new look" at the gender-typing process. Not only does this model describe how gender-role stereotypes might originate very early and persist over time, but it also indicates how these emerging "gender schemas" might contribute to the development of strong gender-role preferences and gender-typed behaviors long before a child may realize that gender is an unchanging attribute.

own-sex schema
detailed knowledge or plans of action that enable a person to perform gender-consistent activities and to enact his or her gender role.

An Integrative Theory

Biological, social-learning, cognitive-developmental, and gender schema perspectives have each contributed in important ways to our understanding of sex differences and gender-role development (Ruble, Martin, & Berenbaum, 2006; Serbin, Powlishta, & Gulko, 1993).

In fact, the processes that different theories emphasize seem to be especially important at different periods. Biological theories account for the major biological developments that occur before birth—the events that induce people to label the child as a boy or a girl and to treat him or her accordingly. The differential reinforcement process that social-learning theorists emphasize seems to account rather well for early gender typing: Young children display gender-consistent behaviors largely because other people encourage these activities and will often discourage behaviors considered more appropriate for members of the other sex. And as Diane Halperin proposes in her psychobiosocial theory, encouraging gender-typed activities and experiences can even affect the ways that boys' and girls' brains are wired, making them even more responsive to different kinds of stimulation.

As a result of early socialization and the growth of categorization skills, 2½- to 3-year-olds acquire a basic gender identity and begin to construct *gender schemas* which tell them (1) what boys and girls are like and (2) how they, as boys and girls, are supposed to think and act. And when they finally understand, at age 6 or 7, that their gender will never change, children begin to pay more and more attention to same-sex models to decide which attitudes, activities, interests, and mannerisms are most appropriate for members of their own sex (Kohlberg's viewpoint). Of course, summarizing developments in an integrative model such as this one (see Table 8.5 for an overview) does not mean that biological forces play no further role after the child is born or that differential reinforcement ceases to affect development once the child acquires a basic gender identity. But an integrative theorist would emphasize that from age 3 on, children are active, *self-socializers* who will try very hard to

Table 8.5 An overview of the gender-typing process from the perspective of an integrative theorist

Developmental Period	Events and Outcomes	Most Pertinent Theory(ies)
Prenatal period	The fetus develops male or female genitalia, which others will react to once the child is born.	Biosocial
Birth to 3 years	Parents and other companions label the child a boy or a girl, frequently remind the child of his or her gender, and begin to encourage gender-consistent behavior while discouraging cross-sex activities. As a result of these social experiences, the neural developments they foster, and the development of very basic classification skills, the young child acquires gender-typed behavioral preferences and the knowledge that he or she is a boy or a girl (basic gender identity).	Social-learning Psychobiosocial
3 to 6 years	Once children acquire a basic gender identity, they begin to seek information about sex differences, form gender schemas, and become intrinsically motivated to perform those acts that are viewed as "appropriate" for their own sex. When acquiring gender schemas, children attend to *both* male and female models. Once their gender schemas are well established, these youngsters are likely to imitate behaviors considered appropriate for their sex, regardless of the gender of the model who displays them.	Gender schema
7 to puberty	Children finally acquire a sense of gender consistency—a firm, future-oriented image of themselves as boys who must necessarily become men or girls who will obviously become women. At this point they begin to rely less exclusively on gender schemas and begin to look to the behavior of same-sex models to acquire those mannerisms and attributes that are consistent with their firm categorization of self as a male or female.	Cognitive-developmental (Kohlberg)
Puberty and beyond	The biological upheavals of adolescence, in conjunction with new social expectations (gender intensification), cause teenagers to reexamine their self-concepts, forming an adult gender identity.	Biosocial/psychobiosocial Social-learning Gender schema Cognitive-developmental

acquire the masculine or feminine attributes that they view as consistent with their male or female self-images. This is why parents who hope to discourage their children from adopting traditional gender roles are often amazed that their sons and daughters seem to become little "sexists" all on their own.

One more point: All theories of gender-role development would agree that what children actually learn about being a male or a female will depend greatly on what their society offers them in the way of a "gender curriculum." In other words, we must view gender-role development through an *ecological* lens and appreciate that there is nothing inevitable about the patterns of male and female development that we see in our society today. (Indeed, recall the gender-role reversals that Mead observed among the Tchambuli tribe of New Guinea.) In another era, in another culture, the gender typing process can produce very different kinds of boys and girls.

Should we in Western cultures be trying to raise different kinds of boys and girls? As we will see in our next section, some theorists would answer this question with a resounding YES!

PSYCHOLOGICAL ANDROGYNY: A PRESCRIPTION FOR THE 21ST CENTURY?

Throughout this chapter, we have used the term *gender-appropriate* to describe the mannerisms and behaviors that societies consider more suitable for members of one sex than the other. Today many developmentalists believe that these rigidly defined gender-role standards are actually harmful because they constrain the behavior of both males and females. Sandra Bem (1978), for example, has stated that her major purpose in studying gender roles is "to help free the human personality from the restrictive prison of sex-role stereotyping and to develop a conception of mental health that is free from culturally imposed definitions of masculinity and femininity."

For many years, psychologists assumed that masculinity and femininity were at opposite ends of a single dimension. If one possessed highly masculine traits, one must be very unfeminine; being highly feminine implied being unmasculine. Bem (1974) challenged this assumption by arguing that individuals of either sex can be characterized by psychological **androgyny**—that is, by a balancing or blending of *both* desirable masculine-stereotyped traits (for example, being assertive, analytical, forceful, and independent) and desirable feminine-stereotyped traits (for example, being affectionate, compassionate, gentle, and understanding). In Bem's model, then, masculinity and femininity are *two separate dimensions* of personality. A male or female who has many desirable masculine-stereotyped traits and few feminine ones is defined as a *masculine gender-typed* person. One who has many feminine—and few masculine-stereotyped traits is said to be *feminine gender-typed*. The androgynous person possesses both masculine and feminine traits, whereas the *undifferentiated* individual lacks both of these kinds of attributes (see Figure 8.6).

androgyny
a gender-role orientation in which the individual has incorporated a large number of both masculine and feminine attributes into his or her personality.

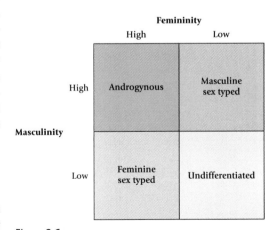

Figure 8.6
Categories of sex-role orientation based on viewing masculinity and femininity as separate dimensions of personality.

Do Androgynous People Really Exist?

Bem (1974) and other investigators (Spence & Helmrich, 1978) have developed self-perception inventories that contain both a masculinity (or instrumentality) scale and a femininity (or expressivity) scale. In one large sample of college students (Spence & Helmreich, 1978), roughly 66 percent of the test takers proved to be either "masculine" men or "feminine" women, about 30 percent were androgynous, and the remaining 7–8 percent were either undifferentiated or "sex-reversed" (masculine gender-typed females or feminine gender-typed males). What is your gender-role orientation? Return to Box 8.1 (on page 242), look at the sum of your scores on traits 1–16 (desirable masculine attributes) and 17–32 (desirable feminine attributes), and divide each sum by 16. Although these traits are not identical to those on the Bem Sex-Role Inventory, if your average score is 3.9 or higher on *both* sets of traits, chances are you would be classified as androgynous on that instrument.

Although the adult gender-role inventories were constructed in the 1970s, they remain valid measures of self-perceived gender-role orientations (Holt & Ellis, 1998). However, since the 1970s women have come to display a greater number of desirable masculine attributes (Spence & Buckner, 2000); so much so that 45 percent of college women in one recent study (as compared to 34 percent of the men) were classified as psychologically androgynous (Morrison & Shaffer, 2003). Janet Boldizar (1991) has developed a gender-role inventory for grade-school children and found that approximately 25–30 percent of third- through seventh-graders can be classified as androgynous. So androgynous individuals do exist, and in sizable numbers.

Are There Advantages to Being Androgynous?

When we think about the idea that a person can be both assertive and sensitive, both independent and understanding, we can't help but think that being androgynous is psychologically healthy. Is it? Bem (1975, 1978) demonstrated that androgynous men and women behave more flexibly than more traditionally gender-typed individuals. For example, androgynous people, like masculine gender-typed people, can display the "masculine" instrumental trait of *independence* by resisting social pressure to judge very unamusing cartoons as funny just because their companions do. Yet they are as likely as feminine gender-typed individuals to display the "feminine" expressive quality of *nurturance* by interacting positively with a baby. Androgynous people do seem to be more highly adaptable, able to adjust their attitudes and behavior to the demands of the situation at hand (Harter, Waters, & Whitesell, 1998; Morrison & Shaffer, 2003; Shaffer, Pegalis, & Cornell, 1992). What's more, college students—both males and females—believe that the ideal person is androgynous (Slavkin & Stright, 2000), and androgynous children and adolescents appear to enjoy higher self-esteem and are perceived as more likable and better adjusted than their traditionally gender-typed peers (Allgood-Merten & Stockard, 1991; Boldizar, 1991; O'Heron & Orlofsky, 1990).

Alternative Viewpoints   Before we conclude that androgyny is something for which everyone should strive, let's consider some qualifications to this idea. First, it seems to be the possession of masculine traits rather than androgyny per se that is most strongly associated with positive social adjustment and high self-esteem (Spence & Hall, 1996; Whitley, 1983). In addition, psychological health and well-being are highest for androgynous individuals who possess predominantly *positive* rather then negative masculine and feminine attributes (Woodhill & Samuels, 2003, 2004).

We might also legitimately wonder whether being androgynous is all that adaptive during childhood, a period of strong gender segregation and heavy peer pressure for gender-appropriate conduct, or even during early adolescence in view of the intensifying gender pressures that young teens face. Indeed, Thalma Lobel and her associates (1997) found that children who strive too hard to express traits considered more appropriate for members of the other sex are at risk of being rejected by peers and experiencing low self-esteem. As noted earlier, gender identity in childhood includes not only the knowledge that "I am a boy/girl and will always be a boy/girl," but also judgments about whether "I am a typical/atypical boy or girl and am contented with being a boy or girl." Clearly, these latter aspects of gender identity truly matter, for Susan Egan and David Perry (2001) found that fourth-through eighth-grade boys and girls enjoyed higher self-esteem and better peer relations when they perceived themselves to be *typical* members of their own sex, were content with being a boy or a girl, and yet felt free to explore cross-gender options if they wanted to. So far from being a constraining straightjacket, feelings of gender typicality and contentment during late childhood and early adolescence appear to be quite adaptive, fostering very positive psychosocial outcomes. Perhaps, then, a child must first be secure in a gender-typical orientation, feeling like one of the regular guys or gals, before he or she can derive many benefits from cross-gender explorations later in life.

In sum, it may be premature to conclude that one is better off in *all* respects to be androgynous rather than masculine or feminine in orientation, particularly during middle childhood and early adolescence. But given the behavioral flexibility that androgynous adults display and the strong contribution that androgyny makes to adult's' perceived self-worth, we can safely assume that it is probably adaptive and certainly not harmful for girls and women to become a little more "masculine," and for boys and men to become a little more like women.

Applications: On Changing Gender-Role Attitudes and Behavior

Today many people believe that the world would be a better place if sexism were eliminated and if boys and girls were no longer pressured to adopt the confining "masculine" or "feminine" roles. In a nonsexist culture, women would no longer suffer from a lack of assertiveness and confidence in the world of work, and men would be freer to display their sensitive, nurturant sides that many now suppress in the interest of appearing "masculine." How might we reduce sexism and encourage children to be more flexible about the interests and attributes they might display?

Bem (1983, 1989) believes that parents must take an active role by (1) teaching their young children about genital anatomy as part of a larger lesson that one's biological sex is unimportant outside the domain of reproduction, and (2) delaying children's exposure to gender stereotypes by encouraging cross-sex as well as same-sex play and by dividing household chores more equitably (with fathers sometimes cooking and cleaning and mothers polishing the car or making repairs). If preschoolers come to think of sex as a purely biological attribute and often see themselves and their parents pursuing cross-sex interests and activities, they should be less inclined to construct the rigid gender stereotypes that might otherwise evolve in a highly sexist early environment. Research suggesting that androgynous parents tend to raise androgynous children is consistent with Bem's prescriptions for change. So too are findings that children whose parents hold nontraditional attitudes toward gender roles or whose fathers routinely perform "feminine" household and child-care tasks are less aware of gender stereotypes and are less likely to display gender-typed interests and ability profiles, compared with youngsters whose parents are more traditional in their gender-role attitudes and behaviors (Sabattini & Leaper, 2004; Turner & Gervai, 1995).

How might we reach children from more traditional backgrounds, who have already received thousands of gender-stereotyped messages from family members, television, and their peers? Researchers are finding that this is a difficult task indeed (Hughes & Seta, 2003). Apparently, interventions that simply show children the benefits of cross-gender cooperation or that praise them for playing with other-sex toys and play partners have no lasting effect: Children soon retreat to same-sex play and continue to prefer same-sex peers after the interventions are over (Maccoby, 1998). One particularly ambitious program (Guttentag & Bray, 1976) exposed kindergarten, fifth-grade, and ninth-grade students to age-appropriate readings and activities designed to teach them about the capabilities of women and about the problems created by stereotyping and sexism.

Box 8.4 Applying Developmental Research

Combating Gender Stereotypes with Cognitive Interventions

During the preschool period when children are constructing gender schemas, their thinking tends to be intuitive and one-dimensional. As we have seen, children who encounter a violation of their gender schemas—learning of a boy who likes to cook, for example—are unlikely to process and retain this information. After all, their one-dimensional, intuitive thinking makes it extremely hard to separate the gender-typed activity (cooking) from the gender category (for girls). So the information doesn't compute and is likely to be distorted or forgotten.

Rebecca Bigler and Lynn Liben (1990, 1992) have devised and compared two cognitive interventions aimed at reducing children's gender-schematic thinking about the occupations that men and women might pursue. The 5- to 11-year-olds who participated in this research were assigned to one of three conditions:

1. *Rule training.* Through a series of problem-solving discussions, children were taught that (1) the most important considerations in deciding who would perform well at such traditionally masculine and feminine occupations as construction worker and beautician are the person's interests and willingness to learn, and (2) that the person's gender was irrelevant.

2. *Classification training.* Children were given multiple classification tasks that required them to sort objects into two categories at once (for example, men and women engaged in masculine and feminine activities). This training was designed to illustrate that objects can be classified in many ways—knowledge that would hopefully help children to see that occupations can be classified independently of the kinds of people who normally enact these roles.

3. *Control group.* Children were simply given lessons on the contributions of various occupations to the community.

Compared to children in the control group, those who either received rule training or who improved in classification skills showed clear declines in occupational stereotyping. Furthermore, later tests of information processing provided further evidence for the weakening of children's stereotypes. Specifically, children who received rule training or who had gained in classification skills after the classification training were much more likely than "control" children to remember counterstereotypic information in stories (for example, recalling that the garbage man in a story was actually a woman). It seems, then, that gender stereotypes can be modified by directly attacking their accuracy (rule training) or by promoting the

Interventions that show men and women participating side by side at traditionally "masculine" or traditionally "feminine" occupations can be highly effective at combating rigid gender stereotypes.

cognitive skills (classification training) that help children to see the fallacies in their own rigid gender schemas.

Unfortunately, teachers may unwittingly foster gender-schematic thinking should they group children on the basis of gender and emphasize gender differences during the first few years of school. In a recent experiment, Bigler (1995) randomly assigned some 6- to 11-year-old summer school students to "gender classrooms" in which teachers created separate boy and girl bulletin boards, seated boys with boys and girls with girls, and often made statements that distinguished boys from girls (for example, "All the boys should be sitting down"; "All the girls put their bubble-makers in the air"). Other children were assigned to classrooms in which teachers were instructed to refer to their pupils only by name and to treat the entire class as a unit. After only four weeks, children in the "gender classrooms" endorsed more gender stereotypes than those in control classrooms, particularly if they were one-dimensional thinkers who have trouble understanding that a person can belong to more than one social category at the same time. So it seems that teachers can help to combat gender stereotyping should they avoid grouping pupils on the basis of gender during the early grades, when young one-dimensional thinkers are otherwise prone to construct rigid gender schemas.

This program worked quite well with the younger children, particularly the girls, who often became outraged about what they had learned about sexism. However, it actually had a boomerang effect among ninth-grade boys, who seemed to resist the new ideas they were being taught and actually expressed more stereotyped views after the training than before. And although ninth-grade girls took many of the lessons to heart, they still tended to cling to the idea that women should run the family and that men should be the primary breadwinners.

This study and others (see Katz & Walsh, 1991, for a review) suggest that efforts to change gender-role attitudes are more effective with younger children than with older ones and possibly more so with girls than with boys. It makes some sense that it is easier to alter children's thinking early on, before their stereotypes have become fully crystallized; and many researchers now favor *cognitive interventions* that either attack the stereotypes directly or remove constraints on children's thinking that permit them to construct these rigid gender schemas. As we see in Box 8.4, these cognitive interventions can be quite effective indeed.

Finally, there is some evidence that programs designed to modify children's gender-stereotyped attitudes and behaviors may be more effective when the adult in charge is a man (Katz & Walsh, 1991). Why? Possibly because men normally make stronger distinctions between "gender-appropriate" and "gender-inappropriate" behaviors than women do (Tennenbaum & Leaper, 2002); thus men may be particularly noteworthy as *agents of change*. In other words, children may feel that cross-gender activities and aspirations are quite legitimate if it is a man who encourages (or fails to discourage) these pursuits.

So new gender-role attitudes can be taught, although it remains to be seen whether such change will persist and generalize to new situations should these attitudes not be reinforced at home or in the culture at large. Sweden is one culture that has made a strong commitment to gender equality: Men and women have the same opportunities to pursue traditionally masculine (or traditionally feminine) careers, and fathers and mothers are viewed as equally responsible for housework and child care. Swedish adolescents still value masculine attributes more highly than feminine characteristics. However, they are much less adamant about it than American adolescents are, and are much more inclined to view gender roles as acquired domains of expertise rather than biologically programmed duties (Intons-Peterson, 1988).

Although our society has not made the commitment to gender equality that Sweden has, it is slowly becoming more egalitarian, and some people believe that these changes are having an impact on children (Tennenbaum & Leaper, 2002). Judith Lorber (1986) sees much hope in her 13-year-old's response to her inquiry about whether a pregnant acquaintance of theirs had delivered a boy or girl: "Why do you want to know?" this child of the modern era asked (p. 567).

SEXUALITY AND SEXUAL BEHAVIOR

sexuality
aspect of self referring to erotic thoughts, actions, and orientation.

Although some preschool and many grade-school children masturbate and partake in such other forms of sexual experimentation as kiss-and-chase games or playing "doctor" that help to groom them for sexual relationships later in life (Larsson & Svedin, 2002; Thorne, 1993), many boys and girls experience their first sexual attraction at about age 10—a point at which the adrenal glands begin to produce increasing amounts of androgen (Herdt & McClintock, 2000). As children approach and experience puberty and secretions of sex hormones increase, they experience strong attractions and sexual urges (Smith, Guthrie, & Oakley, 2005) and become increasingly aware of their own **sexuality**—an aspect of development that can greatly influence their self-concepts. One major hurdle adolescents face is to figure out how to properly manage and express their sexual feelings, an issue that is heavily influenced by the social and cultural contexts in which they live (Weisfeld & Woodward, 2004).

Comstock Images/Jupiter Images

Photo 8.6
At about age 10 or 11, children begin to show more interest in peers of the opposite sex.

Cultural Influences on Sexuality

Societies clearly differ in the education they provide children about sexual matters and in their attempts to encourage them to prepare for their roles as mature sexual beings (Ford & Beach, 1951). Some societies are rather *permissive* about childhood sexuality. In the Mangian culture of the South Pacific, boys are taught about and encouraged to masturbate; at age 13, they learn about sexual techniques and are taught by an older woman how to delay ejaculation until she can achieve orgasm with him (Santrock, 2002). By contrast, *restrictive* societies suppress sexual expression. In New Guinea, for example, Kwoma children are punished for sex play and are not allowed to touch themselves. In fact, a Kwoma boy caught having an erection is likely to have his penis beaten with a stick!

Where do the United States and other Western societies fall on this continuum of sexual permissiveness/restrictiveness? One survey of sexual attitudes in 24 countries (Widmer, Treas, & Newcomb, 1998) classified Germany, Sweden, and Austria as permissive with respect to teenage sexuality, whereas United States, Ireland, Northern Ireland, and Poland were very conservative or nonpermissive toward early teenage sex and premarital sex in general. And several countries, namely the Netherlands, Norway, Czech Republic, Canada, and Spain were classified as "homosexual permissives" because of their relatively high tolerance toward homosexuality. Otherwise, however, these countries were more similar to the sexually restrictive societies. Parents in restrictive societies often elude sexually explicit questions posed by their children (Thorne, 1993) and leave the task of preparing for sexual relations up to the children themselves. And many children and adolescents end up learning from their peers how they should relate to members of the other sex (Whitaker & Miller, 2000).

Adolescent Sexual Explorations, Attitudes, and Behavior

How, then, do Western adolescents, who receive so little guidance from adults, ever learn to manage sexual urges and to incorporate their sexuality into their self-concepts? These tasks have never been easy, and as we see in Box 8.5, can be especially trying for these teenagers who find themselves attracted to members of their own sex. Judging from letters to advice columns, adults seem to think that modern adolescents, driven by raging hormones, are almost obsessed with sex and feel quite free to express their sexuality. How accurate is this portrayal?

Exploring One's Sexuality on the Internet   Aside from their face-to-face contacts with peers, adolescents have often sought information about sex from media outlets such as TV, magazines, and movies (Brown, 2002), and the Internet is certainly no exception (Fraiberg, 2004). In one study of teenagers' use of bulletin boards on the Internet, Suzuki and Calzo (2004) found that teens showed more than twice as much interest in a sexual health bulletin board as in a general teen issues bulletin board. And unlike other media outlets, Internet users can be actively involved in sexual matters, using Internet chat rooms to explore their emerging sexual identities, gain information about other adolescents' attitudes about sexuality, and even engage in cybersexual relationships (Subrahmanyam, Greenfield, & Tynes, 2004). Indeed, research with adolescents from the Czech Republic revealed that about 16 percent of the sample (and as many girls as boys) had tried virtual sex on the Internet, and about a third of the participants revealed that the Internet was the site of their first sexual experience (Smahel, 2003; Smahel & Divinova, 2004, as cited in Subrahmanyam, Smahel, & Greenfield, 2006).

What exactly do teens chat about in the anonymous environment of online chat rooms? One recent study (Subrahmanyam, Smahel, & Greenfield, 2006) revealed that aspects of identity that would be taken for granted in face-to-face conversations (that is, one's age, sex,

On Sexual Orientation and the Origins of Homosexuality

Part of the task of establishing one's sexual identity is becoming aware of one's **sexual orientation**—one's preference for sexual partners of the same or the other sex. Sexual orientation exists on a continuum (Diamond, 2008; Morgan-Thompson & Morgan, 2008) and not all cultures categorize sexual preferences as ours does (Paul, 1993), but we commonly describe people as having primarily heterosexual, homosexual, or bisexual orientations.

Interestingly, about 15 percent of young teens experience some (usually passing) emotional and sexual attraction to members of their own sex (Carver, Egan, & Perry, 2004), although most adolescents establish a heterosexual orientation without much soul-searching. For the 5–9 percent of youths who remain attracted to members of their own sex, the process of accepting that they have a homosexual orientation and establishing a positive identity in the face of negative societal attitudes can be a long and torturous one (Hershberger & D'Augelli, 1995; Diamond & Lucas, 2004). Adolescents who are attracted to members of their own sex often express lower levels of self-esteem than their heterosexual peers (Bos et al., 2008) and may be anxious or even depressed about their gay or lesbian orientation; often this is because they fear rejection from family members or physical and verbal abuse from peers were their orientation to become known (Bos et al., 2008; Dube & Savin-Williams, 1999; Diamond & Lucus, 2004; D'Augelli, 2002). Consequently, they may not gather the courage to "come out" (typically telling a friend or a sibling) until age 16–19 (Savin-Williams, 1998; Savin-Williams & Diamond, 2000) and do not tell their parents until a year or two later, if at all (Savin-Williams & Ream, 2003). Telling anyone may be especially difficult for Asian-American or Latino youth, for members of their subcultural communities tend to be much less accepting of homosexuality than many European Americans are (Dube, Savin-Williams, & Diamond, 2001).

In recent years, a number of social changes have helped gay and lesbian youth to cope more effectively with the challenges they face. Some of the stigma associated with alternative sexual orientations was removed in the 1970s when the American Psychological and Psychiatric Associations proclaimed that homosexuality was not a psychological disorder. Moreover, support groups, consisting of both straight and homosexual students, are becoming more common in American high schools (Savin-Williams, 2008; Scott, 2007), and increasing numbers of positive homosexual role models in the media (for example, Ellen Degeneres; such popular shows as *Queer Eye for the Straight Guy*) help to communicate to people of all sexual orientations that homosexuals are pretty much the same as everyone else except for their sexual orientation. Still, prejudices remain and are often intensified by exposure to homophobic peers (Poteat, 2007) who assume that homosexuals are far more different from them than they really are and experience revulsion over these imputed dissimilarities (Shaffer & Augustine, 2003).

	Identical Twins	Fraternal Twins
Both male twins are gay/bisexual if one is	52%	22%
Both female twins are gay/bisexual if one is	48%	16%

Source: Male figures are from Bailey & Pillard, 1991. Female figures are from Bailey et al., 1993.

How do adolescents become homosexual, bisexual, or heterosexual? One perspective is that this not a choice we make, but rather something that is primarily biological; we simply turn out that way (Money, 1988). Clearly, part of the answer to the sexual orientation mystery does lie in the genetic code. Michael Bailey and his colleagues (Bailey & Pillard, 1991; Bailey et al., 1993; Bailey, Dunne, & Martin, 2000) find that identical twins are more alike in sexual orientation than fraternal twins are. But as we see in the table, only about half of identical twin pairs share the same sexual orientation. This means that environment contributes *at least as much as genes* to the development of sexual orientation.

What environmental factors might help to determine whether a person with a genetic predisposition toward homosexuality comes to be attracted to same-sex companions? We really don't know as yet. The old psychoanalytic view that male homosexuality stems from having a domineering mother and a weak father has received little support (LeVay, 1996). Most homosexuals were raised by heterosexual parents, and there is no evidence that growing up with a gay or lesbian parent influences children's gender typing (Golombok et al., 2003) or their eventual sexual orientation (Bailey et al., 1995; Patterson, 2004). Nor is there any support for the notion that homosexuals were rejected by their fathers or were seduced into the lifestyle by older individuals (Green, 1987). A more promising hypothesis is that hormonal influences in the prenatal environment may be important. For example, women exposed before birth to heightened levels of androgen are more likely than other women to express a bisexual or lesbian orientation—a finding which suggests that high doses of male sex hormones prenatally may dispose at least some females to homosexuality (Berenbaum, 2002; Meyer-Bahlberg et al., 1995). What's more, there is some evidence to suggest that a prenatal environment that is low in androgen may be a factor predisposing some boys to display an erotic attraction to men (Lippa, 2003). However, the fact is that no one yet knows exactly which factors in the prenatal or postnatal environment contribute, along with genes, to a homosexual orientation (Herek, 2000).

and location) were typically exchanged. And there was ample evidence that chatting teenagers were seeking sexual information and exploring sexual identities as well. On average, a sexual comment was made about once per minute, with frequencies being higher among those 18 and older than among 10- to 17-year-olds. About 20 percent of participants in this study had sexualized screen nicknames (for example, "snowbunny"; "sexy dickhead"). Sexualized content differed by gender. Boys were more likely than girls to make explicit

sexual orientation
one's preference for sexual partners of the same or other sex; often characterized as primarily heterosexual, homosexual, or bisexual.

sexual comments (ANY HOT CHICKS WANNA CHAT PRESS 69) as if they were seeking partners, whereas girls were more likely than boys to communicate sexual themes implicitly (he's really hot) or through the use of a sexualized screen name (for example, "innocent angel") as if they were trying to attract partners. Do these findings imply that adolescents are obsessed with sexual matters? Certainly not, for most participants produced no sexual themes in their chats, although all were likely to be exposed to them in the public space of the chat window that was visible to everyone.

So the Internet provides adolescents a multitude of information about sexual matters as well as relatively safe and anonymous opportunities to explore their emerging sexual identities without exposing themselves to risks they might encounter through similar identity explorations in the real world (Subrahmanyam, Smahel, & Greenfield, 2006).

Sexual Attitudes Though they are hardly obsessed with sex, adolescents have become increasingly liberal in their thinking about it throughout the 20th century, with recent attitudes reverting only slightly in a more conservative direction due to fears of contracting AIDS (McKenna, 1997). Yet it is clear that today's youth have changed some of their attitudes about sex while retaining many of the same views held by their parents and grandparents.

What has changed? For one thing, adolescents now firmly believe that premarital *sex with affection* is acceptable, although like people of earlier eras, they think that casual or exploitative sex is wrong even if they have had such experiences (Astin et al., 1994). Still, only a minority of sexually active individuals in one survey (25 percent of the males and 48 percent of the females) cited affection for the partner as the primary reason they first had intercourse (Laumann et al., 1994).

A second major change in adolescent attitudes about sex is the decline of the **double standard**—the idea that many sexual practices viewed as appropriate for males (for example, premarital sex, promiscuity) are less appropriate for females. The double standard hasn't completely disappeared (Simon & Gagnon, 1998). For example, college students still believe that a woman who has many sexual partners is more immoral than an equally promiscuous man (Crawford & Popp, 2003; Robinson et al., 1991). What's more, adolescent boys express more permissive attitudes about premarital sex than adolescent girls do (Lesch & Kruger 2005; Smith, Guthrie, & Oakley, 2005). But Western societies are gradually moving toward a single standard of sexual behavior for both males and females.

Finally, sexual attitudes today are highly variable and seem to reflect an *increased confusion about sexual norms* (Lesch & Kruger, 2005; Welles, 2005). As Philip Dreyer (1982) notes, the "sex with affection" idea is very ambiguous: Must one truly be in love, or is mere liking enough to justify sexual intercourse? It is now up to the individual(s) to decide. Yet these decisions are tough because adolescents receive mixed messages from many sources. On the one hand, they are often told by parents, the clergy, and advice columnists to value virginity and to avoid such consequences as pregnancy and sexually transmitted diseases; yet they are discouraged from and made to feel shameful about masturbating (Halpern et al., 2000; Ponton, 2001). On the other hand, adolescents are encouraged to be popular and attractive, and the more than 12,000 glamorous sexual innuendos and behaviors that they see annually on television (many of which depict promiscuity in a favorable way and occur among *unmarried* couples) may convince them that sexual activity is one means to these ends (Associated Press, 1999). Apparently, the behavior of older siblings adds to the confusion, for younger brothers and sisters of a sexually active sibling tend to be sexually active themselves, often at an earlier age than the older siblings were (East, 1996; East & Jacobson, 2001). In years gone by, norms of appropriate behavior were simpler: Sex was fine if you were married (or perhaps engaged), but it should otherwise be avoided. This is not to say that our parents or grandparents always resisted the temptations they

double standard
the view that sexual behavior that is appropriate for members of one sex is less appropriate for the other.

faced; but they probably had a lot less difficulty than today's adolescents in deciding whether what they were doing was acceptable or unacceptable.

Sexual Behavior Not only have sexual attitudes and modes of sexual exploration changed over the years, but so have patterns of sexual behavior, particularly for girls. Generally, modern adolescents are involved in more intimate forms of sexual activity (petting, intercourse) at earlier ages than adolescents of earlier eras. About 20 percent of European-American and 30 percent of African-American teens have had intercourse by age 15 (Althaus, 2001; DiIorio, 2001). Figure 8.7 shows the percentages of high school students from different historical periods who reported ever having experienced premarital intercourse. Notice that the long-term increase in sexual activity at the high school level may have peaked, for the most

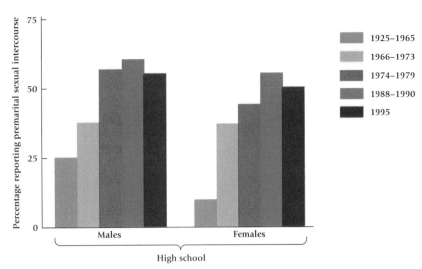

Figure 8.7
Historical changes in the percentages of high school students reporting premarital sexual intercourse. (Data for first three time periods adapted from Dreyer, 1982; data for more recent periods from Baier, Rosenzweig, & Whipple, 1991; (From Reinisch et al., 1992; McKenna, 1997.)

recent data available (in the figure) indicate that about half of high school girls (down from 55 percent in 1990) and 55 percent of high school boys (down from 60 percent in 1990) have ever had intercourse. And it appears that this downward trend in sexual intercourse is continuing today (Centers for Disease Control and Prevention, 2003; Mosher, Chandra, & Jones, 2005). Let's note, however, that this decline in sexual intercourse may simply reflect the higher rates of substitute activities such as oral sex among today's high school students (Prinstein, Meade, & Cohen, 2003). Many teens and even college students do not consider oral-genital contact (or anal-genital contact) to be having sex (Pitts & Rahman, 2001). As one young women put it in a recent class discussion, "If it can't get you pregnant, it doesn't count."

Most sexually active teens become involved at mid-adolescence or later with a single partner. However, girls are more likely than boys to insist that sex and love go together (Darling, Davidson, & Passarello, 1992; Welles, 2005). This attitudinal gap between the sexes can create misunderstandings and hurt feelings, and it may partially explain why girls are less likely than boys to describe their first sexual experience as pleasurable and much more likely than boys to be disappointed (Darling, Davidson, & Passarello, 1992; de Gaston, Weed, & Jensen, 1996; Hyde & DeLamater, 2003).

In sum, both the sexual attitudes and the sexual behaviors of adolescents have changed dramatically in this century—so much so that some kind of sexual involvement is now part of the average adolescent's experience. This is true of all major ethnic groups and social classes, and differences in sexual activity among social groups are shrinking dramatically (Centers for Disease Control and Prevention, 2003; Forrest & Singh, 1990).

Michael Newman/Photo Edit, Inc.

Photo 8.7
Some kind of sexual involvement is now part of the average adolescent's experience.

Personal and Social Consequences of Adolescent Sexual Activity

Who is most inclined to become sexually active early in adolescence and how risky is this activity? Research has identified a number of factors that contribute to early sexual involvement. Teenagers who have intercourse very early tend to be early maturers from low-income families in which fathers are absent; who are having difficulties at school; whose friends are sexually active; and who are already involved in such delinquent activities as alcohol or substance abuse (Bingham & Crockett, 1996; Capaldi et al., 2002; Ellis et al., 2003; Miller, Benson, & Galbraith, 2001). Indeed, the finding that African-American, Native American, and Latino-American adolescents are more likely than adolescents of other ethnicities to be sexually involved at earlier ages probably reflects the fact that more teenagers from these social groups are living with their mothers in poverty, having difficulties at school, and have friends or older siblings who are sexually active (Coley & Chase-Lansdale, 1998; East, 1996).

Sadly, large numbers of sexually active adolescents fail to use contraception (Kaplan et al., 2001), largely because they are (1) uninformed about reproductive issues, (2) too cognitively immature to take seriously the possibility that their behavior could have serious long-term consequences, and (3) concerned that other people (including their partners) will think negatively of them if they appear prepared and thus "ready" to have sex (Coley & Chase-Lansdale, 1998). Peer influences are also important. When friends perceive few costs associated with having sex and engage in unprotected sex, sexually active adolescents become more inclined to have unprotected sex themselves (Henry et al., 2007). Of course, such unsafe sex places them at risk of experiencing two serious consequences: sexually transmitted disease and teenage pregnancy.

Sexually Transmitted Disease in the United States Approximately one in five sexually active adolescents will contract a sexually transmitted disease (STD)—syphilis, gonorrhea, chlamydia, genital herpes, or AIDS—that, left untreated, can cause problems ranging from sterility to death in the infected individual to birth defects and other complications for his or her children (Cates, 1995). Clearly, risk of STD is highest for teenagers who fail to use condoms regularly and for those who have sex with multiple partners (Capaldi et al., 2002).

As the number of cases of AIDS has grown, so too have efforts to educate children and adolescents about how to prevent this deadly disease. The incidence of AIDS in the United States is growing fastest among 13- to 19-year-olds, particularly African-American and Latino adolescents from urban backgrounds (Faden & Kass, 1996). Most states now require some form of AIDS education in the public schools, and there is evidence that these programs can increase grade-school children's knowledge about this disease and how to prevent it (Sigelman et al., 1996). But unfortunately, knowledge about STDs and AIDS transmission and interventions to increase this knowledge have had little effect at modifying risky sexual behaviors (Boyer, Tschann, & Shafer, 1999; National Campaign to Prevent Teen Pregnancy, 2005).

Teenage Pregnancy and Childbearing Adolescents who are sexually active face another important risk: Each year in the United States about 10 percent of (or more than *one million*) 15- to 19-year-old girls become pregnant (Ellis et al., 2003). And although more than half of these pregnancies end in miscarriage or abortion, in any given year nearly half a *million* U.S. babies will be born to adolescent mothers (Miller et al., 1996). The incidence of teenage pregnancy is about twice as high in the United States as in Canada and most European nations, although the good news is that the rates of out of wedlock births have been declining in recent years, especially among very young teens, reaching levels not seen since 1946 (Centers for Disease Prevention and Control, 2004). Out-of-wedlock births are more common among such economically disadvantaged groups as African Americans,

Latinos, and Native Americans, and about two-thirds of these adolescent mothers choose to keep their babies rather than place them up for adoption.

Consequences for Adolescent Mothers   Unfortunately for the adolescent who gives birth, the consequences are likely to include an interrupted education, loss of contact with her social network, and if she is one of the 50 percent who drop out of school, a life of low-paying (or no) jobs that perpetuates her economic disadvantage (Coley & Chase-Lansdale, 1998). In addition, many adolescent girls, particularly younger ones, are not prepared psychologically to become parents, a fact that can greatly affect their babies' developmental outcomes.

Consequences for Babies of Adolescent Mothers   Teenage mothers, particularly those from economically disadvantaged backgrounds, are more likely than older mothers to be poorly nourished, to use alcohol and drugs while pregnant, and to fail to obtain adequate prenatal care. Consequently, many adolescent mothers experience more prenatal and birth complications than older mothers do and are more likely to deliver premature or small-for-date babies (Chomitz, Cheung, & Lieberman, 2000).

   Not only are their babies at risk for getting off to a rocky start, but so too are many adolescent mothers, who are so ill prepared intellectually for the responsibilities of motherhood and who rarely receive adequate financial or social support from a teenage father (Coley & Chase-Lansdale, 1998). Compared to older mothers, adolescent mothers know less about child development, view their infants as more difficult, experience greater parenting stress, and respond to their babies with less sensitivity and affection (Miller et al., 1996). However, recent research indicates that these poor parenting practices of young mothers and poor outcomes for themselves and their babies are *not* due to these mothers' *youth* per se: Poor outcomes are much more apparent among *unmarried* teen mothers from economically disadvantaged backgrounds in which parenting (regardless of the mother's age) is generally less sensitive and stimulating (Kalil & Kunz, 2002; Turley, 2003). Unfortunately, this pattern of parenting from these at-risk teenage mothers can have long-term consequences because their children often show sizable intellectual deficits and emotional disturbances during the preschool years, and poor academic achievement, poor peer relations, and delinquent behaviors later in childhood (Moore & Brooks-Gunn, 2002; Spieker et al., 1999). A teenage mother's life situation and her child's developmental progress may improve later on, especially if she receives social support from her own parents, returns to school, and avoids having more children (Benson, 2004); nevertheless, she (and her children) are at risk of remaining economically disadvantaged compared to peers who postpone parenthood until their 20s (Hardy et al., 1998).

Dealing with the Problem of Teenage Sexuality   How might we delay the onset of sexual behavior and reduce the incidence of teenage pregnancy and STDs? Many developmentalists now believe that the critical first steps to accomplishing this aim should begin at home. Parents consistently underestimate the sexual activity of their teens (particularly younger teens) and are reluctant to communicate just how strongly opposed they are to adolescent sexual activity (Jaccard, Dittus, & Gordon, 1998). Yet it is becoming quite clear that early and frank discussions between parents and their teens (or even preteens) can be a crucial preventive strategy. That is, research consistently reveals that parent/child communications about sexual risk and condom use, undertaken *before* teens begin having sex appear to (1) delay the onset of intercourse and (2) promote regular condom use once teens do become sexually active (Miller et al., 1998; Whitaker & Miller, 2000)—outcomes that clearly lessen the likelihood that adolescents will conceive a child or contract STDs. Supplementing these discussions with a careful monitoring of an adolescent's whereabouts and choice of friends can further reduce the incidence of sexual activity and risky sexual behaviors (Capaldi et al., 2002; Miller, Forehand, & Kotchick, 1999).

Promising interventions from outside the family are also beginning to emerge. One such approach is the privately funded Teen Outreach program now underway at nearly 50 locales around the United States. Adolescents in Teen Outreach perform volunteer service activities (for example, peer tutoring, hospital work) and take part in regular classroom discussions centering on such topics as their volunteer work, future career options, and current and future relationship decisions. An evaluation of Teen Outreach at 25 sites nationwide revealed that the incidence of pregnancy among female participants was less than half that of girls from similar social and family backgrounds who had not participated in the program (Allen et al., 1997). What's more, a similar program in Mexico, focusing heavily on concrete knowledge about contraception and sexual risk and on life-skills training in communication, self-assertion, and social decision making, has produced clear reductions in risky behaviors and teen pregnancies, compared to traditional sex education programs, many of which do little to teach adolescents how to deal with sexual desires and resist sexual advances (Pick, Givaudian, & Poortinga, 2003). Apparently, productively engaged adolescents who have reason to be optimistic about their future and their ability to manage personal relationships are much less likely to become pregnant.

So formal sex education that goes beyond the biological facts of reproduction can be an effective intervention indeed. Programs that focus primarily on abstinence can be effective at transmitting knowledge about reproduction and promoting more adaptive attitudes about sex (see, for example, Thomas & Dimitrov, 2007) but are often ineffective at delaying sexual activity, promoting safe sex, and reducing rates of pregnancy (Kirby, 2002; Peck, in preparation). Programs that are more successful at delaying sexual activity and at increasing contraceptive use among older sexually active adolescents generally rely on a two-pronged approach of (1) teaching and strongly justifying why abstinence is best for preteens and young adolescents, and (2) providing to older teens ample information about contraceptives and about strategies they can use to resist pressures to have sex (Frost & Forrest, 1995; Lowy, 2000; Peck, in preparation). And in light of evidence from Western Europe that free distribution of condoms does *not* encourage sexually inactive teenagers to become sexually active, many educators in this country are calling for similar contraceptive programs in the United States (Lowy, 2000). Those who favor earlier and more extensive sex education and free access to contraception believe that there is little chance of preventing the harmful consequences of teenage sexuality unless more adolescents either postpone sex or practice safer sex.

SUMMARY

- **Gender typing** is the process by which children acquire a gender identity as well as the motives, values, and behaviors considered appropriate in their society for members of their biological sex.

CATEGORIZING MALES AND FEMALES: GENDER-ROLE STANDARDS

- A **gender-role standard** is a motive, value, or behavior considered more appropriate for members of one sex than the other. Many societies are characterized by a gender-based division of labor in which females are encouraged to adopt an **expressive role** and males an **instrumental role**.

SOME FACTS AND FICTIONS ABOUT SEX DIFFERENCES

- Girls outperform boys in many assessments of verbal ability and are more emotionally expressive, compliant, and timid than boys are. Boys are more active and more physically and verbally aggressive than girls, and they display higher self-esteem and tend to outperform girls on tests of arithmetic reasoning and **visual/spatial skills**. In all, however, these sex differences are small, and males and females are far more psychologically similar than they are different.

- Of the many traditional gender-role stereotypes that have no basis in fact are the notions that females are more sociable, suggestible, and illogical and less analytical and achievement-oriented than males. The persistence of these "cultural myths" can create **self-fulfilling prophecies** that promote sex differences in cognitive performance and steer males and females along different career paths.

DEVELOPMENTAL TRENDS IN GENDER TYPING

- By age 2½ to 3, children firmly label themselves as boys or girls, taking the first step in the development of **gender identity.** Between ages 5 and 7, they come to realize that gender is an unchanging aspect of self. Shortly thereafter, they construct such aspects of gender identity as how gender typical they are and how content they feel about being a male or a female.

+ Children begin to learn gender-role stereotypes about the same age that they display a basic gender identity. By age 10–11, children's stereotyping of male and female personality traits rivals that of an adult. At first, stereotypes are viewed as obligatory prescriptions, but children become more flexible in their thinking about gender during middle childhood before becoming somewhat more rigid once again during the adolescent period of **gender intensification.**

+ Even before reaching basic gender identity, many toddlers are displaying gender-typed toy and activity preferences. By age 3, they display **gender segregation** by preferring to spend time with same-sex associates and developing clear prejudices against members of the other sex. Boys face stronger gender-typing pressures than girls do and are quicker to develop gender-typed toy and activity preferences.

THEORIES OF GENDER TYPING AND GENDER-ROLE DEVELOPMENT

+ Evolutionary theorists contend that sex differences and gender-based division of labor have evolved over time because males and females faced different evolutionary pressures and challenges over the course of human history. By contrast, proponents of the **social-roles hypothesis** attribute these differences to variations in the *socially assigned* roles that men and women play.

+ Money and Ehrhardt's biosocial theory emphasizes biological developments that occur before birth and influence the way a child is socialized. Genes contribute to some extent to gender-typed toy and activity preferences and to masculine and feminine self-concepts. The behavior of **androgenized females** implies that prenatal androgen levels also contribute to sex differences in play styles and activity preferences. Yet the development of some children raised as members of the other sex (for example, those with **testicular feminization syndrome**) and cross-cultural comparisons illustrate that social labeling and gender-role socialization play important roles in determining one's gender identity and role preferences. A recent **psychobiosocial model** explains how biological and social influences might interact to produce sex differences in behavior.

+ Freud believed that children become gender typed as they **identify** with the same-sex parent during the **phallic stage** of development in order to resolve their **Oedipus** or **Electra complexes.** However, several lines of research have failed to support Freud's theory.

+ Consistent with social learning theory, children acquire many of their earliest gender-typed toy and activity preferences through **direct tuition** (or differential reinforcement). *Observational learning* also contributes to gender typing as preschool children attend to models of *both sexes* and become increasingly aware of gender stereotypes.

+ Kohlberg's cognitive-developmental theory claims that children are self-socializers who must pass through **basic gender identity** and **gender stability** before reaching **gender consistency,** the point at which they begin to selectively attend to same-sex models and become gender typed. However, research consistently reveals that gender typing begins much earlier than Kohlberg thought and that measures of gender consistency do not predict the strength of gender typing.

+ According to Martin and Halverson's *gender schema* theory, children who have established a basic gender identity construct **"in-group/out group"** and **own-sex gender schemas,** which serve as scripts for processing gender-related information and socializing oneself into a gender role. Schema-consistent information is gathered and retained, whereas schema-inconsistent information is ignored or distorted, thus perpetuating gender stereotypes that have no basis in fact.

+ The best account of gender typing is an eclectic, integrative theory that recognizes that processes emphasized in biosocial, psychobiosocial, social-learning, cognitive-developmental, and gender schema theories all contribute to gender-role development.

PSYCHOLOGICAL ANDROGYNY: A PRESCRIPTION FOR THE 21ST CENTURY?

+ The psychological attributes "masculinity" and "femininity" are generally considered to be at opposite ends of a single dimension. However, one "new look" at gender roles proposes that masculinity and femininity are two separate dimensions and that the **androgynous** person is someone who possesses a fair number of desirable masculine *and* feminine characteristics. Recent research shows that androgynous people do exist, are relatively popular and well adjusted, and may be adaptable to a wider variety of environmental demands than people who are traditionally gender typed. However, androgyny may not be that advantageous in childhood and early adolescence, when such aspects of identity as gender typicality and gender contentment predict adaptive psychosocial outcomes.

+ Parents and teachers (particularly males) may prevent rigid gender typing by emphasizing that one's sex is largely irrelevant outside the domain of reproduction, encouraging and modeling other-sex as well as same-sex activities, and highlighting and discussing the many exceptions to any unfounded gender stereotypes children may have acquired.

SEXUALITY AND SEXUAL BEHAVIOR

+ Hormonal changes beginning before puberty bring about an increase in sexual urges and the need to properly manage one's **sexuality**—a task that may be particularly difficult for teenagers who are sexually attracted to same-sex peers. Sexual attitudes have become increasingly liberal over the years, as a majority of adolescents now think that sex with affection is acceptable and are rejecting the **double standard** for sexual behavior. Teenage sexual activity has also increased, although the sexual behavior of girls has changed more than that of boys.

+ Large numbers of sexually active teenagers fail to use contraception regularly, thus placing themselves at risk of contracting sexually transmitted diseases (STDs) or becoming pregnant.

+ Adolescent pregnancy and childbearing represent a major social problem in the United States. Unmarried teenage mothers, many of whom are poor and ill prepared psychologically to be parents, often drop out of school and perpetuate their economic disadvantage. And their poor parenting contributes to the emotional problems and cognitive deficiencies their children often display.

+ Discussions about sexual matters and reproductive health at home, coupled with reasonable parental monitoring of adolescents' activities, improved sex education and contraceptive services, and programs such as Teen Outreach stressing life-skills training can help to reduce sexual risk and the rate of teenage pregnancy.

CHAPTER 9

Aggression and Antisocial Conduct

Photo 9.1
Seuing-Hui Cho

ON APRIL 16, 2007, over a 2½-hour period Seuing-Hui Cho, a 23-year-old English major at Virginia Tech University, methodically committed the deadliest mass shooting in U.S. history, killing 32 people and wounding 17 others before turning his weapon on himself and taking his own life. After first shooting two students in a dormitory shortly after 7 A.M., Cho left the scene to mail a package of writings, photos, and video recordings to NBC news before returning to a classroom building where he chained the three main entrance doors shut and began shooting horrified and defenseless students and faculty members. Cho had a troubled background characterized by depression and selective mutism—a serious social anxiety disorder that inhibited him from expressing himself. Like many other perpetrators of school shootings, this social misfit had been teased and bullied by peers during middle childhood and early adolescence and had displayed such aberrant behaviors at Virginia Tech as harassing female students and expressing disturbing and occasionally violent themes in his writings and classroom activities. Clearly, Cho was a tortured young man with serious mental health issues (Wikipedia, 2007).

After Cho's horrific rampage, expressions of sympathy and support for the Virginia Tech community poured in from around the world. Yet Cho's actions, while admittedly extreme, may not be all that unusual in that human aggression and other forms of antisocial conduct are pervasive phenomena. We need not look beyond the evening news to observe serious instances of brutality, for kidnappings, shoot-outs, and murders are everyday items for NBC *Nightly News* anchor Brian Williams and his colleagues in the network and local news bureaus. Elliot Aronson (1976) has described a book that surely qualifies as the shortest capsule history of the world, a 10- to 15-page chronological listing of the most important events in human history. Perhaps you can guess how it reads: one war after another, with a few other happenings such as the birth of Jesus Christ and the invention of the printing press sandwiched in between. If an extraterrestrial somehow obtained a copy and deciphered it, he or she would probably conclude that we are extremely hostile, antisocial creatures who should probably be avoided.

What makes humans aggressive? Most vertebrates do not try to kill members of their own species as we sometimes do. Is an inclination to aggress a part of human nature or, rather, something that children must acquire? Is there any hope for peaceful coexistence among people with conflicting interests? If so, how can aggression and other forms of antisocial behavior be prevented, modified, or controlled? These are but a few of the issues that we will consider in the pages that follow.

WHAT IS AGGRESSION?

Most of us have an implicit definition of aggression. Rape is an act that almost everyone would consider violent and aggressive. But the vigorous and passionate lovemaking of consenting partners is generally considered nonaggressive behavior. When the topic of aggression is introduced in classes and students are asked to define the term in their own words, classmates invariably begin to argue about the meaning of aggression and the kinds of behavior that should be considered aggressive. These debates are hardly surprising in view of the fact that social scientists have argued the very same issues for 60 to 70 years. Let's now consider some of the more common definitions of aggression.

Aggression as an Instinct

Could aggression be an instinct—a basic component of human nature? Freud thought so, describing the ***Thanatos*** (or death instinct) as the factor responsible for the generation of

Thanatos
Freud's name for inborn, self-destructive instincts, which were said to characterize all human beings.

aggressive energy in all human beings. Freud held a "hydraulic" view of aggression: Hostile, aggressive energy would build up to a critical level and then be discharged through some form of violent, destructive behavior.

Psychoanalytic theorists are not the only ones who have adopted this viewpoint. The famous ethologist Konrad Lorenz (1966) described aggression as a fighting instinct triggered by certain "eliciting" cues in the environment. In his book *African Genesis,* Robert Ardrey (1967) has gone so far as to imply that the human being "is a predator whose natural instinct is to kill with a weapon" (p. 322). Although there are several important differences between psychoanalytic and ethological perspectives, both schools of thought maintain that aggressive, antisocial conduct results from an inborn propensity for violence.

Behavioral and Intentional Definitions of Aggression

Most behavioral (learning) theorists have rejected an instinctual explanation for violent and destructive acts, choosing instead to think of human aggression and antisocial conduct as a particular category of goal-driven behaviors. Among the more frequently cited **"behavioral" definitions of aggression** is that of Arnold Buss (1961), who characterized an aggressive act as "a response that delivers noxious stimuli to another organism" (p. 3).

Notice that Buss's definition emphasizes the *consequences of action* rather than the intentions of the actor. According to Buss, any act that delivers pain or discomfort to another living organism has to be considered aggressive. Yet how many of us consider our dentists aggressive when they drill our teeth, producing some pain in the process? Is a klutzy dance partner being aggressive when he or she steps on our toes? And is a sniper who misses his target any less aggressive just because no physical harm has been done?

Although you are certainly free to disagree, most people would consider the sniper's behavior aggressive while viewing the dentist's and the dance partner's actions as careless or accidental. In making this pattern of attributions, people are relying on an **intentional definition of aggression,** which implies that an aggressive act is *any form of behavior designed to harm or injure another living being who is motivated to avoid such treatment* (Dodge, Coie, & Lynam, 2006). Note that this intentional definition would classify as aggressive all acts in which harm is intended but not done (for example, a violent kick that misses its target) while excluding accidental injuries or activities such as rough-and-tumble play in which participants are enjoying themselves with no harmful intent.

Aggressive acts are often divided into two categories: **hostile aggression** and **instrumental aggression.** If an actor's major goal is to harm or injure a victim (either physically, psychologically, or by destroying his work or property), his or her actions qualify as hostile aggression. By contrast, instrumental aggression describes those situations in which one person harms another as a means to some other end (for example, knocking a playmate down while trying to take his candy). Clearly, the same overt act could be classified as either hostile or instrumental aggression, depending on the circumstances. If a young boy clobbered his sister and teased her for crying, we might consider this hostile aggression. But these same actions might be labeled instrumental aggression (or a mixture of hostile and instrumental aggression) had the boy also grabbed a toy that his sister was using.

Some have criticized the practice of distinguishing between hostile and instrumental aggression because it is often difficult to tell whether a harm-doer had a harmful intent, let alone to be confident about whether the aggressive behavior of older children, adolescents, or adults is hostile or instrumental in character (Tremblay, Hartup, & Archer, 2005). Bandura (1973), for example, describes a teenage gang that routinely assaulted innocent victims on the street. But gang members did not necessarily attack others for "kicks" (hostile motives); they were required to rough up at least 10 individuals in order to become full-fledged members of the group (an instrumental goal). So even behaviors that appear to be clear instances of hostile aggression may actually be controlled by hidden reinforcement contingencies.

behavioral definition of aggression
any action that delivers noxious stimuli to another organism.

intentional definition of aggression
any action intended to harm or injure another living being, who is motivated to avoid such treatment.

hostile aggression
aggressive acts for which the perpetrator's major goal is to harm or injure a victim.

instrumental aggression
aggressive acts for which the perpetrator's major goal is to gain access to objects, space, or privileges.

In sum, the distinction between hostile and instrumental aggression is not as sharp as many would have us believe. Nevertheless, it is a distinction worth making because developmentalists have found that two kinds of aggression emerge at different times, often have different developmental antecedents, and can have very different implications for one's future personal and social adjustment.

Aggression as a Social Judgment

Although we have talked as if there were a class of intentional behaviors that almost everyone would label "aggressive," such a viewpoint is simply incorrect. Bandura and others (for example, Parke & Slaby, 1983) argue convincingly that "aggression" is really a social label that we apply to various acts, guided by our judgments about the meaning of those acts to us. Presumably, our interpretation of an act as aggressive or nonaggressive will depend on a variety of social, personal, and situational factors such as our own beliefs about aggression (which may vary as a function of our gender, culture, social class, and prior experiences), the context in which the response occurs, the intensity of the response, and the identities and reactions of the people involved, to name a few. Accordingly, a high-intensity response such as a hard right hand to someone's jaw is more likely to be labeled aggressive than a milder version of the same action, which we might interpret as a playful prompt or even as a sign of affection (Costabile et al., 1991). Shooting a deer may be seen as much more violent and aggressive by a pacifist vegetarian than by a carnivorous card-carrying member of the National Rifle Association. Scuffles between children are more likely to be labeled aggressive if someone is hurt in the process (Costabile et al., 1991). And as we see in Box 9.1, the identities of the people involved in an incident can play a major role in determining our impressions of their aggressive intent.

In sum, aggression is to no small extent a *social judgment* that we make about the seemingly injurious or destructive behaviors that we observe or experience. Clearly, we can continue to think of aggression as behavior that is *intended* to frustrate, harm, injure, or deprive someone, as long as we recognize that the basis for inferring whether an actor has a harmful intent can vary dramatically across perceivers, perpetrators, victims, contexts, and situations, thereby ensuring that people will often disagree about what has happened and whether it qualifies as aggression.

✍ THEORIES OF AGGRESSION

By now you may have guessed that each of the preceding definitions of aggression is based on a theory of some sort. In the pages that follow, we will consider several theories that have been offered as explanations of human aggression.

Instinct Theories

Freud's Psychoanalytic Theory
After viewing the horrors of World War I, Freud proposed that humans are born with a death instinct (*Thanatos*) that seeks to end life and underlies all acts of violence and destruction. Presumably, energy derived from food is continually converted to aggressive energy and these aggressive urges must be discharged periodically to prevent them from building to dangerous levels. According to Freud, aggressive energy can be discharged in a socially acceptable fashion through vigorous work or play, or through less desirable activities such as insulting others, fighting, or destroying property. An interesting Freudian notion is that aggressive urges are occasionally directed inward, resulting in some form of self-punishment, self-mutilation, or perhaps even suicide.

Adult Reactions to Roughhousing: Boys Will Be Boys, But Girls Are Aggressors

Imagine that you are walking down the street on a snowy winter afternoon and you happen to notice a child hitting, jumping on, and throwing snowballs at an age-mate. How might you interpret this event? Would your judgment be affected by the identities of the actor and the recipient? What would you think if the children were both boys? Both girls? A boy and a girl?

John Condry and David Ross (1985) conducted an interesting experiment to determine how adults might interpret the rough-and-tumble activities of children they thought to be boys or girls. Subjects first watched a videotape in which two children, whose genders were concealed by snowsuits, played together in the snow. The play soon became quite rough as one child (the target) hit, jumped on, and hurled snowballs at the other (the recipient). Before watching the video, participants were told that these children were both boys, both girls, a boy target and girl recipient, or a girl target and boy recipient. After the video was over, participants were asked to rate the behavior of the target child along

two dimensions: (1) the amount of aggression the target displayed toward the recipient and (2) the extent to which the target's behavior was merely active, playful, and affectionate.

The results were indeed interesting. As we see in scanning the figure, the rough-and-tumble behavior of the target child was much less likely to be interpreted as aggressive and tended to be seen instead as a display of affection when both the target child and the recipient were said to be boys. So, if we see two children "roughhousing" and think that the two are boys, we say, "Boys will be boys" and may fail to intervene. By contrast, boys' roughhousing with girls was definitely interpreted as aggressive behavior. And notice that the high-intensity antics of the girl targets were also seen as highly aggressive, regardless of whether the recipient of those actions was a boy or a girl! In summarizing these data, Condry and Ross say, "It may not be fair, and it certainly is not equal, but from the results of this study, it looks as if boys and girls really are judged differently in terms of what constitutes aggression" (p. 230).

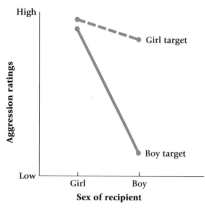

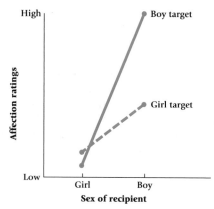

Average ratings of the aggressiveness and the affection of the target child's behavior as a function of the gender of the target and the recipient. (Adapted from Condry, J. C., & Ross, D. F. 1985. Sex and aggression: The influence of gender label on the perception of aggression in children. Child Development, 56, 225–233.) © 1985 by The Society for Research in Child Development. Reprinted by permission of Blackwell Publishing.

Most contemporary psychoanalytic theorists continue to think of aggression as an instinctual drive but reject Freud's notion that we harbor a self-directed death instinct. Presumably, an instinctual tendency to aggress occurs whenever we are frustrated in our attempts at need satisfaction or face some other threat that hinders the functioning of the ego. Viewed in this way, aggressive drives are *adaptive:* They help the individual to satisfy basic needs and thus serve to promote life rather than self-destruction.

Lorenz's Ethological Theory of Aggression A second instinct theory of aggression stems from the work of ethologist Konrad Lorenz. Lorenz (1966) argues that humans and animals have a basic fighting (aggressive) instinct that is directed against members of the same species. Like psychoanalytic theorists, Lorenz views aggression as a hydraulic system that generates its own energy. But he believes that aggressive urges continue to build until relieved by an appropriate *releasing stimulus.*

What kinds of stimuli are likely to trigger aggressive behavior? What functions might these displays of aggression serve? According to Lorenz, all instincts, including aggression, serve a basic evolutionary purpose: *to ensure the survival of the individual and the species.*

Thus, fights that occur when one animal enters another's territory are said to be adaptive; they disperse individuals over a wider area, thereby preventing large numbers of animals from congregating in the same locale, exhausting all sources of food, and starving. An animal may also fight off an intruder in order to protect its young, thereby allowing them to live, mature, and eventually reproduce. Finally, fighting among the males of a species determines which males will mate with available females. Because the stronger males usually win these battles, intraspecies aggression helps to ensure that the hardier members of the lot will be the ones to reproduce.

From an ethological perspective, aggression can help most species survive because they have evolved various "instinctual inhibitions" that prevent them from killing members of their own kind. For example, many species of fish engage in "threat" displays or ritualized aggressive ceremonies in which one of the participants will "win" without seriously injuring an adversary. Birds of the same species could easily kill each other (or peck each other's eyes out) but rarely do so. Wolves normally refrain from killing each other when the loser of a battle "signals" that it has had enough by offering its unprotected throat to the teeth of the victor.

According to Lorenz, human beings kill members of their own species because their aggressive instinct is poorly controlled. Because *Homo sapiens* in prehistoric times lacked the innate equipment to kill (such as claws or fangs), there was little need for the evolution of instinctual inhibitions against maiming or killing other human beings. But humans did evolve intellectually, developed weapons of destruction, and, lacking innate inhibitions, showed little reluctance to use this lethal weaponry to defeat human adversaries. Lorenz points out that this lack of aggressive inhibitions, coupled with the recent development of doomsday weapons, presents a crucial challenge to humanity: We must now work very hard to channel our aggressive urges into socially acceptable pursuits or face the very real possibility of becoming an endangered species.

"Of course, we'll never actually use it against a potential enemy, but it will allow us to negotiate from a position of strength."

According to Lorenz, humans are "lethal" creatures because their aggressive instinct is so poorly controlled.

A Critique of Instinct Theories It is often argued that instinct theories of aggression are of limited explanatory value. For example, the notion that all aggression stems from inborn, instinctual forces cannot easily explain why some societies are more aggressive than others. Cultures such as the Arapesh of New Guinea, the Lepchas of the Himalayas, and the Pygmies of the Congo all use weapons to procure food but rarely show any kind of intraspecies aggression. When invaded by outsiders, these peace-loving people retreat to inaccessible regions rather than stand and fight (Gorer, 1968). Although these observations do not rule out the possibility of biological influences on aggression, they present a strong challenge to any theory that humans are *instinctively* aggressive.

To date, there is no neurophysiological evidence that the body generates or accumulates aggressive energy (Gilbert, 1994; Scott, 1992). Nor is there any solid evidence that human aggression is so widespread because we lack inborn and instinctual inhibitions against harming other humans. In fact, there is evidence to the contrary. Martin Hoffman (2000), for example, claims that our capacity for **empathy,** and the sympathetic emotions it may foster, is itself a product of human evolution and is (or can become) a powerful inhibitor of aggression. And Albert Bandura (1973) points out that humans do not need to bare their throats or rely on other signals of aggressive appeasement like animals do; humans have

empathy
the ability to experience vicariously the same emotions that someone else is experiencing.

evolved a much more intricate system—namely language—for resolving disputes without resorting to aggression.

Human ethologists and modern evolutionary theorists are nowhere near as pessimistic about the prospect of controlling human aggression as Lorenz and Freud were (Buss, 2000; Gilbert, 1994). Consider that ethological studies of children's play groups (Sluckin & Smith, 1977; Strayer, 1980) reveal that even 3- to 5-year-olds form reasonably stable *dominance hierarchies* (determined on the basis of who dominates whom in conflict situations) and know which of their playmates is likely to dominate or submit to them during a conflict. Strayer (1980) proposes that the function of these dominance hierarchies is to *minimize* aggression, just as similar hierarchies minimize fighting and promote the social adaptation of apes and other species. And apparently he is right. In play groups characterized by such dominance hierarchies, children who are attacked or otherwise dominated rarely counterattack or enlist the aid of teachers and peers. Instead, the nondominant child usually terminates the incident by stepping away or making some sort of conciliatory gesture to the dominant peer, such as offering to be his friend, offering to share a disputed possession, or even touching the former adversary in a friendly manner (Sackin & Thelen, 1984). So not only can children successfully resolve most disputes before they escalate into violent, aggressive exchanges, but they are remarkably proficient at doing so at an early age.

Even if human beings were instinctively aggressive, it is likely that an individual's aggressive inclinations would soon be affected by social experiences. If we look at the animal literature, we find that cats will normally kill rats, a behavior that many people have called instinctive. Yet when kittens are raised with rats, they rarely kill them, even after being exposed to a vigorous, rat-killing feline model (Kuo, 1930). This observation nicely illustrates that aggressive behaviors thought to be instinctive can modified substantially or even eliminated through social learning. Largely for this reason, many theorists now believe that human aggressive behaviors, whatever their basic origins, have been so modified by learning that it is simply not helpful to spend much time speculating about their possible bioevolutionary significance (Bandura, 1973; Baron & Richardson, 1994).

Learning Theories

frustration/aggression hypothesis
early learning theory of aggression, holding that frustration triggers aggression and that all aggressive acts can be traced to frustrations.

Disenchanted by instinctual theories of aggression, John Dollard and his associates at Yale University proposed an early and highly influential learning theory of human aggression that came to be known as the **frustration/aggression hypothesis** (Dollard et al., 1939). This model had two basic propositions: (1) Frustration (the thwarting of goal-directed behavior) always produces some form of aggression, and (2) aggression is always caused by some form of frustration.

The problems with this very simple theory soon become apparent. To cite one example, we learned in Chapter 4 that young infants who are frustrated to tears over losing their ability to control objects will become very *angry* and flail their limbs without necessarily intending to harm anyone (Sullivan, Lewis, & Alessandri, 1992; Sullivan & Lewis, 2003). Simply stated, frustration does not invariably result in aggression. Even frustrated 3-year-olds are more inclined to get angry and display unfocused temper tantrums than they are to commit aggressive responses (Goodenough, 1931). And must we assert that all acts of aggression are instigated by some kind of frustration? Leonard Berkowitz certainly didn't think so.

Berkowitz's Revised Frustration/Aggression Hypothesis   Berkowitz (1965) contends that frustration merely makes us angry and creates only a "readiness for aggressive acts." He adds that a variety of other causes of anger—events such as being provoked or attacked, and even previously acquired aggressive habits—may also heighten a person's readiness to aggress. Finally, Berkowitz argues that aggressive responses will not occur, even given one's readiness to aggress, unless there is some "aggressive cue" present in the situation—that is, some stimulus ". . . associated with present or previous anger instigators. . . that *evokes aggressive responses* from [a person who is] primed to make them" (1965, p. 308). So according to Berkowitz, aggressive cues must be present before an angry person will behave aggressively. However, as we see in Figure 9.1, Berkowitz (1974, 1993) later modified his position to acknowledge that an *extremely* angry person may behave aggressively, regardless of whether aggressive cues are present.

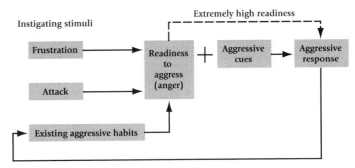

Figure 9.1
Berkowitz's revised frustration/aggression hypothesis. (Adapted from Berkowitz, L. 1974. Some determinants of impulsive aggression: Role of mediated association with reinforcement for aggression. Psychological Review, 81, 165–176.) Adapted by permission of the American Psychological Association.

Notice that Berkowitz's theory anticipates individual differences in aggression: When exposed to aggressive cues, children with well-ingrained aggressive habits should be more inclined to behave aggressively than those whose aggressive habits are not well established. But by far the most provocative of Berkowitz's ideas is the **"aggressive cues" hypothesis,** which implies that exposure to any object or event previously associated with aggression will serve a cuing function and increase the likelihood of aggressive exchanges among young children. Would toys such as guns, tanks, rubber soldiers, and other symbolic implements of destruction have such an effect?

Apparently they can. In one classic study, Seymour Feshbach (1956) exposed 5- to 8-year-olds to structured play sessions in the classroom that revolved around *aggressive* themes such as pirates and soldiers or *neutral* themes such as circuses, farm activities, and running a store. Then, during periods of free play, an adult observer noted any aggressive interactions among these children and labeled each as *thematic* aggression—action that was appropriate in the context of earlier play, such as challenging an enemy pirate—or *inappropriate* aggression—verbal taunts or physical blows that were clearly outside the context of the previous play session. Not surprisingly, thematic aggression was highest for the children who had played with aggressive toys. However, these children were also involved in a greater number of inappropriate aggressive exchanges than classmates who had played with neutral toys (see also, Turner & Goldsmith, 1976; Watson & Peng, 1992). So consistent with the "aggressive cues" hypothesis, toys that encourage the enactment of aggressive themes can indeed increase the likelihood of hostile, aggressive interactions in children's play groups.

In sum, Berkowitz's revised frustration/aggression hypothesis views aggressive behavior as stemming from a combination of *internal forces* (anger, aggressive habits) and external stimuli (aggressive cues). Although this theory may help to explain how aggressive responses are evoked from a person who is angry at the moment, it has little to say about the development of aggressive habits or about how various stimuli become "aggressive cues." Furthermore, other theorists have criticized Berkowitz's model on the grounds that many aggressive acts are committed not out of a sense of anger or outrage, but merely as a means to other nonaggressive ends. And as we will see, the impact of aggressive cues on children's behavior seems to depend more on children's *interpretations* of those stimuli and events (cognitive factors) than on the mere presence of the cues themselves.

"aggressive cues" hypothesis
Berkowitz's notion that the presence of stimuli previously associated with aggression can evoke aggressive responses from an angry individual.

Photo 9.2
Although these young boys seem to be enjoying themselves, toys that encourage the enactment of aggressive themes do increase the likelihood of hostile interactions in children's play groups.

J. Berndt/Stock Boston

Bandura's Social-Learning Theory Bandura's (1973, 1989) social-learning theory of aggression is noteworthy in several respects. It was the first model to stress cognitive influences on aggression. It treats aggression as a class of social behaviors that are acquired through the same processes as any other type of social behavior. And whereas most theorists concentrate on factors that instigate aggression, Bandura proceeds a step further by seeking to explain how aggressive behaviors are *acquired* and *maintained*.

According to Bandura, aggressive responses are acquired in either of two ways. The first and most important method is *observational learning*—a cognitive process whereby children attend to and retain in memory the aggressive responses they see others commit. The now-classic Bandura (1965) experiment that we discussed in Chapter 2 clearly illustrates his point. Recall that children who witnessed an adult model beat up on a Bobo doll clearly *learned* the aggressive responses they had observed and were likely to direct similar acts toward Bobo, as long as they had not seen the model punished for aggression.

Children may also acquire aggressive responses (or aggressive habits) through *direct experience*. A child who is reinforced for aggressive behavior will be more likely to resort to aggression in the future. Consider, for example, a preschool child who discovers that he can easily gain access to attractive toys by simply overpowering his day-care classmates, who cave in to his forceful demands. Clearly, this child's bullying has been reinforced by his control of the desired objects he sought.

How Is Aggression Maintained? According to Bandura (1973), aggressive behaviors are often maintained (and may become habitual) if they are frequently instrumental in procuring benefits for the aggressor or otherwise satisfying his or her objectives. In other words, highly aggressive children have presumably learned that the use of force is an effective and efficient means to other ends.

It turns out that aggressive children do tend to have more positive *expectancies* about the outcomes of aggression; compared to nonaggressive peers, they are (1) more confident that aggression will yield tangible rewards (such as control of a disputed toy), (2) more certain that aggression will be easy for them and successful at terminating others' noxious behavior, and (3) more inclined to believe that aggression will enhance their self-esteem and to callously assume that they do not cause their victims any permanent harm (Crick & Dodge, 1996; Dodge, Coie, & Lynam, 2006; Frick et al., 2003). In addition, aggressive children are more likely than nonaggressive children to *value* the outcomes of aggression; that is, they attach much significance to their ability to dominate and control their victims, and they are not particularly concerned about the suffering they may cause or the possibility of being rejected by their peers (Boldizar, Perry, & Perry, 1989; Crick & Dodge, 1996; Frick et al., 2003; Zakriski & Coie, 1996). Furthermore, highly aggressive youngsters tend to cluster together in cliques (or gangs) that encourage and *reinforce* aggressive solutions to conflict (Dishion, Andrews, & Crosby, 1995; Poulin & Boivin, 2000; Tolan, Gorman-Smith, & Henry, 2003), and they may become so accustomed to dominating others (or attempting to dominate others) that aggression becomes habitual and especially satisfying. Indeed, neuroimaging studies (for example, de Quervain et al., 2004) reveal that the positive consequences of aggression need not be tangible at all and can occur at the neural level. That is, successful aggression activates pleasure centers in the brain, and this pleasant neural activation may be experienced psychologically as the intrinsic satisfaction of exerting dominance or extracting revenge (Dodge, Coie, & Lynam, 2006). In the language of Bandura's theory, these aggressive individuals "have... a *self*-reinforcement system in which aggressive actions are a source of personal pride" (1973, p. 208). A passage from Toch (1969) nicely illustrates how aggression can be self-reinforcing:

> And he said, "F— you, man." And the dude got up and we were both on him, man. And we beat him to a pulp. . . Once we got going we just wasted the dude. . . Sent him on down to

the hospital. And after that I felt like a king, man. It felt like, you know, "I'm the man. You're not going to mess with me." . . . I felt like everybody looking up to me. (pp. 91–92)

In sum, Bandura claims that aggressive habits often persist because they are (1) instrumental to the satisfaction of other goals, (2) useful as a means of terminating other's noxious behaviors, (3) socially sanctioned by aggressive peers, and (4) even intrinsically rewarding for the aggressor.

Internal Arousal and Aggressive Behavior   Notice that Bandura differs from other aggression theorists in a very important way: He depicts human beings as basically rational creatures who typically aggress in order to *satisfy important personal objectives* rather than as a reactive creatures who are "driven" to aggress by such "internal" forces as instincts, frustrations, or anger. Yet Bandura concedes that internal arousal *of any kind* can increase the likelihood of aggression if cues available in a situation might cause one to *interpret* that arousal as frustration or anger. And the available evidence is consistent with Bandura's views. Compared with participants who have not been aroused, those who have experienced nonhostile forms of arousal from exercising, or even from viewing erotica, are likely to display heightened aggression if exposed to insults or some other provocation (Geen, 1998). So it seems that any kind of internal arousal may be more a catalyst for rather than an instigator of aggression.

Evaluating Bandura's Theory   Bandura is a learning theorist who, like all other learning theorists, views aggression as a class of behavior that has some instrumental value for the aggressor. His major contributions to the study of human aggression are his focus on (1) the processes by which aggressive responses are acquired and maintained and (2) the *cognitive* contributors to aggressive behavior, particularly the notion that one's *interpretation* of the social situation (including situational cues to the possible meaning of any arousal one many be experiencing) plays an important role in determining whether he or she will respond aggressively to that situation. However, it appears that Bandura may overstate the case in arguing that virtually all highly aggressive children are highly aggressive because they *value* aggression as an effective *instrumental* strategy for attaining other objectives.

To illustrate, recent research points to two classes of aggressive behavior that highly aggressive children display: *proactive aggression* and *reactive aggression*. Compared to non-aggressive youngsters, **proactive aggressors** are quite confident that aggression will "pay off" in tangible benefits (such as control of a disputed toy), and they are inclined to believe that they can enhance their self-esteem by dominating other children, who will generally submit to them before any serious harm has been done (Crick & Dodge, 1996; Frick et al., 2003; Quiggle et al., 1992). So for proactive aggressors, who sound very much like the highly aggressive youngsters that Bandura describes, shows of force are an *instrumental* strategy by which they achieve personal goals.

By contrast, **reactive aggressors** display high levels of *hostile*, retaliatory aggression. These youngsters are quite suspicious and wary of other people, often viewing them as belligerent adversaries who *deserve* to be dealt with in a forceful manner (Astor, 1994; Crick & Dodge, 1996; Hubbard et al., 2001, 2002). These hot-headed individuals do not as easily fit the mold for a highly aggressive child from the framework of Bandura's social-learning theory, which focuses so heavily on the *instrumental* value of aggression. They are more similar to the angry aggressors that Berkowitz wrote about.

Of all children identified as highly aggressive, about 33 percent are primarily reactively aggressive; another 15–20 percent are mainly proactively aggressive, showing little if any reactive aggression; and the remaining 50 percent display instances of both proactive and reactive aggression (Brendgen et al., 2006; Vitaro & Brendgen, 2005). Interestingly,

proactive aggressors
highly aggressive children who find aggressive acts easy to perform and who rely heavily on aggression as a means of solving social problems or achieving other personal objectives.

reactive aggressors
children who display high levels of hostile, retaliatory aggression because they overattribute hostile intents to others and can't control their anger long enough to seek nonaggressive solutions to social problems.

highly aggressive children display distinct biases in their processing of social information that contribute to their high levels of aggression and to the kinds of aggression they display. And one recent theory of children's aggression—the *social information-processing* approach—anticipates and easily explains these variations in aggressive behavior. Let's take a closer look.

Dodge's Social Information-Processing Theory

Kenneth Dodge (1986; Dodge & Pettit, 2003; Crick & Dodge, 1994) has formulated a social information processing model that seeks to explain how children come to favor aggressive or nonaggressive solutions to social problems. To illustrate, imagine that you are an 8-year-old who is harmed under somewhat ambiguous circumstances: A peer walks by, nudges your work table with his leg and says, "Oops!" as he scatters a puzzle you have been working on for a long time and have nearly completed. As you quickly assess the damage, you really have little information about why this incident may have occurred, although you are certainly aroused by it. So how would you respond?

Dodge proposes that a child's response to this situation will depend on the outcome of six cognitive steps or processes that are illustrated in Figure 9.2. As shown in the figure, the

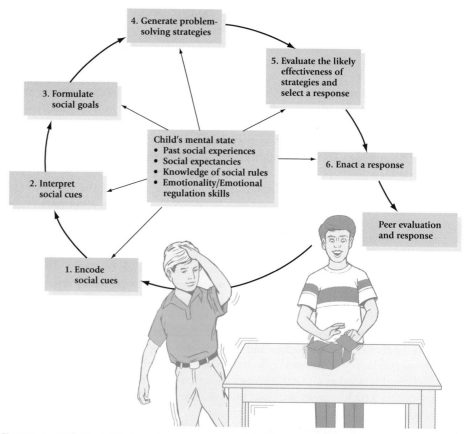

Figure 9.2 Dodge's social information-processing model of the steps children take when deciding how to respond to harm-doing or other social problems. The boy whose creation is destroyed by the other boy's nudging the table must first encode and interpret the social cues (in other words, did he mean it or was it accidental?) and then proceed through the remaining steps to formulate and enact a response to this harmdoing. (Adapted from Crick & Dodge, 1994; Lemerise & Arsenio, 2000.)

youngster who is harmed will first *encode* and *interpret* the immediate cues (How exactly was the damage done? What was the harm-doer's reaction? Did he mean to do it?). After interpreting the cues, the child must then *formulate a goal* (to resolve the incident), *generate* and *evaluate* possible strategies for achieving this goal, and finally, *select and enact* a response. Notice that the model proposes that a child's *mental state*—that is, his past social experiences (especially those involving harm-doing), social expectancies, knowledge of social rules, and ability to regulate emotions—can influence any of the theory's six phases of information processing.

Do young children really proceed through all this mental calculus when reacting to resolve social problems? Typically they do not—at least not in the precise order the model specifies. Many youngsters, particularly younger ones or those who are highly aggressive, take mental shortcuts, skipping certain steps or working on two or more at the same time (Crick & Dodge, 1994; Mayeux & Cillessen, 2003). And as we are about to see, some of these shortcuts and information-processing bias tend to foster aggressive rather than non-aggressive solutions to social problems.

According to Dodge, the mental states of *reactive aggressors,* who have a history of bickering with peers, are likely to include an expectancy that "others are hostile to me." So when harmed under ambiguous circumstances (such as having their puzzle scattered by a careless peer) they are much more inclined then nonaggressive children to (1) search for and find cues compatible with this expectancy, (2) quickly attribute hostile intent to the harm-doer, and (3) become very angry and quickly retaliate in a hostile manner without generating or carefully considering the probable effectiveness of other nonaggressive solutions to this problem. Not only does research consistently indicate that reactive aggressors do overattribute hostile intent to peers (Crick & Dodge, 1996; Dodge, 1980; Hubbard et al., 2001, 2002), but by virtue of their own hostile retaliations, these children will have many negative experiences with teachers and peers (Pellegrini, Bartini, & Brooks, 1999; Poulin & Boivin, 2000), who come to dislike them, thereby reinforcing their expectancy that "others are hostile to me" (see Figure 9.3). Interestingly, girls can be as reactively aggressive as boys, displaying the same kind of **hostile attributional bias** and a strong readiness to react aggressively to imagined or ambiguous harm-doing (Crick & Dodge, 1996; Crick, Grotpeter, & Bigbee, 2002).

Proactive aggressors display a different pattern of social information processing. Because these youngsters do not feel especially disliked, and may even be popular and have many friends (LaFontana & Cillessen, 2002; Rodkin et al., 2000), they are not so inclined to quickly attribute hostile intent to a person who causes them some harm under ambiguous circumstances. However, this does not mean that the proactive aggressor is inclined to let the incident pass. In fact, these youngsters, who often evaluate themselves more favorably than they evaluate peers (Salmivalli et al., 2005), are much more inclined than nonaggressive children to formulate an *instrumental goal* (for example, "I'll teach the careless so-and-so to be more careful around me") and to *coolly and consciously decide* that an aggressive response is likely to be most effective at achieving this aim. Proactive aggressors seem to be skilled at dampening whatever anger they may experience over an ambiguous provocation (Hubbard et al., 2002), appearing almost unemotional and callous (Frick et al., 2003), although they sometimes display such *positive* emotions as pleasure or happiness during aggressive encounters with peers (Arsenio, Cooperman, & Lover, 2000). Their mental states favor aggressive solutions to conflict because they expect positive outcomes to result from their use of force and they feel quite capable about the prospect of dominating their targets (Crick & Dodge, 1996).

Evaluating Dodge's Theory The research cited above provides impressive support for Dodge's social-cognitive theory of aggression. Like Bandura, social

hostile attributional bias tendency to view harm done under ambiguous circumstances as having stemmed from a hostile intent on the part of the harm-doer; characterizes reactive aggressors.

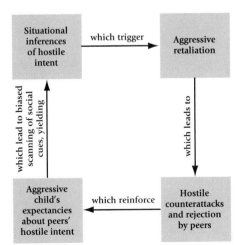

Figure 9.3
A social-cognitive model of the reactive aggressor's biased attributions about ambiguous harm-doing and their behavioral outcomes.

information-processing theorists stress that children's behavioral responses to provocations and other harm-doing depend more on their own cognitive interpretations of the situation than on the amount of objective harm done. However, the social information-processing viewpoint goes far beyond this basic premise to illustrate that children with different mental states and social information-processing biases may interpret and respond to provocations and other harm-doing in very different ways. In other words, it accounts for both Berkowitz's "angry" aggression and the cool, calculating instrumental aggression that Bandura emphasizes.

Despite its clear strengths, this social-cognitive model is most useful in helping to understand why children and adolescents might behave aggressively in particular social situations rather than informing us about why children become aggressive (or nonaggressive) in the first place and how they acquire the information-processing biases that they come to display. Fortunately, social-developmentalists are learning more about the origins of children's information-processing deficits. For example, we will see later in the chapter how the hostile attributional bias that often underlies acts of reactive aggression can emerge very early from interactions with parents and siblings at home.

Another major criticism is that this social-cognitive theory pays insufficient attention to emotions and emotional self-regulation. For example, young children who are difficult temperamentally, displaying such attributes as impulsivity, inattentiveness, negative emotionality, and poor self-regulation, are especially inclined to show deficiencies in information processing and to commit aggressive or other antisocial acts later in childhood and adolescence (see Dodge, Coie, & Lynam, 2006; Eisenberg, Spinrad, et al., 2004; Hill et al., 2006; Lemerise & Arsenio, 2000). So the social information-processing model has provided many new insights but falls far short of offering a complete account of children's aggression and antisocial conduct.

Our survey of the major theories of aggression points mainly to factors that instigate, motivate, and maintain aggressive acts and that help to explain individual differences in aggressive behavior. Now let's look more carefully at age-related changes in aggression before considering some of the biological factors that contribute to it and the social contexts in which aggressive behaviors are acquired and maintained.

DEVELOPMENTAL TRENDS IN AGGRESSION

When do children begin to behave in ways that match our intentional definition of aggression? And how does aggressive behavior change with age? These are the issues we will address in this section of the chapter.

Early Conflict and the Origins of Aggression

Although very young infants do get angry and may occasionally strike people, it is difficult to think of these actions as having an aggressive intent. Piaget (1952) describes an incident in which he frustrated his 7-month-old son Laurent by placing his hand in front of an interesting object that Laurent was trying to reach. Without even looking at his father, Laurent smacked Piaget's hand, as if it merely represented an obstruction that must be removed.

However, the picture soon changes. Marlene Caplan and her associates (1991) found that even 1-year-olds can be quite forceful with each other when one child controls a toy that the other desires. It seemed to Caplan and her colleagues that one child's possession of a toy makes that object a more valuable commodity in the eyes of other infants (a clear social influence), for even when duplicate toys were readily available, 12-month-olds would occasionally ignore these objects and try to overpower a peer in order to control the *other child's* plaything. Clearly the intimidators in these tussles were treating other children as adversaries rather than inanimate obstacles—a finding which implies that the seeds of instrumental aggression have already been sown by the end of the first year (see also Hay, 2005). The appearance of aggression at this particular time even makes some sense when viewed through the lens of Erikson's psychosocial theory, for 1-year-olds have begun their quest for autonomy. As a result, they are more inclined than younger infants to exert their wills in ways that bring them into conflict with their companions (Alink et al., 2006).

Although 2-year-olds have just as many (or more) **conflicts** over toys as 1-year-olds, conflict and aggression are hardly synonymous terms, even for toddlers. Toddlers do become more physically aggressive between their first and second birthdays (Alink et al., 2006). However, they are also becoming better at resolving conflicts in nonaggressive ways. For example, Caplan found that 2-year-olds were much more likely than 1-year-olds to settle their disputes by negotiating with an adversary or by sharing resources than by fighting with each other, especially when toys were in short supply. So it seems that early conflicts need not be training grounds for aggression and can even be adaptive, serving as a context in which infants, toddlers, and preschool children can learn to negotiate and achieve their aims without resorting to shows of force—especially when adults intervene and encourage harmonious means of conflict resolution (NICHD Early Child Care Research Network, 2001a; Perlman & Ross, 1997). Indeed, Japanese mothers are especially intolerant of harm-doing and encourage their children to suppress anger in the interest of promoting social harmony. As a result, Japanese *preschoolers* are already less angered by interpersonal conflicts and less likely to respond aggressively to them than American children are (Zahn-Waxler et at., 1996).

conflict
circumstance in which two (or more) persons have incompatiable needs, desires, or goals.

Age-Related Changes in the Nature of Aggression

Determining whether children become any more or less aggressive over time is not always easy because the aggressive or antisocial acts that 2-year-olds display are not directly comparable to those of a 5-year-old, an 8-year-old, or an adolescent. As a result researchers have chosen to study age-related changes in both the form of aggressive behavior and the situations that elicit aggressive or antisocial conduct.

Aggression During the Preschool Period   Much of what we learned early on about changes in aggression among preschool children came from a handful of studies. One was a project conducted by Florence Goodenough (1931), who asked mothers of 2- to 5-year-olds to keep diaries recording each angry outburst displayed by their children, its apparent causes, and its consequences. A second longitudinal study conducted by Mark Cummings and his associates (1989) recorded the squabbles that occurred among pairs of children at play, once when these children were 2 years old, and again at age 5, in an attempt to determine the stability of children's aggressive inclinations over time. These studies, in conjunction with interview data collected from parents (Alink et al., 2006; Baillageon et al., 2007) and other observations of toddlers, preschoolers, and first-graders playing in laboratories (e.g., Rubin et al., 1998), day-care settings (for example, NICHD Early Child Care Research Network, 2001a, 2004a), and playgrounds (for example, Hartup, 1974) indicate the following:

1. Unfocused temper tantrums diminish during the preschool period and are uncommon after age 4.

2. The incidence of forceful, oppositional behaviors (that is, aggression) normally peaks at about 3 years of age and very gradually declines over the preschool period. However,

Photo 9.3
The squabbles of young children usually center around toys, candy, or other treasured resources and qualify as acts of instrumental aggression.

Robert Pleban

children's tendency to retaliate in response to obvious provocations increases dramatically after age 3.

3. There are at least two ways that aggression changes with age. Two- and 3-year-olds are likely to hit, bite, or kick an adversary. Most of the squabbles among children this young concern toys and other possessions, so that their aggression is usually instrumental in character. Older preschoolers (and young-grade school children) show less and less physical aggression as they choose instead to tease, taunt, tattle, and call their victim uncomplimentary names. And although the majority of older children's tussles involve instrumental objectives (for example, control of toys) an increasing percentage of their aggressive outbursts are *hostile* in character—designed primarily to harm another person.

Why are aggressive exchanges less common among 4-, 5- and 6-year-olds than among 2- and 3-year-olds? One possibility is that older preschoolers are better at regulating anger and other negative emotions and have begun to internalize parental (and day-care providers') rules of conduct (Kochanska, Coy, & Murray, 2001), at least one of which is likely to be the proscription "Be nice, don't fight, and take turns (or share)." What's more, children's language skills grow rapidly between ages 3 and 5, perhaps better enabling older preschoolers to communicate their needs, frustrations, and desires rather than simply lashing out at adversaries (Alink et al., 2006; Dodge, Coie, & Lynam, 2006). And given all of these developments, children are likely to learn from their own experiences that negotiation and sharing can be relatively painless and efficient methods of achieving objectives that they used to attempt through shows of force, without undermining their relationships with playmates (Fabes & Eisenberg, 1992; NICHD Early Child Care Research Network, 2001).

Aggression During the Grade-School Years   Over the course of middle childhood, physical aggression and other forms of overt conduct problems continue to decline as children become less impulsive and increasingly proficient at regulating emotions, complying with rules, and settling disputes more amicably (Eisenberg, et al., 2004; Dodge, Coie, & Lynam, 2006; Loeber & Stouthamer-Loeber, 1998; Shaw et al., 2003).

Photo 9.4
As children mature, an increasing percentage of their aggressive acts qualify as examples of hostile aggression.

Catherine Ursillo/Photo Researchers, Inc.

Yet hostile aggression (especially among boys) shows a slight increase with age, even as instrumental aggression and other forms of disorderly conduct are becoming less frequent. Why is there an increase in hostile aggression? Hartup's (1974) explanation is remarkably straightforward: Older children are becoming more proficient role-takers and thus are better able to infer the motives and intentions of other people. So if a companion behaves in a deliberately harmful way, a grade-school child is more likely than a preschooler to detect the aggressive intent and to retaliate in a hostile manner against the harm-doer (see also Gifford-Smith & Rabiner, 2004).

Research on children's perceptions of harm-doing is generally consistent with Hartup's point of view. Although 3- to 5-year-olds may appropriately infer an actor's aggressive intentions if the relevant cues are clear and made *very obvious* to them, they are nowhere near as proficient at interpreting such information as older children or adolescents are (Nelson-LeGall, 1985). In one study (Dodge, Murphy, & Buchsbaum, 1984), kindergartners, second-graders, and fourth-graders were asked to judge the intentions of a child who had destroyed a peer's tower of blocks accidentally or while portraying either a hostile, a benign, or a prosocial intent. The results were clear: Kindergartners correctly discriminated the actor's true intentions less than half the time (42 percent). Second-graders were more accurate (57 percent correct), but not nearly as skilled at detecting intentional cues as the fourth-graders (72 percent correct).

Yet it is important to note that 7- to 12-year-olds, who can easily discriminate accidental from deliberate harm-doing (see Dodge, 1980), may react aggressively to almost any provocation, even one that they know was unintentional (Sancilio, Plumert, & Hartup, 1989). Why? Because grade-school children (particularly boys) are reluctant to condemn **retaliatory aggression,** often viewing it as a normal (though not necessarily moral) response to provocation (Astor, 1994; Coie et al., 1991). So another reason why hostile aggression increases with age is that peers informally sanction the practice of *fighting back;* they view it as a normal reaction to harm-doing.

retaliatory aggression
aggressive acts elicited by real or imagined provocations.

Perpetrators and Victims of Childhood Aggression   Although most children become less involved in aggressive exchanges over time, longitudinal research conducted at several locales around the world reveals that a small percentage of youngsters, perhaps 4 to 7 percent, become and remain frequent participants in fights and other aggressive or antisocial behaviors (Brody et al., 2003; Nagin & Tremblay, 1999; Shaw et al., 2003). In fact, by age 8 to 12, a small minority of youngsters are most directly involved in a large majority of overtly aggressive episodes. Who is involved? In many groups, the participants are a handful of highly aggressive instigators and the 10–20 percent of their classmates who are regularly abused by these bullies (Olweus, 1993; Perry, Kusel, & Perry, 1988).

Each of us has probably known at least one victimized peer—a youngster who repeatedly serves as a target for other children's hostile acts. Who are these children and who singles them out for abuse?

A nationally representative study of more than 15,000 sixth- through tenth-graders was recently undertaken to document the scope of bullying and victimization in U.S. schools (Nansel et al., 2001), and its findings are noteworthy:

1. Seventeen percent of students reported having been bullied at least "sometimes" during the school year, and 19 percent reported bullying others at least "sometimes." Six percent of these students reported both being a bully and having been bullied.

2. Boys were more likely to be bullies and to be victimized than girls were (although other investigators report no sex differences in bullying and/or victimization; see Kochenderfer-Ladd & Skinner, 2002; Veenstra et al., 2007).

3. Boys were more likely to be physically bullied, whereas girls were more likely to be verbally bullied or abused in psychological ways (for example, socially excluded, victimized by rumors and malicious gossip).

4. Bullying was most frequent early in adolescence (sixth through eighth grades) and was equally common in urban, suburban, and rural areas.

5. Bullies were more likely to smoke, drink alcohol, and be poor students.

Other research finds that bullying (and victimization) may be even more frequent earlier in childhood, although these higher percentages are hard to interpret because children younger than 9 often do not distinguish between bullying episodes and general fighting (Smith et al., 2002). Bullies often hang out with other aggressive peers like themselves, who may egg them on or even assist with and reinforce their bullying activities (Espelage, Holt, & Henkel, 2003). Friendships are very important in sustaining bullying activities. That is, highly aggressive boys and girls have been found to agree upon who is worthy of being victimized, and they tend to pick on the same victims as their best friends do (Card & Hodges, 2006). Interestingly, at least some bullies become quite popular during adolescence, being viewed as "cool" for their ability (or *savoir faire*) at convincing victims (and others) to comply with their wishes (LaFontana & Cillessen, 2002; Rodkin et al., 2000), although the majority of habitual bullies are very much disliked by peers (Veenstra et al., 2005). Habitual bullies have often observed adult conflict and aggression (for example, heated arguments, spouse abuse) at home but have rarely themselves been the target of aggression or abuse (Dodge, Coie, & Lynam, 2006; Schwartz et al., 1997). Some parents of bullies have been very permissive about their children's aggression and may even have encouraged them to be assertive and to strike back at the least provocation (Demaray & Malecki, 2003). All these home experiences suggest that aggression is likely to pay off for the perpetrator, and also suggest that victims are "easy marks" who will surrender tangible resources or otherwise submit to their dominance without putting up much of a fight. So habitual bullies appear to harass their victims for personal or instrumental reasons (Olweus, 1993) and are usually classifiable as *proactive* aggressors.

Although chronic victims are generally disliked by their peers (Boivin & Hymel, 1997; Veenstra et al., 2005, 2007), they are not all alike. Most are **passive victims** who are socially withdrawn, sedentary, physically weak, and reluctant to fight back, and appear to do little (other than being easy marks) to invite the hostilities they receive (Boulton, 1999; Olweus, 1993). Passively victimized boys often have had close, overprotective relationships with their mothers in which they have been encouraged to voice their fears and self-doubts—practices that are generally discouraged of boys as part of masculine gender typing and that are not well received by male classmates (Ladd & Kochenderfer-Ladd, 1998). Indeed, passively victimized boys who appeal to adults (or peers) to assist them are at risk of being viewed as provoking conflicts rather than dealing with them effectively, and are likely to further alienate their peers and contribute to their own continued victimization (Graham & Juvonen, 1998, 2001; Nansel et al., 2004; Kochenderfer-Ladd & Skinner, 2002).

By contrast, a smaller number of victims in many studies (for example, Egan & Perry, 1998; Olweus, 1993; Perry, Kusel, & Perry, 1988) could be described as **provocative victims**—that is, oppositional, restless, and hot-tempered individuals who often irritated peers, were inclined to fight back (often unsuccessfully) when picked on, and who displayed the hostile attributional bias that characterizes reactive aggressors. Indeed, these highly oppositional victims may themselves victimize their more passive peers, becoming **"bully/victims"** who are even more disliked than bullies and passive victims are (Veenstra et al., 2005). Provocative victims have often been physically or emotionally abused or otherwise victimized at home and may have learned from these experiences to view other people as hostile adversaries (Dodge, Coie, & Lynam, 2006; Schwartz et al., 1997).

Many children and adolescents who become chronic victims will continue to be victimized, especially if they blame themselves for their victimization and have no friends to stick up for them and help them acquire social skills and more positive perceptions of their peers (Graham & Juvonen, 1998; Hodges et al., 1999; Ladd & Troop-Gordon, 2003; Schwartz et al., 2000). Unfortunately victimized youth may find it very difficult

passive victims (of aggression) socially withdrawn and anxious children whom bullies torment, even though they appear to have done nothing to trigger such abuse.

provocative victims (of aggression) restless, hot-tempered, and oppositional children who are victimized because they are disliked and often irritate their peers.

bully/victims a small subset of children who are often bullied and who, in turn, often bully their more positive peers.

Photo 9.5
Bullying is widespread among school-age children and has potentially harmful long-term consequences for both bullies and their victims.

Jonathan Nourok/PhotoEdit, Inc.

to make friends; not only are they socially unskilled, but children they may try to befriend often seek to avoid them for fear of losing social status among their classmates or even being victimized themselves (Nansel et al., 2001; Veenstra et al., 2005). So it should come as no surprise that victimized children are at risk for a variety of adjustment problems, including loneliness, anxiety, depression, further erosion of self-esteem, and a growing dislike for and avoidance of school (Egan & Perry, 1998; Hawker & Boulton, 2000; Kochenderfer-Ladd & Wardrop, 2001; Troop-Gordon & Ladd, 2005). Yet even skipping school does not necessarily make things easier for chronic victims, who may often be subjected to such electronic forms of bullying as harassing or threatening e-mails and instant messages, defaming websites, and online "slam books" in which others are invited to post mean or insulting comments about them (Raskauskas & Stoltz, 2007). And the outcomes of Internet bullying can be grim, as illustrated by the recent case of Megan Meier, a depressed 13-year-old who chose to take her own life after being publicly defamed and humiliated online by a new male acquaintance, who actually turned out to be the *mother* of a female rival (Pitts, 2007; and see Table 9.1 for methods of coping with electronic bullying). If all these consequences were not sobering enough, consider that the one commonality that characterizes the vast majority of the perpetrators in the more than 40 school shootings in the United States (including Columbine and Virginia Tech) was their history of long-term harassment and victimization by peers (U.S. Secret Service as cited in Crawford, 2002; Wikipedia, 2007). Clearly, there is a pressing need for programs to stop the abuse—for interventions that not only take strong measures to discourage bullying but that also help victimized children to build self-esteem and develop social skills and supportive friendships that will improve their standing among peers and make them less inviting targets for their tormentors (Dodge, Coie, & Lynam, 2006; Egan & Perry, 1998; Hodges et al., 1999). As we conclude this chapter, we will examine some early returns from interventions undertaken with precisely these objectives in mind.

Aggression and Antisocial Conduct in Adolescence   Major reviews of developmental trends in aggression have concluded that the incidences of fighting and other overt, easily detectable forms of aggression continue to decline from middle childhood throughout adolescence (see, for example, Brody et al., 2003; Loeber & Stouthamer-Loeber, 1998)—a trend that holds for both boys and girls (Bongers et al., 2004). How, then, might we explain the fact that juvenile arrests for assault and other forms of serious violence increase dramatically in adolescence (Dodge, Coie, & Lynam, 2006; Snyder, 2003)? These seemingly inconsistent findings appear to reflect the facts that (1) the 5 to 10 percent of children who are most physically aggressive are at risk of becoming violent young adolescents (see, for

Table 9.1 Strategies for reducing or managing electronic bullying

- ✦ Take Internet harassment seriously. If electronic bullying includes physical threats (including death threats), notify the police immediately.
- ✦ Guard your contact information. Exercise some discretion when deciding to whom you give your cell phone number, instant message name, or e-mail address.
- ✦ If you are harassed online, log out of the site immediately. Immediately mention the incident to an adult you can trust.
- ✦ *Never* reply to harassing messages. If you are bullied through e-mail or instant messaging, block the sender's messages.
- ✦ Save harassing messages and forward them to your Internet or e-mail provider. Most Internet service providers have appropriate-use policies that restrict users from harassing others via the Internet.
- ✦ Speak out when you see others harassing someone online or via cell phones. Most adolescents respond better to criticism from peers than from adults.

Source: Adapted from Raskauskas & Stoltz (2007).

example, Broidy et al., 2003) who (2) often show increases rather than declines in physical aggression as they progress through adolescence (Loeber & Stouthamer-Loeber, 1998; Nagin & Tremblay, 1999). These undercontrolled individuals become dangerous because they growing larger, stronger, and have greater access to weapons than was true during childhood; thus they become ever more likely to inflict *serious* injuries when they act on their aggression inclinations (U.S. Department of Health & Human Resources, 2001).

One final point: Although most adolescents become notably less outwardly aggressive with age, they are not necessarily becoming any better behaved. Not only do more covert forms of social ostracism increase dramatically, especially among girls as they enter adolescence (Cairns et al., 1989; Crick et al., 1999; Galen & Underwood, 1997), but teenage boys (and to a lesser extent girls) become more inclined to act out their anger and frustrations indirectly through such acts as theft, truancy, substance abuse, malicious destruction of property, and sexual misconduct (Broidy et al., 2003; Loeber & Stouthamer-Loeber, 1998; U.S. Department of Health & Human Services, 2001). In American peer culture, defiant and delinquent conduct becomes more socially acceptable during adolescence, and some deviant youth begin to assume a higher status among peers (Miller-Johnson & Costanzo, 2004). Consider that approximately 15 percent of 17-year-old boys in the United States have been arrested for some kind of deviant, antisocial conduct; and yet less than one-third of all offenders are ever apprehended (Dodge, Coie, & Lynam et al., 2006). Girls, to a lesser extent, are also involved. About 28 percent of juvenile arrests involve girls (Snyder, 2003), and as many as 12 percent of American girls report their involvement in at least one violent act by age 17 (Dodge, Coie, & Lynam, 2006). So it seems that adolescents who are becoming less *overtly* aggressive for the most part may simply turn to other forms of antisocial conduct as a means of "fitting in" with peers or expressing their discontents.

Is Aggression a Stable Attribute?

We have seen that the kinds of aggression/antisocial conduct that children display clearly change over time. But what about aggressive (or antisocial) dispositions? Do aggressive toddlers and preschoolers remain highly aggressive throughout the grade-school years? Do highly combative grade-school children become aggressive, antisocial adolescents and young adults?

If we consider population trends, aggression does seem to be a moderately stable attribute even among 1- and 2-year-olds (Alink et al., 2006). Not only are aggressive infants and toddlers likely to remain relatively aggressive as 3-, 4-, and 5-year-olds (Alink et al., 2006; Baillargeon et al., 2007; Cummings, Iannotti, & Zahn-Waxler, 1989; Rubin et al., 2003), but longitudinal research conducted in Finland, Iceland, New Zealand, and the United States reveals that the amount of moody, ill-tempered, and aggressive behavior that children display between ages 3 and 10 is a fairly good predictor of their aggressive or other antisocial conduct later in life (D. Hart et al., 1997; Henry et al., 1996; Kokko & Pulkkinen, 2000; Newman et al., 1997). Rowell Huesmann and his associates (1984), for example, tracked one group of 600 participants for 22 years. As we see in Figure 9.4, highly aggressive 8-year-olds often became relatively hostile 30-year olds who were likely to batter their spouses and children and to be convicted of criminal offenses.

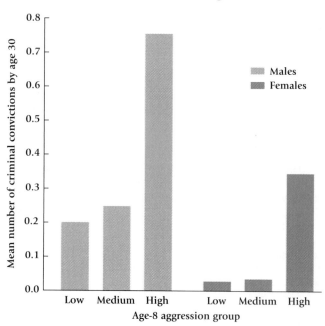

Figure 9.4
Aggression in childhood predicts criminal behavior in adulthood for both males and females. (From Huesmann et al., 1984.)

Of course, these findings reflect group trends and do not imply that all highly aggressive children will remain highly aggressive over time or that all nonaggressive children will remain nonaggressive. In fact, there is a great deal of variability at the individual level, with four life trajectories often being reported in longitudinal studies (for example, Broidy, Nagin, & Tremblay, 2003; Nagin & Tremblay, 1999; Shaw et al., 2003; and see Figure 9.5). A fairly small number of boys (and smaller number of girls) follow a **chronic persistence trajectory,** showing high and gradually escalating levels of aggression throughout childhood and adolescence. These are the children who are at most risk of becoming violent and displaying other forms of antisocial conduct later in life. Other children follow a **high-level desister trajectory,** displaying high initial levels of aggression that decline over time. A third pattern is the **moderate-level desister trajectory** in which moderately aggressive children gradually become less aggressive and antisocial over the course of childhood and adolescence. And some children (more girls than boys) showed a **no-problem trajectory,** displaying low levels of aggression and antisocial conduct throughout childhood and adolescence.

Finally, other investigators have described a fifth, **late-onset (or adolescent-limited) trajectory,** characterizing those individuals who were relatively tranquil as children but who become more aggressive and antisocial as adolescents (Aguilar et al., 2000; Brennan et al., 2003; Loeber & Stouthamer-Loeber, 1998; Moffitt, 1993). Many of these late-onset adolescents engage in mischievous delinquent and other antisocial acts in the context of peer-group activities, although they are not clearly intertwined with a deviant peer culture and are likely to simply drop out of or drift away from delinquent activities over time (Moffitt & Caspi, 2001; Patterson, Capaldi, & Bank, 1991).

In sum, aggression is more stable over time for some people than for others, with stability being greatest for children who displayed the highest and the lowest levels of (predominantly physical) aggression early in life. And we should not be surprised to find that aggression is a reasonably stable attribute for many individuals. Shortly, we will see that some children may be genetically predisposed to behave in ways that are likely to provoke bad feelings and aggressive incidents (Dodge, Coie, & Lynam, 2006). Equally or even more important, we will see how some home settings can serve as "breeding grounds" for the development of aggressive habits. And when a child who has learned to react aggressively to conflicts at home later faces similar problems at school, she may try her forceful tactics on classmates and be reinforced for her aggression, or she may invite snubs, rejections, or counterattacks, which may lead her to assume that "peers are hostile toward me." Before long, such children may find themselves in the vicious cycle portrayed earlier in Figure 9.3—a pattern that seems likely to perpetuate their aggressive inclinations.

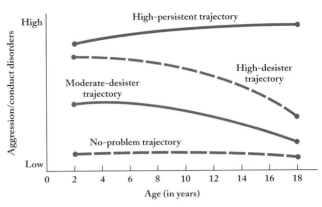

Figure 9.5
Four most commonly reported longitudinal trajectories for aggression/conduct disorders across childhood and adolescence.

chronic persistence trajectory
growth curve of children who are highly aggressive early in life and who display the same high (or escalating) levels of aggression throughout childhood and adolescence.

high-level desister trajectory
growth curve of children who are highly aggressive early in life but who gradually become less aggressive throughout childhood and adolescence.

moderate-level desister trajectory
growth curve of children who are moderately aggressive early in life but who gradually become less aggressive throughout childhood and adolescence.

no-problem trajectory
growth curve of children who are low in aggression throughout childhood and adolescence.

late-onset (or adolescent-limited) trajectory
growth curve of individuals who become more aggressive, usually for a limited time, during adolescence or young adulthood after having been relatively nonaggressive during childhood.

◆ SEX DIFFERENCES IN AGGRESSION

Although aggression is a reasonably stable attribute for many people of each sex, data from more than 100 countries around the world reveal that boys and men are more *overtly* (that is, physically *and* verbally) aggressive than girls and women are (Harris, 1992; Maccoby &

Jacklin, 1974). Furthermore, the magnitude of these sex differences in aggression is greater in studies conducted in the naturalistic environment than in laboratory investigations of aggressive behavior (Blakemore, Berenbaum, & Liben, in press; Hyde, 1984). Why do males and females differ in aggression?

The Biological Viewpoint

According to Maccoby and Jacklin (1974, 1980), there are at least four reasons to suspect that biological factors contribute heavily to sex differences in aggression. First, males are more aggressive than females in almost every society that has been studied. Second, reliable sex differences in physical aggression appear so early—as early as 17 months in one recent study (Baillargeon et al., 2007)—that it is difficult to attribute them solely to social learning or to parental child-rearing practices. Third, males tend to be the more aggressive sex among our closest phylogenetic relatives—species such as baboons and chimpanzees. Finally, heightened levels of male aggression could be attributable to males' higher levels of *testosterone*—the male sex hormone that is thought to promote heightened activity, a readiness to anger, and hence a predisposition to behave aggressively.

The evidence for a testosterone-aggression link seems quite convincing when experiments are conducted with animals. Female rhesus monkeys exposed prenatally to the male hormone testosterone later display patterns of social behavior more characteristic of males: They often threaten other monkeys, initiate rough-and-tumble play, and try to "mount" a partner as males do at the beginning of a sexual encounter (Wallen, 1996; Young, Goy, & Phoenix, 1964). By contrast, genetically male rat pups that are castrated and cannot produce testosterone tend to be passive and to display feminine sexual behavior (Beach, 1965).

What about humans? Dan Olweus and his associates (1980) found that 16-year-old bullies who view themselves as physically and verbally aggressive do have higher testosterone levels than boys who view themselves as nonaggressive, and men with extremely high testosterone levels tend to display higher rates of delinquency, abusiveness, and violence (Dabbs et al., 1995; Dabbs & Morris, 1990). Yet one meta-analysis of 45 studies revealed that links between testosterone and aggression are modest at best (Book, Starzyk, & Quinsey (2001). What's more, there are a number of reasons that we must be cautious in interpreting these correlational data. For one, human beings experience prolonged socialization and are not as likely as animals are to be at the mercy of hormones. Consider what Alan Booth and his associates (2003) found. Among adolescent boys who felt close to and accepted by their parents, testosterone levels were unrelated to antisocial behavior. Only among boys who felt distant from their parents was there positive association between higher levels of testosterone and antisocial conduct. Thus, socialization experiences and hormones interact to influence behavior. What's more, a person's hormonal levels may depend on his or her experiences. To illustrate, Irwin Bernstein and his associates (Rose, Bernstein, & Gordon, 1975) found that the testosterone levels of male rhesus monkeys rose after they had won a fight but fell after they had been defeated. Similarly, human participants who "beat" their opponent at competitive games show an increase in testosterone, whereas losers show a clear decline (see Geen, 1998). What these latter findings imply is that higher concentrations of male sex hormones might be either a cause or an effect of oppositional behavior. Finally, one recent review (Dodge, Coie, & Lynam, 2006) further clouds the picture by concluding that testosterone levels in boys are much more closely related to their levels of social dominance among peers than to their levels of aggressive behavior. Even among boys in deviant peer groups, testosterone levels predict only their *non*aggressive rather than their aggressive conduct problems (Rowe et al., 2004). Clearly, then, we should be skeptical of strong claims that male sex hormones either *cause* one to act aggressively or explain sex differences in aggression (Archer, 1991).

The Social-Learning Viewpoint

Proponents of a social-learning viewpoint are not only critical of the hormonal argument for sex differences in aggression but also point out that very young boys are not always more aggressive than girls (Alink et al., 2006; Hay, Castle, & Davies, 2000). In fact, Marlene Caplan and her associates (1991) found that forceful, aggressive resolutions of disputes over toys were actually more numerous among 1-year-olds when the play groups were dominated *by girls!* Even at age 2, groups dominated by boys were more likely than those dominated by girls to negotiate and share when toys were scarce. Not until age 17 to 18 months are sex differences in aggression reliable (Baillargeon et al., 2007)—and this is clearly enough time for social influences to have steered boys and girls in different directions (Loeber & Stouthamer-Loeber, 1998).

What social influences might conspire to make boys more aggressive than girls? For one, parents play rougher with boys than with girls and react more negatively to the aggressive behaviors of daughters than to those of sons (Ruble, Martin, & Berenbaum, 2006). Furthermore, the ray-guns, tanks, missile launchers, and other symbolic implements of destruction that boys often receive as gifts encourage the enactment of aggressive themes—and actually promote aggressive behavior (Feshbach, 1956; Watson & Peng, 1992). During the preschool years, children came to view physical aggression as a male attribute in their gender schemas (Giles & Heyman, 2005); and by middle childhood, boys expect aggressive acts to provide them with more tangible benefits and to elicit less disapproval from either parents or peers than girls do (Hertzberger & Hall 1993; Perry, Perry, & Weiss, 1989). So even though biological factors may contribute, it is clear that sex differences in aggression depend to no small extent on gender typing and gender differences in social learning.

The Interactive (or Biosocial) Viewpoint

Finally, proponents of an interactive viewpoint believe that sex-linked constitutional factors (biology) interact with social-environmental influences to promote sex differences in aggression. Right from birth, male babies are both more active and more irritable and difficult to comfort than female babies. Clearly, these sex-linked and genetically influenced aspects of temperament could have direct effects on development; but a more likely possibility is that they have indirect or evocative effects on caregivers. For example, parents may be inclined to play more roughly with a highly active son than with a less active daughter; or perhaps they are more inclined to become impatient with an irritable and demanding son who is difficult to comfort. In the first case, parents would be encouraging boys to partake in the kinds of fast-paced, vigorous activities from which anger and aggressive outbursts might emerge. In the second case, parents' greater impatience or irritability with sons than with daughters could also push boys in the direction of becoming quicker to anger and/or somewhat more hostile or resentful toward other people. So it is unlikely that sex differences in aggression (or in any other form of social behavior) are automatic or "biologically programmed." Instead, it seems as if a child's biological predispositions are likely to affect the *behavior* of caregivers and other close companions, which in turn will elicit certain reactions from the child and influence the activities and interests that the child is likely to display. The implication then is that biological factors and social influences are complexly intertwined and are both important contributors to sex differences in aggression.

Box 9.2 Focus on Research

How Girls Are More Aggressive than Boys

Nicki Crick and Jennifer Grotpeter (1995) proposed that both boys and girls can be quite hostile and aggressive, but they display their aggression in very different ways. Boys, who often pursue competitive, instrumental goals, are likely to strike, insult, or display other overt forms of aggression toward others who displease them or who interfere with their objectives. Girls, by contrast, are more likely to focus on *expressive* or *relational* goals—on establishing close, intimate connections with others rather than attempting to compete with or dominate their associates. So Crick and Grotpeter proposed that girls' aggressive behavior would be more consistent with the *social* goals they pursue, consisting largely of covert forms of **relational aggression**—actions such as withdrawing acceptance of an adversary, excluding her from one's social network, or taking some sort of action (for example, spreading rumors) that might damage her friendships or general status in the peer group.

To test this hypothesis, third- through sixth-graders were asked to nominate classmates who often displayed (1) overtly aggressive acts (for example, hitting or insulting others) and (2) *relationally manipulative* acts (for example, withdrawing acceptance, snubbing or excluding others). As we see in the figure, far more boys than girls were viewed as high in overt aggression—a finding that replicates past research. However, far more girls than boys were perceived to be high in relational aggression. Clearly, such subtle or indirect expressions of hostility may be difficult at times for victims to detect and may thus allow the perpetrator to behave aggressively while avoiding open conflict. Even 3- to 5-year-old girls are learning this lesson, for they are already more inclined than preschool boys are to try to exclude rather than to hit a peer who provokes them (Crick, Casas, & Mosher, 1997) and to victimize certain peers in relationally manipulative ways (Crick, Casas, & Ku, 1999). What's more, girls high in relational aggression display the same hostile attributional bias when they think that they are targets of relationally manipulative acts that many aggressive boys do when experiencing ambiguous instrumental provocations (Crick, Grotpeter, & Bigbee, 2002).

Do other children perceive these attempts to undermine a person's status or the quality of his or her personal relationships as clear examples of aggression? Jessica Giles and Gail Heyman (2005) addressed this issue by asking 3- to 5-year-olds to indicate the ways in which peers of each sex try to get back at or "to be mean to" someone who makes them mad. Overwhelmingly,

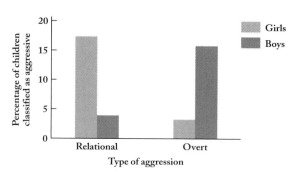

Percentage of girls and boys nominated by classmates as high in relationally manipulative behaviors and overt aggression (physical or verbal assaults) by a sample of third- through sixth-graders. (Adapted from Crick & Grotpeter, 1995.)

children said that boys will hit or insult their adversaries (particularly other boys), whereas they felt that the most likely response for girls was to try to undermine an adversary's (particularly another girl's) social standing. So even preschool children clearly view these relationally manipulative acts as harmful and "aggressive"—a viewpoint that grows ever stronger throughout middle childhood and adolescence (Galen & Underwood, 1997; Park et al., 2005). Relational aggression is also more common among girls than boys in collectivist societies like Indonesia, where maintaining social harmony is so heavily stressed (French, Jansen, & Pidada, 2002). And girls who frequently display relational aggression are often lonely and are rejected by their peers in much the same way that boys high in overt aggression are at risk of poor peer relations (Tomada & Schneider, 1997). However, not all studies find sex differences in relational aggression (see Dodge, Coie, & Lynam, 2006); so perhaps the most apt conclusion is that when sex differences are found, girls are typically more relationally aggressive than boys.

In sum, boys and girls often tend to express their hostilities in very different ways. Because most prior research on children's aggression has focused on physical and verbal assaults and has largely ignored relationally manipulative acts, it clearly underestimates girls' aggressive inclinations.

One other point: Some investigators now believe that boys may appear so much more aggressive than girls because researchers have focused on *overt*, easily detectable aggressive behaviors and have failed to consider *covertly* hostile acts that may be more common among girls than boys. The research in Box 9.2 clearly supports this point of view.

Finally, it is worth noting that even though males remain more heavily represented than females among children identified as displaying serious conduct disorders and adolescents identified as delinquent (Dodge, Coie, & Lynam, 2006), most other sex differences in aggression and oppositional conduct (for example, argumentativeness, defiance, hot-temperedness) are most apparent early in life and fade over time. Figure 9.6 shows age

relational aggression
acts such as snubbing, exclusion, withdrawing acceptance, or spreading rumors that are aimed at damaging an adversary's self-esteem, friendships, or social status.

trends in aggression and oppositional behaviors that emerged in a large longitudinal study of 2600 Dutch children. As we can see, there were steady declines with age in both aggression and oppositional behavior, and the declines were larger for boys—to the point that sex differences that were readily apparent in early and middle childhood had disappeared by age 18 (Bongers et al., 2004). The message: Yes, boys are more overtly aggressive and prone to delinquent antisocial conduct that girls are, but we can get a misleading picture about sex differences by focusing too intently on the small minority of people who remain highly aggressive and antisocial over time. For the vast majority of people, oppositional conduct and (particularly) aggression become less and less common as they mature, to the point that, on an absolute level, most young women *and men* are decidedly nonaggressive.

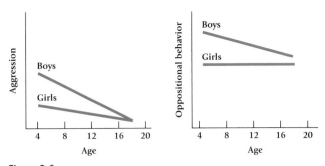

Figure 9.6
Developmental trajectories of aggression and oppositional behavior observed in a longitudinal study of Dutch children. (Adapted from Bongers, Koot, van der Ende & Verhulst, 2004.)

⌒ BIOLOGICAL INFLUENCES ON AGGRESSION

To what extent might biological factors account for individual differences in aggression and antisocial conduct? We have already seen that one heavily biological attribute, testosterone level, is, at best, only weakly related to the incidence of hostile, antisocial conduct. However, the evidence for genetic influences is much stronger.

Genotype and Aggression

In their recent review of the literature, Kenneth Dodge and his associates (2006) claim that the results of more than 100 behavioral genetics studies conducted around the world lead us to an inescapable conclusion: Because identical twins (kinship = 1.00) are routinely found to be more similar in aggression and antisocial conduct than fraternal twins (kinship = .50), our propensities for these attributes are clearly influenced by the genes that we have inherited. How much can aggression be attributed to genetic influence? This varies dramatically across studies, depending on the age of the participants and the kinds of aggression or antisocial conduct assessed, but most studies imply that genes account for 40–50 percent of the variability in aggression, whereas nonshared environmental influences account for another 40 percent, and shared environmental influences common to siblings in the same family account for about 15 percent (see, for example, Rhee & Waldman, 2002). Estimates of genetic influence are higher among samples of younger children than older ones and for aggressive behaviors than for delinquent, antisocial conduct (Dodge, Coie, & Lynam, 2006). Moreover, physical aggression appears to be more genetically influenced than is relational aggression (Brendgen et al., 2005) or our propensities to be proactively or reactively aggressive (Brendgen et al., 2006). Nonetheless, virtually all kinds of aggression and antisocial conduct are influenced to some extent by our genetic predispositions.

Let's note, however, that just because many forms of aggression and antisocial conduct are genetically influenced, this in no way implies that environmental influences are unimportant. Even pairs of identical twins differ in aggression, and because they share 100 percent of their genes, these differences have to be attributable to environmental influences they do *not* share. Differential treatment by a parent is one such nonshared environmental influence, and one recent study of identical twins found that the twin who received the most negative treatment and least warmth from his mother generally becomes the more aggressive of the two twins (Caspi et al., 2004).

It is also important to note that genetic predispositions toward aggression/antisocial conduct do *not* imply that some of us inherit "aggressive" genes coded to produce aggressive or oppositional behaviors. A more likely possibility is that genes and environments interact to influence these attributes. Consider one clear example. To date, only one specific gene has been identified as a likely contributor to conduct disorders. But even so, people who inherit this suspect gene are likely to display serious conduct disorders only if they have also experienced other potent *environmental* adversity such as abuse or neglect from their parents (Caspi et al., 2002; Foley et al., 2004).

Temperament

We have already mentioned another *genetically influenced* contributor to aggression—difficult temperament. Yet temperamental influences on aggression provide another example of genotype/environment interactions. Children with irritable or otherwise difficult temperaments tend to evoke negative reactions from their companions, which in turn may foster the impression that "others are mean to me," thereby inviting aggressive retaliations. Thus, temperamentally influenced aggression may result from what Scarr and McCartney (1983) call *evocative genotype/environment correlations* (see Chapter 3). And as these temperamentally challenged children become more aggressive, they eventually begin to associate mostly with other aggressive children, thereby creating environmental niches that perpetuate their aggressive behavior (an active genotype/environmental correlation). From this point on, association with aggressive friends and peers becomes a potent *environmental* influence. Consider that second- through fourth-graders who hang out with aggressive friends show further increases over time in their own levels of aggression (Werner & Crick, 2004). In fact, the growing influence of peers and other *social* forces beyond the family may help to explain why genetic influences on aggression are highest early in childhood and more modest later in adolescence.

In sum, biological factors clearly contribute to individual differences in aggression and antisocial behavior. However, Albert Bandura, Gerald Patterson, and many other aggression theorists believe that a person's *absolute* level of aggression—that is, how aggressive or antisocial he or she is likely to become—depends very critically on the social environment in which he or she is raised. Let's now consider two important sets of social influences that help to explain why some children and adolescents are more aggressive than others: (1) the norms and values endorsed by their societies and subcultures and (2) the family settings in which they reside.

⌢ CULTURAL AND SUBCULTURAL INFLUENCES ON AGGRESSION

Cross-cultural and ethnographic studies consistently indicate that some societies and subcultures are more violent and aggressive than others (Triandis, 1994). Earlier, we referred to such cultures as the Arapash of New Guineau and the Lepchas of Sikkim—passive, non-aggressive social orders that actively preach collectivist values, strongly discourage fighting and other forms of interpersonal conflict, and will flee rather than fight when their territory is invaded by outsiders (Gorer, 1968). In marked constrast to these groups are the Gebusi of New Guinea, who teach their children to be combative and emotionally unresponsive to the needs of others and who show a murder rate that is more than 50 times higher than that of any industrialized nation (Scott, 1992). The United States is also an "aggressive" society. On a percentage basis, the incidence of rape, homicide, and assault is higher in the United States than in any other industrialized nation, and the United States ranks a close

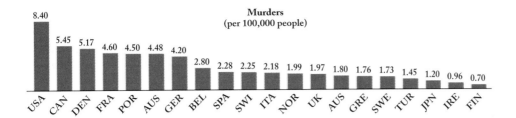

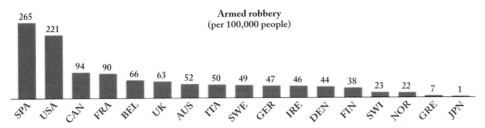

Figure 9.7 Frequencies of two major violent crimes in modern industrialized societies. (Adapted from Wolff, Rutten, & Bayer, 1992.) © 1992 by Michael Wolff & Company, Inc. Originally appeared in *Where We Stand* by Michael Wolff et al., originally published by Bantam Books. Reprinted by permission of Curtis Brown, Ltd.

second to Spain (and far above third-place Canada) in the incidence of armed robbery (Wolff, Rutten, & Bayer, 1992). Firearm homicide rates are more than 12 times higher in the United States than the average rate across other major industrialized societies, largely because of laws that make it so easy to own guns in the United States (Dodge, Coie, & Lynam, 2006). And U.S. children in the five states with the highest levels of gun ownership are three times more likely to die from firearm homicide than are children from the five states with the lowest levels of gun ownership (Miller, Azrael, & Hemenway, 2002).

Subcultural Variations

Studies conducted in England, Canada, and the United States also point to social class differences in aggression: Children and adolescents from the lower socioeconomic strata (particularly poverty-stricken males from larger inner-city urban areas) exhibit more aggressive behavior and higher levels of delinquency than their age-mates from the middle class (Loeber & Stouthamer-Loeber, 1998; NICHD Early Child Care Research Network, 2004a; Tolan, Gorman-Smith, & Henry, 2003). These trends are partially attributable to social class variations in child rearing. For example, parents from lower-income families are more likely than middle-class parents to rely on harsh forms of physical punishment to discipline aggression and noncompliance, thereby *modeling aggression* even as they are trying to suppress it (Dodge, Pettit, & Bates, 1994). Lower-income parents are also more inclined to endorse aggressive solutions to conflict and to encourage their children to respond forcefully when provoked by peers (Dodge, Pettit, & Bates, 1994; Jagers, Bingham, & Hans, 1996)—practices that may foster the development of the *hostile attributional bias* that highly aggressive youngsters so often display. Finally, lower-income parents are often living complex, stressful lives of their own, working at multiple jobs or simply coping with the many stresses associated with low-income living, which may make it difficult for them to manage or monitor their children's whereabouts, activities, and choice of friends. Unfortunately, this lack of parental monitoring is consistently associated with such aggressive or delinquent activities as fighting, destroying property, conduct disorders at school, drug use, and general rule breaking away from home (Dishion, Nelson, & Bullock, 2004; Laird et al., 2003).

Yet parents are not solely responsible for the elevated levels of aggression, antisocial conduct, and delinquency seen among youth from lower-income families (Chung & Steinberg, 2006). Many of these at-risk youth are living in poor, inner-city neighborhoods in which violent crime and other forms of antisocial conduct are high; there are few community services to support effective parenting and keep youth productively occupied; and there is little in the way of **collective efficacy,** or neighborly interconnectiveness in which residents monitor the behavior of neighborhood youth and maintain public order (Tolan, Gorman-Smith, & Henry, 2003). As we will see later in the chapter, the kind of parenting children receive at home can play a major part in shielding children from or pushing them toward the deviant peer groups (and gangs) that often evolve in and inhabit these high-risk communities (Brookmeyer, Heinrich, & Schwab-Stone, 2005; Chung & Steinberg, 2006; Kliewer et al., 2006). Nevertheless, it has become quite apparent that the neighborhoods in which many lower-income families live can contribute meaningfully to the heightened levels of aggression and antisocial conduct often observed among children and adolescents from the lower socioeconomic strata (Farver et al., 2005; Tolan, Gorman-Smith, & Henry, 2003; Walker-Barnes & Mason, 2001), largely by fostering the impression that aggression and violence are acceptable ways to deal with social problems (Guerra, Huesmann, & Spindler, 2003) and by providing children with ample exposure to deviant peers (Chung & Steinberg, 2006).

In sum, a person's aggressive or antisocial inclinations will depend in part on the extent to which one's culture, subculture, or neighborhood encourages and condones such behavior. Yet not all people in pacifistic societies are kind, cooperative, and helpful, and the vast majority of people raised in relatively "aggressive" societies, subcultures, or neighborhoods are not especially prone to violence. One reason that there are dramatic differences in aggression within any social context is that children are raised in very different families. In our next section, we will see how the home setting can sometimes serve as a breeding ground for hostile, antisocial conduct.

⌒ FAMILY INFLUENCES ON AGGRESSION

How might one's family and the family setting contribute to violent and aggressive behavior? In the pages that follow, we will consider two interrelated avenues of influence: (1) the effects of particular child-rearing practices and (2) the more global impact of the family environment on children's aggressive behavior.

Parental Child-Rearing Practices and Children's Aggression

When investigators began to study the development of aggression, they operated under the assumption that parents' attitudes and child-rearing strategies play a major role in shaping children's aggressive inclinations. Clearly, there is some truth to this assumption. Some of the most reliable findings in the child-rearing literature are that *cold* and *rejecting* parents who apply harsh **power-assertive** discipline in an *erratic* fashion and often *permit* their child to express aggressive impulses are likely to raise hostile, aggressive children (Dodge, Pettit, & Bates, 1994; Dodge, Coie, & Lynam, 2006; Olweus, 1980; Rubin et al., 2003). Surely these findings make good sense. Cold and rejecting parents are frustrating their children's emotional needs and modeling a lack of concern for others by virtue of their aloofness. What's more, if these aloof parents often express negative emotions during parent/child interactions, they interfere with the child's ability to properly regulate his or her own emotions—a

collective efficacy
term used to describe neighborhoods in which residents are well connected, neighborly, and tend to monitor events in the neighborhood (including activities of neighborhood youth) to maintain public order.

power-assertion
a form of discipline in which an adult relies on his or her superior power (for example, by administering spankings or withholding privileges) to modify or control a child's behavior.

strong contributor to aggressive behavior (Eisenberg et al., 2003). By ignoring many of the child's aggressive outbursts, a permissive parent is legitimizing combative activities and failing to provide many opportunities for the child to control aggressive impulses. And when aggression or defiance escalates to the point that the parent spanks the child, the adult is serving as a model for the very behavior that he or she is trying to suppress. So it is hardly surprising to find that aloof parents who rely on physical coercion to discipline aggression have children who are highly aggressive outside the home (DeKlyen et al.,1998; Dodge, Coie, & Lynam, 2006). A child who learns that he will be hit, kicked, or shoved when he displeases his parents will probably direct the same kind of responses toward playmates who displease him (Hart, Ladd, & Burleson, 1990).

Photo 9.6
Children who are hit when they displease others are likely to hit others who displease them.

Might the Child Be Influencing the Parent?   Although parental attitudes and child-rearing practices certainly contribute to children's aggression and antisocial conduct, the direction of influence may also flow in the opposite direction, from child to parent. In Dan Olweus's (1980) child-rearing study, the best predictors of aggression among young adolescent males were (1) parents' permissiveness toward, or willingness to tolerate, their boys' aggressive behavior earlier in childhood and (2) parents' cold and rejecting attitudes toward their sons. However, the next best predictor was not a child-rearing variable at all, but rather a measure of the boys' own temperamental impulsivity (highly active, impulsive boys tended to be the most aggressive). According to Olweus, a boy with an active and impetuous temperament may simply "exhaust his mother, resulting in her becoming more permissive of aggression in the boy" (p. 658). And should the impetuous child really anger his mother so that she can no longer ignore his conduct, she may express her negative feelings openly or resort to physical punishment as a control tactic, thereby increasing the likelihood that her boy will behave in a surly and belligerent manner. Although researchers disagree about just how much child characteristics such as temperament contribute to aggressive, antisocial conduct (see, for example, Dodge, 1990; Lytton, 1990), it has become quite apparent that children (by virtue of their temperaments) have a hand in creating the very child-rearing environments that will influence their propensities for aggression (see, for example, Brennan et al., 2003; Frick et al., 2003; Jaffee et al., 2004; Rubin et al., 2003).

Family Climate and Children's Aggression

Developmentalists have long suspected that the emotional climate of the home can and often does influence children's adjustment. One major contributor to a disruptive home environment is a strife-ridden parental relationship.

Parental Conflict and Children's Aggression   How are children influenced by their exposure to parental conflict? A growing body of evidence indicates that they often become extremely distressed when parents fight and that continuing conflict at home increases the likelihood that children will have hostile, aggressive interactions with siblings and peers (Cummings & Davies, 2002; Davies & Cummings, 2006). Indeed, longitudinal studies reveal that even after controlling for earlier levels of child conduct problems, increases over time in parental conflict and marital distress predict similar increases in children's and adolescents' aggression and other problem behaviors (Cui, Conger, & Lorenz, 2005;

Sturge-Apple, Davies, & Cummings, 2006). And, unfortunately, as children of conflict-ridden homes become more unruly and aggressive, their behavior contributes to a vicious cycle: Parents may argue more about child management issues, and this elevated marital conflict promotes further increases in problem behaviors (Cui, Donnellan, & Conger, 2007; Jenkins et al., 2005).

Youngsters are especially likely to be affected by marital conflict when parents show a pattern of attacking and then withdrawing from one another so that children are not exposed to amiable and satisfactory resolutions of heated conflicts (Katz & Woodin, 2002). In fact, recent research finds that parental detachment and withdrawal in the face of conflict is a better predictor of future child problem behaviors than parental conflict per se (Sturge-Apple, Davies, & Cummings, 2006). Why should this be? One reason is that distressed parents who withdraw from each other become more *emotionally unavailable* to their children. That is, they become less warm and supportive and even indifferent, disinterested, or neglectful (Sturge-Apple, Davies, & Cummings, 2006), thus displaying aspects of parenting that we have seen are associated with the development of aggressive behavior. What's more, distressed children in conflict-ridden homes come to display blunted physiological reactivity to parental conflict that may reflect a means of disengaging from or shutting out the unpleasantries they witness; yet this decrease in physiological reactivity is a reliable predictor of their conduct problems (Davies et al., 2007). Why decreased reactivity to stress forecasts future aggressive behavior is not well understood, but one speculation is that these less arousable children may have difficulty acquiring and marshalling the social skills and other adaptive behaviors (for example, emotional regulatory mechanisms) that might enable them to make close friends and settle disputes amicably with peers.

As we will see in Chapter 11, families are complex social systems in which the relationship between any two family members (mother and father, for example) can affect the behavior of all other family members. The literature connecting parental conflict to child aggression and other problem behaviors is a clear example of a family system effect. Now let's consider one broader family climate (or system) effect: the growth of aggression and problem behaviors in coercive home environments.

Coercive Home Environments as "Breeding Grounds" for Aggression   For nearly 30 years, Gerald Patterson (1982; Patterson, Reid, & Dishion, 1992; Snyder, Reid, & Patterson, 2003) has observed patterns of interaction in families that have at least one highly aggressive child. The aggressive children in Patterson's sample seemed "out of control"—they fought a lot at home and at school and were generally unruly and defiant. These families were then compared with other families of the same size and socioeconomic status that had no problem children.

Patterson soon discovered that he could not explain "out of control" behavior by merely focusing on the child-rearing practices that parents use. Instead, it seemed that highly aggressive children were living in rather atypical family environments that were characterized by a social climate that *they had helped to create*. Unlike most homes, where people frequently display approval and affection, the highly aggressive problem child usually lives in a setting in which family members are constantly bickering with one another. They are reluctant to initiate conversations, and when they do talk, they tend to needle, threaten, or otherwise irritate other family members rather than conversing amiably. Patterson called these settings **coercive home environments** because a high percentage of interactions centered on one family member's attempts to force another to stop irritating him or her. He also noted that **negative reinforcement** was important in maintaining these coercive interactions: When one family member is making life unpleasant for another, the second will learn to whine, yell, scream, tease, or hit because these actions often force the antagonist to stop (and thus are reinforced).

coercive home environment
a home in which family members often annoy one another and use aggressive or otherwise antisocial tactics as a method of coping with these aversive experiences.

negative reinforcer
any stimulus whose removal or termination as the consequence of an act will increase the probability that the act will recur.

Consider the following sequence of events, which may be fairly typical in a coercive home environment:

1. A girl teases her older brother, who makes her stop teasing by yelling at her (yelling is negatively reinforced).

2. A few minutes later, the girl calls her brother a nasty name. The boy then chases and hits her.

3. The girl stops calling him names (which negatively reinforces hitting). She then whimpers and hits him back, and he withdraws (negatively reinforcing her hits). The boy then approaches and hits his sister again, and the conflict escalates.

4. At this point, the mother intervenes. However, her children are too emotionally disrupted to listen to reason, so she finds herself applying punitive and coercive tactics to make them stop fighting.

5. The fighting stops (thus reinforcing the mother for using coercive methods). However, the children soon begin to whine, cry, or yell at the mother. These countercoercive techniques are then reinforced if the mother backs off and accepts peace at any price. Unfortunately, backing off is only a temporary solution. The next time the children antagonize each other and become involved in an unbearable conflict, the mother is likely to use even more coercion to get them to stop. The children once again apply their own methods of countercoercion to induce her to "lay off," and the family atmosphere becomes increasingly unpleasant for everyone.

Mothers of problem children rarely use social approval as a means of behavior control, choosing instead to largely ignore prosocial conduct, to interpret many innocuous acts as antisocial, and to rely almost exclusively on coercive tactics to deal with perceived misconduct (Nix et al., 1999; Snyder et al., 2005). Perhaps the overwhelmingly negative treatment that these problem children receive at home (including parents' tendency to label ambiguous or innocuous events as antisocial) helps to explain why they generally mistrust other people and display the *hostile attributional bias* so commonly observed among highly aggressive children (Dishion, 1990; Snyder et al., 2003; Weiss et al., 1992). And ironically, children from highly coercive home environments eventually become resistant to punishment. They have learned to fight coercion with countercoercion and will often do so by defying the parent and *repeating the very act that she is trying to suppress*. Why? Because this is one of the few ways that the child can successfully command the attention of an adult who rarely offers praise or shows any signs of affection. No wonder Patterson calls these children "out of control"! By contrast, children from noncoercive families receive much more positive attention from siblings and parents, so they don't have to irritate other family members to be noticed.

So we see that the flow of influence in the family setting is *multidirectional*: Coercive *interactions* between parents and their children and the children themselves will affect the behavior of *all* parties and contribute to the development of a hostile family environment— a true breeding ground for aggression (Garcia et al., 2000). Unfortunately, these problem families may never break out of this destructive pattern of attacking and counterattacking one another unless they receive help. In Box 9.3, we consider one particularly effective approach to this problem—a method that necessarily focuses on the family as a social system rather than simply on the aggressive child who has been referred for treatment.

Individual Differences in Response to Coercive Parenting   One interesting aspect of Patterson's work is that not all of the children residing in the same coercive family environment displayed the same pattern of aggression and early conduct disorders that Patterson labeled "out of control." Although Patterson does acknowledge that children contribute to

Box 9.3 Applying Developmental Research

Helping Children (and Parents) Who Are "Out of Control"

How does one treat a problem child who is hostile, defiant, and "out of control"? Rather than focusing on the problem child, Gerald Patterson's (1981, 1982) approach is to work with the entire family. Patterson begins by carefully observing the family's interactions and determining just how family members are reinforcing one another's coercive activities. The next step is to describe the nature of the problem to parents and to teach them a new approach to managing their children's behavior. Some of the principles, skills, and procedures that Patterson stresses are the following:

1. Don't give in to the child's coercive behavior.
2. Don't escalate your own coercion when the child becomes coercive.
3. Control the child's coercion with the time-out procedure—a method of discipline in which the child is sent to her room (or some other location) until she calms down and stops using coercive tactics.
4. Identify those of the child's behaviors that are most irritating, and then establish a point system in which the child can earn credits (rewards, privileges) for acceptable conduct or lose them for unacceptable behavior. Parents with older problem children are taught how to formulate "behavioral contracts" that specify how the child is expected to behave at home and at school, as well as how deviations from this behavioral code will be punished. Whenever possible, children should have a say in negotiating these contracts.

5. Be on the lookout for occasions when you can respond to the child's prosocial conduct with warmth and affection. Although this is often difficult for parents who are accustomed to snapping at their children and accentuating the negative, Patterson believes that parental affection and approval will reinforce good conduct and eventually elicit displays of affection from the child—a clear sign that the family is on the road to recovery.

A clear majority of problem families respond quite favorably to these methods. Not only do problem children become less coercive, defiant, and aggressive, but the mother's depression fades as she gradually begins to feel better about herself, her child, and her ability to resolve family crises (Patterson, 1981). Some problem families show an immediate improvement. Others respond more gradually to the treatment and may require periodic "booster shots"—that is, follow-up treatments in which the clinician visits the family, determines why progress has slowed (or broken down), and then retrains the parents or suggests new procedures to correct the problems that are not being resolved. Clearly, this therapy works because it recognizes that "out of control" behavior stems from a *family system* in which both parents and children are influencing each other and contributing to the development of a hostile family environment. Therapies that focus exclusively on the problem child are not enough!

---

the establishment of a coercive home environment, he tended to emphasize how parenting and patterns of parental control shape children's aggression and focused less on child contributions and on differences among siblings in adapting to coercive parenting.

In recent years, it has become clearer why some children are more vulnerable than others to the potentially harmful impacts of aloof, rejecting, and punitive parenting. Studies of longitudinal trajectories in children's aggression, conduct disorders, and delinquency are beginning to converge on the conclusion that temperamentally impetuous, uninhibited, or fearless children who are either callous, unemotional, and nonempathetic and/or deficient at regulating negative emotions are at greatest risk of displaying high levels of aggression and behavioral problems when they experience aloof or rejecting, power-assertive parenting (see, for example, Brennan et al., 2003; Rubin et al., 2003; Shaw et al., 2003). Moreover, these very temperamental attributes often exasperate parents and contribute to the aloofness and coercive discipline parents display. Indeed, it has been argued that temperamentally fearless and dysregulated children who so often struggle with parents, siblings, and peers may never learn to sympathize with others or to acquire strong, internalized moral controls that would otherwise moderate their aggression and antisocial conduct (Frick et al., 2003; Kochanska, 1997; Shaw et al., 2003). Clearly, we are talking here about the combination of an at-risk temperament and coercive parenting placing children at greatest risk because (1) children with more desirable temperaments are less likely to show heightened levels of aggression and conduct disorder in response to coercive parenting (Brennan et al., 2003; Shaw et al., 2003) and (2) parents who are firm but more patient and supportive with temperamentally at-risk children (that is, who provide a "good fit" between their parenting and the child's temperament) have youngsters who are better able to comply with parental rules and requests (Kochanska, 1997) and are less inclined to become (or remain) particularly aggressive and antisocial (Rubin et al., 2003).

Gender Differences?   Coercive family processes were first identified in families with "out of control" boys, but they are also apparent in many families of girls with conduct disorders (Compton et al., 2003). However, boys and girls may react in different ways to different kids of heavy-handed parental disciplinary tactics. In their recent study of parental contributions to aggression in Chinese preschoolers, David Nelson and his associates (2006) found that higher levels of physically coercive discipline best predicted (predominately physical) aggression for boys. However, heavy-handed use of *psychological control*—a coercive attempt to manage behavior by withdrawing affection, making derogatory statements, inducing guilt or shame, or undermining self-worth—was the better predictor of physical and relational aggression for girls, particularly when combined with *low levels* of physical coercion by parents. Whether these results apply to children outside of China is presently unknown. However, they offer the intriguing suggestion that pathways between harsh discipline and childhood aggression may not only differ for boys and girls but also need not be limited to physically coercive parenting practices.

Coercive Home Environments as Contributors to Chronic Delinquency   How serious are the risks faced by children who display early conduct disorders and remain in a coercive home environment? Patterson and his associates (1989) have addressed this issue by reviewing the literature on problem children and drawing some strong conclusions. As shown in Figure 9.8, coercive parenting early in childhood contributes to the development of children's hostile attributional biases; defiant, aggressive behaviors; and general lack of self-restraint, which, by middle childhood, can cause these youngsters to be rejected by grade-school peers, criticized by teachers, and to founder academically (Birch & Ladd, 1998; Dodge, Coie, & Lynam, 2006). These poor outcomes may then cause parents to feel less invested in their children and less inclined to closely monitor their activities (Dishion, Nelson, & Bullock, 2004; Vuchinich, Bank, & Patterson, 1992).

Furthermore, the rejection that problem children experience from peers, coupled with their likely placement in classes or study groups with other academically deficient children, often means that they will have ample exposure to other relatively defiant, aggressive, and socially unskilled youngsters like themselves. By age 11 to 14, these youngsters are associating mainly with other hostile, antisocial classmates, banding together to form *deviant peer cliques* that tend to devalue academics, endorse aggressive solutions to conflict, and promote such dysfunctional adolescent activities as sexual misconduct, substance abuse, dropping out of school, and a variety of other kinds of antisocial or delinquent behaviors

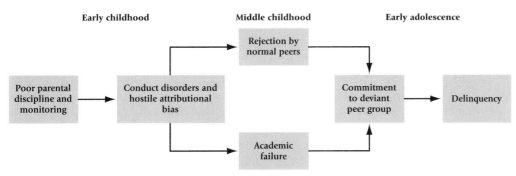

Figure 9.8   A model of the development of chronic antisocial behavior. (Adapted from Patterson, G. R., DeBaryshe, B. D., & Ramsey, E. 1989. A developmental perspective on antisocial behavior. American Psychologist, 44, 329–335.) © 1989 by the American Psychological Association. Reprinted by permission.

Box 9.4 Developmental Issues

Gangs and Antisocial Conduct

Perhaps the strongest potential for negative peer-group influence on adolescents comes from their affiliation with **gangs**—loosely organized groups of teens and young adults, often of the same ethnicity, that identity with their group and may engage in illegal activities and other antisocial conduct (for example, using and selling drugs, fighting, robbery, stealing cars, and so on). Many adolescents join gangs as they make the transition from junior high to high school, and they often do so because they (1) are pressured to by friends, (2) desire companionship and to have a sense of "belonging," and (3) hope to gain some protection from members of rival gangs (Decker, 1996; Walker-Barnes & Mason, 2001).

Teenagers who join gangs are usually already taking part in some delinquent activities and have delinquent friends *prior* to their gang involvement. However, being in a gang appears to increase adolescents' delinquent conduct over and above the levels they displayed before joining the gang (Gordon et al., 2004; Thornberry, Krohn, et al., 2003). A clear majority of serious juvenile crime in American cities is perpetrated by gang members, most of whom are male (Thornberry, Krohn, et al., 2003). However, female gang members face their own set of risks: drug and alcohol abuse, early onset of sexual activity, promiscuity without adequate protection against STDs, prostitution, and so on (Harper & Robinson, 1999). Gangs can emerge anywhere but are most numerous (and influential) in poor, inner-city neighborhoods characterized by a lack of neighborliness and *collective efficacy*, where adolescents are largely unmonitored and, hence, free to do pretty much as they please (Brody et al., 2001; Tolan, Golan-Smith, & Henry, 2003).

When assessing the impact of gangs on adolescents, it is important to distinguish between *gang involvement* and *gang delinquency*. Large numbers of inner-city teens become involved with gangs early in adolescence, hanging out with gang members, wearing gang-sanctioned clothing, and participating in many other nominal gang activities (for example, flashing gang hand signs). Yet researchers are finding that gang involvement declines dramatically over time, with most gang members staying in their gangs for less than one year (Thornberry, Krohn, et al., 2003; Walker-Barnes & Mason, 2001). What may be happening is that nominal gang involvements become less important as adolescents become more involved in legitimate academic or extracurricular activities. It is mainly those gang members who feel most alienated from their

Mark Richards/PhotoEdit, Inc.

Gangs provide many teens with a sense of belonging early in adolescence, although their membership in gangs is often short lived.

families and who were most delinquent and gang-identified to begin with that remain in gangs and become heavily involved in *gang delinquency*.

Parenting can play a significant role in influencing whether adolescents stay in or decrease their gang involvement. For African-American youth, firm but supportive parenting and careful monitoring of children's activities are practices that seem to undermine preadolescents' involvement with deviant peers (Brody et al, 2001) and adolescents' long-term involvement with gangs (Tolan, Golan-Smith, & Henry, 2003; Walker-Barnes & Mason, 2001). By contrast, hostile coercive treatment at home, coupled with lax behavioral monitoring, was associated with *higher* levels of deviant peer involvement and gang delinquency among African-American, Hispanic, and white adolescents (see also Chung & Steinberg, 2006). For many of these latter youths, gangs serve as substitute families, providing them with emotional support that is simply not available at home (Walker-Barnes & Mason, 2001), and it is this kind of hard-core gang involvement that often spells trouble in the months and years ahead.

---

gangs
loosely organized groups of adolescents that hang out, identify as a group, and often partake in delinquent or criminal activities.

(Poulin & Boivin, 2000; Dishion, Andrews, & Crosby, 1995; Dodge, Coie, & Lynam, 2006). Outcomes can be particularly grim should adolescents formally affiliate with and remain members of one of the estimated 31,000 gangs in the United States (Walker-Barnes & Mason, 2001; and see Box 9.4 for a closer look at gang involvement). So to return to the question raised earlier, Patterson claims that living in a coercive home environment poses serious risks indeed, for such an experience is often a crucial first step along the road to chronic aggression and delinquency.

Of course, not all chronically delinquent or antisocial individuals are products of coercive home environments. In their study of more than 4000 Vietnam veterans, Windle and Windle (1995) found that about one veteran in five of those who were classified as highly aggressive were *late-onset types*—men who become aggressive in adulthood without having a history of aggression or a disordered home life earlier in childhood (see also Moffit &

Caspi, 2001). Furthermore, some juvenile and adult offenders who commit mostly *covert* offenses (theft, fraud, and so on) are apparently not the products of coercive home environments. Yet most violent offenders do progress from minor aggression early in childhood to more serious fighting during the middle school and high school years, to such truly violent acts as criminal assault, rape, robbery, and murder later in adolescence and young adulthood, following a pathway consistent with Patterson's coercion model (Lorber & Stouthhamer-Loeber, 1998).

Although boys are more likely than girls to take the chronic-persistence developmental path described in Figure 9.8 (Broidy, Nagin, & Tremblay, 2003; McFadyen-Ketchum et al., 1996), the delinquency "gender gap" is narrowing. Male delinquents still dominate the violent crime statistics; but by age 17, 19 percent of boys and 12 percent of girls report having committed at least one serious act of violence (Dodge, Coie, & Lynam, 2006). Girls are about as likely as boys to be involved in larcenies, sexual misconduct, and substance abuse, and they are more likely than boys to be arrested for such status offenses as running away from home and engaging in prostitution (Snyder, 2003; *Uniform Crime Reports,* 1997). It may take a more disordered home environment to push girls along the path to delinquency, but girls can become just as prone to delinquency as boys (Loeber & Stouthamer-Loeber, 1998), particularly if they view their own parents as hostile and antisocial (Dogan et al., 2007).

Not surprisingly, antisocial male adolescents tend to pair up with antisocial females. Not only are these antisocial couples at risk of experiencing hostile and even abusive romantic relationships (Capaldi & Clark, 1998; Murphy & Blumenthal, 2000), they are also inclined to make an early entry into parenthood, a role that they are ill-prepared to handle. In fact, these young, antisocial parents frequently rely on the same aloof, unresponsive, and coercive child-rearing practices that their parents used with them (Conger et al., 2003; Thornberry, Freeman-Gallant, et al., 2003), thus exposing their own offspring to a home environment that fosters irritable, coercive child behaviors, hostile attributional biases, and all their concomitants (review Figure 9.8). Here, then, is one way in which antisocial inclinations are transmitted from generation to generation.

Family interventions of the kind described in Box 9.3 can be quite effective at modifying the antisocial tendencies of preadolescent (and younger) children. However, once early antisocial patterns continue into adolescence, so many factors conspire to maintain them that interventions are less likely to succeed. Successful programs with adolescents have been reported (see Curtis, Ronan, & Bourdvin, 2004; Dodge, Coie, & Lynam, 2006, for reviews). But one major problem with therapies targeted at families with antisocial adolescents is that parents may have already disengaged from and become less involved with their antisocial offspring, and it is often difficult to get families to complete the therapy (Kazdin, 2003b). In addition, adolescents who derive their emotional support from their deviant-peer or gang "families" are likely to reject parents and other established authorities as legitimate sources of influence. In fact, one study that attempted to modify the antisocial inclinations of groups of deviant adolescents actually backfired, *increasing* their levels of antisocial conduct (Dishion, McCord, & Poulin, 1999). Note the implication here: If bringing deviant individuals together for treatment only makes matters worse, we are undoubtedly wasting time and resources on such currently popular "political" solutions to deviancy as group "boot camps" in reform schools (Dodge, Dishion, & Lansford, 2006) or exposure to even more deviant inmates in correctional institutions, as is done in the Scared Straight program (Petrosino, Turpin-Petrosino, & Finckenauer, 2000). Thus, to better cope with the problem of chronic aggression and delinquency, we must think in terms of *preventive* interventions—ideally, programs that would (1) teach parents of at-risk children more effective child-management techniques, (2) foster children's social skills to prevent them from being rejected by their peers, and (3) provide any academic remediation that may be necessary to keep children on track at school and to lessen the likelihood that they will fall in with deviant peer groups and/or become high school dropouts. Of course, any intervention that makes aggressive, antisocial conduct a less viable or attractive option would be a step in the right direction. Let's now consider some of the procedures that developmentalists have used in attempting to control children's hostilities.

METHODS OF CONTROLLING AGGRESSION AND ANTISOCIAL CONDUCT

What methods other than family therapy might help parents and teachers to suppress the aggressive antics of young children so that antisocial approaches to conflict do not become habitual? Over the years, a variety of solutions have been offered, including procedures to create nonaggressive play environments, eliminate the payoffs for aggression, and foster such cognitive and emotional strengths as anger management and the capacities for empathy and for taking others' perspectives (role-taking) so that they may be less inclined to overattribute hostile intentions to their peers. But few solutions have been so highly touted as the recommendation that we offer children harmless ways to express their anger or frustrations. Let's consider this "popular" alternative first.

Catharsis: A Dubious Strategy

Sigmund Freud believed that hostile, aggressive urges build over time, and he urged people to find harmless ways to release them every now and then (that is, to experience catharsis) before they reach dangerous levels and trigger a truly violent outburst. The implications of this **catharsis hypothesis** are clear: If we encourage young children to vent their anger or frustrations on inanimate objects such as Bobo dolls, they should drain away their aggressive energies and become less inclined to harm other people.

Popular as this **cathartic technique** has been, it does not work and *may even backfire*. In one study (Walters & Brown, 1963), children who had been encouraged to slap, punch, and kick an inflatable Bobo doll were found to be much more aggressive in their later interactions with peers than were classmates who had not had an opportunity to beat on the doll. Other investigators have noted that children who are first angered by a peer and then given an opportunity to aggress against an inanimate object become no less aggressive toward the peer who had angered them in the first place (Mallick & McCandless, 1966). So cathartic techniques do not reduce aggressive urges, in children or in adults (see Geen, 1998). In fact, they may imply to impressionable youngsters that hitting, kicking, and other coercive behaviors are acceptable methods of expressing their anger or frustrations.

Creating Nonaggressive Environments

One simple but effective approach for reducing children's aggression is to create play areas that minimize the likelihood of conflict. For example, parents and teachers might remove (or refuse to buy) such "aggressive" toys as guns, tanks, and rubber knives that provoke violent fantasies and aggressive behaviors (Dunn & Hughes, 2001; Watson & Peng, 1992). Providing ample space for vigorous play also helps to eliminate the accidental bumps, shoves, and trips that often escalate into full-blown hostilities (Hartup, 1974). Finally, shortages of play materials sometimes contribute to conflicts and aggression; yet children are likely to play quite harmoniously if adults have provided enough balls, slides, swings, and other toys to keep them from having to compete for scarce resources (Smith & Connolly, 1980).

How might one reach children who have already become highly aggressive? Developmentalists now recognize that different forms of aggression require different

---

catharsis hypothesis
the notion that aggressive urges are reduced when people witness or commit real or symbolic acts of aggression.

cathartic technique
a strategy for reducing aggression by encouraging children to vent their anger or frustrations on inanimate objects.

kinds of interventions (Crick & Dodge, 1996). Recall that proactive aggressors rely on forceful strategies because they are easy for them to enact and often enable these youngsters to achieve personal goals. An effective intervention for these children might teach them that aggression doesn't pay and that alternative prosocial responses, such as cooperation or sharing, are better ways to achieve their objectives. By contrast, hot-headed reactive aggressors may profit more from social-cognitive interventions that teach them to control their anger and to suppress their tendency to overattribute hostile intentions to companions who displease them. Let's take a closer look at these two kinds of intervention.

Eliminating the Payoffs for Aggression

Parents and teachers can reduce the incidence of *proactive aggression* by identifying and eliminating its reinforcing consequences and by encouraging alternative means of achieving one's objectives. For example, if 4-year-old Lennie were to hit his 3-year-old sister Gail in order to take possession of a toy, Lennie's mother could teach him that this instrumental aggression doesn't pay by simply returning the toy to Gail and denying him his objective. However, this strategy wouldn't work if Lennie is an insecure child who feels neglected and has attacked his sister *in order to attract his mother's attention;* under these circumstances, the mother would be reinforcing Lennie's aggression if she attended to it at all! So what is she to do?

One proven method that she might use is the **incompatible-response technique**—a strategy of ignoring all but the most serious of Lennie's aggressive antics (thereby denying him an "attentional" reward) while reinforcing such acts as cooperation and sharing that are incompatible with aggression. Teachers who have tried this strategy find that it gradually produces an increase in children's prosocial conduct and a corresponding decrease in their hostilities (Brown & Elliot, 1965; Conduct Problems Prevention Research Group, 1999).

And how might adults handle *serious* acts of harm-doing without "reinforcing" them with their attention? One effective approach is the **time-out technique** that Patterson favors—a technique in which the adult removes the offender from the situation in which his aggression is reinforced (for example, by sending him to his room until he is ready to exert some self-control and behave appropriately). Although this approach may generate some resentment, the adult in charge is not physically abusing the child, is not serving as an aggressive model, and is not likely to unwittingly reinforce the child who misbehaves as a means of attracting attention. The time-out procedure is most effective at controlling children's hostilities when adults also reinforce cooperative or helpful acts that are incompatible with aggression (Parke & Slaby, 1983).

incompatible-response technique
a nonpunitive method of behavior modification in which adults ignore undesirable conduct while reinforcing acts that are incompatible with these responses.

time-out technique
a form of discipline in which children who misbehave are removed from the setting until they are prepared to act more appropriately.

Photo 9.7
Time-out can be a most effective means of controlling children's aggression and other misconduct, particularly when adults also strive to reinforce behaviors that are incompatible with aggression.

Social-Cognitive Interventions

Highly aggressive youngsters, particularly those high in *reactive aggression,* can profit from social-cognitive interventions that help them to (1) regulate their anger and (2) to become more skilled at empathizing with and taking others' perspectives so that they will not be so likely to overattribute hostile intentions to their peers (Crick & Dodge, 1996; Rabiner, Lenhart, & Lochman, 1990). In one study (Guerra & Slaby, 1990), a group of violent adolescent offenders were coached in such skills as (1) looking for nonhostile cues that might be associated with harmdoing, (2) controlling their impulses (or anger), and

Jim Pickerell/Stock Boston

(3) generating nonaggressive solutions to conflict. Not only did these violent offenders show dramatic improvements in their social problem-solving skills, but they also became less inclined to endorse beliefs supporting aggression and less aggressive in their interactions with authority figures and other inmates. Michael Chandler (1973) found a similar reduction in the hostile social cognitions and aggressive behaviors of a group of 11 to 13-year-old delinquents who had participated in a 10-week program designed specifically to make them more aware of other people's intentions and feelings (see also Kazdin, 2003a, and Lochman & Wells, 2004, for other successful social-cognitive interventions with aggressive children).

Applications: Preventing Aggression and Violence at School

Violence among young people in the United States is a significant public health problem (Snyder, 2003; U.S. Department of Health and Human Services, 2001). We've all seen attention-grabbing stories about disgruntled youth (such as Cho at Virginia Tech or the Columbine duo in Colorado) who take weapons to school and begin methodically killing their classmates and teachers. Although these incidents are infrequent and children's risk of homicide at school is low, elementary and middle school children in the United States are at significant risk of experiencing nonlethal forms of aggression and violence from bullies (Kaufman et al., 2000; Singer et al., 1999), and the 7 percent of high school students who have taken a weapon to school over the past 30 days (Kann et al., 2000) obviously have the means at their disposal to do great harm. Indeed, while many forms of violent crime have decreased over the past 20 years, arrest rates for aggravated assaults—a type of violence common among youth—are almost 70 percent higher today than they were in 1983 (U.S. Department of Health and Human Services, 2001; see also Dodge, Coie, & Lynam, 2006).

Not surprisingly, social-developmentalists interested in aggression and antisocial conduct have begun to design interventions aimed at preventing aggression and violence at school. These investigators generally favor *comprehensive* preventive interventions, administered universally to all students rather than solely to the highly aggressive children, and incorporating a variety of proven strategies such as reinforcing prosocial conduct, helping children to regulate and control anger, better understand others' feelings and intentions, and seek nonaggressive solutions to conflict.

One such program that has been carefully evaluated is PeaceBuilders, a school-wide violence prevention program undertaken in ethnically-diverse kindergarten through fifth-grade classrooms in Tucson, Arizona (Flannery et al., 2003). PeaceBuilders attempts to alter the school climate by rewarding prosocial conduct and providing children with strategies to avoid reinforcing aggression and other antisocial behaviors. Children learn several basic rules: praise others, avoid putdowns, right wrongs, notice and correct hurts. New lessons and strategies for becoming more prosocial and less antagonistic are introduced regularly. Initial outcomes are very positive. Compared to peers in comparable classrooms that have not participated in PeaceBuilders, those who have participated become more prosocial, less aggressive, and are rated by teachers as significantly more sensitive, empathic, cooperative, and self-controlled (Flannery et al., 2003). What's more, progress made by intervention children after one year was maintained throughout a second year of intervention, and the benefits of the program among third- through fifth-graders were strongest for students who were initially highest in aggression.

Evaluations of two other programs that targeted young elementary school children in New York City and Seattle also found that program participants were significantly less aggressive at school than comparable children in classrooms that did not participate. And there was more: Program participants also showed increases (as rated by teachers) in prosocial behaviors and academic achievement and decreases in internalizing disorders such as anxiety and depression; and the longer classes participated in the program, the more positive the outcomes (see Heinrich, Brown, & Aber, 1999, for an overview of these interventions). A recent follow-up on the New York City Intervention reveals that this Resolving Conflict Creativity Program, with its heavy emphasis on persuading children to communicate, manage anger, overcome their hostile attributional biases, and rely on nonaggressive methods of solving social problems, was continuing to have an impact on preadolescent fifth- and sixth-graders, whose teachers saw them as more prosocial and less aggressive than comparable program nonparticipants (Aber, Brown, & Jones, 2003).

Successful interventions undertaken to date range from those aimed at reducing specific kinds of aggression such as bullying (Frey et al., 2005) to exceptionally comprehensive programs that include virtually all methods known to reduce children's aggression, and even include a parent-training component. Once such ambitious program is Fast Track that targeted low-SES first-graders at high risk for aggression and delinquency. Fast Track not only sought to reduce aggression and prevent antisocial conduct, but also to promote academic achievement and reduce the incidence of high school dropout. Full evaluations of the program are as yet incomplete; but compared to children not participating in the intervention, Fast Track children showed better social skills and less aggressive behavior in first, third, and fifth grades, as well as lower levels of clinically deviant conduct disorders (Conduct Problems Prevention Research Group, 2002, 2004).

So the early returns are quite promising. Yet much more research is needed to identify exactly which aspects of the interventions are most closely tied to longer-term reductions in aggression and antisocial conduct. By doing so, it may be possible to design reasonably *economical* interventions, administered by classroom teachers (or teachers' assistants) as part of "citizenship" curriculum already in place, to improve the social competencies of our grade-school children.

SUMMARY

WHAT IS AGGRESSION?

+ Human aggression is a pervasive phenomenon that has been defined in many different ways. Freud used the term **Thanatos** to describe what he considered to be an inborn aggressive and destructive instinct. Ethnologists also view aggression as a basic part of human nature.

+ Learning theorists have rejected instinct definitions in favor of the **behavioral definition of aggression** and, more recently, an **intentional definition of aggression.** Aggressive acts are often further subdivided into two categories: **Hostile aggression** and **instrumental aggression.** Yet people often disagree whether particular acts are truly aggressive, thus reflecting the notion that aggression is largely a social judgment individuals make about injurious acts, based on the meaning of those acts *to them*.

THEORIES OF AGGRESSION

+ Freud proposed that humans are driven by a destructive instinct, the *Thanatos,* which he considered responsible for the generation of aggression impulses. Ethologists describe aggression as a fighting instinct triggered by certain eliciting cues in the environment. Thus, both schools of thought view humans as instinctively aggressive.

+ From the early and rather simple **frustration/aggression hypothesis** sprang other learning theories of aggression. Berkowitz's revised frustration/aggression theory contends that frustration as well as provocations and previously

acquired aggressive habits increase one's readiness to aggress. But aggressive responses may not occur unless **aggressive cues** are present to evoke them. Bandura's social-learning theory describes how aggressive responses are acquired through direct experience and observational learning and are maintained to become habits. He also broke new ground by claiming that (1) any form of arousal can promote aggression, and (2) our cognitive interpretation of harm-doing is more important in determining our reactions than is the amount of objective harm done.

+ Dodge's social-information processing theory extends Bandura's cognitive emphasis, describing six information-processing phases that children may display as they interpret harm done and formulate a response. This model has helped us to discriminate **proactive aggressors,** for whom aggression is usually a means to other ends, from **reactive aggressors,** who display a **hostile attributional bias** and quickly retaliate after real or imagined provocations.

DEVELOPMENTAL TRENDS IN AGGRESSION

+ Instrumental aggression emerges by the end of the first year as infants begin to quarrel with siblings and peers over toys and other possessions.

+ Over the course of childhood, aggression becomes less physical and increasingly verbal, and somewhat less instrumental and increasingly hostile or **retaliatory** in nature. By middle childhood, a small number of youngsters are responsible for a majority of aggressive incidents. The participants in these exchanges are often bullies and their **passive** and/or **provocative victims.**

+ Overt aggression continues to decline in adolescence, except for the most highly aggressive individuals, who can become truly violent. However, many adolescents, though showing less aggression, are turning to other covert or indirect methods to express their anger or discontent.

+ At the population level, aggressive dispositions are moderately stable over time for both males and females. However, there is variability at the individual level. Children who follow a **chronic-persistence trajectory** are highly aggressive throughout childhood, whereas those displaying a **high-level desister trajectory** are high in aggression early in life and become less aggressive over time. Children displaying a **moderate-level desister trajectory** are moderately aggressive early in childhood but become less aggressive over time, whereas those displaying a **no-problem trajectory** are low in aggression throughout childhood and adolescence. Yet other youth may display a **late-onset trajectory,** becoming more aggressive as adolescents or young adults after a tranquil childhood. Both genetic influences and environmental factors contribute to stability of aggression over time.

SEX DIFFERENCES IN AGGRESSION

+ On an absolute level, males are more *overtly* (physically and verbally) aggressive than females. This well-established sex difference reflects the interactive influence of biological and social forces. However, this research may underestimate female proclivities for aggression, for girls are often found to exceed boys in **relational aggression.**

BIOLOGICAL INFLUENCES ON AGGRESSION

+ Contrary to popular belief, testosterone levels are only weakly related, at best, to the incidence of aggression and antisocial conduct. However, studies from around the world indicate that identical twins are more similar in aggression and delinquency than fraternal twins are—a finding that indicates that our propensities for aggression/antisocial conduct are influenced in part by the genes we have inherited. It is not that some of us inherit "aggressive" genes. A more plausible explanation is that genetically influenced characteristics such as temperament influence the reactions that we evoke from others and the environments we create for ourselves, and these genotype/environment correlations influence how aggressive or antisocial we become.

CULTURAL AND SUBCULTURAL INFLUENCES ON AGGRESSION

+ A person's aggressive inclinations will depend in part on the cultural and subcultural settings in which he or she is raised.

Due in part to social class differences in parenting, and to a greater likelihood of living in high-risk neighborhoods that are low in **collective efficacy,** children and adolescents from disadvantaged backgrounds are more aggressive and display higher rates of delinquency than their middle-class peers.

FAMILY INFLUENCES ON AGGRESSION

+ Cold and rejecting parents who rely on **power assertion** and who often permit aggression are likely to raise highly aggressive children. However, the socialization of aggression is a two-way street, for characteristics of the child (such as temperament or reactions to discipline) can affect parental attitudes and child-rearing practices.

+ Strife-ridden homes appear to be breeding grounds for aggression and violence. Parental conflict at home increases the likelihood that children will have hostile, aggressive interactions with siblings and peers. Many highly aggressive youngsters live in **coercive home environments** in which such hostile behaviors such as bickering and fighting are **negatively reinforced.** Children who are influenced most by a coercive family climate are those with impetuous and fearless temperaments who cannot regulate negative emotions and who often evoke hostile, coercive responses from family members. Family therapy is often necessary to help these out-of-control children, who otherwise are at risk of alienating teachers and peers, falling in with deviant peers, and becoming increasingly antisocial—sometimes to the point of joining **gangs** and graduating to violence and other serious forms of delinquency.

METHODS OF CONTROLLING AGGRESSION AND ANTISOCIAL CONDUCT

+ Contrary to the **catharsis hypothesis, cathartic techniques** are not effective means of reducing children's hostilities. Creating "nonaggressive" play environments is a more fruitful approach.

+ *Proactive* aggressors can benefit when adults rely on such control procedures as the time-out and the **incompatible-response technique,** which teaches them that aggression doesn't pay and that nonaggressive means of problem solving are better ways to achieve their objectives. And all aggressive youngsters, particularly hot-headed *reactive aggressors,* can benefit from social-cognitive interventions that help them regulate their anger and become more skilled at empathizing with and taking others' perspectives, thus becoming less inclined to attribute hostile intents to other people.

+ Comprehensive school-based interventions such as PeaceBuilders, the Resolving Conflict Creatively Program, and Fast Track are achieving some noteworthy success at fostering children's social competencies and reducing levels of aggression at school.

CHAPTER 10

Altruism and Moral Development

SEVERAL YEARS AGO, one of my laboratory classes interviewed first-time parents of newborn infants and asked them, "What would you say is the most important aspect of a child's social development—the lessons that you most hope to instill?" Here is a portion of a highly representative response.

Mother: Well . . . I want him to be a good kid . . . to think not only about himself and his own needs but about other kids too.

Father: Honey, he also has to look out for himself and not get taken advantage of; but (turning to interviewer) to learn to do it in the right way.

Interviewer: What do you mean by the right way?

Father: I mean that he should not bully kids to get his own way. He has to learn how to do his own thing while getting along with other people and following the rules.

Interviewer: What rules?

Father: You know . . . not hurting others; learning to do what we and other adults think is right; paying attention to his teachers; staying out of trouble . . . things like that.

Mother: It's more than that, S_____. We need to teach him *why* he should follow rules and make him feel ashamed of breaking them so that we don't have to look over his shoulder all the time to see that he behaves.

Amazingly, perhaps, 74 percent of the new parents in the sample provided responses that were in many ways similar to this one, indicating that, above all, they hoped that their children would acquire a strong sense of *morality*—right and wrong—to guide their everyday transactions with other people. And when elaborating on the moral principles they hoped to instill, most of their responses fit nicely into one of the following categories (all of which can be seen in the interview above):

1. *Avoid hurting others.* Parents generally hoped their children could learn to become appropriately autonomous and serve their needs without harming others. In fact, unprovoked and intentional acts of harmdoing—or *aggression*—was one class of behavior that most parents said they would try to suppress as they try to instill the principle that it is inappropriate and a violation of another person's rights to purposely attempt to harm that person.

2. *Prosocial concern.* Another value that many parents hoped to instill was a sense of *altruism*—that is, a selfless concern for the welfare of other people and a willingness to act on that concern. In fact, it is not at all unusual for parents to encourage such altruistic acts as sharing, comforting, or helping others, while their children are still in diapers.

3. *A personal commitment to abide by rules.* Finally, almost all of our survey respondents mentioned the importance of persuading children to comply with socially condoned rules of conduct and of monitoring their behavior to ensure that these rules are followed. They felt that the ultimate goal of this *moral socialization* is to help the child acquire a set of *personal* values, or ethical principles, that will enable her to distinguish right from wrong and to do the "right" things, even when there may be no one else present to monitor and evaluate her conduct.

Having covered the topic of aggression in Chapter 9, we will now examine the other two interrelated aspects of social development that people often consider when making judgments about a person's moral character. We will begin by exploring the development of an attribute that is seemingly incompatible with aggression—prosocial concern (or altruism)—as we consider how young and reputedly selfish children might come to make personal sacrifices to benefit others. We will then examine the broader issue of moral development and trace the child's evolution from a seemingly self-indulgent creature who appears to respect no rules to a moral philosopher of sorts who has internalized certain ethical principles to evaluate her own and others' conduct.

Let's now consider how children might become prosocially inclined.

WHAT ARE ALTRUISM AND PROSOCIAL BEHAVIOR?

Prosocial behavior is *any action that is intended to benefit other people,* such as sharing with someone less fortunate that oneself, comforting or rescuing a distressed person, cooperating with or helping someone to achieve an objective, or even simply making others feel good by complimenting them on their appearance or accomplishments (Eisenberg, Fabes, & Spinrad, 2006). Now, before proceeding further, briefly scan the following four statements:

1. John S., a millionaire, makes a $50,000 contribution to AIDS research.
2. Odell W. intervenes to help a young female mugging victim and is stabbed to death.
3. Juan K. donates a pint of blood, receiving $15 for his donation.
4. Sam P. repays his friend Jim for a previous favor by offering to help Jim paint his garage.

Most of us would undoubtedly agree that these acts are examples of *prosocial* behavior. But would you consider each to be *altruistic*? My own students often disagree on whether one or more of these four acts qualify as **altruism.**

Most adults, including the vast majority of students, favor a **motivational/(intentional) view of altruism.** That is, they view as altruistic those kindly acts for which the actor's *primary* motive is to provide a benefit or other positive consequence to another person. Thus, altruism implies some sympathy and/or concern for others' welfare, and few adults would teach children that it is appropriate to serve others only in exchange for rewards or promises of repayment.

Yet a skeptical minority of adults seriously doubts that any form of prosocial conduct is motivated *solely* out of a concern for others without regards for the self. Is John S. in scenario 1 truly altruistic? What would you say upon learning that John S. has AIDS? Even Odell W., who made the supreme sacrifice in scenario 2, could conceivably be seeking adulation (or other anticipated rewards) from the woman he might have rescued. Because it is often difficult to pinpoint a helper's underlying intent, some adults (and developmentalists) favor a **behavioral definition of altruism,** which states that an altruistic act is one that benefits another person *regardless of the actor's motives.* In other words, altruism and prosocial behavior are viewed as roughly synonymous concepts, and any and all of the scenarios described above could be labeled "altruistic."

Interestingly, children as old as 12 seem to favor a behavioral definition of altruism, making few distinctions between actors who helped others out of sympathy from those who helped to repay favors or to obtain tangible rewards (Peterson & Gelfand, 1984). And even though parents generally favor the motivational definition of altruism, neither they nor most developmentalists make sharp distinctions between altruism and prosocial behavior when referring (or responding to) the benevolence of young children. One reason they don't is that people in Western societies (even those as young as second-graders) generally perceive themselves as having less of an obligation to do something nice for others (the positive side of morality) than to inhibit harm-doing and antisocial conduct

Photo 10.1
Might there be any justification for considering this prosocial act nonaltruistic? If so, which definition of altruism do you favor?

David Young-Wolff/PhotoEdit, Inc.

(the negative side of morality; Grusec, 1991; Kahn, 1992). In other words, benevolent acts, although socially sanctioned, often have a *discretionary* quality about them and thus are often *not* viewed as mandatory.[1] So in the interest of promoting such positive but non-obligatory behaviors, parents and teachers are likely to view a variety of benevolent acts as "good" and worthy of praise (even if not wholly altruistic).

THEORIES OF ALTRUISM AND PROSOCIAL DEVELOPMENT

Several theorists have debated the issue of whether the bases for altruism are innate or learned. *Evolutionary* theorists believe that a sense of prosocial concern is a preadapted, genetically programmed attribute—a basic component of human nature—that helps to ensure the survival of the species. By contrast, *psychoanalytic* and *social-learning* theorists argue that a child's prosocial inclinations derive not from his or her genes or evolutionary history but, rather, from experiences with social agents (altruism is acquired). *Cognitive-developmental* theorists can certainly agree with this latter point of view. However, they would add that both the form and the frequency of a child's prosocial conduct will depend in part on his or her level of social-cognitive development.

Biological Theories: Are We "Programmed" for Prosocial Conduct?

In 1965, Donald Campbell argued that altruism is in part instinctive—a basic component of human nature. His argument hinged on the assumption that individuals, be they animal or human, are more likely to receive protection from natural enemies and to satisfy their basic needs if they live together in cooperative social units. If this assumption is correct, then cooperative, altruistic individuals would be most likely to survive and to pass along "altruistic genes" to their offspring. Thus, over thousands of years evolutionary processes would favor the development of innate prosocial motives. Campbell notes that "the tremendous survival value of being social makes innate social motives as likely on *a priori* grounds as self-centered ones" (1965, p. 301; see also Hastings, Zahn-Waxler, & McShane, 2006).

How exactly have we humans evolved that might make us prosocially inclined? Martin Hoffman (1981, 2000) proposes that the capacity for *empathy*—our tendency to become aroused by and vicariously experience the emotions of others—is the biological substrate for altruistic concern. Why else, Hoffman asks, would we set aside our own selfish motives to aid other people or to avoid harming them unless we had the capacity to share their emotions and experience their distress?

Indeed, we noted in Box 3.1 that newborn infants may be displaying a primitive empathic response when they become distressed at the sound of another infant's cries. However, an inborn capacity for empathy does *not* imply that altruism is "automatic" or programmed in any biologically deterministic way, for as Hoffman argues, empathic sensitivities are subject to environmental influence and may be fostered or suppressed by the social environments in which children are raised. This presents a major challenge to evolutionary accounts of prosocial behavior, which pertain to the human species as a whole and do not account for individual differences in empathy and prosocial conduct.

The Behavioral Genetic Viewpoint Behavioral geneticists have argued (and found) that our proclivities for empathy, sympathy, and prosocial activities are influenced to some extent by the genes that we have inherited (see Eisenberg, Fabes, & Spinrad, 2006, and

---

[1]As we will see later in the chapter, people from collectivist societies and subcultures are much more inclined to view prosocial conduct as obligatory or mandatory than are Westerners from individualistic societies.

Knafo & Plomin, 2006, for recent reviews). The results of several twin studies suggest that genes, shared environments, and nonshared environments all contribute to empathic responding and prosocial behavior for preschool and young elementary school children, and that the contributions of genes and nonshared environmental influences become larger with the passage of time.

There are several important implications of these findings. First, the declining contributions of shared environmental influences imply that home environments and parents' attempts to foster empathy and prosocial conduct are most important early in life. Second, the fact that genes influence prosocial conduct does not imply that some of us inherit more "altruistic" genes than others. Instead, genetic contributions to empathy and altruism are most closely linked to differences in temperament. For example, children who are low in negative emotionality and high in effortful control are less likely to become overwhelmed emotionally by another person's distress and thus are more inclined to react sympathetically to that person's plight (see Eisenberg, Fabes, & Spinrad, 2006; Valiente et al., 2004). Finally, it is hardly surprising that nonshared environmental influences have a stronger influence on prosocial behavior over time, for as siblings mature, new environments (for example, day-care placements, peer groups, friendships) that they do not share become increasingly widespread. So if one sibling, for example, develops a long-standing friendship with a highly prosocial peer, it is easy to see how she might become more prosocially inclined than her twin brother who does not share this friendship (Knafo & Plomin, 2006).

In sum, evolutionary processes may well have operated so as to foster empathic capabilities and prosocial motives in human beings, and genetic differences among us humans help to explain individual differences in empathy, sympathy, and prosocial conduct. Nevertheless, behavioral genetics research implies that both shared and nonshared environmental influences contribute very meaningfully to our prosocial inclinations. Now let's turn to other theories that stress environmental contributions to children' prosocial development.

Psychoanalytic Theory: Let Your Conscience Be Your Guide

Recall from our discussion of psychoanalytic theory in Chapter 2 that Sigmund Freud described the young child as a self-serving creature constantly driven by id-based, hedonistic impulses. This characterization of human nature might seem to suggest that the concept of altruism offers a severe challenge to a psychoanalytic account of personality development: How is it possible for a selfish, egoistic child to acquire a sense of altruistic concern that will occasionally dictate that he or she make self-sacrificing responses to benefit others?

The challenge is not as formidable as it first appears. According to proponents of psychoanalytic theory, prosocial norms and principles—for example, the **norm of social responsibility** and the Golden Rule—are but a few of the many parental prescriptions and values that may be internalized during the period of childhood in which the superego develops. We will examine the process of superego development as we take up Freud's theory of Oedipal morality later in the chapter.

norm of social responsibility
the principle that we should help others who are in some way dependent on us for assistance.

Social-Learning Theory: What's In It for Me?

Altruism presents an interesting paradox for social-learning theory (Rosenhan, 1972). A central premise of the social-learning approach is that people repeat behaviors that are reinforced and avoid repeating responses that prove costly or punishing. Yet many prosocial acts seem to defy this view of human nature: Altruists occasionally choose to take dangerous risks, forgo personal rewards, and donate their own valuable resources (thereby incurring a loss) in order to benefit others. The challenge for social-learning theorists is to explain how these self-sacrificial tendencies are acquired and maintained.

Responses to the challenge have been many and varied. On a conceptual level, some learning theorists have taken the position that all prosocial acts, even those that prove extremely costly to the benefactor, are prompted by some form of subtle reward or self-gain. For example, one could argue that the German citizens who risked their lives to rescue Jews from their Nazi tormentors did so in order to increase their self-esteem, win a favorable evaluation from future generations, or reap the benefits afforded to morally righteous people in the afterlife. The major problem with this explanation is its circularity: It is assumed that, because helping behavior occurred, its consequences must have been reinforcing.

Although tangible rewards do not always follow altruistic responses, altruism may still be a function of social learning and reinforcement. Let's consider three ways in which children might learn that altruism "pays off."

Relieving Empathic Responses   Our capacity for empathy may help to explain why we might help, comfort, or share with others in situations where there are no obvious tangible rewards to sustain helping behavior. For example, a person who empathizes with a suffering victim and vicariously experiences the victim's distress may have learned from past experience that if she helps or comforts the victim, she will not only relieve the victim's pain and suffering but her own distress as well. So prosocial responses may often appear to be self-sacrificing when, in fact, they *reinforce* the helper by making her feel good or by relieving empathic distress.

Reinforcing Prosocial Acts   Learning theorists also believe that if parents and teachers often preach the virtues of prosocial conduct and praise children for their acts of kindness, some of the positive affect resulting from the praise will become associated with the prosocial acts so that children will feel good when they behave prosocially. In other words, acts of kindness become *self-reinforcing*. And because children receive periodic praise or recognition for their benevolence, it is not hard to imagine how prosocial acts might retain their "satisfying" qualities over time and become quite resistant to extinction.

Learning by Observation   Finally, Albert Bandura (1989) believes that the most pervasive influence on children's prosocial concern is the behavior of other people—the social models to whom they are exposed. And he may be right, for as we will see, children who witness the charitable acts of altruistic models often become more prosocially inclined, even when the models incur personal costs and receive no tangible benefits for their kindly deeds (Eisenberg, Fabes, & Spinrad, 2006).

Photo 10.2 Children learn many prosocial lessons by observing the behavior of altruistic models.

In sum, learning theorists have offered several plausible explanations for children's willingness to perform prosocial acts that promise few if any tangible rewards and may even be costly. In a later section of the chapter, we will follow up on these ideas by taking a closer look at the contributions of reinforcement, empathy, and social modeling influences to children's prosocial development.

Cognitive Theories of Altruism: Maturity Is the Medium

Both cognitive-developmental theorists and social information-processing theorists assume that prosocial responses such as cooperation, sharing, giving reassurance and comfort, and volunteering to help others should become increasingly apparent over the course of childhood (Eisenberg, Lennon, & Roth, 1983; Kohlberg, 1969; Chapman et al., 1987). The basis for this prediction is straightforward: As children develop intellectually, they will acquire important cognitive skills that will affect both their reasoning about prosocial issues and their motivation to act in the interests of others.

Cognitive theorists have proposed that there are four broad phases of prosocial development. The first phase, in which some sharing and demonstrations of sympathy are observed, begins in the second year of life. This is the period when many toddlers begin to react more predictably to others' distress, often becoming distressed themselves (that is, empathizing) and occasionally trying to cheer a distressed companion (M. L. Hoffman, 2000). The second broad phase of development roughly coincides with Piaget's preoperational period (ages 3–6). Presumably, young preschool children are still relatively egocentric, and their thinking about prosocial issues (as well as their actual behavior) is often self-serving, or hedonistic. Acts that benefit others are considered worth performing if one might expect some comparable benefit in return. During middle childhood and preadolescence (or Piaget's concrete-operational stage), children are becoming less egocentric, are acquiring important role-taking skills, and should now begin to focus on the legitimate needs of others as a justification for prosocial behavior. This is the period when children begin to think that any act of kindness that most people would condone is probably "good" and should be performed. It is also the phase at which sympathetic responses should become a more important contributor to altruism. Finally, adolescents who have reached formal operations have begun to better understand and more readily appreciate the implications of abstract prosocial norms—universal principles such as the norm of social responsibility or the Golden Rule that (1) would encourage them to direct their acts of kindness to a wider range of prospective recipients and (2) may also trigger strong attributions of personal responsibility for prosocial conduct and feelings of guilt or self-condemnation should they callously ignore their obligations (Chapman et al., 1987; Eisenberg, Lennon, & Roth, 1983).

Many cognitively-oriented researchers have chosen to explore the links between particular cognitive skills (for example, role-taking) and children's prosocial behaviors rather than trying to identify broad stages of prosocial development. Yet Nancy Eisenberg and her associates have charted age-related changes in children's reasoning about prosocial issues, and her results are indeed interesting. We will review both these lines in inquiry in a later section of the chapter.

⌇ DEVELOPMENTAL TRENDS IN ALTRUISM

As we noted in opening the chapter, a genuine concern about the welfare of other people and a willingness to act on this concern are attributes that most adults hope their children will acquire. In fact, many parents are already encouraging altruistic acts such as sharing, cooperating, or helping while their children are still in diapers! Experts in child development would once have claimed that these well-intentioned adults were wasting their time, for infants and toddlers were thought so egocentric as to be incapable of considering the needs of anyone other than themselves. But the experts were wrong!

Origins of Prosocial Behavior

Long before children receive any formal moral or religious training, they may act in ways that resemble the prosocial behavior of older people. Twelve- to 18-month-olds, for example, will occasionally offer toys to their companions (Hay et al., 1991) and even attempt to help their mothers with such household chores as sweeping or dusting (Rheingold, 1982). And the prosocial conduct of very young children even has a certain "rationality" about it. For example, 2-year-olds are more likely to offer toys to a peer when playthings are scarce rather than plentiful (Hay et al., 1991) and are more likely to help a regular playmate than a child who is not as familiar to them (Eisenberg, Fabes, & Spinard, 2006).

Are toddlers capable of behaving compassionately toward their companions? Yes, indeed, and these displays of prosocial concern are not all that uncommon (Eisenberg, Fabes, & Spinard, 2006). Carolyn Zahn-Waxler and her colleagues (Zahn-Waxler, Radke-Yarrow, et al., 1992) asked mothers of 13- to 25-month-old toddlers to observe and record their children's reactions to others' distress. As we see in Table 10.1, the most frequent response of the youngest toddlers was to become upset themselves and to turn or move away from a distressed companion. If a 12- to 18-month-old does decide that some comforting is necessary, she is likely to seek her mother or some other adult to tend to the distressed person rather than providing comfort herself (M. L. Hoffman, 2000). But by age 20–23 months, toddlers were more inclined to show concern for someone experiencing distress that they had not caused, and often tried to do something themselves to comfort their companions. Consider the reaction of 21-month-old John to his distressed playmate Jerry:

> Today Jerry was kind of cranky; he just started . . . bawling and he wouldn't stop. John kept coming over and handing Jerry toys, trying to cheer him up. . . . He'd say things like "Here, Jerry," and I said to John "Jerry's sad; he doesn't feel good; he had a shot today." John would look at me with his eyebrows wrinkled together like he really understood that Jerry was crying because he was unhappy. . . . He went over and rubbed Jerry's arm and said, "Nice Jerry," and continued to give him toys [Zahn-Waxler, Radke-Yarrow, & King, 1979, pp. 321–322].

Clearly, John was concerned about his little playmate and did what he could to make him feel better.

Although some 2- to 3-year-olds may regularly attempt to comfort distressed playmates, others rarely do. These individual differences in early compassion are due, in part, to temperamental variations. For example, 2-year-olds who are temperamentally fearful, or behaviorally inhibited, are much more likely than fearless, uninhibited toddlers to become highly upset by others' distress and to turn away from a distressed acquaintance in an attempt to regulate their own *personal* distress (Young, Fox, & Zahn-Waxler, 1999).

Table 10.1 Mothers' reports of the proportion of times their toddlers displayed sympathy, prosocial behavior, aggression, or personal distress to others' distress that they did not cause

Toddler Reaction	13–15 Months	18–20 Months	23–25 Months
Sympathy	.09	.10	.25
Prosocial behavior	.09	.21	.49
Aggressive behavior	.01	.01	.03
Personal distress	.15	.12	.07

Source: Adapted from Zahn-Waxler, Radke-Yarrow, et al. (1992).

Yet individual differences in early compassion also depend on parents' reactions to occasions in which their toddler has harmed another child. Carolyn Zahn-Waxler and her associates (1979) found that mothers of less compassionate toddlers typically used coercive tactics such as verbal rebukes or physical punishment to discipline harm-doing. By contrast, mothers of more compassionate toddlers frequently disciplined harm-doing with simple **affective explanations** that may foster sympathy (and perhaps some remorse) by helping the child to see the relation between his or her own acts and the distress they have caused (for example, "Stop that! You made Doug cry; it's not nice to bite!").

affective explanations
discipline which focuses a child's attention on the harm or distress that his or her conduct has caused others.

Age-Related Changes in Altruism

Although many 2- to 3-year-olds will show some sympathy and compassion toward distressed companions, they are not particularly eager to make truly *self-sacrificial* responses, such as sharing a treasured toy with a peer. Sharing and other benevolent acts are more likely if adults instruct a toddler to consider others' needs (Levitt et al., 1985) or if a peer should actively elicit sharing through a request or a threat of some kind, such as "I won't be your friend if you won't gimme some" (Birch & Billman, 1986). But, on the whole, acts of *spontaneous* self-sacrifice in the interest of others are relatively infrequent among toddlers and young preschool children (Eisenberg, Fabes, & Spinard, 2006). Is this because toddlers are largely oblivious to others' needs and to the good they might do by sharing or helping their companions? Probably not, for at least one observational study in a nursery-school setting found that 2½- to 3½-year-olds often took pleasure at performing acts of kindness to benefit others during *pretend play;* by contrast, 4- to 6-year-olds performed more *real* helping acts and rarely "play-acted" the role of an altruist (Bar-Tal, Raviv, & Goldberg, 1982).

Many studies conducted in cultures from around the world find that sharing, helping, and many other forms of prosocial conduct become more and more common from the early elementary school years onward (see, for example, Eisenberg, Fabes, & Spinard, 2006; Underwood & Moore, 1982; Whiting & Edwards, 1988). One kind of prosocial activity that is much more common in adolescence than at younger ages is *volunteering* for some kind of community service (for example, mentoring a disadvantaged child or working at a homeless shelter), which about half of all adolescents undertake (National Center for Educational Statistics, 1997). Although motives for volunteering may sometimes be personal rather than altruistic, researchers have generally found that adolescents who participate in programs that last for three months or longer experience increases in self-esteem and in feelings of personal responsibility to help others (Eisenberg, Fabes, & Spinard, 2006). Even participating in *required* school-based service activities seems to have a very positive effect on students who were initially less inclined to participate, often increasing their intentions to volunteer and their actual levels of civic service in the years ahead (Metz & Youniss, 2005). Why? Probably for several reasons. For one, young adolescents value the opinions of peers and are particularly sensitive to peer pressures, and exposure to classmates partaking in service activities may signal that the pursuit of prosocial goals is something that the peer group condones and expects of them (Wentzel, Filisetti, & Looney, 2007). What's more, required service activities may allow a young adolescent to experience the emotional rewards of helping and to feel more confident that he or she has the ability to better others' lives (Bandura, 2002; Eisenberg, Fabes, & Spinard, 2006). Finally, required service activities that otherwise reluctant participants successfully complete may foster a change in self-concept, so that they become more inclined to view themselves as concerned, other-oriented individuals (Cialdini & Goldstein,

Photo 10.3
Preschool children are not very altruistic and must often be coaxed to share.

Mary Kate Denny/PhotoEdit, Inc.

2004). Yet a caution is in order, for pressuring college students to volunteer may backfire by undermining their motivation to help (Stukas, Snyder, & Clary, 1999).

Much of the research we will examine seeks to explain *why* older children and adolescents tend to become more prosocially inclined. Before turning to this research, let's address one other issue social-developmentalists have pondered: Are there sex differences in altruism?

Sex Differences?   People commonly assume that girls are (or will become) more helpful, generous, and compassionate than boys. Truth or fiction? Perhaps this stereotype qualifies as a partial truth. Girls are often reported to help, comfort, and share more than boys, although the magnitude of this sex difference is not large (Eisenberg, Fabes, & Spinard, 2006; Russell et al., 2003) and is not apparent in all situations (Grusec, Goodnow, & Cohen, 1996). People believe that girls are more concerned about others' welfare, and girls often emit stronger facial and vocal expressions of sympathy than boys do (Hastings et al., 2000). But these findings are difficult to interpret because boys experience just as much physiological arousal upon encountering someone who is distressed as girls do (Eisenberg, Fabes, & Spinard, 2006). Yet boys are often found to be less cooperative and more competitive than girls. For example, one study found that, by middle childhood, boys were more likely than girls to act so as to hinder another child's chances of winning a prize while playing a game, even when they themselves could easily earn the same prize without regard to how the other player performed (Roy & Benenson, 2002). Thus, it seems as if looking good or attaining status or dominance over others seems to be more important to boys than to girls.[2]

Do girls need or seek help more than boys do? Apparently not. One study found that from first through fifth grades, children of both sexes become less and less dependent on others to accomplish tasks for them, and they were equally likely to favor indirect help (such as hints) that will enable them to master tasks on their own (Shell & Eisenberg, 1996). So the notion that girls are any less capable of accomplishing tasks without direct assistance is probably best described as a cultural myth that has little basis in fact.

⁀) COGNITIVE AND AFFECTIVE CONTRIBUTORS TO ALTRUISM

As we noted earlier, cognitive theories of altruism contend that increases in prosocial behavior throughout middle childhood and early adolescence are closely linked to the development of such attributes as role-taking skills, prosocial moral reasoning, empathy, and even a better understanding of the responsibilities implied should we come to view ourselves as helpful, compassionate, or otherwise altruistic individuals. Let's see whether there is any support for these ideas.

Role-Taking and Altruism

It makes some sense to assume that proficient role-takers might be more altruistic than poor role-takers if their role-taking skills help them to recognize and appreciate the factors that contribute to another person's distress or misfortune. And there is ample support for this notion (Eisenberg, Fabes, & Spinard, 2006; Eisenberg, Zhou, & Koller, 2001). In one study (Hudson, Forman, & Brian-Meisels, 1982), second-graders who had previously

[2]The issue of sex differences in prosocial conduct is far from resolved. Eisenberg and her colleagues (2006) note that differences between boys and girls in both prosocial behavior and empathic/sympathetic responding is much larger when parents or children themselves report prosocial inclinations than in observational or experimental studies. Thus, part of the sex differences in self-report studies may reflect reporters' gender-stereotyped beliefs that girls are more empathic, sympathetic, and prosocially inclined than boys are.

tested high or low in role-taking skills tutored kindergartners at an arts-and-crafts task and were filmed to see how they responded should their younger pupils experience any difficulties. Both the good and the poor role-takers were quite helpful if the younger children *explicitly* asked for help. But if the younger children's needs were *subtle* or their requests *indirect* (for example, frequent glances at the tutor accompanied by frowns), good role-takers recognized them and provided the necessary assistance, whereas poor role-takers usually smiled at their young charges and resumed their own activities without helping.

The study cited here and the majority of other published data provide evidence for a positive *correlation* between role-taking skills and prosocial conduct. Yet evidence for a *causal* link between **social perspective taking** (recognizing what another person is feeling, thinking, or intending) and prosocial behavior is quite clear in studies showing that children and adolescents who receive training that bolsters these role-taking skills subsequently become more charitable, more cooperative, and more concerned about the needs of others when compared with age-mates who receive no training (Chalmers & Townsend, 1990; Iannotti, 1978). However, role-taking is only one of several personal attributes that play a part in the development of altruistic behavior. Three other important contributors are children's level of **prosocial moral reasoning,** their empathic reactions to the distress of other people, and their emerging self-concepts as altruistic individuals.

social perspective taking
the ability to infer others' thoughts, intentions, motives, and attitudes.

Prosocial Moral Reasoning

Over the past 25 years, researchers have charted the development of children's reasoning about prosocial issues and its relationship to altruistic behavior. Nancy Eisenberg and her colleagues, for example, have presented children with stories in which the central character has to decide whether to help or comfort someone when the prosocial act would be personally costly. Here is one such story (Eisenberg-Berg & Hand, 1979):

prosocial moral reasoning
the thinking that people display when deciding whether to help, share with, or comfort others when these actions could prove costly to themselves.

> One day a girl named Mary was going to a friend's birthday party. On her way she saw a girl who had fallen down and hurt her leg. The girl asked Mary to go to her house and get her parents so that [they] could come and take her to a doctor. But if Mary did . . . , she would be late to the party and miss the ice-cream, cake, and all the games. What should Mary do?

As illustrated in Table 10.2, reasoning about these prosocial dilemmas may progress through as many as five levels between early childhood and adolescence. Notice that

Table 10.2 Eisenberg's levels of prosocial moral reasoning

Level	Approximate Age	Brief Description and Typical Response
Hedonistic	Preschool, early elementary school	Concern is for one's own needs. Giving help is most likely if it will benefit the self. *Example:* "I wouldn't help 'cause I'd miss the party."
Needs oriented	Elementary school and a few preschoolers	Others' needs are recognized as a legitimate basis for helping, but there is little evidence of sympathy or guilt for failing to help. *Example:* "I'd help because she needs help."
Stereotyped, approval oriented	Elementary school and some high school students	Concern for approval and stereotyped images of good and bad heavily influence one's thinking. *Example:* "My mother would hug me for helping."
Empathic orientation	Older elementary school and high school students	Judgments now include evidence of sympathetic feelings; vague references are sometimes made to duties and values. *Example:* "I'd feel good about helping because she was in pain."
Internalized values orientation	A small minority of high school students; no elementary school students	Justifications for helping (or not helping) are based on internalized values, norms, convictions, and responsibilities; violating these principles could undermine self-respect. *Example:* "I refused to make a donation because the [charity] wastes too much money fund-raising and gives little to its intended recipients."

Source: Adapted from Eisenberg, Lennon, & Roth, 1983.

preschoolers' responses are frequently *self-serving:* These youngsters often say that Mary should go to the party so as not to miss out on the fun and games. But as children mature, they tend to become increasingly responsive to the needs and wishes of others; so much so that some high school students feel that they could no longer respect themselves were they to ignore the appeal of a person in need in order to pursue their own interests (Eisenberg, Lennon, & Roth, 1983; Eisenberg, Miller, et al., 1991).

Does a child's or adolescent's level of prosocial moral reasoning predict his or her altruistic behavior? Apparently so, and the relationship between reasoning and behavior is stronger for self-sacrificial behaviors than for trivial acts of helping that involve little cost (Eisenberg, Fabes, & Spinard, 2006). For example, preschoolers who have progressed beyond the hedonistic level of prosocial moral reasoning are more likely to help and to *spontaneously* share valuable commodities with their peers than are those who still reason in a self-serving way (Eisenberg-Berg & Hand, 1979; Miller et al., 1996). Studies of older participants tell a similar story. Mature moral reasoners among a high school sample often said they would help someone they *disliked* if that person really needed their help, whereas immature moral reasoners were apt to ignore the needs of a person they disliked (Eisenberg, 1983; Eisenberg, Miller, et al., 1991). Finally, Eisenberg and her associates (1999) found in a 17-year longitudinal study that children who had shown more spontaneous sharing and who had been relatively mature in their levels of prosocial moral reasoning at age 4 to 5 remained more helpful, were more considerate of others, and reasoned more complexly about prosocial issues and social responsibilities throughout childhood, adolescence, and into young adulthood. In fact, young adolescents nominated by peers as highly prosocial have often developed a **benign attributional bias**—a tendency to give the benefit of the doubt to peers who displease them rather than assuming that their behaviors reflect hostile motives (Nelson & Crick, 1999). This willingness to accentuate the positive in others—itself a prosocial characteristic—helps prosocial youngsters to avoid hostilities and to remain cooperative and other-oriented. Taken together, then, these observations imply that prosocial dispositions can be established early and often remain reasonably stable over time (see also Eisenberg et al., 2002).

Why are mature moral reasoners so sensitive to the needs of others—even *disliked* others? Eisenberg's view is that the child's growing ability to *sympathize* with others contributes heavily to mature prosocial reasoning and to the development of a selfless concern for promoting the welfare of whoever might require one's assistance (Eisenberg et al., 1999; Eisenberg, Zhou, & Koller, 2001). Let's now consider what researchers have learned about the relationship between empathy and altruism.

Empathy: An Important Affective Contributor to Altruism

Although infants and toddlers do seem to recognize and often react to (that is, empathize) with the distress of their companions (Zahn-Waxler, Radke-Yarrow, & King, 1979; Zahn-Waxler, Radke-Yarrow, et al., 1992; and see Box 3.1), their responses are not always helpful ones. In fact, many young children exhibit clear signs of *personal distress* upon witnessing the distress or misfortunes of others (this may be the predominant response early in life) and may turn away from a person in need, or even attack him or her, in an attempt to relieve their *own* discomfort. Yet other children (even some young ones) are more inclined to interpret their empathic arousal as concern, or sympathy, for distressed others, and it is this **sympathetic empathic arousal,** rather than **self-oriented distress,** that should eventually come to promote altruism (Batson, 1991; M. L. Hoffman, 2000).

Socialization of Empathy As we noted earlier when discussing the origins of compassion in toddlers, parents can help to promote sympathetic responses by (1) modeling empathic concern and (2) relying on affectively oriented forms of discipline that help

---

benign attributional bias
tendency to give the benefit of the doubt to peers rather than quickly assuming that their displeasing actions reflect a hostile or antisocial intent.

sympathetic empathic arousal
feelings of sympathy or compassion that may be elicited when we experience the emotions of (that is, empathize with) a distressed other; thought to become an important mediator of altruism.

self-oriented distress
feeling of *personal* discomfort or distress that may be elicited when we experience the emotions of (that is, empathize with) a distressed other; thought to inhibit altruism.

young children to understand the harmful effects of any distress they may have caused others (Barnett, 1987; Hastings et al., 2000; Zahn-Waxler, Radke-Yarrow, & King, 1979; Zahn-Waxler, Radke-Yarrow, et al., 1992). Other investigators (for example, Davidov & Grusec, 2006; Zhou et al., 2002) find that parents who are warm and nurturant and who respond sensitively when their child becomes distressed tend to have children who are more empathic and prosocially inclined. Children who receive this kind of parenting experience a positive, supportive family climate in which their own emotional needs are met. And this sense of emotional security helps them to successfully regulate the negative emotions they experience over others' misfortunes, thus making them more inclined to interpret their own empathic arousal as *sympathy* rather than *personal* distress (Davidov & Grusec, 2006).

Age Trends in the Empathy-Altruism Relationship   So what is the relationship between empathy and altruism? The answer depends in part on how empathy is measured and how old the research participants are. In studies that assess empathy by having children report their own feelings about the misfortunes of story characters, researchers have found little association between empathy and altruism. However, teacher ratings and self-ratings of children's empathic sensitivities and children's own *facial* expressions of emotion in response to others' misfortunes are better predictors of prosocial behavior (Chapman et al., 1987; Eisenberg et al., 1990). Overall, it seems that the evidence for a link between empathy and altruism is modest at best for preschool and young grade-school children but stronger for preadolescents, adolescents, and adults (Eisenberg & Miller, 1987; Underwood and Moore, 1982).

One possible explanation for these age trends is that it simply takes some time for children to become better at regulating negative emotionality and suppressing personal distress to others' misfortunes so that they can respond more sympathetically (Eisenberg, Fabes, et al., 1998). And it is likely that social-cognitive development plays an important part in this process, for younger children may lack the role-taking skills and insight about their own emotional experiences to fully understand and appreciate (1) *why* others are distressed and thus (2) *why* they are feeling aroused (Roberts & Strayer, 1996). For example, when kindergartners see a series of slides showing a boy becoming increasingly depressed after his dog runs away, they usually attribute his sadness to an external cause (the dog's disappearance) rather than to a more "personal" or internal one, such as the boy's concern and longing for his pet (Hughes, Tingle, & Sawin, 1981). And, although kindergartners report that they too feel sad after seeing the slides, they usually provide egocentric explanations for their empathic arousal—explanations that seem to reflect *personal distress* (for example, "I might lose my dog"). However, 7- to 9-year-olds are beginning to associate their own empathic emotions with those of the story character as they put themselves in his place and infer the *psychological* basis for his sadness (for example, "I'm sad because he's sad . . . because, if he really liked the dog, then . . ."). So empathy may become a stronger contributor to prosocial behavior once children become better at inferring others' points of view (role-taking) and understanding the causes of their own empathic emotions—causes (for example, "I'm sad because he's sad") that can help them to feel *sympathy* for distressed or needy companions (Eisenberg, Gershoff, et al., 2001; Eisenberg, Fabes, & Spinard, 2006; Roberts & Strayer, 1996).

The Felt-Responsibility Hypothesis   Now an important question: *How* exactly does empathy promote altruism? Clearly, people can feel sympathy for distressed others without feeling compelled to help. So how might empathy promote altruistic *behavior?*

Photo 10.4
As children mature and develop better role-taking skills, they are more likely to sympathize with distressed companions and to provide them with comfort or assistance.

David Young-Wolff/PhotoEdit, Inc.

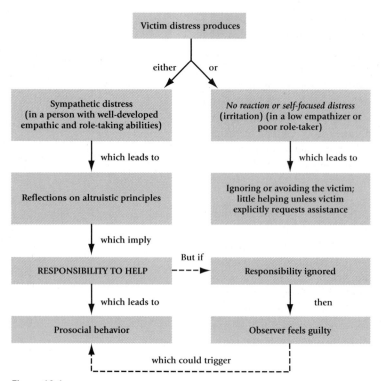

Figure 10.1
How empathy promotes altruism: a "felt responsibility" interpretation.

One possibility is that a child's *sympathetic* empathic arousal causes him to reflect on altruistic lessons he has learned—lessons such as the Golden Rule, the *norm of social responsibility,* or even the knowledge that other people approve of helping behavior. As a result of this reflection, the child is likely to assume some personal *responsibility* for aiding a victim in distress (see Figure 10.1) and would now experience some shame, guilt, or remorse for callously ignoring that obligation (Chapman et al., 1987; Williams & Bybee, 1994). Notice that this **"felt responsibility" hypothesis** is reflected in Eisenberg's higher levels of prosocial moral reasoning (see Table 10.2) and may help to explain why the link between empathy and altruism becomes stronger with age. Because older children are likely to have learned (and internalized) more altruistic principles than younger children, they should have much more to reflect on as they experience empathic arousal. Consequently, they are more likely than younger children to feel responsible for helping a distressed person and to follow through by rendering the necessary assistance.

"felt responsibility" hypothesis
the theory that empathy may promote altruism by causing one to reflect on altruistic norms and thus to feel some obligation to help others who are distressed.

Viewing Oneself as Altruistic

A person's willingness to sacrifice in order to benefit others may also hinge very critically on how altruistic she believes herself to be. Although researchers have been largely unsuccessful at identifying a definable set of altruistic personality traits (Myers, 1996), it nevertheless appears that adolescents and adults who view prosocial concern as an important part of their self-concepts do tend to be more prosocially inclined than those who do not view themselves as particularly compassionate, charitable, or helpful (Clary & Snyder, 1991; Eisenberg et al., 1999; Hart & Fegley, 1995). Could we then promote altruism by persuading youngsters to think of themselves as generous or helpful individuals?

Joan Grusec and Erica Redler (1980) sought to answer these questions by first urging 5- and 8-year-olds to (1) donate marbles to poor children, (2) share colored pencils with classmates who hadn't any, and (3) help an experimenter with a dull and repetitive task. Once children had donated, shared, or begun to work on the repetitive task, they either were told that they were "nice" or "helpful" persons for the good that they had done (self-concept training condition) or nothing was said (control condition). One to two weeks later, the children were asked by another adult to donate drawings and craft materials to help cheer up sick children at a local hospital.

Grusec and Redler found that self-concept training had a much greater effect on the 8-year-olds than the 5-year-olds. The 8-year-olds who had been told that they were "nice" or "helpful" were more likely than those in the control condition to make drawings for and to share their possessions with sick children. Why was the self-concept training so effective with 8-year-olds but not with 5-year-olds? The research we reviewed in Chapter 6 provides a strong clue. Recall that 8-year-olds are just beginning to describe the self in psychological terms and to see these "traits" as *stable* aspects of their character. Thus, when told that they were "nice" or "helpful," Grusec and Redler's 8-year-olds (but not the 5-year-olds) apparently incorporated these trait-like attributions into their self-concepts and were later trying to live up to this new, more altruistic self-image by generously volunteering assistance when help was needed. And, as we have noted, similar changes in one's altruistic self-concept may help to explain why adolescents who participate in community service activities often become even more willing to serve in the future.

So encouraging youngsters to think of themselves as concerned and caring is one way to promote acts of kindness—at least among children old enough to understand and fully appreciate the implications of trait-like attributions. In our next section, we will consider a number of other social and cultural influences that have a bearing on how altruistic children are likely to become.

⌣ CULTURAL AND SOCIAL INFLUENCES ON ALTRUISM

Cultural Influences

Cultures clearly differ in their endorsement or encouragement of altruism. In one interesting cross-cultural study, Beatrice and John Whiting (1975) observed the altruistic behavior of 3- to 10-year-olds in six cultures—Kenya, Mexico, the Philippines, Okinawa, India, and the United States. As we see in Table 10.3, the cultures in which children were most altruistic were the less industrialized societies where people tend to live in large families and children *routinely contribute to the family welfare* by processing food, preparing meals, fetching wood and water, or caring for younger brothers or sisters. Although children in Western industrialized societies are involved in relatively few family-maintenance activities, those who are assigned housework or other tasks that *benefit all family members* are more prosocially inclined than age-mates whose responsibilities consist mainly of *self*-care routines, such as cleaning their own rooms (Grusec, Goodnow, & Cohen, 1996).

Another factor contributing to the low altruism scores of children from Western industrialized nations is the tremendous emphasis these *individualistic societies* place on competition and on individual rather than group goals. By contrast, children from *collectivist societies* (and such collectivist subcultures as Native American tribes in North America or kibbutz-reared children in Israel) are taught to suppress individualism, cooperate with others for the greater good of the group, and avoid interpersonal conflicts (Triandis, 1994, 1995). So for children in many of the world's collectivist societies, prosocial behavior does not have the same "discretionary" quality about it that is true of individualistic societies; instead, giving of oneself for the greater good of the group is every bit as much an *obligation* as resolving not to break moral rules (Chen, 2000; Triandis, 1995). As illustrated in Box 10.1, children from one collectivist society (People's Republic of China) become so attuned to their culture's prosocial ideals that they think it quite inappropriate to call attention to their own good deeds—and may even deny responsibility for their acts of kindness! Yet, as immigrant

Table 10.3 Prosocial behavior in six cultures: Percentages of children in each culture who scored above the median altruism score for the cross-cultural sample as a whole

Type of Society	Percentage Scoring High in Altruism	Type of Society	Percentage Scoring High in Altruism
Nonindustrialized		*Industrialized*	
Kenya	100	Okinawa	29
Mexico	73	India	25
Philippines	63	United States	8

Source: Based on Whiting & Whiting, 1975.

Cultural Differences in Thinking about Prosocial Issues

In Western individualistic societies such as Canada and the United States, children are taught that prosocial acts are laudable and that they should feel good and even take credit for their self-sacrificial behaviors. By contrast, children in the collectivist People's Republic of China not only learn that prosocial conduct is necessary and an obligation, they are also taught to be modest, avoid self-aggrandizement, and thus not seek praise or personal recognition for their own good deeds. In fact, admitting or seeking credit for prosocial conduct is viewed as a violation of both traditional Chinese cultural norms and the government's communist-collectivist doctrine.

How might these teachings affect Chinese children's thinking about prosocial issues? Would they truly seek to downplay their good deeds? Would they be so modest and self-effacing that they might even deny responsibility for (that is, lie about) having performed altruistic acts?

To address these issues, Kang Lee and associates (1997) conducted an interesting cross-cultural study in which 7-, 9-, and 11-year-old children from Canada and the People's Republic of China evaluated four brief stories. To compare Canadian and Chinese children's thinking about *prosocial* issues, two stories involved a child who first carried out a good deed (for example, anonymously donating money to a classmate who otherwise could not go on a field trip) and who then either *truthfully admitted* this prosocial act or who *lied about it* (saying, "I did not do it") when the teacher asked, "Do you know [who is responsible for this act of kindness?]" For comparative purposes, children's thinking about *antisocial* conduct was also assessed. Each participant heard two stories in which the actor committed a misdeed (for example, injuring a classmate by knocking him down) and who then either *truthfully admitted* or who *lied* about this act when questioned by a teacher. After hearing each story, participants evaluated the goodness or naughtiness of both the actor's behavior and his/her statement about that behavior when questioned by the teacher.

Interestingly, there were no major cultural differences in evaluation of either the actor's *antisocial* conduct (which was considered very bad) or evaluations of the actor's statements about it. Both Chinese and Canadian children felt that it was very good for harm-doers to tell the truth about committing transgressions and very bad to lie about them. Similarly, both Chinese and Canadian children evaluated *prosocial* acts quite positively. However, their thinking about lying and telling the truth about prosocial conduct diverged sharply.

As the figure illustrates, Canadian children at all three ages thought that altruists should readily admit (that is, tell the truth and take credit for) their good deeds and that denying responsibility for (lying about) them was bad (or perhaps stupid). By contrast, we see that as Chinese children grow older, they increasingly come to view taking credit for prosocial acts in *less* positive terms and denying responsibility for them much *more* positively. For Chinese children, prosocial conduct is *expected,* not discretionary, and is *not* viewed as worthy of individual praise or recognition in the same way that Canadian children think it is. In fact, the strong emphasis on self-effacement and modesty in Chinese culture eventually overrides children's reluctance to lie, so that Chinese children come to view acting modest about performing behavior expected of them to be more praiseworthy than boldly telling the truth and calling undue attention to acts that any good child should perform (Lee et al., 1997).

Lest you wonder, Chinese children are not necessarily more prone to lying than Canadian children are. Children from both cultures know what lies are and view lying as less than totally virtuous. Yet the contexts in which lies surrounding prosocial issues are considered most and least appropriate clearly differ across the two cultures. Imagine two situations, one in which a person lies to help his team (a collective) achieve an important goal but hurts his friend (by omitting this individual from the team), and a second situation in which the person lies to include the friend on the team, thereby hurting the prospects of the collective. Which lie is worse? When 7-, 9-, and 11-year-olds in one study were asked to evaluate them, Chinese children from a collectivist society increasingly came to evaluate lying to help the collective less negatively than lying to help the individual. But as they grew older, Canadian children from an individualistic culture increasingly thought it better (that is, less inappropriate) to lie to help the individual (their friend) than to lie to help the collective (Fu et al., 2007).

In sum, these interesting cross-cultural studies clearly illustrate that the values that shape people's thinking about prosocial behavior (as well as the circumstances under which little "white lies" might be more or less appropriate) can vary dramatically from culture to culture.

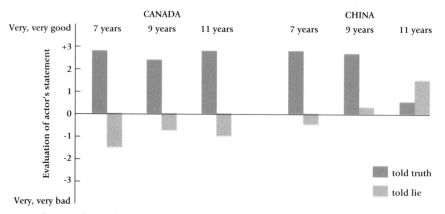

Ratings by Canadian and Chinese children of actors who told the truth or lied about committing good deeds. (Adapted from Lee et al., 1997.)

children from collectivist backgrounds become more acculturated into a Western society, they report lower levels of prosocial behavior (de Guzman & Carlo, 2004).

Although cultures may differ in the emphasis they place on altruism, most people in most societies endorse the norm of social responsibility—the rule of thumb prescribing that one should help others who need help. Let's now consider some of the ways adults might persuade young children to adopt this important value and to become more concerned about the welfare of other people.

Reinforcing Altruism

Many studies (for example, Mills & Grusec, 1989; Yarrow, Scott, & Waxler, 1973) reveal that liked and respected adults can promote prosocial behavior by *verbally reinforcing* children's acts of kindness. A little praise can go a long way because children hope to live up to standards set by a liked and respected individual, and praise that accompanies their kindly acts suggests that they are accomplishing that objective (Kochanska, Coy, & Murray, 2001). However, youngsters who are "bribed" with tangible rewards for their prosocial acts are not particularly altruistic. Why? Because they tend to attribute their kindly behaviors to a desire to earn the incentives rather than to a concern for others' welfare, and they are actually less likely than nonrewarded peers to make sacrifices to benefit others once the rewards stop (Fabes et al., 1989; Grusec, 1991).

altruistic exhortations
verbal encouragement to help, comfort, share, or cooperate with others.

Modeling Influences: Practicing and Preaching Altruism

Social-learning theorists have assumed that adults who encourage altruism and who practice what they preach will affect children in two ways. By behaving altruistically, the adult model may induce the child to perform similar acts of kindness. In addition, regular exposure to the model's **altruistic exhortations** provides the child with opportunities to internalize principles such as the norm of social responsibility that should contribute to the development of a prosocial orientation.

Photo 10.5
Children who are committed to performing prosocial acts often have parents who have encouraged altruism and who have practiced what they preach.

Laboratory experiments consistently indicate that young children who observe charitable or helpful models become more charitable or helpful themselves, especially if the model has established a warm relationship with them, provides a compelling justification, or rationale, for performing acts of kindness, and regularly *practices what he preaches*. In one study (Midlarsky & Bryan, 1972), children were exposed to an adult model who took ten turns at a game, winning five times and losing five times. On winning trials, the model either behaved *charitably*, by donating some of his winnings to a needy children's fund, or *selfishly*, by keeping all of his winnings for himself. On losing trials, the model either preached *charity* and emphasized the positive impact of charitable acts on recipients ("I know that I don't have to give, but it would make some children very happy") or preached *greed* and stressed the undesirable aspects of charity ("I could really use some spending money this week; it makes some children feel bad to get charity"). The child then played the game, won five times, and thus had five opportunities to anonymously donate money to needy children.

Elizabeth Crews/The Image Works

Table 10.4 summarizes the results. As expected, children who observed a charitable model donated a larger percentage of their winnings (35.8 percent) than children who observed a selfish model (14 percent). Furthermore, the model's verbal exhortations had a significant effect; models who exhorted charity elicited larger donations from the children (30.8 percent) than models who exhorted greed (19 percent). So charitable exhortations can increase

Table 10.4 Average percentage of winnings donated by children exposed to charitable or selfish models who preached charity or greed

Model's Behavior	Model's Verbal Preaching		Row Averages
	Charity	Greed	
Charitable	44.0	27.5	35.8
Selfish	17.5	10.5	14.0
Column Averages	30.8	19.0	

Source: Adapted from Midlarsky & Bryan, "Affect expressions and children's initiative altruism." *Journal of Experimental Research in Personality 6:* 195–203, 1972. Reprinted by permission of Elsevier.

children's generosity if they are strongly stated and justified in terms of the needs of prospective recipients. However, the relatively large donations prompted by the charitable model who preached charity serve as a reminder that our inducements to children to share or to perform other prosocial acts are most effective when we practice what we preach.

Now let's turn to the child-rearing literature to see whether the variables that promote altruism in the laboratory have similar effects on children in the natural environment.

Who Raises Altruistic Children?

Studies of Prosocial Activists   Studies of unusually charitable adults indicate that these "altruists" have enjoyed a warm and affectionate relationship with parents who themselves were highly concerned about the welfare of others. For example, Christians who risked their lives to save Jews from the Nazis during World War II reported that they had had close ties to moralistic parents (and other confidants) who always acted in accordance with their ethical principles (London, 1970; Oliner & Oliner, 1988). And interviews with white "freedom riders" from the U.S. civil rights movement of the 1960s revealed that *fully committed activists* (volunteers who gave up their homes or careers to work full-time for the cause) differed from *partially committed (part-time) activists* in two major ways: They had enjoyed warmer relations with their parents and had parents who strongly advocated altruism and who backed up these exhortations by performing many kind and compassionate deeds. By contrast, parents of partially committed activists had often preached but rarely practiced altruism (Rosenhan, 1970; see also Clary & Snyder, 1991). Finally, recent research indicates that adolescents who readily volunteer for community service activities tend to be closely connected to parents who have participated in similar kinds of community service (McLellan & Youniss, 2003). Clearly, these findings are consistent with the laboratory evidence we reviewed, which indicated that a warm and compassionate models who advocate prosocial behaviors and who practice what they preach are especially effective at eliciting prosocial responses from young children.

Parental Disciplinary Practices   Parental reactions to a child's harm-doing also play an important role in the development of altruism. Recall that mothers of less compassionate toddlers react to harm-doing in punitive or forceful ways, whereas mothers of compassionate toddlers rely more heavily on nonpunitive, affective explanations in which they display sympathy for the victim, persuade the child to accept personal responsibility for her harm-doing, and often urge her to direct some sort of comforting or helpful response toward the victim (Zahn-Waxler, Radke-Yarrow, & King, 1979; Zahn-Waxler, Radke-Yarrow et al., 1992). Research with older children paints a similar picture: Parents who continue to rely on rational, nonpunitive disciplinary techniques in which they regularly display sympathy and concern for others (including their own child) tend to raise children who are sympathetic and self-sacrificing, whereas frequent use of forceful and punitive discipline appears to inhibit altruism and lead to the development of self-centered values (Brody & Shaffer, 1982; Davidov & Grusec, 2006; Eisenberg, Fabes, & Spinard, 2006; Hastings et al., 2000).

There are probably several reasons why rational affectively oriented discipline that is heavy on reasoning might inspire children to become more prosocially inclined. First, it encourages the child to assume another person's perspective (role-taking) and to experience that person's distress (empathy training). It also teaches the child to perform helpful or comforting acts that make both the self and the other person feel better. And last but not least, these reparative responses might convince children that they can be "caring" or "helpful" people, thereby fostering a *prosocial self-concept* that children may try to live up to by performing other acts of kindness in the future.

We are now ready to turn to what Sigmund Freud and many other early theorists (for example, McDougall, 1908) claimed to be the most important aspect of socialization—the establishment of a mature sense of morality. In truth, we have been considering the topic of morality since we began Chapter 9, for the process of moral development encompasses both the growth of prosocial values and the inhibition of hostile, antisocial impulses.

◈ WHAT IS MORALITY?

During the course of development, most of us arrive at a point at which we wish to behave responsibly and to think of ourselves (and be thought of by others) as moral individuals (Blasi, 1990; Hoffman, 1988). What is **morality?** College students generally agree that morality implies a capacity to (1) *distinguish right from wrong,* (2) *act on this distinction,* and (3) *experience pride in virtuous conduct and guilt or shame over acts that violate one's standards* (Quinn, Houts, & Grasser, 1994; Shaffer, 1994). And when asked to indicate the particular attributes that *morally mature* individuals display, adults in one Western society (Canada) generally agreed that there are six aspects, or dimensions, of moral maturity, which appear in Table 10.5.

Implicit in college students' consensual definition of morality and the character traits that define moral maturity for adults is the idea that morally mature individuals do not submit to society's dictates because they expect tangible rewards for complying or fear punishments for transgressing. Rather, they eventually internalize the moral principles they have learned and will conform to these ideals, even when authority figures are not present to enforce them. As we will see, virtually all contemporary theorists consider **internalization**—the shift from externally controlled actions to conduct that is governed by internal standards and principles—to be a most crucial milestone along the road to moral maturity.

morality
a set of principles or ideals that help that the individual to distinguish right from wrong, act on the this distinction, and feel pride in virtuous conduct and guilt (or shame) for conduct that violates one's standards.

internalization
the process of adopting the attributes or standards of other people—taking these standards as one's own.

Table 10.5 Six dimensions of character that define moral maturity for Canadian adults

Character Dimension	Sample Traits
1. Principled-idealistic	Has clear values; concerned about doing right; ethical; highly developed conscience; law-abiding
2. Dependable-loyal	Responsible; loyal; reliable; faithful to spouse; honorable
3. Has integrity	Consistent; conscientious; rational; hard-working
4. Caring-trustworthy	Honest; trustful; sincere; kind; considerate
5. Fair	Virtuous; fair; just
6. Confident	Strong; self-assured; self-confident

Source: Walker & Pitts, 1998.

Photo 10.6
Resisting temptation is a difficult feat for young children to accomplish, particularly when there is no one around to help the child exercise willpower.

moral affect
the emotional component of morality, including feelings such as empathy, guilt, shame, and pride in ethical conduct.

moral reasoning
the cognitive component of morality; the thinking that people display when deciding whether various acts are right or wrong.

moral behavior
the behavioral component of morality; actions that are consistent with one's moral standards in situations in which one is tempted to violate them.

How Developmentalists Look at Morality

Developmental theorizing and research have centered on the same three moral components that college students mention in their global definition of morality:

1. An *affective*, or emotional, component that consists of the feelings (guilt, concern for others' feelings, and so on) that surround right or wrong actions and that motivate moral thoughts and actions.

2. A *cognitive* component that centers on the way we conceptualize right and wrong and make decisions about how to behave.

3. A *behavioral component* that reflects how we actually behave when we experience the temptation to lie, cheat, or violate other moral rules.

As it turns out, each of the major theories of moral development has focused on a different component of morality. Psychoanalytic theorists emphasize the affective component, or powerful **moral affects.** They believe that children are motivated to act in accordance with their ethical principles in order to experience positive affects such as pride and to avoid such negative moral emotions as guilt and shame. Cognitive-developmental theorists have concentrated on the cognitive aspects of morality, or **moral reasoning,** and have found that the ways children think about right and wrong may change rather dramatically as they mature. Finally, the research of social-learning and social information-processing theorists has helped us to understand how children learn to resist temptation and to practice **moral behavior,** inhibiting actions such as lying, stealing, and cheating that violate moral norms.

In examining each of these theories and the research it has generated, we will be looking at the relationships among moral affect, moral reasoning, and moral behavior. This information should help us to decide whether a person really has a *unified* "moral character" that is stable over time and across situations. Then we will take an in-depth look at how various child-rearing practices may affect a child's moral development and, in so doing, will attempt to integrate much of the information we have reviewed.

PSYCHOANALYTIC EXPLANATIONS OF MORAL DEVELOPMENT

In Chapter 2, we learned that psychoanalysts view the mature personality as having three components: an irrational *id*, which seeks the immediate gratification of instinctual needs, a rational *ego* that formulates *realistic* plans for meeting these needs, and a moralistic *superego* (or conscience) that monitors the acceptability of the ego's thoughts and deeds. Freud claimed that infants and toddlers lack a superego and will act on their selfish impulses unless parents control their behavior. But once the superego emerges, it was said to function as an *internal* censor—one that has the power to make a child feel proud of his virtuous conduct and guilty or shameful about committing moral transgressions. So children who are morally mature should generally resist temptation to violate moral norms in order to maintain self-esteem and avoid experiencing negative moral affects.

Freud's Theory of Oedipal Morality

According to Freud (1935/1960), the supergeo develops during the phallic stage (ages 3–6), when children were said to experience an emotional conflict with the same-sex parent that stemmed from their incestuous desire for the other-sex parent. To resolve this *Oedipus complex*, a boy was said to *identify* with and pattern himself after his father, particularly if his father is a threatening figure who arouses fear. Not only does he learn his masculine role in this manner, but he also internalizes his father's moral standards. Similarly, a girl resolves her *Electra complex* by identifying with her mother and internalizing her mother's moral standards. However, Freud claimed that because girls do not experience the intense fear of castration that boys do, they will develop weaker superegos than boys do.

Evaluating Freud's Theory We might credit Freud for pointing out that moral emotions such as pride, shame, and guilt are potentially important determinants of ethical conduct and that the internalization of moral principles is a crucial step along the way to moral maturity. Yet the "specifics" of his theory are largely unsupported. For example, threatening and punitive parents do not raise children who are morally mature. Quite the contrary; parents who rely on harsh forms of discipline tend to have children who often misbehave and who rarely express feelings of guilt, remorse, shame, or self-criticism (Brody & Shaffer, 1982; Kochanska et al., 2002). Furthermore, there is simply no evidence that boys develop stronger superegos than girls. In fact, recent research indicates that, if anything, 3- to 5-year-old girls are less likely to break rules and more likely to experience guilt when they think they've committed a transgression than 3- to 5-year-old boys are (Kochanska et al., 2002; Laible & Thompson, 2002). Finally, Freud's proposed age trends for moral development are actually rather pessimistic. As early as 13–15 months of age, some toddlers are already willing complying with requests and even obeying some prohibitions in the absence of external surveillance (Kochanska, Aksan, & Carlson, 2005; Kochanska, Tjebkes, & Forman, 1998). By age 2, more toddlers are beginning to show clear signs of distress that look very much like guilt if they violate rules (Kochanska, Casey, & Fukumoto, 1995; Kochanska et al., 2002), and they will sometimes try to correct any mishaps they think they have caused—*even when no one else is present to tell them to* (Cole, Barrett, & Zahn-Waxler, 1992). In addition, 3-year-olds are already displaying complex emotions that look very much like *pride* when they live up to a standard and *shame* when they fail to do so (Lewis, Alessandri, & Sullivan, 1992; Stipek, Recchia, & McClintic, 1992). These observations imply that the process of moral internalization may have already begun long before young children would have even experienced much of an Oedipus or Electra complex, much less have resolved it. So even though Freud's broader themes about the significance of moral emotions have some merit, perhaps it is time to lay his theory of **Oedipal morality** to rest.

Oedipal morality
Freud's theory that moral development occurs during the phallic period (ages 3 to 6) when children internalize the moral standards of the same-sex parent as they resolve their Oedipus or Electra conflicts.

Newer Ideas about the Early Development of Conscience

In recent years, a number of investigators have taken a new look at the early development of "conscience" from a social-learning or socialization perspective (for example, Kochanska, Coy, & Murray, 2001; Kochanska, Aksan, & Carlson, 2005; Kochanska & Murray, 2000; Laible & Thompson, 2000, 2002), and their findings are quite revealing. It seems that children may begin to form a conscience *as toddlers* if they are *securely attached* to warm and responsive parents who have shared many positive experiences with them, have often cooperated with their wishes during joint play, and who resolve the many conflicts that all parents have with a willful toddler by remaining firm but calm as they openly express their feelings, evaluating the toddler's behavior as wrong and explaining why he or she should feel uneasy about this conduct. By establishing rules in rational, nonthreatening ways, clearly evaluating the child's transgressions, and working to establish *mutual* understandings about what is acceptable and what is not, parents give children a rule system to internalize. And within the context of such a warm, secure climate (rather than a fear-provoking one) toddlers and their parents are likely to develop a **mutually responsive orientation** in which parent and child:

✦ Develop easily flowing routines at meals, bed time, or play.

✦ Show harmonious patterns of communication as both parties become highly proficient at reading each others' social signals and seem to truly enjoy the back and forth exchange of information that promotes their sense of connectedness.

✦ Display a willingness and even an eagerness to cooperate with each other. Conflicts that arise rarely escalate and are quickly resolved.

✦ Often express joy, mutual affection, and humor, while quickly dampening whatever negative affect may arise.

Like attachments, the extent to which parents and their toddlers establish mutually responsive orientations can be measured by observing the quality of their interactions (Aksan, Kochanska, & Ortman, 2006), and Kochanska and her colleagues believe that toddlers who enjoy such warm, responsive relationships will generally come to display **committed compliance**—an orientation in which they are (1) highly motivated to embrace the parent's agenda and to comply with her rules and requests, (2) sensitive to a parent's emotional signals indicating whether they have done right or wrong, and (3) beginning to internalize these parental reactions to their triumphs and transgressions, coming to experience the pride, shame, and guilt that will help them to evaluate and regulate their own conduct (Kochanska, Coy, & Murray, 2001; Kochanska et al., 2002; Kochanska, Aksan, & Carlson, 2005; Laible & Thompson, 2000). By contrast, aloof and impatient parents who rely more on power assertion to resolve conflicts and who have failed to establish a mutually responsive orientation with their toddlers are likely to promote **situational compliance**—generally nonoppositional behavior that stems more from parents' power to control the child's conduct than from the child's eagerness to cooperate or comply.

Evidence is rapidly emerging to support these newer ideas about early development of conscience. Consider, for example, that 2- to 2½-year-old toddlers who have mutually responsive relationships with mothers who resolve conflicts with them calmly and rationally are more likely to resist temptation to touch prohibited toys at age 3 (Laible & Thompson, 2002) and continue to show more signs of having a strong internalized conscience (for example, a willingness to comply with rules when adults are not present, clear signs of guilt when they think they have transgressed) at ages 4½ to 6 than do age-mates whose earlier mother/toddler relationships had been less warm and mutually responsive (Kochanska & Murray, 2000). What's more, boys who show committed compliance to their mothers at 33 months soon come to view themselves as "good" or "moral" individuals (Kochanska, 2002)—a finding which may help to explain why such children are more inclined to cooperate with other adult authority figures (for example, fathers, day-care providers, experimenters) compared to those whose compliance with their mothers is less consistent and more situational in nature (Feldman & Klein, 2003; Kochanska, Coy, & Murray, 2001; Kochanska, Aksan, & Carlson, 2005).

So can we characterize the nature of this "conscience" that emerges during toddlerhood and the preschool period? Yes, indeed. Nazan Aksan and Grazyna Kochanska (2005) have conducted sophisticated statistical analyses of many early indicators of internalized controls, concluding that "conscience" for 33- to 45-months-olds consists of two components: *moral emotions* (for example, empathy, guilt) and *rule-compatible conduct* (for example, internalizing prohibitions, obeying other rules, complying with requests). Though these two components are different aspects of morality, they are already interrelated by 33 months of age, so that children who experience more empathy in response to another person's distress (moral emotion) are also more inclined to follow rules in the absence of external surveillance (rule-compatible behavior). What's more each of these moral components is moderately stable over time, although they become even more closely interrelated by age 45 months, almost as if older preschoolers are developing something akin to the unitary superego that Freud wrote about.

In sum, recent research points quite clearly to the kinds of emotional climates and child-rearing practices that seem to foster or inhibit the early development of an internalized conscience—something that emerges much sooner than Freud had thought. Yet, to date, these researchers have had much less to say about moral development beyond the pre-school period or about the development or *moral reasoning*—the very issue that cognitive-developmentalists emphasize.

COGNITIVE-DEVELOPMENTAL THEORY: THE CHILD AS A MORAL PHILOSOPHER

Cognitive-developmentalists study morality by charting the development of *moral reasoning*—the thinking children display when deciding whether various acts are right or wrong. According to cognitive theorists, both cognitive growth and social experiences help children to develop progressively richer understandings of the meaning of rules, laws, and interpersonal obligations. As children acquire these new understandings, they are said to progress through an *invariant sequence* of moral stages, each of which evolves from and replaces its predecessor and represents a more advanced or "mature" perspective on moral issues. In this portion of the chapter, we will first examine Jean Piaget's early theory of moral development before turning to Lawrence Kohlberg's revision and extension of Piaget's approach.

Piaget's Theory of Moral Development

Piaget's early work on children's moral judgments focused on two aspects of moral reasoning. He studied children's developing *respect for rules* by rolling up his sleeves and playing marbles with Swiss children aged 5 to 13. As they played, Piaget would ask questions such as, "Where do these rules come from? Must everyone obey a rule? Can these rules be changed?" To study children's conceptions of *justice*, Piaget gave them moral-decision stories to ponder. Here is one example:

Story A. A little boy who is called John is in his room. He is called to dinner. He goes into the dining room. But behind the door there was a chair, and on the chair there was a tray with 15 cups on it. John couldn't have known that there was all this behind the door. He goes in, the door knocks against the tray, bang go the 15 cups, and they all get broken.

Story B. Once there was a little boy whose name was Henry. One day when his mother was out he tried to reach some jam out of the cupboard. He climbed onto a chair and stretched out his arm. But the jam was too high up, and he couldn't reach it. . . . While he was trying to get it, he knocked over a cup. The cup fell down and broke. (Piaget, 1932/1965, p. 122]

Having heard the stories, participants were asked such questions as "Which child is naughtier? Why?" and "How should the naughtier child be punished?" Using these research techniques, Piaget formulated theory of moral development that included a premoral period and two moral stages.

The Premoral Period   According to Piaget, preschool children show little concern for or awareness of rules. In a game of marbles, these **premoral** children do not play systematically with the intent of winning. Instead, they seem to make up their own rules, and they think the point of the game is to take turns and have fun.

premoral period
in Piaget's theory, the first five years of life, when children have little respect for or awareness of socially defined rules.

The Stage of Moral Realism, or Heteronomous Morality   Between the ages of 5 and 10, children develop a strong respect for rules as they enter Piaget's stage of **heteronomous morality** ("heteronomous" means "under the rule of another"). Children now believe that rules are laid down by powerful authority figures such as God, the police, or their parents, and they think that these regulations are sacred and unalterable. Try breaking the speed limit with a 6-year-old at your side and you may see what Piaget was talking about. Even if you are rushing to the hospital in a medical emergency, the young child may note that you are breaking a "rule of the road" and consider your behavior unacceptable conduct that deserves to be punished. Heteronomous children think of rules as *moral absolutes*. They believe that there is a "right" side and a "wrong" side to any moral issue, and right always means following the rules.

Heteronomous children are also likely to judge the naughtiness of an act by its objective consequences rather than the actor's intent. For example, many 5- to 9-year-olds judged John, who broke 15 cups while performing a well-intentioned act, to be naughtier than Henry, who broke one cup while stealing jam.

Heteronomous children also favor *expiatory punishment*—punishment for its own sake with no concern for its relation to the nature of the forbidden act. So a 6-year-old might favor spanking a boy who had broken a window rather than making the boy pay for the window from his allowance. Furthermore, the heteronomous child believes in **immanent justice**—the idea that violations of social rules will invariably be punished in one way or another (see, for example, Dennis's warning to Joey in the cartoon). So if a 6-year-old boy were to fall and skin his knee while stealing cookies, he might conclude that this injury was the punishment he deserved for his transgression. Life for the heteronomous child is fair and just.

The Stage of Moral Relativism, or Autonomous Morality   By age 10 or 11, most children have reached Piaget's second moral stage—moral relativism, or **autonomous morality**. Older, autonomous children now realize that social rules are arbitrary agreements that can be challenged and even changed with the consent of the people they govern. They also feel that rules can be violated in the service of human needs. Thus, a driver who speeds during a medical emergency will no longer be considered immoral, even though she is breaking the law. Judgments of right and wrong now depend more on the actor's intent to deceive or to violate social rules rather than the objective consequences of the act itself. So 10-year-olds reliably say that Henry, who broke one cup while stealing some jam (bad intent), is naughtier than John, who broke 15 cups while coming to dinner (good or neutral intent).

When deciding how to punish transgressions, the morally autonomous child usually favors reciprocal punishments—that is, treatments that tailor punitive consequences to the "crime" so that the rule breaker will understand the implications of a transgression and perhaps be less likely to repeat it. So an autonomous child may decide that the boy who deliberately breaks a window should pay for it out of his allowance (and learn that windows cost money) rather than simply submitting to a spanking. Finally, autonomous youngsters no longer believe in immanent justice, because they have learned from experience that violations of social rules often go undetected and unpunished.

"HEY, CAREFUL, JOEY! GOD SEES EVERYTHING WE DO, THEN HE GOES AN' TELLS SANTA CLAUS!"

Dennis the Menace © used by permission of Hank Ketcham and © North American Syndicate. 11/10/1990

Moving from Heteronomous to Autonomous Morality   According to Piaget, progressing from heteronomous to autonomous morality requires both the development of role-taking skills (cognitive maturation) and an important kind of social experience—equal-status contacts with peers. As we noted in Chapter 6, peer contacts are important because they foster role-taking: children must recognize and adapt to peers' divergent perspectives (that is, cooperate and compromise) to resolve disagreements in mutually beneficial ways. These experiences help them to see that there is no one absolute perspective on how things should be done or how conduct should be governed—a morally autonomous outlook on rules—and that they are quite capable of resolving disputes and regulating their own behavior without adult intervention (Carpendale, 2000).

And what role do parents play? Interestingly, Piaget claimed that unless parents relinquish some of their power, they may *slow* the progress of moral development by reinforcing the child's exaggerated respect for rules and authority figures. If, for example, a parent enforces a demand with a threat or a statement such as "Do it because I told you to!", it is easy to see how the young child might conclude that rules are "absolutes" that derive their "teeth" from the parent's power to enforce them.

An Evaluation of Piaget's Theory

Many researchers in many cultures have replicated Piaget's findings when they rely on his research methods. Younger children around the world are more likely than older ones to display such aspects of heteronomous morality as a belief in immanent justice or a tendency to emphasize consequences more than intentions when judging how wrong an act is (Jose, 1990; Lapsley, 1996). In addition, the maturity of children's moral judgments is related to such indications of cognitive development as IQ and role-taking skills (Ambron & Irwin, 1975; Lapsley, 1996). There is even some support for Piaget's "peer participation" hypothesis: Popular children who often take part in peer-group activities and who assume positions of leadership tend to make mature moral judgments (Bear & Rys, 1994; Keasey, 1971).

Nevertheless, there is ample reason to believe that Piaget's theory clearly underestimates the moral capacities of preschool and grade-school children.

Do Younger Children Ignore an Actor's Intentions?   Consider Piaget's claim that children younger than 9 or 10 judge acts as right or wrong based on the consequences the acts produce rather than the intentions that guided them. Unfortunately, Piaget's moral-decision stories were flawed in that they (1) confounded intentions and consequences by asking whether a person who caused little harm with a bad intent was naughtier than one who caused a larger amount of harm while serving good intentions, and (2) made information about the consequences of an act *much clearer* than information about the actor's intentions.

Sharon Nelson (1980) overcame these flaws in an interesting experiment with 3-year-olds. Each child listened to stories in which a character threw a ball to a playmate. The actor's motive was described as *good* (his friend had nothing to play with) or *bad* (the actor was mad at his friend), and the consequences of his act were either *positive* (the friend caught the ball and was happy to play with it) or *negative* (the ball hit the friend in the head and made him cry). To ensure that her 3-year-olds would understand the actor's intentions, Nelson showed them drawings such as Figure 10.2, which depicts a negative intent.

Not surprisingly, the 3-year-olds in this study judged acts that had positive consequences more favorably than those that caused harm. However, as Figure 10.3 shows, they also judged the well-intentioned child who had wanted to play much more favorably than the child who intended to hurt his friend, *regardless of the consequences of his actions*. Indeed, when we discussed the development of theory of mind in Chapter 6, we learned that even 3-year-olds have a pretty fair

Figure 10.2

Example of drawing used by Nelson to convey an actor's intentions to preschool children. (Adapted from Nelson, S. A. 1980. Factors influencing young children's use of motives and outcomes as moral criteria. Child Development, 51, 823–829.) © 1980 by the Society for Research in Child Development. Reprinted by permission of Blackwell Publishing.

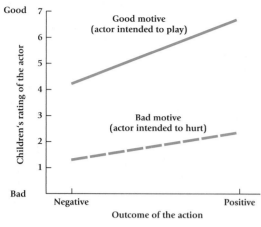

Figure 10.3
Average ratings of an actor's behavior for actors who produced positive or negative outcomes while serving either good or bad intentions. (Adapted from Nelson, S. A. 1980. Factors influencing young children's use of motives and outcomes as moral criteria. *Child Development, 51,* 823–829.) © 1980 by the Society for Research in Child Development. Reprinted by permission of Blackwell Publishing.

moral rules
standards of acceptable and unacceptable conduct that focus on the rights and privileges of individuals.

social-conventional rules
standards of conduct determined by social consensus that indicate what is appropriate within a particular social context.

personal choices
decisions about one's conduct that are (or should be, in the person's view) under personal jurisdiction and not regulated by rules or authority figures (for example, choice of friends or leisure activities).

understanding of others' intentions. And this is about the age that they begin to react more negatively to blatant *lies,* in which the actor presents false information while *intending* to deceive, than to honest mistakes on an actor's part (Siegal & Peterson, 1998). And by age 4, when they acquire a belief-desire theory of mind and recognize that people act on the basis of false beliefs, they may begin to cry and try to avoid punishment with an *intentional* plea such as "I didn't mean to, Mommy!" designed to change their mother's assessment of their conduct. So contrary to Piaget's view, preschool children are quite aware that an actor's intentions should be considered when evaluating his conduct (Chandler, Sokel, & Weinryb, 2000). But Piaget was right in one respect: Younger children do assign more weight to consequences and less weight to intentions than older children do, even though both younger and older children consider both sources of information when evaluating others' behavior (Lapsley, 1996; Zelazo, Helwig, & Lau, 1996).

Do Younger Children Respect All Rules (and Adult Authority)?

According to Piaget, young children think of rules and other adult commandments as sacred and obligatory prescriptions that are laid down by respected authority figures and are not to be questioned or changed. However, Elliot Turiel (1983) notes that children actually encounter two kinds of rules. **Moral rules** focus on the welfare and basic rights of individuals and include prescriptions against hitting, stealing, lying, cheating, or otherwise harming others or violating their rights. By contrast, **social-conventional rules** are determined by social consensus and regulate conduct in particular social situations. These standards are more like rules of social etiquette and include the rules of games as well as school rules that forbid snacking in class or using the restroom without permission. In addition, adults often try to regulate or influence children's **personal choices,** telling them, for example, who or what they can play with, what they can eat, what they should be doing with leisure time, and so on. Do children treat these three kinds of rules or prescriptions as equivalent?

Apparently not. Judith Smetana (1981, 1985, 2006; Yau & Smetana, 2003) reports that even 2½- to 4-year-olds in the United States, Korea, and China consider moral transgressions such as hitting, stealing, and refusing to share to be much more serious and more deserving of punishment than social conventional violations such as snacking in class or not saying "please" when requesting a toy. When asked whether a violation would be okay if there were no rule against it, children said that moral transgressions are always wrong, but social-conventional violations are okay in the absence of any explicit rule (see also Turiel, 2006). Clearly, parents view themselves as responsible for enforcing both moral and social-conventional rules. However, they attend more closely to moral violations and place much more emphasis on the harm such violations do to others (Nucci & Smetana, 1996; Turiel, 2002), perhaps explaining why children understand the need for and importance of *moral* prescriptions by age 2½ to 3—about the time that they begin to show evidence of an emerging conscience.

Yet there is ample evidence that even though preschoolers show more respect for rules than Piaget had thought, they may not value them very highly, particularly those that would thwart their desires (see Zoe's reaction in the cartoon). Indeed, 4-year-olds are much less likely than 7-year-olds to attribute (1) negative emotions (for example, guilt) to someone who satisfies personal desires by violating a rule or (2) positive emotions (for example, pride) to someone who displays willpower by resisting the temptation to break a rule (Lagattuta, 2005). What's more, preschoolers feel obligated to follow rules largely because such authority figures as parents and day-care providers want them to (Kalish & Cornelius, 2006).

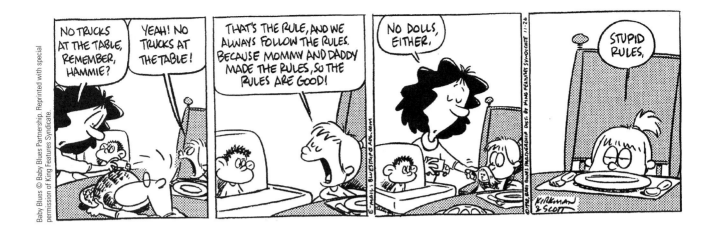

Interestingly, Piaget's theory predicts that 6- to 10-year-old heteronomous children should be even *more* inclined than younger children are to respect pronouncements laid down by adults. Yet children of this age are already quite capable of challenging rules and adult authority. They believe that parents are justified in enforcing rules against stealing and other *moral* transgressions; but they feel that a parent is clearly abusing authority should he or she arbitrarily impose rules that restrict their choice of friends or leisure activities—areas that they perceive as either negotiable or under their own *personal* jurisdiction (Helwig & Kim, 1999; Tisak & Tisak, 1990). In fact, even *preschoolers* in countries as diverse as Columbia, China, and the United States believe that leisure activities and choices of playmates or snacks are primarily personal choices that should not be subjected to strict adult regulation (Ardila-Rey & Killen, 2001; Yau & Smetana, 2003). And perhaps the best illustration that older heteronomous children are not totally cowed by adult authority is this: Ten-year-olds who are relatively religious believe that not even the endorsement of the ultimate authority figure—God—would make a *moral* transgression (such as stealing) morally right (Nucci & Turiel, 1993; and see Perkins & Turiel, 2007, for evidence that adolescents become even more adamant about resisting pressures from authority figures to behave in morally unacceptable ways). So 6- to 10-year-olds, even those in cultures like Korea and China where respect for authority is so highly stressed, have some firm ideas about what constitutes *legitimate* authority, and those ideas are not based solely on an unwavering respect for the sanctity or wisdom of adults as Piaget had assumed (Kim, 1998; Yau & Smetana, 2003).

Do Parents Impede Children's Moral Development? Finally, Piaget was partially right and partially wrong in his views of parents as agents of moral socialization. He was right in assuming that parents can impede moral growth by adopting a heavy-handed, authoritarian approach in which they *challenge* the child's moral reasoning and present their own ideas in a lecture-like format as lessons to be learned (Walker & Taylor, 1991). But he was very wrong in assuming that parents typically operate in this way when discussing moral issues with their children. Consider that 6- to 7-year-olds, who should be at Piaget's heteronomous stage, often make *autonomous* moral judgments—*as long as their parents do* (Leon, 1984). How is this possible? Research by Lawrence Walker and his associates (Walker, Hennig, & Krettenauer, 2000; Walker & Taylor, 1991) suggests an answer: By carefully tailoring their own reasoning to the child's ability to understand, and by presenting new moral perspectives in a supportive (rather than challenging) way, parents may often *promote* their children's moral development.

Developmentalists are indebted to Piaget for suggesting that children's moral reasoning develops in stages that are closely tied to cognitive growth. Even today, his theory continues to stimulate research and new insights—including the findings above, which reveal that children younger than 10 are considerably more sophisticated in their moral reasoning than Piaget made them out to be. But is moral reasoning fully developed by age 10 to 11, as Piaget had assumed? Lawrence Kohlberg certainly didn't think so.

Kohlberg's Theory of Moral Development

Kohlberg (1963, 1984; Colby & Kohlberg, 1987) refined and extended Piaget's theory of moral development by asking 10-, 13-, and 16-year-old boys to resolve a series of "moral dilemmas." Each dilemma challenged the respondent by requiring him to choose between (1) obeying a rule, law, or authority figure and (2) taking some action that conflicts with these rules and commands while serving a human need. The following story is the best known of Kohlberg's moral dilemmas:

> In Europe, a woman was near death from a special kind of cancer. There was one drug that doctors thought might save her. It was a form of radium that a druggist in the same town had recently discovered. The drug was expensive to make, but the druggist was charging $2000, or 10 times the cost of the drug, for a small (possibly life-saving) dose. Heinz, the sick woman's husband, borrowed all the money he could, about $1000, or half of what he needed. He told the druggist that his wife was dying and asked him to sell the drug cheaper or to let him pay later. The druggist replied, "No, I discovered the drug, and I'm going to make money from it." Heinz then became desperate and broke into the store to steal the drug for his wife. Should Heinz have done that?

Kohlberg was actually less interested in the respondent's decision (that is, what Heinz should have done) than in the underlying rationale, or "thought structures," that the individual used to justify his decision. So, if a participant says, "Heinz should steal the drug to save his wife's life," it is necessary to determine why her life is so important. Is it because she cooks and irons for Heinz? Because it's a husband's duty to save his wife? Or because the preservation of life is among the highest of human values? To determine the "structure" of a person's moral reasoning, Kohlberg asked probing questions: Does Heinz have an obligation to steal the drug? If Heinz doesn't love his wife, should he steal it for her? Should Heinz steal the drug for a stranger? Is it important for people to do everything they can to save another life? Is it against the law to steal? Does that make it morally wrong? The purpose of these probes is to clarify how individual participants reason about obedience and authority on the one hand and about human needs, rights, and privileges on the other.

Through his use of these elaborate *clinical interviews*, Kohlberg's first discovery was that moral development extends far beyond Piaget's autonomous stage, becoming progressively more complex throughout adolescence and into young adulthood. Careful analyses of his participants' responses to several dilemmas led Kohlberg to conclude that moral growth progresses through an *invariant sequence* of three moral levels, each of which is composed of two distinct moral stages. According to Kohlberg, the order of these moral levels and stages is invariant because they depend on the development of certain cognitive abilities that evolve in an invariant sequence. Like Piaget, Kohlberg assumed that each succeeding stage evolves from and replaces its predecessor; once the individual has attained a higher stage of moral reasoning, he or she should never regress to earlier stages.

Before examining Kohlberg's moral stages, it is important to emphasize that each stage represents a particular perspective, or *method of thinking* about moral dilemmas, rather than a particular type of moral decision. As we will see, decisions are not very informative in themselves, because people at each

Photo 10.7

Lawrence Kohlberg (1927–1987) formulated a highly influential theory that changed the way developmentalists looked at the growth of moral reasoning.

Courtesy Harvard University Graduate School of Education

moral stage might well endorse either of the alternative courses of action (for example, steal or not steal) when resolving one of these ethical dilemmas. (However, participants at Kohlberg's highest moral level do generally favor serving human needs over complying with rules or laws that would compromise others' welfare.)

The basic themes and defining characteristics of Kohlberg's three moral levels and six stages are as follows:

Level 1: Preconventional Morality Rules are truly external rather than internalized. The child conforms to rules imposed by authority figures to avoid punishment or obtain personal rewards. Morality is self-serving: What is right is what one can get away with or what is personally satisfying.

preconventional morality
Kohlberg's term for the first two stages of moral reasoning, in which moral judgments are based on the tangible punitive consequences (Stage 1) or rewarding consequences (Stage 2) of an act for the actor rather than on the relationship of that act to society's rules and customs.

Stage 1: Punishment-and-Obedience Orientation The goodness or badness of an act depends on its consequences. The child will obey authorities to avoid punishment but may not consider an act wrong if it will not be detected and punished. The greater the harm done or the more severe the punishment is, the more "bad" the act is. The following two responses reflect a "punishment-and-obedience" orientation to the Heinz dilemma:

> *Protheft*: It isn't really bad to take the drug—he did ask to pay for it first. He wouldn't do any other damage or take anything else, and the drug he'd take is only worth $200, not $2000.

> *Antitheft*: Heinz doesn't have permission to take the drug. He can't just go and break through a window. He'd be a bad criminal doing all that damage . . . and stealing anything so expensive would be a big crime.

Stage 2: Naive Hedonism A person at this second stage conforms to rules in order to gain rewards or satisfy personal objectives. There is some concern for the perspective of others, but other-oriented behaviors are ultimately motivated by the hope of benefiting in return. "You scratch my back and I'll scratch yours" is the guiding philosophy. Here are two samples of this hedonistic, self-serving morality (see also Calvin's moral philosophy in the cartoon):

> *Protheft*: Heinz isn't really doing any harm to the druggist, and he can always pay him back. If he doesn't want to lose his wife, he should take the drug.

> *Antitheft*: Hey, the druggist isn't wrong, he just wants to make a profit like everybody else. That's what you're in business for, to make money.

conventional morality
Kohlberg's term for the third and fourth stages of moral reasoning, in which moral judgments are based on a desire to gain approval (Stage 3) or to uphold laws that maintain social order (Stage 4).

postconventional morality
Kohlberg's term for the fifth and sixth stages of moral reasoning, in which moral judgments are based on social contracts and democratic law (Stage 5) or on universal principles of ethics and justice (Stage 6).

Level 2: Conventional Morality The individual now strives to obey rules and social norms in order to win others' approval or to maintain social order. Social praise and the avoidance of blame have now replaced tangible rewards and punishments as motivators of ethical conduct. The perspectives of other people are clearly recognized and given careful consideration.

Stage 3: "Good Boy" or "Good Girl" Orientation Moral behavior is that which pleases, helps, or is approved of by others. Actions are evaluated on the basis of the actor's intent. "He means well" is a common expression of moral approval at this stage. As we see in the responses below, the primary objective of a Stage 3 respondent is to be thought of as a "good" person.

Protheft: Stealing is bad, but Heinz is only doing something that is natural for a good husband to do. You can't blame him for doing something out of love for his wife. You'd blame him if he didn't save her.

Antitheft: If Heinz's wife dies, he can't be blamed. You can't say he is heartless for failing to commit a crime. The druggist is the selfish and heartless one. Heinz tried to do everything he really could.

Stage 4: Social-Order–Maintaining Morality At this stage, the individual considers the perspectives of the generalized other—that is, the will of society as reflected in law. Now what is right is what conforms to the rules of *legal* authority. The reason for conforming is not a fear of punishment, but a belief that rules and laws maintain a social order that is worth preserving. As we see in the following responses, laws ultimately transcend special interests:

Protheft: The druggist is leading the wrong kind of life if he just lets somebody die; so it's Heinz's duty to save [his wife]. But Heinz just can't go around breaking laws—he must pay the druggist back and take his punishment for stealing.

Antitheft: It's natural for Heinz to want to save his wife, but it's still always wrong to steal. You have to follow the rules regardless of your feelings or the special circumstances.

Level 3: Postconventional (or Principled) Morality A person at this third level of moral reasoning now defines right and wrong in terms of broad principles of justice that could conflict with written laws or with the dictates of authority figures. Morally right and legally proper are not always one and the same.

Stage 5: The Social-Contract Orientation At Stage 5, the individual now views laws as instruments for expressing the will of the majority and furthering human values. Laws that accomplish these ends and are impartially applied are viewed as social contracts that one has an obligation to follow; but imposed laws that compromise human rights or dignity are considered unjust and worthy of challenge. Notice how distinctions between what is legal and what is moral begin to appear in the following Stage 5 responses to Heinz's dilemma:

Protheft: Before you say stealing is morally wrong, you've got to consider this whole situation. Of course, the laws are quite clear about breaking into a store. And . . . Heinz would know that there were no *legal* grounds for his actions. Yet it would be reasonable for anybody, in that kind of situation, to steal the drug.

Antitheft: I can see the good that would come from illegally taking the drug. But the ends don't justify the means. The law represents a consensus of how people have agreed to live together, and Heinz has an obligation to respect these agreements. You can't say Heinz would be completely wrong to steal the drug, but even these circumstances don't make it right.

Stage 6: Morality of Individual Principles of Conscience At this "highest" moral stage, the individual defines right and wrong on the basis of the self-chosen ethical principles of his or her own conscience. These principles are not concrete rules such as the Ten Commandments. They are abstract moral guidelines or principles of universal justice (and respect for the rights of *all* human beings) that *transcend* any law or social contract that may conflict with them. Kohlberg (1981) described Stage 6 thinking as a kind of "moral musical chairs" in which the person facing a moral dilemma is able to take the perspective of *each and every person* who could potentially be affected by a decision and arrive at a solution that would be regarded as "just" by all. Here are two Stage 6 responses to the Heinz dilemma:

> *Protheft*: When one must choose between disobeying a law and saving a human life, the higher principle of preserving life makes it morally *right* to steal the drug.

> *Antitheft*: With many cases of cancer and the scarcity of the drug, there may not be enough to go around to everybody who needs it. The correct course of action can only be the one that is "right" by all people concerned. Heinz ought to act not on emotion or the law, but according to what he thinks an ideally just person would do in this case.

Stage 6 is Kohlberg's vision of ideal moral reasoning. But because it is so very rare and virtually no one functions consistently at this level, Kohlberg came to view it as a hypothetical construct—that is, the stage to which people would progress were they to develop beyond Stage 5. In fact, the later versions of Kohlberg's manual for scoring moral judgments no longer attempt to measure Stage 6 reasoning (Colby & Kohlberg, 1987).

Support for Kohlberg's Theory

Although Kohlberg believed that his stages form an invariant and universal sequence of moral growth that is closely tied to cognitive development, he also claimed that cognitive growth, by itself, is not sufficient to guarantee moral development. In order to ever move beyond the preconventional level of moral reasoning, children must be exposed to persons or situations that introduce *cognitive disequilibria*—that is, conflicts between existing moral concepts and new ideas that will force them to reevaluate their viewpoints. So, like Piaget, Kohlberg believed that both cognitive development and *relevant social experiences* underlie the growth of moral reasoning.

How much support is there for these ideas? Let's review the evidence, starting with data bearing on Kohlberg's invariant-sequence hypothesis.

Are Kohlberg's Stages an Invariant Sequence? If Kohlberg's stages represent a true developmental sequence, we should find a strong positive correlation between age and maturity of moral reasoning. This is precisely what researchers have found in studies conducted in the United States, Mexico, the Bahamas, Taiwan, Turkey, Honduras, India, Nigeria, and Kenya (Colby & Kohlberg, 1987). So it seems that Kohlberg's levels and stages of moral reasoning are "universal" structures that are age-related—just as we would expect them to be if they formed a developmental sequence. But do these studies establish that Kohlberg's stages form a fixed, or *invariant*, sequence?

No, they do not! The problem is that participants at each age level in these cross-sectional studies were *different* people, and we cannot be certain that a 25-year-old at Stage 5 has progressed through the various moral levels and stages in the order specified by Kohlberg's theory.

The Longitudinal Evidence Clearly the most compelling evidence for Kohlberg's invariant-sequence hypothesis would be a demonstration that individual children progress through the moral stages in precisely the order that Kohlberg said they should.

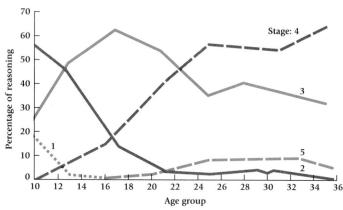

Figure 10.4

Use of Kohlberg's moral stages at ages 10 through 36 by male participants studied longitudinally over a 20-year period. (Adapted from Colby, A., Kohlberg, L., Gibbs, J., & Lieberman, M. 1983. A longitudinal study of moral judgment. Monographs of the Society for Research in Child Development, 48, Nos. 1–2, Serial No. 200.) © 1983 by the Society for Research in Child Development. Reprinted by permission of Blackwell Publishing.

Ann Colby and her associates (1983) have conducted a 20-year longitudinal study of Kohlberg's original research participants, who were reinterviewed five times at three- to four-year intervals. As shown in Figure 10.4, moral reasoning developed very gradually, with use of preconventional reasoning (Stages 1 and 2) declining sharply in adolescence—the same period in which conventional reasoning (Stages 3 and 4) is on the rise. Conventional reasoning remained the dominant form of moral expression in adulthood, with very few participants ever moving beyond it to postconventional morality (Stage 5). But even so, Colby and her colleagues found that participants proceeded through the stages they did attain in precisely the order Kohlberg predicted and that no one ever skipped a stage. Similar results have emerged from longitudinal studies in several countries around the world (Colby & Kohlberg, 1987; Rest et al., 1999). Let's note, however, that people progress in an orderly fashion to *their* highest stage of reasoning (Boom, Brugman, & van der Heijden, 2001) and that Stage 3 or 4 is the end of this developmental journey for most individuals worldwide (Snarey, 1985).

Cognitive Prerequisites for Moral Growth   According to Kohlberg (1963), the young, preconventional child reasons about moral issues from an egocentric point of view. At Stage 1, the child thinks that certain acts are bad because they are punished. At Stage 2, the child shows a limited awareness of the needs, thoughts, and intentions of others but still judges *self-serving* acts as appropriate. However, conventional reasoning clearly requires some role-taking abilities. A person at Stage 3, for example, must necessarily recognize others' points of view before she will evaluate intentions that would win their approval as "good" or morally acceptable. Furthermore, Kohlberg proposed that postconventional moral reasoning requires *formal operations*. A Stage 5 individual who bases moral judgments on abstract principles must be able to reason abstractly rather than simply adhering to the rule of law or concrete moral norms.

These hypotheses have received ample support. Lawrence Walker (1980), for example, found that all 10- to 13-year-olds who had reached Kohlberg's Stage 3 ("good boy—good girl" morality) were quite proficient at mutual role-taking, although not all proficient role-takers had reached Stage 3 in their moral reasoning. Similarly, Carolyn Tomlinson-Keasey and Charles Keasey (1974) and Deanne Kuhn and her associates (1977) found that (1) all participants who showed any evidence of postconventional (Stage 5) moral reasoning had reached formal operations but that (2) most formal operators had not reached Kohlberg's postconventional level of moral reasoning. So good role-taking skills are *necessary but not sufficient* for the development of conventional morality, and formal operations are *necessary but not sufficient* for the development of postconventional morality. This pattern is precisely what Kohlberg had expected, as he viewed cognitive growth as only one prerequisite for moral development. The other prerequisite is *relevant social experience*—exposures to persons or situations that force a person to reevaluate and alter his current moral perspectives.

Evidence for Kohlberg's "Social Experience" Hypothesis   What social experiences might be responsible for furthering moral growth? One important contributor is the discussions about moral issues that children and adolescents may have with parents and peers.

Parental and Peer Influences   Like Piaget, Kohlberg felt that interactions with peers probably contribute more to moral growth than one-sided discussions with adult authority figures. Lawrence Walker and his associates (2000) compared parental and peer influences on moral development by having 11- and 15-year-olds resolve moral dilemmas with a parent and then separately with a friend. Four years later, these participants responded again to moral dilemmas. Earlier discussions with *both* parents and peers influenced participants' moral development, but they did so in somewhat different ways. Friends were much more likely than parents to challenge and disagree with a child's or an adolescent's ideas, and they contributed positively to moral growth when they did confront and challenge. Indeed, other research (for example, Berkowitz & Gibbs, 1983) supports these findings, noting that when groups of peers are asked to reach consensus when resolving moral dilemmas, moral growth typically results if the group discussions are characterized by explicit but nonhostile **transactive interactions**— exchanges in which discussants co-construct shared meanings by challenging each other and hashing out their differences. These are important findings for they reinforce Kohlberg's idea that social experiences promote moral growth by introducing cognitive challenges to one's current reasoning (Turiel, 2006).

Photo 10.8
Discussing weighty ethical issues with peers often promotes the growth of moral reasoning.

transactive interactions
verbal exchanges in which individuals perform mental operations on the reasoning of their discussion partners.

By contrast, parents made bigger contributions to moral growth when they presented their reasoning in a positive, supportive way and asked gentle, probing questions to see whether their children or adolescents were understanding their viewpoints (Walker, Hennig, & Krettenaver, 2000). Direct confrontations by parents, however, did more harm they good, possibly because children and adolescents view a direct parental challenge as hostile criticism, which may make them defensive. The same kind of challenge is much less threatening when voiced by a social equal; in fact, adolescents may be especially inclined to listen carefully and accommodate a peer's position because they are so highly motivated to establish and maintain good relations with peers. So Piaget and Kohlberg were right in calling attention to peers as agents of moral socialization, but they failed to appreciate that parents may also have much to contribute.

Advanced Education   Another kind of social experience that promotes moral growth is receiving an advanced education. Consistently, adults who go on to college and receive many years of education reason more complexly about moral issues than those who are less educated (Speicher, 1994), and differences in the moral reasoning between college students and their nonstudent peers become greater with each successive year of school that the college students complete (Rest & Thoma, 1985). Advanced education may foster moral growth in two ways: (1) by contributing to cognitive growth and (2) by exposing students to diverse moral perspectives that produce cognitive conflict and soul-searching (Kohlberg, 1984; Mason & Gibbs, 1993).

Cultural Influences   Finally, simply living in a complex, diverse, and democratic society can stimulate moral development. Just as we learn the give-and-take of mutual perspective taking by discussing issues with our friends, we learn in a diverse democracy that the opinions of many groups must be weighed and that laws reflect a consensus of the citizens rather than the arbitrary rulings of a dictator. Cross-cultural studies suggest that postconventional moral reasoning emerges primarily in Western democracies and that people in rural villages in many nonindustrialized countries show no signs of it (Harkness, Edwards,

& Super, 1981; Snarey & Keljo, 1991). People in these homogeneous communities may have less experience with the kinds of political conflicts and compromises that take place in a more diverse society and so may never have any need to question conventional moral standards. By adopting a contextual perspective on development, we can appreciate that the conventional (mostly Stage 3) reasoning typically displayed by adults in these societies—with its collectivist emphasis on cooperation and loyalty to the immediate social group—is adaptive and mature within their own social systems (Harkness, Edwards, & Super, 1981; Turiel, 2006).

In sum, Kohlberg has described an invariant sequence of moral stages and has identified some of the cognitive factors and major environmental influences that determine how far an individual progresses in this sequence. Yet critics have offered many reasons for suspecting that Kohlberg's theory is far from a complete account of moral development.

Criticisms of Kohlberg's Approach

Many of the criticisms of Kohlberg's theory have centered on the possibilities that it is biased against certain groups of people, underestimates the moral sophistication of young children, and says much about moral reasoning but little about moral affect and moral behavior.

Is Kohlberg's Theory Biased?

Cultural Bias   Although research indicates that children and adolescents in many cultures proceed through the first three or four of Kohlberg's stages in order, we have seen that postconventional morality as Kohlberg defines it simply does not exist in some societies. Critics have charged that Kohlberg's highest stages reflect a Western ideal of justice and that his stage theory is therefore biased against people who live in non-Western collectivist societies or who otherwise do not value individualism and individual rights highly enough to want to challenge society's rules (Mascolo & Li, 2004; Shweder, Mahapatra, & Miller, 1990). People in collectivist societies that emphasize social harmony and place the good of the group ahead of the good of the individual may be viewed as conventional moral thinkers in Kohlberg's system but may actually have very sophisticated concepts of fairness and justice (Li, 2002; Snarey & Keljo, 1991; Turiel, 2006), including a strong respect for individual rights and such "democratic" principles as decision by majority rule (Helwig et al., 2003). Although there are some aspects of moral development that do seem to be common to all cultures, the research presented in Box 10.2 indicates that other aspects of moral growth can vary considerably from society to society.

Gender Bias   Critics have also charged that Kohlberg's theory, which was developed from responses provided by male participants to dilemmas involving male characters, does not adequately represent female moral reasoning. Carol Gilligan (1977, 1982, 1993), for example, has been disturbed by the fact that, in some early studies, women seemed to be the moral inferiors of men, typically reasoning at Kohlberg's Stage 3 while men usually reasoned at Stage 4. Her response was to argue that differential gender typing causes boys and girls to adopt different moral orientations. According to Gilligan, the strong independence and assertiveness training that boys receive encourages them to view moral dilemmas as inevitable conflicts of interest between *individuals* that laws and other social conventions are designed to resolve. She calls this orientation the **morality of justice**—a perspective that approximates Stage 4 in Kohlberg's scheme. By contrast, girls are taught to be nurturant, empathic, and concerned about others—in short, to define their sense of "goodness" in terms of their interpersonal *relationships*. So for females, morality implies a sense of caring or compassionate concern for human welfare—a **morality of care** that may seem

morality of justice
Gilligan's term for what she presumes to be the dominant moral orientation of males, focusing more on socially defined justice as administered through law than on compassionate concerns for human welfare.

morality of care
Gilligan's term for what she presumes to be the dominant moral orientation for females—an orientation focusing more on compassionate concerns for human welfare than on socially defined justice as administered through law.

Cultural Differences in Moral Reasoning

Is each of the following acts wrong? If so, how serious a violation is it?

1. A young married women is beaten black and blue by her husband after going to a movie without his permission despite having been warned not to do so again.
2. A brother and sister decide to get married and have children.
3. The day after his father died, the oldest son in a family has a haircut and eats chicken.

These are three of 39 acts presented by Richard Shweder, Manamahan Mahapatra, and Joan Miller (1987) to children ages 5 to 13 and adults in India and the United States. You may be surprised to learn that Hindu children and adults rated the son's having a haircut and eating chicken after his father's death as among the very most morally offensive of the 39 acts they rated, and the husband's beating of his disobedient wife as not wrong at all. American children and adults, of course, viewed wife beating as far more serious than breaking seemingly arbitrary rules about appropriate mourning behavior. Although Indians and Americans could agree that a few acts like brother-sister incest were serious moral violations, they did not agree on much else.

Furthermore, Indian children and adults viewed the Hindu ban against behavior disrespectful of one's dead father as a *universal moral rule;* they thought it would be best if *everyone in the world* followed it and strongly disagreed that it would be acceptable to change the rule if most people in their society wanted to change it. Hindus also believed that it is a serious moral offense for a widow to eat fish or wear brightly colored clothes or for a woman to cook food for her family during her menstrual period. To orthodox Hindus, rules against such behavior are required by divinely inspired natural law; they not just arbitrary social conventions created by members of society. Hindus also regard it as morally necessary for a man to beat his disobedient wife in order to uphold his obligations as head of the family.

What effects do cultural beliefs of this sort have on moral development? The developmental trend in moral thinking that Shweder detected in India was very different from the developmental trend he observed in the United States, as the figure shows. With age, Indian children saw more and more issues as matters of universal moral principle, whereas American children saw fewer and fewer issues in the same light (and more and more as matters of arbitrary social convention that can legitimately differ from society to society).

Based on these cross-cultural findings, Shweder calls into question Kohlberg's claims that all children everywhere construct similar moral codes at similar ages and that certain universal moral principles exist. Shweder also questions Turiel's claim that children everywhere distinguish from an early age between moral rules and social-conventional rules, for the concept of social-conventional rules was simply not very meaningful to Indians of any age. Instead, Shweder believes that culture defines for a child exactly what is morally acceptable or unacceptable and then assists the young to adopt that conceptual framework. Indeed, we saw evidence of this very process in Box 10-1: Children from the collectivist People's Republic of China gradually adopt their society's communist-collectivist ideals of behaving prosocially and remaining modest

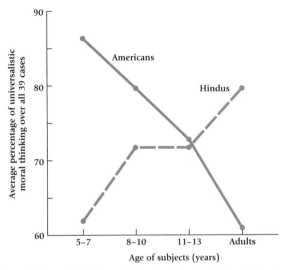

Universalistic moral thinking—the tendency to view rules of behavior as universally valid and unalterable—increases with age among Hindu children in India but decreases with age in the United States. The course of moral development is likely to be different in different societies. (Adapted from Shweder, R. A., Mahapatra, M., & Miller, J. G. 1987. Culture and moral development. In J. Kagan & S. Lamb, Eds., The emergence of morality in young children (pp. 1–83). Chicago: University of Chicago Press.) Reprinted by permission of the University of Chicago Press.

or humble about it—to the point that they think it better to *lie* and deny *personal* responsibility for a good deed than to boldly claim responsibility or seek recognition for their acts of kindness.

Interestingly, there are also important *subcultural* influences on moral reasoning. For example, individuals who occupy a subordinate position within their societies (for example, Arab women and Brazilian children from the lower socioeconomic strata) are more inclined than age-mates of higher status to view themselves as having relatively few personal choices about how to behave and as under greater moral obligation to submit to authority (Nucci, Camino, & Sapiro, 1996; Turiel, 2006; Turiel & Wainryb, 2000).

Clearly, these findings challenge the cognitive-developmental position that *all* important aspects of moral growth are universal. Instead, they tend to support a *contextual* perspective on moral development by suggesting that children's moral judgments are shaped by the culture and subculture in which they live. In Canada, for example, one need not display a strong sense of religiosity or spiritualism to be considered morally mature (Walker & Pitts, 1998), whereas a strong sense of spiritualism and adherence to an "ethics of divinity" is of central importance to Hindus—and seems to explain their tendency to view so many cultural prescriptions as universal moral laws (Shweder, 1997). What then, should we conclude about culture and moral reasoning? Perhaps children all over the world do think in more *cognitively complex* ways about issues of morality and justice as they get older, as Kohlberg claimed, but at the same time adopt different notions about *what* is right and *what* is wrong (or a personal choice versus a moral obligation) as Shweder and others claim.

to represent Stage 3 in Kohlberg's scheme. However, Gilligan insists that the morality of care that females adopt can become quite abstract or "principled," even though Kohlberg's scheme might place it at Stage 3 because of its focus on interpersonal obligations.

Despite the intuitive appeal of Gilligan's ideas, there is little support for her claim that Kohlberg's theory is based against women. In most studies, women reason just as complexly about moral issues as men do when their answers are scored by Kohlberg's criteria (Jaffee & Hyde, 2000; Walker, 1995). When resolving *real-life* moral dilemmas that they have faced, women are somewhat more inclined than men to focus on issues of care and obligations to other people (Jaffe & Hyde, 2000), but this sex difference is very modest and both men and women rely primarily on care-based reasoning when they ponder dilemmas involving relationships and on justice-based reasoning when issues of individual rights arise. The nature of the moral dilemma is far more important than the sex of the moral reasoner (Wark & Krebs, 1996). And when we look at patterns of *interaction* among female elementary school students, the strong forms of social exclusion and other hurtful behaviors that many girls display have caused some to question Gilligan's claim that girls are more fundamentally oriented toward a morality based on relatedness and care (Goodwin, 2002). What's more, there is surprisingly little support for Gilligan's claim that boys and girls are socialized differently in the area of morality (Lollis, Ross, & LeRoux, 1996). Instead, *both* males and females come to view *both* justice-related and care-related attributes as central elements of moral maturity (Walker & Pitts, 1998; and review Table 10.5).

Even though the justice and care orientations are not the sex-specific moralities that Gilligan claimed they were, her work is valuable nonetheless: It has made us more aware that both men and women often think about moral issues—especially real-life as opposed to hypothetical moral issues—in terms of their responsibilities for the welfare of other people. Kohlberg tended to emphasize a very legalistic way of thinking about right and wrong. Yet there seems to be merit in tracing the development of *both* a morality of justice and a morality of care in both males and females (Brabeck, 1983; Moshman, 1999).

Is Kohlberg's Theory Incomplete?   Another major criticism of Kohlberg's theory is that it focuses too heavily on moral reasoning and neglects moral affect and behavior. Indeed, Kohlberg does not emphasize moral affects such as empathy, which provides the motivation for us to take others' perspectives and needs seriously and to act in ways that do not compromise their welfare (M. L. Hoffman, 2000). He also had little to say about other powerful emotions such as pride, shame, and guilt that influence our thoughts and actions (Hart & Chmiel, 1992). However, Kohlberg predicted that mature moral reasoners should be more inclined to behave morally and that the links between moral reasoning and moral behavior would become stronger as individuals progress toward higher levels of moral understanding (Blasi, 1990).

Does Moral Reasoning Predict Moral Conduct?   Most of the available data are consistent with Kohlberg's viewpoint. With few exceptions (for example, Kochanska, Padavich, & Koening, 1996), most researchers have found that the moral judgments of young children do *not* predict their behavior in situations where they are induced to cheat or violate other moral norms (Nelson, Grinder, & Biaggio, 1969; Santrock, 1975; Toner & Potts, 1981). However, studies of older grade-school children, adolescents, and young adults often do find that individuals at higher stages of moral reasoning are more likely than those at lower stages to behave altruistically and conscientiously by living up to their promises and being less likely to cheat or take part in delinquent or criminal activities (Judy & Nelson, 2000; Midlarsky et al., 1999; Rest et al., 1999). Kohlberg, for example, found that only 15 percent of college students who reasoned at the postconventional level actually cheated on a test when given an opportunity, compared with 55 percent of the "conventional" students and 70 percent of those at the preconventional level. Yet the relationship between stage of moral reasoning and moral behavior is only moderate at best (Turiel, 2006). Why? One reason is that people may resolve some moral issues quite automatically, out of habit (for example, having unprotected sex), without much cognitive reflection (Walker, 2000). What's more, situational factors (for example, likelihood that transgressions will be punished or will harm others) also influence moral conduct in daily life. Indeed, Bandura (2002) goes so far as to argue than many of us develop mechanisms of **moral disengagement** that enable us to avoid strong self-condemnation even though we know that our behavior violates important moral norms. For example, moral disengagement may sometimes allow us to conclude that violating our principles is morally right (as in war), or to view a violation as acceptable in context (partaking in peer-sponsored misconduct) or as serving a more critical long-range goal (cheating on a test to earn or maintain a necessary scholarship). Thus, a person's level of moral reasoning may not always predict his conduct because it is only one input (but a meaningful one to be sure) into a complex behavioral equation. The process of moral growth may even contribute to inconsistencies between moral reasoning and moral behavior. Stephen Thoma and James Rest (1999) for example, propose that situational factors may have a stronger influence on a person's conduct than reasoning does if that person is reexamining (and often questioning) her existing moral principles as she begins the transition from one moral stage to the next higher stage.

moral disengagement
the ability to avoid self-condemnation when engaged in immoral behavior by justifying one's actions as appropriate, minimizing their effects, or blaming others for one's conduct.

Kohlberg Underestimates Young Children Finally, Kohlberg's primary focus on legalistic dilemmas that laws were designed to address caused him to overlook other "nonlegalistic" forms of moral reasoning that influence the behavior of grade-school children. To cite one example, we've seen that young elementary school children do often display such "conventional" aspects of moral reasoning as considering the needs of others or doing whatever they think people will approve of when resolving Eisenberg's *prosocial* moral dilemmas—even though these youngsters are hopelessly mired in preconventional morality (Stage 1 or Stage 2) when tested on Kohlberg's legalistic dilemmas (see also Helwig & Jasiobedzka, 2001, and Turiel, 2006, for other notable ways in which Kolberg underestimates the moral sophistication of grade-school children).

In sum, Kohlberg's theory of moral development has become prominent for good reason. It describes a universal sequence of changes in moral reasoning extending from childhood through adulthood. Furthermore, the evidence supports Kohlberg's view that both cognitive growth and social experiences contribute to moral development. However, there is also some merit to the criticisms. Kohlberg's theory does not fully capture the morality of people who live in many collectivist societies or who choose to emphasize a spiritual or a care orientation rather than an orientation centering on individual rights and justice, and it clearly underestimates the moral reasoning of young children. And because Kohlberg concentrated so heavily on moral reasoning, we must rely on other perspectives to help us to understand how moral affect and moral behavior develop, and how thought, emotions, and behavior interact to make us the moral beings that most of us ultimately become.

In our next section, we turn to social-learning and social information-processing perspectives—approaches that attempt to specify some of the important cognitive, social, and emotional influences on children's moral behavior.

Photo 10.9
The process of moral disengagement helps to explain how people will sometimes justify acts that they know violate important moral principles.

Courtesy United States Army

MORALITY AS A PRODUCT OF SOCIAL LEARNING (AND SOCIAL INFORMATION-PROCESSING)

Social-learning theorists such as Albert Bandura (1991, 2002) have been primarily interested in the behavioral component of morality—in what we actually do when faced with temptation. They claim that moral behaviors are learned in the same way that other social behaviors are: through the processes of differential reinforcement and observational learning. They also consider moral behavior to be strongly influenced by the specific situations in which people find themselves. It is not at all surprising, they say, to see a person behave morally in one situation but transgress in another situation, or proclaim that nothing is more important than honesty but then lie or cheat.

How Consistent Are Moral Conduct and Moral Character?

Perhaps the most extensive study of children's moral conduct is one of the oldest—the Character Education Inquiry reported by Hugh Hartshorne and Mark May (1928–1930). The purpose of this five-year project was to investigate the moral "character" of 10,000 children aged 8–16 by tempting them to lie, cheat, or steal in a variety of situations. The most noteworthy finding of this massive investigation was that children tended *not* to be consistent in their moral behavior; a child's willingness to cheat in one situation did not predict his willingness to lie, cheat, or steal in other situations. Of particular interest was the finding that children who cheated in a particular setting were just as likely as those who did not to state that cheating is wrong! Hartshorne and May concluded that "honesty" is largely specific to the situation rather than a stable character trait.

However, modern and more sophisticated analyses of data from the Character Education Inquiry (Burton, 1963) and new studies (for example, M. L. Hoffman, 2000; Kochanska & Murray, 2000) have challenged Hartshorne and May's **doctrine of specificity,** finding that moral behaviors of a *particular kind* (for example, a child's willingness to cheat or not cheat on tests, or to share or not share toys with playmates) are reasonably consistent over time and across situations. What's more, correlations among measures of moral affect (for example, guilt proneness, empathy) moral reasoning, and moral conduct are detectable in toddlerhood and become progressively stronger with age (Aksan & Kochanska, 2005; Blasi, 1990; Kochanska et al., 2002). So there is some consistency or concordance to moral character after all, especially as we become more morally mature. However, we should never expect even the most morally mature individuals to be perfectly consistent across *all* situations, because one's willingness to lie, cheat, or violate other moral norms (or one's feelings and thoughts about doing so) may always depend to some extent on weighty personal and contextual factors, such as the importance of the goal one might achieve by transgressing, the amount of encouragement provided by peers for deviant conduct, or the ease with which we might disengage from our moral principles (Bandura, 2002).

Learning to Resist Temptation

From society's standpoint, one of the more important indexes of morality is the extent to which an individual is able to resist pressures to violate moral norms, *even when the possibility of detection and punishment is remote* (Hoffman, 1970; Kochanska, Aksan, & Joy, 2007). A person who resists temptation in the absence of external surveillance not only has learned a moral rule but is *internally* motivated to

doctrine of specificity
a viewpoint shared by many social-learning theorists that holds that moral affect, moral reasoning, and moral behavior may depend on the situation one faces as much as or more than on an internalized set of moral principles.

Photo 10.10
Sometimes it is difficult to tell whether children are working together, helping each other, or using each other's work. Although there is some consistency to children's moral behavior, a child's conduct in any particular situation is likely to be influenced by factors such as the importance of the goal that might be achieved by breaking a moral rule and the probability of being caught should he or she commit a transgression.

Wayne Miller/Magnum Photos

abide by that rule. How do children acquire moral standards, and what motivates them to obey these learned codes of conduct? Social-learning theorists have attempted to answer these questions by studying the effects of reinforcement, punishment, and social modeling on children's moral behavior.

Reinforcement as a Determinant of Moral Conduct   We have seen on several occasions that the frequency of many behaviors can be increased if these acts are reinforced. Moral behaviors are certainly no exception. When warm, accepting parents set clear and reasonable standards for their children and often *praise* them for behaving well, even toddlers are likely to meet their expectations and to display strong evidence of an internalized conscience by age 4 to 5 (Kochanska et al., 2002; Kochanska, Aksan, & Joy, 2007; Kochanska & Murray, 2000). Children are generally motivated to comply with the wishes of a warm, socially reinforcing adult, and the praise that accompanies their desirable conduct tells them that they are accomplishing that objective.

The Role of Punishment in Establishing Moral Prohibitions   Although reinforcing acceptable behaviors is an effective way to promote desirable conduct, adults will often fail to recognize that a child has *resisted* a temptation and is deserving of praise. By contrast, people may be quick to inform a child of his or her misdeeds by *punishing* moral transgressions. Is punishment an effective way to foster the development of **inhibitory controls?** As we will see, the answer depends very critically on the child's *interpretation* of these aversive experiences.

inhibitory control
an ability to display acceptable conduct by resisting the temptation to commit a forbidden act.

Early Research   Ross Parke (1977) used the *"forbidden toy" paradigm* to study the effects of punishment on children's resistance to temptation. During the first phase of a typical experiment, participants are punished (by hearing a noxious buzzer) whenever they touch an attractive toy; however, nothing happens when they play with unattractive toys. Once the child has learned the prohibition, the experimenter leaves and the child is surreptitiously observed to determine whether he or she plays with the forbidden toys.

Parke soon discovered that not all punishments were equally effective at promoting the development of moral controls. Specifically, he noted that *firm* (rather than mild) punishments, administered *immediately* (rather than later) and *consistently* by a *warm* (rather than an aloof) disciplinarian, proved most effective at inhibiting a child's undesirable conduct. Yet Parke's most important discovery was that all forms of punishment became more effective if accompanied by a cognitive rationale that provides the transgressor with reasons for inhibiting a forbidden act.

Why Are Rationales Important? An Information-Processing Analysis   Why do rationales increase the effectiveness of punishment, even mild or delayed punishments that produce little moral restraint by themselves? According to Martin Hoffman's (1988) information-processing viewpoint, rationales are effective because they specify why a punished act was wrong and why the transgressor should feel guilty, shameful, or otherwise less than virtuous were she to repeat it. So when youngsters who have received such rationales think about committing the forbidden act in the future, they should experience a general uneasiness (stemming from previous disciplinary encounters), should be inclined to make an *internal attribution* for this arousal (for example, "I'd feel guilty were I to harm others"; "I'd violate my positive self-image"), and should now be more likely to inhibit the forbidden act and to feel rather good about their "mature and responsible" conduct (see Figure 10.5). By contrast, children who receive no rationales or who have been exposed to reasoning that focuses their attention on the negative consequences *they* can expect for future transgressions (for example, "You'll be spanked again if you do it") will experience just as much uneasiness when they think about committing the forbidden

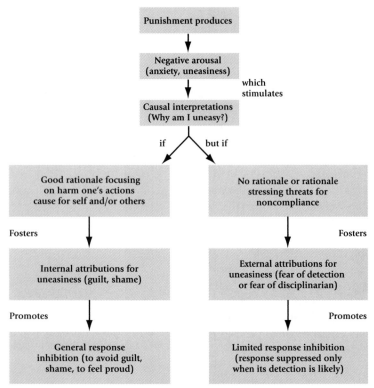

```
Punishment produces
        │
        ▼
Negative arousal
(anxiety, uneasiness)              which
        │                         stimulates
        ▼
Causal interpretations
(Why am I uneasy?)
    if  ╱  ╲  but if
       ╱    ╲
      ▼      ▼
```

Good rationale focusing on harm one's actions cause for self and/or others	No rationale or rationale stressing threats for noncompliance
Fosters ▼	Fosters ▼
Internal attributions for uneasiness (guilt, shame)	External attributions for uneasiness (fear of detection or fear of disciplinarian)
Promotes ▼	Promotes ▼
General response inhibition (to avoid guilt, shame, to feel proud)	Limited response inhibition (response suppressed only when its detection is likely)

Figure 10.5
The social information-processing model of the suppressive effects of punishment.

act. However, these youngsters should tend to make *external attributions* for their emotional arousal (for example, "I'm worried about getting caught and punished")—attributions that might make them comply with moral norms in the presence of authority figures but should do little to inhibit deviant conduct if there is no one around to detect their transgressions.

Of course, it may take many disciplinary encounters that include good rationales before young children come to connect the uneasiness they are experiencing with the information they receive and begin to make the kinds of internal attributions the model anticipates. Nevertheless, it is important to note that mere fear of detection and punishment is not enough to persuade children to resist temptations in the absence of external surveillance. In order to establish truly internalized *self*-controls, adults must structure disciplinary encounters to include an appropriate rationale—one that informs the child why the prohibited act is wrong and why she should feel guilty, shameful, or otherwise less than virtuous were she to repeat it (Hoffman, 1988). Clearly, true self-restraint is largely under *cognitive* control—it depends more on what's in children's heads than on the amount of fear or uneasiness in their guts.

Moral Self-Concept Training If making internal attributions about one's feelings or one's conduct truly promotes moral self-restraint, then we should be able to convince children that they can resist the temptation to break rules or violate moral norms *because* they are "good," "honest," or otherwise "responsible" persons. This kind of *moral self-concept training* really does work. William Casey and Roger Burton (1982) found that 7- to 10-year-olds became much more honest while playing games if being "honest" was stressed and the players had learned to remind themselves to follow the rules. Yet when honesty was *not* stressed, players often cheated. Furthermore, David Perry and his associates (1980) found that 9- to 10-year-olds who had been told that they were especially good at carrying out instructions and following rules (moral self-concept training) behaved very differently after succumbing to a nearly irresistible temptation (leaving a boring task that they had promised to perform to watch an exciting TV show) than did peers who had not been told they were especially good. Specifically, children who had heard positive attributions about themselves were more inclined than control participants to *punish their own transgressions* by giving back many of the valuable prize tokens they had been paid for working at the boring task. So it seems that labeling children as "good" or "honest" may not only increase the likelihood that they will resist temptations, but also contributes to children's feelings of guilt or remorse should they behave inappropriately and violate their positive self-images.

In sum, moral self-concept training, particularly when combined with praise for desirable conduct, can be a most effective alternative to punishment as a means of establishing inhibitory controls—one that should help convince the child that "I'm resisting temptation because I want to do right or live up to my positive self-image," and lead to the development of truly *internalized* controls rather than a response inhibition based on a fear of detection and punishment. Furthermore, this positive, nonpunitive approach should produce none of the undesirable side effects (for example, resentment) that often accompany punishment.

Effects of Social Models on Children's Moral Behavior Might children be influenced by rule-following models who exhibit moral behaviors in a "passive" way by failing to commit forbidden acts? Indeed, they may, as long as they are aware that the "passive" model is resisting the temptation to violate a rule. Joan Grusec and her associates (1979) found that a rule-following model can be particularly effective at inspiring children to behave in kind if he clearly verbalizes that he is following a rule *and* states a good rationale for not committing the deviant act.

Finally, consider what Nace Toner and his associates (1978) found: 6- to 8-year-olds who were persuaded to *serve* as models of moral restraint for other children became more likely than age-mates who had not served as rule-following models to obey other rules during later tests of resistance to temptation. It was almost as if serving as a model had produced a change in children's self-concepts, so that they now defined themselves as "people who follow rules." The implications for child rearing are clear: Perhaps parents could succeed in establishing inhibitory controls in their older children by appealing to their maturity and persuading them to act as models of self-restraint for their younger brothers and sisters.

⤳ WHO RAISES CHILDREN WHO ARE MORALLY MATURE?

Many years ago, Martin Hoffman (1970) reviewed the child-rearing literature to see whether the disciplinary techniques that *parents actually use* have any effect on the moral development of their children. Three major approaches were compared:

1. **Love withdrawal:** withholding attention, affection, or approval after a child misbehaves—or in other words, creating anxiety over a loss of love.

2. **Power assertion:** use of superior power to control the child's behavior (includes techniques such as forceful commands, physical restraint, spankings, and withdrawal of privileges—techniques that may generate fear, anger, or resentment).

3. **Induction:** explaining why a behavior is wrong and should be changed by emphasizing how it affects other people; often suggests how the child might undo any harm done.

Suppose that little Shannon has just terrorized the family cat by chasing her with a lit sparkler during a Fourth of July celebration. Using *love withdrawal,* a parent might say, "How could you? Get away; I can't bear to look at you." Using *power assertion,* a parent might spank Shannon or say, "That's it! No movie for you this Saturday." Using *induction,* the parent might say, "Shannon, stop that! Look how scared Spotz is. You could have set her on fire, and you know how sad we'd all be if she were burned." Induction, then, is a matter of providing rationales that focus special attention on the consequences of one's wrongdoing for oneself or other people (or cats, as the case may be).

Although only a limited number of child-rearing studies had been conducted by 1970, their results suggested that (1) neither love withdrawal nor power assertion were particularly effective at promoting moral maturity, but that (2) induction seemed to foster the development of all three aspects of morality—moral emotions, moral reasoning, and moral behavior (Hoffman, 1970). Table 10.6 summarizes the relationships among the three patterns of parental discipline and various measures of children's moral maturity that emerged from a later review of the literature, which included many more studies (Brody & Shaffer, 1982). Clearly these data confirm Hoffman's conclusions: Parents who rely on inductive discipline tend to have children who are morally mature, whereas frequent use of power assertion is more often associated with moral *immaturity* than with moral maturity. The few cases in which induction was not associated with moral maturity all involved children under age 4. However, recent research indicates that induction can

love withdrawal
a form of discipline in which an adult withholds attention, affection, or approval in order to modify or control a child's behavior.

power assertion
a form of discipline in which an adult relies on his or her superior power (for example, by administering spankings or withholding privileges) to modify or control a child's behavior.

induction
a nonpunitive form of discipline in which an adult explains why a child's behavior is wrong and should be changed by emphasizing its effects on others.

Table 10.6 Relationships between parents' use of three disciplinary strategies and children's moral development

Direction of Relationship Between Parent's Use of a Disciplinary Strategy and Children's Moral Maturity	Type of Discipline		
	Power Assertion	Love Withdrawal	Induction
+ (positive correlation)	7	8	38
− (negative correlation)	32	11	6

Note: Table entries represent the number of occasions on which a particular disciplinary technique was found to be associated (either positively or negatively) with a measure of children's moral affect, reasoning, or behavior.

Source: Adapted from Brody & Shaffer, 1982.

be highly effective with 2- to 5-year-olds, reliably promoting sympathy and compassion for others as well as a willingness to comply with parental requests; by contrast, use of such high-intensity, power-assertive tactics as becoming angry and physically restraining or spanking the child is already associated with and seems to promote noncompliance, defiance, and a lack of concern for others (Crockenberg & Litman, 1990; Eisenberg, Fabes, & Spinard, 2006; Kochanska et al., 2002; Kochanska & Murray, 2000; Laible & Thompson, 2000, 2002; Zahn-Waxler, Radke-Yarrow, & King, 1979; Zahn-Waxler, et al., 1992).

Why is inductive discipline effective? Hoffman cites several reasons. First, it provides chlldren with *cognitive standards* (or rationales) that children can use to evaluate their conduct. Second, this form of discipline helps children to sympathize with others and allows parents to talk about other *moral affects* such as pride, guilt, and shame that are not easily discussed with a child who is made emotionally insecure by love withdrawal or angry and resentful by power-assertive techniques. Finally, parents who use inductive discipline are likely to explain to the child (1) what he or she *should have done* when tempted to violate a prohibition and (2) what he or she *can now do* to make up for a transgression. So induction may be an effective method of moral socialization because it calls attention to the cognitive, affective, and behavioral aspects of morality and may help the child to integrate them.

Finally, it is important to note that few if any parents are totally inductive, love-oriented, or power-assertive in their approach to discipline; most make at least some use of all three disciplinary techniques. In fact, Hoffman (2000) stresses that a little bit of power assertion is useful *now and then*, as long as it does not arouse too much fear, because it can motivate a child to pay close attention to the inductive component of discipline. As he puts it, the winning formula for effective discipline is "a blend of frequent inductions, occasional power assertions, and a lot of affection" (p. 23). The prescription is very similar to the "rationale + mild punishment from a warm disciplinarian" treatment that Parke (1977) found most effective in laboratory studies of resistance to temptation.

' IF YOU'RE TRYIN' TO GET SOMETHING INTO MY HEAD, YOU'RE WORKIN' ON THE WRONG END!"

Dennis the Menace © used by permission of Hank Ketcham and © North American Syndicate.

Criticisms of Hoffman's Ideas about Discipline

Several investigators have wondered whether Hoffman's conclusions about the effectiveness of inductive discipline might not be overstated. For example, inductive discipline used by white, middle-class mothers is consistently associated with measures of children's moral maturity;

however, the same findings don't always hold for fathers or for parents from other socio-economic backgrounds (Brody & Shaffer, 1982; Grusec & Goodnow, 1994). Furthermore, one study found that the positive association between parents' use of power-assertive discipline and children's aggressive, antisocial conduct held for European-American but not for African-American children (Deater-Deckard & Dodge, 1997; and see Walker-Barnes & Mason, 2001). Clearly, more research is needed to establish how culturally-specific Hoffman's ideas may be.

Other critics have raised the *direction-of-effects* issue: Does induction promote moral maturity; or rather, do morally mature children elicit more inductive forms of discipline from their parents? Because child-rearing studies are based on correlational data, either of these possibilities can explain Hoffman's findings. Hoffman (1975) responds by claiming that parents exert far more control over their children's behavior than children exert over parents. In other words, he believes that parental use of inductive discipline promotes moral maturity rather than the other way around. And there is some *experimental* support for Hoffman's claim in that induction is much more effective than other forms of discipline at persuading children to keep their promises and to comply with rules imposed by *unfamiliar* adults (Kuczynski, 1983).

However, children can influence the discipline they receive. A child who has already developed a sense of committed compliance as a toddler may have come to view himself as a "good" or "moral" person and will respond well to induction and be treated that way (Kochanska, 2002). Another child who frequently acts out and defies his parents will often elicit more coercive (and less effective) forms of discipline over time (Dodge, Coie, & Lynam, 2006; Stoolmiller, 2001). And although most youngsters may respond quite favorably to inductive discipline, it is becoming quite clear that there is no one disciplinary style that works best for all children and that the most effective approaches are those that are carefully tailored to the child's attributes and the situation at hand (Grusec, Goodnow, & Kuczynski, 2000). For example, the research presented in Box 10.3 nicely illustrates that different kinds of discipline may be necessary to promote an internal morality for children with different temperaments.

So moral socialization at home is a two-way street: Although inductive discipline often does promote moral maturity, children who respond more favorably to this rational, relatively nonpunitive approach are the ones who are most likely to be treated this way by their parents.

A Child's-Eye View of Discipline

What do children think about various disciplinary strategies? Do they feel (as many developmentalists do) that physical punishment and love withdrawal are ineffective methods of promoting moral restraint? Would they favor inductive techniques, or perhaps prefer that their parents adopt more permissive attitudes about transgressions?

Michael Siegal and Jan Cowen (1984) addressed these issues by asking children and adolescents between the ages of 4 and 18 to listen to stories describing different kinds of misdeeds and to evaluate strategies that mothers had used to discipline these antics. Five kinds of transgressions were described: (1) simple disobedience (the child refused to clean his room), (2) causing physical harm to others (the child punched a playmate), (3) causing physical harm to oneself (ignoring an order not to touch a hot stove), (4) causing psychological harm to others (making fun of a physically disabled person), and (5) causing physical damage (breaking a lamp while roughhousing). The four disciplinary techniques on which mothers were said to have relied were *induction,* (reasoning with the culprit by pointing out the harmful consequences of his or her actions), *physical punishment* (striking the child), *love withdrawal* (saying she wanted nothing more to do with the culprit), and *permissive nonintervention* (ignoring the incident and assuming that the child would

Box 10.3 | Focus on Research

Temperament, Discipline, and Moral Internalization

Several years ago, Grazyna Kochanska (1993, 1997) proposed that the kind of parenting most likely to foster moral internalization depends on a child's temperament. Some children are temperamentally *fearful*—that is, prone to become highly anxious and to burst into tears when they receive a sharp reprimand from their parents. According to Kochanska, fearful children respond much more favorably to gentle, psychological forms of discipline that deemphasize power assertion—something akin to Hoffman's induction. Other children are highly impulsive and temperamentally *fearless*. Kochanska believes that these emotionally nonreactive youngsters may not be sufficiently aroused by mild psychological forms of discipline to pay attention and internalize parental rules or even to stop performing the behavior for which they are being reprimanded! Although their parents may be inclined to become forceful with them when gentle forms of discipline do not work, Kochanska claims that resorting to power assertion proves no more effective with a fearless child than with a fearful one. Instead, she proposes that the route to moral internalization for a fearless child is warm, sensitive parenting of the kind that promotes secure attachments and a mutually cooperative parent/child relationship. Her view is that a secure and mutually positive orientation fosters *committed compliance* from the child, who wants to cooperate with and please his parents.

To test her theory, Kochanska (1995, 1997) classified a sample of 2- to 3-year-olds as temperamentally fearful or fearless. She then observed each of them interacting with their mothers to assess the mothers' warmth and responsiveness to social signals and the kinds of discipline that mothers used. Data on the security of the child's attachment to his or her mother were also available. The strength of children's moral internalization was assessed at three times: ages 2 to 3, 4, and 5. Measures of moral internalization included complying with requests and following rules (that is, refusing to touch prohibited toys) at age 2 to 3, as well as refusing to cheat at games and maturity of moral reasoning at ages 4 and 5.

The results of this longitudinal study provided clear support for Kochanska's theory. For the *fearful* children, use of gentle inductive discipline that was low in power assertion predicted higher levels

of moral internalization at all three ages. Yet this same discipline bore no relationship to the levels of the moral internalization that *fearless* participants displayed. Instead, a secure attachment to a mother who was highly responsive to their social signals is what predicted strength of conscience among fearless children.

Kochanska and her associates (2007) have replicated and extended these parenting × temperament interactions in longitudinal studies that assessed new measures of moral internalization (for example, moral self-concept) in two additional samples of toddlers and preschool children. Thus, we can be much more confident that different kinds of parenting really are more (or less) effective for children with different temperaments. Another finding to emerge from the recent studies was that patterns of parenting displayed *in the child's second year* (rather than the first or third year) had the most influence on children's moral internalization. Why? Possibly because the second year is when children are developing (or failing to develop) the mutually cooperative orientation with parents that influences the likelihood that they will willingly comply with parental demands, resolve conflicts amicably, and develop a strong internalized conscience.

Here then, is another example of how "goodness of fit" between parenting practices and children's temperaments foster adaptive outcomes. Judging from the child-rearing literature, most children probably are sufficiently aroused by gentle, inductive disciplinary techniques to learn moral lessons, although this approach may be essential to foster moral internalization among especially fearful youngsters. However, continued reliance on this same discipline constitutes a poor fit for highly fearless children, who are more likely to internalize moral lessons in the context of a secure relationship with a parent whose discipline is firm and reminds the child of the desirability of maintaining the warm, mutually cooperative relationship they have enjoyed. Finally, Kochanska and her associates (Kochanska, Padavich, & Koenig, 2006; Kochanska et al., 2002; Kochanska, Aksan, & Coy, 2007) find that heavy use of power assertion is associated with low levels of (or no) child guilt after transgressions and few (if any) signs of moral internalization, thus representing a poor disciplinary fit with all temperaments.

---

learn important lessons on his or her own). Each participant heard 20 stories that resulted from pairing each of the four maternal disciplinary strategies with each of the five kinds of transgressions. After listening to or reading each story, the participant indicated whether the mother's approach to the problem was "very wrong," "wrong," "half right—half wrong," "right," or "very right."

Although the perceived appropriateness of each disciplinary technique varied somewhat across transgressions, the most interesting findings overall were that (1) induction was the most preferred disciplinary strategy for participants of all ages (even preschoolers), and (2) physical punishment was the next most favorably evaluated technique. So all participants seemed to favor a rational disciplinarian who relies heavily on reasoning that is occasionally backed by power assertion. By contrast, love withdrawal and permissiveness were favorably evaluated by no age group. In fact, the 4- to 9-year-olds in the sample favored any form of discipline, even love withdrawal, over a permissive attitude on the mother's part (which they viewed as "wrong" or "very wrong"). Apparently young children see the need for adults to step in and restrain their inappropriate conduct, for they were disturbed by stories in which youngsters were generally free to "do their own thing," largely unencumbered by adult constraints.

In sum, the disciplinary style that children favor (induction backed by occasional use of power assertion) is the one most closely associated with measures of moral maturity in the child-rearing studies and with resistance to temptation in the laboratory. Perhaps another reason that inductive discipline may promote moral maturity is simply that children view this approach as the "right" way to deal with transgressions and they may be highly motivated to accept influence from a disciplinarian whose "worldview" matches their own. By contrast, children who favor induction but are usually disciplined in other ways may see little justification for internalizing the values and exhortations of a disciplinarian whose very methods of inducing compliance seem unwise, unjust, and hardly worthy of their respect.

SUMMARY

WHAT ARE ALTRUISM AND PROSOCIAL BEHAVIOR?

+ **Prosocial behavior** consists of actions that are intended to benefit other people. **Altruism,** a form of prosocial behavior, has been defined in two ways. The **motivational, or intentional, definition** contends that an act is altruistic if the helper is acting more out of a concern for others than for any personal benefits that might accrue. By contrast, proponents of a **behavioral definition** think of altruism as any act that benefits others, regardless of the helper's motives.

THEORIES OF ALTRUISM AND PROSOCIAL DEVELOPMENT

+ Evolutionary theorists argue that altruism is a preadapted, genetically programmed motive that evolved because it promotes the survival of the individual and the species, and altruistic concern does appear to be a genetically influenced attribute. By contrast, proponents of psychoanalytic, social-learning, and cognitive-developmental theories believe that children must *acquire* a sense of altruistic concern. Psychoanalytic theorists assume that altruistic values are internalized and become a part of one's superego. Social-learning theorists believe that altruistic habits are acquired and maintained because children learn that prosocial behavior is in some way reinforcing. Cognitive-developmental theorists argue that the growth of altruistic concern depends on fundamental cognitive changes that occur during childhood, including (1) a gradual decline in egocentrism, (2) the development of role-taking skills, and (3) the growth of empathic concern and prosocial moral reasoning.

DEVELOPMENTAL TRENDS IN ALTRUISM

+ Early indications of prosocial conduct, such as sharing toys and comforting distressed companions, appear in infancy and toddlerhood, particularly among youngsters whose mothers emphasize a concern for others as part of their disciplinary strategies.

+ Sharing, helping, and other forms of prosocial behavior become more and more common from the preschool period onward. Volunteering for community service is a noteworthy kind of prosocial activity that many adolescents undertake. Girls tend to be more generous and helpful and less competitive than boys, although these sex differences are small and not apparent in all contexts.

COGNITIVE AND AFFECTIVE CONTRIBUTORS TO ALTRUISM

+ The growth of altruistic concern is linked to the development of **social perspective-taking skills, prosocial moral reasoning, sympathetic empathic arousal,** and establishment of an altruistic self-concept. Although young children often interpret empathic arousal as personal or **self-oriented distress,** they eventually acquire the role-taking skills to interpret their reactions as sympathy for others, which, in conjunction with their learning of prosocial norms, promotes altruism by inducing them to feel responsible for others' welfare (the **"felt responsibility" hypothesis**).

CULTURAL AND SOCIAL INFLUENCES ON ALTRUISM

+ Prosocial conduct is much more apparent in *collectivist* societies, where strongly stressed social goals make it almost obligatory, than in *individualistic* societies, where it has more of a discretionary quality about it.

+ Many other social influences affect one's propensity for altruism. Parents can promote altruistic behavior through their **altruistic exhortations,** by praising their child's kindly deeds, and by practicing themselves the prosocial lessons they have preached. Furthermore, parents who discipline harm-doing with nonpunitive, affective explanations that point out the negative effects of one's misconduct on victims are likely to raise children who become sympathetic, self-sacrificing, and concerned about the welfare of others.

WHAT IS MORALITY?

+ **Morality** has been defined in many ways, although almost everyone agrees that it implies a set of internalized principles or ideals that help the individual to distinguish right from wrong and to act on this distinction. Morality has three basic components: **moral affect, moral reasoning,** and **moral behavior.**

PSYCHOANALYTIC EXPLANATIONS OF MORAL DEVELOPMENT

+ According to Freud's theory of **Oedipal morality,** children internalize the moral standards of the same-sex parent during the phallic stage as they resolve their Oedipus or Electra complexes and form a conscience, or superego.

+ Research has consistently discredited Freud's theory. However, newer ideas and research imply that a conscience can begin to develop in toddlerhood in the context of a warm, **mutually responsive relationship** in which the child shows a strong sense of **committed compliance** (rather than **situational compliance**).

COGNITIVE-DEVELOPMENTAL THEORY: THE CHILD AS A MORAL PHILOSOPHER

✦ Cognitive-developmental theorists have emphasized the cognitive component of morality by studying the development of moral reasoning. Jean Piaget formulated a two-stage model of moral development based on changes that occur in children's conceptions of rules and their sense of social justice. From a **premoral period,** in which children allegedly respect no rules, they progress to **heteronomous morality,** in which they view rules as moral absolutes and believe in **immanent justice,** and finally, to **autonomous morality,** in which they regard rules as flexible and justice as relative rather than absolute.

✦ Piaget identified some important trends in the development of moral reasoning. However, shortcomings of his research methods and his failure to capture children's distinctions between **moral rules, social conventional rules, and personal choices** caused him to underestimate the moral sophistication of preschool and young grade-school children.

✦ Lawrence Kohlberg's revision and extension of Piaget's theory views moral reasoning as progressing through an invariant sequence of three levels, (**preconventional, conventional, and postconventional moralities**), each composed of two distinct stages. According to Kohlberg, the order of progression through the levels and stages is invariant because each of these modes of thinking depends in part on the development of cognitive abilities that evolve in a fixed sequence. Yet Kohlberg also claimed that no moral growth occurs in the absence of social experiences that would cause a person to reevaluate her existing moral concepts.

✦ Research indicates that Kohlberg's stages do form an invariant sequence. Furthermore, both cognitive development and such relevant social experiences as exposure to divergent moral perspectives in the context of **transactive interactions** with parents, peers, and other participants in higher education or democratic activities do contribute to the growth of moral reasoning. However, Kohlberg's theory may not adequately describe the morality of people who live in many non-Westernized societies or who emphasize a **morality of care** rather than a **morality of justice;** and like Piaget, Kohlberg clearly underestimates the moral reasoning of young children. Critics also claim the theory says too little about moral affect and moral behavior.

MORALITY AS A PRODUCT OF SOCIAL LEARNING (AND SOCIAL INFORMATION-PROCESSING)

✦ Although their **doctrine of specificity** is clearly an overstatement, social-learning theorists have helped to explain how children come to resist temptation and inhibit acts that violate moral norms. Among the factors that promote the development of **inhibitory controls** are praise given for virtuous conduct, punishments that include appropriate rationales, moral self-concept training, and exposing the child to (or having children serve as) models of moral restraint.

WHO RAISES CHILDREN WHO ARE MORALLY MATURE?

✦ Child-rearing studies consistently imply that use of **inductive discipline** promotes moral maturity, whereas **love withdrawal** has little effect, and **power assertion** is associated with moral *immaturity.* The effectiveness of induction may vary, however, depending on the child's temperament. But children generally prefer inductive discipline to other approaches, and most seem highly motivated to accept influence from an inductive adult whose methods they can respect.

CHAPTER 11

The Family

I N APRIL OF 1995, at the age of 95 and on the day after her own 75th wedding anniversary, Cora Shaffer attended the 50th wedding anniversary party of her eldest son (then aged 73). Also present at that gathering were Cora's other surviving child, four of her eight grandchildren, eight of her 11 great-grandchildren, and nine of her 11 great-great-grandchildren. Remarkably, Cora could easily recite the most notable dates (birthdays, wedding anniversaries) of *all* of her descendants and could give you a pretty fair account of the most notable current events (for example, recent occupational, educational, or personal attainments) of all these relatives as well. When I asked her how she managed to keep up with all the family doings, she laughed, said she had ample time for family matters since her retirement in 1985 (at age 85!), and quipped that "Alexander Graham Bell must have had folks like me in mind when he invented the telephone." This woman could also expound at length about the lives and times of departed relatives she had known, some of whom had been born in the early 1840s, before the telephone (or even the pony express) had been invented. Clearly, Cora Shaffer valued her ties to past, present, and future generations of Shaffers.

Most of us will never have the opportunity to know and care about as many generations of relatives as my grandmother did, but her emphasis on family ties is not at all unusual. More than 99 percent of children in the United States are raised in a family of one kind or another (U.S. Bureau of the Census, 2002), and the vast majority of children in all societies grow up in a home setting with at least one biological parent or other relative. So virtually all of us are bound to families. We are born into them, work our way toward adulthood in them, start our own as adults, and remain connected to them in old age. We are part of our families, and they are part of us.

Our focus in this chapter is on the family as a *social system*—an institution that both influences and is influenced by its young. What is a family and what functions do families serve? How does the birth of a child affect other family members? Do the existing (or changing) relationships among other members of the family have any effect on the care and training that a young child receives? Are some patterns of parenting better than others? Do parents decide how they will raise their children—or might children be influencing their parents? Does the family's cultural heritage and socioeconomic status affect parenting and parent/child interactions? How important are siblings as socialization agents? How are children affected by the increasing diversity of family life we see today—by growing up with gay or lesbian parents, or by having to adjust to maternal employment, divorce, or a return to the two-parent family when a single parent remarries? And why do some parents abuse their offspring? These are some of the major issues that we will consider as we look at the important roles that families play in the cognitive, social, and emotional development of children and adolescents.

⤳ UNDERSTANDING THE FAMILY

From a developmental perspective, the most important function that families serve in all societies is to care for and socialize their young. **Socialization** refers to the process by which children acquire the beliefs, motives, values, and behaviors deemed significant and appropriate by older members of their society. And the socialization of each successive generation serves society in at least three ways. First, it is a means of regulating children's behavior and controlling their undesirable impulses. Second, socialization promotes the personal growth of the individual. As children interact with and become like other members of their culture, they acquire the knowledge, skills, motives, and aspirations that should enable them to adapt to and function effectively within their communities. Finally,

socialization
the process by which children acquire the beliefs, values, and behaviors considered desirable or appropriate by their culture or subculture.

socialization perpetuates the social order: Appropriately socialized children become competent, adaptive, prosocial adults who will impart what they have learned to their own children.

Of course, families are only one of many institutions involved in the socialization process. Religious institutions, for example, provide important emotional supports and moral guidance that often increase family cohesion (Brody, Stoneman, & Flor, 1996) and expose children and adolescents to trustworthy adult mentors and peers who reinforce parental values, foster the growth of prosocial identities, and promote other healthy developmental outcomes (King & Furrow, 2004; Larson, Hansen, & Moneta, 2006). And as we will see in

Photo 11.1
For many families, religious activities provide an important source of social/emotional support that increases family cohesion and helps promote healthy developmental outcomes.

Chapter 12, such institutions as the schools, the mass media, and children's groups (for example, Boy Scouts and Girl Scouts) frequently supplement the training and emotional support functions served by families. Nevertheless, many children have limited exposure to people outside the family until they are placed in day care or nursery school or begin their formal schooling. So the family has a clear head start on other institutions when it comes to socializing a child. And because the events of the early years are so very important to the child's social, emotional, and intellectual development, it is appropriate to think of the family as society's primary instrument of socialization.

The Family as a Social System

It is not easy to define the term **family** in a way that applies to all cultures, subcultures, or historical eras because many forms of family life have worked and continue to work for humans (Coontz, 2000). By one recent definition, a family is "two or more persons related by birth, marriage, adoption, or choice" who have emotional ties and responsibilities to each other (Allen, Fine, & Demo, 2000, p. 1).

When developmentalists began to study socialization in the 1940s and 1950s, they focused almost entirely on the mother/child relationship, operating under the assumption that mothers (and to a lesser extent fathers) were the agents who molded children's conduct and character (Ambert, 1992). However, modern family researchers have rejected this simple unidirectional model in favor of a more comprehensive "systems" approach—one that is similar to Urie Bronfenbrenner's ecological systems theory that we discussed in Chapter 3 (Bronfenbrenner & Morris, 2006). The systems approach recognizes that parents influence their children. But it also stresses that (1) children influence the behavior and child-rearing practices of their parents, and (2) families are complex **social systems**—that is, networks of *reciprocal* relationships and alliances that are constantly evolving and are greatly affected by community and cultural influences (Parke & Buriel, 2006). Now consider some implications of this systems perspective.

Direct and Indirect Influences

What does it mean to say that a family is a social system? To family systems theorists it means that the family, much like the human body, is a *holistic structure* consisting of

family
two or more persons, related by birth, marriage, adoption, or choice, who have emotional ties and responsibilities to each other.

family social system
the complex network of relationships, interactions, and patterns of influence that characterize a family with three or more members.

The Family   371

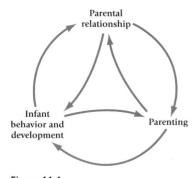

Figure 11.1
A model of the family as a social system. As implied in the diagram, a family is bigger than the sum of its parts. Parents affect infants, who affect each parent and the marital relationship. Of course, the marital relationship may affect the parenting the infant receives, the infant's behavior, and so on. Clearly, families are complex social systems. As an exercise, you may wish to rediagram the patterns of influence within a family after adding a sibling or two. (Belsky, J. 1981. Early human experience: A family perspective. Developmental Psychology, 17, 3–23.) © 1981 by The American Psychological Assn. Reprinted by permission.

traditional nuclear family
a family unit consisting of a wife/mother, a husband/father, and their dependent child(ren).

direct effect
instances in which any pair of family members affects and is affected by each other's behavior.

indirect, or third party, effect
instances in which the relationship between two individuals in a family is modified by the behavior or attitudes of a third family member.

coparenting
circumstance in which parents mutually support each other and function as a cooperative parenting team.

extended family
a group of blood relatives from more than one nuclear family (for example, grandparents, aunts, uncles, nieces, and nephews) who live together, forming a household.

interrelated parts, each of which affects and is affected by every other part, and each of which contributes to the functioning of the whole (Parke & Buriel, 2006).

To illustrate, let's consider the simplest of **traditional nuclear families,** consisting of a mother, a father, and a firstborn child. According to Jay Belsky (1981), even this man/woman/infant "system" is a complex entity. An infant interacting with his or her mother is already involved in a process of *reciprocal influence,* as is evident when we notice that the infant's smile is likely to be greeted by the mother's smile or that a mother's concerned expression often makes her infant wary. These influences, in which any pair of family members affects and is affected by each other's behavior, are called **direct effects.** And what happens when Dad arrives? As shown in Figure 11.1, the mother/infant dyad is suddenly transformed into a "*family system* [comprising] a husband/wife as well as mother/infant and father/infant relationships" (Belsky, 1981, p. 17).

One implication of viewing the family as a system is that interactions between any two family members are likely to be influenced by attitudes and behaviors of a third family member—a phenomenon known as an **indirect, or third party, effect.** To illustrate, fathers clearly influence the mother/infant relationship: Happily married mothers who have close, supportive relationships with their husbands tend to interact much more patiently and sensitively with their infants than mothers who experience marital tension and feel that they are raising their children on their own (Cox et al., 1989, 1992; Parke & Buriel, 2006). Their infants are therefore more likely to be securely attached (Doyle et al., 2000). Meanwhile, mothers directly influence the father/infant relationship: Fathers tend to be more involved and supportive with their children when their relations with their spouses are harmonious (Kitzmann, 2000) and their wives are also highly involved (Flouri & Buchanan, 2003). Overall, children fare best when couples **coparent**—that is, mutually support each other's parenting efforts and function as a cooperative (rather than an antagonistic) team. Unfortunately, effective coparenting is difficult for couples experiencing marital discord and other life stresses (Kitzmann, 2000; McHale, 1995), and disputes between parents over child-rearing issues can be particularly intense (Papp, Cummings, & Goeke-Morey, 2002) and harmful, often forecasting increases in childhood and adolescent adjustment problems over and above those attributable to other aspects of marital conflict (Mahoney, Jouriles, & Scavone, 1997; McHale et al., 2002). Clearly, both mothers and fathers can influence their children *indirectly* through their own interactions.

Of course, children also exert direct and indirect effects on their parents. A highly impulsive child who throws tantrums and shows little inclination to comply with requests may drive a mother to punitive, coercive methods of discipline (a direct "child-to-mother" effect; Stoolmiller, 2001), which in turn may make the child more defiant than ever (a direct "mother-to-child" effect; Crockenberg and Litman, 1990; Donovan, Leavitt, & Walsh, 2000). Alarmed by this state of affairs, the exasperated mother may then criticize her husband for his nonintervention, thereby precipitating an unpleasant discussion about parental obligations and responsibilities (an indirect effect of the child's conduct on the husband/wife relationship (Jenkins et al., 2005).

In short, every person and every relationship within the family affects every other person and relationship through pathways of direct and indirect influence illustrated in Figure 11.1. Now we begin to see why it was rather naive to think we might understand how families influence children by concentrating exclusively on the mother/child relationship.

Now think about how complex the family system becomes with the birth of a second child and the addition of sibling/sibling and sibling/parent relationships. Or consider the complexity of an **extended family household,** a nearly universal practice in some cultures in which parents and their children live with (or in very close proximity to) other kin—grandparents or aunts, uncles, nieces, and nephews. In the United States, African Americans, Hispanic Americans and Native Americans tend to place greater emphasis on extended family bonds than European Americans do (Leyendecker & Lamb, 1999; Parke & Buriel,

2006). And this family arrangement has proved to be highly adaptive for economically disadvantaged African-American mothers, who are likely to become more sensitive, responsive parents should they receive much needed child-rearing assistance and social support from their own mothers or other relatives (Burton, 1990; Taylor, 2000). What's more, disadvantaged African-American school children and adolescents whose families receive ample kinship support usually receive competent parenting at home, which in turn is associated with such positive outcomes as a strong sense of self-reliance, good psychological adjustment, solid academic performance, and fewer behavioral problems (Taylor, 1996; Taylor & Roberts, 1995; Zimmerman, Salem, & Maton, 1995). And in cultures such as the Sudan, where social life is governed by collectivist ideals stressing communal interdependence and intergenerational harmony, children routinely display better patterns of psychological adjustment if raised in extended-family households rather than in Westernized, two-parent nuclear families (Al Awad & Sonuga-Barke, 1992). So it seems that the healthiest family contexts for development will depend very heavily on both the needs of individual families and the values that families (within particular cultural and subcultural contexts) are trying to promote.

Photo 11.2
Older members of extended families serve many useful functions. In addition to providing information and emotional support to young parents, grandmothers and even great-grandmothers may figure prominently in the care and guidance of the family's children.

Families Are Developing Systems

Not only are families complex social systems, they are dynamic systems as well. Consider that every family member is a *developing* individual and that relationships between husband and wife, parent and child, and sibling and sibling will also change in ways that can influence the development of each family member (Parke & Buriel, 2006). Many such changes are planned, as when parents allow toddlers to do more things on their own as a means of encouraging autonomy and the development of individual initiative. Yet a host of unplanned or unforeseen changes (such as the death of a sibling or the souring of the husband/wife relationship and the divorce that may result) can greatly affect family interactions and the growth of its children. So the family is not only a system in which developmental change takes place; its dynamics also change with development of its members.

Families Are Embedded Systems

The social systems perspective also emphasizes that all families are embedded within larger cultural and subcultural contexts and that the ecological niche a family occupies (for example, the family's religion, its socioeconomic status, and the values that prevail within a subculture, a community, or even a neighborhood) can affect family interactions and the development of a family's children (Bronfenbrenner & Morris, 2006). As we will see later in the chapter, economic hardship exerts a strong influence on parenting: Parents often become distressed over their financial situation, which in turn can cause them to become less nurturant toward and involved with their children (Conger et al., 1992, 2002; Parke & Buriel, 2006). And yet economically distressed parents who have close ties to a "community"—a church group, a volunteer organization, or a circle of close friends and other confidants—experience far less stress and less disruption of their parenting routines (Burchinal, Follmer, & Bryant, 1996; MacPhee, Fritz, & Miller-Heyl, 1996). Clearly, the broader social contexts that families experience can greatly affect the ways that family functions are carried out.

In sum, even the simplest of families is a true social system that is much bigger than the sum of its parts. Not only does each family member influence the behavior of every other, but the relationship between any two family members can affect the interactions and relationships of all other family members. And when we consider that family members develop, relationships change, and that all family dynamics are influenced by the broader social contexts in which families are embedded, it becomes quite clear that socialization within the family is best described not as a two-way street between parents and children, but as the busy intersection of many, many avenues of influence.

Changing Family Systems in a Changing World

Not only is the family a complex, developing system, but it exists and develops in a world that is constantly changing. During the last half of the 20th century, several dramatic social changes have affected the makeup of the typical family and the character of family life. Drawing on U.S. census data and other surveys, I'll highlight these changes:

1. *More single adults.* More adults are living as singles today than in the past. Marriage isn't "out," however, as about 90 percent of young adults will eventually marry (Whitehead & Popenoe, 2003).

2. *Postponed marriages.* Many young singles are postponing marriage to pursue educational and career goals. Although the average age of first marriage actually decreased during the first half of the 20th century, it has risen again to about 25 for women and 27 for men (Whitehead & Popenoe, 2003).

3. *Decreased childbearing.* Today's adults are not only waiting longer after they marry to have children, they are having fewer of them—about 1.8 on average (U.S. Bureau of the Census, 2006). The Baby Boom period after World War II was an unusual departure from an otherwise consistent trend toward smaller family sizes. Today, about 19 percent of 40- to 44-year-old women remain childless, many by choice, compared with 10 percent in 1980 (U.S. Bureau of the Census, 2006).

4. *More women are employed.* In 1950, 12 percent of married women with children under age 6 worked outside the home; now the figure is 63 percent, a truly dramatic social change (U.S. Bureau of the Census, 2006). Fewer and fewer children have a mother whose full-time job is that of homemaker.

5. *More divorce.* The divorce rate has been increasing over the past several decades, to the point where an additional one *million* children each year are affected by their parents' divorce (Hetherington, Bridges, & Insabella, 1998). Recent estimates are that between 40 and 50 percent of newly married couples can expect to divorce (Hetherington, Henderson, & Reiss, 1999; Meckler, 2002).

6. *More single-parent families.* Partly because of a rise in births by never-married parents and partly because of divorce, more children today spend at least some time in a **single-parent family.** In 1960, only 9 percent of children lived with one parent, usually a widowed one. In 2002, 28 percent of children under 18 lived with one parent, usually a divorced or never-married one (Whitehead & Popenoe, 2003). Father-headed single-parent homes are more common than they used to be, recently accounting for about 18 percent of all single-parent families (Fields, 2003).

7. *More children living in poverty.* Unfortunately, the increase in the number of single-parent families has contributed to an increase in the proportion of children living below the poverty line. Almost one in five children in the United States lives in poverty today, the highest rate of child poverty among Western industrialized countries (Childstats.gov, 2007a). As seen in Figure 11.2, African-American and Hispanic-American children are about three times more likely to be living in poverty than European-American children.

single-parent family
a family system consisting of one parent (either the mother or the father) and the parent's dependent child(ren).

Figure 11.2
Child poverty rates in 2005 in the United States. Source: U.S. Bureau of the Census, 2007.

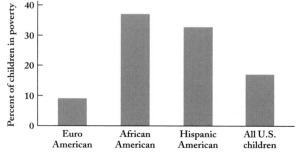

8. *More remarriage.* Because more married couples are divorcing, more adults (about 66 percent of divorced mothers and 75 percent of divorced fathers) are remarrying, forming **blended (or reconstituted) families** that involve at least one child, his or her biological parent, and a stepparent, and that often blend multiple children from two families into a new family system (Hetherington, Henderson, & Reiss, 1999). About 25 percent of American children will spend some time in a stepparent family (Hetherington & Jodl, 1994).

9. *More multigeneration families.* More children today than in the past know their grandparents and even their great-grandparents, and multigenerational bonds in American families are becoming more important (Parke & Buriel, 2006). With the trends toward dual-earner couples and fewer children, we see more *beanpole families,* characterized by more generations, but smaller ones, than in the past.

What these changes tell us is that modern families are much more diverse than ever. Our stereotyped image of the model family—the *Leave It to Beaver* nuclear aggregation with a breadwinning father, a housewife mother, and at least two children—is just that: a stereotype. By one estimate, this "typical" family represented about 50 percent of American households in 1960, but only 12 percent in 1995 (Hernandez, 1997). Although families are no less influential today than they were in previous eras, we must broaden our image of them to include the many dual-career, single-parent, blended, and multigenerational families that exist today and are influencing the development of the *majority* of our children. Bear that in mind as we begin our excursion into family life, seeking to determine how families influence the development of their children.

Photo 11.3
Because divorce and remarriage are so common, many children now live in blended (stepparent) families with stepsiblings.

blended (or reconstituted) families
new families resulting from cohabitation or remarriage that include a parent, one or more children, and step-relations.

∾ PARENTAL SOCIALIZATION DURING CHILDHOOD AND ADOLESCENCE

In previous chapters, we considered the results of a large body of research aimed at understanding how parents might affect the social, emotional, and intellectual development of their infants and toddlers. Recall that this work was remarkably consistent in its implications: Warm and sensitive parents who often talk to their infants and try to stimulate their curiosity are contributing in a positive way to the establishment of secure emotional attachments as well as to the child's willingness to explore, sociability, and intellectual development. It also helps if *both* parents are sensitive, responsive caregivers who can agree on how their infant should be raised and support each other in their roles as parents. Indeed, Jay Belsky (1981) has argued that parental warmth/sensitivity "is the most influential dimension of [parenting] in infancy. It not only fosters healthy psychological functioning during this developmental epoch, but also . . . lays the foundation on which future experience will build" (p. 8).

During the second year, parents continue to be caregivers and playmates, but they also become more concerned with teaching children how to behave (or how *not* to behave) in a variety of situations (Fagot & Kavanaugh, 1993). According to Erik Erikson (1963), this is the period when socialization begins in earnest. Parents must now manage the child's budding autonomy in the hope of instilling a sense of social propriety and self-control, while taking care not to undermine his or her curiosity, initiative, and feelings of personal competence.

Two Major Dimensions of Parenting

Erikson and others (for example, Maccoby & Martin, 1983) claim that two aspects of parenting are especially important throughout childhood and adolescence: *Parental acceptance/responsiveness* and *parental demandingness/control* (sometimes called "permissiveness/restrictiveness").

acceptance/responsiveness
a dimension of parenting that describes the amount of responsiveness and affection that a parent displays toward a child.

Acceptance/responsiveness refers to the amount of support and affection that a parent displays. Parents classified as accepting and responsive often smile at, praise, and encourage their children, expressing a great deal of warmth, even though they can become quite critical when a child misbehaves. By contrast, less accepting and relatively unresponsive parents are often quick to criticize, belittle, punish, or ignore a child; they rarely communicate to children that they are valued or loved.

demandingness/control
a dimension of parenting that describes how restrictive and demanding parents are.

Demandingness/control refers to the amount of regulation or supervision parents undertake with their children. Controlling/demanding parents place limits on their children's freedom of expression by imposing many demands and actively surveying their children's behavior to ensure that these rules are followed. Less controlling/demanding parents are much less restrictive; they make fewer demands and allow children considerable freedom to pursue their interests and to make decisions about their own activities.

I assume that you have little difficulty deciding that parental acceptance and responsiveness are preferable to parental rejection and insensitivity. As we have seen throughout this book, warm, responsive parenting is consistently associated with such positive outcomes as secure emotional attachments, a prosocial orientation and good peer relations, high self-esteem, a strong sense of morality, and many other virtues. Children generally want to please loving parents and so are motivated to do what is expected of them and learn what parents would like them to learn (Forman & Kochanska, 2001; Kochanska, 2002). By contrast, a primary contributor to poor peer relations, clinical depression, and other adjustment problems later in life is a family setting in which one or both parents have treated the child as if he or she were unworthy of their attention and affection (Ge et al., 1996; MacKinnon-Lewis et al., 1997; Scaramella et al., 2002). Children simply do not thrive when they are often ignored or rejected.

Is it better for parents to be highly controlling, or rather should they impose few restrictions and grant their children considerable autonomy? To answer these questions, we need to be more specific about the degrees of control that parents display and to look carefully at patterns of parental acceptance.

Photo 11.4
Warmth and affection are crucial components of effective parenting.

Four Patterns of Parenting

It turns out that the two major parenting dimensions are reasonably independent, so that we find parents who display each of the four possible combinations of acceptance/responsiveness and control/demandingness shown in Figure 11.3. How are these four parenting styles related to a child's or an adolescent's social, emotional, and intellectual development?

Baumrind's Early Research Perhaps the best-known research on parenting styles is Diana Baumrind's (1967, 1971) early studies of preschool children and their parents. Each child in Baumrind's sample was observed on several occasions in nursery school and at home. These data were used to rate the child on such behavioral dimensions as sociability, self-reliance, achievement, moodiness, and self-control. Parents were also interviewed and observed while interacting with their children at home. When Baumrind analyzed the parental data, she found that individual parents generally used one of three parenting styles shown in Figure 11.3 (none of her parents could be classified as "uninvolved"). These three patterns of parenting were described as follows:

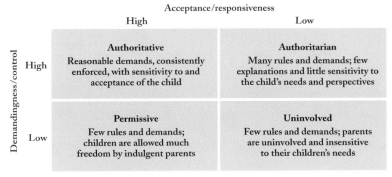

Acceptance/responsiveness

	High	Low
High Demandingness/control	**Authoritative** Reasonable demands, consistently enforced, with sensitivity to and acceptance of the child	**Authoritarian** Many rules and demands; few explanations and little sensitivity to the child's needs and perspectives
Low	**Permissive** Few rules and demands; children are allowed much freedom by indulgent parents	**Uninvolved** Few rules and demands; parents are uninvolved and insensitive to their children's needs

Figure 11.3 Two major dimensions of parenting. When we cross the two dimensions, we come up with four parenting styles: accepting/controlling (or "authoritative"); accepting/uncontrolling (or "permissive"); aloof/controlling (or "authoritarian"); and aloof/uncontrolling (or "uninvolved"). Which parenting style did your parents use? (Based on Maccoby & Martin, 1983.)

Authoritarian parenting: A very restrictive pattern of parenting in which adults impose many rules, expect strict obedience, will rarely if ever explain to the child why it is necessary to comply with all these regulations, and will often rely on punitive, forceful tactics (that is, power assertion or love withdrawal) to gain compliance. Authoritarian parents are not sensitive to a child's conflicting viewpoints, expecting instead for the child to accept their word as law and to respect their authority.

Authoritative parenting: A controlling but flexible style in which parents make many reasonable demands of their children. They are careful to provide rationales for complying with the limits they set and will ensure that their children follow these guidelines. However, they are much more accepting of and responsive to their children's points of view than authoritarian parents are and will often seek their children's participation in family decision making. So authoritative parents exercise control in a *rational, democratic* (rather than a heavy-handed, domineering) way that recognizes and respects their children's perspectives.

Permissive parenting: An accepting but lax pattern of parenting in which adults make relatively few demands, permit their children to freely express their feelings and impulses, do not closely monitor their children's activities, and rarely exert firm control over their behavior.

When Baumrind (1967) linked these three parenting styles to the characteristics of the preschool children who were exposed to each style, she found that children of authoritative parents were developing rather well. They were cheerful, socially responsible, self-reliant, achievement oriented, and cooperative with adults and peers. By contrast, children of authoritarian parents tended to be moody and seemingly unhappy much of the time, easily annoyed and unfriendly, relatively aimless, and generally not very pleasant to be around. Finally, children of permissive parents were often impulsive and aggressive, especially if they were boys. They tended to be bossy and self-centered, lacking in self-control, and quite low in independence and achievement.

Do children of authoritarian or permissive parents eventually "outgrow" whatever shortcomings they displayed as preschoolers? Seeking to answer this question, Baumrind followed up on her child participants when they were 8 to 9 years old. As we see in Table 11.1, children of authoritative parents were still relatively high in both *cognitive competencies* (that is, shows originality in thinking, has high achievement motivation, likes intellectual challenges) and *social skills* (for example, is sociable and outgoing, participates actively and shows leadership in group activities), whereas children of authoritarian parents were generally average to below average in cognitive and social skills, and children of permissive parents were relatively unskilled in both areas. Indeed, the strengths of children exposed to

authoritarian parenting
a restrictive pattern of parenting in which adults set many rules for their children, expect strict obedience, and rely on power rather than reason to elicit compliance.

authoritative parenting
flexible, democratic style of parenting in which warm, accepting parents provide guidance and control while allowing the child some say in deciding how best to meet challenges and obligations.

permissive parenting
a pattern of parenting in which otherwise accepting adults make few demands of their children and rarely attempt to control their behavior.

Table 11.1 Relationships between child-rearing patterns and developmental outcomes in middle childhood and adolescence

	Outcomes	
Child-Rearing Pattern	**Childhood**	**Adolescence**
Authoritative	High cognitive and social competencies	High self-esteem, excellent social skills, strong moral/prosocial concern, high academic achievement
Authoritarian	Average cognitive and social competencies	Average academic performance and social skills; more conforming than adolescents of permissive parents
Permissive	Low cognitive and social competencies	Poor self-control and academic performance; more drug use than adolescents of authoritative or authoritarian parents

Sources: Baumrind, 1977, 1991; Steinberg et al., 1994.

authoritative parenting were still evident in adolescence: Compared to teenagers raised by either permissive or authoritarian parents, those raised by authoritative parents were relatively confident, achievement oriented, and socially skilled, and they tended to stay clear of drug use and other problem behaviors (Baumrind, 1991). The link between authoritative parenting and positive developmental outcomes seems to hold for all racial and ethnic groups studied to date in the United States (Glasgow et al., 1997; Collins & Steinberg, 2006) and in a variety of different cultures as well (Chen, Hastings, et al., 1998; Scott, Scott, & McCabe, 1991; Vazsonyi, Hibbert, & Snider, 2003).

Uninvolved Parenting In recent years, it has become quite clear that the least successful parenting style is what might be termed **uninvolved parenting**—an extremely lax and undemanding approach displayed by parents who have either *rejected* their children or are so overwhelmed with their own stresses and problems that they haven't much time or energy to devote to child rearing (Maccoby & Martin, 1983). By age 3, children of uninvolved parents are already relatively high in aggression and such externalizing behaviors as temper tantrums (Miller et al., 1993). Furthermore, they tend to be disruptive and to perform very poorly in the classroom later in childhood (Eckenrode, Laird, & Doris, 1993; Kilgore, Snyder, & Lentz, 2000), and often become hostile, selfish, and rebellious adolescents who lack meaningful long-range goals and are prone to commit such antisocial and delinquent acts as alcohol and drug abuse, sexual misconduct, truancy, and a wide variety of criminal offenses (Collins & Steinberg, 2006; Kurdek & Fine, 1994; Patterson, Reid, & Dishion, 1992; Pettit et al., 2001). In effect, these youngsters have neglectful, (or even "detached") parents whose actions (or lack thereof) seem to be saying "I don't care about you or about what you do"—a message that undoubtedly breeds resentment and willingness to strike back at these aloof, uncaring adversaries or at other authority figures.

Explaining the Effectiveness of Authoritative Parenting Why is authoritative parenting so consistently associated with positive social, emotional, and intellectual outcomes? Probably for several reasons. First, authoritative parents are warm and accepting—they communicate a sense of *caring concern* that may motivate their children to comply with the directives they receive in a way that children of more aloof and demanding (authoritarian) parents are not. Then there is the issue of how control is exercised. Unlike the authoritarian parent who sets *inflexible* standards and *dominates* the child, allowing little if any freedom of expression, the authoritative parent exercises control in a *rational* way, carefully explaining his or her point of view while also considering the child's viewpoint. Demands that

uninvolved parenting
a pattern of parenting that is both aloof (or even hostile) and overpermissive, almost as if parents neither cared about their children nor about what they may become.

come from a warm, accepting parent and that appear to be fair and reasonable rather than arbitrary and dictatorial are likely to elicit *committed compliance* rather than complaining or defiance (Kochanska, 2002). Finally, authoritative parents are careful to tailor their demands to the child's ability to regulate his or her own conduct. In other words, they set standards that children can *realistically* achieve and allow the child some freedom, or *autonomy*, in deciding how best to comply with these expectations. This kind of **autonomy support** carries a most important message—something like "You are a capable human being whom I trust to be self-reliant and accomplish important objectives" (Steinberg, 2005). Of course, we've seen in earlier chapters that feedback of this sort fosters the growth of self-reliance, achievement motivation, and high self-esteem in childhood, and is the kind of support that adolescents need to feel comfortable about exploring various roles and ideologies to forge a personal identity.

In sum, it appears that authoritative parenting—warmth combined with *moderate* and *rational* parental control—is the parenting style most consistently associated with positive developmental outcomes. Children apparently need love *and* limits—a set of rules that help them to structure and to evaluate their conduct. Without such guidance, they may not learn self-control and may become quite selfish, unruly, and lacking in clear achievement goals, particularly if their parents are also aloof or uncaring (Steinberg et al., 1994). But if they receive too much guidance and are hemmed in by inflexible restrictions, they may have few opportunities to become self-reliant and may lack confidence in their own decision-making abilities (Steinberg, 2005; Steinberg et al., 1994).

autonomy support
parental attempts to foster individuality and self-determination by encouraging children to express their viewpoints, participate in family decisions that affect them, and to have some say in how they will comply with parental demands and directives.

Behavioral Control versus Psychological Control

Brian Barber and his associates (Barber, 1996; Barber, Stolz, & Olsen, 2006) raise another important issue about parental exercise of control that is not captured completely by merely classifying parents as authoritative, authoritatorian, permissive, or uninvolved. They point out that parents may differ in their exercise of **behavioral control**—regulating the child's conduct through firm but reasonable discipline and monitoring of his or her activities. They may also differ in exercise of **psychological control**—attempts to influence a child's or adolescent's behavior by such psychological means as ignoring, discounting, or belittling a child's feelings, withholding affection, or inducing shame or guilt.

Based on research we've covered throughout the text, you can probably guess which form of control is associated with more positive developmental outcomes. As early as the preschool period, parents who rely on firm behavioral control without often resorting to psychological guilt trips tend to have well-behaved children and adolescents who do not become involved in deviant peer activities and generally stay out of trouble; by contrast, heavy use of psychological control (or high levels of *both* behavioral and psychological control) is often associated with such poor developmental outcomes as anxiety and depression, poor academic performance, affiliation with deviant peers, and antisocial conduct (Aunola & Nurmi, 2004, 2005; Galambos, Barker, & Almeida, 2003; Olsen et al., 2002; Pettit et al., 2001; Wang, Pomerantz, & Chen, 2007). These outcomes may reflect the findings that parents who rely on behavioral control, along with ample autonomy support, have generally displayed a pattern of supportive but firm (authoritative) guidance, whereas those who favor psychological control have relied on harsh discipline and attempts to thwart the child's autonomy (Barber & Harman, 2002; Pettit et al., 2001). Indeed, heavy use of psychological control can be construed as a strong intrusion on a child's sense of self and self-worth (Barber, Stolz, & Olsen, 2006). Thus, it may be difficult to feel very autonomous, self-confident and self-reliant when psychologically controlling parents are often sending the message that "you are loathful or shameful for ignoring me and behaving inappropriately"—a message that may depress the child or push her away, perhaps into the arms of a deviant peer group.

behavioral control
attempts to regulate a child's or an adolescent's conduct through firm discipline and monitoring of his or her conduct.

psychological control
attempts to regulate a child's or an adolescent's conduct by such psychological tactics as withholding affection and/or inducing shame or guilt.

Parent Effects or Child Effects?

Social-developmentalists have long been guided by a **parent effects model,** which assumes that influences in families run primarily one way, from parent to child. Proponents of this viewpoint would claim that authoritative parenting fosters (that is, causes) positive developmental outcomes. By contrast, a **child effects model** of family influence claims that children have a major influence on their parents. Proponents of this viewpoint claim that authoritative parenting looks so adaptive because easygoing, manageable, and competent children persuade their parents to become more authoritative.

Diana Baumrind (1983, 1993) favors the parent effects model. She notes that children of authoritative parents often resist parental demands at first. But they eventually comply because their parents are firm in their demands and sufficiently patient to allow their children time to comply without caving in to the children's unreasonable demands or turning to power-assertive tactics. Indeed, longitudinal studies of early parental control strategies used by mothers with their 1½ to 3-year-olds clearly supports Baumrind's parental effects hypothesis. Specifically, authoritative mothers who insisted that their children perform competent actions (or *do*'s) and who dealt firmly but patiently with noncompliance had toddlers who became more compliant over time and displayed few problem behaviors. By contrast, authoritarian mothers whose demands emphasized *don'ts* (don't touch, don't yell) and who used arbitrary, power-assertive control strategies had children who were less compliant and cooperative, and who displayed an increase in problem behaviors over time (Crockenberg & Litman, 1990; Kuczynski & Kochanska, 1995).

So parenting practices clearly matter. What's more, a parents' genes play a role in shaping parenting practices. Jenae Neiderhiser and her colleagues (2004), for example, found that pairs of identical twin mothers were more similar in the degrees of warmth that they displayed toward their children than pairs of fraternal twin mothers were—a finding that clearly illustrates that parenting is affected to some extent by a mother's genetic endowment.

Yet, consistent with the child effects model, children clearly influence the kind of parenting they receive. For example, children who display such genetically influenced aspects of temperament as high activity, impulsivity, and low effortful control often appear stubborn and obstinate, elicit more coercive forms of parenting over time (Jaffee et al., 2004, Parke & Buriel, 2006; Stoolmiller, 2001), and may eventually even wear their parents out, causing them to become more lax, less affectionate, and possibly even hostile and uninvolved (Lytton, 1990; Stoolmiller, 2001). Today, most developmentalists favor a **transactional model** of family influence in which socialization is viewed as a matter of reciprocal influence (Collins et al., 2000; Neiderhiser et al., 2004). Longitudinal studies

Parent effects model

Child effects model

Transactional model

generally imply that patterns of parenting influence children more than children influence parenting (Crockenberg & Litman, 1990; Scaramella et al., 2002; Wakschlag & Hans, 1999). Yet the transactional model recognizes that (1) children can and often do affect their parents, for better or worse, and (2) we simply cannot take it for granted, as John Watson (1928) proclaimed, that parents are almost solely responsible for determining whether their children turn out good or bad.

Social Class and Ethnic Variations in Child Rearing

Associations between authoritative parenting, use of behavioral control, and healthy psychological development have been found in many cultures and subcultures (Barber, Stolz, & Olsen, 2006; Collins & Steinberg, 2006; Wang Pomerantz, & Chen, 2007). Yet people from different social strata and ethnic backgrounds face different kinds of problems, pursue different goals, and adopt different values about what it takes to adapt to their environments, and these ecological considerations often affect their approaches to child rearing.

Social Class Differences in Child Rearing   How, then, do parenting styles differ by social class? Compared to middle-class parents, economically disadvantaged and working-class parents tend to (1) stress obedience and respect for authority; (2) be more restrictive and authoritarian, using more power-assertive discipline; (3) reason with their children less frequently; and (4) show less warmth and affection (Maccoby, 1980; McLoyd, 1998).

According to Eleanor Maccoby (1980), these class-linked differences in parenting have been observed in many cultures and across racial and ethnic groups in the United States. However, we should keep in mind that what we are talking about here are *group trends* rather than absolute contrasts. Some middle-class parents are highly restrictive, power assertive, and aloof in their approach to child rearing, whereas many economically disadvantaged and working-class parents function more like their counterparts in the middle class (Kelley, Power, & Wimbush, 1992; Laosa, 1981). But, on average, it appears that lower-SES and working-class parents are somewhat more critical, more punitive, and more intolerant of disobedience than parents from the middle and upper socioeconomic strata.

Explaining Social Class Differences in Child Rearing   Undoubtedly, many factors contribute to social-class differences in child rearing, and economic considerations seem to head the list. Vonnie McLoyd (1989, 1998), for example, claims that economic hardship creates its own psychological distress—a most pervasive discomfort about life's conditions that makes economically disadvantaged adults more edgy and irritable and more vulnerable to all negative life events (including the daily hassles associated with child rearing), thereby diminishing their capacity to be warm, supportive parents who are highly involved in their children's lives.

Recently, Rand Conger and his associates (1992; Conger, Patterson, & Ge, 1995; Conger et al., 2002; see also Gershoff et al., 2007; NICHD Early Child Care Research Network, 2005a) offered support for this "economic distress" hypothesis by finding clear links between family economic hardships, nonnurturant/uninvolved parenting, and poor child-rearing outcomes. The chain of events, shown in Figure 11.4, goes like this: Parents who are experiencing economic pressure or feeling that they cannot cope with their financial problems tend to become depressed, which increases marital conflict. Marital conflict in turn disrupts each parent's ability to be a supportive, involved parent—largely, perhaps, by undermining feelings of spousal support and coparenting that would help parents to feel efficacious at handling child-rearing problems (see Gondoli & Silverberg, 1997). And parents may have reason for such concern, because their children and adolescents often react negatively to the marital strife and the insensitive parenting they receive, experiencing a loss of *emotional*

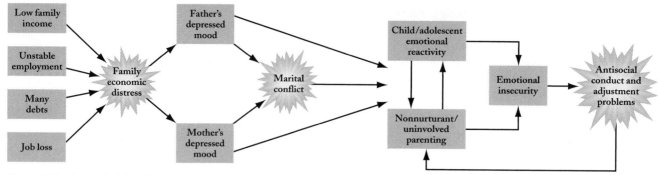

Figure 11.4 A model of the relationships among family economic distress, patterns of parenting, and child/adolescent adjustment. (Adapted from Conger et al., 1992; Davies & Cummings, 1998.)

family distress model
Conger's model of how economic distress affects family dynamics and developmental outcomes.

security, which contributes to such child and adolescent problems as low self-esteem, poor school performance, poor peer relations, and such problem behaviors as depression, hostility, and antisocial conduct (see Cummings et al., 2006; Davies & Cummings, 1998). These child adjustment problems that nonnurtant/coercive parenting help to create may heighten marital conflict and further exasperate parents, causing them to back away and become even less nurturant and less involved in the lives of their children (Jenkins et al., 2005; Rueter & Conger, 1998).

Families living below the poverty line are especially inclined to experience all the maladaptive family dynamics outlined in Conger's **family distress model,** and the deeper the poverty and the longer it lasts, the less favorable the prognosis for developing children and adolescents (Duncan & Brooks-Gunn, 1997, 2000; NICHD, 2005a; Votruba-Drzal, 2006). Unfortunately, federal and state welfare reform programs that require poverty-stricken welfare mothers to work are unlikely to solve the problems faced by the most economically distressed families. A single welfare mother with two children who earns a minimum wage is unlikely to earn enough by working to rise above the federal poverty threshold (Seccombe, 2000); and by current estimates, low-income families making between 100–200 percent of the federal poverty threshold still have insufficient income to overcome the material hardships (for example, insufficient nutrition and health care, residential instability) that would alleviate parental distress and promote the more positive parenting that fosters adaptive developmental outcomes (Gershoff et al., 2007). Of course, we should keep in mind that many low-income adults are able to cope with their problems and parent quite effectively, particularly if their economic and/or marital distresses are not prolonged; they feel optimistic and highly efficacious about parenting; and they receive emotional and parenting support from kin, friends, and other adults living outside the home (Ackerman et al., 1999b; Brody, Dorsey, et al., 2002; Brody, Murry, et al., 2002; Livner, Brooks-Gunn, & Kohen, 2002). Nevertheless, it appears that Maccoby and McLoyd were quite correct in assuming that economic hardships can be a very important contributor to the relatively aloof and coercive style of parenting often observed in low-income, economically distressed families.

Another explanation for the link between social class and parenting styles focuses on the skills needed by workers in white-collar and blue-collar jobs (Arnett, 1995; Kohn, 1979). A large percentage of lower-SES and working-class breadwinners are blue-collar workers who must please a supervisor and defer to his or her authority. So many lower-income parents may emphasize obedience and respect for authority because these are precisely the attributes they view as critical for success in the blue-collar economy. By contrast, middle- and upper-class parents may reason and negotiate more with their children while emphasizing individual initiative, curiosity, and creativity because these are the skills, attributes, and abilities that matter in their own occupations as business executives, white-collar workers, or professionals (Greenberger, O'Neil, & Nagel, 1994).

Many contextual factors other than parenting conspire to differentiate economically disadvantaged children from their more advantaged middle- and working-class peers. One such contextual influence is *family instability*. Family instability refers to circumstances that challenge the daily continuity and cohesiveness of a child's family life—such factors as (1) many changes in residence, (2) a primary caregiver's having had many intimate partners, (3) living in many family arrangements (for example, with a parent, with grandparents, in foster care, and so on), and (4) experiencing many negative life events (for example, serious illness, death of a close relative, job loss by a parent). Brian Ackerman and his associates (1999a, 2002) used these indexes to assess the stability/instability of large numbers of economically disadvantaged families. They were seeking to determine whether family instability was associated with any emotional problems and conduct disorders displayed by the families' 5- to 9-year-old children, even after controlling for the type of parenting these children had received. The results clearly implicated family instability as a potential contributor to developmental difficulties. Specifically, boys from the more unstable families displayed more *externalizing* problems (for example, aggression and disobedient/antisocial conduct), whereas girls from chronically unstable homes were more at risk for *internalizing* disorders (for example, anxiety, depression, social withdrawal). A similar study of adolescent girls yielded similar results: Even after controlling for the quality of relationships they had with their mothers, girls who experienced many residential moves and separations from their mothers experienced significantly more behavioral problems than age-mates whose families' lives were equally disadvantaged but far more stable (Adam & Chase-Lansdale, 2002). So even when economically disadvantaged children have good relationships with their custodial parents and receive adequate parenting, many remain at risk of displaying problem behaviors if their family lives are otherwise unstable.

Homelessness One kind of family instability that may seem horrifying to those of us who grew up in stable families is the plight of those who do not have a place of their own to call "home." In any given year, nearly 800,000 American children are homeless at least part of the time (National Law Center on Homelessness and Poverty, 2004), and as many as 300,000 of these are chronically homeless (Associated Press, 2006). We have all seen tele-

Photo 11.5
Homeless children are at risk of becoming anxious, depressed, and socially withdrawn.

vised examples of homeless nuclear families living in cars or camped out in parks or highway rest stops. However, the typical homeless family is a single mother in her 20s and her one or two children who are residing in a public shelter. How does homelessness affect developing children and adolescents?

John Buckner and his associates (1999) recently compared the behavioral profiles of homeless children aged 6 and older to those of other economically disadvantaged age-mates who had never been homeless. After controlling for other variables that might influence the type of parenting children had received (for example, maternal stress), Brucker and associates found that homeless children living in shelters scored notably higher on such *internalizing* behaviors as

The Family   **383**

anxiety/depression, socially withdrawn behavior, and somatic complaints than did other impoverished children who had never been homeless. It is likely that homelessness contributes to these internalizing disorders because children living in shelters may be painfully aware of the negative social stigma associated with homelessness, are shamed by being homeless, and are ostracized by peers, thus coming to feel depressed, self- critical, and low in self-worth. And not surprisingly perhaps, homeless adolescents, many of whom have been driven from their homes by rejecting or abusive parents, often affiliate with gangs and become involved in illegal activities such as dealing drugs, stealing, or prostitution (Unger et al., 1998). If home is truly where the heart is, the world may seem like a heartless place to homeless children and adolescents.

In sum, family instabilities (including homelessness) may clearly contribute to the less than optimal patterns of development that economically disadvantaged children often display. Unfortunately, many U.S. public assistance programs have recently been cut back in the name of welfare reform—an action that raises the threat of increased economic distress, family instabilities, and homelessness among poor families, particularly those headed by single mothers. As Buckner and associates (1999) point out, adequate economic assistance to needy families (for example, food stamps, housing subsidies, and child care that would allow parents to hold jobs) is absolutely essential to enable more poor children to have stable homes and to improve the odds of avoiding the many harmful consequences of growing up under extreme conditions of poverty.

Our focus on economic disadvantage and maladaptive outcomes might seem to imply that children from affluent families should experience many developmental successes. Yet Suniya Luther's program of research in Box 11.1 clearly challenges this point of view.

Ethnic Variations in Child Rearing   Parents of different ethnicities may also hold distinct child-rearing beliefs and values that are products of their cultural backgrounds or the ecological niches they occupy in society (MacPhee, Fritz, & Miller-Heyl, 1996; McLoyd & Smith, 2002). For example, Native American and Hispanic parents, whose cultural backgrounds are more collectivistic and stress communal rather than individual goals, are more inclined than European-American parents to (1) maintain close ties to a variety of kin and (2) insist that their children display calm, proper, and polite behaviors and a strong respect for authority figures, particularly fathers, rather than independence and competitiveness (Halgunseth, Ipsa, & Rudy, 2006; Harwood et al., 1996; MacPhee, Fritz, & Miller-Heyl, 1996). Mexican-American parents who speak Spanish and are experiencing considerable **acculturation stress** are more controlling than European-American parents are. But this highly controlling form of parenting, when combined with warmth and emotional support, can be adaptive because it gives their children few options about how to behave with a new cultural setting that may seem unusual and highly confusing to them (Hill, Bush, & Roosa, 2003).[1]

Asian and Asian-American parents also tend to stress self-discipline and interpersonal harmony and, if anything, are even more directive and rigidly controlling than parents of other ethnicities (Greenberger & Chen, 1996; Uba, 1994; Wu et al., 2002). Yet this seemingly authoritarian parenting style may mean something quite different for children of East Asian ancestry than for European Americans. Ruth Chao (1994, 2001) notes, for example, that Chinese and Chinese-American children perform very well in school despite the fact that their parents may appear to be highly authoritarian rather than authoritative. In Chinese culture, parents believe that strictness is the best way to express love for children and to train them properly. Children accept longstanding cultural values specifying that they obey elders and honor their families, and they may come to view their parents' strictness and control as signs of parental concern, caring, and involvement. So within the Chinese value system, the strict, controlling parenting that children receive may, when

acculturation stress
anxiety or uneasiness that new residents may feel upon attempting to assimilate a new culture and its traditions.

---

[1]For an expanded discussion of the cultural roots of parenting practices in Latino families, consult Halqunseth, Ipsa, and Rudy (2006).

Developmental Surprises from Affluent Families

Although developmentalists have been studying the effects of social class on parenting and child development since the 1970s, they have largely ignored one social class: the affluent (Luthar & Latendresse, 2005a). Suniya Luthar and associates saw this neglect and began a research program to study affluent families in the 1990s (for example, Luthar & Becker, 2002; Luthar & D'Avanzo, 1999; Luthar & Latendresse, 2005a, 2005b). Since then they have collected data on three large samples of affluent children in suburban areas of the United States and compared them with control groups of children from low-SES urban homes (see the accompanying table for comparisons among these samples). They also compared the affluent children to national norms on variables for which data were available. What they found ran counter to the supposition that affluent parents provide what is best for their children and was actually quite disturbing.

Even though the affluent parents were more likely to use an authoritative parenting style, their children were not faring well. These "rich" kids were more depressed and anxious and were more likely to smoke, drink, and use drugs than was true of children and adolescents in the national normative sample. And these problem behaviors began to surface early—as early as the seventh grade! All of the material advantages available to them did not seem to matter because affluent children were not significantly different from the urban disadvantaged children in the control groups on most developmental outcomes.

Luthar and associates point to several parenting variables that appear to contribute to the poor outcomes that some affluent children display. They include an intense pressure that parents placed on them to succeed academically coupled with an emotional and physical distancing from their children. That is, affluent parents were not home for their kids much of the time, and when they are at home, they are often preoccupied with their careers and high-powered jobs rather than spending time with their children. Surprisingly, perhaps, there were few differences between the very affluent and the low-SES families in many aspects of family life, including children's not feeling close to either of their parents and families not having many meals together as a family.

What's more, even though affluent kids have greater financial access to therapy for their mental health problems or to treatment centers for substance abuse, they are not as likely to receive such help as lower-SES children are. Why? Because affluent parents are more inclined to deny or to be embarrassed by their children's problems, wanting to keep them within the family rather than seeking available help.

Clearly this program of research has revealed an important, but overlooked, population of potentially "needy" children. Financial advantage provides no guarantee of children's developmental successes if parents are so preoccupied with their own career-related or other personal concerns that they fail to provide the warmth, attention, and guidance their children need.

Characteristics of affluent families from research program

Sample	Number of Participants	Minority Ethnicity in Sample	Participants Eligible for Free or Reduced Lunch in School	Median Annual Family Income in the Area (from Census Data)	Adults with Graduate or Professional Degrees in the Area (from Census Data)
Affluent Group 1	264	18	1	$80,000–$102,000	24–37
Low SES Group 1	224	87	86	$35,000	5
Affluent Group 2	302	8	3	$120,000	33
Affluent Group 3	314	7	3	$125,000	33
Low SES Group 2	300	80	79	$27,000	6

Source: Adapted from Luthar & Latendresse, 2005a.

coupled with parental concern, actually come closer to an authoritative than an authoritarian style (Nelson et al., 2006). Nevertheless, a pattern of parenting that is too controlling to work well for European Americans appears highly effective indeed in China (and among Asian immigrant families in the United States).

Although it is difficult to summarize the diversity of child-rearing practices that characterize African-American families, research suggests that urban African-American mothers (particularly if they are single and less educated) are inclined to demand strict obedience from their children and to use coercive forms of discipline to ensure that they get it (Kelley, Power, & Wimbush, 1992; Ogbu, 1994). Were we to quickly assume (as researchers did for years) that one particular pattern of parenting (authoritative) is superior to all others, then we might be tempted to conclude that the **no-nonsense parenting** often seen in African-American families is maladaptive. Yet this somewhat coercive and controlling pattern of parenting may actually be *highly adaptive* for many young mothers who lack caregiving support if it protects children who reside in dangerous neighborhoods

no-nonsense parenting
a mixture of authoritative and authoritarian parenting styles that is associated with favorable outcomes in African-American families.

from becoming victims of crime (Ogbu, 1994) or from associating with antisocial peers (Mason et al., 1996). In fact, use of spanking and other power-assertive tactics does not foster heightened aggression and antisocial conduct in African-American youth in the same way it does for European Americans, possibly because it may be viewed by African-American children as a sign of caring and concern rather than a symptom of parental hostility (Deater-Deckard & Dodge, 1997; Lansford et al., 2004). Furthermore, this "no-nonsense" parenting, which falls somewhere in between the authoritarian and authoritative styles, is adaptive in other ways, for African-American children who are treated in this way tend to be cognitively and socially competent youngsters who display little anxiety, depression, or other internalizing disorders (Brody & Flor, 1998) and who are less inclined as adolescents to become (or to remain) involved in delinquent activities (Walker-Barnes & Mason, 2001).[2]

Considering the findings we have reviewed, one must be careful *not* to assume that a "middle-class" pattern of authoritative parenting that seems to promote favorable outcomes in many contexts is necessarily the most adaptive pattern for all ecological niches. There simply is no single pattern of child rearing that is optimal for all cultures and subcultures. Louis Laosa (1981, p. 159) made this same point nearly 30 years ago, noting that "indigenous patterns of child care throughout the world represent largely successful adaptations to conditions of life that have long differed from one people to another. [Adults] are 'good [parents]' by the only relevant standards, those of their own culture."

The Quest for Autonomy: Renegotiating the Parent/Child Relationship during Adolescence

One of the most important developmental tasks that adolescents face is to achieve a mature and healthy sense of **autonomy**—the capacity to make one's own decisions and to manage life tasks without being overly dependent on other people. If adolescents are "make it" as adults, they can't be rushing home for loving hugs after every little setback. Nor can they continue to rely on parents to get them to work on time or to remind them of their duties and obligations.

So what happens within the family system as children mature and begin to act more autonomously? Sparks fly! In cultures as diverse as China and the United States, conflicts between parents and children about self-governance issues become much more common early in adolescence and gradually decline in frequency (though not necessarily in intensity) from middle through late adolescence (Laursen, Coy, & Collins, 1998; McGue et al., 2005; Shanahan, McHale, Osgood, & Crouter, 2007; Yau & Smetana, 1996). These squabbles, which occur about equally often in families that have immigrated from collectivist cultures as in European-American homes (Fuligni, 1998), are usually neither prolonged nor severe, often centering around such issues as the adolescent's physical appearance, her choice of friends, or her neglect of schoolwork and household chores. And much of the friction stems from the different perspectives that parents and adolescents adopt. Parents view conflicts through a moral or *social-conventional* lens, feeling that they have a responsibility to monitor and regulate their child's conduct, whereas the adolescent, locked in his quest for autonomy, views his nagging parents as infringing on *personal* rights and choices (Collins & Steinberg, 2006; Smetana & Daddis, 2002). As teenagers continue to assert themselves and parents slowly loosen the reins, the parent/child relationship normally evolves from an enterprise in which the parent was dominant to one in which parents and adolescents are on

autonomy
the capacity to make decisions independently, to serve as one's own source of emotional strength, and to otherwise manage one's life tasks without depending on others for assistance; an important developmental task of adolescence.

[2]Let's note that the coercion that characterizes no-nonsense parenting is high by European-American standards, but not extreme by any means. By contrast, extremely coercive parenting and chronically negative patterns of family interactions foster such negative outcomes as depression, poor self-esteem, and antisocial/delinquent conduct about as often for African-American children and adolescents as they do in European-American families (see, for example, Gutman & Eccles, 2007).

a more equal footing (Collins & Steinberg, 2006). Yet how much autonomy parents grant differs across cultures and ethnic groups. For example, Chinese-American and Mexican-American adolescents, particularly those from immigrant families, tend to emphasize family obligations to a greater extent than European Americans do (Hardway & Fuligni, 2006) and expect to be granted limited autonomy. Indeed, Asian parents in the United States and Candada tend to exert their authority far longer than do parents from European backgrounds (Greenberger & Chen, 1996; Yau & Smetana, 1996)—a practice that often bothers and may depress some Asian adolescents (Leung, McBride-Chang, & Lai, 2004), particularly those more acculturated teens whose parents' values seem too closely tied to their countries of origin to suit their tastes (Costigan & Dokis, 2006).

Photo 11.6
As adolescents begin their quest for autonomy, conflicts with parents become more commonplace.

Researchers once believed that the most adaptive route to establishing autonomy was for adolescents to separate from parents by cutting the emotional cords. Indeed, teenagers who perceive their relationships with parents to be very conflictual and nonsupportive do appear to be better adjusted when they distance themselves a bit from their families and can gain the support of a teacher, a "Big Brother/Sister," or another adult mentor from outside the home (Fuhrman & Holmbeck, 1995; Rhodes, Grossman, & Resch, 2000). Yet adolescents who are warmly received at home would be ill-advised to cut the emotional cords. Securely attached adolescents feel freer to disagree with their parents, take independent stands, and become autonomous, without worrying about losing parental warmth and affection (Allen et al., 2003), and those who are best adjusted overall have maintained a close attachment to the parents, even as they gained autonomy and prepared to leave the nest (Allen et al., 2007; Beyers & Goossens, 1999; Collins & Steinberg, 2006). So autonomy *and* attachment, or independence *and* interdependence, are most desirable.

Encouraging Autonomy Adolescents are most likely to become appropriately autonomous, achievement oriented, and otherwise well adjusted if their parents recognize and acknowledge their greater need for autonomy and gradually loosen the reins. A good deal of research indicates that parents should consistently enforce a well-reasoned set of rules while involving their teenagers in discussions and decisions about self-governance issues, monitoring their comings and goings, going easy on the guilt trips (or other forms of psychological control), and continuing to be warm and supportive, even in the face of inevitable conflicts that arise (Barber & Harmon, 2002; Collins & Steinberg, 2006).

Interestingly, young adolescents who are granted too much independence to make their own decisions are often more poorly adjusted than those whose parents exert more control (see, for example, Smetana, Campione-Barr, & Daddis, 2004). Recently, Bart Soenens and his associates (2007) have argued (and found) that parental autonomy support is most effective not when it promotes *independent* decision making but rather when it offers choices to adolescents and helps them to explore various alternatives and *make their own decisions*, guided by their interests, goals, and values. This approach is called **promotion of volitional functioning (PVF)**—a strategy whereby parents guide or scaffold an adolescent's decision making (rather than imposing a solution or ceding control), thereby allowing him or her to experience a sense of *self-*determination when resolving personal issues.

promotion of volitional functioning (PVF)
method of autonomy support in which parents guide adolescents' decision making by suggesting alternatives, tying them to adolescents' values and goals, and permitting them to resolve issues for themselves.

Does this general pattern of parenting practices sound familiar? It should, for this winning combination of parental acceptance and a pattern of flexible behavioral guidance and control that is neither too lax nor overly restrictive is an *authoritative* approach that is consistently associated with healthy developmental outcomes in many contexts. Indeed, adolescents treated this way often interpret parents' questions about their activities and whereabouts as a sign of caring and often willingly disclose such information, thereby preventing parents from having to badger them or snoop in order to know what they are doing (Kerr & Stattin, 2000; Soenens et al., 2006). It is mainly when parents resist a teenager's push for autonomy and become overly controlling or overly permissive and uninvolved that adolescents are likely to experience personal distress and rebel, volunteering little information about their activities and eventually getting into trouble (Barber & Harmon, 2002; Kerr & Stattin, 2000; Soenens et al., 2006). Of course, we must remind ourselves that socialization within the family is a matter of reciprocal influence and that it may be much easier for a parent to respond authoritatively to a responsible, level-headed adolescent than to one who is rude, hostile, and unruly.

In sum, conflicts and power struggles are an almost inevitable consequence of an adolescent's quest for autonomy. Yet most teenagers and their parents are able to resolve these differences while maintaining positive feelings for one another as they renegotiate their relationship so that it becomes more equal (Collins & Steinberg, 2006; Furman & Buhrmester, 1992). As a result, young autonomy seekers become more self-reliant while also developing a more "friend-like" attachment to their parents.

⤳ THE INFLUENCE OF SIBLINGS AND SIBLING RELATIONSHIPS

Although families are getting smaller, the majority of American children still grow up with at least one sibling, and there is certainly no shortage of speculation about the roles that brothers and sisters play in a child's life. Many parents, distressed by the fighting and bickering that their children display, often fear that such rivalrous conduct will undermine the growth of children's prosocial concern and their ability to get along with others. At the same time, the popular wisdom is that "only" children are likely to be lonely, overindulged "brats" who would profit both socially and emotionally from having siblings to teach them that they are not nearly as "special" as they think they are (Falbo, 1992).

Although rivalries among siblings are certainly commonplace, we will see that siblings can play some very positive roles in a child's life, often serving as caregivers, teachers, playmates, and confidants. And yet we will also see that only children may not be nearly as disadvantaged by their lack of sibling relationships as people have commonly assumed.

Changes in the Family Systems When a New Baby Arrives

Judy Dunn and Carol Kendrick (1982; see also Dunn, 1993) have studied how firstborn children adapt to a new baby, and the account they provide is not an entirely cheerful one. After the baby arrives, mothers typically devote less warm and playful attention to the older child, who may respond to this perceived "neglect" by becoming difficult, disruptive, and less securely attached, particularly if he or she is 2 years of age or older and can more readily appreciate that an "exclusive" relationship with caregivers has been undermined by the baby's birth (Teti et al., 1996). Clearly, older children often resent losing the mother's attention, may harbor animosities toward the baby for stealing it, and their own difficult behavior may make matters worse by alienating their parents.

Thus, **sibling rivalry**—a spirit of competition, jealousy, or resentment between siblings— often begins as soon as a younger brother or sister arrives. How can it be minimized? The adjustment process is easier if the firstborn had secure relationships with both parents before the baby arrived and continues to enjoy close ties afterward (Dunn & Kendrick, 1982; Volling

sibling rivalry
the spirit of competition, jealousy, and resentment that may arise between two or more siblings.

& Belsky, 1992). Parents are advised to continue to provide love and attention to their older children and to maintain their normal routines as much as possible. It also helps to encourage older children to become aware of the baby's needs and assist in the care of their new brother or sister (Dunn & Kendrick, 1982).

Sibling Relationships over the Course of Childhood

Fortunately, most older siblings adjust fairly quickly to having a new brother or sister, becoming much less anxious and less inclined to display the problem behaviors that they showed early on. But even in the best of sibling relationships, conflict is normal. Indeed, Judy Dunn (1993) reports that the number of minor skirmishes between very young siblings can range as high as 56 per hour! These sibling squabbles, which tend to center heavily on personal possessions and scripts to be followed during play episodes (Howe et al., 2002; McGuire et al., 2000), are rarely resolved during the heat of battle, when each combatant may feel that she is "right" and has been wronged by her sibling (Wilson et al., 2004). Once negative feelings subside, 4- to 12-year-old siblings are often successful at resolving their differences in constructive ways if the older sib has positive feelings about the younger one and siblings seek means by which each can achieve at least some of their objectives rather than continuing to attack, accuse, and belittle one another while focusing exclusively on their own interests (Ram & Ross, 2001; Ross et al., 2006).

Ursula Markus/Photo Researchers, Inc.

Photo 11.7
Coercive and rivalrous conduct between siblings is a normal aspect of family life.

There are some reliable differences in the behavior of older and younger siblings, with older siblings often becoming the more domineering aggressive parties and younger siblings the more compliant ones (Abramovitch et al., 1986; Erel, Margolin, & John, 1998; Ross et al., 2006). Yet older sibs also initiate more helpful, playful, and other prosocial behaviors, a finding that may reflect the pressure parents place on them to demonstrate their maturity by caring for a younger brother or sister (Brody, 1998; Rogoff, 2003).

In general, siblings are much more likely to get along if their parents get along (Dunn, 1993; Kim et al., 2006; Reese-Weber, 2000). Marital conflict and dissatisfaction is a very good predictor of jealousy and antagonistic sibling interactions, especially if the older sibling has a shaky, insecure relationship with either or both parents who themselves rely heavily on power-assertive discipline (Erel, Margolin, & John, 1998; Volling, McElwain, & Miller, 2002). Marital conflict may put children on edge emotionally and contribute to emotional insecurity (Cummings et al., 2006), whereas parental use of power assertion may communicate to a more powerful older sibling that forceful strategies are the way one deals with associates (particularly smaller, less powerful ones) who displease them.

Sibling relationships are also friendlier if parents make an effort to monitor their children's activities and intervene during conflicts. As noted earlier in Chapter 6, interventions in which parents serve as "judges" to resolve squabbles for their children are much less effective than those in which parents *mediate* disputes by dampening the acrimony and contentiousness, allowing each child to state his or her feelings and goals, fostering mutual understanding and empathy for these opposing viewpoints, and encouraging children to devise their own mutually agreeable solutions to their conflicts (Smith & Ross, 2007). Unfortunately, normal conflicts among young, preschool children can escalate into serious incidents that become habitual if parents often let them pass without intervening (Kramer, Perozynski, & Chung, 1999). In fact, intense, destructive sibling battles that occur against a backdrop of uninvolved parenting are a very strong predictor of aggressive, antisocial behavior outside the home (Garcia et al., 2000; Snyder, Bank, & Burraston, 2005).

Finally, sibling relationships tend to be less conflictual and siblings are better adjusted when mothers and fathers respond warmly and sensitively to *all* their children and do not consistently favor one child over the other (Boyle et al., 2004; Brody, 1998; McHale et al., 2000). Younger siblings are particularly sensitive to unequal treatment (Boyle et al., 2004), often reacting negatively and displaying adjustment problems if they perceive that the older sib is favored by parents. It is not that older siblings are unaffected by differential treatment; but because they are older, they are usually better able to understand that siblings may have different needs and that unequal treatment may be justified, even if that means that parents may sometimes favor a younger sib in certain respects (Kowal & Kramer, 1997; Kowal, Krull, & Kramer, 2004).

But it is easy to overemphasize sibling rivalries. Grade-school children tend to value their relationships with siblings, even though they have many conflicts with them (Furman & Buhrmester, 1985), and adolescents, who now have fewer conflicts with sibs than was true in earlier childhood (Kim et al., 2006), often view brothers and sisters as intimate associates—people to whom they can turn for companionship and emotional support, despite the fact that relations with them have often been stormy (Buhrmester & Furman, 1990; Furman & Buhrmester, 1992). So why do siblings value a relationship that has often been conflictual? The observational record provides one answer: Brothers and sisters often do nice things for one another and resolve most minor disputes amicably, and these prosocial acts are typically much more common than hateful, rivalrous, or destructive conduct (see, for example, Abramovitch et al., 1986; Ram & Ross, 2001).

Positive Contributions of Sibling Relationships

What positive roles might siblings play in one another's lives? One important contribution that older siblings make is to provide *caretaking* services for younger brothers and sisters. One survey of child-rearing practices in 186 societies found that older children were the *principal* caregivers for infants and toddlers in 57 percent of the groups studied (Weisner & Gallimore, 1977). Even in industrialized societies such as the United States, older siblings (particularly girls) are often asked to look after their younger brothers and sisters (Brody, 1998). Of course, their role as caregivers provides older children opportunities to influence their younger siblings in many ways by serving as their teachers, playmates, and advocates, and as important sources of emotional support.

Siblings as Providers of Emotional Support   Do infants become attached to older siblings, viewing them as providers of security? To find out, Robert Stewart (1983) exposed 10- to 20-month-old infants to a variation of Ainsworth's "Strange Situation." Each infant was left with a 4-year-old sibling in a strange room that a strange adult soon entered. The infants typically showed signs of distress as their mothers departed, and they were wary in the company of the stranger. Stewart noted that these distressed infants would often approach their older brother or sister, particularly when the stranger first appeared. And most 4-year-olds will offer some sort of comforting or caregiving to their baby brothers and sisters, particularly if they are securely attached themselves to their mothers (Teti & Ablard, 1989) and have developed the role-taking skills to understand why their younger brother or sister is distressed (Garner, Jones, & Palmer, 1994; Howe & Rinaldi, 2004; Stewart & Marvin, 1984).

As they mature, siblings may frequently protect and confide in each other, often more than they confide in parents (Howe et al., 2000), and may draw strength from the support a sibling provides. For example, children with severe medical problems and those with an alcoholic or mentally ill parent show fewer problem behaviors and better developmental outcomes when their relations with siblings are solid and supportive (Vandell, 2000). An intimate tie to a sibling also helps to minimize the anxiety and adjustment problems that grade-school children often display if they are ignored or rejected by their classmates (Brody & Murry, 2001; East & Rook, 1992; Stormshak et al., 1996) and often promotes the development of social skills that enable them to improve their standing with peers (Downey & Condron, 2004; Kim et al., 2007).

Siblings as Models and Teachers   In addition to the caretaking and emotional support they may provide, older siblings often teach new skills to younger brothers and sisters, either by modeling these competencies or by providing direct instruction (Brody et al., 2003). Even toddlers are quite attentive to older sibs, often choosing to imitate their behaviors as they actively participate with siblings at play, infant care, and other household routines (Maynard, 2002). Younger children often admire their older siblings, who continue to serve as important models and tutors throughout childhood (Buhrmester & Furman, 1990). Given a problem to master, children are likely to learn more when they have an older sibling available to guide them than when they have access to an equally competent older peer (Azmitia & Hesser, 1993). Why? Because (1) older children feel a greater responsibility to teach if the younger pupil is a *sibling*; (2) they provide more detailed instructions and encouragement than older peers do; and (3) younger children are more inclined to seek the older sibling's guidance. This kind of informal instruction clearly pays off: When older siblings play school with younger brothers and sisters, teaching them such lessons as the ABCs, younger siblings have an easier time learning to read (Norman-Jackson, 1982). What's more, older siblings who often tutor younger ones may profit as well, for they score higher on tests of academic aptitude than peers who have not had these tutoring experiences (Paulhus & Shaffer, 1981; Smith, 1990).

Siblings as Contributors to Social-Cognitive Understandings   Finally, the sheer frequency and intensity of sibling interactions imply that these contacts may foster the growth of many social-cognitive competencies. In Chapter 6, for example, we learned that playful interactions among siblings contribute to children's understanding of false beliefs and to the emergence of a belief-desire theory of mind. Even the squabbles can be important; siblings are not at all shy about communicating their wants, needs, and emotional reactions to conflict, thus providing each other with information that fosters the growth of perspective-taking

Photo 11.8
Older siblings often serve as teachers for their younger brothers and sisters.

Dennis MacDonald/PhotoEdit, Inc.

skills, emotional understanding, a capacity for negotiation and compromise, and more mature forms of moral reasoning (Bedford, Volling, & Avioli, 2000; Howe, Petrakos, & Rinaldi, 1998). Clearly, there are many ways in which children may benefit from their experiences with siblings.

Of course, siblings can influence one another in less desirable ways. For example, younger brothers and sisters tend to become more aggressive and to display more problem behaviors over time if their older brothers are highly aggressive and antisocial (Snyder, Bank, & Burraston, 2005; Williams, Conger, & Blozis, 2007). And even after controlling for such family variables as parental mental health and the quality of parent/child relationships, older children and adolescents whose sibling relationships become more conflictual over time often display an increase in depressive symptoms (Kim et al., 2007). So, although it can be advantageous to grow up with brothers and sisters, there are some potential disadvantages as well.

Characteristics of Only Children

Are "only" children who grow up without siblings the spoiled, selfish, overindulged brats that people often presume them to be? Hardly! Two major reviews of hundreds of pertinent studies found that only children are (1) relatively high, on average, in self-esteem and achievement motivation, (2) more obedient and slightly more intellectually competent than children with siblings, and (3) likely to establish very good relations with peers (Falbo, 1992; Falbo & Polit, 1986).

Might these findings simply reflect the fact that parents who prefer to have only one child differ systematically from those who have more children? Probably not. In 1979, the People's Republic of China implemented a one-child family policy in an attempt to control its burgeoning population. So regardless of the number of children parents may have wanted, most Chinese couples, in urban areas at least, have been limited to one child. Contrary to the fears of many critics, there is no evidence that China's one-child policy has produced a generation of spoiled, self-centered brats who behave like "little emperors." Only children in China closely resemble only children in Western countries, scoring slightly higher than children with siblings on measures of intelligence and academic achievement and showing few meaningful differences in personality or personal values (Fuligni & Zhang, 2004; Jaio, Ji, & Jing, 1996; Wang et al., 2000). In fact, only children in China actually report *less* anxiety and depression than children with siblings do, a finding that may reflect China's social condemnation of multichild families and only children's tendency to taunt children with siblings with such remarks as "You shouldn't be here" or "Your parents should have only one child" (Yang et al., 1995).

So evidence from very different cultural settings suggests that only children are hardly disadvantaged by having no brothers and sisters. Apparently, many singletons are able to gain through their friendships and peer alliances whatever they may miss by not having siblings at home.

∽ DIVERSITY IN FAMILY LIFE

As we noted earlier in the chapter, modern families are so diverse today that the *majority* of our children are growing up in dual-career, single-parent, or blended families that may be very different than the two-parent, single-breadwinner aggregation with two or more children that people often think of as the typical family unit. So let's examine some of these variations in family life.

Adoptive Families

If one member of the pair is infertile, couples who hope to become parents often seek to adopt a child. A clear majority of adoptive parents develop secure emotional ties to their genetically unrelated adoptees (Levy-Shiff, Goldschmidt, & Har-Even, 1991; Stams, Juffer, & van IJzendoorn, 2002), and caregiver sensitivity predicts attachment classifications for adoptees in the same way that it does for biologically related children, thus implying that an adult's desire to be a parent is much more important to a child's developmental outcomes than the adult's genetic ties to his or her children.

Nevertheless, because adoptive parents and their children share no genes, the rearing environments adoptive parents provide may not be as closely compatible with an adoptee's own genetic predispositions as they are for a biological child. These environmental incompatibilities—coupled with the fact that many adoptees have been neglected or abused prior to their adoptions, have experienced unstable placements in a series of foster homes, or have other special needs (Juffer, Bakermans-Kranenburg, & van IJzendoorn, 2005; Kirchner, 1998)—may help to explain why adoptees display more learning difficulties, more emotional problems, and higher rates of oppositional behavior and antisocial conduct than their nonadopted peers later in childhood and adolescence (Lewis et al., 2007; Miller et al., 2000; Sharma, McGue, & Benson, 1998).

Don't misunderstand. The vast majority of adopted children and adolescents are quite well adjusted (Jaffari-Bimmel et al., 2006; Stams, Juffer, & van IJzendoorn, 2002) and typically fare much better in adoptive homes than in foster care, where their foster parents may not be very invested in them or their long-range prospects (Brodzinsky, Smith, & Brodzinsky, 1998; Miller et al., 2000). Even *transracially adopted* children from lower socioeconomic backgrounds usually fare quite well intellectually and academically and often display healthy patterns of psychosocial adjustment when raised in supportive middle-class adoptive homes (Brodzinsky et al., 1987; DeBerry, Scarr, & Weinberg, 1996; Sharma, McGue, & Benson, 1998). So adoption is a quite satisfactory arrangement for most adoptive parents and their adoptees.

Adoption practices in the United States are changing from a confidential system, in which the identities of the birth mother and adoptive parents are withheld from each other, to a more open system that allows for varying amounts of direct or indirect contact between birth mothers and members of adoptive families. Because adoptees are often curious about their biological origins and may be upset about the prospect of never knowing their birth parents, more open arrangements may prove beneficial to them. Indeed, research conducted in the United States and a variety of other countries reveals that (1) adopted children are both more curious and more satisfied with information about their biological roots when they can share information or even have contact with their birth mothers (see Leon, 2002, for a review), and (2) the vast majority of birth parents welcome contact with their adopted-away children (Associated Press, 2007). What's more, information about and contact with biological relatives typically help adoptees see that their adoptive parents are their "true" mothers and fathers and to think of their birth parents as "birthgivers" (Leon, 2002). So there is little evidence that providing information about birth parents will confuse children about the meaning of adoption or undermine their self-esteem as some critics of open adoption policies had feared.

Donor Insemination (DI) Families

Rather than adopt, some infertile couples choose to have children through **donor insemination (DI)**—a process by which a fertile woman conceives with the aid of sperm from an unknown donor. Several concerns have been raised about the creation of families in this way. For example, Burns (1990) argued that stresses associated with the couple's

donor insemination
process by which a fertile woman conceives with the aid of sperm from an unknown donor.

infertility may lead to dysfunctional patterns of parenting. Moreover, children conceived in this way do not have genetic ties to their fathers, who may be more distant and less nurturant than genetically related fathers (Turner & Coyle, 2000). Are there reasons for concern then about the development of DI children?

Apparently not. In a 12-year longitudinal study conducted in England, Susan Golombok and her colleagues (2002) compared the developmental progress of children raised in DI families to that of adopted children and children raised by two biological parents. They found that the DI children at age 12 showed no more behavioral problems and were as well adjusted on measures of emotional development, scholastic progress, and peer relations as their adoptive or naturally conceived peers. Mothers of DI children were found to be warmer and more sensitive to their children's needs than mothers of adoptive or naturally conceived children. And although fathers of DI families were less involved in disciplining their children, they were no less involved in other aspects of parenting and were judged just as close to their children as adoptive or biological fathers were. Although this is but one study of a relatively small sample of DI families, it was carefully conducted and suggests that couples who truly want to be parents and who are comfortable with donor insemination need not to be concerned about adverse developmental outcomes in a child of theirs conceived in this way.

Gay and Lesbian Families

In the United States, several million gay men or lesbians are parents, most through previous heterosexual marriages, although some have adopted children or conceived through donor insemination (Flaks et al., 1995; Chan, Raboy, & Patterson, 1998). Historically, many courts have been so opposed to the prospect of lesbians and gay men raising children that they have denied the petitions of homosexual parents in child custody hearings solely on the basis of these parents' sexual orientations. Among the concerns people have are that gay and lesbian parents may be less mentally healthy or that they will molest their children, who in turn are at risk of being stigmatized by peers because of their parents' sexual orientations. But perhaps the greatest concern is the fear that children raised by gay or lesbian parents are likely to become gay or lesbian themselves.

Interestingly, there is virtually no basis for any of these speculations. As shown in Figure 11.5, more than 90 percent of adult children of lesbian mothers or gay fathers develop a heterosexual orientation—a figure that is not significantly different from the percentages of heterosexuals raised by heterosexual parents (see also Patterson, 2004). Furthermore, children of gay and lesbian parents are just as cognitively, emotionally, and morally mature, on average, and are otherwise as well adjusted as children of heterosexual parents (Chan, Rabboy, & Patterson, 1998; Flaks et al., 1995; Golombok et al., 2003; Lambert, 2005). And in response to recent criticisms that children of gay and lesbian parents may be less appropriately gender typed (Stacey & Biblarz, 2001), Susan Golombok and her colleagues (2003) found only that boys from single-parent homes headed by mothers (the vast majority of whom were *heterosexual*) had fewer traditionally masculine activity preferences than boys raised by two parents, whether homosexual or heterosexual. Finally, gay fathers and lesbian mothers are every bit as knowledgeable (or more so) about effective child-rearing practices as heterosexual parents are (Bigner & Jacobsen, 1989; Flaks et al., 1995), and partners of homosexual parents are usually attached to the children and assume some caregiving responsibilities. These

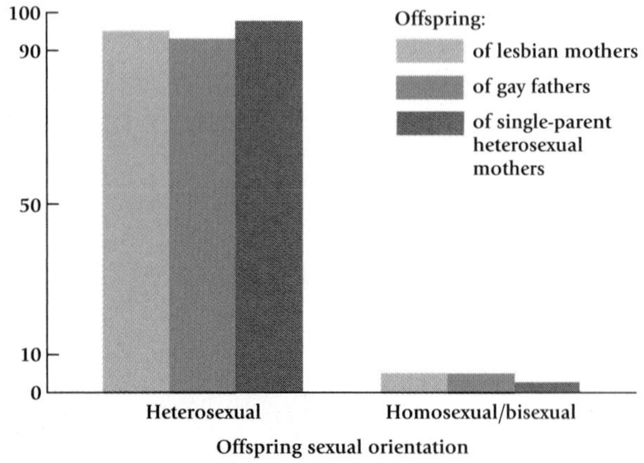

Figure 11.5

Sexual orientation of adult children raised by lesbian mothers, gay fathers, and single-parent heterosexual mothers. (Notice that children with homosexual parents are just as likely to display a heterosexual orientation as children raised by heterosexuals.) (Adapted from Bailey et al., 1995; Golombok & Tasker, 1996.)

are important findings because recent analyses conducted on a national sample of *adolescents* in the United States revealed that positive psychosocial and scholastic outcomes were (1) predicted by *satisfying* parent/adolescent relationships but (2) *unrelated* to family type (that is, whether parents were same-sex or opposite-sex) (Wainwright & Patterson, 2008; Wainright, Russell, & Patterson, 2004).

In sum, there is no credible scientific evidence that would justify denying a person's rights of parenthood on the basis of his or her sexual orientation (Wainright & Patterson, 2008). Children and adolescents raised in gay and lesbian families are virtually indistinguishable from those of heterosexual couples.

Family Conflict and Divorce

Earlier we noted that between 40 and 50 percent of today's marriages will end in divorce and that more than half of all children born in the 1990s and 2000s will spend some time (about five years, on average) in a single-parent home—usually one headed by the mother (Hetherington, Bridges, & Insabella, 1998). What effects might a divorce have on developing children? As we address this issue, let's first note that divorce is *not* a singular life event; instead, it represents a series of stressful experiences for the entire family that often begins with marital conflict before the actual separation and includes a multitude of life changes afterward. As Mavis Hetherington and Kathleen Camara (1984) see it, families must often cope with "the diminution of family resources, changes in residence, assumption of new roles and responsibilities, establishment of new patterns of [family] interaction, reorganization of routines . . . , and [possibly] the introduction of new relationships [that is, stepparent/child and stepsibling relationships] into the existing family" (p. 398).

Before the Divorce: Exposure to Marital Conflict   The period prior to divorce is often accompanied by a dramatic rise in family conflict that may include many heated verbal arguments and even physical violence between parents. How are children influenced by their exposure to marital conflict? A growing body of evidence indicates that they often become extremely distressed and that continuing conflict at home increases the likelihood that children will have hostile, aggressive interactions with siblings and peers (Cummings & Davies, 1994; Cummings et al., 2006). Furthermore, regular exposure to marital discord is a contributor to a number of other child and adolescent adjustment problems, including anxiety, depression, and externalizing conduct disorders (Davies & Cummings, 1998; Parke & Buriel, 2006). Marital discord can have both *direct effects* on children and adolescents by putting them on edge emotionally and undermining the maturity of their behavior (Cummings et al., 2006; Thompson, 2000) as well as *indirect effects* by undermining parental acceptance/sensitivity and the quality of the parent/child relationship (Davies et al., 2003; Erel & Burman, 1995; Parke & Buriel, 2006). Children with secure attachment representations cope somewhat better with parental conflict than those with insecure attachment representations (Davies & Forman, 2002), perhaps because they feel less responsible for precipitating the conflict and/or less concerned that their parents will stop loving them (El-Sheikh & Harger, 2001; Grych et al., 2000; Grych, Harold, & Miles, 2003). But conflict-ridden homes are not healthy contexts for child or adolescent development, and some family researchers believe that children in strife-ridden homes will often fare better in the long run if their parents separate or divorce (Booth & Amato, 2001; Hetherington, Bridges, & Insabella, 1998). Nevertheless, divorce can be a highly unsettling life transition that often has its own effects on the well-being of all family members.

Photo 11.9
Youngsters who live in conflict-ridden nuclear families often suffer physically and emotionally. In the long run, children of divorce are usually better adjusted than those whose unhappily married parents stay together "for the sake of the children."

Michael Newman/PhotoEdit, Inc.

After the Divorce: Crisis and Reorganization   Most families going through a divorce experience a *crisis period* of a year or more in which the lives of all family members are seriously disrupted (Amato, 2000; Hetherington & Kelly, 2002). Typically, both parents experience emotional as well as practical difficulties. The mother, who obtains custody of any children in about 82 percent of divorcing families, may feel angry, depressed, lonely, or otherwise distressed, although often relieved as well. The father is also likely to be distressed, particularly if he did not seek the divorce and feels shut off from his children. Having just become single adults, both parents often feel isolated from former married friends and other bases of social support on which they relied as marrieds. Divorced women with children usually face the added problem of getting by with less money—about 50–75 percent of the family income they had before, on average (Bianchi, Subaiya, & Kahn, 1997). And life may seem especially difficult if they must move to a lower-income neighborhood and try to work and raise young children single-handedly (Emery & Forehand, 1994).

As you might suspect, psychologically distressed adults do not make the best parents. Hetherington and her associates (1982; Hetherington & Kelly, 2002) find that custodial mothers, overwhelmed by responsibilities and by their own emotional reactions to divorce, often become edgy, impatient, and insensitive to their children's needs; and as a result, they frequently begin to rely on coercive methods of child rearing. Indeed, divorced mothers often appear (to their children, at least) to have been transformed into more hostile, less caring parents (Fauber et al., 1990). Meanwhile, noncustodial fathers are likely to change in a different way, becoming somewhat overpermissive and indulging during visits with their children (Amato & Sobolewski, 2004).

Perhaps you can imagine how these changes in parenting are likely to be received. Children of divorce, who are often anxious, angry, or depressed by the family breakup, may react by becoming whiney and argumentative, disobedient, and downright disrespectful. Parent/child relationships during this crisis phase have been described as a vicious circle in which the child's emotional distress and problem behaviors and the adults' ineffective parenting styles feed on each other and make everyone's life unpleasant (Hetherington & Kelly, 2002). However, children's initial reactions to divorce vary somewhat as a function of their ages, temperaments, and sex.

Children's Age   Younger, cognitively immature preschool and grade-school children often display the most visible signs of distress as a divorce unfolds. They may not understand why their parents have divorced and are even inclined to feel guilty if they think they are somehow responsible for the breakup of their families (Hetherington, 1989). Older children and adolescents are better able to understand the personality conflicts and lack of caring that may lead distressed parents to divorce, and may be able to resolve any loyalty conflicts that may arise; however, they often remain highly distressed over their parents' divorce and may react by withdrawing from family members and becoming more involved in such undesirable peer-sponsored activities as truancy, sexual misconduct, substance abuse, and other forms of delinquent behavior (Amato, 2000; Hetherington, Bridges, & Insabella, 1998). So even though they are better able to comprehend the reasons for their parents' divorce and to feel less responsible for having caused it, older children and adolescents seem to suffer no less than younger children do (Hetherington & Clingempeel, 1992).

Children's Temperament and Sex   The stresses associated with parental conflict and divorce hit particularly hard at temperamentally difficult children, who display more immediate and long-range adjustment problems to these events than easy-going children do (Henry et al., 1996; Hetherington & Clingempeel, 1992; Lengua et al., 1999). Often the highly volatile behavior of a temperamentally difficult child elicits more coercive forms of parenting from his impatient and highly distressed caregiver, which in turn represents an extremely "poor fit" with a difficult child's reactive demeanor and contributes substantially to his adjustment difficulties.

Although the finding is by no means universal, many investigators report that the impact of marital strife and divorce is more powerful and enduring for boys than for girls. Even before a divorce, boys are already displaying more overt behavioral problems than girls are (Block, Block, & Gjerde, 1986, 1988). And at least two early longitudinal studies found that girls had largely recovered from their social and emotional disturbances two years after a divorce, whereas boys, who improved dramatically over this same period, were nevertheless continuing to show signs of emotional stress and problems in their relationships with parents, siblings, teachers, and peers (Hetherington, Cox, & Cox, 1982; Wallerstein & Kelly, 1980).

A word of caution on sex differences, however. Most early research focused on mother-headed families and on *overt* problem behaviors that are easy to detect. Subsequent work suggests that boys may fare better when their fathers are the custodial parent (Amato & Keith, 1991; Clarke-Stewart & Hayward, 1996) and that girls in divorced families experience more *covert* distress than boys do, often becoming withdrawn or depressed rather than acting out their anger, fears, or frustrations (Chase-Lansdale, Cherlin, & Kiernan, 1995; Doherty & Needle, 1991). What's more, a disproportionate number of girls from divorced families show precocious sexual activity early in adolescence and a persistent lack of self-confidence in their relationships with boys and men (Cherlin, Kiernan, & Chase-Lansdale, 1995; Ellis et al., 2003; Hetherington, Bridges, & Insabella, 1998). So divorce can strike hard at children of either sex, although it is likely to affect boys and girls in somewhat different ways.

Divorce Effects or Genetic Effects? The finding that child temperament—a genetically influenced attribute—affects children's reactions to divorce suggests an interesting hypothesis: Perhaps many of the negative developmental outcomes associated with divorce are attributable to genes that children share with their divorcing parents and that predispose them to experience conflicts, emotional problems, antisocial behavior, and other adverse consequences (for example, academic difficulties) in response to any kind of major life stress. Indeed, children's reactions to parental conflict in the home appears to be influenced by their genotypes (Harden et al., 2007). Yet a clever and carefully conducted study of families of twin parents who were discordant for divorce (that is, one twin parent divorced and the other didn't) revealed that the poor outcomes displayed by children of divorce— educational difficulties, depression, suicidal thoughts, drug use, early initiation of sexual intercourse, and other emotional problems—were largely attributed *to the divorce itself* (an environmental influence) rather than to any genes that these children shared with their divorcing parents (D'Onofrio et al., 2006). Here, then, is another indication that a divorce and its aftermath can be a most unsettling life transition for *all* children who experience it, regardless of their genotype.

Long-Term Reactions to Divorce The vast majority of children and adolescents whose parents divorce eventually adjust to this family transition to display healthy patterns of psychological adjustment (Hetherington & Kelly, 2002). Nevertheless, even *well-adjusted* children of divorce may show some lingering after-effects. In one longitudinal study, children from divorced families were still very negative in the assessment of the impact of divorce on their lives when interviewed more than 20 years after the divorce (Wallerstein & Lewis, as cited by Fernandez, 1997). As adults, children of divorce report more depressive symptoms and lower levels of life satisfaction (Hetherington & Kelly, 2002; Segrin, Taylor, & Altman, 2005). A common source of dissatisfaction is a perceived loss of closeness with their parents, especially with fathers (Emery, 1999; Woodward, Fergusson, & Belsky, 2000). Another interesting long-term reaction is that adolescents from divorced

Box 11.2 Applying Developmental Research

Smoothing the Road to Recovery from a Divorce

Some individuals adjust rather well to a divorce, whereas others may suffer negative and long-lasting effects. Who is likely to fare well and what factors make the process of adjustment easier for members of divorcing families?

Adequate Financial Support

Families fare better after a divorce if the noncustodial parent pays child support and the family has adequate finances (Amato & Sobolewski, 2004; Marsiglio et al., 2000). The Family Support Act of 1988, passed to clamp down on so-called "deadbeat dads" and make them meet their obligations, is a step in the right direction. However, only about half of noncustodial fathers do pay full child support, thus causing many custodial mothers and their children to struggle to survive (Sorensen, 1997; U.S. Bureau of the Census, 2007).

Good Parenting by the Custodial Parent

The custodial parent plays a crucial role in the family's adjustment to a divorce. If she or he can continue to be warm and authoritative, children are much less likely to experience serious problems (Hetherington & Kelly, 2002). Clearly, it is difficult to be patient and supportive when one is stressed and depressed, but parents who understand the stakes may be better able to give their children the love and attention they need. What's more, interventions can help them. Forgatch and DeGarmo (1999), for example, found that divorced mothers who were randomly assigned to a parenting skills program designed to prevent them from becoming more coercive did come to rely less on coercive tactics, compared to divorced mothers in a control group. And the positive changes in their parenting were tied to improvements in their children's behavior at home and at school.

Social/Emotional Support from the Noncustodial Parent

If divorced parents continue to squabble and are hostile to each other, both are likely to be upset; the custodial parent's parenting is likely to suffer; and children will likely feel "caught in the middle," torn in their loyalties, and will probably have difficulties adjusting (Amato, 1993; Buchanan, Maccoby, & Dornbusch, 1991). Children may also suffer should they lose contact with a noncustodial father, something that happens to more than a quarter of youngsters living with custodial mothers (Demo & Cox, 2000). Yet far more important than the amount of contact children have with their fathers is the quality of the contact. Children fare far better if their fathers are authoritative, emotionally close to their children, and make some effort to support the custodial mother in her parenting role (Amato & Sobolewski, 2004; Marsiglio et al., 2000).

One way of ensuring that children of divorce do not lose contact with a noncustodial parent is to seek *joint physical custody* and have children spend part of the time in each parent's home.

---

families are more likely than those from nondivorced families to fear that their own marriages will be unhappy (Franklin, Janoff-Bulman, & Roberts, 1990). There may well be some basis for this concern, for adults whose parents divorced are more likely than adults from intact families to experience an unhappy marriage and a divorce themselves (Amato, 1996; Segrin, Taylor, & Altman, 2005).

In sum, divorce tends to be a most disruptive and troubling life event—one that few children feel very positive about, even after 20 years have elapsed. But despite the gloomy portrait of divorce we have painted here, there are more encouraging messages. First, researchers are consistently finding that children in *stable,* single-parent (or stepparent) homes are usually better adjusted than those who remain in conflict-ridden two-parent families. Indeed, some of the behavior problems that children display after a divorce are actually evident well *before* the divorce and may often be more closely related to long-standing family conflict than to the divorce itself (Amato & Booth, 1996; Shaw, Winslow, & Flanagan, 1999). Take away the marital discord and the breakdown in parenting often associated with divorce, and the experience, while always stressful, need not always be damaging. So today's conventional wisdom holds that unhappily married couples who have unreconcilable differences might well *divorce* for the good of the children; that is, children are likely to *benefit* in the long run if the ending of a stormy marriage ultimately reduces the stress they experience and enables either or both parents to be more sensitive and responsive to their needs (Booth & Amato, 2001; Hetherington, Bridges, & Insabella, 1998).

A second encouraging message is that not all divorcing families experience all the difficulties we have described. In fact, some adults and children manage this transition quite well and may even grow psychologically as a result of it. Who are these survivors? Box 11.2 provides some clues by exploring the factors that seem to promote a positive adjustment to divorce.

This arrangement can work well if parents get along (Bauserman, 2002); but if their relationship is hostile, their children may feel "caught in the middle"—an impression associated with high levels of stress and poor adjustment outcomes (Buchanan, Maccoby, & Dornbusch, 1991). It really doesn't matter whether families obtain joint custody as long as children are permitted to maintain close affectionate ties to *both* parents, who are committed to *coparenting* and to shielding their children from any continuing conflict between them (Amato, 1993; Coley, 1998).

Additional Social Support

Divorcing adults are often less depressed if they participate in support groups such as Parents without Partners (a national organization with local chapters that attempts to help single parents cope with their problems) or if they have relatives or close confidants to whom they can turn (Emery, 1988; Hetherington, 1989). Children also benefit from the support they receive from close friends (Lustig, Wolchik, & Braver, 1992), as well as from participating in peer-support programs at school, in which they and other children of divorce are encouraged to share their feelings, correct their misconceptions, and learn positive coping skills (Grych & Fincham, 1992; Pedro-Carroll & Cowen, 1985). In sum, friends, peers, school personnel, and other sources of social support outside the nuclear family can do much to help families adjust to divorce.

Minimizing Additional Stress

Generally, families respond more positively to divorce if additional disruptions are kept to a minimum—for example, if parents do not have to go through messy divorce trials and custody hearings, seek new jobs or residences, cope with the loss of their children, and so on. One way to accomplish some of these aims is through *divorce mediation*—meetings prior to the divorce in which a trained professional tries to help divorcing parents reach amicable agreements on disputed issues such as child custody and property settlements. Divorce mediation does appear to be an effective intervention—one that not only increases the likelihood of out-of-court settlements, but also promotes true compromises, cooperation, and better feelings between divorcing adults and increases the likelihood that a noncustodial father will pay child support and remain involved in the lives of his children (Emery et al., 2001; Emery, Sbarra, & Grover, 2005).

Here, then, are some effective first steps in the path toward a positive divorce experience—as well as a better understanding of why divorce is more disruptive for some families than for others. This research also serves as yet another excellent example of the family as a social system embedded in larger social systems. Mother, father, and children will all influence one another's adjustment to divorce, and the family's experience will also depend on the supports available within the neighborhood, the schools, the community, and family members' own social networks.

Remarriage and Reconstituted Families

Within 3 to 5 years after a divorce, about 75 percent of single-parent families experience yet another major change when the custodial parent remarries or *cohabits* with a partner outside of marriage and the children acquire a stepparent—and perhaps new siblings as well (Hetherington & Stanley-Hagan, 2000). Remarriage often improves the financial and other life circumstances of custodial parents, and most newly remarried adults report that they are satisfied with their second marriages. Yet these reconstituted families introduce many new challenges for children, who must now adjust not only to the parenting of an unfamiliar adult, but to the behavior of stepsiblings (if any) and to the possibility of receiving less attention from both their custodial and noncustodial parents (Hetherington & Stanley-Hagan, 2000). In fact, the restabilizing of family roles after the custodial parent remarries often takes considerably longer than was true after a divorce (Hetherington, Henderson, & Reiss, 1999). Furthermore, second marriages are somewhat more likely to end in divorce than first marriages are (Booth & Edwards, 1992). Imagine, then, the stresses experienced by families that find themselves in a recurring cycle of marriage, marital conflict, divorce, single parenthood, and remarriage. Indeed, research indicates that the more marital transitions grade-school children have experienced, the poorer their academic performances and the less well-adjusted they are (Capaldi & Patterson, 1991; Kurdek, Fine, & Sinclair, 1995; and see Figure 11.6).

So how do children fare in relatively *stable* stepparent families? The answer depends in part on their ages and gender and on whether their mother or father has formed the new family.

Mother/Stepfather Families
After an initial period of disruption and confusion that occurs as new family roles iron themselves out, boys often seem to benefit more than girls

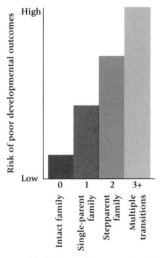

Figure 11.6
Grade-school boys' risk for poor adjustment outcomes (that is, antisocial behavior, low self-esteem, peer rejection, drug use, depression, poor academic performance, and deviant peer associations) as a function of number of marital transitions experienced. (From Capaldi & Patterson, 1991.)

by gaining a *stepfather*. Stepfathers who are warm and accepting offer relief from the coercive cycles that boys may have experienced with a custodial mother, so that these stepsons often enjoy a boost in self-esteem and will eventually overcome many of the adjustment problems they displayed before their mothers remarried (Hetherington, 1989; Vuchinich et al., 1991). Why do girls not fare as well? Certainly *not* because stepfathers are treating stepdaughters any worse than stepsons; in fact, just the opposite is true during the early stages of remarried life. Sometimes, no matter how hard stepfathers try, their stepdaughters often remain rather cool and aloof. Girls often view stepfathers as threats to their relationships with their mothers and may even resent their mothers for remarrying and becoming less attentive to their needs (Hetherington & Stanley-Hagan, 2002; Visher, Visher, & Pasley, 2003).

Father/Stepmother Families Less is known about children's reactions to *stepmothers* because stepmother families are still relatively uncommon (recall that fathers currently receive custody of their children in only about 18 percent of all divorcing families). What research there is indicates that introduction of a stepmother into the family system is somewhat more disruptive initially than the introduction of a stepfather, in part because (1) fathers granted custody typically have very close relations with their children that stepmothers may disrupt (Mekos, Hetherington, & Reiss, 1996), and (2) stepmothers play more active roles as behavior monitors and disciplinarians than stepfathers do (Clarke-Stewart & Bretano, 2005; Hetherington, Bridges, & Insabella, 1998). Furthermore, the transition from a father-custody single-parent home to a two-parent *stepmother* family is once again more disruptive and difficult for girls than for boys, particularly if the biological mother maintains frequent contact with her children (Brand, Clingempeel, & Bowen-Woodward, 1988; Clingempeel & Segal, 1986). Girls are often so closely allied with their mothers that they are bothered by either a stepfather competing for their mother's attention or a stepmother attempting to play a substitute-mother role. However, their adjustment to life in *stable* stepparent families generally improves over time. In one longitudinal study of stepfamilies at 5 to 10 years after remarriage, Mavis Hetherington and her associates (1999) found that girls no longer appeared to be disadvantaged by living in a stepparent home. In fact, they were actually more autonomous and socially responsible (though somewhat lower in self-esteem) than boys were.

Family Composition and Age The composition of a stepparent family often influences how well children adjust to it. Problems of all kinds are more common in **complex stepparent homes**—true "blended" families in which each parent brings at least one biological child to the new family unit. Both mothers and fathers in these complex aggregations tend to show an **ownness effect,** displaying more warmth, support, and involvement with their biological children than with their stepchildren (Hetherington, Henderson, & Reiss, 1999). And children pick up on this differential treatment, often acting out or otherwise reacting negatively to it, siding with their biological parent in disputes about child-rearing issues, which further exacerbates marital conflict, and remaining somewhat more distant and less affectionate over the long run toward their steprelations than toward biological kin (Hetherington, Henderson, & Reiss, 1999; Jenkins et al., 2005; Mekos, Hetherington, & Reiss, 1996) Clearly, it is harder for adults to effectively *coparent* if each parent consistently favors his or her biological children. By contrast, coparenting is much more common in **simple stepparent homes,** particularly if family roles stabilize before the children reach adolescence (Hetherington, Henderson, & Reiss, 1999).

Given the many other changes that occur early in adolescence (for example, pubertal changes, school transitions, heightened needs for autonomy), it may come as no surprise

complex stepparent home
family consisting of two married (or cohabiting) adults, each of whom has at least one biological child living at home.

ownness effect
tendency of parents in complex stepparent homes to favor and be more involved with their biological children than with their stepchildren.

simple stepparent home
family consisting of a parent, his or her biological children, and a stepparent.

to learn that early adolescents of both sexes find it more difficult to adjust to a remarriage than younger children or older adolescents do. In fact, Mavis Hetherington and Glenn Clingempeel (1992) reported that children who were early adolescents at the time of a parent's remarriage were significantly less well-adjusted than age-mates from nondivorced homes and showed little improvement over the 26-month course of their study. Of course, many early adolescents adapt reasonably well to this family transition, and authoritative parenting within stepparent families is consistently associated with more favorable adjustment outcomes for stepchildren of *all* ages (Hetherington, Henderson, & Reiss, 1999; Hetherington & Stanley-Hagan, 2002). Nevertheless, a fair number (perhaps one-third) of young adolescents disengage from their reconstituted families, and the incidence of academic problems, sexual misconduct, and many other delinquent activities is higher among adolescents from stepparent homes (particularly complex stepparent homes) than among age-mates from nondivorced families (see Hetherington, Henderson, & Reiss, 1999 for a review).

But before we get too carried away about the antisocial tendencies of adolescents in stepparent homes, an important truth should be stated here: The vast majority of adolescents who experience this marital transition turn out to be perfectly normal teenagers who may experience some initial problems adjusting but are unlikely to display any prolonged psychopathological tendencies (Emery & Forehand, 1994; Hetherington, Henderson, & Reiss, 1999). In fact, disengagement from a reconstituted family may even be beneficial if a teenager's time away from home is spent at a job or at extracurricular activities that foster constructive, supportive relationships with adult mentors or peers (Hetherington, Bridges, & Insabella, 1998).

Challenges for Working Mothers and Dual-Career Families

In Chapter 5, we learned that a clear majority of mothers in many Western societies now work outside the home and that this arrangement need not and usually does not undermine the emotional security of their infants, toddlers, and preschool children. And research with older children suggests that maternal employment is unlikely to impede a child's social or intellectual development (Burchinal & Clarke-Stewart, 2007; Harvey, 1999). In fact, the opposite may often be true, for children of working mothers (particularly daughters) tend to be more independent, enjoy higher self-esteem, and hold higher educational and occupational aspirations and less stereotyped views of men and women than those whose mothers are not employed (Gottfried, Gottfried, & Bathurst, 2002; L. W. Hoffman, 2000; Richards & Duckett, 1994). Indeed, one study of a national sample of *low-income* families linked maternal employment to children's cognitive *competence:* Second-graders whose mothers had worked regularly outperformed those whose mothers had worked less (if at all) in mathematics, reading, and language achievement (Vandell & Ramanan, 1992).

Maternal Employment and Father Involvement One reason why many children of employed mothers experience favorable outcomes and tend to be socially mature is that a mother's work-related absences often cause the father to play a bigger role in children's lives. When mothers work long hours, fathers become more heavily involved in child rearing (Cabrera et al., 2000) and know more about their children's activities, whereabouts, and companions (Crouter, Helms-Erikson, et al., 1999). This kind of father involvement (whether inspired by a mother's working or other factors) can have a very positive influence on children. Research consistently indicates that grade-school children and adolescents whose fathers are *warm, supportive,* and *emotionally invested* in child rearing are, on average, more academically competent, more socially skilled, and less inclined to display problem behaviors and delinquent conduct compared with age-mates whose

Photo 11.10
Children fare rather well, both socially and academically, if their working parents are authoritative and carefully monitor their activities.

fathers are less nurturant and less involved in their lives (Cabrera et al., 2000; Coley & Medeiros, 2007; Jaffee et al., 2003). Favorable outcomes associated with positive and supportive father involvement characterize all racial and ethnic groups in the United States (Rohner, 2000) and are *unique* in that they still occur after controlling for the impact of other variables known to influence child development, such as family income and mothers' child-rearing practices (Black, Dubowitz, & Starr, 1999; Cabrera et al., 2000; Parke et al., 2004). So maternal employment can be beneficial to children if it prompts sensitive and supportive fathers to play a larger role in their lives.

Of course not all children of working-mother and dual-career families fare so well, especially if their parents experience lots of work pressures and associated stresses that spill over to the home setting and compromise the quality of parent/child interactions (Crouter, Bumpass, et al., 1999; Greenberger, O'Neil, & Nagel, 1994) and parental monitoring of a child's or adolescent's activities and whereabouts (Perry-Jenkins, Repetti, & Crouter, 2000). Not surprisingly, a mother's working conditions clearly matter. Children of single working mothers often experience declines in self-esteem and academic performance and display increases in aggression and other externalizing behaviors if their mothers are employed at unstable, low-paying jobs and work variable shifts and nonstandard hours (Hsueh & Yoshikawa, 2007; Kalil & Ziol-Guest, 2005). Clearly, families experiencing considerable work-related stress and disruption of normal family routines are likely to need help if they are to raise children successfully.

The Importance of Good Day Care Aside from spousal (or partner) *coparenting*, one of the strongest supports workings parents could hope for is *high-quality* day care for their children. Recall that children who enter high-quality day care centers early in life tend to display positive social, emotional, and intellectual outcomes from infancy through early adolescence (Andersson, 1989, 1992; Broberg et al., 1997; Erel, Oberman, & Yirmiya, 2000). Much of the research that points to the long-term benefits of excellent day care comes from Western European countries, where day care for infants, toddlers, and preschool children is often government subsidized, staffed with trained, well-paid child-care professionals, and widely available to all citizens at a modest fee (usually less than 10 percent of an average woman's wages; Scarr, 1998). By comparison, day care in the United States is often woefully inadequate. Typically run as a for-profit enterprise, U.S. day-care centers and day-care homes are generally staffed by poorly compensated caregivers who have little training or experience in early childhood education and who rarely stay in the profession long enough to gain much expertise (Scarr, 1998; Zigler & Gilman, 1993). Furthermore, American day care is expensive; providing *one child* with what is often far less than optimal center-based care often runs $6000 to $8000 per year, or more than 50 percent of the annual income of a minimum-wage worker (U.S. Bureau of the Census, 2007). In 1990, the U.S. Congress passed a bill granting some tax relief to parents to help offset the cost of day care. But the absence of a national day-care policy that would ensure the availability of *high-quality* care at a *reasonable cost* to *all* who may need it means that many American workers will have to struggle to find and finance the kind of alternative care that would help them to optimize the development of their children (Scarr, 1998).

Self-Care   Some developmentalists have become concerned that more and more children of working parents are becoming **self-care (or latchkey) children,** caring for themselves after school with little or no direct adult supervision (Zigler & Finn-Stevenson, 1993). Are these youngsters at risk of becoming victimized, led astray by peers, or experiencing other less than desirable outcomes?

Research designed to answer these questions is often contradictory. Some studies find that self-care children do display higher levels of anxiety, poor academic performance, and more delinquent or antisocial conduct than supervised youngsters do (Marshall et al., 1997; Pettit, Bates, & Dodge, 1997), whereas other studies find no such effects (Galambos & Maggs, 1991; Vandell & Corasantini, 1988). Why the inconsistencies? Let's begin by noting that the risks of self-care do seem to be greater for lower-income children in urban neighborhoods—settings that may present many opportunities for unsupervised children to associate with deviant peer groups and to take part in antisocial conduct (Lord & Mahoney, 2007; Pettit et al., 1999). And regardless of the neighborhood, the way self-care children spend their time is crucial. Grade-school children and adolescents who have received authoritative parenting, who are required to come home after school to complete homework or other chores, and who are monitored at a distance by telephone calls are generally responsible and well-adjusted. By contrast, unmonitored age-mates who are allowed to "hang out" after school are more inclined to be influenced by peers and to engage in antisocial or delinquent conduct (Galambos & Maggs, 1991; Pettit et al., 1999; Steinberg, 1986).

So it appears that there are steps that working parents can take to minimize some of the potential risks of leaving schoolchildren to care for themselves—namely, by requiring them to go home after school, supervising them *in absentia* to ensure that they do, and parenting them in an authoritative manner. Nevertheless, leaving children younger than 8 or 9 to fend for themselves may be asking for trouble (Pettit et al., 1997). Not only is the practice illegal in many states, but 5- to 7-year-olds often lack the cognitive skills to avoid high-risk hazards such as swimming pools or heavy traffic or to cope with such emergencies as personal injuries or fires (Peterson, Ewigman, & Kivlahan, 1993). Younger children in self-care also appear to be more vulnerable to sexual abuse and to harm at the hands of burglars as well (Zigler & Finn-Stevenson, 1993).

Fortunately, organized after-school care for school-aged children is becoming more common in American communities (Mahoney, Lord, & Carryl, 2005). These programs differ in quality, ranging from "social addresses" where children hang out largely unsupervised, to well-run programs with trained staff, reasonable child-to-staff ratios, and curricula that include a variety of age-appropriate activities including sports, games, dance, art projects, music, computer activities, and academic assistance. Not only do children prefer the higher-quality after-school care programs (Rosenthal & Vandell, 1996), but they fare better in these programs as well. Jill Posner and Deborah Vandell (1994), for example, found that 9-year-olds from high-risk neighborhoods who attended *closely supervised* after-school care programs providing ample recreational opportunities and/or academic assistance were more academically competent, rated as better adjusted by teachers, and much *less* likely to be involved in antisocial activities than age-mates who were not supervised after school by an adult. A follow-up on these participants revealed that even after controlling for competencies they displayed in the third grade, children who had spent more time between third and fifth grades in such program-related enrichment activities as theater, music, dance, or other learning projects were rated as better adjusted emotionally by fifth-grade teachers and were performing better academically than unsupervised age-mates, who spent much of their after-school time hanging out or watching television (Posner & Vandell, 1999; see also Mahoney, Lord, & Carryl 2005). Yet these same benefits of after-school care are *not* found if the programs children attend are primarily custodial and provide little stimulation or adult guidance

self-care (or latchkey) children
children who care for themselves after school or in the evenings while their parents are working.

(Kane, 2004; Pierce, Hamm, & Vandell, 1999; U.S. Department of Education, 2003). So the *quality* of day care that children receive is important at all ages. Given the success of the publicly funded programs that Posner and Vandell evaluated, we might encourage politicians and community leaders to look carefully at them as a potentially affordable means of (1) optimizing developmental outcomes and (2) preventing more children of working mothers from having to face the risks of being alone in the afternoon and early evening.

🔊 WHEN PARENTING BREAKS DOWN: THE PROBLEM OF CHILD ABUSE

child abuse
term used to describe any extreme maltreatment of children, involving physical battering; sexual molestations; psychological insults such as persistent ridicule, rejection, and terrorization; and physical or emotional neglect.

Family relationships can be our greatest source of nurturance and support, but they can also be a powerful source of anguish. Nowhere is this more obvious than in cases of **child abuse.** Every day, thousands of infants, children, and adolescents are burned, bruised, beaten, starved, suffocated, sexually molested, or otherwise mistreated by their caregivers. Other children are not targets of these "physical" forms of abuse, but are victims of such *psychological abuse* as rejection, ridicule, or even being terrorized by their parents (Cicchetti & Toth, 2006). Even larger numbers of children (see Figure 11.7) are *neglected* and deprived of the basic care and stimulation that they need to develop normally. Although instances of severe battering are the most visible forms of child abuse and are certainly horrible, many investigators now believe that strong and recurrent psychological abuse and neglect may prove to be even more harmful to children in the long run (Erickson & Egeland, 1996; Lowenthal, 2000).

Child abuse is a very serious problem. About *3 million* reports of child maltreatment are filed each year in the United States, and about a third of these (or just under *1 million*) are substantiated as abuse cases by child protection agencies (Childstats, 2007b; U.S. Department of Health and Human Services, 2005). And because many cases of child abuse are never reported or detected, these figures may represent only the tip of the iceberg. Indeed, one national sampling of families in the United States found that 11 percent of the children had reportedly been kicked, bitten, punched, beaten up, hit with an object, or threatened with a knife or a gun by their parents in the past year (Wolfner & Gelles, 1993), and many cases of sexual abuse are committed by relatives (often fathers, stepfathers, or older siblings) and are never reported (Finkelhor & Dziuba-Leatherman, 1994). It is not a pretty picture, is it? What's more, reports of child abuse have increased over the past 20 years, due in part to increased awareness of the problem and a greater willingness to citizens to report suspected cases, but also to true increases in family violence associated with increased use of illegal drugs, greater poverty, and the disintegration of family-oriented residential areas (Emery & Laumann-Billings, 1998; Garbarino, 1995).

As you might expect, there are many, many factors that contribute to a social problem as widespread as child abuse. Fortunately, we are gaining a better understanding of why abuse occurs by adopting a social systems perspective and recognizing that (1) some adults may be more inclined than others to abuse children; (2) some children may be more likely than others to be abused; and (3) abuse may be more likely to occur in some contexts, communities, and cultures than in others.

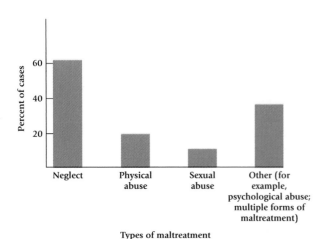

Figure 11.7
Distribution of types of substantiated child maltreatment. The percentages total more than 100 percent because children may be victims of more than one type of abuse. (Source: U.S. Department of Health & Human Services, 2005.)

Who Are the Abusers?

Researchers have found that there is no single "abusive personality syndrome" that accurately characterizes adults who commit child abuse (Wiehe, 1996). Child abusers come from all ethnic groups and social classes, and many of them even appear on the surface to be rather typical, loving parents who would never harm their children.

Yet there are at least some differences between parents who abuse their children and those who do not. Let's first note that about 20 to 40 percent of abusive parents have an alcohol or drug problem that plays a role in precipitating abuse (Emery & Laumann-Billings, 1998). And about 30 percent of maltreated children will abuse their own children when they become parents, thus implying that abusive parenting practices are often passed down from generation to generation (Cicchetti & Toth, 2006; van IJzendoorn, 1992). Many of the "formerly abused" abusive parents are battered women—abused by their husbands or romantic partners (Coohey & Braun, 1997; Stith et al., 2000). They may have learned through their experiences as a battered child or romantic partner that violence is a common reaction to frustration. Abusive mothers are also often young, poverty-stricken, poorly educated, and are raising children without a partner to share their burdens (Wiehe, 1996; Wolfner & Gelles, 1993). And many abusive parents of each sex are *emotionally insecure* individuals with low self-esteem who are likely to interpret a child's irritability or independence in the face of an autonomy conflict as signs that their children are *disrespectful* or are *rejecting* them (Bugental, 2001). These insecure individuals often feel victimized by their child's unpleasant behavior and powerless to control such conduct (Bugental & Beaulieu, 2003; Bugental & Happaney, 2004), which elicits anger, depression, and a tendency to lash out at their children or to back off and neglect them (Bugental & Happaney, 2004).

In sum, abusive parents are often highly stressed younger caregivers with little social support who have a history of abuse, believe that coercive discipline is more effective than reasoning, and find parenting more unpleasant and ego-threatening than nonabusive parents do. Still, there are many, many *nonabusive* parents who display all these characteristics, and it has been difficult to specify in advance exactly who will become a child abuser.

Who Is Abused?

Abusive parents often single out only one child in the family as a target, thus implying that some children may bring out the worst in their parents (Gil, 1970). No one is suggesting that children are to *blame* for this abuse, but some children do appear to be at more risk than others. For example, infants who are emotionally unresponsive, hyperactive, irritable, temperamentally impulsive, or ill are far more likely to be abused than quiet, healthy, and responsive babies who are easy to care for (Bugental & Happaney, 2004; Cicchetti & Toth, 2006). These child risk factors might seem to imply that some children may be targeted for abuse because of genetically influenced characteristics that promote unpleasant behaviors. Yet in a recent twin study, Sara Jaffee and her associates (2004) found no support for the notion that victims of maltreatment actively provoke abusive incidents by virtue of their difficult or otherwise unpleasant demeanor; factors precipitating abuse were more often found within the family environment or the adult abuser. Indeed, most "difficult" children are never abused, while many cheerful and seemingly easy-going children will be mistreated. Just as caregiver characteristics cannot fully predict or explain why abuse occurs, neither can characteristics of children, although it is often the case that the *combination* of a high-risk parent and a high-risk child spells trouble (Bugental & Happaney, 2004).

But even the match between a high-risk child and caregiver does not invariably result in child abuse. The broader social contexts in which families are embedded matter too.

Photo 11.11
The incidence of child abuse is relatively high in deteriorating neighborhoods that offer few services and little if any social support to financially troubled families.

a residential area in which the incidence of child abuse is much higher than in other neighborhoods with the same demographic characteristics.

Contextual Triggers: The Ecology of Child Abuse

Child abuse is most likely to occur in families under stress. Such significant life changes as a divorce, the death of a family member, the loss of a job, or moving to a new home can disrupt social and emotional relationships within a family and contribute to neglectful or abusive parenting (Cicchetti & Toth, 2006; Emery & Laumann-Billings, 1998). Children are also much more likely to be abused or neglected if their parents are unhappily married (Belsky, 1993; Egeland, Jacobvitz, & Sroufe, 1988).

High-Risk Neighborhoods   Families are also embedded in broader social contexts (that is, a neighborhood, a community, and a culture) that can affect a child's chances of being abused. Some residential areas can be labeled **high-risk neighborhoods** because they have much higher rates of child abuse than other neighborhoods with similar demographic characteristics (Coulton et al., 1995). What are these high-risk areas like? They tend to be deteriorating neighborhoods where families are poor, transient, socially isolated, and lacking in *community services* (for example, preschool programs, recreation centers) and *informal* support systems (Garbarino & Kostelny, 1992). Adults in these communities display little *collective efficacy;* they do not look after each other's children and fail to appreciate the notion that "It takes a village to raise a child" (Korbin, 2001). Consequently, socially isolated parents in these neighborhoods often have nowhere to turn for assistance and advice during particularly stressful times, and they often end up taking out their frustrations on their children.

Cultural Influences   Finally, the broader cultural contexts in which families live can affect the likelihood that children will be abused. Some developmentalists believe that child abuse is rampant in the United States because people in the society (1) have a permissive attitude about violence and (2) generally sanction the use of physical punishment as a means of controlling children's behavior. There may well be some truth to these assertions, for cross-cultural studies reveal that children are less often abused in societies that discourage the use

Factors contributing to child abuse and neglect

Contributing Factor	Examples
Parental characteristics	Younger age (under 25); low educational level; depression or other psychological disturbance; history of rejection or abuse; belief in effectiveness of coercive discipline; general insecurity or low ego strength; alcoholism and/or illegal drug use
Child characteristics	Irritable or impulsive temperament; hyperactivity; prematurity; inattentiveness; sickliness or other chronic developmental problems
Family characteristics	Financial strain or poverty; job loss; frequent moves; marital instability; lack of spousal support; many children to care for; divorce
Neighborhood	High-risk areas characterized by few community services and little opportunity for informal social support from friends and relatives
Culture	Approval of coercive methods of resolving conflicts and use of corporal punishment to discipline children

of physical punishment and advocate nonviolent ways of resolving interpersonal conflict (Belsky, 1993; U.S. Department of State, 2002). In fact, several Scandivanian countries have outlawed the use of corporal punishment (spanking), even by parents (Finkelhor & Dziwba-Leatherman, 1994).

Consequences of Abuse and Neglect

Children who are neglected or abused tend to display a number of serious problems, including intellectual deficits, academic difficulties, depression, social anxiety, low self-esteem, and disturbed relationships with teachers and peers (Bolger, Patterson, & Kupersmidt, 1998; Cicchetti & Toth, 2006; Kim & Cicchetti, 2006; Margolin & Gordis, 2000). The behavioral correlates of neglect differ somewhat from those most commonly associated with other forms of abuse. Neglected children are more likely than those who are physically or sexually abused to founder academically (Eckenrode, Laird, & Doris, 1993; Shonk & Cicchetti, 2001) and to have few if any close friends (Bolger, Patterson, & Kupersmidt, 1998). Neglected children may receive very little intellectual or social simulation from nurturing adults that would foster their academic competencies and social skills (Golden, 2000).

By contrast, hostility, overt aggression, and disordered social relationships are more common among physically abused youngsters, who have difficulties regulating negative emotions (Cicchetti & Toth, 2006; Maughan & Cicchetti, 2002), often create disciplinary problems at school (Eckenrode et al., 1993), and are likely to be rejected by peers (Bolger, Patterson, & Kupersmidt, 1998; Salzinger et al., 1993). One of the more disturbing correlates of physical abuse is a lack of normal empathy in response to the distress of peers. When Mary Main and Carol George (1985) observed the responses of abused and non-abused toddlers to the fussing and crying of peers, they found that nonabused children typically attended carefully to the distressed child, showed concern, or even attempted to provide comfort. But as shown in Figure 11.8, not one abused child showed appropriate concern; instead, abused toddlers were likely to become angry and attack the crying child (see also Klimes-Dougan & Kistner, 1990). So it seems that physically abused children are likely to become abusive companions who have apparently learned from their own experiences at home that distress signals are particularly irritating to others and will often elicit angry responses rather than displays of sympathy. Other forms of domestic violence (for example, spouse battering) are also common in families that abuse children (McCloskey, Figuerdo, & Koss, 1995), so that victims of abuse may have few occasions to learn to respond compassionately to others' distress (Shields, Ryan, & Cicchetti, 2001) but many opportunities to learn aggressive solutions to conflict (Bolger & Patterson, 2001). No wonder these children are often rejected by their peers.

Victims of *sexual abuse* are often emotionally deregulated and may experience any of the problems commonly seen in emotionally disturbed individuals, including anxiety, depression, acting out, behavioral withdrawal, and academic difficulties (Kendall-Tackett, Williams, & Finkelhor, 1993; Shipman et al., 2000). Many of these after-effects boil down to strong feelings of shame, lack of attractiveness and self-worth; a pessimistic outlook on life; and a reluctance to trust other people (Bolger, Patterson, & Kupersmidt, 1998; Feiring, Taska, & Lewis, 2002; Vigil, Geary, & Byrd-Craven, 2005). But there are two problems that seem to be closely associated with sexual abuse. First, many victims engage in "sexualized behaviors," acting out sexually by placing objects in their vaginas, masturbating in public, behaving seductively, or, if they are older, early onset of sexual intercourse and sexual promiscuity (Kendall-Tackett, Williams, & Finkelhor, 1993; Vigil, Geary, & Byrd-Craven, 2005). Second, about one-third of sexual abuse victims display partial or full symptoms of **posttraumatic stress disorder,** a clinical syndrome that includes nightmares, flashbacks to the traumatizing events, and feelings of hopelessness and anxiety in the face

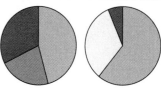
Abused toddlers   Nonabused toddlers

☐ Concern, sadness

☐ Interest, looks, "mechanical" comfort movements

☐ Fearful distress

☐ Threats, diffuse anger, physical assaults

Figure 11.8
Responses to the distress of peers observed in abused and nonabused toddlers in the day-care setting. (The figures show the mean proportion of responses falling in each category for the nine abused and nine nonabused toddlers.) (Adapted from Main & George, 1985.)

posttraumatic stress disorder
a psychological syndrome involving flashbacks to traumatizing events, nightmares, and feelings of anxiety and helplessness in the face of threats; common among soldiers in combat and sexually abused children.

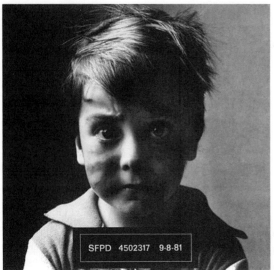

4 out of 5 convicts were abused children.

In the United States, an average of 80% of our prisoners were abused children. That is why we are working so hard to help those children today, before

they develop into a threat to others tomorrow.
With your support, we can have a full staff of trained people available 24 hours a day. Abused

children desperately need us. Please let us be there to help. Write for our free brochure, or send in your tax-deductible donation today.

San Francisco Child Abuse Council, Inc.
4093 24th Street, San Francisco, CA 94114

Courtesy San Francisco Child Abuse Council

Photo 11.12

of threats (Kendall-Tackett, Williams, & Finkelhor, 1993; Saywitz et al., 2000).

Sadly, many maltreated children are victims of more than one type of abuse; and any of the previously mentioned consequences may appear in any particular child who is a victim of severe and prolonged maltreatment, regardless of the types of maltreatment he or she has experienced (Bolger & Patterson, 2001; Bolger, Patterson, & Kupersmidt, 1998). And the harmful social and emotional consequences of abuse and neglect can be long lasting, with some adolescents trying to escape their pain, anxieties, self-doubts, and disordered social lives by attempting to take their own lives (Bagley, 1995; Sternberg et al., 1993). Furthermore, adults who were abused as children are prone to violence, both inside and outside the family, and they show higher than average rates of criminal activity, substance abuse, depression, and other psychological disturbances (Bagley, 1995; Cicchetti & Toth, 2006; Margolin & Gordis, 2000).

The good news is that many abused or neglected youngsters are remarkably resilient, especially if they are able to establish a warm, secure, and supportive relationship with a nonabusive parent, a grandparent, or some other member of the family (Bolger, Patterson, & Kupersmidt, 1998; Egeland, Jacobovitz, & Sroufe, 1988). What's more, some abused children and adolescents may avoid most psychological problems and turn out fine because they have inherited genes that help to protect them from the stress of maltreatment. As shown in Figure 11.9, Avshalom Caspi and his associates (2003) found that maltreatment during childhood increases the risk of clinical depression among abuse victims with a genotype that predisposes them to depression, but not among victims with a genotype known to protect against depression. Indeed, the likelihood of depression among individuals with the "protective" genotype was no greater for maltreated participants than for those who had never been abused! And even though abused children are at risk of becoming abusive parents, it is worth emphasizing once again that a sizable majority of abuse victims show enough resilience to *never* abuse their own children (Cicchetti & Toth, 2006). Abused parents who succeed at breaking the cycle of abuse are more likely than those who do not to (1) have received emotional support from a nonabusive parent (or parent substitute), a therapist, or a spouse and (2) avoided severe stress as adults (Egeland, Jacobovitz, & Sroufe, 1988; Vondra & Belsky, 1993).

Despite our better understanding of the causes of child abuse and observations that its often severe consequences can be lessened or even overcome, we are still a long way from solving the problem. Rather than conclude on that depressing note, Box 11.3 considers some of the promising steps that have been taken to assist the abused child and his or her abusers.

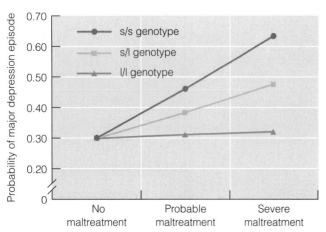

Figure 11.9
Genes interact with child maltreatment to influence the odds of depression as an adult. A short (s) variant of the gene studied increases risk, whereas a long (l) variant protects against depression.
Source: Adapted from Caspi et al. (2003, p. 388, Figure 2).

REFLECTIONS ON THE FAMILY

James Garbarino (1992) characterizes the family as "the basic unit of human experience" (p. 7). To fully appreciate the awesome significance of the family for children and adolescents, think for a moment on how very badly things can go when

Combatting Child Abuse

It can be discouraging to realize that so many factors contribute to the maltreatment of children. Where do we begin to intervene? Just how many problems must we correct before we can prevent or stop the violence and discourage the neglect? Despite the complexity of the problem, progress has been made.

Preventing Abuse and Neglect

Let's first consider the task of preventing child maltreatment before it starts. This requires identifying high-risk families—a task that is greatly aided by the kinds of studies we have reviewed. For example, once neonatal assessment indicates that an infant may be at risk of abuse or neglect because he or she is particularly irritable or unresponsive, it makes some sense to help the child's parents to appreciate and evoke the baby's positive qualities. Indeed, we learned in Box 5.2 that interventions for mothers of high-risk infants can be quite effective at fostering maternal sensitivity as well as secure mother-infant attachments and generally positive developmental outcomes.

Even better, efforts to prevent abuse can be directed at the combination of a high-risk parent and a high-risk child. Daphne Bugental and her associates (Bugental & Beaulieu, 2003; Bugental et al., 2002) focused on parents who felt that they were locked in a power struggle with children who were deliberately trying to annoy or to get the best of them—parents who are likely to become abusive if their child is unresponsive or difficult. Some of the families had high-risk infants who were born prematurely or had scored low on neonatal exams and were at risk for future health problems; other families had infants who displayed no risks. Families were randomly assigned to three conditions. The *empowerment condition* was a home visitation program aimed at empowering mothers as parents by teaching them to analyze the underlying causes of caregiving problems without blaming either themselves or their children and to devise effective solutions to these problems. Other families were either assigned to a second home visitation program without the empowerment training or to a control group in which families were simply referred to regular community services.

After the intervention period, mothers in the empowerment condition were notably less depressed and felt more empowered as effective caregivers than did mothers in the other two conditions. The rate of physical abuse, including slapping and spanking, was only 4 percent in the empowerment group as compared with 23 percent in the other home visitation program and 26 percent in the control group. And the benefits of the program were greatest for the families with high-risk infants. As shown in the accompanying figure, harsh parenting among mothers in the empowerment condition was unlikely regardless of whether their infants were at risk, whereas in the other two conditions, high-risk infants in particular were treated quite harshly by their mothers. Here then is a very successful *experimental* intervention suggesting that home visitations that alter high-risk mothers' malevolent cognitive appraisals of their infants' behavior may go a long way toward preventing physical maltreatment.

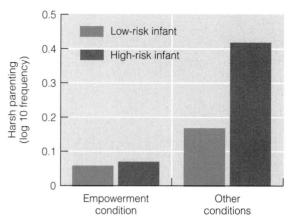

Empowerment training for low-income mothers under stress reduces harsh parenting practices, especially among mothers who are the most at risk of being abusive because their babies had medical problems or were born prematurely. (From D.B. Bugental and D.A. Beaulieu, "A bio-social-cognitive approach to understanding and promoting the outcomes of children with medical and physical disorders" in R.V. Kail, ed. Advanced in Child Development and Behavior, Vol. 31.) Reprinted by permission of Elsevier.

Controlling Abuse

How do we deal with parents who are already abusive? What does seem clear is that a visit or two from a social worker is unlikely to solve the problem. A more promising approach is Parents Anonymous, a self-help program based on Alcoholics Anonymous that helps caregivers to understand and cope with their problems and provides them the emotional support they often lack. Ultimately, however, a comprehensive approach is likely to be more effective. Abusive parents need emotional support *and* opportunities to learn more effective parenting and coping skills, whereas the victims of abuse and neglect need stimulating day-care programs *and* specialized training to help them overcome the cognitive, social, and emotional problems associated with abuse (Malley-Morrison & Hines, 2004; Wiehe, 1996). In short, the ultimate goal in attempting to prevent or control child abuse must be to convert a pathological family system into a healthy one.

Finally, some family systems are more pathological than others and may not respond to supportive interventions. Indeed, it may shock you to learn that between 35 and 50 percent of child maltreatment fatalities occur in cases of *repeated* abuse that are already known to law enforcement and social services agencies. Robert Emery and Lisa Laumann-Billings (1998) speak for the vast majority of developmentalists in saying that cases of severe and repeated maltreatment may call for *coercive* interventions—prosecuting the abuser and removing the victim from an abusive home. The big challenge we face is to become more successful at preventing child maltreatment and controlling it early on so that the difficult decision whether to separate children from their parents can be made far less frequently than it is at present.

the family does not fulfill its important functions. Start with a neglected or physically abused infant who does not experience anything faintly resembling warm, sensitive, and responsive parenting. How is this child to form the secure attachments that serve as foundations for later social and intellectual competencies? Or think about the child whose parents are downright hostile—and who either provide no guidance at all or who hem the child in with rules and punish his every misstep. How is this child to learn how to care about other people, willingly comply with reasonable rules, become appropriately autonomous, and fit into society?

Regina Campos and her associates (Campos, Raffaelli, et al., 1994) have studied homeless street youths in Brazil whose families have failed them by neglecting, abusing, or otherwise dismissing them as unimportant. What were these homeless youngsters like? Compared to age-mates who worked on the streets but lived at home, youths "of the street" are faring very poorly. They struggle daily to survive, often begging, if necessary, to get by. What's more, they live in constant fear of being victimized and are themselves heavily involved in such antisocial behaviors as prostitution, drug abuse, thievery, and a host of other criminal activities (see also Whitbeck, Hoyt, & Bao, 2000). In short, these youngsters who have no family life are pursuing a highly atypical and deviant lifestyle that might seem to place them on the fast track to psychopathology, as we see in one 16-year-old's account of his daily routine:

> When you go to sleep it's about 5 in the morning; we wake up around 2 or 3 in the afternoon . . . get up, wash your face, if you have money you have breakfast [then] go out to steal, then you start to sell the stuff and the money all goes on drugs, because in the street it's all drugs! . . . Then, you get high, you're all set, then you come down and sleep (Campos, Raffaelli, et al., 1994, p. 322).

What happens to these homeless street youths when they grow up? Clearly, there is reason to suspect that their outcomes are likely to be grim, in view of the fact that 80 percent of the prison population of one major Brazilian city consisted of former street youth (Campos, Raffaelli, et al., 1994).

You get the picture. It is often easier to illustrate the grave importance of families by accentuating the negative. Fortunately, most of us have fared much better than this, even though we do not always acknowledge just how significant our families may have been in underwriting our developmental successes. So think about what you have learned in this chapter the next time you gather with the closest members of your own family. Chances are, you will understand why children and adults who are asked to reflect on what or whom is most important in their lives almost invariably speak of their families (Furman & Buhrmester, 1992; Whitbourne, 1986). Although we change and our families change as we get older, it seems that we never cease to affect, or to be affected by, those folks we call "family."

SUMMARY

UNDERSTANDING THE FAMILY

+ The **family** is the primary agent of **socialization**—the context in which children begin to acquire the beliefs, attitudes, values, and behaviors considered appropriate in their society.

+ Whether a **traditional nuclear family** or an **extended family**, families are best viewed as **social systems** in which each family member has **direct effects** and **indirect**, or **third party, effects** on all other family members. Children fare better when adult

members of the family can effectively **coparent**, mutually supporting each other's parenting efforts.

+ Families are also developing social systems embedded in community and cultural contexts that affect how family functions are carried out.

+ Social changes affecting family life today include greater numbers of single adults; later marriages; a decline in childbearing; more female participation in the work force; more divorces, **single parent families**, **blended** or **reconstituted families**, and multigenerational families; and greater numbers of families living in poverty.

PARENTAL SOCIALIZATION DURING CHILDHOOD AND ADOLESCENCE

✦ Parents differ along two broad childrearing dimensions—**acceptance/responsiveness** and **demandingness/control**—that, when considered together, yield four patterns of parenting. Generally speaking, accepting and demanding (or **authoritative**) parents who appeal to reason in order to enforce their demands tend to raise highly competent, well-adjusted children. Children of less accepting but highly demanding (or **authoritarian**) parents and accepting but undemanding (or **permissive**) parents display somewhat less favorable developmental outcomes, and children of unaccepting, unresponsive, and undemanding (or **uninvolved**) parents are often deficient in virtually all aspects of psychological functioning.

✦ Recent research on parental control clearly favors use of **behavioral control** (coupled with ample **autonomy support**) over **psychological control.**

✦ Developmentalists have traditionally assumed that parenting patterns determine developmental outcomes (**parent effects model**). Yet we know that children can influence parenting as well (**child effects model**) and that a complete account of family socialization recognizes reciprocal influences between parents and their children (**transactional model**).

✦ Parents from different cultures, subcultures, and social classes have different values, concerns, and outlooks on life that influence their child-rearing practices. Yet parents from all social backgrounds emphasize the characteristics that contribute to *success as they know it* in their own ecological niches, and it is inappropriate to conclude that one particular style of parenting is somehow "better" or more competent than all others.

✦ Parent/child relationships are renegotiated as adolescents begin to seek **autonomy.** Although family conflict escalates during this period, adolescents are likely to become appropriately autonomous if their parents willingly grant them more freedom, explain the rules and restrictions that they impose, rely more on behavioral control than on psychological control, and continue to be loving and supportive guides.

THE INFLUENCE OF SIBLINGS AND SIBLING RELATIONSHIPS

✦ **Sibling rivalry** is a normal aspect of family life that may begin as soon as a younger sibling arrives. Yet siblings are likely to get along and do many nice things for one another, particularly if parents get along, encourage their children to resolve conflicts amicably, and do not consistently favor one child more than the other(s).

✦ Siblings are typically viewed as intimate associates who can be counted on for support. Older sibs frequently serve as caregivers, security objects, models, and teachers for their younger siblings, and they often profit themselves from the instruction and guidance they provide. Yet sibling relationships are not essential for normal development; only children are just as socially, emotionally, and intellectually competent (or slightly more so), on average, than children with siblings are.

DIVERSITY IN FAMILY LIFE

✦ Infertile couples and single adults who desire to be parents often adopt to start a family. Although adoptees display more emotional and learning problems than biological children do, adoption is a highly satisfactory arrangement for the vast majority of adoptive parents and their children. Adopted children are often more satisfied with their family lives in open adoption systems that permit them to learn about their biological roots.

✦ Despite concerns raised about forming families in this way, children conceived through **donor insemination** are as well adjusted, on average, as children raised by two biological parents.

✦ Gay and lesbian parents are just as effective as heterosexual parents are. Their children tend to be well-adjusted and are overwhelmingly heterosexual in orientation.

✦ Divorce represents a major transition in family life that is stressful and unsettling for children and their parents. Children's initial reactions often include anger, fear, depression, and guilt—feelings that may last more than a year. The emotional upheaval that follows a divorce often influences the parent/child relationship. Children often become cranky, disobedient, or otherwise difficult, while the custodial parent may suddenly become more punitive and controlling. The stresses resulting from a divorce and this new coercive lifestyle often affect the child's peer relations and schoolwork. Visible signs of distress may be most apparent in younger children and those with difficult temperaments, and girls adjust better than boys to life in a single-parent, mother-headed home. Although some effects of divorce can be seen even after 10–20 years have elapsed, children of divorce are usually better adjusted than those who remain in conflict-ridden, two-parent families. Among the factors that help children to make positive adjustments to divorce are adequate financial and emotional support from the noncustodial parent, additional social support (from friends, relatives, and the community) for custodial parents and their children, and a minimum of additional stressors surrounding the divorce itself.

✦ Forming a family after a single parent remarries (or cohabits) is often a stressful transition for all family members. Initially, boys adjust better than girls to having a stepparent, and younger children and older adolescents adjust better than early adolescents do. Adjustment outcomes are better in **simple stepparent homes** than in **complex stepparent homes.** Although the incidence of antisocial conduct is higher in reconstructed families, the vast majority of children and adolescents successfully negotiate this family transition, displaying no psychopathological tendencies.

✦ Maternal employment is often associated with such favorable child outcomes as self-reliance, sociability, competent intellectual and academic performances, and less stereotyped views of men and women, particularly when a mother's work induces warm, supportive fathers to become more involved in their children's lives. Yet child outcomes are much less favorable if mothers work variable shifts and irregular hours at low-paying jobs or otherwise suffer work-related stress that spill over to the home setting and compromise the quality of their parenting. One of the strongest supports that working parents could hope for is stimulating day care for their children, a support system that is woefully inadequate in the United States compared with that provided by many other Western industrialized nations. Large numbers of American grade-school children whose mothers work must care for themselves after school. When monitored from a distance by authoritative parents, these **self-care (or latchkey) children** fare well. After-school day-care programs are becoming more common in the United States, and well-managed ones that offer children meaningful activities can help to optimize developmental outcomes and lessen the chances that children of working mothers will engage in antisocial conduct.

WHEN PARENTING BREAKS DOWN: THE PROBLEM OF CHILD ABUSE

+ **Child abuse** is related to conditions within the family, the community, and the larger culture. Abusers come from all social strata and walks of life, although many of them are young, highly stressed caregivers who favor coercive forms of discipline, feel victimized by their children and powerless to control them, and were themselves abused as children. Highly impulsive children and those who are irritable, emotionally unresponsive, or ill are more vulnerable to abuse than healthy, even-tempered children who are easy to care for. The incidence of child abuse is higher when stressed caregivers are living in **high-risk neighborhoods** where they are isolated from sources of social support, and when the broader culture approves of physical punishment and use of force as a means of resolving conflicts. The long term consequences of abuse can be severe and long lasting. Programs designed to assist abused children and their abusive parents have achieved some noteworthy success. However, we are still a long way from solving the problem.

CHAPTER 12

Extrafamilial Influences I: Television, Computers, and Schooling

In CHAPTER 11, WE CONSIDERED the family a socializing agent, looking at the ways that parents and siblings affect developing children. Although families have an enormous impact on their young, it is only a matter of time before other societal institutions begin to exert their influence. For example, infants, toddlers, and preschool children are often exposed to alternative caregivers and a host of new playmates when their working parents place them in day care or preschool classes. Yet even those toddlers who remain at home soon begin to learn about a world beyond the family once they develop an interest in television. And by age 5 to 6, virtually all children in Western societies are going to elementary school, a setting that requires them to interact with other little people who are similar to themselves and to adjust to rules and practices that may be very dissimilar to those they follow at home.

So as they mature, children are becoming increasingly familiar with the outside world and spend much less time under the watchful eyes of their parents. How do these experiences affect their lives? The next two chapters explore this issue as we consider the impacts of four **extrafamilial influences** on development: television, computers, and the schools (in this chapter) and the society of one's peers (in Chapter 13).

extrafamilial influences
social agencies other than the family that influence a child's or an adolescent's cognitive, social, and emotional development.

🔁 THE EARLY WINDOW: EFFECTS OF TELEVISION ON CHILDREN AND ADOLESCENTS

It seems almost incomprehensible that the average American of only 60 years ago had never seen a television. Now more than 98 percent of American homes have one or more TV sets, and children between the ages of 3 and 11 watch an average of three to four hours of TV a day (Bianchi & Robinson, 1997; Huston et al., 1992; Roberts, Foehr, & Rideout, 1999, 2005). As we see in Figure 12.1, TV viewing begins in infancy, increases until about age 11, and then declines somewhat during adolescence—a trend that holds in Australia, Canada, Japan, Korea, and several European countries, as well as in the United States (Larson & Verma, 1999). By age 18, a child born today will have spent more time watching television—about 20,000 hours, or two full years—than in any other single activity except sleeping (Kail & Cavanaugh, 2007; Liebert & Sprafkin, 1988). Boys watch more TV than girls do, and ethnic minority children living in poverty are especially likely to be heavy viewers (Huston et al., 1999). Is all this time in front of the tube damaging to children's cognitive, social, and emotional development, as many critics have feared? Let's explore this issue by first considering what effects television might have on children's lifestyles.

Figure 12.1
Average number of hours per day that American children and adolescents spent watching television in 1987. (From Robert M. Liebert and Joyce Sprafkin, The early window: Effects of television on children and youth. 1988. Published by Allyn & Bacon: Boston, MA.) Copyright © 1988 by Pearson Education. Reprinted by permission of the publisher.

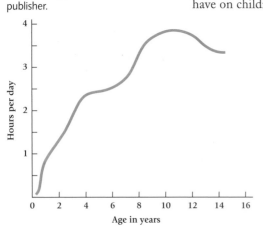

Television and Children's Lifestyles

Has television changed children's lifestyles and the character of family life? In some ways it has. One early survey found that a majority of families altered their sleeping patterns and mealtimes once they had purchased a television (Johnson, 1967). The presence of a TV at home also had the effect of decreasing the amount of time that parents spend with their youngsters in non-TV-related leisure activities such as games and family outings, and most parents at least occasionally used television as an "electronic babysitter." Although family members may spend many hours in close proximity as they watch television together, many critics believe that this form of family interaction is not very meaningful for the younger set—particularly if they are told to sit still or keep their mouths shut until the commercials come on. Urie Bronfenbrenner (1970b) has argued:

> The primary danger of . . . television . . . lies not so much in the behavior it produces—although there is danger there—as in the behavior that it prevents: the talks, games, the family festivities and arguments through which much of the child's learning takes place and through which his character is formed. Turning on the television can turn off the process that transforms children into people.

So is TV viewing as harmful to family life and social development as the early critics maintained? One way to assess the global impact of television is to see whether children who have access to the medium differ systematically from those who live in remote areas not served by television. And one such study of Canadian children gave some cause for concern. Prior to the introduction of television to the isolated town, "Notel," children living there tested higher in creativity and reading proficiency than did age-mates in comparable Canadian towns served by television. Yet, two to four years after television was introduced, the children of Notel showed declines in their reading skills and creativity (to levels shown by peers in other towns), less community involvement, and dramatic increases in aggression and gender stereotyping (Corteen & Williams, 1986; Harrison & Williams, 1986).

Although sobering, these findings may be somewhat misleading. Other investigators report that the biggest impact of the coming of television is to persuade children to substitute TV watching for such other leisure activities as listening to the radio, reading comics, or going to movies (Huston & Wright, 1998; Liebert & Sprafkin, 1988). What's more, there are seasonal variations: Children watch more television in the winter months when the weather is bad and they have nothing better to do (McHale, Crouter, & Tucker, 2001). And as long as TV viewing is not excessive, children and adolescents exposed to the medium show no significant cognitive or academic deficiencies, and spend no less time playing or socializing with peers (Huston et al., 1999; Liebert & Sprafkin, 1988). In fact, one review of the literature reveals that children may actually learn a great deal of useful information from television, particularly educational programming (Anderson et al., 2001).

So in moderate doses, television neither deadens young minds nor impairs children's social development. Yet we will see that this medium does have the potential to do good or harm, depending on *what* children are watching and their ability to understand and interpret what they have seen.

Development of Television Literacy

Television literacy refers to one's ability to understand how information is conveyed on the small screen. It involves the ability to process program content to construct a story line from characters' activities and the sequencing of scenes. It also involves an ability to interpret the *form* of the message—production features such as zooms, fade-outs, split-screens, and sound effects that are often essential to understanding a program's content.

Interestingly, 2-year-olds show a "video deficit": That is, they learn less from models on TV than they do from face-to-face interactions with another person (Anderson & Pempek, 2005; Troseth, Saylor, & Archer, 2006). Why? Probably because video models are not contingently responsive to their audience, and young children thus consider them as less viable sources of information (Troseth, Saylor, & Archer, 2006). Nevertheless, television programming often captures younger audiences, who are potentially influenced in many ways by their interpretations of what they see.

Before age 8 or 9, children process program content in a piecemeal fashion. They are likely to be captivated by zooms, fast-paced action, loud music, and children's (or cartoon

television literacy
one's ability to understand how information is conveyed in television programing and to interpret this information properly.

characters') voices, and will often direct their attention elsewhere during slower scenes that feature adult males or quiet dialogue (Schmitt, Anderson, & Collins, 1999). Consequently, preschool children are often unable to construct a causal chain of events leading from the beginning to the end of a story. Even 6-year-olds have trouble recalling a coherent story line due in part to their tendency to remember the *actions* that characters perform rather than the motives or goals that characters pursue and the events that shaped these goals (McKenna & Ossoff, 1998; van den Broek, Lorch, & Thurlow, 1996). Furthermore, children younger than 7 do not fully grasp the fictional nature of television programming, often thinking that characters retain their roles (and scripted characteristics) in real life (Wright et al., 1994). And even though 8-year-olds may know that TV programming is fiction, they may still view it as an *accurate* portrayal of everyday events (Wright et al., 1995).

Comprehension of TV programming increases sharply from middle childhood throughout adolescence. Experience watching TV helps children to properly interpret the zooms, fade-outs, musical scores, and other production features that help viewers to infer characters' motives and to connect nonadjacent scenes. Furthermore, older children and adolescents are increasingly able to draw accurate inferences about scenes that are widely separated in time (van den Broek, 1997). So if a character were to act nice and gain someone's trust in order to dupe him later, a 10-year-old would eventually recognize the character's deceptive intent and evaluate him negatively. By contrast, a 6-year-old, who focuses more on concrete behaviors than on subtle intentions, will often brand this con artist as a "nice guy" and is likely to evaluate his later self-serving acts much more positively (van den Broek et. al., 1996).

Does their strong focus on actions and general lack of television literacy increase the likelihood that younger children will imitate the particularly vivid behaviors that TV characters display? Yes, indeed, and whether these imitations are beneficial or harmful depends very critically on *what* children happen to be watching.

Televised Violence and Children's Aggression

As early as 1954, complaints raised by parents, teachers, and experts in child development prompted Senator Estes Kefauver, then chairman of the Senate Subcommittee on Juvenile Delinquency, to question the need for violence in television programming. Yet more than 40 years later, the National Television Violence Study, a two—year survey of the frequency, nature, and context of TV violence, revealed that American television programming remains incredibly violent (Mediascope, 1996; Seppa, 1997). Fifty-eight percent of programs broadcast between 6 A.M. and 11 P.M. contained *repeated* acts of overt aggression, and 73 percent contained violence in which the perpetrator neither displayed any remorse nor received any penalty or criticism. In fact, the most violent TV programs are those intended for children, especially cartoons, and nearly 40 percent of the violence on TV is initiated by such heroes as *The Mighty Morphin Power Rangers* or other characters portrayed as attractive role models for children (Seppa, 1997). Furthermore, nearly two-thirds of the violent incidents in children's programming are couched in humor.

Theoretical Perspectives on Media Violence Does a heavy exposure to media violence encourage spectators to behave aggressively or to partake in other kinds of antisocial conduct? Proponents of the *catharsis hypothesis* say no. In fact, Seymour Feshbach (1970) argued that people may often experience *catharsis* (that is, a draining away of aggressive energy) by merely thinking aggressive thoughts (fantasy aggression). If this is the case, exposure to televised violence should *reduce* aggressive impulses by providing fantasy material that viewers can use for cathartic purposes.

By contrast, proponents of social-learning and social information-processing theories (for example, Anderson et al., 2003; Bandura, 1973) offer several reasons for hypothesizing that media violence might *promote* aggressive or antisocial inclinations:

- Actors portraying violence on television serve as *aggressive models* who teach children harmful actions that they may not know about or would not have thought of performing. Here is one example:

  In Los Angeles, a housemaid caught a 7-year-old boy in the act of sprinkling ground glass into a family's lamb stew. There was no malice behind the act. It was purely experimental, having been inspired by curiosity to learn whether it would really work as well as it did on television. (Liebert & Sprafkin, 1988, p. 9)

- Viewing violent action television may increase the cognitive accessibility of the viewer's own aggressive thoughts and feelings, and this aggressive mindset may increase the likelihood that he or she will interpret ambiguous events as involving aggressive intent and respond accordingly.

- Media violence is exciting, creating physiological arousal that might be interpreted as anger and thereby promote aggressive behavior should a viewer soon experience a mild provocation (for example, teasing) or some other unpleasant social event.

- Frequent and long-term exposure to media violence may eventually desensitize viewers to violence; that is, they may gradually become less aroused by the violence they witness and even begin to view aggression and violence as normative, which can make violent thoughts and behavior more likely.

So here are two theories that make opposing predictions about the likely impacts of exposure to TV violence. Which is the more reasonable? Researchers have attempted to answer this question by conducting three kinds of research: laboratory experiments, field experiments, and correlational surveys.

Results of Laboratory Experiments   One method of assessing whether televised violence really can instigate (or reduce) aggression is to expose children to violent programming and then give them an opportunity to commit aggressive acts. By 1972, 18 such laboratory experiments had been conducted, and 16 of them found that children became more aggressive after watching violent sequences on television (Liebert & Baron, 1972).

Despite the consistency of this early experimental research, the laboratory findings have been criticized as highly artificial viewing experiences in which children are encouraged to give their *undivided attention* to program clips that have been edited to pack them with violent incidents, followed immediately by a tailor-made opportunity for children to behave aggressively in an atypical laboratory setting. Is it possible that the instigating effects of TV violence are extremely short-lived and thus are a problem only in a laboratory setting where subjects are "encouraged" to be aggressive by the requirements of the task they face soon after observing unusually violent programming? Certainly not, for as Box 12.1 illustrates, boys who watch an unedited and highly violent program *designed for children* do subsequently become more aggressively inclined when interacting with peers in their natural environment.

Results of Field Experiments   The field experiment would seem to be an excellent method of assessing the impact of televised violence on spectators' behavior because it combines the naturalistic approach of a correlational survey with the more rigorous control of an experiment. In other words, well-conducted field experiments can determine whether real-life exposure to violent television increases the incidence of aggressive behavior in natural settings.

Do the *Mighty Morphin Power Rangers* Promote Children's Aggression?

In recent years, one of the most popular and most violent TV shows for children was *The Mighty Morphin Power Rangers*—a program that aired five to six times a week in many markets and contained in excess of 200 violent acts per hour. The Power Rangers are a racially diverse group of adolescents who are ordered by Zordon, their elderly leader, to transform, or "morph," into superheroes to battle monsters sent to Earth by an evil Asian woman bent on taking control of the planet. Violence occurs not only in battles between the forces of good and evil but in non-battle scenes in which the adolescent heroes practice martial arts on each other. According to the National Coalition on Television Violence, *Power Rangers* is the most violent TV program for children that it has ever studied (Kiesewetter, 1993)—and most of its violence is *hostile,* being intended to harm or kill another character. Do *unedited* versions of this immensely popular program increase the likelihood of aggression among its young viewers as they play in their *natural* environment?

Chris Boyatzis and associates (1995) sought to answer this question in an interesting experiment with 5- to 7-year-olds. Half of the children in this study had been randomly assigned to watch a randomly selected, unedited episode of *The Mighty Morphin Power Rangers* at school, whereas the remaining children in a control group engaged in other activities and did not view the program. After the program had been shown, children in the experimental group were each observed for a set length of time as they played in their classrooms, and instances of aggressive behavior (for example, physical and verbal aggression, taking objects by force) were recorded. Their behavior was then compared to that of children in the control group, who had not viewed the program.

The dramatic results appear in the accompanying figure. Notice that watching *Power Rangers* had no effect on the girls, probably because the majority of the Rangers are boys, and young boys may have identified more strongly with the Rangers than young girls did. However, we see that boys who had watched the show committed seven times the number of aggressive acts during free play as their male counterparts who had not watched this episode.

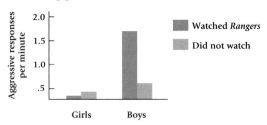

Average number of aggressive responses per minute in the free play of girls and boys who either had or had not watched an episode of *The Mighty Morphin Power Rangers.* (Adapted from Boyatzis, Matillo, & Nesbitt, 1995.)

Here, then, is dramatic evidence that exposure to an *unedited* and *randomly selected* episode of a violent children's show featuring male characters dramatically increases the likelihood of aggression among young male playmates in the *natural environment.* Furthermore, it is worth emphasizing that the boys who became more aggressive had been *randomly assigned* to watch *Power Rangers* and were not merely the most aggressive boys in their classes. Later research suggests that a lack of TV literacy may have contributed strongly to these results, for children younger than 8 or 9 tend not to recall any prosocial causes the Power Rangers are pursuing and usually say "the fights" when asked what they do remember (McKenna & Ossoff, 1998). Clearly, the Boyatzis, Matillo, and Nesbitt (1995) experiment may have somewhat over-dramatized the impact of *Power Rangers* on young boys by observing their play *immediately* after they viewed the show. Nevertheless, the results certainly imply that *repeated exposure* of young, non-TV-literate audiences to this popular and highly accessible program can and probably does increase the frequency of aggressive peer interactions in the natural environment and may lead children (particularly boys) to favor aggressive solutions to conflict as well.

An Experiment with Preschool Children In one well-known field experiment, Lynette Friedrich and Aletha Stein (1973; Stein & Friedrich, 1972) carefully observed a sample of nursery-school children to establish a baseline level of aggression for each child. Then, for the next month at school, children were exposed daily to either a violent TV show (for example, *Batman* or *Superman*) or to a nonviolent program (for example, *Mr. Rogers' Neighborhood*). Following these month-long television diets, the children were observed daily for two additional weeks to measure the effects of the programming. The results were clear: Children who had watched violent programming were subsequently more aggressive in their interactions with nursery-school classmates than were those who had watched nonviolent programming. Although the impact of violent programming was statistically significant only for those youngsters who were above average in aggression on the initial baseline measure, these "initially aggressive" children were by no means extreme or deviant. They simply represented the more aggressive members of a normal nursery-school peer group. Stein and Friedrich remind us that "these effects occurred in [a naturalistic context] that was removed both in time and environmental setting from the viewing experience.

They occurred with a small amount of exposure . . . and they endured during the post viewing period" (1972, p. 247).

An Experiment with Adolescents   Earlier in Box 1.2 (on page 14), we discussed a similar field experiment conducted with Belgian delinquents. Recall that for a period of one week, half of these delinquent inmates saw a different violent movie (for example, *Bonnie & Clyde, The Dirty Dozen*) each evening, whereas the other half watched relatively nonviolent movies (for example, *Lily, La Belle Americane*). Compared to their baseline levels of aggression, inmates who watched violent movies became more physically aggressive, whereas those who watched nonviolent movies did not (Leyens et al., 1975). And in agreement with the Friedrich and Stein (1973) experiment, violent movies promoted larger increases in aggression among inmates who were already relatively high in aggression before the movies were shown.

Despite these and other demonstrations, critics have argued that the results, though usually in the anticipated direction, are very weak in many field experiments (Geen, 1998), and the strongest effects often come from "captive" audiences in correctional institutions—precisely the populations that one might expect to be more heavily influenced by programming advocating and displaying violence (Freedman, 1984). Yet one might anticipate less dramatic results in "non-captive" audiences, whatever their background, simply because it is not always possible to control precisely what they watch. Researchers in the Friedrich and Stein (1973) experiment, for example, could specify what nursery-school children watched at school but not what they watched at home. Their results could well have been even stronger had they had more precise control over the home viewing practices of the children they studied.

Results of Correlational Studies
A positive relationship between exposure to TV violence and aggressive behavior in naturalistic settings has been documented over and over with preschool, grade-school, high school, and adult participants in the United States and with grade-school boys and girls in Australia, Canada, Finland, Great Britain, Israel, and Poland (Bushman & Huesmann, 2001; Geen, 1998). These simple relations are, of course, correlational data which establish only that exposure to televised violence *might be* implicated in promoting aggression.

However, *longitudinal* correlational studies are more revealing. Recently, Rowell Huesmann and his associates (2003) reported a study of 329 individuals followed longitudinally for 15 years, from elementary school to their early 20s. Data collected included the amount of TV violence these individuals had observed as children and as young adults, their interpretations of this violence, their levels of aggression both as children and as adults, and a host of other information, including family socioeconomic status and parents' child-rearing practices.

The results were most interesting. Even after controlling for children's aggressiveness in grade school, socioeconomic status, and parental child-rearing practices, both boys and girls who had watched more TV violence in grade school were subsequently more aggressive 15 years later as young adults (see Figure 12.1, panel A) Interestingly, however, aggressiveness in childhood was only weakly related to adults' preference for violent television, thus implying that early exposure to TV violence is more closely linked to later aggression than early aggression is to later viewing habits. Heavy childhood exposure to TV violence was most closely related to physical aggression for adult males but related to both physical and relational aggression for adult females.

And there is more. As we see in Figure 12.2, children who interpreted TV violence as real (that is, an accurate depiction of everyday life; see panel B) and those who identified more strongly with same-sex perpetrators of aggression (panel C) were the individuals who were most heavily influenced by their exposure to TV violence. Clearly, this is a correlational study that, despite its many controls, cannot definitively demonstrate causality; but its results are quite consistent with the argument that early exposure to a

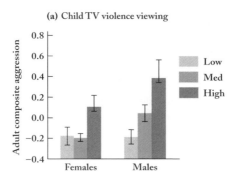

(a) Child TV violence viewing

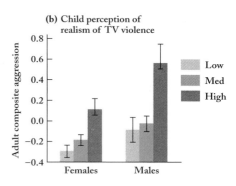

(b) Child perception of realism of TV violence

(c) Child identification with same-sex aggressive TV character

Figure 12.2   Relations between viewing TV violence in childhood and adult aggression (Panel a), adult aggression as a function of childhood perceptions of the realism of TV violence (Panel b), and adult aggression as a function of one's identification in childhood with same-sex aggressive TV characters (Panel c). (Huesmann, L. R., Moise-Titus, J., Podolski, C., & Eron, L. D. 2003. Longitudinal relations between children's exposure to TV violence and their aggressive and violent behavior in young adulthood: 1977–1992. Developmental Psychology, 39, p. 211.) © 2003 by the American Psychological Assn. Reprinted by permission.

mean-world belief
a belief, fostered by televised violence, that the world is a more dangerous and frightening place than is actually the case.

desensitization hypothesis
the notion that people who watch a lot of media violence will become less aroused by aggression and more tolerant of violent and aggressive acts.

Photo 12.1
Heavy exposure to media violence may blunt children's emotional reactions to real-life aggression and convince them that the world is a violent place populated mainly by hostile and aggressive people.

heavy diet of televised violence can lead to the development of hostile, antisocial attitudes and behaviors that persist over time.

Televised Violence as a Desensitizing Agent   Even if young viewers do not act out the aggression they observe on television, they may be influenced by it nonetheless. For example, a steady diet of televised violence can instill **mean-world beliefs**—a tendency to view the world as a violent place inhabited by people who typically rely on aggressive solutions to their interpersonal problems (Comstock, 1993; Slaby et al., 1995). In fact, 7- to 9-year-olds who show the strongest preferences for violent television are the ones most likely to believe that violent shows are an accurate portrayal of everyday life (Huesmann et al., 2003).

In a similar vein, prolonged exposure to televised violence can *desensitize* children—that is, make them less emotionally upset by violent acts and more willing to tolerate them in real life. Margaret Thomas and her colleagues (1977; Drabman & Thomas, 1974) tested this **desensitization hypothesis** with 8- to 10-year-olds. Participants watched either a violent detective show or a nonviolent but exciting sporting event while hooked up to a physiograph that recorded their emotional reactions. Then each participant was told to watch over two kindergartners, visible in the next room on a TV monitor, and to come to get the experimenter should *anything* go wrong. A prepared film then showed the two kindergartners getting into an intense battle that escalated until the video went dead. Participants who had earlier watched the violent program were now less physiologically aroused by the fight they observed and were more inclined to tolerate it (by being much slower to intervene) than their counterparts who had watched an equally arousing but nonviolent sporting event. Apparently, TV violence can desensitize viewers to real-world instances of aggression (see also Huesmann et al., 2003).

What Can We Conclude about Exposure to TV Violence   So does exposure to violent TV fare instigate aggression and cultivate aggressive and antisocial tendencies in children and adolescents? It certainly seems that way. Few social-developmentalists today would blame all our social ills on the fact that our violent and antisocial adults may have watched *Batman* or the *Rambo* movies as youth or would claim that heavy exposure to media violence, by itself, will transform an otherwise well-adjusted viewer into a violent sociopath. Nevertheless, investigators who have carefully conducted large-scale reviews of the correlational, experimental, and field experimental literatures—three approaches to the question that have different strengths that largely offset the other methods' weaknesses—note that the data *converge* on the conclusions that the aggression-instigating effects of TV violence are (1) observed among *both* boys and girls, (2) strongest when the violence appears justified, and (3) sufficiently powerful to desensitize viewers to aggression, create mean-world beliefs, and cultivate aggressive habits and antisocial behavior among heavy viewers (see Anderson et al., 2003; Bushman & Huesmann, 2001; Geen, 1998; Hearold, 1986). Of course we should heed the cautions expressed by these researchers, who have stressed that televised violence is only one of many contributors to children's hostile, antisocial conduct and may be nowhere near as strong a contributor as growing up in a coercive home environment or identifying with deviant and antisocial peers (Geen, 1998; Huesmann et al., 2003). However, it is difficult to argue that a heavy exposure to TV violence has salutary long-term effects on anyone, and its capacity to do harm is substantial (Anderson et al., 2003). Finally, let's note that there is virtually no support for the notion that exposure to media violence leads to a reduction of viewers' aggressive impulses through catharsis.

Other Potentially Undesirable Effects of Television

Aside from its potential for instigating aggressive behavior and cultivating hostile, antisocial attitudes, there are several other undesirable consequences that TV viewing might have for young viewers. Let's briefly consider three such influences.

Television as a Source of Social Stereotypes   Another unfortunate effect that television may have on children is to reinforce a variety of potentially harmful social stereotypes (Huston et al., 1992). In Chapter 8, for example, we noted gender-role stereotyping is common on television and that children who watch a lot of commercial TV are likely to hold more traditional views of men and women than their classmates who watch little television. Unfortunately, the ways in which men and women are portrayed on television can have very real implications for viewers' self-concepts and self-esteem. Consider, for example, that TV programming in Western societies often reinforces the notion that girls and women must be thin to be considered attractive (the *thin ideal*). One recent longitudinal study in Australia found that even 5- to 8-year-old girls are acquiring this thin ideal, and that those who often watched appearance-oriented TV programs such as *Friends* or *Rage* subsequently became more dissatisfied with their own appearance (a primary contributor to declining self-esteem later in adolescence), compared to age-mates who watched such shows less often (Dohnt & Tiggemann, 2006). If television consistently reinforces a thin ideal that few girls and woman can achieve, is it any wonder that adolescents, ready to try an endless number of diets, may, in many cases, become susceptible to such potential life-threatening eating disorders, as *anorexia nervosa* and *bulimia*.[1]

Stereotyped views of minorities are also common on television. Largely due to the influence of the civil rights movement, African Americans now appear on television in a much wider range of occupations, and their numbers equal or exceed their proportion in the population. However, Latinos and other ethnic minorities remain underrepresented. And when non-black minorities do appear, they are usually portrayed in an unfavorable light, often cast as villains or victims (Liebert & Sprafkin, 1988; Staples, 2000).

Although the evidence is limited, it seems that children's ethnic and racial attitudes are influenced by televised portrayals of minority groups. Earlier depictions of African Americans as comical, inept, or lazy led to negative racial attitudes (Graves, 1975; Liebert & Sprafkin, 1988), whereas positive portrayals of minorities in cartoons and on such educational programs as *Sesame Street* appear to reduce children's racial and ethnic stereotypes and increase their likelihood of having ethnically diverse friends (Graves, 1993; Gorn, Goldberg, & Kanungo, 1976). Apparently television has the power to bring people of different racial and ethnic backgrounds closer together—or to drive them further apart—depending on the ways in which these social groups are depicted on the small screen.

Children's Reactions to Commercial Messages   In the United States, the average child is exposed to nearly 20,000 television commercials each year—many of which extol the virtues of toys, fast foods, and sugary treats that adults may not wish to purchase. Nevertheless, young children continue to ask for products that they have seen on television, and conflicts often ensue when parents refuse to honor their requests (Atkin, 1978; Kunkel & Roberts, 1991). Young children may be so persistent because they rarely understand the manipulative (selling) intent of ads, often treating them like public service announcements that are intended to be helpful and informative (Liebert & Sprafkin, 1988; Linn, 2004). By age 8–11, most children realize that ads are designed to persuade and sell, and by 13–14, they will have acquired a healthy skepticism about advertising and product claims (Linn, 2005). Nevertheless, even adolescents are often persuaded by the ads they see, particularly if the product endorser is a celebrity or the appeals are deceptive and misleading (Cialdini, 2001; Huston et al., 1992).

Is it any wonder, then, that many parents are concerned about the impact of commercials on their children? Not only do children's ads often push products that are unsafe or of poor nutritional value, but the many ads for over-the-counter drugs and glamorous depictions of alcohol use could cause children to underestimate the consequences of such risky behaviors as drinking, self-medication, and drug use (Tinsley, 1992). The National Foundation to Improve Television—an organization of parents that works to improve programming for children—considers the potentially harmful influence of TV commercials to be an even greater problem than televised violence!

Television Viewing and Children's Health   Heavy TV viewing can also contribute in subtle ways to undermining children's health and well-being. You have probably been exposed to one (or more) of the many recent reports that the American public is becoming **obese**—a medical term that is applied to people who are 20 percent or more over their ideal weight for their height, age, and sex. Obesity is clearly a threat to physical health—having been implicated as a major contributor to heart disease, high blood pressure, and diabetes—and rates of obesity have been increasing dramatically among all age groups, especially young children (Krishnamoorthy, Hart, & Jelalian, 2006). There are many contributors to

Obesity
a medical term describing individuals who are at least 20 percent above the ideal weight for their height, age, and sex.

---

[1]Anorexia nervosa is a life-threatening eating disorder characterized by self-starvation and a compulsive fear of getting fat. Bulimia is another potentially fatal eating disorder characterized by recurrent eating binges followed by such purging activities as heavy use of laxatives or vomiting. For further discussion of these disorders, see Shaffer & Kipp (2007).

obesity, with hereditary predispositions and poor eating habits being most heavily cited. However, it is also true that many people are obese because they do not get sufficient exercise to burn the calories they've consumed (Cowley, 2001).

Unfortunately, television viewing is an inherently sedentary activity that is less likely to help children burn excess calories than physically active play or even performing household chores. Interestingly, one of the strongest predictors of *future* obesity is the amount of time children spend watching television (Anderson et al., 2001; Cowley, 2001), with young couch potatoes who watch more than five hours a day being most at risk of actually coming to resemble a potato (Gortmaker et al., 1996). Aside from restricting children's physical activity, television viewing also promotes poor eating habits. Not only do children tend to snack while passively watching TV, but the foods they see advertised (and may be snacking on) are mostly high-calorie products containing lots of fat and sugar and few beneficial nutrients (Tinsley, 1992).

Reducing the Harmful Effects of Television Exposure How might concerned parents limit the potentially harmful consequences of watching commercial television? Table 12.1 lists several

Table 12.1 Strategies for Regulating the Effects of TV on Children's Development

Goal	Strategies
Reduce the amount of TV viewing	Work together to keep a time chart of your child's activities, including TV viewing, homework, and play with friends. Then, discuss what you believe to be a balanced set of activities.
	Set a weekly viewing limit. Rule out TV at certain times (before breakfast or on school nights).
	Don't locate a television set in your child's room.
	Remember that if you watch a lot of TV, chances are your child will also.
Limit the effects of violent TV	Judge the amount of violence in the shows your children view by watching several episodes.
	View TV together and discuss the violence with your child. Talk about why the violence happened and how painful it is. Ask the child how conflicts can be solved without violence.
	Explain to your child how violence on an entertainment program is "faked."
	Restrict violent videos.
	Encourage your child to watch programs with characters that cooperate, help, and care for each other. These programs have been shown to have a positive influence on children.
Counteract negative values portrayed on TV	Ask your child to compare what is shown on the screen with real life.
	Discuss with your child what is real and what is make-believe on TV.
	Explain to your child the values you hold about sex, alcohol, and drugs.
	If you own a VCR or DVD player, begin a selective video library specifically for children.
	Before subscribing to cable television, be aware of the variety and types of programming seen on it. Many of these easily accessed channels are for adult viewing only. Ask for a parental "lockout" device from the cable company what will allow you to select channels for your child.
Deal with the effects of TV advertising	Tell your child that advertising is used to sell products to as many viewers as possible.
	Put advertising disclaimers into words children understand.
	On shopping trips, let your child see that advertising claims are often exaggerated. Toys that look big, fast, and exciting on TV may be disappointingly small, slow, and unexciting close up.

Source: Adapted from Murray, J. P., & Lonnborg, B. (2005). *Children and television: Using TV sensibly*. Kansas State University Agricultural Experiment Station and Cooperative Extension Service.

effective strategies recommended by experts, including monitoring of children's home viewing habits to limit their exposure to highly violent or otherwise offensive fare while trying to interest them in programs with prosocial or educational themes. Information about programs that experts consider inappropriate for children can be obtained from The National Foundation to Improve Television, 60 State Street, Boston, MA 02109 (phone: [617] 523-6353).

Although each of the guidelines in Table 12.1 is excellent, a couple of comments are in order. First, the effectiveness of lockout provisions to control what the TV can broadcast was weakened from the start. Producers of violent programming managed to ensure that the content-based rating system for television programming merely reflects age-guideline ratings rather than a more detailed system that would allow parents to make lockout decisions based on a program's sexual or violent content (Huesmann et al., 2003). And unfortunately, recent voluntary content guidelines that have arisen are not used by all networks and are poorly understood by parents (Bushman & Cantor, 2003).

Second, the suggestion that parents help their young non-TV-literate viewers to evaluate what they are watching is particularly important. One reason that younger children are so responsive to aggressive models on TV is that they don't always interpret the violence they see in the same way adults do, often missing subtleties such as an aggressor's antisocial motives and intentions or the unpleasant consequences that perpetrators may suffer as a result of their aggressive acts (Collins, Sobol, & Westby, 1981; Slaby et al., 1995). What's more, young children's tendency to strongly *identify* with aggressive heroes whose violence is socially reinforced makes them even more susceptible to the instigating effects of TV violence—a fact that parents need to know (Huesmann et al., 2003). When adults highlight the information children miss, while strongly disapproving of a perpetrator's conduct, young viewers gain a much better understanding of media violence and are less affected by what they have seen—particularly if the adult commentator also suggests how these perpetrators (or violent heros) might have approached their problems in a more constructive way (Collins, 1983; Liebert & Sprafkin, 1988). Unfortunately, this may be an underutilized strategy, for as Michele St. Peters and her associates (1991) have noted, parent/child co-viewing at home most often occurs *not* during action/adventure shows or other highly violent fare, but during the evening news, sporting events, or prime-time dramas—programming that is not particularly captivating for young children.

Television as an Educational Tool

Thus far, we've cast a wary eye at television, talking mostly about its capacity to do harm. Yet this "early window" could become a most effective way of teaching a number of valuable lessons if only its content were altered to convey such information. Let's examine some of the evidence to support this claim.

Educational Television and Children's Prosocial Behavior   Many TV programs— especially offerings such as *Sesame Street* and *Mister Rogers' Neighborhood*, broadcast on public television—are designed in part to illustrate the benefits of such prosocial activities as cooperation, sharing, and comforting distressed companions. Available research reveals that young children who often watch prosocial programming do become more prosocially inclined (Calvert & Kotler, 2003; Hearold, 1986). However, it is important to emphasize that these programs may have few if any lasting benefits unless an adult monitors the broadcasts and encourages children to rehearse and enact the prosocial lessons they have learned (Friedrich & Stein, 1975; Friedrich-Cofer et al., 1979). Furthermore, young children are more likely to process and enact any prosocial lessons that are broadcast when the programming is free of violent acts that will otherwise compete for their attention. But despite these important qualifications, it seems that the positive effects of prosocial programming greatly outweigh the negatives and that prosocial television actually promotes prosocial behavior to a greater extent than violent television promotes aggression, especially if adults encourage children to pay close attention to episodes that emphasize constructive methods of resolving interpersonal conflicts (Hearold, 1986).

Television as a Contributor to Early Learning and Cognitive Development   In 1968, the U. S. government and a number of private foundations provided funds to create Children's Television Workshop (CTW), an organization committed to producing TV programs that would hold children's interest and promote their intellectual development. CTW's first production, *Sesame Street*, became the world's most popular children's series—seen an average of three times a week by about half of America's preschool children and broadcast to nearly 50 other countries around the world (Liebert & Sprafkin, 1988). Targeted at 3- to 5-year olds, *Sesame Street* attempts to foster important cognitive skills such as counting, recognizing and discriminating numbers and letters, ordering and classifying objects, and solving simple problems. It was hoped that children from disadvantaged backgrounds would be much better prepared for school after viewing this programming on a regular basis.

Evaluating **Sesame Street**   During the first season that *Sesame Street* was broadcast, its impact was assessed by the Educational Testing Service. About 950 3- to 5-year-olds from five areas of the United States took a pretest that measured their cognitive skills and determined what they knew about letters, numbers, and geometric forms. At the end of the season, they took this test again to see what they had learned.

When the data were analyzed, it was clear that *Sesame Street* was achieving its objectives. As shown in Figure 12.3, children who watched *Sesame Street* the most (groups Q3 and Q4, who watched four or more times a week) were the ones who showed the biggest improvements in their total test scores (panel A), their scores on the alphabet test (panel B), and their ability to write their names (panel C). Three-year-olds posted bigger gains than the

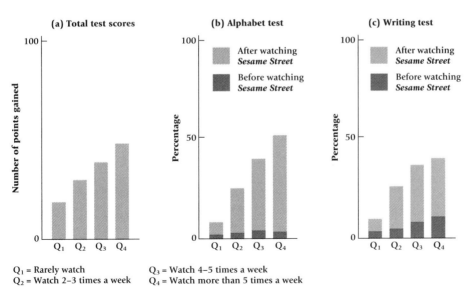

Q₁ = Rarely watch   Q₃ = Watch 4–5 times a week
Q₂ = Watch 2–3 times a week   Q₄ = Watch more than 5 times a week

Figure 12.3   Relationship between amount of viewing of *Sesame Street* and children's abilities: (a) improvement in total test scores for children grouped into different quartiles according to amount of viewing; (b) percentage of children who recited the alphabet correctly, grouped according to quartiles of amount of viewing; (c) percentage of children who wrote their first names correctly, grouped according to quartiles of amount of viewing. (From Liebert & Sprafkin, 1988.)

Children's Television Workshop. Richard Termine

Photo 12.2 Children learn many valuable lessons from educational TV programs such as *Sesame Street.*

5-year-olds, probably because the younger children knew less to begin with. The results of a second similar study that included only urban disadvantaged preschoolers paralleled those of the original study (Bogatz & Ball, 1972), and others have found that regular exposure to *Sesame Street* is associated with impressive gains in preschoolers' vocabularies and prereading skills as well (Rice et al., 1990). Finally, disadvantaged children who had been heavy viewers of *Sesame Street* were later rated by their first-grade teachers as better prepared for school and more interested in school activities than classmates who had rarely watched the program (Bogatz & Ball, 1972).

Other Educational Programs The success of *Sesame Street* has prompted CTW and other noncommercial producers to create programs that teach children subjects such as reading skills (*The Electric Company*), math (*Square One*), logical reasoning (*Think About*), science (*3–2–1 Contact*), and social studies (*Big Blue Marble*). Designed for first- through fourth-graders, *The Electric Company* does produce gains in reading skills, but only when children watch at school, where teachers can help them to apply what they have learned (Ball & Bogatz, 1973).[2] Unfortunately, a number of educational programs produced by commercial networks and aimed at older children have largely failed to attract a wide viewership, although such offerings as ABC's *Science Court* and the syndicated show *Popular Mechanics for Kids* rate as qualified successes (Farhl, 1998).

Unfounded Concerns and Further Benefits of Educational Programming Critics have argued that viewing educational programming is a passive activity that displaces more valuable, growth-enhancing pursuits such as reading and active learning under the guidance of an adult (Singer & Singer, 1990). Indeed, research pointing to the "video deficit" that young

[2]In 1985, *The Electric Company* went off the air. However, episodes are still available to schools on videocassette for classroom use.

children display in learning new material (Troseth, Saylor, & Archer, 2006) might seem to imply that their time might be better spent in alternative activities under adult supervision. Yet this criticism of educational programming seems a bit harsh. Developmentalists have always felt that educational shows could be more effective if they became more lifelike and interactive, and the *Nickelodeon* channel's *Blue's Clues* tried to do just that: The video tutor looks directly at viewers when presenting new materials, asks direct questions of viewers, and then pauses to invite them to answer. What's more, lessons are purposely repeated across episodes to ensure ample opportunities to learn from the video tutors. Clearly, this is not as rich an experience as two-way contingent interaction; but the format captures young children's attention, and evaluations of *Blue's Clues* reveal that preschoolers who watched regularly posted clear gains in cognitive and problem-solving skills and language proficiencies, compared to age-mates who did not watch this program (Anderson, 2004; Linebarger & Walker, 2005).

Even with its inherent limitations, educational programming is a valuable resource. Consider that more time spent watching general audience programs during the preschool period is associated with poor performances on cognitive assessments of children's readiness for school, whereas more time spent watching *educational* programming is associated with *better* performances on these same school-related skills (Anderson et al., 2001; Wright et al., 2001). What's more, parents who encourage their children to watch educational programming are also inclined to provide other educational alternatives to television—experiences that have their own enriching effects and serve to further limit their children's exposure to general-audience programming (Huston et al., 1999).

It was also once feared that *Sesame Street* might actually widen the intellectual gap between economically disadvantaged children and their middle-class peers if middle-class youngsters were more in inclined to watch it (Cook et al., 1975). Yet later research revealed that children from disadvantaged backgrounds not only watch *Sesame Street* about as often as their advantaged peers (Pinon, Huston, & Wright, 1989) but learn just as much from it (Rice et al., 1990). What's more, the impact of this program can be long lasting. Longitudinal research reveals that heavy preschool viewing of *Sesame Street* is associated with better academic performances and (to a lesser extent) increased involvement in creative activities 10 to 13 years later in high school (Anderson et al., 2001). So viewing *Sesame Street* appears to be a potentially valuable experience for *all* preschool children—and a true educational bargain that only costs pennies a day per viewer (Anderson et al., 2001). The formidable task is to convince more parents that *Sesame Street* (and other educational programs) are valuable resources that they and their children should not be missing (Larson, 2001).

In sum, television is a technology that has the capacity to do good or harm, depending primarily on what children happen to be watching. In other words, it is the message, not the medium, that is important. So can we alter television programming to make it a more effective agent of socialization that teaches the attitudes, values, and behaviors that more accurately reflect the mores of a free society? Surely we can, although it remains to be seen whether we will.

⌒ CHILD DEVELOPMENT IN THE COMPUTER AGE

Like television, the computer is a modern technology that has the potential to influence children's learning and lifestyles. But in what ways? If we take our cues from Hollywood, we might be led to believe that young computer users will grow up to be *brainy* but socially inept misfits like those curiously lovable characters from the movie *Revenge of the Nerds*. Indeed, most educators believe that computers contribute positively to children's education by serving as an effective supplement to classroom instruction—a tool that helps children to learn more and to have more fun learning. By 1996, over 98 percent of American public schools were using computers as instructional tools, and by 2003, about 60–70 percent of American homes had computers and more than 50 percent of American families had Internet access. (U.S. Bureau of the Census, 1997; Day, Janus, & Davis, 2003). So computers have been widely available for some time; but do they really help children to learn, think, or create? Is there a danger that young computer users will become so enamored of computer technology and so reclusive or socially unskilled that they risk being ostracized by their peers?

Computers in the Classroom

Are computers useful learning tools in the classroom? A large-scale evaluation of computer use and mathematics achievement among 13,000 fourth- and eighth-grade students conducted by the Educational Testing Service suggests that **computer-assisted instruction** can (but does not always) promote academic performance (Wenglinsky, 1998a). For fourth-graders in this study, more time spent on the computer was associated with *lower* math achievement. Many of these students were performing simple computer-generated drill exercises that other investigators have also found to be of limited usefulness. However, computers were found to have a positive influence on math achievement and promoted more positive attitudes toward learning when used in connection with highly motivating, thought-provoking games that allow children to discover important math concepts and when their teachers had been trained how to incorporate computers effectively in the classroom (Wenglinsky, 1998a).

Results for the eighth-graders were in many ways similar to those for younger children. Math achievement was *enhanced* when computers were used primarily for captivating applications and simulations but was *negatively influenced* when the primary use of computers was for drills (Wenglinsky, 1998a). Once again, students who benefited from using computers were those whose teachers had been trained how to make better use of computers in class. The message: Computers can be useful instructional aids, but only if used properly. Clearly teacher training is essential and must be expanded if we are to optimize the educational potential of computer technology.

Computer Programming and Cognitive Growth Under the guidance of a properly trained instructor, it seems that teaching students to *program* (and thus *control*) a computer can also have such important benefits as fostering mastery motivation and self-efficacy, as well as promoting novel modes of thinking that are unlikely to emerge from computer-assisted academic drills. In his own research, Douglas Clements (1991, 1995) trained first- and third-graders in Logo, a computer language that allows children to take drawings they've made and translate them into input statements so that they eventually succeed at reproducing their creations on the computer monitor. Although Clements's "Logo" children performed no better on achievement tests than age-mates who participated in the more usual kinds of computer-assisted academic exercises, Logo users scored higher on tests of Piagetian concrete-operational abilities, mathematical problem-solving strategies, and creativity (Clements, 1995; Nastasi & Clements, 1994). And because children must detect errors and debug their Logo programs to get them to work, programming fosters thinking about one's own thinking and is associated with gains in **metacognitive knowledge** (Clements, 1990). Finally, increasing numbers of high school teachers and college professors have created Web pages for their courses to stimulate discussion of course material online, a practice that they believe will induce students' to ponder course materials more critically and deeply (Hara, Bonk, & Angeli, 2000; Murray, 2000). Clearly, these findings are all potentially important, for they suggest that computers are useful not only for teaching academic concepts but for helping students to *think* in new ways as well.

computer-assisted instruction (CAI)
use of computers to teach new concepts and practice academic skills.

metacognition
one's knowledge about cognition and about the regulation of cognitive activities.

Social Impacts Are young computer users at risk of becoming reclusive, socially unskilled misfits as some people have feared? Hardly! Children often use home computers as a mechanism for attracting others, as chat mates or as participants in computer games (Crook, 1992). And research conducted in classrooms reveals that students who are learning to solve problems by computer or how to program a computer (1) are likely to seek collaborative solutions to the challenges they face and (2) are more inclined to persist after experiencing problems if they are collaborating with a peer (Nastasi & Clements, 1993, 1994. Conflicts may arise should collaborators disagree about how to approach a problem; yet the strong interest that collaborators frequently display when facing a programming challenge often supersedes their differences and encourages amiable methods of conflict resolution (Nastasi & Clements, 1993). So computers seem to promote (rather than impede) peer interactions—contacts that are often lively, challenging, and that appear to foster the growth of socially skilled behaviors.

Photo 12.3
Learning by computer can be an effective complement to classroom instruction and an experience that can teach young children to collaborate.

Beyond the Classroom: Benefits of Internet Exposure

The widespread availability of computers outside the classroom implies that large numbers of children and adolescents could be influenced in any number of ways by their exposure to computer technology. Let's focus first on three demonstrated benefits of Internet exposure.

Internet Availability and Academic Achievement In addition to research indicating that computer use in the classroom can produce some benefits in cognitive skills and academic achievement, research implies that having a computer at home enables children to search the Internet for information needed to complete school projects and better their academic performance (Pew Internet and American Life Project, 2002; Valkenburg & Soeters, 2001). Unfortunately, there is a broad digital divide in the United States: Underachieving ethnic minority and other economically disadvantaged children are less likely to have home access to computers and the Internet, possibly serving to perpetuate their poor academic performances. Recently, Linda Jackson and her associates (Jackson, von Eye, et al., 2006) explored the impact of Internet use at home on the academic achievement of urban disadvantaged 13- to 14-year-olds who were lagging academically. Each family was provided a computer and free Internet access. The researchers monitored how often these young adolescents used the Internet as well as measures of their reading achievement and grades at school for the next 16 months.

The results were clear. The more often these young teens logged on at home, the better their scores on standardized reading tests six months later and the higher their grade point averages at one year and at 16 months after receiving the computer. More time spent reading online, whether about school-related information or rap stars, probably accounts for the improvement in reading scores, and better reading skills likely helped these teens to achieve higher grades. In addition, Jackson and her associates speculated that compared to reading texts, and other traditional ways of developing academic skills, searching the Internet for information is fun and one can "learn without pain," so that positive academic outcomes may in part be a coincidental effect of having a good time. Yet it is important to note that participants in this study were performing well below average at school prior to receiving their computers, and it remains to be seen whether use of the Internet has similar benefits for youngsters who are already doing well at school.

Social Benefits of Computer Use   One recent survey revealed that 89 percent of American adolescents use the Internet at least once a week, 61 percent log on daily, and that social communications via e-mail or instant messaging (IM) account for most of the time they spend online (Cynkar, 2007a). Contrary to popular belief, most teens spend far more time chatting with friends from school, clubs, or other offline social networks that they do with strangers (Gross, 2004; Valkenburg & Peter, 2007). What's more, adolescents who frequently communicate online feel closer to their friends than those who do not (Valkenburg & Peter, 2007).

Why might online communication promote closer friendships? In their study of Dutch teens, Patti Valkenburg and Jocken Peter (2007) found that adolescents feel freer to share intimate information about themselves online than offline, particularly with members of the opposite sex. They view the Internet as a low-risk venue for disclosing personal information and for posing questions to their partners that would be considered rude in face-to-face interactions. Simply stated, it is easier to talk on the Internet about such topics as being in love or about fears, concerns, or things they are ashamed of; and as we will see in Chapter 13, this sort of intimate self-disclosure is a primary determinant of deep, committed friendships. Moreover, we learned in Chapter 8 that online communication with peers is valuable in another important aspect—helping young adolescents to explore and refine their emerging sexual identities in a relatively anonymous forum that presents fewer risks than similar face-to-face explorations with members of the other sex (Subrahmanyam, Smaehl, & Greenfield, 2006).

Health Benefits of Computer Use   Finally, recent research indicates that adolescents from Western countries such as the United States, Canada, and the United Kingdom often use the Internet as a health information source, especially seeking information about sexual matters and sexual risk (Borzekowski & Rickert, 2001; Gray et al., 2005). Use of the Internet is potentially very important for residents of developing countries in which nutritional disorders are common and communicable diseases are hard to control owing to inadequate medical care. Dina Borzekowski and her associates (Borzekowski, Fobil, & Asante, 2006) have studied Internet use for health purposes in an urban sample of 15- to 18-year-olds in Ghana, West Africa—a country beset with the above-mentioned health problems and where teens are at considerable risk of contracting sexually transmitted diseases, including AIDS. Though few Ghanaians have computers at home, those living in cities have Internet access at a nominal cost in cybercafés. This study found that more than 60 percent of this urban Ghanaian adolescent sample use the Internet, many explicitly seeking health information, which was perceived to be useful, trustworthy, and easy to read. Many adolescents feel more comfortable turning to the Internet than to traditional health providers when seeking answers to personal, sensitive, and embarrassing questions about their bodies, relationships, and health (Suzuki & Calzo, 2004). Though nothing should replace interactions with health providers, it appears that easily accessible, credible, and confidential information on the Internet can help to improve the lives and the choices made by young people the world over.

Concerns about Computers

What are the danger signs of exposing children and adolescents to computer technology? Three concerns are most often raised.

Concerns about Video Games

Grand Theft Auto: Vice City: A video game in which participants ramp up their scores by having sex with a prostitute and gain additional points by killing her. The game includes scenes in which blood splatters out of a woman's body as the player beats her to death. (National Institute on Media and the Family, as cited in Associated Press, 2002b)

One national survey revealed that 80 percent of U.S. adolescents spend two or more hours a week playing computer video games (Williams, 1998), and game playing is the predominant computer activity for grade-school children (Subrahmanyam et al., 2000). It is not that this activity necessarily diverts children from schoolwork or peer activities, as many parents have assumed; time spent playing at the computer is usually a substitute for other leisure activities, most notably TV viewing (Huston et al., 1999). Nevertheless, critics have feared that heavy exposure to such popular and incredibly violent video games as *America's Army, Killzone, Mortal Kombat,* and *Grand Theft Auto* can instigate aggression and cultivate aggressive habits in the same ways that televised violence does.

The critics' concerns are certainly valid. At least three early surveys of fourth- to twelfth-graders found moderate positive correlations between the amount of time spent playing video games and real-world aggressive behaviors (Dill & Dill, 1998). The experimental evidence is even more revealing: One study of third- and fourth-graders (Kirsh, 1998) and another study of college students (Anderson & Dill, 2000) found that participants randomly assigned to play violent video games subsequently displayed a strong hostile attributional bias toward ambiguous provocations and significantly more aggressive behavior than their counterparts who had played nonviolent video games (see also Bushman & Anderson, 2002), and the instigating effects of violent video games are strongest for boys who identify with violent game characters (Konijn, Bijvank, & Bushman, 2007). And because violent game players are *actively* involved in planning and performing aggressive acts and are *reinforced* for their successful symbolic violence, it has been argued that the aggression-instigating effects of violent video games is probably far greater than that of violent television programming, in which children are only passively exposed to aggression and violence (Anderson & Dill, 2000). Clearly, these findings imply that parents should be at least as concerned about what their children are playing on-screen as they are about what children watch.

Concerns about Social Inequalities   Other critics are convinced that the computer revolution may leave some groups of children behind, lacking in skills required in our increasingly computer-dependent society. As noted earlier, children from economically disadvantaged families may be exposed to computers at school but are less likely to have them at home or to have teachers who have been trained to use them most effectively in the classroom (Becker, 2000; Rocheleau, 1995). What's more, when computers were first introduced, boys were more likely than girls to take an interest in them and to sign up for computer camps. Why? Probably because computers were often viewed as involving mathematics, a traditionally masculine subject, and many available computer games are designed with boys in mind (Lepper, 1985; Ogletree & Williams, 1990). Yet this gender gap has essentially closed in the United States (Mayer-Smith, Pedretti, & Woodrow, 2000; Subrahmanyam, Greenfield, & Gross, 2000), largely due to the increasing use of computers to socialize with friends and to foster cooperative classroom learning activities that girls typically enjoy (Collis, 1996; Rocheleau, 1995).

Concerns about Internet Exposure   The proliferation of home computers and online services means that literally millions of children and adolescents around the world may now have unsupervised access to the Internet. Clearly, exposure to information available on the Web can be a boon to students researching topics pertinent to their school assignments. Nevertheless, many parents and teachers are alarmed about potentially unsavory Web influences.

Concerns about Pornography and Sexual Exploitation Finding pornography on the Internet is as easy as Googling the word "sex," and each year about 40 percent of U.S. teens and preteens visit one or more of the 400,000 sexually explicit sites on the Web, many of which require no verification of legal age for entry (DeAngelis, 2007; Wolak, Mitchell, & Finkelhor, 2007). Although research to date on the effects of porn exposure is sparse, the data available reveals some disturbing impacts on sexual attitudes: Children and adolescents who visit porn sites more often are more likely than those who rarely if ever visit to view sex as a purely physical, recreational activity that requires little affection, to objectify women and grow more tolerant of aggression toward them, and to become more accepting of premarital and extramarital sex (DeAngelis, 2007, Greenfield, 2004; Peter & Valkenburg, 2006). Boys, who visit porn sites far more often than girls, are more likely to hold these attitudes, especially if the materials they are viewing are very explicit and are perceived by viewers as realistic depictions of sexual relationships (Peter & Valkenburg, 2006, 2007).

Other Concerns about Internet Exposure Many other concerns of parents and teachers have yet to draw much attention from researchers. For example, the Internet is a primary recruiting tool for a variety of cults as well as hate organizations such as the Ku Klux Klan (Downing, 2003). Moreover, we learned in Chapter 9 that online bullying has become quite common and can have psychological effects on victims that equal or exceed those that victims experience face-to-face at school or in the neighborhood (Raskauskas & Stoltz, 2007). Children are frequently exposed to the same troublesome and deceptive advertising practices online as they are on commercial television (Wartella, Caplovitz, & Lee, 2004). And although use of the Internet serves to bolster offline friendships for most teens, perhaps as many as 15 percent use it to isolate themselves from their families and classmates (that is, to escape from their current circumstances) and to rely on online contact with strangers as their primary means of socializing (Cynkar, 2007a).

What might parents do to address the concerns? In his forthcoming book, Larry Rosen (2008) offers the following suggestions:

1. *Learn the technology.* Learn how MySpace works and what YouTube is and what controls and blocks are available. This may give parents a better idea about which rules and limits may be necessary.

2. *Place computers in rooms the family frequents.* Don't create techno-cocoons where teens can isolate themselves and not participate in family activities.

3. *Plan family activities in advance and include your teen.*

4. *Limit your teen's online time,* stipulating that time on the Internet must be matched by such alternative activities as visiting with family members or friends.

5. *Monitor online activities.* Be aware of what information teens are consuming and whether this content might create discomfort or cause problems. The easiest way to do this is to maintain a line of communication that is respectful and constructive, not punitive.

Summing Up Like television sets, then, computers may prove to have either positive or negative influences on development, depending on how they are used. Outcomes may be less than positive if a young person's primary uses of the machine are to flitter away study time chatting about undesirable topics or gaping at porn on line, or to hole up by himself,

Thinkstock/Jupiter Images

Photo 12.4
Frequent exposure to Internet pornography can create unhealthy attitudes toward women, sex, and the nature of sexual relationships.

conversing with strangers or zapping mutant aliens from space. But the news may be rather positive indeed for youngsters who use computers to learn, create, and collaborate or socialize amicably with their friends.

THE SCHOOL AS A SOCIALIZATION AGENT

Of all the formal institutions that children encounter in their lives away from home, few have as much opportunity to influence their development as the schools they attend. Starting at age 5 or 6, the typical child in the United States spends about five hours of each weekday at school. And children are staying there longer than ever before. In 1870, there were only 200 public high schools in the United States, and only half of all American children were attending during the three to five months that school was in session. Today, the school term is about nine months long (180 school days); more than 75 percent of American youth are still attending high school at age 17; and nearly 50 percent of U.S. high school graduates enroll in some form of higher education (U.S. Bureau of the Census, 2001).

If asked to characterize the mission of the schools, we are likely to think of them as the place where children acquire basic knowledge and academic proficiencies: reading, writing, arithmetic, computer skills, and later, foreign languages, social studies, higher math, and science. But schools also expose children to an **informal curriculum** that teaches them how to fit into their culture. Students are expected to obey rules, cooperate with their classmates, respect authority, and become good citizens. And much of the influence that peers may have on developing children occurs in the context of school-related activities and may depend very critically on the type of school that a child attends and the quality of a child's school experiences (Brody, Dorsey, et al., 2002). So it is quite proper to think of the school as an agent of socialization that is likely to affect children's social and emotional development as well as imparting knowledge and helping to prepare students for a job and economic self-sufficiency.

In this section of the chapter, we will focus on the ways in which schools influence children. First, we will consider whether formal classroom experiences are likely to promote children's intellectual development. Then we will see that schools clearly differ in "effectiveness"—that is, the ability to accomplish both curricular goals and noncurricular objectives that contribute to what educators often call "good citizenship." After reviewing the characteristics of effective schools, we will discuss a few of the obstacles that special-needs students and disadvantaged youth may encounter at school as we consider whether our educational system is currently meeting the needs of our children.

informal curriculum
noncurricular objectives of schooling such as teaching children to cooperate, respect authority, obey rules, and become good citizens.

Does Schooling Promote Cognitive Development?

If you have completed the first two years of college, you may already know far more biology, chemistry, and physics than many of the brightest college professors of only 100 years ago. Clearly, students acquire a vast amount of knowledge about their world from the schooling they receive. But when developmentalists ask, "Do schools promote cognitive growth?" they want to know whether formal education hastens intellectual development or encourages modes of thinking and methods of problem solving that are less likely to develop in the absence of schooling.

To address these issues, researchers have typically studied the intellectual growth of children from developing countries where schooling is not compulsory or not yet available throughout the society. Studies of this type generally find that children who attend school are quicker to reach certain Piagetian milestones (for example, conservation) and perform better on tests of memory and metacognitive knowledge than age-mates from similar backgrounds who do not go to school (Rogoff, 1990; Sharp, Cole, & Lave, 1979). And it seems that the more schooling children complete, the better their cognitive performance. Consider what Frederick Morrison and his associates (1995, 1997) found when comparing the cognitive performance of children who had just made the age cutoff for entering first grade with that of youngsters who had just missed the cutoff and had spent the year in kindergarten. When tested at the end of the school year, the youngest first-graders clearly outperformed the nearly *identically aged* kindergartners in reading, memory, language, and arithmetic skills (see Gormley et al., 2005, for similar education-related boosts in 4-year-old pre-K students). In another study, U.S. school children on an *extended-year* (210-day) calendar tested higher in academic achievement and general cognitive competencies in the fall of the following year than did peers who were equally competent at the beginning of the study but who had attended school on a normal 180-day calendar (Frazier & Morrison, 1998). Finally, Janellen Huttenlocher and her associates (1998) carefully tracked kindergartners' and first-graders' cognitive development at six-month intervals and found that growth was significantly greater during the October-to-April period of heavy schooling than during the April-to-October period when children spent less time in school. So schooling does seem to promote cognitive growth, both by transmitting general knowledge and by teaching children a variety of rules, strategies, and problem-solving skills (including an ability to concentrate and an appreciation for abstraction) that they can apply to many different kinds of information (Ceci, 1991; Ceci & Williams, 1997).

Do these findings imply that we might be serving our children well by starting them in school at an earlier age? As we will see in Box 12.2, there are advantages and some possible disadvantages associated with early entry into a school-like environment.

Determinants of Effective (and Ineffective) Schooling

One of the first questions that parents often ask when searching for a residence in a new town is "Where should we live so that our children will get the best education?" This concern reflects the common belief that some schools are "better" or "more effective" than others. But are they?

Michael Rutter (1983) certainly thinks so. According to Rutter, **effective schools** are those that promote academic achievement, social skills, polite and attentive behavior, positive attitudes toward learning, low absenteeism, continuation of education beyond the age at which attendance is mandatory, and acquisition of skills that will enable students to find and hold a job. Rutter argues that some schools are more successful than others at accomplishing these objectives, regardless of the students' ethnic or socioeconomic backgrounds. Let's examine the evidence for this claim.

effective schools
schools that are generally successful at achieving curricular and noncurricular objectives, regardless of the racial, ethnic, or socioeconomic background of the student population.

Box 12.2 Current Controversies

Should Preschoolers Attend School?

Over the past 15 years, the popular media has let it be known that infants and toddlers are quite capable of learning and that such enrichment activities as reading to babies or exposing them to music can stimulate brain development and intellectual growth (for example, Kulman, 1997). Many parents have bought heavily into this idea and embrace programs such as Bookstart, which claims to help parents promote preliteracy skills in 6- to 9-month-old infants (Hall, 2001)! And already many preschoolers spend 4- to 8-hour days in day-care settings and prekindergarten (pre-K) programs that have a strong academic emphasis (Early et al., 2007). Is this beneficial?

David Elkind (1987), author of *Miseducation: Preschoolers at risk*, certainly doesn't think so. He argues that the current push for earlier and earlier education may be going too far (see also Bruer, 1999) and that many young children today are not given enough time simply to be children—to play and socialize as they choose. Elkind even worries that children may lose their self-initiative and enjoyment of learning if their lives are orchestrated by parents who incessantly push them to achieve.

Several studies (for example, Hart, Burts, et al., 1998; Marcon, 1999; Stipek et al., 1995; Valeski & Stipek, 2001) seem to confirm Elkind's concerns. Three- to 6-year-olds in academically oriented preschools or kindergartens sometimes display an initial advantage in such basic academic competencies as a knowledge of letters and reading skills but often lose it by the end of kindergarten. What's more, students in these highly structured academically oriented programs proved to be *less creative, more stressed, and more anxious about tests, less prideful* about their successes, *less confident* about succeeding in the future and generally *less enthused* about school than children who attended preschool or kindergarten programs that emphasized child-centered social agendas and flexible, hands-on, discovery-based learning. So there seem to be dangers in overemphasizing academics during the preschool period after all.

On the other hand, preschool programs that offer a healthy mix of play and child-initiated discovery learning can be very beneficial to young children, especially to disadvantaged children (Stipek, 2002; Gormley & Gayer, 2005). Although most children

Jennie Woodcock, Reflections Photolibrary/Corbis

Preschools that provide a healthy balance of preacademic and social activities can help children prepare for school.

who attend preschool classes are no more or less intellectually advanced than those who remain at home, *disadvantaged* preschoolers who attend child-centered programs designed to prepare them for school do display more cognitive growth and achieve more later success in school than other disadvantaged youngsters who do not attend these programs (Campbell et al., 2001; Magnusson et al., 2003; Reynolds & Temple, 1998; and see Chapter 7), due in part to increasing involvement by parents in the program participants' education (Reynolds & Robertson, 2003). So as long as preschool programs allow plenty of time for play and for skill building in the context of group social interactions, they can help children from all social backgrounds acquire social, academic, and communication skills, as well as an appreciation of rules and routines, that will smooth the transition from individual learning at home to group learning in an elementary school classroom.

In one large study, Rutter and his associates (1979) conducted extensive interviews and observations in 12 high schools serving lower- to lower-middle income populations in London, England. As the children entered these schools, they were given a battery of achievement tests to measure their prior academic accomplishments. At the end of high school, the pupils took another major exam to assess their academic progress. Other information, such as attendance records and teacher ratings of classroom behavior, was also available. When the data were analyzed, Rutter found that the 12 schools clearly differed in "effectiveness": Students from the "better" schools exhibited fewer problem behaviors, attended school more regularly, and made more academic progress than students from the less effective schools. We get some idea of the importance of these "schooling effects" from Figure 12.4. The "bands" on the graph refer to the pupils' academic accomplishments *at the time they entered* high school (band 3, low achievers; band 1, high achievers). In all three bands, students attending the "more effective" schools outperformed those in the "less effective" schools on the final assessment of academic achievement. Even more revealing is the finding that the initially poor students (band 3) who attended the "better" schools

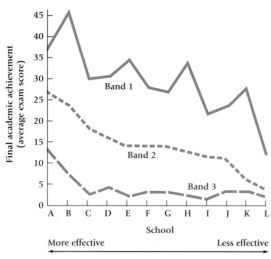

Figure 12.4
Average level of academic achievement in secondary school as a function of initial achievement at the time of entry (bands 1–3) and the school that pupils were attending (schools A–L). Note that pupils in all three bands performed at higher levels on this final academic assessment if they attended the more effective schools. Moreover, students in band 2 performed like band 1 students in the more effective schools but like band 3 students in the least effective schools. (From Rutter et al., 1979.)

ended up scoring just as high on this final index of academic progress as the initially good (band 1) students who attended the least effective schools. Similar findings were obtained in other large studies of elementary and high schools in the United States. Even after controlling for important variables such as the ethnic composition and socioeconomic backgrounds of the student bodies and the type of communities served, some elementary schools were found to be much more "effective" than others (Brookover et al., 1979; Hill, Foster, & Gendler, 1990; see also Eccles & Roeser, 2005).

So the school that children attend can make a difference. And you may be surprised by some of the factors that do and do not have a bearing on how "effective" a school is.

Some Misconceptions about Effective Schooling

Monetary Support Interestingly, a school's level of support may have less to do with the quality of education students receive than one might think. Seriously inadequate funding can undermine the quality of education; but some research shows that as long as a school has qualified teachers and a reasonable level of support, the precise amount of money spent per pupil, the number of books in the school library, teachers' salaries, and teachers' academic credentials play only a minor role in determining student outcomes (Early et al., 2007; Hanushek, 1997; Rutter, 1983). However, other research suggests that increased resources applied directly to classroom instruction can increase student achievement in the earlier grades (Wenglinsky, 1998b). Thus, simply adding money to a school's budget may not improve school effectiveness unless it is invested wisely.

School and Class Size Another factor that has relatively little to do with a school's effectiveness is average class size: In typical elementary- and secondary-school classes ranging from 20 to 35 students, class size has only a modest effect at best on academic achievement (Ehrenberg et al., 2001; NICHD Early Child Care Research Network, 2004b; Rutter & Maughan, 2002). Tutoring students one-on-one or in small groups during the primary grades, particularly those who are economically disadvantaged or have low ability, can significantly improve performances in reading and arithmetic (Blatchford et al., 2002; Finn, 2002). And reducing class sizes to 20 or fewer students can produce meaningful gains in achievement for kindergarteners and first-graders (see NICHD Early Child Care Research Network, 2004b, for a review). But simply reducing classes sizes in all grades across the board may not be worth the large amounts of money it would cost.

There is some evidence that the size of one's school affects older students' participation in structured extracurricular activities—settings in which such aspects of the "informal curriculum" as cooperation, fair play, and healthy attitudes toward competition are likely to be stressed. Although larger high schools offer a greater number of extracurricular activities, students in the smaller schools tend to be (1) more heavily involved, (2) more likely to hold positions of responsibility or leadership, and (3) more satisfied with extracurricular experiences (Barker & Gump, 1964; Jacobs & Chase, 1989). Why? One reason is that students in larger schools receive much less encouragement to participate, often becoming lost in the crowd and feeling a sense of alienation and a lack of connectedness with peers and the academic culture. This is indeed unfortunate, for an early longitudinal study that tracked adolescents from seventh grade through early adulthood found that less competent students with poor social skills were much less likely to drop out of school or to be involved in antisocial activities as young adults if they had maintained a voluntary connection to their school environments by participating in one or more extracurricular activities (Mahoney, 2000; Mahoney & Cairns, 1997; see Figure 12.5). Of course, one potential critique of these findings is that well-adjusted students who are inclined to stay in school are the ones who are drawn to extracurricular activities. Yet longitudinal studies that control for such self-selection variables consistently reveal that a reasonable amount of participation in such activities as after-school clubs and sports, as well as involvement in other organized extracurricular activities (for example, volunteer-ism), does indeed appear to foster such positive outcomes as academic achievement, staying in school, fewer mental health problems, lower levels of alcohol and drug use, and greater involvement in politi-cal and social causes in young adulthood; and the benefits of such participation are detectable for students at all ability levels and from all social classes and ethnic groups (Busseri et al., 2006; Fredricks & Eccles, 2006; Mahoney, Harris, & Eccles, 2006). The implica-tions of these findings are clear: To better accomplish their mission of educating students and properly preparing them for adult life, middle and secondary schools—large and small—might do more to encourage *all* students to participate in extracurricular activities and not be so quick to deny them these opportunities because of marginal academic performances.

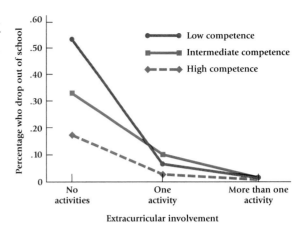

Figure 12.5

Rates of high school dropout as a function of student social/academic competencies and participation in extracurricular activities. Clearly, students of low or intermediate competence are more likely to stay in school if they participate in extracur-ricular activities and maintain a positive and voluntary connec-tion to peers and the school environment. (From Mahoney & Cairns, 1997.)

Ability Tracking   The merits of **ability tracking**—a procedure in which students are grouped by IQ or academic achievement and then taught in classes made up of students of comparable "ability"—have been debated for years. Some educators believe that stu-dents learn more when surrounded by peers of equal ability. Others argue that ability tracking undermines the self-esteem of lower-ability students and contributes to their poor academic achievement and high dropout rate.

Available research suggests that neither ability tracking nor mixed-ability instruction has distinct advantages: Both procedures are common in highly effective and less effec-tive schools (Glass, 2002; Rutter, 1983). Yet there are some qualifications. Ability tracking *can* be beneficial to high-ability students *if* they are exposed to a challenging curriculum carefully tailored to their abilities and learning needs (Glass, 2002; Kulik & Kulik, 1992). However, lower-ability students are unlikely to benefit and may well suffer if ability track-ing denies them access to the best instructors (as it often does), fails to challenge them aca-demically, and stigmatizes them as "dummies" (Mac Iver, Reuman, & Main, 1995; Mehan et al., 1996; Porter & Polikoff, 2007). Hugh Mehan and his colleagues (1996) put it this way: "It is not that dumb kids are placed in slow groups or low tracks; . . . kids are made dumb by being placed in slow groups or low tracks" (p. 230).

In sum, the factors we've discussed thus far do *not* seem to contribute appreciably to effective education. A school that has only adequate financial support, places students in relatively large classes, and practices mixed-ability instruction is often just as "effective" as another school that has abundant resources, small classes, and practices ability tracking.

ability tracking
the educational practice of grouping students according to ability and then educating them in classes with students of comparable educational or intellectual standing.

Factors That Do Contribute to Effective Schooling

Composition of the Student Body   To some extent, the "effectiveness" of a school is a function of what it has to work with. On average, academic achievement is lowest in schools with a preponderance of economically disadvantaged students, and it appears that *any* child is likely to make more academic progress if taught in a school with a higher concentration of intellectually capable peers (Brookover et al., 1979; Portes & MacLeod, 1996). However, this *does not* mean that a school is only as good as the stu-dents it serves, for many schools that draw heavily from disadvantaged populations are highly effective at motivating students and preparing them for jobs or higher education (Reynolds, 1992).

School Climate   Students' perceptions of the school climate, including how safe they feel and how much emotional support and encouragement they receive from teachers and other school personnel, also affects school effectiveness (Hamre & Pianta, 2005; Loukas & Robinson, 2004). When children feel secure and teachers create a positive and supportive emotional climate in the classroom, students achieve more academically, are more likely to enjoy classroom activities, and experience fewer emotional problems (Eccles & Roeser, 2005; Gazelle, 2006; Hamre & Pianta, 2005).

The Scholastic Atmosphere of Successful Schools   So what is it about the *learning* environment of some schools that allows them to accomplish so much? Reviews of the literature (Eccles & Roeser, 2005; National Research Council and Institute of Medicine, 2004; Rutter, 1983) point to the following values and practices that characterize effective schools:

+ *Academic emphases.* Effective schools have a clear focus on academic goals. Children are regularly assigned homework, which is checked, corrected, and discussed with them.

+ *Classroom management.* In effective schools, teachers waste little time getting activities started or dealing with distracting disciplinary problems. Lessons begin and end on time. Pupils are told exactly what is expected of them and receive clear and unambiguous feedback about their academic performance. The classroom atmosphere is comfortable; all students are actively encouraged to work to the best of their abilities, and ample praise acknowledges good work.

+ *Discipline.* In effective schools, the staff is firm in enforcing rules and does so on the spot rather than sending offenders off to the principal's office. Rarely do instructors resort to physical sanctions (slapping or spanking), which contribute to truancy, defiance, and a tense classroom atmosphere.

+ *Challenging and culturally relevant curricula.* Effective schools made an effort to promote students' interest, attention, effort, and attendance by providing at least some learning materials that emphasize their culture and history as well as the developmental issues they are currently facing. By contrast, content that does not challenge students, or that they don't feel they can personally relate to, can undermine academic achievement and alienate students from school (Eccles & Roeser, 2005; Jackson & Davis, 2000).

+ *Teamwork.* Effective schools have faculties that work as a team, jointly planning curricular objectives and monitoring student progress, under the guidance of a principal who provides active, energetic leadership.

In sum, the effective school environment is a comfortable but businesslike setting in which academic successes are expected and students are motivated to learn. And in many ways, effective teachers are like authoritative parents—caring and concerned but firm and controlling (Wentzel, 2002), and research consistently indicates that children and adolescents from many social backgrounds prefer **authoritative instruction** and are more likely to thrive when treated this way than students taught by more **authoritarian** or more **permissive instructors** (Arnold, McWilliams, & Arnold, 1998; Lewin, Lippitt, & White, 1939; Wentzel, 2002).

Finally, one can hardly emphasize strongly enough just how important effective schooling can be for economically disadvantaged students who are not only at risk of academic underachievement but may be living in neighborhoods or in family settings that place them at risk of displaying conduct problems, internalizing disorders (for example, anxiety, depression), and other antisocial behaviors. Gene Brody and his colleagues (Brody, Dorsey, et al., 2002), for example, found that teachers who create an effective classroom

authoritative instruction
a warm but controlling style of instruction in which the teacher makes many demands but also allows some autonomy and individual expression as long as students are staying within the guidelines that the teacher has set.

authoritarian instruction
a restrictive style of instruction in which the teacher makes absolute demands and uses threats or force (if necessary) to ensure that students comply.

permissive instruction
a lax style of instruction in which the teacher makes few demands of students and provides little or no active guidance.

environment help low-income, at-risk 7- to 15-year-olds from single-parent homes to cope with stresses they experience, keep on track at school, and avoid the internalizing and externalizing disorders commonly observed among such populations. What's more, this protective stabilizing effect of effective schooling was quite clear in this study, *even when the parenting that youngsters received was compromised* (that is, low in warmth and involved supervision; (see also Meehan, Hughes, & Cavell, 2003, for similar results with aggressive African-American and Latino students). In a similar vein, Deborah O'Donnell and her colleagues (2002) found that high-risk adolescents living in violent neighborhoods are less subject to deviant peer influences and less involved in substance abuse and other antisocial conduct when they receive the support and encouragement of teachers in effective schools. Findings such as these clearly illustrate just how important effective schooling can be in the socialization process, contributing substantially to positive social and emotional (as well as to positive academic) outcomes.

The "Goodness of Fit" between Students and Schools   There is another important point to make about effective schooling: Characteristics of the student and of the school environment often interact to affect student outcomes—a phenomenon Lee Cronbach and Richard Snow (1977) call **aptitude-treatment interaction (ATI)**. Over the years, much educational research has been based on the assumption that a particular teaching method, philosophy of education, or classroom structure will prove superior for all students, regardless of their abilities, personalities, and cultural backgrounds. This assumption is often wrong. Instead, many approaches to education are highly effective with some kinds of students but quite ineffective with others. The secret to being effective is to find an appropriate fit between learners and educational practices.

For example, teachers tend to get the most out of *high-ability, middle-class* students by moving at a quick pace and insisting on high standards of performance—that is, by challenging these students. By contrast, *low-ability* and *disadvantaged* students often respond more favorably to a teacher who motivates them by providing truly engaging learning exercises and remaining warm and encouraging rather than intrusive and demanding (Good & Brophy, 1994; Sacks & Mergendoller, 1997).

Aside from providing culturally relevant learning materials, sensitivity to students' cultural *traditions* is also crucial for designing an effective instructional program. European-American students come from cultures that stress individual accomplishments, perhaps making them especially well suited for the individual mastery expectations that are emphasized in traditional classrooms. By contrast, ethnic Hawaiians and other students from collectivist cultures that stress cooperation and collaborative approaches to learning often founder in traditional Western classrooms. They pay little attention to the teacher or their lessons and spend a lot of time seeking the attention of classmates—behaviors that are perceived by teachers as reflecting their lack of interest in school (Tharp, 1989). Yet when instruction is made more culturally compatible for these youngsters by having teachers circulate among small groups, instructing each group and encouraging group members to pull together and assist each other to achieve learning objectives, Hawaiian children become much more enthusiastic about school and achieve much more as well (see Figure 12.6).

Unfortunately, young adolescents from any social background may begin to lose interest in academics should they experience a disconnect between their school environments and their changing developmental needs.

For some time now, educators have been concerned about a number of undesirable changes that often occur when emerging adolescents make the transition from elementary school to middle school or junior high school: loss of self-esteem and interest in school, declining grades, and increased troublemaking, to name a few (Eccles et al., 1996; Seidman et al., 1994). Why is this a treacherous move?

aptitude-treatment interaction (ATI) a phenomenon whereby characteristics of the student and of the school environment interact to affect student outcomes, such that any given educational practice may be effective with some students but not with others.

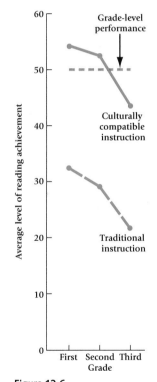

Figure 12.6
Reading achievement of ethnic Hawaiian first- through third-grade students who received traditional or culturally compatible classroom instruction. The students who received culturally compatible instruction read at grade level, whereas those receiving traditional instruction read far below grade level. (Adapted from Tharp & Gallimore, 1988.)

Photo 12.5
Moving from small, close-knit elementary schools to highly bureaucratic and impersonal secondary schools is stressful for adolescents, many of whom lose interest in academics and become more susceptible to peer-group influences.

Part of the problem stems from the fact that young adolescents are often trying to cope with many other stressors (for example, pubertal changes and other life transitions such as family turmoil or a change in residence) at about the time they change schools (Flanagan & Eccles, 1993). Yet Jacquelynne Eccles and her colleagues (Eccles, Lord, & Midgley, 1991; Roeser & Eccles, 1998) think that the character of secondary schools themselves is partially responsible for the adjustment difficulties that transitioning students display. Specifically, they propose a "goodness of fit" hypothesis stating that the transition to a secondary school is likely to be especially difficult when that school, whether a junior high or middle school, is poorly matched to adolescents' developmental needs.

What "mismatches" might be involved? Consider that the transition from elementary school to a middle- or junior high school often involves going from a small school with close student/teacher ties, a good deal of choice regarding learning activities, and gentle discipline to a larger, more bureaucratized environment where student/teacher relationships are impersonal, good grades are emphasized but harder to come by, opportunities for choice in learning activities are limited, and discipline is rigid—*all this at a time when adolescents are seeking more rather than less autonomy* (Andermann & Midgley, 1997).

Eccles and others have demonstrated that the "fit" between developmental needs and school environments is indeed an important influence on adolescent adjustment to school. In one study (Mac Iver & Reuman, 1988), the transition to junior high brought about a decline in intrinsic interest in learning mainly among students who wanted more involvement in classroom decisions but ended up with fewer such opportunities than they had had in elementary school. A second study illustrates just how important a *good* fit between student and schools can be: Students experienced negative changes in their attitudes toward mathematics if their transition to junior high resulted in less personal and supportive relations with math teachers; but for those few students whose transition to junior high involved gaining more supportive teachers than they had in elementary school, interest in academics actually *increased* (Midgley, Feldlauter, & Eccles, 1989). Finally, students in a third study fared better psychologically and academically when they felt that their school encouraged all students to do their best (learning goals) than when competition for grades (that is, performance goals) was emphasized (Roeser & Eccles, 1998).

The message? Declines in academic motivation and performance are not inevitable as students move from elementary to secondary schools. These declines occur primarily when the fit between student and school environment goes from good to poor. How might we improve the fit? Parents can help by recognizing how difficult school transitions can be and communicating this understanding to their teens. One study found that adolescents whose parents were in tune with their developmental needs and who fostered autonomy in decision making generally adjusted well to the transition to junior high and posted *gains* in self-esteem (Lord, Eccles, & McCarthy, 1994). Teachers can also help by stressing mastery goals rather than grades and by seeking parents' opinions about scholastic matters and keeping them involved during this transitional period—a time when collaborative relations between parents and teachers normally decline and adolescents often feel that they are facing the stresses of this new, impersonal academic setting with little social support (Eccles & Harold, 1993). Indeed, specially designed programs to provide these supports for young adolescents do help them to adjust to school transitions and reduce the odds that they will drop out of school (Smith, 1997).

In sum, the "goodness of fit" between students and their classroom environments is a crucial aspect of effective schooling. Education that is carefully tailored to students' cultural backgrounds, personal characteristics, and developmental needs is much more likely to succeed.

Do Our Schools Meet the Needs of All Our Children?

Public education in the United States arose not so much from a desire to educate a work force (most 19th century workers were farmers or unskilled laborers who required little education) as from the need to "Americanize" a nation of immigrants—to bring them into the mainstream of American society (Rudolph, 1965). So our public schools have traditionally been majority-culture, middle-class institutions staffed by white instructors who promote middle-class values.

However, more and more of the students educated in our public schools come from non-white social backgrounds; in fact, for some time now a *majority* of students in California's public schools have come from various "minority" groups (Garcia, 1993). How well are minority students being served by our schools? And how well are today's schools meeting the needs of students with developmental disabilities and other special needs?

Educational Experiences of Ethnic Minorities   In his book *Dark Ghetto*, Kenneth Clark (1965) argued that the American public school classroom represents a "clash of cultures" in which teachers who have adopted middle-class values fail to appreciate the difficulties that minority students face in trying to adjust to the quiet, orderly, Eurocentric atmosphere of the schools. To cite one example of clashing language customs, African-American children are asked fewer questions at home than white children are, and the questions they are asked are typically open-ended prompts that call for them to recount their knowledge or experiences through long, elaborate verbal responses (Brice-Heath, 1982, 1989). Consequently, these youngsters are often hesitant to answer what, for them, are "unusual" knowledge-training questions (requiring brief, factually correct answers) at school and may thus be branded by teachers as unknowledgeable or uncooperative.

Indeed, many lower-income children from ethnic minority groups do have problems at school. We noted in Chapter 7 that these children are often academic underachievers, making poorer grades and scoring lower on standardized achievement tests than European-American classmates. And they are also more likely than their European-American peers to be disciplined by the staff, to be "held back" in one or more grades, and to drop out before completing high school (Associated Press, 2002a; U.S. Bureau of Census, 2007). Why is this? Let's consider three possibilities.

Parental Involvement   Although it was once fashionable to attribute the academic underachievement of ethnic minorities to a failure on their parents' part to value education or to encourage academic achievement, we learned in Chapter 7 that this is a serious misconception.[3] Recall that African-American and Latino-American parents value education at least as much as European-American parents do (Galper, Wigfield, & Seefeldt, 1997) and are actually more inclined to favor such reforms as competency

[3]Let's also recall from Chapter 7 that the underachievements displayed by ethnic minorities are *not* simply attributable to intellectual deficiencies. Even when intelligence (that is, IQ test performance) is equivalent, African-American, Native American, and Latino-American students tend to make lower grades and lower scores on standardized achievement tests than European-American and Asian-American students do.

Photo 12.6
Children are more likely to do well in school if their parents value education and are interested and involved in school activities.

testing for students and a longer school day (Stevenson, Chen, & Uttal, 1990). However, minority parents are often less knowledgeable about the school system and less heavily involved in parent/teacher conferences, PTA meetings, and other school-sponsored activities, and this lack of involvement may partially counteract their message that schooling is important. Yet when minority parents *are* highly involved in school activities, their children feel more confident about mastering academic challenges and tend to do well in school (Luster & McAdoo, 1996; Reynolds & Robertson, 2003). So active parental involvement can make a big difference.

Fortunately, these findings have prompted many schools to implement *kindergarten* transition programs, hoping to get more parents involved early on in school-related activities. Common transition practices include meeting with parents in orientations prior to the start of the school year, visitations to kindergarten classrooms by parents and their preschoolers and by parents after their child has enrolled, and arranging other contacts (home visits, phone consultations) between teachers and parents during the school year. And these transition policies really work. One recent evaluation undertaken in 992 schools around the United States revealed that low-SES, at-risk students, in particular, were displaying notably better academic achievement by the end of kindergarten in schools with extensive transition programs than in schools without such programs, and these academic improvements were attributable in part to greater parent-initiated involvement in their children's learning activities (Schulting, Malone, & Dodge, 2005).

Interfacing Parent and Peer Influences Although minority parents play a crucial role in fostering their children's scholastic competencies, we cannot fully appreciate their impact without also understanding how peers influence academic achievement. Lawrence Steinberg and his colleagues (1992) have conducted a large-scale study of school achievement among African-American, Latino, Asian-American, and European-American high school students. They found that academic success and good personal adjustment are usually associated with *authoritative* parenting. However, this positive parental influence on academic achievement can easily be undermined by African-American peers, who often devalue academic achievement and pressure many African-American students to choose between academic success and peer acceptance (see also Arroyo & Zigler, 1995; Ogbu, 2003).

Latino parents tend to be strict and somewhat authoritarian rather than flexible and authoritative. As a result, many Latino students may have relatively few opportunities at home to act autonomously and acquire decision-making skills that would serve them well in the individualistic context of our schools (Steinberg, Dornbusch, & Brown, 1992). Furthermore, Latino students from low-income areas often associate with peers who do not strongly value academics and who may undercut their parents' efforts to promote academic achievement. By contrast, European-American students are more likely than either African-American or Latino students to have a combination of authoritative parenting *and* peer support for education working in their favor. Yet it is important to note that when

African-American and Latino students associate with supportive peers, feel closely connected to their ethnic group, and believe that academic achievement is part of being a good in-group member, their academic achievement is unlikely to suffer (Altschul, Oyserman, & Bybee, 2006; Gutman, Sameroff, & Eccles, 2002).

Interestingly, high-achieving Asian-American students often experience restrictive, seemingly authoritarian parenting at home. However, this highly controlling pattern, coupled with a *very strong* emphasis on education and the *very high* achievement standards that many Asian-American parents set for their children, actually *fosters* academic success. Why? Because as we noted in Chapter 7, Asian-American children are also taught from a very early age to be respectful and to obey their elders, who have a duty to train them to be socially responsible and competent human beings (Chao, 1994, 2001). Given this kind of socialization in Asian-American homes, it is hardly surprising that the Asian-American peer group strongly endorses education and encourages academic success (Fuligni, 1997). The result? Asian-American students typically spend more hours studying, often with their supportive friends, than other students do, which undoubtedly accounts for much of their academic success (Fuligni, 1997; Steinberg, Dornbusch, & Brown, 1992).

Teacher Evaluations and Expectations   Teachers have tremendous power to influence their student's self-perceptions, as well as their academic achievement and social status, by virtue of the ways that they interpret and evaluate students' behavior. Let's first discuss some of the avenues by which teachers might influence any student's outcomes and then see how these processes might contribute to ethnic variations in adjustment to school.

First, let's note that teachers form distinct impressions of their students' scholastic abilities, and these expectancies can clearly affect children's academic progress. In a landmark study, Robert Rosenthal and Lenore Jacobson (1968) proposed that a teacher's expectancies about a student can influence the child's achievement through what they called the **Pygmalion effect:** A student should perform better when expected to do well than when expected to do poorly, so that teacher expectancies may become *self-fulfilling prophecies*. To demonstrate this, Rosenthal and Jacobson gave each elementary school teacher in their study a list of five students who were supposed to be "rapid bloomers." In fact, the so-called rapid bloomers had been randomly selected from class rosters. The only way they differed from other students is that their teachers expected more of them. Yet planting these high expectancies in the minds of first- and second-grade teachers was sufficient to cause the so-called rapid bloomers to show greater gains in IQ and reading achievement than their unlabeled classmates.

Clearly, the positive or negative expectations that teachers form often reflect *real* ability differences: Those expected to perform well (or poorly) have often performed well (or poorly) in the past. Still, if two students have equal aptitude and academic motivation, the one whose teacher expects great things is likely to outperform the one whose teacher expects less (Jussim & Eccles, 1992). How does the Pygmalion effect work? It seems that teachers are more likely to challenge high-expectancy students and to praise them for answering questions correctly (perhaps leading them to infer that they have high ability). And when high-expectancy students do not answer correctly, they often hear the question rephrased so that they can get it right, thus implying that failures can be overcome by persisting and trying harder (Dweck & Elliot, 1983). Meanwhile, low-expectancy students are not often challenged and are more likely to be criticized when they answer questions incorrectly—a practice that may convince them that they have *little ability* and undermine their motivation to achieve (Brophy, 1983; Dweck & Elliott, 1983). Teacher expectancy effects on academic achievement are largest in the early grades, particularly in classrooms where high- and low-expectancy students reliably receive differential treatment (Kuklinski & Weinstein, 2000, 2001). And these expectations eventually affect student's own academic self-concepts, thus helping to

Pygmalion effect
the tendency of teacher expectancies to become self-fulfilling prophecies, causing students to perform better or worse depending on their teacher's estimation of their potential.

perpetuate the differences in achievement displayed by high- and low-expectancy students (Kuklinksi & Weinstein, 2001).

Teachers as Contributors to Ethnic Variations in Achievement Now let's consider the possibility that the poor academic outcomes that some minority students display might be partially attributable to differential treatment by their teachers. According to social stereotypes, Asian-American students are expected to be bright and hard-working, whereas African-American, Native American, and Latino students from low-income neighborhoods are expected to perform poorly in school. And teachers are hardly immune to these stereotypes. Minority students often feel that white teachers do not understand them and that they could do better in school were they given more respect and understanding (Ford & Harris, 1996). There is also some evidence that students display more positive outcomes, both socially and academically, when they and their teachers share similar backgrounds (Goldwater & Nutt, 1999; Jackson, Barth, et al., 2006; Meehan, Hughes, & Cavell, 2003). Indeed, teachers in one study were asked to select from a checklist those attributes that best described their lower-income, minority pupils. They consistently selected adjectives such as *lazy, fun-loving,* and *rebellious,* thus implying that they did not expect much of these students (Gottlieb, 1966).

Perhaps you can see how teachers who form expectancies based on these stereotypes might unwittingly contribute to ethnic variations in academic achievement. For example, they may subtly communicate to an Asian-American student that he or she is expected to do well by rephrasing questions that the child has missed, thus sending the message that failures can be overcome by *persisting* and *trying harder.* Indeed, we learned in Chapter 7 (see Box 7.2) that Asian-American students often perform better on academic exercises if their Asian-American identity (and presumably, stereotypes about Asian-Americans) are made salient to them. By contrast, a Mexican-American or African-American student from a low-income neighborhood might be tagged by the teacher as a low-ability student, who is then rarely challenged and is even criticized for errors in ways that cause him to doubt his abilities. Even stigmatized minority students who are doing well at school are at risk of becoming underachievers because, by age 6 to 10, they have become quite aware of broadly held negative stereotypes about their own groups and are already beginning to experience the effects of *stereotype threat* (see Box 7.2) that undermine academic performance (McKown & Weinstein, 2003).

In sum, parents' values, styles of parenting, and involvement in school-related activities, peers' level of support for academic achievement, and teacher expectancies and evaluations probably all contribute to ethnic differences in school achievement. Some theorists believe that children from lower-income, minority subcultures are at an immediate disadvantage when they enter a middle-class scholastic setting and that schools must change dramatically if they are to motivate and better educate these children. Researchers have known for years that underachieving ethnic minorities fare much better at school if the experiences they have in class (or read about in their textbooks) include more information about people of their own ethnicity (Jackson & Davis, 2000; Kagan & Zahn, 1975; Stevenson, Chen, & Uttal, 1990), and this knowledge is a large part of the rationale behind recent efforts to make the school experience more culturally relevant for minority students. Among the positive changes we see today are stronger bilingual education programs designed to meet the needs of children from the over 100 distinct language groups in the United States (Winsler et al., 1999) and multicultural education programs that bring the perspectives of many cultural and subcultural groups into the classroom so that all students feel more welcome there (Banks, 1993; Burnette, 1997).

Educating Students with Special Needs One major challenge that educators face is that of successfully educating students with special needs—learning disabilities, mental retardation, physical and sensory handicaps, and other developmental disorders. These youngsters were once placed in separate schools or classrooms—or in some cases, were rejected as unteachable by public schools—until the U.S. Congress passed the *Education for All Handicapped Children Act* in 1975. Revised in 1990, this law requires school districts to provide an education comparable to that received by other children to all youngsters with special needs. The intent of the law was to better prepare children with special needs to participate in society by ensuring that their educational experiences were as similar as possible to pupils in typical public school classrooms. How might the law be served? Many school districts opted for **inclusion** (formerly called *mainstreaming*)—the practice of integrating special-needs children into regular classrooms for all or large parts of the day, as opposed to segregating them in special schools or classrooms.

Has inclusion accomplished its objectives? Not very well, unfortunately. Compared with other special-needs children who attend segregated special-education classes, those who are "mainstreamed" sometimes fare better academically, particularly if their disability is not severe (Holahan & Costenbader, 2000), but they often do not (Buysse & Baily, 1993; Hunt & Goetz, 1997; Manset & Semmel, 1997). Furthermore, their self-esteem often declines because many special-needs children have trouble initiating and sustaining interactions with classmates, who may ridicule them and are reluctant to choose them as friends or playmates (Guralnick & Groom, 1988; Guralnick et al., 2006; Hunt & Goetz, 1997; Taylor, Asher, & Williams, 1987).

Do these findings imply that inclusion has failed? In one sense, it has, for we have learned that simply putting special-needs students into regular classrooms accomplishes little by itself. To work, inclusion must seek to ensure that students from diverse backgrounds and ability levels do, in fact, interact *positively* with other students and learn what they are supposed to be learning. How might we accomplish these objectives?

Robert Slavin and his colleagues (1991, 1996; Stevens & Slavin, 1995a, 1995b; see also Salend, 1999) have had much success with **cooperative learning methods** in which a special-needs child and several classmates are assigned to work teams and are reinforced for performing well *as a team*. For example, each member of a math team is given problems to solve that are appropriate to his or her ability level. Yet members of a work team also monitor one another's progress and offer one another aid when needed. To encourage this cooperation, the teams that complete the most math units are rewarded—for example, with special certificates that designate them as "superteams." Similarly, the "jigsaw method" of instruction developed by Elliot Aronson and his colleagues (1978) to facilitate racial integration involves giving each member of a small learning team one portion of the material to be learned and requiring him or her to teach it to teammates. Here, then, is a formula for ensuring that children of different social backgrounds and ability levels will interact in a context where the efforts of even the least capable team members are important to the *group's* success.

Clearly, these cooperative learning methods work. Special-needs second-through sixth-graders in classrooms stressing cooperative learning come to like school better and to outperform special-needs peers in traditional classrooms in vocabulary, reading and

Inclusion
the educational practice of integrating special needs students into regular classrooms rather than placing them in segregated special education classes.

cooperative learning methods
an educational practice whereby children of different backgrounds or ability levels are assigned to teams; each team member works on problems geared to his or her ability level, and all members are reinforced for "pulling together" and performing well as a team.

Photo 12.7
By stressing teamwork to achieve shared goals, cooperative learning activities make inclusion a more fruitful experience for children of all ability levels.

Richard Hutchings/PhotoEdit, Inc.

language skills, and tests of metacognitive knowledge, posting even bigger advantages in the second year of cooperative learning than in the first (Stevens & Slavin, 1995a). What's more, both special-needs children and gifted children thrive in the cooperative learning classrooms, often displaying clear gains in self-esteem and becoming more fully accepted by peers (Stevens & Slavin, 1995b). So inclusion can succeed if educators deliberately design learning experiences that encourage students from different backgrounds or ability levels to pool their efforts in order to achieve common goals.

◌ HOW WELL EDUCATED ARE OUR CHILDREN? CROSS-CULTURAL COMPARISONS

How successful are our schools at imparting academic skills to their pupils? Large surveys of the reading, writing, and mathematical achievement of 9- to 17-year-old American students reveal that most of them do learn to read during the elementary school years and have acquired such mathematical proficiencies as basic computational skills and graph-reading abilities by the time they finish high school (National Education Goals Panel, 1992). Yet the most recent assessments available from the National Assessment of Educational Progress—the Nation's Report Card—revealed that only 39 percent of fourth-graders and 32 percent of eighth-graders are "proficient" or better in math skills, and barely a third of the students in these two grades are proficient or better at reading (The Education Trust, 2007). More disturbing perhaps is the finding that one in five American students scores below the basic achievement level in these fundamental academic skills. Furthermore, American youth do not write very well; in fact, more than one-third of all 17-year-olds could not produce a well-formed and coherent paragraph. Are these findings cause for alarm?

Both politicians and educators think so. In fact, earlier evidence that substantial percentages of American school children fail to achieve basic academic proficiencies was the main impetus for No Child Left Behind (NCLB), a law passed in 2001 with bipartisan support that seeks to assure that 100 percent of American school children are proficient (at grade level) or higher in reading and math by 2014 (see Box 12.3 on page 449 for the provisions of NCLB and an early assessment of its effectiveness). Aside from the poor marks many American children make on the Nation's Report Card, several cross-national surveys indicate that the average scores obtained by American school children in math, verbal skills, and science are consistently lower, and sometimes much lower, than those made by students in many other industrialized nations (Martin et al., 2000; National Education Goals Panel, 1992; Stevenson, Chen, & Lee, 1993; and see Table 12.2 for cross-national comparisons in eighth-grade math and science achievement).

Cross-cultural research conducted by Harold Stevenson and his colleagues (Chen & Stevenson, 1995; Stevenson, Lee, & Stigler, 1986; Stevenson, Chen, & Lee, 1993) leaves no doubt that schoolchildren in Taiwan, the People's Republic of China, and Japan outperform students in the United States in math, reading, and other school subjects. The gap in math performance is especially striking; in testing of fifth-graders, for example, only 4 percent of Chinese children and 10 percent of Japanese students had scores on a math achievement test as low as those of the *average* American child (Stevenson, Chen, & Lee, 1993). Achievement differences of this sort are evident from the time children enter school and grow larger each year as children progress from first to fifth to eleventh grade (Geary et al., 1996; Stevenson, Chen, & Lee, 1993). Why do these differences exist, and what can they tell us about improving American education?

The problem is not that American students are any less intelligent, for they enter school performing just as well on IQ tests as their Asian counterparts (Stevenson et al., 1985), and

Table 12.2 Average math and science achievement of eighth-grade students in various nations (1999 scores)

Mathematics		Science	
Singapore	604	Chinese Taipei	569
Republic of Korea	587	Singapore	568
Chinese Taipei	585	Hungary	552
Hong Kong SAR	582	Japan	550
Japan	579	Republic of Korea	549
Netherlands	540	Netherlands	545
Hungary	532	Australia	540
Canada	531	Czech Republic	539
Slovenia	530	England	538
Russian Federation	526	Slovenia	533
Australia	525	Canada	533
Czech Republic	520	Hong Kong SAR	530
Malaysia	519	Russian Federation	529
United States	502	United States	515
England	496	New Zealand	510
New Zealand	491	Italy	493
INTERNATIONAL AVERAGE	487	Malaysia	492
Italy	479	INTERNATIONAL AVERAGE	488
Cyprus	476	Thailand	482
Romania	472	Romania	472
Thailand	467	Cyprus	460
Turkey	429	Iran	448
Iran	422	Turkey	433
Chile	392	Chile	420
Philippines	345	Philippines	345
Morocco	337	Morocco	323
South Africa	275	South Africa	243

☐ Average is significantly higher than the U.S. average
▨ Average does not differ significantly from the U.S. average
▩ Average is significantly lower than the U.S. average

Source: Martin et al. (2000).

they score at least as well as Japanese and Chinese students on general information tests covering material not typically taught in school (Stevenson, Chen, & Lee, 1993). Indeed, most of the achievement gap between American and Asian students seems to reflect cultural differences in educational attitudes and practices. For example:

1. *Classroom instruction.* Asian students spend more time being educated than American students do. Elementary school teachers in Asian countries devote more class time to core academic subjects—for example, two to three times as many hours a week on math instruction. The Asian classroom is a comfortable but businesslike setting where little time is wasted. Asian students spend about 95 percent of their time on "on task" activities such as listening to the teacher and completing assignments, whereas American students spend only about 80 percent of their time "on task" (Stigler, Lee, & Stevenson, 1987). Asian students also attend school for more hours per day and more days per year (often attending half the day on Saturdays) than American students do (Fuligni & Stevenson, 1995; Stevenson, Lee, & Stigler, 1986).

Photo 12.8
Children in traditional Asian classrooms are required to stay in their seats working on assignments or paying close attention to their teacher.

Figure 12.7
Percentages of Chinese, Japanese, and American high school students who picked "studying hard" or having "a good teacher" as the most important factor influencing their performance in mathematics. (Adapted from Chen & Stevenson, 1995.)

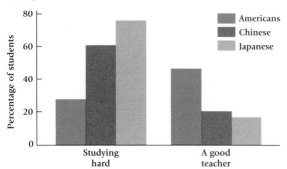

2. *Parental involvement.* Asian parents are strongly committed to the educational process. They hold higher achievement expectancies for their children than American parents do, and even though their children are excelling by American standards, Asian parents are much less likely than American parents to be satisfied with their children's current academic performance (Chen & Stevenson, 1995; Ng, Pomerantz, & Lam, 2007; Stevenson, Chen, & Lee, 1993). Asian parents think that homework is more important than American parents do, and they also receive frequent communications from their children's teachers in notebooks children carry to and from school each day. These communications enable Asian parents to keep close tabs on how their children are progressing and to follow teachers' suggestions about how they can encourage and assist their children at home (Stevenson & Lee, 1990). By contrast, communications between U.S. parents and teachers are often limited to brief annual parent/teacher conferences.

3. *Student involvement.* Not only do Asian students spend more days in class and more class time on academic assignments than American children do, but they are assigned and complete more homework as well (Larson & Verma, 1999; Stevenson, Chen, & Lee, 1993). During the high school years, Asian students continue to devote more time to scholastic activities and spend much less time working, dating, or socializing with friends than American students do (Fuligni & Stevenson, 1995). Much of the socializing that Asian students undertake with peers centers around academics (for example, studying together), and academic achievement is an important contributor to social adjustment and popularity in Asian peer groups (Chen, Chang, & He, 2003).

4. *A strong emphasis on effort.* Another major reason that Asian students apply themselves so diligently to academic activities is that their parents, teachers, and they themselves share the strong belief that all youngsters have the potential to master their studies if they work hard enough; by contrast their American counterparts are more inclined to believe that academic success reflects other factors such as the quality of the child's teachers (see Figure 12.7) or one's native intelligence (Chen & Stevenson, 1995; Stevenson, Chen, & Lee, 1993). East Asian parents are much more likely than American parents to emphasize children's academic failures, taking them as an opportunity to stress an important cultural value—the need to strive for self-improvement by working harder (Ng, Pomerantz, & Lam, 2007). Asian students face especially strong pressures to excel in the classroom because their prospects for obtaining a college education largely depend on the results of competitive exams taken in high school. Yet their strong belief that effort will ultimately pay off in better learning (and higher test scores) helps to explain why Asian youngsters are no more anxious about school or otherwise psychologically maladjusted than American students are (Chen, Chang, & He, 2003; Chen & Stevenson, 1995; Crystal et al., 1994).

Box 12.3 Current Controversies

Can No Child Left Behind Succeed at Leaving No Children Behind?

The No Child Left Behind Act (NCLB) is based on theory of change that politicians hope will raise American students' academic achievement (Porter & Polikoff, 2007). Here are its major provisions:

◆ Create curriculum and content standards to show teachers what they are supposed to teach.

◆ Use student achievement tests to convince teachers to teach the content that will enable students to reach achievement targets.

◆ Make teachers and schools accountable by requiring them to meet adequate yearly progress (AYP) toward achievement targets. Schools failing to meet AYP for six consecutive years must be restructured. What's more, students in schools failing to meet AYP for two consecutive years would be allowed to transfer to schools making better progress.

◆ Disaggregate data on student performance to ensure that special-needs students and those from all ethnic and socioeconomic groups are making AYP.

◆ Set minimum standards to ensure that teachers are qualified and thus up to the task of effectively teaching program-mandated content.

This very complex law has been in force only since 2002, and several of its provisions (for example, the six-year accountability standards defining the need for school restructuring) have yet to come into play. And some interpretive problems have already arisen. Individual states have considerable leeway in defining standards of student proficiency, AYP, and teacher qualifications, and this presents major problems in evaluating NCLB. For example, 21 states have set standards defining "proficiency" so low that they translate to Nation's Report Scores falling just below the "basic" proficiency level. How do we compare progress toward proficiency of students in these states to that of students in states with more ambitious proficiency targets? And although all states require teachers to have a Bachelor's degree to ensure their qualifications to teach, some states require that their teachers score at nearly the 75th percentile in their knowledge of their subject matter to be labeled highly qualified to teach, whereas others require a score below the 25th percentile to be "highly qualified." Thus, proficiency standards, progress toward achieving them, and the qualifications of instructors assisting students to achieve these goals

vary so much that using state-by-state data to evaluate NCLB and make comparisons is akin to comparing apples with oranges.

So what can we say about changes in student achievement since the implementation of NCLB? If we rely on standardized *national* tests—Nation's report card assessments of reading and math proficiencies—it appears that there have been

◆ Modest improvements in the math proficiencies of American students and smaller improvements in the reading proficiencies of elementary school students (Center on Education Policy, 2007; Porter & Polikoff, 2007).

◆ Small improvements at narrowing the achievement gap in reading and math proficiencies between blacks and whites, Latinos and whites, and among students from different socioeconomic backgrounds (Porter & Polikoff, 2007).

◆ Modest gains in teacher qualifications (Desimone, Smith, & Frisvold, 2007).

Is NCLB working then? Few educators would agree that it is the resounding success that President George W. Bush proclaimed it to be (The White House, 2007); in fact many are much less optimistic, saying that although scores are moving in the right direction, (1) it is really too early to draw causal connections between NCLB and improvements made, and (2) given the modest progress to date, it seems clear that *many changes* are necessary to *ever* achieve NCLB's goal of making 100 percent of America's children proficient in math and reading (for a sampling of recommended changes, see Figlio, 2007; Porter & Polikoff, 2007; Schwartz & McCartney, 2007). Others have criticized NCLB for placing all the accountability pressures on teachers and schools, failing to recognize that so many children are at risk of failing because they have not acquired the requisite skills *at home* that would better enable them to succeed at school. And notice that NCLB does not emphasize or fund many of the early childhood interventions—quality preschool education and programs to get parents more involved in their children's learning activities—that we know to have very positive effects on later educational outcomes. So although NCLB may be a step in the right direction, far more will be needed to come close to reaching the ambitious goals that this well-meaning law seeks to achieve.

So the formula for more effective education may not be so mysterious after all, judging from the success of the Chinese and Japanese educational systems. The secret is to get teachers, students, and parents working together to make education a top priority for youth, to set high achievement goals, and to invest the day-by-day effort required to attain those objectives. In response to evidence that American students are being outclassed by those in other countries, many states and local school districts have taken up the challenge. How? By strengthening curricula, tightening standards for teacher certification, raising standards for graduation and promotion from grade to grade, implementing alternative academic calendars to shorten summer vacations and increase student retention in previously learned material, and, most importantly, seeking ways to involve parents as partners with teachers, at both the elementary and secondary school levels, to create more supportive learning environments (Gonzalez, 2000; Zigler, Finn-Stevenson, & Stern, 1997). These educational reformers are well aware that improving the scholastic and vocational preparation of American's youth is crucial if Americans are to maintain a leadership role in an ever-changing and ever more competitive world.

SUMMARY

- This chapter focuses on three **extrafamilial influences** on developing children and adolescents: television, computers, and the schools.

THE EARLY WINDOW: EFFECTS ON TELEVISION ON CHILDREN AND ADOLESCENTS

- Although children spend more time watching television than in any other waking activity, TV viewing, in moderate doses, is unlikely to impair their cognitive growth, academic achievement, or peer relations.

- Prior to age 8 or 9, children are most captivated by visual production features on TV programming and may have difficulty inferring characters' motives and intentions or reconstructing a coherent story line. However, cognitive development and experience watching television leads to increases in **television literacy** during middle childhood and adolescence.

- Three lines of evidence—correlational surveys, laboratory experiments, and field experiments—*converge* on the conclusions that heavy exposure to televised violence can instigate aggressive behavior, cultivate aggressive habits and **mean-world beliefs,** and **desensitize** viewers to instances of real-world aggression. Taken together, this evidence supports the social-learning viewpoint on the effects of televised violence and provides no support for the catharsis hypothesis.

- In addition to the potentially harmful impacts of televised violence, commercial TV programs also present negative stereotypes that influence viewers' beliefs about minority groups and gender issues, and children are easily manipulated by TV commercials that push products that parents are reluctant to purchase. What's more, excessive TV viewing restricts physical activity and contributes to **obesity** and related health problems.

- On the positive side, children are likely to learn prosocial lessons and to put them into practice after watching acts of kindness on television. Parents can help by watching shows such as *Mister Rogers' Neighborhood* with their children and then encouraging them to verbalize or role-play the prosocial lessons they have observed. Educational programs such as *Sesame Street* have been quite successful at fostering basic cognitive skills that enhance children's readiness for school, particularly when children watch with an adult who discusses the material with them and helps them to apply what they have learned.

CHILD DEVELOPMENT IN THE COMPUTER AGE

- Children seem to benefit, both intellectually and socially, from their use of computers. In the hands of knowledgeable teachers who present their pupils with higher-level, thought-provoking academic games and simulations, **computer-assisted instruction** often improves children's achievement. Learning to program a computer can also facilitate cognitive and **metacognitive** development. What's more, computers often promote rather than inhibit social interactions with peers.

- Internet exposure has been shown to have such positive benefits as improving the reading skills of disadvantaged children, providing opportunities for more intimate self-disclosure that leads to closer friendships, and providing information about health issues that allow adolescents to make healthier or less risky decisions about their conduct.

- There are concerns about children's use of computers including (1) data illustrating that violent computer games instigate hostile attributional biases and aggressive behavior, (2) fears that disadvantaged children and girls may reap fewer benefits associated with computer use, and (3) harm may result from exposure to pornography, unrestricted access to sexual predators and other unsavory influences on the Internet.

THE SCHOOL AS A SOCIALIZATION AGENT

- Schools influence many aspects of development. Formal scholastic curricula are intended to impart academic knowledge, and schooling promotes cognitive and metacognitive development by teaching rules and problem-solving strategies that can be applied to many different kinds of information. Schools also pursue an **informal curriculum** that teaches children culturally valued social skills that help them to become good citizens.

- Aside from fostering children's cognitive development, some schools are more "effective" than others at producing positive outcomes such as low absenteeism, an enthusiastic attitude about learning, academic achievement, occupational skills, and socially desirable patterns of behavior. What makes a school effective is not the precise amount of money spent per pupil, average class size, or whether schools practice **ability tracking** or mixed-ability instruction. Instead, **effective schools** are those in which (1) teachers create a classroom environment that is comfortable, task-focused, and engaging; (2) students are motivated to learn; and (3) there are positive **aptitude-treatment interactions**—that is, a "good fit" between students' personal or cultural characteristics and the kinds of instruction they receive. In many ways, effective teachers are like authoritative parents and can contribute positively to their pupils' social, emotional, and academic development. Indeed, students prefer such **authoritative instruction** to more **authoritarian** or **permissive** instructional styles.

- Ethnic differences in adjustments to school and scholastic challenges can often be traced to parental and peer influences and to differential treatment by teachers, as illustrated by teacher expectancy or **Pygmalion effects.**

- At best, the practice of **inclusion** has produced modest improvements (or no improvements) in the academic performance of special-needs students while failing to enhance their self-esteem or peer acceptance. Among the steps that might be taken to better meet the educational needs of all of our students are creating stronger bilingual and multicultural educational programs and making greater use of **cooperative learning methods** in the classroom.

HOW WELL EDUCATED ARE OUR CHILDREN? CROSS-CULTURAL COMPARISONS

- Cross-national surveys of academic achievement clearly brand American students as "underachievers," especially in math and science. The achievement gap that exists between American schoolchildren and those in many other industrialized societies centers around cultural differences in educational attitudes, educational practices, and the involvement of both parents and students in the learning process. No Child Left Behind has produced modest gains in student achievement but needs to be restructured to achieve its lofty objectives.

CHAPTER 13

Extrafamilial Influences II: Peers as Socialization Agents

THROUGHOUT THIS TEXT, we have focused heavily on adults as socializing agents. In their roles as parents, teachers, coaches, scoutmasaters, and religious leaders, adults clearly represent the power, authority, and expertise of a society. However, some theorists, Jean Piaget among them, believe that peers may contribute as much (or even more) to a child's or an adolescent's development as adults do (Harris, 1998, 2000; Sullivan, 1953; Youniss, McLellan, & Strouse, 1994). In effect, they argue that there are "two social worlds of childhood," one involving adult/child transactions and the other involving the society of one's peers, and that these social systems influence development in different ways.

What roles do peers play in a child's or an adolescent's development? If we allow ourselves to be influenced by popular novels and films such as *Lord of the Flies* and *Dead Poets Society*, we might conclude that peers are subversive agents who often undermine the best laid plans of adults and lead the child into a life of rebelliousness and antisocial conduct. However, developmentalists now know that this perspective on peer influences is highly distorted and unnecessarily negative (Hartup & Stevens, 1997). Yes, peers are occasionally "bad influences"; but they clearly have the potential to affect their playmates in a number of positive ways. Consider the viewpoint of a lonely farmer from the Midwestern United States whose own life experiences convinced him that normal peer interactions foster healthy and adaptive developmental outcomes.

> Dear Dr. Moore:
>
> I read the report in the Oct. 30 issue of _____ about your study of only children. I am an only child, now 57 years old, and I want to tell you some things about my life. Not only was I an only child, but I grew up in the country where there were no nearby children to play with . . . [And] from the first year of school, I was teased and made fun of . . . I dreaded to get on the school bus and go to school because the other children on the bus called me "Mommy's baby." In about the second grade I heard the boys use a vulgar word. I asked what it meant and they made fun of me. So I learned a lesson—don't ask questions. This can lead to a lot of confusion to hear talk one doesn't understand and not be able to learn what it means. I never went out with a girl while I was in school—in fact I hardly talked to them. In our school the boys and girls did not play together. Boys were sent to one part of the playground and girls to another. So I didn't learn anything about girls. When we got into high school and boys and girls started dating, I could only listen to their stories about their experiences.
>
> I could tell you a lot more, but the important thing is I have never married or had any children. I have not been very successful in an occupation or vocation. I believe my troubles are not all due to being an only child . . . but I do believe you are right in recommending playmates for . . . school agers and not have them strictly supervised by adults. . . Parents of only children should make special efforts to provide playmates for them.
>
> Sincerely yours, [1]

If we assume that peers are important agents of socialization, there are a number of questions that remain to be answered. For example, who qualifies as a peer? How do peers influence one another? What is it about peer influence that is unique? What are the consequences (if any) of poor peer relations? Is it important to have special peer alliances, or friendships? Do peers eventually become a more potent source of influence than parents or other adults? These are some of the issues that we will explore in the pages that follow.

---

[1]This letter appears with the permission of its author and its recipient, Dr. Shirley G. Moore.

WHO IS A PEER AND WHAT FUNCTIONS DO PEERS SERVE?

Webster's New Collegiate Dictionary defines a **peer** as "one that is of equal standing with another." Developmentalists also think of peers as "*social equals*" or as individuals *who, for the moment at least, are operating at similar levels of behavioral complexity* (Lewis & Rosenblum, 1975). According to this *activity-based* definition, children who differ somewhat in age could still be considered "peers"—as long as they can adjust their behaviors to suit one another's capabilities as they pursue common interests or goals.

peers
two or more persons who are operating at similar levels of behavioral complexity.

The Significance of Peer Interaction

Early research on peer influence was heavily influenced by theorists from the *ethological* tradition, who sought to determine the *adaptive significance* of child/child interactions. You may recall from Chapters 9 and 10 that conflicts among peers when resources (toys) are scarce can help youngsters learn how to resolve their differences amicably by fostering the growth of prosocial modes of conflict resolution, such as sharing (see Caplan et al., 1991). We also noted that even overtly hostile exchanges among 3- to 5-year-olds may prove adaptive by helping to create *dominance hierarchies* that establish the relative power and status of individual group members and thereby *minimize* the likelihood of future aggression within the peer group (see Sackin & Thelen, 1984; Strayer, 1980). Based on such observations, ethologists propose that peer interaction may be a special form of social behavior that has been "selected" over the course of evolution to promote the development of adaptive patterns of social conduct in each successive generation. Let's now consider some of the specific functions that child/child interactions might serve.

Same-Age (or Equal-Status) Interactions We gain some idea why contacts among age-mates may be important by contrasting them to exchanges that occur with parents. A child's interactions with parents are typically lopsided: Because parents are the more powerful associates, children are in a subordinate position at home and must often defer to adult authority. By contrast, age-mates typically have roughly equal status and must learn to appreciate each other's perspectives, negotiate and compromise, and cooperate if they are to play amicably or achieve other joint objectives. Thus, equal-status contacts with peers are likely to contribute to the development of social competencies that are difficult to acquire in the nonegalitarian atmosphere of the home.

Mixed-Age Interactions According to Hartup (1983), interaction among children of *different* ages is also a critically important context for social and personality development. Although **mixed-age interactions** tend to be somewhat *unbalanced*, with one child (typically the elder) possessing more power than the other, these asymmetries may help children to acquire certain social competencies. One cross-cultural survey revealed that the presence of younger peers may foster the development of compassion, caregiving, prosocial inclinations, assertiveness, and leadership skills in older children (Whiting & Edwards, 1988; see also Kowalski et al., 2004). At the same time, younger children benefited from mixed-age interactions by acquiring a variety of new skills from older playmates and by learning how to seek assistance and defer gracefully to these more powerful associates. Older children usually take charge of mixed-age interactions and adjust their behavior to the competencies of their younger companions. Even 2-year-olds show such powers of leadership and accommodation, for they are already more inclined to take the initiative and to display simpler and more repetitive play routines when paired with an 18-month-old toddler than with an age-mate (Brownell, 1990).

mixed-age peer interaction
interactions among children who differ in age by a year or more.

Photo 13.1
Both older and younger children benefit from mixed-age interactions.

Perhaps you have noticed that mixed-age peer interactions are presumed to benefit older and younger children in many of the same ways that sibling interactions benefit older and younger siblings (see Chapter 11). But there is a crucial difference between sibling and peer contacts, for one's status as either a younger or an older sibling is *fixed* by order of birth, whereas one's peer status is more *flexible*, depending on the associates one chooses. So mixed-age *peer* interactions may provide children with experiences they might otherwise miss in their sibling interactions and, in fact, may be the primary context in which (1) an habitually domineering elder sibling learns to be more accommodating (when interacting with older peers); (2) an oppressed younger sib learns to lead and to show compassion (when dealing with even younger children); and (3) an only child (who has no sibs) acquires both sets of social competencies. Viewed in this way, mixed-age peer interactions may be important experiences indeed.

Frequency of Peer Contacts

Between the ages of 2 and 12, children spend more and more time with peers and less and less time with adults (Rubin, Bukowski, & Parker, 2006). This trend is nicely illustrated in Figure 13.1, which summarizes what Sherri Ellis and her colleagues (1981) found while observing 436 children playing in their homes and around the neighborhood. Interestingly, this same study revealed that youngsters of all ages spend *less* time with age-mates (defined as children whose ages were within a year of their own) than with children who were more than a year older or younger than they were. Apparently, we must take seriously the idea that peers are social equals rather than age-mates.

Another finding of Ellis's study is a familiar one: Even 1- to 2-year-olds played more often with same-sex companions than with other-sex companions, and this *gender segregation* became increasingly apparent with age. Once in their sex-segregated worlds, boys and girls experience different kinds of social relationships. Boys tend to form "packs," whereas girls form "pairs"; that is, a boy often plays competitive games or team sports in groups, whereas a girl more often establishes a longer and more cooperative relationship with one or two playmates (Benenson, Apostoleris, & Parnass, 1997; Fabes, Martin, & Hanish, 2003).

Overall, then, children spend an increasing amount of time with peers, and those peers are typically *same-sex* children who are only *roughly similar* in age but who enjoy the same kinds of gender-typed activities.

How Important Are Peer Influences?

To this point, we have speculated that peer interactions may promote the development of many social and personal competencies that are not easily acquired within the decidedly nonegalitarian parent/child relationship. Is there truly any basis for such a claim? And if so, just how important are these peer influences? Developmentalists became very interested in these questions once they learned of Harry Harlow's research with rhesus monkeys.

Harlow's Work with Monkeys Will youngsters who have little or no contact with peers turn out to be abnormal or maladjusted? To find out, Harlow and his associates (Alexander & Harlow, 1965; Suomi & Harlow, 1978) raised rhesus monkeys with their mothers and denied them the opportunity to play with peers. These **"mother-only" monkeys** failed to

"mother-only" monkeys
monkeys who are raised with their mothers and denied any contact with peers.

Figure 13.1
Developmental changes in children's companionship with adults and other children. (Adapted from Ellis, Rogoff, & Cromer, 1981.)

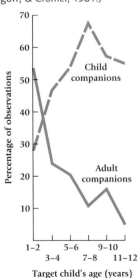

develop normal patterns of social behavior. When finally exposed to age-mates, the peer-deprived youngsters preferred to avoid them. On those occasions when they did approach a peer, these social misfits tended to be highly (and inappropriately) aggressive, and their antisocial tendencies often persisted into adulthood.

Is peer contact, then, the key to normal social development? Not entirely. In later experiments, Harlow and his colleagues separated rhesus monkeys from their mothers and raised them so that they had continuous exposure to their peers. These **"peer-only" monkeys** were observed to cling tenaciously to one another and to form strong mutual attachments. Yet their social development was somewhat atypical in that they became highly agitated over minor stresses or frustrations, and as adults they were unusually aggressive toward monkeys from outside their peer groups.

Courtesy Harlow Primate Center, University of Wisconsin

Photo 13.2
Monkeys raised only with peers form strong mutual attachments and will often attack other monkeys from outside their peer group.

"peer-only" monkeys
monkeys who are separated from their mothers (and other adults) soon after birth and raised with peers.

A Human Parallel   In 1951, Anna Freud and Sophie Dann reported a startling human parallel to Harlow's peer-only monkeys. During the summer of 1945, six 3-year-olds were found living by themselves in a Nazi concentration camp. Soon after these children were born, their parents were put to death. Although they received minimal caregiving from a series of inmates who were periodically executed, these children had, in effect, reared themselves.

When rescued at the war's end, the six orphans were flown to a special treatment center in England, where attempts were made to "rehabilitate" them. How did these "peer-only" children respond to this treatment? They began by breaking nearly all their toys and damaging their furniture. What's more, they often reacted with cold indifference or open hostility toward the staff at the center. And like Harlow's monkeys, these children had no other wish than to be together and became extremely agitated when they were separated . . . even for short periods. They also showed a remarkable prosocial concern for one another.

> There was no occasion to urge the children to "take turns"; they did it spontaneously. They were extremely considerate of each other's feelings. . . . At mealtimes handing food to one's neighbor was of greater importance than eating oneself. [Freud & Dann, 1951, pp. 131–133]

Although these youngsters displayed many signs of anxiety and were highly suspicious of outsiders, they eventually established positive relationships with their adult caregivers and acquired a new language during the first year at the center. The story even has a happy ending, for 35 years later, these orphans were leading effective, productive lives as middle-aged adults (Hartup, 1983).

Taken together, Harlow's monkey research and Freud and Dann's observations of their war orphans suggest that parents and peers each contribute something essential but different and perhaps unique to a child's (or a monkey's) social development. Regular contacts with sensitive, responsive parents not only permit infants to acquire some very basic interactive skills but also provide a sense of *security* that enables them to venture forth to explore the environment and to discover that other individuals can be interesting companions (Hartup, 1989; Rubin, Bukowski, & Parker, 2006). By contrast, contacts with peers may allow children (and young monkeys) to elaborate their basic interactive routines and to develop competent and adaptive patterns of social behavior with associates who are more or less similar to themselves. Indeed, Harlow's "peer-only" monkeys lacked the security of a mother/infant relationship, perhaps explaining why they clutched at one another, were reluctant to explore, and were terrified by (and aggressive toward) outsiders. But *within*

Box 13.1 Current Controversies

Are Peers More Important Than Parents?

One of the more controversial ideas to emerge in recent years is Judith Harris's (1995, 1998, 2000) notion that peers are far more important as socialization agents that parents are. Specifically, Harris claims that:

1. Developmentalists have long assumed that correlations between parenting practices and child outcomes are due to parental influences (that is, socialization) within the family when, in fact, they are largely due to genes shared by parents and their children.

2. Any influence that parents do have is limited to children's behavior at home; such influence is strongest for young children and rarely affects their behaviors away from home.

3. Because adaptive social learning is specific to particular contexts, peers are more important than parents in socializing children for the world outside the home.

Harris states that "Children would develop into the same sort of adults if we left their lives outside the home unchanged and left them in their schools and neighborhoods—but switched all the parents around" (Harris, 1998, p.359). To make her point, she notes that immigrant children quickly acquire a new language and new cultural traditions from peers, even when their parents come from a very different culture and speak a different language.

Harris's ideas were heavily influenced by some of the behavioral genetics research we discussed in Chapter 3. She argues that research claiming that certain parenting styles (for example, authoritative parenting) foster adaptive outcomes fails to control for important genetic influences. For example, if certain parents are genetically predisposed to parent authoritatively, their children may turn out well not because of the parenting they receive but because they may share genes with their parents that foster adaptive development. What's more, Harris correctly notes that siblings raised by the same parents often turn out differently. Why? Because, she argues, they have different genes and genetically influenced attributes that elicit different responses from parents. In effect, parents are said to react to preexisting genetic differences among their children rather than to parent in ways that would create individual differences in developmental outcomes.

Harris goes on to argue that peer socialization makes children from different families alike. As they spend more time with peers and figure out what social groups (based on age, sex, and interest patterns) they belong to, children increasingly want to be like other members of these groups. Thus, they carefully attend to other children and adopt the attitudes, speech patterns, dress codes, and patterns of behavior that prevail within their focal peer groups. And they eventually begin to associate with peers who are more

their own peer groups, they developed competent interactive routines and displayed normal patterns of social behavior (Suomi & Harlow, 1978).

Just how important is it for human beings to establish and maintain *harmonious* relations with their peers? Apparently it is very important. Reviews of more than 30 studies reveal that youngsters who have been rejected by their peers during grade school are much more likely than those who have enjoyed good peer relations to drop out of school, become involved in delinquent or criminal activities, and display serious psychological difficulties later in adolescence and young adulthood (Parker & Asher, 1987, Parker et al., 1995; see also Rubin, Bukowski, & Parker, 2006). So merely having contact with peer associates is not enough to ensure normal developmental outcomes; getting along with peers is important too.

In sum, peers do seem to be important agents of socialization, and the task of becoming *appropriately* sociable with peers is a most important developmental hurdle. In fact, Judith Harris is one theorist who believes that peers and peer interactions are far more important in shaping a child's or an adolescents's developmental outcomes than parents and parenting practices are. In Box 13.1, we examine Harris's controversial claims, and the reactions of her critics to them, before returning to the topic of peer sociability and focusing on some of the factors that influence how appropriately (or inappropriately) sociable a child turns out to be.

☜ THE DEVELOPMENT OF PEER SOCIABILITY

sociability
one's willingness to interact with others and to seek their attention or approval.

Sociability is a term that describes the child's willingness to engage others in social interaction and to seek their attention or approval. In Chapter 5, we noted that even young infants are sociable creatures: Months before forming their first attachments, they are already smiling, cooing, or otherwise trying to attract the attention of caregivers and are likely to protest whenever any *adult* puts them down or walks off and leaves them alone (Schaffer &

psychologically similar to themselves, creating social environments that are largely compatible with their genetic predispositions. So intellectually inclined youngsters associate with the brainiacs (see Iervolino et al., 2002), which reinforces their interest in intellectual pursuits (Kindermann, 2007; Rubin, Bukowski, & Parker, 2006); by contrast, children inclined to be aggressive often associate and identify with other aggressive peers, which perpetuates or even increases their aggressive inclinations (Ellis & Zarbatany, 2007). Over time, then, Harris asserts that parenting practices matter little, and genetic predispositions, in concert with peer influences, largely determine one's developmental outcomes.

Not surprisingly, developmentalists who study family processes have reacted sharply to Harris's theory, charging that she badly overstates her case (Collins et al., 2000; Vandell, 2000). They claim that she lacks any compelling evidence that peers are the primary influence on child or adolescent development. What's more, there is solid evidence that parenting behaviors do matter, even when genetic influences are taken into account. For example, we learned in Chapter 3 that identical twins will show different patterns of development to the extent that they are treated differently by their parents (Asbury et al., 2003). Because these identical twins have identical genes, the differences they display have to be attributable (in part at least) to different parenting. And recall from Chapters 5 and 11 that the caregiving sensitivity (or lack thereof) of adoptive parents largely determines whether their adoptees form secure or insecure attachments with them (Stams, Juffer, & van IJzendoorn, 2002) and influences the character of their social developmental outcomes throughout childhood and adolescence (Jaffari-Bimmel et al., 2006). Again, this reflects a true parental influence because adoptive parents share no genes with their adopted children. What's more, we learned in Box 5.2 that parents of temperamentally difficult infants can be helped to become more sensitive, responsive caregivers and that improvements in caregiver sensitivity are *causally related* to the security of attachments their infants form. Finally, we will see later in this chapter that parents not only influence their children's ability to interact amicably with peers but that their parenting practices also influence the kinds of peers with whom their children are likely to associate.

In sum, Harris is correct in asserting that (1) both genes and peers contribute substantially to our social/personality development, and (2) developmentalists may often have overestimated the role of parenting in shaping child and adolescent outcomes. However, she is wrong in concluding that patterns of parenting don't matter. As we've seen throughout the text (and will see in this chapter as well), *both* parents and peers—as well as siblings, teachers, and other socialization agents operating within specific cultural or subcultural contexts—all contribute substantially to human development (Bronfenbrenner & Morris, 2006; Collins et al., 2000; Vandell, 2000).

Emerson, 1964). But would they be so positively disposed to a peer—that is, an infant or a toddler companion?

Peer Sociability in Infancy and Toddlerhood

It seems that evolution may have equipped human infants not only with a capacity for forming attachments to caregivers but also with a capacity for entering relationships with peers (Nash & Hay, 2003). By 6–7 months of age, babies will often smile, vocalize, and gesture to other babies and occasionally offer them toys (Vandell & Mueller, 1995). And 6- to 10-month-olds are already showing some simple social preferences, for they reliably choose to play with a partner that they have seen help rather than hurt a companion (Hamlin, Wynn, & Bloom, 2007). By the end of the first year, infants may even imitate another child's simple actions with a toy, thus implying that they are trying to share meaning with or to understand the intentions of a peer (Rubin, Bukowski, & Parker, 2006). Nevertheless, many friendly gestures among children this young go unnoticed and unreciprocated.

Between 12 and 18 months of age, toddlers begin to react more appropriately to each other's behavior, often partaking in more complex exchanges in which participants appear to take turns. Here is one example:

> Larry sits on the floor and Bernie turns and looks toward him. Bernie waves his hand and says "da," still looking at Larry. He repeats the vocalization three more times before Larry laughs. Bernie vocalizes again and Larry laughs again. This same sequence is repeated twelve more times before Bernie . . . walks off. (Mueller & Lucas, 1975, p. 241)

Yet there is some question about whether these "action/reaction" episodes qualify as true social discourse, for 12- to 18-month-olds often seem to treat peers as particularly responsive "toys" that they can control by making them look, gesture, smile, and laugh (Brownell, 1986).

Photo 13.3
With age, toddlers' interactions with one another become increasingly skilled and reciprocal.

By 18 months of age, however, almost all infants are beginning to display *coordinated interactions* with age-mates that are clearly social in character. They now take a great delight in *imitating* each other (Asendorph, 2002; Nielsen & Dissanayake, 2003) and will often gaze and smile at their partners as they turn their imitative sequences into social games (Eckerman & Didow, 1996; Eckerman & Stein, 1990; Howes & Matheson, 1992). In fact, 18-month-olds are so highly attentive to peers that they are now more likely to imitate a peer's simple actions than to imitate adult models who perform the same actions (Ryalls, Gul, & Ryalls, 2000).

By age 20–24 months, toddlers' play has a strong verbal component: Playmates often describe their ongoing play activities to each other ("I fall down!" "Me too, I fall down!") or attempt to influence the role their partner should assume ("You go in playhouse.") (Eckerman & Didow, 1996). This coordinated social speech makes it easier for 2- to 2½-year-olds to assume *complementary roles,* such as chaser and chasee in a game of tag, or to cooperate to achieve a shared goal, as illustrated by one child's operating a handle, thereby enabling the second to retrieve attractive toys from a container (Brownell & Carriger, 1990; see also Brownell, Ramani, & Zerwas, 2006).

Both social and cognitive developments contribute to the growth of peer sociability over the first two years. In Chapter 5, we learned that toddlers who are securely attached to their caregivers are generally more outgoing and more attractive as playmates than those who are insecurely attached, thus implying that the sensitive, responsive caregiving that securely attached infants receive contributes in a positive way to development of **social skills.** And 18- to 24-month-olds are beginning to display truly coordinated, reciprocal interactions at precisely the time that they first display self-awareness on the rouge test and can discriminate photographs of themselves from those of peers (see Chapter 6). This may be no accident. Celia Brownell and Michael Carriger (1990) propose that toddlers must first realize that both they and their companions are independent agents who can act on their intentions to make things happen before they are likely to play complementary games or try to coordinate their actions to accomplish a goal. And consistent with their reasoning, they found that toddlers who cooperated successfully to achieve a goal did score higher on a test of self–other differentiation than their less cooperative agemates (see also Brownell, Ramani, & Zerwas, 2006), thus implying that early interactive skills may depend very heavily on social-cognitive development. Indeed, a sense of *intersubjectivity*—the ability to share meaning, intentions, and goals with a social partner—is absolutely essential for the emergence of intricate *pretend play* activities that unfold and become progressively more complex throughout the preschool period (Rubin, Bukowski, & Parker, 2006).

social skills
thoughts, actions, and emotional regulatory activities that enable children to achieve personal or social goals while maintaining harmony with their social partners.

Sociability during the Preschool Period

Between the ages of 2 and 5, children not only become more outgoing but also direct their social gestures to a wider audience. Observational studies suggest that 2- to 3-year-olds are more likely than older children to remain near an adult and to seek physical affection, whereas the sociable behaviors of 4- to 5-year-olds normally consist of playful bids for attention or approval that are directed at *peers* rather than adults (Harper & Huie, 1985; Hartup, 1983).

As children become more peer oriented during the preschool years, the character of their interactions changes as well. In a classic study, Mildred Parten (1932) observed 2½ - to 4-year-olds during free-play periods at nursery school, looking for developmental changes in the *social complexity* of peer interactions. She found that preschoolers' play activities could be placed into four categories, arranged from least to most socially complex:

1. **Nonsocial activity**—children watch others play or engage in their own solitary play and largely ignore what others are doing.

2. **Parallel play**—children play side by side but interact very little and do not try to influence the behavior of other players.

3. **Associative play**—children now share toys and swap materials, but pursue their own agendas and do not cooperate to achieve shared goals.

4. **Cooperative play**—children now act out make-believe themes, assume reciprocal roles, and collaborate to achieve shared goals.

As we see in Figure 13.2, solitary and parallel play declined with age, whereas associative and cooperative play became more common. Parten concluded that her data reflect a three-step developmental sequence in which solitary play emerges first and is least mature, followed by parallel play, which eventually gives way to more mature forms of associative and cooperative play.

Some researchers have challenged Parten's conclusions, noting that solitary play is actually quite common throughout the preschool period and need not be considered immature (Hartup, 1983; Rubin, Bukowski, & Parker, 1983). If solitary play is *functional* in character, involving such cognitively simplistic and repetitive actions as rolling a ball back and forth or running around a room, then it might be properly labeled "immature" (Coplan et al., 2001). However, most of the solitary play of the preschool period is more cognitively complex and *constructive* in nature, as children work alone to build towers of blocks, draw pictures, or complete puzzles. Interestingly, this more passive, constructive solitary play is positively associated with emotional adjustment and social competencies among kindergarten girls, but not among kindergarten boys. Because boys normally play in groups, solitary play and more reticent onlooker behaviors may appear unusual or antisocial to teachers and peers,

nonsocial activity
onlooker behavior and solitary play.

parallel play
largely noninteractive play in which players are in close proximity but do not often attempt to influence each other.

associative play
form of social discourse in which children pursue their own interests but will swap toys or comment on each other's activities.

cooperative play
true social play in which children cooperate or assume reciprocal roles while pursuing shared goals.

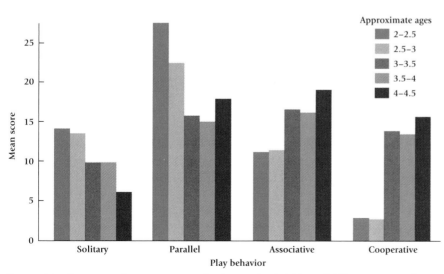

Figure 13.2 Frequency of activities engaged in by preschool children of different ages. With age, solitary and parallel play occur less frequently, whereas associative and cooperative play occur more frequently. (Adapted from Parten, 1932.)

Table 13.1 Changes in play activities from infancy through the preschool period

Play Type	Age of Appearance	Description
Parallel play	6–12 months	Two children perform similar activities without paying any attention to each other.
Parallel aware play	By age 1	Children engage in parallel play while occasionally looking at each other or monitoring each other's activities.
Simple pretend play	1–1½ years	Children engage in similar activities while talking, smiling, sharing toys, or otherwise interacting.
Complementary and reciprocal play	1½–2 years	Children display action-based role reversals in social games such as run-and-chase or peekaboo.
Cooperative social pretend play	2½–3 years	Children play complementary *nonliteral*, or "pretend," roles (for example, mommy and baby), but without any planning or discussion about the meaning of these roles or about the form the play will take.
Complex social pretend play (or sociodramatic play)	3½–4 years	Children actively *plan* their pretend play. They name and explicitly assign roles for each player and propose a play script, and may stop playing to modify the script if play breaks down.

Source: Adapted from Howes & Matheson, 1992.

and may reflect shyness or social anxieties that could cause a boy to be neglected or even shunned by peers in the years ahead (Coplan et al., 2001; Hart, Yang, & Nelson, 2000).

Other researchers believe that the "maturity" of preschool play depends more on its cognitive complexity than on its social or nonsocial character. In a longitudinal study in which the play activities of a group of 1- to 2-year-olds were observed at six-month intervals for three years, Carolee Howes and Catherine Matheson (1992) found that play became more and more cognitively complex with age, as described by the six-category sequence in Table 13.1. What's more, there was a clear relationship between the complexity of a child's play and the child's social competence with peers: Children whose play was more complex at any given age were rated as more outgoing and prosocially inclined and as less aggressive and withdrawn at the next observation period six months later. So it seems that the *cognitive complexity* of a child's play (particularly pretend play) is a reliable predictor of his or her future social competencies with peers.

Cultural Influences   Although cognitively complex forms of social pretend play become more frequent with age in all cultures, the character of preschoolers' play is influenced by cultural values (Goencue, Mistry, & Mosier, 2000). One study comparing the pretend play of American and Korean preschoolers (Farver, Kim, & Lee-Shin, 2000) found that U.S. children liked to play superheros and to act out themes of danger, whereas Korean children generally took on family roles and enacted everyday activities. American children also played up their individual exploits and bossed others around, whereas Korean children were quite attentive to their playmates' activities and more inclined to cooperate. Thus, play was teaching children from an *individualistic* culture (the United States) to assert their identities as individuals, whereas children from a *collectivist* culture (Korea) were learning to keep their own egos and emotions under control to promote group harmony.

Functions of Pretend Play   How important are the pretend-play activities of the preschool period? Carolee Howes (1992) claims that they serve at least three crucial developmental functions. First, pretend play helps children to master ways of sharing meaning with their social equals. In addition, play provides opportunities for young children to learn to *compromise* as they negotiate the roles they will enact in their play and the rules that guide these pretend episodes. Last, but not least, social pretext is a context that permits children to display feelings that may bother them, thereby allowing them opportunities to better understand their own (or their partner's) emotional crises, to receive social support from (or provide it to) playmates, and to develop a sense of trust and even intimate ties to these associates. So pretend play may be a major contributor to the growth of communication skills, emotional understanding, social perspective-taking, and an enhanced capacity for caring. Viewed in this way, it is hardly surprising that preschoolers who are relatively proficient at pretend play activities tend to be favorably received by their peers (Farver, Kim, & Lee-Shin, 2000; Rubin, Bukowski, & Parker, 2006).

The content of a child's pretend play can also point to emotional disturbances that may require adult intervention. For example, preschoolers who persist in immature forms of solitary play (such as wandering around aimlessly without attempting to join playgroups) are at risk of later displaying problem behaviors (such as extreme shyness or social anxiety) that could cause them to be rejected by peers (Coplan, 2000; Coplan et al., 2001; Gazelle et al., 2005). And those who often enact violent fantasy themes are also heading for trouble: They tend to display a lot of anger and aggressive behavior and little prosocial conduct (Dunn & Hughes, 2001). Thus, early play may provide indications of which preschool children might profit from social-skills training (described later in the chapter) that is designed to improve their prospects of being accepted by peers.

Peer Sociability in Middle Childhood and Adolescence

Peer interactions become increasingly sophisticated throughout the grade-school years. Not only do cooperative forms of complex pretend play become more commonplace, but by age 6–10, children have become enthusiastic participants in games (such as T-ball and Monopoly) that are governed by formal sets of rules (Hartup, 1983; Piaget, 1965).

Another very noticeable way that peer interactions change during middle childhood is that contacts among 6- to 10-year-olds more often occur in true **peer groups.** When developmentalists talk about peer groups, they are referring not merely to a collection of playmates but rather to a true confederation that (1) interacts on a regular basis, (2) defines a sense of belonging, (3) formulates its own *norms* that specify how members are supposed to dress, think, and behave, and (4) develops a structure or hierarchical organization (for example, leader and other roles) that enables group members to work together toward the accomplishment of shared goals. Furthermore, elementary school children now clearly *identify* with their groups; to be a Brownie, a Cub Scout or "one of Smitty's gang" is often a source of great personal pride. So between ages 6 and 10, children are exposing themselves to a most potent social context—the *peer group*—in which they are likely to discover the value of teamwork, develop a sense of loyalty and commitment to shared goals, and learn a number of other important lessons about how social organizations pursue their objectives (Hartup, 1983; Sherif et al., 1961).

Emergence of Peer Cliques By early adolescence, youngsters spend more time with peers, particularly with small groups of friends know as **cliques,** than with parents, siblings, or any other agent of socialization (Berndt, 1996; Rubin, Bukowski, & Parker, 2006). Early peer cliques, which initially form late in childhood, usually consist of four to eight same-sex members who share similar values and activity preferences. Membership in early same-sex cliques is often

peer group
a confederation of peers that interact regularly, define a sense of membership, and formulate norms that specify how members are supposed to look, think, and act.

clique
a small group of friends that interacts frequently.

Photo 13.4
Young adolescents spend more time socializing with their peers than with their parents or siblings. Much time is spent with small numbers of same-sex associates who genuinely like each other and prefer similar activities. These same-sex cliques often evolve into mixed-sex (heterosexual) cliques by mid-adolescence.

David Young-Wolff/PhotoEdit, Inc.

unstable, and children or young adolescents, particularly boys, are likely to be members of more then one clique (Degirmencioglu et al., 1998; Kindermann, 2007; Urberg et al., 1995). By midadolescence, boy cliques and girl cliques begin to interact more frequently, eventually forming *heterosexual cliques* (Collins & Laursen, 2004; Dunphy, 1963). Once formed, cliques often develop distinct and colorful dress codes, dialects, and behaviors—norms that set cliques apart from each other and help clique members to establish a firm sense of belongingness, or a group identity (Cairns et al., 1995; Espelage, Holt, & Henkel, 2003).

Emergence of Crowds   By midadolscence, cliques with similar norms and values often become identifiable as a larger, more loosely organized aggregation known as a **crowd** (Connolly, Furman, & Konarski, 2000). Crowds do not replace cliques; membership in a crowd is socially assigned by peers, based on an adolescent's reputation, and individual members of a particular clique may even belong (or be assigned to) different crowds (Urberg et al., 1995). Crowds are defined by the attitudes and activities their members allegedly share, and they come into play mainly as a mechanism for defining an adolescent's niche within the larger social structure of a high school and, occasionally, for organizing such social activities as parties, trips to the football game, and so on. The names may vary, but most schools have crowds of "brains," "populars," "jocks," "druggies," "grungers," "gangstas," and "burnouts," each consisting of a loose aggregation of adolescents who are similar to one another in some fundamental way and different from the adolescents in other crowds (Brown, Mory, & Kinney, 1994; La Greca, Prinstein, & Fetter, 2001). And everyone in the high school seems to recognize these differences: [the brains] "all wear glasses and 'kiss up' to teachers" (Brown, Morey, & Kinney, 1994, p. 128); "The partyers goof off a lot more than the jocks do, but they don't come to school stoned like the burnouts do" (p. 133). Peer cliques and crowds may be universal group structures among high school students. Although the names may vary, crowds similar to those identified in predominantly European-American high schools are also found in majority African-American high schools (Hughes, 2001), and student cliques (and presumably crowds) with very different interests and values have been identified among tenth-graders in Shanghai, China, as well (Chen, Chang, & He, 2003).

Identifying with a clique or a crowd can be harmful, particularly if evolving group norms encourage alcohol or drug use, sexual misconduct, or other kinds of antisocial or delinquent behaviors (Brendgen, Vitaro, & Bukowski, 2000; Brown, 2004; Urberg et al., 1995). Simply stated, adolescents are much more likely to take risks and to focus on the benefits (but not the costs) of risky behaviors when they are with peers than when they are alone (Gardner & Steinberg, 2005). Yet these peer groups serve many useful functions as well. Not only do cliques and crowds permit adolescents to try out new roles and express emerging values as they begin to forge an identity apart from their families, but they also pave the way for the establishment of dating relationships (Connolly, Furman, & Konarski, 2000, 2004; Dunphy, 1963). Gender segregation usually breaks down early in adolescence as members of boys' and girls' cliques begin to interact. Same-sex cliques provide what amounts to a "secure base" for exploring ways to behave toward members of the other sex: Talking to girls when your buddies are there is far less threatening than doing so on your own. And as heterosexual cliques and crowds take shape, adolescents are likely to have many opportunities to get to know members of the other sex in casual social situations, without having to be intimate. Eventually, strong cross-sex friendships develop and couples form, often double-dating or spending time with a small number of other couples (Feiring, 1996). At this point, the old cliques and crowds may gradually begin to disintegrate, having served their purposes of helping adolescents to establish a social identity and bringing the boys and girls together (Brown, 1990; Collins & Steinberg, 2006).

crowd
a large, reputationally based peer group made up of individuals and cliques that share similar norms, interests, and values.

Establishment and Functions of Dating Relationships For most adolescents, the transition to dating is an outgrowth of peer group activities (Collins & Steinberg, 2006). Candice Feiring (1996) has provided an interesting snapshot of typical dating experiences among American 15-year-olds. About 90 percent of teens had dated by age 15, although only 21 percent were currently dating. Most young dating couples double- or group-dated with friends and saw each other or talked on the phone (for an average of 60 minutes) every day. These dating relationships were casual and lasted for an average of only four months. Although partners are drawn to each other, their relationships are more like intense same-sex friendships than adult romantic relationships, with partners serving a companionship function rather than as an object of love or security.

It has been suggested that humans have an evolved tendency to compete with peers for mates and to engage in sexual experimentation with several partners before settling on a long-term partner (Weisfeld & Woodward, 2004). According to Bradford Brown (1999), there may be as many as four phases that adolescents pass through as they progress from those first crushes to mature love relationships.

1. *Initiation phase.* Early in adolescence, the major focus is on the self—on coming to see oneself as someone who can relate in romantic ways to members of the other sex.

2. *Status phase.* By mid-adolescence, having a romantic relationship with the "right kind" of partner is important for status if it brings acceptance in the larger peer group.

3. *Affection phase.* By late adolescence, one's focus is on the relationship itself rather than on the self or the peer status. Romantic relationships are now more personal and caring, and apart from the context of the larger crowd.

4. *Bonding phase.* In emerging adults, emotional intimacies achieved in the affection phase are joined with longer-term commitments to create lasting bonds—true loving attachments.

So it may take some time for adolescents to integrate their various needs for security (satisfied earlier by parents), intimacy and status (obtained earlier from same-sex peers), and sexual gratification (a new need) into a mature love relationship.

Dating serves several developmental functions. It helps adolescents to achieve autonomy from both parents and peers, to gain status as a grown-up, and from an evolutionary perspective, to distance themselves from family members and avoid incestuous relationships (Gray & Steinberg, 1999). So is dating a positive experience for adolescents? It depends. Dating early in adolescence often has more negative then positive effects on social and emotional adjustment, especially for early maturing girls whose boyfriends are likely to be older than they are (Poulin & Pedersen, 2007) and to provide contexts for such risky behaviors as sexual involvement, alcohol and drug use, truancy, shoplifting, and running away from home (Stattin et al., 2005). The impacts of dating also depend, to some extent, on the quality of adolescents' other relationships. For example, poor-quality relationships with parents and insecure attachment representations often spell trouble: These adolescents may fall in "love" and have sex a lot but mistrust or mistreat their partners and fail to make emotional commitments to them (Collins & Steinberg, 2006; Tracy et al., 2003). Yet the news is much better for most adolescents who begin dating later. In their longitudinal study of 10th- and 11th-graders, Patrick Davies and Michael Windle (2000) found that entering a steady dating relationship is good for one's self-esteem and protective in the sense that dating teens were less involved in problem behaviors such as drinking and minor delinquency, and their acceptance by romantic partners can help to compensate for poor relationships with parents (Furman & Shaffer, 2003). However, teens whose steady relationships crash tended to feel unattractive and depressed, and those who dated very casually (or not at all) had closer ties to same-sex friends but higher rates of problem behaviors. But even though steady dating relationships may carry some emotional risks, older adolescents who date tend to be better adjusted emotionally than those who do not (Collins & Steinberg, 2006; Davies & Windle, 2000).

Parental Influences on Peer Sociability

Some children are drawn to peers and seem to thrive on social interaction, whereas others appear rather unsociable or even withdrawn. Recall from our discussion in Chapter 4 that sociability is a basic component of temperament that is influenced to some extent by one's genotype. That is, some children are genetically predisposed to be more sociable and outgoing than others. Nevertheless, it is also clear that the path to positive or negative peer relations often begins at home and that parents may either foster or inhibit peer sociability.

Parents as Booking Agents, Monitors, and Coaches   There are several ways that parents influence the sheer amount of contact their children have with peers. Their choice of a residence is one such influence. If parents choose to live in a neighborhood where there are parks, playgrounds, and many young children, their own sons and daughters may have ample opportunities to interact with peers. By contrast, a decision to reside in a neighborhood with big yards, widely spaced houses, and few playgrounds or available playmates could seriously restrict children's access to peers (Medrich et al., 1982).

When young children cannot easily get together on their own, their contact with peers will depend very heavily on whether parents serve as "booking agents" for peer interaction—whether they arrange visits by playmates, enroll their children in day care or nursery school, or encourage their participation in other organized activities for children. Some debate has emerged about the impacts of alternative care on children's social skills and relations with peers. In the large multisite NICHD longitudinal study, 3-year-olds who had spent more time in alternative care were as competent or more competent in their peer interactions as those who had spent less time in child care (NICHD Early Child Care Research Network, 2001a). The downside, however, was that these same youngsters looked to be somewhat more aggressive and disobedient in the early grade-school years and continued to display more problem behaviors at age 12 if they had spent large amounts of time in group day-care centers (Belsky et al., 2007; NICHD Early Child Care Research Network, 2003a). At face value, these findings might make parents hesitant to enroll their children in day care or nursery school as a means of providing them with peer contacts. However, other investigators who have studied children in excellent day care, where peer contacts are closely monitored by sensitive caregivers, often find more positive results (for example, Love et al., 2003). What's more, we learned in Box 12.2 that children who attend preschool programs that emphasize a social curriculum tend to develop social skills at an earlier age than those who remain at home. Why? Probably for at least three reasons. First, guidance offered by preschool teachers and knowledgeable day-care providers undoubtedly plays a part in improving children's social skills (Howes, Hamilton, & Matheson, 1994). Furthermore, children often become securely attached to warm and responsive teachers and day-care providers, and their positive working models of these individuals may encourage them to be more outgoing with other people in the nursery-school or day-care setting (that is, with their classmates). Carolee Howes and her associates (1998) found that children who had established a secure rather than insecure attachments with a preschool teacher were not only inclined to form close friendships during the preschool period, but were also more likely to have close (as opposed to shaky, nonsupportive) friendships five to seven years later in elementary school. Finally, we must not overlook the possibility that nursery-school children may often become more sociable because they have become more familiar with their classmates and feel more comfortable with them. Indeed, play among preschoolers is much more cooperative, complex, and socially skilled when playmates are familiar companions rather than strangers (Brody, Graziano, & Musser, 1983; Harper & Huie, 1985; Rubin, Bukowski, & Parker, 2006). So for any or all of these reasons, it seems that parents may indeed foster their children's social competence with peers by arranging for them to receive care in a high-quality preschool or child-care program.

Parental Monitoring and Coaching Parents who arrange home visits by playmates are also in a position to influence their child by monitoring his or her peer interactions to ensure that play proceeds smoothly and amicably, without major conflicts. This brings us to an interesting issue.

Should parents closely monitor or intrude upon playful interactions between young children? Gary Ladd and Beckie Golter (1988) attempted to answer this question by asking parents of preschool children how they had supervised any recent interactions their child had had with peers at home. Some parents reported that they had closely watched over the children or had even participated in their play activities (direct monitoring), whereas others said they had checked occasionally on the children without often intruding or becoming involved as a playmate (indirect monitoring). Which form of monitoring is associated with successful and harmonious peer interactions? Ladd and Golter's findings clearly favor *indirect* parental monitoring. As we see in Figure 13.3, preschoolers whose parents had indirectly monitored their peer interactions were much better liked (and less often disliked) by their nursery school classmates than those whose parents closely monitored and often intruded on their play activities.

However, these results could be somewhat misleading. Other investigators find that mothers who believe that their children are not very socially skilled are more likely to intrude in their children's play activities—a finding that implies that conflictual peer interactions may promote direct parental monitoring rather than the other way around (Mize, Pettit, & Brown, 1995). What's more, most mothers report that they will intervene when playmates become aggressive, using power assertion as necessary to end the battle (Colwell et al., 2002). What may be more important in promoting good social skills is not the extent to which parents monitor and intervene in peer play but the quality of those interventions when they occur. If parents coach their children on prosocial strategies for resolving conflicts or for gaining entry into a group of peers at play (for example, making suggestions as to how to request entry into the play activities without disrupting them), and if this coaching is positive, supportive, and optimistic, their children are likely to develop a prosocial orientation that fosters positive peer relationships (Clark & Ladd, 2000; Mize & Pettit, 1997). This kind of coaching should not be limited to peer interactions. Mothers who establish less directive and more egalitarian relations with their children, encouraging them to make reasonable requests and allowing them to influence their behavior are teaching their children how to communicate in ways that will enable them to successfully influence their playmates (Black & Logan, 1995; Guralnick et al., 2007). By contrast, intrusive, controlling parents who become cross and angry and are constantly barking orders and failing to suppress their own negative affect tend to have children who are also poor at regulating negative emotions—and poor emotional regulation is a strong correlate of nonharmonious peer interactions (Denham et al., 2003; Fabes et al., 1999). What's more, these parents may also inhibit peer sociability by teaching their children to be bossy and dictatorial themselves, a style that elicits negative reactions from playmates, which may convince the child that contacts with peers are not all that pleasant (Kochanska, 1992; Guralnick et al., 2007; MacKinnon-Lewis, Rabiner,& Starnes, 1999).

Taken together, the findings we have reviewed imply that parents can foster the development of social skills and positive peer relations by (1) calmly discussing basic social courtesies and teaching their

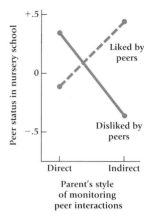

Figure 13.3
Nursery-school children enjoy a more favorable status with peers when parents have indirectly monitored their interactions with playmates. (Based on Ladd & Golter, 1988.)

Photo 13.5
Bossy parents who fail to regulate their own negative emotions tend to have children who establish conflictual relationships with peers.

Vicki Beaver

children prosocial strategies for initiating and maintaining social interactions (Clark & Ladd, 2000; Guralnick et al., 2007; Landry et al., 1998; Mize & Pettit, 1997), (2) indirectly (or nonintrusively) monitoring their children's transactions with peers to ensure that they comply with the rules of social etiquette they have learned, and (3) allowing playmates considerable freedom to structure their own play activities and to resolve most minor disputes on their own (Rubin, Bukowski, & Parker, 2006).

Parent-Child Relationships and Peer Sociability In addition to their roles as initiators and monitors of peer interactions, parents may indirectly influence their children's reactions to peers by virtue of their behavior as caregivers, authority figures, and disciplinarians. In Chapter 5, we learned that different patterns of caregiving during first year are reliably associated with the development of different kinds of attachments. Although attachment behaviors and peer sociability represent different social systems, attachment theorists (Ainsworth, 1979; Bowlby, 1988) argue that the quality of a child's primary attachments will influence his or her reactions to other people later in life. Specifically, they believe that children who are insecurely attached to one or more unresponsive caregivers may be rather anxious and inhibited in the presence of unfamiliar companions and much less sociable than children who are securely attached.

The available evidence is generally consistent with this notion. Recall from our discussion in Chapter 5 that infants who were securely attached to their mothers at 12–18 months of age are more likely than those who were insecurely attached to display socially competent behaviors and to be attractive to peers as playmates or social companions throughout the toddler, preschool, elementary school, and early adolescent periods (see, for example, Allen et al., 2007; Englund et al., 2000; Jaffari-Bimmel et al., 2006; Schneider, Atkinson, & Tardiff, 2001). Furthermore, securely attached 3½- to 6-year-olds already *perceive* peers in more positive ways and have established more friendships with them than children who are insecurely attached (Cassidy et al., 1996), and adults who recall their early attachments as secure are less lonely, less depressed, and are more likely to receive social support from friends and peers than those who portray their childhood attachments as insecure (Allen et al., 2007; Kobak & Sceery, 1988).

Why might secure attachments foster peer sociability and positive peer relations? Bowlby's (1988) viewpoint was that securely attached youngsters have formed positive working models of their sensitive, responsive caregivers, which in turn predispose them to have positive views of other people and to assume that others will welcome their sociable gestures. However, links between attachment security and peer sociability are correlational data that are subject to alternative interpretation. One such interpretation is that children with easy temperaments or who are otherwise socially skilled are the ones who are most likely to establish secure attachments and to be appropriately sociable with peers. Yet a study of 3- to 4-year-olds by Kelly Bost and associates (1998) revealed that (1) the security of children's attachments clearly predicted the character of their social support networks and their social competencies with peers, whereas (2) measures of children's social competencies with peers did *not* predict the character of their social support or the quality of their attachments with their mothers. So it appears that secure attachments do indeed promote social competencies (and favorable relations with peers) rather than the other way around.

Patterns of Childrearing and Peer Sociability Perhaps you have gleaned from our discussion thus far that parents of appropriately sociable children tend to be warm, sensitive companions who both teach and model effective patterns of communication and other social skills and who monitor their children in a nonintrusive way, thereby allowing them considerable autonomy to properly apply the guidelines they have learned in the context of playful interactions with peers. Clearly this pattern of warmth, sensitivity, and moderate control sounds very much like the *authoritative* pattern of child rearing that we have commented favorably upon throughout the text—a pattern that is consistently associated

A Cross-Cultural Examination of Parenting and Children's Social Skills

As we learned in Chapter 4, shyness and socially inhibited behaviors have very different meanings in different cultures. In *individualistic* societies such as the United States and Canada, children are encouraged to become autonomous, outwardly confident, and properly assertive, whereas shyness and a corresponding inability to assert oneself in social situations are taken as indications of social immaturity and considered psychologically maladaptive. By contrast, children in such *collectivist* societies as China, Taiwan, and Korea are encouraged to restrain their personal desires in favor of pursuing group goals. Indeed, both Confucian and Taoist Chinese philosophies seek to instill this communal orientation by stressing that self-restraint and socially inhibited behaviors are crucially important social *skills* rather than weaknesses. So if authoritative parenting or its components (that is, warmth, guidance, and a generally nonpunitive orientation to child rearing) promote socially skilled behaviors, then Western parents who display this profile should tend to raise children who are not very shy or socially inhibited, whereas Chinese parents who display the same pattern of parenting should produce children who are generally reserved or inhibited.

These hypotheses were tested by Xinyin Chen and associates (1998) in a cross-cultural study of 2-year-olds and their mothers from Canada and the People's Republic of China. Each of the toddlers was observed in an unfamiliar play room containing novel toys (for example, a big robot that moved and made strange noises) as well as a friendly stranger wearing a mask, who encouraged the child to join her in play. These observations permitted the researchers to note how wary the child seemed of unfamiliar stimuli and thus to assign him or her a score for behavioral inhibition. In addition, the mothers of these toddlers each completed a questionnaire to assess their child-rearing attitudes and behaviors. Among the dimensions of interest were (1) the mother's acceptance of her child (warmth), (2) her encouragement of mastery or achievement behavior, and

(3) her orientation to punishment (that is, favoritism of power-assertive discipline).

As might be expected from the value placed on social restraint in Chinese culture and its devaluation in Canada, Chinese toddlers proved to be significantly more inhibited than their Canadian counterparts. But there was more. When Chen and associates correlated mothers' scores on the three child-rearing dimensions with their children's scores on the behavioral inhibition measure, strikingly different patterns emerged across cultures. As the correlations in the table indicate, warm, accepting mothers who actively encourage achievement and are reluctant to use power assertion had the more *inhibited* 2-year-olds in China, where inhibition is valued, but the more *uninhibited* toddlers in Canada, where inhibition is *not* a strength but self-assertion is. Not only are these results consistent with the researchers' cross-cultural hypotheses, but they serve as a rather dramatic reminder that even though the parenting styles that foster good social skills may be similar in many respects across cultures, the particular skills they foster may vary dramatically from culture to culture.

Correlations between child-rearing attitudes/behaviors and toddlers' behavioral inhibition in a Chinese and a Canadian sample

Child-Rearing Variable	China	Canada
Acceptance of child	.17	−.22
Encourages achievement	.18	−.21
Punitiveness	−.15	.22

Note: A positive correlation means that mothers high on that child-rearing variable tended to have behaviorally inhibited toddlers, whereas a negative correlation indicates that mothers scoring high on that dimension had relatively *un*inhibited toddlers.

Source: Adapted from C. Chen et al., 1998.

---

with children's socially skilled behaviors and acceptance by peers (Baumrind, 1971; Hart, Newell, & Olsen, 2003; Hinshaw et al., 1997; Mize & Pettit, 1997). By contrast, highly authoritarian (or uninvolved) parents who rely heavily on power assertion as a control tactic tend to raise youngsters who are often aggressive or otherwise socially unskilled when interacting with other children and are likely to be *rejected* by peers (Dekovic & Janssens, 1992; Hart, Nelson, et al., 1998; Yang et al., 2003). Clearly, there is ample evidence that the path to positive (or negative) peer interactions often begins at home.

One final point and an important one: Although authoritative parenting seems to promote good social skills and positive peer relations, Box 13.2 reveals that the particular skills it fosters can vary dramatically from culture to culture.

☙ PEER ACCEPTANCE AND POPULARITY

Perhaps no other aspect of children's social lives has received more attention than **peer acceptance**—the extent to which a child is viewed by peers as a likable companion. As you might expect, there are many factors that determine one's worthiness in the eyes of peers, some of which are specific to a particular group or setting. For example, toughness, hostility, and an ability to handle a motorcycle may make you a valued Hell's Angel, but it is doubtful that these qualities would enhance your standing among the members of your

peer acceptance
a measure of a person's likability (or dislikability) in the eyes of peers.

church youth group. Clearly, different groups value different attributes, and those who are accepted possess the characteristics that are valued by *their* peer groups (Chang, 2004). Nevertheless, there are a number of factors that seem to affect a person's social standing in many kinds of groups, regardless of the age, sex, or sociocultural backgrounds of the members. These are the qualities on which we will focus as we review the determinants of one's standing with his or her peers.

Measuring Children's Acceptance by Peers

Developmentalists generally rely on **sociometric techniques** to assess a child's acceptance by his or her peers. These techniques require children to state their preferences for other group members with respect to some specific criterion. In most sociometric surveys, children in a particular classroom might be asked to nominate several classmates whom they like and several whom they dislike; or they may rate every other child in the group on a 5-point likeability scale (ranging from "really like to play with" to "really don't like to play with") (Cillessen & Bukowski, 2000; Terry & Coie, 1991). Even 3- to 5-year-olds can respond appropriately to sociometric surveys (Denham et al., 1990), and the choices (or ratings) they provide correspond reasonably well to teacher ratings of children's peer acceptance, thus indicating that sociometric surveys provide *valid* assessments of children's social standing in their peer groups (Hymel, 1983; Wu et al., 2001).

Categories of Peer Acceptance When sociometric data are analyzed, it is usually possible to classify children into one of five sociometric categories. **Popular children** are liked by many peers and disliked by few. **Rejected children,** by contrast, are disliked by many peers and liked by few. **Neglected children** receive few nominations as a liked or a disliked individual; they are very low in social impact and almost invisible to their peers. **Controversial children** are those liked by many peers but disliked by many others. Together, these four types of children make up about two-thirds of the pupils in a typical elementary school classroom; the remaining one-third are of **average status,** having received an average number of nominations as a liked or a disliked individual (Coie, Dodge, & Coppotelli, 1982).

Stability of Sociometric Statuses How stable are these sociometric classifications? Is a popular child likely to remain popular? Can initially rejected children become better liked?

In addressing these issues, let's first note that controversial children have not been studied extensively because they make up only about 5 percent of the students in a typical elementary school classroom, and they often do not remain controversial for long. In fact, one study found that nearly 60 percent of children initially classified as controversial had achieved another status in the peer group over intervals as brief as one month (Newcomb & Bukowski, 1984).

Controversial children are controversial for good reason, displaying positive behaviors characteristic of more popular youngsters (for example, cooperation, high sociability) and negative behaviors (for example, aggression, disruptiveness) as well (Bukowski et al., 1993; Rubin, Bukowski, & Parker, 2006). Controversials are often described as arrogant or snobbish (Hatzichristou & Holf, 1996). Interestingly, youngsters with these "mixed" behavioral profiles may not be well liked by many peers but may be described as "popular" based on their sheer social impact or quantity of peer interactions, thus leading some researchers to conclude that sociometric status (based on liking) and peer popularity (based on who is perceived as having prestige or high social status) are somewhat different constructs (LaFontana & Cillessen, 2002; Schwartz et al., 2006).

Calvin and Hobbes   by Bill Watterson

Over relatively brief periods of less than one year, children who are classified as popular (as defined sociometrically as well liked) and as average status tend to retain these statuses, although popular children may not retain their lofty status over longer periods (Newcomb & Bukowski, 1984). However, the rejection status tends to be more stable over time, with rejectees often remaining rejected from year to year (Rubin, Bukowski, & Parker, 2006). One reason for this is that peers often display an unfavorable bias in assessing the causes of a rejectee's behavior. That is, they tend to attribute a rejectee's *antisocial* conduct to stable dispositional causes (for example, "She's mean and nasty"), while attributing *prosocial* behaviors to unstable situational factors (for example, "His mother made him invite me to the party"). By contrast, the prosocial behaviors of liked children are attributed to dispositional causes ("He invited me because he likes me"), whereas their *antisocial* acts are attributed to unstable, situational factors (He didn't invite me because he ran out of invitations) (Hymel, 1986; Hymel et al., 1990). So popular and average-status children receive the benefit of the doubt should they respond negatively to their peers, whereas disliked children are assigned personal responsibility for their negative antics without receiving much credit for any acts of kindness that might help them to overcome their bad reputations and low social status. This social-cognitive bias on the part of peers, coupled with the fact that rejectees do often annoy or anger their peer associates (see below), seems to explain why they often remain rejected over the long run.

Finally, let's note that both neglected children and rejected children are not well received by their peers. Yet it is not nearly as bad to be ignored by other children as to be rejected by them. Neglectees do not feel as lonely as rejectees do (Cassidy & Asher, 1992; Crick & Ladd, 1993), and they are much more likely than rejected children to eventually attain a more favorable sociometric status should they enter a new class at school or a new play group (Coie & Dodge, 1983). Furthermore, rejected children are the ones who face the greater risk of displaying deviant, antisocial behavior and other serious adjustment problems later in life (Dodge & Pettit, 2003; Laird et al., 2001; Parker & Asher, 1987).

Why Are Children Accepted, Neglected, or Rejected by Peers?

At several points throughout the text, we have discussed factors that seem to contribute to children's acceptance by peers. By way of review:

Parenting Styles   As noted earlier in the chapter, warm, sensitive, and authoritative caregivers who rely on reasoning rather than power to guide and control children's conduct tend to raise youngsters who are securely attached and who are liked by both adults and peers. By contrast, highly authoritarian or uninvolved parents who rely heavily on power assertion as a control tactic often have insecurely attached youngsters who are surly, uncooperative, and aggressive and are actively *disliked* by peers.

The fact that parents influence their children's social skills implies that the *long-term* adjustment problems that many rejected children display may stem as much from a rejectee's disordered home life as from poor peer relations. Yet there is clear evidence that once a child becomes rejected, other children begin to pick on or to actively exclude the rejectee from peer group activities, and that this unfavorable treatment by peers often induces rejectees to feel depressed and lonely, retaliate aggressively or withdraw from peer group and classroom activities, and founder academically (Buhs & Ladd, 2001; Flook, Repetti, & Ullman, 2005; Haselager et al., 2002; Ladd, 2006). Thus, peer rejection appears to contribute to poor adjustment outcomes *over and above* whatever problems a child may be experiencing at home.

Temperamental Characteristics Certain aspects of children's temperaments are correlated with and undoubtedly contribute to their sociometric statuses. For example, we learned in Chapter 4 that difficult children who are often irritable and impulsive are at risk for having nonharmonious interactions with peers that could cause them to become rejected. In addition, relatively passive children who are behaviorally inhibited or slow to warm up are at risk (in Western societies, at least) of being neglected or even rejected by peers (see also, Eisenberg, Shepard, et al., 1998; Hart, Newell, & Olsen, 2003).

Cognitive Skills Both cognitive and social-cognitive skills predict children's peer acceptance. Among groups of third- through eighth-graders, the most popular children are those who have well-developed role-taking skills (Kurdek & Krile, 1982; LeMare & Rubin, 1987), and children who have established intimate friendships score higher on tests of role taking than classmates without close friends (McGuire & Weisz, 1982). In addition, popular, average-status, and neglected youngsters also tend to perform better academically and to score higher on IQ tests than rejected children and adolescents do (Bukowski et al. 1993; Chen Chang, & He, 2003; Chen, Rubin, & Li, 1997; Wentzel & Asher, 1995).

Yet these findings are correlational data and do not conclusively establish that poor cognitive or academic skills cause children to be disliked; an equally plausible interpretation is that poor sociometric status contributes to cognitive/academic deficiencies. Indeed, a recent longitudinal study found that a lack of peer acceptance in fourth grade predicted increases in anxiety/depression and decreases in academic self-concept by fifth grade, which in turn undermined children's sixth-grade academic performance (Flook, Repetti, & Ullman, 2005). However, it is likely that peer acceptance and academic performance are reciprocally related, for as we will see, interventions designed to boost children's academic performance often have the effect of bolstering their social status as well.

At least two additional sets of characteristics seem to reliably predict children's and adolescents' standing among their peers: their physical attributes and their patterns of interpersonal behavior.

Physical Correlates of Peer Acceptance

Facial Attractiveness Despite the maxim that "beauty is only skin deep," many of us seem to think otherwise. Even 6-month-old infants can easily discriminate attractive from unattractive faces (Langlois et al., 1991), and 12-month-old infants already prefer to interact with attractive rather than unattractive strangers (Langlois, Roggman, & Rieser-Danner, 1990). By the preschool period, attractive youngsters are often described in more favorable ways (that is, friendlier, smarter) than their less attractive classmates by both teachers and peers (Adams & Crane, 1980; Langlois, 1986). What's more, attractive elementary school children are generally more popular than their unattractive classmates, and this attractiveness bias becomes even stronger among preadolescents and adolescents (Langlois et al., 2000; Xie et al., 2006). The link between facial attractiveness and peer acceptance even begins to make some sense when we consider how attractive and unattractive children interact with their playmates. Although attractive and unattractive 3-year-olds do not yet differ a great deal in the character of their social behaviors, by age 5, unattractive youngsters are more likely than attractive ones to be active and boisterous during play sessions and to respond aggressively toward peers (Langlois & Downs, 1979). So unattractive children do seem to develop patterns of social interaction that could alienate other children.

Why might this happen? Some theorists have argued that parents, teachers, and other children may contribute to a self-fulfilling prophecy by subtly (or not so subtly) communicating their expectancies to attractive youngsters, letting them know that they are capable and are supposed to do well in school, behave pleasantly, and be likable. Information of this sort undoubtedly has an effect on children: Attractive youngsters may become progressively more confident, friendly, and outgoing, whereas unattractive children may resent the less favorable feedback they receive and become more oppositional or aggressive. This is precisely how a "beautiful is good" stereotype could become a reality (Langlois & Downs, 1979).

Body Build Body build (or physique) is another physical attribute that can affect a child's self-concept and popularity with peers. In one classic study (Staffieri, 1967), 6- to 10-year-olds were shown full-length silhouettes of *ectomorphic* (thin, linear), *endomorphic* (soft, rounded, chubby), and *mesomorphic* (athletic and muscular) physiques (see Figure 13.4). After stating which body type they preferred, the children were given a list of adjectives and asked to select those that applied to each body type. Finally, each child listed the names of five classmates who were good friends and three classmates whom he or she didn't like very well.

The results were clear. Not only did children prefer the mesomorphic silhouette, they attributed positive adjectives—for example, brave, strong, neat, and helpful—to this figure while assigning much less favorable adjectives to the ectomorphic and endomorphic figures. Among the children themselves, there was a definite relationship between body build and popularity: The mesomorphs in the class turned out to be the most popular children, whereas endomorphic classmates were least popular (see also Sigelman, Miller, & Whitworth, 1986). Even today, as more American children than ever are obese, endomorphic youngsters are likely to be teased and ostracized by their peers (Davison & Birch, 2002; Krishnamoorthy, Hart, & Jelalian, 2006).

Now think back for a moment to your own adolescence when your body began to change and you first realized that you were rapidly becoming a young man or a young woman. Did this happen to you earlier than to your friends, or later? Do you think that the timing of these events could have influenced your personality or social life?

Timing of puberty does have some meaningful implications, although its impact differs somewhat for boys and girls.

Possible Pubertal Impacts of Boys Some classic longitudinal research conducted at the University of California suggested that boys who mature early enjoy a number of social advantages over boys who mature late. One study followed the development of 16 early-maturing and 16 late-maturing male adolescents over a six-year period and found late maturers to be more eager, anxious, and attention-seeking (they were also rated by teachers as less masculine and less physically attractive) than early maturers (Jones & Bayley, 1950). Early maturers tended to be poised and confident in social settings and were more likely to win athletic honors and election to student offices. Although this study was based on only 32 boys in California, other researchers have also found that early maturers tend to be accepted by (and even popular with) their peers (Bulcroft, 1991). Yet there is a possible downside to being

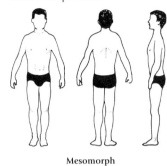

Figure 13.4
The three body types used in Staffieri's experiment.

Mesomorph

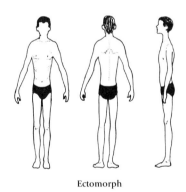

Endomorph

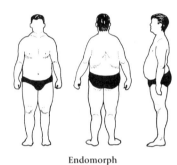

Ectomorph

Photo 13.6
Early-maturing males tend to be poised and confident in social settings and popular with their peers.

Barbara Stitzer/PhotoEdit, Inc.

an early maturer: Later research suggests that early maturing boys are at somewhat greater risk of displaying minor delinquency and misbehavior at school and of using alcohol or other drugs, particularly if they live in economically disadvantaged neighborhoods or have been exposed to harsh, coercive parenting at home (Ge et al., 2002; Kaitiala-Heino et al., 2003). However, research continues to point to social disadvantages among late-maturing boys, who are often somewhat anxious and unsure of themselves and prone to minor adjustment problems (Dorn, Susman, & Ponirakis, 2003). Late-maturing boys also have lower educational aspirations than early maturers do, and they even score lower early in adolescence on school achievement tests (Dubas, Graber, & Petersen, 1991).

Why might the early-maturing boy be socially advantaged? One reason may be that his greater size and strength often make him a more capable athlete, which in turn is apt to bring social recognition from adults and peers (Lease, Kennedy, & Axelrod, 2002; Rodkin et al., 2000). The early maturer's adultlike appearance may also prompt others to overestimate his competencies and to grant him privileges and responsibilities normally reserved for older individuals. Indeed, parents hold higher educational and achievement aspirations for early-maturing than for late-maturing sons (Duke et al., 1982), and they have fewer conflicts with early maturers about issues such as acceptable curfews and the boy's choice of friends (Savin-Williams & Small, 1986). Perhaps you can see how this generally positive, harmonious atmosphere might promote the poise or self-confidence that enables early maturers to become popular and assume positions of leadership within the peer group.

Do these differences between early- and late-maturing boys persist into adulthood? In general, they fade over time. By 12th grade, for example, differences in academic performances between early and late maturers have already disappeared (Dubas, Graber, & Petersen, 1991). However, Jones (1965) found that early maturing boys from the University of California study were still somewhat more sociable and self-confident in their 30s than their peers who had matured later.

Possible Impacts on Girls For girls, maturing early can be a disadvantage. Several studies have found that early-maturing girls are somewhat less outgoing and less popular than their prepubertal classmates (Aro & Taipale, 1987; Clausen, 1975) and are likely to report more symptoms of anxiety and depression as well (Ge, Conger, & Elder, 1996; Stice, Presnell, & Bearman, 2001). Intuitively, these findings make some sense. A girl who matures very early may look very different from female classmates, who may tease her, and from boys in the class, who will not mature for two to three years and are not yet all that enthused about the early maturer's more womanly attributes (Caspi et al., 1993). As a result, early-maturing girls often seek (or are sought out by) older companions, particularly boys, who may often steer them away from academic pursuits and into less desirable activities, such as smoking, drinking, drug use, and sex, that they are not yet prepared to handle (Caspi et al., 1993; Dick et al., 2000; Stattin et al., 2005). Indeed, risks of psychological distress among early-maturing girls are much higher when they attend coed schools and have lots of boys as friends (Caspi et al., 1993; Ge et al., 1996).

Some of the curses of early maturation can be long lasting. One Swedish study, for example, found that early-maturing girls continued to perform less well at school and were more likely to drop out than their late-maturing or on-time classmates (Stattin & Magnusson, 1990). Yet most early-maturing girls fare better over time. By 11th or 12th grade, early-maturing girls are no longer less popular than other girls (Hayward et al., 1997) and may even be admired once their female peers discover that early maturing girls tend to be popular with boys. Long-term negative impacts are most apparent among those early-maturing girls who become heavily involved early on with deviant peers and partake in sexual misconduct and substance abuse—behaviors that present their own harmful consequences (see, for example, Ge et al., 2002).

Overall, then, both the advantages of maturing early and the disadvantages of maturing late are greater for boys than for girls. However, it is important to note that differences in peer acceptance between early and late maturers are not large and are highly variable from child to child, and that many factors other than timing of puberty influence whether this period of life goes smoothly or not.

Behavioral Correlates of Peer Acceptance Although one's physical characteristics and cognitive, scholastic, and athletic prowess are all meaningfully related to peer acceptance, even the brightest and most attractive children may not be well liked if peers consider their behavior inappropriate or antisocial (Dodge, 1983). What behavioral characteristics are most important in influencing a child's standing with peers?

Several studies of preschool, elementary school, and middle school (young adolescent) children report pretty much the same findings. Popular children—at least those nominated as well liked on sociometric surveys—are observed to be relatively calm, outgoing, friendly, and supportive companions who can successfully initiate and maintain interactions and can resolve disputes amicably (Coie, Dodge, & Kupersmidt, 1990; Denham et al., 1990; Rubin, Bukowski, & Parker, 2006; Xie et al., 2006). In both the United States and China, these "sociometric stars" are generally warm, friendly, cooperative, and compassionate individuals who display many prosocial behaviors and are seldom disruptive or aggressive (C. Chen et al., 2000; Rubin, Bukowski, & Parker, 2006).

Neglected children, by contrast, often appear somewhat passive and shy. They are not very talkative; they make fewer attempts than children of average status to enter play groups; they feel that they receive little support from peers; and they seldom call attention to themselves (Coie, Dodge, & Kupersmidt, 1990; Harrist et al., 1997; Wentzel, 2003). Nevertheless, these "neglectees" are no less socially skilled than children of average status; nor are they any more lonely or more distressed about the character of their social relationships (Cassidy & Asher, 1992; Wentzel & Asher, 1995). They are simply not "noticed" by peers because of their general lack of social assertiveness.

There are at least two kinds, or categories, of *rejected* children, each with a distinct behavioral profile. **Aggressive-rejected children** often alienate peers by using a physical force or relationally aggressive tactics to dominate peers or otherwise achieve their objectives (Cillessen & Mayeux, 2004; Hinshaw et al., 1997). These disruptive braggarts tend to be uncooperative and critical of peer group activities and to display very low levels of prosocial behavior (Newcomb, Bukowski, & Pattee, 1993;

aggressive-rejected children
a subgroup of rejected children who display high levels of hostility and aggression in their interactions with peers.

Photo 13.7
Neglected children are often shy and hover on the fringes of a group, making few attempts to enter it.

Michael Newman/PhotoEdit, Inc.

Parkhurst & Asher, 1992). Aggressive-rejected children are prone to interpret others' behavior as hostile, even when it isn't, and to favor retaliation rather than nonaggressive strategies to settle disputes (Troop-Gordon & Asher, 2005); yet they clearly overestimate their social standing, often saying that they are liked just as well as, or better than, most children (Zakriski & Coie, 1996). These are the youngsters who display the greatest risk of retaining their rejectee status over time (Haselager et al., 2002), becoming chronically hostile, and displaying externalizing conduct disorders and even criminal acts of violence later in adolescence and adulthood (Parker et al., 1995; Ladd, 2006; Rubin, Bukowski, & Parker, 2006).

Withdrawn-rejected children, on the other hand, are typically socially awkward companions who display many unusual and immature behaviors and are insensitive to peer group expectations. Like their aggressive-rejected counterparts, withdrawn-rejected children are quick to anger in response to conflicts and would like to retaliate as they quickly abandon prosocial avenues of conflict resolution (Burgess et al., 2006; Troop-Gordon & Ladd, 2005). But unlike aggressive-rejected children, withdrawn-aggressive children tend to be socially anxious and are well aware that other children do not like them, and may eventually begin to withdraw as peers actively exclude them from their activities (Burgess et al., 2006; Gazelle & Ladd, 2003; Harrist et al., 1997; Hymel, Bowker, & Woody, 1993; Zakriski & Coie, 1996). These withdrawn rejectees feel especially lonely and are at risk of experiencing low self-esteem, depression, and other internalizing disorders (Hymel, Bowker, & Woody, 1993; Ladd, 2006; Rabiner, Keane, & MacKinnon-Lewis, 1993). And because of their unusual behaviors, their hypersensitivity to criticism, and their lack of close friends to stick up for them, they are particularly inviting targets for abuse at the hands of bullies (Gazelle et al., 2005; Hodges et al., 1999; Ladd & Burgess, 1999).

withdrawn-rejected children
a subgroup of rejected children who are often passive, socially anxious, socially unskilled, and insensitive to peer-group expectations.

The Direction of Effects Issue   Now let's consider a thorny interpretive problem: Do the behavioral profiles that children display really *cause* them to become accepted, rejected, or neglected by peers? Do children with lofty sociometric status, for example, become so very well liked because they are friendly, cooperative, and nonaggressive? Or is it that children become friendlier, more cooperative, and less aggressive after achieving positive recognition from peers? One way to test these competing hypotheses is to place children in play groups with *unfamiliar* peers and then see whether the behaviors they display will predict their eventual status in the peer group. Several studies of this type have been conducted (Coie & Kupersmidt, 1983; Dodge, 1983; Dodge et al., 1990; Gazelle et al., 2005; Ladd, Price, & Hart, 1988), and the results are reasonably consistent: The patterns of behavior that children display do predict the statuses they will achieve with their peers. Children who are ultimately accepted by unfamiliar peers are highly effective at initiating social interactions and at responding positively to others' bids for attention. When they want to join a group activity, for example, these socially skilled, *soon-to-be-accepted* children will first watch and attempt to understand what is going on, and then comment pleasantly and constructively about the proceedings as they blend smoothly into the group. By contrast, children who are ultimately *rejected* are pushy and self-serving: They will often criticize or disrupt group activities and may even threaten reprisals if they are not allowed to join in. Other children who end up being neglected by their peers tend to hover around the edges of a group, initiating few interactions and shying away from other children's bids for attention. Interestingly, some children who are neglected by familiar playmates will suddenly become quite sociable with *unfamiliar* peers (Coie & Kupersmidt, 1983), whereas other extremely withdrawn neglectees are apt to retain this status or could eventually even become rejected (French, 1988; Rubin, Bukowski, & Parker, 2006).

So is sociometric status merely an epiphenomen—a mere reflection of one's agreeable or disagreeable behavior that has no *unique* implications for future behavior or adjustment outcomes? No—social status does matter! Consider that aggressive-rejected boys who become more accepted over time show sizable declines in aggression *after* their acceptance by peers has improved—a clear demonstration that changes in social status have behavioral implications (Haselager et al., 2002). And in his recent seven-year longitudinal study of children from 5 to 12 years of age, Gary Ladd (2006) found support for an *additive* model in predicting children's adjustment problems. That is, early aggressive and withdrawn behaviors clearly predicted later internalizing and externalizing disorders; yet the peer rejection that resulted from earlier aggressive or withdrawn behavioral profiles had its own independent effect, clearly increasing the likelihood that these disliked children would display serious adjustment problems in the years ahead. So far from begin epiphenomenal, one's sociometric status not only reflects earlier behaviors but has important implications *in its own right* for one's future behavior and psychological well-being (see also Buhs & Ladd, 2001; Gazelle & Ladd, 2003).

Cultural Influences on Peer Acceptance Although most research on correlates and contributors to peer acceptance has been conducted in the United States and Canada, findings similar to those we have discussed have been obtained in countries around the world. Generally speaking, children who are highly aggressive or extremely withdrawn are at risk of being rejected by peers in European countries and in China, whereas those who are friendly, cooperative, or otherwise prosocially inclined are likely to be favorably received by their peers (Attili, Vermigli, & Schneider, 1997; Casiglia, Lo Coco, & Zappula, 1998; Chen, Rubin, & Sun, 1992; Schwartz, Chang, & Farver, 2001).

Yet behaviors most closely associated with various sociometric statuses do vary somewhat across cultures. In Box 4.3, for example, we learned that a somewhat shy, socially unassertive demeanor that might place an American child at risk of being neglected (or even rejected) by peers may actually promote peer acceptance in China, where being quiet, reserved, and self-effacing are more desirable behaviors. It also appears that good academic performance may be a stronger contributor to peer acceptance among Chinese children *and* adolescents than is true for Americans, and that poor academic performances can place Chinese children at risk of being ostracized, rejected, and even victimized by their peers (Chen, Chang, & He, 2003; McCall, Beach, & Lau, 2000; Schwartz, Chang, & Farver, 2001).

Age-Related Changes in Correlates of Peer Status It turns out that the ingredients of peer status also change somewhat with age. For example, even though heightened aggression is generally associated with unfavorable peer status at any age, it becomes less important as a determinant of one's social standing as children approach adolescence (Cillessen & Mayeux, 2004): Now at least some "tough" boys who view themselves as cool, popular, and antisocial are perceived as "popular" (though are not always well liked) by male classmates and are attractive to many girls (Bukowski, Sippola, & Newcomb, 2000; LaFontana & Cillessen, 2002; Rodkin et al., 2000). This seemingly paradoxical finding is due in part to a critical distinction between popularity (as adolescents define it) and sociometric likeability. Adolescents use the term "popularity" to describe peers who have achieved prestige, visibility, and a capacity to influence others, and aggressive or antisocial "populars," who are often quite controversial sociometrically and receive most of their social support and nominations as liked individuals from other aggressive or antisocial peers (Kiesner & Pastore, 2005). Yet their increased "popularity" may be a mixed blessing, for teens whose social standing increases as a consequence of their aggressive or antisocial conduct tend to disengage from school and show declines in academic achievement (Schwartz et al., 2006). By contrast, adolescents who become better liked *sociometrically* (whether they are "populars" or not) show no such pattern of academic disengagement. Thus, popularity and likeability are not one and the same, and it appears to be more adaptive for adolescents to be liked by peers than to have achieved high status (popularity) by virtue of their aggressive or antisocial inclinations.

Photo 13.8
An ability to relate positively to members of the other sex begins to enhance one's social standing in adolescence.

Brand X Pictures/Jupiter Images

A second developmental trend is that, over the course of childhood, withdrawn behavior becomes a *more* important predictor of peer rejection and such internalizing disorders as anxiety and depression (Ladd, 2006; Rubin, Bukowski, & Parker, 2006). By the middle to late elementary school years, the abnormal behavior of many withdrawn children begins to stand out in the eyes of peers, who become increasingly likely to reject them; and these withdrawn rejectees become increasingly alienated from peer group activities and anxious or depressed about their poor social standing.

Finally, let's note that the ability to establish close relationships with members of the other sex begins to *enhance* one's social standing in adolescence, when the boys and the girls come together (Collins & Steinberg, 2006), whereas frequent consorting with "the enemy" violates norms of gender segregation during childhood and can *undermine* one's status with peers (Kovacs, Parker, & Hoffman, 1996; Sroufe et al., 1993).

Clearly, peer acceptance is influenced by many factors. It may help to have a pleasant temperament, an attractive face, and academic competencies, but it is even more important to display good social-cognitive skills and to *behave* in ways considered to be socially competent within one's own culture and peer groups.

Unfortunately, some children who lack these attributes and are rejected by peers often retain their rejected status from grade to grade and are at risk of experiencing any (or all) of the adjustment problems associated with peer rejection (Brendgen et al., 2001; Coie, Dodge, & Kupersmidt, 1990; Ladd, 2006). Let's now examine some of the programs that have helped rejected children to improve their social skills and their prospects for experiencing healthier psychological outcomes.

On Improving the Social Skills of Rejected Children

The finding that peer rejection is a strong predictor of current and future psychological difficulties has prompted many investigators to devise interventions aimed at improving the social skills of less likable children. Here are some of the more effective techniques.

Reinforcement and Modeling Therapies   Many early approaches to social-skills training were based on learning theory and involved (1) reinforcing children (with tokens or praise) for displaying such socially appropriate behaviors as cooperation and sharing or (2) exposing children to social models who display a variety of socially skilled acts. Both approaches have been successful at increasing the frequency of children's socially skilled behaviors. And when teachers and peers participate in the intervention, they are much more likely to notice changes in the rejected child's behavior and are more inclined to change their opinion of him or her (Bierman & Furman, 1984; White & Kistner, 1992). There are several ways for teachers and other adults to structure play environments so that it becomes easier to reinforce children for their appropriate social conduct. For example, they might capitalize on the successful inclusion strategies we discussed in Chapter 12, in which youngsters work at tasks or strive to achieve valuable shared goals that will require cooperation among *all* who are present. What's more, modeling programs work best when the model is similar to the target child and when his socially skillful actions are accompanied by some form of commentary that directs the child's attention to the purposes and benefits of behaving appropriately toward peers (Asher, Renshaw, & Hymel, 1982).

Cognitive Approaches to Social-Skills Training The fact that modeling strategies work better when accompanied by verbal rationales and explanations implies that interventions that prompt the child to imagine the positive consequences of skillful social overtures are likely to be effective. Why? Because the child's active cognitive involvement in the social-skills training may increase her understanding and appreciation of the principles that are taught, thereby persuading her to internalize and then rely on these lessons when interacting with peers.

Coaching is a cognitive social-learning technique in which the therapist displays one or more social skills, carefully explains the rationales for using them, allows children to practice such behavior, and then suggests how the children might improve on their performances. Sherri Oden and Steven Asher (1977) coached third- and fourth-grade social isolates on four important skills: how to make an entry into ongoing play activities, how to take turns and share, how to communicate effectively, and how to give attention and help to peers. Not only did the children who were coached become more outgoing and positive, but follow-up measures a year later revealed that these former isolates had achieved even further gains in social status (see also Mize & Ladd, 1990; Schneider, 1992).

Other cognitive interventions, firmly grounded in cognitive-developmental theory, include attempts to improve children's *role-taking* skills and *social problem-solving abilities*. These techniques can be especially effective with aggressive-rejected children who often display a strong *hostile attributional bias* (a tendency to overattribute hostile intentions to their companions) that has been acquired at home from coercive parents who mistrust other people and endorse aggressive problem-solving strategies (Keane, Brown, & Crenshaw, 1990; Pettit, Dodge, & Brown, 1988). In order to help these aggressive rejectees, the training must not only emphasize that aggression is inappropriate but also help them to generate nonaggressive solutions to conflict. One such approach is the **social problem-solving training** that Myrna Shure and George Spivack (1978; Shure, 1989) devised to help preschoolers generate and then evaluate amicable solutions to interpersonal problems. Over a 10-week period, children role-played conflict scenarios with puppets and were encouraged to discuss the impact of their solutions on the feelings of all parties involved in a conflict. Shure and Spivack found that fewer aggressive solutions were offered the longer the children had participated in the program. What's more, the children's classroom adjustment (as rated by teachers) improved as they became better able to think through the social consequences of their own actions (see also Kazdin, 2003a; Vitaro et al., 1999).

Academic-Skills Training Children who are struggling at school are often rejected by their classmates (Schwartz, Chang, & Farver, 2001; Dishion, Andrews, & Crosby, 1995), which tends to make them anxious or depressed and further erodes their academic performance (Flook, Repetti, & Ullman, 2005). Might we elevate their social status by improving their academic skills and bringing them back into the mainstream of school activities? One research team tried this approach, providing extensive academic-skills training to low-achieving, socially

coaching
method of social-skills training in which an adult displays and explains various socially skilled behaviors, allows the child to practice them, and provides feedback aimed at improving the child's performances.

social problem-solving training
method of social-skills training in which an adult helps children (through role playing or role-taking training) to make less hostile attributions about harm-doing and to generate nonaggressive solutions to conflict.

Photo 13.9
Coaching can be effective at improving the social skills of rejected children.

Lori Adamski Peek/Stone/Getty Images

rejected fourth-graders (Coie & Krehbiel, 1984). This training not only improved the children's reading and math achievement, but their social standing improved as well. One year after the intervention ended, these former rejectees now enjoyed average status in their peer group.

So there are a variety of techniques on which adults might rely to improve the social skills of unpopular children and help them to establish a more favorable standing among their peers. Yet a caution is in order: The long-term success of any intervention could easily be compromised if the new social skills and problem-solving strategies that children have acquired are likely to be undermined by coercive, mistrusting parents or by highly aggressive friends who endorse aggressive solutions to conflict. For these reasons, Gregory Pettit and his associates (1988) favor *preventive* interventions that are undertaken (1) as soon as a child's problems with peers become apparent and (2) are not limited solely to groups of problem children (see also Lavellee et al., 2005). Unfortunately, treatments that center exclusively on groups of adolescent aggressive rejectees, without any involvement by parents or more accepted peers, actually seem to backfire: Participants show little change in sociometric status and often display *increases* in problem behaviors and delinquent conduct (Dishion, McCord, & Poulin, 1999; Dodge, Dishion, & Lansford, 2006). So social-skills training programs are clearly more effective when undertaken early, before rejected youngsters band together into deviant peer cliques that encourage antisocial conduct (Dodge, Dishion, & Lansford, 2006; Kazdin, 2003b).

CHILDREN AND THEIR FRIENDS

friendship
a strong and often enduring relationship between two individuals, characterized by loyalty, intimacy, and mutual affection.

As young children become more outgoing and are exposed to a wider variety of peers, they typically form close ties to one or more playmates—bonds that we think of as **friendships.** Recall from Chapter 6 that children have some pretty firm ideas about what qualifies someone as a friend. Before age 8, the principal basis for friendship is *common activity:* Children view a friend as someone who likes them and who enjoys similar kinds of play activities. By contrast, 8- to 10-year-olds, equipped with more sophisticated role-taking skills, begin to see friends as individuals who are *psychologically similar* and who can be trusted to be loyal, kind, cooperative, and sensitive to each other's feelings and needs (Berndt, 1996). And although adolescents continue to think that loyalty and shared psychological attributes are characteristics that friends display, their conceptions of friendship now focus more on *reciprocal emotional commitments.* That is, friends are viewed as intimate associates who truly understand each other's strengths, can accept each other's weaknesses, and are willing to share their innermost thoughts and feelings (Hartup, 1996).

On the Development of Friendships

Although young children may have many playmates, few of these companions become close friends. How do friendships develop? One way to find out is to randomly pair unacquainted children as playmates and then observe their play over a period of weeks for clues as to why some pairs become friends and others do not. John Gottman (1983) tried this approach with pairs of initially unacquainted 3- to 9-year-olds. Each pair of playmates met in the home of one of the children for several play sessions over a period of four weeks. At the end of the study, mothers responded to a questionnaire on which they indicated whether their children had become friends with their new playmates. Furthermore, observers had recorded children's behavior during the play sessions, hoping to use these observations as a way of determining how the interactions of children who become friends differ from those of eventual nonfriends.

As expected, Gottman found that some of the playmate pairs became fast Friends, whereas others did not. He also found several important differences in the play activities of eventual friends and nonfriends. First, even though eventual friends didn't always initially agree on which play activities to pursue, they were much more successful than eventual nonfriends at *resolving conflicts* and establishing a *common-ground activity*—that is, at agreeing on what and how to play. Eventual friends were also the more successful at *communicating clearly* with each other and *exchanging information*. Some of the information exchanged was very personal in nature, and eventual friends were more likely than children who did not become friends to engage in such **self-disclosure.** So it seemed to Gottman as if children who generally agreed about play activities early on simply "hit it off," thus becoming more inclined to show affection and approval toward their partners and to reveal personal information about themselves—processes that allowed their relationship to gel as a friendship.

Of course, a child's own characteristics may strongly influence his or her ability to become a friend. Judy Dunn and her associates (Dunn & Cutting, 1999; Dunn, Cutting, & Fisher, 2002) report that preschool children who form solid friendships characterized by high levels of cooperative pretend play and other prosocial behaviors tend to display high levels of *social understanding:* They respect rules, understand other's emotions and are good at reading others' thoughts (as assessed by "theory of mind" tasks). This finding should remind us of research we discussed earlier in Chapter 4 indicating that preschoolers who are skilled at emotional understanding and who can regulate their own emotions are perceived as *socially competent* by preschool teachers and are attractive as playmates to their peers. What's more, Dunn and associates (2002) found that socially competent 4-year-olds who had formed *close* friendships found it easier to make new friends later at school. Thus, it is possible that children may be forming early "working models" of friendship during the preschool years that will influence the quality or character of their friendships later in life.

Social Interactions among Friends and Acquaintances

As early as age 1 to 2, children may become attached to a preferred play partner and respond very differently to these "friends" than to other playmates (Howes, 1996). For example, friends display more advanced forms of pretend play than acquaintances do—as well as more affection and more approval (Howes, Droege, & Matheson, 1994; Whaley & Rubenstein, 1994). Friends often do nice things for each other, and many altruistic behaviors may first appear within these early alliances of the preschool era. Frederick Kanfer and his associates (1981), for example, found that 3- to 6-year-olds were generally willing to give up their own valuable play time to perform a dull task if their efforts would benefit a friend; yet this same kind of self-sacrifice was almost never made for a mere acquaintance. Young children also express more sympathy in response to the distress of a friend than to that of an acquaintance, and they are more inclined to try to relieve the friend's distress as well (Costin & Jones, 1992; Farver & Branstetter, 1994). What's more, friends may even *socialize* prosocial behavior. Carolyn Barry and Katherine Wentzel (2006), for example, found that when young adolescents often interact with close friends who are supportive and prosocial, they choose to pursue more prosocial goals themselves and become more prosocially inclined over time.

It is often said that there is a "chemistry" to close friendships and that best friends seem to be "in tune" with each other. Research clearly supports this notion. Casual conversations among pairs of sixth-graders are much more cheerful, playful, and relaxed when the members of these pairings are good friends rather than mere acquaintances (Field et. al., 1992). In fact, a measure of participants' saliva cortisol levels (a physiological correlate of stress) taken after the conversations suggested that casual interactions between acquaintances are more stressful than those between friends. Should they be snubbed or experience some sort of ambiguous harm, most children (even aggressive ones) are much more likely to give

self-disclosure
the act of revealing private or intimate information about oneself to another person.

friends (rather than acquaintances or enemies) the benefit of the doubt, without becoming angry, making hostile attributions, or retaliating in some way (Burgess et al., 2006; Peets et al., 2007). And when collaborating on school assignments, friends tend to be more "in synch," agreeing more readily with each other and spending more time "on task" than collaborating acquaintances do (Hartup, 1996). One reason that interactions among friends may be so synchronous and productive is that friends are more similar than acquaintances are in their interests and attitudes, academic competencies, sociometric status, personality, and levels of prosocial behavior (Chen et al., 2005; Haselager et al., 1998; Rubin, Bukowski, & Parker, 2006). So it seems that birds of a feather really do flock together—a finding that helps to explain why interactions between friends are often characterized by a sense of mutuality and positive regard and do indeed have a favorable "chemistry" about them.

How long do children's friendships last? It may surprise you to learn that even preschool friendships can be highly stable. Carollee Howes (1988), for example, found that children who attend the same day-care center for several years often keep the same close friends for more than a year. Although they may wax and wane in strength, close friendships often remain stable from year to year during middle childhood (Berndt & Hoyle, 1985; Cairns et al., 1995). However, friendship networks (the list of all individuals that a child might nominate as "friends") tend to shrink in size as children approach adolescence (Berndt, Hawkins, & Hoyle, 1986; Berndt & Hoyle, 1985). This loss of friends may simply reflect the young adolescent's growing awareness that the obligations of friendship—which now include the exchange of intimate information and the provision of emotional support—are easier to live up to if one selects a smaller circle of very close friends.

Are There Advantages to Having Friends?

Do friends play a unique role in shaping a child's development? Do children who have established adequate peer relations but no close friends turn out any differently from those who have one or more of these special companions? Although few well-controlled longitudinal studies that are needed to answer these questions have yet been conducted (Hartup, 1996), we can draw some tentative conclusions about the roles friends play as socializing agents.

Friends as Providers of Security and Social Support   One strong clue that friends play an important role in children's lives are the findings that having at least one supportive friend can go a long way toward reducing the loneliness and the victimization of unpopular children who are excluded from the larger peer group (Hodges, Malone, & Perry, 1997; Hodges et al., 1999; Parker & Asher, 1993; Schwartz et al., 2000). One recent longitudinal study found that first-graders who had no friends became more anxious and depressed, were more prone to externalizing behaviors such as fighting, and were even more socially isolated in second grade than they had been in first grade. By contrast, socially isolated first-graders who had managed to make a friend showed no such increases in adjustment problems or social isolation over the same time period (Laursen et al., 2007). How might having a friend buffer a troubled child against the downward spiral of social isolation and maladjustment? Current speculation is that a close friendship provides a context for improving an isolated child's poor social skills while functioning as an emotional safety net—a kind of security that eases the distress arising from poor peer relations (Berndt, 2004; Laursen et al., 2007) and may make other kinds of potentially stressful life challenges a little easier to bear. Gary Ladd and his associates (1987, 1990, 1996), for example, found that children who enter kindergarten along with their friends seem to like school better and have fewer adjustment problems than those who enter school without many friends, and Thomas Berndt and his associates (1999) found that the often difficult transition from elementary school to junior high was much smoother for students who experienced this change along with close friends. Close supportive friendships can play an especially important role in promoting the social competencies of children from non-nurturant, noncohesive families in which parents rely on harsh forms of discipline (Criss et al., 2002; Gauze et al., 1996); and should youngsters from these disordered home environments lose a particularly close, supportive friend, they often experience sizable declines in their feelings of self-worth (Gauze et al., 1996).

So friends are potentially important sources of security and **social support,** and they become increasingly important in fulfilling this role as children grow older. Fourth-graders, for example, say that their parents are their primary sources of social support; however, friends are perceived to be (1) as supportive as parents by seventh-graders and (2) the most frequent providers of social support by 10th-grade adolescents (Buhrmester, 1996; Furman & Buhrmester, 1992). But even though this trend toward deriving more social support from friends and other peers is quite normal, it can be overdone. David DuBois and his associates (2002b), for example, found that adolescents who received ample social support from *both* adults and peers enjoy a strong sense of self-esteem and tend to be well adjusted, whereas those who receive most of their social support from friends (and other peers) and little from parents (and teachers) face a much greater risk of displaying problem behaviors and emotional disorders (see also Dishion & Dodge, 2005; Seidman et al., 1999).

Frederick D. Bodin/Stock Boston

Photo 13.10
Sometimes nothing is as reassuring as the affection and encouragement of a friend.

social support
tangible and intangible resources provided by other people in times of uncertainty or stress.

Friends as Contributors to Social Problem-Solving Skills   Because friendships are usually described as pleasant and rewarding relationships that are worth preserving, children should be highly motivated to resolve any conflicts with these "special" companions (Hartup, 1996). And apparently they are. Because they spend so much time together, friends are more likely than nonfriends to argue; but from the preschool period onward, disagreeing friends are more likely than disagreeing acquaintances to step away before the squabbles become intense, make concessions by accepting equal outcomes, and continue their interactions after the conflict is over (Hartup et al., 1988; Laursen, Finkelstein, & Betts, 2001). By middle childhood, friends are much more inclined than acquaintances are to follow the rules (and not cheat) while playing competitive games and to respect the opinions, needs, and wishes of their partner while negotiating to settle a dispute (Fonzi et al., 1997; Nelson & Aboud, 1985). These experiences amicably resolving conflicts with a friend are undoubtedly important contributors to the growth of mature social problem-solving skills—one of the strongest predictors of a healthy sociometric status with peers (Rubin, Bukowski, & Parker, 2006).

Friendships as Preparation for Adult Romantic Relationships   We've seen that *close* friendships are characterized by increasing intimacy and mutuality from middle childhood through adolescence. Could these relatively intense and intimate ties to what are overwhelmingly same-sex companions be necessary for the development of the deep interpersonal sensitivity and commitment so often observed in stable adult love relationships? Harry Stack Sullivan (1953) thought so. Sullivan reported that many of his lonely, mentally disturbed patients had failed to form close friendships when they were young, and he concluded that the close reciprocal bonds that develop between same-sex friends (or "chums") during preadolescence provide the foundation for a strong sense of self-worth and the growth of caring and compassionate attitudes that a person needs to establish and maintain intimate love relationships later in life. Consistent with Sullivan's ideas, preadolescents who have established *intimate* same-sex friendships are more likely than their friendless age-mates to have broken through the gender segregation barrier and begun to forge closer ties with members of the opposite sex (Connolly, Furman, & Konarski, 2000; George & Hartmann, 1996). What's more, Wyndol Furman and his associates (2002) found that adolescents' views and representations of their romantic relationships are more closely associated with their representations of their friendships than with their representations of their attachments with parents, a finding that is also consistent with Sullivan's and others' ideas (for example, Furman, 1999) that same-sex friendships prepare children and adolescents for intimate romantic relationships.

However, a critic could argue that a strong test of Sullivan's theory would require a longitudinal **prospective study** to see whether preadolescents who are friendless really do turn out any different as adults then age-mates who have at least one close chum. Catherine Bagwell and her associates (1998) conducted such a study. A sample of 11-year-olds completed sociometric measures that indicated their general sociometric status and whether they had established a close reciprocal tie with a best friend. Twelve years later, these same (now 23-year-old) participants completed an extensive set of questionnaires to measure their general self-worth, school and job performances, levels of aspiration for the future, quality of relationships with family members, perceived romantic competence, and depressive and other psychopathological symptoms.

The results provided some support for Sullivan's theory. Preadolescents who had established intimate same-sex friendships were found as young adults to feel more competent with one group of intimate associates (family members), to have a stronger sense of self-esteem, and to report less depressive symptomatology than their counterparts who had been friendless as preadolescents. What's more, these findings were *uniquely attributable* to participants' earlier *friendship* status rather than to their general levels of peer acceptance. Although befriended preadolescents in this study did not view themselves as any more romantically competent 12 years later in their adult romantic relationships than their friendless age-mates, it is possible that the results may have differed had the assessments of romantic competence come from the romantic partners rather than the participants themselves (after all, who among 23-year-olds would like to admit to romantic incompetence?).

Friends versus Peers as Contributors to Adjustment Outcomes Interestingly, Bagwell and her associates (1998) also found that general peer acceptance predicted some adjustment outcomes, but that the outcomes it predicted differed from those forecast by participants' earlier status as a friended or friendless preadolescent. Specifically, preadolescents who had been rejected at age 11 had lower levels of aspiration 12 years later and viewed themselves as less competent in their school and job performances than their counterparts who had enjoyed more favorable sociometric status. Do these findings imply that friends and peer groups play somewhat different or even unique roles in one's social development? Very possibly, but it is really too early to tell. More recent studies with younger children consistently find that friendship status and general peer acceptance each seem to influence many adjustment outcomes and that children seem to be better adjusted overall when they are accepted by peers *and* have one or more close, supportive friendships (Criss et al., 2002; Ladd & Burgess, 2001). Indeed, Bagwell and her associates (1998) found that both earlier peer acceptance and earlier friendship status made important contributions to their participants' overall mental health, such that young adults who had been rejected *and* friendless as preadolescents reported the highest levels of psychopathological symptoms.

Cross-Sex Friendships Teenagers normally begin to make more cross-sex friends as they become members of heterosexual cliques in early to mid-adolescence. Girls generally have more cross-sex friends than boys do, and their cross-sex alliances are more likely than those of boys to be with older partners from outside of their school settings (Feiring, 1999; Poulin & Pedersen, 2007). And even though they can and sometimes do evolve into best

prospective study

study in which the suspected causes or contributors to a developmental outcome are assessed earlier to see whether they accurately forecast the developments they are presumed to influence.

friendships or romantic relationships, most adolescent cross-sex friendships are less intimate than and somewhat secondary to one's same-sex friendships (Poulin & Pedersen, 2007). Consider what Ruth Sharabany and her colleagues (1981) found when they asked 5th, 7th, 9th, and 11th graders to describe their same- and cross-sex friendships in terms of such aspects of emotional intimacy as trust, loyalty, sensitivity to others' feelings, and feelings of emotional attachment. As we see in Figure 13.5, same-sex friendships were described as highly initmate at all ages, whereas cross-sex friendships were not equally intimate until the 11th grade. These data are interesting because they offer additional support for Sullivan's notion that children first learn lessons about intimate peer alliances in their same-sex friendships, lessons that they only apply later to their heterosexual relationships.

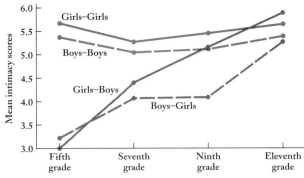

Figure 13.5

Changes during adolescence in the intimacy of same-sex and cross-sex friendships. The "Girls–Boys" scores reflect how girls rated the intimacy of their relationships with boys; "Boys–Girls" scores reflect how boys rated their relationships with girls. Cross-sex friendships clearly become more and more intimate during the adolescent years, ultimately achieving the levels of intimacy that characterize same-sex friendships throughout this developmental period. (Source: Sharabany, Gershoni, & Hoffman, 1981.)

Notice also that girls tended to report higher levels of intimacy in both their same- and cross-sex friendships than boys did, a finding consistently reported in the literature (see Winstead & Griffin, 2001, for a review). And both boys and girls report that they receive more help, support, and encouragement from their female rather than their male friends (Poulin & Pedersen, 2007). This may help to explain why girls are later more likely than boys are to associate the "romance" in a romantic relationship with friend-like qualities such as sharing intimate feelings and providing emotional support (Feiring, 1999).

Some Possible Costs of Friendships

Although we have stressed how friendships might promote positive developmental outcomes, there can be a darker side to having friends—even close supportive friends. Some very close friends are inclined to *co-ruminate*—that is, they tend to excessively discuss and seem to be almost obsessed with their personal problems. In a recent longitudinal study, Amanda Rose, Wendy Carlson, and Erika Waller (2007) found that this kind of intense focus on one another's problems and the ensuing social support provided had the effect of bolstering the perceived quality of older children's and young adolescents' friendships. But for girls, who co-ruminate more than boys, there was an added cost: Even after controlling for adjustment difficulties already present at the beginning of the study, more co-rumination among girls predicted increases over time in anxiety and depression, which in turn fostered increased co-rumination. So it seems that when provision of social support among friends involves excessive hashing and rehashing of one's own or a friend's problems, its impact on emotional adjustment may be negative rather than positive.

Under what other circumstances might having friends prove to be problematic? Let's first note that friendships clearly differ in quality, and the very children who tend to have poor social skills—those who are insecurely attached to their parents, who have highly controlling or uninvolved parents, or who are rejected by peers—also tend to have friendships that are nonsupportive and lacking in trust (Capaldi et al., 2001; Dishion & Dodge, 2005; Kerns, Klepec, & Cole, 1996; Lieberman, Doyle, & Markiewicz, 1999). Socially unskilled children who are insecurely attached or depressed may even select friends who view them and treat them negatively, perhaps helping to perpetuate their negative self-concepts (Cassidy, Aikins, & Chernoff, 2003; Parker et al., 2005). And unfortunately, low-quality friendships tend to be highly conflictual alliances in which children may respond to disagreements with friends by seeking revenge or behaving in a hostile rather than a conciliatory manner (Rose & Asher, 1999). Does the *quality* of a child's friendships influence his or her adjustment and developmental outcomes?

Apparently so. Studies of both kindergartners (Ladd, Kochenderfer, & Coleman, 1996) and seventh- and eighth-grade preadolescents (Berndt & Keefe, 1995) reveal that children who enter a school year with close, supportive friendships typically show an increase in their liking for or involvement with school, whereas students whose friendships are more rivalrous and conflictual display poorer attitudes toward school, often becoming less engaged in scholastic activities and increasingly disruptive. Furthermore, children who are insecurely attached to their parents or who are rejected by the larger peer group are more likely to display poor adjustment outcomes if their social support is provided mainly by their friends (Booth, Rubin, & Rose-Krasnor, 1998; Rubin, Bukowski, & Parker, 2006). This finding seems to reflect the fact that the friendship networks of these children are often comprised of other socially unskilled and antisocial individuals who (1) are not particularly supportive companions and (2) are inclined to talk about and encourage maladaptive patterns of behavior (Dishion & Owen, 2002; Piehler & Dishion, 2007; Rubin, Bukowski, & Parker, 2006). Indeed, it seems that only when best friendships *are* close and nonconflictual do they foster the social competencies and self-esteem of children from nonnurturant and disordered families (Gauze et al., 1996). Finally, adolescents who have close, supportive same-sex friendships are likely to establish relatively intimate and nonconflictual romantic relationships (Connolly, Furman, & Konarski, 2000), whereas those who have more deviant nonsupportive friends are at risk of battering or otherwise mistreating romantic partners (Capaldi et al., 2001; Dishion & Patterson, 2006).

Clearly, these findings are correlational data that cannot conclusively establish that low-quality friendships *cause* adjustment problems and poor developmental outcomes. In truth, longitudinal studies point to more of a *transactional* process: Socially unskilled children with problems tend to band together and form low-quality friendships, often with deviant peers. These deviant friends then engage in lots of deviant talk (for example, "Weed is always a good time" or "All girls really want to do it"), which glamorizes problem behavior, providing a kind of **deviancy training** that exacerbates a child's or an adolescent's antisocial conduct and other adjustment problems (Piehler & Dishion, 2007). In Chapter 9, for example, we learned that already aggressive, antisocial youngsters are the ones most inclined to bond with gang members, which in turn is associated with *increased* delinquency and antisocial conduct (Walker-Barnes & Mason, 2001). Similarly, young adolescents who have begun to smoke and use drugs often select drug-using friends, which fosters even heavier drug use over time (Dishion & Owen, 2002). Interestingly (and consistent with a transactional model of friendship influence), adolescent substance use is less likely to persist over time in high schools where there are few substance-using peers and adolescents have fewer opportunities to select friends who might perpetuate (or intensify) their use of tobacco, alcohol, or drugs (Cleveland & Wiebe, 2003).

In sum, there is now ample evidence that having friendships that are untrustworthy, nonsupportive, and conflictual can indeed contribute to poor developmental outcomes. When we contrast these findings to the crucial roles that intimate, *supportive* friendships can play in one's life, it is easy to see why some researchers have argued that our interventions for at-risk, unpopular children should be broadened to include lessons in how to establish and maintain these supportive intimate ties as well as more general kinds of social-skills training (Rose & Asher, 1999).

deviancy training
interactions among deviant peers that perpetuate and intensify a child's behavior problems and antisocial conduct.

PARENTS AND PEERS AS INFLUENCE AGENTS

As should be clear at this point, developmentalists now know that peer groups and friendship networks become more and more important contributors to child development as children mature. In fact, Judith Harris (1998, 2000) has gone so far as to say that children are socialized into the ways of their culture primarily by their peer groups and would become approximately the same persons even if they lived in different homes with different parents. Consistent with her point of view are observations that immigrant children readily learn local cultural practices and behaviors from peers, even though these customs may be very different from those of their parents (Fuligni, Tseng, & Lam, 1999; Phinney, Ong, & Madden, 2000).

Peers influence each other in many ways. They *reinforce* certain patterns of behavior and discourage or *punish* others. For example, we learned in Chapter 8 that even toddlers contribute to gender segregation by reinforcing gender-typed play activities and disrupting or otherwise discouraging a child who would play with cross-sex toys or playmates. Children also influence one another by serving as *social models* and as objects for *social comparison.* Recall from our discussion in Chapter 6 that grade-school children often reach conclusions about their competencies that contribute greatly to their self-esteem by comparing their behaviors and accomplishments against those of their peers. Peers also influence one another as *critics* and *agents of persuasion.* They discuss and debate issues on which they disagree, often inducing changes in attitudes or behavior in the process (Cohen & Prinstein, 2006). In Chapter 10, for example, we learned that lively challenges and discussions among peers who disagreed with one another are a potent contributor to the growth of moral reasoning.

Although no developmentalist today would deny the importance of peers as agents of socialization, many of them (myself included; and review Box 13.1) think that theorists like Harris overstate the case (see also Jaccard, Blanton, & Dodge, 2005). One reason for this sentiment is that many apparent peer influences may be hidden parental influences because, as we will see, parents can have a major impact on the company their children and adolescents keep.

Increasing Conformity to Peers

A major reason that peers become increasingly important as agents of socialization is that, from middle childhood onward, an increasing percentage of peer interactions occur in true *peer groups*—confederations that influence their members by setting **norms** specifying how group members are supposed to look, dress, think, and act. And children do become increasingly responsive to normative peer pressures as they grow older, although they are hardly blind conformists like people commonly assume.

In his classic study of **peer conformity,** Thomas Berndt (1979) asked 3rd-through 12th-graders to indicate the likelihood that they would bend to peer pressure when peers were advocating various prosocial or antisocial acts. He found that conformity to peer pressure for prosocial behaviors did not change much with age. Instead, the most striking developmental change was a sharp increase in conformity to peers urging *antisocial* behavior. This receptivity to peer-sponsored misconduct peaked in the ninth grade (or about age 14–15; see Figure 13.6) and then declined throughout the high school years (see also Brown, Clasen, & Eicher, 1986; Steinberg & Silverberg, 1986). It is not that susceptible 10- to 14-year-olds are showing a weakening of their principles or internal fortitude; instead, they are facing growing peer pressures to conform, along with implications that there may be adverse social consequences for resisting peer influence (Steinberg & Monahan, 2007). In fact, it is often sociometric stars, who show high psychosocial maturity but have a lot of status to lose, who are most susceptible to peer-sponsored misconduct (Allen et al., 2005), particularly if they are also members of high-status (trendy) peer groups (Ellis & Zarbatany, 2007). So parents may have some grounds for worrying that their 10- to 15-year-olds could wind up in trouble by going along with the crowd. Peer pressure of all kinds is especially strong at this age, and there is nothing worse than being viewed as a "dweeb" who does not fit in (Brown, 2004).

norms
group-defined rules or expectations about how the members of that group are to think or behave.

peer conformity
the tendency to go along with the wishes of peers or to yield to peer-group pressures.

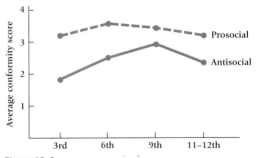

Figure 13.6
Average scores by grade for conformity to peer pressure for prosocial and antisocial behaviors. (Adapted from Berndt, T. J. 1979. Developmental changes in conformity to peers and parents. Developmental Psychology, 15, 608–616.) © 1979 by the American Psychological Assn. Reprinted by permission.

Why does conformity to peer-sponsored misconduct *decrease* by the end of high school? Perhaps this trend reflects the progress older adolescents have made in their quest for autonomy: They are now better able to make their own decisions and are less dependent on the opinions of *either* parents or peers (Steinberg, 2008). According to Lawrence Steinberg and Susan Silverberg (1986), strong conformity to peer pressure early in adolescence may even be a necessary step in the development of autonomy: Young adolescents who are struggling to become less dependent on their parents may need the security that peer acceptance provides before they will develop confidence to take their own stands and stick by them. And they are unlikely to gain such acceptance if they conform too closely to adult rules and values without taking a chance and going along with peers every now and then (Allen, Weissberg, & Hawkins, 1989). Although the parent whose teenager is nabbed with his friends for cherry-bombing mailboxes or deflating tires may not be totally comforted by this thought, it does seem that a period of heavy peer influence may pave the way for later independence.

Children around the world may become more susceptible to peer-group influences as they enter adolescence. But as we will see in Box 13.3, they are not always as susceptible to *peer-sponsored* misconduct as their American counterparts are.

Box 13.3 Cultural Influences

Cultural Variations in Peer-Sponsored Misconduct

As we learned in Chapter 11, early adolescence is a period when children in many cultures experience heightened conflicts with parents as they begin their quest for autonomy. Do younger adolescents around the world suddenly become more susceptible to peer-sponsored misconduct as they begin to experience more hassles with their parents at home?

Although data to address these questions are sparce, a study by Chuansheng Chen and associates (1998) is certainly relevant. The young adolescents who participated in this study were seventh- and eighth-graders from the United States, Taiwan, and the People's Republic of China. Each adolescent confidentially reported how often he or she had been involved (1 = never; 2 = once; 3 = several times; 4 = often) in each of 20 kinds of misconduct (for example, cheated on tests, got in fistfights, drank alcohol, damaged property, lied to parents) since the school year began. They also indicated on 7-point scales the extent to which their peers would (1) admire them for misbehaving or approve of misconduct and (2) think badly of them for their antisocial behavior.

The results of this study appear in the figure. As we see in panel A, adolescents in all three cultures reported *similar levels* of general misconduct. This was true even though the Chinese peer groups in this study were much *less* inclined than European-American peer groups to endorse this kind of behavior (panel B) and were much *more* inclined to disapprove of misconduct. So it seems that young Chinese and Taiwanese adolescents are no better behaved than their American counterparts, even though their peers are less likely than American peers are to encourage such antics.

One limitation of this study is that it sampled middle-class youngsters in all three cultures who reported low to moderate levels of misconduct (indeed, misconduct scores could have ranged as high as 80 on the total misconduct measure). Nevertheless, the finding that Chinese and Taiwanese could be just as mischievous and antisocial as Americans despite experiencing fewer peer pressures (and more negative sanctions) suggests that much of the blame placed

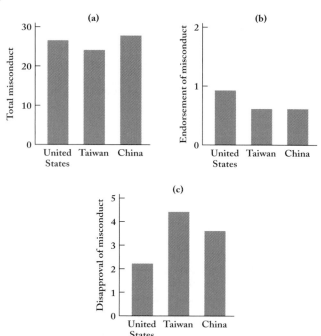

Total self-reported misconduct scores (Panel a), perceived levels of peer endorsements (Panel b), and disapproval of misconduct (Panel c), U.S. data shown here are for European-American adolescents. (Adapted from C. Chen et al., 1998.)

on *peers* for triggering adolescent misconduct may be overstated (see also Jaccard, Blanton, & Dodge, 2005). In the final section of the chapter, we will consider another body of research that makes this same point in a different way.

Are Cross-Pressures a Problem?

In years gone by, adolescence was often characterized as a stormy period when all youths experience **cross-pressures**—strong conflicts that stem from differences in the values or practices advocated by parents and those favored by peers. How accurate is this life portrait of the teenage years? It may have some merit for some adolescents, particularly those "rejected" youths who form deviant peer cliques that endorse and promote antisocial conduct that is likely to alienate their parents, teachers, and most other peers (Broidy et al., 2003; Dishion et al., 1995; Dishion, McCord, & Poulin, 1999; Dodge, Coie, & Lynam, 2006; Fuligni et al., 2001). These youngsters often resolve any cross-pressures they experience by rejecting mainstream adult values in favor of those advocated by deviant peers. But there are several reasons why the so called cross-pressures "problem" is simply not a problem for most adolescents.

One reason that parent/peer conflicts are kept to a minimum is that parents and peers tend to exert their influence in different domains. Hans Sebald (1986), for example, has asked adolescents whether they would seek the advice of their parents or the advice of their peers on a number of different issues. *Peers* were likely to be more influential than parents on such issues as what styles to wear and which clubs, social events, hobbies, and other recreational activities to choose. By contrast, adolescents claimed that they would depend more on their *parents* when the issue involved scholastic or occupational goals or other *future-oriented* decisions. Teenagers are unlikely to be torn between parent and peer pressures as long as parents and peers have different primary areas of influence.

A second and more important reason why parent/peer warfare is typically kept to a minimum is that parents, by virtue of their parenting styles, have a good deal of influence on the company their adolescents keep (Collins et al., 2000; Scaramella et al., 2002). Authoritative parents who are warm, neither too controlling nor too lax, and who are consistent in their discipline generally find that their adolescents are closely attached to them and have internalized their values. These adolescents have little need to rebel or to desperately seek acceptance from peers when they are so warmly received at home (Allen et al., 2007; Brown et al., 1993; Goldstein, Davis-Kean, & Eccles, 2005). Indeed, they tend to associate with friends who share their values, which largely protects them from unhealthy peer influences (Bogenschneider et al., 1998; Fletcher et al., 1995). Even when they encounter deviant peer pressures, adolescents whose parents are supportive, who allow them a reasonable and appropriate amount of autonomy, and who rely on behavioral rather than psychological control are generally able to resist or overcome negative peer influences and remain reasonably well behaved (Galambos, Barker, & Almeida, 2003; Goldstein, Davis-Kean, & Eccles, 2005).

Interestingly, problems for youths who *do* "fall in with the wrong crowd" and display antisocial behavior usually begin at home. One way parents can go wrong is by being too strict and intrusive, failing to adjust to an adolescent's need for greater autonomy. This may cause adolescents to become alienated from parents and overly susceptible to negative peer influences, to the point that they will let schoolwork slide or break parental rules to please their friends (Fuligni et al., 2001; Goldstein, Davis-Kean, & Eccles, 2005). Parents can also go wrong if they are overly permissive or become seemingly hostile or uncaring and rely heavily on psychological control rather than carefully monitoring their children's activities and choice of friends (Galambos, Barker, & Almeida, 2003; Goldstein, Davis-Kean, & Eccles, 2005; Scaramella et al., 2002). So parents have a good deal of power to influence, through their parenting, whether their adolescents end up in "good" or "bad" crowds and are exposed to healthy or unhealthy peer pressures.

Of course, even when parents do everything right, there will be issues for which parental opinions are likely to conflict with those of many peers (for example, opinions about acceptable curfews, conduct on dates, or about the harm involved in experimenting with tobacco,

cross-pressures
conflicts stemming from differences in the values and practices advocated by parents and those advocated by peers.

Photo 13.11
Although teenagers are often characterized as wild and rebellious, typically their norms and values are a reflection of adult society.

alcohol, or marijuana). Yet peer group values are rarely as deviant as adults commonly assume; even at mid-adolescence, when negative peer pressures are greatest, most teenagers report that their friends and associates are more likely to *discourage* antisocial behavior than to condone it (Brown, Clasen, & Eicher, 1986; and review Box 13.3). And on many issues for which parental and peer norms might seem to be in conflict, the adolescent's behavior is actually a product of both parental and peer influences. Consider the following example. Denise Kandel (1973) studied a group of adolescents whose best friends either did or did not smoke marijuana and whose parents either did or did not use psychoactive drugs. Among those teenagers whose parents used drugs but whose friends did not, only 17 percent were marijuana users. When parents did not use drugs but best friends did, 56 percent of the adolescents used marijuana. From these findings, we might conclude that the peer group is more influential than parents over marijuana use. However, the highest rate of marijuana smoking (67 percent) occurred among teenagers whose parents and peers *both* used psychoactive drugs, and a similar pattern emerges when we look at parental and peer influences on use of alcohol, tobacco, and other illicit drugs (Bogenschneider et al., 1998; Chassin et al., 1996, 1998; Newcomb & Bentler, 1989).

In sum, adolescent socialization is not a continual war pitting parents *against* peers; instead, these two important sources of influence are generally complementary rather than contradictory (Bogenschneider et al., 1998; Collins et al., 2000). Most adolescents have cordial relationships with their parents, accept many of their parents' values, and are reluctant to associate with peers who stray too far from these guidelines. And most parents know how important it is for their children and adolescents to establish close relationships with their social equals. They seem to appreciate what the lonely farmer whose letter opened this chapter has learned the hard way: Many of the social competencies that serve people well are the fruits of their alliances with close friends and peers.

SUMMARY

WHO IS A PEER AND WHAT FUNCTIONS DO PEERS SERVE?

+ **Peer** contacts represent a second world for children—a world of equal status interactions that is very different from the nonegalitarian environment of the home. However, **mixed-age peer interactions** are also crucially important socialization contexts that have benefits for both younger and older peer associates.

+ Contacts with peers increase dramatically with age, and during the preschool or early elementary school years, children are spending at least as much of their leisure time with peers as with adults. The "peer group" consists mainly of same-sex associates of somewhat different ages.

+ Research with **mother-only** and **peer-only monkeys** and young children indicates that peer contacts are important for the development of competent and adaptive patterns of social behavior. Children who fail to establish and maintain adequate relations with their peers will run the risk of experiencing any

number of serious adjustment problems later in life. In fact, Judith Harris proposes that peers are more important agents of socialization than adults.

THE DEVELOPMENT OF PEER SOCIABILITY

+ **Sociability** between peers emerges by the middle of the first year. By age 18–24 months, toddlers' sociable interactions are becoming much more complex and coordinated as they reliably imitate each other, assume complementary roles in simple social games, and occasionally coordinate their actions to achieve shared goals.

+ During the preschool years, **nonsocial activities** and **parallel play** become less common, whereas **associative play** and **cooperative play** become more common. Pretend play contributes in many ways to the growth of **social skills**, and the maturity of a preschooler's play activities predict his or her present and future popularity with peers.

- During middle childhood, more peer interactions occur in true peer groups—confederations that associate regularly, define a sense of group membership, and formulate **norms** that specify how group members are supposed to behave. By early adolescence, youngsters are spending even more time with peers—particularly with their closest friends in small **cliques,** and in larger confederations known as **crowds.** Cliques and crowds help adolescents to forge an identity apart from their families and pave the way for the establishment of dating relationships. Early dating relationships are more like friendships and often boost an adolescent's social standing and self-esteem. However, heavy dating early in adolescence can spell trouble, particularly for early-maturing girls who may be drawn by older boys into deviant or antisocial activities.

- Parents influence their children's sociability with peers by virtue of the neighborhood in which they choose to live, their willingness to serve as "booking agents" for peer contacts, and their monitoring of peer interactions. Sensitive, responsive parenting promotes secure attachments, which are associated with positive peer relations. And authoritative parents tend to raise appropriately sociable children who establish good relations with peers, whereas highly authoritarian or uninvolved parents—particularly those who rely on power assertion as a control tactic—tend to raise disruptive, aggressive youngsters whom peers often dislike.

PEER ACCEPTANCE AND POPULARITY

- Children clearly differ in **peer acceptance**—the extent to which other youngsters view them as likable (or dislikable) companions. Using **sociometric techniques,** developmentalists find that there are five categories of peer acceptance: (1) **popular children** (liked by many and disliked by few), (2) **rejected children** (disliked by many and liked by few), (3) **controversial children** (liked by many and disliked by many), (4) **neglected children** (seldom nominated by others as likable or dislikable), and (5) **average-status children** (those who are liked or disliked by a moderate number of peers). Neither neglected children nor rejected children are well received by peers; however, it is the rejected child who is typically the lonelier of the two and at greater risk of displaying serious adjustment problems later in life.

- Although physical characteristics, cognitive prowess, and the parenting one has received may influence a child's sociometric status, one's patterns of social behavior are strong predictors of peer acceptance. Popular children are generally warm, cooperative, and compassionate companions who display many prosocial behaviors and are rarely disruptive or aggressive. Neglected children often have adequate social skills, but they appear shy and reserved and tend to hover at the edge of peer-group activities. Rejected children display many unpleasant and annoying behaviors and few prosocial ones. **Aggressive-rejected** children are hostile, impulsive, highly uncooperative, and aggressive, whereas **withdrawn-rejected** children are socially anxious, awkward, and immature companions who are hypersensitive to criticism and may become targets for abuse by peers. Correlates of peer acceptance are generally similar across cultures, although behaviors most closely associated with particular sociometric classifications vary somewhat across cultures.

- Although sociometric status often reflects one's past behaviors, it has important implications in its own right for one's future behavior and psychological well-being.

- Programs to improve the social skills of rejected children include reinforcement and modeling therapies, such social-cognitive interventions as **coaching** and **social problem-solving training,** and even academic remediation, which keeps children on track at school and reduces their exposure to hostile, antisocial peers. Social-skills training programs work better (1) with younger children than with adolescents and (2) when the target children's teachers and classmates also participate in the intervention.

CHILDREN AND THEIR FRIENDS

- Children typically form close ties, or **friendships,** with one or more members of their play groups. Younger children view a friend as a harmonious playmate, whereas older children and adolescents come to think of friends as close companions who share similar interests and values and are willing to provide them with intimate social and emotional support.

- Children who display high levels of *social understanding* and who can resolve conflicts, agree on joint play activities, and are willing to exchange information through **self-disclosure** are attractive to peers and find it easy to make friends.

- Interactions among friends are warmer, more cooperative, more compassionate, and more synchronous (though not necessarily less conflictual) than those among nonfriend acquaintances.

- Close supportive friendships appear to promote positive developmental outcomes by (1) providing children and adolescents with security and **social support,** (2) promoting the growth of social problem-solving skills and an ability to compromise, and (3) fostering a strong sense of self-worth and caring and compassionate attitudes that are the foundation of intimate love relationships later in life. Yet excessive co-rumination with close friends can promote anxiety and depression. What's more, friendships clearly differ in quality, and children with conflictual, nonsupportive friendships may benefit little from them; in fact, associations with deviant friends often constitute a form of **deviancy training** that can exacerbate maladaptive or antisocial conduct.

PARENTS AND PEERS AS INFLUENCE AGENTS

- Peers become increasingly important as socialization agents as children mature. **Peer conformity** pressures peak at mid-adolescence when teenagers are highly susceptible to peer-group **norms,** including those that endorse misconduct. Ironically, susceptibility to peer influence early in adolescence may help youth to take stands apart from those of parents and to gradually become more autonomous—to the point that they are far less susceptible to either parental or peer influence later in adolescence.

- Strong **cross-pressures** are not a problem for most adolescents who have established warm relations with their parents and have internalized many of their parents' values. What's more, peer-group values are often very similar to those of parents, and peers are more likely to discourage than to condone antisocial conduct. So adolescent socialization is not a continual battle between parents and peers; instead, these two important influences are typically more complementary than contradictory.

CHAPTER 14

Epilogue:
Fitting the Pieces
Together

W E HAVE NOW CONCLUDED our survey of the major theories and empirical issues that comprise the discipline known as social and personality development. The content of this book is based on more than 10,000 empirical studies of developing children and adolescents, and your knowledge base was undoubtedly expanded further by other writings that your instructor asked you to read or presented as part of classroom exercises. Having reached this point in the course, it may be helpful to reflect for a moment on what you have learned and what all this knowledge implies for your role as a parent, prospective parent, or aspiring child-care professional who may one day influence the lives of developing persons.

Were we to fast-forward to one year from today, you might find that you recall fewer than 50 percent of the "facts" that you had at your command upon taking the final exam in this course. Psychologists who study long-term learning and memory tell us that this is to be expected and in no way implies that you haven't profited from taking this class. In fact, I usually mention this to my own students as we near the end of the course and say to them that I'd feel that I'd succeeded as their instructor if they now see the "bigger picture" and can retain and use this knowledge to their own advantage in the years ahead. And what is this bigger picture? I like to define it as a set of broad principles about human development that are relatively timeless and extremely important to keep in mind if we hope to optimize the development of the children and adolescents under our direction. The principles I'll discuss below are not intended as an exhaustive list. In fact, one useful exercise that you and your classmates may wish to undertake is to generate your own list of important principles about human social and personality development and see how closely your list matches the points discussed below. It is likely that you will have some insights that do not appear on my list but should be there. In that event, I'd like to hear from you so that I (and future student cohorts) might benefit from your reasoning.

⌒ MAJOR THEMES IN HUMAN SOCIAL AND PERSONALITY DEVELOPMENT

Human Development Is a Holistic Enterprise

Although this is a second-level or "specialty" course focusing on social and personality development, it is hopefully quite obvious by now that human development is truly a holistic endeavor. For example, the fact that a 7-month-old infant becomes attached to her caregivers is not just a milestone in social development. This infant has developed *cognitive schemes* for the faces of familiar companions and can discriminate them from unfamiliar individuals. She has also developed the *motor capabilities* that permit her to crawl to her attachment objects to maintain the proximity she desires. She protests separations from loved ones, in part because of the growth of *object permanence,* which makes her aware that departing companions continue to exist when they pass from view (and therefore can be summoned). And the emergence of attachment bonds affect development in many other ways—for example, by providing the *security* and social skills that allow toddlers to (1) confidently explore the world around them, thereby developing their motor and problem-solving capabilities and promoting a sense of self-efficacy, as well as (2) encouraging them to strike up social relationships with new associates, which can lead to new attachments that take the form of friendships. In sum, we are at once physical, cognitive, social, and emotional beings, and all these developmental threads are interwoven in the whole developing person.

We Are Active Contributors to Our Own Development

Early developmental theorists tended to view human beings as passively shaped by influences beyond their control. Sigmund Freud saw the child as driven by biological forces but

Photo 14.1
Humans actively contribute to their own development by selecting environmental niches that suit their genetic predispositions and by influencing the character of the social environments that they experience.

Addison Geary/Stock Boston

molded by early experiences in the family. John B. Watson and other early learning theorists portrayed young human beings as *tabula rasae* who develop in positive or negative directions, based primarily on how their parents choose to raise them. Jean Piaget did much to alter this view of child development by emphasizing how children *actively* explore their environments and *actively* construct new understandings of the objects, events, and people they encounter. His viewpoint was echoed (in a different way) by Albert Bandura, who was among the first to claim that children, by virtue of their own behavior, *actively* influence how they are treated by their parents, and by behavioral geneticists, who claim that we *actively* select environmental niches that are "comfortable" for us because they are compatible with our own genetic predispositions. Certainly, we are affected by many people with whom we might not ordinarily choose to interact (for example, day-care providers, teachers, unfriendly classmates, and so on). But just as certainly, we create our own environments, influence those around us, and by so doing, contribute to our own development. It is this ongoing *transaction* between an active person and a changing environment, each influencing the other in a reciprocal way, that steers development.

There Is Both Continuity and Discontinuity in Development

Developmentalists have long grappled with the issue of continuity and discontinuity in human development. Is development stage-like, or does it occur in small, orderly steps? Do early traits carry over into later life, or do they not?

Although some research supports the claims of theorists such as Piaget and Kohlberg, who contend that we progress through qualitatively distinct stages of cognitive development, moral development, and gender identity, we now know that advances in these domains occur gradually, so that transitions from one "stage" to another do not unfold abruptly. What's more, the rate at which children progress through a series of developmental milestones often depends heavily on their environment. (Recall from Chapter 8, for example, that children who have often seen people of both sexes naked may achieve a mature sense of gender constancy 1–2 years before those who lack this experience.) Today, many developmentalists are quite comfortable with assuming that development, within particular domains, may be sequential (or even stagelike), with earlier milestones serving as prerequisites for those that follow. Yet they recognize that the "transitions" we see (and take as stage markers) reflect the culmination of a large number of smaller, incremental changes that prepare a child or adolescent to make these transitions. Viewed in this way, human development seems to be both continuous and discontinuous.

Of course, another important variation on the continuity/discontinuity debate is the issue of whether early developments carry over and have implications for the kinds of persons we become later in life. Here again, the literature points to developmental continuities and discontinuities. In Chapter 4, for example, we learned that the temperamental attribute of *behavioral inhibition* is moderately stable over the course of childhood, such that inhibited youngsters often remained inhibited over a period of 11–15 years, whereas their uninhibited counterparts often remained relatively uninhibited. And yet we also learned that this developmental continuity was most apparent for the 20–25 percent of children who were most highly inhibited (or highly uninhibited) to begin with, and that the remaining 75–80 percent often displayed sizable fluctuations in their behavioral inhibition over time—a developmental *discontinuity*. So if we look at population trends, development often seems continuous, with earlier traits, or earlier developments, predicting later life outcomes. Yet at the *individual* level, development is often discontinuous, and it remains a risky business to try to predict the characterological attributes that a particular adult will display from a knowledge of his or her childhood traits.

There Is Much Plasticity in Human Development

One reason why earlier traits or earlier developments often do *not* forecast later life outcomes is that human beings are resilient organisms who display much *plasticity*—a remarkable capacity to change in response to experience. Thus, infants who have spent their first year in understaffed, impoverished institutions and who show stunted social and intellectual development can overcome at least some of these initial deficiencies if placed in stimulating homes where they receive ample affection and guidance from sensitive caregivers. A hostile grade-school child who has alienated peers and is foundering academically can often be helped to get back on track at school and to achieve a more favorable sociometric status with the assistance of the academic remediation and social-skills training programs that we discussed in Chapter 13. Evidence of such plasticity and change in later life is especially heartening to all of us who would hope to foster healthy development. Contrary to what Freud believed, early experiences, in themselves, rarely make or break us. Instead, there are opportunities throughout life to undo much of the damage done by early traumas, teach new skills, and redirect young lives along more fruitful pathways. True, adverse early experiences that continue or are followed by other adverse experiences are likely to produce maladaptive developmental outcomes. But if potentially damaging early experiences are offset by favorable later experiences, we can expect plastic and resilient young humans to display a strong self-righting tendency and *adaptive* developmental outcomes.

The Nature/Nurture Distinction Is a False Dichotomy

In a very important sense, the nature/nurture issue has been resolved. It is now clear that multiple causal forces, representing *both* nature and nurture, and ranging from changes in cell chemistry to changes in the global economy or the values of one's culture, conspire to direct human development.

Indeed, we learned in Chapter 3 that the genes that each of us inherits play a most important role in influencing the environments each of us experiences. That is, we each display genetically influenced attributes that may *evoke* particular kinds of responses from other people (environmental influences) that will affect our development. Furthermore, we tend to actively seek out experiences, or environmental niches, that are most compatible with our genetically influenced characteristics—niches that clearly influence our development. At the same time, our environments may influence the course of biological development. In Chapter 8, for example, we noted that the different experiences that young boys and girls may have as part of early gender-role socialization is thought to affect the "wiring" of the immature brain: Boys who receive ample visual/spatial experiences, for example, may develop more synaptic connections than girls do in areas of the brain that process spatial information, whereas girls, who tend to receive more varied verbal experiences than boys, may develop more extensive synaptic connections in the areas of the brain that process verbal information. So how much of the sex differences we've observed in visual/spatial skills or in verbal skills is attributable to nature, or to nurture? We now know that this question is nearly impossible to answer, for the forces of nature and nurture on these (and virtually all other aspects of social and personality development) are complexly intertwined and difficult to disentangle. Diane Halpern's (1997) compelling conclusion certainly bears repeating here: When it comes to explaining many aspects of human development, ". . . . biology and environment are as inseparable as conjoined twins who share a common heart" (p. 1097).

Having drawn this conclusion, I would certainly hope that no one who has taken this course would ever attribute the behavior of an oppositional or defiant young son (or pupil) to "bad seed." Yes, genes may influence our reactions to environmental stimulation and, ultimately, our social conduct—but they hardly *determine* that conduct. Social behavior often reflects an intricate interplay that unfolds as other people react to a child's genetically influenced attributes in ways that promote either adaptive or maladaptive responses. Stated another way, nature needs nurture to be expressed behaviorally, and nurture always acts on nature. There would be no development at all without the ongoing contribution of *both*.

Both Normative and Idiosyncratic Developments Are Important

In any human development textbook, there is a tendency to emphasize normative developments that are shared by nearly all individuals—that is, to highlight developmental regularities and commonalities. And we each do share a great deal with our fellow developing humans. But let's not lose sight of the fact that each of us is truly one of a kind who will also display a unique (or idiosyncratic) pattern of development. In fact, the developmental diversities we display are so impressive that it often seems impossible to accurately characterize them.

Individuality is apparent starting at birth if we look closely at each infant's temperament, daily rhythms, and rate of development. Yet young infants are not nearly as diverse as they will become, for early development is strongly channeled by a species-wide maturational blueprint that unfolds in remarkably predictable ways (McCall, 1981). For example, the vast majority of infants worldwide proceed through a predictable sequence of motor skills over the first 10 months, take their first steps and utter their first meaningful word at about age 1 year, and begin to respond more reciprocally to peer playmates and to combine words into simple sentences at about age 18 months. Yet, late in toddlerhood, our unique genetic endowments, in concert with our individualized rearing environments, begin to express themselves more fully. The result? We can tell a good deal about an individual 2-year-old, just by knowing his age, whereas we know much less about a person simply by knowing that he or she is an 8-year-old. And because diversity increases with age, adolescents are much less alike than 8-year-olds or 11-year-olds are.

In sum, no child should ever be expected to emerge as a carbon copy of his parents, an especially competent older sibling, or even a genetically identical co-twin. Development *always* proceeds in normative *and* idiosyncratic directions, and such diversity is even adaptive from an evolutionary point of view, because species with highly diverse characteristics are more likely to survive catastrophic changes in their environments. To truly explain human development, then, we must recognize and appreciate developmental diversities and must seek to understand the forces that underlie both the normative and the idiosyncratic changes that children and adolescents display. Only by doing so will we ever accomplish the aim of that perceptive young sophomore we met in Chapter 1, who claimed that her reason for taking this course was to learn how we all turn out so similar and, at the same time, so different from each other.

We Develop in a Cultural and Historical Context

We have also seen throughout the text that children and adolescents are embedded in a sociocultural context that affects their development. Social and personality development simply takes different forms in different cultures, social classes, and racial and ethnic groups. Furthermore, development in the 12th or 19th century was different from development in the 21st century; and each person's development is influenced by social changes and historical events occurring *during his or her lifetime*. The implication? Our current knowledge of human development is largely culture bound and time bound, for it is most often based on studies of children and adolescents in Western societies in the latter half of the 20th century—and often white middle-class participants at that!

The more developmentalists study cultural, subcultural, and historical variations in development, the more they appreciate the importance of *contextual influences* and the usefulness of such theories as Bronfenbrenner's (1979; Bronfenbrenner & Morris, 2006) *ecological systems model* and Vygotsky's (1978) *sociocultural theory* that emphasize these influences. We know, for example, that shyness can be a social strength, rather than a social liability, in cultures such as China that stress communal rather than individualistic goals and seek to inhibit individual assertiveness and self-aggrandizement. We now know that the somewhat coercive, "no-nonsense" parenting often seen in lower-SES African-American families may be more adaptive than other parenting styles if it helps to shield youngsters from negative peer influences that would undermine academic achievement or promote antisocial conduct. What's more, we should also recognize that changes in the family and in men's and women's roles, not to mention technological and social innovations yet to come, may conspire to make human development in the mid-21st century very different than it is today. Clearly, then, we should disabuse ourselves of the rather dogmatic and ethnocentric notions that a particular set of values, style of childrearing, or pattern of developmental outcomes is "optimal" for everyone. What qualifies as adaptive patterns of development—and the forces that foster or inhibit them—can vary dramatically across cultures and subcultures and is *always* time bound.

Bob Daemmerich/Stock Boston

Photo 14.2
This Guatemalan girl will spend hundreds of hours learning to weave because the livelihood of her people depends on this craft. However, it would be far less sensible for children from industrialized societies to set aside their schoolwork to acquire weaving skills that are unnecessary for their economic self-maintenance. Clearly, what qualifies as adaptive development may vary dramatically from culture to culture.

Development Is Best Viewed from Multiple Perspectives

As we have seen at many points throughout the text, many disciplines have something to contribute to a comprehensive understanding of social and personality development. Behavioral geneticists and endocrinologists, for example, have helped us to understand how genes and hormones might influence our behavior and other people's reactions to it, thereby creating a social "environment" in which the personality develops. Psychologists and family theorists have contributed immensely to our understanding of the relationships and family social systems that influence and are influenced by developing children and adolescents. Meanwhile, anthropologists, sociologists, historians, and even economists have taught us much about the impacts of changing economic and varying sociocultural contexts in which individuals develop.

Not surprisingly, then, the task of understanding something as complex as human social and personality development requires that we take an *eclectic* approach and recognize that many theories have something to offer and that none has a monopoly on the truth. To illustrate, I once asked Carol Lynn Martin (co-author of the Gender Schema theory we reviewed in Chapter 8) if she thought that her new ideas about preschoolers' schematic processing of gender-related information pretty much explained how they come to prefer masculine and feminine gender roles. She replied, "Heavens no!" and proceeded to tell me that while she thought her ideas were somewhat innovative and worth pursuing, she had benefitted immensely from the earlier theories of Bandura, Kohlberg, and people in the social information-processing camp, and that our knowledge of gender-typing would actually be quite impoverished if all we knew was what she had demonstrated in her own research. My own impression was that Dr. Martin was being somewhat self-efficacing and modest in assessing her contributions; yet she was quite correct that biosocial, psychobiosocial, social-learning, and cognitive-developmental theorists have all contributed, and contributed substantially, along with gender schema theorists, to what we now know about the development of gender roles (review Table 8.5, on page 270). And so it goes for every domain of development we have studied: Our knowledge is *always* enriched by integrating the contributions of researchers from many disciplines and diverse theoretical viewpoints.

Patterns of Parenting (and Adult Guidance) Clearly Matter

In Box 3.3, we touched on an interesting debate concerning the importance of parenting and childrearing practices in shaping children's and adolescents' developmental outcomes. Behavioral geneticist Sandra Scarr (1992) argued that patterns of parenting are not all that important. Presumably, humans have evolved in ways that make them responsive and adaptable to a wide range of environments. Thus, given an "average expectable" home environment—that is, one that falls within the broad range of those typical of the human species—children will display normal, adaptive developmental outcomes, regardless of the child-rearing practices their parents (or other guardians) employ. Judith Harris has also argued that patterns of parenting have little influence on who we ultimately become. She asserts that our genes and the socializing influences of our peer groups are the primary influences on social and personality development (see Box 13.1). By contrast, environmentalists such as Diana Baumrind (1993), Martin Hoffman (1988, 2000) and Kenneth Dodge (see Dodge, Coie, & Lynam, 2006) claim that patterns of parenting and adult guidance do matter and that different childrearing styles and practices can produce *very large differences* in children's and adolescents' developmental outcomes. So which viewpoint should we accept?

Quite frankly, my biases are showing here, but the empirical record clearly suggests to me that parenting *does* matter and exerts a most important influence on developing children and adolescents. In fact, the research we have reviewed throughout the text point to two broad conclusions that are strongly supported by existing research.

Children Need Love, Guidance . . . and Limits   At several points, we have noted that developing persons fare much better if they are warmly received by their caregivers, and that a cool, aloof (or rejecting) attitude on caregivers' part often forecasts poor developmental outcomes. Warmth is clearly a crucial component of effective parenting (and effective alternative caregiving and effective instruction during the preschool and early grade-school years). Yet warmth and acceptance alone are not sufficient to guarantee developmental successes. We need only recall the far less than optimal outcomes displayed by children of *permissive* parents, who generally accept their children but provide them with few standards to govern and evaluate their behavior, and do not carefully monitor their conduct.

The pattern of parenting that is most closely associated with adaptive developmental outcomes is one characterized by warm acceptance; provision of guidance, or standards for children to live up to; and a monitoring of the child's or the adolescent's behavior to ensure that he or she is complying with parental guidelines or otherwise meeting those expectations. In other words, developing persons seem to fare best when they receive love, guidance . . . and limits from involved parents who are highly concerned with helping to underwrite their developmental successes. For many families in Western democracies, the *authoritative* pattern of child rearing, with its emphasis on granting youngsters some autonomy in deciding how to satisfy parental expectations, is a particularly effective method of combining love and guidance with reasonable limitations to promote adaptive outcomes. However, this winning combination of love, guidance, and limits can be embodied in other ways that are equally (or more) effective for families within other cultures, subcultures, or ecological niches. For example, the "no-nonsense" parenting often observed in lower-SES African-American families—a style in between Baumrind's authoritative and authoritarian patterns of parenting—is highly effective in shielding youngsters who live in dangerous neighborhoods from deviant peer influences and other forms of harm. And even though no-nonsense parenting is somewhat power-assertive and coercive by white middle-class standards, it does not predict aggression and antisocial conduct in the same way for African-American youth as it does for whites—possibly because it is interpreted as a sign of concern and caring (rather than aloofness and hostility) by African-American children (Deater-Deckard & Dodge, 1997). Similarly, the highly restrictive pattern of parenting displayed by Chinese and immigrant Chinese-American parents is sometimes characterized as rather authoritarian by Western standards. And yet it forecasts highly favorable developmental outcomes because of Chinese cultural values (accepted by both parents and their offspring) stressing that (1) caring, concerned parents have an obligation to be highly controlling and restrictive so as to train their children to become well-socialized members of a collectivist order, and (2) children are obligated to honor their concerned parents by accepting and living up to the guidelines and limitations their parents set for them. So a pattern of child rearing that is too rigid to work very well among families highly acculturated into Western, individualistic democracies is most effective in other contexts, largely because it skillfully interfaces the love, guidance, and limits that developing persons need with other important values that prevail within these contexts (Chao, 1994, 2001).

The message? Yes, love and the provision of guidance . . . and limits are all crucial components of effective parenting. However, there are many ways to incorporate these elements into the caregiving that parents (and other adults) provide, and the pattern that works best largely depends on one's culture and/or the ecological niche occupied by one's family. There is clearly much truth to Louis Laosa's (1981) observation that "indigenous patterns of child care throughout the world represent largely successful adaptations to conditions of life that have long differed from one people to another. [Adults] are good [parents] by the only *relevant* standards, those of their own culture" (p. 159, italics added).

Parents Must Themselves Be Adaptable Let's also note that raising a child successfully is hard work and that there are no magic formulas that provide absolute guarantees of fostering developmental successes. Why not? Perhaps the main reason is because children and adolescents are each unique beings, and practices that work well for one individual may fail miserably with another, even if the two youngsters are siblings raised in the same home by the same adult caregivers!

One clear example of this point is Grazyna Kochanska's (1997) research on temperament and moral internalization that we discussed in Box 10.3. Recall that temperamentally *fearful* youngsters showed greater evidence of acquiring a strong internalized conscience if their parents used gentle, psychological forms of inductive discipline and deemphasized power assertion. However, this same kind of discipline was less effective with highly impulsive, temperamentally *fearless* youngsters, who responded much better to parents who fostered compliance by establishing a warm, mutually cooperative relationship with the child, thus making the fearless youngster eager to cooperate with and please his parents and concerned about undermining a highly satisfying parent/child alliance.

What this study (and many, many others we have reviewed) clearly illustrates is this: Favorable outcomes are more likely to result when parents successfully adapt to *their* child, thereby creating a "goodness of fit" between their parenting practices and their child's unique characteristics. Of course, establishing such "goodness of fit" may sometimes require the patience of a saint, particularly if the child is often cranky, oppositional, or otherwise difficult. And yet, we have seen that parents who can set their preconceived opinions aside and sensitively adapt their caregiving to their own child's difficult demeanor tend to have youngsters who become securely attached to them (van den Boom, 1995) and may no longer be perceived as difficult or suffer any adjustment problems later in childhood and adolescence (Jaffari-Bimmel et al., 2006; Rubin et al., 2003). By contrast, difficult children are likely to remain that way if their parents fail to adapt to their oppositional demeanor, choosing instead to be impatient, demanding, and forceful with them.

In sum, effective parents are those who can sensitively adjust to their own child, creating a good fit between their parenting practices and the child's unique characteristics. As we noted in Chapter 5, one of the reasons that caregiver *sensitivity* predicts attachment security (and many other adaptive outcomes) is that the very notion of *sensitive* care implies an ability to tailor one's routines to whatever characteristics a child (or an adolescent) might display.

Many Social Forces Conspire to Shape Development

Perhaps the major strength of recent contextualist models of social and personality development is their calling our attention to the many extrafamilial influences on developing children and adolescents. We now know that schools are a crucial agent of socialization and that children can be influenced by the goodness of fit between their own background or developmental needs and the characteristics of the schools they attend. We also have learned that such cultural and technological forces as the content of television programming and exposure to personal computers and the Internet have the capacity to influence developing persons in many ways—some good, and some not so good. And we have learned over the past 35 years that the society of one's peers is another important developmental context, not only for acquiring social skills that are valued by one's equals, but also for the growth of such attributes as prosocial concern, cooperation and teamwork, healthy attitudes about competition, a sense of identity and belongingness apart from one's family, and self-esteem (to name a few). So although the family may be the primary agent of socialization, each of us is exposed, either directly or indirectly, to a variety of extrafamilial contexts and experiences than can play a major part in shaping our personalities and social behavior.

Photo 14.3
Although families may be the primary agent of socialization, each of us is exposed to a variety of extrafamilial contexts that play meaningful roles in shaping our personalities and social conduct.

David Young-Wolff/PhotoEdit, Inc.

We've Come a Long Way . . . But Have So Far to Go

In 1979, I dedicated the first edition of this text ". . . to those researchers who have made the study of social and personality development an exciting endeavor" and expressed my belief that this discipline had "come of age." Among the most exciting new thrusts then were (1) emergence of the Bowlby-Ainsworth ethological theory of attachment and of research seeking to identify the long-term implications (if any) of secure and insecure attachments and (2) the movement afoot among many other social-developmentalists to pinpoint the significance (if any) of peers as socializing agents. This was also the time at which Bronfenbrenner's (1979) early version of *ecological systems theory* appeared. And as social-developmentalists began to increasingly incorporate contextual assumptions into their thinking, they started asking new questions that might not have occurred to them in the past. For example, early returns suggesting that good peer relations promoted adaptive developmental outcomes and that peer rejection spelled trouble prompted many investigators to go beyond peer acceptance to see whether establishing special peer alliances, or *friendships,* had any unique impacts on one's social and personality development (such as protecting a child with a negative sociometric status against the maladaptive outcomes associated with peer rejection). At the same time, Bronfenbrenner's emphasis on *mesosystem* influences—the connections among microsystems such as the family and peer groups—prompted researchers to explore such links and to learn that the pathways to positive peer relations and high-quality intimate friendships often begin at home. And the current emphasis on cultural influences on development, which has come to the forefront of our discipline in the past 20 years, largely stemmed from Bronfenbrenner's writings about the developmental significance of *macrosystems,* as well as from empirical observations that the forces that produce one set of outcomes for white, middle-class youngsters in Western societies didn't always have the same effects elsewhere—and from researchers' desire to determine why this is so.

Clearly, we have come a long way since 1979. In fact, a sizable majority of the research citations in this sixth edition of the text date from 1995 to the present and represent knowledge that simply was not available at the time the first edition of this book was written. As we enter the second decade of the 21st century, there can be little doubt that the field of social and personality development is an extremely dynamic one, with our knowledge increasing almost exponentially every few years or so. Yet, as a developing entity, the field is far from mature.

Why do I say this given that we have learned so much about social and personality development in the past 10–15 years? Simply because it often seems to social-developmentalists that the more they learn about a topic, the more they recognize how much more there is to learn. Were you to read articles from our leading journals (and I hope you will), you would find that all of them provide some sort of "answer" for the questions they have raised. And yet, the discussion sections of these same articles usually raise many more interesting questions that their data do *not* address, along with a call for additional research to explore these issues.

For developmentalists, then, there are always more questions than answers. I find this to be both a humbling and inspiring thought. Hopefully, you too will feel inspired as we complete our introduction to social and personality development, for much as you may have learned, there is much, much more to be discovered. And I sincerely hope that you will use what you have learned (and may learn should you take additional courses) to observe more closely your own development and that of those around you, and will seek to steer your own and others' lives in healthier directions.

Glossary

ability tracking the educational practice of grouping students according to ability and then educating them in classes with students of comparable educational or intellectual standing.

acceptance/responsiveness a dimension of parenting that describes the amount of responsiveness and affection that a parent displays toward a child.

accommodation Piaget's term for the process by which children modify their existing schemes in order to incorporate or adapt to new experiences.

acculturation stress anxiety or uneasiness that new residents may feel upon attempting to assimilate a new culture and its traditions.

achievement expectancies cognitive expectations of succeeding or failing at a particular achievement-related activity.

achievement motivation a willingness to strive to succeed at challenging tasks and to meet high standards of accomplishment.

achievement training encouraging children to do things well—that is, to meet or exceed high standards as they strive to accomplish various objectives.

achievement value perceived value of attaining a particular goal should one strive to achieve it.

active genotype/environment correlations the notion that our genotypes affect the types of environments that we prefer and seek out.

activity/passivity issue debate among developmental theorists about whether children are active contributors to their own development or, rather, passive recipients of environmental influence.

adaptation inborn tendency to adjust to the demands of the environment.

adoption design a study in which adoptees are compared with their biological relatives and their adoptive relatives to estimate the heritability of an attribute.

Adult Attachment Interview clinical interview used with adolescents and adults to tap respondents' memories of their childhood relationships with parents in order to assess the character of respondents' attachment representations.

affective explanations discipline which focuses a child's attention on the harm or distress that his or her conduct has caused others.

"aggressive cues" hypothesis Berkowitz's notion that the presence of stimuli previously associated with aggression can evoke aggressive responses from an angry individual.

aggressive-rejected children a subgroup of rejected children who display high levels of hostility and aggression in their interactions with peers.

altruism a concern for the welfare of others that is intrinsically motivated and expressed through such voluntary prosocial acts as sharing, cooperating, and helping.

altruistic exhortations verbal encouragement to help, comfort, share, or cooperate with others.

Amae Japanese term that refers to an infant's feeling of total dependance on his or her mother and presumption of the mother's love and indulgence.

androgenized females females who develop male-like external genitalia because of exposure to male sex hormones during the prenatal period.

androgyny a gender-role orientation in which the individual has incorporated a large number of both masculine and feminine attributes into his or her personality.

aptitude-treatment interaction (ATI) a phenomenon whereby characteristics of the student and of the school environment interact to affect student outcomes, such that any given educational practice may be effective with some students but not with others.

asocial phase (of attachment) approximately the first six weeks of life, in which infants respond in an equally favorable way to interesting social and nonsocial stimuli.

assimilation Piaget's term for the process by which children interpret new experiences by incorporating them into their existing schemes.

associative play form of social discourse in which children pursue their own interests but will swap toys or comment on each other's activities.

attachment a close emotional relationship between two persons, characterized by mutual affection and a desire to maintain proximity.

Attachment Q-set alterative method of assessing attachment security that is based on observations of the child's attachment-related behaviors at home; can be used with infants, toddlers, and preschool children.

attribution retraining therapeutic intervention in which helpless children are persuaded to attribute failures to their lack of effort rather than a lack of ability.

authoritarian instruction a restrictive style of instruction in which the teacher makes absolute demands and uses threats or force (if necessary) to ensure that students comply.

authoritarian parenting a restrictive pattern of parenting in which adults set many rules for their children, expect strict obedience, and rely on power rather than reason to elicit compliance.

authoritative instruction a warm but controlling style of instruction in which the teacher makes many demands but also allows some autonomy and individual expression as long as students are staying within the guidelines that the teacher has set.

authoritative parenting flexible, democratic style of parenting in which warm, accepting parents provide guidance and control while allowing the child some say in deciding how best to meet challenges and obligations.

autonomous morality Piaget's second stage of moral development, in which children realize that rules are arbitrary agreements that can be challenged and changed with the consent of the people they govern.

autonomy the capacity to make decisions independently, to serve as one's own source of emotional strength, and to otherwise manage one's life tasks without depending on others for assistance; an important developmental task of adolescence.

autonomy support   parental attempts to foster individuality and self-determination by encouraging children to express their viewpoints, participate in family decisions that affect them, and to have some say in how they will comply with parental demands and directives.

average-status children   children who receive an average number of nominations as a liked and/or a disliked individual from members of their peer group.

avoidant attachment   an insecure infant/caregiver bond characterized by little separation protest and a tendency of the child to avoid or ignore the caregiver.

baby biography   a detailed record of an infant's growth and development over a period of time.

basic gender identity   the stage of gender identity in which the child first labels the self as a boy or a girl.

behavioral comparisons phase   the tendency to form impressions of others by comparing and contrasting their overt behaviors.

behavioral control   attempts to regulate a child's or an adolescent's conduct through firm discipline and monitoring of his or her conduct.

behavioral definition of aggression   any action that delivers noxious stimuli to another organism.

behavioral definition of altruism   behavior that benefits another person, regardless of the actor's motives.

behavioral genetics   the scientific study of how genotype interacts with environment to determine behavioral attributes such as intelligence, personality, and mental health.

behavioral inhibition   a temperamental attribute reflecting the fearful distress children display and their tendency to withdraw from unfamiliar people and situations.

behavioral schemes   organized patterns of behavior that are used to represent and respond to objects and experiences.

behaviorism   a school of thinking in psychology that holds that conclusions about human development should be based on controlled observations of overt behavior rather than speculation about unconscious motives or other unobservable phenomena; the philosophical underpinning for social-learning theories.

belief-desire theory   theory of mind that develops between ages 3 and 4; the child now realizes that both beliefs and desires may determine behavior and that people will often act on their beliefs, even if they are inaccurate.

benign attributional bias   tendency to give the benefit of the doubt to peers rather than quickly assuming that their displeasing actions reflect a hostile or antisocial intent.

blended (or reconstituted) families   new families resulting from cohabitation or remarriage that include a parent, one or more children, and step-relations.

bully/victims   a small subset of children who are often bullied and who, in turn, often bully their more positive peers.

caregiving hypothesis   Ainsworth's notion that the type of attachment an infant develops with a particular caregiver depends primarily on the kind of caregiving he has received from that person.

case study   a research method in which the investigator gathers extensive information about the life of an individual and then tests developmental hypotheses by analyzing the events of the person's life history.

castration anxiety   in Freud's theory, a young boy's fear that his father will castrate him as punishment for his rivalrous conduct.

categorical self   a person's classification of the self along socially significant dimensions such as age and sex.

catharsis hypothesis   the notion that aggressive urges are reduced when people witness or commit real or symbolic acts of aggression.

cathartic technique   a strategy for reducing aggression by encouraging children to vent their anger or frustrations on inanimate objects.

causal attributions   conclusions drawn about the underlying causes of our own or another person's behavior.

causal attributions   conclusions drawn about the underlying causes of one's own or another person's behavior.

centered thinking (centration)   the tendency to focus on only one aspect of a problem when two or more aspects are relevant.

child abuse   term used to describe any extreme maltreatment of children, involving physical battering; sexual molestations; psychological insults such as persistent ridicule, rejection, and terrorization; and physical or emotional neglect.

child effects model   model of family influence in which children are believed to influence their parents rather than vice versa.

chronic persistence trajectory   growth curve of children who are highly aggressive early in life and who display the same high (or escalating) levels of aggression throughout childhood and adolescence.

chronosystem   in ecological systems theory, changes in the individual or the environment that occur over time and influence the direction development takes.

clinical method   a type of interview in which a participant's response to each successive question (or problem) determines what the investigator will ask next.

clique   a small group of friends that interacts frequently.

coaching   method of social-skills training in which an adult displays and explains various socially skilled behaviors, allows the child to practice them, and provides feedback aimed at improving the child's performances.

coercive home environment   a home in which family members often annoy one another and use aggressive or otherwise antisocial tactics as a method of coping with these aversive experiences.

cognitive development   age-related changes that occur in mental activities such as attending, perceiving, learning, thinking, and remembering.

cognitive operation   an internal mental activity that one performs on objects of thought.

cohort effect   age-related difference among cohorts that is attributable to cultural/historical differences in cohorts' growing-up experiences rather than to true developmental change.

collaborative (or guided) learning   The process of learning or acquiring new skills that occurs as novices participate in activities under the guidance of a more skillful tutor.

collective efficacy   term used to describe neighborhoods in which residents are well connected, neighborly, and tend to monitor events in the neighborhood (including activities of neighborhood youth) to maintain public order.

collectivist (or communal) society   society that values cooperative interdependence, social harmony, and adherence to group norms. These societies generally hold that the group's well-being is more important than that of the individual.

committed compliance   compliance based on the child's eagerness to cooperate with a responsive parent who has been willing to cooperate with him or her.

compensation the ability to consider more than one aspect of a problem at a time (also called decentration).

compensatory interventions special educational programs designed to further the cognitive growth and scholastic achievements of disadvantaged children.

complex stepparent home family consisting of two married (or cohabiting) adults, each of whom has at least one biological child living at home.

computer-assisted instruction (CAI) use of computers to teach new concepts and practice academic skills.

concordance rate the percentage of cases in which a particular attribute is present for one member of a twin pair if it is present for the other.

concrete-operational stage Piaget's third stage of cognitive development, lasting from about ages 7 to 11, when children are acquiring cognitive operations and thinking more logically about tangible objects and experiences.

conflict circumstance in which two (or more) persons have incompatiable needs, desires, or goals.

confounding variable some factor other than the independent variable that, if not controlled by the experimenter, could explain any differences across treatment conditions in participants' performance on the dependent variable.

congenital adrenal hyperplasia (CAH) a genetic anomaly that causes one's adrenal glands to produce unusually high levels of androgen from the prenatal period onward; often has masculinizing effects on female fetuses.

conservation the recognition that the properties of an object or substance do not change when its appearance is altered in some superficial way.

consistency schema attributional heuristic implying that actions that a person consistently performs are likely to be internally caused (reflecting a dispositional characteristic).

constructivist one who gains knowledge by acting or otherwise operating on objects or events to discover their properties.

contextual model view of children as active entities whose developmental paths represent a continuous, dynamic interplay between internal forces (nature) and external influences (nurture).

continuity/discontinuity issue debate among theorists about whether developmental changes are best characterized as gradual and quantitative or, rather, abrupt and qualitative.

controversial children children who receive many nominations as a liked individual and many as a disliked individual from members of their peer group.

conventional morality Kohlberg's term for the third and fourth stages of moral reasoning, in which moral judgments are based on a desire to gain approval (Stage 3) or to uphold laws that maintain social order (Stage 4).

cooperative learning methods an educational practice whereby children of different backgrounds or ability levels are assigned to teams; each team member works on problems geared to his or her ability level, and all members are reinforced for "pulling together" and performing well as a team.

cooperative play true social play in which children cooperate or assume reciprocal roles while pursuing shared goals.

coparenting circumstance in which parents mutually support each other and function as a cooperative parenting team.

correlation coefficient a numerical index, ranging from −1.00 to +1.00, of the strength and direction of the relationship between two variables.

correlational design a type of research design that indicates the strength of associations among variables; though correlated variables are systematically related, these relationships are not necessarily causal.

cross-cultural comparison a study that compares the behavior and/or development of people from different cultural or subcultural backgrounds.

cross-generational problem the fact that long-term changes in the environment may limit conclusions of a longitudinal project to that generation of children who were growing up while the study was in progress.

cross-pressures conflicts stemming from differences in the values and practices advocated by parents and those advocated by peers.

cross-sectional design a research design in which subjects from different age groups are studied at the same point in time.

crowd a large, reputationally based peer group made up of individuals and cliques that share similar norms, interests, and values.

deferred imitation reproduction of a modeled activity that has been witnessed at some point in the past.

demandingness/control a dimension of parenting that describes how restrictive and demanding parents are.

dependent variable the aspect of behavior that is measured in an experiment and assumed to be under the control of the independent variable.

desensitization hypothesis the notion that people who watch a lot of media violence will become less aroused by aggression and more tolerant of violent and aggressive acts.

desire theory an early theory of mind in which a person's actions are thought to be a reflection of her desires rather than other mental states such as beliefs.

development the systematic continuities and changes in the individual that occur between conception (when a sperm penetrates an ovum creating a new organism) and death.

developmental stage a distinct phase within a larger sequence of development; a period characterized by a particular set of abilities, motives, behaviors, or emotions that occur together and form a coherent pattern.

deviancy training interactions among deviant peers that perpetuate and intensify a child's behavior problems and antisocial conduct.

diary study a self-report methodology in which participants respond to standardized questions, in a diary or notebook, at a specified time or whenever they are instructed to respond by prompt from an electronic pager.

difficult temperament temperamental profile in which the child is irregular in daily routines and adapts slowly to new experiences, often responding negatively and intensely.

direct effect instances in which any pair of family members affects and is affected by each other's behavior.

direct tuition teaching young children how to behave by reinforcing "appropriate" behaviors and by punishing or otherwise discouraging inappropriate conduct.

discrete emotions theory a theory of emotions specifying that specific emotions are biologically programmed, accompanied by distinct sets of bodily and facial cues, and discriminable from early in life.

disequilibriums   imbalances or contradictions between one's thought processes and environmental events. By contrast, *equilibrium* refers to a balanced, harmonious relationship between one's cognitive structures and the environment.

disorganized/disoriented attachment   an insecure infant/caregiver bond characterized by the infant's dazed appearance on reunion or a tendency to first seek and then abruptly avoid the caregiver.

doctrine of specificity   a viewpoint shared by many social-learning theorists that holds that moral affect, moral reasoning, and moral behavior may depend on the situation one faces as much as or more than on an internalized set of moral principles.

donor insemination   process by which a fertile woman conceives with the aid of sperm from an unknown donor.

double standard   the view that sexual behavior that is appropriate for members of one sex is less appropriate for the other.

easy temperament   temperamental profile in which the child quickly establishes regular routines, is generally good natured, and adapts easily to novelty.

eclectics   those who borrow from many theories in their attempts to predict and explain human development.

ecological systems theory   Bronfenbrenner's model emphasizing that the developing person is embedded in a series of environmental systems that interact with one another and with the person to influence development (sometimes called **bioecological theory**).

ecological validity   state of affairs in which the findings of one's research are an accurate representation of processes that occur in the natural environment.

effective schools   schools that are generally successful at achieving curricular and noncurricular objectives, regardless of the racial, ethnic, or socioeconomic background of the student population.

effortful control   temperamental attribute that reflects one's ability to focus and/or shift attention as called for by the situation and to suppress dominant or inappropriate responses in favor of those more appropriate for the situation.

ego   psychoanalytic term for the rational component of the personality.

egocentrism   the tendency to view the world from one's own perspective while failing to recognize that others may have different points of view.

Electra complex   female version of Oedipus complex, in which a 3- to 6-year-old girl was believed to envy her father for possessing a penis and to seek him as a sex object in the hope of sharing the organ that she lacks.

emotion   a motivational construct that is characterized by changes in affect (or feelings), physiological responses, cognitions, and overt behavior.

emotional bonding   term used to describe the strong affectional ties that parents may feel toward a neonate; some theorists believe that the strongest bonding occurs shortly after birth, during a sensitive period.

emotional competence   abilities to display predominantly positive (rather than negative) emotions, correctly identify others' emotions and respond appropriately to them, and adjust one's own emotions to appropriate levels of intensity in order to achieve one's goals.

emotional display rules   culturally defined rules specifying which emotions should or should not be expressed under which circumstances.

emotional self-regulation   the process of adjusting one's emotions to appropriate levels of intensity in order to accomplish one's goals.

empathic concern   a measure of the extent to which an individual recognizes the needs of others and is concerned about their welfare.

empathy   the ability to experience vicariously the same emotions that someone else is experiencing.

emulation   reproduction of a modeled outcome by use of means other than those that the model displayed.

entity view of ability   belief that one's ability is a highly stable trait that is not influenced much by effort or practice.

environmental determinism   the notion that children are passive creatures who are molded by their environments.

Eros   Freud's name for instincts such as respiration, hunger, and sex that help the individual (and the species) to survive.

ethnic identity   sense of belonging to an ethnic group and committing oneself to that group's traditions or culture.

ethnography   method in which the researcher seeks to understand the unique values, traditions, and social processes of a culture or subculture by living with its members and making extensive observations and notes.

ethology   the study of the bioevolutionary bases of behavior and development.

evocative genotype/environment correlations   the notion that our heritable attributes affect others' behavior toward us and thus influence the social environment in which development takes place.

exosystem   social systems that children and adolescents do not directly experience but that may nonetheless influence their development; the third of Bronfenbrenner's environmental layers, or contexts.

experimental control   steps taken by an experimenter to ensure that all extraneous factors that could influence the dependent variable are roughly equivalent in each experimental condition; these precautions must be taken before an experimenter can be reasonably certain that observed changes in the dependent variable were caused by the manipulation of the independent variable.

experimental design   a research design in which the investigator introduces some change in the participant's environment and then measures the effect of that change on the participant's behavior.

expressive role   a social prescription, usually directed toward females, that one should be cooperative, kind, nurturant, and sensitive to the needs of others.

extended family   a group of blood relatives from more than one nuclear family (for example, grandparents, aunts, uncles, nieces, and nephews) who live together, forming a household.

extended self   more mature self-representation, emerging between ages 3½ and 5 years, in which children are able to integrate past, present, and unknown future self-representations into a notion of a self that endures over time.

extrafamilial influences   social agencies other than the family that influence a child's or an adolescent's cognitive, social, and emotional development.

extrinsic orientation   a desire to achieve in order to earn external incentives such as grades, prizes, or the approval of others.

false-belief task   method of assessing one's understanding that people can hold inaccurate beliefs that can influence their conduct, wrong as these beliefs may be.

false self-behavior   acting in ways that do not reflect one's true self or the "true me."

falsifiability a criterion for evaluating the scientific merit of theories; a theory is falsifiable when it is capable of generating predictions that could be disconfirmed.

family two or more persons, related by birth, marriage, adoption, or choice, who have emotional ties and responsibilities to each other.

family distress model Conger's model of how economic distress affects family dynamics and developmental outcomes.

family social system the complex network of relationships, interactions, and patterns of influence that characterize a family with three or more members.

"felt responsibility" hypothesis the theory that empathy may promote altruism by causing one to reflect on altruistic norms and thus to feel some obligation to help others who are distressed.

field experiment an experiment that takes place in a naturalistic setting such as the home, the school, or a playground.

fixation arrested development at a particular psychosexual stage, often occurring as a means of coping with existing conflicts and preventing movement to the next stage, where stress may be even greater.

foreclosure identity status characterizing individuals who have prematurely committed themselves to occupations or ideologies without really thinking about these commitments.

formal-operational stage Piaget's fourth and final stage of cognitive development, from age 11 to 12 and beyond, when the individual begins to think more rationally and systematically about abstract concepts and hypothetical events.

friendship a strong and often enduring relationship between two individuals, characterized by loyalty, intimacy, and mutual affection.

frustration/aggression hypothesis early learning theory of aggression, holding that frustration triggers aggression and that all aggressive acts can be traced to frustrations.

functionalist perspective (on emotions) a theory specifying the major purpose of an emotion is to establish, maintain, or change one's relationship with the environment to accomplish a goal; emotions are not viewed as discrete early in life but as entities that emerge with age.

gangs loosely organized groups of adolescents that hang out, identify as a group, and often partake in delinquent or criminal activities.

gender consistency the stage of gender identity in which the child recognizes that a person's gender is invariant despite changes in the person's activities or appearance (also known as gender constancy).

gender identity one's awareness of one's gender and its implications.

gender intensification a magnification of sex differences early in adolescence; associated with increased pressure to conform to traditional gender roles.

gender schemas organized sets of beliefs and expectations about males and females that guide information processing.

gender segregation children's tendency to associate with same-sex playmates and to think of the other sex as an out-group.

gender stability the stage of gender identity in which the child recognizes that gender is stable over time.

gender typing the process by which a child becomes aware of his or her gender and acquires motives, values, and behaviors considered appropriate for members of that sex.

gender-role standard a behavior, value, or motive that members of a society consider more typical or appropriate for members of one sex.

genotype the genetic endowment that an individual inherits.

"goodness-of-fit" model Thomas and Chess's notion that development is likely to be optimized when parents' child-rearing practices are sensitively adapted to the child's temperamental characteristics.

habits well-learned associations between stimuli and responses that represent the stable aspects of one's personality.

heritability the amount of variability in a trait that is attributable to hereditary factors.

heritability coefficient a numerical estimate, ranging from .00 to +1.00, of the amount of variation in an attribute that is due to hereditary factors.

heteronomous morality Piaget's first stage of moral development, in which children view the rules of authority figures as sacred and unalterable.

heuristic value a criterion for evaluating the scientific merit of theories. An heuristic theory is one that continues to stimulate new research and new discoveries.

high-level desister trajectory growth curve of children who are highly aggressive early in life but who gradually become less aggressive throughout childhood and adolescence.

high-risk neighborhood a residential area in which the incidence of child abuse is much higher than in other neighborhoods with the same demographic characteristics.

holistic perspective a unified view of the developmental process that emphasizes the interrelationships among the physical/biological, mental, social, and emotional aspects of human development.

HOME inventory a measure of the amount and type of intellectual stimulation provided by a child's home environment.

hostile aggression aggressive acts for which the perpetrator's major goal is to harm or injure a victim.

hostile attributional bias tendency to view harm done under ambiguous circumstances as having stemmed from a hostile intent on the part of the harm-doer; characterizes reactive aggressors.

hypothesis a theoretical prediction about some aspect of experience.

hypothetico-deductive reasoning a style of problem solving in which all possible solutions to a problem are generated and then systematically evaluated to determine the correct answer(s).

id psychoanalytic term for the inborn component of the personality that is driven by the instincts.

identification Freud's term for the child's tendency to emulate another person, usually the same-sex parent.

identity a mature self-definition; a sense of who one is, where one is going in life, and how one fits into society.

identity achievement identity status characterizing individuals who have carefully considered identity issues and have made firm commitments to an occupation and ideologies.

identity crisis Erikson's term for the uncertainty and discomfort that adolescents experience when they become confused about their present and future roles in life.

identity diffusion identity status characterizing individuals who are not questioning who they are and have not yet committed themselves to an identity.

imaginary audience allegedly a form of adolescent egocentrism that involves confusing one's own thoughts with those of a hypothesized audience and concluding that others share your preoccupations.

immanent justice the notion that unacceptable conduct will invariably be punished and that justice is ever-present in the world.

imprinting an innate or instinctual form of learning in which the young of certain species will follow and become attached to moving objects (usually their mothers).

Inclusion the educational practice of integrating special needs students into regular classrooms rather than placing them in segregated special education classes.

incompatible-response technique a nonpunitive method of behavior modification in which adults ignore undesirable conduct while reinforcing acts that are incompatible with these responses.

incremental view of ability belief that one's ability can be improved through increased effort and practice.

independence training encouraging children to become self-reliant by accomplishing goals without others' assistance.

independent variable the aspect of the environment that an experimenter modifies or manipulates in order to measure its impact on behavior.

indirect, or third party, effect instances in which the relationship between two individuals in a family is modified by the behavior or attitudes of a third family member.

individualistic society society that values personalism and individual accomplishments, which often take precedence over group goals. These societies tend to emphasize ways in which individuals differ from each other.

induction a nonpunitive form of discipline in which an adult explains why a child's behavior is wrong and should be changed by emphasizing its effects on others.

informal curriculum noncurricular objectives of schooling such as teaching children to cooperate, respect authority, obey rules, and become good citizens.

"in-group/out-group" schema one's general knowledge of the mannerisms, roles, activities, and behaviors that characterize males and females.

inhibitory control an ability to display acceptable conduct by resisting the temptation to commit a forbidden act.

innate purity the idea that infants are born with an intuitive sense of right and wrong that is often misdirected by the demands and restrictions of society.

inner experimentation the ability to solve simple problems on a mental, or symbolic, level without having to rely on trial-and-error experimentation.

inner speech internalized private speech; covert verbal thought.

insightfulness caregiver capacity to understand an infant's motives, emotions, and behaviors and to take them into account when responding to the infant; thought to be an important contributor to sensitive caregiving.

instinct an inborn biological force that motivates a particular response or class of responses.

instrumental aggression aggressive acts for which the perpetrator's major goal is to gain access to objects, space, or privileges.

instrumental role a social prescription, usually directed toward males, that one should be dominant, independent, assertive, competitive, and goal-oriented.

intentional definition of aggression any action intended to harm or injure another living being, who is motivated to avoid such treatment.

internal working models cognitive representations of self, others, and relationships that infants construct from their interactions with caregivers.

internalization the process of adopting the attributes or standards of other people—taking these standards as one's own.

intimacy versus isolation the sixth of Erikson's psychosocial conflicts, in which young adults must commit themselves to a shared identity with another person (that is, intimacy) or else remain aloof and unconnected to others.

intrinsic orientation a desire to achieve in order to satisfy one's personal needs for competence or mastery.

introversion/extroversion the opposite poles of a personality dimension: Introverts are shy and anxious around others and tend to withdraw from social situations; extroverts are highly sociable and enjoy being with others.

intuitive thought Piaget's term for reasoning that is dominated by appearances (or perceptual characteristics of objects and events) rather than by rational thought processes.

invariant developmental sequence a series of developments that occur in one particular order because each development in the sequence is a prerequisite for the next.

joint attention the act of attending to the same object at the same time as someone else; a way in which infants share experiences and intentions with their caregivers.

kinship the extent to which two individuals have genes in common.

late-onset (or adolescent-limited) trajectory growth curve of individuals who become more aggressive, usually for a limited time, during adolescence or young adulthood after having been relatively nonaggressive during childhood.

learned helplessness orientation a tendency to give up or to stop trying after failing because these failures have been attributed to a lack of ability that one can do little about.

learned helplessness the failure to learn how to respond appropriately in a situation because of previous exposures to uncontrollable events in the same or similar situations.

learning goal state of affairs in which one's primary objective in a achievement context is to increase one's skills or objectives.

locus of control personality dimension distinguishing people who assume that they are personally responsible for their life outcomes (internal locus) from those who believe that their outcomes depend more on circumstances beyond their control (external locus).

longitudinal design a research design in which one group of subjects is studied repeatedly over a period of months or years.

looking-glass self the idea that a child's self-concept is largely determined by the ways other people respond to him or her.

love withdrawal a form of discipline in which an adult withholds attention, affection, or approval in order to modify or control a child's behavior.

macrosystem the larger cultural or subcultural context in which development occurs; Bronfenbrenner's outermost environmental layer, or context.

mastery motivation an inborn motive to explore, understand, and control one's environment.

mastery orientation a tendency to persist at challenging tasks because of a belief that one has the ability to succeed and/or that earlier failures can be overcome by trying harder.

maternal deprivation hypothesis the notion that socially deprived infants develop abnormally because they have failed to establish attachments to a primary caregiver.

mean-world belief a belief, fostered by televised violence, that the world is a more dangerous and frightening place than is actually the case.

mechanistic model view of children as passive entities whose developmental paths are primarily determined by external (environmental) influences.

mesosystem the interconnections among an individual's immediate settings, or microsystems. The second of Bronfenbrenner's environmental layers, or contexts.

meta-analysis statistical procedure for combining and analyzing the results of several studies on the same topic to test hypotheses and draw conclusions.

metacognition one's knowledge about cognition and about the regulation of cognitive activities.

microgenetic design a research design in which participants are studied intensively over a short period of time as developmental changes occur; attempts to specify how or why those changes occur.

microsystem the immediate settings (including role relationships and activities) that the person actually encounters; the innermost of Bronfenbrenner's environmental layers, or contexts.

mixed-age peer interaction interactions among children who differ in age by a year or more.

moderate-level desister trajectory growth curve of children who are moderately aggressive early in life but who gradually become less aggressive throughout childhood and adolescence.

moral affect the emotional component of morality, including feelings such as empathy, guilt, shame, and pride in ethical conduct.

moral behavior the behavioral component of morality; actions that are consistent with one's moral standards in situations in which one is tempted to violate them.

moral disengagement the ability to avoid self-condemnation when engaged in immoral behavior by justifying one's actions as appropriate, minimizing their effects, or blaming others for one's conduct.

moral reasoning the cognitive component of morality; the thinking that people display when deciding whether various acts are right or wrong.

moral rules standards of acceptable and unacceptable conduct that focus on the rights and privileges of individuals.

morality a set of principles or ideals that help that the individual to distinguish right from wrong, act on the this distinction, and feel pride in virtuous conduct and guilt (or shame) for conduct that violates one's standards.

morality of care Gilligan's term for what she presumes to be the dominant moral orientation for females—an orientation focusing more on compassionate concerns for human welfare than on socially defined justice as administered through law.

morality of justice Gilligan's term for what she presumes to be the dominant moral orientation of males, focusing more on socially defined justice as administered through law than on compassionate concerns for human welfare.

moratorium identity status characterizing individuals who are currently experiencing an identity crisis and are actively exploring occupational and ideological positions in which to invest themselves.

"mother-only" monkeys monkeys who are raised with their mothers and denied any contact with peers.

motivational/intentional definition of altruism beneficial acts for which the actor's primary motive or intent was to address the needs of others.

motive to achieve success (M_s) Atkinson's term for the disposition describing one's tendency to approach challenging tasks and take pride in mastering them; analogous to McClelland's need for achievement.

motive to avoid failure (M_{af}) Atkinson's term for the disposition describing one's tendency to shy away from challenging tasks so as to avoid the embarrassment of failing.

mutually responsive orientation parent/child relationship characterized by establishment of comfortable routines, harmonious patterns of communication, mutual responsiveness to each other's needs and goals, and shared positive affect.

natural (or quasi) experiment a study in which the investigator measures the impact of some naturally occurring event that is assumed to affect people's lives.

natural selection an evolutionary process, proposed by Charles Darwin, stating that individuals with characteristics that promote adaptation to the environment will survive, reproduce, and pass these adaptive characteristics to offspring; those lacking these adaptive charac

naturalistic observation a method in which the scientist tests hypotheses by observing people as they engage in everyday activities in their natural habitats (for example, at home, at school, or on the playground).

nature versus nurture issue debate within developmental psychology over the relative importance of biological predispositions (nature) and environmental influences (nurture) as determinants of human development.

need for achievement (*n* Ach) McClelland's depiction of achievement motivation as a learned motive to compete and to strive for success in situations in which one's performance can be evaluated against some standard of excellence.

negative identity Erikson's term for an identity that is in direct opposition to that which parents and most adults would advocate.

negative reinforcer any stimulus whose removal or termination as the consequence of an act will increase the probability that the act will recur.

neglected children children who receive few nominations as either a liked or a disliked individual from members of their peer group.

neonate a newborn infant from birth to approximately 1 month of age.

no-nonsense parenting a mixture of authoritative and authoritarian parenting styles that is associated with favorable outcomes in African-American families.

nonrepresentative sample a subgroup that differs in important ways from the larger group (or population) to which it belongs.

nonshared environmental influence (NSE) an environmental influence that people living together do not share and that should make these individuals different from one another.

nonsocial activity   onlooker behavior and solitary play.

no-problem trajectory   growth curve of children who are low in aggression throughout childhood and adolescence.

norm of social responsibility   the principle that we should help others who are in some way dependent on us for assistance.

norms   group-defined rules or expectations about how the members of that group are to think or behave.

obesity   a medical term describing individuals who are at least 20 percent above the ideal weight for their height, age, and sex.

object permanence   the realization that objects continue to exist when they are no longer visible or detectable through the other senses.

observational learning   learning that results from observing the behavior of others.

observer influence   tendency of participants to react to an observer's presence by behaving in unusual ways.

Oedipal morality   Freud's theory that moral development occurs during the phallic period (ages 3 to 6) when children internalize the moral standards of the same-sex parent as they resolve their Oedipus or Electra conflicts.

Oedipus complex   Freud's term for the conflict that 3- to 6-year-old boys experience when they develop an incestuous desire for their mothers and, at the same time, a jealous and hostile rivalry with their fathers.

operant learning   a form of learning in which voluntary acts (or operants) become either more or less probable, depending on the consequences they produce.

operational schemes   Piaget's term for schemes that utilize cognitive operations, or mental "actions of the head," that enable one to transform objects of thought and to reason logically.

organismic model   view of children as active entities whose developmental paths are primarily determined by forces from within themselves.

organization   an inborn tendency to combine and integrate available schemes into coherent systems or bodies of knowledge.

original sin   the idea that children are inherently selfish egoists who must by controlled by society.

owness effect   tendency of parents in complex stepparent homes to favor and be more involved with their biological children than with their stepchildren.

own-sex schema   detailed knowledge or plans of action that enable a person to perform gender-consistent activities and to enact his or her gender role.

parallel play   largely noninteractive play in which players are in close proximity but do not often attempt to influence each other.

parent effects model   model of family influence in which parents (particularly mothers) are believed to influence their children rather than vice versa.

parsimony   a criterion for evaluating the scientific merit of theories; a parsimonious theory is one that uses relatively few explanatory principles to explain a broad set of observations.

particularistic development   developmental outcomes that vary from person to person.

passive genotype/environment correlations   the notion that the rearing environments that biological parents provide are influenced by the parents' own genes and hence are correlated with the child's own genotype.

passive victims (of aggression)   socially withdrawn and anxious children whom bullies torment, even though they appear to have done nothing to trigger such abuse.

peer acceptance   a measure of a person's likability (or dislikability) in the eyes of peers.

peer conformity   the tendency to go along with the wishes of peers or to yield to peer-group pressures.

peer group   a confederation of peers that interact regularly, define a sense of membership, and formulate norms that specify how members are supposed to look, think, and act.

peers   two or more persons who are operating at similar levels of behavioral complexity.

"peer-only" monkeys   monkeys who are separated from their mothers (and other adults) soon after birth and raised with peers.

performance goal   state of affairs in which one's primary objective in an achievement context is to display one's competencies (or to avoid looking incompetent).

permissive instruction   a lax style of instruction in which the teacher makes few demands of students and provides little or no active guidance.

permissive parenting   a pattern of parenting in which otherwise accepting adults make few demands of their children and rarely attempt to control their behavior.

person (or trait) praise   praise focusing on desirable personality traits such as intelligence; this praise fosters performance goals in achievement contexts.

personal agency   the recognition that one can be the cause of an event or events.

personal choices   decisions about one's conduct that are (or should be, in the person's view) under personal jurisdiction and not regulated by rules or authority figures (for example, choice of friends or leisure activities).

personal fable   allegedly a form of adolescent egocentrism in which the individual thinks that he and his thoughts and feelings are special or unique.

phallic stage   Freud's third stage of psychosexual development (from 3 to 6 years of age) in which children gratify the sex instinct by fondling their genitals and developing an incestuous desire for the parent of the other sex.

phase of indiscriminate attachments   period between 6 weeks and 6–7 months of age in which infants prefer social to nonsocial stimulation and are likely to protest whenever any adult puts them down or leaves them alone.

phase of multiple attachments   period when infants are forming attachments to companions other than their primary attachment object.

phase of specific attachment   period between 7 and 9 months of age when infants are attached to one close companion (usually the mother).

phenotype   the ways in which a person's genotype is expressed in observable or measurable characteristics.

popular children   children who are liked by many members of their peer group and disliked by very few.

postconventional morality   Kohlberg's term for the fifth and sixth stages of moral reasoning, in which moral judgments are based on social contracts and democratic law (Stage 5) or on universal principles of ethics and justice (Stage 6).

posttraumatic stress disorder a psychological syndrome involving flashbacks to traumatizing events, nightmares, and feelings of anxiety and helplessness in the face of threats; common among soldiers in combat and sexually abused children.

power assertion a form of discipline in which an adult relies on his or her superior power (for example, by administering spankings or withholding privileges) to modify or control a child's behavior.

power-assertion a form of discipline in which an adult relies on his or her superior power (for example, by administering spankings or withholding privileges) to modify or control a child's behavior.

preadapted characteristic an innate attribute that is a product of evolution and serves some function that increases the chances of survival for the individual and the species.

preconventional morality Kohlberg's term for the first two stages of moral reasoning, in which moral judgments are based on the tangible punitive consequences (Stage 1) or rewarding consequences (Stage 2) of an act for the actor rather than on the relationship of that act to society's rules and customs.

premoral period in Piaget's theory, the first five years of life, when children have little respect for or awareness of socially defined rules.

preoperational stage Piaget's second stage of cognitive development, lasting from about ages 2 to 7, when children are thinking at a symbolic level but are not yet using cognitive operations.

present self early self-representation in which 2- and 3-year-olds recognize current representations of self but are largely unaware that past self-representations or self-relevant events have implications for the future.

primary (or basic) emotions the set of emotions present at birth or emerging early in the first year that some theorists believe to be biologically programmed.

primary circular reaction a pleasurable response, centered on the infant's own body, that is discovered by chance and performed over and over.

private self (or I) those inner, or subjective, aspects of self that are known only to the individual and are not available for public scrutiny.

private speech Vygotsky's term for the subset of a child's verbal utterances that serve a self-communicative function and guide the child's activities.

proactive aggressors highly aggressive children who find aggressive acts easy to perform and who rely heavily on aggression as a means of solving social problems or achieving other personal objectives.

process praise praise of effort expended to formulate good ideas and effective problem-solving strategies; this praise fosters learning goals in achievement contexts.

promotion of volitional functioning (PVF) method of autonomy support in which parents guide adolescents' decision making by suggesting alternatives, tying them to adolescents' values and goals, and permitting them to resolve issues for themselves.

proprioceptive feedback sensory information from the muscles, tendons, and joints that helps one to locate the position of one's body (or body parts) in space.

prosocial behavior actions, such as sharing, helping, or comforting, that are intended to benefit other people.

prosocial moral reasoning the thinking that people display when deciding whether to help, share with, or comfort others when these actions could prove costly to themselves.

prospective study study in which the suspected causes or contributors to a developmental outcome are assessed earlier to see whether they accurately forecast the developments they are presumed to influence.

provocative victims (of aggression) restless, hot-tempered, and oppositional children who are victimized because they are disliked and often irritate their peers.

psychobiosocial model perspective on nature/nurture interactions specifying that specific early experiences affect the organization of the brain, which in turn influences one's responsiveness to similar experiences in the future.

psychological comparisons phase tendency to form impressions of others by comparing and contrasting these individuals on abstract psychological dimensions.

psychological constructs phase tendency to base one's impressions of others on the stable traits these individuals are presumed to have.

psychological control attempts to regulate a child's or an adolescent's conduct by such psychological tactics as withholding affection and/or inducing shame or guilt.

psychophysiological methods methods that measure the relationships between physiological processes and aspects of children's physical, cognitive, social, or emotional behavior and development.

psychosexual theory Freud's theory that states that maturation of the sex instinct underlies stages of personality development and that how parents manage children's instinctual impulses will determine the traits children come to display.

psychosocial theory Erikson's revision of Freud's theory, which emphasizes sociocultural (rather than sexual) determinants of development and posits a series of eight psychosocial conflicts that people must resolve successfully to display healthy psychological adjustment.

public self (or me) those aspects of self that others can see or infer.

punisher any consequence of an act that suppresses that act and/or decreases the probability that it will recur.

Pygmalion effect the tendency of teacher expectancies to become self-fulfilling prophecies, causing students to perform better or worse depending on their teacher's estimation of their potential.

random assignment a control technique in which participants are assigned to experimental conditions through an unbiased procedure so that the members of the groups are not systematically different from one another.

reactive aggressors children who display high levels of hostile, retaliatory aggression because they overattribute hostile intents to others and can't control their anger long enough to seek nonaggressive solutions to social problems.

reactive attachment disorder inability to form secure attachment bonds with other people; characterizes many victims of early social deprivation and/or abuse.

reciprocal determinism the notion that the flow of influence between children and their environments is a two-way street; the environment may affect the child, but the child's behavior will also influence the environment.

reinforcer any consequence of an act that increases the probability that the act will recur.

rejected children children who are disliked by many peers and liked by few.

relational aggression acts such as snubbing, exclusion, withdrawing acceptance, or spreading rumors that are aimed at damaging an adversary's self-esteem, friendships, or social status.

relational self-worth feelings of self-worth within a particular relationship context (for example, with parents, with male classmates); may differ across relationship contexts.

reliability the extent to which a measuring instrument yields consistent results, both over time and across observers.

repression a type of motivated forgetting in which anxiety-provoking thoughts and conflicts are forced out of conscious awareness.

resistant attachment an insecure infant/caregiver bond characterized by strong separation protest and a tendency of the child to remain near but resist contact initiated by the caregiver, particularly after a separation.

retaliatory aggression aggressive acts elicited by real or imagined provocations.

reversibility the ability to reverse, or negate, an action by mentally performing the opposite action.

role taking the ability to assume another person's perspective and understand his or her intentions, thoughts, feelings, and behaviors.

rouge test test of self-recognition that involves marking a toddler's face and observing his or her reaction to the mark when he or she is placed before a mirror.

scaffolding process by which an expert, when instructing a novice, responds contingently to the novice's behavior in a learning situation so that the novice gradually increases his or her understanding of a problem.

scheme an organized pattern of thought or action that a child constructs to make sense of some aspect of his or her experience; Piaget sometimes uses the term cognitive structure as a synonym for scheme.

schizophrenia a serious form of mental illness characterized by disturbances in logical thinking, emotional expression, and interpersonal behavior.

scientific method an attitude or value about the pursuit of knowledge that dictates that investigators must be objective and must allow their data to decide the merits of their theorizing.

secondary (or complex) emotions self-conscious or self-evaluative emotions that emerge in the second and third years and depend in part on cognitive development (sometimes called **self-conscious emotions**).

secondary circular reaction a pleasurable response, centered on an object external to the self, that is discovered by chance and performed over and over.

secondary reinforcer an initially neutral stimulus that acquires reinforcement value by virtue of its repeated association with other reinforcing stimuli.

secure attachment an infant/caregiver bond in which the child welcomes contact with a close companion and uses this person as a secure base from which to explore the environment.

secure base use of a caregiver as a base from which to explore the environment and to which to return for emotional support.

selective attrition nonrandom loss of participants during a study, resulting in a nonrepresentative sample.

selective breeding experiment a method of studying genetic influences by determining whether traits can be bred in animals through selective mating.

self the combination of physical and psychological attributes that is unique to each individual.

self-care (or latchkey) children children who care for themselves after school or in the evenings while their parents are working.

self-concept one's perceptions of one's unique combination of attributes.

self-conscious emotions see secondary (or complex) emotions.

self-disclosure the act of revealing private or intimate information about oneself to another person.

self-esteem one's evaluation of one's worth as a person based on an assessment of the qualities that make up the self-concept.

self-fulling prophecy phenomenon whereby people cause others to act in accordance with the expectations they have about those others.

self-oriented distress feeling of *personal* discomfort or distress that may be elicited when we experience the emotions of (that is, empathize with) a distressed other; thought to inhibit altruism.

self-recognition the ability to recognize oneself in a mirror or a photograph, coupled with the conscious awareness that the mirror or photographic image is a representation of "me."

sensitive period period of time that is optimal for the development of particular capacities or behaviors, and in which the individual is particularly sensitive to environmental influences that would foster these attributes.

sensorimotor stage Piaget's first stage of cognitive development, from birth to 2 years, when infants rely on behavioral schemes to adapt to the environment.

separation anxiety a wary or fretful reaction that infants and toddlers often display when separated from persons to whom they are attached.

sequential design a research design in which subjects from different age groups are studied repeatedly over a period of months or years.

seriation a cognitive operation that allows one to order a set of stimuli along a quantifiable dimension such as height or weight.

sexual orientation one's preference for sexual partners of the same or other sex; often characterized as primarily heterosexual, homosexual, or bisexual.

sexuality aspect of self referring to erotic thoughts, actions, and orientation.

shared environmental influences (SE) an environmental influence that people living together share and that should make these individuals similar to one another.

sibling rivalry the spirit of competition, jealousy, and resentment that may arise between two or more siblings.

simple stepparent home family consisting of a parent, his or her biological children, and a stepparent.

single-parent family a family system consisting of one parent (either the mother or the father) and the parent's dependent child(ren).

situational compliance compliance based primarily on a parent's power to control the child's conduct.

slow-to-warm-up temperament temperamental profile in which the child is inactive and moody and displays mild passive resistance to new routines and experiences.

sociability one's willingness to interact with others and to seek their attention or approval.

social cognition the thinking that people display about the thoughts, feelings, motives, and behaviors of themselves and other people.

social comparison the process of defining and evaluating the self by comparing oneself to other people.

social competence the ability to achieve personal goals in social interactions while maintaining positive relationships with others.

social information-processing (or attribution) theory social-cognitive theory stating that the explanations we construct for social experiences largely determine how we react to those experiences.

social perspective taking the ability to infer others' thoughts, intentions, motives, and attitudes.

social problem-solving training method of social-skills training in which an adult helps children (through role playing or role-taking training) to make less hostile attributions about harm-doing and to generate nonaggressive solutions to conflict.

social referencing the use of others' emotional expressions to gain information or infer the meaning of otherwise ambiguous situations.

social skills thoughts, actions, and emotional regulatory activities that enable children to achieve personal or social goals while maintaining harmony with their social partners.

social smile smile directed at people; first appears at 6–10 weeks of age.

social stimulation hypothesis the notion that socially deprived infants develop abnormally because they have had little contact with companions who respond contingently to their social overtures.

social support tangible and intangible resources provided by other people in times of uncertainty or stress.

social-conventional rules standards of conduct determined by social consensus that indicate what is appropriate within a particular social context.

socialization the process by which children acquire the beliefs, values, and behaviors considered desirable or appropriate by their culture or subculture.

social-roles hypothesis the notion that psychological differences between the sexes and other gender-role stereotypes are created and maintained by differences in *socially assigned* roles that men and women play (rather than attributable to biologically evolved dispositions).

sociocultural theory Vygotsky's perspective on development, in which children acquire their culture's values, beliefs, and problem-solving strategies through collaborative dialogues with more knowledgeable members of society.

socioeconomic status (SES) one's position within a society that is stratified according to status and power.

sociometric techniques procedures that ask children to identify those peers whom they like or dislike or to rate peers for their desirability as companions; used to measure children's peer acceptance (or nonacceptance).

stereotype threat a fear that one will be judged to have traits associated with negative social stereotypes about his or her ethnic group.

Strange Situation a series of eight separations and reunion episodes to which infants are exposed in order to determine the quality of their attachments.

stranger anxiety a wary or fretful reaction that infants and toddlers often display when approached by an unfamiliar person.

structured interview or structured questionnaire a technique in which all participants are asked the same questions in precisely the same order so that the responses of different participants can be compared.

structured observation an observational method in which the investigator cues the behavior of interest and observes participants' responses in a laboratory.

superego psychoanalytic term for the component of the personality that consists of one's internalized moral standards.

symbolic function the ability to use symbols (for example, images and words) to represent objects and experiences.

symbolic representations the images and verbal labels that observers generate in order to retain the important aspects of a model's behavior.

symbolic schemes internal mental symbols (such as images or verbal codes) that one uses to represent aspects of experience.

sympathetic empathic arousal feelings of sympathy or compassion that may be elicited when we experience the emotions of (that is empathize with) a distressed other; thought to become an important mediator of altruism.

synchronized routines generally harmonious interactions between two persons in which participants adjust their behavior in response to the partner's actions and emotions.

tabula rasa the idea that the mind of an infant is a "blank slate" and that all knowledge, abilities, behaviors, and motives are acquired through experience.

television literacy one's ability to understand how information is conveyed in television programing and to interpret this information properly.

temperament hypothesis Kagan's view that the Strange Situation measures individual differences in infants' temperaments rather than the quality of their attachments.

temperament a person's characteristic modes of emotional and behavioral responding to environmental events, including such attributes as activity level, irritability, fearful distress, and positive affect.

tertiary circular reaction an exploratory scheme in which infants devise new methods of acting on objects to reproduce interesting results.

testicular feminization syndrome (TFS) a genetic anomaly in which a male fetus is insensitive to the effects of male sex hormones and will develop female-like external genitalia.

Thanatos Freud's name for inborn, self-destructive instincts that were said to characterize all human beings.

theory a set of concepts and propositions designed to organize, describe, and explain an existing set of observations.

theory of mind an understanding that people are cognitive beings with mental states that are not always accessible to others and that often guide their behavior.

time sampling a procedure in which an investigator records the frequencies with which individuals display particular behaviors during the brief time intervals that each participant is observed.

time-out technique a form of discipline in which children who misbehave are removed from the setting until they are prepared to act more appropriately.

timing of puberty effect the finding that people who reach puberty late preform better on visual/spatial tasks than those who mature early.

tools of intellectual adaptation Vygotsky's term for methods of thinking and problem-solving strategies that children internalize from their interactions with more competent members of society.

traditional nuclear family a family unit consisting of a wife/mother, a husband/father, and their dependent child(ren).

trait   a dispositional characteristic that is stable over time and across situations.

transactional model   model of family influence in which parent and child are believed to influence each other reciprocally.

transactive interactions   verbal exchanges in which individuals perform mental operations on the reasoning of their discussion partners.

transitivity   the ability to infer relations among elements in a serial order (for example, if $A > B$ and $B > C$, then $A >$ than C).

trust versus mistrust   the first of Erikson's eight psychosocial stages, in which infants must learn to trust their closest companions or else run the risk of mistrusting other people later in life.

twin design   a study in which sets of twins that differ in zygosity (kinship) are compared to determine the heritability of an attribute.

two-generation interventions   interventions with goals of (1) stimulating children's intellectual development and readiness for school through preschool day care and education and (2) assisting parents to gain parenting skills and move out of poverty.

unconscious motives   Freud's term for feelings, experiences, and conflicts that influence a person's thinking and behavior but lie outside the person's awareness.

uninvolved parenting   a pattern of parenting that is both aloof (or even hostile) and overpermissive, almost as if parents neither cared about their children nor about what they may become.

universal development   normative developments that all individuals display.

validity   the extent to which a measuring instrument accurately reflects what the researchers intended to measure.

verbal mediator   in Bandura's theory, a verbal encoding of modeled behavior that the observer stores in memory.

visual/spatial ability   the ability to mentally manipulate or otherwise draw inferences about pictorial information.

withdrawn-rejected children   a subgroup of rejected children who are often passive, socially anxious, socially unskilled, and insensitive to peer-group expectations.

X-linked recessive trait   an attribute determined by recessive gene that appears only on X chromosomes; because the gene determining these characteristics is recessive (that is, dominated by other genes that might appear at the same location on X chromosomes), such characteristics are more common among males; who have only one X chromosome; also called *sex-linked trait*.

zone of proximal development   Vygotsky's term for the range of tasks that are too complex to be mastered alone but can be accomplished with guidance and encouragement from a more skillful partner.

References

Aber, J. L., Brown, J. L., & Jones, S. M. (2003). Developmental trajectories toward violence in middle childhood: Course, demographic differences, and responses to school-based intervention. *Developmental Psychology, 39*, 324–348.

Aboud, F. E. (1988). *Children and prejudice*. New York: Blackwell.

Aboud, F. E. (2003). The formation of in-group favoritism and out-group prejudice in young children: Are they distinct attitudes? *Developmental Psychology, 39*, 48–60.

Abramovitch, R., Corter, C., Pepler, D. J., & Stanhope, L. (1986). Sibling and peer interaction: A final follow-up and a comparison. *Child Development, 57*, 217–229.

Abravanel, E., & Sigafoos, A. D. (1984). Exploring the presence of imitation during early infancy. *Child Development, 55*, 381–392.

Ackerman, B. P., Brown, E. D., Schoff D'Eramo, K., & Izard, C. E. (2002). Maternal relationship instability and school behavior of children from disadvantaged families. *Developmental Psychology, 38*, 694–704.

Ackerman, B. P., Kogos, J., Youngstrom, E., Schoff, K., & Izard, C. (1999). Family instability and the problem behaviors of children from economically disadvantaged families. *Developmental Psychology, 35*, 258–268.

Ackerman, B. P., Schoff, K., Levinson, K., Youngstrom, E., & Izard, C. E. (1999). The relations between cluster indexes of risk and promotion and the problem behaviors of 6- and 7-year-old children from economically disadvantaged families. *Developmental Psychology, 35*, 1355–1366.

Adam, E. K., & Chase-Lansdale, P. L. (2002). Home sweet home(s): Parental separations, residential moves, and adjustment problems. *Developmental Psychology, 38*, 792–805.

Adams, G. R., Abraham, K. G., & Markstrom, C. A. (1987). The relations among identity development, self-consciousness, and self-focusing during middle and late adolescence. *Developmental Psychology, 23*, 292–297.

Adams, G. R., & Crane, P. (1980). An assessment of parents' and teachers' expectations of preschool children's social preference for attractive or unattractive children and adults. *Child Development, 51*, 224–231.

Adams, R. E., & Passman, R. H. (1980, March). *The effects of advance preparation upon children's behavior during brief separation from their mother*. Paper presented at annual meeting of the Southeastern Psychological Association. Washington, DC.

Adler, A. (1964). *Problems of neurosis*. New York: Harper & Row. (Original work published 1929).

Aguilar, B., Sroufe, L. A., Egeland, B., & Carlson, E. (2000). Distinguishing the life-course-persistent and adolescent-limited antisocial behavior types: From birth to 16 years. *Development and Psychopathology, 12*, 109–132.

Ahnert, L., Rickert, L., & Lamb, M. E. (2000). Shared caregiving: Comparison between home and child-care settings. *Developmental Psychology, 36*, 339–351.

Ainsworth, M. D. S. (1967). *Infancy in Uganda: Infant care and the growth of love*. Baltimore: Johns Hopkins University Press.

Ainsworth, M. D. S. (1979). Attachment as related to mother-infant interaction. In J. S. Rosenblatt, R. A. Hinde, C. Beer, & M. Busnel (Eds.), *Advances in the study of behavior* (Vol. 9). Orlando, FL: Academic Press.

Ainsworth, M. D. S. (1989). Attachments beyond infancy. *American Psychologist, 44*, 709–716.

Ainsworth, M. D. S., Blehar, M. C., Waters, E., & Wall, S. (1978). *Patterns of attachment: A psychological study of the strange situation*. Hillsdale, NJ: Erlbaum.

Aksan, N., & Kochanska, G. (2005). Conscience in childhood: Old questions, new answers. *Developmental Psychology, 41*, 506–516.

Aksan, N., Kochanska, G., & Ortmann, M. R. (2006). Mutually responsive orientation between parents and their young children: Toward methodological advances in the science of relationships. *Developmental Psychology, 42*, 833–848.

Al Awad, A. M. H., & Sonuga-Barke, E. J. S. (1992). Childhood problems in a Sudanese city: A comparison of extended and nuclear families. *Child Development, 63*, 906–914.

Alessandri, S. M., & Lewis, M. (1996). Differences in pride and shame in maltreated and nonmaltreated toddlers. *Child Development, 67*, 1857–1869.

Alexander, B. K., & Harlow, H. F. (1965). Social behavior in juvenile rhesus monkeys subjected to different rearing conditions during the first 6 months of life. *Zoologische Jarbucher Phvsioloqie, 60*, 167–174.

Alexander, G. M., & Hines, M. (1994). Gender labels and play styles: Their relative contribution to children's selection of playmates. *Child Development, 65*, 869–879.

Alexander, K. L., & Entwisle, D. R. (1988). Achievement in the first two years of school: Patterns and processes. *Monographs of the Society for Research in Child Development, 53*, (2, Serial No. 218).

Alfieri, T., Ruble, D. N., & Higgins, E. T. (1996). Gender stereotypes during adolescence: Developmental changes and the transition to junior high school. *Developmental Psychology, 32*, 1129–1137.

Alink, L. R. A., Mesman, J., van Zeijl, J., Stolk, N., Juffer, F., Koot, H. M., Bakermans-Kranenburg, M. J., & van IJzendoorn, M. H. (2006). The early childhood aggression curve: Development of physical aggression in 10- to 50-month-old children. *Child Development, 77*, 954–966.

Allen, J. P., McElhaney, K. B., Kuperminc, G. P., & Jodl, K. M. (2004). Stability and change in attachment security across adolescence. *Child Development, 75*, 1792–1805.

Allen, J. P., McElhaney, K. B., Land, D. J., Kuperminc, G. P., Moore, C. W., O'Beirne-Kelly, H., & Kilmer, S. L. (2003). A secure base in adolescence: Markers of attachment security in the mother-adolescent relationship. *Child Development, 74*, 292–307.

Allen, J. P., Moore, C., Kuperminc, G., & Bell, K. (1998). Attachment and adolescent psychosocial functioning. *Child Development, 69*, 1406–1409.

Allen, J. P., Philliber, S., Herrling, S., & Kuperminc, G. P. (1997). Preventing teen pregnancy and academic failure: Experimental evaluation of a developmentally based approach. *Child Development, 68,* 729–742.

Allen, J. P., Porter, M. R., McFarland, C., Marsh, P., & McElhaney, K. B. (2005). The two faces of adolescents' success with peers: Adolescent popularity, social adaptation, and deviant behavior. *Child Development, 76,* 747–760.

Allen, J. P., Porter, M., McFarland, C., McElhaney, K. B., & Marsh, P. (2007). The relation of attachment security to adolescents' paternal and peer relationships, depression, and externalizing behavior. *Child Development, 78,* 1222–1239.

Allen, J. P., Weissberg, R. P., & Hawkins, J. A. (1989). The relation between values and social competence in early adolescence. *Developmental Psychology, 25,* 458–464.

Allen, K. R., Fine, M. A., & Demo, D. H. (2000). An overview of family diversity: Controversies, questions, and values. In D. H. Demo, K. R. Allen, & M. A. Fine (Eds.), *Handbook of family diversity.* New York: Oxford University Press.

Alley, T. R. (1981). Head shape and the perception of cuteness. *Developmental Psychology, 17,* 650–654.

Allgood-Merten, B., & Stockard, J. (1991). Sex role identity and self-esteem: A comparison of children and adolescents. *Sex Roles, 25,* 129–139.

Almli, C. R., Ball, R. H., & Wheeler, M. E. (2001). Human fetal and neonatal movement patterns: Gender differences and fetal-to-neonatal continuity. *Developmental Psychology, 38,* 252–273.

Altermatt, E. R., Pomerantz, E. M., Ruble, D. N., Frey, K. S., & Greulich, F. K. (2002). Predicting changes in children's perceptions of academic competence: A naturalistic examination of evaluative discourse among classmates. *Developmental Psychology, 38,* 903–917.

Althaus, F. (2001). Levels of sexual experience among U.S. teenagers have declined for the first time in three decades. *Family Planning Perspectives, 33,* 180.

Altschul, I., Oyserman, D., & Bybee, D. (2006). Racial-ethnic identity in mid-adolescence: Content and change as predictors of academic achievement. *Child Development, 77,* 1155–1169.

Alvarez, J. M., Ruble, D. N., & Bolger, N. (2001). Trait understanding or evaluative reasoning: An analysis of children's behavioral predictions. *Child Development, 72,* 1409–1425.

Amato, P. R. (1993). Children's adjustment to divorce: Theories, hypotheses, and empirical support. *Journal of Marriage and the Family, 55,* 23–38.

Amato, P. R. (1996). Explaining the intergenerational transmission of divorce. *Journal of Marriage and the Family, 58,* 628–640.

Amato, P. R. (2000). The consequences of divorce for adults and children. *Journal of Marriage and Family, 62,* 1269–1287.

Amato, P. R., & Booth, A. (1996). A prospective study of divorce and parent-child relationships. *Journal of Marriage and the Family, 58,* 356–365.

Amato, P. R., & Keith, B. (1991). Parental divorce and the well-being of children: A meta-analysis. *Psychological Bulletin, 110,* 26–46.

Amato, P. R., & Sobolewski, J. M. (2004). The effects of divorce on fathers and children: Nonresidential fathers and stepfathers. In M. E. Lamb (Ed.), *The role of the father in child development* (4th ed.). Hoboken, NJ: Wiley.

Ambert, A. (1992). *The effect of children on parents.* New York: Haworth.

Ambron, S. R., & Irwin, D. M. (1975). Role-taking and moral judgment in five- and seven-year-olds. *Developmental Psychology, 11,* 102.

American Psychiatric Association (2000). *Diagnostic and Statistical Manual of Mental Disorders, 4th edition—Text Revision (DSM-IV-TR)* Washington, DC: American Psychiatric Association.

Andermann, E. M., & Midgley, C. (1997). Changes in achievement goal orientation, perceived academic competence, and grades across the transition to middle level schools. *Contemporary Educational Psychology, 2,* 269–298.

Anderson, C. R., & Dill, K. E. (2000). Video games and aggressive thoughts, feelings, and behavior in the laboratory and in life. *Journal of Personality and Social Psychology, 78,* 772–790.

Anderson, D. R. (2004). Watching children watch television and the creation of *Blue's clues.* In H. Hendershot (Ed.), *Nickelodeon nation: The history, politics, and economics of America's only TV Channel for kids* (pp. 241–268). New York: University Press.

Anderson, D. R., Berkowitz, L., Donnerstein, E., Huesmann, L. R., Johnson, J. D., Linz, D., Malamuth, N. M., & Wartella, E. (2003). The influence of media violence on youth. *Psychological Sciences in the Public Interest, 4,* 81–110.

Anderson, D. R., Huston, A. C., Schmitt, K. L., Linebarger, D. L., & Wright, J. C. (2001). Early childhood television viewing and adolescent behavior. *Monographs of the Society of the Research in Child Development, 66,* (1, Serial No. 264).

Anderson, D. R., & Pempek, T. A. (2005). Television and very young children. *American Behavioral Scientist, 48,* 505–522.

Andersson, B. (1989). Effects of public day-care: A longitudinal study. *Child Development, 60,* 857–866.

Andersson, B. (1992). Effects of day-care on cognitive and socioemotional competence of thirteen-year-old Swedish schoolchildren. *Child Development, 63,* 20–36.

Archer, J. (1991). The influence of testosterone on human aggression. *British Journal of Psychology, 92,* 1–28.

Archer, J. (1992). *Ethology and human development.* Hertfordshire, England: Harvester Wheatsheaf.

Archer, S. L. (1982). The lower age boundaries of identity development. *Child Development, 53,* 1551–1556.

Archer, S. L. (1992). A feminist's approach to identity research. In G. R. Adams, T. P. Gullotta, & R. Montemayor (Eds.), *Adolescent identity formation* (Advances in Adolescent Development, Vol. 4). Newbury Park, CA: Sage.

Archer, S. L. (1994). *Interventions for adolescent identity development.* Thousand Oaks, CA: Sage.

Ardila-Ray, A., & Killen, M. (2001). Columbian preschool children's judgments about autonomy and conflict resolution in the classroom setting. *International Journal of Behavioral Development, 25,* 246–255.

Ardrey, R. (1967). *African genesis.* New York: Dell.

Aries, P. (1962). *Centuries of childhood.* New York: Knopf.

Arnett, J. J. (1995). Broad and narrow socialization: The family in the context of a cultural theory. *Journal of Marriage and the Family, 57,* 617–628.

Arnett, J., & Balle-Jensen, L. (1993). Cultural bases of risk behavior: Danish adolescents. *Child Development, 64,* 1842–1855.

Arnold, D. H., McWilliams, L., & Arnold, E. H. (1998). Teacher discipline and child misbehavior in day care: Untangling causality with correlational data. *Developmental Psychology, 34,* 267–287.

Aro, H., & Taipale, V. (1987). The impact of timing of puberty on psychosomatic symptoms among fourteen- to sixteen-year-old Finnish girls. *Child Development, 58,* 261–268.

Aronson, E. (1976). *The social animal.* New York: W. H. Freeman.

Aronson, E., Blaney, N., Stephan, C., Sikes, J., & Snapp, M. (1978). *The jigsaw classroom.* Beverly Hills, CA: Sage.

Aronson, J., Fried, C. B., & Good, C. (2002). Reducing the effects of stereotype threat on African American college students by shaping theories of intelligence. *Journal of Experimental Social Psychology, 38,* 113–125.

Arroyo, C. G., & Zigler, E. (1995). Racial identity, academic achievement, and the psychological well-being of economically disadvantaged adolescents. *Journal of Personality and Social Psychology, 69,* 903–914.

Arsenio, W. F., Cooperman, S., & Lover, A. (2000). Affective predictors of preschooler's aggression and peer acceptance: Direct and indirect effects. *Developmental Psychology, 36,* 438–448.

Asbury, K., Dunn, J. F., Pike, A., & Plomin, R. (2003). Nonshared environmental influences on individual differences in early behavioral development: A monozygotic twin differences study. *Child Development, 74,* 933–943.

Asendorph, J. B. (2002). Self-awareness, other-awareness, and secondary representation. In A. Meltzoff & W. Prinz (Eds.), *The imitative mind: Development, evolution, and brain bases* (pp. 63–73). Cambridge, UK: Cambridge University Press.

Asendorph, J. B., & Baudonniere, P. (1993) Self-awareness and other-awareness: Mirror self-recognition and synchronic imitation among unfamiliar peers. *Developmental Psychology, 29,* 88–95.

Asendorph, J. B., Warkentin, V., & Baudonniere, P. (1996). Self-awareness and other-awareness II: Mirror self-recognition, social contingency awareness, and synchronic imitation. *Developmental Psychology, 32,* 313–321.

Asher, S. R., Renshaw, P. D., & Hymel, S. (1982). Peer relations and the development of social skills. In S. G. Moore (Ed.), *The young child: Reviews of research (Vol. 3).* Washington, DC: National Association for the Education of Young Children.

Associated Press (1999, January 10). TV sex rampant, critics say. *Atlanta Constitution,* pp. D1, D3.

Associated Press (2002a, October 11). Hispanic dropout rate soars. *Athens Banner Herald,* p. D6.

Associated Press (2002b, December 21). Video game warning. *Athens Banner Herald,* p. C1.

Associated Press (2006, Jan 10). *Study: 744,000 homeless people in U.S.* Retrieved from http://www.msnbc.msn.com/id/1654208/

Associated Press (2007, November 12). *Report urges states to open adoptee records.* Retrieved from http://www.msnbc.msn.com/id/21741004

Astin, A. W., Korn, W. S., Sax, L. J., & Mahoney, K. M. (1994). *The American freshman: National norms for Fall 1994.* Los Angeles, CA: Higher Education Research Institute, University of California at Los Angeles.

Astor, R. A. (1994). Children's moral reasoning about family and peer violence: The role of provocation and retribution. *Child Development, 65,* 1054–1067.

Atkin, C. (1978). Observation of parent-child interaction in supermarket decision-making. *Journal of Marketing, 42,* 41–45.

Atkinson, J. W. (1964). *An introduction to motivation.* Princeton, NJ: Van Nostrand.

Attili, G., Vermigli, P., & Schneider, B. H. (1997). Peer acceptance and friendship patterns among Italian school children within a cross-cultural perspective. *International Journal of Behavioral Development, 21,* 277–288.

Aunola, K., & Nurmi, J. (2004). Maternal affection moderates the impact of psychological control on a child's mathematical performance. *Developmental Psychology, 40,* 965–978.

Aunola, K., & Nurmi, J. (2005). The role of parenting styles in children's problem behavior. *Child Development, 76,* 1144–1159.

Aviezer, D., Sagi, A., Joels, T., & Ziv, Y. (1999). Emotional availability and attachment representations in kibbutz infants and their mothers. *Developmental Psychology, 35,* 811–821.

Azmitia, M. (1992). Expertise, private speech, and the development of self-regulation. In R. M. Diaz & L. E. Berk (Eds.), *Private speech: From social interaction to self-regulation.* Hillsdale, NJ: Erlbaum.

Azmitia, M., & Hesser, J. (1993). Why siblings are important agents of cognitive development: A comparison of siblings and peers. *Child Development, 64,* 430–444.

Bagley, C. (1995). *Child sexual abuse and mental health in adolescents and adults.* Aldershot, England: Ashgate Publishing Company.

Bagwell, C. L., Newcomb, A. F., & Bukowski, W. M. (1998). Preadolescent friendship and peer rejection as predictors of adult adjustment. *Child Development, 69,* 140–153.

Baier, J. L., Rosenzweig, M. G., & Whipple, E. (1991). Patterns of sexual behavior, coercion, and victimization of university students. *Journal of College Student Development, 32,* 310–322.

Bailey, J. M., Bechtold, K. T., & Berenbaum, S. A. (2002). Who are tomboys and why should we study them? *Archives of Sexual Behavior, 31,* 333–341.

Bailey, J. M., Browbow, D., Wolfe, M., & Mikach, S. (1995). Sexual orientation of adult sons of gay fathers. *Developmental Psychology, 31,* 124–129.

Bailey, J. M., Dunne, M. P., & Martin, N. G. (2000). Genetic and environmental influences on sexual orientation and its correlates in an Australian twin sample. *Journal of Personality and Social Psychology, 78,* 524–536.

Bailey, J. M., & Pillard, R. C. (1991). A genetic study of male sexual orientation. *Archives of General Psychiatry, 48,* 1089–1096.

Bailey, J. M., Pillard, R. C., Neale, M. C., & Agyei, Y. (1993). Heritable factors influence sexual orientation in women. *Archives of General Psychiatry, 50,* 217–223.

Baillargeon, R. H., Zoccolillo, M., Keenan, K., Cote, S., Perusse, D., Wu, H., Boivin, M., & Tremblay, R. E. (2007). Gender differences in physical aggression: A prospective population-based survey of children before and after 2 years of age. *Developmental Psychology, 43,* 13–26.

Baker, D. P., & Jones, D. P. (1992). Opportunity and performance: A socio-logical explanation for gender differences in academic mathematics. In J. Wrigley (Ed.), *Education and gender equality.* London: The Falmer Press.

Baker, L. A., & Daniels, D. (1990). Nonshared environmental influences and personality differences in adult twins. *Journal of Personality and Social Psychology, 58,* 103–110.

Baker, L. A., Mack, W., Moffitt, T. E., & Mednick, S. (1989). Sex differences in property crime in a Danish adoption cohort. *Behavior Genetics, 19,* 355–370.

Bakermans-Kranenburg, M. J., van IJzendoorn, M. H., & Juffer, F. (2003). Less is more: Meta-analyses of sensitivity and attachment interventions in early childhood. *Psychological Bulletin, 129,* 195–215.

Baldwin, D. A., & Moses, L. J. (1996). The ontogeny of social information gathering. *Child Development, 67,* 1915–1939.

Ball, S., & Bogatz, C. (1973). *Reading with television: An evaluation of The Electric Company*. Princeton, NJ: Educational Testing Service.

Bandura, A. (1965). Influence of models' reinforcement contingencies on the acquisition of imitative responses. *Journal of Personality and Social Psychology, 1*, 589–595.

Bandura, A. (1973). *Aggression: A social learning analysis*. Englewood Cliffs, NJ: Prentice-Hall.

Bandura, A. (1977). Social learning theory. Englewood Cliffs, NJ: Prentice-Hall.

Bandura, A. (1978). The self system in reciprocal determinism. *American Psychologist, 33*, 344–358.

Bandura, A. (1986). *Social foundations of thought and action. A social cognitive theory*. Englewood Cliffs, NJ: Prentice-Hall.

Bandura, A. (1989). Social cognitive theory. In R. Vasta (Ed.), *Annals of child development* (Vol. 6, pp. 1–60). Greenwich, CT: JAI Press.

Bandura, A. (1991). Social cognitive theory of moral thought and action. In W. M. Kurtines & J. L. Gewirtz (Eds.), *Handbook of moral behavior and development* (Vol. 1, pp. 45–103). Hillsdale, NJ: Erlbaum.

Bandura, A. (1992).Perceived self-efficacy in cognitive development and functioning. *Educational Psychologist, 28*, 117–148.

Bandura, A. (2001). Social cognitive theory: An agentic perspective. *Annual Review of Psychology, 52*, 1–26.

Bandura, A. (2002). Selective moral disengagement in the exercise of moral agency. *Journal of Moral Education, 31*, 101–119.

Banerjee, R., & Lintern, V. (2000). Boys will be boys: The effect of social evaluation concerns on gender-typing. *Social Development, 9*, 397–408.

Banks, J. A. (1993). Multicultural education: Historical development, dimensions, and practice. *Review of Educational Research, 19*, 3–49.

Barash, D. P (2002, May 24). Evolution, males and violence. *Chronicle of Higher Education*, pp. B7–B9.

Barber, B. K (1996). Parental psychological control: Revisiting a neglected construct. *Child Development, 67*, 3296–3319.

Barber, B. K., & Harmon, E. (2002). Violating the self: Parental psychological control of children and adolescents. In B. K. Barber (Ed.), *Intrusive parenting: How psychological control affects children and adolescents* (pp. 15–52). Washington, DC: American Psychological Association.

Barber, B. K., Stolz, H. E., & Olsen, J. A. (2006). Parental support, psychological control, and behavioral control: Assessing relevance across time, culture, and method. *Monographs of the Society for Research in Child Development, 70*, Serial No. 282, 1–137.

Barden, R. C., Ford, M. E., Jensen, A. G., Rogers-Salyer, M., & Salyer, K. E. (1989). Effects of craniofacial deformity in infancy on the quality of mother-infant interactions. *Child Development, 60*, 819–824.

Bardwell, J. R., Cochran, S. W., & Walker, S. (1986). Relation of parental education, race, and gender to sex-role stereotyping in five-year-old kindergartners. *Sex Roles, 15*, 275–281.

Barenboim, C. (1981). The development of person perception in childhood and adolescence: From behavioral comparisons to psychological constructs to psychological comparisons. *Child Development, 52*, 129–144.

Barglow, P., Vaughn, B. E., & Molitor, N. (1987). Effects of maternal absence due to employment on the quality of infant-mother attachment in a low-risk sample. *Child Development, 58*, 945–954.

Barker, R. G., & Gump, P. V. (1964). *Big school, small school*. Stanford, CA: Stanford University Press.

Barnett, M. A. (1987). Empathy and related responses in children. In N. Eisenberg & J. Strayer (Eds.), *Empathy and its development*. New York: Cambridge University Press.

Barnett, W. S. (1993). Benefit-cost analysis of preschool education: Findings from a 25-year follow-up. *American Journal of Orthopsychiatry, 63*, 500–508.

Baron, R. A., & Richardson, D. (1994). *Human aggression*. New York: Wiley.

Baron-Cohen, S. (1995). *Mindblindness: An essay on autism and theory of mind*. Cambridge, MA: MIT Press.

Baron-Cohen, S. (2000). Theory of mind and autism. In S. Baron-Cohen, H. Tager-Flusberg, & D. Cohen (Eds.), *Understanding other minds: Perspectives from developmental cognitive neuroscience*. (2nd ed., pp. 3–20). Oxford: Oxford University Press.

Baron-Cohen, S. (2003). *The essential difference: The truth about male and female brains*. New York: Basic Books.

Barr, R., & Hayne, H. (1999). Developmental changes in imitation from television during infancy. *Child Development, 70*, 1067–1081.

Barry, C., & Wentzel, K. R. (2006). Peer influence on prosocial behavior: The role of motivational factors and friendship characteristics. *Developmental Psychology, 42*, 153–163.

Barry, H., III, Bacon, M. K., & Child, I. L. (1957). A cross-cultural survey of some sex differences in socialization. *Journal of Abnormal and Social Psychology, 55*, 327–332.

Bar-Tal, D., Raviv, A., & Goldberg, M. (1982). Helping behavior among preschool children: An observational study. *Child Development, 53*, 396–402.

Bartels, M., van den Oord, E. J. C. G., Hudziak, J. J., Rietveld, M. J. H., van Bejsterveldt, C. E. M., & Boomsma, D. I. (2004). Genetic and environmental mechanisms underlying stability and change in problem behaviors at ages 3, 7, 10, and 12. *Developmental Psychology, 40*, 852–867.

Bartholomew, K., & Horowitz, L. M. (1991). Attachment styles among young adults: A test of a four-category model. *Journal of Personality and Social Psychology, 61*, 226–244.

Bates, J. E., Pettit, G. S., Dodge, K. A., & Ridge, B. (1998). Interaction of temperamental resistance to control and restrictive parenting in the development of externalizing behavior. *Developmental Psychology, 34*, 982–995.

Batson, C. D. (1991). *The altruism question: Toward a social-psychological answer*. Hillsdale, NJ: Erlbaum.

Battle, E. S. (1966). Motivational determinants of academic competence. *Journal of Personality and Social Psychology, 4*, 634–642.

Bauer, P. J., & Mandler, J. M. (1989). One thing follows another: Effects of temporal structure on 1- to 2-year-olds' recall of events. *Developmental Psychology, 25*, 197–206.

Baumeister, R. F., Campbell, J. D., Krueger, J. I., & Vohs, K. E. (2003). Does high self-esteem cause better performance, interpersonal success, happiness, or healthier lifestyles? *Psychological Science in the Public Interest, 4*, 1–44.

Baumrind, D. (1967). Child care practices anteceding three patterns of preschool behavior. *Genetic Psychology Monographs, 75*, 43–88.

Baumrind, D. (1971). Current patterns of parental authority. *Developmental Psychology Monographs, 4* (1, Part 2).

Baumrind, D. (1973). The development of instrumental competence through socialization. In A. Pick (Ed.), *Minnesota symposium on child psychology* (Vol. 7). Minneapolis: University of Minnesota Press.

Baumrind, D. (1977, March). *Socialization determinants of personal agency*. Paper presented at the biennial meeting of the Society for Research in Child Development, New Orleans.

Baumrind, D. (1983). Rejoinder to Lewis's reinterpretation of parental firm control effects: Are authoritative families really harmonious? *Psychological Bulletin, 94,* 132–142.

Baumrind, D. (1991). Effective parenting during the early adolescent transition. In P. A. Cowan & E. M. Hetherington (Eds.), *Family transitions.* Hillsdale, NJ: Erlbaum.

Baumrind, D. (1993). The average expectable environment is not good enough: A response to Scarr. *Child Development, 64,* 1299–1317.

Bauserman, R. (2002). Child adjustment in joint-custody versus sole-custody arrangements: A meta-analytic review. *Journal of Family Psychology, 16,* 91–102.

Beach, F. A. (1965). *Sex and behavior.* New York: Wiley.

Beal, C. R. (1994). *Boys and girls: The development of gender roles.* New York: McGraw-Hill.

Bear, G. G., & Rys, G. S. (1994). Moral reasoning, classroom behavior, and sociometric status among elementary school children. *Developmental Psychology, 30,* 633–638.

Becker, H. J. (2000). Who's wired and who's not: Children's access to and use of computer technology. *The Future of Children, 10,* 44–75.

Beckett, C., Maughan, B., Rutter, M., Castle, J., Colvert, E., Groothues, C., Kreppner, J., Stevens, S., O'Connor, T. G., & Sonuga-Barke, E. J. S. (2006). Do the effects of early severe deprivation on cognition persist into early adolescence? Findings from the English and Romanian adoptees study. *Child Development, 77,* 696–711.

Beckwith, L., Rozga, A., & Sigman, M. (2002). Maternal sensitivity and attachment in atypical groups. In R. V. Kail (Ed.), *Advances in child development and behavior* (Vol. 30). San Diego, CA: Academic press.

Bedford, V. H., Volling, B. L., & Avioli, P. M. (2000). Positive consequences of sibling conflict in childhood and adulthood. *International Journal of Aging and Human Development, 51,* 53–69.

Behne, T., Carpenter, M., Call, J., & Tomasello, M. (2005). Unwilling versus unable: Infants' understanding of intentional action. *Developmental Psychology, 41,* 328–337.

Behrens, K. Y., Hesse, E., & Main, M. (2007). Mothers' attachment status as determined by the Adult Attachment Interview predicts their 6-year-olds' reunion responses: A study conducted in Japan. *Developmental Psychology, 43,* 1553–1567.

Beilin, H. (1992). Piaget's enduring contribution to developmental psychology. *Developmental Psychology, 28,* 191–204.

Bell, R. Q. (1979). Parent, child, and reciprocal influences. *American Psychologist, 34,* 821–826.

Belsky, J. (1981). Early human experience: A family perspective. *Developmental Psychology, 17,* 3–23.

Belsky, J. (1993). Etiology of child maltreatment: A developmental ecological analysis, *Psychological Bulletin, 114,* 413–434.

Belsky, J. (1996). Parent, infant, and social-contextual antecedents of father-son attachment security. *Developmental Psychology, 32,* 905–913.

Belsky, J., Garduque, L., & Hrncir, E. (1984). Assessing performance, competence, and executive capacity in infant play: Relations to home environment and security of attachment. *Developmental Psychology, 20,* 406–417.

Belsky, J., Jaffee, S. R., Sligo, J., Woodward, L., & Silva, P. A. (2005). Intergenerational transmission of warm-sensitive-stimulating parenting: A prospective study of mothers and fathers of 3-year-olds. *Child Development, 76,* 384–396.

Belsky, J., Rosenberger, K., & Crnic, K. (1995). Maternal personality, marital quality, social support, and infant temperament: Their significance for mother-infant attachment in human families. In C. Pryce, R. Martin, & D. Skuse (Eds.), *Motherhood in human and nonhuman primates* (pp. 115–124). Basel, Switzerland, Kruger.

Belsky, J., & Rovine, M. (1988). Nonmaternal care in the first year of life and the security of infant-parent attachment. *Child Development, 59,* 157–167.

Belsky, J., Rovine, M., & Taylor, D. G. (1984). The Pennsylvania Infant and Family Development Project, III: The origins of individual differences in infant-mother attachment—maternal and infant contributions. *Child Development, 55,* 718–728.

Belsky, J., Spritz, B., & Crnic, K. (1996). Infant attachment security and affective-cognitive information processing at age 3. *Psychological Science, 7,* 111–114.

Belsky, J., Vandell, D. L., Burchinal, M., Clarke-Stewart, K. A., McCartney, K., Owen, M. T., and the NICHD Early Child Care Research Network (2007). Are there long-term effects of early child care? *Child Development, 78,* 681-701.

Bem, S. L. (1974). The measurement of psychological androgyny. *Journal of Consulting and Clinical Psychology, 42,* 155–162.

Bem, S. L. (1975). Sex-role adaptability: One consequence of psychological androgyny. *Journal of Personality and Social Psychology, 31,* 634–643.

Bem, S. L. (1978). Beyond androgyny: Some presumptuous prescriptions for a liberated sexual identity. In J. A. Sherman & F. L. Denmark (Eds.), *The psychology of women: Future directions in research.* New York: Psychological Dimensions.

Bem, S. L. (1983). Gender schema theory and its implications for child development: Raising gender aschematic children in a gender-schematic society. *Signs: Journal of Women in Culture and Society, 8,* 598–616.

Bem, S. L. (1989). Genital knowledge and gender constancy in preschool children. *Child Development, 60,* 649–662.

Benbow, C. P., & Arjimand, O. (1990). Predictors of high academic achievement in mathematics and science by mathematically talented students: A longitudinal study. *Journal of Educational Psychology, 82,* 430–441.

Bendig, A. W. (1958). Predictive and postdictive validity of need achievement measures. *Journal of Educational Research, 52,* 119–120.

Benenson, J. F., Apostoleris, N. H., & Parnass, J. (1997). Age and sex differences in dyadic and group interaction. *Developmental Psychology, 33,* 538–543.

Benenson, J. F., & Heath, A. (2006). Boys withdraw more in one-on-one interactions, whereas girls withdraw more in groups. *Developmental Psychology, 42,* 272–282.

Benoit D., & Parker, K. C. H. (1994). Stability and transmission of Attachment across three generations. *Child Development, 65,* 1444–1456.

Benson, M. J. (2004). After the adolescent pregnancy: Parents, teens, and families. *Child and Adolescent Social Work Journal, 21,* 435–455.

Berenbaum, S. A. (1998). How hormones affect behavioral and neural development: Introduction to the special issue on "Gonadal hormones and sex differences in behavior." *Developmental Neuropsychology, 14,* 175–196.

Berenbaum, S. A. (2002). Prenatal androgen and sexual differentiation of behavior. In E. A. Eugster & O. H. Pescovitz (Eds.), *Developmental Endocrinology: From research to clinical practice* (pp. 293–311). Totowa, NJ: Humana Press.

Berenbaum, S. A., & Snyder, A. (1995). Early hormonal influences on childhood sex-typed activity and playmate preferences: Implications for the development of sexual orientation. *Developmental Psychology, 31*, 31–42.

Berkowitz, L. (1965). The concept of aggressive drive: Some additional considerations. In L. Berkowitz (Ed.), *Advances in experimental social psychology* (Vol. 2). Orlando, FL: Academic Press.

Berkowitz, L. (1974). Some determinants of impulsive aggression: Role of mediated association with reinforcement for aggression. *Psychological Review, 81*, 165–176.

Berkowitz, L. (1993). *Aggression.* New York: McGraw-Hill.

Berkowitz, M., & Gibbs, J. C. (1983). Measuring the developmental features of moral discussion. *Merrill-Palmer Quarterly, 29*, 399–410.

Bernal, M. E., & Knight, G. P. (1997). Ethnic identity of Latino children. In J. G. Garcia & M. C. Zea (Eds.), *Psychological interventions and research with Latino populations.* Boston: Allyn & Bacon.

Berndt, T. J. (1979). Developmental changes in conformity to peers and parents. *Developmental Psychology, 15*, 608–616.

Berndt, T. J. (1989). Friendships in childhood and adolescence. In W. Damon (Ed.), *Child development today and tomorrow.* San Francisco: Jossey-Bass.

Berndt, T. J. (1996). Friendship quality affects adolescents' self-esteem and social behavior. In W. M. Bukowski, A. F. Newcomb, & W. W. Hartup (Eds.), *The company they keep: Friendship during childhood and adolescence* (pp. 346–365). New York: Cambridge University Press.

Berndt, T. J. (2004). Children's friendships: Shifts over a half-century in perspective on their development and their effects. *Merrill-Palmer Quarterly, 50*, 206–223.

Berndt, T. J., Hawkins, J. A., & Hoyle, S. G. (1986). Changes in friendship during a school year: Effects on children's and adolescents' impressions of friendship and sharing with friends. *Child Development, 57*, 1284–1297.

Berndt, T. J., Hawkins, J. A., & Jiao, Z. (1999). Influence of friends and friendships on adjustment to junior high school. *Merrill-Palmer Quarterly, 45*, 13–41.

Berndt, T. J., & Hoyle, S. G. (1985). Stability and change in childhood and adolescent friendships. *Developmental Psychology, 21*, 1007–1015.

Berndt, T. J., & Keefe, K. (1995). Friends' influence on adolescents' adjustment to school. *Child Development, 66*, 1312–1329.

Berndt, T. J., & Perry, T. B. (1990). Distinctive features and effects of early adolescent friendships. In R. Montemayor, G. R. Adams, & T. P. Gulotta (Eds.), *From childhood to adolescence: A transitional period.* Newbury Park, CA: Sage.

Berry, J. W. (1967). Independence and conformity in subsistence-level societies. *Journal of Personality and Social Psychology, 7*, 415–418.

Berry, J. W., Poortinga, Y. H., Segall, M. H., & Dasen, P. R. (1992). *Cross-cultural psychology: Research and applications.* New York: Cambridge University Press.

Berzonsky, M. D., & Adams, G. R. (1999). Reevaluating the identity status paradigm: Still useful after 35 years. *Developmental Review, 19*, 557–590.

Berzonsky, M. D., & Kuk, L. S. (2000). Identity status, identify processing style, and the transition to university. *Journal of Adolescent Research, 15*, 81–98.

Best, D. L., & Williams, J. E. (1997). Sex, gender, and culture. In J. W. Berry, M. H. Segall, & C. Kagitcibasi (Eds.), *Handbook of cross-cultural psychology: Vol.3. Social behavior and applications.* Boston: Allyn & Bacon.

Best, D. L., Williams, J. E., Cloud, J. M., Davis, S. W., Robertson, L. S., Edwards, J. R., Giles, H., & Fowlkes, J. (1977). Development of sex-trait stereotypes among young children in the United States, England, and Ireland. *Child Development, 48*, 1375–1384.

Beyers, W., & Goossens, L. (1999). Emotional autonomy, psychosocial adjustment, and parenting: Interactions, moderating, and mediating effects. *Journal of Adolescence, 22*, 753–769.

Beyth-Marom, R., Austin, L., Fischoff, B., Palmgren, C., & Jacobs-Quadrel, (1993). Perceived consequences of risky behaviors: Adolescents and adults. *Developmental Psychology, 29*, 549–563.

Bianchi, S. M., & Robinson, J. (1997). What did you do today? Children's use of time, family composition, and the acquisition of social capital. *Journal of Marriage and the Family, 59*, 332–344.

Bianchi, S. M., Subaiya, L., & Kahn, J. (1997, March). *Economic well-being of husbands and wives after marital disruption.* Paper presented at the annual meeting of the Population Association of America, Washington, DC.

Bierman, K. L., & Furman, W. (1984). The effects of social skills training and peer involvement on the social adjustment of preadolescents. *Child Development, 55*, 157–162.

Bigler, R. S. (1995). The role of classification skill in moderating environmental influences on children's gender stereotyping: A study of the functional use of gender in the classroom. *Child Development, 66*, 1072–1087.

Bigler, R. S., & Liben, L. S. (1990). The role of attitudes and interventions in gender-schematic processing. *Child Development, 61*, 1440–1452.

Bigler, R. S., & Liben, L. S. (1992). Cognitive mechanisms in children's gender stereotyping: Theoretical and educational implications of a cognitive-based intervention. *Child Development, 63*, 1351–1363.

Bigler, R. S., & Liben, L. S. (1993). A cognitive-developmental approach to racial stereotyping and reconstructive memory in Euro-American children *Child Development, 64*, 1507–1518.

Bigner, J. J., & Jacobsen, R. B. (1989). Parenting behaviors of homosexual and heterosexual fathers. *Journal of Homosexuality, 18*, 173–186.

Bingham, C. R., & Crockett, L. J. (1996). Longitudinal adjustment patterns of boys and girls experiencing early, middle, and later sexual intercourse. *Developmental Psychology, 32*, 647–658.

Birch, L. L., & Billman, J. (1986). Preschool children's food sharing with friends and acquaintances. *Child Development, 57*, 387–395.

Birch, S. H., & Ladd, G. W. (1998). Children's interpersonal behaviors and the teacher-child relationship. *Developmental Psychology, 34*, 934–946.

Biringen, Z. (1990). Direct observation of maternal sensitivity and dyadic interactions in the home: Relations to maternal thinking. *Developmental Psychology, 26*, 278–284.

Bjorklund, D. F. (2005). *Children's thinking: Cognitive development and individual differences* (4th ed.). Belmont, CA: Wadsworth.

Bjorklund, D. F., & Bjorklund, B. R. (1992). *Looking at children.* Pacific Grove, CA: Brooks/Cole.

Bjorklund, D. F., & Pellegrini, A. D. (2002). *The origins of human nature: Evolutionary developmental psychology.* Washington, DC.: APA Books.

Black, B., & Logan, A. (1995). Links between communication patterns in mother-child, father-child, and child-peer interactions and children's social status. *Child Development, 66*, 255–271.

Black, M. M., Dubowitz, H., & Starr, R. H., Jr. (1999). African-American fathers in low income urban families: Development, behavior, and home environment of their three-year-old children. *Child Development, 70,* 967–978.

Black-Gutman, D., & Hickson, F. (1996). The relationship between racial attitudes and social-cognitive development in children: An Australian study. *Developmental Psychology, 32,* 448–456.

Blackwell, L. S., Trzesniewski, K. H., & Dweck, C. S. (2007). Implicit theories of intelligence predict achievement across an adolescent transition: A longitudinal study of an intervention. *Child Development, 78,* 246–263.

Blair, C., & Razza, R. P. (2007). Relating effortful control, executive function, and false belief understanding to emerging math and literacy ability in kindergarten. *Child Development, 78,* 647–663.

Blair, R. J. R. (2003). Did Cain fail to represent the thoughts of Abel before he killed him? The relationship between theory of mind and aggression. In B. Repacholi & V. Slaughter (Eds.), *Individual differences in theory of mind: Implications for typical and atypical development.* New York: Psychology Press.

Blakemore, J. E. O. (2003). Children's beliefs about violating gender norms: Boys shouldn't look like girls, and girls shouldn't act like boys. *Sex Roles, 48,* 411–419.

Blakemore, J. E. O., Berenbaum, S. A., & Liben, L. S. (in press). *Gender development.* Philadelphia, PA: Taylor & Francis.

Blakemore, J. E. O., LaRue, A. A., & Olejnik, A. B. (1979). Sex-appropriate toy preference and the ability to conceptualize toys as sex-role related. *Developmental Psychology, 15,* 339–340.

Blasi, A. (1990). Kohlberg's theory and moral motivation. In D. Schrader (Ed.), *New directions for child development* (No. 47, pp. 51–57). San Francisco: Jossey-Bass.

Blatchford, P., Moriatry, V., Edmonds, S., & Martin, C. (2002). Relationships between class size and teaching: A multimethod analysis of English infant schools. *American Educational Research Journal, 39,* 101–132.

Block, J. H. (1976). Issues, problems, and pitfalls in assessing sex differences: A critical review of *The psychology of sex differences.* *Merrill-Palmer Quarterly, 27,* 283–308.

Block, J. H., Block, J., & Gjerde, P. F. (1986). The personality of children prior to divorce: A prospective study. *Child Development, 57,* 827–840.

Block, J. H., Block, J., & Gjerde, P. F. (1988). Parental functioning and the home environment of families of divorce: Prospective and current analyses. *Journal of the American Academy of Child and Adolescent Psychiatry, 27,* 207–213.

Bogatz, G. A., & Ball, S. (1972). *The second year of Sesame Street: A continuing evaluation.* Princeton, NJ: Educational Testing Service.

Bogenschneider, K., Wu, M., Rafaelli, M., & Tsay, J. C. (1998). Parental influences on adolescent peer orientation and substance use: The interface of parenting practices and values. *Child Development, 69,* 1672–1688.

Bohlin, G, & Hagekull, B. (1993). Stranger wariness and sociability in the early years. *Infant Behavior and Development, 16,* 53–67.

Boivin, M., & Hymel, S. (1997). Stranger wariness and sociability in the early years. *Infant Behavior and Development, 16,* 53–67.

Bokhorst, C. L., Bakermans-Kranenburg, M. J., Fearon, R. M. P., van IJzendoorn, M. H., Fonagy, P., & Schuengel, C. (2003). The importance of shared environment in mother-infant attachment security: A behavioral genetic study. *Child Development, 74,* 1769–1782.

Boldizar, J. P. (1991). Assessing sex-typing and androgyny in children: The children's sex-role inventory. *Developmental Psychology, 27,* 505–515.

Boldizar, J. P., Perry, D. G., & Perry, L. C. (1989). Outcome values and aggression. *Child Development, 60,* 571–579.

Bolger, K. E., & Patterson, C. J. (2001). Developmental pathways from child maltreatment to peer rejection. *Child Development, 72,* 549–568.

Bolger, K. E., Patterson, C. J., & Kupersmidt, J. B. (1998). Peer relationships and self-esteem among children who have been maltreated. *Child Development, 69,* 1171–1197.

Bongers, I. L., Koot, H. M., van der Ende, J., & Verhulst, F. C. (2004). Developmental trajectories of externalizing behaviors in childhood and adolescence. *Child Development, 75,* 1523–1537.

Book, A. S., Starzyk, K. B., & Quinsey, V. L. (2001). The relationship between testosterone and aggression: A meta-analysis. *Aggression and Violent Behavior, 6,* 579–599.

Boom, J., Brugman, D., & van der Heijden, P. G. M. (2001). Hierarchical structure of moral stages assessed by a sorting task. *Child Development, 72,* 535–548.

Boone, R. T., & Cunningham, J. G. (1998). Children's decoding of emotion in expressive body movement: The development of cue attunement. *Developmental Psychology, 34,* 1007–1016.

Booth, A., & Amato, P. R. (2001). Parental predivorce relations and offspring postdivorce well-being. *Journal of Marriage and the Family, 63,* 197–212.

Booth, A., & Edwards, J. N. (1992). Starting over: Why remarriages are more unstable. *Journal of Family Issues, 13,* 179–194.

Booth, A., Johnson, D. R., Granger, D. A., Crouter, A. C., & McHale, S. (2003). Testosterone and child adolescent adjustment: The moderating role of parent-child relationships. *Developmental Psychology, 39,* 85–98.

Booth, C. L., Rubin, K. H., & Rose-Krasnor, L. (1998). Perceptions of emotional support from mother and friend in middle childhood: Links with social-emotional adaptation and preschool attachment security. *Child Development, 69,* 427–442.

Bornstein, M. H., & Haynes, O. M. (1998). Vocabulary competence in early childhood: Measurement, latent construct, and predictive validity. *Child Development, 69,* 2910–2929.

Bornstein, M. H., Haynes, O. M., Pascual, L., Painter, K. M., & Galperin, C. (1999). Play in two societies: Pervasiveness of process, specificity of structure. *Child Development, 70,* 317–331.

Bornstein, M. H., & Lamb, M. E. (2005). *Developmental science: An advanced textbook* (5th Ed.). Mahwah, NJ: Lawrence Erlbaum Associates.

Borstelmann, L. J. (1983). Children before psychology: Ideas about children from antiquity to the late 1800s. In P. H. Mussen (Ed.), *Handbook of child psychology* (Vol. 1). New York: Wiley.

Borzekowski, D. L. G., Fobil, J. N., & Asante, K. O. (2006). Online access by adolescents in Accra: Ghanaian teen's use of the Internet for health information. *Developmental Psychology, 42,* 450–458.

Borzekowski, D. L. G., & Rickert, V. I. (2001). Adolescent cyber-surfing for health information: A new resource that crosses barriers. *Archives of Pediatric and Adolescent Medicine, 155,* 813–817.

Boseovski, J. J., & Lee, K. (2006). Children's use of frequency information for trait categorization and behavioral prediction. *Developmental Psychology, 42,* 500–513.

Bosma, H. A., & Kunnen, E. S. (2001). Determinants and mechanisms of ego identity development: A review and synthesis. *Developmental Review, 21,* 39–66.

Bost, K. K., Vaughn, B. E., Washington, W. N., Cielinski, K. L., & Bradbard, M. R. (1998). Social competence, social support, and attachment: Demarcation of construct domains, measurement, and paths of influence for preschool children attending Head Start. *Child Development, 69,* 192–218.

Botkin, D. R., Weeks, M. O. N., & Morris, J. E. (2000). Changing marriage role expectations: 1991–1996. *Sex Roles, 42,* 933–942.

Bouchard, T. J., Jr., Lykken, D. T., McGue, M., Segal, N. L., & Tellegen, A. (1990). Sources of human psychological differences: The Minnesota study of twins reared apart. *Science, 250,* 223–228.

Bouchard, T. J., Jr., & McGue, M. (1981). Family studies of intelligence: A review. *Science, 212,* 1055–1059.

Boulton, M. J. (1999). Concurrent and longitudinal relations between children's playground behavior and other social preferences, victimization, and bullying. *Child Development, 70,* 944–954.

Bower, T. G. R. (1982). *Development in Infancy,* 2nd ed. San Francisco: W. H. Freeman.

Bowlby, J. (1960). Separation anxiety. *International Journal of Psychoanalysis, 41,* 89–113.

Bowlby, J. (1969). *Attachment and loss.* Vol. 1: *Attachment.* London: Hogarth Press.

Bowlby, J. (1973). *Attachment and loss.* Vol. 2: *Separation.* London: Hogarth Press.

Bowbly, J. (1980). *Attachment and loss.* Vol. 3: *Loss, sadness, and depression.* New York: Basic Books.

Bowbly, J. (1988). *A secure base: Clinical applications of attachment theory.* London: Routledge.

Boyatzis, C. J., Matillo, G. M., & Nesbitt, K. M. (1995). Effects of the *Mighty Morphin Power Rangers* on children's aggression with peers. *Child Study Journal, 25,* 44–55.

Boyer, C. B., Tschann, J. M., & Shafer, M. (1999). Predictors of risk for sexually transmitted disease in ninth-grade urban high school students. *Journal of Adolescent Research, 14,* 448–465.

Boyes, M. C., & Chandler, M. (1992). Cognitive development, epistemic doubt, and identity formation in adolescence. *Journal of Youth and Adolescence, 21,* 277–304.

Boyle, M. H., Jenkins, J. M., Georgiades, K., Cairney, J., Duku, E., & Racine, Y. (2004). Differential-maternal parenting behavior: Estimating within-and between-family effects on children. *Child Development, 75,* 1457–1476.

Brabeck, M. (1983). Moral judgment: Theory and research on differences between males and females. *Developmental Review, 3,* 274–291.

Bradbard, M. R., Martin, C. L., Endsley, R. C., & Halverson, C. F. (1986). Influence of sex stereotypes on children's exploration and memory: A competence versus performance distinction. *Developmental Psychology, 22,* 481–486.

Bradley, R. H., & Caldwell, B. M. (1984). The HOME inventory and family demographics, *Developmental Psychology, 20,* 315–320.

Bradley, R. H., Corwyn, R. F., Burchinal, M., McAdoo, H. P., & Coll, C. G. (2001). The home environments of children in the United States: part II: Relations with behavioral development through age thirteen. *Child Development, 72,* 1868–1886.

Bradley, R. H., Corwyn, R. F., McAdoo, H. P., & Coll, C. G. (2001). The home environments of children in the United States part I: Variations by age, ethnicity, and poverty status. *Child Development, 72,* 1844–1867.

Bradley, S. J., Oliver, G. D., Chernick, A. B., & Zucker, K. J. (1998). Experiment of nurture: Ablatio penis at 2 months, sex reassignment at 7 months, and a psychosexual follow-up in young adulthood. *Pediatrics, 102,* 132–133.

Brand, E., Clingempeel, W. G., & Bowen-Woodward, K. (1988). Family relationships and children's psychological adjustment in stepmother and stepfather families: Findings and conclusions from the Philadelphia Stepfamily Research Project. In E. M. Hetherington & J. D. Arasteh (Eds.), *Impact of divorce, single-parenting, and stepparenting on children.* Hillsdale, NJ: Erlbaum.

Braungart, J. M., Plomin, R., DeFries, J. C., & Fulker, D. W. (1992). Genetic influence on tester-rated infant temperament as assessed by Bayley's Infant Behavior Record: Nonadoptive and adoptive siblings and twins. *Developmental Psychology, 28,* 40–47.

Brendgen, M., Dionne, G., Girard, A., Boivin, M., Vitaro, F., & Perusse, D. (2005). Examining genetic and environmental effects on social aggression in 6-year-old twins. *Child Development, 76,* 930–946.

Brendgen, M., Vitaro, F., Boivin, M., Dionne, G., & Perusse, D. (2006). Examining genetic and environmental effects on reactive versus proactive aggression. *Developmental Psychology, 42,* 1299–1312.

Brendgen, M., Vitaro, F., & Bukowski, W. M. (2000). Deviant friends and early adolescents' emotional and behavioral adjustment. *Journal of Research on Adolescence, 10,* 173–189.

Brendgen, M., Vitaro, F., Bukowski, W. M., Doyle, A. B., & Markiewcz, D. (2001). Developmental profiles of peer social preference over the course of elementary school: Associations with trajectories of externalizing and internalizing behavior. *Developmental Psychology, 37,* 308–320.

Brennan, P. A., Hall, J., Bor, W., Najman, J. M., & Williams, G. (2003). Integrating biological and social processes in relation to early-onset persistent aggression in boys and girls. *Developmental Psychology, 39,* 309–323.

Bretherton, I. (1985). Attachment theory: Retrospect and prospect. In I. Bretherton & E. Waters (Eds.), Growing points of attachment theory and research. *Monographs of the Society for Research in Child Development, 50* (Nos. 1–2, Serial No. 209).

Bretherton, I. (1990). Open communication and internal working models: Their role in the development of attachment relationships. In R. A. Thompson (Ed.), Socioemotional development. *Nebraska Symposium on Motivation* (Vol. 36). Lincoln: University of Nebraska Press.

Bretherton, I., Stolberg, U., & Kreye M. (1981). Engaging strangers in proximal interaction: Infants' social initiative. *Developmental Psychology, 17,* 746–755.

Brice-Heath, S. (1982). Questioning at home and at school: A comparative study. In G. Spindler (Ed.), *Doing the ethnography of schooling: Educational anthropology in action.* New York: Holt, Rinehart & Winston.

Brice-Heath, S. (1989). Oral and literate traditions among black Americans living in poverty. *American Psychologist, 44,* 367–373.

Broberg, A. G., Wessels, H., Lamb, M. E., & Hwang, C. P. (1997). Effects of day care on the development of cognitive abilities in 8-year-olds: A longitudinal study. *Developmental Psychology, 33,* 62–69.

Brody, G. H. (1998). Sibling relationship quality: Its causes and consequences. *Annual Review of Psychology, 49,* 1–14.

Brody, G. H., Dorsey, D., Forehand, R., & Armistead, L. (2002). Unique and protective contributions of parenting and classroom processes in the adjustment of African American children living in single parent homes. *Child Development, 73,* 274–286.

Brody, G. H., & Flor, D. L. (1998). Maternal resources, parenting practices, and child competence in rural single-parent African American families. *Child Development, 69,* 803–816.

Brody, G. H., Ge, X., Conger, R. D., Gibbons, F. X., Murry, V. B., Gerrard, M., & Simons, R. L. (2001). The influence of neighborhood disadvantage on African American children's affiliation with deviant peers. *Child Development, 72,* 1231–1246.

Brody, G. H., Graziano, W. G., & Musser, L. M. (1983). Familiarity and children's behavior in same-age and mixed-age peer groups. *Developmental Psychology, 19,* 568–576.

Brody, G. H., Kim, S., Murry, V. B., & Brown, A. C. (2003). Longitudinal direct and indirect pathways linking older sibling competence to the development of younger sibling competence. *Developmental Psychology, 39,* 618–628.

Brody, G. H., & Murry, V. M. (2001). Sibling socialization of competence in rural, single-parent African American families. *Journal of Marriage and the Family, 63,* 996–1008.

Brody, G. H. Murry, V. M., Kim, S., & Brown, A. C. (2002). Longitudinal pathways to competence and psychological adjustment among African American children living in rural single-parent households. *Child Development, 73,* 1505–1516.

Brody, G. H., & Shaffer, D. R. (1982). Contributions of parents and peers to children's moral socialization. *Developmental Review, 2,* 31–75.

Brody, G. H., Stoneman, Z., & Flor, D. (1996). Parental religiosity, family processes, and youth competence in rural, two-parent African American families. *Developmental Psychology, 32,* 696–706.

Brody, L. R. (1999). *Gender, emotion, and the family.* Cambridge, MA: Harvard University Press.

Brodzinsky, D. M., Radice, C., Huffman, L., & Merkler, K. (1987). Prevalence of clinically significant symptomatology in nonclinical samples of adopted and nonadopted children. *Journal of Clinical Child Psychology, 16,* 350–356.

Brodzinsky, D. M., Smith, D. W., & Brodzinsky, A. B. (1998). *Children's adjustment to adoption: Developmental and clinical issues.* London: Sage.

Broidy, L. M., Nagin, D. S., Tremblay, R. E., et al., (2003). Developmental trajectories of childhood disruptive behaviors and adolescent delinquency: A six-site, cross-national study. *Developmental Psychology, 39,* 222–245.

Bronfenbrenner, U. (1970a). *Two worlds of childhood: U.S. and U.S.S.R.* New York: Russell Sage Foundation.

Bronfenbrenner, U. (1970b). *Who cares for America's children?* Invited address presented at the Conference of the National Association for the Education of Young Children, Washington, DC.

Bronfenbrenner, U. (1977). Toward an experimental ecology of human development. *American Psychologist, 32,* 513–531.

Bronfenbrenner, U. (1979). *The ecology of human development.* Cambridge, MA: Harvard University Press.

Bronfenbrenner, U. (1989). Ecological systems theory. In R. Vasta (Ed.). *Annals of child development: Theories of child development: Revised formulations and current issues* (Vol. 6, pp. 187–251). Greenwich, CT: JAI Press.

Bronfenbrenner, U., & Morris, P. A. (2006). The bioecological model of human development. In W. Damon & R. M. Lerner (Series Eds.), and R. M. Lerner (Vol. Ed.), *Handbook of child psychology, Vol. 1. Theoretical models of human development* (6th ed., pp.793–828). New York: Wiley.

Bronfenbrenner, U., & Neville, P. R. (1995). America's children and families: An international perspective. In S. L. Kagan & B. Weissbourd (Eds.), *Putting families first* (pp. 3–27). San Francisco: Jossey-Bass.

Brookmeyer, K. A., Heinrich, C. C., & Schwab-Stone, M. (2005). Adolescents who witness community violence: Can parent support and prosocial cognitions protect them from committing violence? *Child Development, 76,* 917–929.

Brookover, W., Beady, C., Flood, P., Schweitzer, J., & Wisenbaker, J. (1979). *School social systems and student achievement: Schools can make a difference.* New York: Praeger.

Brooks-Gunn, J., Berlin, L. J., & Fuligni, A. S. (2000). Early childhood intervention programs: What about the family? In J. P. Shonkoff, & S. J. Meisels (Eds.), *Handbook of early childhood intervention.* (2nd ed., pp. 549–588). New York: Cambridge University Press.

Brooks-Gunn, J., Han, W., & Waldfogel, J. (2002). Maternal employment and child cognitive outcomes in the first three years of life. The NICHD study of early child care. *Child Development, 73,* 1052–1072.

Brooks-Gunn, J., Klebanov, P. K., & Duncan, G. J. (1996). Ethnic differences in children's intelligence test scores: Role of economic deprivation, home environment, and maternal characteristics. *Child Development, 67,* 396–408.

Brophy, J. E. (1983). Research on the self-fulfilling prophecy and teacher expectations. *Journal of Educational Psychology, 75,* 631–661.

Broverman, I. K., Vogel, S. R., Clarkson, F. E., & Rosenkrantz, P. S. (1972). Sex-role stereotypes: A current appraisal. *Journal of Social Issues, 28,* 59–78.

Brown, A. L. (1997). Transforming schools into communities of thinking and learning about serious matters. *American Psychologist, 52,* 300–313.

Brown, B. B. (1990). Peer groups. In S. Feldman & G. Elliott (Eds.), *At the threshold: The developing adolescent.* Cambridge, MA: Cambridge University Press.

Brown, B. B. (1999). "You're going out with who?" Peer group influences on adolescent romantic relationships. In W. Furman, B. B. Brown, & C. Feiring (Eds.), *The development of romantic relationships in adolescence.* Cambridge, England: Cambridge University Press.

Brown, B. B. (2004). Adolescents' relationships with peers. In R. M. Lerner & L. Steinberg (Eds.), *Handbook of adolescent psychology* (2nd ed., pp. 363–394). New York: Wiley.

Brown, B. B., Clasen, D. R., & Eicher, S. A. (1986). Perceptions of peerpressure, peer conformity dispositions, and self-reported behavior among adolescents. *Developmental Psychology, 22,* 521–530.

Brown, B. B., Mory, M. S., & Kinney, D. (1994). Casting adolescent crowds in a relational perspective: Caricature, channel, and context. In R. Montemayor, G. R. Adams, & T. P. Gulotta (Eds.), *Personal relationships during adolescence.* Thousand Oaks, CA: Sage.

Brown, B. B., Mounts, N., Lamborn, S. D., & Steinberg, L. (1993). Parenting practices and peer group affiliation in adolescence. *Child Development, 64,* 467–482.

Brown, C. S., & Bigler, R. S. (2004). Children's perceptions of gender discrimination. *Developmental Psychology, 40,* 714–726.

Brown, J. D. (1998). *The self.* New York: McGraw-Hill.

Brown, J. D. (2002). Mass media influences on sexuality. *The Journal of Sex Research, 39,* 42–45.

Brown, J. R., & Dunn, J. (1996). Continuities in emotion understanding from three to six years. *Child Development, 67,* 789–802.

Brown, P., & Elliot, R. (1965). Control of aggression in a nursery school class. *Journal of Experimental Child Psychology, 2,* 103–107.

Brownell, C. A. (1986). Convergent developments: Cognitive-developmental correlates of growth in infant/toddler peer skills. *Child Development, 57,* 275–286.

Brownell, C. A. (1990). Peer social skills in toddlers: Competencies and constraints illustrated by same-age and mixed-age interaction. *Child Development, 61,* 838–848.

Brownell, C. A., & Carriger, M. S. (1990). Changes in cooperation and self/other differentiation during the second year. *Child Development, 61,* 1164–1174.

Brownell, C. A., Ramani, G. B., & Zerwas, S. (2006). Becoming a social partner with peers: Cooperation and social understanding in one- and two-year-olds. *Child Development, 77,* 803–821.

Bruer, J. T. (1999). *The myth of the first three years: A new understanding of early brain development and lifelong learning.* New York: Free Press.

Bruer, J. T., (2001). A critical and sensitive period primer. In D. B. Bailey, J. T., Bruer, F. J. Symons, & J. W. Lichtman (Eds.), *Critical thinking about critical periods.* Baltimore, MD: Paul H. Brookes Publishing.

Buchanan, C. M., Eccles, J. S., & Becker, J. B. (1992). Are adolescents the victim of raging hormones?: Evidence for the activational effects of hormones on moods and behavior at adolescence. *Psychological Bulletin, 111,* 62–107.

Buchanan, C. M., Maccoby, E. E., & Dornbusch, S. M. (1991). Caught between parents: Adolescents' experiences in divorced homes. *Child Development, 62,* 1008–1029.

Buckner, J. C., Bassuk, E. L., Weinreb, L. F., & Brooks, M. G. (1999). Homelessness and its relation to the mental health and behavior of low-income school-age children. *Developmental Psychology, 35,* 246–257.

Bugental, D. B. (2001). *Parental cognitions as predictors of dyadic interaction with very young children.* Paper presented at the biennial meeting of the Society for Research Child Development, Minneapolis.

Bugental, D. B., & Beaulieu, D. A. (2003). A bio-social-cognitive approach to understanding and promoting the outcomes of children with medical and physical disorders. In R. V. Kail (Ed.), *Advances in child development and behavior* (Vol. 31). San Diego: Academic Press.

Bugental, D. B., Ellerson, P. C., Lin, E. K., Rainey, B., Kokotovic, A., & O'Hara, N. (2002). A cognitive approach to child abuse prevention. *Journal of Family Psychology, 16,* 243–258.

Bugental, D. B., & Happaney, K. (2004). Predicting infant maltreatment in low-income families: The interactive effects of maternal attributions and child status at birth. *Developmental Psychology, 40,* 234–243.

Buhrmester, D. (1990). Intimacy of friendship, interpersonal competence, and adjustment during preadolescence and adolescence. *Child Development, 61,* 1101–1111.

Buhrmester, D. (1996). Need fulfillment, interpersonal competence, and the developmental contexts of friendship. In. W. M. Bukowski, A. F. Newcomb, & W. M. Hartup (Eds) *The company they keep: Friendship during childhood and adolescence* (pp. 158–185). New York: Cambridge University Press.

Buhrmester, D., & Furman, W. (1990). Perceptions of sibling relationships during middle childhood and adolescence. *Child Development, 61,* 1387–1398.

Buhs, E. S., & Ladd, G. W. (2001). Peer rejection as an antecedent of young children's school adjustment: An examination of mediating processes. *Developmental Psychology, 37,* 550–560.

Bukowski, W. M., Gauze, C., Hoza, B., & Newcomb, A. F. (1993). Differences and consistency between same-sex and other-sex peer relationships during early adolescence. *Developmental Psychology, 29,* 253–263.

Bukowski, W. M., Sippola, L. K., & Newcomb, A. F. (2000). Variations in patterns of attraction to same- and other-sex peers during early adolescence. *Developmental Psychology, 36,* 147–154.

Bulcroft, R. A. (1991). The value of physical change in adolescence: Consequences for the parent-adolescent exchange relationship. *Journal of Youth and Adolescence, 20,* 89–105.

Burack, J. A., Flanagan, T., Peled, T., Sutton, H. M., Zygmuntowicz, C., & Manly, J. T. (2006). Social perspective-taking skills in maltreated children and adolescents. *Developmental Psychology, 42,* 207–217.

Burchinal, M. R., & Clarke-Stewart, K. A. (2007). Maternal employment and child cognitive outcomes: The importance of analytic approach. *Developmental Psychology, 43,* 1140–1153.

Burchinal, M. R., Follmer, A., & Bryant, D. M. (1996). The relations of maternal social support and family structure with maternal responsiveness and child outcomes among African-American families. *Developmental Psychology, 32,* 1073–1083.

Burchinal, M. R., Roberts, J. E., Riggins, R., Jr., Ziesel, S. A., Neebe, E., & Bryant D. (2000). Relating quality of center-based care to early cognitive and language development longitudinally. *Child Development, 71,* 339–357.

Burgess, K. B., Wojslawowicz, J. C., Rubin, K. H., Rose-Krasnor, L., & Booth-LaForce, C. (2006). Social-information processing and coping strategies of shy/withdrawn and aggressive children: Does friendship matter? *Child Development, 77,* 371–383.

Burhans, K. K., & Dweck, C. S. (1995). Helplessness in early childhood: The role of contingent worth. *Child Development, 66,* 1719–1738.

Burn, S., O'Neil, A. K., & Nederend, S. (1996). Childhood tomboyishness and adult androgyny. *Sex Roles, 34,* 419–428.

Burnette, E. (1997). Talking openly about race thwarts racism in children. *Monitor of the American Psychological Association, 28,* 33.

Burns, L. H. (1990). An exploratory study of perceptions of parenting after infertility. *Family Systems Medicine, 8,* 177–189.

Burt, S. A., McGue, M., Iacono, W. G., & Kruger, R. F. (2006). Differential parent-child relationships and adolescent externalizing symptoms: Cross-lagged analyses within a monozygotic twin differences design. *Developmental Psychology, 42,* 1289–1298.

Burton, L. M. (1990). Teenage childrearing as an alternative life-course strategy in multigenerational black families. *Human Nature, 1,* 123–143.

Burton, R. V. (1963). The generality of honesty reconsidered. *Psychological Review, 70,* 481–499.

Bushman, B. J., & Anderson, C. R. (2002). Violent video games and hostile expectancies: A test of the general aggression model. *Personality and Social Psychology Bulletin, 28,* 1679–1686

Bushman, B. J., & Cantor, J.(2003). Media ratings for violence and sex: Implications for policymakers and parents. *American Psychologist, 58,* 130–141.

Bushman, B., J. & Husemann, L. R. (2001). Effects of televised violence on aggression. In D. Singer & J. Singer (Eds.), *Handbook of children and the media* (pp. 223–254). Thousand Oaks, CA: Sage.

Buss, A. H. (1961). *The psychology of aggression.* New York: Wiley.

Buss, A. H., & Plomin, R. (1984). *Temperament: Early developing personality traits.* Hillsdale, NJ: Erlbaum.

Buss, D. M. (1995). Psychological sex differences: Origins through sexual selection. *American Psychologist, 50,* 164–168.

Buss, D. M. (2000). Evolutionary psychology. In A. Kazdin (Ed.), *Encyclopedia of psychology*. Washington, DC, & New York: American Psychological Association and Oxford University Press.

Buss, K. A., & Goldsmith, H.H. (1998). Fear and anger regulation in infancy: Effects on temporal dynamics of affective expression. *Child Development, 69*, 359–374.

Buss, K. A., & Kiel, E. J., (2004). Comparison of sadness, anger, and fear facial expressions when toddlers look at their mothers. *Child Development, 75*, 1761–1773.

Busseri, M. A., Rose-Krasnor, L., Willoughby, T., & Chalmers, H. (2006). A longitudinal examination of breadth and intensity of youth activity involvement and successful development. *Developmental Psychology, 42*, 1313–1326.

Bussey, K. (1992). Lying and truthfulness: Children's definitions, standards, and evaluative reactions. *Child Development, 63*, 129–137.

Bussey, K., & Bandura, A. (1992). Self-regulatory mechanisms governing gender development. *Child Development, 63*, 1236–1250.

Bussey, K., & Bandura, A. (1999). Social cognitive theory of gender development and differentiation. *Psychological Review, 106*, 676–713.

Butler, R., & Ruzany, N. (1993). Age and socialization effects on the development of social comparison motives and normative ability assessment in kibbutz and urban children. *Child Development, 64*, 532–543.

Buysse, V., & Bailey, D. B. (1993). Behavioral and developmental outcomes in young children with disabilities in integrated and segregated settings: A review of comparative studies. *Journal of Special Education, 26*, 434–461.

Byrnes, J. P., & Takahira, S. (1993). Explaining gender differences on SAT math items. *Developmental Psychology, 29*, 805–810.

Cabrera, N. J., Tamis-LeMonda, C. S., Bradley, R. H., Hofferth, S., & Lamb, M. E. (2000). Fatherhood is the twenty-first century. *Child Development, 71*, 127–136.

Cahill, L. (2005, May). His brain, her brain. *Scientific American, 292*, 41–47.

Cairns, R. B., Cairns, B. D., Neckerman, H. J., Ferguson, L. L., & Gariepy, J. (1989). Growth and aggression: 1. Childhood to early adolescence. *Developmental Psychology, 25*, 320–330.

Cairns, R. B., Leung, M., Buchanan, L., & Cairns, B. D. (1995). Friendships and social networks in childhood and adolescence: Fluidity, reliability, and interrelations. *Child Development, 66*, 1330–1345.

Caldera, Y. M., Huston, A. C., & O'Brien, M. (1989). Social interactions and play patterns of parents and toddlers with feminine, masculine, and neutral toys. *Child Development, 60*, 70–76.

Caldwell, B. M. & Bradley, R. H. (1984). *Manual for the Home Observation for Measurement of the Environment*. Little Rock: University of Arkansas Press.

Caldwell, C. H., Zimmerman, M. A., Bernat, D. H., Sellers, R. M., & Notaro, P. C. (2002). Racial identity, maternal support, and psychological distress among African American adolescents. *Child Development, 73*, 1322–1336.

Calkins, S. D., Fox, N. A., & Marshall, T. R. (1996). Behavioral and physiological antecedents of inhibited and uninhibited behavior. *Child Development, 67*, 523–540.

Call, J., Carpenter, M., & Tomasello, M. (2005). Copying results and copying actions in the process of social learning: Chimpanzees (*Pan troglodytes)* and human children *(Homo sapiens)*. *Animal Cognition, 8*, 151–163.

Call, J., & Tomasello, M. (1999). A nonverbal false belief task: Performance of children and great apes. *Child Development, 70*, 381–395.

Calvert, S. L., & Kotler, J. A. (2003). Lessons from children's television: The impact of the Children's Television Act on children's learning. *Journal of Applied Developmental Psychology, 24*, 275–335.

Campbell, D. T. (1965). Ethnocentric and other altruistic motives. In D. Levine (Ed.), *Nebraska Symposium on Motivation* (Vol. 13). Lincoln: University of Nebraska Press.

Campbell, F. A., Pungello, E. P., Miller-Johnson, S., Burchinal, M., & Ramey, C. T. (2001). The development of cognitive and academic abilities: Growth curves from an early childhood education experiment. *Developmental Psychology, 37*, 231–242.

Campbell, F. A., & Ramey, C. T. (1994). Effects of early intervention on intellectual and academic achievement: A follow-up study of children from low-income families. *Child Development, 65*, 684–698.

Campbell, F. A., & Ramey, C. T. (1995). Cognitive and school outcomes for high-risk African-American students at middle adolescence: Positive effects of early intervention. *American Educational Research Journal, 32*, 743–772.

Campbell, S. B., Cohn, J. F., & Meyers, T. (1995). Depression in first-time mothers: Mother-infant interaction and depression chronicity. *Developmental Psychology, 31*, 349–357.

Campos, J. J., Bertenthal, B.I., & Kermoian, R. (1992). Early experience and emotional development: The emergence of wariness of heights. *Psychological Science, 3*, 61–64.

Campos, J. J., Mumme, D. L., Kermoian, R., & Campos, R. G. (1994). A functionalist perspective on the nature of emotion. *Monographs of the Society for Research in Child Development, 59* (2–3, Serial No. 240).

Campos, R., Raffaelli, M., Ude, W., Greco, M., Ruff, A., Rolf, J., Antunes, C., M., Halsley, N., Greco, D., & Associates (1994). Social networks and daily activities of street youth in Belo Horizonte, Brazil. *Child Development, 65*, 319–330.

Campos, R. G. (1989). Soothing pain-elicited distress in infants with swaddling and pacifiers. *Child Development, 60*, 781–792.

Camras, L. A., Oster, H., Campos, J. J., Miyake, K., & Bradshaw, D. (1992). Japanese and American infants' responses to arm restraint. *Developmental Psychology, 28*, 578–583.

Canter, R. J., & Ageton, S. S. (1984). The epidemiology of adolescent sex-role attitudes. *Sex Roles, 11*, 657–676.

Capaldi, D. M., & Clark, S. (1998). Prospective family predictors of aggression toward female partners for at-risk young men. *Developmental Psychology, 34*, 1175–1188.

Capaldi, D. M., Dishion, T. J., Stoolmiller, M., & Yoerger, K. (2001). Aggression toward female partners by at-risk young men: The contribution of male adolescent friendships. *Developmental Psychology, 37*, 61–73.

Capaldi, D. M., & Patterson, G. R. (1991). Relation of parental transitions to boys' adjustment problems: I. A linear hypothesis. II. Mothers at risk for transition and unskilled parenting. *Developmental Psychology, 27*, 489–504.

Capaldi, D. M., Stoolmiller, M., Clark, S., & Owen, L. D. (2002). Heterosexual risk behaviors in at-risk young men from early adolescence to young adulthood: Prevalence, prediction, and association with STD contraction. *Developmental Psychology, 38*, 394–406.

Caplan, M., Vespo, J., Pedersen, J., & Hay, D. F. (1991). Conflict and its resolution in small groups of one- and two-year-olds. *Child Development, 62*, 1513–1524.

Card, N. A., & Hodges, E. V. (2006). Shared targets for aggression by early adolescent friends. *Developmental Psychology, 42,* 1327–1338.

Carlson, E. A. (1998). A prospective longitudinal study of attachment disorganization/disorientation. *Child Development, 69,* 1107–1128.

Carlson, S. M., Mandell, D. J., & Williams, L. (2004). Executive function and theory of mind: Stability and prediction form ages 2 to 3. *Developmental Psychology, 40,* 1105–1122.

Carlson, V., Cicchetti, D., Barnett, D., & Braunwald, K. (1989). Disorganized/disoriented attachment relationships in maltreated infants. *Developmental Psychology, 25,* 525–531.

Carpendale, J. I. M. (2000). Kohlberg and Piaget on stages of moral reasoning. *Developmental Review, 20,* 181–205.

Carpenter, M., Call, J., & Tomasello, M. (2002). Understanding Aprior intentions@ enables two-year-olds to imitatively learn a complex task. *Child Development, 73,* 1431–1441.

Carrick, N., & Quas, J. A., (2006). Effects of discrete emotions on young children's ability to discuss fantasy and reality. *Developmental Psychology, 42,* 1278–1288.

Carstensen, L., Pasupathi, M., Mayr, R., & Nesselroade, J. (2000). Emotional experience in everyday life across the life span. *Journal of Personality and Social Psychology, 79,* 644–655.

Carver, L. J., & Vaccaro, B. G. (2007). 12-month-old infants allocate increased neural resources to stimuli associated with negative adult emotion. *Developmental Psychology, 43,* 54–69.

Carver, P. R., Egan, S. K., & Perry, D. G. (2004). Children who question their heterosexuality. *Developmental Psychology, 40,* 43–53.

Casey, M. B. (1996). Understanding individual differences in spatial ability within females: A nature/nurture interactions framework. *Developmental Review, 16,* 241–260.

Casey, M. B., Nuttall, R. L., & Pezaris, E. (1997). Mediators of gender differences in mathematics college entrance test scores: A comparison of spatial skills with internalized beliefs and anxieties. *Developmental Psychology, 33,* 669–680.

Casey, W. M., & Burton, R. V. (1982). Training children to be consistently honest through verbal self-instructions. *Child Development, 53,* 911–919.

Casiglia, A. C., Lo Coco, A., & Zappulla, C. (1998). Aspects of social reputation and peer relationships in Italian children: A cross-cultural perspective. *Developmental Psychology, 34,* 723–730.

Caspi, A., Elder, G. H., Jr., & Bem, D. J. (1988). Moving away from the world: Life-course patterns of shy children. *Developmental Psychology, 24,* 824–831.

Caspi, A., Lynam, D., Moffitt, T. E., & Silva, P. A. (1993). Unraveling girls' delinquency: Biological, dispositional, and contextual contributors to adolescent misbehavior. *Developmental Psychology, 29,* 19–30.

Caspi, A., McClay, J., Moffitt, T. E., Mill, J., Martin, J., Craig, I. W., et al., (2002). The role of genotype in the cycle of violence in maltreated children. *Science, 297,* 851–854.

Caspi, A., Moffitt, T. E., Morgan, J., Rutter, M., Taylor, A., Arseneault, L., Tully, L., Jacobs, C., Kim-Cohen, J., & Polo-Thomas, M. (2004). Maternal expressed emotion predicts children's antisocial behavior problems: Using monozygotic-twin differences to identify environmental effects on behavioral development. *Developmental Psychology, 40,* 149–161.

Caspi, A., & Silva, P. A. (1995). Temperamental qualities at age three predict personality traits in young adulthood: Longitudinal evidence from a birth cohort. *Child Development, 66,* 486–498.

Caspi, A., Sugden, K., Moffitt, T. E., Taylor, A., Craig, I. W., Harrington, H., et al., (2003, July 18). Influence of life stress on depression: moderation by a polymorphism in the 5-HHT gene. *Science, 301,* 386–389.

Cassidy, J. (2003). Continuity and change in the measurement of infant attachment: Comment on Fraley and Spieker (2003). *Developmental Psychology, 39,* 409–412.

Cassidy, J., Aikins, J. W., & Chernoff, J. J (2003). Children's peer selection: Experiment examination of the role of self-perceptions. *Developmental Psychology, 39,* 495–508.

Cassidy, J., & Asher, S. R. (1992). Loneliness and peer relations in young children. *Child Development, 63,* 350–365.

Cassidy, K. W. (1998). Preschoolers' use of desires to solve theory of mind problems in a pretense context. *Developmental Psychology, 34,* 503–511.

Castelli, L., DeAmicis, L., & Sherman, S. J., (2007). The loyal member effect: On the preference for ingroup members who engage in exclusive relations with the in group. *Developmental Psychology, 43,* 1347–1359.

Cates, W., Jr. (1995). Sexually transmitted diseases. In B. P. Sachs, R. Beard, E. Papiernik, & C. Russell (Eds.), *Reproductive health care for women and babies* (pp. 57–84). New York: Oxford University Press.

Caughy, M. O., O'Campo, P. J., Randolph, S. M., & Nickerson, K. (2002). The influences of racial socialization practices on the cognitive and behavioral competencies of African American preschoolers. *Child Development, 73,* 1611–1625.

Ceci, S. J. (1991). How much does schooling influence general intelligence And its cognitive components? A reassessment of the evidence. *Developmental Psychology, 27,* 703–722.

Ceci, S. J., & Williams, W. W. (1997). Schooling, intelligence, and income, *American Psychologist, 52,* 1051–1058.

Center on Educational Policy (2007). *Answering the question that matters most: Has student achievement increased since No Child Left Behind?* Washington, DC: Author.

Centers for Disease Control and Prevention (2003). *Sexual behavior among high school students—United States, 2001.* Atlanta, GA: Author.

Centers for Disease Control and Prevention (2004). *Births to young teens at lowest levels in almost 60 years.* Retrieved from http//www.cdc.gov/nchs/pressroom/04news/lowbirths.html.

Cervantes, C. A., & Callanan, M. A. (1998). Labels and explanations in mother-child emotion talk: Age and gender differentiation. *Developmental Psychology, 34,* 88–98.

Chalmers, J. B., & Townsend, M. A. R. (1990). The effects of training in social perspective taking on socially maladjusted girls. *Child Development, 61,* 178–190.

Chan, R. W., Raboy, B., & Patterson, C. J. (1998). Psychosocial adjustment among children conceived via donor insemination by lesbian and heterosexual mothers. *Child Development, 69,* 443–457.

Chandler, M., Sokol, B. W., & Wainryb, C. (2000). Beliefs and truth and beliefs about rightness. *Child Development, 71,* 91–97.

Chandler, M. J.(1973). Egocentrism and antisocial behavior: The assessment and training of social perspective taking skills. *Developmental Psychology, 9,* 326–332.

Chandler, M. J., Lalonde, C. E., Sokol, B. W., & Hallett, D. (2003). Personal persistence, identity development, and suicide. *Monographs of the Society for Research in Child Development, 68* (No. 2, Serial No. 273).

Chang, L. (2004). The role of classroom norms in contextualizing the relations of children's social behaviors to peer acceptance. *Developmental Psychology, 40,* 691–702.

Chao, R. K. (1994). Beyond parental control and authoritarian parenting style: Understanding Chinese parenting through the cultural notion of training. *Child Development, 65,* 1111–1119.

Chao, R. K. (2001). Extending research on the consequences of parenting style for Chinese Americans and European Americans. *Child Development, 72,* 1832–1843.

Chapman, M., Zahn-Waxler, C., Cooperman, G., & Iannotti, R. J. (1987). Empathy and responsibility in the motivation of children's helping. *Developmental Psychology, 23,* 140–145.

Charlesworth, W. R. (1992). Darwin and developmental psychology: Past and present. *Developmental Psychology, 28,* 5–16.

Chase-Lansdale, P. L., Cherlin, A. J., & Kiernan, K. E. (1995). The long-term effects of parental divorce on the mental health of young adults: A developmental perspective. *Child Development, 66,* 1614–1634.

Chassin, L., Curran, P. J., Hussong, A. M., & Colder, C. R. (1996). The relation of parent alcoholism to adolescent substance use: A longitudinal follow-up study. *Journal of Abnormal Psychology, 105,* 70–80.

Chassin, L., Presson, C. C., Todd, M., Rose, J. S., & Sherman, S. J. (1998). Maternal socialization of adolescent smoking: The intergenerational transmission of parenting and smoking. *Developmental Psychology, 34,* 1189–1201.

Chavous, T. M., Bernat, D. H., Schmeelk-Cone, K., Caldwell, C. H., Kohn-Wood, L., & Zimmerman, M. A. (2003). Racial identity and academic attainment among African American adolescents. *Child Development, 74,* 1076–1090.

Chen, C., Greenberger, E., Lester, J., Dong, Q., & Guo, M. (1998). A cross-cultural study of family and peer correlates of adolescent misconduct. *Developmental Psychology, 34,* 770–781.

Chen, C., Li, D., Li, Z., Li, B., & Liu, M. (2000). Sociable and prosocial dimensions of social competence in Chinese children: Unique contributions to social, academic, and psychological adjustment. *Developmental Psychology, 36,* 302–314.

Chen, C., & Stevenson, H. W. (1995). Motivation and mathematics achievement: A comparative study of Asian-American, Caucasian-American, and East Asian high school students. *Child Development, 66,* 1215–1234.

Chen, X. (2000). Growing up in a collectivist culture: Socialization and socioemotional development in Chinese Children. In A. L. Comunian & U. P. Gielen (Eds.), *Human development in cross-culture perspective.* Padua, Italy: Cedam.

Chen, X., Cen, G., Li, D., & He, Y. (2005). Social functioning and adjustment in Chinese children: The imprint of historical time. *Child Development, 76,* 182–195.

Chen, X., Chang, L., & He, Y. (2003). The peer group as a context: Mediating and moderating effects on relations between academic achievement and social functioning in Chinese children. *Child Development, 74,* 710–727.

Chen, X., Chang, L., He, Y., & Liu, H. (2005). The peer group as a context: Moderating effects on relations between maternal parenting and social and school adjustment in Chinese children. *Child Development, 76,* 417–434.

Chen, X., Chen, H., Kaspar, V., & Noh, S. (2000). Adolescent social, emotional, and school adjustment in mainland China. *International Journal of Group Tensions, 39,* 51–78.

Chen, X., Dong, Q., & Zhou, H. (1997). Authoritative and authoritarian parenting practices and social and school performance in Chinese children. *International Journal of Behavioral Development, 21,* 855–873.

Chen, X., Hastings, P. D., Rubin, K. H., Chen, H., Cen, G., & Stewart, S. L. (1998). Child-rearing attitudes and behavioral inhibition in Chinese and Canadian toddlers: A cross-cultural study. *Developmental Psychology, 34,* 677–686.

Chen, X., Rubin, K. H., & Li, Z. (1995). Social functioning and adjustment in Chinese children: A longitudinal study. *Developmental Psychology, 31,* 531–539.

Chen, X., Rubin, K. H., & Li, D. (1997). Relation between academic achievement and social adjustment: Evidence from Chinese children. *Developmental Psychology, 33,* 518–525.

Chen, X., Rubin, K. H., & Sun, Y. (1992). Social reputation in Chinese and Canadian children: A cross-cultural study. *Child Development, 63,* 1336–1343.

Cherlin, A. J., Kiernan, K. E., & Chase-Lansdale, P. L. (1995). Parental divorce in childhood and demographic outcomes in young adulthood. *Demography, 32,* 299–318.

Chess, S., & Thomas A. (1999). *Goodness of fit: Clinical applications from infancy through adult life.* Ann Arbor, MI: Edwards Brothers.

Child, I. L. (1954). Socialization. In G. Lindzey (Ed.), *Handbook of social psychology.* Reading, MA: Addison-Wesley.

ChildStats (2007a). *American's children: Key national indicators of well-being, 2007: Child poverty.* Retrieved October 1, 2007, from http//www.childstats.gov/americaschildren/tables/asp.

ChildStats (2007b). *Child maltreatment: Rate of substantiated maltreatment reports of children ages 0–17.* Retrieved October 9, 2007, from http//www.childstats.gov/tables.asp.

Chisholm, K. (1998). A three-year follow-up of attachment and indiscriminate friendliness in children adopted from Romanian orphanages. *Child Development, 69,* 1092–1106.

Choi, J., & Silverman, I. (2003). Processes underlying sex differences in route-learning strategies in children and adolescents. *Personality and Individual Differences, 34,* 1153–1166.

Chomitz, V. R., Cheung, L. W. Y., & Lieberman, E. (2000). The role of lifestyle in preventing low birth weight. In K. L. Freiberg (Ed.), *Human development 00/01* (28th ed., pp. 18–28). Guilford, CT: Duskin/McGraw Hill.

Christopherson, E. R. (1989). Injury control. *American Psychologist, 44,* 237–241.

Chung, H. L., & Steinberg, L. (2006). Relations between neighborhood factors, parenting factors, peer deviance, and delinquency among serious juvenile offenders. *Developmental Psychology, 42,* 319–331.

Cialdini, R. B. (2001). Influence: Science and practice (4th ed.). Boston: Allyn & Bacon.

Cialdini, R. B., & Goldstein, N. (2004). Social influence: Compliance and conformity. *Annual Review of Psychology, 55,* 591–621.

Cicchetti, D., & Toth, S. L. (2006). Developmental psychopathology and preventive intervention. In W. Damon & R. M. Lerner (Series Eds.), & K. A. Renniger & I. E. Siegel, (Vol. Eds.), Handbook of child psychology, Vol. 4. *Child Psychology in practice* (6th ed.,). New York: Wiley.

Cillessen, A. H. N., & Bukowski, W. M. (Eds.) (2000). *New directions for child and adolescent development:* No. 88. *Recent advances in the measurement of acceptance and rejection in the peer system.* San Francisco: Jossey-Bass.

Cillessen, A. H. N., & Mayeux, L. (2004). From censure to reinforcement: Developmental changes in association between aggression and social status. *Child Development, 75,* 147–163.

Clark, E. A., & Hanisee, J. (1982). Intellectual and adaptive performance of Asian children in adoptive American settings. *Developmental Psychology, 18*, 595–599.

Clark, K. B. (1965). *Dark ghetto.* New York: Harper & Row.

Clark, K. E., & Ladd, G. W. (2000). Connectedness and autonomy support in parent-child relationships: Links to children's socioemotional orientation and peer relationships. *Developmental Psychology, 36*, 485–498.

Clark, R., Hyde, J. S., Essex, M. J., & Klein, M. H. (1997). Length of maternity leave and quality of mother-infant interactions. *Child Development, 68*, 364–383.

Clarke, A. M., & Clarke, A. D. B. (2000). *Early experience and the life path.* London: Jessica Kingsley.

Clarke, R., Hyde, J. S., Essex, J., & Klein, M. H. (1997). Length of maternity leave and quality of mother-infant attachment. *Child Development, 68*, 364–383.

Clarke-Stewart, K. A., & Bretano, C. (2005). *Till divorce do us part.* New Haven, CT: Yale University Press.

Clarke-Stewart, K. A., & Hayward, C. (1996). Advantages of father custody and contact for the psychological well-being of school-age children. *Journal of Applied Developmental Psychology, 17*, 239–270.

Clary, E. G., & Snyder, M. (1991). A functional analysis of altruism and prosocial behavior: The case of volunteerism. *Review of Personality and Social Psychology, 12*, 119–148.

Clausen, J. A. (1975). The social meaning of differential physical maturation. In D. Drugastin & G. H. Elder (Eds.), *Adolescence in the life cycle.* New York: Halsted Press.

Clements, D. H. (1990). Metacomponential development in a Logo programming environment. *Journal of Educational Psychology, 82*, 141–149.

Clements, D. H. (1991). Enhancement of creativity in computer environments. *American Educational Research Journal, 28*, 173–187.

Clements, D. H. (1995). Teaching creativity with computers. *Educational Psychology Review, 7*, 141–161.

Cleveland, H. H., & Wiebe, R. P. (2003). The moderation of adolescent-to-peer similarity in tobacco and alcohol use by school levels of substance use. *Child Development, 74*, 279–291.

Clingempeel, W. G., & Segal, S. (1986). Stepparent-stepchild relationships and the psychological adjustment of children in stepmother and stepfather families. *Child Development, 57*, 474–484.

Coates, B., & Hartup, W. W. (1969). Age and verbalization in observational learning. *Developmental Psychology, 1*, 556–562.

Cohen, G. L., & Prinstein, M. J. (2006). Peer contagion of aggression and health risk behavior among adolescent males: An experimental investigation of effects on public conduct and private attitudes. *Child Development, 77*, 967–983.

Coie, J. D., & Dodge, K. A. (1983). Continuities and changes in children's social status: A five-year longitudinal study. *Merrill-Palmer Quarterly, 19*, 261–282.

Coie, J. D., Dodge, K. A., & Coppotelli, H. (1982). Dimensions and types of social status: A cross-age perspective. *Developmental Psychology, 18*, 557–570.

Coie, J. D., Dodge, K. A., & Kupersmidt, J. B. (1990). Peer group behavior And social status. In S. R. Asher & J. D. Coie (Eds.), *Peer rejection in childhood.* Cambridge, England: Cambridge University Press.

Coie, J. D., Dodge, K. A., Terry, R., & Wright, V. (1991). The role of aggression in peer relations: An analysis of aggression episodes in boys' play groups. *Child Development, 62*, 812–826.

Coie, J. D., & Krehbiel, G. (1984). Effects of academic tutoring on the Social status of low-achieving, socially rejected children. *Child Development, 55*, 1465–1478.

Coie, J. D., & Kupersmidt, J. B. (1983). A behavioral analysis of emerging social status in boys' groups. *Child Development, 54*, 1400–1416.

Colapinto, J. (2000). *As nature made him: The boy who was raised a girl.* New York: HarperCollins.

Colby, A., & Kohlberg, L. (1987). *The measurement of moral judgment (Vol. 1): Theoretical foundations and research validation.* Cambridge: Cambridge University Press.

Colby, A., Kohlberg, L., Gibbs, J., & Lieberman, M. (1983). A longitudinal study of moral judgment. *Monographs of the Society for Research in Child Development, 48* (Nos. 1–2, Serial No. 200).

Cole, D. A., Martin, J. M., Peeke, L. A., Seroczynski, A. D., & Fier, J. (1999). Children's over- and underestimation of academic competence: A longitudinal study of gender differences, depression, and anxiety. *Child Development, 70*, 459–473.

Cole, D. A., Maxwell, S. E., Martin, J. M., Peake, L. G. Scoroczynski, A. D., Tram, J. M., Hoffman, K. B., Ruiz, M. D., Jicquez, F., & Maschman, T. (2001). The development of multiple domains of child and adolescent self-concept: A cohort sequential longitudinal design. *Child Development, 72*, 1723–1746.

Cole, P. M., Barrett, K. C., & Zahn-Waxler, C. (1992). Emotion displays in two-year-olds during mishaps. *Child Development, 63*, 314–324.

Cole, P. M., Bruschi, C. J., & Tamang, B. L. (2002). Cultural differences in children's emotional reactions to difficult situations. *Child Development, 73*, 983–996.

Cole, P. M., & Tamang, B. L. (1998). Nepali children's ideas about emotional displays in hypothetical challenges. *Developmental Psychology, 34*, 640–646.

Cole, P. M., Tamang, B. L., & Shrestha, A. (2006). Cultural variations in the socialization of young children's anger and shame. *Child Development, 77*, 1237–1251.

Coleman, J. S., Campbell, E. Q., Hobson, C. J., McPartland, J., Mood, A. M., Weinfeld, F. D., & York, R. L. (1966). *Equality of educational opportunity.* Report from U.S. Office of Education. Washington, DC: U.S. Government Printing Office.

Coley, R. L. (1998). Children's socialization experiences and functioning in single-mother households: The importance of fathers and other men. *Child Development, 69*, 219–230.

Coley, R. L., & Chase-Lansdale, P. L. (1998). Adolescent pregnancy and parenthood: Recent evidence and future directions. *American Psychologist, 53*, 152–166.

Coley, R. L., & Hernandez, D. C. (2006). Predictors of paternal involvement for resident and nonresident low-income fathers. *Developmental Psychology, 42*, 1041–1056.

Coley, R. L., & Medeiros, B. L. (2007). Reciprocal longitudinal relations between nonresident father involvement and adolescent delinquency. *Child Development, 78*, 132–147.

Colley, A., Griffiths, D., Hugh, M., Landers, K., & Jaggli, N. (1996). Childhood play and adolescent leisure preferences: Associations with gender typing and the presence of siblings. *Sex Roles, 35*, 233–245.

Collie, R., & Hayne, H. (1999). Deferred imitation by 6- and 9-month-old infants: More evidence for declarative memory. *Developmental Psychobiology, 35*, 83–90.

Collins, W. A. (1983). Interpretation and inference in children's television viewing. In J. R. Bryant & D. R. Anderson (Eds.), *Children's understanding of television: Research on attention and comprehension.* New York: Academic Press.

Collins, W. A., & Laursen B. (2004). Changing relationships, changing youth: Interpersonal contexts of adolescent development. *Journal of Early Adolescence, 24,* 55–62.

Collins, W. A., Maccoby, E. E., Steinberg, L., Hetherington, E. M., & Bornstein, M. H. (2000). Contemporary research on parenting: The case for nature and nurture. *American Psychologist, 55,* 218–232.

Collins, W. A., Sobol, B. L., & Westby, S. (1981). Effects of adult commentary on children's comprehension and inferences about a televised aggressive portrayal. *Child Development, 52,* 158–163.

Collins, W. A., & Steinberg, L. (2006). Adolescent development in interpersonal context. In W. Damon & R. M. Lerner (Series Eds.) & N. Eisenberg (Vol. Ed.), *Handbook of child psychology: Vol. 3. Social, emotional, and personality development* (6th ed., pp. 1003–1067). New York: Wiley.

Collis, B. A., (1996). *Children and computers at school.* Mahwah, NJ: Erlbaum.

Colwell, M. J., Mize, J., Pettit, G. S., & Laird, R. D. (2002). Contextual determinants of mothers' interventions in young children's peer interactions. *Developmental Psychology, 38,* 492–502.

Compton, K., Snyder, J., Schrepferman, L., Bank, L., & Shortt, J. W. (2003). The contribution of parents and siblings to antisocial and depressive behavior in adolescents: A double-jeopardy coercion model. *Development and Psychopathology, 15,* 163–182.

Comstock, G. A. (1993). The medium and society: The role of television in American life. In G. L. Berry & J. K. Asamen (Eds.), *Children and television: Images in a changing sociocultural world* (pp. 117–131). Newbury Park, CA: Sage.

Condry, J., & Condry, S. (1976). Sex differences: A study in the eye of the beholder. *Child Development, 47,* 812–819.

Condry, J. C., & Ross, D. F. (1985). Sex and aggression: The influence of gender label on the perception of aggression in children. *Child Development, 56,* 225–233.

Conduct Problems Prevention Research Group (1999). Initial impact of the Fast Track Prevention Trial for Conduct Problems: II. Classroom effects. *Journal of Consulting and Clinical Psychology, 67,* 648–657.

Conduct Problems Prevention Research Group (2002). Evaluation of the first 3-years of the Fast Track prevention trial with children at high risk for antisocial conduct problems. *Journal of Abnormal Child Psychology, 30,* 19–35.

Conduct Problems Prevention Research Group (2004). The effects of the Fast Track program on serious problem outcomes at the end of elementary school. *Journal of Clinical Child and Adolescent Psychology, 33,* 650–661.

Conger, R. D., Conger, K. J., Elder, G. H., Jr., Lorenz, F. O., Simons, R. L., & Whitbeck, L. B. (1992). A family process model of economic hardship and adjustment of early adolescent boys. *Child Development, 63,* 527–541.

Conger, R. D., Neppel, T., Kim, K. J., & Scaramella, L. (2003). Angry and aggressive behavior across three generations: A prospective, longitudinal study of parents and children. *Journal of Abnormal Child Psychology, 31,* 143–160.

Conger, R. D., Patterson, G. R., & Ge, X. (1995). It takes two to replicate: A mediational model for the impact of parents' stress on adolescent adjustment. *Child Development, 66,* 80–97.

Conger, R. D., Wallace, L. B., Sun, Y., Simons, R. L., McLoyd, V., & Brody, G. H. (2002). Economic pressure in African American families: A replication and extension of the family stress model. *Developmental Psychology, 38,* 179–193.

Connolly, J., Craig, W., Goldberg, A., & Pepler, D. (2004). Mixed-gender groups, dating, and romantic relationships in early adolescence. *Journal of Research on Adolescence, 14,* 185–207.

Connolly, J., Furman, W., & Konarski, R. (2000). The role of peers in the emergence of heterosexual romantic relationships in adolescence. *Child Development, 71,* 1395–1408.

Connolly, J. A., & Doyle, A. (1984). Relation of social fantasy play to social competence in preschoolers. *Developmental Psychology, 20,* 797–806.

Conway, M., & Vartanian, L. R. (2000). A status account of gender stereotypes: Beyond communality and agency. *Sex Roles, 43,* 181–199.

Coohey, C., & Braun, N. (1997). Toward an integrated framework for understanding child physical abuse. *Child Abuse and Neglect, 21,* 1081–1094.

Cook, T. D., Appleton, H., Conner, R. F., Shaffer, A., Tabkin, G., & Weber, J. S. (1975). *Sesame Street revisited.* New York: Russell Sage Foundation.

Cooley, C. H. (1902). *Human nature and the social order.* New York: Scribner's.

Coontz, S. (2000). Historical perspective on family diversity. In D. H. Demo, K. R. Allen, & M. A. Fine (Eds.), *Handbook of family diversity.* New York: Oxford University Press.

Coopersmith, S. (1967). *The antecedents of self esteem.* New York: W. H. Freeman.

Coplan, R. J. (2000). Assessing nonsocial play in early childhood: Conceptual and methodological approaches. In K. Gitlin-Weiner, A. Sandgrund, & C. Schaefer, (Eds.), *Play diagnosis assessment* (2nd ed., pp. 563–598). New York: Wiley.

Coplan, R. J., Gavinski-Molina, M., Lagace-Sequin, D. G., & Wichmann, C. (2001). When girls versus boys play alone: Nonsocial play and adjustment in kindergarten. *Developmental Psychology, 37,* 464–474.

Corteen, R. S., & Williams, T. (1986). Television and reading skills. In T. Williams (Ed.), *The impact of television: A natural experiment in three communities.* Orlando, FL: Academic Press.

Corter, C. M., Zucker, K. J., & Galligan, R. F. (1980). Patterns in the infant's search for mother during brief episodes. *Developmental Psychology, 16,* 62–69.

Costabile, A., Smith, P. K., Matheson, L., Aston, J., Hunter, T., & Boulton, M. (1991). Cross-national comparison of how children distinguish serious and playful fighting. *Developmental Psychology, 27,* 881–887.

Costigan, C. L., & Dokis, D. P. (2006). Relations between parent-child acculturation differences and adjustment within immigrant Chinese families. *Child Development, 77,* 1252–1267.

Costin, S. E., & Jones, D. C. (1992). Friendship as a facilitator of Emotional responsiveness and prosocial interventions among young children. *Developmental Psychology, 28,* 941–947.

Cote, J. E., & Levine, C. (1988). A critical examination of the ego identity status paradigm. *Developmental Review, 8,* 147–184.

Coulton, C. J., Korbin, J. E., Su, M., & Chow, J. (1995). Community level factors and child maltreatment rates. *Child Development, 66,* 1262–1276.

Courage, M. L., Edison, S. C., & Howe, M. L. (2005). Variability in the early development of visual self-recognition. *Infant Behavior and Development, 27,* 509–532.

Cousins, S. D. (1989). Culture and self-perception in Japan and the United States, *Journal of Personality and Social Psychology, 56*, 124–131.

Cowan, P. A., Powell, D., & Cowan, C. P. (1998). Parenting interventions: A family systems perspective. In I.E., Sigel & A. Renniger (Eds.), *Handbook of child psychology: Vol 4. Child psychology in practice* (5th ed., pp. 3–72). New York: Wiley.

Cowley, G. (2001). Generation XXL. In K. L. Freiberg (Ed.), *Human development* 01/02 (29th ed., pp. 120–121). Guilford, CT: Duskin/McGraw-Hill.

Cox, M. J., Owen, M. T., Henderson, V. K., & Margand, N. A. (1992). Prediction of infant-father and infant-mother attachment. *Developmental Psychology, 28*, 474–483.

Cox, M. J., Owen, M. T., Lewis, J. M., & Henderson, V. K. (1989). Marriage, adult adjustment, and early parenting. *Child Development, 60*, 1015–1024.

Coyle, T. R., & Bjorklund, D. F. (1997). Age differences in, and consequences of, multiple-and variable strategy use on a multitrial sort-recall task. *Developmental Psychology, 33*, 372–380.

Crandall, V. C. (1967). Achievement behavior in young children. In *The young child: Reviews of research*. Washington, DC: National Association for the Education of Young Children.

Crandall, V. C., Katkovsky, W., & Preston, A. A. (1960). A conceptual formulation of some research on children's achievement development. *Child Development, 31*, 787–797.

Crawford, M., & Popp, D. (2003). Sexual double standards: A review and methodological critique of two decades of research. *The Journal of Sex Research, 40*, 13–26.

Crawford, N. (2002). New ways to stop bullying. *Monitor on Psychology, 33*, 64–66.

Crews, F. (1996). The verdict on Freud [Review of *Freud evaluated: The completed arc*]. *Psychological Science, 7*, 63–68.

Crick, N. R. (1996). The role of overt aggression, relational aggression, and prosocial behavior in the prediction of children's future social adjustment. *Child Development, 67*, 2317–2327.

Crick, N. R., Casas, J. F., & Ku, H. (1999). Relational and physical forms of peer victimization in preschool. *Developmental Psychology, 35*, 376–385.

Crick, N. R., Casas, J. F., & Mosher, M. (1997). Relational and overt aggression in preschool. *Developmental Psychology, 33*, 579–588.

Crick, N. R. & Dodge, K. A., (1994). A review and reformulation of social information processing mechanisms in children's social adjustment. *Psychological Bulletin, 115*, 74–101.

Crick, N. R. & Dodge, K. A., (1996). Social information-processing mechanisms in reactive and proactive aggression. *Child Development, 67*, 993–1002.

Crick, N. R., & Grotpeter, J. K. (1995). Relational aggression, gender, and social-psychological adjustment. *Child Development, 66*, 710–722.

Crick, N. R., Grotpeter, J. K., & Bigbee, M. A. (2002). Relationally and physically aggressive children's intent attributions and feelings of distress for relational and instrumental peer provocations. *Child Development, 73*, 1134–1142.

Crick, N. R., & Ladd, G. W. (1993). Children's perceptions of their peer experiences: Attributions, loneliness, social anxiety, and social avoidance. *Developmental Psychology, 29*, 244–254.

Crick, N. R., Werner, N. E., Casas, J. F., O'Brien, K. M., Nelson, D. A., Grotpeter, J. K., & Markon, K. (1998). Childhood aggression and gender: A new look at an old problem. In D. Bernstein (Ed.),

Nebraska Symposium on Motivation: Vol. 45. Lincoln: University of Nebraska Press.

Criss, M. M., Pettit, G. S., Bates, J. E., Dodge, K. A., & Lapp, A. L. (2002). Family adversity, positive peer relationships, and children's externalizing behavior: A longitudinal perspective on risk and resilience. *Child Development, 73*, 1220–1237.

Crockenberg, S. C., & Leerkes, E. M. (2004). Infant and maternal behaviors regulate infant reactivity to novelty at 6 months. *Developmental Psychology, 40*, 1123–1132.

Crockenberg, S., & Litman, C. (1990). Autonomy as competence in 2-year-olds: Maternal correlates of child defiance, compliance, and self-assertion. *Developmental Psychology, 26*, 961–971.

Croft, C., Beckett, C., Rutter, M., Castle, J., Colvert, E., Groothues, C. (2007). Early adolescent outcomes of institutionally deprived and non-deprived adoptees. II: Language as a protective factor and a vulnerable outcome. *Journal of Child Psychology and Psychiatry, 48*, 31–44.

Cronbach, L. J., & Snow, R. E. (1977). *Aptitude and instructional methods: A handbook for research on interactions*. New York: Irvington.

Crook, C. (1992). Cultural artifacts in social development: The case of computers. In H. McGurk (Ed.), *Childhood social development: Contemporary perspectives*. Hove, England: Erlbaum.

Crosnoe, R., & Elder, G. H., Jr. (2002). Adolescent twins and emotional distress: The interrelated influence of nonshared environment and social structure. *Child Development, 73*, 1761–1774.

Cross, W. E. (1985). Black identity: Rediscovering the distinction between personal identity and reference group orientation. In M. B. Spencer, G. K. Brookins, & W. R. Allen (Eds.), *Beginnings: The social and affective development of black children*. Hillsdale, NJ: Erlbaum.

Crouter, A. C., Bumpass, M. F., MacGuire, M. C., & McHale, S. M. (1999). Linking parents' work pressure and adolescents' well-being: Insights into dynamics in dual-career families. *Developmental Psychology, 35*, 1453–1461.

Crouter, A. C., Helms-Erikson, H. Updegraff, K., & McHale, S. M. (1999). Conditions underlying parents' knowledge about children's daily lives in middle childhood: Between- and within-family comparisons. *Child Development, 70*, 246–259.

Crouter, A. C., Manke, B. A., & McHale, S. M. (1995). The family context of gender intensification in early adolescence. *Child Development, 66*, 317–329.

Crowell, J. A., & Feldman, S. S. (1991). Mothers' working models of attachment relationships and mother and child behavior during separation and reunion. *Developmental Psychology, 27*, 597–605.

Crystal, D. S., Chen, C., Fuligni, A. J., Stevenson, H. W., Hsu, C., Ko, H., Kitamura, S., & Kimura, S. (1994). Psychological maladjustment and academic achievement: A cross-cultural study of Japanese, Chinese, and American high school students. *Child Development, 65*, 738–753.

Crystal, D. S., Watanabe, H., Weinfert, K., & Wu, C. (1998). Concepts of human differences: A comparison of American, Japanese and Chinese children and adults. *Developmental Psychology, 34*, 714–722.

Cui, M., Conger, R. D., & Lorenz, F. O. (2005). Predicting change in adolescent adjustment from change in marital problems. *Developmental psychology, 41*, 812–823.

Cui, M., Donnellan, M. B., & Conger, R. D. (2007). Reciprocal influences between parents' marital problems and adolescent internalizing and externalizing behavior. *Developmental Psychology, 43*, 1544–1552.

Cummings, E. M., & Davies, P. T. (1994). *Children and marital conflict: The impact of family dispute and resolution.* New York: Guilford Press.

Cummings, E. M., & Davies, P. T. (2002). Effects of marital conflict on children: Recent advances and emerging themes in process-oriented research. *Journal of Child Psychology and Psychiatry and Allied Disciplines, 43,* 31–63.

Cummings, E. M., Iannotti, R. J., & Zahn-Waxler, C. (1989). Aggression between peers in early childhood: Individual continuity and developmental change. *Child Development, 60,* 887–895.

Cummings, E. M., Schermerhorn, A. C., Davies, P. T., Goeke-Morey, M. C. & Cummings, J. S. (2006). Interparental discord and child adjustment: Prospective investigations of emotional security as an explanatory mechanism. *Child Development, 77,* 132–152.

Curtis, N. M., Ronan, K. R., & Bourduin, C. M. (2004). Multisystemic treatment: A meta-analysis of outcome studies. *Journal of Family Psychology, 18,* 411–419.

Cynkar, A. (2007a). Socially wired. *Monitor on Psychology, 38,* 47–49.

Cynkar, A. (2007b). The changing gender composition of psychology. *Monitor on Psychology, 38,* 46–47.

Crystal, D. S., Watanabe, H., Weinfert, K., & Wu, C. (1998). Concepts of human differences: A comparison of American, Japanese and Chinese children and adolescents. *Developmental Psychology, 34,* 714–722.

Dabbs, J. M., Jr., Carr, T. S., Frady, F. L., & Riad, J. K. (1995). Testosterone, crime, and misbehavior among 692 male prison inmates. *Personality and Individual Differences, 18,* 627–633.

Dabbs, J. M., & Morris, R. (1990). Testosterone, social class, and antisocial behavior in a sample of 4,462 men. *Psychological Science, 1,* 209–211.

Damon, W. (1977). *The social world of the child.* San Francisco: Jossey-Bass.

Damon, W., & Hart, D. (1988). *Self-understanding in childhood and adolescence.* New York: Cambridge University Press.

Daniels, D. (1986). Differential experiences of siblings in the same family as predictors of adolescent sibling personality differences. *Journal of Personality and Social Psychology, 51,* 339–346.

Daniels, D., & Plomin, R. (1985). Differential experience of siblings in the same family. *Developmental Psychology, 21,* 747–760.

Darling, C. A., Davidson, J. K., & Passarello, L. C. (1992). The mystique of first intercourse among college youth: The role of partners, contraceptive practices, and psychological reactions. *Journal of Youth and Adolescence, 21,* 97–117.

Darlington, R. B. (1991). The long-term effects of model preschool programs. In L. Okagaki & R. J. Sternberg (Eds.), *Directors of development. Influences on the development of children's thinking.* Hillsdale, NJ: Erlbaum.

Darwin, C. A. (1877). A biographical sketch of an infant. *Mind, 2,* 285–294.

Darwin, C. (1965). *The expression of emotions in man and animals.* Chicago: University of Chicago Press (Original work published in 1872).

Das Eiden, R., Teti, D. M., & Corns, K. M. (1995). Maternal working models of attachment, marital adjustment, and the parent-child relationship. *Child Development, 66,* 1504–1518.

D'Augelli, A. (2002). Mental health problems among lesbian, gay, and bisexual youths ages 14–21. *Clinical Child Psychology and Psychiatry, 7,* 433–466.

David, H. P. (1992). Born unwanted: Long-term developmental effects of denied abortion. *Journal of Social Issues, 48,* 163–181.

David, H. P. (1994). Reproductive rights and reproductive behavior: Clash or convergence of private values and public policies. *American Psychologist, 49,* 343–349.

David, H. P., Dytrych, Z., Matejcek, Z. (2003). Born unwanted: Observations from the Prague study. *American Psychologist, 58,* 224–229.

Davidov, M., & Grusec, J. E. (2006). Untangling the links of parental responsiveness to distress and warmth to child outcomes. *Child Development, 77,* 44–58.

Davies, P. T., & Cummings, E. M. (1994). Exploring children's emotional insecurity as a mediator of the link between marital relations and child adjustment. *Child Development, 69,* 124–139.

Davies, P. T., & Cummings, E. M. (1998). Exploring children's emotional insecurity as a mediator of the link between marital relations and child adjustment. *Child Development, 69,* 124–139.

Davies, P. T., & Cummings, E. M. (2006). Interparental discord, family process, and developmental psychopathology. In D. Cicchetti & D. J. Cohen, (Eds.), *Developmental Psychopathology: Vol. 3. Risk, disorder, and adaptation* (2nd ed., pp. 86–128). New York: Wiley.

Davies, P. T., & Forman, E. M. (2002). Children's patterns of preserving emotional security in the interparental subsystem. *Child Development, 73,* 1880–1903.

Davies, P. T., Harold, G. T., Goeke-Morley, M. C., & Cummings, E. M. (2003). Child emotional security and interpersonal conflict. *Monographs of the Society for Research in Child Development, 67,* (3, Serial No. 270).

Davies, P. T., Sturge-Apple, M. L., Cicchetti, D., & Cummings, E. M. (2007). The role of child adrenocortical functioning in pathways between interpersonal conflict and child maladjustment. *Developmental Psychology, 43,* 918–930.

Davies, P. T., & Windle, M. (2000). Middle adolescents' dating pathways and psychological adjustment. *Merrill-Palmer Quarterly, 46,* 90–118.

Davis, T. L. (1995). Gender differences in masking negative emotions: Ability or motivation? *Developmental Psychology, 31,* 660–667.

Davison, K. K., & Birch, L. L. (2002). Processes linking weight status and self-concept among girls from ages 5 to 7 years. *Developmental Psychology, 38,* 735–748.

Day, J. C., Janus, A., & Davis, J. (2003). Computer and Internet use in the United States: 2003. *U.S. Census Bureau, current population study.* http://www.census.gov/prod/2003pubs/p-23-208.pdf.

DeAngelis, T. (2007). Web pornography effects on children. *Monitor on Psychology, 38,* 50–52.

Deater-Deckard, K., & Dodge, K. A. (1997). Externalizing behavior problems and discipline revisited: Nonlinear effects and variation by culture, context, and gender. *Psychological Inquiry, 8,* 161–175.

DeBerry, K. M., Scarr, S., & Weinberg, R. (1996). Family racial socialization and ecological competence: Longitudinal assessments of African-American transracial adoptees. *Child Development, 67,* 2375–2399.

Deci, E. L., Koestner, R., & Ryan, R. M. (2001). A meta-analytic review of experiments examining the effects of extrinsic rewards on intrinsic motivation. *Psychological Bulletin, 125,* 627–668.

Decker, S. H. (1996). Collective and normative features of gang violence. *Justice Quarterly, 13,* 243–264.

DeGarmo, D. S., Forgatch, M. S., & Martinez, C. M., Jr. (1999). Parenting of divorced mothers as a link between social status and boys' academic outcomes: Unpacking the effects of socioeconomic status. *Child Development, 70,* 1231–1245.

de Gaston, J. P., Weed, S., & Jensen, L. (1996). Understanding gender differences in adolescent sexuality. *Adolescence, 31,* 217–232.

Degirmencioglu, S. M., Urberg, K. A., Tolson, J. M., & Richard, P. (1998). Adolescent friendship networks: Continuity and change over the school year. *Merrill-Palmer Quarterly, 44,* 313–337.

de Guzman, M. R. T., & Carlo, G. (2004). Family, peer, and acculturative correlates of prosocial development among Latino youth in Nebraska. *Great Plains Research, 14,* 185–202.

DeKlyen, M., Biernbaum, M. A., Speltz, M. L., & Greenberg, M. T., (1998). Fathers and preschool behavior problems. *Developmental Psychology, 34,* 264–275.

Dekovic, M., & Janssens, J. M. A. M. (1992). Parents' child-rearing style and children's sociometric status. *Developmental Psychology, 28,* 925–932.

DeLoache, J. S., Simcock, G., & Macari, S. (2007). Planes, trains, automobiles and tea sets: Extremely intense interests in very young children. *Developmental Psychology, 43,* 1579–1586.

DeLuccie, M. E. (1995). Mothers as gatekeepers: A model of maternal mediators of father involvement. *Journal of Genetic Psychology, 156,* 115–131.

Demaray, M. K., & Malecki, C. K. (2003). Perceptions of the frequency and importance of social support by students classified as victims, bullies, and bully/victims in an urban middle school. *School Psychology Review, 32,* 471–489.

deMause, L. (1974). The evolution of childhood. In L. deMause (Ed.), *The history of childhood.* New York: Harper & Row.

Demo, D. H., & Cox, M. J. (2000). Families with young children: A review of research in the 1990s. *Journal of Marriage and the Family, 62,* 876–895.

DeMulder, E. K., Denham, S., Schmidt, M., & Mitchell, J. (2000). Q-sort assessment of attachment security during the preschool years: Links from home to school. *Developmental Psychology, 36,* 274–282.

Denham, S. A. (1998). *Emotional development in young children.* New York: Guilford Press.

Denham, S. A., & Auerbach, S. (1995). Mother-child dialogue about emotions and preschoolers' emotional competence. *Genetic, Social, and General Psychology Monographs, 121,* 313–337.

Denham, S. A., Blair, K. A., DeMulder, E., Levitas, J., Sawyer, K., Auerbach-Major, S., & Queenan, P. (2003). Preschool emotional competence: Pathway to social competence? *Child Development, 74,* 238–256.

Denham, S. A., McKinley, M., Couchoud, E. A., & Holt, R. (1990). Emotional and behavioral predictors of preschool peer ratings. *Child Development, 61,* 1145–1152.

Denham, S. A., Zoller, D., & Couchoud, E. A. (1994). Socialization of preschoolers' emotion understanding. *Developmental Psychology, 30,* 928–936.

Denissen, J. J. A., Zarrett, N. R., & Eccles, J. S. (2007). I like to do it, I'm able, and I know I am: Longitudinal couplings between domain-specific achievement, self-concept, and interest. *Child Development, 78,* 430–447.

de Quervain, D. J. F., Fischbacker, U., Treyer, V., Schelhammer, M., Schayder, U., & Buck, U. (2004). The neural basis of altruistic punishment. *Science, 305,* 1254–1258.

de Schipper, E. J., Ricksen-Walraven, J. M., & Geurts, S. A. E. (2006). Effects of child-caregiving ratio on the interactions between caregivers and children in child-care centers: An experimental study. *Child Development, 77,* 861–874.

Desimone, L. M., Smith, T. M., & Frisvold, D. (2007). Teacher quality, evidence-based practice, and students in poverty. Standards-based reform and the poverty gap: Lessons for "No Child Left Behind." Washington, DC: Brookings Institute Press.

Despert, J. L. (1965). *The emotionally disturbed child: Then and now.* New York: Brunner/Mazel.

Dewandre, N. (2002). European strategies for promoting women in science. *Science, 295,* 278–279.

De Wolff, M. S., & van IJzendoorn, M. H. (1997). Sensitivity and attachment: A meta-analysis on parental antecedents of infant attachment. *Child Development, 68,* 571–591.

Dewsbury, D. A. (1992). Comparative psychology and ethology: A reassessment, *American Psychologist, 47,* 208–215.

Diamond, L. M. (2008). Female bisexuality from adolescence to adulthood: Results from a 10-year longitudinal study. *Developmental Psychology, 44,* 5–14.

Diamond, L. M., & Lucas, S. (2004). Sexual-minority and heterosexual youths' peer friendships: Experiences, expectations, and implications for well-being. *Journal of Research on Adolescence, 14,* 313–340.

Diamond, M., & Sigmundson, H. K. (1997). Sex reassignment at birth: Long-term review and clinical implications. *Archives of Pediatric and Adolescent Medicine, 151,* 298–304.

Dick, D. M., Rose, R. J., Viken, R. J., & Kapiro, J. (2000). Pubertal timing and substance use: Associations between and within families across late adolescence. *Developmental Psychology, 36,* 180–189.

Diekman, A. B., & Murnen, S. K. (2004). Learning to be little women and little men: The inequitable gender equality of nonsexist children's literature. *Sex Roles, 50,* 373–385.

Diesendruck, G., & haLevi, H. (2006). The role of language, appearance, and culture in children's social category-based induction. *Child Development, 77,* 539–553.

DiIorio, C., Dudley, W. N., Kelly, M., Soet, J. E., Mbwarn, J., & Sharpe Potter, J. (2001). Social cognitive correlates of sexual experience and condom use among 13- through 15-year-old adolescents. *Journal of Adolescent Health, 29,* 208–216.

DiLalla, L. F., Kagan, J., & Reznick, J. S. (1994). Genetic etiology of behavioral inhibition among 2-year-old children. *Infant Behavior and Development, 17,* 405–412.

Dill, K. E., & Dill, J. C. (1998). Video games violence: A review of the empirical literature. *Aggression and Violent Behavior: A Review Journal, 3,* 407–428.

Dishion, T. J. (1990). The family ecology of boys' peer relations in middle childhood. *Child Development, 61,* 874–892.

Dishion, T. J., Andrews, D. W., & Crosby, L. (1995). Antisocial boys and their friends in early adolescence: Relationship characteristics, quality, and interactional processes. *Child Development, 66,* 139–151.

Dishion, T. J., & Dodge, K. A. (2005). Peer contagion in interventions for children and adolescents: Moving toward an understanding of ecology and dynamics of change. *Journal of Abnormal Child Psychology, 33,* 395–400.

Dishion, T. J., McCord, J., & Poulin, F. (1999). When interventions harm: Peer groups and problem behavior. *American Psychologist, 54,* 755–764.

Dishion, T. J., Nelson, S. N., & Bullock, B. M. (2004). Premature adolescent autonomy: Parent disengagement and deviant peer processes in the amplification of problem behavior. *Journal of Adolescence, 27,* 515–530.

Dishion, T. J., & Owen, L. D. (2002). A longitudinal analysis of friendships and substance use: Bidirectional influence from adolescence to adulthood. *Developmental Psychology, 38,* 480–491.

Dishion, T. J., & Patterson, G. R. (2006). The development and ecology of antisocial behavior. In D. Cicchetti & D. J. Cohen (Eds.), *Developmental psychopathology: Risk, disorder, and adaptation.* Vol. 3. New York: Wiley.

Dodge, K. A. (1980). Social cognition and children's aggressive behavior. *Child Development, 51,* 162–170.

Dodge, K. A. (1983). Behavioral antecedents of peer social status. *Child Development, 54,* 1386–1399.

Dodge, K. A. (1986). A social information processing model of social competence in children. In M. Perlmutter (Ed.), *Minnesota symposia on child psychology* (Vol. 18). Hillsdale, NJ: Erlbaum.

Dodge, K. A. (1990). Nature versus nurture in childhood conduct disorder: It is time to ask a different question. *Developmental Psychology, 26,* 698–701.

Dodge, K. A., Coie, J. D., & Lynam, D. (2006). Aggression and antisocial conduct in youth. In W. Damon & R. M. Lerner (Series Eds.), & N. Eisenberg, (Vol. Ed.), *Handbook of child psychology: Vol. 3. Social, emotional, and personality development* (6th ed., pp 719–788). New York: Wiley.

Dodge, K. A., Coie, J. D., Pettit, G. S., & Price, J. M. (1990). Peer status and aggression in boys' groups: Developmental and contextual analyses. *Child Development, 61,* 1289–1309.

Dodge, K. A., Dishion, T. J., & Lansford, J. E. (2006). Deviant peer influences in intervention and pubic policy for youth. *Social Policy Report, 20.* Society for Reaserch in Child Development.

Dodge, K. A., Murphy, R. R., & Buchsbaum, K. (1984). The assessment of intention-cue detection skills in children: Implications for developmental psychopathology. *Child Development, 55,* 163–173.

Dodge, K. A., & Pettit, G. S. (2003). A biopsychosocial model of the development of chronic conduct problems in adolescence. *Developmental Psychology, 39,* 349–371.

Dodge, K. A., Pettit, G. S. & Bates, J. E. (1994). Socialization mediators of the relation between socioeconomic status and child conduct problems. *Child Development, 65,* 649–665.

Dogan, S. J., Conger, R. D., Kim, K. J., & Masyn, K. E. (2007). Cognitive and parenting pathways in the transmission of antisocial behavior from parents to adolescents. *Child Development, 78,* 335–349.

Doherty, W. J., & Needle, R. H. (1991). Psychological adjustment and substance abuse among adolescents before and after a parental divorce. *Child Development, 62,* 328–337.

Dohnt, H., & Tiggemann, M. (2006). The contribution of peer and media influences to the development of body dissatisfaction and self-esteem in young girls: A prospective study. *Developmental Psychology, 42,* 929–936.

Dollard, J., Doob, L. W., Miller, N. E., Mowrer, O. H., & Sears, R. R. (1939). *Frustration and aggression.* New Haven, CT: Yale University Press.

Dondi, M., Simion, F., & Caltran, G. (1999). Can newborns discriminate between their own cry and the cry of another newborn infant? *Developmental Psychology, 35,* 418–426.

Donnellan, M. B., Trzesniewski, K. H., Robins, R. W., Moffitt, T. E., & Caspi, A.(2005). Low self-esteem is related to aggression, antisocial behavior, and delinquency. *Psychological Science, 16,* 328–335.

D'Onofrio, B. M., Turkheimer, E., Emery, R. E., Slutske, W. S., Heath, A. C., Madden, P. A., & Martin, N. G. (2006). A genetically informed study of the processes underlying the association between parental marital instability and offspring adjustment. *Developmental Psychology, 42,* 486–499.

Donovan, W. L., Leavitt, L. A., & Walsh, R. O. (2000). Maternal illusory control predicts socialization strategies and toddler compliance. *Developmental Psychology, 36,* 402–411.

Dorn, L. D., Susman, E. J., & Ponirakis, A. (2003). Pubertal timing and adolescent adjustment and behavior: Conclusions vary by rater. *Journal of Youth and Adolescence, 32,* 157–167.

Downey, D. B., & Condron, D. J. (2004). Playing well with others in kindergarten: The benefit of siblings at home. *Journal of Marriage and the Family, 66,* 333–350.

Downing, L. L. (2003). *Fragile realities: Conversion and commitment in cults and other powerful groups*: State University of New York at Oneonta.

Doyle, A. B., & Aboud, F. E. (1995). A longitudinal study of white children's racial prejudice as a social-cognitive development. *Merrill-Palmer Quarterly, 41,* 209–228.

Doyle, A. B., Markiewicz, D., Brendgen, M., Lieberman, M., & Voss, K. (2000). Child attachment security and self-concept: Associations with mother and father attachment style and marital quality. *Merrill-Palmer Quarterly, 46,* 514–539.

Dozier, M., Stovall, C., Albus, K. E., & Bates B. (2001). Attachment for infants in foster care: The role of caregiver state of mind. *Child Development, 72,* 1467–1477.

Drabman, R. S., & Thomas, M. H. (1974). Does media violence increase children's toleration of real-life aggression? *Developmental Psychology, 10,* 418–421.

Dreyer, P. H. (1982). Sexuality during adolescence. In B. B. Wolman (Ed.), *Handbook of developmental psychology.* New York: Wiley.

Droege, K. L., & Stipek, D. J. (1993). Children's use of dispositions to predict classmates' behavior. *Developmental Psychology, 29,* 646–654.

Dubas, J. S., Graber, J. A., & Petersen, A. C. (1991). The effects of pubertal development on achievement during adolescence. *American Journal of Education, 99,* 444–460.

Dube, E. M., & Savin-Williams, R. C. (1999). Sexual identity development among ethnic sexual-minority male youths. *Developmental Psychology, 35,* 1389–1398.

Dube, E. M., Savin-Williams, R. C., & Diamond, L. M. (2001). Intimacy development, gender, and ethnicity among sexual-minority youth. In A. R. D'Augelli & C. Patterson (Eds.), *Lesbian, gay, and bisexual identities among youth: Psychological perspectives* (pp. 129–152). New York: Oxford University Press.

Dubois, D. L., Burk-Braxton, C., Swenson, L. P., Tevendale, H. D., & Hardesty, J. L. (2002a). Race and gender influences on adjustment in early adolescence: Investigation of an integrative model. *Child Development, 73,* 1573–1592.

DuBois, D. L., Burk-Braxton, C., Swenson, L. P., Tevendale, H. D., Lockerd, E. M., & Moran, B. L. (2002b). Getting by with a little help from self and others: Self-esteem and social support as resources during early adolescence. *Developmental Psychology, 38,* 822–839.

Duke, P. M., Carlsmith, J. M., Jennings, D., Martin, J. A., Dornbusch, S. M., Gross, R. T., & Siegel-Gorelick, B. (1982). Educational correlates of early and late sexual maturation in adolescence. *Journal of Pediatrics, 100,* 633–637.

Duncan, G. J., & Brooks-Gunn, J. (1997). *Growing up poor: Consequences across the life span.* New York: Russell Sage Foundation.

Duncan, G. J., & Brooks-Gunn, J. (2000). Family poverty, welfare reform, and child development. *Child Development, 71,* 188–196.

Duncan, G. J., Dowsett, C. J., Claessens, A., Magnuson, K., Huston, A. C., Klebanov, P., et al. (2007). School readiness and later achievement. *Developmental Psychology, 43,* 1428–1446.

Duncan, G. J., & Magnusson, K. (2007). Penny wise and effect size foolish. *Child Development Perspectives, 1,* 46–51.

Dunham, Y., Baron, A. S., & Banaji, M. R. (2006). From American city to Japanese village: A cross-cultural investigation of implicit race attitudes. *Child Development, 77,* 1268–1281.

Dunn, J. (1993). *Young children's close relationships. Beyond attachment.* Newbury Park, CA: Sage.

Dunn, J., Brown, J. R., & Maguire, M. (1995). The development of children's moral sensibility: Individual differences and emotional understanding. *Developmental Psychology, 31,* 649–659.

Dunn, J., & Cutting, A. (1999). Understanding others, and individual differences in friendship interactions in young children. *Social Development, 8,* 201–219.

Dunn, J., Cutting, A. L., & Fisher, N. (2002). Old friends, new friends: Predictors of children's perspectives on their friends at school. *Child Development, 73,* 621–635.

Dunn, J., & Hughes, C. (2001). "I got some swords and your're dead!" Violent fantasy, antisocial behavior, friendship, and moral sensibililty in young children. *Child Development, 72,* 491–505.

Dunn, J., & Kendrick, C. (1982). *Siblings: Love, envy, and understanding.* Cambridge, MA: Harvard University Press.

Dunn, J., & Plomin, R. (1990). *Separate lives: Why siblings are so different.* New York: Basic Books.

Dunphy, D. C. (1963). The social structure of urban adolescent peer groups. *Sociometry, 26,* 230–246.

Dweck, C. S. (1975). The role of expectations and attributions in the alleviation of learned helplessness. *Journal of Personality and Social Psychology, 31,* 674–685.

Dweck, C. S. (1978). Achievement. In M. E. Lamb (Ed.), *Social and personality development.* New York: Holt, Rinehart and Winston.

Dweck, C. S., (2001). Caution—praise can be dangerous. In K. L. Frieberg (Ed.), *Human development 01/02* (29th ed., pp. 105–109). Guilford, CT: McGraw-Hill/Dushkin.

Dweck, C. S., Davidson, W., Nelson, S., & Enna, B. (1978). Sex differences in learned helplessness: II. The contingencies of evaluative feedback in the classroom; III. An experimental analysis. *Developmental Psychology, 14,* 268–276.

Dweck, C. S., & Elliott, E. S. (1983). Achievement motivation. In P. H. Mussen (Ed.), *Handbook of child psychology. Vol. 4: Socialization, personality, and social development.* New York: Wiley.

Dweck, C. S., & Leggett, E. L. (1988). A social-cognitive approach to motivation and personality. *Psychological Review, 95,* 256–273.

Eagly, A. H. (1995). The science and politics of comparing men and women. *American Psychologist, 50,* 145–158.

Eagly, A. H., Wood, W., & Diekman, A. B. (2000). Social role theory of sex differences and similarities: A current appraisal. In T. Eckes & H. M. Trautner (Eds.), *The developmental social psychology of gender* (pp. 123–174). Mahwah, NJ: Erlbaum.

Early, D. M., Maxwell, K. L., Burchinal, M., Alva, S., Bender, R. H., et al., (2007). Teachers' education, classroom quality, and young children's academic skills: Results from seven studies of preschool programs. *Child Development, 78,* 558–580.

East, P. L. (1996). The younger sisters of childbearing adolescents: Their attitudes, expectations, and behaviors. *Child Development, 67,* 267–282.

East, P. L., & Jacobson, L. J. (2001). The younger siblings of teenage mothers: A follow-up of their pregnancy risk. *Developmental Psychology, 37,* 254–264.

East, P. L., & Rook, K. S. (1992). Compensatory patterns of support among children's peer relationships: A test using school friends, nonschool friends, and siblings. *Developmental Psychology, 28,* 163–172.

Eaton, W. O., & Enns, L. R. (1986). Sex differences in human motor activity level. *Psychological Bulletin, 100,* 19–28.

Eaton, W. O., & Yu, A. P. (1989). Are sex differences in child motor activity level a function of sex differences in maturational status? *Child Development, 60,* 1005–1011.

Eccles, J. S. (2004). Schools, academic motivation, and stage-environment fit. In R. M. Lerner & L. D. Steinberg, (Eds.), *Handbook of adolescent psychology.* (2nd Ed., pp. 125-133). New York: Wiley.

Eccles, J. S., Flanagan, C., Lord, S., & Midgley, C. (1996). Schools, families, and early adolescents: What are we doing wrong and what can we do instead? *Journal of Developmental and Behavioral Pediatrics, 17,* 267–276.

Eccles, J. S., Freeman-Doan, C., Jacobs, J., & Yoon, K. S. (2000). Gender-role socialization in the family: A longitudinal approach. In T. Eckes & H. M. Trautner (Eds.), *The developmental social psychology of gender* (pp. 333–360). Mahwah, NJ: Erlbaum.

Eccles, J. S., & Harold, R. D. (1993). Parent-school involvement during the early adolescent years. *Teachers College Record, 94,* 568–587.

Eccles, J. S., Jacobs, J. E., & Harold, R. D. (1990). Gender role stereotypes, expectancy effects, and parents' socialization of gender differences. *Journal of Social Issues, 46,* 183–201.

Eccles, J. S., Lord, S., & Midgley, C. (1991). What are we doing to early adolescents? The impact of educational contexts on early adolescents. *American Journal of Education, 99,* 521–542.

Eccles, J. S., & Roeser, R. W. (2005). School and community influences on human development. In M. H. Bornstein and M. E. Lamb (Eds.), *Developmental Science: An advanced textbook* (5th ed, pp. 513–555). Mahwah, NJ: Erlbaum.

Eccles, J. S., Wigfield, A., Harold, R. D., & Blumenfeld, P. (1993). Age and gender differences in children's task perceptions during elementary school. *Child Development, 64,* 830–847.

Eckenrode, J., Laird, M., & Doris, J. (1993). School performance and disciplinary problems among abused and neglected children. *Developmental Psychology, 29,* 53–62.

Eckerman, C. O., & Didow, S. M. (1996). Nonverbal imitation and toddlers' mastery of verbal means of achieving coordinated action. *Developmental Psychology, 32,* 141–152.

Eckerman, C. O., & Stein, M. R. (1990). How imitation begets imitation and toddlers' generation of games. *Developmental Psychology, 26,* 370–378.

Eckman, P. (2003). *Emotions revealed.* New York: Times Books.

Eder, R. A. (1989). The emergent personologist: The structure and content of 3½-, 5½-, and 7½-year-olds' concepts of themselves and other persons. *Child Development, 60,* 1218–1228.

Eder, R. A. (1990). Uncovering young children's psychological selves: Individual and developmental differences. *Child Development, 61,* 849–863.

Egan, S. K., & Perry, D. G. (1998). Does low self-regard invite victimization? *Developmental Psychology, 34,* 299–309.

Egan, S. K., & Perry, D. G. (2001). Gender identity: A multidimensional analysis with implications for psychosocial adjustment. *Developmental Psychology, 37,* 451–463.

Egeland, B., Jacobvitz, D., & Sroufe, L. A. (1988). Breaking the cycle of abuse. *Child Development, 59,* 1080–1088.

Ehrenberg, R. G., Brewer, D. J., Gamoran, A., & Willms, J. D. (2001). Class size and student achievement. *Psychological Science in the Public Interest, 2,* 1–30.

Ehrhardt, A. A. (1985). The psychobiology of gender. In A. S. Rossi (Ed.), *Gender and the life course.* New York: Adline.

Ehrhardt, A. A., & Baker, S. W. (1974). Fetal androgens, human central nervous system differentiation, and behavioral sex differences. In R. C. Friedman, R. M. Rickard, & R. L. Van de Wiele (Eds.), *Sex differences in behavior.* New York: Wiley.

Eisenberg, N. (1983). Children's differentiations among potential recipients of aid. *Child Development, 54,* 594–602.

Eisenberg, N., Cumberland, A., Spinrad, T. L., Fabes, R. A., Shepard, S. A., Reiser, M., Murphy, B. C., Losoya, S. H., & Gutherie, I. K. (2001). The relations of regulation and emotionality to children's externalizing and internalizing problem behavior. *Child Development, 72,* 1112–1134.

Eisenberg, N., & Fabes, R. A. (1998). Prosocial development. In W. Damon (Series Ed.) & N. Eisenberg (Vol. Ed.), *Handbook of child psychology: Vol. 3. Social, emotional, and personality development* (5th ed., pp. 701–778). New York: Wiley.

Eisenberg, N., Fabes, R. A., Miller, P. A., Shell, R., Shea, C., & May-Plumlee, T. (1990). Preschoolers' vicarious emotional responding and their situational and dispositional prosocial behavior. *Merrill-Palmer Quarterly, 36,* 507–529.

Eisenberg, N. Fabes, R. A., Shepard, S. A., Murphy, B. C., Jones, S., & Guthrie, I. K. (1998). Contemporaneous and longitudinal prediction of children's sympathy from dispositional regulation and emotionality. *Developmental Psychology, 34,* 910–924.

Eisenberg, N., Fabes, R. A., & Spinrad, T. L. (2006). Prosocial development. In W. Damon & R. M. Lerner (Series Eds.), & N. Eisenberg (Vol. Ed.), *Handbook of child psychology. Vol. 3. Social, emotional, and personality development* (6th ed., pp. 646–717). New York: Wiley.

Eisenberg, N., Gershoff, E. T., Fabes, R. A., Shepard, S. A., Cumberland, A. J., Losoya, S. H., Guthrie, I. K., & Murphy, B. C. (2001). Mothers' emotional expressivity and children's behavior problems and social competence: Mediation through children's regulation. *Developmental Psychology, 37,* 475–490.

Eisenberg, N., Guthrie, I., Cumberland, A., Murphy, B. C., Shepard, S. A., Zhou, Q. et al., (2002). Prosocial development in early childhood: A longitudinal study. *Journal of Personality and Social Psychology, 82,* 993–1006.

Eisenberg, N., Guthrie, I. K., Murphy, B. C., Shepard, S. A., Cumberland, A., & Carlo, G. (1999). Consistency and development of prosocial dispositions. *Child Development, 70,* 1360–1372.

Eisenberg, N., Lennon, R., & Roth, K. (1983). Prosocial development: A longitudinal study. *Developmental Psychology, 19,* 846–855.

Eisenberg, N., Liew, J., & Pidada, S. U. (2004). The longitudinal relations of regulation and emotionality to quality of Indonesian children's socioemotional functioning. *Developmental Psychology, 40,* 790–804.

Eisenberg, N., & Miller, P. (1987). The relation of empathy to prosocial and related behaviors. *Psychological Bulletin, 101,* 91–119.

Eisenberg, N., Miller, P. A., Shell, R., McNalley, S., & Shea, C. (1991). Prosocial development in adolescence: A longitudinal study.

Eisenberg, N., Murray, E., & Hite, T. (1982). Children's reasoning regarding sex-typed toy choices. *Child Development, 53,* 81–86.

Eisenberg, N., Sadovsky, A., Spinrad, T. L., Fabes, R. A., Losoya, S. H., Valiente, C., Reiser, M., Cumberland, A., & Shepard, S. A. (2005). The relations of problems behavior status to children's negative emotionality, effortful control, and impulsivity: Concurrent relations and prediction of change. *Developmental Psychology, 41,* 193–211.

Eisenberg, N., Shepard, S. A., Fabes, R. A., Murphy, B. C., & Guthrie, I. K. (1998). Shyness and children's emotionality, regulation, and coping: Contemporaneous, longitudinal, and cross-context relations. *Child Development, 69,* 767–790.

Eisenberg, N., Spinrad, T. L., Fabes, R. A., Reiser, M., Cumberland, A., Shepard, S. A., Valiente, C., Loyosa, S. H., Guthrie, I. K., & Thompson, M. (2004). The relations of effortful control and impulsivity to children's resiliency and adjustment. *Child Development, 75,* 25–46.

Eisenberg, N., Valiente, C., Morris, A. S., Fabes, R. A., Cumberland, A., Reiser, M., Gershoff, E. T., Shepard, S. A., & Loyosa, S. (2003). Longitudinal relations among parental emotional expressivity, children's' emotional regulation, and quality of socioemotional functioning. *Developmental Psychology, 39,* 3–19.

Eisenberg, N., Zhou, Q., & Koller, S. (2001). Brazilian adolescents' prosocial moral judgment and behavior: Relations to sympathy, perspective-taking, gender-role orientation, and demographic characteristics. *Child Development, 72,* 518–534.

Eisenberg, N., Zhou, Q., Spinrad, T. L., Valiente, C., Fabes, R. A., & Liew, J. (2005). Relations among positive parenting, children's effortful control, and externalizing problems: A three-wave longitudinal study. *Child Development, 76,* 1055–1071.

Eisenberg-Berg, N., & Hand, M. (1979). The relationship of preschoolers' reasoning about prosocial moral conflicts to prosocial behavior. *Child Development, 50,* 356–363.

Elder, G. H., Liker, J. K., & Cross, C. E. (1984). Parent-child behavior in the Great Depression: Life course and intergenerational influences. In P. B. Baltes & O. G. Brim (Eds.), *Life-span development and behavior* (Vol. 6). New York: Academic Press.

Elicker, J., Englund, M., & Sroufe, L. A. (1992). Predicting peer competence and peer relationships in childhood from early parent-child relationships. In R. D. Parke & G. W. Ladd (Eds.), *Family-peer relationships: Modes of linkage.* Hillsdale, NJ: Erlbaum.

Elkind, D. (1967). Egocentrism in adolescence. *Child Development, 38,* 1025–1033.

Elkind, D. (1981). *Children and adolescents: Interpretive essays on Jean Piaget* (3rd ed.), New York: Oxford, University Press.

Elkind, D. (1987). *Miseducation: Preschoolers at risk.* New York: Knopf.

Ellis, B. J., Bates, J. E., Dodge, K. A., Fergusson, D. M., Horwood, L. J., Pettit, G. S., & Woodward L. (2003). Does father absence place daughters at special risk for early sexual activity and teenage pregnancy? *Child Development, 74,* 801–821.

Ellis, S., Rogoff, B., & Cromer, C. C. (1981). Age segregation in children's social interactions. *Developmental Psychology, 17,* 399–407.

Ellis, W. E., & Zarbatany, L. (2007). Peer group status as a moderator of group influence on children's deviant, aggressive, and prosocial behavior. *Child Development, 78,* 1240–1254.

Ellsworth, C. P., Muir, D. W., & Hains, S. M. J. (1993) Social competence and person-object differentiation: An analysis of the still-face effect. *Developmental Psychology, 29,* 63–73.

El-Sheikh, M., & Harger, J. (2001). Appraisals of marital conflict and children's adjustment, health, and physiological reactivity. *Development Psychology, 37,* 875–885.

Emde, R. N., Plomin, R., Robinson, J., Corley, R., DeFries, J., Fulker, D. W., Reznick, J. S., Campos, J., Kagan, J., & Zahn-Waxler, C. (1992). Temperament, emotion, and cognition at fourteen months: The MacArthur longitudinal twin study. *Child Development, 63,* 1437–1455.

Emery, R. E. (1988). *Marriage, divorce, and children's adjustment.* Beverly Hills, CA: Sage.

Emery, R. E. (1999). Post divorce family life for children: An overview of research and some implications for policy. In R. A. Thompson & P. R. Amato (Eds.), *The post divorce family: Children, parenting, and society.* Thousand Oaks, CA: Sage.

Emery, R. E., & Forehand, R. (1994). Parental divorce and children's well-being: A focus on resilience. In R. J. Haggerty, L. R. Sherrod, N. Garmezy, & M. Rutter (Eds.), *Stress, risk, and resilience in children and adolescents* (pp. 64–99). New York: Cambridge University Press.

Emery, R. E., & Laumann-Billings, L. (1998). An overview of the nature, causes, and consequences of abusive family relationships: Toward differentiating maltreatment and violence. *American Psychologist, 53,* 121–135.

Emery, R. E., Laumann-Billings, L., Waldron, M. C., Sbarra, D. A., & Dillon, P. (2001). Child custody mediation and litigation: Custody, contact, and coparenting 12 years after initial dispute resolution. *Journal of Counseling and Clinical Psychology, 69,* 323–332.

Emery, R. E., Sbarra, D., & Grover, T. (2005). Divorce mediation: Research and reflections. *Family Court Review, 43,* 22–37.

Englund, M. M., Levy, A. K., Hyson, D. M., & Sroufe, L. A. (2000). Adolescent social competence: Effectiveness in a group setting. *Child Development, 71,* 1049–1060.

Erel, O., & Burman, B. (1995). Interrelatedness of marital relations and parent-child relations: A meta-analytic review. *Psychological Bulletin, 118,* 108–132.

Erel, O., Margolin, G., & John, R. S. (1998). Observed sibling interaction: Links with the marital and the mother-child relationship. *Developmental Psychology, 34,* 288–298.

Erel, O., Oberman, Y., & Yirmiya, N. (2000). Maternal versus nonmaternal care and seven domains of child development. *Psychological Bulletin, 126,* 727–747.

Erickson, M. F., & Egeland, B. J. (1996). Child neglect. In J. Biere, L. Berliner, J. Bulkey, C. Jenny, & T. Reid (Eds.), *The APSAC handbook on child maltreatment* (pp. 4–20). Thousand Oaks, CA: Sage.

Erikson, E. H. (1963). *Childhood and society* (2nd ed.). New York: Norton.

Erikson, E. H. (1982). *The life cycle completed: A review.* New York: Norton.

Espelage, D., Holt, M., & Henkel, R. (2003). Examination of peer-group contextual effects on aggression during early adolescence. *Child Development, 74,* 205–220.

Eyer, D. E. (1992). *Mother-infant bonding. A scientific fiction.* New Haven, CT: Yale University Press.

Fabes, R. A., & Eisenberg, N. (1992). Young children's coping with interpersonal anger. *Child Development, 63,* 116–128.

Fabes, R. A., Eisenberg, N., Jones, S., Smith, M., Gutherie, I., Poulin, R., Shepard, S., & Friedman, J. (1999). Regulation, emotionality, and preschoolers' socially competent peer interactions. *Child Development, 70,* 432–442.

Fabes, R. A., Eisenberg, N., McCormick, S. E., & Wilson, M. S. (1988). Preschoolers' attributions of the situational determinants of other's naturally occurring emotions. *Developmental Psychology, 24,* 376–385.

Fabes, R. A., Eisenberg, N., Nyman, M., & Michealieu, Q. (1991). Young children's appraisals of others' spontaneous emotional reactions. *Developmental Psychology, 27,* 858–866.

Fabes, R. A., Fultz, J., Eisenberg, N., May-Plumlee, T., & Christopher, F. S. (1989). Effects of rewards on children's prosocial motivation: A socialization study. *Developmental Psychology, 25,* 509–515.

Fabes, R. A., Martin, C. L., & Hanish, L. D. (2003). Young children's play qualities in same-, other-, and mixed-sex peer groups. *Child Development, 74,* 921–933.

Faden, R. R., & Kass, N. E., (1996). *HIV/AIDS, and childbearing.* New York: Oxford University Press.

Fagot, B. I. (1978). The influence of sex of child on parental reactions to toddler children. *Child Development, 49,* 459–465.

Fagot, B. I. (1985a). Beyond the reinforcement principle: Another step toward understanding sex-role development. *Developmental Psychology, 21,* 1097–1104.

Fagot, B. I. (1985b). Changes in thinking about early sex-role development. *Developmental Review, 5,* 83–98.

Fagot, B. I. (1997). Attachment, parenting, and peer interactions of toddler children. *Developmental Psychology, 33,* 489–499.

Fagot, B. I., & Hagan, R. I. (1991). Observations of parent reactions to sex-stereotyped behaviors: Age and sex effects. *Child Development, 62,* 617–628.

Fagot, B. I., & Kavanaugh, K. (1993). Parenting during the second year: Effects of children's age, sex, and attachment classification. *Child Development, 64,* 258–271.

Fagot, B. I., & Leinbach, M. D. (1993). Gender-role development in young children: From discrimination to labeling. *Developmental Review, 13,* 205–224.

Fagot, B. I., Leinbach, M. D., & Hagan, R. (1986). Gender labeling and the adoption of sex-typed behaviors. *Developmental Psychology, 22,* 440–443.

Fagot, B. I., Leinbach, M. D., & O'Boyle, C. (1992). Gender labeling, gender stereotyping, and parenting behaviors. *Developmental Psychology, 28,* 225–230.

Fagot, B. I., Rodgers, C. S., & Leinbach, M. D. (2000). Theories of gender socialization. In T. Eckes & H. M. Trautner (Eds.), *The developmental social psychology of gender* (pp. 65–89). Mahwah, NJ: Erlbaum.

Falbo, T. (1992). Social norms and the one-child family: Clinical and policy implications. In F. Boer & J. Dunn (Eds.), *Children's sibling relationships* (pp. 71–82). Hillsdale, NJ: Erlbaum.

Falbo, T., & Polit, D. F. (1986). Quantitative review of the only child literature: Research evidence and theory development. *Psychological Bulletin, 100,* 176–189.

Farber, S. L. (1981). *Identical twins reared apart: A reanalysis.* New York: Basic Books.

Farhl, P. (1998, January 10). "Educational" TV programs are flunking in viewership. Washington Post report as cited in the *Athens Banner-Herald,* p. A1, A14.

Farrant, K., & Reese, E. (2000). Maternal style and children's participation in reminiscing: Stepping stones to children's autobiographical memory development. *Journal of Cognition and Development, 1,* 193–225.

Farver, J. A. M., Kim, Y. K., & Lee-Shin, Y. (2000). Within cultural differences: Examining individual differences in Korean American and European American preschoolers' social pretend play. *Journal of Cross-Cultural Psychology, 31,* 583–602.

Farver, J. A. M., Xu, Y., Eppe, S., Fernandez, A., & Schwartz, D. (2005). Community violence, family conflict, and preschoolers' socio-emotional functioning. *Developmental Psychology, 41,* 160–170.

Farver, J. M., & Branstetter, W. H. (1994). Preschoolers' prosocial responses to their peers' distress. *Developmental Psychology, 30,* 334–341.

Fauber, R., Forehand, R., Thomas, A. M., & Wierson, M. (1990). A mediational model of the impact of marital conflict on adolescent adjustment in intact and divorced families: The role of disrupted parenting. *Child Development, 61,* 1112–1123.

Fearon, R. M. P., van IJzendoorn, M. H., Fonagy, P., Bakermans-Kranenburg, M. J., Schuengel, C., & Bokhorst, C. L. (2006). In search of shared and nonshared environmental factors in security of attachment: A behavior-genetic study of the association between sensitivity and attachment security. *Developmental Psychology, 42,* 1026–1040.

Fein, G. G. (1986). The affective psychology of play. In A. W. Gottfried & C. C. Brown (Eds.), *Play interactions: The contributions of play material and parental involvement in children's development.* Lexington, MA: Lexington Books.

Feingold, A. (1994). Gender differences in personality: A meta-analysis. *Psychological Bulletin, 116,* 429–456.

Feinman, S. (1992). *Social referencing and the social construction of reality in infancy.* New York: Plenam.

Feiring, C. (1996). Concepts of romance in 15-year-old adolescents. *Journal of Research on Adolescence, 6,* 181–200.

Feiring, C. (1999). Other-sex friendship networks and the development of romantic relationships in adolescence. *Journal of Youth and Adolescence, 28,* 495–512.

Feiring, C., Taska, L., & Lewis, M. (2002). Adjustment following sexual abuse discovery: The role of shame and attributional style. *Developmental Psychology, 38,* 79–92.

Feldman, R. (2006). From biological rhythms to social rhythms: Psychological precursors of mother-infant synchrony. *Developmental Psychology, 42,* 175–188.

Feldman, R., & Klein, P. S. (2003). Toddlers' self-regulated compliance to mothers, caregivers, and fathers: Implications for theories of socialization. *Developmental Psychology, 39,* 680–692.

Feldman, R., Sussman, A. L., & Zigler, E. (2004). Parental leave and work adaptation at the transition to parenthood: Individual, marital, and social correlates. *Journal of Applied Developmental Psychology, 25,* 459–480.

Fernald, A., & Mazzie, C. (1991). Prosody and focus in speech to infants and adults. *Developmental Psychology, 27,* 209–221.

Fernandez, E. (1997, June 3). The grim legacy of divorce. *The Atlanta Constitution,* p. F5.

Feshbach, S. (1956). The catharsis hypothesis and some consequences of interaction with aggressive and neutral play objects. *Journal of Personality, 24,* 449–461.

Feshbach, S. (1970), Aggression. In P. H. Mussen (Ed.), *Carmichael's manual of child psychology (Vol. 2).* New York: Wiley.

Field, T., Greenwald, P., Morrow, C., Healy, B., Foster, T., Guthertz, M., & Frost, P. (1992). Behavior state matching during interactions of preadolescent friends versus acquaintances. *Developmental Psychology, 28,* 242–250.

Field, T. M. (1995). Infants of depressed mothers. *Infant Behavior and Development, 18,* 1–13.

Field, T. M., Woodson, R., Greenberg, R., & Cohen, D. (1982). Discrimination and imitation of facial expressions by neonates. *Science, 218,* 179–181.

Fields, J. (2003). Children's living arrangements and characteristics: March, 2002. *Current Population Reports, P20-S47.* Washington, DC: U.S. Census Bureau. Available at http//www.census.gov/prod/2003pubs/P20-S47.pdf.

Figlio, D. N. (2007). Commentary on Porter and Polikoff. In Porter, A.C., and Polikoff, M.S. (2007). *Social Policy Report, 21.* Society for Research in Child Development.

Fincham, F. D., Hokoda, A., & Sanders, R., Jr. (1989). Learned helplessness, text anxiety, and academic achievement: A longitudinal analysis. *Child Development, 60,* 138–145.

Findley, M. J., & Cooper, H. M. (1983). Locus of control and academic achievement: A literature review. *Journal of Personality and Social Psychology, 44,* 419–427.

Finkelhor, D., & Dziuba-Leatherman, J. (1994). Victimization of children. *American Psychologist, 49,* 173–183.

Finkelstein, N. W., & Ramey, C. T (1977). Learning to control the environment in infancy. *Child Development, 48,* 806–819.

Finn, J. D. (2002). Class size reductions in grades K–3. In A. Molnar (Ed.). *School reform proposals: The research evidence* (pp. 27–48). Greenwich, CT: Information Age Publishing.

Fischer, K. W., & Bidell, T. (1998). Dynamic development of psychological structures in action and thought. In R. M. Lerner (Ed.), *Theoretical models of human development,* Vol. 1 of W. Damon (Gen. Ed.), *Handbook of child psychology* (pp. 467–561). New York: Wiley.

Fisher, L., Ames, E. W., Chisholm, K., & Savoie, L. (1997). Problems reported by parents of Romanian orphans adopted to British Columbia. *International Journal of Behavioral Development, 20,* 67–82.

Fitch, S. A., & Adams, G. R. (1983). Ego identity and intimacy status: Replication and extension. *Developmental Psychology, 19,* 839–845.

Flaks, D. K., Ficher, I., Masterpasqua, F., & Joseph, G. (1995). Lesbians choosing motherhood: A comparative study of lesbian and heterosexual parents and their children. *Developmental Psychology, 31,* 105–114.

Flanagan, C. A., & Eccles, J. S., (1993). Changes in parents' work status and adolescents' adjustment to school. *Child Development, 64,* 246–257.

Flannery, D. J., Vazsonyi, A. T., Liau, A. K., Guo, S., Powell, K. E., Atha, H., Vesterdal, W., & Embry, D. (2003). Initial behavior outcomes for the Peace Builders Universal School-Based Violence Prevention Program. *Developmental Psychology, 39,* 292–308.

Flavell, J. H. (1963). *The Developmental Psychology of Jean Piaget.* New York: Van Nostrand Reingold.

Flavell, J. H. (1996). Piaget's legacy. *Psychological Science, 7,* 200–203.

Flavell, J. H., Miller, P. H., & Miller, S. A. (1993). *Cognitive development* (3rd ed.). Englewood Cliffs, NJ: Prentice Hall.

Fletcher, A. C., Darling, N. E., Steinberg, L., & Dornbusch, S. M. (1995). The company they keep: Relation of adolescents' adjustment and behavior to their friends' perceptions of authoritative parenting in the social network. *Developmental Psychology, 31,* 300–310.

Flom, R., & Bahrick, L. E. (2007). The development of infant discrimination of affect in multimodal and unimodal stimulation: The role of intersensory redundancy. *Developmental Psychology, 43,* 238–252.

Flook, L., Repetti, R. L., & Ullman, J. B. (2005). Classroom social experiences as predictors of academic experience. *Developmental Psychology, 41,* 319–327.

Flouri, E., & Buchanan, A. (2003). What predicts fathers' involvement with their children? A prospective study of intact families. *British Journal of Developmental Psychology, 21,* 81–97.

Fogel, A. (1995). Relational narratives of the prelinguistic self. In P. Rochat (Ed.), *The self in infancy: Theory & research* (pp. 117–139). Amsterdam: North Holland-Elsevier.

Fogel, A., Hsu, H. C., Shapiro, A. F., Nelson-Goens, G., & Secrist, C. (2006). Effects of normal and perturbed social play on the duration and amplitude of different types of infant smiles. *Developmental Psychology, 42,* 459–473.

Foley, D. L., Eaves, L. J., Wormley, B., Silberg, J., Maes, H., & Kuhn, J. (2004). Childhood adversity, monoamine oxidase A genotype, and risk for conduct disorder. *Archives of General Psychology, 61,* 738–744.

Fonagy, P., Steele, H., & Steele, M. (1991). Maternal representations of attachment during pregnancy predict the organization of infant-mother attachment at one year of age. *Child Development, 62,* 891–905.

Fonzi, A., Schneider, B. H., Tani, F., & Tomada, G. (1997). Predicting children's friendship status from their dyadic interaction in structured situations of potential conflict. *Child Development, 68,* 496–506.

Forbes, L. M., Evans, E. M., Moran, G., & Pederson, D. R. (2007). Change in atypical maternal behavior predicts change in attachment disorganization from 12 to 24 months in a high risk sample. *Child Development, 78,* 955–971.

Ford, C. S., & Beach, F. A. (1951). *Patterns of sexual behavior.* New York: Harper.

Ford, D. Y., & Harris, J. J., III (1996). Perceptions and attitudes of black students toward school, achievement, and other educational variables. *Child Development, 67,* 1141–1152.

Fordham, S., & Ogbu, J. (1986). Black students' school success: Coping with the "burden of 'acting white.'" *Urban Review, 18,* 176–206.

Forgatch, M. S., & DeGarmo, D. S. (1999). Parenting through change: An effective prevention program for single mothers. *Journal of Consulting and Clinical Psychology, 67,* 711–724.

Forman, D. R., & Kochanska, G. (2001). Viewing imitation as child responsiveness: A link between teaching and discipline domains of socialization. *Developmental Psychology, 37,* 198–206.

Forrest, J. D., & Singh, S. (1990). The sexual and reproductive behavior of American women, 1982–1988. *Family Planning Perspectives, 22,* 206–214.

Fox, N. A. (2007). Commentary. In J. Kagan, N. Snidman, V. Kahn, & S. Towsley. The preservation of two infant temperaments into adolescence. *Monographs of the Society for Research in Child Development, 72* (pp. 81–91). Serial No. 287.

Fox, N. A., Bell, M. A., & Jones, N. A. (1992). Individual differences in response to stress and cerebral asymmetry. *Developmental Neuropsychology, 8,* 161–184.

Fox, N. A., & Fitzgerald, H. E. (1990). Autonomic functioning in infancy. *Merrill-Palmer Quarterly, 36,* 27–51.

Fox, N. A., Kimmerly, N. L., & Schafer, W. D. (1991). Attachment to mother/attachment to father: A meta-analysis. *Child Development, 62,* 210–225.

Fraiberg, A. (2004). Electronic fans, interpretive flames: Performative sexualities and the Internet.

Fraley, R. C., & Spieker, S. J. (2003). Are infant attachment patterns continuously or categorically distributed? A taxometric analysis of Strange Situation behavior. *Developmental Psychology, 39,* 387–404.

Frankel, K. A., & Bates, J. E. (1990). Mother-toddler problem-solving: Antecedents in attachment, home behavior, and temperament. *Child Development, 61,* 810–819. http://www.usyd.edu.au/social/papers/fraiberg.html.

Franklin, K. M., Janoff-Bulman, R., & Roberts, J. E. (1990). Long-term impact of parental divorce on optimism and trust: Changes in general assumptions or narrow beliefs? *Journal of Personality and Social Personality, 59,* 743–755.

Frazier, J. A., & Morrison, F. J. (1998). The influence of extended-year schooling on the growth of achievement and perceived competence in early elementary school. *Child Development, 69,* 495–517.

Fredricks, J. A., & Eccles, J. S (2002). Children's competence and value beliefs from childhood through adolescence: Growth trajectories in two male sex-typed domains. *Developmental Psychology, 38,* 519–533.

Fredricks, J. A., & Eccles, J. S. (2006). Is extracurricular participation associated with beneficial outcomes? Concurrent and longitudinal relations. *Developmental Psychology, 42,* 698–713.

Freedman, J. L. (1984). Effect of television violence on aggressiveness. *Psychological Bulletin, 96,* 227–246.

French, D. C. (1988). Heterogenity of peer-rejected boys: Aggressive and nonaggressive subtypes. *Child Development, 59,* 976–985.

French, D. C., Jansen, E. A., & Pidada, S. (2002). United States and Indonesian children's and adolescents' reports of relational aggression by disliked peers. *Child Development, 73,* 1143–1150.

French, S. E., Seidman, E., Allen, L., & Aber, J. L. (2006). The development of ethnic identity during adolescence. *Developmental Psychology, 42,* 1–10.

Freud, A., & Dann, S. (1951). An experiment in group upbringing. In R. Eisler, A. Freud, H. Hartmann, & E. Kris (Eds.), *The psychoanalytic study of the child* (Vol. 6). New York: International Universities Press.

Freud, S. (1930). *Three contributions to the theory of sex.* New York: Nervous and Mental Disease Publishing Co. (Original work published 1905).

Freud, S. (1933). *New introductory lectures in psychoanalysis.* New York: Norton.

Freud, S. (1960). *A general introduction to psychoanalysis.* New York: Washington Square Press (Original work published 1935).

Freud, S. (1961). Some physical consequences of the anatomical distinction between the sexes. In J. Strachey (Ed.), *The standard edition of the complete psychological works of Sigmund Freud* (Vol. 19). London: Hogarth Press. (Original work published 1924).

Freud, S. (1964). An outline of psychoanalysis. In J. Strachey (Ed. & Trans). *The standard edition of the complete psychological works of Sigmund Freud* (Vol. 23). London: Hogarth Press. (Original work published 1940).

Frey, K. S., Hirschstein, M. K., Snell, J. L., Edstrom, L. V. S., MacKenzie, E. P., & Broderick, C. J. (2005). Reducing playground bullying and supporting beliefs: An experimental trial of the *Steps to Respect* program. *Developmental Psychology, 42,* 479–491.

Frey, K. S., & Ruble, D. N. (1985). What children say when the teacher is not around: Conflicting goals in social comparison and performance assessment in the classroom. *Journal of Personality and Social Psychology, 48,* 550–562.

Frey, K. S., & Ruble, D. N. (1992). Gender constancy and the cost of sex-typed behavior: A test of the conflict hypothesis. *Developmental Psychology, 28,* 714–721.

Frick, P. J., Cornell, A. H., Bodin, S. D., Dane, H. E., Barry, C. T., & Loney, B. R. (2003). Callous-unemotional traits and developmental pathways to severe conduct disorders. *Developmental Psychology, 39,* 246–260.

Friedrich, L. K., & Stein, A. H. (1973). Aggressive and prosocial television programs and the natural behavior of preschool children. *Monographs of the Society for Research in Child Development, 38* (4, Serial No. 51).

Friedrich, L. K., & Stein, A. H. (1975). Prosocial television and young children: The effects of verbal labeling and role-playing on learning and behavior. *Child Development, 46,* 27–38.

Friedrich-Cofer, L. K., Huston-Stein, A., Kipnis, D. M., Susman, E. J., & Clewett, A. S. (1979). Environmental enhancement of prosocial television content: Effects on interpersonal behavior. *Developmental Psychology, 15,* 637–646.

Frome, P. M., & Eccles, J. S. (1998). Parents' influence on children's achievement-related perceptions. *Journal of Personality and Social Psychology, 74,* 435–452.

Frost, J. J., & Forrest, J. D. (1995). Understanding the impact of effective teenage pregnancy prevention programs. *Family Planning Perspectives, 27,* 188–195.

Fry, C. L. (1996). Age, aging, and culture. In R. H. Binstock & L. K. George (Eds.), *Handbook of aging and the social sciences* (4th ed.). San Diego. Academic.

Fu, G., Xu, F., Cameron, C. A., Heyman, G., & Lee, K. (2007). Cross-cultural differences in children's choices, categorizations, and evaluations of truths and lies. *Developmental Psychology, 43,* 278–293.

Fuchs, D., & Thelan, M. H. (1988). Children's expected interpersonal consequences of communicating their affective state and reported likelihood of expression. *Child Development, 59,* 1314–1322.

Fuhrman, T., & Holmbeck, G. N. (1995). A contextual-moderator analysis of emotional anatomy and adjustment in adolescence. *Child Development, 66,* 793–811.

Fuligni, A. J. (1997). The academic achievement of adolescents from immigrant families: The roles of family background, attitudes, and behavior. *Child Development, 68,* 351–363.

Fuligni, A. J. (1998). Authority, autonomy, and parent-adolescent conflict and cohesion: A study of adolescents from Mexican, Chinese, Filipino, and European backgrounds. *Developmental Psychology, 34,* 782–792.

Fuligni, A. J., Eccles, J. S., Barber, B. L., & Clements, P. (2001). Early adolescent peer orientation and adjustment during high school. *Developmental Psychology, 37,* 28–36.

Fuligni, A. J., & Stevenson, H. W. (1995). Time use and mathematics achievement among American, Chinese, and Japanese high school students. *Child Development, 66,* 830–842.

Fuligni, A. J., Tseng, V., & Lam, M. (1999). Attitudes toward family obligations among American adolescents with Asian, Latin American, and Euro American backgrounds. *Child Development, 70,* 1030–1044.

Fuligni, A. J., Witkow, M., & Garcia, C. (2005). Ethnic identity and the academic adjustment of adolescents from Mexican, Chinese, and European backgrounds. *Developmental Psychology, 41,* 799–811.

Fuligni, A. J., Yip, T., & Tseng, V. (2002). The impact of family obligation on the daily activities and psychological well-being of Chinese American adolescents. *Child Development, 73,* 302–314.

Fuligni, A. J., & Zhang, W. (2004). Attitudes toward family obligation among adolescents in urban and rural China. *Child Development, 74,* 180–192.

Fuller, B., Holloway, S. D., & Liang, X. (1996). Family selection of child-care centers: The influence of household support, ethnicity, and parental practices. *Child Development, 67,* 3320–3337.

Furman, W. (1999). Friends and lovers: The role of peer relationships in adolescent romantic relationships. In W. A. Collins & B. Laursen (Eds.), *Relationships as developmental contexts: The 30th Minnesota Symposia on Child Development* (pp. 133–154). Hillsdale, NJ: Erlbaum.

Furman, W., & Buhrmester, D. (1985). Children's perceptions of the qualities of sibling relationships. *Child Development, 56,* 448–461.

Furman, W., & Buhrmester, D. (1992). Age and sex differences in perceptions of networks of personal relationships. *Child Development, 63,* 103–115.

Furman, W., & Shaffer, L. (2003). The role of romantic relationships in adolescent development. In P. Florsheim (Ed.), *Adolescent romantic relations and sexual behavior: Theory, research, and practical implications.* Mahwah, NJ: Erlbaum.

Furman, W., Simon, V. A., Shaffer, L., & Bouchey, H. A. (2002). Adolescents' working models and styles for relationships with parents, friends, and romantic partners. *Child Development, 73,* 241–255.

Fyans, L. J., Jr., Salili, F., Maehr, M. L., & Desai, K. A. (1983). A cross-cultural exploration into the meaning of achievement. *Journal of Personality and Social Psychology, 44,* 1000–1013.

Galambos, N. L., Almeida, D. M., & Petersen, A. C. (1990). Masculinity, femininity, and sex role attitudes in early adolescence: Exploring gender intensification. *Child Development, 61,* 1905–1914.

Galambos, N. L., Barker, E. T., & Almeida, D. M. (2003). Parents do matter: Trajectories of change in externalizing and internalizing problems in early adolescence. *Child Development, 74,* 578–594.

Galambos, N. L., Barker, E. T., & Krahn, H. J. (2006). Depression, self-esteem, and anger in emerging adulthood: Seven-year trajectories. *Developmental Psychology, 42,* 350–365.

Galambos, N. L., & Maggs, J. L. (1991). Out-of-school care of young adolescents and self-reported behavior. *Developmental Psychology, 27,* 644–655.

Galen, B. R., & Underwood, M. K. (1997). A developmental investigation of social aggression among children. *Developmental Psychology, 33,* 589–600.

Gallagher, J. M., & Firth, C. D. (2003). Functional imaging of "theory of mind." *Trends in Cognitive Sciences, 7,* 77–83.

Gallup, G. G., Jr. (1979). Self-recognition in chimpanzees and man: A developmental and comparative perspective. In M. Lewis & L. A. Rosenblum (Eds.), *Genesis of behavior. Vol. 2: The child and its family.* New York: Plenum.

Galper, A., Wigfield, A., & Seefeldt, C. (1997). Head Start parents' beliefs about their children's abilities, task values, and performances on different activities. *Child Development, 68,* 897–907.

Garbarino, J. (1992). *Children and families in the social environment* (2nd ed.). New York: Aldine de Gruyter.

Garbarino, J. (1995). Growing up in a socially toxic environment: Life for children and families in the 1990s. In G. B. Melton (Ed.), *Nebraska Symposium on Motivation*: Vol. 42. *The individual, the family, and the social good: Personal fulfillment in times of change* (pp. 1–20). Lincoln, NE: University of Nebraska Press.

Garbarino, J., & Kostelny, K. (1992). Child maltreatment as a community problem. *Child Abuse & Neglect, 16,* 455–464.

Garcia, E. E. (1993). Language, culture, and education. *Review of Educational Research, 19,* 51–98.

Garcia, M. M., Shaw, D. S., Winslow, E. B., & Yaggi, K. E. (2000). Destructive sibling conflict and the development of conduct problems in young boys. *Developmental Psychology, 36,* 44–53.

Gardner, M., & Steinberg, L. (2005). Peer influence on risk taking, risk preference, and risky decision making in adolescence and adulthood: An experimental study. *Developmental Psychology, 41,* 625–635.

Garner, P. W., Jones, D. C., & Palmer, D. J. (1994). Social-cognitive correlates of preschool children's sibling caregiving behavior. *Developmental Psychology, 30,* 905–911.

Garner, P. W., & Power, T. G. (1996). Preschoolers' emotional control in the disappointment paradigm and its relation to temperament, emotional knowledge, and family expressiveness. *Child Development, 67,* 1406–1419.

Gauze, C., Bukowski, W. M., Aquan-Assee, J., & Sippola, L. K. (1996). Interactions between family environment and friendship and associations with well-being during early adolescence. *Child Development, 67,* 2201–2216.

Gavin, L. N., & Furman, W. (1996). Adolescent girls' relationships with mothers and best friends. *Child Development, 67,* 375–386.

Gazelle, H. (2006). Class climate moderates peer relations and emotional adjustment in children with an early history of anxious solitude: A child × environment model. *Developmental Psychology, 42,* 1179–1192.

Gazelle, H., & Ladd, G. W. (2003). Anxious solitude and peer exclusion: A diathesis-stress model of internalizing trajectories in childhood. *Child Development, 74,* 247–258.

Gazelle, H., Putallaz, M., Li, Y., Grimes, C. L., Kupersmidt, J. B., & Coie, J. D. (2005). Anxious solitude across contexts: Girls' interactions with familiar and unfamiliar peers. *Child Development, 76,* 227–246.

Ge, X., Best, K. M., Conger, R. D., & Simons, R. L. (1996). Parenting behaviors and the occurrence and co-occurrence of adolescent depressive symptoms and conduct problems. *Developmental Psychology, 32,* 717–731.

Ge, X., Brody, G. H., Conger, R. D., Simons, R. L., & Murry, V. M. (2002). Contextual amplification of pubertal transition effects on deviant peer affiliation and externalizing behavior among African American children. *Developmental Psychology, 38,* 42–54.

Ge, X., Conger, R. D., & Elder, G. H., Jr. (1996). Coming of age too early: Pubertal influences on girls' vulnerability to psychological distress. *Child Development, 67,* 3386–3400.

Geary, D. C. (1999). Evolution and developmental sex differences. *Current Directions in Psychological Science, 8,* 115–120.

Geary, D. C. (2005). *The origin of mind: Evolution of the brain, cognition, and general intelligence.* Washington, DC: American Psychological Association.

Geary, D. C. (2002). Sexual selection and human life history. In R. V. Kail (Ed.), *Advances in child development and behavior* (Vol. 30, pp. 41–102). San Diego, CA: Academic Press.

Geary, D. C., & Bjorklund, D. F. (2000). Evolutionary developmental psychology. *Developmental Psychology, 71,* 57–65.

Geary, D. C., Bow-Thomas, C. C., Liu, F., & Siegler, R. S. (1996). Development of arithmetical competencies in Chinese and American children: Influence of age, language, and schooling. *Child Development, 67,* 2022–2044.

Geen, R. G. (1998). Aggression and antisocial behavior. In D. T. Gilbert, S. T. Fiske, & G. Lindsey (Eds.). *Handbook of Social Psychology* (Vol. 2, pp. 317–356). New York: McGraw-Hill.

George, T. P., & Hartmann, D. P. (1996). Friendship networks of unpopular, average, and popular children. *Child Development, 67,* 2301–2316.

Georgiades, K., Boyle, M. H., & Duku, E. (2007). Contextual influences on children's mental health and school performance: The moderating effects of family immigrant status. *Child Development, 78,* 1572–1591.

Gerard, J. M., & Buehler, C. (2004). Cumulative environmental risk and youth maladjustment: The role of youth attributes. *Child Development, 75,* 1832–1849.

Gergely, G., Bekkering, H., & Kiraly, I. (2002). Rational imitation in preverbal infants. *Nature, 415,* 755.

Gershkoff-Stowe, L., & Smith, L. B (1997). A curvilinear trend in naming errors as a function of early vocabulary growth. *Cognitive Psychology, 34,* 37–71.

Gershoff, E. T., Aber, J. L., Raver, C. C., & Lennon, M. C. (2007). Income is not enough: Incorporating material hardship into models of income associated with parenting and child development. *Child Development, 78,* 70–95.

Gesell, A. (1933). Maturation and the patterning of behavior. In C. Murchison (Ed.), *A handbook of child psychology.* Worcester, MA: Clark University Press.

Gewirtz, J. L., & Pelaez-Nogueras, M. (1992). Skinner, B. F.: Legacy to human infant behavior and development. *American Psychologist, 47,* 1411–1422.

Gewirtz, J. L., & Petrovich, S. B. (1982). Early social and attachment learning in the frame of organic and cultural evolution. In T. M. Field, A. Huston, H. C. Quav, L. Troll, & G. E. Finley (Eds.), *Review of human development.* New York: Wiley.

Giampaoli, S. (2000). Epidemiology of major age-related diseases in women compared to men. *Aging, 12,* 93–105.

Gifford-Smith, M. E., & Rabiner, D. L. (2004). Social information processing and children's social adjustment. In J. Kupersmidt & K. A. Dodge (Eds.), *Children's peer relations: From development to intervention* (pp. 69–84). Washington, DC: American Psychological Association.

Gil, D. G. (1970). *Violence against children.* Cambridge, MA: Harvard University Press.

Gilbert, P. (1994). Male violence: Towards an integration. In J. Archer (Ed.), *Male violence* (pp. 352–389). New York: Routledge.

Giles, J. W., & Heyman, G. D. (2005). Young children's beliefs about the relationship between gender and aggressive behavior. *Child Development, 76,* 107–121.

Gilligan, C. (1977). In a different voice: Women's conceptions of self and morality. *Harvard Educational Review, 47,* 481–517.

Gilligan, C. (1982). *In a different voice: Psychological theory and women's development.* Cambridge, MA: Harvard University Press.

Gilligan, C. (1993). Adolescent development reconsidered. In A. Garrod (Ed.), *Approaches to moral development: New research and emerging themes.* New York: Teachers College Press.

Gilliom, M., Shaw, D. S., Beck, J. E., Schonberg, M. A., & Lukon, J. L. (2002). Anger regulation in disadvantaged preschool boys: Strategies, antecedents, and the development of self-control. *Developmental Psychology, 38*, 222–235.

Ginsburg, G. S., & Bronstein, P. (1993). Family factors related to children's intrinsic/extrinsic motivational orientation and academic performance. *Child Development, 64*, 1461–1474.

Glasgow, K. L., Dornbusch, S. M., Troyer, L., Steinberg, L., & Ritter, P. L. (1997). Parenting style, adolescents' attributions, and educational outcomes in nine heterogeneous high schools. *Child Development, 68*, 507–529.

Glass, G. V. (2002). Grouping students for instruction. In A. Molnar (Ed.), *School reform proposals: The research evidence* (pp. 95–112). Greenwich, CT: Information Age Publishing.

Gleason, T. R. (2002). Social provisions of real and imaginary relationships in early childhood. *Developmental Psychology, 38*, 979–992.

Gleason, T. R., Sebanc, A. M, & Hartup, W. W. (2000). Imaginary companions of preschool children. *Developmental Psychology, 36*, 419–428.

Gnepp, J. (1989). Personalized inferences of emotions and appraisals: Component processes and correlates. *Developmental Psychology, 25*, 277–288.

Gnepp, J., & Klayman, J. (1992). Recognition of uncertainty in emotional inferences: Reasoning about emotionally equivocal situations. *Developmental Psychology, 28*, 145–158.

Goencue, A., Mistry, J., & Mosier, C. (2000). Cultural variations in the play of toddlers. *International Journal of Behavioral Development, 24*, 321–329.

Goldberg, P. (1968). Are women prejudiced against women? *Trans/Action, 5*, 28–30.

Goldfarb, W. (1943). The effects of early institutional care on adolescent personality. *Journal of Experimental Education, 12*, 107–129.

Goldfarb, W. (1947). Variations in adolescent adjustment in institutionally reared children. *Journal of Orthopsychiatry, 17*, 449–457.

Golden, O. (2000). The federal response to child abuse and neglect. *American Psychologist, 55*, 1050–1053.

Goldsmith, H. H., & Alansky, J. A. (1987). Maternal and infant temperamental predictors of attachment: A meta-analytic review. *Journal of Consulting and Clinical Psychology, 55*, 805–816.

Goldsmith, H. H., Buss, K. A., & Lemery, K. S. (1997). Toddler and childhood temperament: Expanded content, stronger genetic evidence, new evidence for the importance of environment. *Developmental Psychology, 33*, 891–905.

Goldsmith, H. H., Lemery, K. S., Buss, K. A., & Campos, J. J. (1999). Genetic analysis of focal aspects of infant temperament. *Developmental Psychology, 35*, 972–985.

Goldstein, S. E., Davis-Kean, P. E., & Eccles, J. S. (2005). Peers, parents, and problem behavior: A longitudinal investigation of the impact of relationship perceptions and characteristics on the development of adolescent problem behavior. *Developmental Psychology, 41*, 401–413.

Goldwater, O. D., & Nutt, R. L. (1999). Teachers' and students' work-culture variables associated with positive school outcome. *Adolescence, 34*, 653–664.

Golombok, S., MacCallum, F., Goodman, E., & Rutter, M. (2002). Families with children conceived by donor insemination: A follow-up at age twelve. *Child Development, 73*, 952–968.

Golombok, S., Perry, B., Burston, A., Murray, C., Mooney-Somers, J., Stevens, M., & Golding, J. (2003). Children with lesbian parents: A community study. *Developmental Psychology, 39*, 20–33.

Golombok, S., & Tasker, F. (1996). Do parents influence the sexual orientation of their children? Findings from a longitudinal study of lesbian families. *Developmental Psychology, 32*, 3–11.

Gondoli, D. M., & Silverberg, S. B. (1997). Maternal emotional distress and diminished responsiveness: The mediating role of parenting efficacy and parental perspective taking. *Developmental Psychology, 33*, 861–868.

Gonzalez, E. (2000, February 27). Education reform bill draws mixed reactions. *Athens Daily News*, pp. C1, C6.

Good, C., Aronson, J., & Inzlicht, M. (2003). Improving adolescents' standardized test performance: An intervention to reduce the effects of stereotype threat. *Journal of Applied Developmental Psychology, 24*, 645–662.

Good, T. L., & Brophy, J. E. (1994). *Looking in classrooms.* (6th ed.), New York: Harper Collins.

Goodenough, F. L. (1931). *Anger in young children.* Minneapolis: University of Minnesota Press.

Goodwin, M. H. (2002). Exclusion in children's peer groups: Ethnographic analysis of language practices on the playground. *Human Development, 45*, 392–415.

Goossens, F. A., & van IJzendoorn, M. H. (1990). Quality of infants' attachments to professional caregivers: Relation to infant-parent attachment and day-care characteristics. *Child Development, 61*, 832–837.

Gorden, C. (1968). Self-conceptions: Configurations of content. In C. Gorden & K. J. Gergen (Eds.), *The self in social interaction.* New York: Wiley.

Gordon, R. A., Lahey, B. B., Kawai, E., Loeber, R., Stouthamer-Loeber, M., & Farrington, D. P. (2004) Antisocial behavior and gang membership: Selection and socialization. *Criminology, 42*, 55–87.

Gorer, G. (1968). Man has no "killer" instinct. In M. F. A. Montague (Ed.), *Man and aggression.* New York: Oxford University Press.

Gormley, W., & Gayer, T. (2005). Promoting school readiness in Oklahoma: Research highlights and policy implications. *Journal of Human Resources, 40*, 533–558.

Gormley, W. T., Jr., Gayer, T., Phillips, D., & Dawson, B. (2005). The effects of universal pre-K on cognitive development. *Developmental Psychology, 41*, 872–884.

Gorn, G. J., Goldberg, M. E., & Kanungo, R. N. (1976). The role of educational television in changing the intergroup attitudes of children. *Child Development, 47*, 277–280.

Gortmaker, S. L., Must, A., Sobol, A. M., Peterson, K., Colditz, G. A., & Dietz, W. H. (1996). Television viewing as a cause of increasing obesity among children in the Unites States, 1986–1990. *Archives of Pediatrics and Adolescent Medicine, 150*, 356–362.

Gottesman, I. I., & Shields, J. (1982). *Schizophrenia: The epigenetic puzzle.* Cambridge, England: Cambridge University Press.

Gottfried, A. E., Fleming, J. S., & Gottfried, A. W. (1998). Role of cognitively stimulating home environment in children's academic intrinsic motivation: A longitudinal study. *Child Development, 69*, 1448–1460.

Gottfried, A. E., Gottfried, A. W., & Bathurst, K. (2002). Maternal and dual-earner employment status and parenting. In M. H. Bornstein (Ed.), *Handbook of parenting* (2nd ed, Vol. 2): *Biology and ecology of parenting* (pp. 207–229). Mahwah, NJ: Erlbaum.

Gottlieb, D. (1966). Teaching and students: The views of Negro and white teachers. *Sociology of Education, 37,* 344–353.

Gottlieb, G. (1991). Experimental canalization of behavioral development: Results. *Developmental Psychology, 27,* 35–39.

Gottlieb, G. (1996). Commentary: A systems view of psychobiological development. In D. Magnusson (Ed.), *The lifespan development of individuals: Behavioral, neurobiological, and psychosocial perspectives: A synthesis.* Cambridge, England: Cambridge University Press.

Gottlieb, G. (2003). Normally occurring environmental and behavioral influences on gene activity. In C. Garcia Coll, E. Bearer, & R. M. Lerner (Eds.), *Nature and nurture: The complex interplay of genetic and environmental influences on human behavior and development.* Mahwah, N. J. Lawrence Erlbaum Associates.

Gottman, J. M. (1983). How children become friends. *Monographs of the Society for Research in Child Development, 48* (3, Serial No. 201).

Gould, S. J. (1978). Sociobiology: The art of story telling. *New Scientist, 80,* 530–533.

Graham, S., & Juvonen, J. (1998). Self-blame and peer victimization in middle school: An attributional analysis. *Developmental Psychology, 34,* 587–599.

Graham, S., & Juvonen, J. (2001). An attributional approach to peer victimization. In J. Juvonen & S. Graham (Eds.), *Peer harassment in school: The plight of the vulnerable and victimized* (pp. 332–351). New York: Guilford Press.

Grandin, T. (1996). *Thinking in pictures: And other reports from my life with autism.* New York: Vintage.

Graves, S. B. (1975, April). *How to encourage positive racial attitudes.* Paper presented at the biennial meeting of the Society for Research in Child Development, Denver.

Graves, S. B. (1993). Television, the portrayal of African Americans, and the development of children's attitudes. In G. L. Berry & J. K. Asamen (Eds.), *Children and television: Images in a changing sociocultural world* (pp. 179–190). Newbury Park, CA: Sage.

Gray, M. R., & Steinberg, L. (1999). Adolescent romance and the parent-child relationship. In W. Furman, B. B. Brown, & C. Feiring (Eds.), *The Development of romantic relationships in adolescence.* Cambridge, England: Cambridge University Press.

Gray, N. J., Klein, J. D., Noyce, P. R., Sesselberg, T. S., & Cantrill, J. A. (2005). Health information-seeking behavior in adolescence: The place of the Internet. *Social Science and Medicine, 60,* 1467–1478.

Gray, W. M., & Hudson, L. M. (1984). Formal operations and the imaginary audience. *Developmental Psychology, 20,* 619–627.

Gray-Little, B., & Hafdahl, A. R. (2000). Factors influencing racial comparisons of self-esteem: A quantitative review. *Psychological Bulletin, 126,* 26–54.

Green, J., & Goldwyn, R. (2002). Attachment disorganization and psychopathology: New findings in attachment research and their potential implications for developmental psychopathology in childhood. *Journal of Child Psychology and Psychiatry and Allied Disciplines, 43,* 835–846.

Green, M. (1987). *Theories of human development: A comparative approach.* Englewood Cliffs, NJ: Prentice Hall.

Green, R. (1987). *The "sissy boy syndrome" and the development of homosexuality.* New Haven, CT: Yale University Press.

Greenberg, G. (2005). The limitations of behavior-genetic analyses: Comment on McGue, Elkins, Walden, and Iacono (2005). *Developmental Psychology, 41,* 989–992.

Greenberg, M. T., Lengua, L. J., Coie, J. D., & Pinderhughes, E. E., and the Conduct Problems Prevention Research Group (1999). Predicting developmental outcomes at school entry using a multiple-risk model: Four American communities. *Developmental Psychology, 35,* 403–417.

Greenberger, A., & Chen, C. (1996). Perceived family relationships and depressed mood in early and late adolescence: A comparison of European and Asian Americans. *Developmental Psychology, 32,* 707–716.

Greenberger, E., O'Neil, R., & Nagel, S. K. (1994). Linking workplace and homeplace: Relations between the nature of adult work and their parenting behavior. *Developmental Psychology, 30,* 990–1002.

Greenfield, P. M. (2004). Inadvertent exposure to pornography on the Internet: Implications of peer-to-peer file-sharing networks for child development and families. *Journal of Applied Developmental Psychology, 25,* 741–750.

Grieser, D. L., & Kuhl, P. K. (1988). Maternal speech to infants in a tonal language: Support for the universal prosodic features in motherese. *Child Development, 59,* 14–20.

Grolnick, W. S., Bridges, L. J., & Connell, J. P. (1996). Emotion regulation in two-year-olds: Strategies and emotional expression in four contexts. *Child Development, 67,* 928–941.

Grolnick, W. S., Gurland, S. T., DeCourcey, W., & Jacob, K. (2002). Antecedents and consequences of mothers' autonomy support: An experimental investigation. *Developmental Psychology, 38,* 143–155.

Gross, E. F. (2004). Adolescent Internet use: What we expect, what teens report. *Journal of Applied Developmental Psychology, 25,* 633–649.

Grossman, F. K., Eichler, L. S., Winickoff, S. A., & Associates (1980). *Pregnancy, birth, and parenthood: Adaptations of mothers, fathers, and infants.* San Francisco: Jossey-Bass.

Grossmann, K., Grossmann, K. E., Spangler, S., Suess, G., & Unzner, L. (1985). Maternal sensitivity and newborn responses as related to quality of attachment in Northern Germany. In I. Bretherton & E. Waters, Growing points of attachment theory. *Monographs of the Society for Research in Child Development, 50,* (1–2, Serial No. 209).

Grotevant, H. D., & Cooper, C. R. (1998). Individuality and connectedness in adolescent development. In E. Skoe & A. vonder Lippe (Eds.), *Personality development in adolescence: A cross-national and life span perspective.* London: Routledge.

Grusec, J. E. (1991). Socializing concern for others in the home. *Developmental Psychology, 27,* 338–342.

Grusec, J. E. (1992). Social learning theory and developmental psychology: The legacies of Robert Sears and Albert Bandura. *Developmental Psychology, 28,* 776–786.

Grusec, J. E., & Goodnow, J. J. (1994). Impact of parental discipline methods on the child's internalization of values: A reconceptualization of current points of view. *Developmental Psychology, 30,* 4–19.

Grusec, J. E., Goodnow, J. J., & Cohen, L. (1996). Household work and the development of concern for others. *Developmental Psychology, 32,* 999–1007.

Grusec, J. E., Goodnow, J. J., & Kuczynski, L. (2000). New directions in analyses of parenting contributions to children's acquisition of values. *Child Development, 71,* 205–211.

Grusec, J. E., Kuczynski, L., Rushton, J. P., & Simutis, Z. (1979). Learning resistance to temptation through observation. *Developmental Psychology, 15,* 233–240.

Grusec, J. E., & Redler, E. (1980). Attribution, reinforcement, and altruism: A developmental analysis. *Developmental Psychology, 16,* 525–534.

Grych, J. H., & Clark, R. (1999). Maternal employment and development of the father-infant relationship in the first year. *Developmental Psychology, 35*, 893–903.

Grych, J. H., & Fincham, F. D. (1992). Interventions for children of divorce: Toward greater integration of research and action. *Psychological Bulletin, 111*, 434–454.

Grych, J. H., Fincham, F. D., Jouriles, E. N., & McDonald, R. (2000). Interparental conflict and child adjustment: Testing the mediational role of appraisals in the cognitive-contextual framework. *Child Development, 71*, 1648–1661.

Grych, J. H., Harold, G. T., & Miles, C. J. (2003). A prospective investigation of appraisals as mediators of the link between interparental conflict and child adjustment. *Child Development, 74*, 1176–1193.

Guerra, N. G., Husemann, L. R., & Spindler, A. (2003). Community violence exposure, social cognition, and aggression among urban elementary school children. *Child Development, 74*, 1561–1576.

Guerra, N. G., & Slaby, R. G. (1990). Cognitive mediators of aggression in adolescent offenders: 2. Intervention. *Developmental Psychology, 26*, 269–277.

Gunnar, M. R., Larson, M. C., Hertsgaard, L., Harris, M. L., & Brodersen, L. (1992). The stressfulness of separation among 9-month-old infants: Effects of social context variables and infant temperament. *Child Development, 63*, 290–303.

Guralnick, M. J., & Groom, J. M. (1988). Friendships of preschool children in mainstreamed playgroups. *Developmental Psychology, 24*, 595–604.

Guralnick, M. J., Hammond, M. A., Connor, R. T., & Neville, B. (2006). Stability, change, and correlates of the peer relationships of young children with mild developmental delays. *Child Development, 77*, 312–324.

Guralnick, M. J., Neville, B., Hammond, M. A., & Connor, R. T. (2002). Linkages between delayed children's social interactions with mothers and peers. *Child Development, 78*, 459–473.

Gurucharri, C., & Selman, R. L. (1982). The development of interpersonal understanding during childhood, preadolescence, and adolescence: A longitudinal follow-up study. *Child Development, 53*, 924–927.

Gutman, L. M., & Eccles, J. S. (2007). Stage-environmental fit during adolescence: Trajectories of family relations and adolescent outcomes. *Developmental Psychology, 43*, 522–537.

Gutman, L. M., Sameroff, A. J., & Eccles, J. S. (2002). The academic achievement of African American students during early adolescence: An examination of multiple risk, promotive, and protective factors. *American Journal of Community Psychology, 30*, 367–400.

Hala, S., & Chandler, M. (1996). The role of strategic planning in accessing false-belief understanding. *Child Development, 67*, 2948–2966.

Halgunseth, L. C., Ispa, J. M., & Ruby, D. (2006). Parental control in Latino families: An integrated review of the literature. *Child Develoment, 77*, 1282–1297.

Hall, E. (2001). Babies, books, and "impact": Problems and possibilities in the evaluation of a Bookstart project. *Educational Review, 53*, 57–64.

Hall, G. S. (1891). The contents of children's minds on entering school. *Pedagogical Seminary, 1*, 139–173.

Hall, G. S. (1904). *Adolescence*. New York: Appleton-Century-Crofts.

Halle, T. G., Kurtz-Costes, B., & Mahoney, J. L. (1997). Family influences on school achievement in low-income African American children. *Journal of Educational Psychology, 89*, 527–537.

Halpern, C. J. T., Udry, J. A., Suchindran, C., & Campbell, B. (2000). Adolescent males' willingness to report masturbation. *Journal of Sex Research, 37*, 327–332.

Halpern, D. F. (1997). Sex differences in intelligence: Implications for education. *American Psychologist, 52*, 1091–1102.

Halpern, D. F. (2004). A cognitive-process taxonomy for sex differences in cognitive abilities. *Current Directions in Psychological Science, 13*, 135–139.

Hamilton, C. E. (2000). Continuity and discontinuity of attachment from infancy through adolescence. *Child Development, 71*, 690–694.

Hamlin, J. K., Wynn, K., & Bloom, P. (2007). Social evaluation by preverbal infants. *Nature, 450*, 557–559.

Hamre, B. K., & Pianta, R. C. (2005). Can instructional and emotional support in the first-grade classroom make a difference for children at risk of school failure? *Child Development, 76*, 949–967.

Han, W-J. (2005). Maternal nonstandard work schedules and child cognitive outcomes. *Child Development, 76*, 137–154.

Haney, P., & Durlak, J. A. (1998). Changing self-esteem in children and adolescents: A meta-analytic review. *Journal of Clinical Child Psychology, 27*, 423–433.

Hankin, B. L., Abramson, L. Y., Moffitt, T. E., Silva, P. A., McGree, R., & Angell, K. E. (1998). Development of depression from preadolescense to young adulthood: Emerging gender differences in a 10-year longitudinal study. *Journal of Abnormal Psychology, 107*, 128–140.

Hankin, B. L., Mermelstein, R., & Roesch. L. (2007). Sex differences in adolescent depression: Stress exposure and reactivity models. *Child Development, 78*, 279–295.

Hanushek, E. A. (1997). Assessing the effects of school resources on student performance: An update. *Educational Evaluation and Policy Analysis, 19*, 141–164.

Hara, N., Bonk, C. J., & Angeli, C. (2001). Content analysis on online discussion in an applied educational psychology course. *Instructional Science, 28*, 115–152.

Harackiewicz, J. M. (1998). Intrinsic motivation and goals. In H. S. Friedman (Ed.), *Encyclopedia of mental health* (Vol. 2). San Diego: Academic Press.

Harden, K. P., Turkheimer, E., Emery, R. E., D'Onofrio, B. M., Slutske, W. S., Heath, A. C., & Martin, N. G. (2007). Martial conflict and conduct problems in children of twins. *Child Development, 78*, 1–18.

Hardway, C., & Fuligni, A. J. (2006). Dimensions of family connectedness among adolescents with Mexican, Chinese, and European backgrounds. *Developmental Psychology, 42*, 1246–1258.

Hardy, J. B., Astone, H. M., Brooks-Gunn, J., Shapiro, S., & Miller, T. L. (1998). Like mother, like child: Intergenerational patterns of age at first birth and associations with childhood and adolescent characteristics and outcomes in the second generation. *Developmental Psychology, 34*, 1220–1232.

Harkness, S., Edwards, C. P., & Super, C. M. (1981). Social roles and moral reasoning: A case study in a rural African community. *Developmental Psychology, 17*, 595–603.

Harlow, H. F., & Zimmerman, R. R. (1959). Affectional responses in the infant monkey. *Science, 130*, 421–432.

Harper, G. W., & Robinson, W. L. (1999). Pathways to risk among inner-city African American adolescent females: The influence of gang membership. *American Journal of Community Psychology, 27*, 383–404.

Harper, L. V., & Huie, K. S. (1985). The effects of prior group experience, age, and familiarity on the quality and organization of preschoolers' social relationships. *Child Development, 56*, 704–717.

Harris, J. R. (1995). Where is the child's environment? A group socialization theory of development. *Psychological Review, 102,* 458–489.

Harris, J. R. (1998). *The nurture assumption: Why children turn out the way they do.* New York: Free Press.

Harris, J. R. (2000). Socialization, personality development, and the child's environments: A comment on Vandell (2000). *Developmental Psychology, 36,* 711–723.

Harris, N. B. (1992). Sex, race, and the experience of aggression. *Aggressive Behavior, 18,* 201–217.

Harrison, L. F., & Williams, T. (1986). Television and cognitive development. In T. Williams (Ed.), *The impact of television: A natural experiment in three communities.* Orlando, FL: Academic.

Harrison, L. J., & Ungerer, J. A. (2002). Maternal employment and mother-infant attachment security at 12 months postpartum. *Development Psychology, 38,* 758–773.

Harrist, A. W., Zaia, A. F., Bates, J. E., Dodge, K. A., & Pettit, G. S. (1997). Subtypes of social withdrawal in early childhood: Sociometric status and social-cognitive differences across four years. *Child Development, 68,* 278–294.

Hart, C. H., Burts, D. C., Durland, M. A., Charlesworth, R., DeWolf, M., & Fleege, P.O. (1998). Stress behaviors and activity type participation of preschoolers in more or less developmentally appropriate classrooms: SES and sex differences. *Journal of Research in Childhood Education, 12,* 176–196.

Hart, C. H., Ladd, G. W., & Burleson, B. R. (1990). Children's expectations of the outcomes of social strategies: Relations with socioeconomic status and maternal disciplinary styles. *Child Development, 61,* 127–137.

Hart, C. H., Nelson, D., Robinson, C. C., Olsen, S. F., & McNeilly-Choque, M. K. (1998). Overt and relational aggression in Russian nursery-school-age children: Parenting style and marital linkages. *Developmental Psychology, 34,* 687–697.

Hart, C. H., Newell, L. D., & Olsen, S. F. (2003). Parenting skills and social-communicative competence in childhood. In J. D. Greene & B. R. Burleson (Eds.), *Handbook of Communication and Social Interaction Skills* (pp. 753–800). Mahwah, NJ: Erlbaum.

Hart, C. H., Olsen, S. F., Robinson, C. C., & Mandleco, B. L. (1997). The development of social and communicative competence in childhood: Review and a model of personal, familial, and extrafamilial processes. *Communication Yearbook, 20,* 305–373.

Hart, C. H., Yang, C., Nelson, L. J., et al., (2000). Peer acceptance in early childhood and subtypes of socially withdrawn behavior in China, Russia, and the United States. *International Journal of Behavioral Development, 24,* 73–81.

Hart, D., & Chmiel, S. (1992). Influence of defense mechanisms on moral judgment development: A longitudinal study. *Developmental Psychology, 28,* 722–730.

Hart, D., & Fegley, S. (1995). Prosocial behavior and caring in adolescence: Relations to self-understanding and social judgment. *Child Development, 66,* 1346–1359.

Hart, D., Hofmann, V., Edelstein, W., & Keller, M. (l997). The relation of childhood personality types to adolescent behavior and development: A longitudinal study of Icelandic children. *Developmental Psychology, 33,* 195–205.

Harter, S. (1981). A new self-report scale of intrinsic versus extrinsic orientation in the classroom: Motivational and informational components. *Developmental Psychology, 17,* 300–312.

Harter, S. (1982). The perceived competence scale for children. *Child Development, 53,* 87–97.

Harter, S. (1983). Developmental perspectives on the self-system. In P. H. Mussen (Ed.), *Handbook of child psychology. Vol. 4: Socialization, personality and social development.* New York: Wiley.

Harter, S. (1999). *The cognitive and social construction of the developing self.* New York: Guilford.

Harter, S. (2005). Self-concepts and self-esteem, children and adolescents. In C. B. Fisher & R. M. Lerner (Eds.), *Encyclopedia of applied developmental science* (Vol. 2, pp. 972–977). Thousand Oaks, CA: Sage.

Harter, S., Marold, D. B., Whitesell, N. R., & Cobbs, G. (1996). A model of the effects of perceived parent and peer support on adolescent false self-behavior. *Child Development, 67,* 360–374.

Harter, S., & Monsour, A. (1992). Developmental analysis of conflict caused by opposing attributes in the adolescent self-portrait. *Developmental Psychology, 28,* 251–260.

Harter, S., & Pike, R. (1984). The pictorial scale of perceived competence and social acceptance for young children. *Child Development, 55,* 1969–1982.

Harter, S., Waters, P., & Whitesell, N. R. (1998). Relational self-worth: Differences in perceived worth as a person across interpersonal contexts among adolescents. *Child Development, 69,* 756–766.

Harter, S., Waters, P. I., Whitesell, N. R., & Kastelic, D. (1998). Level of voice among female and male high school students: Relational context, support, and gender orientation. *Developmental Psychology, 34,* 892–901.

Harter, S., & Whitesell, N. (1989). Developmental changes in children's understanding of simple, multiple, and blended emotion concepts. In C. Saarni & P. Harris (Eds.), *Children's understanding of emotion.* Cambridge, England: Cambridge University Press.

Hartshorne, H., & May, M. S. (1928–1930). *Studies in the nature of character. Vol. 1: Studies in deceit.* Vol. 2: *Studies in self-control.* Vol. 3: *Studies in the organization of character.* New York: Macmillan.

Hartung, B., & Sweeney, K. (1991). Why adult children return home. *Social Science Journal, 28,* 467–480.

Hartup, W. W. (1974). Aggression in childhood: Developmental perspectives. *American Psychologist, 29,* 336–341.

Hartup, W. W. (1983). Peer relations. In P. H. Mussen (Ed.), *Handbook of child psychology. Vol. 4: Socialization, personality, and social development* (pp. 103–196). New York: Wiley.

Hartup, W. W. (1989). Social relationships and their developmental significance. *American Psychologist, 44,* 120–126.

Hartup, W. W. (1992). Friendships and their developmental significance. In H. McGurk (Ed.), *Childhood social development: Contemporary perspectives.* Hove, England: Erlbaum.

Hartup, W. W. (1996). The company they keep: Friendships and their developmental significance. *Child Development, 67,* 1–13.

Hartup, W. W., Laursen, B., Stewart, M. I., & Eastenson, A. (1988). Conflict and friendship relations of young children. *Child Development, 59,* 1590–1600.

Hartup, W. W., & Stevens, N. (1997). Friendships and adaptation in the life course. *Psychological Bulletin, 121,* 355–370.

Harvey, E. (1999). Short-term and long-term effects of early parental employment on children of the National Longitudinal Survey of Youth. *Developmental Psychology, 35,* 445–459.

Harwood, R. L., Schoelmerich, A., Ventura-Cook, E., Schulze, P. A., & Wilson, S. P. (1996). Culture and class influences on Anglo and Puerto Rican mothers' beliefs regarding long-term socialization goals and child behavior. *Child Development, 67,* 2446–2461.

Haselager, G. J. T., Cillessen, A. H. N., Van Lieshout, C. F. M., Riksen-Walraven, J. M. A., & Hartup, W. W. (2002). Heterogeneity among peer-rejected boys across middle childhood: Developmental pathways of social behavior. *Developmental Psychology, 38,* 446–456.

Haselager, G. J. T, Hartup, W. W., van Lieshout, C. F. M., & Riksen-Walraven, J. M. A. (1998). Similarities between friends and non-friends in middle childhood. *Child Development, 69,* 1198–1208.

Haskett, M. E., & Kistner, J. A. (1991). Social interactions and peer perceptions of young physically abused children. *Child Development, 62,* 979–990.

Hastings, P. D., Zahn-Waxler, C., & McShane, K. (2006). We are, by nature, moral creatures: Biological bases of concern for others. In M. Killen & J. Smetana (Eds.), *Handbook of moral development* (pp. 483–516). Hillside, NJ: Erlbaum.

Hastings, P. D., Zahn-Waxler, C. Z., Robinson, J., Usher, B., & Bridges, D. (2000). The development of concern for others in children with behavior problems. *Developmental Psychology, 36,* 531–546.

Hatzichristou, C., & Holf, D. (1996). A multiperspective comparison of peer sociometric status groups in childhood and adolescence. *Child Development, 67,* 1085–1102.

Hausen-Corn, P. (1995). Mastery motivation in toddlers with developmental disabilities. *Child Development, 66,* 236–248.

Haviland, J. M., & Lelwica, M. (1987). The induced affect response: 10-week-old infants' responses to three emotion expressions. *Developmental Psychology, 23,* 97–104.

Hawker, D. S. J., & Boulton, M. J. (2000). Twenty years' research on peer victimization and psychosocial maladjustment: A meta-analytic review of cross-sectional studies. *Journal of Child Psychology and Psychiatry and Allied Disciplines, 41,* 441–455.

Hay, D. F. (2005). The beginnings of aggression in infancy. In R. E. Tremblay, W. W. Hartup, & J. Archer (Eds.), *Developmental origins of aggression* (pp. 107–132). New York: Guilford Press.

Hay, D. F., Caplan, M., Castle, J., & Stimson, C. A. (1991). Does sharing become increasingly "rational" in the second year of life? *Developmental Psychology, 27,* 987–993.

Hay, D. F., Castle, J., & Davies, L. (2000). Toddlers' use of force against familiar peers: A precursor of serious aggression? *Child Development, 71,* 457–467.

Hayward, C., Killen, J. D, Wilson, D. M., Hammer, L. D., Litt, I. F., Kraemer, H. C., Haydel, F., Varady, M., & Taylor, C. B. (1997). Psychiatric risk associated with puberty in adolescent girls. *Journal of the American Academy of Child and Adolescent Psychiatry, 36,* 255–262.

Hearold, S. (1986). A synthesis of 1043 effects of television on social behavior. In G. Comstock (Ed.), *Public communications and behavior: Volume I* (pp. 65–133). New York: Academic Press.

Hebb, D. O. (1980). *Essay on mind.* Hillsdale, NJ: Erlbaum.

Heckhausen, J., & Dweck, C. S. (1999). *Motivation and self-regulation across the life-span.* New York: Cambridge University Press.

Heider, F. (1958). *The psychology of interpersonal relations.* New York: Wiley.

Heine, S. J., Lehman, D. R., Markus, H. R., & Kitayama, S. (1999). Is there a universal need for positive self-regard? *Psychological Review, 106,* 766–794.

Helwig, C. C., Arnold, M., Dingliang, T., & Boyd, D. (2003). Chinese adolescents' reasoning about democratic and authority-based decision making in peer, family, and school contexts. *Child Development, 74,* 783–800.

Helwig, C. C., Jasiobedzka, U. (2001). The relation between law and morality: Children's reasoning about socially beneficial and unjust laws. *Child Development, 72,* 1382–1393.

Helwig, C. C., & Kim S. (1999). Children's evaluations of decision-making procedures in peer, family, and school contexts. *Child Development, 70,* 502–512.

Henrich, C. C., Brown, J. L., & Aber, J. L. (1999). Evaluating the effectiveness of school-based violence prevention: Developmental approaches. *Society for Research in Child Development Social Policy Report, 13,* Number 3.

Henry, B., Caspi, A., Moffitt, T. E., & Silva, P. A. (1996). Temperamental and familial predictors of violent and nonviolent criminal convictions: Age 3 to age 18. *Developmental Psychology, 32,* 614–623.

Henry, D. B., Schoeny, M. E., Deptula, D. P., & Slavick, J. T. (2007). Peer selection and socialization effects on adolescent intercourse without a condom and attitudes about the costs of sex. *Child Development, 78,* 825–838.

Herdt, G. H., & Davidson, J. (1988). The Sambia "turnim-man": Sociocultural and clinical aspects of gender formation in male pseudohermaphrodites with 5-alpha-reductase deficiency in Papua New Guinea. *Archives of Sexual Behavior, 17,* 33–56.

Herdt, G., & McClintock, M. (2000). The magical age of 10. *Archives of Sexual Behavior, 29,* 587–606.

Herek, G. (2000). Homosexuality. In A. Kazdin (Ed.), *Encyclopedia of psychology.* Washington, DC, & New York: American Psychological Association and Oxford University Press.

Hernandez, D. J. (1997). Child development and the social demography of childhood. *Child Development, 68,* 149–169.

Hershberger, S. L., & D'Augelli, A. R. (1995). The impact of victimization on the mental health and suicidality of lesbian, gay, and bisexual youths. *Developmental Psychology, 31,* 65–74.

Hertzberger, S. D., & Hall, J. A. (1993). Consequences of retaliatory aggression against siblings and peers: Urban minority children's expectations. *Child Development, 64,* 1773–1785.

Hesse, E. (1999). The adult attachment interview: Historical and current perspectives. In J. Cassidy & P. R. Shaver (Eds.), *Handbook of attachment: Theory, research, and clinical applications* (pp. 395–493). New York: Guilford.

Hetherington, E. M. (1989). Coping with family transitions: Winners, losers, and survivors. *Child Development, 60,* 1–14.

Hetherington, E. M., Bridges, M., & Insabella, G. M. (1998). What matters? What does not? Five perspectives on the association between marital transitions and children's adjustment. *American Psychologist, 53,* 167–184.

Hetherington, E. M., & Camara, K. A. (1984). Families in transition: The processes of dissolution and reconstitution. In R. D. Parke (Ed.), *Review of child development research. Vol. 7: The family.* Chicago: University of Chicago Press.

Hetherington, E. M. & Clingempeel, W. G. (1992). Coping with marital transitions. *Monographs of the Society for Research in Child Development, 57,* (2–3, Serial No. 227).

Hetherington, E. M., Cox, M., & Cox, R. (1982). Effects of divorce on parents and children. In M. E. Lamb (Ed.), *Nontraditional families.* Hillsdale, NJ: Erlbaum.

Hetherington, E. M., & Frankie, G. (1967). Effect of parental dominance, warmth, and conflict on imitation in children. *Journal of Personality and Social Psychology, 6,* 119–125.

Hetherington, E. M., Henderson, S. H., & Reiss, D. (1999). Adolescent siblings in stepfamilies: Family functioning and adolescent adjustment. *Monographs of the Society for Research in Child Development, 64*, (4, Serial No. 259).

Hetherington, E. M., & Jodl, K. M. (1994). Stepfamilies as settings for child development. In A. Booth & J. Dunn (Eds.), *Stepfamilies: Who benefits? Who does not?* (pp. 55–79). Hillsdale, NJ: Erlbaum.

Hetherington, E. M., & Kelly, J. (2002). *For better or for worse: Divorce reconsidered.* New York: W. W. Norton.

Hetherington, E. M., & Parke, R. D. (1975). *Child psychology: A contemporary viewpoint.* New York: McGraw-Hill.

Hetherington, E. M., & Stanley-Hagan, M. S. (2000). Diversity among stepfamilies. In D. H. Demo, K. R. Allen, & M. A. Fine (Eds.), *Handbook of family diversity.* New York: Oxford University Press.

Hetherington, E. M., & Stanley-Hagan M. S. (2002). Parenting in divorced and remarried families. In M. Bornstein (Ed.), *Handbook of parenting.* Vol. 3 (2nd ed., pp. 233–255). Mahwah, NJ: Erlbaum.

Hewlett, B. S., Lamb, M. E., Shannon, D., Leyendecker, B., & Scholmerich, A. (1998). Culture and early infancy among central African foragers and farmers. *Developmental Psychology, 34,* 653–661.

Heyman, G. D., Gee, C. L., & Giles, J. W. (2003). Preschool children's reasoning about ability. *Child Development, 74,* 516–534.

Heyman, G. D., & Gelman, S. A. (1998). Young children use motive information to make trait inferences. *Developmental Psychology, 34,* 310–321.

Heyman, G. D., & Legare, C. H. (2005). Children's evaluation of sources of information about traits. *Developmental Psychology, 41,* 579–597.

Higgins, E. T. (1987). Self-discrepancy: A theory relating self and affect. *Psychological Review, 94,* 319–340.

Higgins, E. T., & Parsons, J. E. (1983). Stages as subcultures: Social-cognitive development and the social life of the child. In E. T. Higgins, W. W. Hartup, & D. N. Ruble (Eds.), *Social cognition and social development: A sociocultural perspective.* New York: Cambridge University Press.

Hill, A. L., Degnan, K. A., Calkins, S. D., & Keane, S. P. (2006). Profiles of externalizing behavior for boys and girls across preschool: The roles of emotion regulation and attention. *Developmental Psychology, 42,* 913–928.

Hill, J. L., Waldfogel, J., Brooks-Gunn, J., & Han, W-J. (2005). Maternal employment and child development: A fresh look using newer methods. *Developmental Psychology, 41,* 833–850.

Hill, J. P., & Lynch, M. E. (1983). The intensification of gender-related role expectations during early adolescence. In J. Brooks-Gunn & A. C. Petersen (Eds.), *Girls at puberty. Biological and psychosocial perspectives.* New York: Plenum.

Hill, N. E., Bush, K. R., & Roosa, M. W. (2003). Parenting and family socialization strategies and children's mental health: Low-income Mexican American and Euro American mothers and children. *Child Development, 74,* 189–204.

Hill, N. E., Castellino, D. R., Lansford, J. E., Nowlin, P., Dodge, K. A., Bates, J. E., & Pettit, G. S. (2004). Parental involvement as related to school behavior, achievement, and aspirations: Demographic variations across adolescence. *Child Development, 75,* 1491–1509.

Hill, P. T., Foster, G. E., & Gendler, T. (1990). *High schools with character: Alternatives to bureaucracy.* Santa Monica, CA: Rand Corporation.

Hill, S. D., & Tomlin, C. (1981). Self-recognition in retarded children. *Child Development, 53,* 1320–1329.

Hinde, R. A. (1989). Ethological and relationships approaches. In R. Vasta (Ed.), *Annals of child development. Vol. 6: Theories of child development: Revised formulations and current issues.* Greenwich, CT: JAI Pres.

Hines, M. (2004). *Brain gender.* New York: Oxford University Press.

Hines, M., Golombok, S., Rust, J., Johnston, K. J., Golding, J., and the Avon Longitudinal Study of Parents and Children Study Team (2002). Testosterone during pregnancy and gender role behavior of preschool children: A longitudinal, population study. *Child Development, 73,* 1678–1687.

Hinshaw, S. P., Zupan, B. A., Simmel, C., Nigg, J. T., & Melnick, S. (1997). Peer status in boys with attention-deficit hyperactivity disorder: Predictions from overt and covert antisocial behavior, social isolation, and authoritative parenting beliefs. *Child Development, 68,* 880–896.

Hobbes, T. (1904). *Leviathan.* Cambridge: Cambridge University Press. (Original work published 1651).

Hodges, E. V. E., Boivin, M., Vitaro, F., & Bukowski, W. M. (1999). The power of friendship: Protection against an escalating cycle of peer victimization. *Developmental Psychology, 35,* 94–104.

Hodges, E. V. E., Malone, M. J., & Perry, D. G. (1997). Individual risk and social risk as interacting determinants of victimization in the peer group. *Developmental Psychology, 33,* 1032–1039.

Hoffman. L. W. (1989). Effects of maternal employment in the two-parent family. *American Psychologist, 44,* 283–292.

Hoffman, L. W. (1991). The influence of the family environment on personality: Accounting for sibling differences. *Psychological Bulletin, 108,* 187–203.

Hoffman, L. W. (1994). Commentary on Plomin, R. (1994): A proof and a disproof questioned. *Social Development, 3,* 60–63.

Hoffman, L. W. (2000). Maternal employment: Effects of social context. In R. D. Taylor & M. C. Wang (Eds.), *Resilience across contexts: Family, work, culture, and community.* Mahwah, NJ: Erlbaum.

Hoffman, M. L. (1970). Moral development. In P. H. Mussen (Ed.), *Carmichael's manual of child psychology* (Vol. 2). New York: Wiley.

Hoffman, M. L. (1975). Moral internalization, parental power, and the nature of parent-child interaction. *Developmental Psychology, 11,* 228–239.

Hoffman, M. L. (1981). Is altruism part of human nature? *Journal of Personality and Social Psychology, 40,* 121–137.

Hoffman, M. L. (1988). Moral development. In M. H. Bornstein & M. E. Lamb

(Eds.), *Developmental Psychology: An advanced textbook* (2nd ed., pp. 497–548). Hillsdale, NJ: Erlbaum.

Hoffman, M. L. (2000). *Empathy and moral development: Implications for caring and justice.* Cambridge, England: Cambridge University Press.

Holahan, A., & Costenbader, V. (2000). A comparison of developmental gains for preschool children with disabilities in inclusive and self-contained classrooms. *Topics in Early Childhood Special Education, 20,* 224–235.

Holden, C. (2005). Sex and the suffering brain. *Science, 308,* 1574–1577.

Holt, C. L., & Ellis, J. B. (1998). Assessing the current validity of the Bem Sex-Role Inventory. *Sex Roles, 39,* 929–941.

Horney, K. (1967). *Feminine psychology.* New York: Norton. (Original work published 1923–1937).

Hornik, R., & Gunner, M. R. (1988). A descriptive analysis of social referencing. *Child Development, 59,* 626–634.

Horowitz, F. D. (1992). John B. Watson's legacy: Learning and environment. *Developmental Psychology, 28,* 360–367.

Horstmann, G. (2003). What do facial expressions convey: Feeling states, behavioral intentions, or action requests? *Emotion, 3,* 150–166.

Howe, N., Aquan-Assee, J., Bukowski, W. M., Rinaldi, C. M., & Lehoux, P. M. (2000). Sibling self-disclosure in early adolescence. *Merrill-Palmer Quarterly, 46,* 653–671.

Howe, N., Petrakos, H., & Rinaldi, C. M. (1998). "All the sheeps are dead. He murdered them": Sibling pretense, negotiation, internal state language, and relationship quality. *Child Development, 69,* 182–191.

Howe, N., & Rinaldi, C. M. (2004). "You be the big sister": Maternal-preschool internal state discourse, perspective-taking, and sibling caretaking. *Infant & Child Development, 13,* 217–234.

Howe, N., Rinaldi, C. M., Jennings, M., & Petrakos, H. (2002). *"No! The lambs can stay out because they got cozies"*: Constructive and destructive sibling conflict, pretend play, and social understanding. *Child Development, 73,* 1460–1473.

Howes, C. (1988). Peer interaction of young children. *Monographs of the society for Research in Child Development, 53* (1, Serial No. 217).

Howes, C. (1990). Can the age of entry into child care and the quality of child care predict adjustment in kindergarten? *Developmental Psychology, 26,* 292–303.

Howes, C. (1992). *The collaborative construction of pretend.* Albany: State University of New York Press.

Howes, C. (1996). The earliest friendships. In W. M. Bukowski, A. F. Newcomb, & W. W. Hartup (Eds.), *The company they keep: Friendships in childhood and adolescence* (pp. 66–86). Cambridge, England: Cambridge University Press.

Howes, C. (1997). Children's experiences in center-based child care as a function of teacher background and adult:child ratio. *Merrill-Palmer Quarterly, 43,* 404–425.

Howes, C., Droege, K., & Matheson, C. C. (1994). Play and communicative processes within long-term and short-term friendship dyads. *Journal of Social and Personal Relationships, 11,* 401–410.

Howes, C., Hamilton, C. E., & Matheson, C. C. (1994). Children's relationships with peers: Differential associations with aspects of the parent-child relationship. *Child Development, 65,* 253–263.

Howes, C., Hamilton, C. E., & Philipsen, L. C. (1998). Stability and continuity of child-caregiver and child-peer relationships. *Child Development, 69,* 418–426.

Howes, C., & Matheson, C. C. (1992). Sequences in the development of competent play with peers: Social and social pretend play. *Developmental Psychology, 28,* 961–974.

Howes, P., & Markman, H. J. (1989). Marital quality and child functioning: A longitudinal investigation. *Child Development, 60,* 1044–1051.

Hrdy, S. B., & Batten, M. (2007, June 18). Daddy dearest. *Time, 169,* 60–61.

Hsueh, J., & Yoshikawa, H. (2007). Working nonstandard schedules and variable shifts in low-income families: Associations with parental psychological well-being, family functioning, and child well-being. *Developmental Psychology, 43,* 620–632.

Hubbard, J. A. (2001). Emotion expression processes in children's peer interaction: The role of peer rejection, aggression, and gender. *Child Development, 72,* 1426–1438.

Hubbard, J. A., Dodge, K. A., Cillessen, A. H. N., Coie, J. D., & Schwartz, D. (2001). The dyadic nature of boys' social information processing in boys' reactive and proactive aggression. *Journal of Personality and Social Psychology, 80,* 268–280.

Hubbard, J. A., Smithmyer, C. M., Ramsden, S. R., Parker, E. H., Flanagan, K. D., Dearing, K. F., Relyea, N., & Simons, R. F. (2002). Observational, physiological, and self-report measures of children's anger: Relations to reactive versus proactive aggression. *Child Development, 73,* 1101–1118.

Hudson, L. M., Forman, E. R., & Brion-Meisels, S. (1982). Role-taking as a predictor of prosocial behavior in cross-age tutors. *Child Development, 53,* 1320–1329.

Huesmann, L. R., Eron, L. D., Lefkowitz, M. M., & Walder, L. O. (1984). Stability of aggression over time and generations. *Developmental Psychology, 20,* 1120–1134.

Huesmann, L. R., Moise-Titus, J., Podolski, C., & Eron, L. D. (2003). Longitudinal relations between children's exposure to TV violence and their aggressive and violent behavior in young adulthood: 1977–1992. *Developmental Psychology, 39,* 201–221.

Hughes, C., & Dunn, J. (1998). Understanding mind and emotion: Longitudinal associations with mental-state talk between young friends. *Developmental Psychology, 34,* 1026–1037.

Hughes, D., Rodriquez, T., Smith, E. P., Johnson, D. J., Stevenson, H. C., & Spicer, P. (2006). Parent's ethnic-racial socialization practices: A review of research and directions for future study. *Developmental Psychology, 42,* 747–770.

Hughes, F. M., & Seta, C. E. (2003). Gender stereotypes: Children's perceptions of compensatory social behavior following violations of gender roles. *Sex Roles, 49,* 685–691.

Hughes, J. M., Bigler, R. S., & Levy, S. R. (2007). Consequences of learning about historical racism among European American and African American children. *Child Development, 78,* 1689–1705.

Hughes, P. (2001). *Crowd structures in African American student bodies.* Unpublished data, University of Georgia.

Hughes, R., Jr., Tingle, B. A., & Sawin, D. B. (1981). Development of empathic understanding in children. *Child Development, 52,* 122–128.

Hunt, P., & Goetz, L. (1997). Research on inclusive educational programs, practices, and outcomes for students with severe disabilities. *Journal of Special Education, 31,* 3–29.

Hussong, A. M., Zucker, R. A., Wong, M. M., Fitzgerald, H. E., & Puttler, L. I. (2005). Social competence in children of alcoholic parents over time. *Developmental Psychology 41,* 747–759.

Huston, A. C. (1983). Sex-typing. In P. H. Mussen (Ed.), *Handbook of child psychology. Vol. 4: Socialization, personality, and social development* (4th ed., pp. 387–467). New York: Wiley.

Huston, A. C., Donnerstein, E., Fairchild, H., Feshbach, N. D., Katz, P. A., Murray, J. P., Rubinstein, E. A., Wilcox, B. L., & Zuckerman, D. (1992). *Big world, small screen.* Lincoln, NB: University of Nebraska Press.

Huston, A. C., & Rosenkrantz Aronson, S. (2005). Mothers' time with infant and time in employment as predictors of mother-child relationships and children's early development. *Child Development, 76,* 467–482.

Huston, A. C., & Wright, J. C. (1998). Mass media and children's development. In W. Damon (Series Ed.) & I. E. Sigel & K. A. Renninger (Vol. Eds.), *Handbook of child psychology. Vol. 4: Child psychology in practice* (5th ed., pp. 999–1058). New York: Wiley.

Huston, A. C., Wright, J. C., Marquis, J., & Green, S. B. (1999). How children spend their time: Television and other activities. *Developmental Psychology, 35,* 912–925.

Hutt, C. (1972). *Males and females.* Baltimore: Penguin Books.

Huttenlocher, J., Levine, S., & Vevea, J. (1998). Environmental input and cognitive growth: A study using time-period comparisons. *Child Development, 69,* 1012–1029.

Huttenlocher, P. R. (2002). *Neural plasticity: The effects of environment on the development of the cerebral cortex.* Cambridge, MA: Harvard University Press.

Hyde, J. S. (1984). How large are sex differences in aggression? A developmental meta-analysis. *Developmental Psychology, 20,* 722–736.

Hyde, J. S., & DeLamater, J. (2003). *Understanding human sexuality* (8th ed.). New York: McGraw-Hill.

Hyde, J. S., Fennema, E., & Lamon, S. J. (1990). Gender differences in mathematics performance: A meta-analysis. *Psychological Bulletin, 107,* 139–155.

Hyde, J. S., & Plant, E. A. (1995). Magnitude of psychological gender differences: Another side to the story. *American Psychologist, 50,* 159–161.

Hymel, S. (1983). Preschool children's peer relations: Issues in sociometric assessment. *Merrill-Palmer Quarterly, 19,* 237–260.

Hymel, S. (1986). Interpretations of peer behavior: Affective bias in childhood and adolescence. *Child Development, 57,* 431–445.

Hymel, S., Bowker, A., & Woody, E. (1993). Aggressive versus withdrawn unpopular children: Variations in peer and self-perceptions in multiple domains. *Child Development, 64,* 879–896.

Hymel, S., Rubin, K. H., Rowden, L., & Le Mare, L. (1990). Children's peer relationships: Longitudinal prediction of internalizing and externalizing problems from middle to late childhood. *Child Development, 61,* 2004–2021.

Iacoboni, M. (2005). Neural mechanisms of imitation. *Current Opinion in Neurobiology, 15,* 631–637.

Iannotti, R. J. (1978). Effect of role-taking experiences on role-taking, empathy, altruism, and aggression. *Developmental Psychology, 14,* 119–124.

Iervolino, A. C., Hines, M., Golombok, S. E., Rust, J., & Plomin, R. (2002). Genetic and environmental influences on sex-typed behavior during the preschool years. *Child Development, 76,* 826–840.

Imperato-McGinley, J., Peterson, R. E., Gautier, T., & Sturla, E. (1979). Androgyns and the evolution of male gender identity among male pseudohermaphrodites with 5a-reducase deficiency. *New England Journal of Medicine, 300,* 1233–1237.

Inhelder, B., Piaget, J. (1958). *The growth of logical thinking from childhood to adolescence.* New York: Basic Books.

Intons-Peterson, M. J. (1988). *Gender concepts of Swedish and American youth.* Hillsdale, NJ: Erlbaum.

Intons-Peterson, M. J., & Reddel, M. (1984). What do people ask about a neonate? *Developmental Psychology, 20,* 358–359.

Isabella, R. A. (1993). Origins of attachment: Maternal interactive behavior across the first year. *Child Development, 64,* 605–621.

Isabella, R. A., & Belsky, J. (1991). Interactional synchrony and the origins of infant-mother attachment. *Child Development, 62,* 373–384.

Izard, C. E. (1982). *Measuring emotions in infants and children.* New York: Cambridge University Press.

Izard, C. E. (1993). Four systems for emotion activation: Cognitive and noncognitive processes. *Psychological Review, 100,* 68–90.

Izard, C. E., Ackerman, B. P., Schoff, K. M., & Fine, S. E. (2000). Self-organization of discrete emotions, emotion patterns, and emotion-cognition relations. In M. Lewis & I. Granie (Eds.), *Emotion, development, and self-organization: Dynamic system approaches to emotional development* (pp. 15–36). New York, NY: Cambridge University Press.

Izard, C. E., Fantauzzo, C. A., Castle, J. M., Haynes. O. M., Rayias, M. F., & Putnam, P. H. (1995). The ontogeny and significance of infants' facial expressions in the first 9 months of life. *Developmental Psychology, 31,* 997–1013.

Izard, C. E., Hembree, E. A., & Huebner, R. R. (1987). Infants' emotion expressions to acute pain: Developmental change and stability of individual differences. *Developmental Psychology, 23,* 105–113.

Jaccard, J., Blanton, H., & Dodge, T. (2005). Peer influences on risk behavior: An analysis of the effects of a close friend. *Developmental Psychology, 41,* 135–147.

Jaccard, J., Dittus, P. J., & Gordon, V. V. (1998). Parent-adolescent congruency in reports of adolescent sexual behavior and in communications about sexual behavior. *Child Development, 69,* 247–261.

Jacklin, C. N., & Maccoby, E. E. (1978). Social behavior at 33 months in same-sex and mixed-sex dyads. *Child Development, 49,* 557–569.

Jackson, A. W., & Davis, G. A. (2000). *Turning points 2000: Educating adolescents in the 21st century.* New York: Teachers College Press.

Jackson, J. F. (1993). Human behavioral genetics, Scarr's theory and her views on intervention: A critical review and commentary on their implications for African-American children. *Child Development, 63,* 1318–1332.

Jackson, L. A., von Eye, A., Biocca, F. A., Barbatsis, G., Zhao, Y., & Fitzgerald, H. E. (2006). Does home Internet use influence the academic performance of low-income children? *Developmental Psychology, 42,* 429–435.

Jackson, M. F., Barth, J. M., Powell, N., & Lochman J. E. (2006). Classroom contextual effects of race on children's peer nominations. *Child Development, 77,* 1325–1337.

Jacobs, J. E., Lanza, S., Osgood, D. W., Eccles, J. S., & Wigfield, A. (2002). Changes in children's self-competence and values: Gender and domain differences across grades one through twelve. *Child Development, 73,* 509–527.

Jacobs, L. C., & Chase, C. I. (1989). Student participation in and attitudes toward high school activities. *The High School Journal, 22,* 175–181.

Jacobsen, T., & Hofmann, V. (1997). Children's attachment representations: Longitudinal relations to school behavior and academic competency in middle childhood and adolescence. *Developmental Psychology, 33,* 703–710.

Jacobson, J. L., & Wille, D. E. (1986). The influence of attachment pattern On developmental changes in peer interaction from the toddler to the preschool period. *Child Development, 57,* 338–347.

Jacques, S., & Zelazo, P. D. (2001). The Flexible Item Selection Task (FIST): A measure of executive function in preschoolers. *Developmental Neuropsychology, 20,* 573–591.

Jaffari-Bimmel, N., Juffer, F., van IJzendoorn, M. H., Bakersmans-Kranenburg, M. J., & Mooijart, A. (2006). Social development from infancy to adolescence: Longitudinal and concurrent factors in an adoption sample. *Developmental Psychology, 42,* 1143–1153.

Jaffee, S. R., Caspi, A., Moffitt, T. E., Polo-Thomas, M., Price, T. S., & Taylor, A. (2004). The limits of child effects: Evidence for genetically mediated child effects on corporal punishment but not on physical maltreatment. *Developmental Psychology, 40,* 1047–1058.

Jaffee, S. R., & Hyde, J. S. (2000). Gender differences in moral orientation: A meta-analysis. *Psychological Bulletin, 126*, 703-726.

Jaffee, S. R., Moffitt, T. E., Caspi, A., & Taylor, A. (2003). Life with (or without) father: The benefits of living with two biological parents depend on the father's antisocial behavior. *Child Development, 74*, 109–126.

Jagers, R. J., Bingham, K., & Hans, S. L. (1996). Socialization and social judgments among inner-city African-American kindergartners. *Child Development, 67*, 140–150.

Jahromi, L. B., Putnam, S. P., & Stifter, C. A. (2004). Maternal regulation of infant reactivity from 2 to 6 months. *Developmental Psychology, 40*, 477–487.

Jaio, S., Ji, G., & Jing, Q. (1996). Cognitive development of Chinese urban only children and children with siblings. *Child Development, 67*, 387–395.

Jenkins, J. M., Simpson, A., Dunn, J., Rasbash, J., & O'Connor, T. G. (2005). Mutual influence of martial conflict and children's behavior problems: Shared and nonshared family risks. *Child Development, 76*, 24–39.

Jenkins, J. M., Turrell, S. L., Kogushi, Y., Lollis, S., & Ross, H. S. (2003). A longitudinal investigation of the dynamics of mental state talk in families. *Child Development, 74*, 905–920.

Jennings, K. D., & Dietz, L. J. (2003). Mastery motivation and goal persistence in young children. In M. H. Bornstein & L. Davidson (Eds.), *Well-being: Positive development across the life course.* (pp. 295–309). Mahwah, NJ: Erlbaum.

Jodl, K. M., Michael, A., Malanchuk, O., Eccles, J. S., & Sameroff, A. (2001). Parents' roles in shaping early adolescents' occupational aspirations. *Child Development, 72*, 1247–1265.

Johnson, D. W., & Johnson, R. T. (1989). *Cooperation and competition: Theory and research.* Edina, MN: Interaction.

Johnson, M. H., (1998). The neural basis of cognitive development. In W. Damon (Series Ed.), D. Kuhn & R. S. Siegler (Vol. Eds.), *Handbook of child psychology. Vol. 2: Cognition, perception, and language* (5th ed., pp. 1–49). New York: Wiley.

Johnson, N. (1967). *How to talk back to your television.* Boston: Little, Brown.

Johnson, W., Emde, R. N., Pannabecker, B., Stenberg, C., & Davis, M. (1982). Maternal perception of infant emotion from birth through 18 months. *Infant Behavior and Development, 5*, 313–322.

Jones, D. C. (2004). Body image among adolescent boys and girls: A longitudinal study. *Developmental Psychology, 40*, 823–835.

Jones, D. C., Abbey, B. B., & Cumberland, A. (1998). The development of display rule knowledge: Linkages with family expressiveness and social competence. *Child Development, 69*, 1209–1222.

Jones, M. C. (1965). Psychological correlates of somantic development. *Child Development, 36*, 899–911.

Jones, M. C., & Bayley, N. (1950). Physical maturing among boys as related to behavior. *Journal of Educational Psychology, 41*, 129–148.

Jones, R. A., Hendrick, C., & Epstein, Y. (1979). *Introduction to social psychology.* Sunderland, MA: Sinauer.

Jones, S. S. (1996). Imitation or exploration?: Young children's matching of adults' oral gestures. *Child Development, 67*, 1952–1969.

Jordyn, M., & Byrd, M. (2003). The relationship between the living arrangements of university students and their identity development. *Adolescence, 38*, 267–278.

Jose, P. M. (1990). Just world reasoning in children's immanent justice arguments. *Child Development, 61*, 1024–1033.

Judy, B., & Nelson, E. S. (2000). Relations between parents, peers, morality, and theft in an adolescent sample. *High School Journal, 83*, 31–42.

Juffer, F., Bakermans-Kranenburg, M. J., & van IJzendoorn, M. H. (2005). The importance of parenting in the development of disorganized attachment: Evidence from a preventive intervention study in adoptive families. *Journal of Child Psychology and Psychiatry, 46*, 263–274.

Jussim, L., & Eccles, J. S. (1992). Teacher expectations II: Construction and reflection of student achievement. *Journal of Personality and Social Psychology, 63*, 947–961.

Kagan, J. (1972). Do infants think? *Scientific American, 226*, 74–82.

Kagan, J. (1976). Emergent themes in human development. *American Scientist, 64*, 186–196.

Kagan, J. (1984). *The nature of the child.* New York: Basic Books.

Kagan, J. (1989). *Unstable ideas: Temperament, cognition. and self.* Cambridge, MA: Cambridge University Press.

Kagan, J. (1991). Continuity and discontinuity. In S. E. Brauth, W. S. Hall, & R. J. Dooling (Eds.), *Plasticity of development.* Cambridge, MA: Bradford/MIT Press.

Kagan, J. (1992). Behavior, biology, and the meaning of temperamental constructs. *Pediatrics, 90*, 510–513.

Kagan, J. (1998). Biology and the child. In W. Damon (Series Ed.,) & N. Eisenberg (Vol. Ed.), *Handbook of child psychology. Vol. 3: Social, emotional, and personality development* (5th ed., pp. 177–235). New York: Wiley.

Kagan, J. (2003). Biology, context, and developmental inquiry. *Annual Review of Psychology, 54*, 1–23.

Kagan, J., Kearsley, R. B., & Zelazo, P. R. (1978). *Infancy: Its place in human development.* Cambridge, MA: Harvard University Press.

Kagan, J., & Moss, H. A. (1962). *Birth to maturity.* New York: Wiley.

Kagan, J., Snidman, N., Kahn, V., & Towsley, S. (2007). The preservation of two infant temperaments into adolescence. *Monographs of the Society for Research in Child Development, 72*, (2, Serial No. 287).

Kagan, J., Snidman, N., Zenter, M., & Peterson, E. (1999). Infant temperament and anxious symptoms in school age children. *Development and Psychopathology, 11*, 209–224.

Kagan, S., & Masden, M. C. (1971). Cooperation and competition of Mexican, Mexican-American, and Anglo-American children of two ages and four instructional sets. *Developmental Psychology, 5*, 32–39.

Kagan, S., & Masden, M. C. (1972). Rivalry in Anglo-American and Mexican children of two ages. *Journal of Personality and Social Psychology, 24*, 214–220.

Kagan, S., & Zahn, G. L. (1975). Field dependence and the school achievement gap between Anglo-American and Mexican-American children. *Journal of Educational Psychology, 67*, 643–650.

Kahn, P. H., Jr. (1992). Children's obligatory and discretionary moral judgments. *Child Development, 63*, 416–430.

Kail, R. V., & Cavanaugh, J. C. (2007). *Human development: A lifespan view* (4th ed.). Belmont, CA: Wadsworth.

Kaitiala-Heino, R., Marttunen, M., Rantanen, P., & Rimpela, M. (2003). Early puberty is associated with mental health problems in middle adolescence. *Social Science Medicine, 57*, 1055–1064.

Kaitz, M., Meschulach-Safaty, O., Auerbach, J., & Eidelman, A. (1988). A reexamination of newborns' ability to imitate facial expressions. *Developmental Psychology, 24*, 3–7.

Kalil, A., & Kunz, J. (2002). Teenage childbearing, marital status, and depressive symptoms in later life. *Child development, 73,* 1748–1760.

Kalil, A., & Zoil-Guest, M. (2005). Single mothers' employment dynamics and adolescent well-being. *Child Development, 76,* 196–211.

Kalish, C. W., & Cornelius, R. (2006). What is to be done? Children's ascriptions of conventional obligations. *Child Development, 78,* 859–878.

Kamerman, S. B. (2000). Parental leave policies: An essential ingredient in early childhood education and care policies. *Social Policy Report* (Vol. 14, No. 2). Ann Arbor: Society for Research in Child Development.

Kamins, M. L., & Dweck , C. S. (1999). Person versus process praise and criticism: Implications for contingent self-worth and coping. *Developmental Psychology, 35,* 835–847.

Kandel, D. (1973). Adolescent marijuana use: Role of parents and peers. *Science, 181,* 1067–1070.

Kane, T. J. (2004). *The impact of after-school programs: Interpreting the results of four recent evaluations. New York: W. T. Grant Foundation.*

Kanfer, F. H., Stifter, E., & Morris, S. J. (1981). Self-control and altruism: Delay of gratification for another. *Child Development, 52,* 674–682.

Kann, L., Kinchen, S. A., Williams, B. I., Ross, J. G., Lowry, R., Grunbaum, J. A., et al. (2000, June 9). Youth risk behavior surveillance—United States, 1999. *Morbidity and Mortality Weekly Surveillance Summary* (Centers for Disease Control), *49,* 1–96.

Kaplan, D. W., Feinstein, R. A., Fisher, M. M., Klein, J. D., Olmedo, L. F., Rome, E. S., & Yancy, S. (2001). Condom use by adolescents. *Pediatrics, 107,* 1463–1469.

Kaplan, P. S., Jung, P. C., Ryther, J. S., & Zarlengo-Strouse, P. (1996). Infant-directed versus adult-directed speech as signals for faces, *Developmental Psychology, 32,* 880–891.

Karoly, L. A., Greenwood, P. W., Everingham, S. S., Hoube, J., Kilburn, M. R., Rydell, C. P., Sanders, M., & Chiesa, J. (1998). *Investing in our children: What we know and don't know about the costs and benefits of early childhood interventions.* RAND Distribution Services.

Katcher, A. (1955). The discrimination of sex differences by young children. *Journal of Genetic Psychology, 87,* 131–143.

Katz, L. F., & Woodin, E. M. (2002). Hostility, hostile detachment, and conflict engagement in marriages: Effects on child and family functioning. *Child Development, 73,* 636–652.

Katz, P. A. (1979). The development of female identity. *Sex Roles, 5,* 155–178.

Katz, P. A., & Walsh, P. V. (1991). Modification of children's gender-stereo-typed behavior. *Child Development, 62,* 338–351.

Kaufman, P., Chen, X., Choy, S. P., Ruddy, S. A., Miller, A. K., Fleury, J. K., et al. (2000). *Indicators of school crime and safety, 2000 (NCES 2001–017/NCJ–184176).* Washington, DC: U.S. Department of Education, National Center for Education Statistics and U.S. Department of Justice, Bureau of Justice Statistics.

Kazdin, A. E. (2003a). Problem-solving skills training and parent management training for conduct disorder. In A. E. Kazdin & J. R. Weisz (Eds.), *Evidence-based psychotherapies for children and adolescents* (pp. 241–262). New York: Guilford Press.

Kazdin, A. E. (2003b). Psychotherapy for children and adolescents. *Annual Review of Psychology, 54,* 253–276.

Kean, A. W. G. (1937). The history of the criminal liability of children. *Law Quarterly Review, 3,* 364–370.

Keane, S. P., Brown, K. P., & Crenshaw, T. M. (1990). Children's intention-cue detection as a function of maternal social behavior: Pathways to social rejection. *Developmental Psychology, 26,* 1004–1009.

Keasey, C. B. (1971). Social participation as a factor in the moral development of preadolescents. *Developmental Psychology, 5,* 216–220.

Keating, D., & Clark, L. V. (1980). Development of physical and social reasoning in adolescence. *Developmental Psychology, 16,* 23–30.

Keenan T. (2003). Individual differences in theory of mind. The preschool years and beyond. In B. Repacholi & V. Slaughter (Eds.), *Individual differences in theory of mind: Implications for typical and atypical development.* New York: Psychology Press.

Keith, J. (1985). Age in anthropological research. In R. H. Binstock & E. Shanus (Eds.), *Handbook of aging and the social sciences* (2nd ed.). New York: Van Nostrand Reinhold.

Keller, H., Lohas, A., Volker, S., Cappenberg, M., & Chasiotis, A. (1999). Temporal contingency as an independent component of parenting behavior. *Child Development, 70,* 474, 485.

Keller, H., & Scholmerich, A. (1987). Infant vocalizations and parental reactions during the first four months of life. *Developmental Psychology, 23,* 62–67.

Keller, H., Yovsi, R., Borke, J., Kurtner, J., Jensen, H., & Papligoura, Z. (2004). Developmental consequences of early parenting experiences: Self-recognition and self-regulation in three cultural communities. *Child Development, 75,* 1745–1760.

Kelley, H. H. (1973). The process of causal attribution. *American Psychologist, 28,* 107–128.

Kelley, M. L., Power, T. G., & Wimbush, D. D. (1992). Determinants of disciplinary practices in low-income black mothers. *Child Development, 63,* 573–582.

Kelly, S. A., Brownell, C. A., & Campbell, S. E. (2000). Mastery motivation and self-evaluative affect in toddlers: Longitudinal relations with maternal behavior. *Child Development, 71,* 1061–1071.

Kendall-Tackett, K. A., Williams, L. M., & Finkelhor, D. (1993). Impact of sexual abuse on children: A review and synthesis of recent empirical studies. *Psychological Bulletin, 113,* 164–180.

Kenney-Benson, G. A., Pomerantz, E. M., Ryan, A. M., & Patrick, H. (2006). Sex differences in math performance: The role of children's approach to schoolwork. *Developmental Psychology, 42,* 11–26.

Kerns, K. A., Klepec, L., & Cole, A. (1996). Peer relationships and preadolescents' perceptions of security in the child-mother relationship. *Developmental Psychology, 32,* 457–466.

Kerr, M., Lambert, W. W., & Bem, D. J. (1996). Life course sequelae of childhood shyness in Sweden: Comparison with the United States. *Developmental Psychology, 32,* 1100–1105.

Kerr, M., Lambert, W. W., Stattin, H., & Klackbengerg-Larsson, I. (1994). Stability of inhibition in a Swedish longitudinal sample. *Child Development, 65,* 138–146.

Kerr, M., & Stattin, H. (2000). What parents know, how they know it, and several forms of adolescent adjustment: Further support for a reinterpretation of monitoring. *Developmental Psychology, 36,* 366–380.

Kerwin, C., Ponterotto, J. G., Jackson, B. L., & Harris, A. (1993). Racial identity in biracial children: A qualitative investigation. *Journal of Counseling Psychology, 40,* 221–231.

Kessen, W. (1975). *Childhood in China.* New Haven, CT: Yale University Press.

Kett, J. F. (1977). *Rites of passage. Adolescence in America, 1790 to the present.* New York: Basic Books.

Kiang, L., Yip, T., Gonzales-Backen, M., Witkow, M., & Fuligni, A. J. (2006). Ethnic identity and daily psychological well-being of adolescents from Mexican and Chinese backgrounds. *Child Development, 77,* 1338–1350. New York: Basic Books.

Kiel, E. J., & Buss, K. A. (2006). Maternal accuracy in predicting toddlers' behaviors and associations with toddlers' fearful temperament. *Child Development, 77,* 355–370.

Kiesewetter, J. (1993, Dec. 17). Top kids' show also ranks as most violent. *The Cincinnati Enquirer,* A1.

Kiesner, J., & Pastore, M. (2005). Differences in the relations between antisocial behavior and peer acceptance across contexts and adolescence. *Child Development, 76,* 1278–1293.

Kilgore, K., Snyder, J., & Lentz, C. (2000). The contribution of parental discipline, parental monitoring, and school risk to early-onset conduct problems in African American boys and girls. *Developmental Psychology, 36,* 835–845.

Killen, M., Pisacane, K., Lee-Kim, J., & Ardila-Rey, A. (2001). Fairness or stereotypes? Young children's priorities when evaluating group exclusion and inclusion. *Developmental Psychology, 37,* 587–596.

Kim, J., & Cicchetti, D. (2006). Longitudinal trajectories of self-system processes and depressive symptoms among maltreated and nonmaltreated children. *Child Development, 77,* 624–639.

Kim, J., McHale, S. M., Crouter, A. C., & Osgood, D. W. (2007). Longitudinal linkages between sibling relationships and adjustment from middle childhood through adolescence. *Developmental Psychology, 43,* 960–973.

Kim, J., McHale, S. M., Osgood, D. W., & Crouter, A. C. (2006). Longitudinal course and family correlates of sibling relationships from childhood through adolescence. *Child Development, 77,* 1746–1761.

Kim, J. M. (1998). Korean children's concepts of adult and peer authority and moral reasoning. *Developmental Psychology, 34,* 947–955.

Kindermann, T. A. (2007). Effects of naturally existing peer groups on changes in academic enegagment in a cohort of sixth graders. *Child Development, 78,* 1186–1203.

King, P. E., & Furrow, J. (2004). Religion as a resource for positive youth development: Religion, social capital, and moral outcomes. *Developmental Psychology, 40,* 703–713.

King, V., Harris, K. M., & Heard, H. E. (2004). Racial and ethnic diversity in nonresident involvement. *Journal of Marriage and the Family, 66,* 1–21.

Kirby, D. (2002). *Do abstinence-only problems delay the initiation of sex among young people and reduce teen pregnancy?* Washington, DC: National Campaign to Prevent Teen Pregnancy.

Kirchner, J. (1998, January 25). State making adoption process easier. Associated Press, as reported in the *Athens Banner Herald,* p. 4A.

Kirsh, S. J. (1998). Seeing the world through Mortal Kombat-colored glasses: Violent games and the development of a short-term hostile attributional bias. *Childhood, 5,* 177–184.

Kitzmann, K. M. (2000). Effects of marital conflict on subsequent triadic family interactions and parenting. *Developmental Psychology, 36,* 3–14.

Klaus, M. H., & Kennell, J. H., (1976). *Maternal-infant bonding.* St. Louis: Mosby.

Klaus, M. H., & Kennell, J. H. (1982). *Parent-infant bonding.* St. Louis: Mosby.

Klebanov, P. K., Brooks-Gunn, J., McCarton, C., & McCormick, M. C. (1998). The contribution of neighborhood and family income to developmental test scores over the first three years of life. *Child Development, 69,* 1420–1436.

Kliewer, W., Parrish, K. A., Taylor, K. W., Jackson, K., & Walker, J. M., & Shivy, V. A. (2006). Socialization of coping with community violence: Influences of caregiver coaching, modeling, and family context. *Child Development, 77,* 605–623.

Klimes-Dougan, B., & Kistner, J. (1990). Physically abused preschoolers' responses to peers' distress. *Developmental Psychology, 26,* 599–602.

Kling, K. C., Hyde, J. S., Showers, C. J., & Buswell, B. N. (1999). Gender differences in self-esteem: A meta-analysis. *Psychological Bulletin, 125,* 470–500.

Klinnert, M. D., Emde, R. N., Butterfield, P., & Campos, J. J. (1986). Social referencing: The infant's use of emotional signals from a friendly adult with mother present. *Developmental Psychology, 22,* 427–432.

Knafo, A., & Plomin, R. (2006). Prosocial behavior from early to middle childhood: Genetic and environmental influences on stability and change. *Developmental Psychology, 42,* 771–786.

Knickmeyer, R. C., Wheelwright, S., Taylor, K., Raggatt, P., Hackett, G., & Baron-Cohen, S. (2005). Gender-typed play and amniotic testosterone. *Developmental Psychology, 41,* 517–528.

Kobak, R. R., & Sceery, A. (1988). Attachment in late adolescence: Working models, affect regulation and representation of self and others. *Child Development, 59,* 135–146.

Kochanska, G. (1991). Socialization and temperament in the development of guilt and conscience. *Child Development, 62,* 1379–1392.

Kochanska, G. (1992). Children's interpersonal influence with mothers and peers. *Developmental Psychology, 28,* 491–499.

Kochanska, G. (1993). Toward a synthesis of parental socialization and child temperament in the early development of conscience. *Child Development, 64,* 325–347.

Kochanska, G. (1995). Children's temperament, mothers' discipline, and the security of attachment: Multiple pathways to emerging internalization. *Child Development, 66,* 597–615.

Kochanska, G. (1997). Multiple pathways to conscience for children with different temperaments: From toddlerhood to age 5. *Developmental Psychology, 33,* 228–240.

Kochanska, G. (1998). Mother-child relationship, child fearfulness, and emerging attachment: A short-term longitudinal study. *Developmental Psychology, 34,* 480–490.

Kochanska, G. (2001). Emotional development in children with different attachment histories: The first three years. *Child Development, 72,* 474–490.

Kochanska, G. (2002). Committed compliance, moral self, and internalization: A mediational model. *Developmental Psychology, 38,* 339–351.

Kochanska, G., Aksan, N., & Carlson, J. J. (2005). Temperament, relationships, and young children's receptive cooperation with their parents. *Developmental Psychology, 41,* 648–660.

Kochanska, G., Aksan, N., & Joy, M. E. (2007). Children's fearfulness as a moderator of parenting in early socialization: Two longitudinal studies. *Developmental Psychology, 43,* 222–237.

Kochanska, G., Casey, R. J., & Fukumoto, A. (1995). Toddlers' sensitivity to standard violations. *Child Development, 66,* 643–656.

Kochanska, G., & Coy, K. C. (2002). Child emotionality and maternal responsiveness as predictors of reunion behaviors in the Strange Situation: Links mediated and unmediated by separation distress. *Child Development, 73,* 228–240.

Kochanska, G., Coy, K. C., & Murray, K. T. (2001). The development of self-regulation in the first four years of life. *Child Development, 72,* 1091–1111.

Kochanska, G., Gross, J. N., Lin, M., & Nichols, K. E. (2002). Guilt in young children: Development, determinants, and relations with a broader system of standards. *Child Development, 73,* 461–482.

Kochanska, G., & Murray, K. T. (2000). Mother-child mutually responsive orientation and conscience development: From toddler to early school age. *Child Development, 71,* 417–431.

Kochanska, G., Murray, K. T., & Harlan, E. T. (2000). Effortful control in early childhood: Continuity and change, antecedents, and implications for social development. *Developmental Psychology, 36,* 220–232.

Kochanska, G., Padavich, D. L., & Koenig, A. L. (1996). Children's narratives about hypothetical moral dilemmas and objective measures of their conscience: Mutual relations and socialization antecedents. *Child Development, 69,* 1378–1389.

Kochanska, G., Tjebkes, T. L., & Forman, D. R. (1998). Children's emerging regulation of conduct: Restraint, compliance, and internalization from infancy to the second year. *Child Development, 69,* 1378–1389.

Kochenderfer-Ladd, B., & Skinner, K. (2002). Children's coping strategies: Moderators of the effects of peer victimization? *Developmental Psychology, 38,* 267–278.

Kochenderfer-Ladd, B., & Wardrop, J. L. (2001). Chronicity and instability of children's peer victimization experiences as predictors of loneliness and social satisfaction trajectories. *Child Development, 72,* 134–151.

Kohen, D. E., Brooks-Gunn, J., Leventhal, T., & Hertzman, C. (2002). Neighborhood income and physical and social disorders in Canada: Associations with young children's competencies. *Child Development, 73,* 1844–1860.

Kohlberg, L. (1963). The development of children's orientations toward a moral order: I. Sequence in the development of moral thought. *Vita Humana, 6,* 11–33.

Kohlberg, L. (1966). A cognitive-developmental analysis of children's sex-role concepts and attitudes. In E. E. Maccoby (Ed.), *The development of sex differences.* Stanford, CA: Stanford University Press.

Kohlberg, L. (1969). Stage and sequence: The cognitive-developmental approach to socialization. In D. A. Goslin (Ed.), Handbook of socialization theory and research. Skokie, IL: Rand McNally.

Kohlberg, L. (1975, June). The cognitive-developmental approach to moral education. *Phi Delta Kappa,* pp. 670–677.

Kohlberg, L. (1981). *Essays on moral development. Vol. 1. The philosophy of moral development.* San Francisco: Harper & Row.

Kohlberg, L. (1984). *Essays on moral development. Vol. 2. The psychology of moral development.* San Francisco: Harper & Row.

Kohn, M. L. (1979). The effects of social class on parental values and practices. In D. Reiss & H. A. Hoffman (Eds.), *The American family: Dying or developing?* (pp. 49–68). New York: Plenum.

Kokko, K., & Pulkkinen, L. (2000). Aggression in childhood and long-term unemployment in adulthood: A cycle of maladaptation and some protective factors. *Developmental Psychology, 36,* 463–472.

Konijn, E. A., Bijvank, M. N., & Bushman, B. J. (2007). I wish I were a warrior: The role of wishful identification in the effects of violent video games on aggression in adolescent boys. *Developmental Psychology, 43,* 1038–1044.

Korbin, J. E. (2001). Context and meaning in neighborhood studies of children and families. In A. Booth & A. C. Crouter (Eds.). *Does it take a village? Community effects on children, adolescents, and families.* Mahwah, NJ: Erlbaum.

Koren-Karie, N., Oppenheim, D., Doley, S., Sher, E., & Etzion-Carasso, A. (2002). Mothers' insightfulness regarding their infants' internal experience: Relations with maternal sensitivity and infant attachment. *Development Psychology, 38,* 534–542.

Kovacs, D. M., Parker, J. G., & Hoffman, L. W. (1996). Behavioral, affective, and social correlates of involvement in cross-sex friendships in elementary school. *Child Development, 67,* 2269–2286.

Kowal, A., & Kramer, L. (1997). Children's understanding of parental differential treatment. *Child Development, 68,* 113–126.

Kowal, A. K., Krull, J. L., & Kramer, L. (2004). How the differential treatment of siblings is linked to parent-child relationship quality. *Journal of Family Psychology, 18,* 658–665.

Kowalski, H. S., Wyver, S. R., Massolos, G., & DeLacey, P. (2004). Toddlers' emerging symbolic play: A first-born advantage? *Early Child Development & Care, 174,* 389–400.

Kramer, L. Perozynski, L. A., & Chung, T. (1999). Parental responses to sibling conflict: The effects of development and parent gender. *Child Development, 70,* 1401–1414.

Kreppner, J. M., Rutter, M., Beckett, C., Castle, J., Colvert, J., Groothnes, C., Hawkins, A., O'Connor, T. G., Stevens, S., & Sonuga-Barke, E. J. S. (2007). Normality and impairment following profound early institutional deprivation: A longitudinal follow-up into early adolescence. *Developmental Psychology, 43,* 931–946.

Krishnamoorthy, J. S., Hart, C., & Jelalian, E. (2006). The epidemic of childhood obesity: Review of research and implications for pubic policy. *Social Policy Report, 19.* Society for Research in Child Development.

Kroger, J. (2005). Identity statuses. In C. B. Fisher & R. M. Lerner (Eds.), *Encyclopedia of applied developmental science* (Vol. 1, pp. 567–568). Thousand Oaks, CA: Sage.

Kuchuk, A., Vibbert, M., & Bornstein, M. H. (1986). The perception of smiling and its experiential correlates in three-month-old infants. *Child Development, 57,* 1054–1061.

Kuczynksi, L. (1983). Reasoning, prohibitions, and motivations for compliance. *Developmental Psychology, 19,* 126–134.

Kuczynski, L., & Kochanska, G. (1995). Function and content of maternal demands: Developmental significance of early demands for competent action. *Child Development, 66,* 616–628.

Kuczynski, L., Zahn-Waxler, C., & Radke-Yarrow, M. (1987). Development and content of imitation in the second and third years of life: A socialization perspective. *Developmental Psychology, 23,* 276–282.

Kuebli, J., Butler, S., & Fivush, R. (1995). Mother-child talk about past emotions: Relations of maternal language and child gender over time. *Cognition and Emotion, 9,* 265–283.

Kuhn, D., Nash, S. C., & Brucken, L. (1978). Sex-role concepts of two- and three-year-olds. *Child Development, 49,* 445–451.

Kuhn, D., Kohlberg, L., Langer, J., & Haan, N. (1977). The development of formal operations in logical and moral judgment. *Genetic Psychology Monographs, 95,* 97–188.

Kuklinski, M. R., & Weinstein, R. S. (2000). The stability of teacher expectations and perceived differential teacher treatment. *Learning Environments Research, 3,* 1–34.

Kuklinski, M. R., & Weinstein, R. S. (2001). Classroom and developmental differences in a path model of teacher expectancy effects. *Child Development, 72,* 1554–1578.

Kulik, J. A., & Kulik, C. C. (1992). Meta-analytic findings on grouping programs. *Gifted Child Quarterly, 36,* 73–77.

Kulman, L. (1997, March 10). The prescription for smart kids. *U.S. News and World Report,* p. 10.

Kunkel, D., & Roberts, D. (1991). Young minds and marketplace value: Issues in children's advertising. *Journal of Social Issues, 47,* 57–72.

Kuo, Z. Y. (1930). The genesis of the cat's response to the rat. *Journal of Comparative and Physiological Psychology, 11,* 1–35.

Kurdek, L. A., & Fine, M. A. (1994). Family acceptance and family control as predictors of adjustment in young adolescents: Linear, curvilinear, or interactive effects? *Child Development, 65,* 1137–1146.

Kurdek, L. A., Fine, M. A., & Sinclair, R. J. (1995). School adjustment in sixth graders: Parenting transitions, peer climate, and peer norm effects. *Child Development, 66,* 430–445.

Kurdek, L. A., & Krile, D. (1982). A developmental analysis of the relation between peer acceptance and both interpersonal understanding and perceived social self-competence. *Child Development, 53,* 1485–1491.

La Barbera, J. D., Izard, C. E., Vietze, P. & Parisi, S. A. (1976). Four- and six-month-old infants' visual responses to joy, anger, and neutral expressions. *Child Development, 47,* 535–538.

Ladd, G. W. (1990). Having friends, keeping friends, making friends, and being liked by peers in the classroom: Predictors of children's early school adjustment. *Child Development, 61,* 1081–1100.

Ladd, G. W. (2006). Peer rejection, aggressive or withdrawn behavior, and psychological maladjustment from ages 5 to 12: An examination of four predictive models. *Child Development, 77,* 822–846.

Ladd, G. W., Birch, S. H., & Buhs, E. S. (1999). Children's social and scholastic lives in kindergarten: Related spheres of influence? *Child Development, 70,* 1373–1400.

Ladd, G. W., & Burgess, K. B. (1999). Charting the relationship trajectories of aggressive, withdrawn, and aggressive/withdrawn children during early grade school. *Child Development, 70,* 910–929.

Ladd, G. W., & Burgess, K. B. (2001). Do relational risks and protective factors moderate the linkages between childhood aggression and early psychological and school adjustment? *Child Development, 72,* 1579–1601.

Ladd, G. W., & Golter, B. S. (1988). Parents' management of preschoolers' peer relations: Is it related to children's social competence? *Developmental Psychology, 24,* 109–117.

Ladd, G. W., Kochenderfer, B. J., & Coleman, C. C. (1996). Friendship quality as a predictor of young children's early school adjustment. *Child Development, 67,* 1103–1118.

Ladd, G. W., & Kochenderfer-Ladd, B. (1998). Parenting behaviors and parent-child relationships: Correlates of peer victimization in kindergarten? *Developmental Psychology, 34,* 1450–1458.

Ladd, G. W., & Price, J. M. (1987). Predicting children's social and school adjustment following the transition from preschool to kindergarten. *Child Development, 58,* 1168–1189.

Ladd, G. W., Price, J. M., & Hart, C. H. (1988). Predicting preschoolers' play status from their playground behaviors. *Child Development, 59,* 986–992.

Ladd, G. W., & Troop-Gordon, W. (2003). The role of chronic peer difficulties in the development of children's psychological adjustment problems. *Child Development, 74,* 1344–1367.

LaFontana, K. M., & Cillessen, A. H. N. (2002). Children's perceptions of popular and unpopular peers: A multimethod assessment. *Developmental Psychology, 38,* 635–647.

La Freniere, P., Strayer, F. F., & Gauthier, R. (1984). The emergence of same-sex affiliative preferences among preschool peers: A developmental ethological perspective. *Child Development, 55,* 1958–1965.

Lagattuta, K. H. (2005). When you shouldn't do what you want to do: Young children's understanding of desires, rules, and emotions. *Child Development, 76,* 713–733.

Lagattuta, K. H., & Wellman, H. M. (2001). Thinking about the past: Early knowledge about links between past experience, thinking, and emotion. *Child Development, 72,* 82–102.

Lagattuta, K. H., & Wellman, H. M. (2002). Differences in early parent-child conversations about negative versus positive emotions: Implications for the development of psychological understanding. *Developmental Psychology, 38,* 564–580.

Lagattuta, K. H., Wellman, H. M., & Flavell, J. H. (1997). Preschoolers' understanding of the link between thinking and feeling: Cognitive cuing and emotional change. *Child Development, 68,* 1081–1104.

La Greca, A. M., Prinstein, M. J., & Fetter, M. D. (2001). Adolescent peer crowd affiliation: Linkages with health-risk behaviors and close friendships. *Journal of Pediatric Psychology, 26,* 131–143.

Laible, D. (2004a). Mother-child discourse about a child's past behavior at 30 months and early socioemotional development at age 3. *Merrill-Palmer Quarterly, 50,* 159–180.

Laible, D. (2004b). Mother-child discourse in two contexts: Links with child temperament, attachment security, and socioemotional competence. *Developmental Psychology, 40,* 979–992.

Laible, D., & Thompson, R. (2000). Mother-child discourse attachment security, shared positive affect, and early conscience development. *Child Development, 71,* 1424–1440.

Laible, D. J., & Thompson, R. A. (2002). Mother-child conflict in the early toddler years: Lessons in emotion, morality, and relationships. *Child Development, 73,* 1187–1203.

Laird, R. D., Jordan, K., Dodge, K. A., Pettit, G. S., & Bates, J. E. (2001). Peer rejection in childhood, involvement with antisocial peers in early adolescence, and the development of externalizing problems. *Development and Psychopathology, 13,* 337–354.

Laird, R. D., Pettit, G. S., Bates, J. E., & Dodge, K. A. (2003). Parents' monitoring-relevant knowledge and adolescents' delinquent behavior: Evidence for correlated developmental changes and reciprocal influences. *Child Development, 74,* 752–768.

Lamb, M. E. (1975). Fathers: Forgotten contributors to child development. *Human Development, 18,* 245–266.

Lamb, M. E. (1997). *The role of the father in child development* (3rd ed.). New York: Wiley.

Lamborn, S. D., Mounts, N. S., Steinberg, L., & Dornbusch, S. M. (1991). Patterns of competence and adjustment among adolescents from authoritative, authoritarian, indulgent, and neglectful families. *Child Development, 62,* 1049–1065.

Landry, S. H., Smith, K. E., Miller-Loncar, C. L., & Swank, P. R. (1998). The relation of change in maternal interactive styles to the developing social competence of full-term and preterm children. *Child Development, 69,* 105–123.

Langlois, J. H. (1986). From the eye of the beholder to behavioral reality: Development of social behaviors and social relations as a function of physical attractiveness. In C. P. Herman, M. P. Zanna, & E. T. Higgins (Eds.), *Physical appearance. stigma. and social behavior: The Ontario Symposium* (Vol. 3). Hillsdale, NJ: Erlbaum.

Langlois, J. H., & Downs, A. C. (1979). Peer relations as a function of physical attractiveness: The eye of the beholder or behavioral reality. *Child Development, 50,* 409–418.

Langlois, J. H., Kalakanis, L., Rubenstein, A. J., Larson, A., Hallam, M., & Smoot, M. (2000). Maxims or myths of beauty: A meta-analytic and theoretical review. *Psychological Bulletin, 126,* 390–423.

Langlois, J. H., Ritter, J. M., Casey, R. J., & Sawin, D. B. (1995). Infant attractiveness predicts maternal behaviors and attitudes. *Developmental Psychology, 31,* 464–472.

Langlois, J. H., Ritter, J. M., Roggman, L. A., & Vaughn, L. S. (1991). Facial diversity and infant preferences for attractive faces. *Developmental Psychology, 27,* 79–84.

Langlois, J. H., Roggman, L. A., & Rieser-Danner, L. A. (1990). Infants' differential social responses to attractive and unattractive faces. *Developmental Psychology, 26,* 153–159.

Lansford, J. E., Deater-Deckard, K., Dodge, K. A., Bates, J. E., & Pettit, G. S. (2004). Ethnic differences in the link between physical discipline and later adolescent externalizing behaviors. *Journal of Child Psychology and Psychiatry, 45,* 801–812.

Laosa, L. M. (1981). Maternal behavior: Sociocultural diversity in modes of family interaction. In R. W. Henderson (Ed.), *Parent-child interaction: Theory, research, and prospects.* Orlando, FL: Academic Press.

Lapsley, D. K. (1996). *Moral psychology.* Boulder, CO: Westview.

LeCapitaine, J. E. (1987). The relationship between emotional development and moral development and the differential impact of three psychological interventions on children. *Psychology in the Schools, 24,* 372–378.

Lapsley, D. K., Milstead, M., Quintana, S. M., Flannery, D., & Buss, R. R. (1986). Adolescent egocentrism and formal operations: Tests of a theoretical assumption. *Developmental Psychology, 22,* 800–807.

Larose, S., Bernier, A., & Tarabulsy, G. M., (2005). Attachment state of mind, learning dispositions, and academic performance during the college transition. *Developmental Psychology, 41,* 281–289.

Larson, R. (2001). Commentary. In D. R. Anderson, A. C. Huston, K. L. Schmitt, D. L. Linebarger, & J. C. Wright. Early childhood television viewing and adolescent behavior. *Monographs of the Society for Research in Child Development, 66,* (1, Serial No. 264).

Larson, R. W., & Lampman-Petraitis, C. (1989). Daily emotional states reported by children and adolescents. *Child Development, 60,* 1250–1260.

Larson, R. W., Hansen, D. M., & Moneta, G. (2006). Differing profiles of developmental experiences across types of organized youth activities. *Developmental Psychology, 42,* 849–863.

Larson, R. W., Moneta, G., Richards, M. H., & Wilson, S. (2002). Continuity, stability, and change in daily emotional experience across adolescence. *Child Development, 73,* 1151–1165.

Larson, R. W., & Verma, S. (1999). How children and adolescents spend time across the world: Work and play opportunities. *Psychological Bulletin, 125,* 701–736.

Larsson, I., & Svedin, C. (2002). Sexual experiences in childhood: Young adults' recollections. *Archives of Sexual Behavior, 31,* 263–273.

Laumann, E. O., Gagnon, J. H., Michael, R. T., & Michaels, S. (1994). *The social organization of sexuality: Sexual practices in the United States.* Chicago: University of Chicago Press.

Laursen, B., Bukowski, W. M., Aunola, K., & Nurmi, J. (2007). Friendship moderates prospective associations between social isolation and adjustment problems in young children. *Child Development, 78,* 1395–1404.

Laursen, B., Coy., K. C., & Collins, W. A. (1998). Reconsidering changes in parent-child conflict across adolescence: A meta-analysis. *Child Development, 69,* 817–832.

Laursen, B., Finklestein, B. D., & Betts, N. T. (2001). A developmental meta-analysis of peer conflict resolution. *Development Review, 21,* 423–449.

Lavellee, K. L., Bierman, K. L., Nix, R. L., & the Conduct Problems Prevention Research Group (2005). The impact of first-grade "friendship group" experiences on child social outcomes in the Fast Track Program. *Journal of Abnormal Child Psychology, 33,* 307–324.

Lavelli, M., & Fogel, A. (2002). Developmental changes in mother-infant face-to-face communication: Birth to 3 months. *Developmental Psychology, 38,* 288–305.

Lavelli, M., & Fogel, A. (2005). Developmental changes in the relationship between the infant's attention to emotion during face-to-face communication: The 2-month transition. *Developmental Psychology, 41,* 265–280.

Leaper, C. (1994). *New directions for child development. Vol. 65: Childhood gender segregation: Causes and consequences.* San Francisco: Jossey-Bass.

Leaper, C. (2000). Gender, affiliation, assertion, and the interactive context of parent-child play. *Developmental Psychology, 36,* 381–393.

Leaper, C., Anderson, K. J., & Sanders, P. (1998). Moderators of gender effects on parents' talk to their children. *Developmental Psychology, 34,* 3–27.

Leaper, C., Tennenbaum, H. R., & Shaffer, T. G. (1999). Communication patterns in African American girls and boys from low-income urban backgrounds. *Child Development, 70,* 1489–1503.

Lease, A. M., Kennedy, C. A., & Axelrod, J. L. (2002). Children's social constructions of popularity. *Social Development, 11,* 87–109.

Lee, K., Cameron, C. A., Xu, F., Fu, G., & Board, J. (1997). Chinese and Canadian children's evaluation of lying and truth telling: Similarities and differences in the context of pro- and antisocial behaviors. *Child Development, 68,* 924–934.

Legerstee, M. (1991). The role of people and objects in early imitation. *Journal of Experimental Child Psychology, 51,* 423–433.

Legerstee, M. Anderson, D., & Schaffer, A. (1998). Five-and-eight-month-old infants recognize their faces and voices as familiar social stimuli. *Child Development, 69,* 37–50.

Legerstee, M., Barna, J., & DiAdamo, C. (2000). Precursors to the development of intention at 6 months: Understanding people and their actions. *Developmental Psychology, 36,* 627–634.

Legerstee, M., & Varghese, J. (2001). The role of maternal affect mirroring on social expectancies in three-month-old infants. *Child Development, 72,* 1301–1313.

Leinbach, M. D., & Fagot, B. I. (1986). Acquisition of gender labeling: A test for toddlers. *Sex Roles, 15,* 655–666.

Leinbach, M. D., & Fagot, B. I. (1993). Categorical habituation to male and female faces: Gender schematic processing in infancy. *Infant Behavior and Development, 16,* 317–322.

LeMare, L. J., & Rubin, K. H. (1987). Perspective taking and peer interaction: Structural and developmental analyses. *Child Development, 58,* 306–315.

Lemelin, J., Boivin, M., Forget-Dubois, N., Dionne, G., Seguin, J. R., Brendgen, M., et al., (2007). The genetic-environmental etiology of cognitive school readiness and later academic achievement in early childhood. *Child Development, 78,* 1855–1869.

Lemerise, E. A., & Arsenio, W. F. (2000). An integrated model of emotion processes and cognition in social information processing. *Child Development, 71,* 107–118.

Lemery, K. S., Goldsmith, H. H., Klinnert, M. D., & Mrazek, D. A. (1999). Development models of infant and childhood temperament. *Developmental Psychology, 35,* 189–204.

Lengua, L. J. (2006). Growth of temperament and parenting as predictors of adjustment during children's transition to adolescence. *Developmental Psychology, 42,* 819–832.

Lengua, L. J., Sandler, I. N., West, S. G., Wolchik, S. A., & Curran, P. J. (1999). Emotionally and self-regulation, threat appraisal, and coping in children of divorce. *Development and Psychopathology, 11,* 15–37.

Leon, I. G. (2002). Adoption losses: Naturally occurring or socially constructed? *Child Development, 73,* 652–663.

Leon, M. (1984). Rules mothers and sons use to integrate intent and damage information in their moral judgments. *Child Development, 55,* 2106–2113.

Leppanen, J. M., Moulson, M. C., Vogel-Farley, V. K., & Nelson, C. A. (2007). An ERP study of emotional face processing in the adult and infant brain. *Child Development, 78,* 232–245.

Lepper, M. R. (1985). Microcomputers in education: Motivation and social issues. *American Psychologist, 40,* 1–18.

Lerner, R. M. (1991). Changing organism-context relations as the basic process of development: A developmental contextual perspective. *Developmental Psychology, 27,* 27–32.

Lerner, R. M. (1996). Relative plasticity, integration, temporality, and diversity in human development: A developmental contextual perspective about theory, process, and method. *Developmental Psychology, 32,* 781–786.

Lesch, E., & Kruger, L. M. (2005). Mothers, daughters, and sexual agency in one low-income South African community. *Social Science and Medicine, 61,* 1072–1082.

Lester, B. M., Kotelchuck, M., Spelke, E., Sellers, M. J., & Klein, R. E. (1974). Separation protest in Guatemalan infants: Cross-cultural and cognitive findings. *Developmental Psychology, 10,* 79–85.

Leung, C. Y. W., McBride-Chang, C., & Lai, B. Y. P. (2004). Relations among maternal parenting style, academic competence, and life satisfaction in Chinese early adolescents. *Journal of Early Adolescence, 24,* 113–143.

LeVay, S. (1996). *Queer science: The use and abuse of research into homosexuality.* Cambridge, MA: MIT Press.

Leve, L. D., & Fagot, B. I. (1997). Gender-role socialization and discipline processes in one- and two-parent families. *Sex Roles, 36,* 1–21.

Levin, I., & Druyan, S. (1993). When sociocognitive transaction among peers fails: The case of misconceptions in science. *Child Development, 64,* 1571–1591.

LeVine, R. A., Dixon, S., LeVine, S., Richman, A., Liederman, P. H., Keefer, C. H., & Brazelton, T. B. (1994). *Child care and culture: Lessons from Africa.* New York: Cambridge University Press.

Levitt, M. J., Weber, R. A., Clark, M. C., & McDonnell, P. (1985). Reciprocity of exchange in toddler sharing behavior. *Developmental Psychology, 21,* 122–123.

Levy, G. D., Taylor, M. G., & Gelman, S. A. (1995). Traditional and evaluative aspects of flexibility in gender roles, social conventions, moral rules, and physical laws. *Child Development, 66,* 515–531.

Levy-Shiff, R., Goldschmidt, I., & Har-Even, D. (1991). Transition to parenthood in adoptive families. *Developmental Psychology, 27,* 131–140.

Lewin, K., Lippitt, R., & White, R. K. (1939). Patterns of aggressive behavior in experimentally created "social climates." *Journal of Social Psychology, 10,* 271–299.

Lewin, L. M., Hops, H., Davis, B., & Dishion, T. J. (1993). Multimethod comparison of similarity in school adjustment of siblings and unrelated children. *Developmental Psychology, 24,* 963–969.

Lewis, E. E., Dozier, M., Ackerman, J. & Sepulvada-Kozakowski, S. (2007). The effect of placement instability on adopted children's inhibitory control abilities and oppositional behavior. *Developmental Psychology, 43,* 1415–1427.

Lewis, M. (1998). Emotional competence and development, In D. Pushkar, W. M. Bukowski, A. E. Schwartzman, D. M. Stack, & D. R. White (Eds.), *Improving competence across the lifespan* (pp. 27–36). New York: Plenum.

Lewis, M., Alessandri, S. M., & Sullivan, M. W. (1990). Violation of expectancy, loss of control and anger expressions in young infants. *Developmental Psychology, 26,* 745–751.

Lewis, M., Alessandri, S. M., & Sullivan, M. W. (1992). Differences in shame and pride as a function of children's gender and task difficulty. *Child Development, 63,* 630–638.

Lewis, M., & Brooks-Gunn, J. (1979). *Social cognition and the acquisition of self.* New York: Plenum Press.

Lewis, M., Feiring, C., & Rosenthal, S. (2000). Attachment over time. *Child Development, 71,* 707–720.

Lewis, M., & Ramsay D. (2002). Cortisol responses to embarrassment and shame. *Child Development, 73,* 1034–1045.

Lewis, M., & Ramsay, D. (2004). Development of self-recognition, personal pronoun use, and pretend play during the 2nd year. *Child Development, 75,* 1821–1831.

Lewis, M., & Ramsay, D. (2005). Infant emotional and cortisol responses to goal blockage. *Child Development, 76,* 518–530.

Lewis, M., & Rosenblum, M. A. (1975). *Friendship and peer relations.* New York: Wiley.

Lewis M., Stanger, C., & Sullivan, M. W. (1989). Deception in 3-year-olds. *Developmental Psychology, 24,* 434–440.

Lewis, M., Sullivan, M. W., Stanger, C., & Weiss, M. (1989). Self-development and self-conscious emotions. *Child Development, 60,* 146–156.

Leyendecker, B., & Lamb, M. E. (1999). Latino families. In M. E. Lamb (Ed.), *Parenting and child development in "nontraditional" families.* Mahwah, NJ: Erlbaum.

Leyens, J. P., Parke, R. D., Camino, L., & Berkowitz, L. (1975). Effects of movie violence on aggression in a field setting as a function of group dominance and cohesion. *Journal of Personality and Social Psychology, 32,* 346–360.

Li, J. (2002). Learning models in different cultures. In J. Bempechat & J. G. Elliot (Eds.), Learning in culture and context. *New Directions for Child Development* (No. 96, pp. 45–63). San Fransisco: Jossey-Bass.

Li, J. (2006). Self in learning: Chinese adolescents' goals and sense of agency. *Child Development, 77*, 482–501.

Liben, L. S., & Signorella, M. L. (1993). Gender-schematic processing in children: The role of initial interpretations of stimuli. *Developmental Psychology, 29*, 141–149.

Lieberman, M., Doyle, A. B., & Markiewicz, D. (1999). Developmental patterns of security of attachment to mother and father in late childhood and early adolescence: Association with peer relations. *Child Development, 70*, 202–213.

Liebert, R. M., & Baron, R. A. (1972). Some immediate effects of televised violence on children's behavior. *Developmental Psychology, 6*, 469–475.

Liebert, R. M., & Sprafkin, J. (1988). *The early window: Effects of television on children and youth* (3rd ed.). New York: Pergamon Press.

Li-Grining, C. P. (2007). Effortful control among low-income preschoolers in three cities: Stability, change, and individual differences. *Developmental Psychology, 43*, 208–231.

Lin, C. C., & Fu, V. R. (1990). A comparison of child-rearing practices among Chinese, immigrant Chinese, and Caucasian-American parents. *Child Development, 61*, 429–433.

Linebarger, D. L., & Walker, D. (2005). Infants' and toddlers' television viewing and language outcomes. *American Behavioral Scientist, 48*, 624–645.

Linn, M. C., & Petersen, A. C. (1985). Emergence and characterization of sex differences in spatial ability: A meta-analysis. *Child Development, 56*, 1479–1498.

Linn, S. (2004). *Consuming kids: The hostile takeover of childhood.* New York: New Press.

Linn, S. (2005). The commercialization of childhood. In S. Oldman (Ed.), *Childhood lost: How American culture is failing our kids* (pp. 107–122). Westport, CT: Praeger.

Lippa, R. A. (2003). Are 20:40 finger-length ratios related to sexual orientation? Yes for men, no for women. *Journal of Personality and Social Psychology, 85*, 179–188.

Lips, H. M. (2004). The gender gap in possible selves: Divergence of academic self-views among high school and university students. *Sex Roles, 50*, 357–372.

Lips, H. M. (2006). *A new psychology of women: Gender, culture, and ethnicity* (3rd ed.). New York: McGraw-Hill.

Littenberg, R., Tulkin, S., & Kagan, J. (1971). Cognitive components of separation anxiety. *Developmental Psychology, 4*, 387–388.

Liu, D., Gelman, S. A., & Wellman, H. M. (2007). Components of young children's trait understanding: Behavior-to-trait inferences and trait-to-behavior predictions. *Child Development, 78*, 1543–1558.

Livesley, W. J., & Bromley, D. B. (1973). *Person perception in childhood and adolescence.* London: Wiley.

Livner, M. R., Brooks-Gunn, J., & Kohen, D. E. (2002). Family processes as pathways from income to young children's development. *Developmental Psychology, 38*, 719–734.

Lobel, T. E., Gruber, R., Govrin, N., & Mashraki-Pedhatzur, S. (2001). Children's gender-related inferences and judgments: A cross-cultural study. *Developmental Psychology, 37*, 839–846.

Lobel, T. E., Slone, M., & Winch, G. (1997). Masculinity, popularity, and self-esteem among Israeli preadolescent girls. *Sex Roles, 36*, 395–408. and Development Series, Vol. 2). Newbury Park, CA: Sage.

Lochman, J. E., & Wells, K. C. (2004). The coping power program for preadolescent aggressive boys and their parents: Outcome effects at the 1-year follow-up. *Journal of Consulting and Clinical Psychology, 72*, 571–578.

Lockart, K. L., Chang, B., & Story, T. (2002). Young children's beliefs about the stability of traits: Protective optimism? *Child Development, 73*, 1408–1430.

Locke, J. (1913). *Some thoughts concerning education.* Sections 38 and 40. London: Cambridge University Press. (Original work published 1690).

Loeber, R., & Stouthamer-Loeber, M. (1998). Development of juvenile aggression and violence: Some common misconceptions and controversies. *American Psychologist, 53*, 242–259.

Loehlin, J. C. (1992). *Genes and environment in personality development.* Newbury Park, CA: Sage.

Lollis, S., Ross, H., & Leroux, L. (1996). An observational study of parents' socialization of moral orientation during sibling conflicts. *Merrill-Palmer Quarterly, 42*, 475–494.

London, P. (1970). The rescuers: Motivational hypotheses about Christians who saved Jews from the Nazis. In J. Macaulay & L. Berkowitz (Eds.), *Altruism and helping behavior.* Orlando, FL: Academic Press.

Lorber, J. (1986). Dismantling Noah's ark. *Sex Roles, 14*, 567–580.

Lord, H., & Mahoney, J. L. (2007). Neighborhood crime and self-care: Risks for aggression and lower academic performance. *Developmental Psychology, 43*, 1321–1333.

Lord, S. E., Eccles, J. S., & McCarthy, K. A. (1994). Surviving the junior high school transition: Family processes and self-perceptions as protective and risk factors. *Journal of Early Adolescence, 14*, 162–199.

Lorenz, K. Z. (1937). The companion in the bird's world. *Auk, 54*, 245–273.

Lorenz, K. Z. (1943). Die angeboren Formen moglicher Erfahrung [The innate forms of possible experience]. *Zeitschrift für Tierpsychologie, 5*, 233–409.

Lorenz, K. Z. (1966). *On aggression.* San Diego: Harcourt Brace Jovanovich.

Lorenz, K. Z. (1981). *The foundations of ethology.* New York: Springer-Verlag.

Loukas, A., & Robinson, S. (2004). Examining the moderating role of perceived school climate in early adolescent adjustment. *Journal of Research on Adolescence, 14*, 209–233.

Love, J. M., Harrison, L., Sagi-Schwartz, A., et al., (2003). Child care quality matters: How conclusions may vary with context. *Child Development, 74*, 1021–1033.

Love, J. M., Kisker, E. E., Ross, C., Raikes, H., Constantine, J., Boller, K., Brooks-Gunn, J., Chazan-Cohen, R., Tarullo, L. B., Brady-Smith, C., Fulgini, A. S., Schochet, P.Z., Paulsell, D., & Vogel, C. (2005). The effectiveness of Early Head Start for 3-year-old children and their parents: Lessons for policy and programs. *Developmental Psychology, 41*, 885–901.

Lowenthal, B. (2000). Effects of maltreatment and ways to promote children's resiliency. In K. L. Freiberg (Ed.), *Human development 00/01* (28th ed., pp. 151–154). Guilford, CT: Duskin/McGraw-Hill.

Lowy, J. (2000, February 24). U.S. teen pregnancy rate still high. *Atlanta Constitution*, p. E2.

Luecke-Aleksa, D., Anderson, D. R., Collins, P. A., & Schmitt, K. L. (1995). Gender constancy and television viewing. *Developmental Psychology, 31*, 773–780.

Lueptow, L. B., Garovich-Szabo, L., & Leuptow, M. B. (2001). Social changes and the persistence of sex-typing: 1974–1997. *Social Forces, 80*, 1–36.

Lummis, M., & Stevenson, H. W. (1990). Gender differences in beliefs and achievement: A cross-cultural study. *Developmental Psychology, 26*, 254–263.

Luster, T., & McAdoo, H. (1996). Family and child influences on educational attainment: A secondary analysis of the High/Scope Perry preschool data. *Developmental Psychology, 32*, 26–39.

Lustig, J. L., Wolchik, S. A., & Braver, S. L. (1992). Social support in chumships and adjustment in children of divorce. *American Journal of Community Psychology, 20*, 393–399.

Luthar, S. S., & Becker, B. E. (2002). Privileged but pressured: A study of affluent youth. *Child Development, 73*, 1593–1610.

Luthar, S. S., & D'Avanzo, K. (1999). Contextual factors in substance use: A study of suburban and inner-city adolescents. *Development and Psychopathology, 11*, 845–867.

Luthar, S. S., & Latendresse, S. J. (2005a). Children of the affluent: Challenges to well-being. *Current Directions in Psychological Science, 14*, 49–53.

Luthar, S. S., & Latendresse, S. J. (2005b). Comparable "risks" at the socioeconomic extremes. Preadolescents' perceptions of parenting. *Development and Psychopathology, 17*, 207–231.

Lyons-Ruth, K., Alpern, L., & Repacholi, B. (1993). Disorganized infant attachment classification and maternal psychosocial problems as predictors of hostile-aggressive behavior in the preschool classroom. *Child Development, 64*, 572–585.

Lyons-Ruth, K., Connell, D. B., Grunebaum, H., & Botein, S. (1990). Infants at social risk: Maternal depression and family support services as mediators of infant development and security of attachment. *Child Development, 61*, 85–98.

Lyons-Ruth, K., Easterbrooks, M. A., & Cibelli, C.D., (1997). Infant attachment strategies, infant mental lag, and maternal depressive symptoms: Predictors of internalizing and externalizing problems at age 7. *Developmental Psychology, 33*, 681-692.

Lytton, H. (1990). Child and parent effects in boys' conduct disorder: A reinterpretation. *Developmental Psychology, 26*, 683–697.

Lytton, H., & Romney, D. M. (1991). Parents' differential socialization of Boys and girls: A meta-analysis. *Psychological Bulletin, 109*, 267–296.

Maccoby, E. E. (1980). *Social development*. San Diego: Harcourt Brace Jovanovich.

Maccoby, E. E. (1998). *The two sexes: Growing up apart, coming together*. Cambridge, MA: Harvard University Press.

Maccoby, E. E., & Jacklin, C. N. (1974). *The psychology of sex differences*. Stanford, CA: Stanford University Press.

Maccoby, E. E., & Jacklin, C. N. (1980). Sex differences in aggression: A rejoinder and reprise. *Child Development, 51*, 964–980.

Maccoby, E. E., & Martin, J. A. (1983). Socialization in the context of the family: Parent-child interaction. In E. M. Hetherington (Ed.) & (P. H. Mussen, Gen. Ed.), *Handbook of child psychology. Vol. 4: Socialization, personality, and social development* (4th Ed.). New York: Wiley.

MacFarlane, A. (1977). *The psychology of childbirth*. Cambridge, MA: Harvard University Press.

Mac Iver, D., & Reuman, D. A. (1988, April). *Decision-making in the classroom and early adolescents' valuing of mathematics*. Paper presented at the annual meeting of the American Educational Research Association, New Orleans, LA.

Mac Iver, D. J., Reuman, D. A., & Main, S. R. (1995). Social structuring of the school: Studying what is, illuminating what could be. *Annual Review of Psychology, 46*, 375–400.

MacKinnon-Lewis, C., Rabiner, D., & Starnes, R. (1999). Predicting boys' social acceptance and rejection: Role of mother-child interactions and boys' beliefs about peers. *Developmental Psychology, 35*, 632–639.

MacKinnon-Lewis, C., Starnes, R., Volling, B., & Johnson, S. (1997). Perceptions of parenting as predictors of boys' sibling and peer relations. *Developmental Psychology, 33*, 1024–1031.

MacPhee, D., Fritz, J., & Miller-Heyl, J. (1996). Ethnic variations in personal social networks and parenting. *Child Development, 67*, 3278–3295.

Madigan, S., Moran, G., & Pederson, D. R. (2006). Unresolved states of mind, attachment relationships, and disrupted interactions of adolescent mothers and their infants. *Developmental Psychology, 42*, 293–304.

Magnusson, K., Meyers, M., Rhum C., & Waldfogel, J. (2003). *Inequality in preschool education and school readiness*. New York: Columbia University, School of Social Work.

Mahler, M. S., Pine, F., & Bergman, A. (1975). *The psychological birth of the infant*. New York: Basic Books.

Mahoney, A., Jouriles, E. N., & Scavone, J. (1997). Marital adjustment and marital discard over childrearing, and child problems: Moderating effects of child age. *Journal of Clinical Child Psychology, 26*, 415–423.

Mahoney, J. L. (2000). School extracurricular activity participation as a moderator in the development of antisocial patterns. *Child Development, 71*, 502–516.

Mahoney, J. L., & Cairns, R. B. (1997). Do extracurricular activities protect against early school dropout? *Developmental Psychology, 33*, 241–253.

Mahoney, J. L., Harris, A. L., & Eccles, J. S. (2006). Organized activity participation, positive youth development, and the over-scheduling hypothesis. *Social Policy Report, 20*. Society for Research in Child Development.

Mahoney, J. L., Lord, H., & Carryl, E. (2005). An ecological analysis of after-school program participation in the development of academic performance and motivational attributes for disadvantaged children. *Child Development, 76*, 811–825.

Main, M., & Cassidy, J. (1988). Categories of response to reunion with the parent at age 6: Predictable from infant attachment classifications and stable over a 1-month period. *Developmental Psychology, 24*, 415–426.

Main, M., & George, C. (1985). Responses of abused and disadvantaged toddlers to distress in agemates: A study in the day-care setting. *Developmental Psychology, 21*, 407–412.

Main, M., & Goldwyn, R. (1994). *Interview-based adult attachment classifications: Related to infant-mother and infant-father attachment*. Unpublished manuscript, University of California, Berkeley.

Main, M., & Solomon, J. (1990). Procedures for identifying infants as disorganized/disoriented during the Ainsworth Strange Situation. In M. T. Greenberg, D. Cicchetti, & E. M. Cummings (Eds.), *Attachment in the preschool years: Theory, research, and intervention*. Chicago: University of Chicago Press.

Main, M., & Weston, D. R. (1981). The quality of the toddler's relationship to mother and to father: Related to conflict and the readiness to establish new relationships. *Child Development, 52*, 932–940.

Malatesta, C. Z., Culver, C., Tesman, J. R., & Shepard, B. (1989). The development of emotion expression during the first two years of life. *Monographs of the Society for Research in Child Development, 54,* (1–2, Serial No. 219).

Malatesta, C. Z., Grigoryev, P., Lamb, C., Albin, M., & Culver, C. (1986). Emotional socialization and expressive development in pre-term and full-term infants. *Child Development, 57,* 316–330.

Malatesta, C. Z., & Haviland, J. M., (1982). Learning display rules: The socialization of emotion expression in infancy. *Child Development, 53,* 991–1003.

Malley-Morrison, K., & Hines, D. A. (2004). *Family violence in a cultural perspective: Defining, understanding, and combating abuse.* Thousand Oaks, CA: Sage,

Mallick, S. K., & McCandless, B. R. (1966). A study of the catharsis of aggression. *Journal of Personality and Social Psychology, 4,* 591–596.

Mangelsdorf, S. C. (1992). Developmental changes in infant-stranger interaction. *Infant Behavior and Development, 15,* 191–208.

Mangelsdorf, S. C., Shapiro, J. R., & Marzolf, D. (1995). Developmental and temperamental differences in emotion regulation in infancy. *Child Development, 66,* 1817–1828.

Manset, G., & Semmel, M. I. (1997). Are inclusive programs for students with mild disabilities effective? A comparative review of model programs. *Journal of Special Education, 31,* 155–180.

Marcia, J. E. (1980). Identity in adolescence. In J. Adelson (Ed.), *Handbook of adolescent psychology.* New York: Wiley.

Marcia, J. E., Waterman, A. S., Matteson, D., Archer, S. C., & Orlofsky, J. L. (1993). *Ego identity: A handbook for psychosocial research.* New York: Springer-Verlag.

Marcon, R. A. (1999). Differential impact of preschool models on development and early learning of inner-city children: A three-cohort study. *Developmental Psychology, 35,* 358–375.

Marcovitch, S., Goldberg, S., Gold, A., Washington, J., Wasson, C., Krekwich, K., & Handley-Derry, M. (1997). Determinants of behavioral problems in Romanian children adopted in Ontario. *International Journal of Behavioral Development, 20,* 17–31.

Margolin, G., & Gordis, E. B. (2000). The effects of family and community violence on children. *Annual Review of Psychology, 51,* 445–479.

Markovits, H., & Dumas, C. (1999). Developmental patterns in the understanding of social and physical transitivity. *Journal of Experimental Child Psychology, 73,* 95–114.

Markstrom-Adams, C. (1992). A consideration of intervening factors in adolescent identity formation. In G. R. Adams, T. P., Gullotta, & R. Montemayer (Eds.), *Adolescent identity formation* (Advances in Adolescent Development, Vol. 4). Newbury Park, CA: Sage.

Markus, H., & Kitayama, S. (1994). A collective fear of the collective: Implications for selves and theories of selves. *Personality and Social Psychology Bulletin, 20,* 568–579.

Marsh, H. W., & Ayotte, V. (2003). Do multiple dimensions of self-concept become more differentiated with age? The differential distinctiveness hypothesis. *Journal of Educational Psychology, 81,* 70–85.

Marsh, H. W., Craven, R., & Debus, R. (1998). Structure, stability, and development of children's self-concepts: A multicohort-multioccasion study. *Child Development, 69,* 1030–1053.

Marsh, H. W., Ellis, L. A., & Craven, R. G. (2002). How do preschool children feel about themselves? Unraveling the measurement and multidimensional self-concept structure. *Developmental Psychology, 38,* 376–393.

Marsh, H. W., & Hau, K. (2003). The big fish-little pond effect on academic self-concept: A cross-cultural (26 country) test on the negative effects of academically selective schools. *American Psychologist, 58,* 364–376.

Marshall, N. L., Coll, C. G., Marx, F., McCartney, K., Keefe, N., & Ruh, J. (1997). After-school time and children's behavioral adjustment. *Merrill-Palmer Quarterly, 43,* 497–514.

Marsiglio, W., Amato, P. R., Day, R. D., & Lamb, M. E. (2000). Scholarship on fathering in the 1990s and beyond. *Journal of Marriage and the Family, 62,* 1173–1191.

Martin, C. L. (1990). Attitudes and expectations about children with non-traditional gender roles. *Sex Roles, 22,* 151–165.

Martin, C. L. (1994). Cognitive influences on the development and maintenance of gender segregation. *New directions for Child Development, 65,* 35–51.

Martin, C. L., Eisenbud, L., & Rose, H. (1995). Children's gender-based reasoning about toys. *Child Development, 66,* 1453–1471.

Martin, C. L., & Fabes, R. A. (2001). The stability and conse-quences of young children's same-sex peer interactions. *Developmental Psychology, 37,* 431–446.

Martin, C. L., & Halverson, C. F., Jr. (1981). A schematic processing model of sex typing and stereotyping in children. *Child Development, 52,* 1119–1134.

Martin, C. L., & Halverson, C. F., Jr. (1983). The effects of sex-typing schemas on young children's memory. *Child Development, 54,* 563–574.

Martin, C. L., & Halverson, C. F., Jr. (1987). The roles of cognition in sex-roles and sex-typing. In D. B. Carter (Ed.), *Current conceptions of sex roles and sex-typing: Theory and Research.* New York: Praeger.

Martin, C. L., & Ruble, D. N. (2004). Children's search for gen-der cues: Cognitive perspectives on gender development. *Current Directions in Psychological Science, 13,* 67–70.

Martin, G. B., & Clark, R. D., III. (1982). Distress crying in neo-nates: Species and peer specificity. *Developmental Psychology, 18,* 3–9.

Martin, M. O., et al. (2000). TIMSS 1999 *International Science Report: Findings from IEA's Report of the Third International Mathematics and Science Study at the Eighth Grade.* Chestnut Hill, MA: Boston College.

Martin, N. G., & Jardine, R. (1986). Eysenck's contributions to behavior genetics. In S. Modgil & C. Modgil (Eds.), *Hans Eysenck: Consensus and controversy.* Philadelphia: Falmer.

Mascolo, M. F., & Li, J. (2004). *New directions in child and adolescent development: Beyond dichotomization-culture and developing selves.* San Francisco: Jossey-Bass.

Masden, A. S., Coatsworth, J. D., Neeman, J., Gest, J. D., Tellegen, A., & Garmezy, N. (1995). The structure and coherence of compe-tence from childhood through adolescence. *Child Development, 66,* 1635–1659.

Mason, C. A., Cauce, A. M., Gonzales, N., & Hiraga, Y. (1996). Neither too sweet nor too sour: Problem peers, maternal control, and problem behavior in African-American adolescents. *Child Development, 67,* 2115–2130.

Mason, M. G., & Gibbs, J. C. (1993). Social perspective taking and moral judgment among college students. *Journal of Adolescent Research, 8,* 109–123.

Masters, J. C., Ford, M. E., Arend, R., Grotevant, H. D., & Clark, L. V. (1979). Modeling and labeling as integrated determinants of children's sex-typed imitative behavior. *Child Development, 50,* 364–371.

Matejcek, Z., Dytrych, Z., & Schuller, V. (1979). The Prague study of children born from unwanted pregnancies. *International Journal of Mental Health, 7,* 63–74.

Matias, R., & Cohn, J. F. (1993). Are Max-specified infant facial expressions during face-to-face interaction consistent with differential emotions theory? *Developmental Psychology, 29,* 524–531.

Matsumoto, D. (2000). *Culture and psychology* (2nd ed.). Belmont, CA: Wadsworth.

Matthews, K. A., Batson, C. D., Horn, J., & Rosenman, R. H. (1981). "Principles in his nature which interest him in the fortune of others": The heritability of empathic concern for others. *Journal of Personality, 49,* 237–247.

Maughan, A., & Cicchetti, D. (2002). Impact of child maltreatment and interadult violence on children's emotional regulation abilities and socioemotional adjustment. *Child Development, 73,* 1525–1542.

Mayer-Smith, J., Pedretti, E., & Woodrow, J. (2000). Closing of the gender gap in technology-enriched science education: A case study. *Computers and Education, 35,* 51–63.

Mayeux, L., & Cillessen, A. H. N. (2003). Development of social problem solving in early childhood: Stability, change, and associations with social competence. *Journal of Genetic Psychology, 164,* 153–173.

Maynard, A. E. (2002). Cultural teaching: The development of teaching skills in Maya sibling interactions. *Child Development, 73,* 969–982.

McCabe, M. P., & Ricciardelli, L. A. (2005). A longitudinal study of body image and strategies to lose weight and increase muscles among children. *Applies Developmental Psychology, 26,* 559–577.

McCall, R. B. (1977). Challenges to a science of developmental psychology. *Child Development, 48,* 333–344.

McCall, R. B. (1981). Nature-nurture and the two realms of development: A proposed integration with respect to mental development. *Child Development, 52,* 1–12.

McCall, R. B., Beach, S. R., & Lau, S. (2000). The nature and correlates of underachievement among elementary school children in Hong Kong. *Child Development, 71,* 785–801.

McCartney, K., Harris, M. J., & Bernieri, F. (1990). Growing up and growing apart: A developmental meta-analysis of twin studies. *Psychological Bulletin, 107,* 226–237.

McClelland, D. C. (1961). *The achieving society.* New York: Free Press.

McClelland, D. C., Atkinson, J. W., Clark, R. A., & Lowell, E. L. (1953). *The achievement motive.* New York: Appleton-Century-Crofts.

McCloskey, L. A., Figueredo, A. J., & Koss, M. P. (1995). The effects of systematic family violence on children's mental health. *Child Development, 66,* 1239–1261.

McConaghy, M. (1979). Gender permanence and the genital basis of gender: Stages in the development of constancy and gender identity. *Child Development, 50,* 1223–1226.

McDougall, W. (1908). *An introduction to social psychology.* London: Methuen.

McFadyen-Ketchum, S. A., Bates, J. E., Dodge, K. A., & Pettit, G. S. (1996). Patterns of change in early childhood aggressive-disruptive behavior: Gender differences in predictions from early coercive and affectionate mother-child interactions. *Child Development, 67,* 2417–2433.

McGhee, P. E., & Frueh, T. (1980). Television viewing and the learning of sex-role stereotypes. *Sex Roles, 6,* 179–188.

McGrath, E. P., & Repetti, R. L. (2000). Mothers' and fathers' attitudes toward their children's academic performance and children's perceptions of their academic competence. *Journal of Youth and Adolescence, 29,* 713–723.

McGue, M., Elkins, I., Walden, B., & Iacono, W. G. (2005). Perceptions of the parent-adolescent relationship: A longitudinal investigation. *Developmental Psychology, 41,* 971–984.

McGuire, K. D., & Weisz, J. R. (1982). Social cognition and behavioral correlates of preadolescent chumship. *Child Development, 53,* 1478–1484.

McGuire, S., Manke, G., Eftekhari, A., & Dunn, J. (2000). Children's perception of sibling conflict during middle childhood. Issues and sibling (dis) similarity. *Social Development, 9,* 173–190.

McHale, J. P. (1995). Coparenting and triadic interactions during infancy: The roles of marital distress and child gender. *Developmental Psychology, 31,* 985–996.

McHale, J. P., Lauretti, A., Talbut, J., & Pouquette, C. (2002). Retrospect and prospect in the psychological study of coparenting and family group process. In J. P. McHale & W. S. Grolnick (Eds.), *Retrospect and prospect in the psychological study of families.* (pp. 127–165). Mahwah, NJ: Erlbaum.

McHale, S. M., & Crouter, A. C. (2003). How do children exert an impact on family life. In A. C. Crouter & A. Booth (Eds.), *Children's influence on family dynamics: The neglected side of family relationships* (pp. 207–220). Mahwah, NJ: Erlbaum.

McHale, S. M., Crouter, A. C., Kim, J., Burton, L. M., Davis, K. D., Dotterer, A. M., & Swanson, D. P. (2006). Mothers' and fathers' racial socialization in African American families: Implications for youth. *Child Development, 77,* 1387–1402.

McHale, S. M., Crouter, A. C., & Tucker, C. J. (1999). Family context and gender role socialization in middle childhood: Comparing girls to boys and sisters to brothers. *Child Development, 70,* 990–1004.

McHale, S. M., Crouter, A. C., & Tucker, C. (2001). Free-time activities in middle childhood: Links with adjustment in early adolescence. *Child Development, 72,* 1764–1778.

McHale, S. M., Kim, J., Whiteman, S., & Crouter, A. C. (2004). Links between sex-typed time use in middle childhood and gender development in early adolescence. *Developmental Psychology, 40,* 868–881.

McHale, S. M., Shanahan, L., Updegraff, K. A., Crouter, A. C., & Booth, A. (2004). Developmental and individual differences in girls sex-typed activities in middle childhood and adolescence. *Child Development, 75,* 1575–1593.

McHale, S. M., Updegraff, K. A., Helms-Erikson, H., & Crouter, A. C. (2001). Sibling influences on gender development in middle childhood and early adolescence: A longitudinal study. *Developmental Psychology, 37,* 115–125.

McHale, S. M., Updegraff, K. A., Jackson-Newsom, J., Tucker, C. J., & Crouter, A. C. (2000). When does parents' differential treatment have negative implications for siblings. *Social Development, 9,* 149–172.

McKenna, M. A. J. (1997, May 2). U.S., Georgia gets welcome news on teenagers and sex. *Atlanta Constitution,* D1.

McKenna, M. W., & Ossoff, E. P. (1998). Age differences in children's comprehension of a popular television program. *Child Study Journal, 28,* 53–68.

McKown, C., & Weinstein, R. S. (2003). The development and consequences of stereotype consciousness in middle childhood. *Child Development, 74,* 516–534.

McKown, C., & Weinstein, R. S. (2003). The development and consequences of stereotype consciousness in middle childhood. *Child Development, 74,* 498–515.

McLaughlin, A. E., Campbell, F. A., Pungello, E. P., & Skinner, M. (2007). Depressive symptoms in young adults: The influences of early home environment and early educational child care. *Child Development, 78*, 746–756.

McLean, K. C., & Thorne, A. (2003). Late adolescents self-defining memories about relationships. *Developmental Psychology, 39*, 635–645.

McLellan, J. A., & Youniss, J. (2003). Two systems of youth service: Determinants of voluntary and required youth community service. *Journal of Youth and Adolescence, 32*, 47–58.

McLoyd, V. C. (1989). Socialization and development in a changing economy: The effects of paternal job and income loss on children. *American Psychologist, 44*, 293–302.

McLoyd, V. C. (1998). Socioeconomic disadvantage and child development. *American Psychologist, 53*, 185–204.

McLoyd, V. C., & Smith, J. (2002). Physical discipline and behavior problems in African American, European American, and Hispanic children: Emotional support as a moderator. *Journal of Marriage and the Family, 64*, 40–53.

Mead, G. H. (1934). *Mind, self, and society*. Chicago: University of Chicago Press.

Mead, M. (1935). *Sex and temperament in three primitive societies*. New York: William Morrow.

Measelle, J. R., Albow, J. C., Cowan, P., & Cowan, C. P. (1998). Assessing young children's views of their academic, social, and emotional lives: An evaluation of the self-perception scales of the Berkeley Puppet Interview. *Child Development, 69*, 1556–1576.

Meckler, L. (2002, July 25). When wedding bells clank: Detailed Centers for Disease Control survey outlines factors for divorce, success. *Denver Post*, p. A2.

Mediascope, Inc. (1996). *National Television Violence Study: Executive summary* 1994–1995. Studio City, CA: Author.

Medrich, E. A., Rosen, J., Rubin, V., & Buckley, S. (1982). *The serious business of growing up*. Berkeley: University of California Press.

Meehan, B. T., Hughes, J. N., & Cavell, T. A. (2003). Teacher-student relationships as compensatory resources for aggressive children. *Child Development, 74*, 1145–1157.

Meeks, W., Iedema, J., Helson, M., & Vollebergh, W. (1999). Patterns of adolescents identity development: Review of literature and longitudinal analysis. *Developmental Review, 19*, 419–461.

Meeus, W., Iedema, J., Helson, M., & Vollebergh, W. (1999). Patterns of adolescent identity development: Review of literature and longitudinal analysis. *Developmental Review, 19*, 419–461.

Mehan, H., Villanueva, I., Hubbard, L., & Lintz, A. (1996). *Constructing school success: The consequences of untracking low-achieving students*. New York: Cambridge University Press.

Meilman, P. W. (1979). Cross-sectional age changes in ego identity status during adolescence. *Developmental Psychology, 15*, 230–231.

Meins, E., Fernyhough, C., Wainwright, R., Das Gupta, M., Fradley, E., & Tuckey, M. (2002). Maternal mind-mindedness and attachment security as predictors of theory of mind understanding. *Child Development, 73*, 1715–1726.

Mekos, D., Hetherington, E. M., & Reiss, D. (1996). Sibling differences in problem behavior and parental treatment in nondivorced and remarried families. *Child Development, 67*, 2148–2165.

Melson, G. F., Peet, S., & Sparks, C. (1991). Children's attachments to their pets: Links to socioemotional development. *Children's Environmental Quarterly, 8*, 55–65.

Meltzoff, A. N. (1988a). Imitation of televised models by infants. *Child Development, 59*, 1221–1229.

Meltzoff, A. N. (1988b). Infant imitation and memory: Nine-month-olds in immediate and deferred tests. *Child Development, 59*, 217–225.

Meltzoff, A. N. (1990a). Foundations for developing a concept of self: The role of imitation in relating self to other and the value of social mirroring, social modeling, and self-practice in infancy. In D. Cicchetti & M. Beeghly (Eds.), *The self in transition: Infancy to childhood* (pp. 139–164), Chicago: University of Chicago Press.

Meltzoff, A. N. (1990b). Towards a developmental cognitive science. *Annals of the New York Academy of Sciences, 608*, 1–37.

Meltzoff, A. N. (1995). Understanding the intentions of others: Re-enactment of intended acts by 18-month-old children. *Developmental Psychology, 31*, 838–850.

Meltzoff, A. N., & Moore, M. K. (1977). Imitation of facial and manual gestures by human neonates. *Science, 198*, 75–78.

Meltzoff, A. N., & Moore, M. K. (1989). Imitation in newborn infants: Exploring the range of gestures imitated and the underlying mechanisms. *Developmental Psychology, 25*, 954–962.

Meltzoff, A. N., & Moore, M. K. (1992). Early imitation within a functional framework: The importance of person, identity, movement, and development. *Infant Behavior and Development, 15*, 479–505.

Menon, M., Tobin, D. D., Corby, B. C., Menon, M., Hodges, E. V. E., & Perry, D. G. (2007). The developmental costs of high self-esteem for antisocial children. *Child Development, 78*, 1627–1639.

Messinger, D. S., Fogel, A., & Dickson, K. L. (2001). All smiles are positive, but some smiles are more positive than others. *Developmental Psychology, 37*, 642–653.

Metz, E., & Youniss, J. (2005). Longitudinal gains in civic development through school-based required service. *Political Psychology, 26*, 413–437.

Meyer-Bahlberg, H. F. L., Ehrhardt, A. A., Rosen, L. R., Gruen, R. S., Veridiano, N. P., Vann, F. H., & Neuwalder, H. F. (1995). Prenatal estrogens and the development of homosexual orientation. *Developmental Psychology, 31*, 12–21.

Michalson, L., & Lewis, M. (1985). What do children know about emotions and when do they know it? In M. Lewis & C. Saarni (Eds.), *The socialization of emotions* (pp. 117–139). New York: Plenum.

Midgley, C., Feldlaufer, H., & Eccles, J. S. (1989). Student/teacher relations and attitudes toward mathematics before and after the transition to junior high school. *Child Development, 60*, 981–992

Midlarksy, E., & Bryan, J. H. (1972). Affect expressions and children's initiative altruism. *Journal of Experimental Research in Personality, 6*, 195–203.

Midlarsky, E., Kahana, E., Corley, R., Nemeroff, R., & Schonbar, R. A. (1999). Altruistic moral judgement among older adults. *International Journal of Aging and Human Development, 49*, 27–41.

Miller, B. C., Benson, B., & Galbraith, K. A. (2001). Family relationships and adolescent pregnancy risk: A research synthesis. *Developmental Review, 21*, 1–38.

Miller, B. C., Fan, X., Christensen, M., Grotevant, H. D., & Van Dulmen, M. (2000). Comparisons of adopted and nonadopted adolescents in a large, nationally representative sample. *Child Development, 71*, 533–541.

Miller, C. L. (1983). Developmental changes in male/female voice classification by infants. *Infant Behavior and Development, 6*, 313–330.

Miller, C. L., Miceli, P. J., Whitman, T. L., & Borkowski, J. G. (1996). Cognitive readiness to parent and intellectual-emotional development in children of adolescent mothers. *Developmental Psychology, 32*, 533–541.

Miller, K. S., Forehand R., & Kotchick, B. A. (1999). Adolescent sexual behavior in two ethnic minority samples: The role of family variables. *Journal of Marriage and the Family, 61*, 85–98.

Miller, K. S., Levin, M. L., Whitaker, D. J., & Xu, X. (1998). Patterns of condom use among adolescents: The impact of mother-adolescent communication. *American Journal of Public Health, 88*, 1542–1544.

Miller, M., Azrael, D., & Hemenway, D. (2002). Firearm availability and unintentional firearm deaths, suicide, and homicide among 5- to 14-year-olds. *Journal of Trauma—Injury, Infection, Critical Care, 52*, 267–275.

Miller, N. B., Cowan, P. A., Cowan, C. P., Hetherington, E. M., & Clingempeel, W. G. (1993). Externalizing in preschoolers and early adolescents: A cross-study replication of a family model. *Developmental Psychology, 29*, 3–18.

Miller, P. A., Eisenberg, N., Fabes, R. A., & Shell, R. (1996). Relations of moral reasoning and vicarious emotion to young children's prosocial behavior toward peers and adults. *Developmental Psychology, 32*, 210–219.

Miller, P. H. (2002). *Theories of developmental psychology* (4th ed.). New York: Worth.

Miller, P. H., & Aloise, P. A. (1989). Young children's understanding of the psychological causes of behavior: A review. *Child Development, 60*, 257–285.

Miller-Johnson, S., & Costanzo, P. (2004). If you can't beat them . . . Induce them to join you: Peer-based interventions during adolescence. In J. Kupersmidt & K. A. Dodge (Eds.), *Children's peer relations: From development to intervention* (pp. 209–222). Washington, DC: American Psychological Association.

Milligan, K., Astington, J. W., & Dack, L. A (2007). Language and theory of mind: Meta-analysis of the relation between language ability and false-belief understanding. *Child Development, 78*, 622–646.

Mills, R. S. L., & Grusec, J. E. (1989). Cognitive, affective, and behavioral consequences of praising altruism. *Merrill-Palmer Quarterly, 35*, 299–326.

Minor, C. A., & Neel, R. G. (1958). The relationship between achievement motive and occupational preference. *Journal of Counseling Psychology, 5*, 39–43.

Mitchell, J. E., Baker, L. A., & Jacklin, C. N. (1989). Masculinity and femininity in twin children: Genetic and environmental factors. *Child Development, 60*, 1475–1485.

Mitchell, P. (1997). *Introduction to theory of mind: Children, autism, and apes.* London: Arnold.

Miyazaki, M., & Hiraki, K. (2006). Delayed intermodal contingency affects young children's recognition of their current self. *Child Development, 77*, 736–750.

Mize, J., & Ladd, G. W. (1990). A cognitive-social learning approach to Social skill training with low-status preschool children. *Developmental Psychology, 26*, 388–397.

Mize, J. & Pettit, G. S. (1997). Mother's social coaching, mother-child relationship style, and children's peer competence: Is the medium the message? *Child Development, 68*, 312–322.

Mize, J., Pettit, G. S., & Brown, E. G. (1995). Mothers' supervision of their children's peer play: Relations with beliefs, perceptions, and knowledge. *Developmental Psychology, 31*, 311–321.

Moffitt, T. E. (1993). Adolescent-limited and life-course-persistent antisocial behavior: A developmental taxonomy. *Psychological Review, 100*, 674–701.

Moffitt, T. E., & Caspi, A. (2001). Childhood predictors differentiate life-course persistent and adolescent-limited antisocial pathways among males and females. *Developmental Psychopathology, 13*, 355–375.

Moll, H., & Tomasello, M. (2007). How 14- and 18-month-olds know what others have experienced. *Developmental Psychology, 43*, 309–317.

Money, J. (1965). Psychosexual differentiation. In J. Money (Ed.), *Sex research: New developments.* New York: Holt, Rinehart, and Winston.

Money, J. (1985). Pediatric sexology and hermaphrodism. *Journal of Sex and Marital Therapy, 11*, 139–156.

Money, J. (1988). *Gay, straight, and in-between: The sexology of erotic orientation.* New York: Oxford University Press.

Money, J., & Ehrhardt, A. (1972). *Man and woman, boy and girl.* Baltimore: Johns Hopkins University Press.

Money, J., & Tucker, P. (1975). *Sexual signatures: On being a man or a woman.* Boston: Little, Brown.

Montemayor, R., & Eisen, M. (1977). The development of self-conceptions from childhood to adolescence. *Developmental Psychology, 13*, 314–319.

Moore, E. G. J. (1986). Family socialization and the IQ test performance of traditionally and transracially adopted black children. *Developmental Psychology, 22*, 317–326.

Moore, G. A., Cohn, J. F., & Campbell, S. B. (2001). Infant affective responses to mothers still face at 6 months differentially predict externalizing and internalizing behaviors at 18 months. *Developmental Psychology, 37*, 706–714.

Moore, M. R., & Brooks-Gunn, J. (2002). Adolescent parenthood. In M. H. Borstein (Ed.), *Handbook of parenting. Vol. 3: Being and becoming a parent* (2nd ed., pp. 173–214). Mahwah, NJ: Erlbaum.

Morgan, G. A., & Ricciuti, H. N. (1969). Infants' responses to strangers during the first year. In B. M. Foss (Ed.), *Determinants of infant behavior* (Vol. 4). London: Methuen.

Morgan-Thompson, E., & Morgan, E. M. (2008). "Mostly straight" young women: Variations in sexual behavior and identity development. *Developmental Psychology, 44*, 15–21.

Morrison, F. J., Griffith, E. M., & Alberts, D. M. (1997). Native-nurture in the classroom: Entrance age, school readiness, and learning in children. *Developmental Psychology, 33*, 254–262.

Morrison, F. J., Smith, L., & Dow-Ehrensberger, M. (1995). Education and cognitive development: A natural experiment. *Developmental Psychology, 31*, 789–799.

Morrison, M. M., & Shaffer, D. R. (2003). Gender-role congruence and self-referencing as determinants of advertising effectiveness. *Sex Roles, 49*, 265–275.

Morrongiello, B. A., & Hogg, K. (2004). Mothers' reactions to children's misbehaving in ways that can lead to injury: Implications for gender differences in children's risk taking and injuries. *Sex Roles, 50*, 1003–1018.

Moses, L. J., Coon, J. A., & Wusinich, N. (2000). Young children's understanding of desire information. *Developmental Psychology, 36*, 77–90.

Mosher, W. D., Chandra, A., & Jones, J. (2005). *Sexual behavior and selected health measures: Men and women 15–44 years of age, United States, 2002.* Advance Data: Centers for Disease Control.

Moshman, D. (1999). *Adolescent psychological development: Rationality, morality, and identity*. Mahwah, NJ: Erlbaum.

Moss, E., Cyr, C., Bureau, J. F., Tarabulsy, G. M., & Dubois-Comtois, K. (2005). Stability of attachment during the preschool period. *Developmental Psychology, 41*, 773–783.

Moss, E., & St-Laurent, D. (2001). Attachment at school age and academic performance. *Developmental Psychology, 37*, 863–874.

Mostow, A. J., Izard, C. E., Fine, S., & Trentacosta, J. (2002). Modeling emotional, cognitive, and behavioral predictors of peer acceptance. *Child Development, 73*, 1775–1787.

Mroczek, D., & Kolarz, C. (1998). The effect of age on positive and negative affect: A developmental perspective on happiness. *Journal of Personality and Social Psychology, 75*, 1333–1349.

Mueller, C. M., & Dweck, C. S. (1998). Praise for intelligence can undermine children's motivation and performances. *Journal of Personality and Social Psychology, 75*, 33–52.

Mueller, E., & Lucas, T. (1975). A developmental analysis of peer interactions among toddlers. In M. Lewis & L. Rosenblum (Eds.), *Friendship and peer relations*. New York: Wiley.

Mumme, D. L., & Fernald, A. (2003). The infant as onlooker: Learning from emotional reactions observed in a television scenario. *Child Development, 74*, 221–237.

Mumme, D. L., Fernald, A., & Herrera, C. (1996). Infants' responses to facial and vocal emotional signals in a social referencing paradigm. *Child Development, 67*, 3219–3237.

Munro, G., & Adams, G R. (1977). Ego-identity formation in college students and working youth. *Developmental Psychology, 13*, 523–524.

Munroe, R. H., Shimmin, H. S., & Munroe, R. L. (1984). Gender understanding and sex-role preferences in four cultures. *Developmental Psychology, 20*, 673–682.

Murphy, C. M., & Blumenthal, D. R. (2000). The mediating influence of interpersonal problems on the intergenerational transmission of relationship aggression. *Personal Relationships, 7*, 203–218.

Murray, B. (2000). Reinventing class discussion online. *Monitor on Psychology, 31*, 54–56.

Murray, H. (1938). *Explorations in personality*. New York: Oxford University Press.

Murray, J. P., & Lonnborg, B. (2005). *Children and television: Using TV sensibly*. Kansas State University Agricultural Experiment Station and Cooperative Extension Service.

Murray, L., Fiori-Cowley, A., Hooper, R., & Cooper, P. (1996). The impact of postnatal depression and associated adversity on early mother-infant interactions and later infant outcome. *Child Development, 67*, 2512–2526.

Muzzatti, B., & Agnoli, F. (2007). Gender and mathematics: Attitudes and stereotype threat susceptibility in Italian children. *Developmental Psychology, 43*, 747–759.

Myers, D. G. (1996). *Social psychology* (5th ed.). New York: McGraw-Hill.

Nagin, D. S., & Tremblay, R. E. (1999). Trajectories of boys' physical aggression, opposition, and hyperactivity on the path to physically violent and nonviolent juvenile delinquency. *Child Development, 70*, 1181–1196.

Nansel, T. R., Craig, W., Overpeck, M. D., Saluja, G., Ruan, W. J., & The Health Behavior in School-Aged Children Bullying Analysis Working Group (2004). Cross-national consistency in the relationship between bullying behaviors and psychosocial adjustment. *Archives of Pediatrics and Adolescent Medicine, 158*, 730–736.

Nansel, T. R., Overpeck, M., Pilla, R. S., Ruan, W. J., Simons-Morton, B., & Scheidt, P. (2001). Bullying behaviors among U.S. Youths: Prevalence and association with psychosocial adjustment. *Journal of the American Medical Association, 285*, 2094–2100.

Nash, A., & Hay, D. F. (2003). Social relations in infancy: Origins and evidence. *Human Development, 46*, 222–232.

Nastasi, B. K., & Clements, D. H. (1993). Motivational and social outcomes of cooperative computer education environments. *Journal of Computing in Childhood Education, 4*, 15–43.

Nastasi, B. K., & Clements, D. H. (1994). Effectance motivation, perceived scholastic competence, and higher-order thinking in two cooperative computer environments. *Journal of Educational Computing Research, 10*, 249–275.

National Campaign to Prevent Teen Pregnancy. (2005). *Science says: Teens and oral sex*. Washington, DC: Author.

National Center for Educational Statistics (1997). *1996 National Household Education Survey: Student participation in community service activity*. Washington, DC: U.S. Department of Education (NCES 97–331).

National Council for Research on Women. (2002). *Balancing the equation: Where are women and girls in science, engineering, and technology?* New York: Author.

National Education Goals Panel. (1992). *The National Education Goals Report. 1992*. Washington, DC: U.S. Department of Education.

National Law Center on Homelessness and Poverty. (2004). *Homelessness in America*. Retrieved 11/1/07 from http://www.policyalmanac.org/social_welfare/homeless.shtml

National Research Council and Institute for Medicine. (2000). *From neurons to neighborhoods: The science of child development*. Washington, DC: National Academy of Science Press.

National Research Council and Institute for Medicine. (2004). *Engaging schools*. Washington, DC: National Academies Press.

Neiderhiser J. M., Reiss, D., Pedersen, N. L., Lichtenstein, P., Spotts, E. L., Hansen, K., Cederblad, M., & Ellhammer, O. (2004). Genetic and environmental influences on mothering of adolescents: A comparison of two samples. *Developmental Psychology, 40*, 335–351.

Neisser, U., Boodoo, G., Bouchard, T. J., Jr., Boykin, A. W., Brody, N., Ceci, S. J., Halpern, D. F., Loehlin, J. C., Perloff, R., Sternberg, R. J., & Urbina, S. (1996). Intelligence: Knowns and unknowns. *American Psychologist, 51*, 77–101.

Nelson, C. A. (2007). A neurobiological perspective on early human deprivation. *Child Development Perspectives, 1*, 13–18.

Nelson, D. A., & Crick, N. R. (1999). Rose-colored glasses: Examining the social information-processing of prosocial young adolescents. *Journal of Early Adolescence, 19*, 17–38.

Nelson, D. A., Hart, C. H., Yang, C., Olsen, J. A., & Jin, S. (2006). Aversive parenting in China: Associations with child physical and relational aggression. *Child Development, 77*, 554–572.

Nelson, E. A., Grinder, R. E., & Biaggio, A. M. B. (1969). Relationships between behavioral, cognitive-developmental, and self-report measures of morality and personality. *Multivariate Behavioral Research, 4*, 483–500.

Nelson, J., & Aboud, F. E. (1985). The resolution of social conflict among friends. *Child Development, 56*, 1009–1017.

Nelson, S. A. (1980). Factors influencing young children's use of motives and outcomes as moral criteria. *Child Development, 51*, 823–829.

Nelson-LeGall, S. A. (1985). Motive-outcome matching and outcome foreseeability: Effects on attribution of intentionality and moral judgments. *Developmental Psychology, 21,* 332–337.

Nesdale, D., Maass, A., Durkin, K., & Griffiths, J. (2005). Group norms, threat, and children's racial prejudice. *Child Development, 76,* 652–663.

Newcomb, A. F., & Bukowski, W. M. (1984). A longitudinal study of the utility of social preference and social impact sociometric classification schemes. *Child Development, 55,* 1434–1447.

Newcomb, A. F., Bukowski, W. M., & Pattee, L. (1993). Children's peer relations: A meta-analytic review of popular, rejected, neglected, controversial, and average sociometric status. *Psychological Bulletin, 113,* 99–128.

Newcomb, M. D., & Bentler, P. M. (1989). Substance use and abuse among children and teenagers. *American Psychologist, 44,* 242–248.

Newcombe, N., & Dubas, J. S. (1987). Individual differences in cognitive ability: Are they related to timing of puberty? In R. M. Lerner & T. T. Foch (Eds.), *Biological-psychosocial interactions in early adolescence: A life-span perspective.* Hillsdale, NJ: Erlbaum.

Newcombe, N., & Dubas, J. S. (1992). A longitudinal study of predictors of spatial ability in adolescent females. *Child Development, 63,* 37–46.

Newman, D. L., Caspi, A., Moffitt, T. E., & Silva, P. A. (1997). Antecedents of adult interpersonal functioning: Effects of individual differences in age 3 temperament. *Developmental Psychology, 33,* 206–217.

Ng, F. F., Pomerantz, E. M., & Lam, S. (2007). European American and Chinese parents' responses to children's success and failure: Implications for children's responses. *Developmental Psychology, 43,* 1239–1255.

NICHD Early Child Care Research Network (1997). The effects of infant child care on mother-infant attachment security: Results of the NICHD study of early child care. *Child Development, 68,* 860–879.

NICHD Early Child Care Research Network (1998a). Early child care and self-control, compliance, and problem behavior at twenty-four and thirty-six months. *Child Development, 69,* 1145–1170.

NICHD Early Child Care Research Network (1998b). Relations between family predictors and child outcomes: Are they weaker for children in child care? *Developmental Psychology, 34,* 1119–1128.

NICHD Early Child Care Research Network (1999). Child care and mother-infant interaction in the first 3 years of life. *Developmental Psychology, 35,* 1399–1413.

NICHD Early Child Care Research Network (2000). The relation of child care to cognitive and language development. *Child Development, 71,* 960–980.

NICHD Early Child Care Research Network (2001a). Child care and children's peer interaction at 24 and 36 months: The NICHD study of early child care. *Child Development, 72,* 1478–1500.

NICHD Early Child Care Research Network (2001b). Child-care and family predictors of preschool attachment and stability from infancy. *Developmental Psychology, 37,* 847–862.

NICHD Early Child Care Research Network (2003a). Does amount of time spent in child care predict socioemotional adjustment during the transition to kindergarten? *Child Development, 74,* 976–1005.

NICHD Early Child Care Research Network (2003b). Does quality of child care affect child outcomes at age 42? *Developmental Psychology, 39,* 451–469.

NICHD Early Child Care Research Network (2004a). Trajectories of physical aggression from toddlerhood to middle childhood. *Monographs of the Society for Research in Child Development, 69,* (4, Serial No. 278).

NICHD Early Child Care Research Network (2004b). Does class size in first grade relate to children's academic and social performance or observed classroom processes? *Developmental Psychology, 40,* 651–664.

NICHD Early Child Care Research Network (2005a). Duration and developmental timing of poverty and children's cognitive and social development from birth through third grade. *Child Development, 76,* 795–810.

NICHD Early Child Care Research Network (2005b). Early child care and children's development in the primary grades: Results from the NICHD Study of Early Child Care. *American Educational Research Journal, 43,* 537–570.

NICHD Early Child Care Research Network (2006). Infant-mother attachment classification: Risk and protection in relation to changing maternal caregiving quality. *Developmental Psychology, 42,* 38–58.

Nicholls, J. G. (1989). *The competitive ethos and democratic education.* Cambridge, MA: Harvard University Press.

Nicholls, J. G., & Miller, A. T. (1984). Reasoning about the ability of self-and others: A developmental study. *Child Development, 55,* 1990–1999.

Nichols, M. R. (1993). Parental perspectives on the childbirth experience. *Maternal-Child Nursing Journal, 21,* 99–108.

Nielsen, M. (2006). Coping actions and coping outcomes: Social learning through the second year. *Developmental Psychology, 42,* 555–565.

Nielson, M., Suddendorf, T., & Slaughter V. (2006). Mirror self-recognition beyond the face. *Child Development, 77,* 176–185.

Nielson, M., & Dissanayke, C. (2003). A longitudinal study of immediate, deferred, and synchronic imitation through the second year. *The Interdisciplinary Journal of Artificial Intelligence and the Simulation of Behavior, 1,* 305–318.

Ninio, A., & Rinott, N. (1988). Fathers' involvement in the care of their infants and their attributions of cognitive competence to infants. *Child Development, 59,* 652–663.

Nix, R. L., Pinderhughes, E. E., Dodge, K. A., Bates, J. E., Pettit, G. S., & McFadyen-Ketchum, S. A. (1999). The relation between mothers' hostile attribution tendencies and children's externalizing behavior problems: The mediating role of mothers' harsh discipline practices. *Child Development, 70,* 896–909.

Norman-Jackson, J. (1982). Family interactions, language development, and primary reading achievement of black children in families of low income. *Child Development, 53,* 349–358.

Nucci, L., Camino, C., & Sapiro, C. M. (1996). Social class effects on northeastern Brazilian children's conceptions of areas of personal choice and social regulation. *Child Development, 67,* 1223–1242.

Nucci, L., & Smetana, J. G. (1996). Mothers' concepts of young children's areas of personal freedom. *Child Development, 67,* 1870–1886.

Nucci, L., & Turiel, E. (1993). God's word, religious rules, and their relation to Christian and Jewish children's concepts of morality. *Child Development, 64,* 1475–1491.

O'Connor, B. P. (1995). Identity development and perceived parental behavior as sources of adolescent egocentrism. *Journal of Youth and Adolescence, 24,* 205–227.

O'Connor, B. P., & Nikolic, J. (1990). Identity development and formal operations as sources of adolescent egocentrism. *Journal of Youth and Adolescence, 19,* 149–158.

O'Connor, T. G., & Croft, C. M. (2001). A twin study of attachment in preschool children. *Child Development, 72,* 1501–1511.

O'Connor, T. G., Marvin, R. S., Rutter, M., Olrick, J. T., & Britner, P. A. (2003). Child-parent attachment following early institutional deprivation. *Developmental Psychopathology, 15,* 19–38.

Oden, S., & Asher, S. R. (1977). Coaching children in social skills for friendship making. *Child Development, 48,* 495–506.

O'Donnell, D. A., Schwab-Stone, M. E., & Muyeed, A. Z. (2002). Multidimensional resilience in urban children exposed to community violence. *Child Development, 73,* 1265–1282.

Ogbu, J. U. (1988). Black education: A cultural-ecological perspective. In H. P. McAdoo (Ed.), *Black families.* Beverly Hills: Sage.

Ogbu, J. U. (1994). From cultural differences to differences in cultural frames of reference. In P. M. Greenfield & R. R. Cocking (Eds.), *Cross-cultural roots of minority child development* (pp. 365–391). Hillsdale, NJ: Erlbaum.

Ogbu, J. U. (2003). *Black American students in an affluent suburb: A study of academic disengagement.* Mahwah, NJ: Erlbaum

Ogletree, S. M., Martinez, C. N., Turner, T. R., & Mason, B. (2004). Pokeman: Exploring the role of gender. *Sex Roles, 50,* 851–859.

Ogletree, S. M., & Williams, S. W. (1990). Sex and sex-typing effects on computer attitudes and aptitude. *Sex Roles, 23,* 703–712.

O'Heron, C. A., & Orlofsky, J. L. (1990). Stereotypic and nonstereotypic sex role trait and behavior orientations, gender identity, and psychological adjustment. *Journal of Personality and Social Psychology, 58,* 134–143.

Oliner, S. P., & Oliner, P. M. (1988). *The altruistic personality: Rescuers of Jews in Nazi Europe.* New York: Free Press.

Olsen, S. F., Yang, C., Hart, C. H., et al., (2002). Maternal psychological control and preschool children's behavioral outcomes in China, Russia, and the United States. In B. K. Barber (Ed.), *Intrusive parenting: How psychological control affects children and adolescents* (pp. 235–262). Washington, DC: American Psychological Association.

Olweus, D. (1980). Familial and temperamental determinants of aggressive behavior in adolescent boys: A causal analysis. *Developmental Psychology, 16,* 644–660.

Olweus, D. (1993). *Bullying at school.* Oxford: Blackwell.

Olweus, D., Mattsson, A., Schalling, D., & Low, H. (1980). Testosterone, aggression, physical and personality dimensions in normal adolescent males. *Psychosomatic Medicine, 42,* 253–269.

O'Mahoney, J. F. (1989). Development of thinking about things and people: Social and nonsocial cognition during adolescence. *Journal of Genetic sychology, 150,* 217–224.

O'Neill, D. K. (1996). Two-year-old children's sensitivity to a parent's knowledge state when making requests. *Child Development, 67,* 659–667.

Opfer, J. E., & Gelman, S. A. (2001). Children's and adults' models of teleological action: The development of biology-based models. *Child Development, 72,* 1367–1381.

Oppenheim, D., Koren-Karie, N., & Sagi-Schwartz, A. (2007). Emotion dialogues between mothers and children at 4.5 and 7.5 years: Relations with children's attachment at 1 year. *Child Development, 78,* 38–52.

Oppenheim, D., Sagi, A., & Lamb, M. E. (1988). Infant-adult attachments on the kibbutz and their relation to socioemotional development 4 years later. *Developmental Psychology, 24,* 427–433.

Overbeek, G., Stattin, H., Vermulst, A., Ha, T., & Engles, R. C. M. E. (2007). Parent-child relationships, partner relationships, and emotional adjustment: A birth-to-maturity prospective study. *Child Development, 78,* 429–437.

Overton, W. F. (1984). World views and their influence on psychological theory and research: Kuhn-Lakotes-Lunden. In H. W. Reese (Ed.), *Advances in child development and behavior* (Vol. 18). New York: Academic.

Pahl, K., & Way, N. (2006). Longitudinal trajectories of ethnic identity among urban black and Latino adolescents. *Child Development, 77,* 1403–1415.

Paikoff, R. L., Brooks-Gunn, J. (1991). Do parent-child relationships change at puberty? *Psychological Bulletin, 110,* 47–66.

Palkovitz, R. (1984). Parental attitudes and fathers' interactions with their 5-month-old infants. *Developmental Psychology, 20,* 1054–1060.

Papp, L. M., Cummings, E. M., & Goeke-Morey, M. C. (2002). Marital conflicts in the home when children are present versus absent. *Developmental Psychology, 38,* 774–783.

Park, J., Essex, M. J., Zahn-Waxler, C., Armstrong, J. M., Klein, M. H., & Goldsmith, H. H. (2005). Relational and overt aggression in middle childhood: Early child and family risk factors. *Early Education and Development, 16,* 233–257.

Park, S., Belsky, J., Putnam, S., & Crnic, K. (1997). Infant emotionality, parenting, and 3-year inhibition: Exploring stability and lawful discontinuity in a male sample. *Developmental Psychology, 33,* 218–227.

Parke, R. D. (1977). Some effects of punishment on children's behavior—revisited. In E. M. Hetherington & R. D. Parke (Eds.), *Contemporary readings in child psychology.* New York: McGraw Hill.

Parke, R. D. (2002). Fathers and families. In M. H., Bornstein, (Ed.), *Handbook of parenting, Vol 3: Being and becoming a parent* (pp. 27–73). Mahwah, NJ: Erlbaum.

Parke, R. D., & Buriel, R. (2006). Socialization in the family: Ethnic and ecological perspectives. In W. Damon & R. M. Lerner (Series Eds.), & N. Eisenberg, (Vol. Ed.), *Handbook of child psychology.* Vol. 3. Social, emotional, and personality development (6th ed., pp. 429–504). New York: Wiley.

Parke, R. D., Cotrane, S., Duffy, S., Buriel, R., Dennis, J., Powers, J., French, S., & Widaman, K. F. (2004). Economic stress, parenting, and child adjustment in Mexican American and European American Families. *Child Development, 75,* 1632–1656.

Parke, R. D., & Slaby, R. G. (1983). The development of aggression. In P. H. Mussen (Ed.), *Handbook of child psychology. Vol. 4: Socialization, personality, and social development.* New York: Wiley.

Parker, J. G., & Asher, S. R. (1987). Peer relations and later adjustment: Are low-accepted children "at risk"? *Psychological Bulletin, 102,* 357–389.

Parker, J. G., & Asher, S. R. (1993). Friendship and friendship quality in middle childhood: Links with peer group acceptance and feelings of loneliness and social dissatisfaction. *Developmental Psychology, 29,* 611–621.

Parker, J. G., Low, C. M., Walker, A. R., & Gamm, B. K. (2005). Friendship jealousy in young adolescents: Individual differences and links to sex, self-esteem, aggression, and social adjustment. *Developmental Psychology, 41,* 235–250.

Parker, J. G., Rubin, K. H., Price, J., & DeRosier, E. (1995). Peer relationships, child development, and adjustment. A developmental psychopathology perspective. In D. Cicchetti & E. Cohen (Eds.), *Developmental psychopathology. Vol. 2: Risk, disorder, and adaptation* (pp. 96–161). New York: Wiley.

Parkhurst, J. T., & Asher, S. R. (1992). Peer rejection in middle school: Subgroup differences in behavior, loneliness, and interpersonal concerns. *Developmental Psychology, 28,* 231–241.

Parsons, J. E., Adler, T. F., & Kaczala, C. M. (1982). Socialization of achievement attitudes and beliefs: Parental influences. *Child Development, 53,* 310–321.

Parsons, T. (1955). Family structure and the socialization of the child. In T. Parsons & R. F. Bales (Eds.), *Family socialization and interaction processes.* New York: Free Press.

Parten, M. (1932). Social participation among preschool children. *Journal of Abnormal and Social Psychology, 27,* 243–269.

Partridge, T. (2005). Are genetically informed designs genetically informative? Comment on McGue, Elkins, Walden, and Iacono (2005) and quantitative behavioral genetics. *Developmental Psychology, 41,* 985–988.

Passman, R. H., & Longeway, K. P. (1982). The role of vision in maternal attachment: Giving 2-year-olds a photograph of their mother during separation. *Developmental Psychology, 18,* 530–533.

Passman, R. H., & Weisberg, P. (1975). Mothers and blankets as agents for promoting play and exploration by young children in a novel environment: The effects of social and nonsocial attachment objects. *Developmental Psychology, 11,* 170–177.

Pasterski, V. L., Geffner, M. E., Brain, C., Hindmarsh, P., Brook, C., & Hines, M. (2005). Prenatal hormones and postnatal socialization by parents as determinants of male-typical toy play in girls with congenital adrenal hyperplasia. *Child Development, 76,* 264–278.

Patel, N., Power, T. G., & Bhavnagri, N. P. (1996). Socialization values and practices of Indian immigrant parents: Correlates of modernity and acculturation. *Child Development, 67,* 303–313.

Patterson, C. J. (2004). Gay fathers. In M. E. Lamb (Ed.), *The role of the father in child development* (4th ed.). Hoboken, NJ: Wiley.

Patterson, C. J., Kupersmidt, J. B., & Vaden, N.A. (1990). Income level, gender, ethnicity, and household composition as predictors of children's school-based competence. *Child Development, 61,* 485–494.

Patterson, G. R. (1981). Mothers: The unacknowledged victims. *Monographs of the Society for Research in Child Development, 45* (5, Serial No. 186).

Patterson, G. R. (1982). *Coercive family processes.* Eugene, OR: Castilia Press.

Patterson, G. R., Capaldi, D. & Bank, L. (1991). An early starter model for predicting delinquency. In D. Pepler & K. H. Rubin (Eds.), *The development and treatment of childhood aggression* (pp. 139–168). Hillsdale, NJ: Erlbaum

Patterson, G. R., DeBaryshe, B. D., & Ramsey, E. (1989). A developmental perspective on antisocial behavior. *American Psychologist, 44,* 329–335.

Patterson, G. R., Reid, J. B., & Dishion, T. (1992). *Antisocial boys.* Eugene, OR: Castalia Publishing.

Patterson, M. M., & Bigler, R. S. (2006). Preschool children's attention to environmental messages about groups: Social categorization and the origins of intergroup bias. *Child Development, 77,* 847–860.

Paul, J. P. (1993). Childhood cross-gender behavior and adult homosexuality: The resurgence of biological models of sexuality. *Journal of Homosexuality, 24,* 41–54.

Paulhus, D., & Shaffer, D. R. (1981). Sex differences in the impact of number of older and number of younger siblings on scholastic aptitude. *Social Psychology Quarterly, 44,* 363–368.

Paulussen-Hoogeboom, M. C., Stams, G. J. J. M., Hermanns, J. M. A., & Peetsma, T. T. D. & (2007). Child negative emotionality and parenting from infancy to preschool: A meta-analytic review. *Developmental Psychology, 42,* 438–453.

Paxton, S. J., Eisenberg, M. E., & Neumark-Sztainer, D. (2006). Prospective predictors of body dissatisfaction in adolescent girls and boys: A five-year longitudinal study. *Developmental Psychology, 42,* 888–899.

Peck, S. (in preparation). *On the effectiveness of sex education in America.*

Pederson, D. R., Gleason, K. E., Moran, G., & Bento, S. (1998). Maternal attachment representations, maternal sensitivity, and the mother-infant attachment relationship. *Developmental Psychology, 34,* 925–933.

Pedro-Carroll, J. L., & Cowen, E. L. (1985). The children of divorce inter-vention program: An investigation of the efficacy of a school-based prevention program. *Journal of Consulting and Clinical Psychology, 53,* 603–611.

Peets, K., Hodges, E. V. E., Kikis, E., & Salmivalli, C. (2007). Hostile attributions and behavioral strategies in children: Does relationship type matter. *Developmental Psychology, 43,* 889–900.

Pellegrini, A. D., Bartini, M., & Brooks, F. (1999). School bullies, victims, and aggressive victims: Factors relating to group affiliation and victimization in early adolescence. *Journal of Educational Psychology, 91,* 216–224.

Pellegrini, A. D., & Bjorklund, D. F. (2004). The ontogeny and phylogeny of children's object and fantasy play. *Human Nature, 15,* 23–43.

Pellegrini, A. D., & Smith, P. K. (1998). Physical activity play: the nature and function of a neglected aspect of play. *Child Development, 69,* 577–598.

Pellegrini, D. S. (1985). Social cognition and competence in middle childhood. *Child Development, 56,* 253–264.

Perkins, S. A., & Turiel, E. (2007). To lie or not to lie: To whom and under what circumstances. *Child Development, 78,* 609–621.

Perlman, M., & Ross, H. S. (1997). The benefits of parent intervention in children's disputes: An examination of concurrent changes in children's fighting styles. *Child Development, 68,* 690–700.

Perry, D. G., Kusel, S. J., & Perry, L. C. (1988). Victims of peer aggression. *Developmental Psychology, 24,* 807–814.

Perry, D. G., Perry, L. C., Bussey, K., English, D., & Arnold, G. (1980). Processes of attribution and children's self-punishment following misbehavior. *Child Development, 51,* 545–551.

Perry, D. G., Perry, L. C., & Weiss, R. J. (1989). Sex differences in the consequences that children anticipate for aggression. *Developmental Psychology, 25,* 312–319.

Perry-Jenkins, M., Repetti, R. L., & Crouter, A. C. (2000). Work and family in the 1990s. *Journal of Marriage and the Family, 62,* 981–998.

Peskin, J. (1992). Ruse and representations: On children's ability to conceal information. *Developmental Psychology, 28,* 84–89.

Peter, J., & Valkenburg, P. M. (2006). Adolescents' exposure to sexually explicit online material and recreational attitudes toward sex. *Journal of Communication, 56,* 639–660.

Peter, J., & Valkenburg, P. M. (2007). Adolescents' exposure to a sexualized media environment and notions of women as sex objects. *Sex Roles, 56,* 381–395.

Petersen, A. C., Compas, B. E., Brooks-Gunn, J., Stemmler, M., Ey, S., & Grant, K. E. (1993). Depression in adolescence. *American Psychologist, 48*, 155–164.

Peterson, C., & Steen, T. A. (2002). Optimistic explanatory style. In C. R. Snyder & S. J. Lopez (Eds.)., *Handbook of positive psychology* (pp. 244–256). New York: Oxford University Press.

Peterson, C. C., & Siegal, M. (2000). Insights into a theory of mind from deafness and autism. *Mind and Language, 15*, 123–145.

Peterson, C. C., Wellman, H. M., & Liu, D. (2005). Steps in theory-of-mind development for children with deafness or autism. *Child Development, 76*, 502–517.

Peterson, L., Ewigman, B., & Kivlahan, C. (1993). Judgments regarding appropriate child supervision to prevent injury: The role of environmental risk and child age. *Child Development, 64*, 934–950.

Peterson, L., & Gelfand, D. M. (1984). Causal attributions of helping as a function of age and incentives. *Child Development, 55*, 504–511.

Petrosino, A., Turpin-Petrosino, C., & Finckenauer, J. O. (2000). Well-meaning programs can have harmful effects! Lessons from experiments in Scared Straight and other like programs. *Crime and Delinquency, 46*, 354–379.

Pettit, G. S., Bates, J. E., & Dodge, K. A. (1997). Supportive parenting, ecological context, and children's adjustment: A seven-year longitudinal study. *Child Development, 68*, 908–923.

Pettit, G. S., Bates, J. E., Dodge, K. A., & Messe, D. W. (1999). The impact of after-school peer contact on early adolescent externalizing problems is moderated by parental monitoring, perceived neighborhood safety, and prior adjustment. *Child Development, 70*, 768–778.

Pettit, G. S., Dodge, K. A., & Brown, M. M. (1988). Early family experience, social problem solving patterns, and children's social competence. *Child Development, 59*, 107–120.

Pettit, G. S., Laird, R. D., Bates, J. E., & Dodge, K. A. (1997). Patterns of after-school care in middle childhood: Risk factors and developmental outcomes. *Merrill-Palmer Quarterly, 43*, 515–538.

Pettit, G. S., Laird, R. D., Dodge, K. A., Bates, J. E., & Criss, M. M. (2001). Antecedents and behavior-problem outcomes of parental monitoring and psychological control in early adolescence. *Child Development, 72*, 583–598.

Pew Internet and American Life Project (2002). *The digital disconnect: The widening gap between internet savvy students and their schools.* http://www.pewinternet.org

Pfeifer, J. H., Brown, C. S., & Juvonen, J. (2007). Teaching tolerance in schools: Lessons learned since *Brown v. Board of Education* about the development and reduction of children's prejudice. *Social Policy Report, 21*. Chicago: Society for Research in Child Development.

Pfeifer, J. H., Ruble, D. N., Bachman, M. A., Alvarez, J. M., Cameron, J. A., & Fuligni, A. J. (2007). Social identities and intergroup bias in immigrant and nonimmigrant children. *Developmental Psychology, 43*, 496–507.

Pfeifer, M., Goldsmith, H. H., Davidson, R. J., & Rickman, M. (2002). Continuity and change in inhibited and uninhibited children. *Child Development, 73*, 1474–1485.

Phillips, D. (1984). The illusion of incompetence among academically competent children. *Child Development, 55*, 2000–2016.

Phinney, J. S. (1993). A three-stage model of ethnic identity development in adolescence. In M. E. Bernal & G. P. Knight (Eds.), *Ethnic identity: Formation and transmission among Hispanics and other minorities*. Albany, NY: State University of New York Press.

Phinney, J. S. (1996). When we talk about American ethnic groups, what do we mean? *American Psychologist, 51*, 918–927.

Phinney, J. S., Ferguson, D. L., & Tate, J. D., (1997). Intergroup attitudes among ethnic minority adolescents: A casual model. *Child Development, 68*, 955–969.

Phinney, J. S., Ong, A., & Madden, T. (2000). Cultural values and intergenerational value discrepancies in immigrant and nonimmigrant families. *Child Development, 71*, 528–539

Phinney, J. S., & Rosenthal, D. A. (1992). Ethnic identity in adolescence: Process, context, and outcome. In G. R. Adams, T. P. Gullotta, & R. Montemayor (Eds.), *Adolescent identity formation* (Advances in Adolescent Development, Vol. 4). Newbury Park, CA: Sage.

Piaget, J. (1950). *The psychology of intelligence.* San Diego, CA: Harcourt Brace Jovanovich.

Piaget, J. (1951). *Play, dreams, and imitation in childhood.* New York: Norton.

Piaget, J. (1952). *The origins of intelligence in children.* New York: International Universities Press.

Piaget, J. (1954). *The construction of reality in the child. New* York: Basic Books.

Piaget, J. (1965). *The moral judgment of the child.* New York: Free Press. (Original work published 1932).

Piaget, J. (1970). Piaget's theory. In P. H. Mussen (Ed.), *Carmichael's manual of child psychology* (Vol. 1). New York: Wiley.

Pick, S., Givaudian, M., & Poortinga, Y. H. (2003). Sexuality and life skills education: A multistrategy intervention in Mexico. *American Psychologist, 58*, 230–234.

Piehler, T. F., & Dishion, T. J. (2007). Interpersonal dynamics within adolescent friendships: Dyadic mutuality, deviant talk, and patterns of antisocial behavior. *Child Development, 78*, 1611–1624.

Pierce, K. M., Hamm, J. V., & Vandell, D. L. (1999). Experiences in after-school programs and children's adjustment in first-grade classrooms. *Child Development, 70*, 756–767.

Pinon, M., Huston, A. C., & Wright, J. C. (1989). Family ecology and child characteristics that predict young children's educational television viewing. *Child Development, 60*, 846–856.

Pipp, S., Easterbrooks, M. A., & Harmon, R. J. (1992). The relation between attachment and knowledge of self and mother in one- to three-year-old infants. *Child Development, 63*, 738–750.

Pitts, L. (2007, November 26). If you want a good laugh, read here about Megan. *Athens Banner Herald*, A6.

Pitts, M., & Rahman, Q. (2001). Which behaviors constitute "having sex" among university students in UK? *Archives of Sexual Behavior, 30*, 169–176.

Pleck, J. H., & Masciadrelli, B. P. (2004). Paternal involvement by U. S. resident fathers: Levels, sources, and consequences. In M. E. Lamb (Ed.), *The role of the father in child development*, 4th ed. (pp. 222–271). New York: Wiley

Plomin, R. (1990). *Nature and nurture.* Pacific Grove, CA: Brooks/Cole.

Plomin, R. (1994). *Genetics and experience: The interplay between nature and nurture*, Thousand Oaks, CA: Sage.

Plomin, R., DeFries, J. C., McClearn, G. E., & McGuffin, P. (2001). *Behavioral genetics* (4th ed.). New York: Worth.

Plomin, R., Reiss, D., Hetherington, E. M., & Howe, G. W. (1994). Nature and nurture: Genetic contributions to measures of the family environment. *Developmental Psychology, 30*, 32–43.

Plomin, R., & Rende, R. (1991). Human behavioral genetics. *Annual Review of Psychology, 42*, 161–190.

Plomin, R., & Rutter, M. (1998). Child development, molecular genetics, and what to do with genes once they are found. *Child Development, 69,* 1223–1242.

Poehlmann, J., & Fiese, B. H. (2001). The interaction of maternal and infant vulnerabilities on developing attachment relationships. *Development and Psychopathology, 13,* 1–11.

Polak, A., & Harris, P. L. (1999). Deception by young children following noncompliance. *Developmental Psychology, 35,* 561–568.

Pomerantz, E. M., & Dong, W. (2006). Effects of mothers' perceptions of children's competence: The moderating role of mothers' theories of competence. *Developmental Psychology, 42,* 950–961.

Pomerantz, E. M., & Ruble, D. N. (1997). Distinguishing multiple dimensions and conceptions of ability: Implications for self-evaluation. C*hild Development, 68,* 1165–1180.

Pomerantz, E. M., & Ruble, D. N. (1998). The role of maternal control in the development of sex differences in child self-evaluative factors. *Child Development, 69,* 458–478.

Pomerantz, E. M., Ruble, D. N., Frey, K. S., & Grenlich, F. (1995). Meeting goals and confronting conflict: Children's changing perceptions of social comparison. *Child Development, 66,* 723–738.

Pomerleau, A., Bolduc, D., Malcuit, G., & Cossette, L. (1990). Pink or blue: Environmental gender stereotypes in the first two years of life. *Sex Roles, 22,* 359–367.

Ponton, L. (2001). *The sex lives of teenagers: Revealing the secret world of adolescent boys and girls.* New York: Plume.

Porter, A. C., & Polikoff, M. S. (2007). NCLB: State interpretations, early effects, and suggestions for reauthorization. *Social Policy Report, 21. Chicago: Society for Research in Child Development.*

Portes, A., & MacLeod, D. (1996). Educational progress of children of immigrants: The roles of class, ethnicity, and school context. *Sociology of Education, 69,* 255–275.

Posada, G., Carbonell, O. A., Alzate, G., & Plata, S. J. (2004). Through Columbian lenses: Ethnographic and conventional analyses of maternal care and their associations with secure base behavior. *Developmental Psychology, 40,* 508–518.

Posada, G., & Jacobs, A. (2001). Child-mother attachment relationships and culture. *American Psychologist, 56,* 821–822.

Posner, J. K., & Vandell, D. L. (1994). Low-income children's after-school care: Are there beneficial effects of after-school programs? *Child Development, 65,* 440–456.

Posner, J. K., & Vandell, D. L. (1999). After-school activities and the development of low-income urban children: A longitudinal study. *Developmental Psychology, 35,* 868–879.

Poteat, V. P. (2007). Peer group socialization of homophobic attitudes and behavior during adolescence. *Child Development, 78,* 1830–1842.

Poulin, F., & Boivin, M. (2000). The role of proactive and reactive aggression in the formation and development of boy's friendships. *Developmental Psychology, 36,* 233–240.

Poulin, F., & Pedersen, S. (2007). Developmental changes in gender composition of friendship networks in adolescent girls and boys. *Developmental Psychology, 43,* 1484–1496.

Poulin-Dubois, D., Serbin, L. A., Kenyon, B., & Derbyshire, A. (1994). Infants' intermodal knowledge about gender. *Developmental Psychology, 30,* 436–442.

Povinelli, D. J., Landau, K. R., & Perilloux, H. K. (1996). Self-recognition In young children using delayed versus live feedback: Evidence of a developmental asynchrony. *Child Development, 67,* 1540–1554.

Povinelli, D. J., Landry, A. M., Theall, L. A., Clark, B. R., & Castile, C. M. (1999). Development of young children's understanding that the recent past is casually bound to the present. *Developmental Psychology, 35,* 1426–1439.

Povinelli, D. J., & Simon, B. B., (1998). Young children's understanding of briefly versus extremely delayed images of the self: Emergence of the autobiographical stance. *Developmental Psychology, 34,* 188–194.

Powlishta, K. K. (1995). Intergroup processes in childhood: Social categorization and sex role development. *Developmental Psychology, 31,* 781–788.

Prentice, D. A., & Carranza, E. (2002). What women and men should be, shouldn't be, are allowed to be, and don't have to be: The contents of prescriptive gender stereotypes. *Psychology of Women Quarterly, 26,* 269–281.

Priel, B., & deSchonen, S. (1986). Self-recognition: A study of a population without mirrors. *Journal of Experimental Child Psychology, 41,* 237–250.

Prinstein, M. J., Meade, C. S., & Cohen, G. L. (2003). Adolescent oral sex, peer popularity, and perceptions of best friends' sexual behavior. *Journal of Pediatric Psychology, 28,* 243–249.

Provence, S., & Lipton, R. C. (1962). *Infants in institutions.* New York: International Universities Press.

Putallaz, M., Kupersmidt, J. B., Coie, J. D., McKnight, K., & Grimes, C. L. (2004). A behavioral analysis of girls' aggression and victimization. In M. Putallaz & K. L. Bierman (Eds.), *Aggression, antisocial behavior and violence among girls: A developmental perspective.* New York: Guilford Press.

Quiggle, N. L., Garber, J., Panak, W. F., & Dodge, K. A. (1992). Social information processing in aggressive and depressed children. *Child Development, 63,* 1305–1320.

Quinn, R. A., Houts, A. C., & Graesser, A. C. (1994). Naturalistic conceptions of morality: A question-answering approach. *Journal of Personality, 62,* 260–267.

Rabiner, D. L., Keane, S. P., & MacKinnon-Lewis, C. (1993). Children's Beliefs about familiar and unfamiliar peers in relation to their sociometric status. *Developmental Psychology, 29,* 236–243.

Rabiner, D. L., Lenhart, L., & Lochman, J. E. (1990). Automatic versus reflective social problem solving in relation to children's sociometric status. *Developmental Psychology, 26,* 1010–1016.

Radke-Yarrow, M., Cummings, E. M., Kuczynski, L., & Chapman, M. (1985). Patterns of attachment in two- and three-year-olds in normal families and families with parental depression. *Child Development, 56,* 884–893.

Ram, A., & Ross, H. S. (2001). Problem solving, contention, and struggle: How siblings resolve a conflict of interest. *Child Development, 72,* 1710–1722.

Ramey, C. T., & Ramey, S. L. (1998). Early intervention and early experience. *American Psychologist, 53,* 109–120.

Raskauskas, J., & Stoltz, A. D. (2007). Involvement in traditional and electronic bullying among adolescents. *Developmental Psychology, 43,* 564–575.

Raver, C. C., Gershoff, E. T., & Aber, J. L. (2007). Testing equivalence of mediating models of income, parenting, and school readiness for White, Black, and Hispanic children in a national sample. *Child Development, 78,* 96–115.

Raynor, J. O. (1970). Relationships between achievement-related motives, future orientation, and academic performance. *Journal of Personality and Social Psychology, 15,* 28–33.

Raz, S., Goldstein, R., Hopkins, T. L., Lauterbach, M. D., Shah, F., Porter, C. L., Riggs, W. W., Magill, L. H., & Sander, C. J. (1994). Sex differences in early vulnerability to cerebral injury and their neurobehavioral implications. *Psychobiology, 22,* 244–253.

Raz, S., Lauterbach, M. D., Hopkins, T. L., Glogowski, B. K., Porter, C. L., Riggs, W. W., & Sander, C. J. (1995). A female advantage in cognitive recovery from early cerebral insult. *Developmental Psychology, 31,* 958–966.

Reese-Weber, M. (2000). Middle and late adolescents' conflict resolution skills with siblings: Associations with interparental and parent-adolescent conflict resolution. *Journal of Youth and Adolescence, 29,* 697–711.

Reinisch, J. M., Sanders, S. A., Hill, C. A., & Ziemba-Davis, M. (1992). High-risk sexual behavior among heterosexual undergraduates at a Midwestern university. *Family Planning Perspectives, 24,* 116.

Reiss, D., Neiderhiser, J. M., Hetherington, E. M., & Plomin, R. (2000). *The relationship code: Deciphering genetic and social influences on adolescent development.* Cambridge, MA: Harvard University Press.

Reissland, N. (1988). Neonatal imitation in the first hour of life: Observations in rural Nepal. *Developmental Psychology, 24,* 464–469.

Remley, A. (1988, October). The great parental value shift: From obedience to independence. *Psychology Today,* pp. 56–59.

Repacholi, B. M., & Gopnik, A. (1997). Early reasoning about desires: Evidence from 14- and 18-month-olds. *Developmental Psychology, 33,* 12–21.

Repacholi, B. M., & Meltzoff, A. N. (2007). Emotional eavesdropping: Infants selectivity respond to indirect emotional signals. *Child Development, 78,* 503–521.

Repacholi, B., & Slaughter, V. (2003). *Individual differences in theory of mind: Implications for typical and atypical development.* New York: Psychology Press.

Rest, J., Narvaez, D., Bebeau, M. J., & Thoma, S. J. (1999). *Postconventional moral reasoning: A neo-Kohlbergian approach.* Mahwah, NJ: Erlbaum.

Rest, J. R., & Thoma, S. J. (1985). Relation of moral judgment development to formal education. *Developmental Psychology, 21,* 709–714.

Reynolds, A. J., Ou, S., & Topitzes, J. W. (2004). Paths of effects of early childhood intervention on educational attainment and delinquency: A confirmatory analysis of the Chicago child-parent centers. *Child Development, 75,* 1299–1328.

Reynolds, D. (1992). School effectiveness and school improvement: An updated review of the British literature. In D. Reynolds & P. Cuttance (Eds.), *School effectiveness: Research, policy, and practice.* London, England: Cassell.

Rhee, S. H., & Waldman, I. D. (2002). Genetic and environmental influences on antisocial behavior: A meta-analysis of twin and adoption studies. *Psychological Bulletin, 128,* 490–529.

Rheingold, H. L. (1982). Little children's participation in the work of adults, a nascent prosocial behavior. *Child Development, 53,* 114–125.

Rhodes, J. E., Grossman, J. B., & Resch, N. L. (2000). Agents of change: Pathways through which relationships influence adolescents' academic adjustment. *Child Development, 71,* 1662–1671.

Rholes, W. S., & Ruble, D. N. (1984). Children's understanding of dispositional characteristics of others. *Child Development, 55,* 550–560.

Ribble, M. (1943). *The rights of infants.* New York: Columbia University Press.

Rice, M. L., Huston, A. C., Truglio, R., & Wright, J. (1990). Words from *Sesame Street:* Learning vocabulary while viewing. *Developmental Psychology, 26,* 421–428.

Richards, M. H., Crowe, P. A., Larson, R., & Swarr, A. (1998). Developmental patterns and gender differences in the experience of peer companionship during adolescence. *Child Development, 69,* 154–163.

Richards, M. H., & Duckett, E. (1994). The relationship of maternal employment to early adolescent daily experience with and without parents. *Child Development, 65,* 225–236.

Richardson, J. G., & Simpson, C. H. (1982). Children, gender, and social structure: An analysis of the contents of letters to Santa Claus. *Child Development, 53,* 429–436.

Richman, E. L., & Shaffer, D. R. (2000). "If you let me play sports": How might sport participation influence the self-esteem of adolescent females? *Psychology of Women Quarterly, 24,* 189–199.

Rivers, I., Poteat, V. P., & Noret, N. (2008). Victimization, social support, and psychosocial functioning among children of same-sex and opposite-sex couples in the United Kingdom. *Developmental Psychology, 44,* 127–134.

Roberts, D. F., Foehr, U. G., & Rideout, V. (2005). *Generation M: Media in the lives of 8–18 year olds.* Menlo Park, CA: Henry J. Kaiser Foundation.

Roberts, L. R., Sarigiani, P. A., Petersen, A. C., & Newman, J. L. (1990). Gender differences in the relationship between achievement and self-image during early adolescence. *Journal of Early Adolescence, 10,* 159–175.

Roberts, W., & Strayer, J. (1996). Empathy, emotional expressiveness, and prosocial behavior. *Child Development, 67,* 449–470.

Robins, R. W., Trzesniewski, K. H., Tracey, J. L., Gosling, S. D., & Potter, J. (2002). Global self-esteem across the life span. *Psychology and Aging, 17,* 423–434.

Robinson, C. C., & Morris, J. T. (1986). The gender-stereotyped nature of Christmas toys received by 36-, 48-, and 60-month-old children: A comparison between nonrequested vs. requested toys. *Sex Roles, 15,* 21–32.

Robinson, I., Ziss, K., Ganza, B., Katz, S., & Robinson, E. (1991). Twenty years of sexual revolution, 1965–1985: An update. *Journal of Marriage and the Family, 53,* 216–220.

Robinson, J. L., Kagan, J., Reznick, J. S., & Corley, R. (1992). The heritability of inhibited and uninhibited behavior: A twin study. *Developmental Psychology, 28,* 1030–1037.

Rochat, P., & Morgan, R. (1995). Spatial determinants of the perception of self-produced leg movements by 3- to 5-month-old infants. *Developmental Psychology, 31,* 626–636.

Rochat, P., & Striano, T. (2002). Who's in the mirror? Self-other discrimination in specular images by four- and nine-month old infants. *Child Development, 73,* 35–46.

Rocheleau, B. (1995). Computer use by school-age children: Trends, patterns, and predictors. *Journal of Educational Computing Research, 12,* 1–17.

Rock, A., Trainor, L. J., & Addison, T. L. (1999). Distinctive messages in infant-directed lullabies and play songs. *Developmental Psychology, 35,* 527–534.

Rodkin, P. C., Farmer, T. W., Pearl, R., & Van Acker, R. (2000). Heterogeneity of popular boys: Antisocial and prosocial configurations. *Developmental Psychology, 36,* 14–24.

Roeser, R. W., & Eccles, J. S. (1998). Adolescents' perceptions of middle school: Relation to longitudinal changes in academic and psychological adjustment. *Journal of Research in Adolescence, 8,* 123–158.

Rogoff, B. (1990). *Apprenticeship in thinking: Cognitive development in social context.* New York: Oxford University Press.

Rogoff, B. (1998). Cognition as a collaborative process. In D. Kuhn & R. S. Siegler (Eds.), Cognition language, and perceptual development, Vol. 2. In B. Damon (Gen. Ed.), *Handbook of child psychology,* New York: Wiley.

Rogoff, B. (2003). *The cultural nature of human development.* New York: Oxford University Press.

Rogoff, B., Mistry, J., Goncu, A., & Mosier, C. (1993). Guided participation in cultural activity by toddlers and caregivers. *Monographs of the Society for Research in Child Development, 58* (8, Serial No. 236).

Rohner, R. P. (2000). Father love and child development: History and current evidence. In K. L. Freiberg (Ed.), *Human development* 00/01 (28th ed., pp. 124–128). Guilford, CT: Duskin/McGraw-Hill.

Roisman, G. I., & Fraley, R. C. (2006). The limits of genetic influence: A behavior-genetic analysis of infant-caregiver relationship quality and temperament. *Child Development, 77,* 1656–1667.

Roopnarine, J. L., Fouts, H. N., Lamb, M. E., & Lewis-Elligan, T. Y. (2005). Mothers' and fathers' behaviors toward their 3- to 4-month-old infants in lower, middle, and upper socioeconomic African American families. *Developmental Psychology, 41,* 723–732.

Rose, A. J., & Asher, S. R. (1999). Children's goals and strategies in response to conflicts within a friendship. *Developmental Psychology, 35,* 69–79.

Rose, A. J., Carlson, W., & Waller, E. M. (2007). Prospective associations of co-rumination with friendship and emotional adjustment: Considering the socioemotional trade-offs of co-rumination. *Developmental Psychology, 43,* 1019–1031.

Rose, R. M., Bernstein, I. S., & Gordon, T. P. (1975). Consequences of social conflict on plasma testosterone levels in rhesus monkeys. *Psychosomatic Medicine, 37,* 50–61.

Rosen, B. C., & D'Andrade, R. (1959). The psychological origins of achievement motivation. *Sociometry, 22,* 185–218.

Rosen, K. S., & Rothbaum, F. (1993). Quality of parental caregiving and security of attachment. *Developmental Psychology, 29,* 358–367.

Rosen, L. (2008). *Me, My Space, and I: Parenting the net generation.* New York: Palgrave MacMillian.

Rosen, W. D., Adamson, L. B., & Bakeman, R. (1992). An experimental investigation of infant social referencing: Mothers' messages and gender differences. *Developmental Psychology, 28,* 1172–1178.

Rosenblum, G. D., & Lewis, M. (1999). The relations among body images, physical attractiveness, and body mass in adolescents. *Child Development, 70,* 50–64.

Rosenhan, D. L. (1970). The natural socialization of altruistic autonomy. In J. Macaulay & L. Berkowitz (Eds.), *Altruism and helping behavior.* New York: Academic Press.

Rosenhan, D. L. (1972). Learning theory and prosocial behavior. *Journal of Social Issues, 28,* 151–163.

Rosenholtz, S. J., & Simpson, C. (1984). The formation of ability conceptions: Developmental trend or social construction? *Review of Educational Research, 54,* 31–63.

Rosenthal, R., & Jacobson, L. (1968). *Pygmalion in the classroom.* New York: Holt, Rinehart and Winston.

Rosenthal, R., & Vandell, D. L. (1996). Quality of care at school-aged child-care programs: Regulatable features, observed experiences, child perspectives, and parent perspectives. *Child Development, 67,* 2434–2445.

Ross, H., Ross, M., Stein, N., & Trabasso, T. (2006). How siblings resolve their conflicts: The importance of first offers, planning, and limited opposition. *Child Development, 77,* 1730–1745.

Rothbart, M. K., Ahadi, S. A., Hershey, K. L., & Fisher, P. (2001). Investigators of temperament at three to seven years: The Children's Behavior Questionnaire. *Child Development, 72,* 1394–1408.

Rothbart, M. K., & Bates, J. E. (1998). Temperament. In W. Damon (Series Ed.), & N. Eisenberg (Vol. Ed.), *Handbook of child psychology. Vol. 3: Social, emotional, and personality development* (5th ed., pp. 105–176), New York: Wiley.

Rothbart, M. K., & Bates, J. E. (2006). Temperament. In W. Damon & R. M. Lerner (Series Eds.) & N. Eisenberg, (Vol. Ed.), *Handbook of child psychology, Vol. 3: Social, emotional, and personality* development (6th ed., pp. 99–106). New York: Wiley.

Rothbaum, F., Pott, M., Azuma, H., Miyake, K., & Weisz, J. (2000). The development of close relationships in Japan and the United States: Paths of symbiotic harmony and generative tension. *Child Development, 71,* 1121–1142.

Rothbaum, F., Weisz, J., Pott, M., Miyake, K., & Morelli, G. (2000). Attachment and culture: Security in the United States and Japan. *American Psychologist, 35,* 1093–1104.

Rousseau, J. J. (1955). *Emile.* New York: Dutton. (Original work published 1762).

Rovee-Collier, C. (1995). Time windows in cognitive development. *Developmental Psychology, 31,* 147–169.

Rowe, D. C. (1994). *The limits of family influence: Genes, experience, and behavior.* New York: Guilford.

Rowe, D. C., & Plomin, R. (1981). The importance of nonshared (E_1) environmental influences in behavioral development. *Developmental Psychology, 17,* 517–531.

Rowe, R., Maughan, B., Worthman, C. M., Costello, E. J., & Angold, A. (2004). Testosterone, antisocial behavior, and social dominance in boys: Pubertal developmental and biosocial interaction. *Biological Psychiatry, 55,* 546–552.

Roy, R., & Benenson, J. F. (2002). Sex and contextual effects on children's use of interference competition. *Developmental Psychology, 38,* 306–312.

Rubin, K. H., Bukowski, W. M., & Parker, J. G. (1998). Peer interactions, relationships, and groups. In W. Damon (Series Ed.) & N. Eisenberg (Vol. Ed.), *Handbook of Child Psychology: Vol. 3. Social, emotional, and personality development* (5th ed., pp. 619–700). New York: Wiley.

Rubin, K. H., Bukowski, W., & Parker, J. G. (2006). Peer interactions, relationships, and groups. In W. Damon & R. M. Lerner (Series Eds.) & N. Eisenberg (Vol. Ed.), *Handbook of child psychology. Vol. 3: Social, emotional, and personality development* (6th ed. pp. 571–645). New York: Wiley.

Rubin, K. H., Burgess, K. B., Dwyer, K. M., & Hastings, P. D. (2003). Predicting preschoolers' externalizing behaviors from toddler temperament, conflict, and maternal negativity. *Developmental Psychology, 39,* 164–176.

Rubin, K. H., Burgess, K. B., & Hastings, P. D. (2002). Stability and social-behavioral consequences of toddler's inhibited temperament and parenting behaviors. *Child Development, 73,* 483–495.

Rubin, K. H., Hastings, P., Chen, X., & Vandenberg, B. (1998). Interpersonal and maternal correlates of aggression, conflict, and externalizing problems in toddlers. *Child Development, 69,* 1614–1629.

Ruble, D. N., Balaban, T., & Cooper, J. (1981). Gender constancy and the Effects of sex-typed televised toy commercials. *Child Development, 52,* 667–673.

Ruble, D. N., & Dweck, C. S. (1995). Self-conceptions, person conceptions, and their development. In N. Eisenberg (Ed.), *Social development.* Thousand Oaks, CA: Sage.

Ruble, D. N., & Martin, C. L. (1998). Gender development. In N. Eisenberg (Ed.) & W. Damon (Series Ed.), *Handbook of child psychology. Vol. 3: Social, emotional, and personality development* (5th ed., pp. 933–1016). New York: Wiley.

Ruble, D. N., Martin, C., & Berenbaum, S. (2006). Gender development. In W. Damon & R. M. Lerner (Series Eds.), and N. Eisenberg (Vol. Ed.), *Handbook on child psychology: Vol.3. Social, emotional, and personality development* (pp. 858–932). New York: Wiley.

Ruble, D. N., Taylor, L. J., Cyphers, L., Greulich, F. K., Lurye, L. E., & Shrout, P. E. (2007). The role of gender constancy in early gender development. *Child Development, 78,* 1121–1136.

Ruble, T. L. (1983). Sex stereotypes: Issues of change in the 1970s. *Sex Roles, 9,* 397–402.

Rudolph, F. (1965). *Essays on early education in the republic.* Cambridge, MA: Harvard University Press.

Rudolph, K. D., Caldwell, M. S., & Conley, C. S. (2005). Need for approval and children's well-being. *Child Development, 76,* 309–323.

Rueter, M. A., & Conger, R. D. (1998). Reciprocal influences between parenting and adolescent problem-solving behavior. *Developmental Psychology, 34,* 1470–1482.

Ruffman, T. K., Olson, D. R., Ash, T., & Keenan, T. (1993). The ABCs of deception: Do young children understand deception in the same way as adults? *Developmental Psychology, 29,* 74–87.

Ruffman, T., Perner, J., Naito, M., Parkin, L., & Clements, W. A. (1998). Older (but not younger) siblings facilitate false belief understanding. *Developmental Psychology, 34,* 161–174.

Ruffman, T., Slade, L., & Crowe, E. (2002). The relation between children's and mother's mental state language and theory of mind understanding. *Child Development, 73,* 734–751.

Russell, A., Hart, C. H., Robinson, C. C., & Olsen, S. F. (2003). Children's sociable and aggressive behavior with peers: A comparison of the U.S. and Australia, and contributions of temperament and parenting styles. *International Journal of Behavioral Development, 27,* 74–86.

Rust, J., Golombok, S., Hines, M., Johnston, K., & Golding, J. (2000). The role of brothers and sisters in the gender development of preschool children. *Journal of Experimental Child Psychology, 77,* 292–303.

Rutland, A., Cameron, L., Milne, A., & McGeorge, P. (2005). Social norms and self-presentation: Children's implicit and explicit intergroup attitudes. *Child Development, 76,* 451–466.

Rutter, M. (1979). Protective factors in children's responses to stress and disadvantage. In M. W. Kent & J. E. Rolf (Eds.), *Primary prevention of psychopathology. Vol. 3: Social competence in children.* Hanover, NH: University Press of New England.

Rutter, M. (1983). School effects on pupil progress: Research findings and policy implications. *Child Development, 54,* 1–29.

Rutter, M. (2006). The psychological effects of early institutional rearing. In P. J. Marshall & N. A. Fox (Eds.), *The development of psychological engagement: Neurobiological perspectives* (pp. 355–391). New York & Oxford, UK: Oxford University Press.

Rutter, M., & Maughan, B. (2002). School effectiveness findings 1979–2002. *Journal of School Psychology, 50,* 451–475.

Rutter, M., Maughan, B., Mortimore, P., Ouston, J., & Smith, A. (1979). *Fifteen thousand hours: Secondary schools and their effects on children.* Cambridge, MA: Harvard University Press.

Ryalls, B. O., Gul, R. E., & Ryalls, K. R. (2000). Infant imitation of peer and adult models: Evidence for a peer model advantage. *Merrill-Palmer Quarterly, 46,* 188–202.

Ryan, A. M., (2001). The peer group as a context for the development of young adolescent motivation and achievement. *Child Development, 72,* 1135–1150.

Ryan, C. S., McCall, R. B., Robinson, D. R., Groark, C. J., Mulvey, L., & Plemons, B. W. (2002). Benefits of a comprehensive child development program as a function of AFDC receipt and SES. *Child Development, 73,* 315–328.

Saarni, C. (1984). An observational study of children's attempts to monitor their expressive behavior. *Child Development, 55,* 1504–1513.

Saarni, C. (1990). Emotional competence: How emotions and relationships become integrated. In R. A. Thompson (Ed.), Socioemotional development. *Nebraska Symposium on Motivation* (Vol 36). Lincoln: University of Nebraska Press.

Saarni, C. (1999). *The development of emotional competence.* New York: Guilford.

Saarni, C., Mumme, D. L., & Campos, J. J. (1998). Emotional development: Action, communication, and understanding. In W. Damon (Series Ed.) & N. Eisenberg (Vol. Ed.), *Handbook of child psychology. Vol. 3: Social, emotional, and personality development* (5th Ed., pp. 237–309). New York: Wiley.

Sabattini, L., & Leaper, C. (2004). The relation between mothers' and fathers' parenting styles and their division of labor in the home: Young adults' retrospective reports. *Sex Roles, 50,* 217–225.

Sackin, S., & Thelen, E. (1984). An ethological study of peaceful associative outcomes to conflict in preschool children. *Child Development, 55,* 1098–1102.

Sackin, S., & Thelen, E. (1984). An ethological study of peaceful associative outcomes to conflict in preschool children. *Child Development, 55,* 1098–1102.

Sacks, C. H., & Mergendoller, J. R. (1997). The relationship between teachers' theoretical orientation toward reading and student outcomes in kindergarten children with different initial reading abilities. *American Educational Research Journal, 34,* 721–739.

Sagi, A., & Hoffman, M. L. (1976). Empathic distress in newborns. *Developmental Psychology, 12,* 175–176.

Salend, S. J. (1999). Facilitating friendship among diverse students. *Intervention in School and Clinic, 35,* 9–15.

Salmivalli, C., Ojanen, T., Haanpaa, J., & Peets, K. (2005). "I'm OK but you're not" and other peer-relational schemas: Explaining individual differences in children's social goals. *Developmental Psychology, 41,* 363–375.

Salzinger, S., Feldman, R. S., Hammer, M., & Rosario, M. (1993). The effects of physical abuse on children's social relationships. *Child Development, 64,* 169–187.

Samuels, C. (1986). Bases for the infant's development of self-awareness. *Human Development, 29,* 36–48.

Sancilio, M. F. M., Plumert, J. M., & Hartup, W. W. (1989). Friendship and aggressiveness as determinants of conflict outcomes in middle childhood. *Developmental Psychology, 25,* 812–819.

Sanson, A., Hemphill, S. A., & Smart, D. (2004). Connections between temperament and social development: A review. *Social Development, 13,* 142–170.

Santrock, J. W. (1975). Moral structure: The interrelations of moral behavior, moral judgment, and moral affect. *Journal of Genetic Psychology, 127,* 201–213.

Santrock, J. W. (2002). *A topical approach to life-span development.* New York: McGraw-Hill.

Savin-Williams, R. C. (1998). The disclosure to families of same-sex attractions by lesbian, gay, and bisexual youths. *Journal of Research on Adolescence, 8,* 49–68.

Savin-Williams, R. C. (2008). Then and now: Recruitment, definition, diversity, and positive attributes of same-sex populations. *Developmental Psychology, 44,* 135–138.

Savin-Williams, R. C., & Diamond, L. M. (2000). Sexual identity trajectories among sexual-minority youths: Gender comparisons. *Archives of Sexual Behavior, 29,* 419–440.

Savin-Williams, R. C., & Ream, G. L. (2003). Sex variations in the disclosure to parents of same-sex attractions. *Journal of Family Psychology, 17,* 429–438.

Savin-Williams, R. C., & Small, S. A. (1986). The timing of puberty and its relationship to adolescent and parent perceptions of family interactions. *Developmental Psychology, 22,* 342–347.

Saxe, R., Carey, S., & Kanwisher, N. (2004). Understanding other minds: Linking developmental psychology and functional neuroimaging. *Annual Review of Psychology, 55,* 87–124.

Saywitz, K. J., Mannarino, A. P., Berliner, L., & Cohen, J. A. (2000). Treatment for sexually abused children and adolescents. *American Psychologist, 55,* 1040–1049.

Scaramella, L. V., Conger, R. D., Spoth, R., & Simons, R. L. (2002). Evaluation of a social contextual model of delinquency: A cross-study replication. *Child Development, 73,* 175–195.

Scarr, S., (1992). Developmental theories for the 1990s: Development and individual differences. *Child Development, 63,* 1–19.

Scarr, S. (1998). American child care today. *American Psychologist, 53,* 95–108.

Scarr, S., & McCartney, K. (1983). How people make their own environments: A theory of genotype → environment effects. *Child Development, 54,* 424–435.

Scarr, S., Webber, P. L., Weinberg, R. A., & Wittig, M. A. (1981). Personality resemblance among adolescents and their parents in biologically related and adoptive families. *Journal of Personality and Social Psychology, 40,* 885–898.

Scarr, S., & Weinberg, R. A. (1978). The influence of family background on intellectual attainment. *American Sociological Review, 43,* 674–692.

Scarr, S., & Weinberg, R. A. (1983). The Minnesota adoption studies: Genetic differences and malleability. *Child Development, 54,* 260–267.

Schaffer, H. R. (1977). *Mothering.* Cambridge, MA: Harvard University Press.

Schaffer, H. R. (1991). *Making decisions about children: Psychological questions and answers.* Cambridge, MA: Basil Blackwell.

Schaffer, H. R., & Emerson, P. E. (1964). The development of social attachments in infancy. *Monographs of the Society for Research in Child Development, 29* (3, Serial No. 94).

Schaie, K. W. (1986). Beyond calendar definitions of age, time, and cohort: The general developmental model revisited. *Developmental Review, 6,* 252–277.

Schaie, K. W. (1990). Intellectual development in adulthood. In E. J. Birren & K. W. Schaie (Eds.). *The handbook of the psychology of aging* (3rd ed.). San Diego, CA: Academic Press.

Schick, B., de Villiers, P., de Villers, J., & Hoffmeister, B. (2007). Language and theory of mind: A study of deaf children. *Child Development, 78,* 376–396.

Schmitt, K. L., Anderson, D. R., & Collins, P. A. (1999). Form and content: Looking at visual features of television. *Developmental Psychology, 35,* 1156–1167.

Schneider, B. H. (1992). Didactic methods for enhancing children's peer relations: A quantitative review. *Clinical Psychology Review, 12,* 363–382.

Schneider, B. H., Atkinson, L., & Tardif, C. (2001). Child-parent attachment and children's peer relations: A quantitative review. *Developmental Psychology, 37,* 86–100.

Schneiders, J., Nicolson, N. A., Berkhof, J., Feron, F. J., deVines, J., & deVines, M. W. (2006). Mood reactivity to daily negative events in early adolescence: Relationship to risk for psychopathology. *Developmental Psychology, 42,* 543–554.

Schoon, I., Bynner, J., Joshi, H., Parsons, S., Wiggins, R. D., & Sacker, A. (2002). The influence of context, timing, and duration of risk experiences for the passage from childhood to midadulthood. *Child Development, 73,* 1486–1504.

Schulting, A. B., Malone, P. S., & Dodge, K. A. (2005). The effect of school-based kindergarten transition policies and practices on child achievement outcomes. *Developmental Psychology, 41,* 860–871.

Schwartz, C. E., Snidman, N., & Kagan, J. (1999). Adolescent social anxiety as an outcome of inhibited temperament in childhood. *Journal of the American Academy of Child and Adolescent Psychiatry, 38,* 1008–1015.

Schwartz, D., Chang, L., & Farver, J. M. (2001). Correlates of victimization in Chinese children's peer groups. *Developmental Psychology, 37,* 520–532.

Schwartz, D., Dodge, K. A., Pettit, G. S., & Bates, J. E. (1997). The early socialization of aggressive victims of bullying. *Child Development, 68,* 665–675.

Schwartz. D., Dodge, K. A., Pettit, G. S., & Bates, J. E., & the Conduct Problems Prevention Research Group (2000). Friendship as a moderating factor in the pathway between early harsh home environment and later victimization in the peer group. *Developmental Psychology, 36,* 646–662.

Schwartz, D., Gorman, A. H., Nakamoto, J., & McKay, T. (2006). Popularity, social acceptance, and aggression in adolescent peer groups: Links with academic performance and school attendance. *Developmental Psychology, 42,* 1116–1127.

Schwartz, J. E., Wright, C. I., Shin, L. M., Kagan, J., & Rauch, S. L. (2003). Inhibited and uninhibited infants "grown up": Adult amygdalar response to novelty. *Science, 300,* 1952–1953.

Schwartz, R., & McCartney, K. (2007). Commentary on Porter and Polikoff. In Porter, A. C., and Polikoff, M S. (2007). *Social Policy Report, 21.* Chicago: Society for Research in Childhood Development.

Scott, A. (2007, May 12). Support groups for lesbigay students on the rise in our schools. *Athens Banner Herald,* p. A1–A6.

Scott, J. P. (1992). Aggression: Functions and control in social systems. *Aggressive Behavior, 18,* 1–20.

Scott, W. A., Scott, R., & McCabe, M. (1991). Family relationships and children's personality: A cross-cultural, cross-source comparison. *British Journal of Social Psychology, 30,* 1–20.

Sears, R. R. (1963). Dependency motivation. In M. Jones (Ed.), *Nebraska Symposium on Motivation* (Vol. 11). Lincoln: University of Nebraska Press.

Seaton, E. K., Scottham, K. M., & Sellers, R. M. (2006). The status model of racial identity development in African American adolescents: Evidence of structure, trajectories, and well-being. *Child Development, 77,* 1416–1426.

Sebald, H. (1986). Adolescents' shifting orientation toward parents and peers: A curvilinear trend over recent decades. *Journal of Marriage and the Family, 48,* 5–13.

Seccombe, K. (2000). Families in poverty in the 1990's: Trends, causes, consequences, and lessons learned. *Journal of Marriage and the Family, 62,* 1094–1113.

Secord, P. H., Peevers, D. H. (1974). The development and attribution of person concepts. In T. Michel (Ed.), *Understanding other persons*. Totowa, N.J.: Rowman & Littlefield.

Segal, U. A. (1991). Cultural variables in Asian Indian families. *Families in society: The Journal of Contemporary Human Services, 72,* 233–242.

Segrin, C., Taylor, M. E., & Altman, J. (2005). Social cognitive mediators and relational outcomes associated with parental divorce. *Journal of Social and Personal Relationships, 22,* 361–377.

Seidman, E., Allen, L., Aber, J. L., Mitchell, C., & Feinman, J. (1994). The impact of school transitions in early adolescence on the self-system and perceived social context of poor urban youth. *Child Development, 65,* 507–522.

Seidman, E., Chesir-Teran, D., Friedman, J. L., Yoshikawa, H., Allen, L. & Roberts, A. (1999). The risk and protective functions of perceived family and peer microsystems among urban adolescents in poverty. *American Journal of Community Psychology, 27,* 211–237.

Seitz, V., & Apfel, N. H. (1994). Parent-focused intervention: Diffusion effects on siblings. *Child Development, 65,* 677–683.

Seitz, V., Rosenbaum, L. K., & Apfel, N. H. (1985). Effects of family support intervention: A ten-year follow-up. *Child Development, 56,* 376–391.

Seligman, M. E. P. (1993). *What you can change and what you can't: The complete guide to successful self-improvement.* New York: Fawcett.

Selman, R. L. (1976). Social-cognitive understanding: A guide to educational and clinical practice. In T. Lickona (Ed.), *Moral development and behavior: Theory, research, and social issues*. New York: Holt, Rinehart and Winston.

Selman, R. L. (1980). *The growth of interpersonal understanding*. Orlando, FL: Academic Press.

Seppa, N. (1997). Children's TV remains steeped in violence. *Monitor of the American Psychological Association, 28,* 36.

Serbin, L. A., Powlishta, K. K., & Gulko, J. (1993). The development of sex typing in middle childhood. *Monographs of the Society for Research in Child Development, 58* (2, Serial No. 232).

Servin, A., Nordenstrom, A., Larsson, A., & Bohlin, G. (2003). Prenatal androgens and gender-typed behavior: A study of girls with mild and severe forms of congenital adrenal hyperplasia. *Developmental Psychology, 39,* 440–450.

Shaffer, D. R. (1973). *Children's responses to a hypothetical proposition*. Paper presented at the annual meeting of the Midwestern Psychological Association: Chicago.

Shaffer, D. R. (1994). Do naturalistic conceptions of morality provide any [novel] answers? *Journal of Personality, 62,* 263–268.

Shaffer, D. R., & Augustine, M. L. (2003). Affective mediation of homophobic reactions to homosexual males. *Journal of Psychology and Human Sexuality, 14,* 67–85.

Shaffer, D. R., & Kipp, K. (2007). *Developmental psychology: Childhood and adolescence* (7th ed.). Belmont, CA: Wadsworth.

Shaffer, D. R., Pegalis, L. J., & Cornell, D. P. (1992). Gender and self-disclosure revisited: Personal and contextual variations in self-disclosure to same-sex acquaintances. *Journal of Social Psychology, 132,* 307–315.

Shaffer, D. R., & Wittes, E., (2006). Women's precollege sports participation, enjoyment of sports, and self-esteem. *Sex Roles, 55,* 225–233.

Shanahan, L., McHale, S. M., Crouter, A. C., & Osgood, D. W. (2007). Warmth with mothers and fathers from middle childhood to late adolescence: Within and between family comparisons. *Developmental Psychology, 43,* 551–563.

Shanahan, L., McHale, S. M., Osgood, D. W., & Crouter, A. C. (2007). Conflict frequency with mothers and fathers from middle childhood to late adolescence: Within and between families comparisons. *Developmental Psychology, 43,* 539–550.

Shantz, C. U. (1983). Social cognition. In P. H. Mussen (Ed.), *Handbook of child psychology*. Vol. 3: *Cognitive development*. New York: Wiley.

Sharabany, R., Gershoni, R., & Hoffman, J. E. (1981). Girlfriend, boyfriend: Age and sex differences in intimate friendship. *Developmental Psychology, 17,* 800–808.

Sharma, A. R., McGue, M. K., & Benson, P. L. (1998). The psychological adjustment of United States adopted adolescents and their nonadopted siblings. *Child Development, 69,* 791–802.

Sharp, D., Cole, M., & Lave, C. (1979). Education and cognitive development: The evidence from experimental research. *Monographs of the Society for Research in Child Development, 44* (1–2, Serial No. 78).

Shaw, D. S., Gilliom, M., Ingoldsby, E. M., & Nagin, D. S. (2003). Trajectories leading to school-age conduct problems. *Developmental Psychology, 39,* 189–200.

Shaw, D. S., Winslow, E. E., & Flanagan, C. (1999). A prospective study of the effects of marital status and family relations on young children's adjustment among African American and European American families. *Child Development, 70,* 742–755.

Sheldon, K. M., & Kasser, T. (2001). Getting older, getting better? Personal strivings and psychological maturity across the life span. *Developmental Psychology, 37,* 491–501.

Shell, R. M., & Eisenberg, N. (1996). Children's reactions to the receipt of direct and indirect help. *Child Development, 67,* 1391–1405.

Sherif, M., Harvey, O. J., White, B. J., Hood, W. R., & Sherif, C. W. (1961). *Intergroup conflict and cooperation: The Robber's Cave experiment*. Norman, OK: University of Oklahoma Press.

Shields, A., Ryan , R. M., & Cicchetti, D. (2001). Narrative representations of caregivers and emotional dysregulation as predictors of maltreated children's rejection by peers. *Developmental Psychology, 37,* 321–337.

Shih, M., Pittinsky, T. L., & Ambady, N. (1999). Stereotype susceptibility: Identity salience and shifts in quantitative performance. *Psychological Science, 10,* 80–93.

Shipman, K., Zeman, J., Penza, S., & Champion, K. (2000). Emotion management skills in sexually maltreated and nonmalreated girls: A developmental psychopathology perspective. *Development and Psychpathology, 12,* 47–62.

Shonk, S. M., & Cicchetti, D. (2001). Maltreatment, competency deficits, and risk for academic and behavioral maladjustment. *Developmental Psychology, 37,* 3–17.

Shulman, S., Elicker, J., & Sroufe, A. (1994). Stages of friendship growth in preadolescence as related to attachment history. *Journal of Social and Personal Relationships, 11,* 341–361.

Shultz, T. R., & Wells, D. (1985). Judging the intentionly of action-outcomes. *Developmental Psychology, 21,* 83–89.

Shure, M. B. (1989). Interpersonal competence training. In W. Damon (Ed.), *Child development today and tomorrow.* San Francisco: Jossey-Bass.

Shure, M. B., & Spivack, G. (1978). *Problem-solving techniques in childrearing.* San Francisco: Jossey-Bass.

Shweder, R. A. (1997, April). Varieties of moral intelligence: Autonomy, community, divinity. In L. A. Jensen (Chair), *Shweder's ethics of autonomy, community, and divinity: Theory and research.* Symposium presented at the biennial meeting of the Society for Research in Child Development, Washington, DC.

Shweder, R. A., Mahapatra, M., & Miller, J. G. (1987). Culture and moral development. In J. Kagan & S. Lamb (Eds.), *The emergence of morality in young children* (pp. 1–83). Chicago: University of Chicago Press.

Shweder, R. A., Mahapatra, M., & Miller, J. G. (1990). Culture and moral development. In J. W. Stigler, R. A. Shweder, & G. Herdt (Eds.), *Cultural psychology. Essays on comparative human development.* Cambridge, England: Cambridge University Press.

Siegal, M., & Cowen, J. (1984). Appraisals of intervention: The mother's versus the culprit's behavior as determinants of children's evaluations of discipline techniques. *Child Development, 55,* 1760–1766.

Siegal, M., & Peterson, C. C. (1998). Preschoolers' understanding of lies and innocent and negligent mistakes. *Developmental Psychology, 34,* 332–341.

Siegler, R. S., & Jenkins, E. A. (1989). *How children discover new strategies.* Hillsdale, NJ: Erlbaum.

Siegler, R. S., & Svetina, M. (2002). A microgenetic/cross-sectional study of matrix completion: Comparing short-term and long-term change. *Child Development, 73,* 793–809.

Sigelman, C. K., Carr, M. B., & Begley, N. L. (1986). Developmental changes the influence of sex-role stereotypes on person perception. *Child Study Journal, 16,* 191–205.

Sigelman, C. K., Derenowski, E., Woods, T., Makai, T., Alfred-Livo, L., Durazo, O., & Maddock, A. (1996). Mexican-American and Anglo-American children's responsiveness to a theory-centered AIDS education program. *Child Development, 67,* 253–266.

Sigelman, C. K., Miller, T. E., & Whitworth, L. A. (1986). The early development of stigmatizing reactions to physical differences. *Journal of Applied Developmental Psychology, 7,* 17–32.

Sigelman, C. K., & Rider, E. (2006). *Life-span human development* (5th ed.). Belmont, CA: Wadsworth.

Signorella, M. L., Bigler, R. S., & Liben, L. S. (1993). Developmental differences in children's gender schemata about others: A meta-analytic review. *Developmental Review, 13,* 147–183.

Signorella, M. L., Jamison, W., & Krupa, M. H. (1989). Predicting spatial performance from gender stereotyping in activity preferences and in self-concept. *Developmental Psychology, 25,* 89–95.

Signorielli, N., & Kahlenberg, S. (2001). Television's world of work in the nineties. *Journal of Broadcasting & Electronic Media, 45,* 4–22.

Signorielli, N., & Lears, M. (1992). Children, television, and conceptions about chores: Attitudes and behaviors. *Sex Roles, 27,* 157–170.

Simmons, R. G., Burgeson, R., Carlton-Ford, S., & Blyth, D. A. (1987). The impact of cumulative change in early adolescence. *Child Development, 58,* 1220–1234.

Simpkins, S. D., Davis-Kean, P. E., & Eccles, J. S. (2006). Math and science motivation: A longitudinal examination of the links between choices and beliefs. *Developmental Psychology, 42,* 70–83.

Singelis, T. M. (1994). The measurement of independent and inter-dependent self-construal. *Personality and Social Psychology Bulletin, 20,* 580–591.

Singer, D. G., & Singer, J. L. (1990). The house of make-believe: Children's play and the developing imagination. Cambridge, MA: Harvard University Press.

Singer, L. M. Brodzinsky, D. M., Ramsay, D., Steir, M., & Waters, E. (1985). Mother-infant attachments in adoptive families. *Child Development, 56,* 1543–1551.

Singer, M., Miller, D. B., Guo, S., Flannery, D. J., Frierson, T., & Slovak, K. (1999). Contributors to violent behavior among elementary and middle school children. *Pediatrics, 104,* 878–884.

Skinner, B. F. (1953). *Science and human behavior.* New York: Macmillan.

Slaby, R. G., & Frey, K. S. (1975). Development of gender constancy and selective attention to same-sex models. *Child Development, 46,* 849–856.

Slaby, R. G., Roedell, W. C., Arezzo, D., & Hendrix, K. (1995). *Early violence prevention.* Washington, DC: National Association for the Education of Young Children.

Slade, A., Belsky, J., Aber, J. L., & Phelps, J. L. (1999). Mothers' representations of their relationships with their toddlers: Links to adult attachment and observed mothering. *Developmental Psychology, 35,* 611–619.

Slaughter-Defoe, D. T., Nakagawa, K., Takanishi, R., & Johnson, D. L. (1990). Toward cultural/ecological perspectives on schooling and achievement in African- and Asian-American children. *Child Development, 61,* 363–383.

Slavin, R. E. (1991). Cooperative learning and group contingencies. *Journal of Behavioral Education, 1,* 105–115.

Slavin, R. E. (1996). Research on cooperative learning and achievement: What we know, what we need to know. *Contemporary Educational Psychology, 21,* 43–69.

Slavkin, M., & Stright, A. D. (2000). Gender role differences in college students from one- and two-parent families. *Sex Roles, 42,* 23–37.

Sluckin, A. M., & Smith, P. K. (1977). Two approaches to the concept of dominance in preschool children. *Child Development, 48,* 917–923.

Smetana, J. G. (1981). Preschool children's conceptions of moral and social rules. *Child Development, 52,* 1333–1336.

Smetana, J. G. (1985). Preschool children's conceptions of transgressions: Effects of varying moral and conventional domain-related attributes. *Developmental Psychology, 21,* 18–29.

Smetana, J. G. (2006). Social domain theory: Consistencies and variations in children's moral and social judgments. In M. Killen & J. G. Smetana (Eds.), *Handbook of moral development* (pp. 119–153). Mahwah, NJ: Erlbaum.

Smetana, J. G., Campione-Barr, N., & Daddis, C. (2004). Longitudinal development of family decision making: Defining healthy behavioral autonomy for middle-class African American adolescents. *Child Development, 75,* 1418–1434.

Smetana, J. G., & Daddis, C. (2002). Domain-specific antecedents of parental psychological control and monitoring: The role of parenting beliefs and practices. *Child Development, 73,* 563–580.

Smetana, J. G., & Gaines, C. (1999). Adolescent-parent conflict in middle-class African American families. *Child Development, 70,* 1447–1463.

Smith, C. L., Calkins, D. S., Keane, S. P., Anastopoulous, A. D., & Shelton, T. L. (2004). Predicting stability and change in toddler behavior problems: Contributions of maternal behavior and child gender. *Developmental Psychology, 40,* 29–42.

Smith, J., & Ross, H. (2007). Training parents to mediate sibling disputes affects children's negotiations and conflict understanding. *Child Development, 78,* 790–805.

Smith, J. B., (1997). Effects of eighth-grade transition programs on high school retention and experiences. *Journal of Educational Research, 90,* 144–152.

Smith, L. H., Guthrie, B. J., & Oakley, D. J. (2005). Studying adolescent male sexuality: Where are we? *Journal of Youth and Adolescence, 34,* 361–377.

Smith, P. K., & Connolly, K. J. (1980). *The ecology of preschool behavior.* New York: Cambridge University Press.

Smith, P. K., Cowie, H., Olafsson, R. F., & Liefooghe, A. P. D. (2002). Definitions of bullying: A comparison of terms used, and age and gender differences, in a fourteen-country international comparison. *Child Development, 73,* 1119–1133.

Smith, P. K., & Daglish, L. (1977). Sex differences in parent and infant behavior in the home. *Child Development, 48,* 1250–1254.

Smith, T. W. (1990). Academic achievement and teaching younger siblings. *Social Psychology Quarterly, 53,* 352–363.

Smoll, F. L., & Schutz, R. W. (1990). Quantifying gender differences in physical performance: A developmental perspective. *Developmental Psychology, 26,* 360–369.

Smyke, A. T., Dumitrescu, A., & Zeanah, C. H. (2002). Disturbances of attachment in young children. I: The continuum of caretaking casualty. *Journal of the American Academy of Child and Adolescent Psychiatry, 41,* 972–982.

Snarey, J. R. (1985). Cross-cultural universality of social-moral development: A critical review of Kohlbergian research. *Psychological Bulletin, 97,* 202–232.

Snarey, J. R., & Keljo, K. (1991). In a gemeinschaft voice: The cross-cultural expansion of moral development theory. In W. M. Kurtines & J. L. Gewirtz (Eds.), *Handbook of moral behavior and development* (Vol. 1, pp. 395–424). Hillsdale, NJ: Erlbaum.

Snow, M. E., Jacklin, C. N., & Maccoby, E. E. (1983). Sex-of-child differences in father-child interaction at one year of age. *Child Development, 54,* 227–232.

Snyder, H. N. (2003). *Juvenile arrests 2001.* Washington, DC: U.S. Department of Justice. Office of Justice Programs. Office of Juvenile Justine and Delinquency Prevention.

Snyder, J., Bank, L., & Burraston, B. (2005). The consequences of antiosocial behavior in older male siblings for younger brothers and sisters. *Journal of Family Psychology, 19,* 643–653.

Snyder, J., Cramer, A., Afrank, J., & Patterson, G. R. (2005). The contributions of ineffective discipline and parental hostile attributions of child misbehavior to the development of conduct problems at home and school. *Developmental Psychology, 41,* 30–41.

Snyder, J., Reid, J. B., & Patterson, G. R. (2003). A social learning model of child and adolescent antisocial behavior. In B. B. Lahey, T. E. Moffitt, & A. Caspi (Eds.), *The causes of conduct disorder and juvenile delinquency* (pp. 27–48). New York: Guilford Press.

Sodian, B., Taylor, C., Harris, P. L., & Perner, J. (1991). Early deception and the child's theory of mind: False trails and genuine markers. *Child Development, 62,* 468–483.

Soenens, B., Vansteenkiste, M., Lens, K., Luyckx, K., Goossens, L., Byers, W., & Ryan, R. M. (2007). Conceptualizing parental autonomy support: Adolescent perceptions of promotion of independence versus promotion of volitional functioning. *Developmental Psychology, 43,* 633–646.

Soenens, B., Vansteenkiste, M., Luyckx, K., & Goossens. L. (2006). Parenting and adolescent problem behavior: An integrated model with adolescent self-disclosure and perceived parental knowledge as intervening variables. *Developmental Psychology, 42,* 305–318.

Soken, N., H., & Pick, A. D. (1999). Infants' perception of dynamic affective expressions: Do infants distinguish specific emotions? *Child Development, 70,* 1275–1282.

Sorensen, E. (1997). A national profile of nonresident fathers and their ability to pay child support. *Journal of Marriage and the Family, 59,* 785–797.

Speicher, B. (1994). Family patterns of moral judgment during adolescence and early adulthood. *Developmental Psychology, 30,* 624–632.

Speltz, M. L., Endriga, M. C., Fisher, P. A., & Mason, C. A. (1997). Early predictors of attachment in infants with cleft lip/or palate. *Child Development, 68,* 12–25.

Spence, J. T., & Buckner, C. E. (2000). Instrumental and expressive traits, trait stereotypes, and sexist attitudes: What do they signify? *Psychology of Women Quarterly, 24,* 44–62.

Spence, J. T., & Hall, S. K. (1996). Children's gender-related self-perceptions, activity preferences, and occupational stereotypes: A test of three models of gender constructs. *Sex Roles, 35,* 659–691.

Spence, J. T., & Helmreich, R. L. (1978). *Masculinity and femininity: Their psychological dimensions, correlates, and antecedents.* Austin: TX: University of Texas Press.

Spencer, M. B. (1988). Self-concept development. In D. T. Slaughter (Ed.), *Black children in poverty: Developmental perspectives.* San Francisco: Jossey-Bass.

Spencer, M. B., & Markstrom-Adams, C. (1990). Identity processes among racial and ethnic minority children in America. *Child Development, 61,* 290–310.

Spieker, S. J., Larson, N. C., Lewis, S. M., Keller, T. E., & Gilchrist, L. (1999). Developmental trajectories of disruptive behavior problems in preschool children of adolescent mothers. *Child Development, 70,* 443–458.

Spinrad, T. L., Eisenberg, N., Gaertner, B., Popp, T., Smith, C. L., Kupfer, K., Liew, J., & Hofer, C. (2007). Relations of maternal socialization and toddlers' effortful control to children's adjustment and social competence. *Developmental Psychology, 43,* 1170–1186.

Spitz, R. A. (1945). Hospitalism: An inquiry into the genesis of psychiatric conditions in early childhood. In A. Freud (Ed.), *The psychoanalytic study of the child* (Vol. 1). New York: International Universities Press.

Spitz, R. A. (1949). Motherless infants. *Child Development, 20,* 145–155.

Spitz, R. A. (1965). *The first year of life: A psychoanalytic study of normal and deviant object relations.* New York: International Universities Press.

Sroufe, L. A. (1977). Wariness of strangers and the study of infant development. *Child Development, 48,* 1184–1199.

Sroufe, L. A. (1985). Attachment classification from the perspective of infant-caregiver relationships and infant temperament. *Child Development, 56,* 1–14.

Sroufe, L. A. (1995). *Emotional development: The organization of emotional life in the early years*. Cambridge, England: Cambridge University Press.

Sroufe, L. A. (2003). Attachment categories as reflections of multiple dimensions: Comment on Fraley and Spieker (2003). *Developmental Psychology, 39*, 413–416.

Sroufe, L. A., Bennett, C., Englund, M., Urban, J., & Shulman, S. (1993). The significance of gender boundaries in preadolescence: Contemporary correlates and antecedents of boundary violation and maintenance. *Child Development, 64*, 455–466.

Sroufe, L. A., Egeland, B., & Kreutzer, T. (1990). The fate of early experience following developmental change: Longitudinal approaches to individual adaptation in childhood. *Child Development, 61*, 1363–1373.

Sroufe, L. A., & Waters, E. (1976). The ontogenesis of smiling and laughter: A perspective on the organization of development in infancy. *Psychological Review, 83*, 173–189.

Sroufe, L. A., Waters, E., & Matas, L. (1974). Contextual determinants of infant affectional response. In M. Lewis & L. A. Rosenblum (Eds.), *The origins of fear*. New York: Wiley.

Stacey, J., & Biblarz, T. (2001). (How) Does the sexual orientation of parents matter? *American Sociological Review, 66*, 159–183.

Staffieri, J. R. (1967). A study of social stereotype of body image in children. *Journal of Personality and Social Psychology, 7*, 101–104.

Stams, G. J. M., Juffer, F., & van IJzendoorn, M. H. (2002). Maternal sensitivity, infant attachment, and temperament in early childhood predict adjustment in middle childhood: The case of adopted children and their biologically unrelated parents. *Developmental Psychology, 38*, 806–821.

Staples, G. B. (2000, November 15). Television in black and white: Report on the Children Now survey on ethnic representation in television programming. *Atlanta Constitution*, pp. D1–D2.

Stattin, J., Kerr, M., Mahoney, J. L., Persson, A., & Magnusson, D. (2005). Explaining why a leisure context is bad for some girls but not for others. In J. L. Mahoney, R. W. Larson, & J. Eccles (Eds.), *Organized activities as contexts for development: Extracurricular activities, after-school and community programs* (pp. 211–234). Mahwah, NJ: Erlbaum.

Stattin, H., & Magnusson, D. (1990). *Paths through life. Vol. 2: Pubertal maturation in female development*. Hillsdale, NJ: Erlbaum.

Steele, B. F., & Pollack, C. B. (1974). A psychiatric study of parents who abuse infants and small children In R. E. Helfer & C. H. Kempe (Eds.), *The battered child*. Chicago: University of Chicago Press.

Steele, C. M. (1997). A threat in the air: How stereotypes shape intellectual identity and performance. *American Psychologist, 52*, 613–629.

Steele, C. M., & Aronson, J. (1995). Stereotype threat and the intellectual test performance of African Americans. *Journal of Personality and Social Psychology, 69*, 797–811.

Steele, H., Steele, M., & Fonagy, P. (1996). Associations among attachment classifications of mothers, fathers, and their infants. *Child Development, 67*, 541–555.

Stein, A. H., & Friedrich, L. K. (1972). Television content and young children's behavior. In J. P Murray, E. A. Rubinstein, & G. A. Comstock (Eds.), *Television and social behavior. Vol. 2: Television and social learning*. Washington, DC: U.S. Government Printing Office.

Steinberg, L. (1986). Latchkey children and susceptibility to peer pressure: An ecological analysis. *Developmental Psychology, 22*, 433–439.

Steinberg, L. (1996). Adolescence (4th ed.), New York: McGraw-Hill.

Steinberg, L (2005). Psychological control: Style or substance? In J. Smetana (Ed.), *New directions for child and adolescent development* (Serial No. 108, pp. 71–78). San Francisco: Jossey-Bass.

Steinberg, L. (2008). *Adolescence* (8th ed.). New York: McGraw-Hill.

Steinberg, L., Dornbusch, S. M., & Brown, B. B. (1992). Ethnic differences in adolescent achievement: An ecological perspective. *American Psychologist, 47*, 723–729.

Steinberg, L., Lamborn, S. D., Darling, N., Mounts, N. S., & Dornbusch, S. M. (1994). Over-time changes in adjustment and competence among adolescents from authoritative, authoritarian, indulgent, and neglectful families. *Child Development, 65*, 754–770.

Steinberg, L., & Monahan, K. C. (2007). Age differences in resistance to peer influence. *Developmental Psychology, 43*, 1531–1543.

Steinberg, L., & Silverberg, S. B. (1986). The vicissitudes of autonomy in early adolescence. *Child Development, 57*, 841–851.

Stennes, L. M., Burch, M. M., Sen, M. G., & Bauer, P. J. (2005). Longitudinal study of gendered vocabulary and communicative action in young children. *Developmental Psychology, 41*, 75–88.

Stern, D. (1977). *The first relationship: Infant and mother*. Cambridge, MA: Harvard University Press.

Stern, D. N. (1995). Self/other differentiation in the domain of intimate socio-affective interaction: Some considerations. In P. Rochat (Ed.), *The self in infancy: Theory and research* (pp. 419–429). Amsterdam: North Holland-Elsevier.

Sternberg, K. J., Lamb, M. E., Greenbaum, C., Cicchetti, D., Dawud, S., Cortes, R. M., Krispin, O., & Lorey, F. (1993). Effects of domestic violence on children's behavior problems and depression. *Developmental Psychology, 29*, 44–52.

Stetsenko, A., Little, T. D., Gordeeva, T., Grasshof, M., & Oettingen, G. (2000). Gender effects in children's beliefs about school performance: A cross-cultural study. *Child Development, 71*, 517–527.

Stevens, R. J., & Slavin, R. E. (1995a). Effects of a cooperative learning approach in reading and writing on academically handicapped and nonhandicapped students. *Elementary School Journal, 95*, 241–262.

Stevens, R. J., & Slavin, R. E., (1995b). The cooperative elementary school: Effects on students' achievement, attitudes, and social relations. *American Educational Research Journal, 32*, 321–351.

Stevenson, H. W., Chen, C., & Lee, S. (1993). Mathematics achievement of Chinese, Japanese, and American children: Ten years later. *Science, 259*, 53–58.

Stevenson, H. W., Chen, C., & Uttal, D. H. (1990). Beliefs and achievement: A study of black, white, and Hispanic children. *Child Development, 61*, 508–523.

Stevenson, H. W., & Lee, S. Y. (1990). Contexts of achievement: A study of American, Chinese, and Japanese children. *Monographs of the Society for Research in Child Development, 55*, (1–2, Serial No. 221).

Stevenson, H. W., Lee, S. Y., & Stigler, J. W. (1986). Mathematics achievement of Chinese, Japanese, and American children. *Science, 231*, 693–699.

Stevenson, H. W., Stigler, J. W., Lee, S. Y., Lucker, G. W., Litamura, S., & Hsu, C. (1985). Cognitive performance and academic achievement of Japanese, Chinese, and American children. *Child Development, 56*, 718–734.

Stewart, R. B. (1983). Sibling attachment relationships: Child-infant interactions in the strange situation. *Developmental Psychology, 19*, 192–199.

Stewart, R. B., & Marvin, R. S. (1984). Sibling relations: The role of conceptual perspective-taking in the ontogeny of sibling caregiving. *Child Development, 55,* 1322–1332.

Stice, E., & Bearman, S. K. (2001). Body-image and eating disturbances prospectively predict increases in depressive symptoms in adolescent girls: A growth curve analysis. *Developmental Psychology, 73,* 597–607.

Stice, E., Presnell, K., & Bearman, S. K. (2001). Relation of early menarche to depression, eating disorders, substance abuse, and comorbid psychopathology among adolescent girls. *Developmental Psychology, 37,* 608–619.

Stigler, J. W., Lee, S. Y., & Stevenson, H. W. (1987). Mathematics class-rooms in Japan, Taiwan, and the United States. *Child Development, 58,* 1272–1285.

Stipek, D. J. (2002). At what age should children enter kindergarten? A question for policy makers and parents. *Society for Research in Child Development Social Policy Report, 16,* No. 2.

Stipek, D., Feiler, R., Daniels, D., & Milbern, S. (1995). Effects of different instructional approaches on young children's achievement and motivation. *Child Development, 66,* 209–233.

Stipek, D., Gralinski, H., & Kopp, C. (1990) Self-concept development in the toddler years. *Developmental Psychology, 26,* 972–977.

Stipek, D., & Mac Iver, D. (1989). Developmental change in children's assessment of intellectual competence. *Child Development, 60,* 521–538.

Stipek, D. J., Recchia, s. & McClintic, S. (1992). Self-evaluation in young children. *Monographs of the Society for Research in Child Development, 57* (l, Serial No. 226).

Stipek, D. J., & Ryan, R. H. (1997). Economically disadvantaged pre-schoolers: Ready to learn but further to go. *Developmental Psychology, 33,* 711–723.

Stith, S. M., Rosen, K. H., Middleton, K. A., Busch, A. L., Lundeberg, K., & Carlton, R. P. (2000). The intergenerational transmission of spouse abuse: A meta-analysis. *Journal of Marriage and the Family, 62,* 640–654.

Stoolmiller, M. (2001). Synergistic interaction of child manageability problems and parent-discipline tactics in predicting future growth in externalizing behavior for boys. *Developmental Psychology, 37,* 814–825.

Stormshak, E. A., Bellanti, C. J., Bierman, K. L., & the Conduct Problems Prevention Research Group (1996). The quality of sibling relationships and the development of social competence and behavioral control in aggressive children. *Developmental Psychology, 32,* 79–89.

St. Peters, M., Fitch, M., Huston, A. C., Wright. J. C., & Eakins, D. J. (1991). Television and families: What do young children watch with their parents? *Child Development, 62,* 1409–1423.

Strayer, F. F. (1980). Social ecology of the preschool peer group. In W. A. Collins (Ed.), *Minnesota Symposia on Child Psychology. Vol. 13: Development of cognition, affect, and social relations.* Hillsdale, NJ: Erlbaum.

Stricker, J. M., Miltenberger, R. G., Garlinghouse, M. A., Deaver, C. M., & Anderson, C. A. (2001). Evaluation of an awareness enhancement device for the treatment of thumbsucking in children. *Journal of Applied Behavioral Analysis, 34,* 77–80.

Strough, J., & Berg, C. A. (2000). Goals as a mediator of high affiliation dyadic conversations. *Developmental Psychology, 36,* 117–125.

Stukas, A. A., Snyder, M., & Clary, E. G. (1999). The effects of "mandatory volunteerism" on intentions to volunteer. *Psychological Science, 10,* 59–64.

Stumpf, H., & Stanley, J. C. (1996). Gender-related differences on the College Board's Advanced Placement and Achievement Tests, 1982–1992. *Journal of Educational Psychology, 88,* 353–364.

Sturge-Apple, M. L., Davies, P. T., & Cummings, E. M. (2006). Impact of hostility and withdrawal in interparental conflict on parental emotional unavailability and children's adjustment difficulties. *Child Development, 77,* 1623-1641.

Subrahmanyam, K., Greenfield, P. M., & Tynes, B. (2004). Constructing sexuality and identity in an online teen chatroom. *Journal of Applied Developmental Psychology, 25,* 651–666.

Subrahmanyam, K., Kraut, R. E., Greenfield, P. M., & Gross, E. F. (2000). The impact of home computer use on children's activities and development. *The Future of Children, 10,* 123–144.

Subrahmanyam, K., Smahel, D., & Greenfield, P. M. (2006). Connecting developmental constructions to the Internet: Identity presentation and sexual exploration in online teen chat rooms. *Developmental Psychology, 42,* 395–406.

Sullivan, H. S. (1953). *The interpersonal theory of psychiatry.* New York: Norton.

Sullivan, M. W., & Lewis, M. (2003). Contextual determinants of anger and other negative expressions in young infants. *Developmental Psychology, 39,* 693–705.

Sullivan, M. W., Lewis, M., & Alessandri, S. M. (1992). Cross-age stability in emotional expressions during learning and extinction. *Developmental Psychology, 28,* 58–63.

Suomi, S. J., & Harlow, H. F. (1978). Early experience and social development in rhesus monkeys. In M. E. Lamb (Ed.), *Social and personality development.* New York: Holt, Rinehart and Winston.

Supple, A. J., Ghazarian, S. R., Frabutt, J. M., Plunkett, S. W., & Sands, T. (2006). Contextual influences on Latino adolescent ethnic identity and academic outcomes. *Child Development, 77,* 1427–1433.

Suzuki, L. K., & Calzo, J. P (2004). The search for peer advice in cyberspace: An examination of online teen health bulletin boards. *Journal of Applied Developmental Psychology, 25,* 685–698.

Szkrybalo, J., & Ruble, D. N. (1999). "God made me a girl": Sex-category constancy judgments and explanations revisited. *Developmental Psychology, 35,* 392–402.

Takahashi, K. (1986). Examining the Strange-Situation procedure with Japanese mothers and 12-month-old infants. *Developmental Psychology, 22,* 265–270.

Talwar, V., Gordon, H. M., & Lee, K. (2007). Lying in the elementary school years: Verbal deception and its relation to second-order belief understanding. *Developmental Psychology, 43,* 804–810.

Tangney, J. P., & Dearing, R. (2002). *Shame and guilt.* New York: Guilford Press.

Tanner, J. M. (1990). *Foetus into man: Physical growth from conception to maturity* (2nd ed.). Cambridge, MA: Harvard University Press.

Tarabulsy, G. M., Bernier, A., Provost, M. A., Maranda, J., Larose, S., Moss, E., Larose, M., & Tessier, R. (2005). Another look inside the gap: Ecological contributions to the transmission of attachment in a sample of adolescent mother-infant dyads. *Developmental Psychology, 41,* 212–224.

Taumoepeau, M., & Ruffman, T. (2006). Mother and infant talk about mental states relates to desire language and emotion understanding. *Child Development, 77,* 465–481.

Taylor, A. R., Asher, S. R., & Williams, G. A. (1987). The social adaptation of mainstreamed mildly retarded children. *Child Development, 58,* 1321–1334.

Taylor, M., & Carlson, S. M. (1997). The relation between individual differences in fantasy and theory of mind. *Child Development, 68,* 436–455.

Taylor, M. G. (1996). The development of children's beliefs about social and biological aspects of gender differences. *Child Development, 67,* 1555–1571.

Taylor, R. D. (1996). Adolescents' perceptions of kinship support and family management practices: Association with adolescent adjustment in African-American families. *Developmental Psychology, 32,* 687–695.

Taylor, R. D. (2000). Diversity within African American families. In D. H. Demo, K. R. Allen, & M. A. Fine (Eds.), *Handbook of family diversity.* New York: Oxford University Press.

Taylor, R. D., & Roberts, D. (1995). Kinship support and maternal and adolescent well-being in economically disadvantaged African-American families. *Child Development, 66,* 1585–1597.

Teeven. R. C., & McGhee, P. E. (1972). Childhood development of fear of failure motivation. *Journal of Personality and Social Psychology, 21,* 345–348.

Teichman, Y. (2001). The development of Israeli children's images of Jews and Arabs and their expression in human figure drawings. *Developmental Psychology, 37,* 749–761.

Tennenbaum, H. R., & Leaper, C. (2002). Are parents' gender schemas related to their children's gender-related cognitions? *Developmental Psychology, 38,* 615–630.

Tennenbaum, H. R., & Leaper, C. (2003). Parent-child conversations about science: The socialization of gender inequities? *Developmental Psychology, 39,* 34–47.

Terry, R., & Coie, J. D. (1991). A comparison of methods for defining sociometric status among children. *Developmental Psychology, 27,* 867–880.

Teti, D. M., & Ablard, K. E. (1989). Security of attachment and infant-sibling relationships: A laboratory study. *Child Development, 60,* 1519–1528.

Teti, D. M., & Gelfand, D. M., Messinger, D. S., & Isabella, R. (1995). Maternal depression and the quality of early attachment: An examination of infants, preschoolers, and their mothers. *Developmental Psychology, 31,* 364–376.

Teti, D. M., Sakin, J. W., Kucera, E., Corns, K. M., & Das Eiden, R. (1996). And baby makes four: Predictors of attachment security among preschool-age first-borns during the transition to siblinghood. *Child Development, 67,* 579–596.

Tharp, R. G. (1989). Psychocultural variables and constants: Effects on teaching and learning in schools. *American Psychologist, 44,* 349–359.

Tharp, R. G., & Gallimore, R. (1988). *Rousing minds to life: Teaching. learning, and schooling in social context.* Cambridge, England: Cambridge University Press.

The Education Trust. (2007). *EdTrust statement on the 2007 math and reading results from the Nation's Report Card.* Retrieved November 19, 2007, from http://www2.edtrust.org/EdTrust/Press+Room/NAEP2007.htm

The White House. (2007). *Fact sheet: 2007 Nation's Report Card shows minority students posting all time highs: No Child Left Behind is helping students achieve record success.* Retrieved November 20, 2007, from http://www.whitehouse.gov/news/releases/20070920070926-2.html

Thoma, S. J., & Rest, J. R. (1999). The relationship between moral decision making and patterns of consolidation and transition in moral judgment development. *Developmental Psychology, 35,* 323–334.

Thomas, A., & Chess, S. (1977). *Temperament and development.* New York: Brunner/Mazel.

Thomas, A., Chess, S., & Birch, H. G. (1970). The origin of personality. *Scientific American, 223,* 102–109.

Thomas, C. L., & Dimitrov, D. M. (2007). Effects of a teen pregnancy prevention program on teens' attitudes toward sexuality: A latent trait modeling approach. *Developmental Psychology, 43,* 173–185.

Thomas, M. H., Horton, R. W., Lippincott, E. C., & Drabman, R. S. (1977). Desensitization to portrayals of real-life aggression as a function of exposure to television violence. *Journal of Personality and Social Psychology, 35,* 450–458.

Thompson, R. A. (1994). Emotion regulation: A theme in search of definition. In N. A. Fox (Ed.), The development of emotion regulation: Biological and behavioral considerations. *Monographs of the Society for Research in Child Development, 59* (Nos. 2–3, Serial No. 240).

Thompson, R. A. (1998). Early sociopersonality development. In N. Eisenberg (Ed.) & W. Damon (Series Ed.), *Handbook of child psychology. Vol. 3: Social, emotional, and personality development* (5th ed., pp. 23–104). New York: Wiley.

Thompson, R. A. (2000). The legacy of early attachments. *Child Development, 71,* 145–152.

Thompson, S. K. (1975). Gender labels and early sex-role development. *Child Development, 46,* 339–347.

Thompson, T., Caruso, M., & Ellerbeck, K. (2003). Sex matters in autism and Other developmental disabilities. *Journal of Learning Disabilities, 7,* 345–362.

Thorne, A., & Michaelieu, Q. (1996). Situating adolescent gender and self-esteem with personal memories. *Child Development, 67,* 1374–1390.

Thorne, B. (1993). *Gender play. Girls and boys in school.* New Brunswick, NJ: Rutgers University Press.

Thornberry, T. P., Freeman-Gallant, A., Lizotte, A. J., Krohn, M. D., & Smith, C. A. (2003). Linked lives: The intergenerational transmission of antisocial behavior. *Journal of Abnormal Child Psychology, 31,* 171–184.

Thornberry, T. P., Krohn, M. D., Lizotte, A. J., Smith, C. A., & Tobin, K. (2003). *Gangs and delinquency in developmental perspective.* Cambridge: Cambridge University Press.

Thurber, C. A. (1995). The experience and expression of homesickness in preadolescent and adolescent boys. *Child Development, 66,* 1162–1178.

Tinbergen, N. (1973). *The animal in its world: Explorations of an ethologist, 1932–1972* (Vols. 1 & 2). Cambridge, MA: Harvard University Press.

Tinsley, B. J. (1992). Multiple influences on the acquisition and socialization of children's health attitudes and behavior: An integrative review. *Child Development, 63,* 1043–1069.

Tisak, M. S., & Tisak, J. (1990). Children's conceptions of parental authority, friendship, and sibling relations. *Merrill-Palmer Quarterly, 36,* 347–368.

Toch, H. (1969). *Violent men.* Hawthorne, NY: Aldine.

Tolan, P. H., Gorman-Smith, D., & Henry, D. B. (2003). The developmental ecology of urban males' youth violence. *Developmental Psychology, 39,* 274–291.

Tomada, G., & Schneider, B. H. (1997). Relational aggression, gender, and peer acceptance: Invarance across culture, stability over time, and concordance among informants. *Developmental Psychology, 33,* 601–609.

Tomasello, M. (1999). *The cultural origins of human cognition.* Cambridge, MA: Harvard University Press.

Tomasello, M., Call, J., & Hare, B. (2003). Chimpanzees understand psychological states: The question is which ones and to what extent. *Trends in Cognitive Sciences, 7,* 153–156.

Tomasello, M., Carpenter, M., & Liszkowski, U. (2007). A new look at infant pointing. *Child Development, 78,* 705–722.

Tomlinson-Keasey, C., & Keasey, C. B. (1974). The mediating role of cognitive development in moral judgment. *Child Development, 45,* 291–298.

Toner, I. J., Moore, L. P., & Ashley, P. K. (1978). The effect of serving as a model of self-control on subsequent resistance to deviation in children. *Journal of Experimental Child Psychology, 26,* 85–91.

Toner, I. J., & Potts, R. (1981). Effect of modeled rationales on moral behavior, moral choice, and level of moral judgment in children. *Journal of Psychology, 107,* 153–162.

Tracy, J. L., Shaver, P. R., Albino, A. W., & Cooper, M. L. (2003). Attachment styles and adolescent sexuality. In P. Florsheim (Ed.), *Adolescent romantic relations and sexual behavior: Theory, research, and practical implications.* Mahwah, NJ: Erlbaum.

Tran, H., & Weinraub, M. (2006). Child care effects in context: Quality stability and multiplicity in nonmaternal child care arrangements in the first 15 months of life. *Developmental Psychology, 42,* 566–582.

Trautwein, U., Ludtke, O., Kastens, C., & Koller, O. (2006). Effort on homework in grades 5–9: Development, motivational antecedents, and the association with effort on classwork. *Child Development, 77,* 1094–1111.

Tremblay, R. E., Hartup, W. W., & Archer, J. (2005). *The developmental origins of aggression.* New York: Guilford Press.

Triandis, H. C. (1994). *Culture and social behavior.* New York: McGraw-Hill.

Triandis, H. C. (1995). *Individualism and collectivism.* Boulder, CO: Westview Press.

Tronick, E. Z. (1989). Emotions and emotional communications in infants. *American Psychologist, 44,* 112–119.

Tronick, E., Als, H., Adamson, L., Wise, S., & Brazelton, T. B. (1978). The infant's response to entrapment between contradictory messages in face-to-face interaction. *Journal of the American Academy of Child Psychiatry, 17,* 1–13.

Tronick, E. Z., Morelli, G. A., & Ivey, P. K. (1992). The Efe forager infant and toddler's pattern of social relationships: Multiple and simultaneous. *Developmental Psychology, 28,* 568–577.

Troop-Gordon, W., & Asher, S. R. (2005). Modifications in children's goals when encountering obstacles to conflict resolution. *Child Development, 76,* 568–582.

Troop-Gordon, W., & Ladd, G. W. (2005). Trajectories of peer victimization and perceptions of the self and schoolmates: Precursors to internalizing and externalizing problems. *Child Development, 76,* 1072–1091.

Troseth, G. L., Saylor, M. M., & Archer, A. H. (2006). Young children's use of video as a source of socially relevant information. *Child Development, 77,* 786–799.

True, M. M., Pisani, L., & Oumar, F. (2001). Mother-infant attachment among the Dogon of Mali. *Child Development, 72,* 1451–1466.

Tryon, R. C. (1940). Genetic differences in maze learning in rats. *Yearbook of the National Society for Studies in Education, 39,* 111–119.

Trzesniewski, K. H., Donnellan, M. B., Moffitt, T. E., Robins, R. W., Poulton, R., & Caspi, A. (2006). Low self-esteem during adolescence predicts poor health, criminal behavior, and limited economic prospects during adulthood. *Developmental Psychology, 42,* 381–390.

Trzesniewski, K. H., Donnellan, M. B., & Robins, R. W. (2003). Stability of self-esteem across the life span. *Journal of Personality and Social Psychology, 84,* 205–220.

Tseng, V. (2006). Unpacking immigration in youths' academic and occupational pathways. *Child Development, 77,* 1434–1455.

Tudge, J. R. H. (1992). Processes and consequences of peer collaboration: A Vygotskian analysis. *Child Development, 63,* 1364–1379.

Turiel, E. (1983). *The development of social knowledge: Morality and convention.* Cambridge, England: Cambridge University Press.

Turiel, E. (2002). *The culture of morality: Social development, context, and conflict.* Cambridge, England: Cambridge University Press.

Turiel, E. (2006). The development of morality. In W. Damon & R. M. Lerner (Series Eds.) & N. Eisenberg (Vol. Ed.), *Handbook of child psychology. Vol. 3: Social, emotional, and personality development* (6th ed., pp.789–857). New York: Wiley.

Turiel, E., & Wainryb, C. (2000). Social life in culture: Judgments, conflict, and subversion. *Child Development, 71,* 250–256.

Turley, R. N. L. (2003). Are children of young mothers disadvantaged because of their mother's age or family background? *Child Development, 74,* 465–474.

Turner, A. J., & Coyle, A. (2000). What does it mean to be a donor offspring? The identity experiences of adults conceived by donor insemination and the implications of counseling and therapy. *Human Reproduction, 15,* 2041–2051.

Turner, C. W., & Goldsmith, D. (1976). Effects of toy guns and airplanes on children's antisocial free play behavior. *Journal of Experimental Child Psychology, 21,* 303–315.

Turner, P. J., & Gervai, J. (1995). A multidimensional study of gender typing in preschool children and their parents: Personality, attitudes, preferences, behavior, and cultural differences. *Developmental Psychology, 31,* 759–772.

Turner-Bowker, D. M. (1996). Gender stereotyped descriptions in children's picture books: Does "curious Jane" exist in the literature? *Sex Roles, 35,* 461–488.

Twenge, J. M. (1997). Changes in masculine and feminine traits over time: A meta-analysis. *Sex Roles, 36,* 305–325.

Twenge, J. M., Crocker, J. (2002). Race and self-esteem: Meta-analysis comparing whites, blacks, Hispanics, Asians, and American Indians and comment on Gray-Little and Hafdahl (2000). *Psychological Bulletin, 128,* 371–408.

Twenge, J. M., & Nolen-Hoeksma, S. (2002). Age, gender, race, socioeconomic status, and birth cohort differences on the children's depression inventory: A meta-analysis. *Journal of Abnormal Psychology, 111,* 578–588.

Tyson, P., & Tyson, R. L. (1990). *Psychoanalytic theories of development: An integration.* New Haven, CT: Yale University Press.

Uba, L. (1994). *Asian Americans: Personality patterns, identity, and mental health.* New York: The Guilford Press.

Udry, J. R. (1990). Hormonal and social determinants of adolescent sexual initiation. In J. Bancroft & J. M. Reinisch (Eds.), *Adolescence and puberty* (pp. 70–87). New York: Oxford University Press.

Umana-Taylor, A., Diversi, M., & Fine, M. (2002). Ethnic identity and self-esteem among Latino adolescents: Distinctions among Latino populations. *Journal of Adolescent Research, 17,* 303–327.

Underwood, B., & Moore, B. (1982). Perspective-taking and altruism. *Psychological Bulletin, 91,* 143–173.

Underwood, M. K., Coie, J. D., & Herbsman, C. R. (1992). Display rules for anger and aggression in school-age children. *Child Development, 63,* 366–380.

Underwood, M. K., Hurley, J. C., Johnson, C. A., & Mosley, J. E. (1999). An experimental observational study of children's responses to peer provocation: Developmental and gender differences in middle childhood. *Child Development, 70,* 1428–1446.

Underwood, M. K., Schockner, A. E., & Hurley, J. C. (2001). Children's response to same- and other-gender peers: An experimental investigation with 8-, 10- and 12-year-olds. *Developmental Psychology, 37,* 362–372.

Unger, J. B., Simon, T. R., Newman, T. L., Montgomery, S. B., Kipke, M. D., & Abornoz, M. (1998). Early adolescent street youth: An overlooked population with unique problems and service needs. *Journal of Early Adolescence, 18,* 325–348.

Uniform Crime Reports for the United States. (1997). Federal Bureau of investigation. Washington, D.C.: U.S. Government Printing Office.

Updegraff, K., McHale, S. M., & Crouter, A. C. (1996). Gender roles in marriage: What do they mean for girls' and boys' school achievement? *Journal of Youth and Adolescence, 25,* 73–88.

Urberg, K. A. (1979). Sex-role conceptualization in adolescents and adults. *Developmental Psychology, 15,* 90–92.

Urberg, K. A., Degirmencioglu, S. M., Tolson, J. M., & Halliday-Scher, K. (1995). The structure of adolescent peer networks. *Developmental Psychology, 31,* 540–547.

U.S. Bureau of the Census. (1997). *Statistical Abstract of the United States* (117th ed.). Washington, DC: U.S. Government Printing Office.

U.S. Bureau of the Census. (2001). *Statistical Abstract of the United States* (121st ed.). Washington, DC: U.S. Government Printing Office.

U.S. Bureau of the Census. (2002). *Statistical abstract of the United States.* (122nd ed.). Washington, DC: U.S. Government Printing Office.

U.S. Bureau of the Census. (2006). *Statistical abstract of the United States* (126th ed.). Washington, DC.: U.S. Government Printing Office.

U.S. Bureau of the Census. (2007). *Statistical abstract of the United States:* 2007 (127th ed.). Washington, DC.: U.S. Government Printing Office.

U.S. Department of Education. (2003). *When schools stay open late: The National Evaluation of the 21st Century Learning Centers Program, first year findings.* Washington, DC: Author.

U.S. Bureau of the Census. (2007). Statistical abstract of the United States: 2007 (127th ed.). Washington, DC: U.S. Government Printing Office.

U.S. Department of Education. (2003). When schools stay open late: the National Evaluation of the 21st Century Learning Centers Program, first year findings. Washington, DC.: Author.

U.S. Department of Health and Human Services. (2001). *Youth violence: A report to the Surgeon General.* Rockville, MD: U.S. Public Health Service, Office of the Surgeon General.

U.S. Department of Health and Human Services. (2005). *Child maltreatment 2004: Summary of key findings.* Washington, DC.: National Clearinghouse on Child Abuse.

U.S. Department of State. (2002). *Country reports on human rights practices, 2001.* Retrieved from http://www.state.gov/gdrl/rls/hrrpt/2001/

Valeski, T. N., & Stipek, D. J. (2001). Young children's feelings about school. *Child Development, 72,* 1198–1213.

Valiente, C., Eisenberg, N., Fabes, R. A., Shepard, S. A., Cumberland, A., & Losoya, S. H. (2004). Prediction of children's empathy-related responding from their effortful control and parents' expressivity. *Developmental Psychology, 40,* 911–926.

Valkenburg, P. M., & Peter, J. (2007). Preadolescent's and adolescents' online communication and their closeness to friends. *Developmental Psychology, 43,* 267–277.

Valkenburg, P. M., & Soeters, K. E. (2001). Children's positive and negative experiences with the Internet: An exploration survey. *Communication Research, 28,* 652–675.

van Bakel, H. J. A., & Riksen-Walraven, M. (2002). Parenting and development of one-year-olds: Links with parental, contextual, and child characteristics. *Child Development, 73,* 256–273.

Vandell, D. L. (2000). Parents, peer groups, and other socializing influences. *Developmental Psychology, 36,* 699–710.

Vandell, D. L., & Corasantini, M. A. (1988). The relation between third graders' after-school care and social, academic, and emotional functioning. *Child Development, 59,* 868–875.

Vandell, D. L., & Mueller, E. C. (1995). Peer play and friendships during the first two years. In H. C. Smith, A. J. Chapman, & J. R. Smith (Eds.), *Friendship and social relations in children* (pp. 181–208). New Brunswick, NJ: Transaction.

Vandell, D. L., & Ramanan, J. (1992). Effects of early and recent maternal employment on children from low-income families. *Child Development, 63,* 938–949.

van den Boom, D. C. (1994). The influence of temperament and mothering on attachment and exploration: An experimental manipulation of sensitive responsiveness among lower-class mothers with irritable infants. *Child Development, 65,* 1457–1477.

van den Boom, D. C., (1995). Do first-year intervention efforts endure? Follow-up during toddlerhood of a sample of Dutch irritable infants. *Child Development, 66,* 1798–1816.

van den Broek, P. W. (1997). Discovering the element of the universe: The development of event comprehension from childhood to adulthood. In P. van den Broek, P. Bauer, & T. Bourg (Eds.), *Developmental spans in event comprehension: Bridging fictional and actual events* (pp. 321–342). Mahwah, NJ: Erlbaum.

van den Broek, P., Lorch, E. P., & Thurlow, R. (1996). Children's and adults' memory for television stories: The role of causal factors, story-grammar categories, and hierarchical level. *Child Development, 67,* 3010–3028.

van Doorninck, W. J., Caldwell, B. M., Wright, C., & Frankenberg, W. K. (1981). The relationship between twelve-month home stimulation and school achievement. *Child Development, 52,* 1080–1083.

Van Egeren, L. A., Barratt, M.S., & Roach, M. A. (2001). Mother-infant responsiveness: Timing, mutual regulation, and interactional context. *Developmental Psychology, 37,* 684–697.

van IJzendoorn, M. H. (1992). Intergenerational transmission of parenting: A review of studies in nonclinical populations. *Developmental Review, 12,* 76–99.

van IJzendoorn, M. H. (1995). Adult attachment representations, parental responsiveness, and infant attachment: A meta-analysis on the predictive validity of the Adult Attachment interview. *Psychological Bulletin, 177,* 387–403.

van IJzendoorn, M. H., & De Wolff, M. S. (1997). In search of the absent father—meta-analysis of infant-father attachment: A rejoinder to our discussants. *Child Development, 68,* 604–609.

van IJzendoorn, M. H., Goldberg, S., Kroonenberg, P. M., & Frenkel, O. J. (1992). The relative effects of maternal and child problems on the quality of attachment: A meta-analysis of attachment in clinical samples. *Child Development, 63,* 840–858.

van Ijzendoorn, M. H., & Sagi, A. (1999). Cross-cultural patterns of attachment: Universal and contextual dimensions. In J. Cassidy & P. R. Shaver (Eds.), *Handbook of attachment: Theory, research, and clinical applications.* (pp. 713–734). New York: Guilford Press.

van IJzendoorn, M. H., Vereijken, C. M. J. L., Bakermans-Kranenburg, M. J., & Riksen-Walraven, J. (2004). Assessing attachment security with the attachment Q sort: Meta-analytic evidence for the validity of the observer AQS. *Child Development, 75,* 1188–1213.

Vansteenkiste, M., Simons, J., Lens, W., Soenens, D., & Matos, L. (2005). Examining the motivational impact of intrinsic versus extrinsic goal framing and autonomy-supportive versus internally controlling communication style on early adolescents' academic achievement. *Child Development, 76,* 483–501.

Vartanian, L. R., & Powlishta, K. K. (1996). A longitudinal examination of the social-cognitive foundations of adolescent egocentrism. *Journal of Early Adolescence, 16,* 157–178.

Vazsonyi, A. T., Hibbert, J. R., & Snider, J. B. (2003). Exotic enterprise no more? Adolescent reports of family and parenting processes from youth in four countries. *Journal of Research on Adolescence, 13,* 129–160.

Veenstra, R., Lindenberg, S., Oldehinkel, A., De Winter, A. F., Verhulst, F. C., & Ormel, J. (2005). Bullying and victimization in elementary schools: A comparison of bullies, victims, bully/victims, and uninvolved preadolescents. *Developmental Psychology, 41,* 672–682.

Veenstra, R., Lindenberg, S., Zijlstra, B. J. H., De Winter, A. F., Verhulst, F. C., & Ormel, J. (2007). The dyadic nature of bullying and victimization: testing a dual-perspective theory. *Child Develoment, 78,* 1843–1854.

Verschuren, K., Buyck, P., & Marcoen, A. (2001). Self-representations and socioemotional competence in young children: A 3-year-longitudinal study. *Developmental Psychology, 37,* 126–134.

Verschueren, K., & Marcoen, A. (1999). Representation of self and socioemotional competence in kindergarten: Combined and differential effects of attachment to mother and to father. *Child Development, 70,* 183–201.

Verschueren, K., Marcoen, A., & Schoefs, V. (1996). The internal working model of self, attachment, and competence in five-year-olds. *Child Development, 67,* 2493–2511.

Vigil, J. M., Geary, D. C., & Byrd-Craven, J. (2005). A life history assessment of early childhood sexual abuse in women. *Developmental Psychology, 41,* 553–561.

Vinden, P. G. (1996). Junin Quechua children's understanding of mind. *Child Development, 67,* 1707–1716.

Vinden, P. G., & Astington, J. W. (2000). Culture and understanding others' minds. In S. Baron-Cohen, H. Tager-Flusberg, & D. J. Cohen (Eds.), *Understanding other minds: Perspectives from developmental cognitive neuroscience* (2nd ed.). Oxford: Oxford University Press.

Vinter, A. (1986). The role of movement in eliciting early imitations. *Child Development, 57,* 66–71.

Visher, E. B., Visher, J. S., & Pasley, K. (2003). Remarriage families and step parenting. In F. Walsh, (Ed.), *Normal family processes,* (pp. 153–175). New York: Guilford.

Vitaro, F., & Brendgen, M. (2005). Proactive and reactive aggression: A developmental perspective. In R. E. Tremblay, W. W. Hartup, & J. Archer (Eds.), *The developmental origins of aggression* (pp. 178–201). New York: Guilford Press.

Vitaro, F., Brendgen, M., Pagani, L., Tremblay, R. E., & McDuff, P. (1999). Disruptive behavior, peer association, and conduct disorder: Testing the developmental links through early intervention. *Development and Psychopathology, 11,* 287–304.

Vobejda, B. (1991, September 15). The future deferred. Longer road from adolescence to adulthood often leads back through parents' home. *The Washington Post,* pp. A1, A29.

Volling, B. L., & Belsky, J. (1992). The contribution of mother-child and father-child relationships to the quality of sibling interaction: A longitudinal study. *Child Development, 63,* 1209–1222.

Volling, B. L., McElwain, N. L., & Miller, A. L. (2002). Emotion regulation in context: The jealousy complex between young siblings and its relations with child and family characteristics. *Child Development, 73,* 581–600.

Vondra, J., & Belsky, J. (1993). Developmental origins of parenting: Personality and relationship factors. In T. Luster & L. Okagaki (Eds.), *Parenting. An ecological perspective.* Hillsdale, NJ: Erlbaum.

Votruba-Drzal, E. (2006). Economic disparities in middle childhood development: Does income matter? *Developmental Psychology, 42,* 1154–1167.

Voyer, D., Voyer, S., & Bryden, M. P. (1995). Magnitude of sex differences in spatial abilities: A meta-analysis and consideration of critical variables. *Psychological Bulletin, 117,* 250–270.

Vuchinich, S., Bank, L., & Patterson, G. R. (1992). Parenting, peers, and the stability of antisocial behavior in preadolescent boys. *Developmental Psychology, 28,* 510–521.

Vuchinich, S., Hetherington, E. M., Vuchinich, R. A., & Clingempeel, W. G. (1991). Parent-child interaction and gender differences in early adolescents' adaptation to stepfamilies. *Developmental Psychology, 27,* 618–626.

Vygotsky, L. S. (1962). *Thought and language* (E. Hanfmann & G. Vakar, Eds. & Trans.). Cambridge, MA: MIT Press. (Original work published in 1934).

Vygotsky, L. S. (1978). *Mind in society: The development of higher psychological processes.* Cambridge, MA: Harvard University Press (Original work published 1930, 1933, 1935).

Wade, C., & Tavris, C. (1999). Gender and culture. In L. A. Peplau, S. C. DeBro, R. Veniegas, & P. L. Taylor (Eds.), *Gender, culture, and ethnicity: Current research about women and men* (pp. 15–22). Mountain View, CA: Mayfield.

Wainright, J. L., & Patterson, C. J. (2008). Peer relations among adolescents with female same-sex parents. *Developmental Psychology, 44,* 117–126.

Wainright, J. L., Russell, S. T., & Patterson, C.J. (2004). Psychosocial adjustment, school outcomes, and romantic relationships of adolescents with same-sex parents. *Child Development, 75,* 1886–1898.

Wakschlag, L. S., & Hans, S. L. (1999). Relation of maternal responsiveness during infancy to the development of behavior problems in high-risk youths. *Developmental Psychology, 35,* 569–579.

Walden, T. A., & Baxter, A. (1989). The effect of context and age on social referencing. *Child Development, 60,* 1511–1518.

Waldman, I. D., Weinberg, K. A., & Scarr, S. (1994). Racial-group differences in IQ in the Minnesota Transracial Adoption Study: A reply to Levin and Lynn. *Intelligence, 19,* 29–44.

Walker, J. S. (2000). Choosing biases, using power, and practicing resistance: Moral development in a world without certainty. *Human Development, 43,* 135–156.

Walker, L. J. (1980). Cognitive and perspective-taking prerequisites for moral development. *Child Development, 51,* 131–139.

Walker, L. J. (1995). Sexism in Kohlberg's moral psychology: In W. M. Kurtines & J. L. Gewirtz (Eds.), *Moral development: An introduction* (pp. 83–107). Boston: Allyn & Bacon.

Walker, L. J., Hennig, K. H., & Kettenauer, T. (2000). Parent and peer contexts for children's moral reasoning development. *Child Development, 71,* 1033–1048.

Walker, L. J., & Pitts, R. C. (1998). Naturalistic conceptions of moral maturity. *Developmental Psychology, 34,* 403–419.

Walker, L. J., & Taylor, J. H. (1991). Family interactions and the development of moral reasoning. *Child Development, 62,* 264–283.

Walker-Barnes, C. J., & Mason, C. A. (2001). Ethnic differences in the effect of parenting on gang involvement and gang delinquency: A longitudinal, hierarchical linear modeling perspective. *Child Development, 72,* 1814–1831.

Wallen, K. (1996). Nature needs nurture: The interaction of hormonal and social influences on the development of behavioral sex differences in rhesus monkeys. *Hormones and Behavior 30,* 364–378.

Wallerstein, J. S., & Kelly, J. B. (1980). *Surviving the breakup: How children and parents cope with divorce.* New York: Basic Books.

Walters, R. H., & Brown, M. (1963). Studies of reinforcement of aggression: Transfer of responses to an interpersonal situation. *Child Development, 34,* 562–571.

Wang, D., Kato, N., Inaba, Y., Tango, T., Yoshida, Y., Kusaka, Y., et al. (2000). Physical and personality traits of preschool children in Fuzhou, China: Only child vs. sibling. *Child: Care, Health, and Development, 26,* 49–60.

Wang, Q., Pomerantz, E. M., & Chen, H. (2007). The role of parents' control in early adolescents' psychological functioning: A longitudinal investigation in the United States and China. *Child Development, 78,* 1592–1610.

Want, S. C., & Harris, P. L. (2001). Learning from other people's mistakes. Causal understanding in learning to use a tool. *Child Development, 72,* 431–443.

Warin, J. (2000). The attainment of self-consistency through gender in young children. *Sex Roles, 42,* 209–231.

Wark, G. R., & Krebs, D. L. (1996). Gender and dilemma differences in real-life moral judgments. *Developmental Psychology, 32,* 220–230.

Warneken, F., Chen, F., & Tomasello, M. (2006). Cooperative activities in young children and chimpanzees. C*hild Development, 77,* 640–663.

Wartella, E., Caplovitz, A. G., & Lee, J. H. (2004). From Baby Einstein to Leapfrog, from doom to the sims, from instant messaging to Internet chat rooms: Public interest in the role of interactive media in children's lives. *Social Policy Report, 23.* Chicago: Society For Research in Child Development.

Wartner, U. G., Grossmann, K., Fremmer-Bombik, E., & Suess, G. (1994). Attachment patterns at age six in south Germany: Predictability from infancy and implications for preschool behavior. *Child Development, 65,* 1014–1027.

Waterman, A. S. (1982). Identity development from adolescence to adulthood: An extension of theory and a review of research. *Developmental Psychology, 18,* 341–358.

Waterman, A. S., & Archer, S. L. (1990). A life-span perspective on identity formation: Developments in form, function, and process. In P. B. Baltes, D. L. Featterman, & R. M. Lerner (Eds.), *Life-span development and behavior.* (Vol. 10). Hillsdale, NJ: Erlbaum.

Waters, E., & Cummings, E. M. (2000). A secure base from which to explore close relationships. *Child Development, 71,* 164–172.

Waters, E., Merrick, S., Treboux, D., Crowell, J., & Albersheim, L. (2000). Attachment security in infancy and early adulthood: A twenty-year longitudinal study. *Child Development, 51,* 208–216.

Waters, E., Vaughn, B. E., Posada, G., & Kondo-Ikemura, K. (1995). Caregiving, cultural, and cognitive perspectives on secure-base behavior and working models: New growing points of attachment theory and research. *Monographs of the Society for Research in Child Development, 60,* (2–3, Serial No. 244).

Waters, E., Wippman, J., & Sroufe, L. A. (1979). Attachment, positive affect, and competence in the peer group: Two studies in construct validation. *Child Development, 50,* 821–829.

Watson, J. B. (1913). Psychology as the behaviorist views it. *Psychological Review, 20,* 158–177.

Watson, J. B. (1925). *Behaviorism.* New York: Norton.

Watson, J. B. (1928). *Psychological care of infant and child.* New York: Norton.

Watson, J. B., & Raynor, R. (1920). Conditioned emotional reactions, *Journal of Experimental Psychology, 3,* 1–14.

Watson, M. W., & Peng, Y. (1992). The relation between toy gun play and children's aggressive behavior. *Early Education and Development, 3,* 370–389.

Watt, H. M. G. (2004). Development of adolescents' self-perceptions, values, and task perceptions according to gender and domain in 7th- through 11th-grade Australian students. *Child Development, 75,* 1556–1574.

Weinberg, M. K., Tronick, E. Z., Cohn, J., & Olson, K. L. (1999). Gender differences in emotional expressivity and self-regulation during early infancy. *Developmental Psychology, 35,* 175–188.

Weiner, B. (1974). *Achievement and attribution theory.* Morristown, NJ: General Learning Press.

Weiner, B. (1982). An attribution theory of motivation and emotion. In H. Krohne & L. Laux (Eds.), *Achievement, stress, and anxiety.* Washington, DC: Hemisphere.

Weiner, B. (1986). *An attributional theory of motivation and emotion.* New York: Springer-Verlag.

Weinraub, M. M, & Lewis, M. (1977). The determinants of children's responses to separation. *Monographs of the Society for Research in Child Development, 42,* (4, Serial No. 172).

Weisfeld, G. E., & Woodward, L. (2004). Current evolutionary perspectives on romantic relationships and sexuality. *Journal of the American Academy of Child and Adolescent Psychiatry, 43,* 11–19.

Weisner, T. S., & Gallimore, R. (1977). My brother's keeper: Child and sibling caretaking. *Current Anthropology, 18,* 169–190.

Weisner, T. S., & Wilson-Mitchell, J. E. (1990). Nonconventional family lifestyles and sex typing in six-year-olds. *Child Development, 61,* 1915–1933.

Weiss, B., Dodge, K. A., Bates, J. E., & Pettit, G. S. (1992). Some consequences of early harsh discipline: Child aggression and a maladaptive social information processing style. *Child Development, 63,* 1321–1335.

Weisz, J. R., Chaiyasit, W., Weiss, B., Eastman, K. L., & Jackson, E. W. (1995). A multimethod study of problem behavior among Thai and American children in school: Teacher reports versus direct observations. *Child Development, 66,* 402–415.

Welch-Ross, M. K., & Schmidt, C. R. (1996). Gender-schema development and children's constructive story memory: Evidence for a developmental model. *Child Development, 67,* 820–835.

Welles, C. E. (2005). Breaking the silence surrounding female adolescent sexual desire. *Women & Therapy, 28*, 31–45.

Wellman, H. M., Cross, D., & Watson, J. (2001). Meta-analysis of theory-of-mind development: The truth about false belief. *Child Development, 72*, 655–684.

Wellman, H. M., Hollander, M., & Schult, C. A. (1996). Young children's understanding of thought bubbles and of thoughts. *Child Development, 67*, 768–788.

Wellman, H. M., & Liu, D. (2004). Scaling of theory-of-mind tasks. *Child Development, 75*, 523–541.

Wellman, H. M., Phillips, A. T., & Rodriquez, T. (2000). Young children's understanding of perception, desire, and emotion. *Child Development, 71*, 895–912.

Wells, L. E. (1989). Self-enhancement through delinquency: A conditional test of self-derogation theory. *Journal of Research in Crime and Delinquency, 26*, 226–252.

Wenglinsky, H. (1998a). *Does it compute? The relationship between educational technology and student achievement in mathematics.* Princeton, NJ: Educational Testing Service.

Wenglinsky, H. (1998b). Finance equalization and within-school equity: The relationship between education spending and the social distribution of achievement. *Educational Evaluation and Policy Analysis, 20*, 269–283.

Wentzel, K. R. (2002). Are effective teachers like good parents? Teaching styles and student achievement in early adolescence. *Child Development, 73*, 287–301.

Wentzel, K. R. (2003). Sociometric status and adjustment in middle school: A longitudinal study. *Journal of Early Adolescence, 23*, 5–28.

Wentzel, K. R., & Asher, S. R. (1995). The academic lives of neglected, rejected, popular, and controversial children. *Child Development, 66*, 754–763.

Wentzel, K. R., Filisetti, L., & Looney, L. (2007). Adolescent prosocial behavior: The role of self-processes and contextual cues. *Child Development, 78*, 895–910.

Werner, N. E., & Crick, N. (2004). Maladaptive peer relationships and the development of relational and physical aggression during middle childhood. *Social Development, 13*, 495–514.

Wertsch, J. V., & Tulviste, P. (1992). L. S. Vygotsky and contemporary developmental psychology. *Developmental Psychology, 28*, 548–557.

Whaley, K. L., & Rubenstein, T. S. (1994). How toddlers "do" friendship: A descriptive analysis of naturally occurring friendships in a group child care setting. *Journal of Social and Personal Relationships, 11*, 383–400.

Wheeler, C. S., & Petty, R. E. (2001). The effects of stereotype activation on behavior: A review of possible mechanisms. *Psychological Bulletin, 127*, 797–826.

Whipp, B. J., & Ward, S. A. (1992). Will woman soon outrun men? *Nature, 355*, 25.

Whitaker, D. J., & Miller, K. S. (2000). Parent-adolescent discussion about sex and condoms: Input of peer influences on sexual risk behavior. *Journal of Adolescent Research, 15*, 251–272.

Whitbeck, L. B., Hoyt, D. R., & Bao, W. (2000). Depressive symptoms and co-occurring depressive symptoms, substance abuse, and conduct problems among runaway and homeless adolescents. *Child Development, 71*, 721–732.

Whitbourne, S. K. (1986). *The me I know: A study of adult identity.* New York: Springer-Verlag.

White, K. J., & Kistner, J. (1992). The influence of teacher feedback on young children's peer preferences and perceptions. *Developmental Psychology, 28*, 933–940.

White, R. W. (1959). Motivation reconsidered: The concept of competence. *Psychological Review, 66*, 297–333.

White, S. H. (1992). G. Stanley Hall: From philosophy to developmental psychology. *Developmental Psychology, 28*, 25–34.

Whitehead, B. D., & Popenoe, D. (2003). *The state of the union: The social health of marriage in America 2003. Essay: Marriage and children: Coming together again?* The National Marriage Project, Rutgers University. Available from http://www.marriage.rutgers.edu/publications/print/print500u2003.htm

Whitesell, N. R., Mitchell, C. M., Kaufman, C. E., Spicer, P., and the Voices of Indian Teens Project Team (2006). Developmental trajectories of personal and collective self-concept among American Indian adolescents. *Child Development, 77*, 1487–1503.

Whiting, B. B., & Edwards, C. P. (1988). *Children of different worlds: The formation of social behavior.* Cambridge, MA: Harvard University Press.

Whiting, B. B., & Whiting, J. W. M. (1975). *Children of six cultures.* Cambridge, MA: Harvard University Press.

Whitley, B. E., Jr. (1983). Sex-role orientation and self-esteem: A critical meta-analytic review. *Journal of Personality and Social Psychology, 44*, 765–778.

Wichstrom, L. (1999). The emergence of gender differences in depressed mood during adolescence: The role of intensified gender socialization. *Developmental Psychology, 35*, 232–245.

Wicks-Nelson, R., & Israel, A. C. (2006). *Behavior disorders of childhood* (6th ed), Upper Saddle River, NJ: Prentice-Hall.

Widen, S. C., & Russell, J. A. (2003). A closer look at preschoolers' freely produced labels for facial expressions. *Developmental Psychology, 39*, 114–128.

Widmer, E. D., Treas, J., & Newcomb, R. (1998). Attitudes toward nonmarital sex in 24 countries. *Journal of Sex Research, 35*, 349–358.

Wiehe, V. R. (1996). *Working with child abuse and neglect.* Thousand Oaks, CA: Sage.

Wiggam, A. E. (1923). *The new decalogue of science.* Indianapolis: Bobbs-Merrill.

Wikipedia (2007). *Virginia Tech Massacre.* Retrieved September 4, 2007, from http//en.wikipedia.org/wiki/Virginia_Tech_massacre

Williams, J. E., Bennett, S. M., & Best, D. L. (1975). Awareness and expression of sex stereotypes in young children. *Developmental Psychology, 11*, 635–642.

Willems, E. P., & Alexander, J. L. (1982). The naturalistic perspective in research. In B. B. Wolman (Ed.), *Handbook of developmental psychology.* Englewood Cliffs, NJ: Prentice-Hall.

Williams, B. (1998; January 19). Stricter controls on Internet access sorely needed, parents fear. *Atlanta Constitution*, pp. A1, A15.

Williams, C., & Bybee, J. (1994). What do children feel guilty about? Developmental and gender differences. *Developmental Psychology, 30*, 617–623.

Williams, J. E., & Best, D. L. (1990). *Measuring sex stereotypes: A Multination study* (rev. ed.). Newbury Park, CA: Sage.

Williams, J. E., Satterwhite, R.C., & Best, D. L. (1999). Pancultural gender stereotypes revisited: The five factor model. *Sex Roles, 40*, 513–525.

Williams, S. T., Conger, K. J., & Blozis, S. A. (2007). The development of interpersonal aggression during adolescence: The importance of parents, siblings, and family economics. *Child Development, 78*, 1526–1542.

Williamson, R. A., & Markman, E. M. (2006). Precision of imitation as a function of preschoolers' understanding of the goal of demonstration. *Developmental Psychology, 42,* 723–731.

Williamson, R. A., Meltzoff, A. N., & Markman, E. M. (2008). Prior experience and perceived efficacy influence 3-year-olds' imitation. *Developmental Psychology, 44,* 275–285.

Wilson, A. E., Smith, M. D., Ross, H. S., & Ross, M. (2004). Young children's personal accounts of their sibling disputes. *Merrill-Palmer Quarterly, 50,* 39–60.

Windle, R. C. & Windle, M. (1995). Longitudinal patterns of physical aggression: Associations with adult social, psychiatric, and personality functioning and testosterone levels. *Development and Psychopathology, 7,* 563–585.

Winerman, L. (2005). The mind's mirror. *Monitor on Psychology, 36,* 48–57.

Winsler, A., Diaz, R. M., Espinoza, A., & Rodiquez, J. L. (1999). When learning a second language does not mean losing the first: Bilingual language development in low-income, Spanish-speaking children attending bilingual preschool. *Child Development, 70,* 349–362.

Winstead, B. A., & Griffin, J. L. (2001). Friendship styles. In J. Worell (Ed.), *Encyclopedia of women and gender.* (pp. 481–492). Boston: Academic Press.

Winter, D. G. (1996). *Personality: Analysis and interpretation of lives.* New York: McGraw-Hill.

Winterbottom, M. (1958). The relation of need for achievement to learning experiences in independence and mastery. In J. Atkinson (Ed.), *Motives in fantasy, action, and society.* Princeton, NJ: Van Nostrand.

Witherington, D. C., Campos, J. J., & Hertenstein, M. J. (2001). Principles of emotion and its development in infancy. In G. Bremner & A. Fogel (Eds.), *Blackwell handbook of infant development* (pp. 427–464). Malden, MA: Blackwell.

Wolak, J., Mitchell, K., & Finkelhor, D. (2007). Unwanted and wanted exposure to online pornography in a national sample of youth Internet users. *Pediatrics, 119,* 247–257.

Wolff, M., Rutten, P., & Bayer, A. F., III (1992). *Where we stand: Can America make it in the race for health, wealth, and happiness?* New York: Bantam Books.

Wolfner, G. D., & Gelles, R. J. (1993). A profile of violence toward children: A national study. *Child Abuse and Neglect, 17,* 197–212.

Woo, E. (1995, December 11). Can racial stereotypes psych out students? *Los Angeles Times.*

Woodhill, B. M., & Samuels, C. A. (2003). Positive and negative androgyny and their relationship with psychological health and well-being. *Sex Roles, 49,* 555–565.

Woodhill, B. M., & Samuels, C. A. (2004). Desirable and undesirable androgyny: A prescription for the twenty-first century. *Journal of Gender Studies, 13,* 15–28.

Woodward, L., Fergusson, D. M., & Belsky, J. (2000). Timing of parental separation and attachment to parents in adolescence: Results of a prospective study from birth to age 16. *Journal of Marriage and the Family, 62,* 162–174.

Woodward, S. A., McManis, M. H., Kagan, J., Dedlin, P., Snidman, N., Lewis, M., & Kahn, V. (2001). Infant temperament and the brainstem auditory evoked response in later childhood. *Child Development, 37,* 533–538.

Woolfe, T., Want, S. C., & Siegal, M. (2002). Signposts to development: Theory of mind in deaf children. *Child Development, 73,* 768–778.

Wright, J. C., Huston, A. C., Reitz, A. L., & Piemyat, S. (1994). Young children's perception of television reality: Determinants and developmental differences. *Developmental Psychology, 30,* 229–239.

Wright, J. C., Huston, A. C., Murphy, K. C., St. Peters, M., Pinon, M., Scantlin, R., & Kotler, J. (2001). The relations of early television viewing to school readiness and vocabulary of children from low-income families: The Early Window Project. *Child Development, 72,* 1347–1366.

Wright, J. C., Huston, A. C., Truglio, R., Fitch, M. Smith, E., & Piemyat, S. (1995). Occupational portrayals on television: Children's role schemata, career aspirations, and perceptions of reality. *Child Development, 66,* 1706–1718.

Wright Cassidy, K., Shaw Fineberg, D., Brown, K., & Perkins, A. (2005). Theory of mind may be contagious, but you don't catch it from your twin. *Child Development, 76,* 97–106.

Wu, P., Robinson, C. C., Yang, C., Hart, C. H., et al. (2002). Similarities and differences of mothers' parenting of preschoolers in China and the United States. *International Journal of Behavioral Development, 26,* 481–491.

Wu, X., Hart, C. H., Draper, T. W., & Olsen, J. A. (2001). Peer and teacher sociometrics for preschool children: Cross-informant concordance, temporal stability, and reliability. *Merrill-Palmer Quarterly, 47,* 416–443.

Xie, H., Li, Y., Boucher, S. M., Hutchins, B. C., & Cairns, B. D. (2006). What makes a girl (or a boy) popular (or unpopular)? African American children's perceptions and developmental differences. *Developmental Psychology, 42,* 599–612.

Yang, B., Ollendick, T. H., Dong, Q., Xia, Y., & Lin, L. (1995). Only children and children with siblings in the People's Republic of China: Levels of fear, anxiety, and depression. *Child Development, 66,* 1301–1311.

Yang, C., Hart, C. H., Porter, C. L., Olsen, S. F., Robinson, C. C., & Jin, S. (2003). Fathering in a Beijing Chinese sample: Associations with boys' and girls' negative emotionality and aggression. In R. Day & M. E. Lamb (Eds.), *Measuring father involvement* (pp. 185–215). Mahwah, NJ: Erlbaum.

Yarrow, M. R., Scott, P. M., & Waxler, C. Z. (1973). Learning concern for others. *Developmental Psychology, 8,* 240–260.

Yau, J., & Smetana, J. G. (1996). Adolescent-parent conflict among Chinese adolescents in Hong Kong. *Child Development, 67,* 1262–1275.

Yau, J., & Smetana, J. G. (2003). Conceptions of moral, social-conventional, and personal events among Chinese preschoolers in Hong Kong. *Child Development, 74,* 647–658.

Yeates, K. O., & Selman, R. L. (1989). Social competence in the schools: Toward an integrative developmental model for intervention. *Developmental Review, 9,* 64–100.

Yeung, W. J., Sandberg, J. F., Davis-Kean, P. E., & Hofferth, S. L. (2001). Children's time with fathers in intact families. *Journal of Marriage and the Family, 63,* 136–154.

Yip, T., & Fuligni, A. J. (2002). Daily variation in ethnic identity, ethnic behaviors, and psychological well-being among American adolescents of Chinese descent. *Child Development, 73,* 1557–1572.

Yip, T., Seaton, E. K., & Sellers, R. M. (2006). African American racial identity across the lifespan: Identity status, identity content, and depressive symptoms. *Child Development, 77,* 1504–1517.

Young, S. K., Fox, N. A., & Zahn-Waxler, C. (1999). The relations between temperament and empathy in 2-year-olds. *Developmental Psychology, 35,* 1189–1197.

Young, W. C., Goy, R. W., & Phoenix, C. H. (1964). Hormones and sexual behavior. *Science, 143,* 212–218.

Youniss, J., McLellan, J. A., & Strouse, D. (1994). "We're popular, but we're not snobs": Adolescents describe their crowds. In R. Montemayor, G. R. Adams, & T. P. Gullotta (Eds.), *Personal relationships in adolescence. Vol. 6: Advances in adolescent development.*

Yuill, N., & Pearson, A. (1998). The development of bases for trait attribution: Children's understanding of traits as casual mechanisms based on desire. *Developmental Psychology, 34,* 574–586.

Zahn-Waxler, C., Friedman, R. J., Cole, P. M., Mizuta, I., & Himura, N. (1996). Japanese and United States preschool children's responses to conflict and distress. *Child Development, 67,* 2462–2477.

Zahn-Waxler, C., Radke-Yarrow, M., & King, R. A. (1979). Child rearing and children's prosocial initiations towards victims of distress. *Child Development, 50,* 319–330.

Zahn-Waxler, C., Radke-Yarrow, M., Wagner, E., & Chapman, M. (1992). Development of concern for others. *Developmental Psychology, 28,* 126–136.

Zahn-Waxler, C., Robinson, J. L., & Emde, R. N. (1992). The development of empathy in twins. *Developmental Psychology, 28,* 1038–1047.

Zakriski, A. L., & Coie, J. D. (1996). A comparison of aggressive-rejected and nonaggressive-rejected children's interpretations of self-directed and other-directed rejection. *Child Development, 67,* 1048–1070.

Zeanah, C. H., Smyke, A. T., Koga, S. F., Carlson, E., & the Bucharest Early Intervention Project Care Group. (2005). Attachment in institutionalized and community children in Romania. *Child Development, 76,* 1015–1028.

Zelazo, P. D., Helwig, C. C., & Lau, A. (1996). Intention, act, and outcome in behavioral prediction and moral judgment. *Child Development, 67,* 2478–2492.

Zeman, J., & Garber, J. (1996). Display rules for anger, sadness, and pain: It depends on who is watching. *Child Development, 67,* 957–973.

Zeman, J., & Shipman, K. (1997). Social-contextual influences on expectancies for managing anger and sadness: The transition from middle childhood to adolescence. *Developmental Psychology, 33,* 917–924.

Zern, D. S. (1984). Relationships among selected child-rearing variables in a cross-cultural sample of 110 societies. *Developmental Psychology, 20,* 683–690.

Zhou, Q., Eisenberg, N., Losoya, S. H., Fabes, R. A., Reiser, M., Guthrie, I. K., Murphy, B. C., Cumberland, A. J., & Shepard, S. A. (2002). The relations of parental warmth and positive expressiveness to children's empathy-related responding and social functioning: A longitudinal study. *Child Development, 73,* 893–915.

Zhou, Q., Hofer, C., Eisenberg, N., Reiser, M., Spinrad, T. L., & Fabes, R. A. (2007). The developmental trajectories of attention focusing, attentional and behavioral persistence, and externalizing problems during school-age years. *Developmental Psychology, 43,* 369–385.

Ziegert, D. I., Kistner, J. A., Castro, R., & Robertson, B. (2001). Longitudinal study of young children's responses to challenging achievement situations. *Child Development, 72,* 609–624.

Zigler, E. F., & Finn-Stevenson, M. F. (1993). *Children in a changing world: Development and social issues.* Pacific Grove, CA: Brooks/Cole.

Zigler, E. F., & Finn-Stevenson, M. F. (1996). Funding child care and public education. *The Future of Children, 6,* 104–121.

Zigler, E., Finn-Stevenson, M., & Stern, B. M. (1997). Supporting children and families in the schools: The school of the 21st century. *American Journal of Orthopsychiatry, 67,* 396–407.

Zigler, E. F., & Gilman, E. (1993). Day care in America: What is needed. *Pediatrics, 91,* 175–178.

Zimmerman, M. A., Salem, D. A., & Maton, K. I. (1995). Family structure and psychosocial correlates among urban African-American adolescent males. *Child Development, 66,* 1598–1613.

Name Index

Banaji, M. R., 196
Bandura, A., 46, 47, 49, 50, 73, 86, 254, 265, 266, 286, 289–290, 292–293, 328, 331, 359, 360, 417
Banerjee, R., 251
Bank, L., 303, 313, 315, 390, 392
Banks, J. A., 444
Bao, W., 410
Barash, D. P., 244
Barbatsis, G., 429
Barber, B. K., 379, 381, 387, 388
Barber, B. L., 487
Barden, R. C., 142
Bardwell, J. R., 255
Barenboim, C., 198
Barglow, P., 164
Barker, E. T., 185, 186, 379, 487
Barker, R. G., 436
Barna, J., 176
Barnett, D., 148
Barnett, M. A., 335
Barnett, W. S., 231
Baron, A. S., 196
Baron, R. A., 24, 25, 26, 290, 417
Baron-Cohen, S., 178, 245, 261
Barr, R., 48
Barratt, M.S., 107
Barrett, K. C., 342
Barry, C., 479
Barry, H. III, 241
Bar-Tal, D., 331
Bartels, M., 81, 128
Barth, J. M., 444
Bartholomew, K., 156, 157
Bartini, M., 295
Bassuk, E. L., 383, 384
Bates B., 161
Bates, J. E., 126, 127, 129, 131, 154, 230, 280, 300, 309, 310, 313, 317, 379, 386, 397, 403, 469, 473, 474, 480, 481, 482
Bathurst, K., 401
Batson, C. D., 78, 334
Batten, M., 152
Battle, E. S., 215
Baudonniere, P., 174
Bauer, P. J., 94, 253
Baumeister, R. F., 186
Baumrind, D., 85, 234–235, 376–378, 380, 467, 496
Bauserman, R., 399
Baxter, A., 113
Bayer, A. F. III, 309
Bayley, N., 471
Beach, F. A., 275, 304
Beach, S. R., 475
Beady, C., 436, 437
Beal, C. R., 265
Bear, G. G., 347
Bearman, S. K., 186, 472
Beaulieu, D. A., 405, 409
Bebeau, M. J., 354, 358
Bechtold, K. T., 255

Beck, J. E., 124
Becker, B. E., 385
Becker, H. J., 431
Becker, J. B., 112
Beckett, C., 160, 161
Beckwith, L., 148
Bedford, V. H., 392
Begley, N. L., 252
Behne, T., 176
Behrens, K. Y., 147, 157
Beilin, H., 64
Bekkering, H., 48
Bell, K., 155
Bell, M. A., 128
Bell, R. Q., 50
Bellanti, C. J., 391
Belsky, J., 88, 89, 127, 137, 147, 148, 149, 153, 156, 157, 162, 164, 232, 372, 375, 388–389, 397, 406, 407, 464
Bem, D. J., 130–131
Bem, S. L., 41, 264, 268, 271, 272, 273
Benbow, C. P., 248
Bender, R. H., 435, 436
Bendig, A. W., 213
Benenson, J. F., 254, 332, 454
Bennett, C., 253, 476
Bennett, S. M., 16
Benoit, D., 157
Benson, B., 280
Benson, M. J., 281
Benson, P. L., 393
Bentler, P. M., 488
Bento, S., 157
Berenbaum, S., 244, 245, 246, 254, 255, 256, 258, 261, 268, 269, 277, 304, 305
Berg, C. A., 245
Bergman, A., 170
Berkhof, J., 112
Berkowitz, L., 26, 290–291, 417, 419, 421
Berkowitz, M., 355
Berlin, L. J., 230
Berliner, L., 408
Bernal, M. E., 193, 194
Bernat, D. H., 189, 193, 194
Berndt, T. J., 202, 461, 478, 480, 484, 485
Bernier, A., 155, 157
Bernieri, F., 83
Bernstein, I. S., 304
Berry, J. W., 224
Bertenthal, B. I., 21
Berzonsky, M. D., 192
Best, D. L., 16, 241, 242, 251
Betts, N. T., 481
Beyers, W., 387
Beyth-Marom, R., 64
Bhavnagri, N. P., 20–21
Biaggio, A. M. B., 358
Bianchi, S. M., 396, 414
Biblarz, T., 394
Bidell, T., 64
Bierman, K. L., 391, 476, 478
Biernbaum, M. A., 311

Bigbee, M. A., 306
Bigler, R. S., 174, 196, 197, 252, 253, 274
Bigner, J. J., 394
Bijvank, M. N., 431
Billman, J., 331
Bingham, C. R., 280
Bingham, K., 309
Biocca, F. A., 429
Birch, H. G., 129
Birch, L. L., 331, 471
Birch, S. H., 124, 315
Biringen, Z., 149
Bjorklund, B. R., 6
Bjorklund, D. F., 6, 31, 56, 58, 65, 70, 71, 72, 177
Black, B., 465
Black, M. M., 154, 402
Black-Gutman, D., 196
Blackwell, L. S., 219, 222, 237
Blair, C., 131
Blair, K. A., 123, 124, 465
Blair, R. J. R., 200
Blakemore, J. E. O., 244, 245, 246, 250, 251, 252, 253, 254, 258, 304
Blaney, N., 445
Blanton, H., 485, 486
Blasi, A., 341, 358, 360
Blatchford, P., 436
Blehar, M. C., 144
Block, J., 397
Block, J. H., 244, 397
Bloom, P., 457
Blozis, S. A., 392
Blumenfeld, P., 183, 248
Blumenthal, D. R., 317
Blyth, D. A., 186
Board, J., 338
Bodin, S. D., 292, 293, 295, 311, 314
Bogatz, C., 426
Bogatz, G. A., 426
Bogenschneider, K., 487, 488
Bohlin, G., 108, 261
Boivin, M., 235, 292, 293, 295, 297, 300, 301, 302, 304, 305, 307, 316, 474, 480
Bokhorst, C. L., 151
Boldizar, J. P., 252, 272, 292
Bolduc, D., 240
Bolger, K. E., 407, 408
Bolger, N., 95, 197, 200
Boller, K., 231
Bongers, I. L., 301, 307
Bonk, C. J., 428
Boodoo, G., 215, 225, 229
Book, A. S., 304
Boom, J., 354
Boomsma, D. I., 81, 128
Boone, R. T., 115
Booth, A., 252, 255, 304, 395, 398, 399
Booth, C. L., 484
Booth-LaForce, C., 474, 480
Bor, W., 303, 311, 314
Borke, J., 183

Cameron, C. A., 338
Cameron, J. A., 196, 197
Cameron, L., 196
Camino, C., 357
Camino, L., 26, 419
Campbell, B., 278
Campbell, D. T., 326
Campbell, E. Q., 217
Campbell, F. A., 231, 435
Campbell, J. D., 186
Campbell, S. B., 107, 136, 148
Campbell, S. E., 234
Campione-Barr, N., 387
Campos, J. J., 21, 103, 104, 105, 106, 107, 113, 115
Campos, R., 410
Campos, R. G., 104, 119
Camras, L. A., 105
Canter, R. J., 255
Cantor, J., 424
Cantrill, J. A., 430
Capaldi, D., 303
Capaldi, D. M., 280, 281, 317, 399, 483, 484
Caplan, M., 296–297, 305, 330, 453
Caplovitz, A. G., 417, 421, 432
Cappenberg, M., 137
Carbonell, O. A., 20
Card, N. A., 300
Carey, S., 178
Carlo, G., 334, 336, 339
Carlsmith, J. M., 472
Carlson, E., 159, 303
Carlson, E. A., 148
Carlson, J. J., 342, 344
Carlson, S. M., 131, 177
Carlson, V., 148
Carlson, W., 483
Carlton, R. P., 405
Carlton-Ford, S., 186
Carpendale, J. I. M., 347
Carpenter, M., 48, 94, 171, 176
Carr, M. B., 252
Carr, T. S., 304
Carranza, E., 242
Carrick, N., 120
Carriger, M. S., 174, 458
Carryl, E., 403
Carstensen, L., 112
Caruso, M., 244
Carver, L. J., 21, 113
Carver, P. R., 277
Casas, J. F., 244, 302, 306
Casey, M. B., 243
Casey, R. J., 142, 342
Casey, W. M., 362
Casiglia, A. C., 475
Caspi, A., 29, 84, 128, 130, 186, 302, 303, 307, 308, 311, 316–317, 380, 396, 402, 405, 408, 472
Cassidy, J., 145, 155, 466, 469, 473, 483
Cassidy, K. W., 176, 177

Castelli, L., 196
Castellino, D. R., 230
Castile, C. M., 173
Castle, J., 160, 161, 305, 330
Castle, J. M., 105, 107
Castro, R., 220, 221
Cates, W. Jr., 280
Cauce, A. M., 386
Caughy, M. O., 194
Cavanaugh, J. C., 414
Cavell, T. A., 439, 444
Ceci, S. J., 215, 225, 229, 434
Cederblad, M., 380
Cen, G., 130, 378, 486
Cervantes, C. A., 245
Chaiyasit, W., 130
Chalmers, H., 437
Chalmers, J. B., 333
Champion, K., 407
Chan, R. W., 394
Chandler, M., 59, 177, 192, 348
Chandler, M. J., 192, 320
Chandra, A., 279
Chang, B., 95
Chang, L., 88, 225, 227, 448, 462, 468, 470, 475, 477, 480
Chao, R. K., 183, 189, 226, 235n. 1, 384, 443, 497
Chapman, M., 148, 329, 330, 334, 335, 336, 340, 364
Charlesworth, R., 435
Charlesworth, W. R., 7
Chase, C. I., 436
Chase-Lansdale, P. L., 280, 281, 383, 397
Chasiotis, A., 137
Chassin, L., 488
Chavous, T. M., 193
Chazan-Cohen, R., 231
Chen, C., 225, 226, 384, 387, 442, 444, 446, 447, 448, 473
Chen, F., 174
Chen, H., 378, 379, 381, 486
Chen, X., 88, 130, 225, 227, 235, 297, 320, 337, 378, 448, 462, 470, 475, 480, 486
Cherlin, A. J., 397
Chernick, A. B., 262
Chernoff, J. J., 466, 483
Chesir-Teran, D., 481
Chess, S., 129, 130, 150
Cheung, L. W. Y., 281
Chiesa, J., 231
Child, I. L., 2, 241
Chisholm, K., 159, 160
Chmiel, S., 358
Choi, J., 243
Chomitz, V. R., 281
Choy, S. P., 320
Christensen, M., 393
Christopher, F. S., 339
Christopherson, E. R., 244
Chung, H. L., 310, 316
Chung, T., 390

Cialdini, R. B., 331–332, 422
Cibelli, C. D., 154
Cicchetti, D., 122, 124, 148, 312, 404, 405, 406, 407, 408
Cielinski, K. L., 466
Cillessen, A. H. N., 23, 293, 295, 300, 468, 470, 473, 474, 475
Claessens, A., 235
Clark, B. R., 173
Clark, E. A., 161
Clark, K. B., 441
Clark, K. E., 465, 466
Clark, L. V., 201, 266
Clark, M. C., 331
Clark, R., 153, 165
Clark, R. A., 209, 213, 234
Clark, R. D. III, 73
Clark, S., 280, 281, 317
Clarke, A. D. B., 161
Clarke, A. M., 161
Clarke, R., 89
Clarke-Stewart, K. A., 162, 164, 397, 400, 401, 464
Clarkson, F. E., 242
Clary, E. G., 332, 336, 340
Clasen, D. R., 485, 488
Clausen, J. A., 472
Clements, D. H., 428, 429
Clements, P., 487
Clements, W. A., 178
Cleveland, H. H., 484
Clewett, A. S., 424
Clingempeel, W. G., 89, 378, 396, 400, 401
Cloud, J. M., 251
Coates, B., 49
Coatsworth, J. D., 185
Cobbs, G., 180
Cochran, S. W., 255
Cohen, D., 47, 56
Cohen, G. L., 279, 485
Cohen, J. A., 408
Cohen, L., 332, 337
Cohn, J., 119
Cohn, J. F., 105, 107, 136, 148
Coie, J. D., 50, 122, 225, 286, 292, 293, 295, 296, 298, 299, 300, 301, 302, 303, 304, 306, 307, 309, 310, 311, 316, 317, 320, 365, 461, 468, 469, 473, 474, 476, 478, 487, 496
Colapinto, J., 262
Colby, A., 350, 353, 354
Colder, C. R., 488
Colditz, G. A., 423
Cole, A., 88, 483
Cole, D. A., 185, 248
Cole, M., 434
Cole, P. M., 122, 123, 297, 342
Coleman, C. C., 480, 484
Coleman, J. S., 217
Coley, R. L., 153, 154, 280, 281, 399, 402
Coll, C. G., 226, 228, 230, 233, 234, 403

Colley, A., 266
Collie, R., 48, 55n.1
Collins, P. A., 267, 416
Collins, W. A., 112, 378, 380, 381, 386, 387, 388, 424, 457, 462, 463, 476, 487, 488
Collis, B. A., 431
Colvert, E., 160, 161
Colvert, J., 160, 161
Colwell, M. J., 465
Compton, K., 315
Comstock, G. A., 420
Condron, D. J., 391
Condry, J., 247
Condry, J. C., 288
Condry, S., 247
Conger, K. J., 229, 373, 381, 392
Conger, R. D., 229, 311, 312, 316, 317, 373, 376, 381, 382, 472, 473, 487
Conley, C. S., 186
Connell, D. B., 89, 150
Connell, J. P., 120
Conner, R. F., 427
Connolly, J., 462, 482, 484
Connolly, J. A., 58
Connolly, K. J., 318
Connor, R. T., 445
Constantine, J., 231
Conway, M., 241
Coohey, C., 405
Cook, T. D., 427
Cooley, C. H., 169, 183, 204
Coon, J. A., 176
Coontz, S., 371
Cooper, C. R., 192
Cooper, H. M., 217
Cooper, J., 266
Cooper, M. L., 463
Cooper, P., 149
Cooperman, G., 329, 335, 336
Cooperman, S., 295
Coopersmith, S., 188
Coplan, R. J., 459, 460, 461
Coppotelli, H., 468
Corasantini, M. A., 403
Corby, B. C., 188
Corley, R., 127, 128, 358
Cornelius, R., 348
Cornell, A. H., 292, 293, 295, 311, 314
Cornell, D. P., 272
Corns, K. M., 157, 388
Corteen, R. S., 415
Corter, C., 389, 390
Corter, C. M., 110
Cortes, R. M., 408
Corwyn, R. F., 226, 228, 230, 233, 234
Cossette, L., 240
Costabile, A., 287
Costanzo, P., 302
Costello, E. J., 304
Costenbader, V., 445
Costigan, C. L., 387
Costin, S. E., 479

Cote, J. E., 193
Cote, S., 297, 302, 304, 305
Cotrane, S., 402
Couchoud, E. A., 115, 468, 473
Coulton, C. J., 406
Courage, M. L., 31, 32
Cousins, S. D., 182
Cowan, C. P., 89, 183, 378
Cowan, P., 183
Cowan, P. A., 89, 378
Cowen, E. L., 399
Cowen, J., 365
Cowie, H., 299
Cowley, G., 423
Cox, M., 396, 397
Cox, M. J., 88, 149, 153, 372, 398
Cox, R., 396, 397
Coy, K. C., 112, 151, 298, 339, 342, 344, 386
Coyle, A., 394
Coyle, T. R., 31
Craig, I. W., 308, 408
Craig, W., 300
Cramer, A., 313
Crandall, V. C., 210, 214, 215, 216
Crane, P., 470
Craven, R., 183
Craven, R. G., 183
Crawford, M., 278
Crawford, N., 301
Crenshaw, T. M., 477
Crews, F., 41
Crick, N., 308
Crick, N. R., 23, 244, 292, 293, 294, 295, 302, 306, 318–319, 334, 469
Criss, M. M., 379, 481, 482
Crnic, K., 88, 127, 156
Crockenberg, S., 364, 372, 380, 381
Crockenberg, S. C., 119
Crocker, J., 189
Crockett, L. J., 280
Croft, C., 160
Croft, C. M., 151
Cromer, C. C., 454
Cronbach, L. J., 439
Crook, C., 429
Crosby, L., 292, 316, 474, 487
Crosnoe, R., 80
Cross, C. E., 9
Cross, D., 176, 177
Cross, W. E., 174
Crouter, A. C., 194, 249, 252, 253, 255, 265, 266, 304, 386, 389, 390, 391, 392, 401, 402, 415
Crowe, E., 178
Crowe, P. A., 185
Crowell, J., 155, 157
Crowell, J. A., 149
Crystal, D. S., 183, 448
Cui, M., 311, 312
Culver, C., 119, 120
Cumberland, A., 121, 123, 124, 131, 296, 298, 311, 327, 334, 336

Cumberland, A. J., 122, 335
Cummings, E. M., 122, 146, 148, 297, 302, 311–312, 312, 372, 382, 389, 395
Cummings, J. S., 382, 389, 395
Cunningham, J. G., 115
Curran, P. J., 396, 488
Curtis, N. M., 317
Cutting, A., 479
Cutting, A. L., 124, 479
Cynkar, A., 249, 430, 432
Cyphers, L., 268
Cyr, C., 157

Dabbs, J. M., 304
Dabbs, J. M. Jr., 304
Dack, L. A, 178
Daddis, C., 386, 387
Daglish, L., 253
Damon, W., 175, 179, 199, 202, 251, 252
D'Andrade, R., 234
Dane, H. E., 292, 293, 295, 311, 314
Daniels, D., 80, 435
Dann, S., 4
Darling, C. A., 279
Darling, N., 379
Darling, N. E., 487
Darlington, R. B., 231
Darwin, C. A., 7, 103
Das Eiden, R., 157, 388
Das Gupta, M., 178
Dasen, P. R., 224
D'Augelli, A., 277
D'Avanzo, K., 385
David, H. P., 149
Davidov, M., 335, 341
Davidson, J., 262
Davidson, J. K., 279
Davidson, R. J., 128
Davidson, W., 221
Davies, L., 305
Davies, P. T., 122, 311–312, 312, 382, 389, 395, 463
Davis, B., 78
Davis, G. A., 438, 444
Davis, J., 428
Davis, K. D., 194
Davis, S. W., 251
Davis, T. L., 121
Davis-Kean, P. E., 151, 243, 248, 487
Davison, K. K., 471
Dawson, B., 434
Dawud, S., 408
Day, J. C., 428
Day, R. D., 398
de Gaston, J. P., 279
de Guzman, M. R. T., 339
de Quervain, D. J. F., 292
de Schipper, E. J., 162
de Villers, J., 178
de Villiers, P., 178
De Winter, A. F., 299, 300, 301
De Wolff, M. S., 147, 153

DeAmicis, L., 196
DeAngelis, T., 432
Dearing, K. F., 293, 295
Dearing, R., 111
Deater-Deckard, K., 365, 386, 497
Deaver, C. M., 46
DeBaryshe, B. D., 315
DeBerry, K. M., 194, 393
Debus, R., 183
Deci, E. L., 210
Decker, S. H., 316
DeCourcey, W., 2002
Dedlin, P., 128
DeFries, J., 127
DeFries, J. C., 75, 81, 82, 84, 127
DeGarmo, D. S., 230, 398
Degirmencioglu, S. M., 462
Degnan, K. A., 124, 296
DeKlyen, M., 311
Dekovic, M., 467
DeLacey, P., 453
DeLamater, J., 279
DeLoache, J. S., 254
DeLuccie, M. E., 153
Demaray, M. K., 300
deMause, L., 6, 7
Demo, D. H., 371, 398
DeMulder, E., 123, 124, 465
DeMulder, E. K., 155
Denham, S., 155
Denham, S. A., 115, 118, 119, 123, 124,
    465, 468, 473
Denissen, J. J. A., 249
Dennis, J., 402
Deptula, D. P., 280
Derbyshire, A., 250
Derenowski, E., 280
DeRosier, E., 456, 474
Desai, K. A., 208
deSchonen, S., 172
Desimone, L. M., 449
Despert, J. L., 7
deVines, J., 112
deVines, M. W., 112
Dewandre, N., 248
DeWolf, M., 435
Dewsbury, D. A., 68
DiAdamo, C., 176
Diamond, L. M., 277
Diamond, M., 262
Diaz, R. M., 444
Dick, D. M., 472
Dickson, K. L., 106, 142
Didow, S. M., 458
Diekman, A. B., 242, 258, 266
Diesendruck, G., 196
Dietz, L. J., 208
Dietz, W. H., 423
DiIorio, C., 279
DiLalla, L. F., 128
Dill, J. C., 431
Dill, K. E., 431

Dillon, P., 399
Dimitrov, D. M., 282
Dingliang, T., 356
Dionne, G., 235, 293, 307
Dishion, T., 312, 378
Dishion, T. J., 78, 292, 310, 313, 315, 316,
    317, 474, 478, 481, 483, 484, 487
Dissanayke, C., 458
Dittus, P. J., 281
Diversi, M., 189
Dixon, S., 20, 119, 260
Dodge, K. A., 88, 129, 230, 280, 286, 292,
    293, 294, 295, 296, 298, 299, 300, 301,
    302, 303, 304, 306, 307, 309, 310, 311,
    313, 316, 317, 318–319, 320, 365, 379,
    386, 397, 403, 442, 468, 469, 473, 474,
    476, 477, 478, 480, 481, 482, 483, 487,
    496, 497
Dodge, T., 485, 486
Dogan, S. J., 317
Doherty, W. J., 397
Dohnt, H., 421
Dokis, D. P., 387
Doley, S., 147
Dollard, J., 290
Dondi, M., 73, 170
Dong, Q., 235, 392, 473
Dong, W., 236, 237
Donnellan, M. B., 186, 312
Donnerstein, E., 414, 417, 421, 422
D'Onofrio, B. M., 397
Donovan, W. L., 372
Doob, L. W., 290
Doris, J., 378, 407
Dorn, L. D., 472
Dornbusch, S. M., 88, 188, 226, 227, 235,
    378, 379, 398, 399, 442, 443, 472, 487
Dorsey, D., 382, 433, 438
Dotterer, A. M., 194
Dow-Ehrensberger, M., 434
Downey, D. B., 391
Downing, L. L., 432
Downs, A. C., 470
Dowsett, C. J., 235
Doyle, A., 58
Doyle, A. B., 154, 196, 372, 483
Dozier, M., 161, 393
Drabman, R. S., 420
Draper, T. W., 468
Dreyer, P. H., 278, 279
Droege, K., 479
Droege, K. L., 195, 219
Druyan, S., 93
Dubas, J. S., 260, 472
Dube, E. M., 277
DuBois, D. L., 188, 193, 481
Dubois-Comtois, K., 157
Dubowitz, H., 154, 402
Duckett, E., 401
Dudley, W. N., 279
Duffy, S., 402
Duke, P. M., 472

Duku, E., 227, 390
Dumas, C., 61
Dumitrescu, A., 159
Duncan, G. J., 225, 229, 230, 231, 235, 382
Dunham, Y., 196
Dunn, J., 80, 117, 121, 122, 124, 177, 312,
    318, 372, 382, 388, 389, 400, 461, 479
Dunn, J. F., 80, 457
Dunne, M. P., 277
Dunphy, D. C., 462
Durazo, O., 280
Durkin, K., 196
Durlak, J. A., 187
Durland, M. A., 435
Dweck, C. S., 195, 215, 219, 221, 222, 234,
    237, 443
Dwyer, K. M., 129, 130, 302, 310, 311, 314,
    315, 498
Dytrych, Z., 149
Dziuba-Leatherman, J., 404, 407

Eagly, A. H., 242, 246, 258
Eakins, D. J., 424
Early, D. M., 435, 436
East, P. L., 278, 280, 391
Eastenson, A., 481
Easterbrooks, M. A., 154, 173
Eastman, K. L., 130
Eaton, W. O., 244
Eaves, L. J., 308
Eccles, J. S., 112, 183, 185, 186, 188, 219,
    223, 227, 236, 243, 247, 248, 249, 386n.2,
    436, 437, 438, 439, 440, 443, 487
Eckenrode, J., 378, 407
Eckerman, C. O., 458
Eckman, P., 103
Edelstein, W., 302
Eder, R. A., 96, 175, 195
Edison, S. C., 31, 32
Edmonds, S., 436
Edstrom, L. V. S., 321
Edwards, C. P., 253, 331, 355, 356, 453
Edwards, J. N., 399
Edwards, J. R., 251
Eftekhari, A., 389
Egan, S. K., 250, 273, 277, 300, 301
Egeland, B., 158, 303, 406, 408
Egeland, B. J., 404
Ehrenberg, R. G., 436
Ehrhardt, A., 259, 261
Ehrhardt, A. A., 258, 261, 262, 277
Eicher, S. A., 485, 488
Eichler, L. S., 135
Eidelman, A., 47, 56
Eisen, M., 179, 180
Eisenberg, M. E., 186
Eisenberg, N., 115, 122, 124, 131, 245, 254,
    280, 296, 298, 311, 325, 326, 327, 328,
    329, 330, 331, 332, 334, 335, 336, 339,
    341, 364, 465, 470
Eisenberg-Berg, N., 333, 334
Eisenbud, L., 266, 269

Elder, G. H., 9
Elder, G. H. Jr., 80, 130, 229, 373, 376, 381, 472
Elicker, J., 88, 155
Elkind, D., 63, 255, 435
Elkins, I., 80, 386
Ellerbeck, K., 244
Ellerson, P. C., 409
Ellhammer, O., 380
Elliot, R., 319
Elliott, E. S., 443
Ellis, B. J., 280, 397
Ellis, J. B., 272
Ellis, L. A., 183
Ellis, S., 454
Ellis, W. E., 457, 485
Ellsworth, C. P., 106, 138
El-Sheikh, M., 395
Embry, D., 320
Emde, R. N., 78, 104, 113, 127
Emerson, P. E., 108, 137, 140, 456–457
Emery, R. E., 396, 397, 399, 401, 404, 405, 406, 409
Endriga, M. C., 142
Endsley, R. C., 269
Engles, R. C. M. E., 155
English, D., 362
Englund, M., 155, 253, 476
Englund, M. M., 155, 466
Enna, B., 221
Enns, L. R., 244
Entwisle, D. R., 226
Eppe, S., 310
Epstein, Y., 3
Erel, O., 389, 395, 402
Erickson, M. F., 404
Erikson, E. H., 41–43, 154, 155, 175, 185, 189, 191, 192, 297, 375
Eron, L. D., 302, 419, 420, 421, 424
Espelage, D., 300, 462
Espinoza, A., 444
Essex, J., 89
Essex, M. J., 165, 306
Etzion-Carasso, A., 147
Evans, E. M., 148, 157
Everingham, S. S., 231
Ewigman, B., 191, 403
Eyer, D. E., 135

Fabes, R. A., 115, 122, 124, 131, 245, 253, 254, 265, 280, 296, 298, 311, 325, 326, 327, 328, 330, 331, 332, 334, 335, 339, 341, 364, 454, 465, 470
Faden, R. R., 280
Fagot, B. I., 154, 250–251, 253, 265, 266, 375
Fairchild, H., 414, 421, 422
Falbo, T., 388, 392
Fan, X., 393
Fantauzzo, C. A., 105, 107
Farber, S. L., 83
Farhl, P., 426
Farmer, T. W., 300, 472, 475

Farrant, K., 173
Farrington, D. P., 316
Farver, J. A. M., 310, 460, 461
Farver, J. M., 475, 477, 479
Fauber, R., 396
Fearon, R. M. P., 151
Fegley, S., 336
Feiler, R., 435
Fein, G. G., 58
Feingold, A., 244, 245
Feinman, J., 439
Feinman, S., 108, 113
Feinstein, R. A., 280
Feiring, C., 157, 407, 462, 463, 482, 483
Feldlaufer, H., 440
Feldman, R., 137, 165, 344
Feldman, R. S., 407
Feldman, S. S., 149
Fennema, E., 243
Ferguson, D. L., 193
Ferguson, L. L., 302
Fergusson, D. M., 280, 397
Fernald, A., 113, 114
Fernandez, A., 310
Fernandez, E., 397
Fernyhough, C., 178
Feron, F. J., 112
Feshbach, N. D., 414, 421, 422
Feshbach, S., 291, 305, 416
Fetter, M. D., 462
Ficher, I., 394
Field, T., 479
Field, T. M., 47, 56, 107, 148
Fields, J., 374
Fier, J., 248
Fiese, B. H., 148
Figlio, D. N., 449
Figueredo, A. J., 407
Filisetti, L., 331
Fincham, F. D., 220, 395, 399
Finckenauer, J. O., 317
Findley, M. J., 217
Fine, M., 189
Fine, M. A., 371, 378, 399
Fine, S., 124
Fine, S. E., 103
Finkelhor, D., 404, 407, 408, 432
Finkelstein, N. W., 161
Finklestein, B. D., 481
Finn, J. D., 436
Finn-Stevenson, M., 449
Finn-Stevenson, M. F., 166, 403
Fiori-Cowley, A., 149
Firth, C. D., 178
Fischbacker, U., 292
Fischer, K. W., 64
Fischoff, B., 64
Fisher, L., 159
Fisher, M. M., 280
Fisher, N., 124, 479
Fisher, P., 126
Fisher, P. A., 142

Fitch, M., 416, 424
Fitch, S. A., 191
Fitzgerald, H. E., 17, 21, 429
Fivush, R., 245
Flaks, D. K., 394
Flanagan, C., 398, 439
Flanagan, C. A., 440
Flanagan, K. D., 293, 295
Flanagan, T., 204
Flannery, D., 64
Flannery, D. J., 320
Flavell, J. H., 59, 64, 116, 176
Fleege, P. O., 435
Fleming, J. S., 230, 233
Fletcher, A. C., 487
Fleury, J. K., 320
Flom, R., 113
Flood, P., 436, 437
Flook, L., 469, 470, 477
Flor, D., 371
Flor, D. L., 386
Flouri, E., 372
Fobil, J. N., 430
Foehr, U. G., 414
Fogel, A., 105, 106, 135, 142, 171
Foley, D. L., 308
Follmer, A., 373
Fonagy, P., 151, 157
Fonzi, A., 481
Forbes, L. M., 148, 157
Ford, C. S., 275
Ford, D. Y., 227, 444
Ford, M. E., 142, 266
Fordham, S., 227
Forehand, R., 281, 382, 396, 401, 433, 438
Forgatch, M. S., 230, 398
Forget-Dubois, N., 235
Forman, D. R., 342, 376
Forman, E. M., 395
Forman, E. R., 332
Forrest, J. D., 279, 282
Foster, G. E., 436
Foster, T., 479
Fouts, H. N., 256
Fowlkes, J., 251
Fox, N. A., 21, 128, 153, 330
Frabutt, J. M., 193
Fradley, E., 178
Frady, F. L., 304
Fraiberg, A., 276
Fraley, R. C., 145, 151
Frankel, K. A., 154
Frankenberg, W. K., 232
Frankie, G., 265
Franklin, K. M., 398
Frazier, J. A., 434
Fredricks, J. A., 185, 248, 249, 437
Freedman, J. L., 419
Freeman-Doan, C., 247, 248, 249
Freeman-Gallant, A., 317
Fremmer-Bombik, E., 155
French, D. C., 306, 474

French, S., 402
French, S. E., 193
Freud, A., 4
Freud, S., 19–20, 39–41, 154, 264, 285–286, 287–288, 342–343
Frey, K. S., 60, 188, 219, 255, 266, 268, 321
Frick, P. J., 292, 293, 295, 311, 314
Fried, C. B., 229
Friedman, J., 465
Friedman, J. L., 481
Friedman, R. J., 297
Friedrich, L. K., 26, 418, 419, 424
Friedrich-Cofer, L. K., 424
Frierson, T., 320
Frisvold, D., 449
Fritz, J., 373, 384
Frome, P. M., 236, 248
Frost, J. J., 282
Frost, P., 479
Frueh, T., 266
Fry, C. L., 33
Fu, G., 338
Fu, V. R., 235
Fuchs, D., 245
Fuhrman, T., 387
Fukumoto, A., 342
Fuligni, A. J., 183, 193, 194, 196, 197, 225, 227, 230, 231, 386, 387, 392, 443, 447, 448, 485, 487
Fulker, D. W., 127
Fuller, B., 163
Fultz, J., 339
Furman, W., 88, 202, 388, 390, 391, 410, 462, 463, 476, 481, 482, 484
Furrow, J., 371
Fyans, L. J., 208

Gaertner, B., 131
Gagnon, J. H., 278
Gaines, C., 112
Galambos, N. L., 185, 186, 252, 379, 403, 487
Galbraith, K. A., 280
Galen, B. R., 302, 306
Gallagher, J. M., 178
Galligan, R. F., 110
Gallimore, R., 390, 439
Gallup, G. G. Jr., 173
Galper, A., 226, 441
Galperin, C., 240, 264
Gamm, B. K., 483
Gamoran, A., 436
Ganza, B., 278
Garbarino, J., 404, 406, 408
Garber, J., 123, 293
Garcia, C., 193, 194
Garcia, E. E., 441
Garcia, M. M., 313, 390
Gardner, M., 64, 462
Garduque, L., 232
Gariepy, J., 302

Garlinghouse, M. A., 46
Garmezy, N., 185
Garner, P. W., 121, 391
Garovich-Szabo, L., 242
Gauthier, R., 253
Gautier, T., 262
Gauze, C., 253, 468, 470, 481, 484
Gavin, L. N., 88
Gavinski-Molina, M., 459, 460, 461
Gayer, T., 434, 435
Gazelle, H., 438, 461, 474, 475
Ge, X., 229, 316, 376, 381, 472, 473
Geary, D. C., 72, 141, 257, 407, 446
Gee, C. L., 218, 219
Geen, R. G., 293, 419, 421
Geffner, M. E., 261
Gelfand, D. M., 148, 325
Gelles, R. J., 404, 405
Gelman, S. A., 52, 195, 196, 198, 252, 253
Gendler, T., 436
George, C., 407
George, T. P., 482
Georgiades, K., 227, 390
Gerard, J. M., 186, 189
Gergely, G., 48
Gerrard, M., 316
Gershkoff-Stowe, L., 31
Gershoff, E. T., 122, 226, 229, 335, 381, 382
Gershoni, R., 483
Gervai, J., 254, 266
Gesell, A., 68
Gest, J. D., 185
Geurts, S. A. E., 162
Gewirtz, J. L., 46, 140
Ghazarian, S. R., 193
Giampaoli, S., 243
Gibbons, F. X., 316
Gibbs, J., 354
Gibbs, J. C., 355
Gifford-Smith, M. E., 298
Gil, D. G., 405
Gilbert, P., 289, 290
Gilchrist, L., 281
Giles, H., 251
Giles, J. W., 218, 219, 305, 306
Gilligan, C., 356
Gilliom, M., 124, 298, 299, 314
Gilman, E., 402
Ginsburg, G. S., 235
Girard, A., 307
Givaudian, M., 282
Gjerde, P. F., 397
Glasgow, K. L., 235, 378
Glass, G. V., 437
Gleason, K. E., 157
Gleason, T. R., 58
Glogowski, B. K., 244
Gnepp, J., 117, 204
Goeke-Morley, M. C., 372, 382, 389, 395
Goencue, A., 460
Goetz, L., 445

Gold, A., 159
Goldberg, M., 331
Goldberg, M. E., 422
Goldberg, P., 247
Goldberg, S., 159
Golden, O., 407
Goldfarb, W., 158, 160
Golding, J., 261, 266, 277, 394
Goldschmidt, I., 135, 393
Goldsmith, D., 291
Goldsmith, H. H., 120, 121, 127, 128, 131, 151, 306
Goldstein, N., 331–332
Goldstein, R., 244
Goldstein, S. E., 487
Goldwater, O. D., 444
Goldwyn, R., 145, 148, 157
Golombok, S., 261, 266, 277, 394
Golombok, S. E., 260, 457
Golter, B. S., 465
Goncu, A., 93
Gondoli, D. M., 381
Gonzales, N., 386
Gonzales-Backen, M., 193
Gonzalez, E., 449
Good, C., 229
Good, T. L., 439
Goodenough, F. L., 290, 297
Goodman, E., 394
Goodnow, J. J., 332, 337, 365
Goodwin, M. H., 358
Goossens, F. A., 151
Goossens, L., 387, 388
Gopnik, A., 115, 176, 195
Gordeeva, T., 245, 248
Gorden, C., 169
Gordis, E. B., 407, 408
Gordon, H. M., 177
Gordon, R. A., 316
Gordon, T. P., 304
Gordon, V. V., 281
Gorer, G., 289, 308
Gorman, A. H., 468, 475
Gorman-Smith, D., 292, 309, 310, 316
Gormley, W., 435
Gormley, W. T. Jr., 434
Gorn, G. J., 422
Gortmaker, S. L., 423
Gosling, S. D., 185, 186, 245
Gottesman, I. I., 81
Gottfried, A. E., 230, 233, 401
Gottfried, A. W., 230, 233, 401
Gottlieb, D., 444
Gottlieb, G., 11, 73, 85, 86
Gottman, J. M., 478
Gould, S. J., 72
Govrin, N., 252
Goy, R. W., 304
Graber, J. A., 472
Graesser, A. C., 341
Graham, S., 300
Gralinski, H., 174

Jaccard, J., 281, 485, 486
Jacklin, C. N., 243, 246, 247, 254, 260, 265, 303–304
Jackson, A. W., 438, 444
Jackson, B. L., 194
Jackson, E. W., 130
Jackson, J. F., 85
Jackson, K., 310
Jackson, L. A., 429
Jackson, M. F., 444
Jackson-Newsom, J., 390
Jacob, K., 2002
Jacobs, A., 147
Jacobs, C., 307
Jacobs, J., 247, 248, 249
Jacobs, J. E., 185, 219, 248, 249
Jacobs, L. C., 436
Jacobsen, R. B., 394
Jacobsen, T., 232
Jacobson, J. L., 154
Jacobson, L., 443
Jacobson, L. J., 278
Jacobs-Quadrel, M., 64
Jacobvitz, D., 406, 408
Jacques, S., 131
Jaffari-Bimmel, N., 128, 129, 135, 155, 393, 457, 466, 498
Jaffee, S. R., 84, 157, 311, 358, 380, 402, 405
Jagers, R. J., 309
Jaggli, N., 266
Jahromi, L. B., 119
Jaio, S., 392
Jamison, W., 260
Janoff-Bulman, R., 398
Jansen, E. A., 306
Janssens, J. M. A. M., 467
Janus, A., 428
Jardine, R., 78
Jasiobedzka, U., 359
Jelalian, E., 422, 471
Jenkins, E. A., 31
Jenkins, J. M., 122, 178, 312, 372, 382, 390, 400
Jennings, D., 472
Jennings, K. D., 208
Jennings, M., 389
Jensen, A. G., 142
Jensen, H., 183
Jensen, L., 279
Ji, G., 392
Jiao, Z., 480
Jicquez, F., 185
Jin, S., 315, 385, 467
Jing, Q., 392
Jodl, K. M., 155, 236, 375
John, R. S., 389
Johnson, C. A., 122
Johnson, D. J., 189, 194
Johnson, D. L., 226
Johnson, D. R., 304
Johnson, D. W., 92

Johnson, J. D., 417, 421
Johnson, M. H., 264
Johnson, N., 414
Johnson, R. T., 92
Johnson, W., 104
Johnston, K., 266
Johnston, K. J., 261
Jones, D. C., 121, 123, 255, 391, 479
Jones, D. P., 245
Jones, J., 279
Jones, M. C., 471, 472
Jones, N. A., 128
Jones, R. A., 3
Jones, S., 335, 465
Jones, S. M., 321
Jones, S. S., 56
Jordan, K., 469
Jordyn, M., 192
Jose, P. M., 347
Joseph, G., 394
Joshi, H., 228, 229
Jouriles, E. N., 372, 395
Joy, M. E., 360, 361, 366
Judy, B., 358
Juffer, F., 128, 129, 135, 150, 155, 161, 297, 298, 302, 304, 393, 457, 466, 498
Jung, P. C., 113
Jussim, L., 249, 443
Juvonen, J., 197, 300

Kaczala, C. M., 248
Kagan, J., 13, 29, 108, 109, 110, 127, 128, 150, 162
Kagan, S., 224, 444
Kahana, E., 358
Kahlenberg, S., 266
Kahn, J., 396
Kahn, P. H. Jr., 326
Kahn, V., 128
Kail, R. V., 414
Kaitiala-Heino, R., 472
Kaitz, M., 47, 56
Kalakanis, L., 471
Kalil, A., 281, 402
Kalish, C. W., 348
Kamerman, S. B., 164, 165
Kamins, M. L., 222
Kandel, D., 488
Kane, T. J., 404
Kanfer, F. H., 479
Kann, L., 320
Kanungo, R. N., 422
Kanwisher, N., 178
Kapiro, J., 472
Kaplan, D. W., 280
Kaplan, P. S., 113
Karoly, L. A., 231
Kass, N. E., 280
Kasser, T., 43
Kastelic, D., 184
Kastens, C., 210
Katcher, A., 264

Katkovsky, W., 210
Kato, N., 392
Katz, L. F., 312
Katz, P. A., 253, 255, 274, 275, 414, 421, 422
Katz, S., 278
Kaufman, C. E., 194
Kaufman, P., 320
Kavanaugh, K., 375
Kawai, E., 316
Kazdin, A. E., 317, 320, 477, 478
Kean, A. W. G., 7
Keane, S. P., 124, 245, 296, 319, 474, 477
Kearsley, R. B., 108, 162
Keasey, C. B., 347, 354
Keating, D., 201
Keefe, K., 484
Keefe, N., 403
Keefer, C. H., 20, 119, 260
Keenan, K., 297, 302, 304, 305
Keenan, T., 59, 121, 177
Keith, B., 397
Keith, J., 9
Keljo, K., 355–356
Keller, H., 105, 137, 142, 183
Keller, M., 302
Keller, T. E., 281
Kelley, H. H., 94, 95
Kelley, M. L., 381, 385
Kelly, J., 396, 397, 398
Kelly, J. B., 397
Kelly, M., 279
Kelly, S. A., 234
Kendall-Tackett, K. A., 407, 408
Kendrick, C., 388, 389
Kennedy, C. A., 472
Kennell, J. H., 135
Kenney-Benson, G. A., 243, 249
Kenyon, B., 250
Kermoian, R., 21, 104
Kerns, K. A., 88, 483
Kerr, M., 128, 130–131, 388, 463, 472
Kerwin, C., 194
Kessen, W., 160
Kett, J. F., 9
Kettenauer, T., 349, 355
Kiang, L., 193
Kiel, E. J., 120, 128
Kiernan, K. E., 397
Kiesewetter, J., 418
Kiesner, J., 475
Kikis, E., 480
Kilburn, M. R., 231
Kilgore, K., 378
Killen, J. D., 473
Killen, M., 253, 349
Kilmer, S. L., 387
Kim, J., 194, 266, 389, 390, 391, 392, 407
Kim, J. M., 349
Kim, K. J., 317
Kim, S., 299, 301, 349, 382, 391

Kim, Y. K., 460, 461
Kim-Cohen, J., 307
Kimmerly, N. L., 153
Kimura, S., 448
Kinchen, S. A., 320
Kindermann, T. A., 227, 457, 462
King, P. E., 371
King, R. A., 331, 334, 335, 340, 364
King, V., 256
Kinney, D., 462
Kipke, M. D., 384
Kipnis, D. M., 424
Kipp, K., 422n.1
Kiraly, I., 48
Kirby, D., 282
Kirchner, J., 393
Kirsh, S. J., 431
Kisker, E. E., 231
Kistner, J., 407, 476
Kistner, J. A., 18, 220, 221
Kitamura, S., 448
Kitayama, S., 182, 189
Kitzmann, K. M., 372
Kivlahan, C., 191, 403
Klaus, M. H., 135
Klayman, J., 117
Klebanov, P., 235
Klebanov, P. K., 225, 229
Klein, J. D., 280, 430
Klein, M. H., 89, 165, 306
Klein, P. S., 344
Klein, R. E., 141
Klepec, L., 88, 483
Kliewer, W., 310
Klimes-Dougan, B., 407
Kling, K. C., 245
Klinnert, M. D., 113, 128
Knafo, A., 326–327
Knickmeyer, R. C., 261
Knight, G. P, 193, 194
Ko, H., 448
Kobak, R. R., 466
Kochanska, G., 121, 131, 151, 152, 154,
    245, 298, 314, 315, 339, 342, 344, 358,
    360, 361, 364, 365, 366, 376, 379, 380,
    465, 497
Kochenderfer, B. J., 480, 484
Kochenderfer-Ladd, B., 299, 300, 301
Koenig, A. L., 358, 366
Koestner, R., 210
Koga, S. F., 159
Kogos, J., 383
Kogushi, Y., 178
Kohen, D. E., 230, 382
Kohlberg, L., 64, 266–268, 270, 329,
    350–359, 354
Kohn, M. L., 382
Kohn-Wood, L., 193
Kokko, K., 302
Kokotovic, A., 409
Kolarz, C., 112
Koller, O., 210

Koller, S., 332, 334
Konarski, R., 462, 482, 484
Kondo-Ikemura, K., 145
Konijn, E. A., 431
Koot, H. M., 297, 298, 301, 302,
    304, 307
Kopp, C., 174
Korbin, J. E., 406
Koren-Karie, N., 147, 155
Korn, W. S., 278
Koss, M. P., 407
Kostelny, K., 406
Kotchick, B. A., 281
Kotelchuck, M., 141
Kotler, J., 427
Kotler, J. A., 424
Kovacs, D. M., 253, 254, 476
Kowal, A., 390
Kowal, A. K., 390
Kowalski, H. S., 453
Kraemer, H. C., 473
Krahn, H. J., 185, 186
Kramer, L., 390
Kraut, R. E., 431
Krebs, D. L., 358
Krehbiel, G., 478
Krekwich, K., 159
Kreppner, J., 160, 161
Kreppner, J. M., 160, 161
Kreutzer, T., 158
Kreye, M., 109
Krile, D., 470
Krishnamoorthy, J. S., 422, 471
Krispin, O., 408
Kroger, J., 190, 191, 192
Krohn, M. D., 316, 317
Krueger, J. I., 186
Kruger, L. M., 278
Kruger, R. F., 80
Krull, J. L., 390
Krupa, M. H., 260
Ku, H., 302, 306
Kucera, E., 388
Kuchuk, A., 113
Kuczynski, L., 19, 48, 148, 363, 365, 380
Kuebli, J., 245
Kuhl, P. K., 113
Kuhn, D., 250, 354
Kuhn, J., 308
Kuk, L. S., 192
Kuklinski, M. R., 443, 444
Kulik, C. C., 437
Kulik, J. A., 437
Kulman, L., 435
Kunkel, D., 422
Kunnen, E. S., 192, 193
Kunz, J., 281
Kuo, Z. Y., 290
Kuperminc, G., 155
Kuperminc, G. P., 155, 282, 387
Kupersmidt, J. B., 50, 225, 228, 407, 408,
    461, 473, 474, 476

Kupfer, K., 131
Kurdek, L. A., 378, 399, 470
Kurtner, J., 183
Kurtz-Costes, B., 236
Kusaka, Y., 392
Kusel, S. J., 299, 300

La Barbera, J. D., 113
La Freniere, P., 253
La Greca, A. M., 462
Ladd, G. W., 124, 300, 301, 311, 315,
    465, 466, 469, 470, 474, 475, 476, 477,
    480, 484
LaFontana, K. M., 23, 295, 300, 468, 475
Lagace-Sequin, D. G., 459, 460, 461
Lagattuta, K. H., 115, 116, 117, 120, 348
Lahey, B. B., 316
Lai, B. Y. P., 387
Laible, D., 115, 118, 342, 344, 364
Laird, M., 378, 407
Laird, R. D., 310, 379, 465, 469
Lalonde, C. E., 192
Lam, M., 485
Lam, S., 226, 448
Lamb, C., 119
Lamb, M. E., 11, 21, 119, 153, 154, 160,
    162, 163, 164, 256, 372, 398, 401,
    402, 408
Lambert, W. W., 130–131
Lamborn, S. D., 188, 235, 379, 487
Lamon, S. J., 243
Lampman-Petraitis, C., 112
Land, D. J., 387
Landau, K. R., 173
Landers, K., 266
Landry, A. M., 173
Landry, S. H., 466
Langer, J., 354
Langlois, J. H., 142, 470, 471
Lansford, J. E., 230, 317, 386, 478
Lanza, S., 185, 219, 248, 249
Laosa, L. M., 381, 386, 497
Lapp, A. L., 481, 482
Lapsley, D. K., 64, 347, 348
Larose, M., 157
Larose, S., 155, 157
Larson, A., 471
Larson, M. C., 143
Larson, N. C., 281
Larson, R., 185, 427
Larson, R. W., 16, 112, 371, 414, 448
Larsson, A., 261
Larsson, I., 275
LaRue, A. A., 253, 254
Latendresse, S. J., 385
Lau, A., 348
Lau, S., 475
Laumann, E. O., 278
Laumann-Billings, L., 399, 404, 405,
    406, 409
Lauretti, A., 372
Laursen, B., 112, 386, 462, 480, 481

Maccoby, E. E., 240, 243, 246, 247, 251–252, 253, 254, 265, 273, 303–304, 376, 377, 378, 380, 381, 398, 399, 457, 487, 488
MacFarlane, A., 240
MacGuire, M. C., 402
Mack, W., 81
MacKenzie, E. P., 321
MacKinnon-Lewis, C., 319, 376, 465, 474
MacLeod, D., 437
MacPhee, D., 373, 384
Madden, P. A., 397
Madden, T., 485
Maddock, A., 280
Madigan, S., 148, 149
Maehr, M. L., 208
Maes, H., 308
Maggs, J. L., 403
Magill, L. H., 244
Magnusson, D., 463, 472, 473
Magnusson, K., 231, 235, 435
Maguire, M., 121
Mahapatra, M., 356, 357
Mahler, M. S., 170
Mahoney, A., 372
Mahoney, J. L., 236, 403, 437, 463, 472
Mahoney, K. M., 278
Main, M., 64, 145, 148, 153, 154, 155, 157, 407
Main, S. R., 437
Makai, T., 280
Malamuth, N. M., 417, 421
Malanchuk, O., 236
Malatesta, C. Z., 105, 119, 120
Malcuit, G., 240
Malecki, C. K., 300
Malley-Morrison, K., 409
Mallick, S. K., 318
Malone, M. J., 480
Malone, P. S., 88, 230, 442
Mandell, D. J., 131
Mandler, J. M., 94
Mangelsdorf, S. C., 109, 119–120
Manke, B. A., 252
Manke, G., 389
Manly, J. T., 204
Mannarino, A. P., 408
Manset, G., 445
Maranda, J., 157
Marcia, J. E., 190, 191
Marcoen, A., 154, 181, 182
Marcon, R. A., 435
Marcovitch, S., 159
Margand, N. A., 88, 153
Margolin, G., 389, 407, 408
Markiewicz, D., 154, 372, 483
Markman, E. M., 48
Markman, H. J., 149
Markovits, H., 61
Markstrom, C. A., 191
Markstrom-Adams, C., 174, 192, 193, 194
Markus, H., 182

Markus, H. R., 189
Marold, D. B., 180
Marquis, J., 414, 415, 427, 431
Marsh, H. W., 182, 183, 185
Marsh, P., 155, 387, 466, 485, 487
Marshall, N. L., 403
Marshall, T. R., 128
Marsiglio, W., 398
Martin, C., 256, 268, 269, 305, 436
Martin, C. L., 246, 247, 251, 253, 254, 255, 265, 266, 268, 269, 454, 495
Martin, G. B., 73
Martin, J., 308
Martin, J. A., 376, 377, 378, 472
Martin, J. M., 185, 248
Martin, N. G., 78, 277, 397
Martinez, C. M. Jr., 230
Martinez, C. N., 266
Marttunen, M., 472
Marvin, R. S., 160, 391
Marx, F., 403
Marzolf, D., 119–120
Maschman, T., 185
Masciadrelli, B. P., 153, 154
Mascolo, M. F., 356
Masden, A. S., 185
Masden, M. C., 224
Mashraki-Pedhatzur, S., 252
Mason, B., 266
Mason, C. A., 142, 310, 315, 316, 365, 386, 484
Mason, M. G., 355
Massolos, G., 453
Masterpasqua, F., 394
Masters, J. C., 266
Masyn, K. E., 317
Matas, L., 109
Matejcek, Z., 149
Matheson, C. C., 29, 58, 458, 460, 464, 479
Matheson, L., 287
Matias, R., 105
Matillo, G. M., 418
Maton, K. I., 373
Matos, L., 210, 223
Matsumoto, D., 193
Matteson, D., 191
Matthews, K. A., 78
Mattsson, A., 304
Maughan, A., 122, 124, 407
Maughan, B., 160, 161, 304, 435, 436
Maxwell, K. L., 435, 436
Maxwell, S. E., 185
May, M. S., 360
Mayer-Smith, J., 431
Mayeux, L., 295, 473, 475
Maynard, A. E., 391
May-Plumlee, T., 335, 339
Mayr, R., 112
Mazzie, C., 113
Mbwarn, J., 279
McAdoo, H., 88, 442

McAdoo, H. P., 226, 228, 230, 233, 234
McBride-Chang, C., 387
McCabe, M., 188, 378
McCabe, M. P., 255
McCall, R. B., 25, 230, 475, 494
McCandless, B. R., 318
McCarthy, K. A., 440
McCartney, K., 82, 83, 84, 85, 162, 164, 308, 403, 449, 464
McCarton, C., 229
McClay, J., 308
McClearn, G. E., 75, 81, 82, 84
McClelland, D. C., 209, 210, 213, 234
McClintic, S., 94, 110, 111, 211, 342
McClintock, M., 275
McCloskey, L. A., 407
McConaghy, M., 60
McCord, J., 317, 478, 487
McCormick, M. C., 229
McCormick, S. E., 115
McDonald, R., 395
McDonnell, P., 331
McDougall, W., 341
McDuff, P., 477
McElhaney, K. B., 155, 387, 466, 485, 487
McElwain, N. L., 389
McFadyen-Ketchum, S. A., 313, 317
McFarland, C., 155, 387, 466, 485, 487
McGeorge, P., 196
McGhee, P. E., 234, 266
McGrath, E. P., 235
McGree, R., 112
McGue, M., 77, 80, 83, 386
McGue, M. K., 393
McGuffin, P., 75, 81, 82, 84
McGuire, K. D., 470
McGuire, S., 389
McHale, J. P., 372
McHale, S., 304
McHale, S. M., 194, 249, 252, 253, 255, 265, 266, 386, 389, 390, 391, 392, 401, 402, 415
McKay, T., 468, 475
McKenna, M. A. J., 278, 279
McKenna, M. W., 416, 418
McKinley, M., 468, 473
McKnight, K., 50
McKown, C., 229, 444
McLaughlin, A. E., 231
McLean, K. C., 188
McLellan, J. A., 340, 452
McLoyd, V., 373, 381
McLoyd, V. C., 229, 381, 384
McManis, M. H., 128
McNalley, S., 334
McNeilly-Choque, M. K., 467
McPartland, J., 217
McShane, K., 326
McWilliams, L., 438
Mead, G. H., 169, 204
Mead, M., 33, 263
Meade, C. S., 279

Measelle, J. R., 183
Meckler, L., 374
Medeiros, B. L., 154, 402
Mednick, S., 81
Medrich, E. A., 464
Meehan, B. T., 439, 444
Meeus, W., 191
Mehan, H., 437
Meilman, P. W., 190
Meins, E., 178
Mekos, D., 400
Melnick, S., 467, 473
Melson, G. F., 245
Meltzoff, A. N., 47, 48, 56, 114, 170, 177
Menon, M., 188
Mergendoller, J. R., 439
Merkler, K., 393
Mermelstein, R., 16, 112, 186
Merrick, S., 155, 157
Meschulach-Safaty, O., 47, 56
Mesman, J., 297, 298, 302, 304
Messe, D. W., 403
Messinger, D. S., 106, 142, 148
Metz, E., 331
Meyer-Bahlberg, H. F. L., 277
Meyers, M., 435
Meyers, T., 107, 148
Miceli, P. J., 280, 281, 334
Michael, A., 236
Michael, R. T., 278
Michaelieu, Q., 185, 188
Michaels, S., 278
Michalson, L., 115
Michealieu, Q., 115, 245
Middleton, K. A., 405
Midgley, C., 439, 440
Midlarsky, E., 339, 358
Mikach, S., 277, 394
Milbern, S., 435
Miles, C. J., 395
Mill, J., 308
Miller, A. K., 320
Miller, A. L., 389
Miller, A. T., 219
Miller, B. C., 280, 393
Miller, C. L., 250, 280, 281, 334
Miller, D. B., 320
Miller, J. G., 356, 357
Miller, K. S., 276, 281
Miller, M., 309
Miller, N. B., 378
Miller, N. E., 290
Miller, P., 335
Miller, P. A., 280, 334, 335
Miller, P. H., 9, 94, 176
Miller, S. A., 176
Miller, T. E., 471
Miller, T. L., 281
Miller-Heyl, J., 373, 384
Miller-Johnson, S., 231, 302, 435
Miller-Loncar, C. L., 466
Milligan, K., 178

Mills, R. S. L., 339
Milne, A., 196
Milstead, M., 64
Miltenberger, R. G., 46
Minor, C. A., 213
Mistry, J., 93, 460
Mitchell, C., 439
Mitchell, C. M., 194
Mitchell, J., 155
Mitchell, J. E., 260
Mitchell, K., 432
Mitchell, P., 178
Miyake, K., 105, 146, 147
Miyazaki, M., 173
Mize, J., 465, 466, 467, 477
Mizuta, I., 297
Moffitt, T. E., 29, 81, 84, 112, 128, 186, 302, 303, 307, 308, 311, 316–317, 380, 396, 402, 405, 408, 472
Moise-Titus, J., 419, 420, 421, 424
Molitor, N., 164
Moll, H., 176
Moneta, G., 16, 112, 371
Money, J., 259, 261, 262, 277
Monsour, A., 180
Montemayor, R., 179, 180
Montgomery, S. B., 384
Mood, A. M., 217
Mooijart, A., 128, 129, 135, 155, 393, 457, 466, 498
Mooney-Somers, J., 277, 394
Moore, B., 331, 335
Moore, C., 155
Moore, C. W., 387
Moore, E. G. J., 226
Moore, G. A., 136
Moore, L. P., 363
Moore, M. K., 47, 56
Moore, M. R., 281
Moran, B. L., 188, 481
Moran, G., 148, 149, 157
Morelli, G., 146
Morelli, G. A., 160
Morgan, E. M., 277
Morgan, G. A., 108
Morgan, J., 307
Morgan, R., 171
Morgan-Thompson, E., 277
Moriatry, V., 436
Morris, A. S., 311
Morris, J. E., 242
Morris, J. T., 266
Morris, P. A., 87, 149, 371, 373, 457, 495
Morris, R., 304
Morris, S. J., 479
Morrison, F. J., 434
Morrison, M. M., 272
Morrongiello, B. A., 244
Morrow, C., 479
Mortimore, P., 435
Mory, M. S., 462
Moses, L. J., 114, 176

Mosher, M., 244, 306
Mosher, W. D., 279
Moshman, D., 358
Mosier, C., 93, 460
Mosley, J. E., 122
Moss, E., 155, 157, 232
Moss, H. A., 29
Mostow, A. J., 124
Moulson, M. C., 21, 113
Mounts, N., 487
Mounts, N. S., 188, 235, 379
Mowrer, O. H., 290
Mrazek, D. A., 128
Mroczek, D., 112
Mueller, C. M., 222
Mueller, E., 457
Mueller, E. C., 457
Muir, D. W., 106, 138
Mulvey, L., 230
Mumme, D. L., 103, 104, 106, 113, 114, 115
Munro, G., 192
Munroe, R. H., 267
Munroe, R. L., 267
Murnen, S. K., 266
Murphy, B. C., 122, 124, 334, 335, 336, 470
Murphy, C. M., 317
Murphy, K. C., 427
Murphy, R. R., 299
Murray, B., 428
Murray, C., 277, 394
Murray, E., 254
Murray, H., 212
Murray, J. P., 414, 421, 422, 423
Murray, K. T., 131, 298, 339, 342, 344, 360, 361, 364
Murray, L., 149
Murry, V. B., 299, 301, 316, 391
Murry, V. M., 382, 391, 472, 473
Musser, L. M., 464
Must, A., 423
Muyeed, A. Z., 439
Muzzatti, B., 229
Myers, D. G., 336

Nagel, S. K., 88, 383, 402
Nagin, D. S., 298, 299, 301–302, 302, 303, 314, 317, 487
Naito, M., 178
Najman, J. M., 303, 311, 314
Nakagawa, K., 226
Nakamoto, J., 468, 475
Nansel, T. R., 299, 300, 301
Narvaez, D., 354, 358
Nash, A., 457
Nash, S. C., 250
Nastasi, B. K., 428, 429
Neale, M. C., 277
Neckerman, H. J., 302
Nederend, S., 253, 255
Neebe, E., 162, 163, 164
Needle, R. H., 397

Pellegrini, A. D., 58, 70, 71, 244, 295
Pellegrini, D. S., 202
Pempek, T. A., 415
Peng, Y., 291, 305, 318
Penza, S., 407
Pepler, D. J., 389, 390
Perilloux, H. K., 173
Perkins, A., 179
Perkins, S. A., 349
Perlman, M., 297
Perloff, R., 215, 225, 229
Perner, J., 177, 178
Perozynski, L. A., 390
Perry, B., 277, 394
Perry, D. G., 188, 250, 273, 277, 292, 299,
    300, 301, 305, 362, 480
Perry, L. C., 292, 299, 300, 305, 362
Perry-Jenkins, M., 402
Persson, A., 463, 472
Perusse, D., 293, 297, 302, 304, 305, 307
Peskin, J., 121
Peter, J., 430, 432
Petersen, A. C., 244, 252, 253, 472
Peterson, C., 234
Peterson, C. C., 178, 348
Peterson, K., 423
Peterson, L., 191, 325, 403
Peterson, R. E., 262
Petrakos, H., 389, 392
Petrosino, A., 317
Petrovich, S. B., 140
Pettit, G. S., 129, 230, 280, 294, 300, 309,
    310, 313, 317, 379, 386, 397, 403, 465,
    466, 467, 469, 473, 474, 477, 478, 480,
    481, 482
Petty, R. E., 228
Pezaris, E., 243
Pfeifer, J. H., 196, 197
Pfeifer, M., 128
Phelps, J. L., 157
Philipsen, L. C., 464
Philliber, S., 282
Phillips, A. T., 176
Phillips, D., 215, 220, 434
Phinney, J. S., 193, 485
Phoenix, C. H., 304
Piaget, J., 17, 18, 48, 51–65, 59, 61, 68, 200,
    202, 296, 329, 345, 348, 461
Pianta, R. C., 438
Pick, A. D., 113
Pick, S., 282
Pidada, S., 306
Pidada, S. U., 124
Piehler, T. F., 484
Piemyat, S., 416
Pierce, K. M., 404
Pike, A., 80, 457
Pike, R., 183
Pilla, R. S., 299, 301
Pillard, R. C., 76, 277
Pinderhughes, E. E., 225, 313
Pine, F., 170

Pinon, M., 427
Pipp, S., 154, 173
Pisacane, K., 253
Pisani, L., 148
Pittinsky, T. L., 229
Pitts, L., 301
Pitts, M., 279
Pitts, R. C., 357, 358
Plant, E. A., 246
Plata, S. J., 20
Pleck, J. H., 153, 154
Plemons, B. W., 230
Plomin, R., 75, 76, 77, 78, 79, 80, 81, 82, 84,
    86, 127, 260, 326–327, 457
Plumert, J. M., 299
Plunkett, S. W., 193
Podolski, C., 419, 420, 421, 424
Poehlmann, J., 148
Polak, A., 121
Polikoff, M. S., 437, 449
Polit, D. F., 392
Pollack, C. B., 149
Polo-Thomas, M., 84, 307, 311, 380, 405
Pomerantz, E. M., 188, 219, 226, 236, 237,
    241, 243, 248, 249, 379, 381, 448
Pomerleau, A., 240
Ponirakis, A., 472
Ponterotto, J. G., 194
Ponton, L., 278
Poortinga, Y. H., 224, 282
Popenoe, D., 374
Popp, D., 278
Popp, T., 131
Porter, A. C., 437, 449
Porter, C. L., 244, 467
Porter, M., 155, 387, 466, 487
Porter, M. R., 485
Portes, A., 437
Posada, G., 20, 145, 147
Posner, J. K., 403
Poteat, V. P., 277
Pott, M., 146, 147
Potter, J., 185, 186, 245
Potts, R., 358
Poulin, F., 292, 295, 316, 317, 463, 478, 482,
    483, 487
Poulin, R., 465
Poulin-Dubois, D., 250
Poulton, R., 186
Pouquette, C., 372
Povinelli, D. J., 173, 174
Powell, D., 89
Powell, K. E., 320
Powell, N., 444
Power, T. G., 20–21, 121, 381, 385
Powers, J., 402
Powlishta, K. K., 64, 251, 253, 254, 269
Prentice, D. A., 242
Presnell, K., 472
Presson, C. C., 488
Preston, A. A., 210
Price, J., 456, 474

Price, J. M., 474
Price, T. S., 84, 311, 380, 405
Priel, B., 172
Prinstein, M. J., 279, 462, 485
Provence, S., 158
Provost, M. A., 157
Pulkkinen, L., 302
Pungello, E. P., 231, 435
Putallaz, M., 50, 461, 474
Putnam, P. H., 105, 107
Putnam, S., 127
Putnam, S. P., 119

Quas, J. A., 120
Queenan, P., 123, 124, 465
Quiggle, N. L., 293
Quinn, R. A., 341
Quinsey, V. L., 304
Quintana, S. M., 64

Rabiner, D., 465
Rabiner, D. L., 298, 319, 474
Raboy, B., 394
Racine, Y., 390
Radice, C., 393
Radke-Yarrow, M., 48, 148, 330, 331, 334,
    335, 340, 364
Raffaelli, M., 410, 487, 488
Raggatt, P., 261
Rahman, Q., 279
Raikes, H., 231
Rainey, B., 409
Ram, A., 389, 390
Ramanan, J., 401
Ramani, G. B., 174, 458
Ramey, C. T., 161, 162, 230, 231, 435
Ramey, S. L., 162, 230
Ramsay, D., 107, 110, 135, 172, 173,
    174, 212
Ramsden, S. R., 293, 295
Ramsey, E., 315
Randolph, S. M., 194
Rantanen, P., 472
Rasbash, J., 122, 312, 372, 382, 400
Raskauskas, J., 301, 432
Rauch, S. L., 128
Raver, C. C., 226, 229, 381, 382
Raviv, A., 331
Rayias, M. F., 105, 107
Raynor, J. O., 215
Raynor, R., 45
Raz, S., 244
Razza, R. P., 131
Ream, G. L., 277
Recchia, S., 94, 110, 111, 211, 342
Reddel, M., 240
Redler, E., 336
Reese, E., 173
Reese-Weber, M., 389
Reid, J. B., 312, 313, 378
Reinisch, J. M., 279
Reiser, M., 124, 131, 296, 298, 311, 335

Strayer, F. F., 253, 290
Strayer, J., 335
Striano, T., 171, 172
Stricker, J. M., 46
Stright, A. D., 272
Strough, J., 245
Strouse, D., 452
Stukas, A. A., 332
Stumpf, H., 243
Sturge-Apple, M. L., 311–312, 312
Sturla, E., 262
Subaiya, L., 396
Subrahmanyam, K., 276, 278, 430, 431
Suchindran, C., 278
Suddendorf, T., 173
Suess, G., 146, 155
Sugden, K., 408
Sullivan, H. S., 43, 452, 481
Sullivan, M. W., 105, 106, 107, 110, 121, 171,
    212, 290, 342
Sun, Y., 130, 373, 381, 475
Suomi, S. J., 454, 456
Super, C. M., 355, 356
Supple, A. J., 193
Susman, E. J., 424, 472
Sussman, A. L., 165
Sutton, H. M., 204
Suzuki, L. K., 276, 430
Svedin, C., 275
Svetina, M., 31
Swank, P. R., 466
Swanson, D. P., 194
Swarr, A., 185
Sweeney, K., 9
Swenson, L. P., 188, 193, 481
Szkrybalo, J., 250, 267

Tabkin, G., 427
Taipale, V., 472
Takahashi, K., 146
Takahira, S., 243
Takanishi, R., 226
Talbut, J., 372
Talwar, V., 177
Tamang, B. L., 122, 123
Tamis-LeMonda, C. S., 154, 164, 401, 402
Tangney, J. P., 111
Tango, T., 392
Tani, F., 481
Tanner, J. M., 23, 187
Tarabulsy, G. M., 155, 157
Tardif, C., 155, 466
Tarullo, L. B., 231
Taska, L., 407
Tasker, F., 394
Tate, J. D., 193
Taylor, A., 84, 307, 311, 380, 402,
    405, 408
Taylor, A. R., 445
Taylor, C., 177

Taylor, C. B., 473
Taylor, D. G., 148
Taylor, J. H., 349
Taylor, K., 261
Taylor, K. W., 310
Taylor, L. J., 268
Taylor, M., 177
Taylor, M. E., 397, 398
Taylor, M. G., 252, 253, 257
Taylor, R. D., 373
Teeven. R. C., 234
Teichman, Y., 196, 197
Tellegen, A., 83, 185
Tennenbaum, H. R., 245, 247, 249, 255,
    256, 275
Terry, R., 299, 468
Tesman, J. R., 120
Tessier, R., 157
Teti, D. M., 148, 157, 388, 391
Tevendale, H. D., 188, 193, 481
Tharp, R. G., 439
Theall, L. A., 173
Thelan, M. H., 245
Thelen, E., 290, 453
Thoma, S. J., 354, 355, 358, 359
Thomas, A., 129, 130, 150
Thomas, A. M., 396
Thomas, C. L., 282
Thomas, M. H., 420
Thompson, M., 296, 298
Thompson, R., 118, 342, 344, 364
Thompson, R. A., 120, 121, 157, 171, 395
Thompson, S. K., 250
Thompson, T., 244
Thornberry, T. P., 316, 317
Thorne, A., 185, 188
Thorne, B., 275, 276
Thurber, C. A., 108
Thurlow, R., 416
Tiggemann, M., 421
Tinbergen, N., 69
Tingle, B. A., 335
Tinsley, B. J., 422, 423
Tisak, J., 349
Tisak, M. S., 349
Tjebkes, T. L., 342
Tobin, D. D., 188
Tobin, K., 316
Toch, H., 292–293
Todd, M., 488
Tolan, P. H., 292, 309, 310, 316
Tolson, J. M., 462
Tomada, G., 306, 481
Tomasello, M., 48, 94, 171, 174, 176, 178
Tomlin, C., 173
Tomlinson-Keasey, C., 354
Toner, I. J., 358, 363
Topitzes, J. W., 231
Toth, S. L., 404, 405, 406, 407, 408
Townsend, M. A. R., 333
Towsley, S., 128
Trabasso, T., 389

Tracey, J. L., 185, 186, 245
Tracy, J. L., 463
Tram, J. M., 185
Tran, H., 162
Trautwein, U., 210
Treas, J., 276
Treboux, D., 155, 157
Tremblay, R. E., 286, 297, 299, 301–302, 302,
    303, 304, 305, 317, 477, 487
Trentacosta, J., 124
Treyer, V., 292
Triandis, H. C., 182, 209, 224, 308, 337
Tronick, E., 107
Tronick, E. Z., 114, 119, 136, 160
Troop-Gordon, W., 300, 301, 474
Troseth, G. L., 415, 427
Troyer, L., 235, 378
True, M. M., 148
Truglio, R., 416, 426, 427
Tryon, R. C., 74
Trzesniewski, K. H., 185, 186, 219, 222,
    237, 245
Tsay, J. C., 487, 488
Tschann, J. M., 280
Tseng, V., 183, 225, 227, 485
Tucker, C., 252, 415
Tucker, C. J., 265, 390
Tucker, P., 262
Tuckey, M., 178
Tudge, J. R. H., 92, 93
Tulkin, S., 110
Tully, L., 307
Tulviste, P., 90, 92
Turiel, E., 348, 349, 355, 356, 357, 359
Turkheimer, E., 397
Turley, R. N. L., 281
Turner, A. J., 394
Turner, C. W., 291
Turner, P. J., 254, 266
Turner, T. R., 266
Turner-Bowker, D. M., 266
Turpin-Petrosino, C., 317
Turrell, S. L., 178
Twenge, J. M., 112, 189, 242
Tynes, B., 276, 431
Tyson, P., 43
Tyson, R. L., 43

Uba, L., 384
Ude, W., 410
Udry, J. A., 278
Udry, J. R., 112
Ullman, J. B., 469, 470, 477
Umana-Taylor, A., 189
Underwood, B., 331, 335
Underwood, M. K., 122, 253, 302, 306
Unger, J. B., 384
Ungerer, J. A., 163, 164
Unzner, L., 146
Updegraff, K., 249, 401
Updegraff, K. A., 252, 255, 390
Urban, J., 253, 476

Subject Index

Aggression (*continued*)
 biological influences on, 307–308
 as child abuse effect, 407
 cultural influences on, 308–310
 day care and, 162
 definition of, 285–287
 developmental trends in, 296–303
 family influence on, 310–318
 gender differences in, 244
 methods of controlling, 318–321
 observational learning and, 47
 in operant learning theory, 45
 parenting style and, 377
 parents' desired moral principles and, 324
 self-esteem and, 188
 sex differences in, 303–307
 siblings and, 392
 stability of, 302–303
 temperaments and, 296, 311, 314
 theories of, 287–296
 TV viewing and, 24–25, 26, 416–421, 424
 video games and, 431
Aggressive cues hypothesis, 291
Aggressive models, 417
Aggressive-rejected children, 473–475
AIDS, 280
Alcoholism
 attachment and, 148
 child abuse and, 405
 of gang members, 316
 hereditary contributions to, 81
 sibling support and, 391
 television advertising and, 422
Altruism
 cognitive and affective contributors to, 332–337
 cultural differences in, 337–341, 355–356
 definition of, 72, 325
 developmental trends in, 329–332
 discipline strategies to promote, 339, 343–344, 363–367
 in ethology, 72
 origins of, 330–331
 parents' desire for, 324
 as part of human nature, 73
 psychoanalytic theories of, 326, 327, 342–345
 sex differences in, 332
 television viewing and, 424–425
Altruistic exhortations, 339
American children. *See also* specific
 minority groups
 achievement in, 224
 altruism in, 337*t*
 school success of, 446–449
 self-concept in, 182–183
 sexuality of, 276
American parenting, 146
American Psychiatric Association, 159, 277
Anal stage, of psychosexual development, 40, 42
Androgen, 258, 260–261, 275
Androgenized females, 261
Androgyny, 271–275

Anger
 aggression theories and, 290–291
 attachment and, 148
 cathartic expression of, 318
 development of emotional understanding and, 114
 divorce and, 397
 emotional display rules for, 121–122
 gender differences in, 245
 in infants' emotional displays, 107
 peer rejection and, 474
 in preschoolers, 298
Animal aggression, 289
Anorexia, 421–422
Anti-bias/social-cognitive programs, 197
Antisocial behavior. *See* Aggression;
 Behavior, inappropriate
Antisocial peer groups, 227, 379
Anxiety, 40, 107–110
Approval of others, 210, 211
Approval seeking phase, of achievement, 211
Approval-oriented level, of prosocial moral reasoning, 333*t*
Aptitude-treatment interaction (ATI), 439
AQS (Attachment Q-set), 145
Arapesh tribe, 33
Arctic Eskimo people, 224
Armed robbery, 309
Asian cultures
 achievement motivation and, 225, 226, 443
 parental involvement in, 448
 parenting styles in, 384, 387
 self-concept in, 182–183
 self-esteem in, 189
 teachers' expectations of students from, 444
Asian orphans, 161
Asocial phase, of attachment, 138
Assimilation, 53
Associated Press, 278, 383, 393, 431
Associative play, 459
ATI (aptitude-treatment interaction), 439
Attachment Q-set (AQS), 145
Attachments
 achievement and, 232
 adolescent autonomy and, 387
 altruism theories and, 343–344
 characteristics of, 135–137
 day care and, 161–163
 definition of, 134, 135
 of deprived children, 158–161
 divorce and, 395
 ethnographic studies of, 20
 fathers and, 152–154
 of hospitalized toddlers, 134
 individual differences in, 143–147
 influences on, 147–152
 interventions to foster, 150
 later development and, 154–158
 measurement of, 144–146
 peer sociability and, 464, 466
 process of, 137–142
 self-concept development and, 173

 self-esteem and, 181–182
 separation anxiety and, 108
 to siblings, 390–391
 theories of, 139–142, 156
 working mothers and, 161–166
Attention span, 126
Attention-getting behavior, 319
Attitudes, sexual, 278–279
Attractiveness, 470–473
Attribution retraining, 221–223
Attributional theory. *See* Social information-processing theory
Australian children, 196
Austrian culture, 276
Authoritarian instruction, 438
Authoritarian parenting style, 377–378, 467
Authoritative instruction, 438
Authoritative parenting style
 achievement motivation and, 235
 adolescent autonomy and, 388
 discipline strategies in, 377–379
 peer sociability and, 466–467
Autism, 178
Autobiographical memories, 173–174
Autonomous morality, 346–347
Autonomy
 adolescents' establishment of, 386–388
 definition of, 386
 parenting style and, 378
 peer-parent cross-pressures and, 487
Autonomy support, 379
Autonomy versus shame and doubt stage, 42
Average status, 468
Avoidant attachment
 child abuse and, 148
 internal working models and, 156
 measurement of, 145
 temperaments and, 150, 151

Babies. *See* Infants
Baby biographies, 7–8, 19, 35
Baby, birth of, 388–389
Baby Boom period, 374
Basic gender identity stage, 267
Basic trust versus mistrust stage, 42, 43
Battered women, 405, 407
Beanpole families, 375
Behavior disorders, 81–82, 308
Behavior, human, 93–95. *See also* *specific behaviors*
Behavior, inappropriate
 attachment and, 154, 157, 162
 of bullies, 299–300
 day care and, 162
 gender differences in, 244
 in latchkey children, 403
 of neglected/rejected children, 469
 parenting style and, 377
 as result of friendships, 484–486
 self-conscious emotions and, 111
 sex differences regarding, 241–242
 uninvolved parenting and, 378

Cognitive development (*continued*)
schooling's effects on, 434
self-concept and, 173, 181
self-recognition and, 173
sociocultural theory and, 90–92
stages of, 53–64
television's contribution to, 425–427
Cognitive disequilibria, 353
Cognitive immaturity, 96
Cognitive interventions, 274, 275
Cognitive operations, 57
Cognitive social learning theory
criticisms of, 50–51
imitation and observational learning
in, 46–49
premise of, 46
reciprocal determinism in, 49–50
Cognitive theories. *See also specific theories*
of altruism/prosocial behavior, 326, 329
of attachment, 140–141
cognitive structures in, 53
criticisms of, 64–65
definition of, 38
developmental stages in, 53–64
of gender typing, 267–268
infants' fears and, 109–110
microgenetic designs and, 31
origin of, 51–52
person perception and, 199–200
schemes in, 52–53
separation anxiety and, 143
worldview behind, 97, 98, 99
Cohort effects, 28, 36
Collaborative learning
benefits of, 92
computers and, 429
criticisms of, 93
cross-ethnic groups for, 229
definition of, 91
in sociocultural theory, 91–92
Collective efficacy, 310, 316, 406
Collectivist societies
achievement in, 208, 209, 224–225
altruism in, 337–338, 356
attachments in, 146
effective schooling in, 439
emotional self-regulation in, 122
gender stereotypes in, 252
identity formation in, 194
inhibited children in, 467
preschool play in, 460
self-concept and, 181, 182–183
self-esteem in, 189
College
altruism theories and, 355
gender stereotypes and, 249
identity formation in, 192
Commercials, television, 422
Committed compliance, 344, 378
Common activities, 202
Common-ground activities, 479
Community ties, 373, 406

Compassion, 453
Compensation, 60
Compensatory interventions, 230–231
Competency appraisals, 182–184, 185
Competent emotional expressivity, 123
Competent emotional knowledge, 123
Competent emotional regulation, 123
Competition
achievement motivation and, 225
and infant and toddler achievement, 212
self-esteem and, 187, 188
Complex emotions, 110–111
Complex stepparent homes, 400
Compliance, 245
Computer-assisted instruction, 428
Computers
in classrooms, 428–429
concerns about, 430–433
families with access to, 428
parenting concerns and, 432
Conceptual perspective taking, 59
Concordance rates, 76
Concrete-operational stage
definition of, 60
description of, 60–61, 66
timing of, 53
Condoms, 280, 281
Conduct Problems Prevention Research
Group, 319
Conflict resolution, 479
Conflicts. *See also specific types*
aggression and, 297
among friends, 203–204
with autonomy-seeking adolescents,
386–388
in coercive home environments, 312–318
definition of, 297
parental monitoring and, 465
between parents, 311–312
prevention programs for, 320–321
between siblings, 204, 388–390
Conformity, peer, 485–486
Confounding variables, 24
Congenital adrenal hyperplasia (CAH),
260–261
Connectiveness, 13
Conservation, 59–60, 199
Consistency schema, 95
Constructivists, 52
Consumerism, 422
Contact comfort, 140
Contextual model, 97
Continuity/discontinuity issue
description of, 12–13
worldviews behind, 98–99
Controlling parents, 192, 235, 376
Controversial children, 468
Conventional morality, 352, 354
Converging evidence, 34
Conversations
about sexuality, 281
to decrease prejudice, 197

to develop emotional understanding,
117–118
emotional self-regulation and, 120
Internet's benefits to, 430
self-concept development and, 173–174
theory of mind and, 177–178
Cooperative learning
to decrease prejudice, 197
special needs children and, 445–446
Cooperative play
description of, 460
preschoolers' peer sociability and, 459
self-recognition and, 174
Coordinated interactions, 458
Coparenting
in blended families, 400
definition of, 372
divorce and, 399
in dual-career families, 402
Correlation coefficients, 23, 36, 76
Correlational designs
benefits and drawbacks of, 27
description of, 22–23, 36
Co-ruminating friends, 483
Creativity, 415
Crime statistics, 308–309
Crime, U.S., 308–309
Criminal behavior
child abuse and, 408
coercive home environments and, 315–318
divorce and, 396
of gangs, 316
gender differences in, 244
of homeless, parentless children, 410
identity crises and, 192
increase in, during adolescence, 301–303
methods of controlling, 318–321
parenting styles and, 378, 379
peer influences on, 485–488
self-esteem and, 186
sexual activity and, 280
Crisis period, 396
Critical period, 70, 261–263
Cross-cultural studies, 32–34, 36
Cross-generational problem, 29
Cross-pressures, 487–488
Cross-sectional designs
benefits of, 32
description of, 27–28, 36
drawbacks of, 28, 32
Cross-sex friendships, 482–483
Cross-sex mannerisms, 252
Crowds, 462
CTW (Children's Television Workshop),
425–426
Cults, 432
Culture
achievement and, 208, 209, 224–226,
442–443
aggression and, 308–310
altruism and, 337–341, 355–356
attachment and, 146–147

Emotional development
    fathers' contribution to, 153–154
    sequencing of, 105–112
    theories of, 103–104
Emotional dialogues, 117–118, 120–121
Emotional display rules, 121–123
Emotional expressivity/sensitivity, 244–245
Emotional self-regulation
    components of, 118–119
    definition of, 118
    development of, 118–122
    effortful control and, 131
    first signs of, 104
    social competence and, 123–125
Emotionally bonded parents, 135
Emotionally unavailable parents, 312
Emotions. *See also specific emotions*
    components of, 102–103
    definition of, 102
    infants' initial display of, 104–105
    theories of, 103–104
Emotions, of others
    identification and interpretation of,
        112–118
    social competence and, 123–125
Empathic orientation level, of prosocial moral
    reasoning, 333*t*
Empathy
    age trends in, 335
    child abuse and, 407
    as contributor to altruism, 334–336
    definition of, 73
    gender differences in, 245
    hereditary contributions to, 78
    origin of, 289
    theories of altruism and, 326, 328
    understanding of others, 117
Employment benefits, 164–165
Emulation, 48
Endomorphs, 471
Engineering degrees, 249
Entity view of ability, 219, 220, 236
Environment
    achievement and, 225, 232–234
    aggression and, 300, 311–318
    altruism theories and, 327, 343–344
    attachment security and, 143–147
    bullying and, 300
    child abuse and, 406
    criticisms of behavioral genetics and,
        85–86
    definition of, 86, 87
    ecological systems theory and, 87–90
    of effective schools, 438, 440
    good parenting as, 85
    heritability's codevelopment with, 82–84
    of high-quality day care, 163
    homosexuality origins and, 277
    IQ scores and, 225
    mathematical calculations to determine,
        76–78
    mental health and, 78–82

nature versus nurture debate in, 11
peer sociability and, 464
personality traits and, 78–82
separation anxiety and, 109, 143
social referencing and, 114
temperament and, 127
in twin studies, 75–77
Environmental determinism, 49–50
Epistemology, 51
Eros, 39
ERP (event-related potential), 21, 113
Essentialist bias, 257
Ethnic identity, 193–194, 229
Ethnographies
    benefits and drawbacks of, 22
    description of, 20–21, 35
Ethology
    aggression and, 288–289
    assumptions of, 69
    attachment and, 141–142, 156
    versus behavioral genetics, 74
    criticisms of, 72–74
    definition of, 68
    description of, 100
    infants and, 69–70
    modern version of, 70–72
    origin of, 68
    peer interaction and, 453
    separation anxiety and, 143
    worldview behind, 97, 98
Evaluative embarrassment, 110
Evaluative reasoning, 197, 198
Event-related potential (ERP), 21, 113
Evocative genotype/environment correlations,
    82, 308
Evolutionary history, 7, 103
Evolutionary theories. *See also specific theories*
    of aggression, 288–290
    of altruism/prosocial behavior, 326–327
    of attachment, 141–142
    versus behavioral genetics, 74
    criticisms of, 72–74
    of gender typing, 257–258
    infant fears and, 109
    modern version of, 70–72
    overview of, 68
    theory of mind and, 177, 178
    worldview behind, 97
Exosystem, 88, 89
Expectancies. *See* Achievement
    expectancies
Experimental control, 25
Experimental designs, 23–27
Expiatory punishments, 346
Explorations in Personality (Murray), 212
Expressive roles, 241, 242
Extended family household, 372–373
Extended self, 173
Extended-year schools, 434
External attributions, 362
External cause, of behavior, 93
External stimuli, 46

Externalizing problems, 383
Extrafamilial influences, 414. *See also
    specific types*
Extrinsic orientation, for achievement,
    210–211
Extroversion, 78

Face recognition, 171
Facial attractiveness, 470–471
Facial expressions
    development of emotional understanding
        and, 113–115
    discrete emotions theory and, 103
    empathy-altruism link and, 335
    infant attachment and, 136
    initial appearance of infant emotions and,
        104–105
Facial features, 141–142
Failure
    blame for, 219
    fear of, 214, 215
    learned helplessness and, 219–223
    locus of control and, 217–218
    persistence in face of, 219–220
    praise guidelines and, 222
False self-behaviors, 180
False-belief tasks, 176–177
Falsifiability, 10, 35
Families. *See also specific types*
    behavioral genetics studies methods with,
        75–77, 100
    changes in makeup of, 374–375
    compensatory interventions for, 230–231
    computer access of, 428
    crises in, 383, 384
    cultural variances in systems of, 372–373
    definition of, 371
    drawbacks of longitudinal studies of, 29
    effects of TV viewing on, 414–415
    gangs as, 316
    homosexuality and, 277
    as influence on achievement motivation,
        232–237
    as influence on aggression, 310–318
    instability in, 383–384
    parent versus child effects model in, 380
    parental leave for, 164–166
    socialization functions of, 370–375
    supportive teachers' effects on, 439
    transactional model in, 380–381
Family conflicts
    adolescents' negative emotions and, 112
    divorce and, 395
    between siblings, 204, 388–389
Family distress model, 382
Family instability, 383
Family and Medical Leave Act (1993),
    164, 165
Family Support Act (1988), 398
Family systems, 314
Fantasy aggression, 416
Fast Track program, 321

Fathers
    attachment and, 139, 152–154
    discounted role of, 152
    divorced, 396, 398
    for donor insemination families,
        393–394
    gender typing of, 256
    as head of single-parent home, 374
    origin of homosexuality and, 277
    remarriage of, 400
    who commit child abuse, 405
    working mothers and, 401–402
Favoritism, of child, 390, 400
Fear
    attachment and, 148, 152
    of failure, 214, 215
    gender differences in, 244
    in infants' emotional development,
        107–110
    moral development and, 366
    self-regulation of, 120
    temperament and, 126, 128
Feeding practices, 139, 140, 142
Felt responsibility hypothesis, 336
Feminine gender-typed people, 271–275
Field experiments, 26, 27, 36
Fighting. *See* Aggression
Finland, 165
Fixation, 40
Folktales, 179
Forbidden toy paradigm, 361
Foreclosure, 190, 192
Formal operations
    altruism theories and, 354
    description of, 61, 66
    person perception and, 199–200
Formal-operational stage
    description of, 61–64, 66
    timing of, 53
Fraternal twins, 78, 83, 151
Free association, 39
Friendships. *See also* Peer groups
    versus acquaintance, 479–480
    adolescents' negative emotions
        and, 112
    advantages of, 480–483
    attachment effects on, 154
    bullying and, 300–301
    conflicts in, 203–204
    definition of, 478
    development of, 478–479
    drawbacks of, 483–484
    gender segregation in, 253–254
    Internet concerns and, 432
    length of, 480
    person perception and, 198, 202,
        203–204
    self-concept and, 179–180, 188
    self-esteem and, 184–185
Frustration/aggression hypothesis, 290–291
Fully committed activists, 340
Functionalist perspective, on emotion, 104

Gangs, 286, 292, 316
Gay and lesbian parents, 394–395
Gazing, 136
Gender bias, 356, 358
Gender consistency stage, 267, 268
Gender differences. *See* Sex differences
Gender identity
    of adrogenized girls, 261
    definition of, 249
    development of, 250, 256t, 267
Gender intensification, 252–253
Gender roles
    androgyny and, 271–275
    biosocial theory and, 259–261
    cross-cultural studies of, 33
    cultural influences on, 241–243
    description of, 241
    evolutionary theory and, 258
    television stereotypes of, 421–422
    theories of, 257–271
Gender schema theory, 268–269
Gender segregation, 253–254, 454
Gender stability stage, 267
Gender stereotypes
    actual differences versus, 243–246
    cultural influences on, 254–257
    current state of, 242
    description of, 246
    development of, 250–253, 256t
    effects of, 247–249
    elimination of, 273–274
    gender segregation and, 254
    neonates and, 240
    studies of, 16, 17
Gender typing
    cultural norms and, 241–242
    definition of, 240
    developmental trends in, 249–257
    homosexuality and, 277
    overview of, 256t
    theories of, 257–271
Gender-role standards, 241–243
Generalizability
    of case studies, 20
    cross-cultural studies and, 33
    definition of, 20
    importance of, 32
Generativity versus stagnation stage, 42
Genetics
    achievement motivation and, 235
    aggression and, 307–308
    altruism and, 326–327
    biosocial theory and, 259–261
    child abuse and, 405, 408
    divorce and, 397
    homosexuality and, 277
    human uniqueness and, 3
    importance of peer interactions
        and, 456
    intelligence performance and, 76–77
    modern evolutionary theory and, 70–71
    parenting effects and, 380

sex differences and, 240
    temperament and, 127
Genital stage, of psychosexual development,
    40, 42
Genitalia, 258–261, 273
Genotypes
    criticisms of behavioral genetics and,
        85–86
    definition of, 74
    gender roles and, 259–260
    in heritability/environment
        codevelopment, 82–84
    in selective breeding experiments, 74
    twin studies and, 75
German culture, 276
German parents, 146, 165
Ghana, 430
Girls. *See also* Sex differences
    in blended families, 399–400
    development of negative emotions in, 112
    emotional self-regulation development
        in, 119
    family crises and, 383
    in gangs, 316
    gender-based interactions with, 240
    gender-role standards for, 241
    identity formation in, 190
    peer interactions of, 454
    puberty of, 187, 472–473
    rough play by, 288
    self-esteem of, 186
    sports participation of, 187
    television stereotypes of, 421–422
    temperament and, 130–131
Global self-worth, 182–183, 185
Goal-directed behavior, 54–55
Goals
    as emotional component, 102
    motivation achievement and, 210–211,
        214–215
    using aggression to meet, 292–293,
        295, 306
Golden Rule, 329, 336
"Good boy"/"good girl" orientation, 352
Goodness-of-fit model, 129, 152
Grade achievement, 215
Graduate degrees, 249
Grand Theft Auto (video game), 431
Grandparents, 375
Group trends, 381
Guided learning, 91–93
Guilt
    altruism theories and, 344
    as control mechanism, 379
    development of, 111
    mastery orientation and, 235
    versus shame, 111
Gun ownership, 309

Habits, 44–46
Happiness, early displays of, 105–106
Hate organizations, 432

No Child Left Behind (NCLB) Act (2001), 197, 446, 449
Nomadic tribes, 172–173
No-nonsense parenting, 385–386
Nonrepresentative samples, 29
Nonshared environmental influence (NSE), 77, 80–82, 327
Nonsocial activities, 459
No-problem trajectory, 303
Norm of social responsibility, 327, 336
Norway, 276
Novel responses, 55
NSE (nonshared environmental influence), 77, 80–82
Nurturing behavior, 241

Obedient behavior
    cultural variances in, 384, 385
    gender differences in, 245
    gender roles and, 241
Obese children, 422–423, 471
Object permanence
    attachment and, 141
    description of, 55–57, 58
Objectivity
    in clinical method, 18
    in ethnographic studies, 21
    in psychoanalytic studies, 44
    in scientific method, 15
Observational learning
    in altruism theories, 328
    definition of, 46
    developmental trends in, 46–47
    example of, 47
    of gender roles, 266–267
    origins of, 47–49
    to promote prosocial behavior, 339–340
    reciprocal determinism and, 49–50
Observational research
    for baby biographies, 7–8
    methodologies for, 18–19
Observer influence, 18
Occupations, 249, 252
Oedipal morality, 343
Oedipus complex, 40, 264, 343
Online communication, 430
Only children, 388, 392
Open adoption, 393
Operant learning theory, 45–46
Operational schemes, 52
Oppositional attributes, 180
Oral sex, 279
Oral stage, of psychosexual development, 40, 42
Organismic model, 97, 98–99
Organization, definition of, 53, 65
Organizational effect, 247
Original sin, 10, 11
Orphaned children, 4, 79
    attachment and, 158–161
    peer interactions of, 455

Ownness effect, 400
Own-sex schema, 269

Parallel play, 459, 460
Parent effects model, 380
Parental involvement, in schooling, 441–442, 448
Parental leave, 164–165
Parental monitoring, 465–466
Parenting. *See also* Caregiving
    achievement motivation and, 225, 226, 227, 229
    of adolescents seeking autonomy, 386–388
    after divorce, 398
    aggression in boys and, 304, 305
    altruism theories and, 327, 343–344, 347, 349–350, 355
    behavioral versus psychological control in, 379
    behaviorism and, 45
    biosocial theory and, 259
    cultural differences of, and attachment, 146–147
    development of emotional understanding and, 117–118
    dimensions of, 376
    of divorced parents, 396
    in dual-career families, 401–402
    early philosophical differences regarding, 10–11
    to eliminate sexism, 273
    emotional self-regulation development and, 119, 120–121
    empathy development and, 335
    of gay/lesbian parents, 394–395
    gender stereotypes and, 248–249, 252–253
    good versus good enough, 85
    heritability/environment correlations and, 82–84
    identity development and, 192
    Internet concerns and, 432
    of latchkey children, 403
    learned helplessness and, 220–223
    marital quality and, 149
    moral development and, 363–367
    neonates' emotional attachment and, 135–136
    of out of control children, 313–314
    patterns of, 376–379, 496–498
    in premodern times, 6–7
    to promote prosocial behavior, 339, 343–344, 363–367
    role-taking influence of, 204
    self-conscious emotions and, 111
    self-esteem development and, 188
    sexuality and, 281
    of sibling rivals, 388–390
    in stimulating versus nonstimulating homes, 232–233
    of teenage mothers, 281
    television viewing regulation and, 423–424
    temperament and, 127, 366
    that breeds aggression, 312–318

Parenting classes, 89, 90, 409
Parenting styles
    academic achievement and, 226, 442
    aggression and, 310–311
    children's effect on, 380–381
    cultural variances in, 384–386
    to foster autonomy, 386–388
    identity formation and, 192
    mastery orientation and, 234–235
    of minority groups, 384–386
    parent versus child effects model of, 380
    peer sociability and, 466–467
    peer-parent cross-pressures and, 487
    rejected/neglected children and, 469–470
    self-esteem and, 188, 379
    socioeconomic effects on, 381–384, 385
Parents
    of altruistic children, 340–341
    conflict between, 311–312
    employment benefits of, 164–165
    importance of, versus peers, 456
    moral desires of, 324
    peer sociability and, 464–467
    socialization function of, 375–388
    young and coercive types of, 317
Parents Anonymous program, 409
Parsimony, 10, 35
Particularistic development, 13–14
Part-time activists, 340
Passive genotype/environment correlations, 82, 83
Passive learning, 98–99
Passive victims, 300
Passive-observation conditions, 49
Patience, 129, 148
PeaceBuilders program, 320
Peer groups. *See also* Friendships
    achievement and, 227–228, 442–443
    aggression in boys and, 304
    altruism theories and, 347, 355
    cross-cultural school success and, 448
    definition of, 461
    as influencers of aggression, 308, 315–316
    influential importance of, 452, 454–456
    rejection from, 315
    types of influence of, 485
Peer-only monkeys, 455
Peers
    acceptance from, 467–478, 485–486
    conformity to, 485–486
    cross-pressures with, 487–488
    definition of, 453
    frequency of contact with, 454
    functions of, 453–456
    importance of, versus parents, 456
    significance of interaction with, 453–454
    sociability development and, 456–467
Peer-sponsored misconduct, 486
Pendulum problem, 61–63
Perceptual perspective-taking, 59
Perfection, 149
Performance goals, 222, 223

Permanent withdrawal from human relationships phase, 134
Permissive instruction, 438
Permissive parenting
    aggression and, 310–311
    of bullies, 300
    description of, 377–378
    moral development and, 365, 366
Permissive societies, 276
Persistence, 126
Person perception
    age trends in, 195–199
    theories of, 199–204
Person praise, 222
Personal agency, 171
Personal choices, 348, 349, 386
Personal fables, 63
Personal values, 324
Personality traits
    behavioral genetics and, 78–82
    social information-processing theory and, 93–95
Persuasion, agents of, 485
Peruvian people, 179
Pew Internet and American Life Project, 429
Phallic stage, of psychosexual development, 40, 42, 264
Phase of despair, 134
Phase of indiscriminate attachment, 138
Phase of multiple attachments, 139
Phenotypes, 74
Philippines, 337t
Physical appearance
    attachment and, 141–142
    peer acceptance and, 470–473
    self-concept development and, 174–175, 179
    self-recognition and, 174–175
    television stereotypes of, 421–422
Physical coercion, 315
Physical punishment, 365, 366, 386
Physiological correlates, 102
Plasticity, 264, 493
Play
    aggressive types of, 288, 291, 305
    of androgenized females, 261
    categories of, 459
    to decrease aggression, 318–319
    dominance hierarchies in, 290
    in effective preschool programs, 435
    fathers' role in, 153
    gender differences in, 244
    gender segregation and, 254
    gender stereotypes during, 251–252, 254–255
    gender theories and, 268–269
    gender-typed behavior in, 254–255
    in high-quality day care, 162–163
    importance of, 58–59
    infant attachment and, 139, 153
    preschoolers' peer sociability and, 459–461
    role taking and, 202–203

Polish children, 276
Popularity, with peers
    behavioral correlates of, 473–476
    cognitive abilities and, 470
    holistic development and, 98–99
    measurement of, 468–469
    parenting styles and, 469–470
    physical appearance and, 470–473
    temperament and, 470
Pornography, 432
Positive affect, 126
Positive attitude, 163–164
Positive emotions
    emotional display rules for, 121
    infants' initial display of, 104–105
    sequencing of, 105–106
    social competence and, 125
Positive reinforcement, 313, 314
Positively toned attributes, 127
Postconventional morality, 352–353
Posttraumatic stress disorder, 407–408
Poverty
    achievement motivation and, 228–232
    attachment and, 149, 150
    increase in, 374
    parenting style and, 381–384
    sexual activity and, 280
    television viewing and, 427
Power-assertive discipline
    aggression and, 310–311
    ethnic variances in, 385
    moral development and, 363, 364
Praise
    altruism theories and, 361
    cautions regarding, 222
    learned helplessness and, 221
    mastery orientation and, 234
Preadapted characteristics, 141
Preconventional morality, 351, 354, 358–359
Predicting behaviors, 94–95
Pregnancy, unplanned, 149, 280–282
Premodern times, 6–7
Premoral period, 345
Prenatal period, 270t
Preoperational stage
    altruism theories related to, 329
    description of, 57–60, 66
    person perception and, 199
    timing of, 53
Preschool children
    achievement motivation in, 218
    aggression in, 297–298, 305
    attachments' effects on, 155
    compensatory education for, 231
    development of emotional understanding in, 115–117
    divorce and, 396
    dominance hierarchies of, 290
    early school start for, 435
    emotional development of, 110, 111
    emotional self-regulation of, 120–121
    gender identity development of, 250

gender schema theory and, 268–269
    gender segregation of, 253
    gender stereotyping of, 251, 254–255
    lack of altruism in, 331, 345, 348
    peer sociability in, 458–461
    person perception in, 195–198, 202
    prejudice in, 196–197
    prosocial moral reasoning in, 333t, 334
    same-sex modeling and, 266
    self-concept in, 173, 174–175, 176, 177
    self-esteem of, 181–182, 183
    social information-processing theory and, 94–95, 96
    TV viewing of, 418–419, 425–426, 427
Present self, 173
Pretend play
    description of, 460
    development of, 57–59
    friendship influences of, 479
    functions of, 460–461
    longitudinal studies involving, 29
    moral development through, 331
    theory of mind and, 177, 178–179
Pride
    achievement motivation and, 209, 210
    development of, 110
    self-regulation development and, 121
Primary circular reactions, 54, 58
Private self, 175
Private speech, 91
Proactive aggressors, 293, 295, 300, 319
Problem solving
    in cognitive development theory, 54–64
    friendship benefits and, 481
    gender differences in, 243
    in social-skills training, 477
    in sociocultural theory, 93
Process praise, 222, 223
Programming, computer, 428
Promotion of volitional functioning (PVF), 387
Proprioceptive feedback, 170, 171
Prosocial behavior
    cognitive and affective contributors to, 332–337
    cultural differences in, 337–341, 355–356
    definition of, 325
    developmental trends in, 329–332
    interventions to foster, 320–321
    origins of, 330–331
    parenting to promote, 339, 343–344, 363–367
    peer acceptance and, 473
    psychoanalytic theories of, 326, 327, 342–345
    of siblings, 389
    television viewing and, 424–425
Prosocial moral reasoning, 333–334
Prospective studies, 482
Protest phase, 134
Provocative victims, 300
Psychoanalytic theory
    of aggression, 285–286, 287–288
    of altruism/prosocial behavior, 326, 327, 342–345

Social experiences
   altruism theories and, 354–355
   as contributor to role taking, 202–204
Social information-processing theory
   of achievement motivation, 216–223
   of aggression, 294–296
   of altruism/prosocial behavior, 328
   contributions and criticisms of, 96
   description of, 93–95
   TV viewing and, 417
   worldview behind, 97, 99
Social initiations, 18–19
Social judgment, 287
Social learning, 91, 97, 305
Social learning theories
   of altruism/prosocial behavior, 327–329,
      360–363
   attachment and, 139–140, 142
   of gender typing, 265–267
   TV viewing and, 417
   worldview behind, 98
Social models, 485
Social ostracism, 302
Social perspective taking, 333
Social problem-solving training, 477
Social referencing, 108, 113–114
Social skills, 458, 476–478
Social smiles, 105–106
Social stimulation hypothesis, 160–161
Social support, 480–481
Social systems
   definition of, 370, 371
   divorce and, 399
   family as, 371–375
Social understanding, 479
Social-contract orientation, 352
Social-conventional rules, 348
Social-informational role taking, 201
Socialization
   basic aims of, 208
   definition of, 2, 35, 370
   function of, 2–3
Social-labeling influences, 261–264
Socially mediated activities, 65
Socially transmitted memory, 91
Social-order–maintaining morality, 352
Social-roles hypothesis, 258
Societal role taking, 201
Sociocultural theory
   contributions and criticisms of, 92–93
   definition of, 65, 90
   description of, 100
   origins of early competencies in, 91–92
   role of culture in, 90–91
   worldview behind, 97
Sociodramatic play, 460
Socioeconomic status (SES)
   achievement variances related to, 225, 226,
      228–232
   aggression and, 309–310
   computer concerns regarding, 429, 431
   definition of, 228

effective schools and, 436, 437, 438–439
   gender typing and, 255–256
   latchkey children and, 403
   parenting styles and, 381–384, 385
   school transitions and, 442
   sexual activity and, 280
   of teenage mothers, 281
Sociometric techniques, 468
Solitary play, 459, 461
Spain, 276, 309
Spanking, 385, 409
Spatial abilities, 243, 244
Specific attachment phase, 138
Sports participation, 187
Stability, of attributes
   achievement motivation and, 216–219
   description of, 28
   in social information-processing theory,
      94, 95
Status phase, of relationships, 463
STDs (sexually transmitted diseases), 280, 316
Stepparents. See Blended families
Stereotype threat, 228–229, 444
Stigmatized groups, 228–229
Story writing, 213
Story-telling
   through television, 415–416
   understanding of others' emotions and,
      115–116, 118
Stranger anxiety
   attachment security and, 143–144
   description of, 107–110
   siblings and, 390–391
Stress
   adolescent self-esteem and, 186
   adolescents' negative emotions and, 112
   attachment and, 149, 157–158
   child abuse and, 405
   communities ties and, 373
   of divorced parents, 396
   emotional self-regulation development
      and, 120
   identity formation and, 193–194
   of immigrant families, 384
   parenting style and, 378
   quality of day care and, 163
Structured interviews, 16
Structured observations, 19, 22
Structured questionnaires, 16
Subsidized day care, 165–166
Success-only therapy, 221
Sudanese children, 373
Superego, 39, 342, 343
Swedish culture, 276
Swedish infants, 163, 165
Symbolic function, 57–59
Symbolic representations, 46–47, 55
Symbolic schemes, 52
Sympathetic empathic arousal, 334, 336
Sympathy, 334–336
Synchronized routines, 136–137
Systematic observations. See specific types

Tabula rasa, 2, 11
Tahitian children, 263
Taiwanese children, 252, 486
Tchambuli tribe, 33
Teachers
   computer-assisted instruction by, 428
   cross-cultural school success comparisons
      and, 447–449
   in effective schools, 436, 437, 438
   expectations of, 443–444
   gender stereotyping by, 249
   of minority students, 444
   standards for, 449
Teamwork, 438, 445
Teen Outreach program, 282
Teenagers. See Adolescence
Television literacy, 415–416
Television viewing
   aggression and, 24–25, 26, 416–421, 424
   childhood obesity and, 422–423
   of commercials, 422
   educational benefits of, 424–427
   effects of, on children's lifestyles, 414–415,
      422–423
   gender typing and, 266–267
   parental regulation of, 423–424
   rate of, 414
   social stereotypes and, 421–422
Temme people, 224
Temper tantrums, 297, 378
Temperament hypothesis, 151
Temperaments
   aggression and, 296, 308, 311, 314
   attachment and, 137, 150–152
   child abuse and, 405
   cultural differences and, 130–131
   definition of, 102, 126
   dimensions of, 126
   divorce and, 396–397
   genetic and environmental
      influences on, 127
   interactional synchronicity and, 137
   measures of, 126–127
   moral development and, 365, 366
   parenting and, 129–130, 366
   of rejected/neglected peers, 470
   stability of, 127–128
Temporal stability, 15, 186
Temptation, resisting, 360–363
Tertiary circular reactions, 55, 58
Test Anxiety Questionnaire
   (McClelland), 215
Test performance, 228–229, 243, 245
Testicular feminization syndrome (TFS),
   259, 262
Testosterone, 258, 261, 304–305
Thanatos, 39, 285–286, 287
Thematic aggression, 291
Theories, 8–10, 38. See also specific theories
Theory of mind
   cultural influences on, 179
   definition of, 175